OVERSEAS MATCHES 2007/08

Edited by John Bryant

Scorecards compiled from the CricketArchive database

First published in Great Britain by
Association of Cricket Statisticians and Historians
Cardiff CF11 9XR
© ACS, 2010

British Library Cataloguing-in-Publication Data.
A catalogue record for this book is available from the British Library.

ISBN: 978 1 905138 91 3
Typeset by Limlow Books

Contents

Preface

Full scores of first-class matches in England and Wales are printed in each year's *Wisden Cricketers' Almanack*, but for matches overseas, statisticians have traditionally relied upon a range of national cricket annuals. Unfortunately, however, not every cricketing nation has been able to sustain a regular annual and in recent years this problem has become worse. The long-running *Indian Cricket* annual ceased to appear after the 2004 edition, while the most recent annuals for such major cricketing nations as Australia and Pakistan covered the 2004/05 and 2003/04 seasons respectively.

The Association of Cricket Statisticians and Historians responded to these developments by publishing in September 2009 the first edition of the ACS *Overseas First-Class Annual*, which brought together in a single volume all first-class matches played throughout the world during the 2008/09 season. The reception accorded to this new venture demonstrated that there remains an appetite for match scores in print form, even though they are now also available on the internet.

The new Overseas Annual means that, from 2008/09 onwards, it is possible to maintain a full printed record of the modern first-class game by making only two purchases each year: *Wisden Cricketers' Almanack*, for matches in England and Wales; and the new Annual, for matches elsewhere. In warmly welcoming the full coverage of the 2008/09 season provided by the new Annual, however, several statisticians pointed out the great difficulty of obtaining printed versions of most overseas scores from other recent seasons.

The ACS has therefore issued the current publication, which contains the full score of all 559 first-class matches played in 2007/08. Note that it contains no matches played in England and Wales, for which reference should be made to the relevant edition of *Wisden*. Nor does it include the 24 matches played outside England and Wales in the 2008 season: these are found in the 2009 edition of the *Overseas First-Class Annual*.

Matches are grouped according to the country in which they were played, starting with Australia and finishing with Zimbabwe. Within each country's section, matches are given in date order. In other words, the order is the same as in the first-class match register that appears in each edition of the ACS *International Cricket Year Book*.

A full index of matches will be found at the end of the book.

Abandoned matches are noted at the appropriate point in each country's season. The Zimbabwean home fixtures in the South African SuperSport series, which were announced by Cricket South Africa after the series had already begun only to be revoked after less than a week following objections, are of such an ephemeral nature that they are not treated as abandoned games for this purpose. For the record the dates were as follows.

  Zimbabwe v Eagles, Queens Sports Club, Bulawayo, 22, 23, 24, 25 November 2007
  Zimbabwe v Dolphins, Queens Sports Club, Bulawayo, 20, 21, 22, 23 December 2007
  Zimbabwe v Cape Cobras, Harare Sports Club, 27, 28, 29, 30 December 2007
  Zimbabwe v Warriors, Harare Sports Club, 3, 4, 5, 6 January 2008
  Zimbabwe v Titans, Harare Sports Club, 31 January, 1, 2, 3 February 2008

To keep the bulk and price of the present volume within reasonable bounds despite the very large number of matches to be accommodated, space has been at a premium throughout. This has meant the exclusion of material that is available in other works. In particular, this book has been prepared on the assumption that purchasers are likely already to own (or can readily acquire) the 2009 editions of *Wisden Cricketers' Almanack* and the ACS *International Cricket Year Book*.

Part Four of the 2009 *Wisden*, 'Overseas cricket', provides a narrative account of the 2007/08 domestic season in each ICC member country, together with league tables for the various competitions and averages of leading players. For complete averages of the 2007/08 and 2008 seasons, however, together with full names and other details of all players, plus a register of matches and grounds and a wealth of other material, the reader is referred to the 2009 ACS *Year Book*, which is available from ACS Publications priced £16.00.

The ACS will continue its coverage of the modern first-class game in September 2010 with the second edition of the *Overseas First-Class Annual*, which will cover the 2009/10 season. This means that full first-class scores will have been published for three consecutive overseas seasons – 2007/08 to 2009/10 – containing between them more than 1,600 matches most of which would otherwise have been almost impossible to find in print.

John Bryant
Editor
April 2010

Acknowledgments

This book could not have been produced without the support of Peter Griffiths and Philip Bailey, who allowed access to the comprehensive CricketArchive database at cricketarchive.com, from which the scores are derived. The ACS expresses its appreciation for this support as well as for their advice and encouragement throughout. The ACS also acknowledges the essential role of Robin Abrahams, Chaminda de Silva, Dinar Gupte, Ghulam Mustafa Khan, I.U. Khan, Rajesh Kumar, Francis Payne, Andrew Samson, Saqib Irfan, Ian Smith, Sohel Awrangzeb, Sudhir Vaidya, Charlie Wat, and CricketArchive's other contributors throughout the world. The ACS is also grateful to Zahra Ridge for the cover design.

QUEENSLAND v TASMANIA

Played at Brisbane Cricket Ground, Woolloongabba, Brisbane, October 12, 13, 14, 15, 2007.
Pura Cup 2007/08
Match drawn.   (Points: Queensland 2, Tasmania 0)

TASMANIA

1	M.J.Di Venuto	c Perren b Swan	0	(2) c Broad b Cutting	178
2	T.D.Paine	b Noffke	12	(1) c Maher b Noffke	0
3	M.G.Dighton	lbw b Noffke	3	c Simpson b Noffke	4
4	T.R.Birt	c Maher b Noffke	36	c Sullivan b Simpson	72
5	G.J.Bailey	c Nye b Noffke	4	c Bragg b Sullivan	76
6	*D.J.Marsh	c Bragg b Noffke	0	not out	92
7	†S.G.Clingeleffer	run out (Moller)	27	not out	24
8	B.Geeves	c Moller b Swan	15		
9	B.G.Drew	c Swan b Cutting	28		
10	C.J.Duval	lbw b Cutting	1		
11	A.R.Griffith	not out	10		
	Extras	b 6, lb 9, w 6, nb 1	22	lb 6, w 1, nb 4	11
			158	**(5 wickets)**	**457**

FoW (1): 1-1 (1), 2-14 (3), 3-21 (2), 4-25 (5), 5-25 (6), 6-71 (4), 7-108 (8), 8-116 (9), 9-122 (10), 10-158 (9)
FoW (2): 1-0 (1), 2-4 (3), 3-142 (4), 4-296 (5), 5-373 (2)

QUEENSLAND

1	G.D.Moller	c Duval b Geeves	78
2	R.A.Broad	c Paine b Geeves	94
3	C.T.Perren	c Clingeleffer b Drew	63
4	*J.P.Maher	c Drew b Geeves	26
5	A.J.Nye	c Geeves b Marsh	46
6	C.P.Simpson	not out	107
7	†M.C.Bragg	c Clingeleffer b Geeves	8
8	A.A.Noffke	not out	100
9	C.R.Swan		
10	B.C.J.Cutting		
11	G.J.Sullivan		
	Extras	b 4, lb 13, w 1, nb 4	22
		(6 wickets, declared)	**544**

FoW (1): 1-144 (1), 2-189 (2), 3-242 (4), 4-292 (3), 5-325 (5), 6-341 (7)

Queensland Bowling

	O	M	R	W			O	M	R	W	
Noffke	20	7	33	5			43	9	114	2	1nb
Swan	15	5	32	2			16	3	59	0	1w
Cutting	8.5	1	35	2	6w,1nb	(4)	22	1	94	1	3nb
Sullivan	8	1	26	0		(3)	22	4	82	1	
Simpson	5	2	13	0			39	11	102	1	
Nye	1	0	4	0							

Tasmania Bowling

	O	M	R	W	
Griffith	33	7	101	0	
Geeves	43	13	124	4	
Drew	33	4	141	1	
Duval	25	8	73	0	1w,4nb
Marsh	21	9	69	1	
Dighton	10	5	19	0	

Umpires: S.D.Fry and D.L.Orchard.   Referee: G.N.Williams.   Toss: Queensland

Close of Play: 1st day: Queensland (1) 136-0 (Moller 75*, Broad 57*, 37 overs); 2nd day: Queensland (1) 359-6 (Simpson 18*, Noffke 11*, 133 overs); 3rd day: Tasmania (2) 201-3 (Di Venuto 95*, Bailey 24*, 62 overs).

Man of the Match: A.A.Noffke.

C.P.Simpson's 107 took 183 balls in 232 minutes and included 7 fours and 1 six. A.A.Noffke's 100 took 125 balls in 171 minutes and included 6 fours and 3 sixes. M.J.Di Venuto's 178 took 350 balls in 447 minutes and included 22 fours.

SOUTH AUSTRALIA v VICTORIA

Played at Adelaide Oval, October 14, 15, 16, 17, 2007.
Pura Cup 2007/08
Victoria won by 270 runs.   (Points: South Australia 0, Victoria 6)

VICTORIA

#	Batsman	First innings		Second innings	
1	R.J.Quiney	run out (J.D.Borgas)	25	(2) c Manou b Gillespie	20
2	N.Jewell	lbw b Cosgrove	20	(1) b R.J.Harris	12
3	M.Klinger	c Gillespie b Cullen	27	c Adcock b R.J.Harris	0
4	D.J.Hussey	b Gillespie	104	not out	74
5	*C.L.White	c Manou b R.J.Harris	76	c Adcock b Cullen	38
6	A.B.McDonald	c Elliott b R.J.Harris	32		
7	†M.S.Wade	c and b Adcock	83	(6) not out	5
8	G.J.Denton	c D.J.Harris b Cullen	1		
9	B.E.McGain	lbw b R.J.Harris	0		
10	P.M.Siddle	c Cosgrove b Bailey	17		
11	D.P.Nannes	not out	31		
	Extras	b 5, lb 10, w 7	22	lb 8, w 1	9
			438	**(4 wickets, declared)**	**158**

FoW (1): 1-47 (1), 2-48 (2), 3-111 (3), 4-263 (4), 5-263 (5), 6-318 (6), 7-319 (8), 8-320 (9), 9-363 (10), 10-438 (7)
FoW (2): 1-23 (1), 2-27 (3), 3-51 (2), 4-150 (5)

SOUTH AUSTRALIA

#	Batsman	First innings		Second innings	
1	M.T.G.Elliott	c Wade b Nannes	42	(2) c Hussey b Siddle	10
2	J.D.Borgas	c Wade b Denton	1	(1) c Wade b Denton	8
3	C.J.Borgas	c Wade b Denton	0	c Wade b Nannes	0
4	M.J.Cosgrove	c Jewell b McGain	34	lbw b Nannes	0
5	D.J.Harris	c Quiney b White	16	c Quiney b Denton	6
6	*N.T.Adcock	c White b Nannes	8	(7) b Siddle	0
7	†G.A.Manou	c Quiney b Denton	16	(8) c Hussey b Siddle	0
8	C.B.Bailey	c Hussey b Siddle	34	(9) not out	17
9	R.J.Harris	c Wade b Nannes	13	(10) lbw b Siddle	8
10	J.N.Gillespie	c Hussey b Siddle	49	(6) b Siddle	18
11	D.J.Cullen	not out	20	c McDonald b McGain	2
	Extras	b 5, lb 4, w 5, nb 2	16	lb 6, nb 2	8
			249		**77**

FoW (1): 1-10 (2), 2-10 (3), 3-56 (4), 4-98 (1), 5-106 (6), 6-116 (5), 7-134 (7), 8-156 (9), 9-188 (8), 10-249 (10)
FoW (2): 1-12 (1), 2-15 (3), 3-15 (4), 4-25 (5), 5-35 (2), 6-35 (7), 7-35 (8), 8-64 (6), 9-72 (10), 10-77 (11)

South Australia Bowling

	O	M	R	W			O	M	R	W	
Gillespie	32	6	97	1	7w		8	3	21	1	1w
R.J.Harris	35	11	81	3			9	3	21	2	
Cosgrove	13	3	42	1							
Cullen	37	3	125	2		(3)	12	0	43	1	
Bailey	16	2	66	1		(4)	10	0	37	0	
D.J.Harris	1	0	12	0							
Adcock	0.1	0	0	1		(5)	6	0	28	0	

Victoria Bowling

	O	M	R	W			O	M	R	W	
Denton	14	5	42	3			13	4	20	2	1nb
Nannes	22	6	60	3	5w,1nb		11	6	11	2	
Siddle	14.1	2	46	2	1nb		10	4	27	5	1nb
McGain	25	11	58	1			5.5	4	13	1	
White	11	2	34	1							
Hussey	1	1	0	0							

Umpires: S.J.Davis and B.N.J.Oxenford. Referee: R.B.Woods.   Toss: Victoria

Close of Play: 1st day: Victoria (1) 291-5 (McDonald 16*, Wade 6*, 96 overs); 2nd day: South Australia (1) 162-8 (Bailey 18*, Gillespie 2*, 57 overs); 3rd day: South Australia (2) 27-4 (Elliott 5*, Gillespie 1*, 18 overs).

Man of the Match: D.J.Hussey.
D.J.Hussey's 104 took 178 balls in 236 minutes and included 14 fours and 1 six.

WESTERN AUSTRALIA v NEW SOUTH WALES

Played at Western Australia Cricket Association Ground, Perth, October 14, 15, 16, 17, 2007.
Pura Cup 2007/08
New South Wales won by 275 runs.   (Points: Western Australia 0, New South Wales 6)

NEW SOUTH WALES

1	E.J.M.Cowan	c Ronchi b Magoffin	3	(2) c Heal b Magoffin	56
2	P.A.Jaques	c Langer b Dorey	13	(1) c Bandy b Heal	167
3	P.J.Forrest	c Ronchi b Magoffin	4	c Marsh b Heal	64
4	*S.M.Katich	c Voges b Bandy	50		
5	D.J.Thornely	b Edmondson	4	not out	4
6	G.M.Lambert	b Dorey	5		
7	†D.L.R.Smith	c Ronchi b Edmondson	1	(4) not out	7
8	B.Casson	b Edmondson	51		
9	M.J.Nicholson	not out	106		
10	M.A.Cameron	lbw b Heal	2		
11	D.E.Bollinger	b Edmondson	17		
	Extras	b 8, lb 2, nb 1	11	w 1, nb 1	2
			267	**(3 wickets, declared)**	**300**

FoW (1): 1-16 (2), 2-16 (1), 3-23 (3), 4-28 (5), 5-51 (6), 6-53 (7), 7-89 (4), 8-182 (8), 9-222 (10), 10-267 (11)
FoW (2): 1-94 (2), 2-288 (1), 3-293 (3)

WESTERN AUSTRALIA

1	C.J.L.Rogers	c Smith b Cameron	9	lbw b Lambert	17
2	J.L.Langer	c Jaques b Cameron	7	c Jaques b Bollinger	1
3	S.E.Marsh	c Smith b Bollinger	10	lbw b Bollinger	34
4	*A.C.Voges	b Cameron	1	c Smith b Lambert	0
5	L.A.Pomersbach	b Cameron	0	not out	102
6	D.C.Bandy	b Bollinger	16	c Nicholson b Bollinger	0
7	†L.Ronchi	c Lambert b Cameron	5	c Smith b Bollinger	0
8	A.K.Heal	c Smith b Nicholson	13	c Lambert b Nicholson	21
9	B.R.Dorey	c Casson b Nicholson	0	c Cowan b Casson	2
10	S.J.Magoffin	not out	27	c Smith b Bollinger	4
11	B.M.Edmondson	c Smith b Bollinger	4	b Thornely	0
	Extras	lb 1, w 2, nb 4	7	b 4, lb 4, nb 4	12
			99		**193**

FoW (1): 1-10 (2), 2-24 (1), 3-29 (4), 4-30 (5), 5-30 (3), 6-38 (7), 7-51 (8), 8-52 (9), 9-91 (6), 10-99 (11)
FoW (2): 1-3 (2), 2-39 (1), 3-39 (4), 4-78 (3), 5-78 (6), 6-78 (7), 7-136 (8), 8-144 (9), 9-167 (10), 10-193 (11)

Western Australia Bowling

	O	M	R	W			O	M	R	W	
Magoffin	32	17	61	2			25	4	94	1	1nb
Dorey	18	7	37	2			21	10	35	0	1w
Edmondson	26.5	5	84	4	1nb		1.4	0	10	0	
Bandy	4.5	1	17	1							
Pomersbach	0.1	0	0	0		(4)	1.2	0	1	0	
Heal	21	7	40	1		(5)	29	1	134	2	
Voges	4	0	18	0		(6)	11	0	26	0	

New South Wales Bowling

	O	M	R	W			O	M	R	W	
Bollinger	11.5	2	33	3			16	3	38	5	
Cameron	11	1	33	5	2w,4nb		9	1	33	0	4nb
Nicholson	7	2	24	2			9	4	17	1	
Casson	3	0	8	0			19	4	72	1	
Lambert						(5)	9	3	25	2	
Thornely						(6)	0.1	0	0	1	

Umpires: I.H.Lock and P.D.Parker. Referee: R.J.Evans.   Toss: New South Wales
Close of Play: 1st day: New South Wales (1) 238-9 (Nicholson 85*, Bollinger 13*, 96 overs); 2nd day: New South Wales (2) 145-1 (Jaques 71*, Forrest 17*, 45 overs); 3rd day: Western Australia (2) 139-7 (Pomersbach 54*, Dorey 1*, 50 overs).
Man of the Match: M.A.Cameron.
M.J.Nicholson's 106 took 209 balls in 252 minutes and included 14 fours. P.A.Jaques's 167 took 250 balls in 311 minutes and included 25 fours. L.A.Pomersbach's 102 took 111 balls in 172 minutes and included 14 fours and 3 sixes. D.E.Bollinger took a hat-trick in the Western Australia second innings (Marsh, Bandy, Ronchi).

NEW SOUTH WALES v QUEENSLAND

Played at Sydney Cricket Ground, October 26, 27, 28, 29, 2007.
Pura Cup 2007/08
Match drawn.   (Points: New South Wales 2, Queensland 0)

QUEENSLAND

1	R.A.Broad	c Haddin b Bracken	6	c Haddin b Clark	45
2	M.L.Hayden	c Bracken b Clark	179	b Clark	20
3	C.T.Perren	c and b MacGill	49	c Haddin b Clark	0
4	*J.P.Maher	c Clarke b MacGill	23	c Jaques b Clark	10
5	A.Symonds	c Haddin b Clark	44	c Katich b Bracken	57
6	C.P.Simpson	c Lambert b Clark	2	st Haddin b MacGill	120
7	A.A.Noffke	lbw b Clarke	50	c sub (B.Casson) b Thornely	78
8	†C.D.Hartley	c Thornely b Clarke	34	not out	17
9	M.G.Johnson	c Haddin b Clarke	33	not out	34
10	D.J.Doran	c Clarke b MacGill	16		
11	G.J.Sullivan	not out	8		
	Extras	lb 8, w 8, nb 7	23	b 3, lb 5, w 5, nb 4	17
			467	**(7 wickets, declared)**	**398**

FoW (1): 1-12 (1), 2-141 (3), 3-193 (4), 4-311 (5), 5-320 (2), 6-321 (6), 7-409 (8), 8-410 (7), 9-449 (10), 10-467 (9)
FoW (2): 1-33 (2), 2-33 (3), 3-51 (4), 4-132 (1), 5-138 (5), 6-330 (6), 7-352 (7)

NEW SOUTH WALES

1	E.J.M.Cowan	c Hartley b Noffke	16	(2) not out	12
2	P.A.Jaques	c Hartley b Sullivan	34	(1) not out	22
3	*S.M.Katich	c Sullivan b Noffke	306		
4	M.J.Clarke	run out (Broad)	23		
5	D.J.Thornely	st Hartley b Symonds	64		
6	†B.J.Haddin	lbw b Noffke	123		
7	B.Lee	b Noffke	11		
8	N.W.Bracken	c Sullivan b Noffke	6		
9	S.R.Clark	not out	12		
10	G.M.Lambert				
11	S.C.G.MacGill				
	Extras	lb 4, w 1, nb 1	6		
		(8 wickets, declared)	**601**	**(no wicket)**	**34**

FoW (1): 1-38 (1), 2-54 (2), 3-119 (4), 4-235 (5), 5-569 (3), 6-579 (6), 7-586 (7), 8-601 (8)

New South Wales Bowling

	O	M	R	W			O	M	R	W	
Lee	27	4	113	0	6w,5nb		23	8	75	0	5w,1nb
Bracken	19	7	42	1	1w	(4)	21	9	69	1	
Clark	27	7	79	3	1w,2nb	(2)	24	7	71	4	1nb
Lambert	5	1	20	0		(7)	1	0	7	0	
MacGill	36	1	183	3		(3)	19	1	97	1	1nb
Clarke	12.3	3	22	3							
Thornely						(5)	12	3	53	1	1nb
Katich						(6)	2	0	18	0	

Queensland Bowling

	O	M	R	W			O	M	R	W
Johnson	32	4	134	0	1w	(2)	4	0	21	0
Noffke	35.3	8	108	5		(1)	3	0	9	0
Sullivan	14	2	51	1	1nb					
Simpson	21	4	113	0						
Doran	9	0	66	0						
Symonds	31	5	125	1		(3)	1	0	4	0

Umpires: R.L.Parry and S.J.A.Taufel.   Referee: R.A.French.   Toss: Queensland
Close of Play: 1st day: Queensland (1) 192-2 (Hayden 103*, Maher 22*, 62 overs); 2nd day: New South Wales (1) 151-3 (Katich 70*, Thornely 7*, 45 overs); 3rd day: Queensland (2) 23-0 (Broad 9*, Hayden 14*, 12 overs).
Man of the Match: S.M.Katich.
M.L.Hayden's 179 took 225 balls in 378 minutes and included 20 fours and 2 sixes. S.M.Katich's 306 took 351 balls in 461 minutes and included 30 fours and 9 sixes. B.J.Haddin's 123 took 213 balls in 247 minutes and included 10 fours and 2 sixes. C.P.Simpson's 120 took 123 balls in 135 minutes and included 18 fours and 2 sixes.

VICTORIA v WESTERN AUSTRALIA

Played at Melbourne Cricket Ground, October 26, 27, 28, 29, 2007.
Pura Cup 2007/08
Western Australia won by 288 runs.   (Points: Victoria 0, Western Australia 6)

WESTERN AUSTRALIA

1	M.E.K.Hussey	lbw b Denton	0	c Hodge b White	59
2	J.L.Langer	c Wade b Nannes	27	run out	49
3	S.E.Marsh	lbw b Quiney	29	c Nannes b Harwood	67
4	*A.C.Voges	c Wade b Nannes	33	c Nannes b White	16
5	L.A.Pomersbach	c Wade b Denton	89	c and b McGain	28
6	†A.C.Gilchrist	c and b McGain	29	b McGain	0
7	G.B.Hogg	b Harwood	0	not out	58
8	D.J.Wates	c Wade b Denton	32	not out	3
9	S.J.Magoffin	lbw b Harwood	8		
10	T.P.Kelly	c Wade b Quiney	0		
11	M.W.H.Inness	not out	12		
	Extras	b 4, lb 12, w 2	18	b 2, lb 3, w 1, nb 3	9
			277	(6 wickets, declared)	**289**

FoW (1): 1-0 (1), 2-41 (2), 3-86 (3), 4-120 (4), 5-172 (6), 6-177 (7), 7-241 (5), 8-254 (9), 9-255 (10), 10-277 (8)
FoW (2): 1-81 (2), 2-132 (1), 3-166 (4), 4-209 (5), 5-209 (6), 6-276 (3)

VICTORIA

1	N.Jewell	c Gilchrist b Magoffin	0	lbw b Hogg	34
2	B.J.Hodge	b Inness	2	c Pomersbach b Inness	0
3	R.J.Quiney	lbw b Inness	19	c Langer b Magoffin	6
4	D.J.Hussey	c Gilchrist b Magoffin	15	c Gilchrist b Magoffin	62
5	*C.L.White	run out (Voges)	46	c Pomersbach b Hogg	10
6	M.Klinger	c Marsh b Hogg	19	b Kelly	20
7	†M.S.Wade	run out (Kelly)	4	c Voges b Hogg	3
8	S.M.Harwood	lbw b Hogg	1	c Langer b Hogg	0
9	G.J.Denton	c Marsh b Magoffin	1	lbw b Wates	7
10	B.E.McGain	not out	0	not out	14
11	D.P.Nannes	b Hogg	2	b Hogg	1
	Extras	lb 2, nb 3	5	b 4, lb 2, w 1	7
			114		**164**

FoW (1): 1-0 (1), 2-2 (2), 3-38 (4), 4-38 (3), 5-99 (6), 6-104 (7), 7-106 (8), 8-112 (5), 9-112 (9), 10-114 (11)
FoW (2): 1-8 (2), 2-16 (3), 3-74 (1), 4-98 (5), 5-122 (4), 6-137 (7), 7-137 (6), 8-137 (8), 9-163 (9), 10-164 (11)

Victoria Bowling

	O	M	R	W		O	M	R	W	
Denton	24.2	6	58	3	2w	10	0	39	0	
Nannes	17	4	41	2		13	5	28	0	2nb
Harwood	24	4	61	2		14	2	47	1	1nb
Quiney	12	4	22	2		2	0	10	0	
McGain	17	0	63	1		27	4	95	2	
White	5	0	13	0		10	0	41	2	1w
Hussey	1	0	3	0		3	0	24	0	

Western Australia Bowling

	O	M	R	W			O	M	R	W	
Magoffin	20	11	27	3			16	7	24	2	
Inness	13	4	15	2	1nb		10	3	22	1	1w
Wates	9	1	33	0	2nb		9	3	22	1	
Hogg	12.4	2	21	3		(5)	18.5	4	62	5	
Kelly	6	0	16	0		(4)	11	4	24	1	
Voges						(6)	3	0	4	0	

Umpires: D.L.Orchard and P.R.Reiffel.   Referee: M.M.Smith.   Toss: Victoria

Close of Play: 1st day: Western Australia (1) 272-9 (Wates 31*, Inness 9*, 96 overs); 2nd day: Western Australia (2) 81-1 (Hussey 29*, 25.4 overs); 3rd day: Victoria (2) 116-4 (Hussey 62*, Klinger 2*, 41 overs).

Man of the Match: G.B.Hogg.

TASMANIA v SOUTH AUSTRALIA

Played at Bellerive Oval, Hobart, October 29, 30, 31, November 1, 2007.
Pura Cup 2007/08
Tasmania won by six wickets.   (Points: Tasmania 6, South Australia 2)

SOUTH AUSTRALIA

1	M.T.G.Elliott	b Geeves	55	(2) lbw b Griffith	2
2	S.A.Deitz	c Marsh b Geeves	18	(1) lbw b Hilfenhaus	15
3	*N.T.Adcock	lbw b Geeves	4	c Clingeleffer b Griffith	11
4	M.J.Cosgrove	c Clingeleffer b Geeves	0	b Griffith	76
5	D.S.Lehmann	c Clingeleffer b Geeves	10	c Bailey b Geeves	47
6	A.H.Delmont	lbw b Hilfenhaus	0	c Ponting b Griffith	56
7	†G.A.Manou	lbw b Dighton	190	not out	16
8	R.J.Harris	c Marsh b Hilfenhaus	60	c Hilfenhaus b Geeves	1
9	J.N.Gillespie	not out	118	not out	0
10	D.J.Cullen	lbw b Marsh	12		
11	S.W.Tait	c sub (C.J.Duval) b Marsh	0		
	Extras	b 4, lb 9, w 1, nb 1	15	lb 2, nb 3	5
			482	(7 wickets, declared)	229

FoW (1): 1-61 (2), 2-69 (3), 3-69 (4), 4-87 (5), 5-88 (6), 6-92 (1), 7-204 (8), 8-454 (7), 9-482 (10), 10-482 (11)
FoW (2): 1-8 (2), 2-28 (1), 3-28 (3), 4-102 (5), 5-193 (4), 6-218 (6), 7-222 (8)

TASMANIA

1	M.J.Di Venuto	lbw b Cullen	138	(2) c Adcock b Cosgrove	33
2	M.G.Dighton	c Lehmann b Harris	21	(1) b Cullen	77
3	*R.T.Ponting	c Manou b Tait	96	b Lehmann	124
4	T.R.Birt	lbw b Gillespie	29	b Harris	28
5	G.J.Bailey	b Gillespie	8	not out	69
6	D.J.Marsh	not out	21	not out	7
7	†S.G.Clingeleffer	c Cosgrove b Cullen	11		
8	L.R.Butterworth	not out	11		
9	B.Geeves				
10	B.W.Hilfenhaus				
11	A.R.Griffith				
	Extras	b 8, lb 4, w 2, nb 14	28	b 5, lb 2, w 1, nb 3	11
		(6 wickets, declared)	363	(4 wickets)	349

FoW (1): 1-78 (2), 2-258 (1), 3-286 (3), 4-301 (5), 5-327 (4), 6-345 (7)
FoW (2): 1-83 (2), 2-134 (1), 3-213 (4), 4-332 (3)

Tasmania Bowling

	O	M	R	W		O	M	R	W	
Hilfenhaus	42	6	150	2	1w,1nb	17	5	48	1	
Griffith	32	7	90	0		24	3	79	4	2nb
Butterworth	31	3	106	0	(4)	1	0	10	0	
Geeves	15	1	49	5	(3)	14	2	64	2	1nb
Marsh	17.5	4	39	2		7	1	19	0	
Dighton	12	1	35	1		1	0	7	0	

South Australia Bowling

	O	M	R	W		O	M	R	W	
Tait	27	2	117	1	1w,11nb	12	1	68	0	
Gillespie	22	5	74	2	1w,1nb	12	1	69	0	1w,2nb
Harris	14	1	70	1	1nb	15	2	74	1	
Cosgrove	5	2	21	0	1nb	6	0	25	1	1nb
Cullen	18	3	47	2		12	1	44	1	
Adcock	2	0	7	0	(7)	3	0	15	0	
Lehmann	6	0	15	0	(6)	9.5	0	47	1	

Umpires: S.J.Davis and T.P.Laycock. Referee: R.T.Widows.   Toss: Tasmania

Close of Play: 1st day: South Australia (1) 303-7 (Manou 99*, Gillespie 48*, 96 overs); 2nd day: Tasmania (1) 183-1 (Di Venuto 99*, Ponting 50*, 40 overs); 3rd day: South Australia (2) 171-4 (Cosgrove 66*, Delmont 26*, 42 overs).
Man of the Match: R.T.Ponting.

G.A.Manou's 190 took 315 balls in 403 minutes and included 22 fours. J.N.Gillespie's 118 took 248 balls in 310 minutes and included 14 fours. M.J.Di Venuto's 138 took 178 balls in 258 minutes and included 25 fours. R.T.Ponting's 124 took 152 balls in 200 minutes and included 10 fours.

QUEENSLAND v SRI LANKANS

Played at Allan Border Field, Brisbane, November 2, 3, 4, 2007.
Sri Lanka in Australia 2007/08
Queensland won by four wickets.

SRI LANKANS

1	M.S.Atapattu	c Noffke b Johnson	48	lbw b Noffke		7
2	S.T.Jayasuriya	c Simpson b Noffke	1	c Perren b Noffke		2
3	M.G.Vandort	c Bichel b Noffke	4	c Hartley b Kasprowicz		26
4	*D.P.M.D.Jayawardene	lbw b Noffke	0	c Hartley b Johnson		35
5	T.T.Samaraweera	c Hartley b Kasprowicz	7	c Maher b Bichel		3
6	L.P.C.Silva	run out (Simpson/Kasprowicz)	0	c Maher b Noffke		4
7	†H.A.P.W.Jayawardene	not out	58	c Maher b Kasprowicz		22
8	M.F.Maharoof	c Simpson b Noffke	20	c Perren b Kasprowicz		8
9	W.P.U.J.C.Vaas	c and b Noffke	13	c Simpson b Doran		84
10	C.M.Bandara	c Noffke b Kasprowicz	43	c Perren b Bichel		15
11	S.L.Malinga			not out		15
	Extras	b 4, lb 8, nb 4	16	b 2, lb 2, nb 1		5
		(9 wickets, declared)	**210**			**226**

FoW (1): 1-2 (2), 2-12 (3), 3-14 (4), 4-41 (5), 5-45 (6), 6-81 (1), 7-115 (8), 8-139 (9), 9-210 (10)
FoW (2): 1-2 (2), 2-11 (1), 3-52 (3), 4-55 (5), 5-64 (6), 6-82 (4), 7-104 (8), 8-133 (7), 9-208 (10), 10-226 (9)

QUEENSLAND

1	*J.P.Maher	lbw b Malinga	4	(2) c D.P.M.D.Jayawardene b Maharoof	12
2	R.A.Broad	b Maharoof	12	(1) c H.A.P.W.Jayawardene b Maharoof	26
3	C.T.Perren	lbw b Vaas	25	not out	62
4	A.Symonds	c H.A.P.W.Jayawardene b Maharoof	22	c D.P.M.D.Jayawardene b Maharoof	3
5	C.P.Simpson	c Samaraweera b Malinga	0	lbw b Malinga	1
6	A.J.Bichel	c Silva b Bandara	125	lbw b Malinga	0
7	A.A.Noffke	c D.P.M.D.Jayawardene b Bandara	34	(8) not out	21
8	†C.D.Hartley	c H.A.P.W.Jayawardene b Maharoof	8	(7) st H.A.P.W.Jayawardene b Bandara	8
9	M.G.Johnson	c H.A.P.W.Jayawardene b Jayasuriya	50		
10	D.J.Doran	c Silva b Jayasuriya	2		
11	M.S.Kasprowicz	not out	0		
	Extras	lb 3, nb 10	13	lb 1, nb 8	9
			295	**(6 wickets)**	**142**

FoW (1): 1-5 (1), 2-26 (2), 3-59 (4), 4-60 (5), 5-89 (3), 6-169 (7), 7-191 (8), 8-285 (6), 9-294 (9), 10-295 (10)
FoW (2): 1-35 (2), 2-41 (1), 3-48 (4), 4-51 (5), 5-51 (6), 6-78 (7)

Queensland Bowling

	O	M	R	W		O	M	R	W	
Johnson	13	3	39	1		18	3	47	1	
Noffke	14	3	36	5	4nb	13	4	21	3	
Kasprowicz	13.2	5	28	2 ·		14	4	29	3	1nb
Bichel	10	1	49	0		11	3	34	2	
Symonds	5	1	22	0		7	1	38	0	
Doran	7	1	21	0		10.5	0	53	1	
Simpson	1	0	3	0						

Sri Lankans Bowling

	O	M	R	W		O	M	R	W	
Vaas	14	3	52	1	6nb	9	4	22	0	
Malinga	20	5	54	2	2nb	11	1	49	2	2nb
Maharoof	20	7	72	3	2nb	9	0	33	3	6nb
Bandara	19	0	89	2		7	0	34	1	
Jayasuriya	6.2	1	25	2						
Samaraweera					(5)	1.1	0	3	0	

Umpires: A.R.Curran and N.S.McNamara.

Toss: Queensland

Close of Play: 1st day: Queensland (1) 60-4 (Perren 19*, Bichel 0*, 18.2 overs); 2nd day: Sri Lankans (2) 62-4 (D.P.M.D.Jayawardene 22*, Silva 2*, 29 overs).

A.J.Bichel's 125 took 169 balls in 241 minutes and included 11 fours and 7 sixes.

AUSTRALIA v SRI LANKA

Played at Brisbane Cricket Ground, Woolloongabba, Brisbane, November 8, 9, 10, 11, 12, 2007.
Sri Lanka in Australia 2007/08 - 1st Test
Australia won by an innings and 40 runs.

AUSTRALIA

1	P.A.Jaques	st H.A.P.W.Jayawardene b Muralitharan	100	
2	M.L.Hayden	c Muralitharan b Vaas	43	
3	*R.T.Ponting	st H.A.P.W.Jayawardene b Muralitharan	56	
4	M.E.K.Hussey	c Atapattu b Fernando	133	
5	M.J.Clarke	not out	145	
6	A.Symonds	not out	53	
7	†A.C.Gilchrist			
8	B.Lee			
9	M.G.Johnson			
10	S.R.Clark			
11	S.C.G.MacGill			
	Extras	b 4, lb 12, w 1, nb 4	21	
		(4 wickets, declared)	551	

FoW (1): 1-69 (2), 2-183 (3), 3-216 (1), 4-461 (4)

SRI LANKA

1	M.S.Atapattu	c Jaques b Johnson	51	c Gilchrist b Symonds	16
2	S.T.Jayasuriya	c Gilchrist b Lee	7	c Ponting b Lee	39
3	M.G.Vandort	c Gilchrist b Lee	0	b MacGill	82
4	*D.P.M.D.Jayawardene	c Gilchrist b Clark	14	c Gilchrist b Johnson	49
5	T.T.Samaraweera	c Gilchrist b Johnson	13	c Hussey b Johnson	20
6	L.P.C.Silva	c Clarke b Clark	40	c Hussey b Lee	43
7	†H.A.P.W.Jayawardene	lbw b Lee	37	lbw b Clark	1
8	M.F.Maharoof	b Symonds	21	b Lee	18
9	W.P.U.J.C.Vaas	b MacGill	8	not out	11
10	C.R.D.Fernando	c Johnson b Lee	7	b Lee	4
11	M.Muralitharan	not out	6	b Clark	4
	Extras	lb 1, nb 6	7	b 4, lb 3, nb 6	13
			211		300

FoW (1): 1-7 (2), 2-11 (3), 3-45 (4), 4-65 (5), 5-119 (6), 6-153 (1), 7-181 (8), 8-198 (9), 9-198 (7), 10-211 (10)
FoW (2): 1-53 (1), 2-65 (2), 3-167 (4), 4-213 (3), 5-215 (5), 6-226 (7), 7-259 (8), 8-281 (6), 9-290 (10), 10-300 (11)

Sri Lanka Bowling

	O	M	R	W	
Vaas	28	6	102	1	
Maharoof	34	6	107	0	4nb
Fernando	34	3	130	1	1w
Muralitharan	50	4	170	2	
Jayasuriya	4	0	18	0	
Samaraweera	1	0	8	0	

Australia Bowling

	O	M	R	W			O	M	R	W	
Lee	17.5	9	26	4	2nb		27	7	86	4	
Johnson	18	2	49	2			19	5	47	2	
MacGill	25	5	79	1		(5)	25	3	64	1	
Clark	16	4	46	2	4nb	(3)	22.2	3	75	2	2nb
Symonds	5	3	10	1		(4)	6	1	21	1	

Umpires: A.L.Hill and R.E.Koertzen.   Third umpire: P.D.Parker.   Referee: M.J.Procter.   Toss: Sri Lanka

Close of Play: 1st day: Australia (1) 242-3 (Hussey 28*, Clarke 5*, 76 overs); 2nd day: Sri Lanka (1) 31-2 (Atapattu 19*, D.P.M.D.Jayawardene 5*, 16 overs); 3rd day: Sri Lanka (2) 80-2 (Vandort 15*, D.P.M.D.Jayawardene 8*, 22 overs); 4th day: Sri Lanka (2) 218-5 (Silva 5*, H.A.P.W.Jayawardene 0*, 78 overs).

Man of the Match: B.Lee.
P.A.Jaques's 100 took 203 balls in 280 minutes and included 14 fours. M.E.K.Hussey's 133 took 249 balls in 351 minutes and included 13 fours and 2 sixes. M.J.Clarke's 145 took 249 balls in 333 minutes and included 14 fours and 1 six.

SOUTH AUSTRALIA v NEW SOUTH WALES

Played at Adelaide Oval, November 9, 10, 11, 12, 2007.
Pura Cup 2007/08
New South Wales won by seven wickets.   (Points: South Australia 0, New South Wales 6)

SOUTH AUSTRALIA

1	M.T.G.Elliott	b Bracken	6	(2) c Haddin b Bracken	31
2	S.A.Deitz	c Haddin b Bollinger	15	(1) c Nicholson b Bollinger	18
3	C.J.Borgas	lbw b Bollinger	0	c Lambert b Nicholson	13
4	C.J.Ferguson	c Haddin b Casson	83	c Katich b Bracken	59
5	*N.T.Adcock	c Cowan b Nicholson	4	lbw b Bracken	23
6	A.H.Delmont	lbw b Bollinger	16	c Haddin b Bollinger	40
7	†G.A.Manou	c Haddin b Bollinger	4	c Haddin b Nicholson	17
8	M.F.Cleary	c Katich b Bracken	2	(11) c Haddin b Bracken	23
9	R.J.Harris	c Cowan b Bracken	7	(8) not out	42
10	J.N.Gillespie	not out	19	(9) b Nicholson	6
11	D.J.Cullen	c Haddin b Bracken	7	(10) c Nicholson b Lambert	0
	Extras	b 1, lb 4, w 8, nb 2	15	b 6, lb 5, w 3, nb 5	19
			178		**291**

FoW (1): 1-19 (1), 2-23 (2), 3-24 (3), 4-36 (5), 5-80 (6), 6-85 (7), 7-102 (8), 8-120 (9), 9-171 (4), 10-178 (11)
FoW (2): 1-42 (1), 2-52 (2), 3-101 (3), 4-150 (4), 5-153 (5), 6-190 (7), 7-229 (6), 8-247 (9), 9-248 (10), 10-291 (11)

NEW SOUTH WALES

1	G.M.Lambert	c Manou b Cleary	8	(2) c Borgas b Harris	1
2	E.J.M.Cowan	c Adcock b Cullen	14	(1) c Adcock b Cullen	6
3	P.J.Forrest	c Manou b Cleary	36	c Manou b Gillespie	2
4	B.Casson	c Delmont b Cleary	34		
5	*S.M.Katich	lbw b Harris	117	(4) not out	63
6	D.J.Thornely	lbw b Harris	7	(5) not out	80
7	†B.J.Haddin	st Manou b Adcock	19		
8	M.J.Nicholson	c Manou b Cullen	44		
9	N.M.Hauritz	run out (Harris/Manou)	0		
10	N.W.Bracken	c Gillespie b Cullen	2		
11	D.E.Bollinger	not out	0		
	Extras	b 10, lb 13, w 4, nb 1	28	b 5, lb 1, nb 4	10
			309	**(3 wickets)**	**162**

FoW (1): 1-21 (1), 2-27 (2), 3-86 (4), 4-126 (3), 5-160 (6), 6-204 (7), 7-287 (8), 8-288 (9), 9-309 (10), 10-309 (5)
FoW (2): 1-1 (2), 2-9 (3), 3-13 (1)

New South Wales Bowling

	O	M	R	W			O	M	R	W	
Bollinger	21	4	63	4	5w,2nb	(2)	20	2	60	2	1w,3nb
Nicholson	16	3	45	1	3w	(4)	19	6	51	3	1w
Bracken	20	7	50	4		(1)	26.1	7	57	4	1nb
Hauritz	2	0	3	0		(3)	10	2	46	0	
Lambert	8	5	7	0			16	5	31	1	1w,1nb
Casson	3	1	5	1			12	3	35	0	

South Australia Bowling

	O	M	R	W			O	M	R	W	
Harris	30.4	9	101	2	1w		13.2	7	23	1	
Gillespie	31	12	51	0	2w		14	4	35	1	4nb
Cleary	14	3	40	3	1w,1nb						
Cullen	28	4	75	3		(3)	14	1	71	1	
Adcock	5	0	16	1		(4)	7	0	27	0	
Ferguson	2	0	3	0							

Umpires: S.D.Fry and I.H.Lock. Referee: R.B.Woods.   Toss: South Australia

Close of Play: 1st day: New South Wales (1) 35-2 (Forrest 3*, Casson 0*, 22 overs); 2nd day: South Australia (2) 24-0 (Deitz 7*, Elliott 17*, 5 overs); 3rd day: South Australia (2) 275-9 (Harris 33*, Cleary 19*, 100 overs).

Man of the Match: S.M.Katich.

S.M.Katich's 117 took 182 balls in 278 minutes and included 13 fours.

VICTORIA v TASMANIA

Played at Melbourne Cricket Ground, November 9, 10, 11, 12, 2007.
Pura Cup 2007/08
Victoria won by an innings and 4 runs.   **(Points: Victoria 6, Tasmania 0)**

TASMANIA

1	M.J.Di Venuto	c McDonald b McGain	22	(2) c White b Harwood	20
2	M.G.Dighton	c Quiney b Denton	25	(1) lbw b Denton	2
3	T.R.Birt	c and b McGain	37	lbw b Harwood	51
4	G.J.Bailey	c Denton b Harwood	6	lbw b Denton	0
5	*D.J.Marsh	b McGain	25	b Harwood	35
6	L.R.Butterworth	c Wade b Harwood	11	c Wade b Denton	17
7	†S.G.Clingeleffer	c McDonald b McGain	6	c Wade b Denton	14
8	B.Geeves	lbw b Denton	19	lbw b Denton	3
9	J.J.Krejza	not out	42	not out	9
10	A.R.Griffith	b Denton	10	c Quiney b McGain	2
11	B.W.Hilfenhaus	c McDonald b McGain	23	b Denton	1
	Extras	b 1, lb 6, nb 2	9	b 1, lb 7, nb 2, pen 5	15
			235		**169**

FoW (1): 1-39 (1), 2-62 (2), 3-77 (4), 4-114 (3), 5-129 (5), 6-133 (6), 7-141 (7), 8-183 (8), 9-200 (10), 10-235 (11)
FoW (2): 1-2 (1), 2-71 (2), 3-74 (4), 4-84 (3), 5-133 (5), 6-133 (6), 7-156 (8), 8-157 (7), 9-160 (10), 10-169 (11)

VICTORIA

1	R.J.Quiney	lbw b Hilfenhaus	0
2	N.Jewell	c Krejza b Geeves	41
3	B.J.Hodge	lbw b Krejza	93
4	D.J.Hussey	c Krejza b Griffith	52
5	*C.L.White	c Butterworth b Krejza	5
6	A.B.McDonald	c Birt b Butterworth	70
7	†M.S.Wade	c Clingeleffer b Marsh	95
8	S.M.Harwood	c Marsh b Hilfenhaus	1
9	G.J.Denton	c Marsh b Krejza	37
10	B.E.McGain	b Krejza	1
11	A.B.Wise	not out	0
	Extras	lb 10, nb 3	13
			408

FoW (1): 1-0 (1), 2-80 (2), 3-181 (4), 4-186 (5), 5-201 (3), 6-307 (6), 7-309 (8), 8-405 (7), 9-407 (9), 10-408 (10)

Victoria Bowling

	O	M	R	W			O	M	R	W	
Denton	24	6	77	3	1nb		20.1	8	32	6	
Harwood	24	9	41	2			15	3	40	3	2nb
Wise	21	7	27	0	1nb	(4)	4	0	12	0	
McGain	32.5	8	68	5		(3)	13	1	60	1	
White	5	0	15	0			3	0	12	0	
Quiney	1	1	0	0							

Tasmania Bowling

	O	M	R	W	
Hilfenhaus	33	11	77	2	1nb
Griffith	17	2	77	1	
Geeves	31	6	85	1	1nb
Krejza	29.2	6	91	4	1nb
Butterworth	9	1	26	1	
Marsh	16	4	42	1	

Umpires: B.N.J.Oxenford and J.D.Ward. Referee: M.M.Smith.   Toss: Tasmania

Close of Play: 1st day: Tasmania (1) 200-8 (Krejza 30*, Griffith 10*, 96 overs); 2nd day: Victoria (1) 240-5 (McDonald 31*, Wade 13*, 82 overs); 3rd day: Tasmania (2) 129-4 (Marsh 31*, Butterworth 17*, 40 overs).

Man of the Match: G.J.Denton.

WESTERN AUSTRALIA v QUEENSLAND

Played at Western Australia Cricket Association Ground, Perth, November 9, 10, 11, 12, 2007.
Pura Cup 2007/08
Western Australia won by an innings and 170 runs.   (Points: Western Australia 6, Queensland 0)

QUEENSLAND
1	R.A.Broad	b Magoffin	1	(2) b Magoffin	12
2	*J.P.Maher	c Langer b Magoffin	111	(7) c Ronchi b Hogg	32
3	M.L.Love	c Langer b Magoffin	0	(1) c Marsh b Kelly	10
4	C.T.Perren	c Ronchi b Inness	30	(3) c Voges b Magoffin	3
5	J.R.Hopes	b Magoffin	8	(4) c Langer b Magoffin	0
6	C.P.Simpson	c Ronchi b Kelly	16	(5) c Pomersbach b Hogg	14
7	A.A.Noffke	c Ronchi b Inness	34	(6) c Ronchi b Hogg	44
8	A.J.Bichel	b Inness	0	b Kelly	29
9	†C.D.Hartley	c and b Inness	5	c and b Hogg	3
10	D.J.Doran	lbw b Inness	2	lbw b Hogg	4
11	G.J.Sullivan	not out	0	not out	0
	Extras	b 4, lb 6, w 7, nb 4	21	b 5, lb 9, w 2	16
			228		**167**

FoW (1): 1-6 (1), 2-6 (3), 3-101 (4), 4-115 (5), 5-148 (6), 6-220 (2), 7-220 (7), 8-221 (8), 9-227 (10), 10-228 (9)
FoW (2): 1-24 (1), 2-28 (2), 3-28 (4), 4-29 (3), 5-85 (5), 6-104 (6), 7-145 (8), 8-154 (9), 9-166 (10), 10-167 (7)

WESTERN AUSTRALIA
1	C.J.L.Rogers	lbw b Noffke	47
2	J.L.Langer	c Hartley b Simpson	42
3	S.E.Marsh	not out	166
4	*A.C.Voges	c Hartley b Hopes	6
5	L.A.Pomersbach	c Broad b Doran	176
6	D.C.Bandy	c Hartley b Hopes	7
7	†L.Ronchi	not out	105
8	G.B.Hogg		
9	S.J.Magoffin		
10	M.W.H.Inness		
11	T.P.Kelly		
	Extras	b 1, lb 8, w 5, nb 2	16
	(5 wickets, declared)		565

FoW (1): 1-72 (1), 2-110 (2), 3-138 (4), 4-406 (5), 5-416 (6)

Western Australia Bowling
	O	M	R	W		O	M	R	W	
Magoffin	30	16	40	4		18	7	27	3	
Inness	31.4	19	38	5	1nb	16	10	25	0	
Kelly	20	3	69	1	7w,3nb	13	3	24	2	2w
Bandy	7	5	6	0						
Hogg	19	2	65	0	(4)	25.1	7	77	5	

Queensland Bowling
	O	M	R	W	
Bichel	27	6	84	0	1w
Noffke	28	3	89	1	1w
Hopes	32	11	48	2	2nb
Sullivan	16	3	101	0	3w
Simpson	23	4	109	1	
Doran	16	1	125	1	

Umpires: J.K.Brookes and P.R.Reiffel. Referee: R.J.Evans.   Toss: Western Australia

Close of Play: 1st day: Queensland (1) 220-5 (Maher 111*, Noffke 34*, 96 overs); 2nd day: Western Australia (1) 227-3 (Marsh 71*, Pomersbach 52*, 82 overs); 3rd day: Queensland (2) 77-4 (Simpson 14*, Noffke 34*, 35 overs).

Man of the Match: L.A.Pomersbach.

J.P.Maher's 111 took 296 balls in 388 minutes and included 17 fours. S.E.Marsh's 166 took 321 balls in 456 minutes and included 23 fours and 1 six. L.A.Pomersbach's 176 took 207 balls in 255 minutes and included 22 fours and 8 sixes. L.Ronchi's 105 took 54 balls in 61 minutes and included 6 fours and 11 sixes.

AUSTRALIA v SRI LANKA

Played at Bellerive Oval, Hobart, November 16, 17, 18, 19, 20, 2007.
Sri Lanka in Australia 2007/08 - 2nd Test
Australia won by 96 runs.

AUSTRALIA

1	P.A.Jaques	c Fernando b Jayasuriya	150	c Vandort b Malinga	68
2	M.L.Hayden	c H.A.P.W.Jayawardene b Fernando	17	lbw b Muralitharan	33
3	*R.T.Ponting	c D.P.M.D.Jayawardene b Muralitharan	31	not out	53
4	M.E.K.Hussey	lbw b Fernando	132	not out	34
5	M.J.Clarke	c H.A.P.W.Jayawardene b Malinga	71		
6	A.Symonds	not out	50		
7	†A.C.Gilchrist	not out	67		
8	B.Lee				
9	M.G.Johnson				
10	S.R.Clark				
11	S.C.G.MacGill				
	Extras	b 5, lb 1, w 1, nb 17	24	b 2, lb 1, nb 19	22
		(5 wickets, declared)	542	(2 wickets, declared)	210

FoW (1): 1-48 (2), 2-133 (3), 3-285 (1), 4-410 (4), 5-447 (5)
FoW (2): 1-83 (2), 2-154 (1)

SRI LANKA

1	M.S.Atapattu	c Clarke b Lee	25	c Jaques b Lee	80
2	M.G.Vandort	b Lee	14	c sub (R.J.G.Lockyear) b Johnson	4
3	K.C.Sangakkara	c Hussey b Johnson	57	c Ponting b Clark	192
4	*D.P.M.D.Jayawardene	c Clarke b Lee	104	b Lee	0
5	S.T.Jayasuriya	b MacGill	3	c Gilchrist b Lee	45
6	L.P.C.Silva	c Gilchrist b MacGill	4	c Ponting b Johnson	0
7	†H.A.P.W.Jayawardene	c Gilchrist b Clark	0	lbw b Johnson	0
8	M.F.Maharoof	run out (sub [R.J.G.Lockyear]/Gilchrist)	19	c Lee b MacGill	4
9	C.R.D.Fernando	c Gilchrist b Lee	2	run out	2
10	S.L.Malinga	b Clark	1	not out	42
11	M.Muralitharan	not out	1	b Lee	15
	Extras	lb 7, nb 9	16	b 1, lb 6, w 6, nb 13	26
			246		410

FoW (1): 1-41 (2), 2-54 (1), 3-127 (3), 4-134 (5), 5-152 (6), 6-163 (7), 7-196 (8), 8-207 (9), 9-243 (10), 10-246 (4)
FoW (2): 1-15 (2), 2-158 (1), 3-158 (4), 4-265 (5), 5-272 (6), 6-272 (7), 7-284 (8), 8-290 (9), 9-364 (3), 10-410 (11)

Sri Lanka Bowling

	O	M	R	W			O	M	R	W	
Malinga	35	6	156	1	8nb		12	0	61	1	11nb
Maharoof	23	4	82	0	8nb						
Fernando	26	4	134	2	1w	(2)	12	1	50	0	6nb
Muralitharan	46	4	140	1		(3)	20	1	90	1	
Jayasuriya	9	1	24	1		(4)	2	0	6	0	

Australia Bowling

	O	M	R	W			O	M	R	W	
Lee	23.2	4	82	4	8nb		26.3	3	87	4	1w,4nb
Johnson	17	3	44	1			28	4	101	3	1w,1nb
Clark	16	6	32	2	1nb		24	5	103	1	4nb
MacGill	25	5	81	2			20	1	102	1	4nb
Clarke						(5)	6	1	10	0	

Umpires: Aleem Dar and R.E.Koertzen. Third umpire: P.D.Parker. Referee: M.J.Procter.   Toss: Australia

Close of Play: 1st day: Australia (1) 329-3 (Hussey 101*, Clarke 8*, 90 overs); 2nd day: Sri Lanka (1) 30-0 (Atapattu 18*, Vandort 12*, 12 overs); 3rd day: Australia (2) 111-1 (Jaques 53*, Ponting 7*, 20 overs); 4th day: Sri Lanka (2) 247-3 (Sangakkara 109*, Jayasuriya 33*, 70 overs).

Man of the Match: B.Lee.
P.A.Jaques's 150 took 237 balls in 329 minutes and included 18 fours. M.E.K.Hussey's 132 took 220 balls in 281 minutes and included 18 fours and 1 six. D.P.M.D.Jayawardene's 104 took 194 balls in 267 minutes and included 13 fours. K.C.Sangakkara's 192 took 282 balls in 429 minutes and included 27 fours and 1 six.

QUEENSLAND v VICTORIA

Played at Brisbane Cricket Ground, Woolloongabba, Brisbane, November 18, 19, 20, 21, 2007.
Pura Cup 2007/08
Victoria won by 276 runs.   **(Points: Queensland 2, Victoria 6)**

VICTORIA

1	R.J.Quiney	lbw b Noffke	31	(2) c sub (D.J.Doran) b Nye	32
2	N.Jewell	c Bichel b Noffke	0	(1) c sub (W.J.Townsend) b Swan	188
3	B.J.Hodge	c Maher b Bichel	5	(4) not out	286
4	D.J.Hussey	c Hartley b Noffke	9	(5) c sub (W.J.Townsend) b Swan	18
5	*C.L.White	c Nye b Sullivan	11	(6) c and b Sullivan	40
6	A.B.McDonald	c Hartley b Noffke	2		
7	†M.S.Wade	c Hartley b Sullivan	22		
8	C.J.McKay	c Hartley b Noffke	15		
9	G.J.Denton	c Maher b Noffke	7	(3) b Nye	0
10	B.E.McGain	c Hartley b Sullivan	4		
11	A.B.Wise	not out	1		
	Extras	lb 2, w 2, nb 2	6	b 1, lb 9, w 6, nb 1	17
			113	**(5 wickets, declared)**	**581**

FoW (1): 1-3 (2), 2-16 (3), 3-43 (4), 4-50 (1), 5-61 (5), 6-71 (6), 7-87 (8), 8-99 (9), 9-112 (7), 10-113 (10)
FoW (2): 1-73 (2), 2-73 (3), 3-452 (1), 4-495 (5), 5-581 (6)

QUEENSLAND

1	S.R.Watson	c Wade b Denton	0	c Wise b Denton	0
2	R.A.Broad	c Hussey b McKay	6	(8) c Quiney b White	1
3	C.T.Perren	lbw b McKay	49	lbw b McKay	0
4	*J.P.Maher	c Hussey b Denton	33	(2) c Hussey b McKay	10
5	A.J.Nye	c Wade b Denton	57	(4) b McKay	11
6	C.P.Simpson	c sub (M.Klinger) b Wise	7	(5) c White b McKay	4
7	A.A.Noffke	c Hussey b Wise	82	b Denton	5
8	†C.D.Hartley	c Hussey b Wise	33	(6) c Wade b Denton	26
9	C.R.Swan	b McGain	23	b McGain	13
10	G.J.Sullivan	b McGain	22	not out	4
11	A.J.Bichel	not out	12	absent hurt	0
	Extras	b 4, lb 10, w 1, nb 2	17	lb 3	3
			341		**77**

FoW (1): 1-0 (1), 2-12 (2), 3-90 (4), 4-94 (3), 5-113 (6), 6-211 (5), 7-274 (7), 8-285 (8), 9-322 (9), 10-341 (10)
FoW (2): 1-0 (1), 2-9 (3), 3-10 (2), 4-14 (5), 5-41 (4), 6-59 (6), 7-60 (7), 8-73 (8), 9-77 (9)

Queensland Bowling

	O	M	R	W			O	M	R	W	
Noffke	18	3	33	6	2nb						
Bichel	6	0	28	1	1w						
Swan	18	8	32	0		(2)	40	7	148	2	2w
Sullivan	5.5	2	18	3	1w	(1)	38	3	212	1	4w,1nb
Broad						(3)	2.4	1	6	0	
Nye						(4)	27.2	3	89	2	
Simpson						(5)	28	2	116	0	

Victoria Bowling

	O	M	R	W			O	M	R	W	
Denton	25	10	65	3	1w		13	5	26	3	
McKay	32	12	78	2			10	2	31	4	
Wise	32	14	63	3	2nb		6	3	13	0	
McGain	20	1	96	2			1.1	1	0	1	
Quiney	7	0	25	0							
White						(5)	1	0	4	1	

Umpires: N.S.McNamara and R.J.Tucker. Referee: G.N.Williams.   Toss: Queensland

Close of Play: 1st day: Queensland (1) 100-4 (Nye 8*, Simpson 1*, 42 overs); 2nd day: Victoria (2) 73-2 (Jewell 40*, Hodge 0*, 19 overs); 3rd day: Victoria (2) 426-2 (Jewell 182*, Hodge 202*, 115 overs).
Man of the Match: B.J.Hodge.
N.Jewell's 188 took 335 balls in 462 minutes and included 23 fours. B.J.Hodge's 286 took 385 balls in 456 minutes and included 34 fours and 4 sixes.

NEW SOUTH WALES v TASMANIA

Played at Sydney Cricket Ground, November 20, 21, 22, 23, 2007.
Pura Cup 2007/08
New South Wales won by an innings and 35 runs.   (Points: New South Wales 6, Tasmania 0)

NEW SOUTH WALES

1	E.J.M.Cowan	c Birt b Hilfenhaus	2
2	P.J.Hughes	c Geeves b Krejza	51
3	P.J.Forrest	lbw b Drew	177
4	*S.M.Katich	c Di Venuto b Butterworth	51
5	D.J.Thornely	c Birt b Hilfenhaus	8
6	†B.J.Haddin	c Clingeleffer b Butterworth	100
7	G.M.Lambert	c Krejza b Geeves	32
8	B.Casson	not out	34
9	M.J.Nicholson	not out	34
10	N.W.Bracken		
11	D.E.Bollinger		
	Extras	b 1, lb 8, w 5, nb 9	23
		(7 wickets, declared)	512

FoW (1): 1-2 (1), 2-114 (2), 3-205 (4), 4-226 (5), 5-346 (3), 6-426 (6), 7-443 (7)

TASMANIA

1	M.G.Dighton	b Lambert	63	b Bollinger	0
2	M.J.Di Venuto	lbw b Bollinger	5	c Haddin b Bollinger	0
3	T.R.Birt	b Bollinger	0	b Bollinger	77
4	*D.J.Marsh	c Haddin b Bollinger	0	lbw b Bollinger	0
5	G.J.Bailey	c Haddin b Bollinger	86	c Hughes b Bollinger	0
6	L.R.Butterworth	c Katich b Bracken	29	b Bracken	116
7	†S.G.Clingeleffer	b Bollinger	0	c Nicholson b Bollinger	6
8	B.Geeves	c Katich b Bollinger	15	b Bracken	20
9	J.J.Krejza	b Bracken	10	not out	14
10	B.G.Drew	c Hughes b Casson	1	b Bracken	4
11	B.W.Hilfenhaus	not out	0	c Nicholson b Bracken	4
	Extras	lb 2, nb 3	5	b 16, lb 2, w 1, nb 3	22
			214		263

FoW (1): 1-6 (2), 2-6 (3), 3-10 (4), 4-154 (1), 5-156 (5), 6-156 (7), 7-189 (8), 8-211 (6), 9-214 (9), 10-214 (10)
FoW (2): 1-0 (1), 2-7 (2), 3-7 (4), 4-11 (5), 5-150 (3), 6-167 (7), 7-231 (8), 8-242 (6), 9-255 (10), 10-263 (11)

Tasmania Bowling

	O	M	R	W	
Hilfenhaus	30	5	117	2	1w,2nb
Geeves	30	5	114	1	5nb
Butterworth	22	9	57	2	4w,2nb
Drew	16	1	76	1	
Krejza	25	3	114	1	
Marsh	7	2	25	0	

New South Wales Bowling

	O	M	R	W			O	M	R	W	
Bollinger	21	7	68	6	3nb		16	5	63	6	1w,1nb
Bracken	17	8	24	2			24.1	10	53	4	
Nicholson	6	1	25	0		(4)	10	8	5	0	
Casson	21.2	6	66	1		(5)	29	5	98	0	
Lambert	13	4	29	1		(3)	5	1	26	0	2nb

Umpires: R.D.Goodger and I.H.Lock. Referee: R.A.French.   Toss: New South Wales

Close of Play: 1st day: New South Wales (1) 360-5 (Haddin 55*, Lambert 0*, 96 overs); 2nd day: Tasmania (1) 165-6 (Butterworth 3*, Geeves 4*, 59 overs); 3rd day: Tasmania (2) 141-4 (Birt 68*, Butterworth 62*, 46 overs).

Man of the Match: D.E.Bollinger.

P.J.Forrest's 177 took 246 balls in 367 minutes and included 25 fours and 2 sixes. B.J.Haddin's 100 took 169 balls in 201 minutes and included 12 fours and 1 six. L.R.Butterworth's 116 took 230 balls in 302 minutes and included 15 fours.

SOUTH AUSTRALIA v WESTERN AUSTRALIA

Played at Adelaide Oval, November 23, 24, 25, 2007.
Pura Cup 2007/08
South Australia won by nine wickets.   (Points: South Australia 6, Western Australia 0)

WESTERN AUSTRALIA

1	C.J.L.Rogers	c Manou b Gillespie	14	(2) lbw b Harris	8
2	L.M.Davis	lbw b Gillespie	8	(1) lbw b Adcock	42
3	J.L.Langer	c Manou b Rofe	34	lbw b Adcock	37
4	*A.C.Voges	b Gillespie	58	c Manou b Rofe	35
5	T.P.Doropoulos	b Lehmann	23	c Manou b Lehmann	8
6	†L.Ronchi	c Adcock b Gillespie	9	run out	0
7	G.B.Hogg	b Cosgrove	68	st Manou b Adcock	35
8	A.K.Heal	c Elliott b Gillespie	0	lbw b Rofe	5
9	S.J.Magoffin	not out	5	c Lehmann b Cullen	4
10	M.W.H.Inness	b Gillespie	5	c Lehmann b Gillespie	7
11	B.M.Edmondson	c Elliott b Gillespie	0	not out	2
	Extras	lb 7, nb 5	12	b 3, lb 2, w 1, nb 1	7
			236		**190**

FoW (1): 1-10 (2), 2-32 (1), 3-88 (3), 4-145 (5), 5-154 (6), 6-199 (4), 7-199 (8), 8-231 (7), 9-236 (10), 10-236 (11)
FoW (2): 1-22 (2), 2-88 (3), 3-97 (1), 4-118 (5), 5-121 (6), 6-150 (4), 7-160 (8), 8-181 (7), 9-181 (9), 10-190 (10)

SOUTH AUSTRALIA

1	M.T.G.Elliott	lbw b Magoffin	58	(2) not out	5
2	M.J.Cosgrove	lbw b Inness	0	(1) b Inness	17
3	C.J.Ferguson	c Ronchi b Inness	81	not out	4
4	D.S.Lehmann	b Inness	167		
5	*N.T.Adcock	c Doropoulos b Edmondson	13		
6	A.H.Delmont	b Inness	28		
7	†G.A.Manou	c Davis b Inness	4		
8	R.J.Harris	c Rogers b Inness	2		
9	J.N.Gillespie	not out	16		
10	D.J.Cullen	lbw b Edmondson	5		
11	P.C.Rofe	c Voges b Edmondson	7		
	Extras	lb 4, w 2, nb 10	16	lb 4	4
			397	**(1 wicket)**	**30**

FoW (1): 1-4 (2), 2-124 (1), 3-188 (3), 4-217 (5), 5-337 (6), 6-363 (4), 7-367 (8), 8-372 (7), 9-388 (10), 10-397 (11)
FoW (2): 1-22 (1)

South Australia Bowling

	O	M	R	W		O	M	R	W	
Harris	16	7	47	0		16	3	28	1	
Gillespie	20	6	58	7	5nb	18.2	6	29	1	1w,1nb
Rofe	14	4	37	1	(4)	11	2	41	2	
Cullen	12	2	40	0	(3)	20	4	42	1	
Cosgrove	5	1	12	1						
Lehmann	6	1	35	1		5	0	15	1	
Adcock					(5)	11	3	30	3	

Western Australia Bowling

	O	M	R	W		O	M	R	W	
Magoffin	15	1	82	1	1w,3nb					
Inness	20	4	83	6	(1)	2.2	0	11	1	
Edmondson	22.4	0	106	3	7nb	(2)	2	0	15	0
Hogg	29	6	79	0	1w					
Heal	18	4	43	0						

Umpires: D.L.Orchard and R.L.Parry. Referee: R.B.Woods.   Toss: Western Australia

Close of Play: 1st day: South Australia (1) 75-1 (Elliott 27*, Ferguson 43*, 20 overs); 2nd day: Western Australia (2) 15-0 (Davis 11*, Rogers 4*, 9 overs).

Man of the Match: D.S.Lehmann.
The match was scheduled for four days but completed in three. D.S.Lehmann's 167 took 185 balls in 225 minutes and included 21 fours and 4 sixes.

QUEENSLAND v SOUTH AUSTRALIA

Played at Brisbane Cricket Ground, Woolloongabba, Brisbane, November 30, December 1, 2, 2007.
Pura Cup 2007/08
South Australia won by six wickets.   (Points: Queensland 0, South Australia 6)

QUEENSLAND

1	S.R.Watson	c Elliott b Tait	0	c Adcock b Harris	15
2	N.J.Kruger	c Ferguson b Harris	11	c Ferguson b Tait	0
3	C.T.Perren	run out (Ferguson/Harris)	41	c Deitz b Tait	4
4	*J.P.Maher	b Rofe	16	lbw b Tait	1
5	J.R.Hopes	c Deitz b Tait	59	(6) c sub (D.J.Harris) b Tait	6
6	C.P.Simpson	c Deitz b Tait	89	(7) b Harris	16
7	A.A.Noffke	c Tait b Adcock	37	(8) b Tait	60
8	†C.D.Hartley	c Adcock b Gillespie	1	(9) lbw b Tait	5
9	M.G.Johnson	b Adcock	6	(10) c Deitz b Rofe	13
10	D.J.Doran	b Gillespie	15	(5) c sub (D.J.Cullen) b Tait	4
11	M.S.Kasprowicz	not out	17	not out	2
	Extras	b 5, lb 5, w 1, nb 5	16	b 4, lb 6, w 1	11
			308		**137**

FoW (1): 1-0 (1), 2-39 (2), 3-71 (3), 4-96 (4), 5-214 (5), 6-237 (6), 7-246 (8), 8-268 (9), 9-279 (7), 10-308 (10)
FoW (2): 1-7 (2), 2-19 (1), 3-20 (4), 4-24 (5), 5-25 (3), 6-34 (6), 7-83 (7), 8-100 (9), 9-128 (10), 10-137 (8)

SOUTH AUSTRALIA

1	M.T.G.Elliott	c Hartley b Noffke	78	(2) c Watson b Noffke	4
2	S.A.Deitz	c Hartley b Noffke	58	(1) c Watson b Johnson	10
3	C.J.Ferguson	c Perren b Johnson	20	c Perren b Johnson	1
4	*N.T.Adcock	c Perren b Noffke	10	not out	49
5	A.H.Delmont	c Kruger b Kasprowicz	64	c Kruger b Johnson	4
6	†G.A.Manou	c and b Doran	43	not out	5
7	R.J.Harris	c Simpson b Doran	6		
8	M.J.Cosgrove	c Hopes b Johnson	54		
9	J.N.Gillespie	c Maher b Kasprowicz	13		
10	S.W.Tait	c Watson b Noffke	0		
11	P.C.Rofe	not out	0		
	Extras	lb 15, w 1, nb 4	20	b 4, lb 3	7
			366	**(4 wickets)**	**80**

FoW (1): 1-141 (1), 2-154 (2), 3-176 (3), 4-184 (4), 5-242 (6), 6-248 (7), 7-336 (8), 8-361 (5), 9-366 (9), 10-366 (10)
FoW (2): 1-10 (2), 2-11 (3), 3-30 (1), 4-42 (5)

South Australia Bowling

	O	M	R	W		O	M	R	W	
Tait	19	4	69	3	2nb	16.1	5	29	7	
Gillespie	20.3	4	54	2	1nb	13	2	36	0	
Harris	18	3	62	1	1w	14	7	19	2	
Rofe	19	4	72	1	2nb	9	0	43	1	1w
Cosgrove	1	0	15	0						
Adcock	4	0	26	2						

Queensland Bowling

	O	M	R	W		O	M	R	W	
Johnson	26	2	127	2	1w	10	5	33	3	
Noffke	27.2	5	73	4	1nb	6	1	15	1	
Hopes	15	6	29	0						
Kasprowicz	16	4	78	2	3nb	(3) 3.1	0	25	0	
Doran	8	0	44	2						

Umpires: D.L.Orchard and J.D.Ward. Referee: G.N.Williams.   Toss: South Australia

Close of Play: 1st day: South Australia (1) 33-0 (Elliott 17*, Deitz 16*, 10 overs); 2nd day: Queensland (2) 24-4 (Perren 4*, 7 overs).

Man of the Match: S.W.Tait.

The match was scheduled for four days but completed in three.

VICTORIA v NEW SOUTH WALES

Played at Melbourne Cricket Ground, November 30, December 1, 2, 3, 2007.
Pura Cup 2007/08
Match drawn.　(Points: Victoria 2, New South Wales 0)

NEW SOUTH WALES

#	Batsman	1st innings	R	2nd innings	R
1	G.J.Mail	lbw b Denton	43	(2) c Hussey b McGain	125
2	P.J.Hughes	c Hodge b Nannes	0	(1) c Hodge b McGain	51
3	P.J.Forrest	c Wade b Denton	0	run out	2
4	*S.M.Katich	c McDonald b Nannes	141	c Wade b McGain	10
5	D.J.Thornely	lbw b Denton	0	not out	76
6	†B.J.Haddin	c Hodge b McGain	43	b Denton	11
7	B.Casson	b Denton	18	(9) not out	6
8	M.J.Nicholson	b Nannes	0	(7) c Quiney b McGain	20
9	N.W.Bracken	not out	0		
10	S.R.Clark	b Nannes	0	(8) b McGain	6
11	D.E.Bollinger	not out	0		
	Extras	lb 6, nb 2	8	b 8, lb 6, w 1, nb 1	16
		(9 wickets, declared)	253	(7 wickets, declared)	323

FoW (1): 1-0 (2), 2-1 (3), 3-102 (1), 4-102 (5), 5-194 (6), 6-240 (7), 7-245 (8), 8-252 (4), 9-252 (10)
FoW (2): 1-101 (1), 2-111 (3), 3-145 (4), 4-235 (2), 5-254 (6), 6-281 (7), 7-301 (8)

VICTORIA

#	Batsman	1st innings	R	2nd innings	R
1	R.J.Quiney	c Haddin b Bollinger	8	(2) not out	52
2	N.Jewell	lbw b Bracken	25	(1) c Mail b Casson	49
3	*B.J.Hodge	c Haddin b Bracken	32	lbw b Nicholson	4
4	D.J.Hussey	c Casson b Mail	95		
5	A.B.McDonald	b Bracken	6		
6	M.Klinger	b Thornely	21		
7	†M.S.Wade	c Haddin b Clark	8		
8	S.M.Harwood	c Katich b Bracken	17		
9	G.J.Denton	not out	4		
10	B.E.McGain	not out	19		
11	D.P.Nannes				
	Extras	b 5, lb 2, nb 14	21	b 8, lb 2, nb 2	12
		(8 wickets, declared)	256	(2 wickets)	117

FoW (1): 1-19 (1), 2-57 (2), 3-106 (3), 4-124 (5), 5-204 (4), 6-204 (6), 7-227 (7), 8-233 (8)
FoW (2): 1-96 (1), 2-117 (3)

Victoria Bowling	O	M	R	W			O	M	R	W	
Denton	17	3	54	4		(3)	14	4	38	1	
Nannes	15	3	49	4	1nb		14	3	57	0	
Harwood	20	7	38	0	1nb	(1)	22	5	80	0	1nb
McGain	15	2	59	1			41	12	112	5	
Quiney	15	4	39	0			10	2	19	0	
Hussey	2	1	5	0							
Hodge	2	1	3	0							
Jewell						(6)	2	0	3	0	1w

New South Wales Bowling	O	M	R	W			O	M	R	W	
Clark	25	4	75	1	7nb		11	1	29	0	
Bollinger	16	3	60	1	7nb		8	0	26	0	2nb
Bracken	25	12	40	4			7	3	14	0	
Nicholson	15	2	42	0		(6)	3	0	8	1	
Casson	3	0	13	0		(4)	10	1	28	1	
Mail	7.4	3	12	1							
Thornely	5	2	7	1		(5)	3	2	2	0	

Umpires: R.L.Parry and A.P.Ward.　Referee: M.M.Smith.　　　　　Toss: Victoria

Close of Play: 1st day: Victoria (1) 19-1 (Jewell 2*, 7.1 overs); 2nd day: New South Wales (2) 20-0 (Hughes 16*, Mail 3*, 3 overs); 3rd day: New South Wales (2) 281-6 (Thornely 48*, 98.1 overs).
Man of the Match: S.M.Katich.
S.M.Katich's 141 took 239 balls in 326 minutes and included 17 fours. G.J.Mail's 125 took 276 balls in 341 minutes and included 8 fours.

TASMANIA v WESTERN AUSTRALIA

Played at Bellerive Oval, Hobart, December 3, 4, 5, 6, 2007.
Pura Cup 2007/08
Match drawn.   (Points: Tasmania 0, Western Australia 2)

WESTERN AUSTRALIA

1	C.J.L.Rogers	c Clingeleffer b Butterworth	123	(2) c Clingeleffer b Hilfenhaus	87
2	J.L.Langer	c Geeves b Hilfenhaus	0	(1) c Di Venuto b Drew	121
3	S.E.Marsh	c and b Marsh	17	not out	66
4	M.E.K.Hussey	run out (Di Venuto)	7	not out	59
5	*A.C.Voges	lbw b Drew	180		
6	†A.C.Gilchrist	lbw b Drew	86		
7	G.B.Hogg	c Di Venuto b Drew	4		
8	D.J.Wates	not out	33		
9	S.J.Magoffin	c Butterworth b Geeves	45		
10	M.W.H.Inness	not out	0		
11	B.M.Edmondson				
	Extras	b 3, lb 10, w 2, nb 1	16	b 2, lb 10, w 7, nb 1	20
		(8 wickets, declared)	511	(2 wickets, declared)	353

FoW (1): 1-1 (2), 2-40 (3), 3-57 (4), 4-225 (1), 5-386 (6), 6-402 (7), 7-435 (5), 8-511 (9)
FoW (2): 1-208 (1), 2-218 (2)

TASMANIA

1	M.J.Di Venuto	c Hussey b Wates	61	(2) not out	50
2	M.G.Dighton	c Voges b Magoffin	12	(1) c Gilchrist b Wates	9
3	T.R.Birt	c Gilchrist b Magoffin	0	not out	13
4	D.J.Anderson	c sub (S.M.Ervine) b Inness	39		
5	G.J.Bailey	c Langer b Magoffin	68		
6	*D.J.Marsh	not out	117		
7	L.R.Butterworth	c Gilchrist b Magoffin	0		
8	†S.G.Clingeleffer	b Wates	15		
9	B.Geeves	c Gilchrist b Magoffin	14		
10	B.G.Drew	lbw b Voges	9		
11	B.W.Hilfenhaus	c Rogers b Inness	0		
	Extras	b 2, lb 3, nb 3	8	b 3	3
			343	(1 wicket)	75

FoW (1): 1-17 (2), 2-21 (3), 3-101 (1), 4-127 (4), 5-237 (5), 6-241 (7), 7-267 (8), 8-293 (9), 9-342 (10), 10-343 (11)
FoW (2): 1-44 (1)

Tasmania Bowling	O	M	R	W			O	M	R	W	
Hilfenhaus	31	5	138	1			18	1	61	1	
Geeves	24.2	5	101	1			23	3	64	0	1w
Drew	27	4	94	3	1w		22	2	98	1	
Marsh	25	6	60	1							
Butterworth	23	0	105	1	1w,1nb	(4)	14	2	48	0	6w,1nb
Dighton						(5)	4	0	19	0	
Birt						(6)	3	1	18	0	
Bailey						(7)	4	0	19	0	
Anderson						(8)	6	1	14	0	

Western Australia Bowling	O	M	R	W			O	M	R	W	
Inness	25.5	4	72	2			6	2	13	0	
Magoffin	26	12	53	5	1nb						
Edmondson	4	2	11	0	1nb						
Wates	21	2	76	2	1nb	(2)	7	1	39	1	
Hogg	32	1	95	0							
Voges	6	0	9	1		(3)	5	2	7	0	
Hussey	3	0	22	0		(4)	2	0	11	0	
Marsh						(5)	2	0	2	0	

Umpires: S.D.Fry and B.N.J.Oxenford. Referee: R.T.Widows.   Toss: Tasmania
Close of Play: 1st day: Western Australia (1) 245-4 (Voges 80*, Gilchrist 11*, 73.4 overs); 2nd day: Tasmania (1) 147-4 (Bailey 27*, Marsh 3*, 53 overs); 3rd day: Western Australia (2) 146-0 (Langer 86*, Rogers 54*, 37 overs).
C.J.L.Rogers's 123 took 199 balls in 260 minutes and included 14 fours and 1 six. A.C.Voges's 180 took 260 balls in 329 minutes and included 25 fours and 1 six. D.J.Marsh's 117 took 193 balls in 276 minutes and included 10 fours and 1 six. J.L.Langer's 121 took 144 balls in 197 minutes and included 16 fours.

TASMANIA v VICTORIA

Played at Bellerive Oval, Hobart, December 10, 11, 12, 2007.
Pura Cup 2007/08
Victoria won by eight wickets. (Points: Tasmania 0, Victoria 6)

TASMANIA

1	M.J.Di Venuto	b Harwood	4	(2) c Wade b Nannes		6
2	M.G.Dighton	c Klinger b Siddle	19	(1) b Nannes		11
3	T.R.Birt	b Siddle	11	c McDonald b Siddle		60
4	*D.J.Marsh	c Wade b Nannes	12	c Wade b Siddle		36
5	G.J.Bailey	b Nannes	40	c Hussey b Siddle		4
6	L.R.Butterworth	c Wade b Harwood	15	run out		1
7	†T.D.Paine	c Klinger b Harwood	0	c Wade b Nannes		62
8	J.J.Krejza	lbw b McDonald	15	c Klinger b Siddle		49
9	B.Geeves	not out	16	not out		26
10	C.J.Duval	c Wade b Harwood	27	c Wade b Siddle		6
11	B.W.Hilfenhaus	c Wade b Siddle	0	st Wade b McGain		6
	Extras	b 1, lb 5, nb 3	9	b 2, lb 8		10
			168			**277**

FoW (1): 1-4 (1), 2-29 (2), 3-44 (3), 4-54 (4), 5-85 (6), 6-85 (7), 7-121 (8), 8-121 (5), 9-157 (10), 10-168 (11)
FoW (2): 1-18 (2), 2-23 (1), 3-118 (3), 4-121 (4), 5-122 (6), 6-123 (5), 7-239 (8), 8-239 (7), 9-260 (10), 10-277 (11)

VICTORIA

1	R.J.Quiney	lbw b Geeves	55	(2) b Hilfenhaus		0
2	N.Jewell	lbw b Krejza	42	(1) c Krejza b Hilfenhaus		2
3	M.Klinger	c Marsh b Hilfenhaus	60	not out		11
4	*D.J.Hussey	c Birt b Hilfenhaus	103	not out		31
5	A.B.McDonald	c Duval b Krejza	57			
6	A.C.Blizzard	c Bailey b Marsh	30			
7	†M.S.Wade	c Marsh b Krejza	16			
8	S.M.Harwood	c Paine b Duval	9			
9	P.M.Siddle	c Duval b Geeves	3			
10	B.E.McGain	not out	3			
11	D.P.Nannes	lbw b Geeves	0			
	Extras	lb 8, w 2, nb 11	21	b 1, nb 2		3
			399	(2 wickets)		**47**

FoW (1): 1-100 (2), 2-114 (1), 3-275 (3), 4-276 (4), 5-337 (6), 6-376 (7), 7-388 (8), 8-392 (5), 9-399 (9), 10-399 (11)
FoW (2): 1-1 (2), 2-2 (1)

Victoria Bowling

	O	M	R	W		O	M	R	W	
Harwood	18	7	53	4	1nb	13	5	35	0	
Nannes	14	2	45	2		23	4	84	3	
Siddle	14.4	3	33	3		23	8	61	5	
McDonald	9	0	31	1	2nb	13	4	39	0	
McGain					(5)	20.5	5	46	1	
Hussey					(6)	2	1	2	0	

Tasmania Bowling

	O	M	R	W		O	M	R	W	
Hilfenhaus	33	6	97	2	1nb	4.2	0	31	2	1nb
Geeves	25.1	6	73	3	5nb	4	0	15	0	1nb
Duval	26	4	91	1	1w,4nb					
Butterworth	10	2	46	0	1w,1nb					
Krejza	24	4	82	3						
Marsh	2	0	2	1						

Umpires: J.K.Brookes and T.P.Laycock.   Referee: R.T.Widows.   Toss: Victoria

Close of Play: 1st day: Victoria (1) 111-1 (Quiney 55*, Klinger 4*, 40 overs); 2nd day: Tasmania (2) 10-0 (Dighton 5*, Di Venuto 2*, 1.3 overs).

Man of the Match: D.J.Hussey.
The match was scheduled for four days but completed in three. D.J.Hussey's 103 took 115 balls in 159 minutes and included 15 fours and 1 six.

QUEENSLAND v NEW SOUTH WALES

Played at Brisbane Cricket Ground, Woolloongabba, Brisbane, December 14, 15, 16, 17, 2007.
Pura Cup 2007/08
New South Wales won by 260 runs.　　**(Points: Queensland 0, New South Wales 6)**

NEW SOUTH WALES

1	P.A.Jaques	c Watson b Noffke	38	c Watson b Noffke	63
2	G.J.Mail	c Hartley b Noffke	9	lbw b Swan	7
3	P.J.Forrest	c Hartley b Watson	12	c Hartley b Watson	18
4	*S.M.Katich	c Hartley b Noffke	86	c sub (G.J.Sullivan) b Doran	54
5	D.J.Thornely	c Hartley b Noffke	15	b Noffke	2
6	P.J.Hughes	c Hartley b Watson	53	(7) not out	18
7	†D.L.R.Smith	c Watson b Kasprowicz	42	(6) c Maher b Nye	34
8	G.M.Lambert	c sub (S.A.Brant) b Noffke	86		
9	M.J.Nicholson	c Hartley b Swan	80	(8) c Swan b Doran	4
10	S.R.Clark	c Hartley b Doran	2		
11	D.E.Bollinger	not out	0		
	Extras	lb 7, w 7, nb 1	15	b 4, lb 2, w 1, nb 2	9
			438	**(7 wickets, declared)**	**209**

FoW (1): 1-19 (2), 2-52 (3), 3-74 (1), 4-124 (5), 5-204 (4), 6-225 (6), 7-281 (7), 8-421 (9), 9-434 (10), 10-438 (8)
FoW (2): 1-29 (2), 2-85 (3), 3-109 (1), 4-117 (5), 5-171 (6), 6-203 (4), 7-209 (8)

QUEENSLAND

1	R.A.Broad	c Smith b Bollinger	40	c Hughes b Nicholson	24
2	S.R.Watson	c Katich b Bollinger	13	c Katich b Bollinger	0
3	C.T.Perren	lbw b Clark	2	c Smith b Lambert	31
4	*J.P.Maher	c Lambert b Nicholson	12	b Bollinger	12
5	A.J.Nye	b Bollinger	61	c Smith b Bollinger	9
6	A.A.Noffke	c Clark b Lambert	51	c Forrest b Lambert	8
7	†C.D.Hartley	not out	19	c Smith b Clark	23
8	D.J.Doran	c Smith b Bollinger	6	c Smith b Nicholson	15
9	C.P.Simpson	c Forrest b Clark	0	not out	0
10	C.R.Swan	b Nicholson	6	b Thornely	9
11	M.S.Kasprowicz	c Clark b Thornely	8	c Smith b Nicholson	1
	Extras	b 2, lb 4, nb 12	18	b 4, lb 12, w 1, nb 2	19
			236		**151**

FoW (1): 1-15 (2), 2-25 (3), 3-47 (4), 4-94 (1), 5-192 (5), 6-198 (6), 7-216 (8), 8-217 (9), 9-227 (10), 10-236 (11)
FoW (2): 1-4 (2), 2-64 (1), 3-79 (3), 4-79 (4), 5-98 (5), 6-102 (6), 7-140 (7), 8-140 (8), 9-150 (10), 10-151 (11)

Queensland Bowling

	O	M	R	W			O	M	R	W	
Noffke	32.5	5	115	5			11	2	38	2	
Swan	30	12	92	1	1w		7	2	14	1	1w
Kasprowicz	25	4	81	1	5w,1nb		10	0	28	0	2nb
Watson	22	4	74	2	1w	(5)	7	1	43	1	
Simpson	3	0	9	0							
Doran	11	0	60	1		(4)	10.2	0	58	2	
Nye						(6)	4	0	22	1	

New South Wales Bowling

	O	M	R	W			O	M	R	W	
Clark	21	8	44	2			13	6	18	1	
Bollinger	19	6	55	4	7nb		12	5	25	3	
Lambert	9	3	38	1	1nb	(5)	13	4	56	2	1w,2nb
Nicholson	13	1	46	2			8.5	3	25	3	
Mail	6	3	12	0	3nb						
Thornely	9.4	2	35	1	1nb	(3)	6	3	11	1	

Umpires: I.H.Lock and P.R.Reiffel.　Referee: G.N.Williams.　　　　Toss: Queensland

Close of Play: 1st day: New South Wales (1) 319-7 (Lambert 33*, Nicholson 23*, 96 overs); 2nd day: Queensland (1) 210-6 (Hartley 13*, Doran 2*, 66 overs); 3rd day: Queensland (2) 79-3 (Maher 12*, 27.1 overs).

Man of the Match: M.J.Nicholson.

WESTERN AUSTRALIA v SOUTH AUSTRALIA

Played at Western Australia Cricket Association Ground, Perth, December 14, 15, 16, 2007.
Pura Cup 2007/08
Western Australia won by seven wickets.   (Points: Western Australia 6, South Australia 0)

SOUTH AUSTRALIA

1	M.T.G.Elliott	c Rogers b Inness	26	(2) b Inness	6
2	S.A.Deitz	c Langer b Magoffin	1	(1) run out	26
3	M.J.Cosgrove	lbw b Inness	23	c Pomersbach b Dorey	55
4	C.J.Ferguson	b Dorey	15	c Doropoulos b Inness	56
5	*N.T.Adcock	lbw b Dorey	0	b Dorey	21
6	A.H.Delmont	c Ronchi b Magoffin	7	c Marsh b Dorey	7
7	†G.A.Manou	c Ronchi b Inness	2	c Inness b Magoffin	5
8	R.J.Harris	b Dorey	12	c Voges b Magoffin	15
9	J.N.Gillespie	not out	51	c Voges b Dorey	0
10	D.J.Cullen	b Inness	33	c Ronchi b Dorey	8
11	P.C.Rofe	c Pomersbach b Inness	4	not out	0
	Extras	lb 10	10	lb 9	9
			184		**208**

FoW (1): 1-11 (2), 2-27 (1), 3-74 (4), 4-74 (3), 5-74 (5), 6-83 (6), 7-83 (7), 8-111 (8), 9-174 (10), 10-184 (11)
FoW (2): 1-28 (2), 2-45 (1), 3-127 (3), 4-163 (4), 5-172 (5), 6-181 (6), 7-185 (7), 8-198 (9), 9-208 (10), 10-208 (8)

WESTERN AUSTRALIA

1	J.L.Langer	b Gillespie	109	c Manou b Harris	6
2	C.J.L.Rogers	c Adcock b Harris	51	b Gillespie	6
3	S.E.Marsh	b Rofe	10	not out	23
4	*A.C.Voges	c Adcock b Harris	5	b Gillespie	4
5	L.A.Pomersbach	c Cosgrove b Rofe	75	not out	18
6	T.P.Doropoulos	c Manou b Harris	1		
7	†L.Ronchi	c Manou b Gillespie	62		
8	A.K.Heal	c Cosgrove b Rofe	7		
9	B.R.Dorey	c Manou b Harris	1		
10	S.J.Magoffin	c Elliott b Gillespie	1		
11	M.W.H.Inness	not out	3		
	Extras	b 2, lb 3, w 2	7	lb 4	4
			332	(3 wickets)	**61**

FoW (1): 1-142 (2), 2-167 (1), 3-171 (3), 4-197 (4), 5-215 (6), 6-304 (5), 7-322 (8), 8-326 (7), 9-328 (9), 10-332 (10)
FoW (2): 1-8 (1), 2-12 (2), 3-24 (4)

Western Australia Bowling

	O	M	R	W		O	M	R	W
Magoffin	17	10	30	2		20.2	6	56	2
Inness	17.4	5	59	5		18	7	61	2
Dorey	19	6	53	3		25	6	82	5
Heal	6	0	20	0					
Doropoulos	4	1	12	0					

South Australia Bowling

	O	M	R	W		O	M	R	W	
Harris	28	10	77	4	1w	8	1	20	1	
Gillespie	23	3	85	3	1w	8	2	27	2	
Rofe	21	1	95	3		4	1	10	0	
Cullen	15	0	70	0						

Umpires: P.D.Parker and R.J.Tucker. Referee: R.J.Evans.   Toss: South Australia

Close of Play: 1st day: Western Australia (1) 103-0 (Langer 76*, Rogers 27*, 27 overs); 2nd day: South Australia (2) 53-2 (Cosgrove 15*, Ferguson 1*, 16 overs).

Man of the Match: J.L.Langer.

The match was scheduled for four days but completed in three. J.L.Langer's 109 took 157 balls in 202 minutes and included 14 fours.

VICTORIA v INDIANS

Played at St Kilda Cricket Ground, Melbourne, December 20, 21, 22, 2007.
India in Australia 2007/08
Match drawn.

INDIANS

1	W.Jaffer	c Finch b Wise	0
2	R.S.Dravid	not out	38
3	V.V.S.Laxman	c Wade b Wise	1
4	S.R.Tendulkar	b Wise	19
5	S.C.Ganguly	c Blizzard b Wise	59
6	Yuvraj Singh	not out	6
7	I.K.Pathan		
8	*†M.S.Dhoni		
9	I.Sharma		
10	R.P.Singh		
11	Pankaj Singh		
	Extras	lb 1, nb 9	10
		(4 wickets)	133

FoW (1): 1-3 (1), 2-10 (3), 3-38 (4), 4-121 (5)

VICTORIA

1	N.Jewell
2	R.J.Quiney
3	A.C.Blizzard
4	*D.J.Hussey
5	A.J.Finch
6	A.B.McDonald
7	J.W.Hastings
8	†M.S.Wade
9	B.E.McGain
10	P.M.Siddle
11	A.B.Wise

Victoria Bowling

	O	M	R	W	
Siddle	15	1	43	0	6nb
Wise	15	4	37	4	3nb
McDonald	6	1	11	0	
Hastings	6	2	17	0	
McGain	6	2	24	0	

Umpires: P.R.Reiffel and J.D.Ward.   Toss: Indians

Close of Play: 1st day: Indians (1) 110-3 (Dravid 33*, Ganguly 51*, 38 overs); 2nd day: Indians (1) 133-4 (Dravid 38*, Yuvraj Singh 6*, 48 overs).

There was no play on the final day.

AUSTRALIA v INDIA

Played at Melbourne Cricket Ground, December 26, 27, 28, 29, 2007.
India in Australia 2007/08 - 1st Test
Australia won by 337 runs.

AUSTRALIA

1	P.A.Jaques	st Dhoni b Kumble	66	c and b Kumble		51
2	M.L.Hayden	c Dravid b Khan	124	c Ganguly b Harbhajan Singh		47
3	*R.T.Ponting	b Khan	4	c Dravid b Harbhajan Singh		3
4	M.E.K.Hussey	lbw b Kumble	2	c Tendulkar b R.P.Singh		36
5	M.J.Clarke	c Laxman b R.P.Singh	20	st Dhoni b Kumble		73
6	A.Symonds	c sub (K.D.Karthik) b Kumble	35	lbw b Khan		44
7	†A.C.Gilchrist	c Tendulkar b Kumble	23	c R.P.Singh b Harbhajan Singh		35
8	G.B.Hogg	c Dravid b Khan	17	not out		35
9	B.Lee	lbw b Kumble	0	not out		11
10	M.G.Johnson	not out	15			
11	S.R.Clark	c Harbhajan Singh b Khan	21			
	Extras	lb 5, w 2, nb 9	16	lb 3, nb 13		16
			343	(7 wickets, declared)		**351**

FoW (1): 1-135 (1), 2-162 (3), 3-165 (4), 4-225 (5), 5-241 (2), 6-281 (6), 7-288 (7), 8-294 (9), 9-312 (8), 10-343 (11)
FoW (2): 1-83 (2), 2-89 (3), 3-139 (1), 4-161 (4), 5-243 (6), 6-288 (5), 7-316 (7)

INDIA

1	W.Jaffer	c Gilchrist b Lee	4	(2) c Gilchrist b Lee	15
2	R.S.Dravid	lbw b Clark	5	(1) lbw b Symonds	16
3	V.V.S.Laxman	c Ponting b Lee	26	c Clarke b Clark	42
4	S.R.Tendulkar	b Clark	62	c Gilchrist b Lee	15
5	S.C.Ganguly	b Hogg	43	c Ponting b Hogg	40
6	Yuvraj Singh	c Gilchrist b Clark	0	lbw b Hogg	5
7	†M.S.Dhoni	lbw b Clark	0	c Gilchrist b Johnson	11
8	*A.Kumble	c Gilchrist b Lee	27	c Gilchrist b Johnson	8
9	Harbhajan Singh	c Clarke b Hogg	2	run out	0
10	Z.Khan	c Gilchrist b Lee	11	not out	0
11	R.P.Singh	not out	2	b Johnson	2
	Extras	b 4, lb 3, nb 7	14	b 1, nb 6	7
			196		**161**

FoW (1): 1-4 (1), 2-31 (2), 3-55 (3), 4-120 (4), 5-122 (6), 6-122 (7), 7-166 (5), 8-173 (9), 9-193 (8), 10-196 (10)
FoW (2): 1-26 (2), 2-54 (1), 3-77 (4), 4-118 (3), 5-125 (6), 6-144 (7), 7-157 (8), 8-157 (9), 9-157 (5), 10-161 (11)

India Bowling

	O	M	R	W		O	M	R	W	
Khan	23.4	1	94	4	1w,8nb	20	2	93	1	12nb
R.P.Singh	20	3	82	1	1w	16	1	50	1	
Harbhajan Singh	20	3	61	0	(4)	26	0	101	3	
Ganguly	3	1	15	0	1nb					
Kumble	25	4	84	5	(3)	25	2	102	2	
Tendulkar	1	0	2	0	(5)	1	0	2	0	

Australia Bowling

	O	M	R	W		O	M	R	W	
Lee	19.5	6	46	4	6nb	14	3	43	2	4nb
Johnson	13	5	25	0	1nb	15	6	21	3	2nb
Symonds	3	1	8	0	(5)	13	5	25	1	
Clark	15	4	28	4	(3)	15	9	20	1	
Hogg	21	3	82	2	(4)	17	3	51	2	

Umpires: M.R.Benson and B.F.Bowden. Third umpire: S.J.Davis. Referee: M.J.Procter.   Toss: Australia

Close of Play: 1st day: Australia (1) 337-9 (Johnson 10*, Clark 21*, 90 overs); 2nd day: Australia (2) 32-0 (Jaques 10*, Hayden 22*, 8 overs); 3rd day: India (2) 6-0 (Dravid 3*, Jaffer 2*, 8 overs).

Man of the Match: M.L.Hayden.

The match was scheduled for five days but completed in four. M.L.Hayden's 124 took 183 balls in 268 minutes and included 9 fours.

AUSTRALIA v INDIA

Played at Sydney Cricket Ground, January 2, 3, 4, 5, 6, 2008.
India in Australia 2007/08 - 2nd Test
Australia won by 122 runs.

AUSTRALIA

1	P.A.Jaques	c Dhoni b R.P.Singh	0	c Yuvraj Singh b Kumble	42
2	M.L.Hayden	c Tendulkar b R.P.Singh	13	c Jaffer b Kumble	123
3	*R.T.Ponting	lbw b Harbhajan Singh	55	c Laxman b Harbhajan Singh	1
4	M.E.K.Hussey	c Tendulkar b R.P.Singh	41	not out	145
5	M.J.Clarke	lbw b Harbhajan Singh	1	c Dravid b Kumble	0
6	A.Symonds	not out	162	c Dhoni b R.P.Singh	61
7	†A.C.Gilchrist	c Tendulkar b R.P.Singh	7	c Yuvraj Singh b Kumble	1
8	G.B.Hogg	c Dravid b Kumble	79	c Dravid b Harbhajan Singh	1
9	B.Lee	lbw b Kumble	59	not out	4
10	M.G.Johnson	c Ganguly b Kumble	28		
11	S.R.Clark	lbw b Kumble	0		
	Extras	b 2, lb 9, w 4, nb 3	18	b 3, lb 8, w 3, nb 9	23
			463	**(7 wickets, declared)**	**401**

FoW (1): 1-0 (1), 2-27 (2), 3-119 (3), 4-119 (4), 5-121 (5), 6-134 (7), 7-307 (8), 8-421 (9), 9-461 (10), 10-463 (11)
FoW (2): 1-85 (1), 2-90 (3), 3-250 (2), 4-250 (5), 5-378 (6), 6-393 (7), 7-395 (8)

INDIA

1	W.Jaffer	b Lee	3	(2) c Clarke b Lee	0
2	R.S.Dravid	c Hayden b Johnson	53	(1) c Gilchrist b Symonds	38
3	V.V.S.Laxman	c Hussey b Hogg	109	lbw b Clark	20
4	S.R.Tendulkar	not out	154	b Clark	12
5	S.C.Ganguly	c Hussey b Hogg	67	c Clarke b Lee	51
6	Yuvraj Singh	lbw b Lee	12	c Gilchrist b Symonds	0
7	†M.S.Dhoni	c Gilchrist b Lee	2	lbw b Symonds	35
8	*A.Kumble	c Gilchrist b Lee	2	not out	45
9	Harbhajan Singh	c Hussey b Johnson	63	c Hussey b Clarke	7
10	R.P.Singh	c Gilchrist b Clark	13	lbw b Clarke	0
11	I.Sharma	c and b Lee	23	c Hussey b Clarke	0
	Extras	b 4, lb 13, w 6, nb 8	31	nb 2	2
			532		**210**

FoW (1): 1-8 (1), 2-183 (2), 3-185 (3), 4-293 (5), 5-321 (6), 6-330 (7), 7-345 (8), 8-474 (9), 9-501 (10), 10-532 (11)
FoW (2): 1-3 (2), 2-34 (3), 3-54 (4), 4-115 (1), 5-115 (6), 6-137 (5), 7-185 (7), 8-210 (9), 9-210 (10), 10-210 (11)

India Bowling	O	M	R	W		O	M	R	W	
R.P.Singh	26	3	124	4	1w,1nb	16	2	74	1	2w
Sharma	23	3	87	0	3w,2nb	14	2	59	0	1w,2nb
Ganguly	6	1	13	0						
Harbhajan Singh	27	3	108	2	(3)	33	6	92	2	
Kumble	25.3	0	106	4	(4)	40	3	148	4	7nb
Tendulkar	5	0	14	0	(5)	2	0	6	0	
Yuvraj Singh					(6)	2	0	11	0	

Australia Bowling	O	M	R	W		O	M	R	W	
Lee	32.2	5	119	5	7nb	13	3	34	2	1nb
Johnson	37	2	148	2	5w,1nb	11	4	33	0	1nb
Clark	25	3	80	1	1w	12	4	32	2	
Symonds	7	1	19	0	(5)	19	5	51	3	
Hogg	30	2	121	2	(4)	14	2	55	0	
Clarke	7	1	28	0		1.5	0	5	3	

Umpires: M.R.Benson and S.A.Bucknor. Third umpire: B.N.J.Oxenford. Referee: M.J.Procter. Toss: Australia
Close of Play: 1st day: Australia (1) 376-7 (Symonds 137*, Lee 31*, 89 overs); 2nd day: India (1) 216-3 (Tendulkar 9*, Ganguly 21*, 62 overs); 3rd day: Australia (2) 13-0 (Jaques 8*, Hayden 5*, 5 overs); 4th day: Australia (2) 282-4 (Hussey 87*, Symonds 14*, 83 overs).
Man of the Match: A.Symonds.
A.Symonds's 162 took 226 balls in 344 minutes and included 18 fours and 2 sixes. V.V.S.Laxman's 109 took 142 balls in 218 minutes and included 18 fours. S.R.Tendulkar's 154 took 243 balls in 404 minutes and included 14 fours and 1 six. M.L.Hayden's 123 took 196 balls in 291 minutes and included 12 fours. M.E.K.Hussey's 145 took 259 balls in 355 minutes and included 16 fours.

AUSTRALIA v INDIA

Played at Western Australia Cricket Association Ground, Perth, January 16, 17, 18, 19, 2008.
India in Australia 2007/08 - 3rd Test
India won by 72 runs.

INDIA

1	W.Jaffer	c Gilchrist b Lee	16	c Hussey b Clark	11
2	V.Sehwag	c Gilchrist b Johnson	29	b Clark	43
3	R.S.Dravid	c Ponting b Symonds	93	(4) c Gilchrist b Lee	3
4	S.R.Tendulkar	lbw b Lee	71	(5) lbw b Lee	13
5	S.C.Ganguly	c Hussey b Johnson	9	(6) c Clarke b Johnson	0
6	V.V.S.Laxman	c Tait b Lee	27	(7) c Gilchrist b Lee	79
7	†M.S.Dhoni	lbw b Clark	19	(8) c Gilchrist b Symonds	38
8	I.K.Pathan	lbw b Johnson	28	(3) c Ponting b Clark	46
9	*A.Kumble	c Rogers b Clark	1	c Clarke b Symonds	0
10	R.P.Singh	c Hussey b Johnson	0	c Gilchrist b Clark	30
11	I.Sharma	not out	0	not out	4
	Extras	lb 19, w 9, nb 9	37	lb 14, w 5, nb 8	27
			330		**294**

FoW (1): 1-57 (2), 2-59 (1), 3-198 (4), 4-214 (5), 5-278 (3), 6-284 (6), 7-328 (7), 8-330 (8), 9-330 (9), 10-330 (10)
FoW (2): 1-45 (1), 2-79 (2), 3-82 (4), 4-116 (5), 5-125 (6), 6-160 (3), 7-235 (8), 8-235 (9), 9-286 (10), 10-294 (7)

AUSTRALIA

1	P.A.Jaques	c Laxman b Pathan	8	(2) c Jaffer b Pathan	16
2	C.J.L.Rogers	lbw b Pathan	4	(1) c Dhoni b Pathan	15
3	*R.T.Ponting	c Dravid b Sharma	20	c Dravid b Sharma	45
4	M.E.K.Hussey	c Dhoni b Singh	0	lbw b Singh	46
5	M.J.Clarke	c Dhoni b Sharma	23	st Dhoni b Kumble	81
6	A.Symonds	c Dravid b Kumble	66	lbw b Kumble	12
7	†A.C.Gilchrist	c Dhoni b Singh	55	b Sehwag	15
8	B.Lee	c Dhoni b Singh	11	c Laxman b Sehwag	0
9	M.G.Johnson	not out	6	not out	50
10	S.R.Clark	c Dhoni b Singh	0	c Dhoni b Pathan	32
11	S.W.Tait	c and b Kumble	8	b Singh	4
	Extras	b 4, lb 1, w 4, nb 2	11	lb 6, w 8, nb 10	24
			212		**340**

FoW (1): 1-12 (2), 2-13 (1), 3-14 (4), 4-43 (3), 5-61 (5), 6-163 (6), 7-192 (7), 8-195 (8), 9-195 (10), 10-212 (11)
FoW (2): 1-21 (1), 2-43 (2), 3-117 (3), 4-159 (4), 5-177 (6), 6-227 (7), 7-229 (8), 8-253 (5), 9-326 (10), 10-340 (11)

Australia Bowling

	O	M	R	W		O	M	R	W	
Lee	24	5	71	3	1w,6nb	20.4	4	54	3	1w,4nb
Johnson	28.2	7	86	4	2w	10	0	58	1	
Clark	17	4	45	2	1w	19	4	61	4	2w
Tait	13	1	59	0	1w,3nb	8	0	33	0	2w,4nb
Symonds	10	1	36	1	(6)	10	2	36	2	
Clarke	6	1	14	0	(5)	13	2	38	2	

India Bowling

	O	M	R	W		O	M	R	W	
Singh	14	2	68	4	1w	21.5	4	95	2	3w
Pathan	17	2	63	2	2w	16	2	54	3	
Sharma	7	0	34	2	1w	17	0	63	1	1w,7nb
Kumble	12	1	42	2	2nb	24	2	98	2	3nb
Sehwag					(5)	8	1	24	2	

Umpires: Asad Rauf and B.F.Bowden. Third umpire: B.N.J.Oxenford. Referee: M.J.Procter.   Toss: India

Close of Play: 1st day: India (1) 297-6 (Dhoni 8*, Pathan 8*, 84 overs); 2nd day: India (2) 52-1 (Sehwag 29*, Pathan 2*, 11 overs); 3rd day: Australia (2) 65-2 (Ponting 24*, Hussey 5*, 15 overs).

Man of the Match: I.K.Pathan.

The match was scheduled for five days but completed in four.

TASMANIA v QUEENSLAND

Played at Bellerive Oval, Hobart, January 21, 22, 23, 24, 2008.
Pura Cup 2007/08
Tasmania won by nine wickets.   (Points: Tasmania 6, Queensland 0)

TASMANIA

1	M.J.Di Venuto	lbw b Noffke	0		
2	D.G.Dawson	c Watson b Kasprowicz	0	(1) c Broad b Kasprowicz	0
3	T.R.Birt	b Watson	10	(2) not out	31
4	G.J.Bailey	c Simpson b Noffke	104	(3) not out	51
5	*D.J.Marsh	c Kasprowicz b Noffke	134		
6	L.R.Butterworth	c Hopes b Noffke	70		
7	†T.D.Paine	not out	65		
8	J.J.Krejza	c Broad b Noffke	7		
9	B.Geeves	c Hopes b Kasprowicz	16		
10	C.J.Duval	lbw b Doran	25		
11	B.W.Hilfenhaus	c Hartley b Doran	2		
	Extras	lb 8, nb 13	21	lb 3, nb 3	6
			454	**(1 wicket)**	**88**

FoW (1): 1-0 (2), 2-0 (1), 3-39 (3), 4-194 (4), 5-317 (6), 6-337 (5), 7-345 (8), 8-380 (9), 9-452 (10), 10-454 (11)
FoW (2): 1-10 (1)

QUEENSLAND

1	R.A.Broad	c Paine b Geeves	24	(2) c Di Venuto b Butterworth	35
2	G.D.Moller	b Geeves	10	(1) lbw b Butterworth	51
3	*J.P.Maher	c Paine b Duval	1	c Birt b Krejza	0
4	S.R.Watson	c Dawson b Krejza	44	run out	0
5	C.T.Perren	c Paine b Butterworth	4	lbw b Duval	71
6	C.P.Simpson	b Hilfenhaus	6	c Butterworth b Hilfenhaus	31
7	J.R.Hopes	c Butterworth b Krejza	87	c Marsh b Krejza	84
8	A.A.Noffke	lbw b Geeves	6	c Hilfenhaus b Marsh	47
9	†C.D.Hartley	lbw b Geeves	4	c Paine b Hilfenhaus	5
10	D.J.Doran	not out	6	not out	7
11	M.S.Kasprowicz	c Bailey b Geeves	1	c Paine b Krejza	1
	Extras	lb 3, nb 4	7	lb 8, nb 1	9
			200		**341**

FoW (1): 1-24 (2), 2-30 (3), 3-53 (1), 4-69 (5), 5-85 (6), 6-131 (4), 7-140 (8), 8-169 (9), 9-197 (7), 10-200 (11)
FoW (2): 1-89 (1), 2-90 (3), 3-90 (4), 4-91 (2), 5-159 (6), 6-236 (5), 7-309 (8), 8-325 (9), 9-339 (7), 10-341 (11)

Queensland Bowling

	O	M	R	W		O	M	R	W	
Noffke	30	9	79	5	3nb	6	2	10	0	
Kasprowicz	27	4	101	2	8nb	5	1	16	1	3nb
Hopes	21	8	56	0	2nb					
Watson	25	5	62	1		2.3	0	9	0	
Doran	15	0	108	2		2.3	0	12	0	
Simpson	9	0	40	0	(3)	5.3	0	38	0	

Tasmania Bowling

	O	M	R	W			O	M	R	W	
Hilfenhaus	17	5	29	1	1nb		28	8	51	2	
Geeves	23.2	4	51	5	2nb		27	6	79	0	
Krejza	19	3	66	2		(5)	31.1	5	114	3	
Duval	8	2	31	1	1nb	(3)	14	5	35	1	1nb
Butterworth	7	0	20	1		(4)	12	6	25	2	
Marsh						(6)	15	3	29	1	

Umpires: S.D.Fry and R.L.Parry. Referee: R.T.Widows.   Toss: Tasmania

Close of Play: 1st day: Tasmania (1) 333-5 (Marsh 132*, Paine 1*, 96 overs); 2nd day: Queensland (1) 154-7 (Hopes 49*, Hartley 4*, 63 overs); 3rd day: Queensland (2) 207-5 (Perren 60*, Hopes 24*, 82 overs).

Man of the Match: D.J.Marsh.
G.J.Bailey's 104 took 189 balls in 223 minutes and included 11 fours and 3 sixes. D.J.Marsh's 134 took 190 balls in 285 minutes and included 17 fours and 1 six.

VICTORIA v SOUTH AUSTRALIA

Played at St Kilda Cricket Ground, Melbourne, January 21, 22, 23, 24, 2008.
Pura Cup 2007/08
Victoria won by four wickets.　　(Points: Victoria 6, South Australia 2)

SOUTH AUSTRALIA

1	M.T.G.Elliott	c Wade b Siddle	34	(2) c Hussey b Siddle	32
2	S.A.Deitz	b Harwood	30	(1) c Wade b McDonald	26
3	M.J.Cosgrove	lbw b McDonald	32	c Wade b Siddle	37
4	C.J.Ferguson	b McDonald	11	c White b Siddle	0
5	D.T.Christian	c Hodge b McDonald	1	lbw b Siddle	55
6	*N.T.Adcock	c Hussey b Wise	20	run out	3
7	†G.A.Manou	not out	105	b McGain	9
8	M.F.Cleary	c McDonald b McGain	31	b Harwood	18
9	R.J.Harris	c Jewell b McGain	14	not out	37
10	J.N.Gillespie	lbw b Siddle	1	b Siddle	18
11	P.C.Rofe	c Hussey b McDonald	24	c Hodge b Siddle	0
	Extras	b 10, lb 6, w 1	17	b 1, lb 3, nb 5	9
			320		**244**

FoW (1): 1-50 (2), 2-102 (3), 3-102 (1), 4-103 (5), 5-122 (4), 6-152 (6), 7-201 (8), 8-237 (9), 9-255 (10), 10-320 (11)
FoW (2): 1-44 (1), 2-87 (2), 3-87 (4), 4-103 (3), 5-123 (6), 6-146 (7), 7-179 (8), 8-194 (5), 9-244 (10), 10-244 (11)

VICTORIA

1	R.J.Quiney	c Christian b Harris	2	(2) c Christian b Cleary	21
2	N.Jewell	c Manou b Gillespie	5	(1) not out	91
3	P.M.Siddle	c Manou b Harris	0	lbw b Harris	28
4	B.J.Hodge	b Christian	64	lbw b Harris	2
5	D.J.Hussey	b Rofe	27	b Cleary	53
6	*C.L.White	lbw b Cleary	32	b Cleary	0
7	A.B.McDonald	c Elliott b Cleary	139	c Deitz b Harris	36
8	†M.S.Wade	b Rofe	7	not out	13
9	S.M.Harwood	b Christian	0		
10	B.E.McGain	not out	10		
11	A.B.Wise	b Cleary	4		
	Extras	lb 4, nb 7	11	b 9, lb 9, nb 2	20
			301	**(6 wickets)**	**264**

FoW (1): 1-2 (1), 2-2 (3), 3-14 (2), 4-52 (5), 5-87 (6), 6-112 (8), 7-271 (4), 8-273 (9), 9-297 (7), 10-301 (11)
FoW (2): 1-37 (2), 2-79 (3), 3-83 (4), 4-168 (5), 5-168 (6), 6-231 (7)

Victoria Bowling

	O	M	R	W			O	M	R	W	
Harwood	19	4	84	1			14	3	35	1	1nb
Wise	18	10	20	1		(3)	12	2	40	0	1nb
McDonald	21.5	5	69	4	1w	(4)	14	3	45	1	
Siddle	19	3	71	2		(2)	20.3	3	57	6	3nb
McGain	12	1	60	2		(6)	17	4	48	1	
Quiney						(5)	3	1	15	0	

South Australia Bowling

	O	M	R	W			O	M	R	W	
Harris	17	2	61	2			19	1	65	3	
Gillespie	24	9	53	1			17	3	59	0	
Cleary	19	4	61	3	2nb		20.1	5	56	3	1nb
Rofe	16	3	55	2	2nb		19	7	37	0	1nb
Cosgrove	4	1	14	0		(6)	1	0	4	0	
Adcock	4	0	26	0							
Christian	5	1	27	2	3nb	(5)	6	2	25	0	

Umpires: P.R.Reiffel and A.P.Ward. Referee: M.M.Smith.　　Toss: Victoria
Close of Play: 1st day: Victoria (1) 9-2 (Jewell 3*, Hodge 4*, 4 overs); 2nd day: South Australia (2) 20-0 (Deitz 11*, Elliott 8*, 5 overs); 3rd day: Victoria (2) 44-1 (Jewell 17*, Siddle 5*, 16 overs).
Man of the Match: A.B.McDonald.
G.A.Manou's 105 took 161 balls in 206 minutes and included 7 fours and 4 sixes. A.B.McDonald's 139 took 183 balls in 277 minutes and included 22 fours. B.J.Hodge retired not out in the Victoria first innings having scored 4 (team score 9-2) - he returned when the score was 112-6 (called up for possible international duty overnight).

AUSTRALIA v INDIA

Played at Adelaide Oval, January 24, 25, 26, 27, 28, 2008.
India in Australia 2007/08 - 4th Test
Match drawn.

INDIA

1	V.Sehwag	c Hayden b Lee	63	c Gilchrist b Symonds	151
2	I.K.Pathan	c Gilchrist b Johnson	9	lbw b Johnson	0
3	R.S.Dravid	c Ponting b Johnson	18	retired hurt	11
4	S.R.Tendulkar	c Hogg b Lee	153	run out	13
5	S.C.Ganguly	lbw b Hogg	7	c Hussey b Johnson	18
6	V.V.S.Laxman	c Gilchrist b Lee	51	c Gilchrist b Lee	12
7	†M.S.Dhoni	c Symonds b Johnson	16	c Hayden b Lee	20
8	*A.Kumble	c Gilchrist b Johnson	87	not out	9
9	Harbhajan Singh	c Gilchrist b Symonds	63	c Ponting b Hogg	7
10	R.P.Singh	c Johnson b Clarke	0		
11	I.Sharma	not out	14	(10) not out	2
	Extras	b 8, lb 21, w 3, nb 13	45	b 9, lb 9, w 3, nb 5	26
			526	(7 wickets, declared)	269

FoW (1): 1-34 (2), 2-82 (3), 3-122 (1), 4-156 (5), 5-282 (6), 6-336 (7), 7-359 (4), 8-466 (9), 9-468 (10), 10-526 (8)
FoW (2): 1-2 (2), 2-128 (4), 3-162 (5), 4-186 (6), 5-237 (7), 6-253 (1), 7-264 (9)

AUSTRALIA

1	P.A.Jaques	b Kumble	60
2	M.L.Hayden	b Sharma	103
3	*R.T.Ponting	b Sehwag	140
4	M.E.K.Hussey	b Pathan	22
5	M.J.Clarke	c Laxman b Sharma	118
6	A.Symonds	b Sharma	30
7	†A.C.Gilchrist	c Sehwag b Pathan	14
8	G.B.Hogg	not out	16
9	B.Lee	c Dhoni b Pathan	1
10	M.G.Johnson	c Sharma b Harbhajan Singh	13
11	S.R.Clark	b Sehwag	3
	Extras	b 10, lb 12, w 10, nb 11	43
			563

FoW (1): 1-159 (1), 2-186 (2), 3-241 (4), 4-451 (3), 5-490 (5), 6-506 (7), 7-527 (6), 8-528 (9), 9-557 (10), 10-563 (11)

Australia Bowling	O	M	R	W		O	M	R	W	
Lee	36	4	101	3	6nb	27	3	74	2	3nb
Johnson	37.5	6	126	4	3w,3nb	16	1	33	2	3w,2nb
Clark	31	6	92	0		(4) 12	3	37	0	
Hogg	31	2	119	1		(5) 12	3	53	1	
Clarke	10	0	39	1		(6) 1	0	2	0	
Symonds	7	0	20	1		(3) 22	4	52	1	

India Bowling	O	M	R	W	
R.P.Singh	4	0	14	0	
Pathan	36	2	112	3	3w
Sharma	40	6	115	3	4w,8nb
Harbhajan Singh	48	5	128	1	
Kumble	30	4	109	1	2nb
Sehwag	19	2	51	2	
Tendulkar	1	0	6	0	
Ganguly	3	1	6	0	1nb

Umpires: Asad Rauf and B.F.Bowden. Third umpire: S.J.Davis. Referee: M.J.Procter. Toss: India
Close of Play: 1st day: India (1) 309-5 (Tendulkar 124*, Dhoni 6*, 86 overs); 2nd day: Australia (1) 62-0 (Jaques 21*, Hayden 36*, 21 overs); 3rd day: Australia (1) 322-3 (Ponting 79*, Clarke 37*, 111 overs); 4th day: India (2) 45-1 (Sehwag 31*, Dravid 11*, 17 overs).
Man of the Match: S.R.Tendulkar.
S.R.Tendulkar's 153 took 205 balls in 338 minutes and included 13 fours and 3 sixes. M.L.Hayden's 103 took 200 balls in 271 minutes and included 10 fours and 1 six. R.T.Ponting's 140 took 266 balls in 396 minutes and included 10 fours. M.J.Clarke's 118 took 243 balls in 315 minutes and included 8 fours. V.Sehwag's 151 took 236 balls in 354 minutes and included 11 fours and 2 sixes. R.S.Dravid retired hurt in the India second innings having scored 11 (team score 57-1).

NEW SOUTH WALES v WESTERN AUSTRALIA

Played at Sydney Cricket Ground, January 25, 26, 27, 28, 2008.
Pura Cup 2007/08
New South Wales won by nine wickets.   (Points: New South Wales 6, Western Australia 0)

WESTERN AUSTRALIA

1	C.J.L.Rogers	c Haddin b Bollinger	16	(2) lbw b Casson		9
2	L.M.Davis	lbw b Bollinger	116	(1) lbw b Bollinger		2
3	J.L.Langer	c Haddin b Bollinger	54	lbw b Bollinger		14
4	A.C.Voges	c and b Bollinger	84	c Katich b Casson		2
5	L.A.Pomersbach	b Bollinger	10	b Bracken		81
6	*M.J.North	c Haddin b Casson	32	(7) c and b Thornely		37
7	A.K.Heal	lbw b Casson	2	(6) c Casson b Bollinger		1
8	†L.Ronchi	c Hughes b Nicholson	34	b Thornely		6
9	S.J.Magoffin	c Haddin b Nicholson	2	c Haddin b Bollinger		9
10	M.W.H.Inness	lbw b Nicholson	16	not out		1
11	B.M.Edmondson	not out	0	lbw b Bollinger		0
	Extras	b 4, lb 11, w 1, nb 7	23	b 4, lb 2, nb 2		8
			389			**170**

FoW (1): 1-31 (1), 2-125 (3), 3-278 (2), 4-288 (4), 5-305 (5), 6-312 (7), 7-357 (8), 8-365 (9), 9-385 (6), 10-389 (10)
FoW (2): 1-13 (1), 2-27 (3), 3-29 (2), 4-36 (4), 5-45 (6), 6-115 (7), 7-129 (8), 8-151 (9), 9-169 (5), 10-170 (11)

NEW SOUTH WALES

1	G.J.Mail	c Pomersbach b Edmondson	18	(2) c Rogers b Magoffin		9
2	P.J.Hughes	c Ronchi b Edmondson	44	(1) not out		54
3	P.J.Forrest	c Magoffin b Heal	46	not out		14
4	*S.M.Katich	b Edmondson	189			
5	D.J.Thornely	c Ronchi b Inness	5			
6	†B.J.Haddin	c Rogers b North	13			
7	S.P.D.Smith	c Ronchi b North	33			
8	B.Casson	not out	72			
9	M.J.Nicholson	c and b Voges	8			
10	N.W.Bracken	b Edmondson	30			
11	D.E.Bollinger	c Voges b North	3			
	Extras	b 10, lb 6, nb 8	24	b 1		1
			485	**(1 wicket)**		**78**

FoW (1): 1-41 (1), 2-64 (2), 3-179 (3), 4-192 (5), 5-225 (6), 6-324 (7), 7-388 (4), 8-413 (9), 9-461 (10), 10-485 (11)
FoW (2): 1-32 (2)

New South Wales Bowling

	O	M	R	W			O	M	R	W	
Bollinger	28	9	78	5	1w,3nb		16.5	3	48	5	2nb
Bracken	25	7	68	0			14	6	18	1	
Casson	29	5	85	2		(4)	18	5	54	2	
Nicholson	19.3	5	69	3		(3)	1	1	0	0	
Smith	8	1	25	0			2	0	9	0	
Mail	7	1	28	0	4nb						
Thornely	6	3	21	0		(6)	12	3	35	2	

Western Australia Bowling

	O	M	R	W			O	M	R	W
Inness	20	4	71	1		(3)	5	1	11	0
Magoffin	28	10	64	0	2nb		5	0	22	1
Heal	32	4	111	1		(5)	2	0	15	0
Edmondson	29	6	110	4	6nb	(1)	5	1	14	0
North	24.5	3	77	3		(4)	3	0	15	0
Voges	7	0	36	1						

Umpires: R.J.Tucker and J.D.Ward. Referee: R.A.French.   Toss: Western Australia

Close of Play: 1st day: Western Australia (1) 312-6 (North 13*); 2nd day: New South Wales (1) 213-4 (Katich 82*, Haddin 8*); 3rd day: Western Australia (2) 45-4 (Pomersbach 13*, Heal 1*).
Man of the Match: D.E.Bollinger.
L.M.Davis's 116 took 239 balls in 313 minutes and included 16 fours and 1 six. S.M.Katich's 189 took 303 balls in 373 minutes and included 27 fours.

SOUTH AUSTRALIA v TASMANIA

Played at Adelaide Oval, February 8, 9, 10, 11, 2008.
Pura Cup 2007/08
Match drawn.   (Points: South Australia 0, Tasmania 2)

SOUTH AUSTRALIA

1	M.T.G.Elliott	c Birt b Geeves	13	c Paine b Geeves	27
2	D.J.Harris	c Krejza b Butterworth	120	lbw b Geeves	12
3	M.J.Cosgrove	lbw b Geeves	0	c Birt b Geeves	12
4	C.J.Ferguson	b Butterworth	35	c and b Geeves	54
5	D.T.Christian	lbw b Butterworth	26	c Marsh b Duval	47
6	S.A.Deitz	c Paine b Hilfenhaus	59	c Dawson b Krejza	8
7	*†G.A.Manou	c Di Venuto b Hilfenhaus	6	c Duval b Geeves	98
8	R.J.Harris	c Paine b Geeves	33	c Duval b Hilfenhaus	36
9	J.N.Gillespie	not out	29	c Paine b Marsh	5
10	D.J.Cullen	c Paine b Hilfenhaus	9	not out	10
11	P.C.Rofe	b Hilfenhaus	0	not out	0
	Extras	lb 6, w 3, nb 5	14	lb 7, nb 2	9
			344	**(9 wickets, declared)**	**318**

FoW (1): 1-13 (1), 2-13 (3), 3-77 (4), 4-139 (5), 5-246 (6), 6-262 (7), 7-304 (2), 8-306 (8), 9-340 (10), 10-344 (11)
FoW (2): 1-27 (2), 2-53 (3), 3-56 (1), 4-141 (5), 5-162 (6), 6-184 (4), 7-255 (8), 8-270 (9), 9-318 (7)

TASMANIA

1	M.J.Di Venuto	c Elliott b R.J.Harris	73	(2) c Cosgrove b Cullen	66
2	D.G.Dawson	c Christian b R.J.Harris	0	(1) c Manou b R.J.Harris	1
3	T.R.Birt	c Manou b R.J.Harris	48	c Christian b Cullen	14
4	G.J.Bailey	b R.J.Harris	32	lbw b Gillespie	57
5	*D.J.Marsh	b R.J.Harris	109	run out	41
6	L.R.Butterworth	c Cosgrove b Rofe	7	c Manou b Gillespie	0
7	†T.D.Paine	c Manou b R.J.Harris	57	c D.J.Harris b R.J.Harris	31
8	J.J.Krejza	c Manou b Gillespie	19	not out	7
9	B.Geeves	b R.J.Harris	0	lbw b Cullen	0
10	C.J.Duval	c Ferguson b Rofe	5	not out	0
11	B.W.Hilfenhaus	not out	17		
	Extras	b 3, lb 7, w 6	16	b 4, lb 4, w 7	15
			383	**(8 wickets)**	**232**

FoW (1): 1-7 (2), 2-119 (3), 3-134 (1), 4-168 (4), 5-196 (6), 6-329 (7), 7-360 (5), 8-360 (8), 9-362 (9), 10-383 (10)
FoW (2): 1-6 (1), 2-33 (3), 3-137 (4), 4-153 (2), 5-153 (6), 6-217 (5), 7-220 (7), 8-221 (9)

Tasmania Bowling

	O	M	R	W				O	M	R	W	
Hilfenhaus	27.2	8	80	4	1w	(2)		22	1	103	1	
Geeves	32	12	68	3	1w,4nb	(1)		24	6	79	5	2nb
Duval	12	1	41	0	1w,1nb	(4)		6	0	29	1	
Butterworth	22	5	70	3		(5)		5	1	18	0	
Krejza	17	4	61	0		(3)		15	3	53	1	
Marsh	6	3	18	0				16	8	29	1	

South Australia Bowling

	O	M	R	W				O	M	R	W	
R.J.Harris	32	7	108	7				17	4	63	2	5w
Gillespie	24	8	62	1	6w			11	2	51	2	1w
Cullen	29	5	91	0				17	1	76	3	1w
Rofe	24.3	5	87	2				6	1	32	0	
Christian	3	0	16	0								
Cosgrove	4	1	9	0			(5)	1	0	2	0	

Umpires: S.D.Fry and I.H.Lock. Referee: R.B.Woods.   Toss: South Australia

Close of Play: 1st day: South Australia (1) 284-6 (D.J.Harris 119*, R.J.Harris 14*, 96 overs); 2nd day: Tasmania (1) 228-5 (Marsh 50*, Paine 13*, 72 overs); 3rd day: South Australia (2) 196-6 (Manou 22*, R.J.Harris 6*, 46 overs).

Man of the Match: R.J.Harris.
D.J.Harris's 120 took 317 balls in 410 minutes and included 16 fours. D.J.Marsh's 109 took 192 balls in 309 minutes and included 12 fours.

QUEENSLAND v WESTERN AUSTRALIA

Played at Brisbane Cricket Ground, Woolloongabba, Brisbane, February 11, 12, 13, 14, 2008.
Pura Cup 2007/08
Match drawn. **(Points: Queensland 2, Western Australia 0)**

QUEENSLAND

1	G.D.Moller	c Ronchi b Edmondson	45	(2) c Marsh b Inness	6
2	R.A.Broad	b Edmondson	19	(1) b Magoffin	4
3	M.L.Love	c Ronchi b Edmondson	8	c Davis b Edmondson	15
4	*J.P.Maher	c Pomersbach b Edmondson	9	c Ronchi b Inness	2
5	S.R.Watson	c Langer b Edmondson	80	c North b Dorey	39
6	C.P.Simpson	c Magoffin b Edmondson	61	c Ronchi b Dorey	10
7	A.A.Noffke	c Langer b Inness	48	c North b Magoffin	34
8	†C.D.Hartley	not out	31	not out	14
9	G.J.Sullivan	c Ronchi b Inness	0	c Ronchi b Magoffin	0
10	M.S.Kasprowicz	b Edmondson	0	not out	29
11	S.A.Brant	not out	0		
	Extras	lb 1, nb 8	9	lb 2, nb 1	3
		(9 wickets, declared)	310	(8 wickets, declared)	156

FoW (1): 1-53 (2), 2-74 (1), 3-75 (3), 4-84 (4), 5-197 (6), 6-247 (5), 7-294 (7), 8-294 (9), 9-309 (10)
FoW (2): 1-12 (1), 2-12 (2), 3-18 (4), 4-48 (3), 5-78 (6), 6-79 (5), 7-119 (7), 8-119 (9)

WESTERN AUSTRALIA

1	C.J.L.Rogers	c Hartley b Noffke	16	lbw b Simpson	116
2	L.M.Davis	c Moller b Kasprowicz	19	run out	51
3	J.L.Langer	not out	51	c Hartley b Brant	27
4	S.E.Marsh	not out	20	c Love b Brant	5
5	L.A.Pomersbach			lbw b Simpson	21
6	*M.J.North			c Maher b Simpson	0
7	†L.Ronchi			c Brant b Kasprowicz	1
8	B.R.Dorey			c Hartley b Kasprowicz	0
9	S.J.Magoffin			not out	33
10	M.W.H.Inness			c Watson b Kasprowicz	4
11	B.M.Edmondson			not out	11
	Extras	lb 3, nb 6	9	lb 4, w 1, nb 4	9
		(2 wickets, declared)	115	(9 wickets)	278

FoW (1): 1-40 (1), 2-40 (2)
FoW (2): 1-111 (2), 2-156 (3), 3-168 (4), 4-209 (5), 5-215 (6), 6-228 (1), 7-229 (7), 8-229 (8), 9-233 (10)

Western Australia Bowling

	O	M	R	W			O	M	R	W	
Magoffin	29	9	68	0	3nb		10	3	28	3	1nb
Inness	25	6	67	2	1nb		9	1	23	2	
Dorey	28	8	74	0	3nb	(7)	5	1	19	2	
Edmondson	28	8	95	7	1nb	(6)	8	1	42	1	
North	2	0	5	0		(3)	2	0	2	0	
Pomersbach						(4)	1	1	0	0	
Marsh						(5)	9	2	40	0	

Queensland Bowling

	O	M	R	W			O	M	R	W	
Noffke	12	3	34	1	2nb		20	2	80	0	
Brant	9	4	17	0	2nb		19	5	49	2	
Kasprowicz	7	1	20	1	2nb		17	4	57	3	4nb
Sullivan	5	0	41	0		(5)	4	0	28	0	1w
Simpson						(4)	19	4	60	3	

Umpires: T.P.Laycock and D.L.Orchard. Referee: G.N.Williams. Toss: Queensland

Close of Play: 1st day: Queensland (1) 270-6 (Noffke 38*, Hartley 3*, 83.3 overs); 2nd day: No play; 3rd day: Queensland (2) 27-3 (Love 6*, Watson 7*, 13 overs).

Man of the Match: B.M.Edmondson.

C.J.L.Rogers's 116 took 170 balls in 240 minutes and included 12 fours.

NEW SOUTH WALES v VICTORIA

Played at Sydney Cricket Ground, February 15, 16, 17, 18, 2008.
Pura Cup 2007/08
Match drawn.   (Points: New South Wales 1, Victoria 1)

VICTORIA

#	Batsman	Dismissal	Score	2nd innings	Score
1	L.R.Mash	c Smith b Cameron	23	(2) lbw b Cameron	5
2	N.Jewell	b Bollinger	1	(1) c and b Thornely	34
3	B.J.Hodge	c Smith b Casson	119	b Cameron	4
4	D.J.Hussey	c Smith b Thornely	86	(7) c Smith b Cameron	9
	R.J.Quiney				
5	*C.L.White	b Cameron	54	(4) lbw b Casson	49
6	A.B.McDonald	b Cameron	40	(5) not out	64
7	†M.S.Wade	b Cameron	6	(8) c Cameron b Casson	36
8	C.J.McKay	c Smith b Cameron	12	(9) c Thornely b Casson	13
9	D.J.Pattinson	c Mail b Cameron	5	(10) c sub (A.C.Bird) b Cameron	4
10	P.M.Siddle	c Smith b Casson	14	(6) b Casson	13
11	B.E.McGain	not out	9	c sub (A.C.Bird) b Casson	1
	Extras	b 8, lb 3, w 5, nb 9	25	b 4, lb 1, w 1, nb 2	8
			394		**240**

FoW (1): 1-12 (2), 2-43 (1), 3-228 (4), 4-259 (3), 5-316 (5), 6-333 (7), 7-356 (8), 8-371 (6), 9-382 (9), 10-394 (10)
FoW (2): 1-14 (2), 2-18 (3), 3-77 (1), 4-103 (4), 5-126 (6), 6-143 (7), 7-203 (8), 8-223 (9), 9-237 (10), 10-240 (11)

NEW SOUTH WALES

#	Batsman	Dismissal	Score	2nd innings	Score
1	P.A.Jaques	c Wade b Siddle	2	c Mash b McDonald	29
2	G.J.Mail	c Wade b McGain	68	c sub (R.J.Quiney) b McGain	4
3	P.J.Forrest	c White b McGain	36	c sub (R.J.Quiney) b McDonald	11
4	*S.M.Katich	c McDonald b Hodge	71	lbw b McGain	21
5	D.J.Thornely	lbw b White	24	not out	23
6	B.Casson	c Wade b Pattinson	29	not out	11
7	Usman Khawaja	run out (Hodge)	85		
8	†D.L.R.Smith	c Wade b McKay	9		
9	M.C.Henriques	c Wade b Hodge	47		
10	M.A.Cameron	not out	1		
11	D.E.Bollinger	c Wade b McGain	2		
	Extras	b 7, lb 8, nb 5	20	b 15, lb 8	23
			394	**(4 wickets)**	**122**

FoW (1): 1-3 (1), 2-77 (3), 3-151 (2), 4-204 (4), 5-214 (5), 6-276 (6), 7-301 (8), 8-391 (7), 9-391 (9), 10-394 (11)
FoW (2): 1-31 (2), 2-53 (1), 3-60 (3), 4-92 (4)

New South Wales Bowling	O	M	R	W		O	M	R	W	
Bollinger	25	4	72	1	5w,3nb	3	1	6	0	
Cameron	33	5	101	6	5nb	25	5	86	4	2nb
Henriques	20	2	69	0	(4)	3	0	9	0	
Casson	24	7	98	2	(3)	38.2	11	97	5	
Mail	3	0	19	0	(6)	2	0	9	0	
Thornely	9	3	24	1	1nb (5)	11	5	24	1	1w
Katich					(7)	1	0	4	0	

Victoria Bowling	O	M	R	W		O	M	R	W	
McKay	22	5	53	1		7	3	7	0	
Siddle	18	2	58	1	2nb					
Pattinson	17	5	49	1	(2)	4	0	10	0	
McGain	36.5	7	100	3		18	2	54	2	
McDonald	14	1	33	0	1nb (3)	9	4	16	2	
Hussey	2	0	14	0	2nb	3	2	2	0	
White	11	1	34	1						
Hodge	17	5	38	2	(5)	4	0	10	0	
Mash					(7)	1	1	0	0	

Umpires: J.K.Brookes and J.D.Ward. Referee: R.A.French.   Toss: Victoria
Close of Play: 1st day: Victoria (1) 340-6 (McDonald 22*, McKay 4*, 96 overs); 2nd day: New South Wales (1) 211-4 (Thornely 23*, Casson 3*, 76 overs); 3rd day: Victoria (2) 108-4 (McDonald 7*, Siddle 3*, 34 overs).
Man of the Match: M.A.Cameron.
R.J.Quiney was a full substitute for Victoria, replacing D.J.Hussey (called up for Australia squad after play on day 2 but later returned to the match when not required to play). B.J.Hodge's 119 took 212 balls in 268 minutes and included 17 fours.

SOUTH AUSTRALIA v QUEENSLAND

Played at Adelaide Oval, February 29, March 1, 2, 3, 2008.
Pura Cup 2007/08
Queensland won by an innings and 9 runs.   (Points: South Australia 0, Queensland 6)

SOUTH AUSTRALIA

1	D.J.Harris	c Watson b Brant	4	(2) lbw b Brant	3
2	J.M.Brown	c Simpson b Noffke	10	(1) c Simpson b Watson	11
3	A.H.Delmont	b Swan	25	c Hartley b Brant	0
4	C.J.Ferguson	c Moller b Noffke	25	c Love b Noffke	16
5	D.T.Christian	c Hartley b Noffke	1	c Hartley b Noffke	72
6	S.A.Deitz	c Watson b Swan	14	c Moller b Watson	5
7	*†G.A.Manou	c Hartley b Watson	7	c Hartley b Noffke	12
8	M.F.Cleary	c Hartley b Brant	57	c Maher b Simpson	21
9	R.J.Harris	not out	55	c Broad b Simpson	1
10	J.N.Gillespie	c Love b Brant	1	c Watson b Doran	51
11	D.J.Cullen	b Broad	27	not out	4
	Extras	lb 2, nb 9	11	lb 9, nb 5	14
			237		210

FoW (1): 1-14 (2), 2-16 (1), 3-65 (3), 4-69 (5), 5-76 (4), 6-93 (6), 7-100 (7), 8-176 (8), 9-178 (10), 10-237 (11)
FoW (2): 1-14 (2), 2-14 (3), 3-35 (4), 4-35 (1), 5-46 (6), 6-63 (7), 7-98 (8), 8-104 (9), 9-204 (10), 10-210 (5)

QUEENSLAND

1	R.A.Broad	b Gillespie	35
2	G.D.Moller	c Manou b R.J.Harris	3
3	M.L.Love	c Deitz b Cleary	62
4	*J.P.Maher	c Manou b Cleary	32
5	S.R.Watson	lbw b Cleary	190
6	C.P.Simpson	b R.J.Harris	10
7	A.A.Noffke	b R.J.Harris	2
8	†C.D.Hartley	lbw b R.J.Harris	95
9	D.J.Doran	not out	2
10	C.R.Swan		
11	S.A.Brant		
	Extras	b 9, lb 10, w 3, nb 3	25
		(8 wickets, declared)	456

FoW (1): 1-15 (2), 2-92 (1), 3-134 (3), 4-167 (4), 5-188 (6), 6-190 (7), 7-452 (5), 8-456 (8)

Queensland Bowling

	O	M	R	W			O	M	R	W	
Noffke	26	6	43	3	4nb		21.1	7	41	3	3nb
Brant	22	9	53	3	1nb		10	5	21	2	
Swan	13	2	40	2							
Watson	10	2	28	1	4nb	(3)	10	5	15	2	2nb
Doran	5	0	32	0		(4)	26	4	101	1	
Simpson	12	0	34	0		(5)	13	4	23	2	
Broad	1.2	0	5	1							

South Australia Bowling

	O	M	R	W	
R.J.Harris	39.2	9	93	4	
Gillespie	35	12	97	1	3w
Cullen	39	9	108	0	
Cleary	33	11	83	3	
Christian	14	1	53	0	3nb
D.J.Harris	4	2	3	0	

Umpires: I.H.Lock and P.R.Reiffel. Referee: R.B.Woods.   Toss: South Australia

Close of Play: 1st day: Queensland (1) 8-0 (Broad 2*, Moller 2*, 4 overs); 2nd day: Queensland (1) 245-6 (Watson 69*, Hartley 17*, 100 overs); 3rd day: South Australia (2) 131-8 (Christian 49*, Gillespie 1*, 38 overs).

Man of the Match: S.R.Watson.

S.R.Watson's 190 took 323 balls in 430 minutes and included 19 fours and 3 sixes.

TASMANIA v NEW SOUTH WALES

Played at Bellerive Oval, Hobart, February 29, March 1, 2, 3, 2008.
Pura Cup 2007/08
Match drawn.   (Points: Tasmania 2, New South Wales 0)

TASMANIA

1	M.J.Di Venuto	c Thornely b Casson	144	(2) c Thornely b Cameron		38
2	D.J.Anderson	c Hughes b Thornely	28	(1) b Cameron		15
3	T.R.Birt	c Nicholson b Cockley	15	lbw b Cameron		0
4	G.J.Bailey	run out (Nicholson)	6	c and b Casson		79
5	*D.J.Marsh	b Cameron	15	c Smith b Cameron		59
6	L.R.Butterworth	lbw b Casson	13	b Casson		8
7	†T.D.Paine	run out (Forrest)	72	lbw b Casson		36
8	J.J.Krejza	c Katich b Thornely	65	not out		28
9	B.Geeves	c Smith b Cameron	4	c Katich b Casson		15
10	B.W.Hilfenhaus	not out	4	c Hughes b Cockley		0
11	T.P.Macdonald	c Smith b Cameron	8			
	Extras	b 2, lb 6, w 6, nb 10	24	b 2, lb 2, nb 1		5
			398	(9 wickets, declared)		283

FoW (1): 1-125 (2), 2-167 (3), 3-174 (4), 4-204 (5), 5-240 (6), 6-243 (1), 7-372 (8), 8-378 (9), 9-386 (7), 10-398 (11)
FoW (2): 1-26 (1), 2-30 (3), 3-75 (2), 4-170 (4), 5-184 (6), 6-223 (5), 7-243 (7), 8-277 (9), 9-283 (10)

NEW SOUTH WALES

1	P.A.Jaques	c Paine b Geeves	4	(2) b Hilfenhaus		22
2	P.J.Hughes	c Paine b Geeves	73	(1) not out		58
3	P.J.Forrest	c Paine b Hilfenhaus	8	b Hilfenhaus		0
4	*S.M.Katich	c Paine b Macdonald	129	c Bailey b Krejza		40
5	B.Casson	lbw b Krejza	25			
6	D.J.Thornely	c Marsh b Hilfenhaus	10	(5) not out		30
7	Usman Khawaja	lbw b Geeves	5			
8	†D.L.R.Smith	c and b Macdonald	27			
9	M.J.Nicholson	b Geeves	5			
10	M.A.Cameron	not out	5			
11	B.T.Cockley	not out	4			
	Extras	lb 2, nb 1	3	nb 3		3
		(9 wickets, declared)	298	(3 wickets)		153

FoW (1): 1-5 (1), 2-27 (3), 3-160 (2), 4-233 (5), 5-250 (6), 6-252 (4), 7-274 (7), 8-284 (9), 9-294 (8)
FoW (2): 1-39 (2), 2-47 (3), 3-106 (4)

New South Wales Bowling

	O	M	R	W			O	M	R	W	
Cameron	34.1	5	111	3	6w		16	2	56	4	
Nicholson	23	6	62	0			17	3	72	0	
Thornely	28	6	58	2	3nb	(5)	6	0	18	0	
Cockley	19	3	69	1	7nb	(3)	12.4	2	51	1	1nb
Casson	31	5	90	2		(4)	24	3	82	4	
Usman Khawaja	1	1	0	0							

Tasmania Bowling

	O	M	R	W			O	M	R	W	
Hilfenhaus	22	6	59	2	1nb		12	2	42	2	
Geeves	25	6	92	4			9	0	45	0	3nb
Macdonald	19	4	60	2			7	2	24	0	
Butterworth	7	2	27	0							
Krejza	23	5	58	1		(4)	10	2	29	1	
Marsh						(5)	3	0	13	0	

Umpires: P.D.Parker and J.D.Ward. Referee: R.T.Widows.   Toss: New South Wales

Close of Play: 1st day: Tasmania (1) 291-6 (Paine 25*, Krejza 23*, 96 overs); 2nd day: New South Wales (1) 172-3 (Katich 86*, Casson 0*, 54 overs); 3rd day: Tasmania (2) 198-5 (Marsh 42*, Paine 11*, 52 overs).

Man of the Match: M.J.Di Venuto.
M.J.Di Venuto's 144 took 218 balls in 303 minutes and included 18 fours and 2 sixes. S.M.Katich's 129 took 206 balls in 281 minutes and included 17 fours and 1 six.

WESTERN AUSTRALIA v VICTORIA

Played at Western Australia Cricket Association Ground, Perth, February 29, March 1, 2, 3, 2008.
Pura Cup 2007/08
Western Australia won by 120 runs.   (Points: Western Australia 6, Victoria 0)

WESTERN AUSTRALIA

1	J.L.Langer	lbw b Wise	14	(7) not out		23
2	C.J.L.Rogers	c White b McGain	166	(1) c McDonald b Harwood		2
3	S.E.Marsh	c Wade b Harwood	53	b Wise		96
4	*M.J.North	lbw b McDonald	42	c Mash b McGain		4
5	L.A.Pomersbach	lbw b McGain	13	c Hussey b Harwood		4
6	A.C.Voges	c McDonald b Wise	42	not out		79
7	†L.Ronchi	c Hodge b Harwood	7	(2) c McDonald b McGain		61
8	S.J.Magoffin	c Mash b McKay	30			
9	B.R.Dorey	b McKay	35			
10	M.W.H.Inness	not out	15			
11	B.M.Edmondson	not out	2			
	Extras	b 2, lb 5, w 2	9	b 1, lb 2, w 5		8

(9 wickets, declared)   428   (5 wickets, declared)   277

FoW (1): 1-27 (1), 2-173 (3), 3-271 (2), 4-291 (4), 5-291 (5), 6-308 (7), 7-354 (8), 8-400 (6), 9-417 (9)
FoW (2): 1-3 (1), 2-97 (2), 3-103 (4), 4-112 (5), 5-218 (3)

VICTORIA

1	L.R.Mash	c Ronchi b Magoffin	30	(2) c Marsh b Magoffin		9
2	N.Jewell	lbw b Magoffin	0	(1) c Ronchi b Inness		14
3	B.J.Hodge	b Inness	0	c Magoffin b Dorey		45
4	D.J.Hussey	c Ronchi b Magoffin	84	c Voges b Edmondson		35
5	*C.L.White	c Ronchi b Magoffin	61	not out		149
6	A.B.McDonald	c Marsh b Magoffin	0	c Ronchi b Dorey		0
7	†M.S.Wade	c Edmondson b Inness	2	lbw b North		35
8	C.J.McKay	c Ronchi b Dorey	20	c Edmondson b Voges		1
9	B.E.McGain	c Ronchi b Edmondson	16	lbw b North		17
10	S.M.Harwood	run out (Voges/Ronchi)	16	c Langer b North		5
11	A.B.Wise	not out	0	lbw b Inness		0
	Extras	b 4, lb 6, nb 12	22	b 6, lb 7, w 1, nb 10		24

251   334

FoW (1): 1-1 (2), 2-2 (3), 3-114 (1), 4-129 (4), 5-129 (6), 6-136 (7), 7-171 (8), 8-223 (5), 9-250 (9), 10-251 (10)
FoW (2): 1-17 (2), 2-27 (1), 3-88 (4), 4-132 (3), 5-132 (6), 6-248 (7), 7-249 (8), 8-305 (9), 9-323 (10), 10-334 (11)

Victoria Bowling

	O	M	R	W		O	M	R	W	
McKay	26	3	98	2	1w	12	2	25	0	
Harwood	23	5	82	2	1w	10	1	37	2	
Wise	22	5	57	2		13.5	2	53	1	
McDonald	21	3	88	1		11	1	57	0	5w
McGain	21	4	67	2		17	1	77	2	
White	4	0	29	0		8	2	25	0	

Western Australia Bowling

	O	M	R	W		O	M	R	W	
Magoffin	20	3	67	5	4nb	15	7	49	1	3nb
Inness	13	3	40	2		21	5	88	2	1nb
Dorey	17.1	4	58	1	4nb	18	2	57	2	1w,3nb
Edmondson	18	5	60	1	4nb	12	2	50	1	1nb
Voges	7	0	14	0	(6) 9	4	24	1	
North	3	2	2	0	(5) 20	6	53	3	2nb

Umpires: R.L.Parry and R.J.Tucker. Referee: R.J.Evans.   Toss: Victoria

Close of Play: 1st day: Western Australia (1) 362-7 (Voges 27*, Dorey 3*, 95 overs); 2nd day: Victoria (1) 217-7 (White 56*, McGain 8*, 68 overs); 3rd day: Victoria (2) 17-0 (Jewell 6*, Mash 9*, 9 overs).

Man of the Match: C.J.L.Rogers.
C.J.L.Rogers's 166 took 221 balls in 289 minutes and included 26 fours and 1 six. C.L.White's 149 took 196 balls in 256 minutes and included 22 fours and 4 sixes.

NEW SOUTH WALES v SOUTH AUSTRALIA

Played at Sydney Cricket Ground, March 7, 8, 9, 2008.
Pura Cup 2007/08
New South Wales won by an innings and 162 runs.   (Points: New South Wales 6, South Australia 0)

SOUTH AUSTRALIA

1	D.J.Harris	c Thornely b MacGill	11	(2) lbw b Casson	71
2	J.M.Brown	st Haddin b MacGill	9	(1) c Haddin b Cameron	7
3	C.J.Ferguson	c Haddin b Lambert	13	c Usman Khawaja b Cameron	25
4	D.T.Christian	c Haddin b Nicholson	19	b Cameron	1
5	S.A.Deitz	lbw b MacGill	21	c Jaques b MacGill	0
6	*†G.A.Manou	c Katich b Nicholson	3	lbw b Cameron	54
7	C.B.Bailey	c Nicholson b MacGill	26	lbw b Casson	19
8	M.F.Cleary	b MacGill	0	lbw b Casson	1
9	R.J.Harris	c Katich b Lambert	3	c Jaques b Casson	18
10	D.J.Cullen	c Haddin b Cameron	13	absent hurt	0
11	P.C.Rofe	not out	0	(10) not out	0
	Extras	b 4, lb 2, w 1, nb 3	10	b 3, lb 2, nb 2	7
			128		**203**

FoW (1): 1-24 (1), 2-31 (2), 3-45 (3), 4-81 (4), 5-85 (6), 6-90 (5), 7-90 (8), 8-93 (9), 9-122 (10), 10-128 (7)
FoW (2): 1-7 (1), 2-48 (3), 3-62 (4), 4-63 (5), 5-144 (6), 6-173 (2), 7-179 (8), 8-190 (7), 9-203 (9)

NEW SOUTH WALES

1	P.A.Jaques	c Manou b Cullen	24
2	P.J.Hughes	c Christian b Cleary	35
3	Usman Khawaja	c D.J.Harris b Cullen	7
4	*S.M.Katich	lbw b Cullen	0
5	D.J.Thornely	not out	169
6	†B.J.Haddin	c R.J.Harris b Cullen	113
7	G.M.Lambert	b Rofe	31
8	B.Casson	c Manou b Rofe	99
9	M.J.Nicholson		
10	M.A.Cameron		
11	S.C.G.MacGill		
	Extras	b 7, lb 5, nb 3	15
		(7 wickets, declared)	493

FoW (1): 1-59 (2), 2-65 (1), 3-65 (4), 4-66 (3), 5-244 (6), 6-302 (7), 7-493 (8)

New South Wales Bowling

	O	M	R	W			O	M	R	W	
Cameron	14	8	19	1	1nb	(2)	18	7	34	4	2nb
Nicholson	10	3	17	2		(1)	12	2	25	0	
MacGill	17.4	6	49	5	1w,1nb		17	2	76	1	
Lambert	10	3	23	2	1nb		4	0	15	0	
Casson	4	1	14	0			13.4	3	48	4	

South Australia Bowling

	O	M	R	W	
R.J.Harris	31	7	92	0	
Rofe	28	7	84	2	
Cleary	18	4	54	1	
Cullen	16	5	58	4	
Bailey	41	2	154	0	1nb
Christian	10	2	26	0	2nb
Brown	1	0	1	0	
D.J.Harris	3	0	6	0	
Deitz	1	0	6	0	

Umpires: R.L.Parry and P.R.Reiffel. Referee: R.A.French.   Toss: South Australia

Close of Play: 1st day: New South Wales (1) 76-4 (Thornely 4*, Haddin 5*, 21 overs); 2nd day: New South Wales (1) 446-6 (Thornely 146*, Casson 75*, 133 overs).
Man of the Match: D.J.Thornely.
The match was scheduled for four days but completed in three. D.J.Thornely's 169 took 395 balls in 502 minutes and included 12 fours and 4 sixes. B.J.Haddin's 113 took 159 balls in 206 minutes and included 11 fours and 2 sixes.

VICTORIA v QUEENSLAND

Played at Melbourne Cricket Ground, March 7, 8, 9, 2008.
Pura Cup 2007/08
Victoria won by six wickets. (Points: Victoria 6, Queensland 0)

QUEENSLAND

#	Batsman	Dismissal 1	Score 1	Dismissal 2	Score 2
1	R.A.Broad	b McKay	75	(2) b McGain	107
2	N.J.Kruger	c Jewell b Nannes	9	(1) c Hussey b McKay	11
3	A.J.Nye	c Hussey b Pattinson	20	b McKay	0
4	S.R.Watson	lbw b Nannes	26	c Crosthwaite b Pattinson	32
5	N.J.Reardon	lbw b McDonald	18	lbw b McDonald	1
6	*C.P.Simpson	lbw b McKay	4	lbw b McDonald	0
7	†C.D.Hartley	c Crosthwaite b McKay	1	c White b Nannes	17
8	D.J.Doran	c White b McKay	4	c Quiney b McGain	23
9	B.Laughlin	c Jewell b McDonald	10	b McKay	1
10	G.J.Sullivan	b Pattinson	13	run out	1
11	S.A.Brant	not out	0	not out	4
	Extras	b 1, lb 8, w 1, nb 1	11	b 2, lb 4, w 1, nb 1	8
			191		205

FoW (1): 1-17 (2), 2-56 (3), 3-113 (4), 4-150 (5), 5-157 (1), 6-164 (7), 7-168 (8), 8-169 (6), 9-191 (9), 10-191 (10)
FoW (2): 1-17 (1), 2-17 (3), 3-64 (4), 4-71 (5), 5-71 (6), 6-118 (7), 7-165 (8), 8-172 (9), 9-178 (10), 10-205 (2)

VICTORIA

#	Batsman	Dismissal 1	Score 1	Dismissal 2	Score 2
1	D.J.Pattinson	c Nye b Brant	0		
2	N.Jewell	run out (Laughlin)	4	(1) b Sullivan	7
3	R.J.Quiney	b Brant	13	(2) c Kruger b Sullivan	14
4	B.J.Hodge	c Simpson b Watson	15	(3) lbw b Brant	7
5	D.J.Hussey	c Doran b Watson	92	(4) c Nye b Brant	6
6	*C.L.White	c Hartley b Laughlin	73	(5) not out	28
7	A.B.McDonald	not out	63	(6) not out	13
8	†A.J.Crosthwaite	c Laughlin b Brant	29		
9	C.J.McKay	c Hartley b Brant	9		
10	B.E.McGain	run out (Sullivan/Hartley)	17		
11	D.P.Nannes	not out	0		
	Extras	lb 3, w 2, nb 2	7	nb 1	1
		(9 wickets, declared)	322	(4 wickets)	76

FoW (1): 1-0 (1), 2-6 (2), 3-27 (3), 4-36 (4), 5-201 (6), 6-201 (5), 7-237 (8), 8-251 (9), 9-322 (10)
FoW (2): 1-9 (1), 2-20 (3), 3-34 (4), 4-34 (2)

Victoria Bowling

	O	M	R	W			O	M	R	W	
Nannes	17	4	52	2			15	7	31	1	
McKay	20	9	35	4	1w		16	1	69	3	1w,1nb
Pattinson	19.5	8	40	2		(4)	7	2	17	1	
McDonald	21	7	31	2	1nb	(3)	8	3	18	2	
McGain	15	7	24	0			18.5	5	47	2	
White						(6)	8	2	17	0	

Queensland Bowling

	O	M	R	W			O	M	R	W	
Brant	22	9	59	4	1nb		8	3	19	2	1nb
Sullivan	12	1	45	0	1w		7	2	33	2	
Laughlin	16	2	60	1	1nb	(4)	2	0	5	0	
Watson	12	3	42	2							
Doran	9	0	39	0		(3)	3	0	19	0	
Simpson	20	2	69	0							
Reardon	1	0	5	0	1w						

Umpires: I.H.Lock and R.J.Tucker. Referee: M.M.Smith. Toss: Victoria

Close of Play: 1st day: Victoria (1) 0-1 (Jewell 0*, 1 over); 2nd day: Queensland (2) 12-0 (Kruger 8*, Broad 3*, 3 overs).

Man of the Match: R.A.Broad.
The match was scheduled for four days but completed in three. R.A.Broad's 107 took 222 balls in 292 minutes and included 14 fours and 3 sixes.

WESTERN AUSTRALIA v TASMANIA

Played at Western Australia Cricket Association Ground, Perth, March 7, 8, 9, 10, 2008.
Pura Cup 2007/08
Western Australia won by 222 runs.   (Points: Western Australia 6, Tasmania 0)

WESTERN AUSTRALIA

1	J.L.Langer	lbw b Hilfenhaus	131	c Krejza b Geeves		23
2	C.J.L.Rogers	c Paine b Hilfenhaus	16	c Marsh b Butterworth		41
3	S.E.Marsh	c Birt b Butterworth	63	b Geeves		4
4	*M.J.North	b Butterworth	0	b Butterworth		69
5	L.A.Pomersbach	c Paine b Krejza	58	c Birt b Hilfenhaus		68
6	A.C.Voges	b Butterworth	12	c Di Venuto b Krejza		5
7	†L.Ronchi	not out	61	c Geeves b Macdonald		93
8	S.J.Magoffin	c Butterworth b Macdonald	4	c Di Venuto b Macdonald		6
9	B.R.Dorey	c Di Venuto b Macdonald	3	not out		1
10	M.W.H.Inness	lbw b Macdonald	0			
11	B.M.Edmondson	b Geeves	4			
	Extras	b 5, lb 10, w 4, nb 1	20	b 2, lb 2, w 2, nb 2		8
			372	**(8 wickets, declared)**		**318**

FoW (1): 1-23 (2), 2-215 (3), 3-215 (4), 4-237 (1), 5-256 (6), 6-309 (5), 7-330 (8), 8-334 (9), 9-334 (10), 10-372 (11)
FoW (2): 1-50 (1), 2-65 (3), 3-77 (2), 4-193 (5), 5-198 (6), 6-253 (4), 7-299 (8), 8-318 (7)

TASMANIA

1	M.J.Di Venuto	c Pomersbach b Edmondson	64	lbw b Inness	45
2	D.J.Anderson	c Ronchi b Inness	4	c Langer b North	47
3	T.R.Birt	b Inness	16	b North	17
4	G.J.Bailey	lbw b Dorey	11	c Ronchi b Inness	33
5	*D.J.Marsh	c Langer b Edmondson	51	c North b Dorey	4
6	L.R.Butterworth	c Langer b Dorey	25	c and b Voges	79
7	†T.D.Paine	c Dorey b Edmondson	6	b Inness	5
8	J.J.Krejza	c Ronchi b Dorey	19	c Ronchi b Edmondson	5
9	B.Geeves	lbw b Inness	8	c Inness b Edmondson	13
10	B.W.Hilfenhaus	c Ronchi b Dorey	1	(11) not out	0
11	T.P.Macdonald	not out	1	(10) lbw b Inness	2
	Extras	nb 1	1	b 4, lb 3, w 1, nb 3	11
			207		**261**

FoW (1): 1-6 (2), 2-42 (3), 3-63 (4), 4-145 (1), 5-148 (5), 6-158 (7), 7-188 (8), 8-205 (9), 9-206 (10), 10-207 (6)
FoW (2): 1-62 (1), 2-106 (3), 3-138 (2), 4-156 (4), 5-156 (5), 6-161 (7), 7-180 (8), 8-215 (9), 9-261 (6), 10-261 (10)

Tasmania Bowling

	O	M	R	W			O	M	R	W	
Hilfenhaus	17	3	89	2	1w		15	2	55	1	1w,1nb
Geeves	16	0	78	1	1nb	(3)	9	1	50	2	1nb
Macdonald	14	2	44	3	1w	(2)	8.5	2	54	2	
Butterworth	16	2	48	3	2w		16	3	70	2	1w
Krejza	18	2	98	1			27	8	82	1	
Marsh						(6)	2	1	3	0	

Western Australia Bowling

	O	M	R	W			O	M	R	W	
Magoffin	17	6	37	0			16	4	63	0	1w,2nb
Inness	18	3	62	3			19	8	44	4	
Dorey	11.5	2	45	4	1nb		14	6	38	1	
Edmondson	11	3	29	3		(5)	10	2	41	2	1nb
North	16	4	34	0		(4)	18	3	50	2	
Voges						(6)	4	1	18	1	

Umpires: B.N.J.Oxenford and P.D.Parker.   Referee: R.J.Evans.   Toss: Tasmania

Close of Play: 1st day: Tasmania (1) 29-1 (Di Venuto 17*, Birt 8*, 9 overs); 2nd day: Western Australia (2) 119-3 (North 23*, Pomersbach 24*, 29 overs); 3rd day: Tasmania (2) 148-3 (Bailey 28*, Marsh 1*, 45 overs).

Man of the Match: J.L.Langer.

J.L.Langer's 131 took 162 balls in 215 minutes and included 19 fours and 2 sixes.

43

NEW SOUTH WALES v VICTORIA

Played at Sydney Cricket Ground, March 15, 16, 17, 18, 19, 2008.
Pura Cup 2007/08 - Final
New South Wales won by 258 runs.

NEW SOUTH WALES

1	P.A.Jaques	lbw b Siddle	53	(2) lbw b McGain		23
2	P.J.Hughes	c Hussey b Siddle	6	(1) c McGain b White		116
3	*S.M.Katich	c Jewell b McGain	86	run out		92
4	M.J.Clarke	lbw b Nannes	13	c Crosthwaite b Siddle		64
5	D.J.Thornely	c Crosthwaite b Harwood	9	b Siddle		21
6	†B.J.Haddin	lbw b Siddle	63	b Siddle		4
7	B.Casson	c Crosthwaite b Siddle	17	b McGain		89
8	B.Lee	b Nannes	8	c and b Siddle		97
9	N.W.Bracken	c Hussey b Siddle	0	not out		15
10	S.R.Clark	c Harwood b Nannes	13			
11	S.C.G.MacGill	not out	1			
	Extras	b 1, lb 6, nb 5	12	b 21, lb 19, nb 2		42
			281	(8 wickets, declared)		563

FoW (1): 1-10 (2), 2-127 (1), 3-163 (3), 4-163 (4), 5-189 (5), 6-241 (7), 7-266 (8), 8-266 (6), 9-271 (9), 10-281 (10)
FoW (2): 1-75 (2), 2-220 (1), 3-302 (3), 4-320 (4), 5-324 (6), 6-355 (5), 7-531 (7), 8-563 (8)

VICTORIA

1	L.R.Mash	c Haddin b Bracken	20	(2) b MacGill		19
2	N.Jewell	run out (Thornely)	26	(1) lbw b Clark		99
3	B.J.Hodge	b MacGill	84	c Hughes b MacGill		0
4	D.J.Hussey	c Katich b Clarke	22	c Casson b Lee		31
5	*C.L.White	b Clark	19	c Bracken b Clark		57
6	A.B.McDonald	not out	19	c Katich b Casson		4
7	†A.J.Crosthwaite	c Haddin b MacGill	3	b Casson		50
8	P.M.Siddle	c Haddin b Lee	0	run out		18
9	B.E.McGain	b Lee	4	c Jaques b Casson		25
10	S.M.Harwood	c Casson b Lee	2	not out		15
11	D.P.Nannes	lbw b Lee	0	lbw b Casson		30
	Extras	b 4, lb 4, nb 9	17	b 16, lb 2, nb 4		22
			216			370

FoW (1): 1-44 (1), 2-68 (2), 3-127 (4), 4-166 (5), 5-184 (3), 6-188 (7), 7-193 (8), 8-199 (9), 9-211 (10), 10-216 (11)
FoW (2): 1-44 (2), 2-44 (3), 3-99 (4), 4-214 (5), 5-222 (6), 6-222 (1), 7-262 (8), 8-311 (7), 9-320 (9), 10-370 (11)

Victoria Bowling

	O	M	R	W			O	M	R	W	
Nannes	21.1	4	58	3		(2)	29	4	112	0	
Siddle	22	5	66	5	3nb	(1)	24.3	6	101	4	
Harwood	14	5	37	1	2nb	(5)	24	2	77	0	2nb
McGain	15	4	44	1		(3)	38	11	107	2	
McDonald	14	3	43	0		(7)	12	5	23	0	
Hodge	5	0	17	0		(4)	11	2	36	0	
White	3	1	9	0		(6)	15	2	49	1	
Hussey						(8)	12	2	18	0	

New South Wales Bowling

	O	M	R	W			O	M	R	W	
Lee	19	3	72	4	6nb		15	0	68	1	2nb
Clark	21	4	68	1	2nb		10	3	29	2	
MacGill	16	4	36	2	1nb		19	1	118	2	2nb
Bracken	10	4	21	1			4	1	11	0	
Clarke	5	1	11	1							
Casson						(5)	29.3	5	126	4	

Umpires: R.L.Parry and R.J.Tucker. Third umpire: B.N.J.Oxenford. Referee: R.A.French.   Toss: New South Wales
Close of Play: 1st day: New South Wales (1) 266-8 (Bracken 0*, 89.1 overs); 2nd day: New South Wales (2) 23-0 (Hughes 10*, Jaques 12*, 6 overs); 3rd day: New South Wales (2) 352-5 (Thornely 19*, Casson 12*, 96 overs); 4th day: Victoria (2) 96-2 (Jewell 44*, Hussey 31*, 18 overs).
Man of the Match: S.M.Katich.
P.J.Hughes's 116 took 175 balls in 240 minutes and included 16 fours and 1 six.

BARISAL DIVISION v CHITTAGONG DIVISION

Played at Shaheed Chandu Stadium, Bogra, October 19, 20, 21, 22, 2007.
Ispahani Mirzapore Tea National Cricket League 2007/08
Barisal Division won by five wickets. (Points: Barisal Division 14, Chittagong Division 4)

CHITTAGONG DIVISION

1	Tamim Iqbal	c Shahin Hossain b Sajidul Islam	9	lbw b Tariqul Islam	60
2	Gazi Salahuddin	c Shahin Hossain b Talha Jubair	11	run out	26
3	Nafees Iqbal	c Shahin Hossain b Sajidul Islam	3	lbw b Talha Jubair	34
4	Aftab Ahmed	c Shahin Hossain b Talha Jubair	61	c Shahriar Nafees b Tariqul Islam	22
5	Nazimuddin	b Arafat Salahuddin	47	lbw b Sajidul Islam	79
6	*Ehsanul Haque	c Shahin Hossain b Talha Jubair	0	b Sajidul Islam	28
7	†Dhiman Ghosh	c and b Sajidul Islam	8	c Shahin Hossain b Talha Jubair	22
8	Shabbir Khan	b Sajidul Islam	5	b Sajidul Islam	0
9	Ashiqur Rahman	run out (Nasiruddin Faruque)	1	(11) c Shahin Hossain b Talha Jubair	6
10	Tareq Aziz	lbw b Tariqul Islam	0	(9) c Shahin Hossain b Talha Jubair	14
11	Saju Datta	not out	0	(10) not out	3
	Extras	b 8, lb 7, w 8, nb 8	31	b 2, lb 4, w 6, nb 11	23
			176		**317**

FoW (1): 1-26 (1), 2-28 (2), 3-36 (3), 4-140 (4), 5-140 (6), 6-163 (5), 7-171 (7), 8-172 (9), 9-176 (8), 10-176 (10)
FoW (2): 1-68 (2), 2-103 (1), 3-148 (3), 4-175 (4), 5-264 (6), 6-279 (5), 7-279 (8), 8-300 (7), 9-307 (9), 10-317 (11)

BARISAL DIVISION

1	*Shahriar Nafees	c Nazimuddin b Shabbir Khan	79	c Dhiman Ghosh b Tareq Aziz	1
2	Hannan Sarkar	c Dhiman Ghosh b Tareq Aziz	7	lbw b Saju Datta	49
3	Imran Ahmed	c Tamim Iqbal b Ashiqur Rahman	2	c Tamim Iqbal b Ashiqur Rahman	19
4	Raqibul Hasan	lbw b Tareq Aziz	21	st Dhiman Ghosh b Saju Datta	55
5	Nasiruddin Faruque	lbw b Tareq Aziz	10	(7) not out	10
6	Raisul Islam	lbw b Tareq Aziz	2	(5) not out	54
7	Arafat Salahuddin	lbw b Saju Datta	20	(6) lbw b Saju Datta	0
8	†Shahin Hossain	c Dhiman Ghosh b Tareq Aziz	2		
9	Talha Jubair	b Ashiqur Rahman	35		
10	Sajidul Islam	not out	64		
11	Tariqul Islam	run out (Tareq Aziz)	5		
	Extras	b 10, lb 3, w 1, nb 13	27	b 14, lb 3, w 7, nb 8	32
			274	(5 wickets)	**220**

FoW (1): 1-24 (2), 2-48 (3), 3-124 (1), 4-124 (4), 5-126 (6), 6-147 (5), 7-158 (8), 8-174 (7), 9-228 (9), 10-274 (11)
FoW (2): 1-2 (1), 2-49 (3), 3-117 (2), 4-170 (4), 5-170 (6)

Barisal Division Bowling

	O	M	R	W			O	M	R	W	
Talha Jubair	16	5	57	3	1w,2nb		31.3	10	80	4	2w
Sajidul Islam	18	3	42	4	3w	(3)	24	4	68	3	
Arafat Salahuddin	14	4	30	1		(2)	17	1	54	0	
Tariqul Islam	13.4	5	30	1	5nb		32	6	88	2	11nb
Raqibul Hasan	1	0	2	0							
Raisul Islam						(5)	10	4	21	0	

Chittagong Division Bowling

	O	M	R	W			O	M	R	W	
Tareq Aziz	22.1	1	80	5	7nb		21.5	4	63	1	2nb
Ashiqur Rahman	28.3	6	63	2	1w,2nb		16	4	37	1	2w,5nb
Aftab Ahmed	14	3	39	0		(4)	10	3	10	0	
Shabbir Khan	17	3	53	1		(5)	2	0	20	0	
Saju Datta	8	2	20	1		(6)	22	3	61	3	1w
Ehsanul Haque	2	0	6	0		(3)	4	0	12	0	4w

Umpires: Enamul Haque and Syed Mahabubullah. Referee: Akhtar Ahmed. Toss: Barisal Division

Close of Play: 1st day: Barisal Division (1) 61-2 (Shahriar Nafees 37*, Raqibul Hasan 3*, 20.2 overs); 2nd day: Chittagong Division (2) 34-0 (Tamim Iqbal 17*, Gazi Salahuddin 16*, 16 overs); 3rd day: Chittagong Division (2) 307-9 (Saju Datta 0*, Ashiqur Rahman 0*, 106 overs).

Man of the Match: Sajidul Islam.

DHAKA DIVISION v KHULNA DIVISION

Played at Shere Bangla National Stadium, Mirpur, October 19, 20, 21, 22, 2007.
Ispahani Mirzapore Tea National Cricket League 2007/08
Match drawn. (Points: Dhaka Division 5, Khulna Division 11)

KHULNA DIVISION

1	Nazmus Sadat	c Anwar Hossain b Mohammad Sharif	2	c Mehrab Hossain b Shahadat Hossain	3
2	Imrul Kayes	c Mehrab Hossain b Nadif Chowdhury	9	lbw b Mohammad Sharif	0
3	Tushar Imran	c Nadif Chowdhury			
		b Mosharraf Hossain	36	(4) c and b Mosharraf Hossain	43
4	*Habibul Bashar	c Mohammad Ashraful			
		b Mohammad Rafique	1	(3) lbw b Mosharraf Hossain	67
5	Shakib Al Hasan	c Mehrab Hossain			
		b Mohammad Ashraful	78	st Anwar Hossain b Mohammad Rafique	2
6	†Saghir Hossain	run out	24	c Shahadat Hossain b Mosharraf Hossain	15
7	Jamaluddin Ahmed	lbw b Mosharraf Hossain	0	b Mohammad Sharif	0
8	Mashrafe Mortaza	c Anwar Hossain b Shahadat Hossain	35	c Mohammad Rafique	
				b Mohammad Sharif	31
9	Abdur Razzak	not out	78	c Mohammad Ashraful	
				b Mohammad Sharif	4
10	Dolar Mahmud	b Shahadat Hossain	13	b Mohammad Rafique	9
11	Syed Rasel	not out	11	not out	3
	Extras	b 1, lb 3, w 7, nb 5	16	b 2, lb 3, w 2	7
		(9 wickets, declared)	303		184

FoW (1): 1-3 (1), 2-31 (2), 3-36 (4), 4-64 (3), 5-150 (6), 6-150 (7), 7-170 (5), 8-234 (8), 9-258 (10)
FoW (2): 1-4 (2), 2-6 (1), 3-90 (4), 4-101 (5), 5-133 (6), 6-135 (3), 7-145 (7), 8-171 (8), 9-180 (9), 10-184 (10)

DHAKA DIVISION

1	Javed Omar	lbw b Syed Rasel	5	c Saghir Hossain b Shakib Al Hasan	45
2	Mehrab Hossain	lbw b Mashrafe Mortaza	2	(5) not out	62
3	†Anwar Hossain	c and b Mashrafe Mortaza	8	(2) lbw b Syed Rasel	4
4	Mohammad Sharif	c Saghir Hossain b Mashrafe Mortaza	7	(9) lbw b Syed Rasel	1
5	*Mohammad Ashraful	lbw b Shakib Al Hasan	23	(4) c Abdur Razzak b Mashrafe Mortaza	85
6	Al Sahariar	c Nazmus Sadat b Mashrafe Mortaza	0	(3) c Dolar Mahmud b Abdur Razzak	24
7	Nadif Chowdhury	b Abdur Razzak	8	c Saghir Hossain b Mashrafe Mortaza	10
8	Mahmudullah	not out	28	(6) lbw b Dolar Mahmud	14
9	Mohammad Rafique	b Syed Rasel	58	(8) lbw b Syed Rasel	1
10	Mosharraf Hossain	c Habibul Bashar b Abdur Razzak	16	not out	8
11	Shahadat Hossain	c Mashrafe Mortaza b Abdur Razzak	0		
	Extras	b 1, lb 5, nb 13	19	b 12, lb 9, nb 9	30
			174	(8 wickets)	284

FoW (1): 1-6 (2), 2-15 (1), 3-24 (3), 4-34 (4), 5-34 (6), 6-54 (7), 7-72 (5), 8-138 (9), 9-174 (10), 10-174 (11)
FoW (2): 1-14 (2), 2-65 (3), 3-121 (1), 4-197 (4), 5-229 (6), 6-249 (7), 7-250 (8), 8-254 (9)

Dhaka Division Bowling	O	M	R	W			O	M	R	W	
Shahadat Hossain	12	0	67	2	1w,5nb		15	4	49	1	1w
Mohammad Sharif	13	2	38	1	1w		20	4	38	4	1w
Nadif Chowdhury	2	0	7	1	5w						
Mohammad Rafique	16	1	57	1		(3)	14.3	4	26	2	
Mosharraf Hossain	17	3	60	2		(4)	18	5	32	3	
Mahmudullah	8	1	21	0							
Mohammad Ashraful	13	0	47	1		(5)	8	0	34	0	
Mehrab Hossain	1	0	2	0							

Khulna Division Bowling	O	M	R	W			O	M	R	W	
Mashrafe Mortaza	14	2	36	4	8nb		27	5	71	2	4w
Syed Rasel	11	3	28	2	4nb		29	6	65	3	3w
Abdur Razzak	19.5	4	44	3		(4)	25	3	67	1	
Dolar Mahmud	8.4	2	26	0		(3)	19	8	38	1	2w
Shakib Al Hasan	8.2	3	23	1			13	6	20	1	
Jamaluddin Ahmed	6	2	11	0			1	0	2	0	

Umpires: Nadir Shah and Showkatur Rahman. Referee: Hemayat Ahmed. Toss: Dhaka Division
Close of Play: 1st day: Dhaka Division (1) 17-2 (Anwar Hossain 2*, Mohammad Sharif 0*, 6 overs); 2nd day: Khulna Division (2) 58-2 (Habibul Bashar 22*, Tushar Imran 29*, 26 overs); 3rd day: Dhaka Division (2) 72-2 (Javed Omar 29*, Mohammad Ashraful 3*, 30 overs).
Man of the Match: Abdur Razzak.

RAJSHAHI DIVISION v SYLHET DIVISION

Played at Bir Shrestha Shahid Captain Mohiuddin Jahangir Stadium, Rajshahi, October 19, 20, 21, 22, 2007.
Ispahani Mirzapore Tea National Cricket League 2007/08
Rajshahi Division won by eight wickets.   (Points: Rajshahi Division 15, Sylhet Division 4)

SYLHET DIVISION

1	Imtiaz Hossain	c Khaled Mashud		c Junaid Siddique	
		b Mohammad Shahzada	35	b Mohammad Shahzada	23
2	Golam Rahman	b Farhad Reza	14	c Junaid Siddique b Farhad Reza	15
3	Golam Mabud	lbw b Delwar Hossain	9	run out	12
4	*Rajin Saleh	c Rafiqul Islam b Farhad Reza	13	c Khaled Mashud	
				b Mohammad Shahzada	68
5	Alok Kapali	c Junaid Siddique			
		b Mohammad Shahzada	5	c Farhad Reza b Delwar Hossain	35
6	†Mushfiqur Rahim	c Rafiqul Islam b Delwar Hossain	32	lbw b Suhrawadi Shuvo	27
7	Rezaul Haque	c Delwar Hossain b Suhrawadi Shuvo	5	c Khaled Mashud	
				b Mohammad Shahzada	18
8	Tapash Baisya	b Farhad Reza	6	b Suhrawadi Shuvo	9
9	Enamul Haque	c Khaled Mashud b Mushfiqur Rahman	3	c Khaled Mashud b Suhrawadi Shuvo	1
10	Nazmul Hossain	not out	9	b Suhrawadi Shuvo	14
11	Nabil Samad	c Jahurul Islam b Delwar Hossain	0	not out	19
	Extras	lb 7, w 2, nb 1	10	b 7, lb 4, w 6	17
			141		258

FoW (1): 1-18 (2), 2-36 (3), 3-65 (4), 4-77 (5), 5-82 (1), 6-95 (7), 7-120 (8), 8-123 (9), 9-139 (6), 10-141 (11)
FoW (2): 1-36 (1), 2-42 (2), 3-58 (3), 4-115 (5), 5-183 (6), 6-208 (4), 7-218 (7), 8-219 (9), 9-222 (8), 10-258 (10)

RAJSHAHI DIVISION

1	Jahurul Islam	run out (Tapash Baisya)	67	not out	39
2	Junaid Siddique	c Mushfiqur Rahim b Rezaul Haque	34	c Mushfiqur Rahim b Tapash Baisya	2
3	Farhad Reza	c Rajin Saleh b Enamul Haque	0	st Mushfiqur Rahim b Enamul Haque	27
4	Naeem Islam	c Mushfiqur Rahim b Tapash Baisya	20	not out	23
5	Anisur Rahman	c Mushfiqur Rahim b Tapash Baisya	0		
6	Rafiqul Islam	run out (Rajin Saleh)	6		
7	*†Khaled Mashud	b Rezaul Haque	82		
8	Mushfiqur Rahman	lbw b Enamul Haque	10		
9	Suhrawadi Shuvo	lbw b Alok Kapali	12		
10	Delwar Hossain	c Alok Kapali b Nabil Samad	40		
11	Mohammad Shahzada	not out	12		
	Extras	b 2, lb 2, w 1, nb 13	18	b 4, lb 3, nb 1	8
			301	(2 wickets)	99

FoW (1): 1-62 (2), 2-64 (3), 3-115 (4), 4-115 (5), 5-134 (6), 6-139 (1), 7-159 (8), 8-190 (9), 9-270 (10), 10-301 (7)
FoW (2): 1-6 (2), 2-57 (3)

Rajshahi Division Bowling	O	M	R	W			O	M	R	W	
Mohammad Shahzada	18	11	16	2			27	6	70	3	2w
Delwar Hossain	17.4	6	31	3	1w		16	6	35	1	
Farhad Reza	16	4	33	3			21	10	17	1	
Suhrawadi Shuvo	20	6	42	1	1nb		37.1	11	93	4	
Mushfiqur Rahman	6	1	12	1	1w	(6)	3	1	15	0	
Naeem Islam						(5)	8	2	17	0	

Sylhet Division Bowling	O	M	R	W			O	M	R	W	
Nazmul Hossain	16	4	36	0	1w		5	1	15	0	
Tapash Baisya	20	3	53	2	3nb		5	1	11	1	
Rezaul Haque	21.5	8	38	2			1	0	8	0	
Enamul Haque	40	7	82	2	7nb		7	1	23	1	1nb
Nabil Samad	12	2	43	1	3nb		6	1	19	0	
Alok Kapali	18	8	42	1			2	0	7	0	
Golam Rahman	1	0	3	0							
Imtiaz Hossain						(7)	2	0	9	0	

Umpires: Anisur Rahman and Ashiqur Rahman. Referee: Raqibul Hasan.   Toss: Rajshahi Division
Close of Play: 1st day: Sylhet Division (1) 141 all out; 2nd day: Rajshahi Division (1) 229-8 (Khaled Mashud 50*, Mohammad Shahzada 16*, 98 overs); 3rd day: Sylhet Division (2) 167-4 (Rajin Saleh 53*, Mushfiqur Rahim 22*, 63 overs).
Man of the Match: Delwar Hossain.

DHAKA DIVISION v SYLHET DIVISION

Played at Shaheed Chandu Stadium, Bogra, October 26, 27, 28, 2007.
Ispahani Mirzapore Tea National Cricket League 2007/08
Dhaka Division won by an innings and 34 runs.   (Points: Dhaka Division 16, Sylhet Division 3)

DHAKA DIVISION

1	Javed Omar	lbw b Nazmul Hossain	1
2	†Anwar Hossain	b Alok Kapali	54
3	Shamsur Rahman	c Tapash Baisya b Alok Kapali	30
4	*Al Sahariar	c Rezaul Haque b Imtiaz Hossain	54
5	Mehrab Hossain	c Mushfiqur Rahim b Nazmul Hossain	60
6	Marshall Ayub	b Nazmul Hossain	23
7	Nadif Chowdhury	lbw b Tapash Baisya	1
8	Mosharraf Hossain	not out	35
9	Mohammad Rafique	c sub (Saif Mahmud) b Imtiaz Hossain	39
10	Mohammad Sharif	c Tapash Baisya b Enamul Haque	7
11	Mahbubul Alam	not out	3
	Extras	b 5, lb 15, w 22, nb 2	44

(9 wickets, declared) 351

FoW (1): 1-6 (1), 2-95 (3), 3-116 (2), 4-194 (4), 5-256 (6), 6-257 (7), 7-268 (5), 8-334 (9), 9-347 (10)

SYLHET DIVISION

1	Imtiaz Hossain	c Marshall Ayub b Mahbubul Alam	0	(2) c Anwar Hossain b Mohammad Sharif	11
2	Golam Rahman	c Anwar Hossain b Mahbubul Alam	6	(1) b Mehrab Hossain	24
3	Rezaul Haque	b Mohammad Sharif	10	(7) c Marshall Ayub b Mosharraf Hossain	0
4	*Rajin Saleh	c Anwar Hossain b Mahbubul Alam	6	lbw b Mehrab Hossain	32
5	Alok Kapali	b Mahbubul Alam	0	c Anwar Hossain b Mahbubul Alam	29
6	Sharifullah	c Al Sahariar b Mohammad Rafique	1	c Javed Omar b Mosharraf Hossain	15
7	†Mushfiqur Rahim	c Marshall Ayub b Mosharraf Hossain	36	(3) c Shamsur Rahman b Mehrab Hossain	1
8	Tapash Baisya	c Anwar Hossain b Mohammad Sharif	0	c Nadif Chowdhury b Mehrab Hossain	0
9	Nazmul Hossain	c Al Sahariar b Mohammad Rafique	25	not out	45
10	Enamul Haque	c Marshall Ayub b Mohammad Rafique	7	c Shamsur Rahman b Mehrab Hossain	36
11	Hasibul Hossain	not out	0	c and b Mosharraf Hossain	6
	Extras	lb 4, w 1	5	b 13, lb 6, w 1, nb 2	22

96   221

FoW (1): 1-0 (1), 2-11 (2), 3-23 (4), 4-23 (5), 5-26 (6), 6-26 (3), 7-26 (8), 8-73 (9), 9-94 (10), 10-96 (7)
FoW (2): 1-18 (2), 2-27 (3), 3-48 (1), 4-103 (5), 5-124 (6), 6-124 (4), 7-124 (8), 8-125 (7), 9-204 (10), 10-221 (11)

Sylhet Division Bowling

	O	M	R	W	
Nazmul Hossain	23	5	51	3	1w
Tapash Baisya	13	4	32	1	1w
Alok Kapali	21	7	47	2	
Rezaul Haque	15	2	58	0	1w
Hasibul Hossain	12	2	35	0	1w,1nb
Enamul Haque	26.2	7	64	1	1nb
Imtiaz Hossain	13	6	26	2	
Golam Rahman	3	0	14	0	
Rajin Saleh	2	0	4	0	

Dhaka Division Bowling

	O	M	R	W			O	M	R	W	
Mahbubul Alam	11	6	14	4			13	2	33	1	
Mohammad Sharif	10	5	16	2	1w		9	2	23	1	1w
Mohammad Rafique	19	5	36	3							
Mosharraf Hossain	6.5	0	26	1		(3)	29.3	4	86	3	2nb
Mehrab Hossain						(4)	18	7	43	5	
Marshall Ayub						(5)	3	1	17	0	

Umpires: S.B.Chowdhury and Showkatur Rahman.   Referee: Aliul Islam.   Toss: Sylhet Division

Close of Play: 1st day: Dhaka Division (1) 237-4 (Mehrab Hossain 49*, Marshall Ayub 15*, 91 overs); 2nd day: Sylhet Division (2) 1-0 (Golam Rahman 1*, Imtiaz Hossain 0*, 0.2 overs).
Man of the Match: Mehrab Hossain.
The match was scheduled for four days but completed in three.

KHULNA DIVISION v CHITTAGONG DIVISION

Played at Bir Shrestha Shahid Flight Lieutenant Motiur Rahman Stadium, Khulna, October 26, 27, 28, 29, 2007.
Ispahani Mirzapore Tea National Cricket League 2007/08
Match drawn.   (Points: Khulna Division 12, Chittagong Division 7)

KHULNA DIVISION

1	Nazmus Sadat	c Dhiman Ghosh b Ashiqur Rahman	15	c Dhiman Ghosh b Tareq Aziz	4
2	Imrul Kayes	c Ashiqur Rahman b Saju Datta	52	c Dhiman Ghosh b Tareq Aziz	7
3	*Habibul Bashar	b Ehsanul Haque	22	lbw b Tareq Aziz	11
4	Tushar Imran	c Tareq Aziz b Saju Datta	51	b Rubel Hossain	26
5	Shakib Al Hasan	c Ehsanul Haque b Ashiqur Rahman	108	c Ehsanul Haque b Ashiqur Rahman	50
6	Saghir Hossain	b Saju Datta	47	b Ehsanul Haque	23
7	Mashrafe Mortaza	c Nazimuddin b Ashiqur Rahman	21	c Ashiqur Rahman b Ehsanul Haque	30
8	†Mohammad Salim	b Tareq Aziz	39	lbw b Saju Datta	3
9	Ziaur Rahman	c Dhiman Ghosh b Tareq Aziz	8	c Faisal Hossain b Saju Datta	23
10	Murad Khan	b Tareq Aziz	4	(11) b Tareq Aziz	6
11	Syed Rasel	not out	8	(10) not out	9
	Extras	b 16, lb 7, nb 12	35	b 3, lb 3, nb 6	12
			410		204

FoW (1): 1-59 (1), 2-99 (3), 3-116 (2), 4-212 (4), 5-314 (5), 6-340 (6), 7-354 (6), 8-365 (9), 9-375 (10), 10-410 (8)
FoW (2): 1-4 (1), 2-19 (2), 3-35 (3), 4-78 (4), 5-119 (5), 6-157 (7), 7-164 (6), 8-170 (8), 9-189 (9), 10-204 (11)

CHITTAGONG DIVISION

1	Tamim Iqbal	c Habibul Bashar b Mashrafe Mortaza	1	b Shakib Al Hasan	81
2	Nafees Iqbal	b Murad Khan	35	c Mohammad Salim b Ziaur Rahman	27
3	Gazi Salahuddin	c Mashrafe Mortaza b Syed Rasel	4	c Imrul Kayes b Ziaur Rahman	0
4	Nazimuddin	c Ziaur Rahman b Murad Khan	30	c Mohammad Salim b Syed Rasel	56
5	*Ehsanul Haque	lbw b Murad Khan	11	(6) lbw b Mashrafe Mortaza	13
6	Faisal Hossain	b Murad Khan	85	(5) c and b Mashrafe Mortaza	48
7	†Dhiman Ghosh	run out (Imrul Kayes)	46	b Syed Rasel	0
8	Ashiqur Rahman	not out	1	not out	5
9	Tareq Aziz	lbw b Syed Rasel	13	not out	2
10	Saju Datta	lbw b Syed Rasel	0		
11	Rubel Hossain	lbw b Syed Rasel	0		
	Extras	b 5, w 5, nb 12	22	b 1, lb 9, w 4, nb 6	20
			248	(7 wickets)	252

FoW (1): 1-2 (1), 2-21 (3), 3-65 (2), 4-75 (4), 5-128 (5), 6-227 (7), 7-229 (6), 8-243 (9), 9-243 (10), 10-248 (11)
FoW (2): 1-51 (2), 2-51 (3), 3-149 (1), 4-228 (5), 5-228 (4), 6-228 (7), 7-247 (6)

Chittagong Division Bowling

	O	M	R	W			O	M	R	W	
Rubel Hossain	21	1	93	0	5nb	(2)	11	1	44	1	3nb
Tareq Aziz	24.2	6	82	3	4nb	(1)	13	2	25	4	2nb
Ashiqur Rahman	16	1	71	3	2nb		9	0	31	1	1nb
Saju Datta	31	9	79	3			25	7	52	2	
Ehsanul Haque	10	0	57	1	1nb		9	1	46	2	
Faisal Hossain	1	0	5	0							

Khulna Division Bowling

	O	M	R	W			O	M	R	W	
Mashrafe Mortaza	17	3	49	1	1w,6nb		23	7	67	2	
Syed Rasel	12.1	3	48	4	2nb		23	5	59	2	2w,5nb
Murad Khan	22	2	69	4			18	9	39	0	
Ziaur Rahman	12	5	27	0	4nb	(5)	12	7	20	2	1nb
Shakib Al Hasan	12	3	45	0		(4)	22	8	32	1	
Tushar Imran	2	0	5	0			5	0	25	0	

Umpires: Afzalur Rahman and Enamul Haque.   Referee: Raqibul Hasan.   Toss: Chittagong Division

Close of Play: 1st day: Khulna Division (1) 361-7 (Mohammad Salim 10*, Ziaur Rahman 4*, 90 overs); 2nd day: Chittagong Division (1) 231-7 (Ashiqur Rahman 0*, Tareq Aziz 2*, 71 overs); 3rd day: Chittagong Division (2) 25-0 (Tamim Iqbal 9*, Nafees Iqbal 13*, 12 overs).

Man of the Match: Shakib Al Hasan.
Shakib Al Hasan's 108 took 140 balls in 190 minutes and included 13 fours and 1 six.

RAJSHAHI DIVISION v BARISAL DIVISION

Played at Bir Shrestha Shahid Captain Mohiuddin Jahangir Stadium, Rajshahi, October 26, 27, 28, 29, 2007.
Ispahani Mirzapore Tea National Cricket League 2007/08
Rajshahi Division won by eight wickets.   (Points: Rajshahi Division 15, Barisal Division 4)

RAJSHAHI DIVISION

1	Jahurul Islam	c Arafat Salahuddin b Sajidul Islam	4	lbw b Sajidul Islam	5
2	Rabiul Karim	lbw b Sajidul Islam	1	not out	1
3	Rafiqul Islam	c Shahriar Nafees b Talha Jubair	13	b Talha Jubair	0
4	Naeem Islam	lbw b Talha Jubair	0	not out	1
5	*†Khaled Mashud	c Iftekhar Nayem b Talha Jubair	89		
6	Mushfiqur Rahman	c Raqibul Hasan b Arafat Salahuddin	67		
7	Anisur Rahman	b Raqibul Hasan	32		
8	Farhad Reza	c Arafat Salahuddin b Abul Bashar	52		
9	Delwar Hossain	c Iftekhar Nayem b Arafat Salahuddin	1		
10	Mohammad Shahzada	c Hannan Sarkar b Ali Arman	19		
11	Suhrawadi Shuvo	not out	3		
	Extras	b 8, lb 6, w 1, nb 5	20	b 1, lb 1	2
			301	(2 wickets)	9

FoW (1): 1-9 (1), 2-10 (2), 3-11 (4), 4-46 (3), 5-178 (6), 6-208 (5), 7-235 (7), 8-236 (9), 9-285 (10), 10-301 (8)
FoW (2): 1-7 (1), 2-8 (3)

BARISAL DIVISION

1	*Shahriar Nafees	c Mohammad Shahzada b Farhad Reza	19	b Delwar Hossain	12
2	Hannan Sarkar	run out		c Khaled Mashud b Mohammad Shahzada	3
		(sub [Farhad Hossain]/Rabiul Karim)	4		
3	Abul Bashar	b Farhad Reza	7	c Khaled Mashud b Farhad Reza	5
4	Raqibul Hasan	c Rabiul Karim b Farhad Reza	0	lbw b Suhrawadi Shuvo	24
5	Iftekhar Nayem	c Khaled Mashud b Naeem Islam	13	c Rabiul Karim b Suhrawadi Shuvo	7
6	Raisul Islam	b Suhrawadi Shuvo	0	c and b Suhrawadi Shuvo	52
7	Arafat Salahuddin	c Rafiqul Islam b Suhrawadi Shuvo	5	b Farhad Reza	0
8	†Shahin Hossain	b Naeem Islam	7	lbw b Mohammad Shahzada	29
9	Ali Arman	c Rabiul Karim b Naeem Islam	2	c Khaled Mashud b Mushfiqur Rahman	29
10	Talha Jubair	c Mushfiqur Rahman b Suhrawadi Shuvo	4	st Rabiul Karim b Naeem Islam	45
11	Sajidul Islam	not out	10	not out	9
	Extras	b 7, lb 8, w 1	16	b 5, lb 1, w 1	7
			87		222

FoW (1): 1-9 (2), 2-36 (1), 3-42 (4), 4-47 (3), 5-54 (6), 6-61 (7), 7-67 (5), 8-70 (8), 9-75 (9), 10-87 (10)
FoW (2): 1-15 (2), 2-15 (1), 3-43 (3), 4-52 (4), 5-61 (5), 6-62 (7), 7-134 (6), 8-142 (8), 9-199 (10), 10-222 (9)

Barisal Division Bowling	O	M	R	W		O	M	R	W	
Talha Jubair	29	11	70	3	1nb	1.5	0	3	1	
Sajidul Islam	31	11	64	2	2nb	1	0	4	1	
Arafat Salahuddin	28	13	52	2	1nb					
Hannan Sarkar	5	1	12	0	1w,1nb					
Ali Arman	21	9	39	1						
Raqibul Hasan	8	1	29	1						
Raisul Islam	2	0	5	0						
Abul Bashar	5.1	0	13	1						
Iftekhar Nayem	1	0	3	0						

Rajshahi Division Bowling	O	M	R	W			O	M	R	W	
Mohammad Shahzada	7	2	9	0			16	6	29	2	1w
Delwar Hossain	4	1	4	0			14	3	39	1	
Mushfiqur Rahman	4	1	6	0		(6)	4.5	1	10	1	
Farhad Reza	14	7	15	3		(3)	19	5	47	2	
Suhrawadi Shuvo	17.4	7	31	3	1w	(4)	34	11	66	3	
Naeem Islam	5	2	7	3		(5)	10	0	25	1	

Umpires: Anisur Rahman and Ziaul Islam. Referee: Samiur Rahman.   Toss: Barisal Division

Close of Play: 1st day: Rajshahi Division (1) 187-5 (Khaled Mashud 86*, Anisur Rahman 0*, 90 overs); 2nd day: Barisal Division (1) 77-9 (Talha Jubair 3*, Sajidul Islam 1*, 47 overs); 3rd day: Barisal Division (2) 216-9 (Ali Arman 23*, Sajidul Islam 9*, 96 overs).
Man of the Match: Khaled Mashud.

CHITTAGONG DIVISION v RAJSHAHI DIVISION

Played at Bir Shrestha Shahid Ruhul Amin Stadium, Chittagong, November 2, 3, 4, 5, 2007.
Ispahani Mirzapore Tea National Cricket League 2007/08
Match drawn.   (Points: Chittagong Division 6, Rajshahi Division 8)

RAJSHAHI DIVISION

1	Jahurul Islam	c Nafees Iqbal b Ehsanul Haque	32	lbw b Saju Datta	24
2	Junaid Siddique	c and b Tareq Aziz	78	c and b Tareq Aziz	4
3	Farhad Reza	c Aftab Ahmed b Tareq Aziz	7	(7) not out	69
4	Naeem Islam	c Dhiman Ghosh b Yasin Arafat	4	c Dhiman Ghosh b Saju Datta	43
5	*†Khaled Mashud	run out (Saju Datta)	18	c Dhiman Ghosh b Yasin Arafat	18
6	Mushfiqur Rahman	run out (Faisal Hossain)	18	not out	50
7	Anisur Rahman	b Tareq Aziz	1		
8	Farhad Hossain	lbw b Tareq Aziz	0	(3) run out	12
9	Mohammad Shahzada	c Tareq Aziz b Saju Datta	0		
10	Delwar Hossain	not out	9		
11	Saqlain Sajib	b Tareq Aziz	7		
	Extras	b 4, lb 9, w 1, nb 4	18	b 7, lb 2, nb 3	12
			192	**(5 wickets, declared)**	**232**

FoW (1): 1-68 (1), 2-87 (3), 3-106 (4), 4-138 (5), 5-164 (2), 6-173 (7), 7-173 (8), 8-174 (9), 9-176 (6), 10-192 (11)
FoW (2): 1-21 (2), 2-43 (1), 3-50 (3), 4-104 (4), 5-126 (5)

CHITTAGONG DIVISION

1	Masumud Dowla	lbw b Farhad Reza	21	lbw b Mushfiqur Rahman	33
2	Nafees Iqbal	b Mohammad Shahzada	2	c Farhad Hossain b Mohammad Shahzada	4
3	Nazimuddin	b Mohammad Shahzada	10	c Farhad Hossain b Saqlain Sajib	23
4	Aftab Ahmed	c Jahurul Islam b Mohammad Shahzada	0	not out	45
5	*Ehsanul Haque	c Mushfiqur Rahman b Mohammad Shahzada	5		
6	Faisal Hossain	c Farhad Hossain b Delwar Hossain	3	(5) not out	17
7	†Dhiman Ghosh	c Jahurul Islam b Farhad Reza	5		
8	Shabbir Khan	c Jahurul Islam b Farhad Reza	21		
9	Yasin Arafat	run out	3		
10	Tareq Aziz	c Jahurul Islam b Mohammad Shahzada	35		
11	Saju Datta	not out	2		
	Extras	lb 7, nb 1	8	b 6, w 1, nb 1	8
			115	**(3 wickets)**	**130**

FoW (1): 1-3 (2), 2-22 (3), 3-24 (4), 4-40 (1), 5-44 (5), 6-53 (6), 7-53 (7), 8-60 (9), 9-109 (10), 10-115 (8)
FoW (2): 1-5 (2), 2-42 (3), 3-96 (1)

Chittagong Division Bowling	O	M	R	W		O	M	R	W	
Tareq Aziz	21	9	39	5	4nb	17	3	45	1	3nb
Aftab Ahmed	9	4	19	0		8	5	12	0	
Yasin Arafat	23	7	47	1		14	2	60	1	
Ehsanul Haque	9	3	14	1	1w					
Shabbir Khan	14	5	34	0		15	5	50	0	
Saju Datta	15	6	26	1	(4)	24	8	50	2	
Faisal Hossain					(6)	1	0	6	0	

Rajshahi Division Bowling	O	M	R	W		O	M	R	W	
Mohammad Shahzada	17	5	24	5		5	1	25	1	1w
Delwar Hossain	9	2	20	1	1nb	2	1	3	0	
Farhad Reza	18.1	6	20	3	(4)	7	2	20	0	
Saqlain Sajib	10	2	39	0	(3)	12	2	24	1	1nb
Farhad Hossain	1	0	5	0		3	0	13	0	
Mushfiqur Rahman					(6)	3	2	4	1	
Naeem Islam					(7)	3	0	16	0	
Anisur Rahman					(8)	3	2	14	0	
Khaled Mashud					(9)	2	0	5	0	

Umpires: A.F.M.Akhtaruddin and Mahbubur Rahman.   Referee: Hemayat Ahmed.   Toss: Rajshahi Division
Close of Play: 1st day: Rajshahi Division (1) 191-9 (Delwar Hossain 8*, Saqlain Sajib 7*, 90 overs); 2nd day: No play; 3rd day: Rajshahi Division (2) 78-3 (Naeem Islam 26*, Khaled Mashud 6*, 29 overs).
Man of the Match: Mohammad Shahzada.

DHAKA DIVISION v BARISAL DIVISION

Played at Shere Bangla National Stadium, Mirpur, November 2, 3, 4, 5, 2007.
Ispahani Mirzapore Tea National Cricket League 2007/08
Match drawn.   (Points: Dhaka Division 5, Barisal Division 11)

DHAKA DIVISION

1	Javed Omar	c Imran Ahmed b Talha Jubair	33	run out	24
2	†Anwar Hossain Piju	lbw b Sajidul Islam	2	(7) lbw b Sajidul Islam	8
3	Al Sahariar	c Raqibul Hasan b Arafat Salahuddin	4	c Shahin Hossain b Sajidul Islam	17
4	*Mohammad Ashraful	lbw b Arafat Salahuddin	17	b Talha Jubair	28
5	Mehrab Hossain	c Shahin Hossain b Sajidul Islam	49	(2) c Shahin Hossain b Arafat Salahuddin	19
6	Mahmudullah	b Sajidul Islam	0	b Tariqul Islam	39
7	Shamsur Rahman	c Shahin Hossain b Tariqul Islam	16	(5) c Talha Jubair b Raqibul Hasan	66
8	Mosharraf Hossain	c Shahin Hossain b Raqibul Hasan	1	lbw b Talha Jubair	10
9	Mohammad Sharif	lbw b Sajidul Islam	6	c sub b Talha Jubair	14
10	Anwar Hossain Monir	run out (Tariqul Islam)	0	(11) b Tariqul Islam	2
11	Mahbubul Alam	not out	6	(10) not out	14
	Extras	b 2, lb 3, w 4, nb 9, pen 5	23	b 1, w 6, nb 9	16
			157		**257**

FoW (1): 1-4 (2), 2-19 (3), 3-56 (4), 4-80 (1), 5-81 (6), 6-130 (7), 7-131 (8), 8-146 (9), 9-150 (5), 10-157 (10)
FoW (2): 1-27 (1), 2-58 (2), 3-64 (3), 4-100 (4), 5-206 (6), 6-206 (5), 7-222 (7), 8-227 (8), 9-244 (9), 10-257 (11)

BARISAL DIVISION

1	*Shahriar Nafees	lbw b Mosharraf Hossain	33	c Mahmudullah b Mahbubul Alam	6
2	Hannan Sarkar	lbw b Mohammad Sharif	85	c Anwar Hossain Piju b Mahbubul Alam	3
3	Imran Ahmed	c Al Sahariar b Mohammad Ashraful	35	c Anwar Hossain Piju b Mohammad Sharif	1
4	Raqibul Hasan	c Mohammad Sharif b Mohammad Ashraful	10	lbw b Mahbubul Alam	2
5	Nasiruddin Faruque	run out (Mahmudullah/Anwar Hossain)	34	lbw b Mahbubul Alam	0
6	Raisul Islam	c Mohammad Ashraful b Mosharraf Hossain	35	c Anwar Hossain Piju b Mohammad Sharif	19
7	Arafat Salahuddin	c Mohammad Ashraful b Mosharraf Hossain	13	c Mahmudullah b Mosharraf Hossain	20
8	†Shahin Hossain	lbw b Mohammad Sharif	13	b Mosharraf Hossain	30
9	Talha Jubair	not out	29	b Mohammad Sharif	1
10	Sajidul Islam	lbw b Mahbubul Alam	0	not out	0
11	Tariqul Islam	not out	0	not out	0
	Extras	b 6, lb 5, w 3, nb 3	17	b 10, lb 3, w 2, nb 6	21
		(9 wickets, declared)	**304**	(9 wickets)	**103**

FoW (1): 1-63 (1), 2-132 (3), 3-158 (4), 4-174 (2), 5-226 (5), 6-253 (7), 7-256 (6), 8-292 (8), 9-295 (10)
FoW (2): 1-10 (2), 2-11 (1), 3-14 (1), 4-15 (5), 5-23 (4), 6-38 (6), 7-101 (7), 8-102 (8), 9-102 (9)

Barisal Division Bowling	O	M	R	W		O	M	R	W	
Talha Jubair	17.1	4	51	1	2w,3nb	24	6	87	3	1w,4nb
Sajidul Islam	16	7	40	4	1w,1nb	25	7	73	2	3w,1nb
Arafat Salahuddin	12	3	25	2	1w,1nb (4)	14	5	29	1	2w
Tariqul Islam	14	3	27	1	4nb (3)	18.3	2	45	2	4nb
Raqibul Hasan	4	2	4	1		6	2	22	1	

Dhaka Division Bowling	O	M	R	W		O	M	R	W	
Mahbubul Alam	24	9	53	1	1nb	13	1	29	4	6nb
Mohammad Sharif	24	4	45	2	3w	12.4	2	33	3	1w
Mosharraf Hossain	37	22	40	3		5	1	9	2	
Anwar Hossain	10	2	21	0	1nb	2	0	9	0	1w
Mohammad Ashraful	29	4	86	2	(6)	2	0	5	0	
Mehrab Hossain	16	5	26	0	1nb					
Mahmudullah	8	2	22	0		0.2	0	0	0	
Shamsur Rahman					(5)	1	0	5	0	

Umpires: Mesbahuddin Ahmed and Ziaul Islam. Referee: Akhtar Ahmed.   Toss: Dhaka Division

Close of Play: 1st day: Barisal Division (1) 27-0 (Shahriar Nafees 19*, Hannan Sarkar 6*, 17 overs); 2nd day: Barisal Division (1) 215-4 (Nasiruddin Faruque 27*, Raisul Islam 14*, 111 overs); 3rd day: Dhaka Division (2) 155-4 (Shamsur Rahman 35*, Mahmudullah 24*, 51 overs).
Man of the Match: Sajidul Islam.

KHULNA DIVISION v SYLHET DIVISION

Played at Narayanganj Osmani Stadium, Fatullah, November 2, 3, 4, 5, 2007.
Ispahani Mirzapore Tea National Cricket League 2007/08
Match drawn.   (Points: Khulna Division 10, Sylhet Division 7)

KHULNA DIVISION

1	Imrul Kayes	c sub (Imtiaz Hossain)	
		b Enamul Haque	127
2	Nahidul Haque	lbw b Golam Rahman	16
3	*Habibul Bashar	c Alok Kapali b Enamul Haque	33
4	Tushar Imran	c Golam Rahman b Tapash Baisya	10
5	Shakib Al Hasan	b Enamul Haque	59
6	†Saghir Hossain	c Mushfiqur Rahim b Rashedur Rahman	2
7	Jamaluddin Ahmed	c Mushfiqur Rahim b Rashedur Rahman	0
8	Mashrafe Mortaza	c Sadiqur Rahman b Enamul Haque	7
9	Ziaur Rahman	lbw b Tapash Baisya	1
10	Abdur Razzak	c sub (Imtiaz Hossain) b Enamul Haque	7
11	Syed Rasel	not out	1
	Extras	b 3, lb 4, w 1, nb 3	11
			274

	(6) st Mushfiqur Rahim	
	b Enamul Haque	36
	(1) b Rezaul Haque	8
	(4) c Golam Mabud b Enamul Haque	73
	(3) c Mushfiqur Rahim b Rezaul Haque	0
	c Tapash Baisya b Rezaul Haque	16
	(7) not out	14
	(2) run out	4
	(11) c sub b Sadiqur Rahman	1
	(8) st Mushfiqur Rahim b Alok Kapali	8
	(9) b Alok Kapali	6
	(10) b Golam Mabud	1
	b 1, lb 2, w 1, nb 3	7
		174

FoW (1): 1-46 (2), 2-133 (3), 3-166 (4), 4-222 (1), 5-237 (6), 6-241 (7), 7-256 (8), 8-266 (5), 9-270 (9), 10-274 (10)
FoW (2): 1-9 (1), 2-9 (3), 3-19 (2), 4-43 (5), 5-126 (6), 6-149 (4), 7-160 (8), 8-168 (9), 9-169 (10), 10-174 (11)

SYLHET DIVISION

1	Golam Rahman	lbw b Mashrafe Mortaza	7
2	Golam Mabud	b Mashrafe Mortaza	3
3	*Rajin Saleh	c Saghir Hossain b Ziaur Rahman	54
4	†Mushfiqur Rahim	c Shakib Al Hasan b Syed Rasel	63
5	Alok Kapali	b Ziaur Rahman	59
6	Sharifullah	lbw b Syed Rasel	0
7	Sadiqur Rahman	c Saghir Hossain b Syed Rasel	0
8	Rezaul Haque	c Saghir Hossain b Ziaur Rahman	0
9	Tapash Baisya	b Syed Rasel	0
10	Enamul Haque	c Saghir Hossain b Ziaur Rahman	11
11	Rashedur Rahman	not out	5
	Extras	b 6, lb 7, w 1, nb 9	23
			225

FoW (1): 1-9 (2), 2-27 (1), 3-105 (3), 4-200 (5), 5-203 (6), 6-205 (7), 7-208 (4), 8-208 (8), 9-212 (9), 10-225 (10)

Sylhet Division Bowling

	O	M	R	W			O	M	R	W	
Tapash Baisya	17	4	61	2	3nb	(2)	5	0	26	0	3w
Rashedur Rahman	17	5	33	2		(3)	5	3	11	0	1nb
Rezaul Haque	7	0	41	0		(1)	10	1	49	3	
Golam Rahman	7	1	19	1	1w	(7)	4	4	0	0	
Enamul Haque	25.1	2	65	5		(4)	19	7	30	2	
Alok Kapali	4	0	14	0		(5)	16	1	50	2	
Golam Mabud	3	0	14	0		(6)	6	4	5	1	
Rajin Saleh	2	0	20	0							
Sadiqur Rahman						(8)	1.4	1	0	1	

Khulna Division Bowling

	O	M	R	W	
Mashrafe Mortaza	22	8	53	2	
Syed Rasel	21	5	52	4	11w,8nb
Ziaur Rahman	18.4	5	48	4	1nb
Abdur Razzak	17	3	53	0	
Shakib Al Hasan	2	0	6	0	

Umpires: Sailab Hossain and Syed Mahabubullah.   Referee: Obaydul Haque.   Toss: Sylhet Division

Close of Play: 1st day: No play; 2nd day: Sylhet Division (1) 6-0 (Golam Rahman 3*, Golam Mabud 0*, 3 overs); 3rd day: Sylhet Division (1) 174-3 (Mushfiqur Rahim 54*, Alok Kapali 39*, 60.2 overs).
Man of the Match: Imrul Kayes.
Imrul Kayes's 127 took 208 balls in 275 minutes and included 16 fours and 2 sixes.

BARISAL DIVISION v SYLHET DIVISION

Played at Narayanganj Osmani Stadium, Fatullah, November 10, 11, 12, 13, 2007.
Ispahani Mirzapore Tea National Cricket League 2007/08
Barisal Division won by two wickets.   (Points: Barisal Division 13, Sylhet Division 7)

SYLHET DIVISION

1	Golam Rahman	c Imran Ahmed b Arafat Salahuddin	33	c sub b Talha Jubair		5
2	Imtiaz Hossain	c Talha Jubair b Arafat Salahuddin	16	c and b Sajidul Islam		0
3	†Mithun Ali	b Arafat Salahuddin	9	c Raqibul Hasan b Arafat Salahuddin		24
4	*Rajin Saleh	c Talha Jubair b Arafat Salahuddin	82	c Imran Ahmed b Sajidul Islam		12
5	Alok Kapali	c Shahin Hossain b Talha Jubair	168	c Sajidul Islam b Talha Jubair		32
6	Golam Mabud	b Sajidul Islam	10	c Shahin Hossain b Sajidul Islam		5
7	Saif Mahmud	lbw b Sajidul Islam	2	(8) c Hannan Sarkar b Talha Jubair		0
8	Rezaul Haque	not out	5	(7) b Arafat Salahuddin		5
9	Nabil Samad	c Arafat Salahuddin b Talha Jubair	0	c Shahin Hossain b Arafat Salahuddin		0
10	Rashedur Rahman	c Shahriar Nafees b Sajidul Islam	1	c Shahin Hossain b Talha Jubair		1
11	Subashis Roy			not out		0
	Extras	lb 3, w 5, nb 1	9	b 4, lb 3, w 2, nb 2		11
		(9 wickets, declared)	**335**			**95**

FoW (1): 1-36 (2), 2-57 (3), 3-60 (1), 4-283 (4), 5-319 (6), 6-329 (5), 7-333 (7), 8-334 (9), 9-335 (10)
FoW (2): 1-1 (2), 2-13 (1), 3-46 (3), 4-46 (4), 5-60 (6), 6-93 (5), 7-94 (8), 8-94 (7), 9-95 (9), 10-95 (10)

BARISAL DIVISION

1	*Shahriar Nafees	c Golam Rahman b Rashedur Rahman	14	(8) b Golam Mabud		5
2	Hannan Sarkar	b Subashis Roy	6	c Mithun Ali b Rashedur Rahman		1
3	Imran Ahmed	b Subashis Roy	0	(1) c Saif Mahmud b Subashis Roy		0
4	Raqibul Hasan	c Mithun Ali b Rashedur Rahman	28	c Rashedur Rahman b Golam Mabud		57
5	Raisul Islam	b Subashis Roy	83	run out		4
6	†Shahin Hossain	c Mithun Ali b Rezaul Haque	10	(3) lbw b Subashis Roy		0
7	Abul Bashar	c Golam Mabud b Subashis Roy	56	(6) c Alok Kapali b Subashis Roy		0
8	Arafat Salahuddin	b Rashedur Rahman	8	(7) c Subashis Roy b Nabil Samad		76
9	Taposh Ghosh	not out	4	not out		13
10	Talha Jubair	c Mithun Ali b Rashedur Rahman	7	not out		12
11	Sajidul Islam	c Mithun Ali b Rezaul Haque	18			
	Extras	b 6, lb 10, w 3, nb 6	25	b 2, lb 3, nb 3		8
			259	**(8 wickets)**		**176**

FoW (1): 1-13 (2), 2-17 (3), 3-41 (1), 4-66 (4), 5-108 (6), 6-206 (5), 7-223 (8), 8-229 (7), 9-236 (10), 10-259 (11)
FoW (2): 1-0 (1), 2-0 (3), 3-2 (2), 4-15 (5), 5-17 (6), 6-143 (7), 7-150 (8), 8-155 (4)

Barisal Division Bowling	O	M	R	W			O	M	R	W	
Talha Jubair	27	8	82	2	1w,1nb	(2)	13.2	6	34	4	1nb
Sajidul Islam	23.1	5	69	3	2w	(1)	10	3	28	3	
Arafat Salahuddin	25	5	94	4			12	5	20	3	1nb
Taposh Ghosh	9	2	32	0			1	0	6	0	1w
Abul Bashar	7	2	18	0							
Raqibul Hasan	5	1	28	0							
Hannan Sarkar	3	0	9	0	2w						

Sylhet Division Bowling	O	M	R	W			O	M	R	W	
Subashis Roy	29	12	64	4	4nb		14	1	47	3	2nb
Rezaul Haque	11.2	2	36	2	1w	(4)	6	2	13	0	
Saif Mahmud	15	4	30	0	2w,1nb		5	3	9	0	
Golam Rahman	1	0	6	0							
Rashedur Rahman	21	8	54	4	1nb	(2)	15	5	24	1	
Alok Kapali	4	1	12	0							
Nabil Samad	22	6	39	0		(5)	13.5	2	55	1	1nb
Golam Mabud	1	0	2	0		(6)	10	3	23	2	

Umpires: Afzalur Rahman and S.B.Chowdhury.   Referee: Belayet Hossain.   Toss: Barisal Division

Close of Play: 1st day: Sylhet Division (1) 316-4 (Alok Kapali 157*, Golam Mabud 10*, 90 overs); 2nd day: Barisal Division (1) 215-6 (Abul Bashar 56*, Arafat Salahuddin 1*, 78 overs); 3rd day: Barisal Division (2) 41-5 (Raqibul Hasan 21*, Arafat Salahuddin 13*, 17 overs).
Man of the Match: Arafat Salahuddin.
Alok Kapali's 168 took 230 balls in 273 minutes and included 27 fours and 2 sixes.

DHAKA DIVISION v CHITTAGONG DIVISION

Played at Shere Bangla National Stadium, Mirpur, November 10, 11, 12, 13, 2007.
Ispahani Mirzapore Tea National Cricket League 2007/08
Dhaka Division won by three wickets.   (Points: Dhaka Division 16, Chittagong Division 5)

CHITTAGONG DIVISION

1	Tamim Iqbal	c Mohammad Sharif b Mohammad Rafique	38	c sub (Sajjad Kadir) b Mehrab Hossain	70
2	Masumud Dowla	c Mehrab Hossain b Mohammad Sharif	3	run out	19
3	Nazimuddin	b Mosharraf Hossain	38	c Mahmudullah b Mosharraf Hossain	2
4	Aftab Ahmed	c Shamsur Rahman b Mosharraf Hossain	11	c Al Sahariar b Mohammad Ashraful	32
5	*Ehsanul Haque	c Mahmudullah b Mohammad Ashraful	21	lbw b Mahbubul Alam	56
6	Faisal Hossain	c and b Mohammad Rafique	12	b Mohammad Rafique	25
7	†Dhiman Ghosh	lbw b Mohammad Sharif	41	c Anwar Hossain b Mohammad Sharif	20
8	Tareq Aziz	b Mosharraf Hossain	13	not out	31
9	Saju Datta	c Mahbubul Alam b Mohammad Ashraful	5	(10) lbw b Mehrab Hossain	0
10	Kamrul Islam	not out	5	(9) c sub (Sajjad Kadir) b Mosharraf Hossain	5
11	Rubel Hossain	lbw b Mahbubul Alam	2	c and b Mohammad Ashraful	2
	Extras	b 2, lb 6, w 1, nb 2	11	b 5, lb 6, nb 5	16
			200		278

FoW (1): 1-6 (2), 2-48 (1), 3-71 (4), 4-115 (3), 5-130 (5), 6-130 (6), 7-156 (8), 8-167 (9), 9-195 (7), 10-200 (11)
FoW (2): 1-67 (2), 2-80 (3), 3-126 (4), 4-126 (1), 5-179 (6), 6-225 (7), 7-237 (5), 8-250 (9), 9-255 (10), 10-278 (11)

DHAKA DIVISION

1	Javed Omar	c Tamim Iqbal b Faisal Hossain	101	run out	16
2	†Anwar Hossain	c Masumud Dowla b Saju Datta	62	c Dhiman Ghosh b Kamrul Islam	13
3	Al Sahariar	run out (Saju Datta)	44	c Dhiman Ghosh b Kamrul Islam	0
4	*Mohammad Ashraful	c Rubel Hossain b Faisal Hossain	35	c Masumud Dowla b Kamrul Islam	4
5	Mehrab Hossain	not out	45	not out	22
6	Shamsur Rahman	b Ehsanul Haque	6	c Dhiman Ghosh b Kamrul Islam	0
7	Mahmudullah	lbw b Saju Datta	28	b Saju Datta	27
8	Mosharraf Hossain	c Dhiman Ghosh b Rubel Hossain	4		
9	Mohammad Rafique	c Faisal Hossain b Rubel Hossain	0	(8) c Faisal Hossain b Saju Datta	0
10	Mohammad Sharif	lbw b Saju Datta	2	(9) not out	8
11	Mahbubul Alam	b Faisal Hossain	16		
	Extras	b 16, lb 4, w 1, nb 12	33	b 3, lb 4, w 5, nb 1	13
			376	(7 wickets)	103

FoW (1): 1-104 (2), 2-198 (3), 3-255 (4), 4-268 (1), 5-286 (6), 6-333 (7), 7-344 (8), 8-346 (9), 9-351 (10), 10-376 (11)
FoW (2): 1-27 (2), 2-31 (3), 3-35 (4), 4-42 (1), 5-46 (6), 6-85 (7), 7-85 (8)

Dhaka Division Bowling	O	M	R	W			O	M	R	W	
Mahbubul Alam	11.4	2	41	1			16	4	37	1	1nb
Mohammad Sharif	14	5	42	2			18	6	42	1	
Mohammad Rafique	29	8	48	2	2w	(4)	27	1	72	1	1nb
Mosharraf Hossain	21	6	38	3		(3)	24	5	65	2	3nb
Mohammad Ashraful	7	0	23	2	1w		8.5	1	28	2	
Mehrab Hossain						(6)	8	3	23	2	

Chittagong Division Bowling	O	M	R	W			O	M	R	W	
Rubel Hossain	21	4	65	2	1w,5nb		8	1	25	0	3w
Tareq Aziz	21	9	35	0	3nb		4.5	1	16	0	1w,1nb
Kamrul Islam	18	8	32	0			7	2	19	4	1w
Saju Datta	31	3	103	3			7	1	20	2	
Ehsanul Haque	12	6	56	1		(6)	2	0	6	0	
Faisal Hossain	23.3	6	54	3		(5)	2	0	10	0	
Aftab Ahmed	4	1	11	0							

Umpires: A.F.M.Akhtaruddin and Mahbubur Rahman. Referee: Asaduzzaman.   Toss: Chittagong Division

Close of Play: 1st day: Dhaka Division (1) 17-0 (Javed Omar 0*, Anwar Hossain 16*, 5 overs); 2nd day: Dhaka Division (1) 300-5 (Mehrab Hossain 21*, Mahmudullah 9*, 95 overs); 3rd day: Chittagong Division (2) 165-4 (Ehsanul Haque 18*, Faisal Hossain 17*, 50.2 overs).
Man of the Match: Javed Omar.
Javed Omar's 101 took 241 balls in 325 minutes and included 14 fours.

KHULNA DIVISION v RAJSHAHI DIVISION

Played at Bir Shrestha Shahid Flight Lieutenant Motiur Rahman Stadium, Khulna, November 10, 11, 12, 13, 2007.
Ispahani Mirzapore Tea National Cricket League 2007/08
Khulna Division won by two wickets. (Points: Khulna Division 13, Rajshahi Division 4)

RAJSHAHI DIVISION

1	†Jahurul Islam	b Dolar Mahmud	8	lbw b Shakib Al Hasan	29
2	Junaid Siddique	lbw b Dolar Mahmud	14	lbw b Ziaur Rahman	22
3	Farhad Hossain	c Saghir Hossain b Dolar Mahmud	22	lbw b Shakib Al Hasan	49
4	Naeem Islam	c Saghir Hossain b Dolar Mahmud	0	(6) run out	28
5	Mushfiqur Rahman	c Saghir Hossain b Dolar Mahmud	1	(9) c Tushar Imran b Dolar Mahmud	11
6	*Khaled Mashud	c Saghir Hossain b Murad Khan	35	(7) run out	62
7	Anisur Rahman	c Saghir Hossain b Murad Khan	29	(4) c Dolar Mahmud b Syed Rasel	10
8	Farhad Reza	not out	48	c Nazmus Sadat b Murad Khan	7
9	Suhrawadi Shuvo	c Nazmus Sadat b Dolar Mahmud	11	(5) c Saghir Hossain b Murad Khan	0
10	Mohammad Shahzada	b Dolar Mahmud	6	lbw b Syed Rasel	6
11	Alamgir Kabir	lbw b Ziaur Rahman	9	not out	2
	Extras	b 7, lb 5, nb 8	20	b 6, lb 4, w 1, nb 4	15
			203		**241**

FoW (1): 1-14 (1), 2-23 (2), 3-23 (4), 4-27 (5), 5-72 (3), 6-113 (6), 7-130 (7), 8-154 (9), 9-160 (10), 10-203 (11)
FoW (2): 1-51 (2), 2-55 (1), 3-80 (4), 4-87 (5), 5-129 (6), 6-180 (3), 7-187 (8), 8-204 (9), 9-214 (10), 10-241 (7)

KHULNA DIVISION

1	Nazmus Sadat	lbw b Mohammad Shahzada	95	st Jahurul Islam b Naeem Islam	52
2	Imrul Kayes	c Anisur Rahman b Farhad Reza	5	c Suhrawadi Shuvo b Naeem Islam	41
3	*Habibul Bashar	lbw b Farhad Reza	31	c Mohammad Shahzada b Suhrawadi Shuvo	35
4	Tushar Imran	c Jahurul Islam b Alamgir Kabir	4	c Farhad Reza b Suhrawadi Shuvo	34
5	Shakib Al Hasan	b Alamgir Kabir	2	run out	5
6	Mostafizur Rahman	c Jahurul Islam b Suhrawadi Shuvo	6	(7) c Jahurul Islam b Farhad Reza	19
7	†Saghir Hossain	b Suhrawadi Shuvo	34	(9) lbw b Farhad Reza	2
8	Ziaur Rahman	c Mushfiqur Rahman b Farhad Reza	4	(6) b Mushfiqur Rahman	26
9	Dolar Mahmud	run out	3	(8) not out	12
10	Syed Rasel	not out	5	not out	2
11	Murad Khan				
	Extras	b 4, lb 10, nb 1	15	b 6, lb 3, w 5	14
		(9 wickets, declared)	**204**	(8 wickets)	**242**

FoW (1): 1-6 (2), 2-78 (3), 3-96 (4), 4-100 (5), 5-122 (6), 6-182 (1), 7-190 (7), 8-198 (9), 9-204 (8)
FoW (2): 1-80 (2), 2-108 (1), 3-167 (4), 4-176 (5), 5-177 (3), 6-223 (7), 7-225 (6), 8-228 (9)

Khulna Division Bowling	O	M	R	W			O	M	R	W	
Syed Rasel	23	8	41	0	2nb		19	4	46	2	2nb
Dolar Mahmud	21	6	52	7	5nb		19	0	63	1	1nb
Ziaur Rahman	13	5	20	1			14	3	30	1	1w,1nb
Murad Khan	21	4	43	2	1nb	(5)	15	4	34	2	
Shakib Al Hasan	20	7	31	0		(4)	27	6	46	2	
Tushar Imran	3	0	4	0		(7)	2	0	7	0	
Habibul Bashar						(6)	1	0	5	0	

Rajshahi Division Bowling	O	M	R	W			O	M	R	W	
Alamgir Kabir	22	4	59	2	1nb	(2)	8	2	25	0	
Farhad Reza	12.1	5	29	3		(4)	18.5	1	72	2	1w
Mohammad Shahzada	17	5	31	1		(1)	6	3	18	0	
Suhrawadi Shuvo	15	1	37	2		(6)	8	0	48	2	3w
Farhad Hossain	2	0	5	0			10	3	16	0	
Mushfiqur Rahman	13	5	20	0		(7)	2	0	8	1	1w
Naeem Islam	5	1	9	0		(3)	16	3	46	2	

Umpires: Enamul Haque and Nadir Shah. Referee: Aliul Islam. Toss: Rajshahi Division

Close of Play: 1st day: Rajshahi Division (1) 174-9 (Farhad Reza 26*, Alamgir Kabir 3*, 90 overs); 2nd day: Khulna Division (1) 190-7 (Ziaur Rahman 2*, 76.2 overs); 3rd day: Rajshahi Division (2) 192-7 (Khaled Mashud 29*, Mushfiqur Rahman 5*, 78 overs).
Man of the Match: Dolar Mahmud.
Dolar Mahmud took a hat-trick in the Rajshahi Division first innings (Junaid Siddique, Naeem Islam, Mushfiqur Rahim).

BARISAL DIVISION v KHULNA DIVISION

Played at Shaheed Chandu Stadium, Bogra, November 18, 19, 20, 21, 2007.
Ispahani Mirzapore Tea National Cricket League 2007/08
Khulna Division won by an innings and 3 runs. (Points: Barisal Division 4, Khulna Division 16)

KHULNA DIVISION

1	Nazmus Sadat	c Raqibul Hasan b Talha Jubair	3
2	Imrul Kayes	c Abul Bashar b Sajidul Islam	0
3	*Habibul Bashar	retired hurt	13
4	Tushar Imran	c Abul Bashar b Sajidul Islam	165
5	Shakib Al Hasan	c Talha Jubair b Abul Bashar	81
6	Mostafizur Rahman	c Shahin Hossain b Arafat Salahuddin	29
7	†Saghir Hossain	run out (Abul Bashar)	1
8	Mashrafe Mortaza	b Talha Jubair	17
9	Ziaur Rahman	st Shahin Hossain b Abul Bashar	58
10	Syed Rasel	run out (Raisul Islam)	3
11	Murad Khan	not out	0
	Extras	b 7, lb 10, w 5, nb 4	26
			396

FoW (1): 1-5 (2), 2-25 (1), 3-159 (5), 4-218 (6), 5-233 (7), 6-276 (8), 7-384 (9), 8-396 (4), 9-396 (10)

BARISAL DIVISION

1	Hannan Sarkar	lbw b Syed Rasel	9	lbw b Syed Rasel	15
2	*Shahriar Nafees	lbw b Syed Rasel	4	c Nazmus Sadat b Syed Rasel	0
3	Imran Ahmed	c Shakib Al Hasan b Murad Khan	60	c Ziaur Rahman b Mashrafe Mortaza	15
4	Raqibul Hasan	c Shakib Al Hasan b Murad Khan	38	run out	57
5	Abul Bashar	lbw b Murad Khan	16	b Murad Khan	7
6	Raisul Islam	c Syed Rasel b Murad Khan	6	c Habibul Bashar b Syed Rasel	35
7	Arafat Salahuddin	c Imrul Kayes b Murad Khan	25	c Mashrafe Mortaza b Murad Khan	3
8	†Shahin Hossain	c Saghir Hossain b Murad Khan	4	c Saghir Hossain b Mashrafe Mortaza	19
9	Talha Jubair	b Murad Khan	6	b Syed Rasel	11
10	Sajidul Islam	lbw b Tushar Imran	13	c Shakib Al Hasan b Mashrafe Mortaza	8
11	Tariqul Islam	not out	2	not out	0
	Extras	b 4, lb 7, w 2, nb 10	23	b 6, lb 4, w 3, nb 4	17
			206		187

FoW (1): 1-10 (2), 2-27 (1), 3-121 (4), 4-128 (3), 5-138 (6), 6-164 (5), 7-180 (8), 8-188 (9), 9-189 (7), 10-206 (10)
FoW (2): 1-1 (2), 2-23 (3), 3-62 (1), 4-84 (5), 5-128 (4), 6-133 (7), 7-158 (8), 8-175 (9), 9-187 (10), 10-187 (6)

Barisal Division Bowling

	O	M	R	W	
Talha Jubair	27	8	51	2	3w,2nb
Sajidul Islam	22.2	5	69	2	1w,1nb
Arafat Salahuddin	27	5	92	1	
Tariqul Islam	25	4	99	0	1nb
Hannan Sarkar	5	1	24	0	1w
Abul Bashar	8	0	29	2	
Raqibul Hasan	3	0	15	0	

Khulna Division Bowling

	O	M	R	W		O	M	R	W	
Mashrafe Mortaza	16	4	50	0	1w,5nb	19	2	64	3	1w,1nb
Syed Rasel	13	1	38	2	1w,5nb	19.2	7	33	4	1w,2nb
Ziaur Rahman	13	5	33	0		7	2	12	0	1w,1nb
Murad Khan	31	10	53	7	(5)	21	12	30	2	
Shakib Al Hasan	10	2	21	0	(4)	10	3	30	0	
Tushar Imran	0.3	0	0	1		5	2	8	0	

Umpires: Enamul Haque and Mizanur Rahman. Referee: Hemayat Ahmed. Toss: Barisal Division

Close of Play: 1st day: Khulna Division (1) 312-6 (Tushar Imran 122*, Ziaur Rahman 20*, 90 overs); 2nd day: Barisal Division (1) 159-5 (Abul Bashar 14*, Arafat Salahuddin 13*, 60 overs); 3rd day: Barisal Division (2) 133-6 (Raisul Islam 24*, 63.3 overs).

Man of the Match: Tushar Imran.
Tushar Imran's 165 took 317 balls in 427 minutes and included 25 fours and 1 six. Habibul Bashar retired hurt in the Khulna Division first innings having scored 13 (team score 31-2, 13 ov).

CHITTAGONG DIVISION v SYLHET DIVISION

Played at Bir Shrestha Shahid Ruhul Amin Stadium, Chittagong, November 18, 19, 20, 21, 2007.
Ispahani Mirzapore Tea National Cricket League 2007/08
Chittagong Division won by six wickets.   (Points: Chittagong Division 15, Sylhet Division 4)

CHITTAGONG DIVISION

1	Gazi Salahuddin	b Tapash Baisya	138	c Rajin Saleh b Enamul Haque	25
2	Nafees Iqbal	b Rashedur Rahman	9	c Mushfiqur Rahim b Enamul Haque	34
3	Nazimuddin	c Imtiaz Hossain b Rashedur Rahman	0	c Golam Rahman b Enamul Haque	0
4	Aftab Ahmed	b Nabil Samad	46	c sub (Sadiqur Rahman) b Enamul Haque	6
5	*Ehsanul Haque	c Mushfiqur Rahim b Nabil Samad	30	not out	34
6	Faisal Hossain	c sub (Sadiqur Rahman) b Alok Kapali	11		
7	†Dhiman Ghosh	lbw b Nabil Samad	7	(6) not out	47
8	Yasin Arafat	c Imtiaz Hossain b Nabil Samad	1		
9	Tareq Aziz	c Rajin Saleh b Enamul Haque	5		
10	Kamrul Islam	st Golam Mabud b Enamul Haque	17		
11	Saju Datta	not out	10		
	Extras	b 7, lb 12, w 1, nb 14	34	b 9, nb 6	15
			308	(4 wickets)	161

FoW (1): 1-18 (2), 2-30 (3), 3-131 (4), 4-188 (5), 5-224 (6), 6-233 (7), 7-243 (8), 8-258 (9), 9-280 (1), 10-308 (10)
FoW (2): 1-54 (1), 2-54 (3), 3-60 (4), 4-82 (2)

SYLHET DIVISION

1	Imtiaz Hossain	c Dhiman Ghosh b Tareq Aziz	7	st Dhiman Ghosh b Tareq Aziz	4
2	Golam Rahman	c Dhiman Ghosh b Tareq Aziz	20	c Nafees Iqbal b Yasin Arafat	20
3	*Rajin Saleh	lbw b Yasin Arafat	21	c sub (Masumud Dowla) b Yasin Arafat	13
4	Mushfiqur Rahim	b Saju Datta	14	(7) c Dhiman Ghosh b Kamrul Islam	43
5	Alok Kapali	c Dhiman Ghosh b Kamrul Islam	12	(4) c Kamrul Islam b Yasin Arafat	36
6	†Golam Mabud	b Saju Datta	5	b Saju Datta	110
7	Sharifullah	c Dhiman Ghosh b Kamrul Islam	10	(5) c Faisal Hossain b Yasin Arafat	17
8	Tapash Baisya	lbw b Saju Datta	5	c sub (Mahbubul Karim) b Saju Datta	1
9	Enamul Haque	lbw b Saju Datta	15	run out	25
10	Nabil Samad	c sub (Masumud Dowla) b Kamrul Islam	5	lbw b Ehsanul Haque	33
11	Rashedur Rahman	not out	0	not out	22
	Extras	b 3, lb 1, w 6, nb 3	13	b 6, lb 4, w 3, nb 2	15
			127		339

FoW (1): 1-27 (1), 2-55 (3), 3-55 (2), 4-72 (5), 5-79 (6), 6-86 (8), 7-111 (9), 8-111 (7), 9-117 (10), 10-127 (4)
FoW (2): 1-4 (1), 2-35 (2), 3-48 (3), 4-66 (5), 5-137 (4), 6-224 (7), 7-242 (8), 8-261 (6), 9-296 (9), 10-339 (10)

Sylhet Division Bowling	O	M	R	W		O	M	R	W	
Tapash Baisya	20	7	47	1	3nb	7	2	18	0	
Rashedur Rahman	22	4	75	2	7nb	9	2	29	0	1nb
Golam Rahman	4	0	15	0	1w					
Enamul Haque	22.1	1	74	2	4nb	14.5	2	62	4	5nb
Nabil Samad	24	7	60	4	(3)	9	3	28	0	
Alok Kapali	9	2	18	1						
Imtiaz Hossain					(5)	2	0	15	0	

Chittagong Division Bowling	O	M	R	W		O	M	R	W	
Tareq Aziz	15	5	49	2	3nb	14	1	50	1	2nb
Kamrul Islam	14	2	34	3	5w	15	2	35	1	3w
Yasin Arafat	7	2	17	1	(4)	37	9	107	4	
Saju Datta	7.5	1	23	4	(5)	40	6	107	2	
Aftab Ahmed					(3)	2	0	10	0	
Ehsanul Haque					(6)	7	2	20	1	

Umpires: Anisur Rahman and Syed Mahabubullah. Referee: Samiur Rahman. Toss: Chittagong Division

Close of Play: 1st day: Chittagong Division (1) 289-9 (Kamrul Islam 8*, Saju Datta 7*, 92 overs); 2nd day: Sylhet Division (2) 76-4 (Alok Kapali 11*, Golam Mabud 3*, 32 overs); 3rd day: Chittagong Division (2) 11-0 (Gazi Salahuddin 9*, Nafees Iqbal 1*, 7 overs).
Man of the Match: Gazi Salahuddin.
Gazi Salahuddin's 138 took 269 balls in 315 minutes and included 12 fours and 1 six. Golam Mabud's 110 took 199 balls in 253 minutes and included 11 fours and 2 sixes. Mushfiqur Rahim retired hurt in the Sylhet Division first innings having scored 3 (team score 76-4) - he returned when the score was 111-7 (28 ov).

RAJSHAHI DIVISION v DHAKA DIVISION

Played at Bir Shrestha Shahid Captain Mohiuddin Jahangir Stadium, Rajshahi, November 18, 19, 20, 21, 2007.
Ispahani Mirzapore Tea National Cricket League 2007/08
Rajshahi Division won by 70 runs.   (Points: Rajshahi Division 13, Dhaka Division 5)

RAJSHAHI DIVISION

1	†Jahurul Islam	c Anwar Hossain b Niaz Morshed	18	run out	0
2	Junaid Siddique	c Mosharraf Hossain			
		b Mohammad Sharif	18	lbw b Mahbubul Alam	5
3	Farhad Hossain	lbw b Mahbubul Alam	55	b Mahbubul Alam	17
4	Naeem Islam	c Al Sahariar b Mohammad Sharif	19	lbw b Mohammad Sharif	1
5	*Khaled Mashud	c and b Mosharraf Hossain	73	b Niaz Morshed	12
6	Mushfiqur Rahman	c Anwar Hossain b Mosharraf Hossain	65	c Anwar Hossain b Mahbubul Alam	21
7	Alamgir Kabir	c Anwar Hossain b Mahbubul Alam	3	(11) not out	4
8	Farhad Reza	not out	32	(7) lbw b Mahbubul Alam	98
9	Anisur Rahman	c Anwar Hossain b Mahbubul Alam	0	(8) c Al Sahariar b Mosharraf Hossain	31
10	Mohammad Shahzada	b Mahbubul Alam	2	(9) b Mahbubul Alam	20
11	Saqlain Sajib	run out (Mosharraf Hossain)	0	(10) run out (Mosharraf Hossain)	2
	Extras	lb 5, w 2, nb 6	13	b 5, lb 9, w 1, nb 3	18
			298		**229**

FoW (1): 1-33 (2), 2-49 (1), 3-88 (4), 4-124 (3), 5-248 (6), 6-263 (7), 7-263 (8), 8-264 (9), 9-270 (10), 10-298 (11)
FoW (2): 1-0 (1), 2-10 (2), 3-11 (4), 4-26 (5), 5-59 (3), 6-66 (6), 7-133 (8), 8-195 (9), 9-223 (10), 10-229 (7)

DHAKA DIVISION

1	Javed Omar	lbw b Farhad Reza	36	c Farhad Hossain b Farhad Reza	20
2	†Anwar Hossain	c Khaled Mashud b Alamgir Kabir	0	(8) c Mohammad Shahzada	
				b Alamgir Kabir	8
3	Al Sahariar	c Khaled Mashud b Alamgir Kabir	20	(2) st Khaled Mashud b Saqlain Sajib	44
4	*Mohammad Ashraful	c Anisur Rahman b Alamgir Kabir	27	c Saqlain Sajib b Farhad Reza	58
5	Mehrab Hossain	c Farhad Reza b Mushfiqur Rahman	43	lbw b Saqlain Sajib	20
6	Shamsur Rahman	c Farhad Reza b Saqlain Sajib	55	c and b Saqlain Sajib	5
7	Mahmudullah	c Naeem Islam b Saqlain Sajib	3	(3) c Khaled Mashud b Alamgir Kabir	24
8	Mosharraf Hossain	lbw b Saqlain Sajib	6	(7) lbw b Saqlain Sajib	0
9	Mohammad Sharif	not out	4	not out	42
10	Mahbubul Alam	b Saqlain Sajib	0	c Jahurul Islam b Saqlain Sajib	11
11	Niaz Morshed	not out	0	lbw b Farhad Reza	4
	Extras	lb 8, w 1, nb 2	11	b 8, lb 3, w 1, nb 4	16
		(9 wickets, declared)	**205**		**252**

FoW (1): 1-4 (2), 2-39 (3), 3-82 (4), 4-96 (1), 5-184 (5), 6-189 (7), 7-199 (6), 8-204 (8), 9-204 (10)
FoW (2): 1-25 (1), 2-86 (3), 3-114 (2), 4-166 (4), 5-173 (5), 6-177 (7), 7-180 (6), 8-209 (8), 9-227 (10), 10-252 (11)

Dhaka Division Bowling	O	M	R	W		O	M	R	W	
Mahbubul Alam	25	3	53	4	3nb	22.1	2	47	5	2nb
Mohammad Sharif	14	3	51	2	1w,1nb	17	3	45	1	1w
Niaz Morshed	17	6	40	1		13	5	20	1	
Mosharraf Hossain	30	9	75	2	2nb	25	1	72	1	1nb
Mohammad Ashraful	8	0	30	0	1w	10	0	27	0	
Mahmudullah	5	1	22	0						
Mehrab Hossain	8	1	22	0	(6) 1	0	4	0		

Rajshahi Division Bowling	O	M	R	W		O	M	R	W	
Mohammad Shahzada	18	7	48	0		9	2	30	0	
Alamgir Kabir	16	2	65	3	1w,1nb	15	4	46	2	1w
Farhad Reza	14	5	30	1		16.5	4	45	3	
Saqlain Sajib	12	3	34	4	1nb	(5) 33	9	92	5	4nb
Mushfiqur Rahman	8	3	8	1	(4) 3	0	16	0		
Naeem Islam	2	0	11	0						
Farhad Hossain	1	0	1	0	(6) 6	1	12	0		

Umpires: Mahfuzur Rahman and Nadir Shah. Referee: Raqibul Hasan.   Toss: Dhaka Division

Close of Play: 1st day: Rajshahi Division (1) 257-5 (Khaled Mashud 68*, Alamgir Kabir 2*, 90 overs); 2nd day: Dhaka Division (1) 205-9 (Mohammad Sharif 4*, Niaz Morshed 0*, 71 overs); 3rd day: Rajshahi Division (2) 229-9 (Farhad Reza 98*, Alamgir Kabir 4*, 88 overs).
Man of the Match: Farhad Reza.

CHITTAGONG DIVISION v BARISAL DIVISION

Played at Bir Shrestha Shahid Ruhul Amin Stadium, Chittagong, November 27, 28, 29, 30, 2007.
Ispahani Mirzapore Tea National Cricket League 2007/08
Chittagong Division won by seven wickets. (Points: Chittagong Division 16, Barisal Division 5)

BARISAL DIVISION

1	Hannan Sarkar	c and b Tareq Aziz	10	c Dhiman Ghosh b Kamrul Islam	0
2	*Shahriar Nafees	c Ehsanul Haque b Yasin Arafat	108	c Dhiman Ghosh b Ehsanul Haque	9
3	Imran Ahmed	c Ehsanul Haque b Kamrul Islam	12	b Kamrul Islam	0
4	Raqibul Hasan	lbw b Saju Datta	24	c Nazimuddin b Kamrul Islam	43
5	Raisul Islam	c Dhiman Ghosh b Tareq Aziz	40	lbw b Dhiman Ghosh	21
6	Humayun Kabir	c Saju Datta b Faisal Hossain	23	c Ehsanul Haque b Dhiman Ghosh	26
7	Arafat Salahuddin	lbw b Tareq Aziz	9	(8) b Tareq Aziz	31
8	†Shahin Hossain	b Kamrul Islam	1	(7) lbw b Tareq Aziz	0
9	Talha Jubair	c Tareq Aziz b Kamrul Islam	7	(10) c Dhiman Ghosh b Tareq Aziz	6
10	Sajidul Islam	not out	31	(9) c Dhiman Ghosh b Yasin Arafat	37
11	Tariqul Islam	b Saju Datta	11	not out	0
	Extras	b 1, lb 6, w 1, nb 9	17	b 4, lb 7, w 5, nb 3	19
			293		**192**

FoW (1): 1-20 (1), 2-39 (3), 3-135 (4), 4-169 (2), 5-205 (6), 6-227 (7), 7-235 (8), 8-235 (5), 9-252 (9), 10-293 (11)
FoW (2): 1-0 (1), 2-0 (3), 3-51 (2), 4-61 (4), 5-112 (5), 6-115 (7), 7-117 (6), 8-186 (8), 9-188 (9), 10-192 (10)

CHITTAGONG DIVISION

1	Gazi Salahuddin	c Humayun Kabir b Talha Jubair	17	c Shahriar Nafees b Arafat Salahuddin	60
2	Nafees Iqbal	c Arafat Salahuddin b Tariqul Islam	153	run out	25
3	Nazimuddin	c Tariqul Islam b Arafat Salahuddin	57	c Shahin Hossain b Arafat Salahuddin	4
4	Aftab Ahmed	c Hannan Sarkar b Talha Jubair	15	(5) not out	2
5	*Ehsanul Haque	c Humayun Kabir b Raisul Islam	42		
6	Faisal Hossain	lbw b Sajidul Islam	13		
7	†Dhiman Ghosh	c Shahin Hossain b Sajidul Islam	1	(4) not out	33
8	Kamrul Islam	c Hannan Sarkar b Tariqul Islam	16		
9	Tareq Aziz	not out	10		
10	Saju Datta	b Sajidul Islam	2		
11	Yasin Arafat	not out	1		
	Extras	b 5, lb 6, w 3, nb 11	25	b 6, lb 7	13
		(9 wickets, declared)	**352**	(3 wickets)	**137**

FoW (1): 1-29 (1), 2-128 (3), 3-165 (4), 4-243 (5), 5-283 (6), 6-285 (7), 7-328 (2), 8-349 (8), 9-351 (10)
FoW (2): 1-76 (2), 2-91 (3), 3-107 (3)

Chittagong Division Bowling	O	M	R	W			O	M	R	W	
Tareq Aziz	23	4	89	3	8nb	(2)	21.5	5	58	3	2w,3nb
Kamrul Islam	23	4	94	3	1w	(1)	17	1	39	3	2w
Yasin Arafat	24	7	39	1		(5)	17	7	29	1	
Saju Datta	24.4	5	42	2			18	6	32	0	
Ehsanul Haque	2	0	7	0		(3)	5	1	14	1	
Faisal Hossain	2	0	15	1							
Nazimuddin						(6)	1	0	2	0	
Dhiman Ghosh						(7)	4	2	7	2	

Barisal Division Bowling	O	M	R	W			O	M	R	W	
Talha Jubair	25.1	4	67	2	2w,10nb		5	0	26	0	
Sajidul Islam	28	3	85	3			5	0	20	0	
Arafat Salahuddin	23	8	56	1	1w	(4)	9	2	42	2	
Tariqul Islam	29	5	95	2		(3)	9	1	36	0	
Raqibul Hasan	3	0	11	0							
Humayun Kabir	1	0	8	0							
Raisul Islam	4	0	19	1							

Umpires: Anisur Rahman and Mahfuzur Rahman. Referee: Belayet Hossain. Toss: Barisal Division
Close of Play: 1st day: Barisal Division (1) 264-9 (Sajidul Islam 8*, Tariqul Islam 7*, 90 overs); 2nd day: Chittagong Division (1) 270-4 (Nafees Iqbal 118*, Faisal Hossain 9*, 77.1 overs); 3rd day: Barisal Division (2) 117-7 (Arafat Salahuddin 2*, Sajidul Islam 0*, 53 overs).
Man of the Match: Nafees Iqbal.
Shahriar Nafees's 108 took 141 balls in 222 minutes and included 16 fours. Nafees Iqbal's 153 took 293 balls in 417 minutes and included 20 fours.

KHULNA DIVISION v DHAKA DIVISION

Played at Bir Shrestha Shahid Flight Lieutenant Motiur Rahman Stadium, Khulna, November 27, 28, 29, 30, 2007.
Ispahani Mirzapore Tea National Cricket League 2007/08
Match drawn. (Points: Khulna Division 10, Dhaka Division 7)

KHULNA DIVISION

1	Nazmus Sadat	c Anwar Hossain b Mosharraf Hossain	61	lbw b Mahbubul Alam	6
2	Imrul Kayes	c Mehrab Hossain		lbw b Mosharraf Hossain	48
		b Mohammad Ashraful	19		
3	Mostafizur Rahman	c Mosharraf Hossain		c Mehrab Hossain	
		b Mohammad Ashraful	62	b Mohammad Ashraful	42
4	Tushar Imran	st Anwar Hossain			
		b Mohammad Ashraful	54	b Mahmudullah	92
5	Shakib Al Hasan	c and b Mohammad Sharif	9	not out	103
6	Nahidul Haque	c Mahmudullah b Mosharraf Hossain	7	(7) not out	13
7	†Saghir Hossain	lbw b Shahadat Hossain	13		
8	*Mashrafe Mortaza	b Mahbubul Alam	2	(6) b Mahmudullah	3
9	Ziaur Rahman	lbw b Mahbubul Alam	0		
10	Manjural Islam	b Mahbubul Alam	6		
11	Murad Khan	not out	0		
	Extras	b 4, lb 12, w 1, nb 3	20	b 2, lb 7, w 4, nb 7	20
			253	**(5 wickets, declared)**	**327**

FoW (1): 1-64 (2), 2-113 (1), 3-176 (3), 4-213 (5), 5-228 (6), 6-232 (4), 7-237 (8), 8-239 (9), 9-253 (7), 10-253 (10)
FoW (2): 1-7 (1), 2-84 (3), 3-114 (2), 4-266 (4), 5-270 (6)

DHAKA DIVISION

1	Al Sahariar	lbw b Mashrafe Mortaza	1		
2	Mehrab Hossain	lbw b Murad Khan	26	run out	75
3	Mahmudullah	c Nahidul Haque b Shakib Al Hasan	51	(4) c and b Murad Khan	27
4	*Mohammad Ashraful	c Tushar Imran b Manjural Islam	9	(3) run out	67
5	Shamsur Rahman	b Shakib Al Hasan	19	not out	51
6	Nadif Chowdhury	b Mashrafe Mortaza	27	not out	4
7	Mosharraf Hossain	lbw b Mashrafe Mortaza	9		
8	†Anwar Hossain	not out	27	(1) c Imrul Kayes b Shakib Al Hasan	40
9	Mohammad Sharif	b Mashrafe Mortaza	8		
10	Shahadat Hossain	c Saghir Hossain b Ziaur Rahman	5		
11	Mahbubul Alam	b Shakib Al Hasan	0		
	Extras	b 5, lb 8, nb 9	22	b 9, lb 2	11
			204	**(4 wickets)**	**275**

FoW (1): 1-1 (1), 2-65 (2), 3-84 (4), 4-113 (3), 5-122 (5), 6-140 (7), 7-174 (6), 8-197 (9), 9-203 (10), 10-204 (11)
FoW (2): 1-97 (1), 2-133 (2), 3-174 (4), 4-232 (3)

Dhaka Division Bowling	O	M	R	W		O	M	R	W	
Mahbubul Alam	14.1	2	38	3		8.1	0	42	1	4nb
Mohammad Sharif	15	5	27	1	(3)	7	0	34	0	
Shahadat Hossain	17	4	41	1	3nb	(2)	7	0	44	0	3nb
Mahmudullah	3	0	7	0	(7)	9	0	32	2	
Mosharraf Hossain	30	4	68	2	(4)	26	5	97	1	
Mohammad Ashraful	15	1	56	3	1w	(5)	16	2	64	1	1w
Nadif Chowdhury					(6)	2	0	5	0	
Mehrab Hossain					(8)	1	1	0	0	

Khulna Division Bowling	O	M	R	W		O	M	R	W	
Ziaur Rahman	17	2	33	1		8	3	12	0	
Mashrafe Mortaza	20	5	44	4	9nb					
Manjural Islam	20	6	32	1	(2)	10	1	40	0	
Murad Khan	18	3	48	1	(3)	24	3	85	1	
Shakib Al Hasan	23	11	32	3	(4)	17	3	53	1	
Tushar Imran	1	0	2	0	(5)	7	1	20	0	
Nazmus Sadat					(6)	10	1	43	0	
Nahidul Haque					(7)	2	0	11	0	

Umpires: S.B.Chowdhury and Showkatur Rahman. Referee: Samiur Rahman. Toss: Khulna Division
Close of Play: 1st day: Khulna Division (1) 239-7 (Saghir Hossain 5*, Ziaur Rahman 0*, 90 overs); 2nd day: Dhaka Division (1) 173-6 (Nadif Chowdhury 27*, Anwar Hossain 14*, 83 overs); 3rd day: Khulna Division (2) 288-5 (Shakib Al Hasan 82*, Nahidul Haque 4*, 72 overs).
Man of the Match: Tushar Imran. Shakib Al Hasan's 103 took 136 balls in 185 minutes and included 9 fours.

RAJSHAHI DIVISION v SYLHET DIVISION

Played at Narayanganj Osmani Stadium, Fatullah, November 27, 28, 29, 30, 2007.
Ispahani Mirzapore Tea National Cricket League 2007/08
Match drawn. (Points: Rajshahi Division 11, Sylhet Division 8)

RAJSHAHI DIVISION

1	†Jahurul Islam	b Tapash Baisya	2	(6) b Alok Kapali		0
2	Junaid Siddique	lbw b Tapash Baisya	8	lbw b Enamul Haque		12
3	Farhad Hossain	run out (Ezaz Ahmed)	106	lbw b Alok Kapali		13
4	Anisur Rahman	c Rajin Saleh b Alok Kapali	114	(8) c Enamul Haque b Alok Kapali		47
5	Naeem Islam	b Enamul Haque	2	(4) b Enamul Haque		50
6	Mushfiqur Rahman	c sub b Alok Kapali	13	(5) c Ezaz Ahmed b Alok Kapali		6
7	Alamgir Kabir	c and b Nazmul Hossain	14	(11) not out		0
8	Farhad Reza	c Rashedur Rahman b Enamul Haque	55	(9) c Nazmul Hossain b Sadiqur Rahman		36
9	*Khaled Mashud	lbw b Enamul Haque	33	(7) c Sadiqur Rahman b Enamul Haque		30
10	Mohammad Shahzada	c Nazmul Hossain b Enamul Haque	32	b Sadiqur Rahman		5
11	Saqlain Sajib	not out	12	(1) lbw b Alok Kapali		8
	Extras	b 18, lb 4, w 1, nb 3	26	b 17, lb 2, w 1, nb 1		21
			417			**228**

FoW (1): 1-8 (1), 2-16 (2), 3-221 (3), 4-229 (5), 5-256 (6), 6-276 (4), 7-276 (7), 8-364 (9), 9-371 (8), 10-417 (10)
FoW (2): 1-20 (2), 2-22 (1), 3-71 (3), 4-87 (5), 5-87 (6), 6-100 (4), 7-170 (7), 8-210 (8), 9-227 (9), 10-228 (10)

SYLHET DIVISION

1	Imtiaz Hossain	c Naeem Islam b Alamgir Kabir	69			
2	†Kuntal Chandra	c Farhad Hossain b Saqlain Sajib	1			
3	Sadiqur Rahman	c Jahurul Islam b Alamgir Kabir	18	(2) not out		2
4	*Rajin Saleh	c Jahurul Islam b Alamgir Kabir	13			
5	Alok Kapali	c Junaid Siddique b Alamgir Kabir	2			
6	Golam Mabud	not out	82			
7	Ezaz Ahmed	c and b Saqlain Sajib	65			
8	Nazmul Hossain	c Farhad Hossain b Saqlain Sajib	6	(1) b Farhad Hossain		8
9	Enamul Haque	c Khaled Mashud b Saqlain Sajib	12			
10	Rashedur Rahman	c Mohammad Shahzada b Saqlain Sajib	1	(3) c Mohammad Shahzada b Farhad Hossain		8
11	Tapash Baisya	absent hurt	0			
	Extras	b 5, lb 12, w 3, nb 4	24	b 1		1
			293	**(2 wickets)**		**19**

FoW (1): 1-23 (2), 2-92 (1), 3-110 (3), 4-112 (5), 5-121 (4), 6-256 (7), 7-264 (8), 8-291 (9), 9-293 (10)
FoW (2): 1-9 (1), 2-19 (3)

Sylhet Division Bowling	O	M	R	W		O	M	R	W	
Tapash Baisya	4.3	1	14	2	2nb					
Rashedur Rahman	24	5	70	0	1w	6	0	22	0	
Alok Kapali	27.3	5	89	2		34	6	77	5	
Nazmul Hossain	18	3	53	1		(1) 11	4	14	0	
Enamul Haque	47.1	12	107	4	1nb	(4) 32	13	57	3	1nb
Sadiqur Rahman	9	2	23	0		(5) 5	1	21	2	1w
Golam Mabud	11	2	39	0						
Ezaz Ahmed						(6) 3	0	12	0	
Imtiaz Hossain						(7) 2	0	6	0	

Rajshahi Division Bowling	O	M	R	W		O	M	R	W	
Mohammad Shahzada	19	6	51	0	2w					
Alamgir Kabir	31	12	74	4	3nb					
Saqlain Sajib	27.5	8	55	5	1nb					
Farhad Reza	17	7	47	0	1w					
Mushfiqur Rahman	8	2	38	0		(1) 2	0	13	0	
Farhad Hossain	9	3	11	0		(2) 1.4	1	5	2	

Umpires: Mahbubur Rahman and Sailab Hossain. Referee: Akhtar Ahmed. Toss: Sylhet Division
Close of Play: 1st day: Rajshahi Division (1) 256-5 (Alamgir Kabir 6*, 89.2 overs); 2nd day: Sylhet Division (1) 88-1 (Imtiaz Hossain 65*, Sadiqur Rahman 9*, 37 overs); 3rd day: Rajshahi Division (2) 24-2 (Farhad Hossain 1*, Naeem Islam 2*, 13 overs).
Man of the Match: Anisur Rahman.
Farhad Hossain's 106 took 252 balls in 290 minutes and included 12 fours. Anisur Rahman's 114 took 232 balls in 330 minutes and included 13 fours. Anisur Rahman retired hurt in the Rajshahi Division first innings having scored 102 (team score 243-4) - he returned when the score was 256-5 (86 ov).

CHITTAGONG DIVISION v KHULNA DIVISION

Played at Bir Shrestha Shahid Ruhul Amin Stadium, Chittagong, December 5, 6, 7, 8, 2007.
Ispahani Mirzapore Tea National Cricket League 2007/08
Match drawn.   (Points: Chittagong Division 12, Khulna Division 8)

CHITTAGONG DIVISION

1	Gazi Salahuddin	lbw b Nahidul Haque	94	lbw b Robiul Islam	12	
2	Nafees Iqbal	lbw b Murad Khan	40	c Mohammad Salim b Ziaur Rahman	9	
3	Mahbubul Karim	lbw b Robiul Islam	61	c sub b Murad Khan	26	
4	Nazimuddin	b Murad Khan	12	not out	121	
5	*Ehsanul Haque	c Fariduddin b Murad Khan	78	(6) c Habibul Bashar b Robiul Islam	15	
6	Faisal Hossain	c Habibul Bashar b Fariduddin	19	(7) b Murad Khan	0	
7	†Dhiman Ghosh	b Robiul Islam	5	(5) b Ziaur Rahman	5	
8	Mohammad Younus	b Ziaur Rahman	5	(11) not out	14	
9	Kamrul Islam	c and b Ziaur Rahman	3	(8) c Mohammad Salim b Nahidul Haque	11	
10	Yasin Arafat	not out	15	c Habibul Bashar b Fariduddin	4	
11	Saju Datta	b Robiul Islam	0	(9) c Mohammad Salim b Ziaur Rahman	4	
	Extras	b 11, lb 7, w 1, nb 8	27	b 2, lb 4, w 1, nb 1	8	
			359	**(9 wickets, declared)**	**229**	

FoW (1): 1-67 (2), 2-188 (3), 3-215 (4), 4-219 (1), 5-251 (6), 6-275 (7), 7-284 (8), 8-316 (9), 9-358 (5), 10-359 (11)
FoW (2): 1-18 (1), 2-37 (2), 3-62 (3), 4-74 (5), 5-98 (6), 6-98 (7), 7-131 (8), 8-134 (9), 9-165 (10)

KHULNA DIVISION

1	Nazmus Sadat	c Dhiman Ghosh b Kamrul Islam	91	c Faisal Hossain b Yasin Arafat	36	
2	Imrul Kayes	c Kamrul Islam b Mohammad Younus	15	c Kamrul Islam b Ehsanul Haque	10	
3	Mostafizur Rahman	run out (Nazimuddin)	10	c Mohammad Younus b Yasin Arafat	13	
4	*Habibul Bashar	c Gazi Salahuddin b Yasin Arafat	35	b Yasin Arafat	50	
5	Nahidul Haque	c Nazimuddin b Mohammad Younus	37	c and b Saju Datta	37	
6	Sanjay Chakrabarty	b Yasin Arafat	0	not out	30	
7	†Mohammad Salim	c Gazi Salahuddin b Yasin Arafat	7			
8	Ziaur Rahman	run out (Mohammad Younus)	18			
9	Fariduddin	b Mohammad Younus	38	(7) not out	7	
10	Murad Khan	not out	10			
11	Robiul Islam	lbw b Yasin Arafat	0			
	Extras	b 12, lb 5, w 2, nb 2	21	b 1, w 1, nb 3	5	
			282	**(5 wickets)**	**188**	

FoW (1): 1-65 (2), 2-87 (3), 3-142 (1), 4-174 (4), 5-178 (6), 6-204 (7), 7-228 (5), 8-228 (8), 9-281 (9), 10-282 (11)
FoW (2): 1-32 (2), 2-50 (1), 3-68 (3), 4-143 (5), 5-167 (4)

Khulna Division Bowling	O	M	R	W		O	M	R	W	
Ziaur Rahman	21	2	68	2	1w,3nb	22	5	74	3	1w,1nb
Robiul Islam	25	2	102	3	3nb	17.3	2	63	2	
Murad Khan	30	5	85	3		20	10	46	2	
Sanjay Chakrabarty	1	0	4	0						
Fariduddin	16	4	51	1	(4)	11	1	35	1	
Nazmus Sadat	2	0	14	0						
Nahidul Haque	6	1	17	1	(5)	5	1	5	1	

Chittagong Division Bowling	O	M	R	W		O	M	R	W	
Kamrul Islam	28	3	100	1	2w,1nb	6	1	27	0	
Ehsanul Haque	6	0	31	0	1nb	8	0	31	1	1nb
Mohammad Younus	23	9	37	3		16	3	31	0	2nb
Yasin Arafat	32.1	13	62	4		16	2	54	3	
Saju Datta	20	3	31	0		11	1	39	1	
Faisal Hossain	1	0	4	0						
Dhiman Ghosh					(6)	2	0	5	0	

Umpires: Jahangir Alam and Manzur Rahman.   Referee: Belayet Hossain.   Toss: Chittagong Division

Close of Play: 1st day: Chittagong Division (1) 322-8 (Ehsanul Haque 56*, Yasin Arafat 2*, 90 overs); 2nd day: Khulna Division (1) 216-6 (Nahidul Haque 33*, Ziaur Rahman 11*, 77 overs); 3rd day: Chittagong Division (2) 134-7 (Nazimuddin 48*, Saju Datta 2*, 54 overs).

Man of the Match: Nazimuddin.
Nazimuddin's 121 took 183 balls in 280 minutes and included 11 fours and 6 sixes.

DHAKA DIVISION v SYLHET DIVISION

Played at Narayanganj Osmani Stadium, Fatullah, December 5, 6, 7, 8, 2007.
Ispahani Mirzapore Tea National Cricket League 2007/08
Match drawn.   (Points: Dhaka Division 8, Sylhet Division 11)

SYLHET DIVISION

1	Golam Rahman	run out (Al Sahariar)	43	lbw b Mahmudullah		23
2	Imtiaz Hossain	lbw b Mohammad Sharif	20	c Anwar Hossain b Mahmudullah		148
3	Sadiqur Rahman	c Anwar Hossain b Mohammad Sharif	4	c and b Mohammad Rafique		1
4	*Rajin Saleh	c Al Sahariar b Mohammad Rafique	36	c Anwar Hossain b Mahbubul Alam		71
5	Alok Kapali	lbw b Mahbubul Alam	1	c Mahbubul Alam b Mohammad Rafique		8
6	†Golam Mabud	not out	75	c Mohammad Sharif b Mosharraf Hossain		31
7	Ezaz Ahmed	c Anwar Hossain b Mahbubul Alam	54	c Mehrab Hossain b Mahmudullah		3
8	Rezaul Haque	lbw b Mohammad Sharif	20	(9) not out		7
9	Enamul Haque	run out (Anwar Hossain)	38	(8) c Mahbubul Alam		
					b Mohammad Rafique	7
10	Nabil Samad	lbw b Mohammad Sharif	4			
11	Rashedur Rahman	lbw b Mohammad Rafique	0			
	Extras	b 6, lb 2, nb 9	17	b 4, lb 2, nb 1		7
			312	(8 wickets, declared)		**306**

FoW (1): 1-31 (2), 2-35 (3), 3-98 (1), 4-108 (5), 5-112 (4), 6-176 (7), 7-206 (8), 8-289 (9), 9-311 (10), 10-312 (11)
FoW (2): 1-48 (1), 2-49 (3), 3-212 (4), 4-221 (5), 5-287 (6), 6-293 (2), 7-298 (7), 8-306 (8)

DHAKA DIVISION

1	Uttam Sarkar	b Golam Rahman	0	(6) c Golam Rahman b Alok Kapali		23
2	†Anwar Hossain	b Nabil Samad	31	(8) run out		0
3	Mahmudullah	b Rashedur Rahman	8	(5) not out		60
4	Mehrab Hossain	b Nabil Samad	36	(9) not out		13
5	*Al Sahariar	c Alok Kapali b Nabil Samad	2	(1) b Golam Rahman		12
6	Shamsur Rahman	c Golam Mabud b Enamul Haque	36	(7) c Enamul Haque b Golam Mabud		18
7	Nadif Chowdhury	c Enamul Haque b Nabil Samad	29	(4) c Golam Mabud b Golam Rahman		7
8	Mosharraf Hossain	not out	67			
9	Mohammad Sharif	lbw b Enamul Haque	24	(3) b Rashedur Rahman		5
10	Mohammad Rafique	c Enamul Haque b Imtiaz Hossain	19	(2) b Rashedur Rahman		37
11	Mahbubul Alam	lbw b Enamul Haque	0			
	Extras	b 10, lb 7, w 1, nb 3	21	b 6, lb 1, w 3, nb 3		13
			273	(7 wickets)		**188**

FoW (1): 1-1 (1), 2-10 (3), 3-81 (4), 4-87 (5), 5-96 (2), 6-150 (7), 7-189 (6), 8-243 (9), 9-273 (10), 10-273 (11)
FoW (2): 1-35 (1), 2-60 (2), 3-63 (3), 4-69 (4), 5-116 (6), 6-148 (7), 7-149 (8)

Dhaka Division Bowling	O	M	R	W			O	M	R	W	
Mahbubul Alam	23	6	74	2	9nb	(2)	10	0	51	1	1nb
Mohammad Sharif	23	8	60	4		(1)	15	3	40	0	
Mohammad Rafique	41	8	110	2			30.3	4	97	3	
Mosharraf Hossain	28	5	60	0		(5)	24	6	66	1	
Mahmudullah	1	1	0	0		(4)	11	0	42	3	
Mehrab Hossain						(6)	1	0	4	0	

Sylhet Division Bowling	O	M	R	W			O	M	R	W	
Rashedur Rahman	10	2	34	1			7	0	37	2	1nb
Golam Rahman	5	3	2	1		(3)	5	0	41	2	2w
Rezaul Haque	7	1	22	0							
Sadiqur Rahman	3	0	14	0							
Nabil Samad	34	16	60	4	1w,1nb						
Enamul Haque	37.1	10	88	3	2w	(4)	10	1	39	0	1nb
Alok Kapali	10	3	27	0		(5)	6	0	26	1	
Golam Mabud	2	0	7	0		(6)	4	0	21	1	
Imtiaz Hossain	1	0	2	1							
Ezaz Ahmed						(2)	1	0	17	0	1w,1nb

Umpires: Abdul Awal and Enamul Haque. Referee: Zahid Razzak.   Toss: Sylhet Division
Close of Play: 1st day: Sylhet Division (1) 223-7 (Golam Mabud 24*, Enamul Haque 10*, 90 overs); 2nd day: Dhaka Division (1) 148-5 (Shamsur Rahman 27*, Nadif Chowdhury 29*, 66 overs); 3rd day: Sylhet Division (2) 142-2 (Imtiaz Hossain 69*, Rajin Saleh 43*, 44 overs).
Man of the Match: Golam Mabud.
Imtiaz Hossain's 148 took 236 balls in 357 minutes and included 13 fours and 3 sixes.

RAJSHAHI DIVISION v BARISAL DIVISION

Played at Shaheed Chandu Stadium, Bogra, December 5, 6, 7, 8, 2007.
Ispahani Mirzapore Tea National Cricket League 2007/08
Rajshahi Division won by six wickets. (Points: Rajshahi Division 13, Barisal Division 4)

BARISAL DIVISION

1	Hannan Sarkar	b Alamgir Kabir	14	c Khaled Mashud b Saqlain Sajib	23
2	*Shahriar Nafees	b Alamgir Kabir	7	not out	65
3	Imran Ahmed	b Alamgir Kabir	43	c Farhad Hossain b Mohammad Shahzada	6
4	Raqibul Hasan	run out (Saqlain Sajib)	15	c Naeem Islam b Mohammad Shahzada	8
5	Raisul Islam	run out (Saqlain Sajib)	14	(6) c Naeem Islam b Saqlain Sajib	27
6	Kamrul Islam	c Khaled Mashud b Alamgir Kabir	26	(7) lbw b Saqlain Sajib	0
7	Arafat Salahuddin	lbw b Mohammad Shahzada	1	(8) lbw b Saqlain Sajib	5
8	†Shahin Hossain	not out	31	(9) st Khaled Mashud b Mahbub Alam	5
9	Sajidul Islam	lbw b Mohammad Shahzada	4	(10) c Khaled Mashud b Mahbub Alam	8
10	Talha Jubair	c Saqlain Sajib b Alamgir Kabir	1	(11) c Jahurul Islam b Alamgir Kabir	4
11	Tariqul Islam	run out (Saqlain Sajib)	14	(5) b Mohammad Shahzada	9
	Extras	b 5, lb 4, w 3	12	b 5, lb 4	9
			182		**169**

FoW (1): 1-22 (2), 2-29 (1), 3-62 (4), 4-98 (3), 5-98 (5), 6-100 (7), 7-145 (6), 8-160 (9), 9-161 (10), 10-182 (11)
FoW (2): 1-42 (1), 2-46 (3), 3-55 (4), 4-64 (5), 5-128 (6), 6-128 (7), 7-134 (8), 8-145 (9), 9-162 (10), 10-169 (11)

RAJSHAHI DIVISION

1	Jahurul Islam	b Arafat Salahuddin	31	c Shahin Hossain b Sajidul Islam	74
2	Rafiqul Islam	lbw b Talha Jubair	1	lbw b Sajidul Islam	6
3	Farhad Hossain	c Raqibul Hasan b Sajidul Islam	9	not out	37
4	Anisur Rahman	b Sajidul Islam	3	(5) c Kamrul Islam b Sajidul Islam	3
5	*†Khaled Mashud	c sub (Abul Bashar) b Arafat Salahuddin	18		
6	Naeem Islam	lbw b Tariqul Islam	68	not out	9
7	Mushfiqur Rahman	lbw b Sajidul Islam	7		
8	Mahbub Alam	lbw b Tariqul Islam	27	(4) b Talha Jubair	1
9	Mohammad Shahzada	b Raisul Islam	0		
10	Saqlain Sajib	b Raisul Islam	6		
11	Alamgir Kabir	not out	0		
	Extras	b 15, lb 10, nb 9	34	b 4, lb 11, w 1, nb 2	18
			204	(4 wickets)	**148**

FoW (1): 1-6 (2), 2-42 (3), 3-61 (4), 4-61 (1), 5-91 (5), 6-130 (7), 7-195 (8), 8-196 (9), 9-198 (6), 10-204 (10)
FoW (2): 1-20 (2), 2-114 (1), 3-115 (4), 4-127 (5)

Rajshahi Division Bowling

	O	M	R	W			O	M	R	W
Mohammad Shahzada	21	5	63	2	3w	(2)	16	3	45	3
Alamgir Kabir	22	7	52	5		(1)	15.4	3	48	1
Mushfiqur Rahman	10	4	29	0		(4)	3	1	4	0
Saqlain Sajib	11.1	1	22	0		(3)	19	4	29	4
Mahbub Alam	8	3	7	0		(6)	4	1	5	2
Farhad Hossain	1	1	0	0		(5)	13	2	29	0

Barisal Division Bowling

	O	M	R	W			O	M	R	W	
Talha Jubair	19	3	63	1	7nb		16	7	36	1	1w,2nb
Sajidul Islam	21	5	40	3			16	7	28	3	
Arafat Salahuddin	19	8	37	2			7	3	16	0	
Tariqul Islam	13	6	16	2	2nb		10	0	32	0	
Kamrul Islam	2	0	15	0			4	0	15	0	
Raisul Islam	0	0	8	2			1.4	0	6	0	

Umpires: Syed Mahabubullah and Ziaul Islam. Referee: Hemayat Ahmed. Toss: Barisal Division

Close of Play: 1st day: Rajshahi Division (1) 39-1 (Jahurul Islam 20*, Farhad Hossain 8*, 11.4 overs); 2nd day: Barisal Division (2) 48-2 (Raqibul Hasan 2*, Tariqul Islam 2*, 17 overs); 3rd day: Rajshahi Division (2) 99-1 (Jahurul Islam 65*, Farhad Hossain 19*, 33 overs).
Man of the Match: Alamgir Kabir.
Shahriar Nafees retired hurt in the Barisal Division second innings having scored 11 (team score 27-0) - he returned when the score was 55-3).

DHAKA DIVISION v BARISAL DIVISION

Played at Shere Bangla National Stadium, Mirpur, December 14, 15, 16, 17, 2007.
Ispahani Mirzapore Tea National Cricket League 2007/08
Dhaka Division won by 217 runs.   (Points: Dhaka Division 14, Barisal Division 4)

DHAKA DIVISION

1	Uttam Sarkar	b Tariqul Islam	16	b Talha Jubair	10
2	†Anwar Hossain	b Arafat Salahuddin	8	lbw b Sajidul Islam	10
3	Mehrab Hossain	c and b Sajidul Islam	33	lbw b Tariqul Islam	37
4	*Al Sahariar	lbw b Tariqul Islam	16	b Tariqul Islam	92
5	Mahmudullah	b Talha Jubair	12	not out	81
6	Nadif Chowdhury	c Kamrul Islam b Sajidul Islam	39	c Imran Ahmed b Tariqul Islam	50
7	Sajjad Kadir	c Shahin Hossain b Tariqul Islam	20		
8	Mosharraf Hossain	c Shahriar Nafees b Arafat Salahuddin	40	(7) not out	2
9	Mohammad Sharif	c Shahin Hossain b Raisul Islam	57		
10	Mohammad Rafique	c Nasiruddin Faruque b Talha Jubair	0		
11	Mahbubul Alam	not out	0		
	Extras	b 6, lb 4, w 2, nb 9	21	b 3, lb 3, w 2, nb 4	12
			262	(5 wickets, declared)	294

FoW (1): 1-27 (2), 2-27 (1), 3-52 (4), 4-69 (5), 5-129 (6), 6-132 (3), 7-228 (8), 8-229 (10), 9-262 (7), 10-262 (9)
FoW (2): 1-16 (2), 2-24 (1), 3-144 (3), 4-172 (4), 5-285 (6)

BARISAL DIVISION

1	*Shahriar Nafees	lbw b Mahmudullah	48	c Mahmudullah b Mohammad Sharif	7
2	Nasiruddin Faruque	b Mahbubul Alam	61	st Anwar Hossain b Mosharraf Hossain	16
3	Imran Ahmed	c Mahmudullah b Mosharraf Hossain	16	b Mahbubul Alam	9
4	Raqibul Hasan	c Anwar Hossain b Mohammad Sharif	11	b Mahbubul Alam	46
5	Raisul Islam	b Mohammad Rafique	3	b Mosharraf Hossain	9
6	Kamrul Islam	c Mohammad Sharif b Mohammad Rafique	0	lbw b Mosharraf Hossain	9
7	Tariqul Islam	b Mahbubul Alam	6	(11) run out	0
8	Arafat Salahuddin	c Mahmudullah b Mohammad Rafique	2	(7) c Mohammad Rafique b Mosharraf Hossain	0
9	†Shahin Hossain	b Mohammad Sharif	21	(8) b Mosharraf Hossain	4
10	Sajidul Islam	c Mosharraf Hossain b Mahbubul Alam	11	(9) not out	26
11	Talha Jubair	not out	0	(10) c Nadif Chowdhury b Mahbubul Alam	6
	Extras	b 6, lb 3, w 3, nb 2	14	b 4, lb 4, nb 6	14
			193		146

FoW (1): 1-100 (1), 2-127 (2), 3-144 (3), 4-149 (5), 5-149 (4), 6-149 (6), 7-152 (8), 8-166 (7), 9-191 (10), 10-193 (9)
FoW (2): 1-9 (1), 2-25 (3), 3-46 (2), 4-66 (5), 5-86 (6), 6-86 (7), 7-90 (8), 8-134 (4), 9-146 (10), 10-146 (11)

Barisal Division Bowling	O	M	R	W		O	M	R	W	
Talha Jubair	28	9	46	2	4nb	7	1	25	1	
Sajidul Islam	25	6	45	2	2w,1nb	8	0	32	1	
Arafat Salahuddin	27	8	57	2		21	2	74	0	
Tariqul Islam	25	4	85	3	4nb	35	3	110	3	41nb
Raqibul Hasan	4	0	18	0	(6)	3	0	10	0	
Raisul Islam	1.1	0	1	1	(5)	10	3	20	0	
Nasiruddin Faruque					(7)	3	0	17	0	

Dhaka Division Bowling	O	M	R	W		O	M	R	W	
Mahbubul Alam	14	2	47	3	2nb	11	0	46	3	6nb
Mohammad Sharif	15.5	2	50	2	3w	9	2	18	1	
Mosharraf Hossain	20	10	26	1		20	8	27	5	
Mohammad Rafique	26	10	47	3		22	7	36	0	
Mahmudullah	7	1	14	1		3	1	11	0	

Umpires: Ashiqur Rahman and Nadir Shah.   Referee: Raqibul Hasan.   Toss: Barisal Division
Close of Play: 1st day: Dhaka Division (1) 215-6 (Mosharraf Hossain 35*, Mohammad Sharif 30*, 83 overs); 2nd day: Barisal Division (1) 152-7 (Tariqul Islam 0*, Shahin Hossain 0*, 62 overs); 3rd day: Dhaka Division (2) 205-4 (Mahmudullah 35*, Nadif Chowdhury 15*, 67 overs).
Man of the Match: Mosharraf Hossain.
Sajjad Kadir retired hurt in the Dhaka Division first innings having scored 9 (team score 147-6, 54ov) - he returned when the score was 229-8.

KHULNA DIVISION v SYLHET DIVISION

Played at Bir Shrestha Shahid Flight Lieutenant Motiur Rahman Stadium, Khulna, December 14, 15, 16, 17, 2007.
Ispahani Mirzapore Tea National Cricket League 2007/08
Match drawn.   (Points: Khulna Division 12, Sylhet Division 8)

SYLHET DIVISION

1	Golam Rahman	c Saghir Hossain b Aslam Khan	85			
2	Imtiaz Hossain	lbw b Aslam Khan	15	(1) c Saghir Hossain b Murad Khan	57	
3	†Kuntal Chandra	lbw b Murad Khan	19	c Saghir Hossain b Murad Khan	8	
4	*Rajin Saleh	lbw b Robiul Islam	2	(5) not out	131	
5	Alok Kapali	c Nahidul Haque b Murad Khan	36	(6) c Murad Khan b Saghir Hossain	111	
6	Golam Mabud	c Mostafizur Rahman b Robiul Islam	53	(7) not out	9	
7	Ezaz Ahmed	c sub (Mohammad Salim) b Aslam Khan	6			
8	Saif Mahmud	c Fariduddin b Murad Khan	12	(2) b Aslam Khan	3	
9	Enamul Haque	lbw b Murad Khan	7	(4) c Ziaur Rahman b Murad Khan	29	
10	Nabil Samad	c Saghir Hossain b Robiul Islam	25			
11	Rashedur Rahman	not out	23			
	Extras	b 13, lb 1, nb 3	17	b 12, lb 1, nb 1	14	
			300	(5 wickets)	**362**	

FoW (1): 1-20 (2), 2-70 (3), 3-74 (4), 4-128 (5), 5-211 (6), 6-218 (7), 7-239 (1), 8-240 (8), 9-260 (9), 10-300 (10)
FoW (2): 1-14 (2), 2-38 (3), 3-77 (1), 4-166 (4), 5-334 (6)

KHULNA DIVISION

1	Nazmus Sadat	c Kuntal Chandra b Enamul Haque	47
2	Imrul Kayes	c Kuntal Chandra b Nabil Samad	138
3	Mostafizur Rahman	lbw b Enamul Haque	43
4	*Habibul Bashar	b Rashedur Rahman	0
5	Nahidul Haque	c Kuntal Chandra b Nabil Samad	58
6	†Saghir Hossain	c Saif Mahmud b Alok Kapali	54
7	Fariduddin	b Enamul Haque	33
8	Ziaur Rahman	c Saif Mahmud b Alok Kapali	3
9	Murad Khan	not out	4
10	Aslam Khan	lbw b Enamul Haque	1
11	Robiul Islam	b Enamul Haque	6
	Extras	b 19, lb 6, w 4, nb 5	34
			421

FoW (1): 1-96 (1), 2-204 (3), 3-207 (4), 4-299 (2), 5-317 (5), 6-382 (7), 7-397 (8), 8-406 (6), 9-409 (10), 10-421 (11)

Khulna Division Bowling	O	M	R	W			O	M	R	W	
Ziaur Rahman	15	4	37	0		(5)	3	0	14	0	
Aslam Khan	29	5	63	3			13	1	33	1	
Robiul Islam	26.3	5	60	3	3nb	(1)	16	4	46	0	
Murad Khan	33	10	79	4		(3)	31	6	93	3	1nb
Fariduddin	20	8	46	0		(4)	12	2	37	0	
Nazmus Sadat	1	0	1	0		(7)	11	0	35	0	
Nahidul Haque						(6)	11	0	44	0	
Mostafizur Rahman						(8)	2	0	14	0	
Habibul Bashar						(9)	1	0	9	0	
Saghir Hossain						(10)	2	0	24	1	

Sylhet Division Bowling	O	M	R	W	
Rashedur Rahman	22	4	84	1	1w,2nb
Saif Mahmud	4	0	18	0	3nb
Golam Rahman	12	1	40	0	1w
Nabil Samad	33	7	68	2	
Imtiaz Hossain	1	0	13	0	
Enamul Haque	40	4	126	5	
Alok Kapali	15	4	37	2	
Golam Mabud	3	0	10	0	

Umpires: Sharfuddoula and Tanvir Ahmed.   Referee: Obaydul Haque.   Toss: Sylhet Division
Close of Play: 1st day: Sylhet Division (1) 227-6 (Golam Rahman 78*, Saif Mahmud 5*, 90 overs); 2nd day: Khulna Division (1) 193-1 (Imrul Kayes 87*, Mostafizur Rahman 38*, 56 overs); 3rd day: Sylhet Division (2) 39-2 (Imtiaz Hossain 27*, Enamul Haque 0*, 14 overs).
Man of the Match: Imrul Kayes.
Imrul Kayes's 138 took 261 balls in 350 minutes and included 14 fours and 2 sixes. Rajin Saleh's 131 took 220 balls in 271 minutes and included 14 fours and 1 six. Alok Kapali's 111 took 110 balls in 122 minutes and included 12 fours and 2 sixes.

RAJSHAHI DIVISION v CHITTAGONG DIVISION

Played at Bir Shrestha Shahid Captain Mohiuddin Jahangir Stadium, Rajshahi, December 14, 15, 16, 17, 2007.
Ispahani Mirzapore Tea National Cricket League 2007/08
Chittagong Division won by 21 runs. (Points: Rajshahi Division 4, Chittagong Division 12)

CHITTAGONG DIVISION

1	Gazi Salahuddin	c Khaled Mashud b Alamgir Kabir	0	lbw b Shafiul Islam	49
2	Masumud Dowla	c Khaled Mashud b Shafiul Islam	10	c Farhad Hossain b Mahbub Alam	28
3	Mahbubul Karim	lbw b Shafiul Islam	4	b Mahbub Alam	3
4	Nazimuddin	b Mohammad Shahzada	13	c Farhad Hossain b Alamgir Kabir	52
5	†Dhiman Ghosh	c Khaled Mashud		(7) c Mohammad Shahzada	
		b Mohammad Shahzada	50	b Shafiul Islam	39
6	*Ehsanul Haque	c Khaled Mashud			
		b Mohammad Shahzada	66	c Rabiul Karim b Mohammad Shahzada	48
7	Faisal Hossain	b Mohammad Shahzada	5	(5) c Naeem Islam b Mushfiqur Rahman	25
8	Kamrul Islam	c Mahbub Alam b Farhad Hossain	11	lbw b Mohammad Shahzada	2
9	Yasin Arafat	c and b Mahbub Alam	7	not out	34
10	Tareq Aziz	not out	14	b Farhad Hossain	15
11	Mohammad Younus	b Shafiul Islam	11	c Mushfiqur Rahman b Farhad Hossain	2
	Extras	b 2, lb 2, nb 3	7	b 2, lb 1, w 1	4
			198		**301**

FoW (1): 1-0 (1), 2-7 (3), 3-27 (2), 4-29 (4), 5-145 (5), 6-150 (6), 7-155 (7), 8-164 (9), 9-191 (8), 10-198 (11)
FoW (2): 1-76 (1), 2-81 (2), 3-82 (3), 4-136 (5), 5-175 (4), 6-237 (6), 7-245 (8), 8-258 (7), 9-290 (10), 10-301 (11)

RAJSHAHI DIVISION

1	Jahurul Islam	c Dhiman Ghosh b Tareq Aziz	9	(7) lbw b Mohammad Younus	5
2	Rabiul Karim	lbw b Kamrul Islam	8	c Kamrul Islam b Tareq Aziz	4
3	Farhad Hossain	c Dhiman Ghosh b Tareq Aziz	11	b Yasin Arafat	83
4	Shakil Haider	b Mohammad Younus	21	(1) c Dhiman Ghosh b Ehsanul Haque	76
5	Alamgir Kabir	lbw b Yasin Arafat	9	(10) not out	29
6	*†Khaled Mashud	b Mohammad Younus	25	(5) c Masumud Dowla b Yasin Arafat	0
7	Naeem Islam	c Dhiman Ghosh b Ehsanul Haque	14	(4) b Yasin Arafat	48
8	Mushfiqur Rahman	not out	3	(6) c Mahbubul Karim b Yasin Arafat	47
9	Mahbub Alam	c Gazi Salahuddin b Mohammad Younus	0	(8) c Mahbubul Karim	
				b Mohammad Younus	11
10	Shafiul Islam	c Tareq Aziz b Mohammad Younus	9	(11) c Dhiman Ghosh b Ehsanul Haque	29
11	Mohammad Shahzada	c Dhiman Ghosh b Tareq Aziz	0	(9) c Mahbubul Karim b Tareq Aziz	15
	Extras	b 3, lb 1, nb 5	9	b 6, lb 2, w 3, nb 2	13
			118		**360**

FoW (1): 1-18 (1), 2-18 (2), 3-39 (3), 4-56 (4), 5-69 (5), 6-106 (7), 7-106 (6), 8-106 (9), 9-118 (10), 10-118 (11)
FoW (2): 1-5 (2), 2-146 (1), 3-203 (3), 4-203 (5), 5-248 (4), 6-261 (7), 7-275 (8), 8-294 (9), 9-313 (6), 10-360 (11)

Rajshahi Division Bowling	O	M	R	W			O	M	R	W	
Alamgir Kabir	14	2	56	1	3nb		11	1	37	1	
Shafiul Islam	23.4	2	70	3			26	3	76	2	
Mohammad Shahzada	21	9	36	4		(4)	21	6	53	2	
Mushfiqur Rahman	7	4	8	0		(6)	10	2	34	1	
Farhad Hossain	8	2	16	1		(3)	12.3	1	42	2	
Mahbub Alam	3	1	8	1		(5)	14	2	44	2	
Shakil Haider						(7)	1	0	4	0	
Naeem Islam						(8)	2	0	6	0	
Khaled Mashud						(9)	1	0	2	0	1w

Chittagong Division Bowling	O	M	R	W			O	M	R	W	
Tareq Aziz	18.2	3	53	3	5nb		20	4	63	2	1w,1nb
Kamrul Islam	19	5	29	1			13	1	58	0	1w
Mohammad Younus	11	5	22	4			25	2	88	2	
Ehsanul Haque	8	5	10	1		(5)	9.1	2	38	2	1w,1nb
Yasin Arafat	1	1	0	1		(4)	26	4	96	4	
Faisal Hossain						(6)	1	0	9	0	

Umpires: Afzalur Rahman and Mahbubur Rahman. Referee: Samiur Rahman. Toss: Rajshahi Division
Close of Play: 1st day: Rajshahi Division (1) 24-2 (Farhad Hossain 2*, Shakil Haider 3*, 9.2 overs); 2nd day: Chittagong Division (2) 113-3 (Nazimuddin 19*, Faisal Hossain 13*, 35 overs); 3rd day: Rajshahi Division (2) 115-1 (Shakil Haider 57*, Farhad Hossain 52*, 24 overs).
Man of the Match: Ehsanul Haque.

BARISAL DIVISION v SYLHET DIVISION

Played at Shaheed Chandu Stadium, Bogra, December 27, 28, 29, 30, 2007.
Ispahani Mirzapore Tea National Cricket League 2007/08
Barisal Division won by an innings and 34 runs.   (Points: Barisal Division 16, Sylhet Division 1)

SYLHET DIVISION

1	Imtiaz Hossain	c Imran Ahmed b Sumon Saha	25	c Raisul Islam b Abul Bashar	57
2	Golam Rahman	c Shahin Hossain b Arafat Salahuddin	45	c Shahin Hossain b Arafat Salahuddin	3
3	Sadiqur Rahman	b Hannan Sarkar	0	c Shahin Hossain b Arafat Salahuddin	0
4	*Alok Kapali	b Monir Hossain	39	(5) c Raqibul Hasan b Monir Hossain	3
5	Sharifullah	c Shahin Hossain b Arafat Salahuddin	12	(7) c Nasiruddin Faruque	
				b Arafat Salahuddin	10
6	†Golam Mabud	c Hannan Sarkar b Arafat Salahuddin	5	c Shahin Hossain b Monir Hossain	57
7	Ezaz Ahmed	c Sumon Saha b Monir Hossain	8	(8) c Monir Hossain b Arafat Salahuddin	0
8	Rezaul Haque	run out (Abul Bashar)	32	(9) c Shahin Hossain b Monir Hossain	0
9	Nabil Samad	lbw b Sumon Saha	5	(4) b Arafat Salahuddin	6
10	Rashedur Rahman	b Monir Hossain	10	not out	11
11	Rinku Sarkar	not out	0	c Arafat Salahuddin b Raqibul Hasan	14
	Extras	lb 1, nb 1	2	b 1, lb 4	5
			183		166

FoW (1): 1-34 (1), 2-45 (3), 3-90 (4), 4-120 (2), 5-126 (6), 6-127 (5), 7-135 (7), 8-141 (9), 9-174 (10), 10-183 (8)
FoW (2): 1-4 (2), 2-4 (3), 3-40 (4), 4-43 (5), 5-89 (1), 6-117 (7), 7-117 (8), 8-126 (9), 9-145 (6), 10-166 (11)

BARISAL DIVISION

1	Humayun Kabir	b Rashedur Rahman	0
2	Nasiruddin Faruque	c Alok Kapali b Imtiaz Hossain	77
3	Hannan Sarkar	c Rinku Sarkar b Alok Kapali	70
4	Raqibul Hasan	c Golam Mabud b Alok Kapali	36
5	*Imran Ahmed	not out	70
6	Raisul Islam	lbw b Nabil Samad	16
7	Abul Bashar	not out	82
8	†Shahin Hossain		
9	Monir Hossain		
10	Arafat Salahuddin		
11	Sumon Saha		
	Extras	b 20, lb 7, nb 5	32
		(5 wickets, declared)	383

FoW (1): 1-0 (1), 2-106 (3), 3-188 (4), 4-193 (2), 5-233 (6)

Barisal Division Bowling

	O	M	R	W			O	M	R	W
Sumon Saha	23.1	10	52	2			12	3	40	0
Arafat Salahuddin	22	8	48	3			20	9	44	5
Hannan Sarkar	3	1	13	1	1nb	(5)	2	2	0	0
Monir Hossain	21	5	45	3		(3)	21	4	51	3
Abul Bashar	4	0	24	0		(4)	6	1	17	1
Raqibul Hasan						(6)	1	0	9	1

Sylhet Division Bowling

	O	M	R	W	
Rashedur Rahman	16	2	76	1	2nb
Rinku Sarkar	10	3	34	0	
Golam Rahman	8	3	19	0	
Rezaul Haque	12	3	47	0	
Nabil Samad	22	5	62	1	3nb
Alok Kapali	25	2	97	2	
Sadiqur Rahman	4	2	2	0	
Imtiaz Hossain	7	2	19	1	

Umpires: Abdul Awal and Sailab Hossain. Referee: Akhtar Ahmed.   Toss: Barisal Division

Close of Play: 1st day: Sylhet Division (1) 149-8 (Rezaul Haque 9*, Rashedur Rahman 0*, 60 overs); 2nd day: Barisal Division (1) 118-2 (Nasiruddin Faruque 35*, Raqibul Hasan 6*, 36 overs); 3rd day: Sylhet Division (2) 4-2 (Imtiaz Hossain 1*, Nabil Samad 0*, 6 overs).
Man of the Match: Arafat Salahuddin.

CHITTAGONG DIVISION v DHAKA DIVISION

Played at Bir Shrestha Shahid Ruhul Amin Stadium, Chittagong, December 27, 28, 29, 30, 2007.
Ispahani Mirzapore Tea National Cricket League 2007/08
Match drawn.   (Points: Chittagong Division 6, Dhaka Division 11)

CHITTAGONG DIVISION

1	Gazi Salahuddin	c Anwar Hossain b Mahbubul Alam	11	(7) lbw b Mahmudullah	21
2	Masumud Dowla	c Arafat Sunny b Mohammad Sharif	5	(1) b Mosharraf Hossain	118
3	Mahbubul Karim	lbw b Mohammad Sharif	2	(2) lbw b Mosharraf Hossain	4
4	Nazimuddin	c Nadif Chowdhury b Mahbubul Alam	0	(5) c Nazmul Hossain b Arafat Sunny	80
5	†Dhiman Ghosh	lbw b Mosharraf Hossain	10	(8) lbw b Mohammad Sharif	43
6	*Ehsanul Haque	b Arafat Sunny	36	c Mahbubul Alam b Nazmul Hossain	117
7	Mazharuddin	c Anwar Hossain b Mosharraf Hossain	3	(3) b Arafat Sunny	1
8	Kamrul Islam	b Arafat Sunny	4	(9) not out	12
9	Yasin Arafat	not out	20	(4) run out	1
10	Tareq Aziz	b Arafat Sunny	2	c Anwar Hossain b Nadif Chowdhury	9
11	Saju Datta	c Nazmul Hossain b Mohammad Sharif	1	c Arman Hossain b Mosharraf Hossain	6
	Extras	lb 4	4	b 16, lb 5, nb 3	24
			98		**436**

FoW (1): 1-16 (2), 2-18 (3), 3-18 (1), 4-23 (4), 5-43 (5), 6-63 (7), 7-71 (6), 8-76 (8), 9-84 (10), 10-98 (11)
FoW (2): 1-18 (2), 2-19 (3), 3-20 (4), 4-160 (5), 5-311 (1), 6-356 (7), 7-391 (6), 8-416 (8), 9-429 (10), 10-436 (11)

DHAKA DIVISION

1	†Anwar Hossain	c Ehsanul Haque b Saju Datta	38	(4) st Dhiman Ghosh b Yasin Arafat	46
2	Arman Hossain	b Tareq Aziz	33	(1) c Nazimuddin b Ehsanul Haque	43
3	Mehrab Hossain	c Mazharuddin b Yasin Arafat	2		
4	Shamsur Rahman	lbw b Saju Datta	35		
5	Mahmudullah	lbw b Yasin Arafat	48	(3) b Saju Datta	0
6	Nadif Chowdhury	c Ehsanul Haque b Yasin Arafat	23	(5) not out	1
7	Mosharraf Hossain	c Dhiman Ghosh b Tareq Aziz	4		
8	*Mohammad Sharif	b Tareq Aziz	0		
9	Nazmul Hossain	not out	95	(2) c Kamrul Islam b Saju Datta	23
10	Arafat Sunny	c Dhiman Ghosh b Tareq Aziz	7		
11	Mahbubul Alam	b Tareq Aziz	2		
	Extras	b 15, lb 3, w 4, nb 7	29	b 6, lb 4, w 4, nb 3	17
			316	**(4 wickets)**	**130**

FoW (1): 1-46 (2), 2-50 (3), 3-109 (1), 4-118 (4), 5-151 (6), 6-178 (7), 7-178 (8), 8-212 (5), 9-259 (10), 10-316 (11)
FoW (2): 1-39 (2), 2-39 (3), 3-125 (4), 4-130 (1)

Dhaka Division Bowling	O	M	R	W		O	M	R	W	
Mahbubul Alam	9	2	23	2	(2)	26	4	88	0	2nb
Mohammad Sharif	9.3	5	11	3	(1)	20	5	60	1	
Nazmul Hossain	2	1	1	0	(8)	1	0	1	1	
Mosharraf Hossain	14	3	31	2	(3)	53.3	9	109	3	
Arafat Sunny	12	4	28	3	(4)	38	10	79	2	
Mahmudullah					(5)	19	4	57	1	
Nadif Chowdhury					(6)	6	1	17	1	1nb
Mehrab Hossain					(7)	2	1	4	0	

Chittagong Division Bowling	O	M	R	W		O	M	R	W	
Tareq Aziz	25.4	8	89	5	1w,5nb	8	0	42	0	3nb
Kamrul Islam	20	6	62	0	2w,2nb	3	0	21	0	1w
Yasin Arafat	30	10	63	3		(4)	3	0	13	1	
Saju Datta	28	8	53	2		(3)	5	0	30	2	
Ehsanul Haque	7	1	23	0			2.4	0	14	1	3w
Mazharuddin	3	1	6	0						
Nazimuddin	1	0	2	0						

Umpires: Anisur Rahman and S.B.Chowdhury. Referee: Samiur Rahman.   Toss: Chittagong Division
Close of Play: 1st day: Dhaka Division (1) 88-2 (Anwar Hossain 30*, Shamsur Rahman 15*, 41 overs); 2nd day: Chittagong Division (2) 26-3 (Masumud Dowla 14*, Nazimuddin 2*, 14 overs); 3rd day: Chittagong Division (2) 259-4 (Masumud Dowla 100*, Ehsanul Haque 51*, 104 overs).
Man of the Match: Masumud Dowla.
Masumud Dowla's 118 took 366 balls in 498 minutes and included 13 fours. Ehsanul Haque's 117 took 265 balls in 371 minutes and included 10 fours and 1 six.

RAJSHAHI DIVISION v KHULNA DIVISION

Played at Bir Shrestha Shahid Captain Mohiuddin Jahangir Stadium, Rajshahi, December 27, 28, 29, 30, 2007.
Ispahani Mirzapore Tea National Cricket League 2007/08
Rajshahi Division won by 29 runs.   (Points: Rajshahi Division 11, Khulna Division 4)

RAJSHAHI DIVISION

1	Jahurul Islam	lbw b Aslam Khan	3	c Saghir Hossain b Ziaur Rahman		61
2	Shakil Haider	c Saghir Hossain b Aslam Khan	61	c Saghir Hossain b Robiul Islam		14
3	Farhad Hossain	c Saghir Hossain b Ziaur Rahman	1	c Nahidul Haque b Robiul Islam		4
4	Rafiqul Islam	c Saghir Hossain b Robiul Islam	11	(5) run out		28
5	Naeem Islam	c Saghir Hossain b Ziaur Rahman	0	(7) c Mostafizur Rahman b Ziaur Rahman		0
6	†Khaled Mashud	c Nahidul Haque b Fariduddin	13	c sub (Mohammad Salim) b Murad Khan		48
7	*Mushfiqur Rahman	lbw b Jamaluddin Ahmed	33	(9) c Saghir Hossain b Murad Khan		10
8	Anisur Rahman	not out	25	not out		64
9	Delwar Hossain	b Jamaluddin Ahmed	4	(10) c and b Ziaur Rahman		18
10	Shafiul Islam	c and b Robiul Islam	13	(11) b Ziaur Rahman		7
11	Saqlain Sajib	c Aslam Khan b Jamaluddin Ahmed	0	(4) lbw b Ziaur Rahman		8
	Extras	b 6, lb 10, w 2, nb 6	24	lb 12, w 6, nb 4		22
			188			**284**

FoW (1): 1-3 (1), 2-6 (3), 3-58 (4), 4-66 (5), 5-102 (2), 6-123 (6), 7-160 (7), 8-168 (9), 9-187 (10), 10-188 (11)
FoW (2): 1-35 (2), 2-43 (3), 3-99 (1), 4-100 (4), 5-174 (5), 6-174 (7), 7-196 (6), 8-216 (9), 9-265 (10), 10-284 (11)

KHULNA DIVISION

1	Nazmus Sadat	lbw b Delwar Hossain	11	lbw b Saqlain Sajib		24
2	Imrul Kayes	c Delwar Hossain b Naeem Islam	48	c Farhad Hossain b Saqlain Sajib		24
3	Mostafizur Rahman	c Rafiqul Islam b Delwar Hossain	1	(4) c Khaled Mashud b Shafiul Islam		57
4	Jamaluddin Ahmed	b Farhad Hossain	29	(5) b Saqlain Sajib		86
5	*Nahidul Haque	c Jahurul Islam b Delwar Hossain	29	(6) lbw b Saqlain Sajib		3
6	†Saghir Hossain	c Anisur Rahman b Farhad Hossain	19	(7) c Naeem Islam b Saqlain Sajib		8
7	Fariduddin	c Jahurul Islam b Farhad Hossain	4	(8) not out		41
8	Ziaur Rahman	b Saqlain Sajib	1	(9) st Khaled Mashud b Farhad Hossain		1
9	Murad Khan	not out	3	(3) lbw b Farhad Hossain		0
10	Robiul Islam	lbw b Farhad Hossain	0	c Farhad Hossain b Saqlain Sajib		0
11	Aslam Khan	not out	0	lbw b Mushfiqur Rahman		27
	Extras	b 5, lb 1	6	b 12, lb 5, w 1, nb 3		21
		(9 wickets, declared)	**151**			**292**

FoW (1): 1-15 (1), 2-17 (3), 3-77 (4), 4-111 (2), 5-142 (5), 6-147 (7), 7-148 (8), 8-150 (6), 9-150 (10)
FoW (2): 1-41 (1), 2-53 (3), 3-61 (2), 4-146 (4), 5-151 (6), 6-187 (7), 7-234 (5), 8-235 (9), 9-237 (10), 10-292 (11)

Khulna Division Bowling

	O	M	R	W		O	M	R	W	
Ziaur Rahman	10	4	28	2	1w,2nb	18.4	5	39	5	1nb
Aslam Khan	12	1	44	2		18	3	67	0	1nb
Robiul Islam	9	1	26	2	1w,4nb	22	2	63	2	5w,2nb
Murad Khan	12	0	44	0		20	5	67	2	
Fariduddin	5	1	15	1						
Jamaluddin Ahmed	8.1	1	15	3		6	2	18	0	
Nazmus Sadat					(5)	6	0	18	0	

Rajshahi Division Bowling

	O	M	R	W		O	M	R	W	
Shafiul Islam	12	2	35	0		9	0	41	1	1w
Delwar Hossain	11	2	38	3		15	3	39	0	
Mushfiqur Rahman	2	0	10	0	(6)	5.4	0	13	1	
Saqlain Sajib	16.5	5	45	1		43	7	101	6	3nb
Farhad Hossain	8	3	13	4	(3)	26	1	80	2	
Naeem Islam	3	1	4	1	(5)	1	0	1	0	

Umpires: Mahfuzur Rahman and Nadir Shah.   Referee: Hemayat Ahmed.   Toss: Khulna Division

Close of Play: 1st day: Khulna Division (1) 21-2 (Imrul Kayes 5*, Jamaluddin Ahmed 0*, 7 overs); 2nd day: Rajshahi Division (2) 62-2 (Jahurul Islam 39*, Saqlain Sajib 1*, 12 overs); 3rd day: Khulna Division (2) 56-2 (Imrul Kayes 19*, Mostafizur Rahman 3*, 15 overs).

Man of the Match: Saqlain Sajib.

CHITTAGONG DIVISION v SYLHET DIVISION

Played at Narayanganj Osmani Stadium, Fatullah, January 4, 5, 6, 7, 2008.
Ispahani Mirzapore Tea National Cricket League 2007/08
Chittagong Division won by seven wickets.   **(Points: Chittagong Division 15, Sylhet Division 8)**

SYLHET DIVISION

1	Imtiaz Hossain	c Ehsanul Haque			
		b Mohammad Younus	130	c Kamrul Islam b Mohammad Younus	30
2	Golam Rahman	lbw b Mohammad Younus	36	(7) c Ehsanul Haque b Tareq Aziz	5
3	Saif Mahmud	run out (Rezaul Karim)	9	(2) lbw b Kamrul Islam	0
4	*Alok Kapali	c Tareq Aziz b Mohammad Younus	30	(5) lbw b Kamrul Islam	14
5	†Golam Mabud	c Dhiman Ghosh b Kamrul Islam	37	(4) c Dhiman Ghosh b Tareq Aziz	0
6	Sharifullah	lbw b Mohammad Younus	10	b Kamrul Islam	2
7	Ezaz Ahmed	lbw b Ehsanul Haque	37	(8) lbw b Mohammad Younus	29
8	Sadiqur Rahman	not out	29	(9) lbw b Tareq Aziz	1
9	Rezaul Haque	c Dhiman Ghosh b Yasin Arafat	6	(3) b Kamrul Islam	25
10	Nabil Samad	c Ehsanul Haque b Kamrul Islam	0	lbw b Tareq Aziz	37
11	Rashedur Rahman	c Dhiman Ghosh b Tareq Aziz	1	not out	29
	Extras	b 16, lb 5, w 1, nb 7	29	b 16, lb 4, w 4, nb 5	29
			354		**201**

FoW (1): 1-99 (2), 2-139 (3), 3-206 (4), 4-216 (1), 5-230 (6), 6-237 (7), 7-311 (5), 8-332 (9), 9-349 (10), 10-354 (11)
FoW (2): 1-11 (2), 2-51 (1), 3-51 (4), 4-81 (5), 5-85 (6), 6-90 (3), 7-94 (7), 8-96 (9), 9-141 (8), 10-201 (10)

CHITTAGONG DIVISION

1	Gazi Salahuddin	c Golam Mabud b Rezaul Haque	21	c Nabil Samad b Rezaul Haque	42
2	Masumud Dowla	c Rezaul Haque b Rashedur Rahman	12	c Rashedur Rahman b Rezaul Haque	32
3	Rezaul Karim	c Golam Mabud b Rezaul Haque	12	not out	54
4	Nazimuddin	b Alok Kapali	31	lbw b Nabil Samad	65
5	*Ehsanul Haque	lbw b Alok Kapali	54	not out	34
6	Faisal Hossain	b Imtiaz Hossain	32		
7	†Dhiman Ghosh	c Golam Mabud b Rashedur Rahman	82		
8	Yasin Arafat	c Golam Mabud b Saif Mahmud	23		
9	Kamrul Islam	c Imtiaz Hossain b Alok Kapali	2		
10	Tareq Aziz	b Rezaul Haque	12		
11	Mohammad Younus	not out	6		
	Extras	b 13, lb 10, w 3, nb 6	32	b 3, lb 6, w 1, nb 2	12
			319	**(3 wickets)**	**239**

FoW (1): 1-34 (1), 2-49 (2), 3-72 (3), 4-97 (4), 5-161 (6), 6-201 (5), 7-258 (8), 8-297 (9), 9-299 (7), 10-319 (10)
FoW (2): 1-79 (1), 2-85 (2), 3-154 (4)

Chittagong Division Bowling	O	M	R	W			O	M	R	W	
Tareq Aziz	21.3	6	86	1	4nb	(2)	19.1	4	54	4	4nb
Kamrul Islam	16	2	53	2	1w	(1)	21	4	37	4	3w,1nb
Ehsanul Haque	11	2	49	1	2nb		14	1	32	0	1w
Mohammad Younus	27	6	81	4			8	0	41	2	
Yasin Arafat	15	3	44	1			11	4	17	0	
Rezaul Karim	4	1	20	0	1nb						

Sylhet Division Bowling	O	M	R	W			O	M	R	W	
Rashedur Rahman	23	5	51	2	1w,1nb		9	0	57	0	1nb
Golam Rahman	2	0	6	0							
Rezaul Haque	11	2	41	3	2w		11	1	43	2	
Alok Kapali	24	2	84	3		(5)	2	1	16	0	
Saif Mahmud	14	4	45	1	4nb	(2)	5	0	13	0	1w,1nb
Nabil Samad	15	0	52	0	1nb	(4)	14	3	50	1	
Imtiaz Hossain	3	0	9	1		(6)	6	0	24	0	
Sadiqur Rahman	1	0	8	0							
Golam Mabud						(7)	3.4	0	27	0	

Umpires: Jahangir Alam and Mahfuzur Rahman.   Referee: Raqibul Hasan.   Toss: Chittagong Division

Close of Play: 1st day: Sylhet Division (1) 348-8 (Sadiqur Rahman 28*, Nabil Samad 0*, 90 overs); 2nd day: Chittagong Division (1) 288-7 (Dhiman Ghosh 72*, Kamrul Islam 1*, 83 overs); 3rd day: Sylhet Division (2) 201 all out.
Man of the Match: Imtiaz Hossain.
Imtiaz Hossain's 130 took 144 balls in 215 minutes and included 17 fours and 1 six.

DHAKA DIVISION v RAJSHAHI DIVISION

Played at Shere Bangla National Stadium, Mirpur, January 4, 5, 6, 7, 2008.
Ispahani Mirzapore Tea National Cricket League 2007/08
Dhaka Division won by three wickets. (Points: Dhaka Division 14, Rajshahi Division 8)

RAJSHAHI DIVISION

1	†Jahurul Islam	c Mahmudullah b Mohammad Sharif	23	b Mahbubul Alam	12
2	Shakil Haider	c Anwar Hossain b Mohammad Sharif	4	c Anwar Hossain b Mohammad Sharif	0
3	Farhad Hossain	b Mahbubul Alam	1	(4) b Mosharraf Hossain	3
4	Rafiqul Islam	c Anwar Hossain b Mahbubul Alam	9	(3) b Mohammad Rafique	17
5	*Khaled Mashud	b Mohammad Rafique	52	b Mosharraf Hossain	2
6	Anisur Rahman	b Mohammad Sharif	20	(8) c Anwar Hossain b Mosharraf Hossain	5
7	Mushfiqur Rahman	c Anwar Hossain b Mohammad Sharif	0	(6) lbw b Mosharraf Hossain	0
8	Naeem Islam	c Mohammad Sharif b Mosharraf Hossain	104	(7) not out	15
9	Mohammad Shahzada	b Mohammad Sharif	109	c Anwar Hossain b Mohammad Sharif	6
10	Alamgir Kabir	not out	15	c Anwar Hossain b Mosharraf Hossain	6
11	Saqlain Sajib	not out	0	c Arafat Sunny b Mosharraf Hossain	0
	Extras	b 6, lb 8, nb 14	28	b 3, lb 4, w 1, nb 3	11
		(9 wickets, declared)	365		77

FoW (1): 1-12 (2), 2-13 (3), 3-41 (4), 4-44 (1), 5-79 (6), 6-79 (7), 7-149 (5), 8-321 (8), 9-365 (9)
FoW (2): 1-6 (2), 2-21 (1), 3-30 (4), 4-39 (5), 5-39 (6), 6-39 (3), 7-46 (8), 8-59 (9), 9-77 (10), 10-77 (11)

DHAKA DIVISION

1	†Anwar Hossain	run out (Saqlain Sajib)	3	(2) c Rafiqul Islam b Alamgir Kabir	8
2	Mehrab Hossain Opee	c Alamgir Kabir b Farhad Hossain	33	(4) lbw b Mohammad Shahzada	0
3	Arafat Sunny	c Shakil Haider b Saqlain Sajib	10		
4	Mehrab Hossain jun	c Jahurul Islam b Alamgir Kabir	51	(3) c sub (Mahbub Alam) b Mohammad Shahzada	39
5	Javed Omar	c Alamgir Kabir b Farhad Hossain	3	(1) c Farhad Hossain b Saqlain Sajib	21
6	Mahmudullah	b Saqlain Sajib	41	(5) not out	25
7	*Mohammad Sharif	c Jahurul Islam b Alamgir Kabir	2	(9) not out	23
8	Nazmul Hossain	b Alamgir Kabir	93	(6) c sub (Mahbub Alam) b Alamgir Kabir	3
9	Mosharraf Hossain	c and b Farhad Hossain	34	(7) c Anisur Rahman b Saqlain Sajib	2
10	Mahbubul Alam	b Farhad Hossain	9		
11	Mohammad Rafique	not out	9	(8) c Mohammad Shahzada b Saqlain Sajib	4
	Extras	b 15, lb 3, nb 7	25	b 1, lb 1, nb 3	5
			313	(7 wickets)	130

FoW (1): 1-14 (1), 2-50 (2), 3-54 (3), 4-61 (5), 5-147 (4), 6-152 (7), 7-163 (6), 8-242 (9), 9-255 (10), 10-313 (8)
FoW (2): 1-10 (2), 2-68 (3), 3-68 (4), 4-76 (1), 5-81 (6), 6-87 (7), 7-91 (8)

Dhaka Division Bowling	O	M	R	W		O	M	R	W	
Mahbubul Alam	18	2	70	2	10nb	6	1	21	1	3nb
Mohammad Sharif	21.4	6	70	5		11	3	24	2	1w
Mosharraf Hossain	40	11	79	1		15.3	6	13	6	
Mohammad Rafique	31	5	95	1		9	4	12	1	
Arafat Sunny	10	2	22	0						
Mehrab Hossain	2	1	1	0						
Mahmudullah	6	1	14	0						

Rajshahi Division Bowling	O	M	R	W			O	M	R	W	
Alamgir Kabir	32.4	2	88	3	5nb		11	2	22	2	
Mohammad Shahzada	12	2	19	0		(5)	5	1	8	2	
Saqlain Sajib	36	8	90	2	2nb	(2)	16	0	62	3	3nb
Farhad Hossain	21	2	75	4		(3)	3.4	1	21	0	
Mushfiqur Rahman	6	2	23	0		(6)	2	0	7	0	
Naeem Islam						(4)	1	0	8	0	

Umpires: Nadir Shah and Sharfuddoula. Referee: Asaduzzaman.   Toss: Rajshahi Division
Close of Play: 1st day: Rajshahi Division (1) 264-7 (Naeem Islam 82*, Mohammad Shahzada 57*, 90 overs); 2nd day: Dhaka Division (1) 132-4 (Mehrab Hossain 40*, Mahmudullah 31*, 49 overs); 3rd day: Rajshahi Division (2) 59-7 (Naeem Islam 5*, Mohammad Shahzada 6*, 29 overs).
Man of the Match: Mosharraf Hossain.
Naeem Islam's 104 took 236 balls in 315 minutes and included 14 fours. Mohammad Shahzada's 109 took 237 balls in 268 minutes and included 9 fours and a six.

KHULNA DIVISION v BARISAL DIVISION

Played at Bir Shrestha Shahid Flight Lieutenant Motiur Rahman Stadium, Khulna, January 4, 5, 6, 7, 2008.
Ispahani Mirzapore Tea National Cricket League 2007/08
Khulna Division won by 63 runs.   (Points: Khulna Division 12, Barisal Division 5)

KHULNA DIVISION

1	Nazmus Sadat	c Arafat Salahuddin b Talha Jubair	6	lbw b Abul Bashar		32
2	Imrul Kayes	lbw b Talha Jubair	21	c Hannan Sarkar b Talha Jubair		0
3	Mostafizur Rahman	b Talha Jubair	1	c Abul Bashar b Talha Jubair		34
4	Jamaluddin Ahmed	c Shahin Hossain b Talha Jubair	0	(5) run out		48
5	*Nahidul Haque	run out (Abul Bashar)	58	(6) c Nasiruddin Faruque		
					b Monir Hossain	52
6	†Saghir Hossain	c Abul Bashar b Monir Hossain	11	(4) c Monir Hossain b Arafat Salahuddin		8
7	Fariduddin	c Tariqul Islam b Abul Bashar	38	c Nasiruddin Faruque b Tariqul Islam		61
8	Ziaur Rahman	b Arafat Salahuddin	38	c Monir Hossain b Talha Jubair		32
9	Murad Khan	not out	10	st Shahin Hossain b Abul Bashar		21
10	Robiul Islam	c Imran Ahmed b Abul Bashar	0	(11) not out		12
11	Aslam Khan	b Talha Jubair	1	(10) lbw b Tariqul Islam		3
	Extras	b 1, lb 1, w 1, nb 6	9	b 4, lb 8, w 5, nb 5		22
			193			**325**

FoW (1): 1-6 (1), 2-11 (3), 3-11 (4), 4-45 (2), 5-92 (6), 6-101 (5), 7-174 (8), 8-186 (7), 9-186 (10), 10-193 (11)
FoW (2): 1-7 (2), 2-64 (6), 3-74 (4), 4-80 (3), 5-177 (6), 6-206 (5), 7-263 (8), 8-303 (9), 9-310 (10), 10-325 (7)

BARISAL DIVISION

1	Hannan Sarkar	b Aslam Khan	6	c Nazmus Sadat b Jamaluddin Ahmed		18
2	Nasiruddin Faruque	lbw b Jamaluddin Ahmed	44	st Saghir Hossain b Jamaluddin Ahmed		60
3	*Imran Ahmed	st Saghir Hossain b Aslam Khan	7	b Murad Khan		23
4	Raqibul Hasan	b Jamaluddin Ahmed	9	b Robiul Islam		53
5	Tariqul Islam	c Jamaluddin Ahmed b Murad Khan	11	(10) lbw b Ziaur Rahman		4
6	Raisul Islam	b Murad Khan	28	(5) lbw b Murad Khan		6
7	Abul Bashar	lbw b Murad Khan	12	(6) c Imrul Kayes b Murad Khan		3
8	Arafat Salahuddin	b Jamaluddin Ahmed	28	(7) c Saghir Hossain b Aslam Khan		14
9	†Shahin Hossain	not out	23	(8) c Fariduddin b Robiul Islam		29
10	Monir Hossain	c Saghir Hossain b Robiul Islam	27	(9) lbw b Aslam Khan		0
11	Talha Jubair	b Aslam Khan	13	not out		6
	Extras	b 4, lb 2, w 1, nb 2	9	b 8, lb 2, w 6, nb 6		22
			217			**238**

FoW (1): 1-12 (1), 2-28 (3), 3-59 (4), 4-76 (2), 5-90 (5), 6-112 (7), 7-141 (6), 8-157 (8), 9-193 (10), 10-217 (11)
FoW (2): 1-75 (2), 2-98 (1), 3-120 (3), 4-135 (5), 5-139 (6), 6-187 (4), 7-213 (7), 8-213 (9), 9-231 (5), 10-238 (10)

Barisal Division Bowling	O	M	R	W			O	M	R	W	
Talha Jubair	18	5	48	5	1w,3nb		22	7	77	3	
Arafat Salahuddin	10	3	35	1			19	5	49	1	3w
Abul Bashar	8	2	27	2		(6)	7	1	23	2	1nb
Tariqul Islam	9	1	33	0	1nb		24.2	2	63	2	4nb
Monir Hossain	22	11	36	1			22	4	76	1	
Raqibul Hasan	4	1	12	0		(7)	1	0	5	0	
Hannan Sarkar						(3)	9	5	20	0	

Khulna Division Bowling	O	M	R	W			O	M	R	W	
Ziaur Rahman	13	3	33	0	2nb	(3)	4.1	1	19	1	1nb
Aslam Khan	18.3	3	66	3			11	0	42	2	1w
Robiul Islam	6	0	27	1	1w	(1)	18	4	54	2	1w,4nb
Jamaluddin Ahmed	19	8	35	3			25	8	39	2	1nb
Murad Khan	26	8	50	3			30	5	52	3	
Nazmus Sadat						(6)	3	0	15	0	
Fariduddin						(7)	4	2	7	0	

Umpires: Anisur Rahman and Manzur Rahman.   Referee: Akhtar Ahmed.   Toss: Khulna Division

Close of Play: 1st day: Barisal Division (1) 62-3 (Nasiruddin Faruque 35*, Tariqul Islam 0*, 17 overs); 2nd day: Khulna Division (2) 73-2 (Mostafizur Rahman 31*, Saghir Hossain 8*, 22 overs); 3rd day: Barisal Division (2) 20-0 (Hannan Sarkar 3*, Nasiruddin Faruque 16*, 5 overs).

Man of the Match: Jamaluddin Ahmed.

BANGLADESH v SOUTH AFRICA

Played at Shere Bangla National Stadium, Mirpur, February 22, 23, 24, 25, 2008.
South Africa in Bangladesh 2007/08 - 1st Test
South Africa won by five wickets.

BANGLADESH

1	Tamim Iqbal	c and b Steyn	0	b Steyn	2	
2	Junaid Siddique	c Boucher b Steyn	1	c Boucher b Kallis	74	
3	Shahriar Nafees	c Smith b Morkel	25	lbw b Steyn	16	
4	Habibul Bashar	c McKenzie b Morkel	11	lbw b Steyn	2	
5	*Mohammad Ashraful	c and b Botha	34	c Boucher b Ntini	24	
6	Aftab Ahmed	c Ntini b Botha	44	lbw b Steyn	24	
7	Shakib Al Hasan	c de Villiers b Morkel	30	c Boucher b Kallis	3	
8	†Mushfiqur Rahim	b Morkel	7	c Boucher b Kallis	2	
9	Mohammad Rafique	lbw b Morkel	0	b Kallis	14	
10	Mashrafe Mortaza	b Steyn	29	c Smith b Kallis	11	
11	Shahadat Hossain	not out	0	not out	1	
	Extras	b 2, lb 4, w 2, nb 3	11	lb 4, w 1, nb 4	9	
			192		**182**	

FoW (1): 1-0 (1), 2-3 (2), 3-32 (4), 4-60 (3), 5-82 (5), 6-152 (6), 7-152 (7), 8-152 (9), 9-192 (8), 10-192 (10)
FoW (2): 1-3 (1), 2-25 (3), 3-29 (4), 4-85 (5), 5-148 (2), 6-148 (6), 7-151 (8), 8-169 (9), 9-181 (10), 10-182 (7)

SOUTH AFRICA

1	N.D.McKenzie	lbw b Shahadat Hossain	5	c Habibul Bashar b Shahadat Hossain	26	
2	*G.C.Smith	b Shahadat Hossain	10	lbw b Mohammad Rafique	62	
3	H.M.Amla	lbw b Mohammad Rafique	25	c Junaid Siddique b Mohammad Rafique	46	
4	J.H.Kallis	b Mohammad Rafique	17	c Mashrafe Mortaza b Shahadat Hossain	7	
5	A.G.Prince	run out				
		(Shakib Al Hasan/Mushfiqur Rahim)	10	lbw b Shahadat Hossain	38	
6	J.Botha	lbw b Shahadat Hossain	25			
7	A.B.deVilliers	c and b Mohammad Ashraful	46	(6) not out	19	
8	†M.V.Boucher	lbw b Shahadat Hossain	11	(7) not out	2	
9	M.Morkel	c Mushfiqur Rahim b Shahadat Hossain	1			
10	D.W.Steyn	b Shahadat Hossain	7			
11	M.Ntini	not out	3			
	Extras	b 1, lb 5, w 1, nb 3	10	b 2, lb 2, w 1	5	
			170	**(5 wickets)**	**205**	

FoW (1): 1-12 (2), 2-19 (1), 3-54 (3), 4-69 (4), 5-77 (5), 6-145 (7), 7-156 (6), 8-158 (9), 9-163 (8), 10-170 (10)
FoW (2): 1-52 (1), 2-125 (2), 3-144 (3), 4-144 (4), 5-193 (5)

South Africa Bowling

	O	M	R	W		O	M	R	W	
Steyn	11.4	2	27	3		18	2	48	4	1w
Ntini	13	2	47	0	2w	16	4	35	1	
Morkel	13	2	50	5	3nb	17	3	43	0	3nb
Kallis	5	2	5	0		14	4	30	5	
Botha	12	0	57	2		6	0	18	0	1nb
McKenzie					(6)	2	0	4	0	

Bangladesh Bowling

	O	M	R	W		O	M	R	W	
Mashrafe Mortaza	9	1	43	0	1w	12	0	47	0	
Shahadat Hossain	15.3	8	27	6	2nb	19	0	70	3	1w
Mohammad Rafique	25	6	55	2	1nb	27.5	6	54	2	
Shakib Al Hasan	10	6	30	0		7	0	24	0	
Mohammad Ashraful	1	0	9	1		2	0	6	0	

Umpires: Aleem Dar and S.A.Bucknor. Third umpire: A.F.M.Akhtaruddin. Referee: R.S.Madugalle.   Toss: Bangladesh

Close of Play: 1st day: South Africa (1) 76-4 (Prince 9*, Botha 5*, 24 overs); 2nd day: Bangladesh (2) 125-4 (Junaid Siddique 64*, Aftab Ahmed 13*, 48 overs); 3rd day: South Africa (2) 178-4 (Prince 24*, de Villiers 8*, 57 overs).

Man of the Match: J.H.Kallis.
The match was scheduled for five days but completed in four.

BANGLADESH v SOUTH AFRICA

Played at Bir Shrestha Shahid Ruhul Amin Stadium, Chittagong, February 29, March 1, 2, 3, 2008.
South Africa in Bangladesh 2007/08 - 2nd Test
South Africa won by an innings and 205 runs.

SOUTH AFRICA
1	N.D.McKenzie	b Shahadat Hossain	226
2	*G.C.Smith	b Abdur Razzak	232
3	H.M.Amla	lbw b Shahadat Hossain	38
4	J.H.Kallis	not out	39
5	A.G.Prince	b Shahadat Hossain	2
6	A.B.deVilliers	b Shakib Al Hasan	1
7	†M.V.Boucher	c Shakib Al Hasan	
		b Mohammad Rafique	21
8	R.J.Peterson	c Junaid Siddique b Mohammad Rafique	4
9	D.W.Steyn		
10	M.Morkel		
11	M.Ntini		
	Extras	b 10, lb 7, w 1, nb 2	20
		(7 wickets, declared)	583

FoW (1): 1-415 (2), 2-514 (1), 3-515 (3), 4-519 (5), 5-524 (6), 6-579 (7), 7-583 (8)

BANGLADESH
1	Tamim Iqbal	c de Villiers b Steyn	14	c Steyn b Peterson	9
2	Junaid Siddique	c Boucher b Steyn	18	c Boucher b Steyn	0
3	Shahriar Nafees	c Smith b Steyn	69	c Kallis b Peterson	31
4	*Mohammad Ashraful	c Boucher b Steyn	0	c Boucher b Steyn	4
5	Abdur Razzak	c Prince b Peterson	33	(7) not out	32
6	Aftab Ahmed	retired hurt	21	absent hurt	0
7	Shakib Al Hasan	c Boucher b Ntini	40	(5) c McKenzie b Steyn	2
8	†Mushfiqur Rahim	c Boucher b Ntini	15	(6) c Kallis b Peterson	4
9	Mohammad Rafique	c Smith b Ntini	10	(8) c and b Peterson	0
10	Mashrafe Mortaza	c Boucher b Ntini	1	c McKenzie b Morkel	4
11	Shahadat Hossain	not out	13	(9) c Prince b Peterson	24
	Extras	lb 11, w 1, nb 13	25	b 6, lb 1, nb 2	9
			259		119

FoW (1): 1-39 (1), 2-49 (2), 3-49 (4), 4-118 (5), 5-176 (3), 6-232 (8), 7-241 (7), 8-246 (9), 9-259 (10)
FoW (2): 1-0 (2), 2-44 (1), 3-45 (3), 4-49 (4), 5-54 (5), 6-58 (6), 7-58 (8), 8-114 (9), 9-119 (10)

Bangladesh Bowling
	O	M	R	W	
Mashrafe Mortaza	28	6	92	0	
Shahadat Hossain	25	1	107	3	2nb
Mohammad Rafique	44.1	5	132	2	1w
Abdur Razzak	31	1	129	1	
Shakib Al Hasan	25	4	68	1	
Mohammad Ashraful	3	0	20	0	
Aftab Ahmed	5	0	18	0	

South Africa Bowling
	O	M	R	W			O	M	R	W	
Steyn	22	7	66	4	5nb	(2)	11	2	35	3	
Ntini	13.4	3	35	4		(1)	5	3	10	0	
Morkel	13	0	71	0	8nb		4.5	1	21	1	2nb
Peterson	16	2	61	1		(5)	13	2	33	5	
Kallis	6	1	15	0	1w	(4)	6	3	13	0	

Umpires: Aleem Dar and S.A.Bucknor. Third umpire: Nadir Shah. Referee: R.S.Madugalle.   Toss: South Africa

Close of Play: 1st day: South Africa (1) 405-0 (McKenzie 169*, Smith 223*, 90 overs); 2nd day: Bangladesh (1) 60-3 (Shahriar Nafees 7*, Abdur Razzak 8*, 16 overs); 3rd day: Bangladesh (2) 54-5 (Mushfiqur Rahim 4*, Abdur Razzak 0*, 25.3 overs).
Man of the Match: G.C.Smith.
The match was scheduled for five days but completed in four. N.D.McKenzie's 226 took 388 balls in 518 minutes and included 28 fours and 3 sixes. G.C.Smith's 232 took 277 balls in 406 minutes and included 33 fours and 1 six. Aftab Ahmed retired hurt in the Bangladesh first innings having scored 21 (team score 176-5, 45.2 overs).

INDIA A v SOUTH AFRICA A

Played at Feroz Shah Kotla, Delhi, September 13, 14, 15, 2007.
South Africa A in India 2007/08
India A won by an innings and 242 runs.

INDIA A

1	C.A.Pujara	c Tsolekile b de Wet	8
2	A.S.Chopra	not out	239
3	*M.Kaif	lbw b de Wet	0
4	†P.A.Patel	run out (Dippenaar)	110
5	M.K.Tiwary	c Amla b Kleinveldt	2
6	S.Badrinath	not out	200
7	A.M.Makda		
8	P.P.Ojha		
9	A.Mishra		
10	I.Sharma		
11	Pankaj Singh		
	Extras	b 5, lb 6, w 1, nb 17	29
		(4 wickets, declared)	588

FoW (1): 1-13 (1), 2-13 (3), 3-172 (4), 4-178 (5)

SOUTH AFRICA A

1	†M.N.van Wyk	c Kaif b Sharma	67	c Patel b Ojha	12
2	W.L.Coetsee	c Kaif b Ojha	18	lbw b Pankaj Singh	6
3	H.M.Amla	run out (Mishra)	8	b Ojha	7
4	*H.H.Dippenaar	c Pujara b Mishra	26	(5) c Chopra b Ojha	29
5	A.G.Prince	c Patel b Sharma	4	(6) c Kaif b Pankaj Singh	16
6	J.L.Ontong	c and b Ojha	4	(7) c Kaif b Ojha	36
7	T.L.Tsolekile	c Chopra b Mishra	0	(8) not out	63
8	R.K.Kleinveldt	c and b Mishra	4	(9) c Kaif b Ojha	5
9	F.de Wet	b Ojha	0	(10) c Makda b Mishra	1
10	C.K.Langeveldt	not out	0	(11) c Ojha b Mishra	1
11	A.N.Petersen	absent hurt	0	(4) lbw b Sharma	6
	Extras	b 2, nb 12	14	b 5, lb 4, nb 10	19
			145		201

FoW (1): 1-55 (2), 2-76 (3), 3-122 (1), 4-134 (5), 5-141 (4), 6-141 (7), 7-143 (6), 8-145 (8), 9-145 (9)
FoW (2): 1-14 (2), 2-26 (1), 3-28 (3), 4-52 (4), 5-79 (5), 6-96 (6), 7-162 (7), 8-175 (9), 9-198 (10), 10-201 (11)

South Africa A Bowling

	O	M	R	W	
Langeveldt	27	8	53	0	6nb
de Wet	24	2	84	2	1w,1nb
Kleinveldt	22	3	92	1	9nb
Ontong	17	0	103	0	1nb
Coetsee	45	4	186	0	
Amla	15.3	1	59	0	

India A Bowling

	O	M	R	W			O	M	R	W	
Pankaj Singh	10	1	53	0		(2)	9	2	16	2	
Sharma	11	0	48	2	11nb	(5)	10	3	29	1	1nb
Ojha	16.4	4	29	3			23	5	66	5	
Mishra	6	2	10	3	1nb		18.2	2	63	2	9nb
Makda	2	0	3	0		(1)	8	2	18	0	

Umpires: A.M.Saheba and S.L.Shastri. Third umpire: A.K.Chowdhury. Referee: K.Bhaskar Pillai.   Toss: India A

Close of Play: 1st day: India A (1) 354-4 (Chopra 137*, Badrinath 77*, 89 overs); 2nd day: South Africa A (1) 93-2 (van Wyk 53*, Dippenaar 3*, 26 overs).

The match was scheduled for four days but completed in three. A.S.Chopra's 239 took 461 balls in 623 minutes and included 19 fours and 4 sixes. P.A.Patel's 110 took 118 balls in 164 minutes and included 17 fours. S.Badrinath's 200 took 307 balls in 400 minutes and included 17 fours and 3 sixes.

INDIA A v SOUTH AFRICA A

Played at Himachal Pradesh Cricket Association Stadium, Dharmasala, September 19, 20, 21, 22, 2007.
South Africa A in India 2007/08
Match drawn.

SOUTH AFRICA A

1	†M.N.van Wyk	lbw b Sharma	9
2	A.N.Petersen	st Patel b Ojha	109
3	H.M.Amla	c Kaif b Ojha	49
4	*H.H.Dippenaar	lbw b Mishra	49
5	A.G.Prince	not out	17
6	J.L.Ontong	not out	22
7	W.L.Coetsee		
8	F.de Wet		
9	R.J.Peterson		
10	Y.A.Abdulla		
11	D.W.Steyn		
	Extras	lb 6, nb 3	9
		(4 wickets)	264

FoW (1): 1-9 (1), 2-125 (3), 3-214 (2), 4-231 (4)

INDIA A

1	A.S.Chopra
2	C.A.Pujara
3	*M.Kaif
4	†P.A.Patel
5	M.K.Tiwary
6	S.Badrinath
7	V.Y.Mahesh
8	I.Sharma
9	Pankaj Singh
10	P.P.Ojha
11	A.Mishra

India A Bowling

	O	M	R	W	
Pankaj Singh	6	1	30	0	
Sharma	14	5	35	1	
Ojha	24	3	98	2	1nb
Mahesh	10	2	41	0	2nb
Mishra	16	4	54	1	

Umpires: G.A.Pratapkumar and S.K.Tarapore.   Third umpire: D.Sharma.   Referee: P.Thakur.   Toss: South Africa A

Close of Play: 1st day: South Africa A (1) 264-4 (Prince 17*, Ontong 22*, 70 overs); 2nd day: No play; 3rd day: No play.

There was no play on the final day. A.N.Petersen's 109 took 163 balls in 203 minutes and included 17 fours and 2 sixes.

REST OF INDIA v MUMBAI

Played at Madhavrao Scindia Cricket Ground, Rajkot, October 6, 7, 8, 9, 2007.
Irani Cup 2007/08
Rest of India won by nine wickets.

MUMBAI

1	S.O.Kukreja	run out (Badrinath)	110	run out (Badrinath)		14
2	A.M.Rahane	lbw b Bose	52	c Chopra b Sharma		27
3	W.Jaffer	c Kaif b Bose	8	b M.M.Patel		25
4	*A.A.Muzumdar	lbw b Ojha	8	c Chopra b Bose		4
5	P.T.Naik	lbw b Sharma	12	lbw b M.M.Patel		13
6	A.M.Nayar	c Sharma b Ojha	118	c Chopra b M.M.Patel		8
7	R.R.Powar	c P.A.Patel b Sharma	45	b M.M.Patel		0
8	A.B.Agarkar	c Raina b Bose	4	not out		11
9	†O.D.Gurav	c P.A.Patel b Sharma	0	(10) c P.A.Patel b Sharma		0
10	Iqbal Abdulla	not out	56	(9) c Mishra b Sharma		0
11	R.P.Verma	lbw b Mishra	9	c P.A.Patel b M.M.Patel		0
	Extras	b 2, lb 9, w 3, nb 17	31	lb 1, nb 3		4
			453			106

FoW (1): 1-91 (2), 2-109 (3), 3-150 (4), 4-164 (5), 5-336 (1), 6-338 (6), 7-343 (8), 8-359 (9), 9-410 (7), 10-453 (11)
FoW (2): 1-43 (1), 2-43 (2), 3-50 (4), 4-74 (5), 5-82 (6), 6-82 (7), 7-103 (3), 8-104 (9), 9-105 (10), 10-106 (11)

REST OF INDIA

1	A.S.Chopra	c Naik b Verma	0	st Gurav b Iqbal Abdulla	7
2	†P.A.Patel	c and b Iqbal Abdulla	179	not out	59
3	*M.Kaif	lbw b Agarkar	18	not out	22
4	S.K.Raina	b Verma	17		
5	S.Badrinath	lbw b Iqbal Abdulla	29		
6	M.K.Tiwary	b Verma	130		
7	A.Mishra	c Gurav b Verma	22		
8	P.P.Ojha	c and b Verma	4		
9	R.R.Bose	lbw b Nayar	19		
10	M.M.Patel	lbw b Iqbal Abdulla	31		
11	I.Sharma	not out	0		
	Extras	lb 11, w 9, nb 3	23	lb 2, nb 1	3
			472	(1 wicket)	91

FoW (1): 1-4 (1), 2-33 (3), 3-64 (4), 4-150 (5), 5-351 (2), 6-405 (7), 7-415 (8), 8-418 (6), 9-472 (10), 10-472 (9)
FoW (2): 1-39 (1)

Rest of India Bowling

	O	M	R	W			O	M	R	W	
M.M.Patel	19.5	0	96	0	10nb	(4)	7.3	2	25	5	
Bose	25.1	4	106	3	2w	(1)	11	1	42	1	
Sharma	22	7	63	3	1w,3nb	(2)	11	3	31	3	2nb
Ojha	21	0	114	2							
Mishra	8.2	0	43	1	3nb	(3)	4	1	7	0	1nb
Badrinath	5	0	20	0							

Mumbai Bowling

	O	M	R	W		O	M	R	W	
Agarkar	21	2	101	1	3w,2nb	3.5	0	31	0	1nb
Verma	30	3	97	5	3w,1nb	3	0	29	0	
Nayar	27.3	6	73	1	2w	6	1	11	0	
Powar	14	0	87	0						
Iqbal Abdulla	26	4	100	3	(4)	6	0	18	1	
Rahane	1	0	3	0						

Umpires: K.Hariharan and S.K.Tarapore. Third umpire: R.M.Deshpande. Referee: M.Nayyar.   Toss: Mumbai

Close of Play: 1st day: Mumbai (1) 385-8 (Powar 28*, Iqbal Abdulla 16*, 86 overs); 2nd day: Rest of India (1) 292-4 (P.A.Patel 161*, Tiwary 56*, 70 overs); 3rd day: Mumbai (2) 98-6 (Jaffer 21*, Agarkar 7*, 31 overs).

The match was scheduled for five days but completed in four. S.O.Kukreja's 110 took 210 balls in 331 minutes and included 17 fours. A.M.Nayar's 118 took 108 balls in 131 minutes and included 20 fours and 1 six. P.A.Patel's 179 took 235 balls in 339 minutes and included 27 fours. M.K.Tiwary's 130 took 184 balls in 274 minutes and included 12 fours and 5 sixes.

GOA v HARYANA

Played at Dr Rajendra Prasad Stadium, Margao, November 3, 4, 5, 6, 2007.
Ranji Trophy 2007/08 - Plate Group B
Goa won by 26 runs.   (Points: Goa 5, Haryana 0)

GOA

1	S.K.Kamat	c Viswanathan b Vashisht	40	c Rana b Mishra	60
2	R.D.Asnodkar	c Rana b Badhwar	20	c Rana b Badhwar	0
3	A.K.Desai	c Rana b Badhwar	0	lbw b J.Sharma	2
4	*J.Arunkumar	b Mishra	55	lbw b J.Sharma	0
5	M.V.Joglekar	lbw b J.Sharma	4	c Badhwar b Mishra	36
6	†A.Ratra	b Mishra	15	lbw b Badhwar	86
7	R.R.D'Souza	c Sandeep Singh b Mishra	10	st Sandeep Singh b Mishra	5
8	S.B.Jakati	c Rana b J.Sharma	25	(9) c Viswanathan b Mishra	4
9	A.R.Angle	not out	56	(8) lbw b Mishra	9
10	R.S.D'Souza	c Sandeep Singh b J.Sharma	27	b Mishra	1
11	H.H.Gadekar	c Sandeep Singh b J.Sharma	3	not out	8
	Extras	b 2, lb 2, w 5, nb 7	16	b 3, lb 1, w 4, nb 2	10
			271		221

FoW (1): 1-55 (2), 2-56 (3), 3-74 (1), 4-81 (5), 5-119 (6), 6-154 (4), 7-159 (7), 8-201 (8), 9-266 (10), 10-271 (11)
FoW (2): 1-20 (2), 2-30 (3), 3-30 (4), 4-96 (1), 5-133 (5), 6-151 (7), 7-175 (8), 8-181 (9), 9-189 (10), 10-221 (6)

HARYANA

1	V.Sahni	c Ratra b Jakati	27	lbw b Jakati	0
2	M.R.Beerala	c Gadekar b Jakati	31	st Ratra b Jakati	37
3	S.Sharma	c Joglekar b Jakati	52	(4) lbw b R.R.D'Souza	13
4	S.S.Viswanathan	b R.R.D'Souza	0	(5) lbw b R.R.D'Souza	11
5	S.Rana	c Ratra b Jakati	44	(6) c Gadekar b Jakati	67
6	J.Sharma	c R.R.D'Souza b R.S.D'Souza	7	(7) b R.R.D'Souza	16
7	†Sandeep Singh	c Ratra b Jakati	36	(8) b R.R.D'Souza	0
8	*A.Mishra	lbw b Gadekar	1	(9) b Jakati	19
9	G.Vashisht	c and b Gadekar	21	(3) c Ratra b R.S.D'Souza	47
10	S.Badhwar	b Jakati	2	not out	2
11	P.Huda	not out	2	lbw b Gadekar	0
	Extras	b 8, lb 3, w 3, nb 9	23	b 1, lb 3, w 3, nb 1	8
			246		220

FoW (1): 1-62 (2), 2-70 (1), 3-71 (4), 4-150 (5), 5-165 (6), 6-176 (3), 7-183 (8), 8-228 (9), 9-243 (10), 10-246 (7)
FoW (2): 1-0 (1), 2-85 (2), 3-87 (3), 4-111 (4), 5-112 (5), 6-162 (7), 7-162 (8), 8-217 (6), 9-219 (9), 10-220 (11)

Haryana Bowling

	O	M	R	W			O	M	R	W	
J.Sharma	24.1	5	66	4	1nb		15	4	57	2	
Badhwar	18	5	44	2	5w,4nb		5.3	3	9	2	2w
Rana	10	4	40	0	2nb	(5)	4	0	11	0	
Vashisht	16	7	49	1		(3)	14	2	41	0	2w
Mishra	25	10	52	3		(4)	20	3	75	6	2nb
Huda	5	1	16	0			5	0	24	0	

Goa Bowling

	O	M	R	W			O	M	R	W	
Gadekar	22	10	46	2	1w	(2)	16	3	34	1	
R.S.D'Souza	14	3	37	1	2w,8nb	(3)	9	2	13	1	1nb
R.R.D'Souza	25	6	69	1	1w	(4)	19	4	59	4	
Jakati	29.2	13	52	6		(1)	40	13	94	4	1w
Angle	7	0	31	0			4	0	16	0	

Umpires: A.Bhattacharjee and S.Rao.   Referee: J.N.Jadeja.   Toss: Goa

Close of Play: 1st day: Goa (1) 258-8 (Angle 54*, R.S.D'Souza 21*, 90 overs); 2nd day: Haryana (1) 205-7 (Sandeep Singh 17*, Vashisht 11*, 79 overs); 3rd day: Haryana (2) 6-1 (Beerala 2*, Vashisht 4*, 3 overs).

GUJARAT v ASSAM

Played at Sardar Patel Stadium, Motera, Ahmedabad, November 3, 4, 5, 6, 2007.
Ranji Trophy 2007/08 - Plate Group A
Gujarat won by 248 runs.   (Points: Gujarat 5, Assam 0)

GUJARAT

1	N.D.Modi	c Tarjinder Singh b K.S.Das	17	(2) not out	151
2	H.R.Joshipura	lbw b Suresh	14	(1) c R.N.Das b Goswami	1
3	*†P.A.Patel	c Tarjinder Singh b Goswami	49	c R.N.Das b Suresh	62
4	N.K.Patel	c R.N.Das b K.S.Das	31	c Tarjinder Singh b Goswami	124
5	B.D.Thaker	c R.N.Das b K.S.Das	15	(6) not out	10
6	D.M.Popat	c Tarjinder Singh b K.S.Das	63	(5) b Goswami	5
7	T.K.Patel	c R.N.Das b Suresh	2		
8	N.M.Rawal	b Suresh	0		
9	M.B.Parmar	b Konwar	5		
10	A.M.Makda	lbw b Suresh	1		
11	S.K.Trivedi	not out	22		
	Extras	lb 6, nb 3	9	b 8, lb 3, w 2, nb 1	14
			228	(4 wickets, declared)	**367**

FoW (1): 1-23 (2), 2-61 (1), 3-88 (3), 4-120 (5), 5-134 (4), 6-145 (7), 7-145 (8), 8-152 (9), 9-155 (10), 10-228 (6)
FoW (2): 1-1 (1), 2-118 (3), 3-333 (4), 4-341 (5)

ASSAM

1	S.Bhagawati	c P.A.Patel b Trivedi	1	c Joshipura b Trivedi	4
2	S.K.Das	c N.K.Patel b Makda	0	lbw b Rawal	1
3	N.H.Bordoloi	lbw b Makda	13	c Popat b Parmar	36
4	Tarjinder Singh	c P.A.Patel b T.K.Patel	19	(6) b Trivedi	10
5	S.Ramesh	run out (Makda/P.A.Patel)	43	lbw b Parmar	9
6	*S.Sharath	b Parmar	18	(7) c Thaker b Trivedi	27
7	S.Suresh	lbw b T.K.Patel	25	(8) c Thaker b Parmar	5
8	†R.N.Das	not out	14	(4) c P.A.Patel b T.K.Patel	35
9	D.S.Goswami	c Modi b T.K.Patel	0	c Joshipura b Parmar	5
10	A.Konwar	b Makda	22	c Joshipura b Parmar	4
11	K.S.Das	c Popat b T.K.Patel	20	not out	13
	Extras	b 6, lb 2, nb 6	14	b 5, lb 3, nb 1	9
			189		**158**

FoW (1): 1-2 (1), 2-2 (2), 3-29 (3), 4-56 (4), 5-91 (6), 6-126 (5), 7-142 (7), 8-142 (9), 9-167 (10), 10-189 (11)
FoW (2): 1-6 (1), 2-15 (2), 3-80 (4), 4-82 (3), 5-89 (5), 6-127 (6), 7-134 (8), 8-140 (9), 9-144 (10), 10-158 (7)

Assam Bowling

	O	M	R	W		O	M	R	W	
K.S.Das	19.3	4	73	4		23	5	86	0	
Goswami	10	3	30	1		24	4	80	3	1w
Suresh	16	3	46	4		19	4	59	1	
Konwar	20	5	66	1	3nb	32	7	78	0	1nb
Tarjinder Singh	1	0	7	0	(6)	9	2	32	0	1w
Bhagawati					(5)	1	0	1	0	
S.K.Das					(7)	4	0	20	0	

Gujarat Bowling

	O	M	R	W		O	M	R	W	
Trivedi	23	7	52	1		13.1	4	28	3	
Makda	21	9	47	3		13	5	24	0	
Rawal	9	4	19	0	(4)	5	1	14	1	
Parmar	8	1	25	1	(5)	20	6	52	5	
T.K.Patel	11.5	1	38	4	6nb	(3) 13	3	32	1	1nb

Umpires: S.Dendapani and V.N.Kulkarni. Referee: S.Chaturvedi.   Toss: Assam

Close of Play: 1st day: Assam (1) 56-4 (Ramesh 16*, Sharath 0*, 24 overs); 2nd day: Gujarat (2) 85-1 (Modi 35*, P.A.Patel 48*, 39 overs); 3rd day: Assam (2) 15-2 (Bordoloi 7*, R.N.Das 0*, 15 overs).

N.D.Modi's 151 took 322 balls in 471 minutes and included 16 fours. N.K.Patel's 124 took 192 balls in 237 minutes and included 15 fours and 2 sixes.

HIMACHAL PRADESH v SAURASHTRA

Played at Himachal Pradesh Cricket Association Stadium, Dharmasala, November 3, 4, 5, 6, 2007.
Ranji Trophy 2007/08 - Elite Group A
Match drawn.   (Points: Himachal Pradesh 1, Saurashtra 3)

SAURASHTRA

1	†S.D.Jogiyani	b Malik	32	(2) c Bisla b Thakur	24
2	K.M.Vaghela	c Dogra b Thakur	40	(1) lbw b Thakur	0
3	S.H.Kotak	c S.Sharma b Thakur	38	c Bhatia b Malik	13
4	C.A.Pujara	c Bhatia b Thakur	64	b Malik	109
5	*J.N.Shah	c Dogra b Sarandeep Singh	23	lbw b Thakur	4
6	P.S.Mehta	c Bisla b Sarandeep Singh	8	c Bisla b Thakur	5
7	F.U.Bambhaniya	b Malik	23	c Bisla b Sarandeep Singh	5
8	R.V.Dhruve	c Bisla b Thakur	27	lbw b Thakur	48
9	K.R.Makwana	not out	3	not out	19
10	S.P.Jobanputra	c S.Sharma b Thakur	5	c Mannu b Bhatia	14
11	S.M.Maniar	c Bisla b Thakur	0	c Gupta b Bhatia	8
	Extras	b 16, lb 2, nb 10	28	b 4, lb 11, w 2, nb 7	24
			291		**273**

FoW (1): 1-50 (1), 2-110 (3), 3-196 (2), 4-205 (4), 5-228 (6), 6-237 (5), 7-284 (7), 8-285 (8), 9-291 (10), 10-291 (11)
FoW (2): 1-0 (1), 2-42 (3), 3-73 (2), 4-77 (5), 5-83 (6), 6-116 (7), 7-226 (4), 8-232 (8), 9-253 (10), 10-273 (11)

HIMACHAL PRADESH

1	M.Gupta	lbw b Jobanputra	0	c Bambhaniya b Makwana	104
2	*S.Sharma	lbw b Dhruve	82	c Mehta b Jobanputra	7
3	Sangram Singh	c Pujara b Makwana	50	c Jogiyani b Makwana	19
4	P.Dogra	c Makwana b Dhruve	15	(5) not out	15
5	†M.S.Bisla	lbw b Dhruve	0	(6) not out	2
6	A.Mannu	not out	14	(4) c Bambhaniya b Makwana	57
7	V.Bhatia	lbw b Makwana	3		
8	M.Sharma	lbw b Makwana	0		
9	Sarandeep Singh	b Makwana	0		
10	A.K.Thakur	st Jogiyani b Makwana	1		
11	V.Malik	c Jogiyani b Makwana	4		
	Extras	b 4, lb 4, w 4	12	b 6, lb 1, w 7, nb 2	16
			181	**(4 wickets)**	**220**

FoW (1): 1-12 (1), 2-131 (3), 3-156 (4), 4-156 (5), 5-157 (2), 6-171 (7), 7-171 (8), 8-171 (9), 9-177 (10), 10-181 (11)
FoW (2): 1-19 (2), 2-74 (5), 3-194 (1), 4-200 (4)

Himachal Pradesh Bowling

	O	M	R	W		O	M	R	W	
Thakur	30.5	9	73	6		24	7	53	5	1nb
Malik	24	7	67	2	8nb	24	3	79	2	2w,6nb
Sangram Singh	6	1	20	0						
Sarandeep Singh	29	8	67	2	(3)	29	9	68	1	
Bhatia	13	4	46	0	2nb	(4) 21.4	7	49	2	
S.Sharma					(5)	1	0	9	0	

Saurashtra Bowling

	O	M	R	W		O	M	R	W	
Jobanputra	10	3	39	1	3w	11	1	45	1	6w
Maniar	14	2	56	0		10	2	33	0	
Vaghela	6	3	7	0						
Dhruve	23	13	28	3		13	5	30	0	1w,2nb
Makwana	21	11	41	6	(3)	22	5	81	3	
Kotak	2	1	2	0		5	3	8	0	
Pujara					(5)	3	0	16	0	

Umpires: N.R.S.Prabhu and S.M.Raju. Referee: A.Kaypee.   Toss: Saurashtra

Close of Play: 1st day: Saurashtra (1) 262-6 (Bambhaniya 13*, Dhruve 21*, 90 overs); 2nd day: Himachal Pradesh (1) 175-8 (Mannu 13*, Thakur 0*, 71 overs); 3rd day: Saurashtra (2) 216-6 (Pujara 103*, Dhruve 39*, 83 overs).
C.A.Pujara's 109 took 200 balls in 275 minutes and included 11 fours. M.Gupta's 104 took 144 balls in 210 minutes and included 20 fours. R.V.Dhruve retired hurt in the Saurashtra first innings having scored 27 (team score 271-6) - he returned when the score was 284-7.

JHARKHAND v MADHYA PRADESH

Played at Keenan Stadium, Jamshedpur, November 3, 4, 5, 6, 2007.
Ranji Trophy 2007/08 - Plate Group B
Madhya Pradesh won by 170 runs.   (Points: Jharkhand 0, Madhya Pradesh 5)

MADHYA PRADESH

1	M.A.Pasha	lbw b Rao	6	lbw b Rao		8
2	†N.V.Ojha	c Vardhan b Sharma	1	b Rao		15
3	Jatin S.Saxena	not out	125	c Nadeem b Rao		22
4	D.Bundela	c Ghosh b Rao	1	b Yadav		39
5	*B.R.Tomar	c Ratan Kumar b Gupta	19	run out		17
6	Jalaj S.Saxena	b Yadav	0	(7) not out		21
7	R.N.Bakshi	c Ratan Kumar b Sharma	56	(6) not out		66
8	S.M.Dholpure	c Ghosh b Sharma	0			
9	S.P.Pandey	c and b Sharma	2			
10	A.Rajan	c Yadav b Rao	2			
11	Asif Ali	lbw b Rao	0			
	Extras	lb 8, w 2, nb 1	11	b 8, lb 1, w 1, nb 5		15
			223	(5 wickets, declared)		203

FoW (1): 1-1 (2), 2-20 (1), 3-33 (4), 4-100 (5), 5-100 (6), 6-202 (7), 7-208 (8), 8-216 (9), 9-219 (10), 10-223 (11)
FoW (2): 1-14 (1), 2-40 (3), 3-49 (2), 4-89 (5), 5-134 (4)

JHARKHAND

1	R.Prasad	c Ojha b Rajan	0	b Rajan	0
2	*M.S.Vardhan	c Ojha b Rajan	47	c and b Jalaj S.Saxena	23
3	Ratan Kumar	b Rajan	7	(4) c Pandey b Asif Ali	27
4	A.Hashmi	lbw b Dholpure	16	(5) c Jatin S.Saxena b Jalaj S.Saxena	5
5	S.S.Tiwary	lbw b Asif Ali	11	(3) c Ojha b Pandey	1
6	S.Nadeem	c sub (Murtuza Ali) b Jalaj S.Saxena	1	(8) c Ojha b Asif Ali	27
7	†S.Ghosh	c sub (Murtuza Ali) b Jalaj S.Saxena	0	(6) c Bakshi b Asif Ali	1
8	S.Gupta	c sub (Murtuza Ali) b Rajan	20	(7) c Ojha b Asif Ali	13
9	K.Sharma	c Asif Ali b Pandey	1	c Asif Ali b Jalaj S.Saxena	8
10	S.S.Rao	not out	8	lbw b Jalaj S.Saxena	1
11	R.K.Yadav	c Bakshi b Pandey	1	not out	4
	Extras	b 2, lb 10, w 3, nb 12	27	b 2, nb 5	7
			139		117

FoW (1): 1-8 (1), 2-16 (3), 3-50 (4), 4-82 (5), 5-83 (6), 6-83 (7), 7-108 (2), 8-128 (8), 9-130 (9), 10-139 (11)
FoW (2): 1-2 (1), 2-5 (3), 3-44 (2), 4-54 (5), 5-55 (6), 6-74 (4), 7-85 (7), 8-106 (9), 9-111 (10), 10-117 (8)

Jharkhand Bowling

	O	M	R	W			O	M	R	W	
Sharma	24	10	38	4	1nb	(2)	14.3	4	47	0	1nb
Rao	29.4	6	66	4		(1)	19	3	59	3	1w
Yadav	21	7	49	1	2w		13	2	32	1	
Nadeem	13	1	29	0			15	3	35	0	
Gupta	8	0	33	1			6	1	21	0	
Vardhan	1	1	0	0							

Madhya Pradesh Bowling

	O	M	R	W			O	M	R	W	
Pandey	17.2	9	25	2			7	5	4	1	
Rajan	17	1	51	4	3w,9nb		8	4	9	1	1nb
Dholpure	8	2	24	1	2nb	(4)	4	0	13	0	4nb
Jalaj S.Saxena	9	3	16	2		(3)	18	4	54	4	
Asif Ali	6	1	11	1			12.4	2	35	4	

Umpires: A.Y.Gokhale and H.S.Sekhon.   Referee: C.R.Vijayaraghavan.   Toss: Jharkhand

Close of Play: 1st day: Madhya Pradesh (1) 100-4 (Jatin S.Saxena 69*, Jalaj S.Saxena 0*, 50.3 overs); 2nd day: Jharkhand (1) 83-5 (Vardhan 34*, Ghosh 0*, 33.5 overs); 3rd day: Madhya Pradesh (2) 165-5 (Bakshi 44*, Jalaj S.Saxena 10*, 62 overs).

Jatin S.Saxena's 125 took 281 balls in 430 minutes and included 9 fours.

MUMBAI v KARNATAKA

Played at Wankhede Stadium, Mumbai, November 3, 4, 5, 6, 2007.
Ranji Trophy 2007/08 - Elite Group A
Match drawn.   (Points: Mumbai 3, Karnataka 1)

KARNATAKA

1	B.M.Rowland	c Samant b Agarkar	0	b Verma	40
2	K.B.Pawan	c Rahane b Agarkar	11	c Samant b Nayar	80
3	R.S.Dravid	c Muzumdar b Powar	40	c Rahane b Iqbal Abdulla	214
4	C.Raghu	c Samant b Nayar	31	c Samant b Powar	13
5	Y.K.T.Goud	st Samant b Powar	5	c Nayar b Iqbal Abdulla	1
6	†V.S.T.Naidu	c Samant b Verma	33	not out	34
7	B.Akhil	c Samant b Agarkar	57	st Samant b Iqbal Abdulla	1
8	S.B.Joshi	lbw b Powar	6	not out	0
9	*A.Kumble	c Rahane b Powar	0		
10	R.Vinay Kumar	c Samant b Powar	4		
11	N.C.Aiyappa	not out	2		
	Extras	lb 3, nb 3	6	b 5, lb 1, w 3, nb 5	14
			195	(6 wickets, declared)	397

FoW (1): 1-0 (1), 2-23 (2), 3-72 (3), 4-78 (5), 5-97 (4), 6-145 (6), 7-164 (8), 8-166 (9), 9-172 (10), 10-195 (7)
FoW (2): 1-69 (1), 2-227 (2), 3-281 (4), 4-290 (5), 5-390 (3), 6-396 (7)

MUMBAI

1	S.O.Kukreja	c Naidu b Aiyappa	66	lbw b Vinay Kumar	23
2	W.Jaffer	b Aiyappa	55	b Vinay Kumar	17
3	A.M.Rahane	lbw b Joshi	0	not out	22
4	*A.A.Muzumdar	lbw b Kumble	23	not out	4
5	P.T.Naik	run out (Vinay Kumar)	78		
6	A.M.Nayar	lbw b Joshi	24		
7	R.R.Powar	c Raghu b Joshi	10		
8	A.B.Agarkar	lbw b Vinay Kumar	24		
9	†V.R.Samant	c Naidu b Vinay Kumar	24		
10	Iqbal Abdulla	lbw b Vinay Kumar	18		
11	R.P.Verma	not out	1		
	Extras	b 2, lb 3, nb 9	14	w 1, nb 3	4
			337	(2 wickets)	70

FoW (1): 1-118 (2), 2-121 (3), 3-125 (1), 4-173 (4), 5-217 (6), 6-231 (7), 7-274 (5), 8-306 (8), 9-331 (9), 10-337 (10)
FoW (2): 1-37 (1), 2-46 (2)

Mumbai Bowling

	O	M	R	W			O	M	R	W	
Agarkar	15.5	4	25	3	1nb		16	3	50	0	2nb
Verma	20	6	42	1	1nb		18	4	49	1	2nb
Powar	29	6	69	5	1nb	(4)	33	4	122	1	1nb
Nayar	12	4	17	1		(3)	25	3	84	1	1w
Iqbal Abdulla	17	4	39	0			38	11	73	3	2w
Rahane						(6)	1	0	1	0	
Naik						(7)	4	0	12	0	

Karnataka Bowling

	O	M	R	W			O	M	R	W	
Vinay Kumar	21	6	50	3			7	3	20	2	
Aiyappa	16	3	60	2	6nb		4	0	25	0	1w,2nb
Akhil	12	1	45	0							
Kumble	24	2	90	1	3nb	(3)	6	0	25	0	1nb
Joshi	20	1	67	3							
Raghu	3	0	20	0							

Umpires: A.K.Chowdhury and K.Hariharan.   Referee: S.Mukherjee.   Toss: Karnataka

Close of Play: 1st day: Karnataka (1) 189-9 (Akhil 53*, Aiyappa 1*, 91 overs); 2nd day: Mumbai (1) 302-7 (Agarkar 20*, Samant 13*, 85 overs); 3rd day: Karnataka (2) 195-1 (Pawan 76*, Dravid 77*, 77 overs).

R.S.Dravid's 214 took 330 balls in 437 minutes and included 21 fours and 5 sixes.

ORISSA v UTTAR PRADESH

Played at Barabati Stadium, Cuttack, November 3, 4, 5, 2007.
Ranji Trophy 2007/08 - Elite Group B
Uttar Pradesh won by an innings and 10 runs.   (Points: Orissa 0, Uttar Pradesh 6)

ORISSA

#	Batsman	Dismissal	Runs	2nd innings	Runs
1	R.R.Parida	b Tyagi	1	(3) b Tyagi	1
2	S.S.Das	lbw b Tyagi	75	c S.S.Shukla b Tyagi	9
3	N.J.Behera	lbw b Tyagi	1	absent hurt	0
4	S.S.Biswal	c Amir Khan b Tyagi	0	b Mishra	23
5	*P.M.Mullick	b Abid Khan	16	b Chawla	2
6	P.Jayachandra	c Amir Khan b Chawla	55	b Chawla	50
7	†H.M.Das	c Amir Khan b Tyagi	14	b Tyagi	71
8	D.S.Mohanty	c Chawla b S.S.Shukla	27	(1) c S.S.Shukla b Abid Khan	1
9	S.K.Satpathy	c Amir Khan b Tyagi	0	(8) c Amir Khan b Tyagi	3
10	S.P.Khatua	c Mishra b S.S.Shukla	7	(9) b Chawla	35
11	P.Das	not out	1	(10) not out	11
	Extras	b 8, lb 9, w 1, nb 1	19	b 4, lb 6, nb 6	16
			216		**222**

FoW (1): 1-2 (1), 2-8 (3), 3-8 (4), 4-25 (5), 5-111 (6), 6-154 (7), 7-195 (2), 8-195 (9), 9-215 (8), 10-216 (10)
FoW (2): 1-7 (1), 2-11 (2), 3-15 (3), 4-34 (5), 5-62 (4), 6-119 (6), 7-122 (8), 8-196 (9), 9-222 (7)

UTTAR PRADESH

#	Batsman	Dismissal	Runs
1	R.B.Elahi	lbw b Khatua	7
2	S.S.Shukla	c Mohanty b P.Das	35
3	T.M.Srivastava	lbw b Mohanty	6
4	*M.Kaif	b P.Das	4
5	S.K.Raina	c Behera b Khatua	203
6	R.U.Shukla	b Mullick	46
7	†Amir Khan	c Mullick b Khatua	37
8	P.P.Chawla	lbw b P.Das	69
9	R.L.Mishra	c H.M.Das b P.Das	12
10	Abid Khan	b P.Das	10
11	S.Tyagi	not out	0
	Extras	b 11, lb 7, w 1	19
			448

FoW (1): 1-11 (1), 2-27 (3), 3-35 (4), 4-89 (2), 5-230 (6), 6-337 (7), 7-360 (5), 8-432 (8), 9-443 (9), 10-448 (10)

Uttar Pradesh Bowling

	O	M	R	W		O	M	R	W	
Abid Khan	14	8	33	1		13	3	29	1	2nb
Tyagi	16.5	6	46	6	1w	16.4	3	46	4	4nb
Mishra	11	1	36	0	1nb	9	1	29	1	
R.U.Shukla	4	0	24	0						
Chawla	14.1	5	44	1	(4)	20	2	89	3	
S.S.Shukla	4	0	16	2	(5)	3	0	19	0	

Orissa Bowling

	O	M	R	W	
Mohanty	33	5	94	1	
Khatua	23	5	109	3	1w
P.Das	21	5	63	5	
Jayachandra	11	4	31	0	
Satpathy	20	2	92	0	
Behera	5	1	28	0	
Mullick	3.4	0	13	1	

Umpires: S.J.Phadkar and S.D.Ranade.   Toss: Orissa

Close of Play: 1st day: Uttar Pradesh (1) 84-3 (S.S.Shukla 35*, Raina 27*, 26 overs); 2nd day: Uttar Pradesh (1) 410-7 (Chawla 59*, Mishra 1*, 102 overs).

The match was scheduled for four days but completed in three. S.K.Raina's 203 took 217 balls in 374 minutes and included 27 fours and 2 sixes.

PUNJAB v ANDHRA

Played at Gandhi Sports Complex Ground, Amritsar, November 3, 4, 5, 6, 2007.
Ranji Trophy 2007/08 - Elite Group B
Match drawn. (Points: Punjab 3, Andhra 1)

ANDHRA

1	H.H.Watekar	lbw b Goel	137	retired hurt		100
2	L.N.P.Reddy	lbw b Gagandeep Singh	8	not out		114
3	A.S.Verma	c Dharmani b Gagandeep Singh	6	not out		58
4	Y.Gnaneswara Rao	c Goel b Gagandeep Singh	1			
5	*†M.S.K.Prasad	b Kakkar	51			
6	B.A.Sumanth	c Goel b Amanpreet Singh	35			
7	G.Shankar Rao	c Gagandeep Singh b Gony	26			
8	Mohammad Faiq	lbw b Gagandeep Singh	37			
9	D.Kalyankrishna	c Dharmani b Kakkar	17			
10	I.Raju	not out	4			
11	P.D.Vijaykumar	lbw b Kakkar	0			
	Extras	b 1, lb 5, nb 6	12	b 9, nb 6		15
			334	(no wicket)		**287**

FoW (1): 1-9 (2), 2-17 (3), 3-19 (4), 4-161 (5), 5-244 (1), 6-258 (6), 7-311 (8), 8-317 (7), 9-334 (9), 10-334 (11)

PUNJAB

1	R.S.Ricky	c Prasad b Raju	5
2	K.Goel	lbw b Kalyankrishna	0
3	R.Inder Singh	c Prasad b Raju	18
4	U.Kaul	run out (Sumanth)	144
5	*†P.Dharmani	lbw b Mohammad Faiq	94
6	C.Madan	c Prasad b Raju	2
7	A.Kakkar	b Watekar	48
8	M.S.Gony	c Watekar b Shankar Rao	7
9	Gagandeep Singh	not out	15
10	Amanpreet Singh	lbw b Shankar Rao	6
11	Sarabjit Singh	not out	0
	Extras	b 12, lb 14, w 1, nb 6	33
		(9 wickets, declared)	372

FoW (1): 1-7 (2), 2-16 (1), 3-56 (3), 4-237 (5), 5-248 (6), 6-307 (4), 7-331 (8), 8-361 (7), 9-370 (10)

Punjab Bowling

	O	M	R	W			O	M	R	W	
Gagandeep Singh	25.4	7	53	4							
Gony	30	4	107	1	1nb	(1)	13	2	38	0	4nb
Amanpreet Singh	21	3	76	1		(2)	13	1	53	0	
Sarabjit Singh	10	0	52	0	5nb	(5)	27	0	75	0	2nb
Kakkar	17.3	6	34	3		(3)	24	0	79	0	
Goel	1.2	0	6	1		(4)	8	2	33	0	

Andhra Bowling

	O	M	R	W	
Kalyankrishna	26	8	61	1	1w,2nb
Vijaykumar	33	10	56	0	
Raju	22	3	63	3	
Watekar	24	4	65	1	4nb
Mohammad Faiq	22	6	44	1	
Shankar Rao	29	10	51	2	
Gnaneswara Rao	6	2	6	0	

Umpires: S.N.Bandekar and S.Dua. Referee: R.Bhatia.   Toss: Andhra

Close of Play: 1st day: Andhra (1) 294-6 (Shankar Rao 21*, Mohammad Faiq 23*, 90 overs); 2nd day: Punjab (1) 173-3 (Kaul 79*, Dharmani 63*, 72 overs); 3rd day: Punjab (1) 372-9 (Gagandeep Singh 15*, Sarabjit Singh 0*, 162 overs).

H.H.Watekar's 137 took 239 balls in 346 minutes and included 13 fours and 1 six. U.Kaul's 144 took 384 balls in 523 minutes and included 16 fours. H.H.Watekar's 100 took 146 balls in 194 minutes and included 10 fours and 1 six. L.N.P.Reddy's 114 took 284 balls in 325 minutes and included 11 fours and 1 six. H.H.Watekar retired hurt in the Andhra second innings having scored 100 (team score 151-0, 49 overs).

RAILWAYS v JAMMU AND KASHMIR

Played at Karnail Singh Stadium, Delhi, November 3, 4, 5, 2007.
Ranji Trophy 2007/08 - Plate Group B
Railways won by an innings and 88 runs.   (Points: Railways 6, Jammu and Kashmir 0)

JAMMU AND KASHMIR

1	I.Dev Singh	c Pagnis b Yadav	62	run out	7
2	Sajjad Shaikh	c Pagnis b Harvinder Singh	40	c Rawat b Harvinder Singh	3
3	Hardeep Singh	c Khote b Saxena	16	c Yadav b Harvinder Singh	0
4	Majid Dar	c Khote b Harvinder Singh	0	b Saxena	13
5	Inderjit Singh	b Saxena	1	lbw b Khote	4
6	†Sarabjit Singh	lbw b Yadav	0	not out	44
7	*V.Sharma	not out	34	b Yadav	19
8	S.Beigh	c Rawat b Harvinder Singh	16	c Khote b Bangar	18
9	S.Khajuria	c Rawat b Harvinder Singh	3	(10) lbw b Bangar	0
10	Shafqat Malik	c Rawat b Yadav	9	(9) c Pagnis b Bangar	6
11	Jagtar Singh	b Yadav	0	c Rawat b Bangar	0
	Extras	b 5, lb 1, nb 7	13	lb 5, w 1, nb 3	9
			194		123

FoW (1): 1-104 (1), 2-113 (2), 3-113 (4), 4-123 (5), 5-124 (6), 6-126 (3), 7-160 (8), 8-170 (9), 9-187 (10), 10-194 (11)
FoW (2): 1-13 (2), 2-13 (3), 3-14 (1), 4-19 (5), 5-39 (4), 6-63 (7), 7-103 (8), 8-119 (9), 9-121 (10), 10-123 (11)

RAILWAYS

1	S.S.Joshi	b Sharma	27
2	A.A.Pagnis	lbw b Shafqat Malik	49
3	*S.B.Bangar	c Sarabjit Singh b Beigh	48
4	H.D.Rawle	c Dev Singh b Beigh	15
5	S.C.Sanyal	c Sarabjit Singh b Beigh	46
6	†M.Rawat	c Shafqat Malik b Beigh	0
7	K.V.Sharma	b Beigh	120
8	M.A.Khote	c Sharma b Inderjit Singh	9
9	Harvinder Singh	b Khajuria	38
10	S.R.Saxena	c Sarabjit Singh b Inderjit Singh	11
11	M.S.Yadav	not out	0
	Extras	b 21, lb 10, w 5, nb 6	42
			405

FoW (1): 1-47 (1), 2-116 (2), 3-146 (4), 4-169 (3), 5-169 (6), 6-242 (5), 7-279 (8), 8-382 (9), 9-401 (10), 10-405 (7)

Railways Bowling

	O	M	R	W		O	M	R	W	
Harvinder Singh	24	3	97	4	5nb	15	4	36	2	
Saxena	14	5	36	2	1nb	(3) 6	2	14	1	1w
Bangar	6	2	15	0	1nb	(6) 8.5	0	29	4	
Khote	11	4	18	0		(2) 7	0	26	1	3nb
Yadav	22.3	12	22	4		(4) 6	1	12	1	
Sharma						(5) 3	2	1	0	

Jammu and Kashmir Bowling

	O	M	R	W	
Sharma	24	3	63	1	1nb
Beigh	43.4	11	115	5	2w,4nb
Khajuria	18	4	54	1	1nb
Shafqat Malik	15	0	59	1	2w
Jagtar Singh	18	4	57	0	
Majid Dar	4	1	9	0	1w
Inderjit Singh	4	0	17	2	

Umpires: K.Murali and M.R.Singh.   Referee: V.Narayanan Kutty.   Toss: Jammu and Kashmir

Close of Play: 1st day: Railways (1) 39-0 (Joshi 21*, Pagnis 7*, 10 overs); 2nd day: Railways (1) 307-7 (Sharma 68*, Harvinder Singh 11*, 94.2 overs).

The match was scheduled for four days but completed in three. K.V.Sharma's 120 took 232 balls in 318 minutes and included 17 fours.

TAMIL NADU v MAHARASHTRA

Played at M.A.Chidambaram Stadium, Chepauk, Chennai, November 3, 4, 5, 6, 2007.
Ranji Trophy 2007/08 - Elite Group A
Match drawn.   (Points: Tamil Nadu 1, Maharashtra 1)

MAHARASHTRA
1	H.H.Khadiwale	c Prasanna b Mahesh	126
2	†V.V.More	c Karthik b Ashwin	26
3	K.M.Jadhav	c Karthik b Vasudevadas	35
4	*Y.Venugopal Rao	c Karthik b Ashwin	8
5	Y.V.Takawale	c Karthik b Ganapathy	79
6	V.R.Bhilare	c Karthik b Ashwin	40
7	S.S.Mundhe	c Vasudevadas b Ashwin	12
8	S.A.Agharkar	c Vasudevadas b Ashwin	33
9	A.B.Suryawanshi	c Srinivasan b Vasudevadas	46
10	M.M.Patel	c Vasudevadas b Ashwin	3
11	W.S.Sayyed	not out	0
	Extras	b 3, lb 4, w 5, nb 10	22
			430

FoW (1): 1-69 (2), 2-142 (3), 3-155 (4), 4-261 (1), 5-302 (5), 6-344 (7), 7-345 (6), 8-427 (8), 9-429 (9), 10-430 (10)

TAMIL NADU
1	A.Srikkanth	c Venugopal Rao b Sayyed	21
2	M.Vijay Krishna	b Sayyed	4
3	R.Prasanna	c Jadhav b Patel	16
4	†K.D.Karthik	c More b Agharkar	56
5	C.Ganapathy	c More b Patel	4
6	K.Vasudevadas	run out (Mundhe)	33
7	*S.Badrinath	retired hurt	72
8	R.Srinivasan	c More b Venugopal Rao	62
9	R.Ashwin	not out	51
10	V.Y.Mahesh	not out	6
11	P.Amarnath		
	Extras	b 4, lb 3, w 3, nb 3	13
		(7 wickets)	338

FoW (1): 1-12 (2), 2-39 (1), 3-58 (3), 4-65 (5), 5-132 (4), 6-173 (6), 7-306 (8)

Tamil Nadu Bowling
	O	M	R	W	
Ganapathy	24	5	61	1	2nb
Mahesh	30	8	81	1	1w,6nb
Amarnath	23	3	72	0	1nb
Ashwin	50.3	10	133	6	
Vasudevadas	12	2	40	2	1nb
Badrinath	5	1	12	0	
Prasanna	13	3	24	0	

Maharashtra Bowling
	O	M	R	W	
Patel	22	9	29	2	
Agharkar	31	5	118	1	
Sayyed	20	5	57	2	3nb
Mundhe	15	4	32	0	1w
Suryawanshi	13	1	60	0	
Khadiwale	1	0	4	0	
Jadhav	1	0	9	0	
Venugopal Rao	13	5	22	1	

Umpires: S.Asnani and R.D.Risodkar.   Referee: S.Luthra.   Toss: Maharashtra

Close of Play: 1st day: Maharashtra (1) 261-4 (Takawale 52*, 86.4 overs); 2nd day: Maharashtra (1) 272-4 (Takawale 60*, Bhilare 0*, 90 overs); 3rd day: Tamil Nadu (1) 58-3 (Karthik 13*, Ganapathy 0*, 22 overs).

H.H.Khadiwale's 126 took 263 balls in 392 minutes and included 12 fours. S.Badrinath retired hurt in the Tamil Nadu first innings having scored 72 (team score 239-6, 75.2 overs).

TRIPURA v SERVICES

Played at Maharaja Bir Bikram College Stadium, Agartala, November 3, 4, 5, 6, 2007.
Ranji Trophy 2007/08 - Plate Group A
Match drawn.   (Points: Tripura 3, Services 1)

SERVICES

1	S.Chatarjee	c Dutta b Chanda	5	(2) c Dutta b Manoj Singh	38
2	Tahir Khan	b Chanda	0	(1) c Dutta b Saha	66
3	D.S.Israni	c and b Debnath	46	c Jain b Chowdhury	10
4	Jasvir Singh	c Debnath b Manoj Singh	7	b Jain	29
5	Mumtaz Qadir	b Saha	1	(6) b Jain	0
6	*Yashpal Singh	c Roy b Debnath	1	(5) c Muhuri b Saha	103
7	†K.G.Chawda	lbw b Jain	5	b Jain	0
8	A.K.Mohanty	c Dutta b Jain	0	st Dutta b Debnath	23
9	A.Sharma	not out	24	c Chowdhury b Saha	22
10	Fazil Mohammad	c Chowdhury b Debnath	0	not out	0
11	A.Hariprasad	b Debnath	0	st Dutta b Saha	0
	Extras	b 1, nb 12	13	b 4, lb 11, w 1, nb 14	30
			102		**321**

FoW (1): 1-5 (2), 2-8 (1), 3-36 (4), 4-51 (5), 5-52 (6), 6-66 (7), 7-66 (8), 8-98 (3), 9-102 (10), 10-102 (11)
FoW (2): 1-65 (2), 2-104 (3), 3-144 (1), 4-175 (4), 5-175 (6), 6-181 (7), 7-235 (8), 8-321 (5), 9-321 (9), 10-321 (11)

TRIPURA

1	Manoj Singh	lbw b Hariprasad	35	lbw b Hariprasad	3
2	S.S.Roy	c Chatarjee b Mohanty	9	lbw b Hariprasad	8
3	S.D.Chowdhury	c Chatarjee b Mohanty	34	lbw b Sharma	7
4	N.S.Shetty	c Israni b Fazil Mohammad	32	c Chawda b Mohanty	20
5	*T.K.Chanda	lbw b Fazil Mohammad	2	c Tahir Khan b Mohanty	2
6	R.D.Banik	lbw b Hariprasad	2	lbw b Yashpal Singh	52
7	K.S.Muhuri	lbw b Hariprasad	0	lbw b Sharma	6
8	†R.K.Dutta	lbw b Sharma	7	c Yashpal Singh b Hariprasad	30
9	T.S.Saha	c Chawda b Mohanty	36	c Chawda b Hariprasad	15
10	V.Jain	c Israni b Yashpal Singh	13	not out	3
11	J.S.Debnath	not out	0	not out	13
	Extras	b 9, lb 3, w 2, nb 14	28	b 15, lb 3, w 3, nb 22	43
			198	(9 wickets)	**202**

FoW (1): 1-19 (2), 2-77 (3), 3-95 (1), 4-105 (5), 5-133 (6), 6-133 (4), 7-133 (8), 8-166 (8), 9-189 (10), 10-198 (9)
FoW (2): 1-13 (2), 2-19 (1), 3-53 (4), 4-53 (3), 5-60 (5), 6-83 (7), 7-154 (6), 8-172 (8), 9-177 (9)

Tripura Bowling

	O	M	R	W			O	M	R	W	
Jain	12	3	41	2	3nb		27	4	76	3	3nb
Chanda	8	2	19	2	7nb		12	2	32	0	9nb
Manoj Singh	5	1	9	1		(6)	20	9	32	1	1w
Saha	11	4	19	1	1nb	(3)	51.4	19	89	4	
Debnath	11.4	6	13	4	1nb	(4)	18	1	48	1	1nb
Shetty						(5)	7	2	11	0	
Chowdhury						(7)	12	1	18	1	1nb

Services Bowling

	O	M	R	W			O	M	R	W	
Fazil Mohammad	18	4	52	2	1w,4nb		9	2	23	0	1nb
Hariprasad	12.1	0	35	3	1w,9nb		16	2	50	4	15nb
Sharma	18	2	36	1		(4)	24	5	39	2	2nb
Mohanty	21.1	5	53	3	1w,1nb	(3)	19	4	55	2	1w,4nb
Yashpal Singh	3	0	10	1			8	2	17	0	

Umpires: P.Bhanu Prakash and K.G.Lakshminarayan. Referee: T.B.Arothe.   Toss: Tripura

Close of Play: 1st day: Tripura (1) 93-2 (Manoj Singh 35*, Shetty 2*, 40 overs); 2nd day: Services (2) 116-2 (Tahir Khan 60*, Jasvir Singh 2*, 52 overs); 3rd day: Services (2) 308-7 (Yashpal Singh 94*, Sharma 18*, 142 overs).

Yashpal Singh's 103 took 214 balls in 326 minutes and included 9 fours and 1 six.

VIDARBHA v KERALA

Played at Vidarbha Cricket Association Ground, Nagpur, November 3, 4, 5, 6, 2007.
Ranji Trophy 2007/08 - Plate Group A
Kerala won by 150 runs.   (Points: Vidarbha 0, Kerala 5)

KERALA

1	*S.K.Cheruvathur	c Afzal b Gandhe	24	(2) lbw b Wagh	49
2	S.K.Sarma	b Naidu	11	(1) b Acharya	79
3	V.A.Jagadeesh	b Gandhe	21	c Shitoot b Singh	1
4	S.R.Nair	run out (Paradkar)	20	c Fazal b Shitoot	72
5	R.M.Fernandez	lbw b Khare	17	b Shitoot	19
6	P.Rohan Prem	lbw b Shitoot	23	c Fazal b Shitoot	1
7	P.Prasanth	c Wagh b Gandhe	17	b Shitoot	50
8	†V.G.Nair	lbw b Khare	5	not out	25
9	T.Yohannan	lbw b Gandhe	3	(10) not out	5
10	S.Anish	b Singh	21	(9) c Acharya b Singh	3
11	P.Chandran	not out	0		
	Extras	lb 4, nb 3	7	b 9, lb 13, nb 6	28
			169	(8 wickets, declared)	332

FoW (1): 1-29 (2), 2-53 (1), 3-68 (3), 4-93 (5), 5-98 (4), 6-116 (7), 7-125 (8), 8-138 (9), 9-169 (10), 10-169 (6)
FoW (2): 1-112 (2), 2-113 (3), 3-162 (1), 4-195 (5), 5-197 (6), 6-290 (7), 7-313 (4), 8-319 (9)

VIDARBHA

1	†A.V.Deshpande	c V.G.Nair b Chandran	3	(2) lbw b Chandran	30
2	F.Y.Fazal	b Anish	24	(1) c V.G.Nair b Anish	40
3	A.S.Naidu	lbw b Chandran	9	run out	52
4	H.V.Shitoot	b Yohannan	1	(6) c S.R.Nair b Cheruvathur	0
5	O.S.Afzal	c Chandran b Yohannan	0	c Cheruvathur b Anish	8
6	R.S.Paradkar	c Cheruvathur b Anish	22	(7) not out	29
7	M.S.Acharya	c Jagadeesh b Anish	20	(4) lbw b Cheruvathur	26
8	S.A.Khare	b Yohannan	0	c S.R.Nair b Anish	2
9	*P.V.Gandhe	c Yohannan b Anish	5	b Cheruvathur	26
10	S.B.Wagh	st V.G.Nair b Anish	11	b Cheruvathur	2
11	S.R.Singh	not out	0	b Anish	0
	Extras	b 4, lb 1, nb 14	19	b 4, lb 1, nb 17	22
			114		237

FoW (1): 1-4 (1), 2-28 (3), 3-31 (4), 4-34 (5), 5-68 (2), 6-73 (6), 7-78 (8), 8-93 (9), 9-104 (7), 10-114 (10)
FoW (2): 1-76 (1), 2-84 (2), 3-146 (4), 4-162 (5), 5-163 (6), 6-175 (3), 7-179 (8), 8-232 (9), 9-234 (10), 10-237 (11)

Vidarbha Bowling

	O	M	R	W			O	M	R	W	
Singh	11	3	21	1			26	6	83	2	4nb
Wagh	9	1	18	0	3nb		17	2	66	1	1nb
Naidu	10	2	14	1		(4)	2	0	10	0	
Acharya	16	3	34	0		(5)	17	5	41	1	
Gandhe	28	9	53	4		(3)	28	8	55	0	
Khare	13	4	22	2			11	4	17	0	
Shitoot	1.1	0	3	1			15	4	38	4	

Kerala Bowling

	O	M	R	W			O	M	R	W	
Prasanth	1	1	0	0		(5)	14	6	28	0	2nb
Chandran	10	2	22	2	4nb		10	0	54	1	1nb
Yohannan	11	0	46	3	10nb	(1)	14	2	38	0	11nb
Cheruvathur	6	2	14	0		(3)	15	3	36	4	2nb
Jagadeesh	3	1	7	0		(7)	1	0	3	0	
Anish	10	3	20	5		(4)	30.1	8	52	4	
S.R.Nair						(6)	6	1	18	0	1nb
Rohan Prem						(8)	2	1	3	0	

Umpires: M.Inder Singh and C.R.Mohite.   Referee: D.Vasu.   Toss: Vidarbha

Close of Play: 1st day: Vidarbha (1) 0-0 (Deshpande 0*, Fazal 0*, 1 over); 2nd day: Kerala (2) 92-0 (Sarma 35*, Cheruvathur 45*, 45 overs); 3rd day: Vidarbha (2) 42-0 (Fazal 20*, Deshpande 16*, 16 overs).

BENGAL v HYDERABAD

Played at Eden Gardens, Kolkata, November 4, 5, 6, 7, 2007.
Ranji Trophy 2007/08 - Elite Group B
Match drawn.   (Points: Bengal 3, Hyderabad 1)

BENGAL

1	A.P.Chakraborty	c Ravi Teja b Ojha	25
2	A.S.Das	lbw b Lalith Mohan	25
3	A.P.Majumdar	c Habeeb Ahmed b Arjun	25
4	M.K.Tiwary	st Habeeb Ahmed b Ojha	203
5	Safi Ahmed	c Manohar b Shinde	14
6	*L.R.Shukla	c Pai b Shinde	0
7	†W.P.Saha	not out	111
8	S.S.Lahiri	st Habeeb Ahmed b Lalith Mohan	21
9	M.Y.Lodhgar	c Pai b Shinde	10
10	R.R.Bose	c Ravi Teja b Ojha	3
11	S.S.Paul	lbw b Ojha	2
	Extras	b 5, lb 13, w 1, nb 3	22
			461

FoW (1): 1-45 (2), 2-67 (1), 3-126 (3), 4-221 (5), 5-221 (6), 6-398 (4), 7-433 (8), 8-452 (9), 9-459 (10), 10-461 (11)

HYDERABAD

1	D.S.Manohar	c Saha b Bose	8	c Paul b Lodhgar	7
2	D.B.Ravi Teja	c Saha b Paul	39	c Das b Lodhgar	47
3	*V.V.S.Laxman	c Saha b Paul	0	c Lahiri b Lodhgar	18
4	S.A.Pai	b Lahiri	8	not out	119
5	A.S.Yadav	c Tiwary b Lodhgar	0	c sub (S.S.Sarkar) b Lodhgar	53
6	A.J.Shinde	st Saha b Lahiri	90	c Safi Ahmed b Lahiri	33
7	†Habeeb Ahmed	b Lahiri	23	c Saha b Lodhgar	4
8	M.P.Arjun	b Paul	0	not out	8
9	P.P.Ojha	b Tiwary	35		
10	Shoaib Ahmed	lbw b Lahiri	12		
11	A.Lalith Mohan	not out	0		
	Extras	b 4, lb 2, w 1, nb 5	12	b 1, lb 5, nb 7	13
			227	(6 wickets)	302

FoW (1): 1-16 (1), 2-21 (3), 3-54 (2), 4-56 (4), 5-56 (5), 6-96 (7), 7-99 (8), 8-173 (9), 9-212 (10), 10-227 (6)
FoW (2): 1-37 (1), 2-71 (2), 3-81 (3), 4-154 (5), 5-226 (6), 6-256 (7)

Hyderabad Bowling

	O	M	R	W	
Arjun	15	2	51	1	1nb
Shoaib Ahmed	18	3	49	0	1w,2nb
Ojha	51.1	14	151	4	
Lalith Mohan	35	6	95	2	
Shinde	25	2	95	3	
Ravi Teja	1	0	2	0	

Bengal Bowling

	O	M	R	W		O	M	R	W	
Bose	19	4	83	1	1w	18	6	45	0	
Paul	20	8	37	3		15	3	46	0	
Lahiri	20.1	5	65	4		31	4	100	1	
Lodhgar	11	3	13	1	3nb	40	12	68	5	7nb
Tiwary	9	2	23	1	2nb	7	0	23	0	
Majumdar					(6)	3	0	10	0	
Shukla					(7)	1	0	4	0	

Umpires: V.D.Nerurkar and S.K.Tarapore. Referee: P.N.Desai.   Toss: Bengal

Close of Play: 1st day: Bengal (1) 289-5 (Tiwary 147*, Saha 34*, 95 overs); 2nd day: Hyderabad (1) 65-5 (Shinde 7*, Habeeb Ahmed 1*, 25 overs); 3rd day: Hyderabad (2) 86-3 (Pai 5*, Yadav 5*, 32 overs).

M.K.Tiwary's 203 took 283 balls in 358 minutes and included 28 fours and 2 sixes. W.P.Saha's 111 took 194 balls in 269 minutes and included 15 fours and 1 six. S.A.Pai's 119 took 262 balls in 371 minutes and included 13 fours.

DELHI v RAJASTHAN

Played at Feroz Shah Kotla, Delhi, November 4, 5, 6, 7, 2007.
Ranji Trophy 2007/08 - Elite Group A
Delhi won by 172 runs. (Points: Delhi 5, Rajasthan 0)

DELHI

1	A.S.Chopra	c Jhalani b Pankaj Singh	16	lbw b Mathur	32
2	S.Dhawan	lbw b Mohammad Aslam	35	c Shafiq Khan b Pankaj Singh	14
3	M.Tehlan	run out (Mohammad Aslam)	4	(7) c Jhalani b Pankaj Singh	9
4	V.Kohli	c Jhalani b Mathur	19	b Gehlot	106
5	*M.Manhas	b Pankaj Singh	4	b Pankaj Singh	100
6	R.Bhatia	lbw b Mathur	0	c Jhalani b Gehlot	83
7	†P.Bisht	lbw b Pankaj Singh	5	(3) c Jhalani b Pankaj Singh	0
8	C.Nanda	lbw b Pankaj Singh	10	lbw b Gehlot	1
9	P.Sangwan	c Jhalani b Pankaj Singh	10	lbw b Gehlot	14
10	Kunal Lal	not out	2	c sub (N.S.Doru) b Pankaj Singh	9
11	A.Bhandari	b Mathur	2	not out	0
	Extras	lb 7, nb 5	12	b 4, lb 6, w 1, nb 8	19
			119		387

FoW (1): 1-33 (1), 2-62 (2), 3-67 (3), 4-79 (5), 5-84 (6), 6-93 (4), 7-97 (7), 8-115 (9), 9-116 (8), 10-119 (11)
FoW (2): 1-24 (2), 2-24 (3), 3-102 (1), 4-194 (4), 5-332 (5), 6-342 (7), 7-355 (8), 8-372 (6), 9-379 (9), 10-387 (10)

RAJASTHAN

1	V.A.Saxena	c Bisht b Sangwan	35	lbw b Sangwan	0
2	A.P.Sharma	c Kohli b Bhandari	6	(3) lbw b Sangwan	26
3	G.K.Khoda	lbw b Bhandari	0	(2) c Dhawan b Nanda	71
4	R.D.Bist	lbw b Kunal Lal	14	c and b Bhandari	69
5	Shafiq Khan	b Kunal Lal	5	c Kunal Lal b Bhandari	3
6	R.J.Kanwat	c Chopra b Bhatia	5	c Kohli b Bhandari	0
7	†R.B.Jhalani	c Bisht b Bhatia	5	b Nanda	3
8	Pankaj Singh	c Bhandari b Bhatia	5	lbw b Nanda	19
9	S.G.Gehlot	c Bisht b Sangwan	0	lbw b Manhas	47
10	S.O.Mathur	not out	4	(11) not out	1
11	*Mohammad Aslam	c Bhandari b Sangwan	0	(10) c Kunal Lal b Manhas	0
	Extras	b 1, lb 2, nb 3	6	b 4, lb 2, nb 4	10
			85		249

FoW (1): 1-6 (2), 2-7 (3), 3-32 (4), 4-38 (5), 5-52 (6), 6-64 (7), 7-73 (8), 8-73 (9), 9-85 (1), 10-85 (11)
FoW (2): 1-0 (1), 2-69 (3), 3-116 (2), 4-123 (5), 5-123 (6), 6-146 (7), 7-174 (8), 8-245 (9), 9-245 (10), 10-249 (4)

Rajasthan Bowling

	O	M	R	W		O	M	R	W	
Pankaj Singh	15	3	43	5		30.5	9	110	5	
Gehlot	8	1	29	0	4nb	30	5	97	4	5nb
Mathur	12.3	2	32	3	(4)	21	7	62	1	1nb
Mohammad Aslam	3	1	8	1	(3)	15	1	65	0	
Kanwat					(5)	10	0	34	0	
Khoda					(6)	3	0	9	0	1w,2nb

Delhi Bowling

	O	M	R	W		O	M	R	W	
Sangwan	11.5	3	29	3	3nb	18	5	45	2	1nb
Bhandari	9	2	22	2		10.1	3	17	3	
Bhatia	11	7	16	3		9	2	32	0	1nb
Kunal Lal	4	0	15	2		11	1	46	0	1nb
Nanda					(5)	24	7	72	3	1nb
Manhas					(6)	8	1	26	2	
Chopra					(7)	1	0	5	0	

Umpires: A.Y.Dandekar and R.Radhakrishnan. Referee: K.D.Mokashi.   Toss: Rajasthan

Close of Play: 1st day: Delhi (2) 6-0 (Chopra 4*, Dhawan 0*, 0.5 overs); 2nd day: Delhi (2) 317-4 (Manhas 86*, Bhatia 65*, 90.3 overs); 3rd day: Rajasthan (2) 188-7 (Bist 50*, Gehlot 10*, 61 overs).

V.Kohli's 106 took 192 balls in 231 minutes and included 18 fours. M.Manhas's 100 took 161 balls in 249 minutes and included 12 fours.

ANDHRA v UTTAR PRADESH

Played at Rural Development Trust Stadium, Anantapur, November 15, 16, 17, 18, 2007.
Ranji Trophy 2007/08 - Elite Group B
Match drawn.　(Points: Andhra 3, Uttar Pradesh 1)

UTTAR PRADESH

1	R.P.Srivastava	c Prasad b Kalyankrishna	7	c Prasad b Kalyankrishna	42
2	S.S.Shukla	c Gnaneswara Rao b Vijaykumar	27	c Mohammad Faiq b Shankar Rao	18
3	T.M.Srivastava	c Verma b Raju	30	c Watekar b Shankar Rao	59
4	*M.Kaif	c Gnaneswara Rao b Vijaykumar	34	not out	122
5	S.K.Raina	c Watekar b Vijaykumar	13	c Suresh b Shankar Rao	28
6	R.U.Shukla	not out	99	c sub (S.ArjunKumar) b Vijaykumar	5
7	†Amir Khan	c Watekar b Raju	22		
8	P.P.Chawla	c Vijaykumar b Kalyankrishna	23	(7) c and b Shankar Rao	6
9	R.L.Mishra	c Prasad b Vijaykumar	7		
10	Abid Khan	lbw b Shankar Rao	7		
11	S.Tyagi	lbw b Shankar Rao	0		
	Extras	lb 10, w 8, nb 11	29	b 3, lb 10, w 4	17
			298	(6 wickets, declared)	**297**

FoW (1): 1-26 (1), 2-47 (2), 3-108 (4), 4-126 (5), 5-126 (3), 6-196 (7), 7-234 (8), 8-248 (9), 9-298 (10), 10-298 (11)
FoW (2): 1-59 (2), 2-78 (1), 3-217 (3), 4-257 (5), 5-274 (6), 6-297 (7)

ANDHRA

1	H.H.Watekar	c Amir Khan b Tyagi	11	c Kaif b Tyagi	5
2	L.N.P.Reddy	b Tyagi	132	not out	103
3	A.S.Verma	c Mishra b Abid Khan	61	c Kaif b Abid Khan	89
4	*†M.S.K.Prasad	lbw b Tyagi	32	c Amir Khan b Tyagi	0
5	Y.Gnaneswara Rao	c Amir Khan b Tyagi	10	(6) not out	1
6	Mohammad Faiq	c Abid Khan b Tyagi	5		
7	M.Suresh	lbw b Chawla	17		
8	G.Shankar Rao	c Amir Khan b Tyagi	5	(5) c Amir Khan b Tyagi	0
9	D.Kalyankrishna	c Raina b R.U.Shukla	21		
10	I.Raju	not out	7		
11	P.D.Vijaykumar	b Chawla	1		
	Extras	b 5, lb 11, w 3, nb 5	24	b 9, lb 2, w 1, nb 3	15
			326	(4 wickets)	**213**

FoW (1): 1-26 (1), 2-150 (3), 3-214 (4), 4-259 (5), 5-268 (2), 6-273 (6), 7-279 (8), 8-312 (9), 9-318 (9), 10-326 (11)
FoW (2): 1-10 (1), 2-204 (3), 3-208 (4), 4-208 (5)

Andhra Bowling	O	M	R	W		O	M	R	W	
Kalyankrishna	26	5	77	2	2w,4nb	9	3	33	1	
Vijaykumar	29	7	75	4	5w,4nb	17	2	68	1	1w
Raju	19	3	70	2	(4)	5	0	31	0	
Gnaneswara Rao	7	1	29	0	1w,2nb	(7) 2	0	7	0	
Shankar Rao	8.5	3	10	2		21.4	4	72	4	2w
Watekar	3	1	10	0	1nb					
Mohammad Faiq	3	0	10	0		(3) 14	0	60	0	1w
Suresh	2	0	7	0		(6) 6	2	13	0	

Uttar Pradesh Bowling	O	M	R	W		O	M	R	W	
Abid Khan	30	11	53	1	2nb	(2) 14	2	46	1	1nb
Tyagi	41	12	95	6	3w,2nb	(1) 16	3	68	3	1w,1nb
Mishra	21	7	45	0	1nb	(5) 3	0	22	0	1nb
R.P.Srivastava	5	2	15	0						
Chawla	21.3	4	59	2		(3) 11	0	56	0	
S.S.Shukla	5	2	12	0						
R.U.Shukla	12	3	31	1		(4) 4	1	10	0	

Umpires: R.M.Deshpande and K.Hariharan.　Referee: S.Banerjee.　Toss: Andhra

Close of Play: 1st day: Uttar Pradesh (1) 269-8 (R.U.Shukla 77*, Abid Khan 5*, 90 overs); 2nd day: Andhra (1) 201-2 (Reddy 88*, Prasad 26*, 81 overs); 3rd day: Uttar Pradesh (2) 105-2 (T.M.Srivastava 17*, Kaif 23*, 33 overs).

L.N.P.Reddy's 132 took 319 balls in 450 minutes and included 16 fours. M.Kaif's 122 took 172 balls in 1 minutes and included 11 fours and 3 sixes. L.N.P.Reddy's 103 took 156 balls in 191 minutes and included 16 fours.

ASSAM v VIDARBHA

Played at Nehru Stadium, Guwahati, November 15, 16, 17, 18, 2007.
Ranji Trophy 2007/08 - Plate Group A
Match drawn. (Points: Assam 1, Vidarbha 1)

ASSAM

1	P.M.Das	c Deshpande b Mohammad Hashim	10
2	S.Suresh	c Deshpande b Mohammad Hashim	6
3	N.H.Bordoloi	not out	28
4	S.Ramesh	c Fazal b Singh	13
5	*S.Sharath	c Shitoot b Gandhe	60
6	Tarjinder Singh	b Singh	11
7	†R.N.Das	c Shitoot b Singh	0
8	D.S.Goswami	c Deshpande b Naidu	36
9	A.Konwar	c Fazal b Gandhe	24
10	B.M.Mahanta	st Deshpande b Gandhe	4
11	K.S.Das	lbw b Gandhe	2
	Extras	b 8, lb 5, w 1, nb 8	22
			——
			216

FoW (1): 1-8 (2), 2-30 (1), 3-65 (4), 4-91 (6), 5-91 (7), 6-153 (8), 7-191 (9), 8-207 (10), 9-210 (5), 10-216 (11)

VIDARBHA

1	F.Y.Fazal	run out (K.S.Das)	31
2	H.V.Shitoot	c R.N.Das b K.S.Das	11
3	A.S.Naidu	c Tarjinder Singh b Mahanta	48
4	M.S.Acharya	lbw b Goswami	0
5	†A.V.Deshpande	not out	20
6	R.S.Paradkar	c Ramesh b Goswami	7
7	S.N.Binkar	not out	4
8	S.R.Singh		
9	Mohammad Hashim		
10	H.S.Joshi		
11	*P.V.Gandhe		
	Extras	lb 4, nb 1	5
			——
		(5 wickets)	126

FoW (1): 1-20 (2), 2-94 (1), 3-94 (3), 4-94 (4), 5-106 (6)

Vidarbha Bowling

	O	M	R	W	
Singh	22	4	59	3	4nb
Mohammad Hashim	17	3	43	2	1w
Naidu	16	7	30	1	
Fazal	3	0	14	0	4nb
Gandhe	15.4	4	20	4	
Acharya	5	0	22	0	
Shitoot	5	1	15	0	

Assam Bowling

	O	M	R	W	
Goswami	9	3	19	2	
K.S.Das	6	0	30	1	
Suresh	6	1	25	0	
Konwar	11	3	42	0	1nb
Mahanta	6	4	6	1	

Umpires: M.G.Mandale and S.K.Tarapore. Referee: A.K.Sharma.   Toss: Vidarbha

Close of Play: 1st day: Assam (1) 65-2 (Bordoloi 25*, Ramesh 13*, 29 overs); 2nd day: No play; 3rd day: No play.

N.H.Bordoloi retired hurt in the Assam first innings having scored 25 (team score 65-2) - he returned when the score was 210-9.

BARODA v BENGAL

Played at Moti Bagh Stadium, Vadodara, November 15, 16, 17, 18, 2007.
Ranji Trophy 2007/08 - Elite Group B
Baroda won by an innings and 59 runs. (Points: Baroda 6, Bengal 0)

BENGAL

1	A.P.Majumdar	run out (Shah)	103	lbw b Pathan		0
2	A.S.Das	c Bilakhia b Pawar	117	c Parab b Pathan		6
3	*L.R.Shukla	c Bilakhia b Pathan	0	(6) b Pawar		1
4	M.K.Tiwary	c Singh b Pathan	37	lbw b Pathan		0
5	†W.P.Saha	c Shah b Singh	17	b Pathan		45
6	R.P.Chowdhary	b Singh	11	(7) b Singh		23
7	K.H.Mondal	c Panchal b Singh	28	(3) c Bilakhia b Pawar		4
8	S.S.Lahiri	c Williams b Pathan	9	lbw b Pawar		4
9	M.Y.Lodhgar	c Williams b Pathan	5	(11) not out		0
10	R.R.Bose	not out	10	(9) lbw b Pawar		2
11	S.S.Paul	c and b Pathan	1	(10) c Parab b Pathan		0
	Extras	b 15, lb 9, nb 8	32	lb 1		1
			370			86

FoW (1): 1-221 (1), 2-221 (3), 3-262 (2), 4-276 (4), 5-303 (6), 6-317 (5), 7-333 (8), 8-339 (9), 9-369 (7), 10-370 (11)
FoW (2): 1-1 (1), 2-10 (2), 3-10 (3), 4-10 (4), 5-13 (6), 6-49 (7), 7-66 (8), 8-70 (9), 9-83 (10), 10-86 (5)

BARODA

1	S.S.Parab	c Chowdhary b Lahiri	37
2	*C.C.Williams	c Tiwary b Lodhgar	15
3	A.A.Bilakhia	lbw b Lodhgar	7
4	R.K.Solanki	run out (Majumdar)	186
5	†P.R.Shah	c Das b Lahiri	23
6	A.R.Chauhan	c Chowdhary b Lahiri	23
7	Y.K.Pathan	c Majumdar b Lahiri	183
8	K.N.Panchal	b Shukla	1
9	R.V.Pawar	run out (Bose)	9
10	V.M.Parmar	lbw b Shukla	9
11	S.M.Singh	not out	0
	Extras	b 4, lb 4, w 1, nb 13	22
			515

FoW (1): 1-34 (2), 2-59 (3), 3-67 (1), 4-135 (5), 5-180 (6), 6-456 (7), 7-471 (8), 8-485 (9), 9-508 (10), 10-515 (4)

Baroda Bowling

	O	M	R	W			O	M	R	W
Singh	26	3	75	3		(3)	8	1	12	1
Chauhan	12	1	25	0						
Panchal	6	2	25	0	3nb					
Pawar	36	8	112	1	4nb	(1)	16	7	23	4
Pathan	35.1	9	83	5		(2)	19.4	9	36	5
Parmar	13	3	26	0	1nb	(4)	3	0	14	0

Bengal Bowling

	O	M	R	W	
Bose	21	2	84	0	1w
Paul	16	5	37	0	
Lahiri	56	11	184	4	4nb
Lodhgar	16	4	66	2	5nb
Tiwary	9	1	46	0	
Mondal	9	0	61	0	4nb
Shukla	10.5	0	29	2	

Umpires: S.Dendapani and A.V.Jayaprakash.   Referee: D.V.Pardeshi.   Toss: Bengal

Close of Play: 1st day: Bengal (1) 262-2 (Das 117*, Tiwary 28*, 91 overs); 2nd day: Baroda (1) 129-3 (Solanki 43*, Shah 21*, 52 overs); 3rd day: Bengal (2) 1-1 (Das 1*, 1.3 overs).

A.P.Majumdar's 103 took 221 balls in 278 minutes and included 15 fours. A.S.Das's 117 took 273 balls in 362 minutes and included 18 fours. R.K.Solanki's 186 took 335 balls in 458 minutes and included 22 fours and 1 six. Y.K.Pathan's 183 took 150 balls in 223 minutes and included 24 fours and 4 sixes.

DELHI v SAURASHTRA

Played at Roshanara Club Ground, Delhi, November 15, 16, 17, 18, 2007.
Ranji Trophy 2007/08 - Elite Group A
Match drawn.   (Points: Delhi 3, Saurashtra 1)

DELHI

1	A.S.Chopra	lbw b Jobanputra	6	not out		124
2	S.Dhawan	c Jogiyani b Vaghela	38	st Jogiyani b Dhruve		114
3	M.Tehlan	c Mehta b Jobanputra	17	lbw b Jobanputra		9
4	V.Kohli	lbw b Vaghela	1	not out		40
5	*M.Manhas	c Jogiyani b Jobanputra	62			
6	R.Bhatia	c Jogiyani b Jobanputra	36			
7	†P.Bisht	c Pujara b Jobanputra	35			
8	C.Nanda	run out (Pujara)	4			
9	P.Sangwan	b Jadeja	18			
10	A.Bhandari	b Mehta	18			
11	I.Sharma	not out	0			
	Extras	lb 5, w 2, nb 2	9	lb 6, w 1, nb 1		8
			244	(2 wickets, declared)		295

FoW (1): 1-10 (1), 2-47 (3), 3-54 (4), 4-82 (2), 5-162 (6), 6-165 (5), 7-177 (8), 8-217 (7), 9-238 (9), 10-244 (10)
FoW (2): 1-199 (2), 2-219 (3)

SAURASHTRA

1	K.M.Vaghela	b Sharma	3	b Sangwan		0
2	†S.D.Jogiyani	c Chopra b Sharma	25	b Sangwan		35
3	S.H.Kotak	c Dhawan b Bhatia	77	lbw b Sangwan		6
4	C.A.Pujara	lbw b Bhatia	11	not out		148
5	*J.N.Shah	c Bisht b Bhatia	0	c Bisht b Sangwan		0
6	P.S.Mehta	c Bisht b Bhandari	27	lbw b Sharma		1
7	R.A.Jadeja	c Bisht b Sangwan	1	c Kohli b Sharma		13
8	R.V.Dhruve	lbw b Bhatia	21	(9) c Kohli b Bhatia		2
9	K.R.Makwana	c Dhawan b Sharma	13	(8) b Sharma		0
10	S.P.Jobanputra	b Sharma	7	b Manhas		35
11	S.M.Maniar	not out	2	not out		5
	Extras	b 11, lb 6, w 2, nb 7	26	b 1, lb 1, w 3, nb 4		9
			213	(9 wickets)		254

FoW (1): 1-4 (1), 2-61 (2), 3-83 (4), 4-83 (5), 5-156 (3), 6-156 (6), 7-175 (7), 8-195 (8), 9-204 (10), 10-213 (9)
FoW (2): 1-0 (1), 2-33 (3), 3-56 (2), 4-60 (5), 5-63 (6), 6-101 (7), 7-101 (8), 8-106 (9), 9-225 (10)

Saurashtra Bowling

	O	M	R	W			O	M	R	W	
Jobanputra	27	7	73	5	1w,1nb		15	1	77	1	1nb
Maniar	21	6	58	0	1nb		12	0	64	0	
Vaghela	12	6	27	2	1w		12	2	42	0	1w
Dhruve	3	0	15	0		(6)	2	0	15	1	
Makwana	5	0	23	0			13	3	40	0	
Jadeja	17	7	37	1		(4)	15	2	51	0	
Mehta	0.2	0	6	1							

Delhi Bowling

	O	M	R	W			O	M	R	W	
Sangwan	24	5	69	1	4nb		23	4	70	4	1w,1nb
Sharma	28.1	6	72	4	2w,1nb		24	8	79	3	1nb
Bhandari	14	7	22	1	1nb		11	2	30	0	2nb
Bhatia	17	8	16	4	1nb	(5)	11	2	25	1	2w
Nanda	8	1	16	0		(4)	9	1	26	0	
Manhas	1	0	1	0			7	0	22	1	

Umpires: C.K.Nandan and R.Subramanyam.   Referee: V.Yadav.   Toss: Saurashtra

Close of Play: 1st day: Delhi (1) 244-10 (Sharma 0*, 85.2 overs); 2nd day: Saurashtra (1) 175-7 (Dhruve 12*, 77.2 overs); 3rd day: Delhi (2) 295-2 (Chopra 124*, Kohli 40*, 69 overs).

A.S.Chopra's 124 took 211 balls in 291 minutes and included 16 fours. S.Dhawan's 114 took 139 balls in 209 minutes and included 17 fours and 2 sixes. C.A.Pujara's 148 took 244 balls in 354 minutes and included 27 fours.

GOA v RAILWAYS

Played at Dr Rajendra Prasad Stadium, Margao, November 15, 16, 17, 18, 2007.
Ranji Trophy 2007/08 - Plate Group B
Match drawn. (Points: Goa 3, Railways 1)

GOA

1	R.D.Asnodkar	c Rawat b Harvinder Singh	2	(3) b Harvinder Singh	0
2	S.A.Asnodkar	not out	254	c Pagnis b Harvinder Singh	5
3	S.S.Dhuri	lbw b Khote	6		
4	*J.Arunkumar	c Joshi b Yadav	77	not out	26
5	M.V.Joglekar	c Rawle b Sharma	9		
6	†A.Ratra	c Bangar b Yadav	27		
7	S.B.Jakati	c Pagnis b Khote	40		
8	R.R.D'Souza	st Rawat b Yadav	40		
9	S.S.Bandekar	b Khote	48		
10	A.R.Angle	c Rawat b Yadav	4	(1) not out	20
11	H.H.Gadekar				
	Extras	b 12, lb 8, nb 8	28	lb 2	2
		(9 wickets, declared)	535	(2 wickets)	53

FoW (1): 1-11 (1), 2-25 (3), 3-178 (4), 4-200 (5), 5-247 (6), 6-347 (7), 7-438 (8), 8-524 (9), 9-535 (10)
FoW (2): 1-5 (2), 2-5 (3)

RAILWAYS

1	S.S.Joshi	lbw b Gadekar	1
2	A.A.Pagnis	run out (Dhuri/Ratra)	12
3	*S.B.Bangar	c R.D.Asnodkar b Gadekar	8
4	H.D.Rawle	lbw b Gadekar	102
5	S.C.Sanyal	c Joglekar b Angle	54
6	†M.Rawat	c Jakati b D'Souza	96
7	K.V.Sharma	not out	70
8	M.A.Khote	lbw b Dhuri	20
9	Harvinder Singh	c Ratra b D'Souza	5
10	K.S.Parida	c Ratra b Dhuri	22
11	M.S.Yadav	c R.D.Asnodkar b D'Souza	0
	Extras	b 14, lb 1, w 6, nb 14	35
			425

FoW (1): 1-2 (1), 2-14 (2), 3-47 (3), 4-134 (5), 5-266 (4), 6-348 (6), 7-369 (8), 8-378 (9), 9-424 (10), 10-425 (11)

Railways Bowling

	O	M	R	W			O	M	R	W
Khote	29	6	76	3	1nb	(2)	5	2	6	0
Harvinder Singh	24	5	80	1	4nb	(1)	6	1	27	2
Yadav	44.4	6	136	4		(4)	3	2	1	0
Bangar	15	2	47	0	3nb					
Parida	32	5	95	0			4	2	5	0
Sanyal	7	1	23	0		(3)	2	1	8	0
Sharma	14	2	58	1		(6)	3	2	4	0

Goa Bowling

	O	M	R	W	
Bandekar	32	3	114	0	11nb
Gadekar	17	4	53	3	2w,2nb
D'Souza	26.1	9	60	3	1w
Jakati	37	7	93	0	1w
Angle	20	3	57	1	
Dhuri	19	7	30	2	2w
Joglekar	1	0	3	0	

Umpires: S.N.Bandekar and A.Y.Dandekar.   Toss: Goa

Close of Play: 1st day: Goa (1) 279-5 (S.A.Asnodkar 125*, Jakati 16*, 91 overs); 2nd day: Railways (1) 31-2 (Bangar 3*, Rawle 13*, 13 overs); 3rd day: Railways (1) 291-5 (Rawat 83*, Sharma 12*, 103 overs).

S.A.Asnodkar's 254 took 452 balls in 663 minutes and included 28 fours. H.D.Rawle's 102 took 277 balls in 371 minutes and included 11 fours.

GUJARAT v TRIPURA

Played at Sardar Patel Stadium, Motera, Ahmedabad, November 15, 16, 17, 18, 2007.
Ranji Trophy 2007/08 - Plate Group A
Gujarat won by an innings and 72 runs.   (Points: Gujarat 6, Tripura 0)

TRIPURA

1	Manoj Singh	c P.A.Patel b Trivedi	33	c P.A.Patel b Makda	73
2	S.S.Roy	c N.K.Patel b T.K.Patel	19	c Popat b Makda	24
3	S.D.Chowdhury	run out (Thaker)	1	c T.K.Patel b Trivedi	16
4	N.S.Shetty	b Parmar	17	(5) lbw b Makda	80
5	*T.K.Chanda	b Parmar	0	(7) b Makda	28
6	R.D.Banik	lbw b Parmar	18	(4) lbw b Makda	22
7	K.S.Muhuri	lbw b T.K.Patel	10	(6) c T.K.Patel b Majmudar	10
8	†R.K.Dutta	c Modi b T.K.Patel	0	(9) lbw b Parmar	8
9	T.S.Saha	c Modi b T.K.Patel	1	(8) c sub (R.K.Tabiyar) b Makda	0
10	V.Jain	c Parmar b T.K.Patel	1	not out	2
11	J.S.Debnath	not out	2	lbw b Makda	2
	Extras	b 5, lb 5, nb 4	14	b 3, lb 5, nb 9	17
			116		**282**

FoW (1): 1-28 (2), 2-43 (3), 3-69 (1), 4-76 (5), 5-89 (4), 6-110 (7), 7-112 (6), 8-112 (8), 9-113 (9), 10-116 (10)
FoW (2): 1-68 (2), 2-100 (3), 3-141 (1), 4-150 (4), 5-176 (6), 6-235 (7), 7-235 (8), 8-272 (9), 9-280 (5), 10-282 (11)

GUJARAT

1	H.R.Joshipura	c Banik b Chanda	10
2	N.D.Modi	b Chanda	0
3	*†P.A.Patel	lbw b Saha	158
4	N.K.Patel	st Dutta b Saha	42
5	B.D.Thaker	not out	154
6	D.M.Popat	c sub (A.B.Dey) b Shetty	40
7	T.K.Patel	c Chanda b Saha	25
8	M.B.Parmar	not out	7
9	S.K.Trivedi		
10	A.M.Makda		
11	H.A.Majmudar		
	Extras	b 12, lb 3, nb 19	34
		(6 wickets, declared)	470

FoW (1): 1-0 (2), 2-34 (1), 3-138 (4), 4-293 (3), 5-372 (6), 6-429 (7)

Gujarat Bowling

	O	M	R	W			O	M	R	W	
Trivedi	11	8	16	1			23	5	54	1	
Makda	12	3	20	0			31.4	7	90	7	1nb
Majmudar	5	2	18	0	4nb	(4)	12	1	47	1	7nb
T.K.Patel	11.4	4	15	5		(3)	12	1	30	0	1nb
Parmar	17	6	37	3			31	7	53	1	
N.K.Patel						(6)	1	1	0	0	

Tripura Bowling

	O	M	R	W	
Jain	25	8	61	0	4nb
Chanda	23	3	82	2	11nb
Debnath	31	5	81	0	1nb
Saha	37	2	137	3	
Manoj Singh	11	1	43	0	
Shetty	10	1	24	1	
Chowdhury	4	0	27	0	

Umpires: N.R.S.Prabhu and R.Radhakrishnan.   Referee: P.M.Pankule.   Toss: Gujarat

Close of Play: 1st day: Gujarat (1) 84-2 (P.A.Patel 48*, N.K.Patel 11*, 31 overs); 2nd day: Gujarat (1) 380-5 (Thaker 102*, T.K.Patel 1*, 121 overs); 3rd day: Tripura (2) 154-4 (Shetty 7*, Muhuri 1*, 68 overs).

P.A.Patel's 158 took 258 balls in 361 minutes and included 17 fours. B.D.Thaker's 154 took 276 balls in 373 minutes and included 13 fours and 3 sixes.

JAMMU AND KASHMIR v MADHYA PRADESH

Played at Gandhi Memorial Science College Ground, Jammu, November 15, 16, 17, 18, 2007.
Ranji Trophy 2007/08 - Plate Group B
Madhya Pradesh won by four wickets.   (Points: Jammu and Kashmir 0, Madhya Pradesh 5)

JAMMU AND KASHMIR

1	I.Dev Singh	b Dholpure	104	b Pitre	16
2	Sajjad Shaikh	c Murtuza Ali b Pitre	0	c Ojha b Rajan	1
3	Hardeep Singh	lbw b Pitre	1	(5) c Ojha b Dholpure	14
4	Majid Dar	c Ojha b Dholpure	80	lbw b Rajan	0
5	†Sarabjit Singh	run out (Pitre)	25	(6) lbw b Rajan	0
6	Inderjit Singh	lbw b Rajan	3	(3) lbw b Pitre	0
7	*V.Sharma	b Pitre	17	c Ojha b Rajan	4
8	S.Beigh	lbw b Pitre	0	b Dholpure	0
9	S.Khajuria	b Pitre	12	b Rajan	3
10	Sameer Ali	c Ojha b Pitre	4	b Rajan	32
11	Jagtar Singh	not out	0	not out	3
	Extras	b 7, lb 8, w 2, nb 18	35	b 4, lb 5, nb 9	18
			281		91

FoW (1): 1-1 (2), 2-19 (3), 3-161 (1), 4-207 (5), 5-226 (6), 6-259 (7), 7-259 (8), 8-265 (4), 9-272 (10), 10-281 (9)
FoW (2): 1-18 (1), 2-18 (2), 3-23 (3), 4-28 (4), 5-37 (6), 6-47 (7), 7-47 (5), 8-48 (8), 9-82 (9), 10-91 (10)

MADHYA PRADESH

1	†N.V.Ojha	b Beigh	27	b Sameer Ali	4
2	Jalaj S.Saxena	c Sarabjit Singh b Beigh	0	not out	57
3	Jatin S.Saxena	lbw b Sharma	10	b Sameer Ali	0
4	D.Bundela	c Sajjad Shaikh b Beigh	80	lbw b Sameer Ali	0
5	*B.R.Tomar	c Sarabjit Singh b Sameer Ali	7	(7) c Dev Singh b Khajuria	11
6	R.N.Bakshi	c Sharma b Sameer Ali	38	b Khajuria	10
7	Murtuza Ali	c Sarabjit Singh b Sharma	11	(8) not out	29
8	S.M.Dholpure	c Dev Singh b Jagtar Singh	38		
9	S.K.Pitre	lbw b Khajuria	4	(5) b Jagtar Singh	12
10	A.Rajan	c Beigh b Jagtar Singh	5		
11	Asif Ali	not out	0		
	Extras	b 9, w 1, nb 12	22	b 3, lb 5, nb 2	10
			242	(6 wickets)	133

FoW (1): 1-2 (2), 2-33 (3), 3-41 (1), 4-64 (5), 5-133 (6), 6-162 (7), 7-224 (4), 8-231 (9), 9-241 (10), 10-242 (8)
FoW (2): 1-7 (1), 2-15 (3), 3-15 (4), 4-41 (5), 5-65 (6), 6-85 (7)

Madhya Pradesh Bowling

	O	M	R	W		O	M	R	W	
Pitre	25.2	9	60	6	1w	9	4	22	2	
Rajan	28	7	80	1	1w,6nb	15.1	2	45	6	7nb
Dholpure	18	5	41	2	11nb	7	1	15	2	2nb
Bundela	6	2	9	0	1nb					
Asif Ali	16	4	41	0						
Jalaj S.Saxena	13	2	23	0						
Murtuza Ali	4	0	12	0						

Jammu and Kashmir Bowling

	O	M	R	W			O	M	R	W	
Sharma	21	6	44	2	1w,6nb	(4)	4	2	6	0	1nb
Beigh	27	6	73	3	3nb	(1)	11.3	2	40	0	
Sameer Ali	13	1	60	2	2nb	(2)	9	2	34	3	1nb
Jagtar Singh	18	7	31	2		(3)	5	2	8	1	
Khajuria	9	1	25	1	1nb		6	1	27	2	
Inderjit Singh						(6)	2	0	5	0	
Majid Dar						(7)	2	0	5	0	

Umpires: V.D.Nerurkar and S.M.Raju. Referee: S.K.Singh.   Toss: Madhya Pradesh

Close of Play: 1st day: Jammu and Kashmir (1) 230-5 (Majid Dar 62*, Sharma 3*, 85.3 overs); 2nd day: Madhya Pradesh (1) 159-5 (Bundela 49*, Murtuza Ali 11*, 52 overs); 3rd day: Madhya Pradesh (2) 18-3 (Jatin S.Saxena 11*, Pitre 1*, 4.4 overs).

I.Dev Singh's 104 took 175 balls in 248 minutes and included 17 fours.

JHARKHAND v HARYANA

Played at Keenan Stadium, Jamshedpur, November 15, 16, 17, 18, 2007.
Ranji Trophy 2007/08 - Plate Group B
Haryana won by 131 runs.   (Points: Jharkhand 0, Haryana 5)

HARYANA

1	V.Sahni	c Sharma b Rao	58	run out	54
2	M.R.Beerala	lbw b Rao	20	b Nadeem	75
3	S.Sharma	c Tantubhai b Yadav	14	c Yadav b Vidyarthi	63
4	S.S.Viswanathan	run out (Gupta)	60	c Tantubhai b Nadeem	6
5	S.Rana	c Nadeem b Sharma	24	b Nadeem	3
6	J.Sharma	c Vardhan b Nadeem	29	run out	48
7	†Sandeep Singh	c Sharma b Nadeem	0	(8) not out	0
8	*A.Mishra	lbw b Rao	23	(7) not out	27
9	G.Vashisht	c Tantubhai b Yadav	7		
10	S.Badhwar	not out	24		
11	P.Huda	run out (Sharma)	5		
	Extras	b 1, lb 2, w 1, nb 5	9	b 4, lb 2, w 2, nb 2	10
			273	(6 wickets, declared)	286

FoW (1): 1-33 (2), 2-71 (3), 3-127 (1), 4-166 (5), 5-211 (6), 6-213 (4), 7-213 (7), 8-241 (9), 9-245 (8), 10-273 (11)
FoW (2): 1-101 (2), 2-152 (1), 3-163 (4), 4-181 (5), 5-230 (3), 6-286 (6)

JHARKHAND

1	*M.S.Vardhan	c Rana b J.Sharma	0	(2) b Badhwar	106
2	Ratan Kumar	c Rana b Badhwar	0	(1) lbw b J.Sharma	3
3	A.K.Vidyarthi	c Sandeep Singh b J.Sharma	0	lbw b Rana	14
4	S.S.Tiwary	c Viswanathan b Mishra	14	st Sandeep Singh b Mishra	19
5	A.Hashmi	c Sandeep Singh b Vashisht	50	lbw b Vashisht	14
6	S.Gupta	c S.Sharma b Rana	51	b Rana	16
7	†M.M.Tantubhai	b Vashisht	4	b Badhwar	7
8	S.Nadeem	b Rana	57	lbw b Mishra	0
9	S.S.Rao	b Badhwar	0	b Rana	3
10	K.Sharma	b Rana	5	c Sandeep Singh b J.Sharma	3
11	R.K.Yadav	not out	0	not out	8
	Extras	b 6, lb 6, w 9, nb 3	24	b 9, lb 11, w 4, nb 6	30
			205		223

FoW (1): 1-5 (1), 2-5 (2), 3-5 (3), 4-58 (4), 5-91 (5), 6-101 (7), 7-186 (6), 8-195 (9), 9-204 (8), 10-205 (10)
FoW (2): 1-5 (1), 2-41 (3), 3-81 (4), 4-110 (5), 5-171 (6), 6-197 (7), 7-198 (2), 8-199 (8), 9-208 (10), 10-223 (9)

Jharkhand Bowling

	O	M	R	W			O	M	R	W	
Sharma	15.3	3	58	1	1nb	(2)	21	4	78	0	1w,1nb
Rao	27	6	66	3	1w,1nb	(1)	14	1	59	0	1w
Yadav	23	6	50	2	3nb		8	1	36	0	
Nadeem	26	5	46	2			22	3	61	3	1nb
Gupta	15	4	39	0			8	0	38	0	
Vidyarthi	3	0	9	0			2	0	8	1	
Vardhan	1	0	2	0							

Haryana Bowling

	O	M	R	W		O	M	R	W	
J.Sharma	15	3	36	2	1w,2nb	18	9	37	2	1nb
Badhwar	18	2	57	2	2w	16	5	36	2	4w,2nb
Rana	13.1	5	24	3	2w	16	5	47	3	
Mishra	17	3	52	1	1nb	23	9	40	2	3nb
Vashisht	12	6	24	2		9	1	31	1	
Huda	1	1	0	0		5	0	12	0	

Umpires: S.Asnani and S.Dua. Referee: V.Narayanan Kutty.   Toss: Haryana

Close of Play: 1st day: Haryana (1) 228-7 (Mishra 10*, Vashisht 0*, 90 overs); 2nd day: Jharkhand (1) 179-6 (Gupta 50*, Nadeem 39*, 64 overs); 3rd day: Haryana (2) 286-6 (Mishra 27*, 74.4 overs).

M.S.Vardhan's 106 took 213 balls in 300 minutes and included 15 fours.

KARNATAKA v HIMACHAL PRADESH

Played at M.Chinnaswamy Stadium, Bangalore, November 15, 16, 17, 2007.
Ranji Trophy 2007/08 - Elite Group A
Karnataka won by an innings and 126 runs. (Points: Karnataka 6, Himachal Pradesh 0)

KARNATAKA

1	B.M.Rowland	c Bisla b Malik	7
2	K.B.Pawan	b Bhatia	56
3	R.S.Dravid	b Malik	121
4	C.Raghu	c M.Sharma b Bhatia	58
5	Y.K.T.Goud	c Dogra b Bhatia	23
6	†V.S.T.Naidu	b Bhatia	105
7	B.Akhil	c and b Bhatia	22
8	S.B.Joshi	c Thakur b Bhatia	14
9	*A.Kumble	b Malik	1
10	R.Vinay Kumar	not out	11
11	N.C.Aiyappa	not out	6
	Extras	b 16, lb 4, w 2, nb 6	28

(9 wickets, declared) 452

FoW (1): 1-19 (1), 2-150 (2), 3-242 (3), 4-257 (4), 5-342 (5), 6-403 (7), 7-423 (8), 8-427 (9), 9-434 (6)

HIMACHAL PRADESH

1	M.Gupta	c Naidu b Joshi	42	c Vinay Kumar b Aiyappa	28
2	*S.Sharma	c Dravid b Aiyappa	21	c Naidu b Vinay Kumar	0
3	Sangram Singh	c Dravid b Kumble	7	b Vinay Kumar	5
4	P.Dogra	lbw b Vinay Kumar	3	lbw b Akhil	10
5	A.Mannu	c Kumble b Vinay Kumar	18	c Naidu b Vinay Kumar	9
6	†M.S.Bisla	not out	43	c Pawan b Kumble	32
7	M.Sharma	lbw b Vinay Kumar	0	lbw b Joshi	32
8	V.Bhatia	run out (Rowland)	3	lbw b Kumble	5
9	Sarandeep Singh	c Dravid b Kumble	14	not out	9
10	A.K.Thakur	c Vinay Kumar b Kumble	0	c Akhil b Kumble	0
11	V.Malik	c Vinay Kumar b Joshi	5	c and b Joshi	4
	Extras	b 8, lb 10, pen 5	23	b 13	13

179   147

FoW (1): 1-47 (2), 2-76 (3), 3-79 (4), 4-90 (1), 5-120 (5), 6-124 (7), 7-135 (8), 8-174 (9), 9-174 (10), 10-179 (11)
FoW (2): 1-1 (2), 2-33 (3), 3-43 (1), 4-50 (4), 5-64 (5), 6-125 (7), 7-129 (6), 8-136 (8), 9-138 (10), 10-147 (11)

Himachal Pradesh Bowling

	O	M	R	W	
Thakur	33	5	82	0	2nb
Malik	36	11	103	3	3nb
Sangram Singh	4	1	12	0	
Sarandeep Singh	19	3	90	0	
Bhatia	45	10	129	6	2w,1nb
M.Sharma	1	0	10	0	
S.Sharma	1	0	6	0	

Karnataka Bowling

	O	M	R	W		O	M	R	W
Vinay Kumar	15	6	26	3		10	2	32	3
Aiyappa	13	4	41	1		9	3	29	1
Kumble	16	3	55	3	(4)	13	1	41	3
Joshi	14.5	5	18	2	(5)	12.4	2	22	2
Akhil	10	5	16	0	(3)	6	3	10	1

Umpires: P.S.Godbole and S.D.Ranade. Referee: S.Paul.   Toss: Karnataka

Close of Play: 1st day: Karnataka (1) 271-4 (Goud 8*, Naidu 7*, 91 overs); 2nd day: Himachal Pradesh (1) 117-4 (Mannu 16*, Bisla 11*, 40 overs).

The match was scheduled for four days but completed in three. R.S.Dravid's 121 took 180 balls in 251 minutes and included 14 fours and 4 sixes. V.S.T.Naidu's 105 took 137 balls in 228 minutes and included 16 fours and 1 six.

101

KERALA v SERVICES

Played at Fort Maidan, Palakkad, November 15, 16, 17, 18, 2007.
Ranji Trophy 2007/08 - Plate Group A
Match drawn.   (Points: Kerala 3, Services 1)

KERALA

1	S.K.Sarma	b Fazil Mohammad	1
2	*S.K.Cheruvathur	run out (Tahir Khan)	13
3	V.A.Jagadeesh	b Hariprasad	109
4	S.R.Nair	not out	306
5	R.M.Fernandez	lbw b Hariprasad	0
6	P.Rohan Prem	c Jasvir Singh b Mohanty	70
7	P.Prasanth	c and b Sharma	49
8	†V.G.Nair	not out	0
9	T.Yohannan		
10	S.Anish		
11	P.Chandran		
	Extras	b 1, lb 3, w 6, nb 8	18
		(6 wickets, declared)	566

FoW (1): 1-15 (1), 2-16 (2), 3-318 (3), 4-318 (5), 5-476 (6), 6-566 (7)

SERVICES

1	S.Chatarjee	b Yohannan	4	c and b Anish	16
2	D.S.Israni	c V.G.Nair b S.R.Nair	115	(3) run out	33
3	Tahir Khan	c V.G.Nair b Yohannan	100	(2) c Sarma b Prasanth	19
4	Jasvir Singh	not out	68	c Fernandez b Anish	43
5	*Yashpal Singh	c and b Cheruvathur	9	c S.R.Nair b Anish	43
6	S.Upadhyay	b Anish	9	c Sarma b Anish	38
7	†K.G.Chawda	c Yohannan b Chandran	13	c V.G.Nair b Anish	2
8	A.K.Mohanty	c Jagadeesh b Yohannan	1	not out	13
9	A.Sharma	b Yohannan	0	lbw b Anish	0
10	Fazil Mohammad	c Rohan Prem b Chandran	0	not out	12
11	A.Hariprasad	c V.G.Nair b Yohannan	4		
	Extras	b 1, lb 2, w 9, nb 15	27	b 2, lb 3, nb 9	14
			350	(8 wickets)	233

FoW (1): 1-9 (1), 2-207 (3), 3-267 (2), 4-293 (5), 5-306 (6), 6-331 (7), 7-333 (8), 8-335 (9), 9-343 (10), 10-350 (11)
FoW (2): 1-36 (1), 2-36 (2), 3-105 (3), 4-131 (4), 5-196 (5), 6-206 (7), 7-211 (6), 8-211 (9)

Services Bowling	O	M	R	W	
Fazil Mohammad	23	7	68	1	1w,4nb
Hariprasad	19	2	75	2	1w,4nb
Mohanty	48	5	154	1	2w
Sharma	43	9	115	1	
Yashpal Singh	21	1	87	0	2w
Chatarjee	2	0	10	0	
Upadhyay	9	0	41	0	
Jasvir Singh	2	0	12	0	

Kerala Bowling	O	M	R	W			O	M	R	W	
Yohannan	18	4	57	5	2w,8nb		6	0	20	0	5nb
Chandran	17	2	63	2	1nb		6	2	12	0	
Cheruvathur	28	6	89	1	3w,3nb		15	6	35	0	1nb
Prasanth	8	0	23	0		(6)	11	4	35	1	3nb
Anish	29	10	62	1			34	5	113	6	
Jagadeesh	4	1	10	0							
S.R.Nair	11	0	43	1	3nb		1	0	1	0	
Sarma						(4)	3	0	12	0	

Umpires: R.D.Risodkar and B.Sharma.   Referee: M.Y.Ranade.   Toss: Services

Close of Play: 1st day: Kerala (1) 293-2 (Jagadeesh 101*, S.R.Nair 169*, 90 overs); 2nd day: Services (1) 33-1 (Israni 11*, Tahir Khan 15*, 12 overs); 3rd day: Services (1) 325-5 (Jasvir Singh 56*, Chawda 8*, 102 overs).
V.A.Jagadeesh's 109 took 281 balls in 387 minutes and included 14 fours. S.R.Nair's 306 took 462 balls in 634 minutes and included 37 fours. D.S.Israni's 115 took 235 balls in 335 minutes and included 16 fours. Tahir Khan's 100 took 183 balls in 264 minutes and included 18 fours.

PUNJAB v HYDERABAD

Played at Punjab Cricket Association Ground, Mohali, November 15, 16, 17, 18, 2007.
Ranji Trophy 2007/08 - Elite Group B
Match drawn.   (Points: Punjab 1, Hyderabad 3)

HYDERABAD

1	D.S.Manohar	c Madan b Goel	119	b Birinder Singh		8
2	D.B.Ravi Teja	b Gony	55	lbw b Amanpreet Singh		111
3	*V.V.S.Laxman	c Inder Singh b Kakkar	38	(9) c Sarabjit Singh b Gony		26
4	S.A.Pai	lbw b Kakkar	10	(3) b Birinder Singh		2
5	A.S.Yadav	b Birinder Singh	16	(4) c Dharmani b Gony		14
6	A.J.Shinde	c Madan b Gony	36	(5) c Madan b Kakkar		48
7	†Habeeb Ahmed	b Goel	9	(6) c Inder Singh b Sarabjit Singh		19
8	P.P.Ojha	b Kakkar	7	(7) c Inder Singh b Sarabjit Singh		11
9	Shoaib Ahmed	b Gony	32	(8) b Sarabjit Singh		2
10	Abdul Khader	not out	16	c Madan b Sarabjit Singh		23
11	A.D.Yadav	c Amanpreet Singh b Kakkar	17	not out		0
	Extras	b 10, lb 6, w 3, nb 5	24	b 3, lb 4, w 1, nb 4		12
			379			**276**

FoW (1): 1-128 (2), 2-203 (3), 3-223 (4), 4-256 (1), 5-256 (5), 6-269 (7), 7-280 (8), 8-317 (6), 9-352 (9), 10-379 (11)
FoW (2): 1-44 (1), 2-50 (3), 3-95 (4), 4-160 (2), 5-206 (6), 6-210 (5), 7-222 (7), 8-233 (8), 9-272 (9), 10-276 (10)

PUNJAB

1	R.S.Ricky	c and b Ojha	37	b A.D.Yadav		7
2	K.Goel	c Pai b Abdul Khader	75	c Habeeb Ahmed b A.D.Yadav		29
3	R.Inder Singh	c sub (V.G.Sharma) b Ojha	20	lbw b Ojha		3
4	*P.Dharmani	c Habeeb Ahmed b A.D.Yadav	52			
5	U.Kaul	b Ojha	46	(4) not out		18
6	†C.Madan	lbw b A.D.Yadav	8	(5) c Habeeb Ahmed b A.D.Yadav		7
7	A.Kakkar	run out (Shoaib Ahmed)	45	(6) not out		9
8	M.S.Gony	c sub (V.G.Sharma) b Shoaib Ahmed	48			
9	Birinder Singh	c A.S.Yadav b Manohar	1			
10	Amanpreet Singh	c Pai b Manohar	1			
11	Sarabjit Singh	not out	4			
	Extras	b 4, lb 10, nb 5	19	lb 1, nb 1		2
			356	**(4 wickets)**		**75**

FoW (1): 1-88 (1), 2-142 (3), 3-150 (2), 4-216 (4), 5-236 (6), 6-268 (5), 7-339 (7), 8-340 (9), 9-342 (10), 10-356 (8)
FoW (2): 1-37 (2), 2-38 (1), 3-46 (3), 4-63 (5)

Punjab Bowling

	O	M	R	W			O	M	R	W	
Amanpreet Singh	20	5	66	0		(3)	10	1	42	1	
Gony	28	8	86	3		(1)	17	2	50	2	1w,3nb
Birinder Singh	17	1	77	1		(2)	15	2	55	2	1nb
Ricky	1	0	8	0	2w						
Kakkar	22.3	5	55	4	1nb	(4)	18	3	43	1	
Sarabjit Singh	7	1	37	0			12.5	5	30	4	
Goel	10	0	34	2		(5)	13	0	49	0	

Hyderabad Bowling

	O	M	R	W			O	M	R	W	
Shoaib Ahmed	19	9	33	1	1nb		8	4	12	0	
Abdul Khader	13	3	40	1			5	1	19	0	
Ojha	47	9	127	3			9	4	11	1	
Shinde	13	4	32	0							
A.D.Yadav	25	7	75	2	4nb	(4)	6	0	32	3	1nb
Ravi Teja	3	0	20	0							
Manohar	4	0	15	2							

Umpires: A.Y.Gokhale and M.S.Pathak. Referee: H.R.Wasu.   Toss: Punjab

Close of Play: 1st day: Hyderabad (1) 310-7 (Shinde 29*, Shoaib Ahmed 7*, 89 overs); 2nd day: Punjab (1) 216-3 (Dharmani 52*, Kaul 22*, 71 overs); 3rd day: Hyderabad (2) 85-2 (Ravi Teja 61*, A.S.Yadav 10*, 31 overs).
D.S.Manohar's 119 took 215 balls in 298 minutes and included 16 fours. D.B.Ravi Teja's 111 took 169 balls in 236 minutes and included 13 fours.

RAJASTHAN v MAHARASHTRA

Played at K.L.Saini Ground, Jaipur, November 15, 16, 17, 2007.
Ranji Trophy 2007/08 - Elite Group A
Maharashtra won by eight wickets. (Points: Rajasthan 0, Maharashtra 5)

RAJASTHAN

1	R.G.Sharma	b Patel	2	b Sayyed	6
2	G.K.Khoda	c Mohan b Patel	43	c More b Sayyed	60
3	R.J.Kanwat	b Sayyed	6	lbw b Bahutule	16
4	V.A.Saxena	c More b Khadiwale	10	lbw b Bahutule	99
5	R.D.Bist	c Venugopal Rao b Patel	5	c Jadhav b Bahutule	0
6	R.K.Bishnoi	c Mohan b Patel	4	lbw b Sayyed	42
7	†R.B.Jhalani	lbw b Khadiwale	5	c Bhilare b Bahutule	16
8	Afroz Khan	not out	21	c Takawale b Patel	20
9	Pankaj Singh	b Bahutule	0	c Bahutule b Patel	4
10	*Mohammad Aslam	b Bahutule	3	run out	0
11	S.O.Mathur	c Takawale b Bahutule	1	not out	3
	Extras	lb 4, nb 1	5	b 12, lb 13, w 6, nb 6	37
			105		303

FoW (1): 1-16 (1), 2-31 (3), 3-45 (4), 4-57 (5), 5-67 (6), 6-72 (7), 7-84 (2), 8-85 (9), 9-89 (10), 10-105 (11)
FoW (2): 1-23 (1), 2-78 (3), 3-78 (5), 4-163 (6), 5-203 (7), 6-253 (2), 7-286 (8), 8-294 (9), 9-295 (10), 10-303 (4)

MAHARASHTRA

1	†V.V.More	c Saxena b Afroz Khan	32	c Bishnoi b Pankaj Singh	12
2	H.H.Khadiwale	c Bist b Pankaj Singh	57	c Jhalani b Pankaj Singh	19
3	K.M.Jadhav	c Jhalani b Afroz Khan	8	not out	37
4	*Y.Venugopal Rao	b Pankaj Singh	80	not out	45
5	Y.V.Takawale	c Jhalani b Pankaj Singh	44		
6	V.R.Bhilare	b Kanwat	31		
7	D.Mohan	lbw b Kanwat	5		
8	S.V.Bahutule	b Pankaj Singh	5		
9	S.A.Agharkar	not out	4		
10	M.M.Patel	b Mathur	1		
11	W.S.Sayyed	b Mathur	4		
	Extras	b 9, lb 1, w 3, nb 3	16	b 6, w 2, nb 2	10
			287	(2 wickets)	123

FoW (1): 1-69 (1), 2-84 (3), 3-113 (2), 4-180 (5), 5-253 (6), 6-265 (7), 7-275 (8), 8-282 (4), 9-283 (10), 10-287 (11)
FoW (2): 1-14 (1), 2-48 (2)

Maharashtra Bowling

	O	M	R	W			O	M	R	W	
Patel	16	4	54	4			26	6	76	2	
Sayyed	7	2	26	1			20	2	68	3	2w,5nb
Khadiwale	10	3	19	2	1nb	(4)	5	2	6	0	1nb
Bahutule	2.4	2	2	3		(3)	30.2	4	96	4	
Agharkar						(5)	15	2	32	0	

Rajasthan Bowling

	O	M	R	W			O	M	R	W	
Pankaj Singh	25	6	83	4			13	2	42	2	2w,1nb
Mathur	19.5	0	78	2			6	2	21	0	
Mohammad Aslam	20	4	42	0			5	0	35	0	
Afroz Khan	16	4	54	2	3w,3nb		3	0	19	0	1nb
Kanwat	7	1	20	2							

Umpires: K.Murali and I.Shivram. Referee: S.Luthra. Toss: Maharashtra

Close of Play: 1st day: Maharashtra (1) 155-3 (Venugopal Rao 26*, Takawale 26*, 47 overs); 2nd day: Rajasthan (2) 160-3 (Saxena 38*, Bishnoi 41*, 45 overs).

The match was scheduled for four days but completed in three. G.K.Khoda retired hurt in the Rajasthan second innings having scored 34 (team score 60-1) - he returned when the score was 203-5.

TAMIL NADU v MUMBAI

Played at India Cement Limited Guru Nanak College Ground, Chennai, November 15, 16, 17, 2007.
Ranji Trophy 2007/08 - Elite Group A
Mumbai won by eight wickets.   (Points: Tamil Nadu 0, Mumbai 5)

TAMIL NADU

1	†K.D.Karthik	lbw b Powar	76	b Agarkar	28
2	M.Vijay Krishna	run out (Powar)	17	c Samant b Powar	2
3	R.Prasanna	lbw b Salvi	3	(5) lbw b Powar	0
4	*S.Badrinath	b Salvi	0	b Salvi	32
5	K.Vasudevadas	c Samant b Nayar	4	(7) b Salvi	47
6	R.Srinivasan	not out	66	b Salvi	11
7	R.Ashwin	c and b Iqbal Abdulla	19	(8) run out	51
8	R.Ramkumar	c Jaffer b Powar	7	(9) c Iqbal Abdulla b Powar	16
9	R.Naresh	c Kukreja b Powar	4	(10) c Jaffer b Powar	0
10	V.Y.Mahesh	c Rahane b Powar	3	(3) b Powar	14
11	P.Amarnath	b Agarkar	0	not out	0
	Extras	b 1, lb 3, nb 3	7	b 11, nb 2	13
			206		214

FoW (1): 1-47 (2), 2-57 (3), 3-57 (4), 4-62 (5), 5-119 (1), 6-153 (7), 7-171 (8), 8-185 (9), 9-205 (10), 10-206 (11)
FoW (2): 1-16 (2), 2-30 (1), 3-75 (3), 4-75 (5), 5-93 (4), 6-98 (6), 7-189 (7), 8-206 (8), 9-211 (10), 10-214 (9)

MUMBAI

1	S.O.Kukreja	c Karthik b Amarnath	30		
2	W.Jaffer	c Amarnath b Ramkumar	50	(1) c Prasanna b Ramkumar	17
3	A.M.Rahane	c Karthik b Naresh	4	(2) b Ramkumar	28
4	*A.A.Muzumdar	lbw b Ramkumar	43	not out	2
5	P.T.Naik	run out (Naresh)	8	(3) not out	57
6	A.M.Nayar	c Vasudevadas b Ashwin	105		
7	A.B.Agarkar	b Amarnath	22		
8	R.R.Powar	c Vijay Krishna b Ramkumar	0		
9	†V.R.Samant	not out	39		
10	Iqbal Abdulla	c Amarnath b Ramkumar	8		
11	A.M.Salvi	c Prasanna b Ashwin	0		
	Extras	b 3, lb 3, w 1, nb 1	8		
			317	(2 wickets)	104

FoW (1): 1-57 (1), 2-66 (3), 3-127 (2), 4-138 (4), 5-155 (5), 6-227 (7), 7-228 (8), 8-302 (6), 9-316 (10), 10-317 (11)
FoW (2): 1-28 (1), 2-79 (2)

Mumbai Bowling

	O	M	R	W		O	M	R	W	
Agarkar	13	4	36	1	1nb	15	4	38	1	1nb
Salvi	18.4	5	43	2	2nb	16	6	27	3	1nb
Nayar	17	2	41	1	(4)	14	7	34	0	
Powar	19	4	55	4	(3)	21.2	4	68	5	
Iqbal Abdulla	9.2	2	27	1		10	3	36	0	

Tamil Nadu Bowling

	O	M	R	W		O	M	R	W	
Mahesh	17	6	52	0	1w,1nb	3	0	21	0	
Amarnath	21	5	66	2		4	1	18	0	
Naresh	12	4	31	1		2	1	2	0	
Ashwin	15	0	58	2	(5)	3	0	31	0	
Ramkumar	23	3	88	4	(4)	7	2	32	2	
Badrinath	2	0	16	0						

Umpires: S.J.Phadkar and M.S.S.Ranawat.   Referee: M.Nayyar.   Toss: Tamil Nadu

Close of Play: 1st day: Mumbai (1) 20-0 (Kukreja 17*, Jaffer 3*, 11 overs); 2nd day: Tamil Nadu (2) 30-1 (Karthik 28*, Mahesh 0*, 8 overs).

The match was scheduled for four days but completed in three. A.M.Nayar's 105 took 85 balls in 136 minutes and included 13 fours and 2 sixes.

INDIA v PAKISTAN

Played at Feroz Shah Kotla, Delhi, November 22, 23, 24, 25, 26, 2007.
Pakistan in India 2007/08 - 1st Test
India won by six wickets.

PAKISTAN

1	Salman Butt	b Khan	1	c Dravid b Kumble	67
2	Yasir Hameed	b Kumble	29	c Laxman b Kumble	36
3	Younis Khan	c Patel b Khan	7	lbw b Kumble	23
4	Mohammad Yousuf	lbw b Ganguly	27	c and b Harbhajan Singh	18
5	Misbah-ul-Haq	run out (Karthik)	82	(7) c Karthik b Ganguly	45
6	*Shoaib Malik	c Dhoni b Patel	0	(5) b Harbhajan Singh	11
7	†Kamran Akmal	b Kumble	30	(6) c sub (Yuvraj Singh) b Khan	21
8	Sohail Tanvir	lbw b Harbhajan Singh	4	c Harbhajan Singh b Khan	13
9	Shoaib Akhtar	b Kumble	2	(10) not out	0
10	Mohammad Sami	not out	28	(9) c Jaffer b Ganguly	5
11	Danish Kaneria	b Kumble	0	run out	0
	Extras	b 6, lb 12, w 2, nb 1	21	lb 6, nb 2	8
			231		247

FoW (1): 1-13 (1), 2-35 (3), 3-59 (2), 4-76 (4), 5-83 (6), 6-122 (7), 7-137 (8), 8-142 (9), 9-229 (5), 10-231 (11)
FoW (2): 1-71 (2), 2-114 (3), 3-149 (4), 4-155 (1), 5-161 (5), 6-213 (6), 7-229 (8), 8-243 (7), 9-247 (9), 10-247 (11)

INDIA

1	W.Jaffer	lbw b Shoaib Akhtar	32	(2) c Salman Butt b Shoaib Akhtar	53
2	K.D.Karthik	c Kamran Akmal b Shoaib Akhtar	9	(1) c Kamran Akmal b Shoaib Akhtar	1
3	R.S.Dravid	b Sohail Tanvir	38	b Shoaib Akhtar	34
4	S.R.Tendulkar	run out		not out	56
		(Kamran Akmal/Mohammad Yousuf)	1		
5	S.C.Ganguly	b Sohail Tanvir	8	c Sohail Tanvir b Shoaib Akhtar	48
6	V.V.S.Laxman	not out	72	not out	6
7	†M.S.Dhoni	c Kamran Akmal b Danish Kaneria	57		
8	*A.Kumble	c Younis Khan b Danish Kaneria	24		
9	Harbhajan Singh	b Sohail Tanvir	1		
10	Z.Khan	c Shoaib Akhtar b Danish Kaneria	9		
11	M.M.Patel	lbw b Danish Kaneria	0		
	Extras	b 11, lb 8, w 1, nb 5	25	b 1, lb 3, nb 1	5
			276	(4 wickets)	203

FoW (1): 1-15 (2), 2-71 (1), 3-73 (4), 4-88 (5), 5-93 (3), 6-208 (7), 7-262 (8), 8-263 (9), 9-276 (10), 10-276 (11)
FoW (2): 1-2 (1), 2-84 (2), 3-93 (3), 4-181 (5)

India Bowling

	O	M	R	W		O	M	R	W	
Khan	20	5	45	2	2w,1nb	18	4	45	2	1nb
Patel	24	5	61	1		10	2	48	0	
Kumble	21.2	6	38	4		27.1	8	68	3	1nb
Ganguly	14	5	28	1		9	2	20	2	
Harbhajan Singh	15	1	37	1		17	4	56	2	
Tendulkar	2	0	4	0		2	0	4	0	

Pakistan Bowling

	O	M	R	W		O	M	R	W	
Shoaib Akhtar	16	2	44	2	1nb	18.1	4	58	4	1nb
Sohail Tanvir	24	5	83	3	3nb	12	4	26	0	
Mohammad Sami	17	1	71	0	(4)	15	1	65	0	
Danish Kaneria	21.4	3	59	4	1w (3)	16	2	50	0	

Umpires: B.R.Doctrove and S.J.A.Taufel. Third umpire: S.L.Shastri. Referee: R.S.Madugalle.   Toss: Pakistan

Close of Play: 1st day: Pakistan (1) 210-8 (Misbah-ul-Haq 71*, Mohammad Sami 20*, 85.4 overs); 2nd day: India (1) 228-6 (Laxman 57*, Kumble 7*, 63.2 overs); 3rd day: Pakistan (2) 212-5 (Kamran Akmal 21*, Misbah-ul-Haq 29*, 65.5 overs); 4th day: India (2) 171-3 (Tendulkar 32*, Ganguly 48*, 54.5 overs).

Man of the Match: A.Kumble.

ASSAM v KERALA

Played at Satindra Mohan Dev Stadium, Silchar, November 23, 24, 25, 26, 2007.
Ranji Trophy 2007/08 - Plate Group A
Assam won by 32 runs.   (Points: Assam 5, Kerala 0)

ASSAM

1	S.Suresh	c and b Yohannan	57	c Cheruvathur b Gomez	45
2	S.K.Das	c V.G.Nair b Chandran	0	(4) lbw b Yohannan	4
3	P.M.Das	c V.G.Nair b Cheruvathur	23	c Anish b Chandran	8
4	S.Ramesh	c Rohan Prem b Anish	27	(5) b Yohannan	13
5	*S.Sharath	lbw b Yohannan	17	(6) b Yohannan	14
6	Tarjinder Singh	c Gomez b Yohannan	2	(2) lbw b Cheruvathur	6
7	†R.N.Das	c Rohan Prem b S.R.Nair	30	lbw b S.R.Nair	12
8	D.S.Goswami	c Rohan Prem b S.R.Nair	18	c Chandran b S.R.Nair	18
9	A.Konwar	lbw b Prasanth	9	c Anish b S.R.Nair	10
10	B.M.Mahanta	b S.R.Nair	0	c Sarma b Anish	7
11	B.B.Baruah	not out	6	not out	1
	Extras	b 4, lb 2, nb 3	9	b 1, lb 5, nb 8	14
			198		**152**

FoW (1): 1-0 (2), 2-70 (3), 3-99 (4), 4-109 (1), 5-125 (6), 6-150 (5), 7-175 (8), 8-182 (7), 9-182 (10), 10-198 (9)
FoW (2): 1-16 (2), 2-33 (3), 3-54 (4), 4-81 (1), 5-83 (5), 6-105 (6), 7-120 (7), 8-136 (9), 9-143 (8), 10-152 (10)

KERALA

1	S.K.Sarma	lbw b Goswami	0	lbw b Goswami	9
2	*S.K.Cheruvathur	lbw b Suresh	6	c R.N.Das b Baruah	30
3	V.A.Jagadeesh	c R.N.Das b Goswami	0	lbw b Goswami	1
4	S.R.Nair	c S.K.Das b Goswami	2	lbw b Mahanta	6
5	R.V.Gomez	c Tarjinder Singh b Suresh	12	lbw b Suresh	8
6	P.Rohan Prem	lbw b Goswami	20	c R.N.Das b Suresh	53
7	P.Prasanth	b Suresh	2	c S.K.Das b Goswami	83
8	†V.G.Nair	c Ramesh b Suresh	3	c S.K.Das b Baruah	12
9	S.Anish	not out	19	st R.N.Das b Baruah	4
10	T.Yohannan	b Konwar	2	not out	7
11	P.Chandran	b Baruah	7	b Baruah	6
	Extras	b 8, lb 4	12	b 6, lb 6, w 2	14
			85		**233**

FoW (1): 1-0 (1), 2-0 (3), 3-8 (2), 4-10 (4), 5-23 (5), 6-29 (7), 7-39 (8), 8-54 (6), 9-61 (10), 10-85 (11)
FoW (2): 1-22 (1), 2-24 (3), 3-49 (4), 4-58 (5), 5-64 (2), 6-200 (6), 7-204 (7), 8-219 (8), 9-223 (9), 10-233 (11)

Kerala Bowling

	O	M	R	W			O	M	R	W	
Yohannan	16	3	40	3	2nb		14	4	46	3	5nb
Chandran	14	6	26	1			10	3	32	1	
Cheruvathur	8	1	37	1			6	2	14	1	
Prasanth	8.5	1	26	1	1nb	(6)	5	1	11	0	3nb
Anish	15	3	50	1		(8)	1.3	1	0	1	
S.R.Nair	5	2	13	3		(7)	7	4	11	3	
Gomez						(4)	5	0	27	1	
Jagadeesh						(5)	1	0	5	0	

Assam Bowling

	O	M	R	W			O	M	R	W	
Goswami	17	8	24	4			30	10	65	3	1w
Suresh	20	8	23	4			37	7	83	2	1w
Baruah	2.2	1	2	1		(4)	18	8	13	4	
Konwar	13	5	24	1		(5)	15	7	18	0	
Mahanta						(3)	17	5	33	1	
S.K.Das						(6)	4	0	4	0	
Tarjinder Singh						(7)	5	2	5	0	

Umpires: R.Y.Deshmukh and S.J.Phadkar.   Referee: R.Jolly.   Toss: Assam

Close of Play: 1st day: Kerala (1) 23-5 (Rohan Prem 3*, 22.3 overs); 2nd day: Kerala (2) 11-0 (Sarma 3*, Cheruvathur 8*, 4 overs); 3rd day: Kerala (2) 200-6 (Prasanth 80*, 100.3 overs).

GOA v MADHYA PRADESH

Played at Dr Rajendra Prasad Stadium, Margao, November 23, 24, 25, 26, 2007.
Ranji Trophy 2007/08 - Plate Group B
Match drawn.   (Points: Goa 1, Madhya Pradesh 3)

MADHYA PRADESH

1	†N.V.Ojha	c Ratra b Bandekar	63	c Jakati b Gadekar	93
2	Jalaj S.Saxena	c Jakati b Bandekar	17	run out	58
3	Jatin S.Saxena	lbw b Bandekar	103	(5) not out	16
4	D.Bundela	c Jakati b Gadekar	12	(3) c Arunkumar b Bandekar	0
5	R.N.Bakshi	c Gadekar b D'Souza	14	(4) c Jakati b Gadekar	16
6	*B.R.Tomar	c R.D.Asnodkar b Bandekar	0	not out	18
7	Murtuza Ali	c and b Bandekar	88		
8	A.C.Jadhav	not out	93		
9	S.K.Pitre	c and b Jakati	14		
10	S.P.Pandey	c Arunkumar b Angle	37		
11	A.Rajan	c Ratra b Bandekar	2		
	Extras	b 3, lb 11, w 5, nb 13	32	b 6, lb 2, w 2, nb 6	16
			475	(4 wickets, declared)	217

FoW (1): 1-40 (2), 2-127 (1), 3-149 (4), 4-172 (5), 5-177 (6), 6-259 (3), 7-353 (7), 8-388 (9), 9-464 (10), 10-475 (11)
FoW (2): 1-146 (1), 2-149 (3), 3-176 (4), 4-186 (2)

GOA

1	S.K.Kamat	c Murtuza Ali b Pitre	30	c Jadhav b Jalaj S.Saxena	19
2	S.A.Asnodkar	b Pandey	73	c Bakshi b Rajan	90
3	A.R.Angle	c Tomar b Pitre	4		
4	*J.Arunkumar	c Bakshi b Pandey	35	c Jatin S.Saxena b Jalaj S.Saxena	33
5	S.S.Bandekar	b Pandey	13		
6	M.V.Joglekar	lbw b Pandey	0	not out	9
7	†A.Ratra	b Pandey	62	(5) c Jadhav b Rajan	37
8	R.D.Asnodkar	c Tomar b Pandey	0	(3) lbw b Pandey	1
9	S.B.Jakati	st Ojha b Jalaj S.Saxena	14		
10	R.R.D'Souza	c Tomar b Jalaj S.Saxena	35	(7) not out	2
11	H.H.Gadekar	not out	0		
	Extras	b 3, lb 9, w 3, nb 12	27	b 13, lb 4, w 1, nb 8	26
			293	(5 wickets)	217

FoW (1): 1-70 (1), 2-81 (3), 3-145 (4), 4-176 (5), 5-176 (6), 6-177 (2), 7-177 (8), 8-209 (9), 9-293 (7), 10-293 (10)
FoW (2): 1-40 (1), 2-51 (3), 3-108 (4), 4-174 (2), 5-204 (5)

Goa Bowling

	O	M	R	W			O	M	R	W	
Bandekar	34.5	2	144	6	1w,13nb		14	0	73	1	2w,6nb
Gadekar	23	4	76	1	3w		11	0	45	2	
D'Souza	26	1	101	1	1w		2	0	15	0	
Jakati	36	5	92	1			12	0	58	0	
Angle	10	0	41	1			4	0	18	0	
Arunkumar	2	0	7	0							

Madhya Pradesh Bowling

	O	M	R	W			O	M	R	W	
Pandey	21	7	46	6	2nb (3)		14	2	45	1	4nb
Rajan	18	0	90	0	1w,10nb		14	4	40	2	4nb
Pitre	16	5	37	2	2w (1)		11	2	30	0	1w
Jalaj S.Saxena	22.2	4	55	2			24	5	54	2	
Jadhav	14	1	49	0			6	0	21	0	
Jatin S.Saxena	0.2	0	4	0							
Murtuza Ali					(6)		5	2	10	0	

Umpires: R.M.Deshpande and M.G.Mandale.   Referee: M.Nayyar.   Toss: Madhya Pradesh

Close of Play: 1st day: Madhya Pradesh (1) 334-6 (Murtuza Ali 75*, Jadhav 28*, 90 overs); 2nd day: Goa (1) 145-3 (S.A.Asnodkar 64*, Bandekar 0*, 45 overs); 3rd day: Madhya Pradesh (2) 186-4 (Jatin S.Saxena 5*, 39.1 overs).

Jatin S.Saxena's 103 took 171 balls in 251 minutes and included 14 fours.

HARYANA v RAILWAYS

Played at Chaudhary Bansi Lal Cricket Stadium, Lahli, Rohtak, November 23, 24, 25, 2007.
Ranji Trophy 2007/08 - Plate Group B
Railways won by an innings and 86 runs. (Points: Haryana 0, Railways 6)

HARYANA

1	V.Sahni	b Bangar	1	b Sanyal	32
2	M.R.Beerala	c Pagnis b Bangar	13	lbw b Bangar	8
3	S.Sharma	b Bangar	34	c Rawat b Bangar	25
4	S.S.Viswanathan	c Rawat b Sanyal	10	c Pagnis b Sanyal	9
5	S.Rana	lbw b Sanyal	5	c Rawle b Sanyal	0
6	J.Sharma	c Rawle b Yadav	1	b Yadav	0
7	*A.Mishra	lbw b Bangar	33	b Parida	5
8	†Sandeep Singh	b Harvinder Singh	14	c Pagnis b Parida	9
9	G.Vashisht	c Bangar b Parida	59	b Parida	0
10	S.Badhwar	st Joshi b Yadav	2	not out	0
11	J.Billa	not out	11	c Rawat b Parida	0
	Extras	b 4, lb 2, w 1, nb 3	10	b 8, lb 3, w 1, nb 6	18
			193		106

FoW (1): 1-13 (1), 2-20 (2), 3-47 (4), 4-57 (5), 5-64 (6), 6-71 (3), 7-100 (8), 8-128 (7), 9-131 (10), 10-193 (9)
FoW (2): 1-20 (2), 2-69 (3), 3-86 (4), 4-86 (5), 5-87 (1), 6-91 (6), 7-97 (7), 8-97 (9), 9-106 (8), 10-106 (11)

RAILWAYS

1	S.S.Joshi	c Mishra b Rana	36
2	A.A.Pagnis	b J.Sharma	59
3	*S.B.Bangar	lbw b Mishra	64
4	H.D.Rawle	c and b Rana	16
5	S.C.Sanyal	b Rana	40
6	†M.Rawat	c Beerala b J.Sharma	55
7	K.V.Sharma	b Billa	20
8	M.A.Khote	st Sandeep Singh b Mishra	34
9	Harvinder Singh	not out	13
10	K.S.Parida	b Mishra	1
11	M.S.Yadav	not out	1
	Extras	b 9, lb 22, w 1, nb 14	46
		(9 wickets, declared)	385

FoW (1): 1-99 (1), 2-121 (2), 3-166 (4), 4-247 (3), 5-247 (5), 6-305 (7), 7-370 (8), 8-378 (6), 9-382 (10)

Railways Bowling

	O	M	R	W			O	M	R	W	
Harvinder Singh	14	3	45	1		(2)	6	1	20	0	2nb
Bangar	22	5	56	4	1nb	(1)	13	4	26	2	1w,2nb
Khote	0.4	0	1	0	1w	(4)	4	2	2	0	1nb
Sanyal	9.2	4	22	2	2nb	(7)	5	4	4	3	
Yadav	17	4	47	2		(6)	10	2	13	1	
Parida	4.4	0	16	1		(3)	14.3	5	26	4	
Sharma						(5)	1	0	4	0	

Haryana Bowling

	O	M	R	W	
J.Sharma	23	5	74	2	1w,6nb
Badhwar	10	0	39	0	
Billa	26	6	67	1	5nb
Rana	26	11	54	3	
Vashisht	21	3	51	0	
Mishra	38	17	59	3	2nb
Viswanathan	4	1	10	0	1nb

Umpires: A.Y.Dandekar and I.Shivram. Referee: Umesh Kumar.   Toss: Haryana

Close of Play: 1st day: Railways (1) 80-0 (Joshi 34*, Pagnis 39*, 20 overs); 2nd day: Railways (1) 272-5 (Rawat 10*, Sharma 11*, 109.4 overs).

The match was scheduled for four days but completed in three. Siddarth Joshi kept wicket after 39 overs

HIMACHAL PRADESH v MAHARASHTRA

Played at Himachal Pradesh Cricket Association Stadium, Dharmasala, November 23, 24, 25, 2007.
Ranji Trophy 2007/08 - Elite Group A
Maharashtra won by ten wickets.   (Points: Himachal Pradesh 0, Maharashtra 6)

MAHARASHTRA

1	†V.V.More	b Malik	1			
2	H.H.Khadiwale	c S.Sharma b Malik	16	(1) not out		11
3	K.M.Jadhav	c Bisla b Mehta	18			
4	*Y.Venugopal Rao	c Bisla b Thakur	112	(2) not out		6
5	Y.V.Takawale	c Bisla b Thakur	12			
6	V.R.Bhilare	c Bisla b Malik	8			
7	D.Mohan	b Malik	0			
8	S.V.Bahutule	lbw b Thakur	74			
9	S.A.Agharkar	c S.Sharma b Mehta	46			
10	S.M.Fallah	not out	4			
11	W.S.Sayyed	b Mehta	2			
	Extras	b 5, lb 7, nb 5	17	b 1, lb 4		5
			310	(no wicket)		22

FoW (1): 1-2 (1), 2-37 (2), 3-41 (3), 4-65 (5), 5-81 (6), 6-81 (7), 7-232 (8), 8-300 (4), 9-304 (9), 10-310 (11)

HIMACHAL PRADESH

1	M.Gupta	c Venugopal Rao b Sayyed	4	b Fallah		1
2	*S.Sharma	c Mohan b Fallah	19	c Takawale b Fallah		10
3	B.Sharma	c More b Sayyed	0	(5) lbw b Bahutule		14
4	P.Dogra	lbw b Bahutule	10	(7) b Fallah		38
5	A.Mannu	lbw b Fallah	0	(4) c More b Sayyed		89
6	†M.S.Bisla	not out	23	lbw b Agharkar		12
7	M.Sharma	c Sayyed b Bahutule	7	(3) lbw b Fallah		56
8	V.Bhatia	c Mohan b Khadiwale	7	not out		8
9	A.K.Thakur	c Jadhav b Bahutule	5	(10) b Fallah		6
10	V.Malik	lbw b Bahutule	0	(9) c More b Sayyed		0
11	J.Mehta	b Bahutule	0	b Fallah		0
	Extras	b 6, lb 2	8	lb 12, w 1		13
			83			247

FoW (1): 1-4 (1), 2-14 (3), 3-32 (2), 4-32 (5), 5-38 (4), 6-48 (7), 7-64 (8), 8-81 (9), 9-83 (10), 10-83 (11)
FoW (2): 1-7 (1), 2-12 (2), 3-120 (3), 4-148 (5), 5-167 (6), 6-231 (7), 7-235 (4), 8-235 (9), 9-247 (10), 10-247 (11)

Himachal Pradesh Bowling

	O	M	R	W		O	M	R	W	
Thakur	34	11	86	3	1nb	2	1	1	0	
Malik	28	9	69	4	2nb	2	0	12	0	
Mehta	28	7	88	3		0.2	0	4	0	
Bhatia	16	3	36	0	2nb					
B.Sharma	3	0	14	0						
S.Sharma	1	0	5	0						

Maharashtra Bowling

	O	M	R	W		O	M	R	W	
Sayyed	11	8	7	2		21	3	51	2	1w
Fallah	15	3	34	2		22.5	10	49	6	
Bahutule	18	6	29	5		27	3	68	1	
Khadiwale	7	4	5	1		7	2	15	0	
Agharkar					(5)	15	4	39	1	
Venugopal Rao					(6)	5	0	13	0	

Umpires: A.Bhattacharjee and V.N.Kulkarni. Referee: S.Chaturvedi.   Toss: Himachal Pradesh

Close of Play: 1st day: Maharashtra (1) 249-7 (Venugopal Rao 92*, Agharkar 12*, 90 overs); 2nd day: Himachal Pradesh (2) 41-2 (M.Sharma 25*, Mannu 4*, 15 overs).

The match was scheduled for four days but completed in three. Y.Venugopal Rao's 112 took 275 balls in 384 minutes and included 18 fours and 1 six.

HYDERABAD v BARODA

Played at Rajiv Gandhi International Stadium, Uppal, Hyderabad, November 23, 24, 25, 26, 2007.
Ranji Trophy 2007/08 - Elite Group B
Match drawn.   (Points: Hyderabad 1, Baroda 3)

HYDERABAD

1	D.S.Manohar	c and b Pawar	71	c Shah b I.K.Pathan	0
2	D.B.Ravi Teja	c Shah b I.K.Pathan	72	c Pawar b Y.K.Pathan	54
3	S.A.Pai	c Shah b Singh	62	b I.K.Pathan	16
4	Mohammad Shakeer	c Shah b Pawar	17	(6) not out	29
5	*A.S.Yadav	c Shah b Y.K.Pathan	6	(4) not out	101
6	A.J.Shinde	b I.K.Pathan	11	(5) c Solanki b Y.K.Pathan	57
7	†Habeeb Ahmed	b I.K.Pathan	0		
8	P.P.Ojha	not out	2		
9	Shoaib Ahmed	c I.K.Pathan b Singh	1		
10	A.D.Yadav	lbw b I.K.Pathan	0		
11	A.Lalith Mohan	b Singh	5		
	Extras	lb 9, w 4, nb 1	14	b 6, lb 8, w 1	15
			261	(4 wickets)	272

FoW (1): 1-131 (2), 2-180 (1), 3-208 (4), 4-217 (5), 5-238 (6), 6-246 (7), 7-253 (3), 8-255 (9), 9-256 (10), 10-261 (11)
FoW (2): 1-0 (1), 2-46 (3), 3-86 (2), 4-221 (5)

BARODA

1	*C.C.Williams	c Mohammad Shakeer b Lalith Mohan	153
2	S.S.Parab	c Shinde b Ojha	24
3	A.A.Bilakhia	c Pai b Ojha	68
4	R.K.Solanki	c Mohammad Shakeer b A.D.Yadav	78
5	Y.K.Pathan	b Ojha	28
6	†P.R.Shah	c Shoaib Ahmed b Lalith Mohan	68
7	I.K.Pathan	lbw b Shinde	26
8	A.R.Chauhan	lbw b Lalith Mohan	12
9	K.N.Panchal	not out	8
10	R.V.Pawar	c Ojha b Lalith Mohan	2
11	S.M.Singh		
	Extras	b 5, lb 2, nb 2	9
		(9 wickets, declared)	476

FoW (1): 1-46 (2), 2-178 (3), 3-314 (1), 4-354 (5), 5-354 (4), 6-425 (7), 7-456 (8), 8-467 (6), 9-476 (10)

Baroda Bowling

	O	M	R	W		O	M	R	W	
I.K.Pathan	25	4	71	4	1w,1nb	26	6	67	2	
Singh	16.2	3	39	3	3w	11	2	36	0	
Chauhan	5	1	17	0						
Pawar	27	8	55	2		21.4	7	57	0	
Y.K.Pathan	28	6	69	1	(3)	32	10	80	2	1w
Panchal	2	1	1	0						
Solanki					(5)	4	0	18	0	

Hyderabad Bowling

	O	M	R	W	
Shoaib Ahmed	15	4	52	0	1nb
A.D.Yadav	24	3	71	1	
Lalith Mohan	39.1	6	132	4	
Ojha	44	8	139	3	1nb
Shinde	21	3	68	1	
A.S.Yadav	2	0	7	0	

Umpires: S.Asnani and M.S.S.Ranawat. Referee: C.Sharma.   Toss: Hyderabad

Close of Play: 1st day: Hyderabad (1) 220-4 (Pai 41*, Shinde 2*, 91 overs); 2nd day: Baroda (1) 191-2 (Williams 91*, Solanki 6*, 75 overs); 3rd day: Hyderabad (2) 40-1 (Ravi Teja 27*, Pai 12*, 17 overs).

C.C.Williams's 153 took 329 balls in 451 minutes and included 11 fours and 1 six. A.S.Yadav's 101 took 207 balls in 300 minutes and included 9 fours and 2 sixes.

JAMMU AND KASHMIR v JHARKHAND

Played at Gandhi Memorial Science College Ground, Jammu, November 23, 24, 25, 26, 2007.
Ranji Trophy 2007/08 - Plate Group B
Jharkhand won by 250 runs.   (Points: Jammu and Kashmir 0, Jharkhand 5)

JHARKHAND

1	†S.Ghosh	lbw b Sharma	0	c Bhatt b Khajuria	43
2	*M.S.Vardhan	lbw b Beigh	14	c Bhatt b Beigh	79
3	A.K.Vidyarthi	lbw b Sharma	0	c Jehangir Ahmed b Khajuria	8
4	S.S.Tiwary	b Beigh	10	st Sarabjit Singh b Khajuria	169
5	Santosh Lal	c Sarabjit Singh b Sameer Ali	1	b Dutta	20
6	A.Hashmi	c Sarabjit Singh b Sharma	20	c Bhatt b Majid Dar	12
7	S.Gupta	lbw b Beigh	3	c Bhatt b Sameer Ali	13
8	S.Nadeem	c Majid Dar b Sharma	12	c Majid Dar b Sameer Ali	15
9	S.S.Rao	c Sarabjit Singh b Beigh	12	c Sarabjit Singh b Beigh	1
10	K.Sharma	not out	24	b Sameer Ali	4
11	S.R.Roy	b Sharma	4	not out	4
	Extras	b 2, lb 1, nb 2	5	b 15, lb 9, w 6, nb 5	35
			105		403

FoW (1): 1-0 (1), 2-0 (3), 3-20 (4), 4-25 (5), 5-29 (2), 6-37 (7), 7-60 (6), 8-75 (8), 9-75 (9), 10-105 (11)
FoW (2): 1-107 (1), 2-125 (3), 3-154 (2), 4-193 (5), 5-217 (6), 6-253 (7), 7-277 (8), 8-291 (9), 9-310 (10), 10-403 (4)

JAMMU AND KASHMIR

1	I.Dev Singh	b Sharma	0	c Vardhan b Rao	0
2	Jehangir Ahmed	b Rao	20	c Vidyarthi b Rao	5
3	A.Bhatt	lbw b Rao	5	lbw b Roy	43
4	Kavaljit Singh	c Gupta b Sharma	5	c Ghosh b Sharma	25
5	Majid Dar	c Ghosh b Sharma	0	c Ghosh b Santosh Lal	21
6	†Sarabjit Singh	run out (Ghosh)	13	lbw b Rao	11
7	Sameer Ali	c Roy b Rao	16	(10) b Santosh Lal	0
8	*V.Sharma	b Nadeem	26	(7) not out	5
9	S.Beigh	not out	33	(8) c Ghosh b Santosh Lal	0
10	R.Dutta	c Ghosh b Roy	1	(11) lbw b Santosh Lal	6
11	S.Khajuria	b Roy	0	(9) c Ghosh b Rao	0
	Extras	b 3, lb 8, nb 3	14	b 1, lb 2, w 1, nb 5	9
			133		125

FoW (1): 1-1 (1), 2-19 (3), 3-38 (4), 4-38 (2), 5-52 (5), 6-62 (6), 7-78 (7), 8-126 (8), 9-133 (10), 10-133 (11)
FoW (2): 1-1 (1), 2-10 (2), 3-61 (4), 4-82 (3), 5-113 (6), 6-115 (5), 7-115 (8), 8-116 (9), 9-117 (10), 10-125 (11)

Jammu and Kashmir Bowling

	O	M	R	W			O	M	R	W	
Sharma	11.1	4	20	5	2nb	(4)	13	2	66	0	2nb
Beigh	14	2	50	4		(1)	29	7	83	2	5w,1nb
Sameer Ali	7	2	19	1		(2)	26	4	57	3	
Khajuria	1	0	13	0		(5)	32.2	6	100	3	1nb
Dutta						(3)	16	3	44	1	
Majid Dar						(6)	7	1	12	1	
Dev Singh						(7)	3	0	17	0	1nb

Jharkhand Bowling

	O	M	R	W			O	M	R	W	
Sharma	14	1	57	3	1nb	(2)	21.1	12	34	1	5nb
Rao	14	1	56	3	2nb	(1)	19	6	32	4	
Nadeem	3	1	3	1		(4)	2	1	1	0	
Santosh Lal	2	0	6	0		(3)	12.3	1	48	4	1w
Roy	0.3	0	0	2			4	1	7	1	

Umpires: C.K.Nandan and B.Sharma. Referee: R.J.Bhatt.   Toss: Jharkhand

Close of Play: 1st day: Jharkhand (2) 12-0 (Ghosh 6*, Vardhan 1*, 7 overs); 2nd day: Jharkhand (2) 278-7 (Tiwary 64*, Rao 0*, 90 overs); 3rd day: Jammu and Kashmir (2) 85-4 (Majid Dar 6*, Sarabjit Singh 0*, 38.3 overs).

S.S.Tiwary's 169 took 279 balls in 411 minutes and included 21 fours and 2 sixes.

MUMBAI v DELHI

Played at Wankhede Stadium, Mumbai, November 23, 24, 25, 26, 2007.
Ranji Trophy 2007/08 - Elite Group A
Match drawn.   (Points: Mumbai 1, Delhi 3)

MUMBAI

1	S.O.Kukreja	b Sangwan	4	c Chopra b Sangwan		199
2	A.M.Rahane	b Sharma	8	c Bisht b Sangwan		20
3	R.G.Sharma	lbw b Sangwan	10	(5) c Bisht b Sangwan		0
4	*A.A.Muzumdar	c Kohli b Bhatia	8	lbw b Sangwan		7
5	P.T.Naik	c Sangwan b Narender Singh	40	(3) lbw b Narender Singh		23
6	A.M.Nayar	c Manhas b Sehwag	2	b Sangwan		93
7	A.B.Agarkar	c Nanda b Narender Singh	32	c Narender Singh b Bhatia		60
8	†V.R.Samant	c Sharma b Sangwan	12	b Sharma		6
9	R.R.Powar	c Sangwan b Sharma	20	c Manhas b Bhatia		3
10	B.P.Patel	not out	4	not out		8
11	A.M.Salvi	b Sharma	0	not out		4
	Extras	lb 12, w 7, nb 7	26	b 22, lb 13, w 3, nb 10		48
			166	(9 wickets, declared)		471

FoW (1): 1-4 (1), 2-23 (2), 3-32 (3), 4-64 (4), 5-67 (6), 6-120 (7), 7-133 (8), 8-159 (9), 9-165 (5), 10-166 (11)
FoW (2): 1-91 (2), 2-137 (3), 3-174 (4), 4-186 (5), 5-360 (6), 6-390 (1), 7-399 (8), 8-408 (9), 9-467 (7)

DELHI

1	A.S.Chopra	lbw b Salvi	12	lbw b Salvi	81
2	G.Gambhir	lbw b Nayar	89	not out	137
3	*V.Sehwag	c Samant b Nayar	16	lbw b Salvi	0
4	V.Kohli	c Samant b Salvi	19	lbw b Nayar	0
5	M.Manhas	run out (Agarkar)	4	not out	16
6	R.Bhatia	c Samant b Agarkar	49		
7	†P.Bisht	c Muzumdar b Patel	35		
8	Narender Singh	run out (Rahane)	1		
9	C.Nanda	c Samant b Salvi	9		
10	P.Sangwan	c Kukreja b Agarkar	0		
11	I.Sharma	not out	3		
	Extras	lb 9, nb 5	14	lb 5, w 6, nb 7	18
			251	(3 wickets)	252

FoW (1): 1-42 (1), 2-76 (3), 3-127 (4), 4-133 (5), 5-169 (2), 6-232 (7), 7-237 (8), 8-238 (6), 9-238 (10), 10-251 (9)
FoW (2): 1-188 (1), 2-188 (3), 3-189 (4)

Delhi Bowling

	O	M	R	W			O	M	R	W	
Sangwan	12	3	38	3	2w,1nb		27	4	102	5	2w,1nb
Sharma	10.3	1	60	3	1w,5nb		27	6	73	1	1w,5nb
Bhatia	7	2	7	1	1nb		10	2	28	2	1nb
Sehwag	6	0	21	1		(5)	14	0	63	0	
Nanda	4	2	2	0		(4)	22	3	105	0	
Narender Singh	5	2	26	2			11	1	60	1	
Manhas						(7)	1	0	5	0	

Mumbai Bowling

	O	M	R	W			O	M	R	W	
Agarkar	17	5	52	2	2nb	(2)	14	7	16	0	3nb
Salvi	20.4	5	44	3	3nb	(1)	17	5	31	2	4nb
Nayar	23	8	52	2		(4)	19	4	57	1	2w
Powar	14	1	62	0		(3)	26	4	77	0	
Patel	9	2	25	1			15	1	42	0	
Sharma	3	0	7	0			3	0	6	0	
Naik						(7)	2	0	18	0	

Umpires: G.A.Pratapkumar and S.K.Tarapore.   Referee: S.Banerjee.   Toss: Mumbai

Close of Play: 1st day: Delhi (1) 159-4 (Gambhir 81*, Bhatia 18*, 43 overs); 2nd day: Mumbai (2) 154-2 (Kukreja 89*, Muzumdar 2*, 44 overs); 3rd day: Delhi (2) 59-0 (Chopra 33*, Gambhir 22*, 20 overs).
S.O.Kukreja's 199 took 272 balls in 282 minutes and included 25 fours and 1 six. G.Gambhir's 137 took 278 balls in 378 minutes and included 13 fours and 1 six.

ORISSA v ANDHRA

Played at Barabati Stadium, Cuttack, November 23, 24, 25, 26, 2007.
Ranji Trophy 2007/08 - Elite Group B
Andhra won by 102 runs.   (Points: Orissa 0, Andhra 5)

ANDHRA

1	H.H.Watekar	lbw b Mohanty		2	b P.Das	19
2	L.N.P.Reddy	c S.S.Das b Jayachandra		23	c H.M.Das b Jayachandra	6
3	A.S.Verma	c H.M.Das b Mohanty		1	b Mullick	38
4	*†M.S.K.Prasad	b Jayachandra		21	b Mohanty	22
5	Y.Gnaneswara Rao	c Pati b Behera		28	c S.S.Das b P.Das	2
6	A.G.Pradeep	run out (Mullick)		1	c Behera b Mohanty	60
7	M.Suresh	c H.M.Das b Jayachandra		1	(10) not out	7
8	G.Shankar Rao	c R.R.Das b Jayachandra		73	(7) b P.Das	91
9	Mohammad Faiq	lbw b Jayachandra		13	(8) run out	8
10	D.Kalyankrishna	lbw b Jayachandra		0	(9) run out	0
11	P.D.Vijaykumar	not out		0		
	Extras	b 3, lb 6, nb 7		16	b 11, lb 15, nb 8	34
				179	(9 wickets, declared)	287

FoW (1): 1-5 (1), 2-7 (3), 3-52 (4), 4-53 (2), 5-63 (6), 6-65 (7), 7-127 (5), 8-176 (9), 9-176 (10), 10-179 (8)
FoW (2): 1-25 (1), 2-31 (2), 3-82 (4), 4-86 (5), 5-137 (3), 6-245 (6), 7-267 (8), 8-268 (9), 9-287 (7)

ORISSA

1	B.S.Pati	lbw b Gnaneswara Rao		6	lbw b Suresh	10
2	S.S.Das	c Pradeep b Vijaykumar		22	st Prasad b Shankar Rao	27
3	N.J.Behera	lbw b Watekar		31	lbw b Kalyankrishna	66
4	S.S.Biswal	c Kalyankrishna b Shankar Rao		12	(5) c and b Watekar	7
5	*P.M.Mullick	c Verma b Watekar		11	(4) c Pradeep b Kalyankrishna	6
6	P.Jayachandra	c Verma b Watekar		3	(7) b Kalyankrishna	18
7	R.R.Das	c Vijaykumar b Watekar		8	(8) c Prasad b Shankar Rao	18
8	†H.M.Das	st Prasad b Watekar		30	(6) run out	2
9	D.S.Mohanty	c Watekar b Suresh		5	run out	46
10	S.P.Khatua	lbw b Gnaneswara Rao		0	b Shankar Rao	5
11	P.Das	not out		1	not out	0
	Extras	b 10, nb 1		11	b 9, lb 10	19
				140		224

FoW (1): 1-23 (1), 2-41 (2), 3-62 (4), 4-83 (3), 5-90 (5), 6-93 (6), 7-100 (7), 8-118 (9), 9-131 (10), 10-140 (8)
FoW (2): 1-36 (2), 2-61 (1), 3-84 (4), 4-101 (5), 5-111 (6), 6-144 (3), 7-149 (7), 8-187 (8), 9-224 (9), 10-224 (10)

Orissa Bowling	O	M	R	W			O	M	R	W	
Mohanty	15	3	34	2	3nb		21	6	50	2	4nb
Khatua	12	3	33	0		(6)	10	0	32	0	
P.Das	12	0	37	0	4nb	(2)	20.3	5	53	3	4nb
Jayachandra	12.3	1	37	6		(3)	12	1	31	1	
Behera	21	9	25	1			17	4	49	0	
Mullick	7	4	4	0		(4)	8	1	25	1	
Biswal						(7)	2	0	7	0	
S.S.Das						(8)	3	0	14	0	

Andhra Bowling	O	M	R	W			O	M	R	W	
Kalyankrishna	5	1	12	0			15	6	22	3	
Vijaykumar	9	4	14	1			4	1	14	0	
Shankar Rao	16	12	15	1			25.1	8	54	3	
Mohammad Faiq	13	3	19	0		(6)	19	4	43	0	
Gnaneswara Rao	8	3	15	2			2	0	12	0	
Suresh	11	5	22	1		(4)	17	10	23	1	
Watekar	12.4	3	32	5	1nb		15	4	33	1	
Reddy	2	1	1	0							
Verma						(8)	2	1	4	0	

Umpires: M.S.Mahal and S.Rao.   Referee: S.C.Gudge.   Toss: Andhra

Close of Play: 1st day: Orissa (1) 21-0 (Pati 5*, S.S.Das 10*, 8 overs); 2nd day: Andhra (2) 67-2 (Verma 20*, Prasad 15*, 21 overs); 3rd day: Orissa (2) 32-0 (Pati 8*, S.S.Das 23*, 13 overs).

PUNJAB v UTTAR PRADESH

Played at Punjab Cricket Association Ground, Mohali, November 23, 24, 25, 26, 2007.
Ranji Trophy 2007/08 - Elite Group B
Match drawn.   (Points: Punjab 3, Uttar Pradesh 1)

PUNJAB

1	R.S.Ricky	b Tyagi	3	(6) not out	111
2	K.Goel	c Amir Khan b Kumar	2	b Kumar	10
3	S.Sohal	c Raina b Tyagi	8	(1) lbw b R.P.Srivastava	33
4	*P.Dharmani	lbw b Kumar	46	c Amir Khan b Kumar	15
5	†U.Kaul	c Amir Khan b Abid Khan	162	lbw b Tyagi	0
6	R.Inder Singh	c Amir Khan b Kumar	45	(3) c Amir Khan b Chawla	62
7	A.Kakkar	c Kaif b Chawla	3	c Kaif b Chawla	17
8	M.S.Gony	lbw b Kumar	8	b Chawla	10
9	Charanjeet Singh	c Kaif b Tyagi	40	c Amir Khan b Abid Khan	64
10	Birinder Singh	b Chawla	19	(11) not out	0
11	V.R.Singh	not out	11	(10) b Chawla	11
	Extras	b 22, lb 7, w 1, nb 4	34	b 8, lb 2, w 3, nb 5	18
			381	**(9 wickets, declared)**	**351**

FoW (1): 1-3 (1), 2-11 (3), 3-17 (2), 4-103 (4), 5-224 (6), 6-229 (7), 7-240 (8), 8-343 (9), 9-347 (5), 10-381 (10)
FoW (2): 1-37 (2), 2-48 (1), 3-91 (4), 4-92 (5), 5-166 (3), 6-192 (7), 7-218 (8), 8-334 (9), 9-351 (10)

UTTAR PRADESH

1	R.P.Srivastava	c Kaul b V.R.Singh	40	c Inder Singh b Gony	24
2	S.S.Shukla	c Dharmani b V.R.Singh	25	c Inder Singh b Gony	10
3	T.M.Srivastava	c Goel b V.R.Singh	4	c Dharmani b V.R.Singh	66
4	*M.Kaif	lbw b V.R.Singh	66	c V.R.Singh b Charanjeet Singh	71
5	S.K.Raina	c and b Birinder Singh	123	c V.R.Singh b Charanjeet Singh	5
6	R.U.Shukla	c Dharmani b V.R.Singh	1	not out	23
7	†Amir Khan	c Kaul b Gony	16		
8	P.P.Chawla	c Kaul b V.R.Singh	34		
9	P.Kumar	not out	38	(7) not out	15
10	Abid Khan	lbw b Gony	0		
11	S.Tyagi	c Dharmani b V.R.Singh	0		
	Extras	b 11, lb 6, w 3, nb 8	28	b 1, lb 3, w 4, nb 8	16
			375	**(5 wickets)**	**230**

FoW (1): 1-61 (2), 2-67 (3), 3-91 (1), 4-244 (4), 5-256 (6), 6-294 (7), 7-324 (5), 8-356 (8), 9-358 (10), 10-375 (11)
FoW (2): 1-36 (1), 2-36 (2), 3-164 (4), 4-174 (5), 5-203 (3)

Uttar Pradesh Bowling

	O	M	R	W			O	M	R	W	
Kumar	25.2	6	60	4			14	5	28	2	
Tyagi	30.4	5	107	3	1w,2nb		24	4	97	1	2w,1nb
Abid Khan	26	4	96	1	2nb		19	0	74	1	2nb
R.U.Shukla	2	0	5	0							
Chawla	21	2	84	2			30	9	75	4	2nb
R.P.Srivastava					(4)	16	6	42	1	1w
S.S.Shukla					(6)	8	0	25	0	

Punjab Bowling

	O	M	R	W			O	M	R	W	
V.R.Singh	21.1	2	112	7	2w,5nb		15	1	82	1	3w,4nb
Birinder Singh	10	1	54	1	2nb	(3)	5	0	29	0	
Gony	16	3	78	2	1w,1nb	(2)	11	3	31	2	1w
Kakkar	3	0	29	0		(5)	5	0	21	0	
Charanjeet Singh	14	1	54	0		(4)	15	1	63	2	
Goel	6	0	31	0							

Umpires: K.G.Lakshminarayan and C.R.Mohite. Referee: S.Mukherjee.   Toss: Uttar Pradesh

Close of Play: 1st day: Punjab (1) 324-7 (Kaul 151*, Charanjeet Singh 29*, 90 overs); 2nd day: Uttar Pradesh (1) 352-7 (Chawla 30*, Kumar 20*, 66 overs); 3rd day: Punjab (2) 238-7 (Ricky 76*, Charanjeet Singh 8*, 83 overs).

U.Kaul's 162 took 257 balls in 370 minutes and included 22 fours. S.K.Raina's 123 took 130 balls in 184 minutes and included 19 fours and 2 sixes. R.S.Ricky's 111 took 227 balls in 314 minutes and included 14 fours.

RAJASTHAN v SAURASHTRA

Played at K.L.Saini Ground, Jaipur, November 23, 24, 25, 26, 2007.
Ranji Trophy 2007/08 - Elite Group A
Saurashtra won by 200 runs.   (Points: Rajasthan 0, Saurashtra 5)

SAURASHTRA

1	†S.D.Jogiyani	c Bishnoi b Nishan Singh	21	(2) lbw b Mohammad Aslam	20
2	K.M.Vaghela	c Doru b Pankaj Singh	5	(1) c Afroz Khan b Mohammad Aslam	51
3	S.H.Kotak	c Jhalani b Mohammad Aslam	58	c Saxena b Mohammad Aslam	0
4	C.A.Pujara	c Mohammad Aslam b Afroz Khan	32	not out	151
5	P.S.Mehta	lbw b Afroz Khan	4		
6	*J.N.Shah	c Jhalani b Pankaj Singh	71	(5) not out	21
7	R.A.Jadeja	lbw b Pankaj Singh	18		
8	R.V.Dhruve	not out	46		
9	K.R.Makwana	lbw b Mohammad Aslam	13		
10	S.P.Jobanputra	lbw b Mohammad Aslam	6		
11	S.M.Maniar	c Bist b Pankaj Singh	5		
	Extras	b 7, lb 6, w 3, nb 12	28	b 1, lb 5, nb 4	10
			307	**(3 wickets, declared)**	**253**

FoW (1): 1-16 (2), 2-49 (1), 3-109 (4), 4-120 (5), 5-158 (3), 6-227 (7), 7-247 (6), 8-275 (9), 9-288 (10), 10-307 (11)
FoW (2): 1-29 (2), 2-29 (3), 3-201 (1)

RAJASTHAN

1	†R.B.Jhalani	c Jogiyani b Maniar	8	c Makwana b Maniar	1
2	G.K.Khoda	lbw b Dhruve	44	c Jogiyani b Dhruve	26
3	N.S.Doru	run out (Makwana)	29	st Jogiyani b Dhruve	32
4	V.A.Saxena	b Jobanputra	26	c Pujara b Jadeja	12
5	R.D.Bist	b Dhruve	21	lbw b Jobanputra	26
6	R.K.Bishnoi	b Jobanputra	5	c sub (N.R.Rathod) b Dhruve	36
7	Afroz Khan	lbw b Jobanputra	4	c and b Pujara	12
8	Shamsher Singh	c Makwana b Maniar	6	c Jogiyani b Dhruve	0
9	Pankaj Singh	lbw b Jobanputra	0	c Jobanputra b Pujara	17
10	*Mohammad Aslam	c Jogiyani b Maniar	1	c Jogiyani b Shah	15
11	Nishan Singh	not out	7	not out	5
	Extras	b 8, lb 7, w 4, nb 2	21	b 4, lb 1, nb 1	6
			172		**188**

FoW (1): 1-19 (1), 2-92 (2), 3-92 (3), 4-140 (5), 5-144 (4), 6-149 (6), 7-160 (7), 8-160 (9), 9-161 (10), 10-172 (8)
FoW (2): 1-7 (1), 2-39 (2), 3-70 (4), 4-72 (3), 5-128 (5), 6-137 (6), 7-137 (8), 8-159 (7), 9-170 (9), 10-188 (10)

Rajasthan Bowling

	O	M	R	W		O	M	R	W	
Pankaj Singh	29.4	4	91	4		20	3	59	0	
Nishan Singh	32	8	68	1	3w,10nb	15	4	39	0	1nb
Afroz Khan	18	4	33	2	2nb	10	2	49	0	3nb
Bishnoi	2	0	8	0	(6)	2	0	5	0	
Mohammad Aslam	27	11	54	3	(4)	18	7	51	3	
Shamsher Singh	12	2	40	0	(5)	10	4	44	0	

Saurashtra Bowling

	O	M	R	W		O	M	R	W	
Jobanputra	19	5	47	4	4w,1nb	12	3	45	1	1nb
Maniar	17.5	5	35	3	1nb	7	5	5	1	
Vaghela	4	1	10	0						
Dhruve	13	3	35	2	(3)	23	6	68	4	
Jadeja	8	2	20	0	(4)	15	4	33	1	
Makwana	2	0	10	0	(5)	5	0	20	0	
Pujara					(6)	2	1	4	2	
Shah					(7)	1.2	0	8	1	

Umpires: A.K.Chowdhury and R.Radhakrishnan.   Referee: S.Dutta.   Toss: Saurashtra

Close of Play: 1st day: Saurashtra (1) 220-5 (Shah 62*, Jadeja 13*, 90 overs); 2nd day: Rajasthan (1) 155-6 (Afroz Khan 4*, Shamsher Singh 2*, 55 overs); 3rd day: Saurashtra (2) 253-3 (Pujara 151*, Shah 21*, 75 overs).

C.A.Pujara's 151 took 190 balls in 261 minutes and included 23 fours and 2 sixes.

SERVICES v GUJARAT

Played at Palam A Ground, Model Sports Complex, Delhi, November 23, 24, 25, 2007.
Ranji Trophy 2007/08 - Plate Group A
Gujarat won by an innings and 193 runs.   (Points: Services 0, Gujarat 6)

GUJARAT

1	N.D.Modi	run out	51
2	H.R.Joshipura	c Israni b Pankaj Kumar	0
3	*†P.A.Patel	c Jasvir Singh b Mohanty	23
4	N.K.Patel	c Upadhyay b Mohanty	145
5	B.D.Thaker	st Israni b Patwal	121
6	D.M.Popat	lbw b Mohanty	3
7	T.K.Patel	c Jasvir Singh b Mohanty	8
8	M.B.Parmar	c Chatarjee b Sharma	0
9	A.M.Makda	c Israni b Mohanty	4
10	S.K.Trivedi	not out	51
11	N.Chaudhary	lbw b Yashpal Singh	0
	Extras	b 12, lb 6, w 3, nb 10	31
			437

FoW (1): 1-8 (2), 2-50 (3), 3-125 (1), 4-305 (4), 5-309 (6), 6-318 (7), 7-320 (8), 8-325 (9), 9-432 (5), 10-437 (11)

SERVICES

1	S.Chatarjee	lbw b Parmar	6	lbw b Makda	3
2	Tahir Khan	c Popat b Trivedi	11	b Makda	9
3	†D.S.Israni	c P.A.Patel b Makda	11	lbw b Makda	40
4	Jasvir Singh	lbw b Parmar	4	c T.K.Patel b Parmar	52
5	*Yashpal Singh	st P.A.Patel b Parmar	44	c Thaker b Parmar	18
6	S.Upadhyay	b Parmar	0	st P.A.Patel b Chaudhary	6
7	A.K.Mohanty	c Popat b Parmar	0	st P.A.Patel b Parmar	0
8	A.Sharma	b Trivedi	2	b Makda	1
9	S.S.Patwal	c P.A.Patel b Makda	14	b Parmar	4
10	Pankaj Kumar	lbw b Parmar	0	(11) not out	6
11	A.Hariprasad	not out	4	(10) b Parmar	0
	Extras	lb 1	1	b 4, lb 3, nb 1	8
			97		147

FoW (1): 1-13 (2), 2-29 (3), 3-29 (1), 4-38 (4), 5-38 (6), 6-38 (7), 7-51 (8), 8-85 (9), 9-93 (5), 10-97 (10)
FoW (2): 1-12 (2), 2-13 (1), 3-94 (3), 4-129 (4), 5-130 (5), 6-130 (7), 7-136 (6), 8-141 (9), 9-141 (8), 10-147 (10)

Services Bowling

	O	M	R	W	
Hariprasad	23	6	64	0	5nb
Pankaj Kumar	22	3	78	1	
Mohanty	38	8	113	5	3w,2nb
Sharma	35	6	89	1	3nb
Patwal	16	1	65	1	
Yashpal Singh	3.4	0	10	1	

Gujarat Bowling

	O	M	R	W		O	M	R	W	
Trivedi	9	2	19	2		9	2	31	0	
Makda	12	4	23	2		10	1	42	4	
Parmar	17	6	44	6		17.2	7	22	5	
Chaudhary	3	2	4	0	(5)	9	3	22	1	
T.K.Patel	1	0	6	0	(4)	3	1	23	0	1nb

Umpires: P.BhanuPrakash and P.S.Godbole.   Referee: M.InderSingh.   Toss: Services

Close of Play: 1st day: Gujarat (1) 230-3 (N.K.Patel 107*, Thaker 35*, 80 overs); 2nd day: Services (1) 40-6 (Yashpal Singh 7*, Sharma 0*, 26.4 overs).

The match was scheduled for four days but completed in three. N.K.Patel's 145 took 290 balls in 387 minutes and included 22 fours. B.D.Thaker's 121 took 262 balls in 379 minutes and included 16 fours. Pankaj Kumar retired hurt in the Services first innings having scored 0 (team score 85-8) - he returned when the score was 93-9.

TAMIL NADU v KARNATAKA

Played at M.A.Chidambaram Stadium, Chepauk, Chennai, November 23, 24, 25, 26, 2007.
Ranji Trophy 2007/08 - Elite Group A
Match drawn.   (Points: Tamil Nadu 3, Karnataka 1)

TAMIL NADU

1	A.Srikkanth	lbw b Vinay Kumar	0	c Uthappa b Aiyappa	11
2	M.Vijay Krishna	c Naidu b Aiyappa	32	c Akhil b Appanna	47
3	A.Mukund	run out (Vinay Kumar)	108	c Naidu b Aiyappa	0
4	*S.Badrinath	c Shinde b Joshi	143	c Joshi b Vinay Kumar	46
5	K.Vasudevadas	c Shinde b Joshi	12	c Akhil b Aiyappa	23
6	R.Srinivasan	c Vinay Kumar b Aiyappa	27	not out	50
7	†H.Gopinath	c Goud b Aiyappa	3	c Uthappa b Joshi	9
8	R.Ramkumar	c Akhil b Vinay Kumar	65	c Naidu b Vinay Kumar	20
9	V.Y.Mahesh	lbw b Joshi	0	lbw b Aiyappa	7
10	C.Suresh	not out	7	c Akhil b Joshi	12
11	P.Amarnath	c Pawan b Vinay Kumar	8		
	Extras	b 7, lb 5, w 2, nb 2	16	b 5, lb 4, w 3	12
			421	(9 wickets, declared)	237

FoW (1): 1-0 (1), 2-67 (2), 3-206 (3), 4-223 (5), 5-282 (6), 6-294 (7), 7-377 (8), 8-390 (9), 9-407 (4), 10-421 (11)
FoW (2): 1-17 (1), 2-17 (3), 3-93 (4), 4-128 (2), 5-139 (5), 6-155 (7), 7-185 (8), 8-204 (9), 9-237 (10)

KARNATAKA

1	R.V.Uthappa	c Gopinath b Mahesh	15	(2) c Vijay Krishna b Ramkumar	30
2	K.B.Pawan	b Amarnath	3	(1) c Mukund b Amarnath	13
3	S.P.Shinde	b Ramkumar	45	c Gopinath b Vasudevadas	35
4	C.Raghu	lbw b Ramkumar	6	not out	66
5	*Y.K.T.Goud	c Gopinath b Amarnath	34	not out	19
6	†V.S.T.Naidu	c Srikkanth b Ramkumar	36		
7	B.Akhil	lbw b Amarnath	33		
8	S.B.Joshi	lbw b Amarnath	33		
9	R.Vinay Kumar	c Suresh b Amarnath	5		
10	K.P.Appanna	not out	5		
11	N.C.Aiyappa	lbw b Ramkumar	2		
	Extras	w 1, nb 3	4	lb 1, nb 6	7
			221	(3 wickets)	170

FoW (1): 1-8 (2), 2-30 (1), 3-58 (4), 4-78 (3), 5-140 (6), 6-144 (5), 7-202 (8), 8-213 (7), 9-214 (9), 10-221 (11)
FoW (2): 1-38 (1), 2-53 (2), 3-115 (3)

Karnataka Bowling

	O	M	R	W		O	M	R	W	
Vinay Kumar	30.2	12	74	3	1w,2nb	20	3	64	2	2w
Aiyappa	23	1	73	3		17	5	45	4	1w
Akhil	15	3	52	0	1w (4)	7	1	19	0	
Joshi	37	10	103	3	(3)	11.3	4	38	2	
Appanna	16	0	73	0		18	1	62	0	
Raghu	11	1	34	0						

Tamil Nadu Bowling

	O	M	R	W		O	M	R	W	
Mahesh	16.3	3	56	1	1w,3nb (2)	13	1	71	0	6nb
Amarnath	21.3	8	74	5	(1)	13	6	25	1	
Mukund	1	0	6	0						
Ramkumar	27.2	8	65	4	(3)	14	4	34	1	
Suresh	5	1	20	0		17	8	16	0	
Vasudevadas					(4)	11	2	23	4	

Umpires: S.N.Bandekar and S.D.Ranade. Referee: J.N.Jadeja.   Toss: Tamil Nadu

Close of Play: 1st day: Tamil Nadu (1) 289-5 (Badrinath 93*, Gopinath 3*, 90 overs); 2nd day: Karnataka (1) 144-6 (Akhil 1*, 44.1 overs); 3rd day: Tamil Nadu (2) 185-6 (Srinivasan 17*, Ramkumar 20*, 61 overs).

A.Mukund's 108 took 176 balls in 266 minutes and included 13 fours. S.Badrinath's 143 took 304 balls in 421 minutes and included 14 fours and 2 sixes.

VIDARBHA v TRIPURA

Played at Vidarbha Cricket Association Ground, Nagpur, November 23, 24, 25, 26, 2007.
Ranji Trophy 2007/08 - Plate Group A
Vidarbha won by 13 runs.   (Points: Vidarbha 5, Tripura 0)

VIDARBHA

1	F.Y.Fazal	c and b T.S.Saha	110	c Dutta b Manoj Singh		23
2	H.V.Shitoot	c Chowdhury b Jain	0	run out		50
3	A.S.Naidu	c Dutta b Chanda	87	c Manoj Singh b T.S.Saha		15
4	M.S.Acharya	c Dutta b Jain	0	(7) c Chanda b Shetty		7
5	†A.V.Deshpande	b Jain	17	(4) c Chowdhury b Shetty		2
6	R.S.Paradkar	c Banik b Chanda	24	(8) st Dutta b T.S.Saha		41
7	S.N.Binkar	c Banik b Chanda	6	(6) c Manoj Singh b T.S.Saha		11
8	H.S.Joshi	c Manoj Singh b Debnath	5	(5) c Debnath b Shetty		8
9	*P.V.Gandhe	c sub (A.B.Dey) b T.S.Saha	28	b Jain		3
10	S.R.Singh	c Shetty b Chanda	11	run out		3
11	Mohammad Hashim	not out	4	not out		2
	Extras	lb 4, w 3, nb 16	23	b 1, lb 3, w 13, nb 4		21
			315			**186**

FoW (1): 1-2 (2), 2-162 (1), 3-197 (4), 4-216 (3), 5-232 (5), 6-241 (7), 7-250 (8), 8-300 (6), 9-304 (9), 10-315 (10)
FoW (2): 1-58 (1), 2-92 (3), 3-101 (4), 4-104 (2), 5-113 (5), 6-124 (7), 7-151 (6), 8-161 (9), 9-182 (10), 10-186 (8)

TRIPURA

1	Manoj Singh	lbw b Singh	5	c Acharya b Singh	62
2	S.S.Roy	c Deshpande b Acharya	12	c Shitoot b Mohammad Hashim	2
3	R.H.Saha	c Fazal b Singh	58	lbw b Shitoot	21
4	S.D.Chowdhury	c Deshpande b Acharya	2	(7) run out	28
5	N.S.Shetty	b Acharya	16	(4) c Acharya b Singh	130
6	*T.K.Chanda	c Naidu b Singh	9	c Paradkar b Gandhe	0
7	R.D.Banik	b Naidu	14	(5) c Deshpande b Singh	6
8	†R.K.Dutta	not out	47	b Singh	9
9	T.S.Saha	b Gandhe	11	run out	8
10	V.Jain	c Naidu b Mohammad Hashim	4	b Singh	5
11	J.S.Debnath	c Deshpande b Mohammad Hashim	7	not out	0
	Extras	b 4, lb 10, nb 2	16	lb 8, nb 8	16
			201		**287**

FoW (1): 1-15 (1), 2-23 (2), 3-29 (4), 4-59 (5), 5-68 (6), 6-109 (7), 7-142 (3), 8-161 (9), 9-171 (10), 10-201 (11)
FoW (2): 1-9 (2), 2-67 (3), 3-141 (1), 4-164 (5), 5-166 (6), 6-241 (7), 7-260 (8), 8-274 (9), 9-280 (10), 10-287 (4)

Tripura Bowling

	O	M	R	W			O	M	R	W	
Jain	26	6	51	3	2nb		6	0	33	1	4nb
Chanda	27.4	7	68	4	1w,13nb		6	0	39	0	
Manoj Singh	20	9	34	0	2w		5	0	19	1	
T.S.Saha	37	10	98	2			15.3	0	60	3	5w
Debnath	15	5	45	1	1nb						
Shetty	2	1	4	0		(5)	13	1	31	3	3w
Chowdhury	5	2	11	0							

Vidarbha Bowling

	O	M	R	W			O	M	R	W	
Singh	29.4	12	43	3			24.2	4	90	5	4nb
Mohammad Hashim	17.4	4	60	2	2nb		7	2	16	1	1nb
Naidu	13.2	4	28	1			4	2	6	0	
Acharya	20	8	29	3			9	2	35	0	
Gandhe	12	0	26	1			22	1	82	1	2nb
Shitoot	1	0	1	0		(7)	10	2	38	1	
Joshi						(6)	3	1	12	0	

Umpires: S.Lakshmanan and S.M.Raju. Referee: Vidya Bhaskar.   Toss: Vidarbha

Close of Play: 1st day: Vidarbha (1) 227-4 (Deshpande 17*, Paradkar 0*, 90 overs); 2nd day: Tripura (1) 80-5 (R.H.Saha 22*, Banik 3*, 45 overs); 3rd day: Vidarbha (2) 150-6 (Binkar 11*, Paradkar 16*, 39 overs).
F.Y.Fazal's 110 took 237 balls in 286 minutes and included 19 fours and 1 six. N.S.Shetty's 130 took 137 balls in 226 minutes and included 13 fours and 1 six.

119

INDIA v PAKISTAN

Played at Eden Gardens, Kolkata, November 30, December 1, 2, 3, 4, 2007.
Pakistan in India 2007/08 - 2nd Test
Match drawn.

INDIA

1	W.Jaffer	c Kamran Akmal b Sohail Tanvir	202	b Danish Kaneria		56
2	K.D.Karthik	c Younis Khan b Sohail Tanvir	1	c Misbah-ul-Haq b Danish Kaneria		28
3	R.S.Dravid	c Kamran Akmal b Danish Kaneria	50	(5) not out		8
4	S.R.Tendulkar	b Danish Kaneria	82			
5	S.C.Ganguly	c Sohail Tanvir b Salman Butt	102	(4) b Shoaib Akhtar		46
6	V.V.S.Laxman	not out	112			
7	†M.S.Dhoni	not out	50	(3) b Shoaib Akhtar		37
8	*A.Kumble					
9	Harbhajan Singh					
10	Z.Khan					
11	M.M.Patel					
	Extras	b 8, lb 5, w 1, nb 3	17	lb 3, nb 6		9
		(5 wickets, declared)	616	(4 wickets, declared)		184

FoW (1): 1-2 (2), 2-138 (3), 3-313 (4), 4-375 (1), 5-538 (5)
FoW (2): 1-75 (2), 2-95 (1), 3-166 (3), 4-184 (4)

PAKISTAN

1	Salman Butt	c Dravid b Harbhajan Singh	42	(3) lbw b Kumble	11
2	Yasir Hameed	lbw b Kumble	21	(1) c and b Khan	14
3	*Younis Khan	c Dhoni b Patel	43	(4) not out	107
4	Mohammad Yousuf	b Harbhajan Singh	6	(6) not out	44
5	Misbah-ul-Haq	not out	161	b Patel	6
6	Faisal Iqbal	lbw b Kumble	0		
7	†Kamran Akmal	b Harbhajan Singh	119	(2) b Kumble	14
8	Mohammad Sami	c Jaffer b Laxman	38		
9	Sohail Tanvir	c Dravid b Kumble	0		
10	Shoaib Akhtar	c Dravid b Harbhajan Singh	0		
11	Danish Kaneria	b Harbhajan Singh	0		
	Extras	b 8, lb 7, w 1, nb 10	26	b 8, lb 6, nb 4	18
			456	(4 wickets)	214

FoW (1): 1-38 (2), 2-77 (1), 3-85 (4), 4-134 (3), 5-150 (6), 6-357 (7), 7-448 (8), 8-449 (9), 9-452 (10), 10-456 (11)
FoW (2): 1-22 (1), 2-37 (2), 3-65 (3), 4-78 (5)

Pakistan Bowling	O	M	R	W		O	M	R	W	
Shoaib Akhtar	24	2	84	0	1w	12.4	0	46	2	5nb
Sohail Tanvir	39	6	166	2	1nb	9	0	41	0	1nb
Mohammad Sami	29	2	99	0	2nb	5	1	28	0	
Danish Kaneria	50	7	194	2		15	0	61	2	
Yasir Hameed	4	0	24	0						
Salman Butt	6.5	0	36	1	(5)	1	0	5	0	

India Bowling	O	M	R	W			O	M	R	W	
Khan	25.2	8	69	0	5nb		8	0	32	1	3nb
Patel	21	4	85	1	1w	(3)	10	3	21	1	
Harbhajan Singh	45.5	9	122	5	1nb	(4)	31	5	67	0	
Kumble	47	14	122	3	3nb	(2)	25	4	73	2	1nb
Tendulkar	7	1	32	0			3	0	7	0	
Ganguly	4	1	9	0							
Laxman	1	0	2	0							

Umpires: B.R.Doctrove and R.E.Koertzen. Third umpire: A.M.Saheba. Referee: R.S.Madugalle. Toss: India
Close of Play: 1st day: India (1) 352-3 (Jaffer 192*, Ganguly 17*, 84.3 overs); 2nd day: Pakistan (1) 50-1 (Salman Butt 26*, Younis Khan 3*, 16 overs); 3rd day: Pakistan (1) 358-6 (Misbah-ul-Haq 108*, Mohammad Sami 0*, 104 overs); 4th day: India (2) 141-2 (Dhoni 28*, Ganguly 24*, 36 overs).
Man of the Match: W.Jaffer.
W.Jaffer's 202 took 274 balls in 401 minutes and included 34 fours. S.C.Ganguly's 102 took 156 balls in 245 minutes and included 14 fours. V.V.S.Laxman's 112 took 178 balls in 264 minutes and included 15 fours. Misbah-ul-Haq's 161 took 351 balls in 542 minutes and included 13 fours and 1 six. Kamran Akmal's 119 took 210 balls in 259 minutes and included 20 fours. Younis Khan's 107 took 182 balls in 211 minutes and included 14 fours.

ASSAM v SERVICES

Played at Nehru Stadium, Guwahati, December 1, 2, 3, 4, 2007.
Ranji Trophy 2007/08 - Plate Group A
Assam won by six wickets.   (Points: Assam 5, Services 0)

SERVICES

1	S.Chatarjee	b K.S.Das	5	c Bordoloi b Baruah		19
2	Tahir Khan	c Goswami b Konwar	142	c and b Konwar		55
3	†D.S.Israni	c R.N.Das b Suresh	15	run out		44
4	Jasvir Singh	c Baruah b K.S.Das	23	(5) not out		13
5	*Yashpal Singh	c R.N.Das b Konwar	40	(4) c sub b Baruah		14
6	Mumtaz Qadir	b Baruah	37	not out		4
7	A.Sharma	c Ramesh b K.S.Das	10			
8	A.K.Mohanty	lbw b Goswami	57			
9	S.S.Patwal	b K.S.Das	34			
10	A.Hariprasad	c R.N.Das b Goswami	9			
11	Rakesh Kumar	not out	6			
	Extras	b 12, lb 14, w 1, nb 1	28	b 8, lb 1		9
			406	(4 wickets, declared)		**158**

FoW (1): 1-25 (1), 2-65 (3), 3-137 (4), 4-220 (5), 5-263 (2), 6-284 (7), 7-298 (6), 8-384 (9), 9-394 (8), 10-406 (10)
FoW (2): 1-37 (1), 2-121 (3), 3-141 (4), 4-146 (2)

ASSAM

1	S.Suresh	run out (Mumtaz Qadir)	49			
2	P.M.Das	lbw b Rakesh Kumar	19	(1) c Israni b Mohanty		35
3	N.H.Bordoloi	b Rakesh Kumar	0	run out		1
4	S.Ramesh	c Jasvir Singh b Sharma	1	(2) c Yashpal Singh b Sharma		97
5	M.D.Talukdar	lbw b Mohanty	17	c Tahir Khan b Sharma		32
6	*S.Sharath	c Mumtaz Qadir b Sharma	9	(4) not out		94
7	†R.N.Das	c Israni b Rakesh Kumar	49	(6) not out		19
8	D.S.Goswami	lbw b Mohanty	10			
9	A.Konwar	not out	22			
10	B.B.Baruah	b Rakesh Kumar	12			
11	K.S.Das	lbw b Rakesh Kumar	12			
	Extras	b 23, lb 13, w 6, nb 17	59	b 6, lb 9, w 1, nb 8, pen 5		29
			259	(4 wickets)		**307**

FoW (1): 1-75 (2), 2-79 (3), 3-91 (4), 4-111 (1), 5-133 (6), 6-139 (5), 7-179 (8), 8-206 (7), 9-236 (10), 10-259 (11)
FoW (2): 1-116 (1), 2-123 (3), 3-193 (2), 4-260 (5)

Assam Bowling

	O	M	R	W			O	M	R	W	
Goswami	18.4	1	61	2	1w,1nb	(2)	4	1	15	0	
K.S.Das	29	10	81	4		(1)	6	3	11	0	
Konwar	33	5	98	2		(4)	11	1	50	1	
Suresh	13	2	43	1		(5)	3	1	15	0	
Baruah	36	13	73	1		(3)	11	0	58	2	
Talukdar	6	1	24	0							

Services Bowling

	O	M	R	W			O	M	R	W	
Rakesh Kumar	29	7	82	5	2w,4nb		9	0	32	0	
Hariprasad	12	2	42	0	3nb		5	0	10	0	1nb
Sharma	26	13	40	2	7nb		25	2	92	2	1w,2nb
Mohanty	17	9	35	2	3nb		24	3	86	1	3nb
Patwal	7	0	24	0			6	1	24	0	2nb
Yashpal Singh	1	1	0	0		(7)	5.4	0	34	0	
Chatarjee						(6)	2	0	9	0	

Umpires: K.Murali and S.K.Sharma. Referee: R.Jadhav.   Toss: Services

Close of Play: 1st day: Services (1) 272-5 (Mumtaz Qadir 25*, Sharma 5*, 88.1 overs); 2nd day: Assam (1) 92-3 (Suresh 40*, Talukdar 0*, 31 overs); 3rd day: Services (2) 83-1 (Tahir Khan 22*, Israni 33*, 25.2 overs).

Tahir Khan's 142 took 254 balls in 322 minutes and included 19 fours.

BENGAL v PUNJAB

Played at Kanchanjungwa Krirangan, Siliguri, December 1, 2, 3, 4, 2007.
Ranji Trophy 2007/08 - Elite Group B
Bengal won by nine wickets.   (Points: Bengal 5, Punjab 0)

PUNJAB

1	R.S.Ricky	c Saha b Bose	23	c Tiwary b Bose		19
2	K.Goel	b Dinda	56	lbw b Dinda		21
3	R.Inder Singh	c sub b Dinda	1	c Saha b Sarkar		33
4	*P.Dharmani	b Sarkar	42	c Ghosh b Sarkar		43
5	†U.Kaul	c sub (P.I.Mukherjee) b Sarkar	35	c Tiwary b Bose		38
6	S.Sohal	c Dinda b Mondal	2	c Ghosh b Dinda		95
7	A.Kakkar	not out	34	c Saha b Bose		7
8	Gagandeep Singh	c Saha b Bose	9	c Ghosh b Dinda		14
9	Charanjeet Singh	c Saha b Bose	8	lbw b Lahiri		18
10	M.S.Gony	b Dinda	5	b Sarkar		17
11	V.R.Singh	b Dinda	0	not out		2
	Extras	b 9, lb 10, w 2, nb 5	26	b 2, lb 2, w 1, nb 3		8
			241			315

FoW (1): 1-78 (1), 2-79 (3), 3-124 (2), 4-177 (4), 5-184 (5), 6-187 (6), 7-202 (8), 8-232 (9), 9-241 (10), 10-241 (11)
FoW (2): 1-36 (2), 2-66 (1), 3-78 (3), 4-158 (4), 5-176 (5), 6-199 (7), 7-220 (8), 8-251 (9), 9-270 (10), 10-315 (6)

BENGAL

1	A.P.Majumdar	c Dharmani b Gagandeep Singh	99	not out	29
2	A.S.Das	lbw b Gagandeep Singh	103	c Kaul b Gony	5
3	S.M.Ghosh	lbw b V.R.Singh	16	not out	9
4	M.K.Tiwary	c sub (Sarabjit Singh) b Goel	138		
5	†W.P.Saha	lbw b Gony	8		
6	*L.R.Shukla	b Kakkar	74		
7	K.H.Mondal	not out	37		
8	S.S.Lahiri				
9	S.S.Sarkar				
10	A.B.Dinda				
11	R.R.Bose				
	Extras	b 7, lb 7, w 1, nb 23	38	lb 1, nb 1	2
		(6 wickets, declared)	513	(1 wicket)	45

FoW (1): 1-194 (1), 2-242 (3), 3-247 (2), 4-275 (5), 5-398 (6), 6-513 (4)
FoW (2): 1-8 (2)

Bengal Bowling

	O	M	R	W			O	M	R	W	
Bose	31	13	56	3	1w		27	8	55	3	
Sarkar	29	11	82	2	1nb		23	7	81	3	
Dinda	24	8	42	4	1w		23	1	117	3	1w
Shukla	4	2	15	0	1nb						
Lahiri	9	1	23	0	3nb	(4)	10	1	36	1	3nb
Mondal	1	0	4	1							
Majumdar						(5)	3	0	22	0	

Punjab Bowling

	O	M	R	W			O	M	R	W	
Gagandeep Singh	26	5	93	2	2nb		5.3	1	16	0	1nb
V.R.Singh	24	5	97	1	1w,13nb						
Gony	29	5	107	1	6nb	(2)	5	0	28	1	
Inder Singh	12	2	44	0							
Charanjeet Singh	18	1	72	0	1nb						
Kakkar	24	5	68	1							
Goel	2.2	0	18	1							

Umpires: R.M.Deshpande and S.S.Hazare. Referee: D.Vasu.   Toss: Punjab

Close of Play: 1st day: Punjab (1) 210-7 (Kakkar 14*, Charanjeet Singh 2*, 85 overs); 2nd day: Bengal (1) 231-1 (Das 93*, Ghosh 12*, 72.3 overs); 3rd day: Punjab (2) 64-1 (Ricky 19*, Inder Singh 21*, 27 overs).
A.S.Das's 103 took 227 balls in 330 minutes and included 14 fours. M.K.Tiwary's 138 took 183 balls in 234 minutes and included 17 fours.

GUJARAT v VIDARBHA

Played at Sardar Vallabhai Patel Stadium, Valsad, December 1, 2, 3, 4, 2007.
Ranji Trophy 2007/08 - Plate Group A
Gujarat won by 50 runs.   (Points: Gujarat 5, Vidarbha 0)

GUJARAT

1	*†P.A.Patel	st Deshpande b Gandhe	31	c Deshpande b Naidu	12
2	N.D.Modi	c Shitoot b Naidu	22	lbw b Mohammad Hashim	0
3	N.K.Patel	c Naidu b Singh	93	c and b Singh	71
4	B.D.Thaker	run out (Shrivastava)	61	(6) lbw b Gandhe	17
5	J.D.Desai	st Deshpande b Gandhe	19	(4) c Deshpande b Singh	8
6	D.M.Popat	c Fazal b Mohammad Hashim	19	(5) lbw b Naidu	0
7	T.K.Patel	c Deshpande b Singh	20	b Singh	2
8	M.B.Parmar	c Fazal b Mohammad Hashim	9	c Deshpande b Naidu	1
9	A.M.Makda	c Deshpande b Mohammad Hashim	1	(10) lbw b Naidu	0
10	Amit Singh	not out	5	(9) run out	4
11	H.A.Majmudar	c Deshpande b Mohammad Hashim	17	not out	0
	Extras	b 1, lb 5, nb 9	15	b 1, nb 5	6
			312		**121**

FoW (1): 1-49 (2), 2-63 (1), 3-197 (4), 4-227 (3), 5-238 (5), 6-272 (7), 7-284 (6), 8-286 (9), 9-292 (8), 10-312 (11)
FoW (2): 1-2 (2), 2-35 (1), 3-48 (4), 4-52 (5), 5-94 (6), 6-99 (7), 7-116 (3), 8-117 (8), 9-117 (10), 10-121 (9)

VIDARBHA

1	F.Y.Fazal	b Parmar	44	c Parmar b Amit Singh	78
2	H.V.Shitoot	c Thaker b Majmudar	0	(4) lbw b Makda	0
3	A.S.Naidu	c T.K.Patel b Parmar	34	b Makda	0
4	†A.V.Deshpande	c N.K.Patel b T.K.Patel	24	(2) c P.A.Patel b Makda	9
5	R.L.Jangid	c P.A.Patel b Makda	61	run out	15
6	S.U.Shrivastava	not out	26	c Thaker b Parmar	0
7	M.S.Acharya	c T.K.Patel b Amit Singh	5	c P.A.Patel b Parmar	38
8	H.S.Joshi	b Amit Singh	0	c P.A.Patel b Amit Singh	12
9	*P.V.Gandhe	c N.K.Patel b Amit Singh	0	c P.A.Patel b Amit Singh	2
10	S.R.Singh	c Desai b Amit Singh	0	(11) not out	0
11	Mohammad Hashim	b Majmudar	0	(10) c P.A.Patel b Makda	2
	Extras	lb 5, w 2, nb 7	14	b 9, lb 7, nb 3	19
			208		**175**

FoW (1): 1-1 (2), 2-77 (3), 3-84 (1), 4-148 (4), 5-202 (5), 6-207 (7), 7-207 (8), 8-207 (9), 9-207 (10), 10-208 (11)
FoW (2): 1-40 (2), 2-40 (3), 3-46 (4), 4-84 (5), 5-86 (6), 6-158 (7), 7-160 (1), 8-162 (9), 9-171 (10), 10-175 (8)

Vidarbha Bowling

	O	M	R	W			O	M	R	W	
Singh	27	2	83	2	8nb		20	7	40	3	5nb
Mohammad Hashim	20.5	3	63	4	1nb		10	3	34	1	
Naidu	12	4	31	1			13.1	6	18	4	
Gandhe	27	7	63	2			10	3	24	1	
Shitoot	3	1	21	0							
Acharya	7	2	17	0		(5)	1	0	4	0	
Jangid	1	0	7	0							
Joshi	7	2	21	0							

Gujarat Bowling

	O	M	R	W				O	M	R	W	
Majmudar	19.4	9	25	2	4nb	(2)		8	2	20	0	1nb
Makda	17	6	43	1	2w	(1)		21	8	41	4	
Amit Singh	22	8	57	4	2nb			20.5	8	27	3	
Parmar	25	7	47	2				24	10	56	2	
T.K.Patel	10	2	28	1	1nb			3	0	15	0	2nb
Popat	1	0	3	0								

Umpires: U.L.Dubey and A.V.Jayaprakash.   Toss: Vidarbha

Close of Play: 1st day: Gujarat (1) 270-5 (Popat 12*, T.K.Patel 19*, 92 overs); 2nd day: Vidarbha (1) 189-4 (Jangid 57*, Shrivastava 16*, 75 overs); 3rd day: Vidarbha (2) 31-0 (Fazal 20*, Deshpande 6*, 11 overs).

HIMACHAL PRADESH v DELHI

Played at Himachal Pradesh Cricket Association Stadium, Dharmasala, December 1, 2, 3, 4, 2007.
Ranji Trophy 2007/08 - Elite Group A
Match drawn.   (Points: Himachal Pradesh 3, Delhi 1)

HIMACHAL PRADESH

1	M.Gupta	c Bhandari b Nanda	49	lbw b Nanda		6
2	*S.Sharma	lbw b Sharma	9	lbw b Sharma		0
3	M.Sharma	lbw b Nanda	40	c sub (V.Kohli) b Sharma		0
4	A.Mannu	c Bisht b Bhandari	4	lbw b Sharma		11
5	B.Sharma	lbw b Nanda	22	(7) not out		21
6	P.Dogra	b Nanda	81	(5) lbw b Sharma		0
7	†M.S.Bisla	c Bisht b Awana	50	(6) not out		24
8	Sarandeep Singh	b Chopra	37			
9	V.Bhatia	b Sharma	2			
10	A.K.Thakur	run out (Bhatia)	0			
11	V.Malik	not out	0			
	Extras	b 8, lb 8, nb 33	49	b 4, nb 17		21
			343	(5 wickets)		83

FoW (1): 1-32 (2), 2-103 (1), 3-108 (4), 4-151 (5), 5-154 (3), 6-253 (7), 7-338 (8), 8-343 (9), 9-343 (6), 10-343 (10)
FoW (2): 1-2 (2), 2-9 (3), 3-21 (1), 4-22 (5), 5-34 (4)

DELHI

1	G.Gambhir	lbw b Thakur	13	c Bisla b Thakur		103
2	*V.Sehwag	b Thakur	9	c Bisla b Thakur		32
3	A.S.Chopra	c S.Sharma b Malik	7	c Mannu b Sarandeep Singh		215
4	S.Dhawan	lbw b Malik	5	b Thakur		13
5	R.Bhatia	c Bisla b Malik	7	(6) st Bisla b Bhatia		39
6	†P.Bisht	c Bisla b Thakur	9	(7) not out		17
7	M.Manhas	c S.Sharma b Malik	0	(5) c S.Sharma b Malik		24
8	C.Nanda	lbw b Thakur	5			
9	A.Bhandari	not out	4			
10	I.Sharma	b Malik	1			
11	P.Awana	b Malik	0			
	Extras	lb 5, nb 10	15	b 12, lb 7, w 4, nb 16		39
			75	(6 wickets, declared)		482

FoW (1): 1-25 (2), 2-28 (1), 3-38 (3), 4-48 (5), 5-51 (4), 6-59 (7), 7-64 (8), 8-74 (6), 9-75 (10), 10-75 (11)
FoW (2): 1-53 (2), 2-283 (1), 3-310 (4), 4-367 (5), 5-442 (6), 6-482 (3)

Delhi Bowling

	O	M	R	W			O	M	R	W	
Bhandari	19	7	39	1	3nb	(4)	2	0	12	0	3nb
Sharma	32	6	103	2	28nb	(1)	15	3	44	4	10nb
Awana	22	7	42	1		(2)	4	2	8	0	
Bhatia	8	3	18	0							
Nanda	39.3	15	74	4	2nb	(3)	11	5	14	1	
Sehwag	21	6	50	0		(5)	2	1	1	0	
Chopra	1	0	1	1		(6)	1	1	0	0	

Himachal Pradesh Bowling

	O	M	R	W			O	M	R	W	
Thakur	12	0	45	4	7nb		17	2	72	3	6nb
Malik	11.3	5	25	6	2nb		30	8	84	1	5nb
Bhatia						(3)	39	4	140	1	2w,5nb
B.Sharma						(4)	3	0	13	0	2w
Sarandeep Singh						(5)	44.2	4	131	1	
Dogra						(6)	10	2	17	0	
S.Sharma						(7)	2	0	6	0	

Umpires: P.Bhanu Prakash and S.Dendapani.   Referee: B.Raghunath.   Toss: Delhi

Close of Play: 1st day: Himachal Pradesh (1) 228-5 (Dogra 32*, Bisla 39*, 90 overs); 2nd day: Delhi (2) 38-0 (Gambhir 3*, Sehwag 31*, 4 overs); 3rd day: Delhi (2) 335-3 (Chopra 146*, Manhas 10*, 94 overs).
G.Gambhir's 103 took 199 balls in 302 minutes and included 11 fours. A.S.Chopra's 215 took 448 balls in 448 minutes and included 21 fours and 2 sixes.

HYDERABAD v ORISSA

Played at Rajiv Gandhi International Stadium, Uppal, Hyderabad, December 1, 2, 3, 4, 2007.
Ranji Trophy 2007/08 - Elite Group B
Orissa won by nine wickets.   (Points: Hyderabad 0, Orissa 5)

HYDERABAD

1	D.S.Manohar	c Behera b Sehgal	41	b Jayachandra		22
2	D.B.Ravi Teja	c H.M.Das b D.S.Mohanty	81	c D.S.Mohanty b Sehgal		37
3	S.A.Pai	c Behera b Jayachandra	6	c Parida b D.S.Mohanty		48
4	*A.S.Yadav	c S.S.Das b Sehgal	7	c Behera b D.S.Mohanty		17
5	A.J.Shinde	c Parida b D.S.Mohanty	2	(6) c Pati b Behera		7
6	B.S.K.Yadav	lbw b D.S.Mohanty	2	(5) c Sehgal b R.K.Mohanty		6
7	M.P.Arjun	c S.S.Das b D.S.Mohanty	19	c H.M.Das b D.S.Mohanty		3
8	†Habeeb Ahmed	c D.S.Mohanty b Sehgal	0	c H.M.Das b D.S.Mohanty		10
9	P.P.Ojha	c Sehgal b D.S.Mohanty	33	not out		4
10	A.D.Yadav	not out	28	lbw b D.S.Mohanty		0
11	A.LalithMohan	lbw b Sehgal	9	lbw b Sehgal		0
	Extras	b 1, lb 7, w 1, nb 3	12	lb 1, w 1, nb 4		6
			240			160

FoW (1): 1-97 (2), 2-114 (3), 3-137 (1), 4-140 (4), 5-142 (5), 6-143 (6), 7-144 (8), 8-184 (7), 9-218 (9), 10-240 (11)
FoW (2): 1-54 (1), 2-72 (2), 3-100 (4), 4-118 (5), 5-139 (6), 6-143 (3), 7-150 (7), 8-159 (8), 9-159 (10), 10-160 (11)

ORISSA

1	B.S.Pati	c Habeeb Ahmed b A.D.Yadav	24	run out		52
2	*S.S.Das	c Ravi Teja b Ojha	38	not out		40
3	N.J.Behera	st Habeeb Ahmed b Ojha	103	not out		0
4	R.R.Parida	c Shinde b Ojha	44			
5	P.Jayachandra	b A.D.Yadav	29			
6	R.R.Das	c Arjun b Ojha	25			
7	†H.M.Das	lbw b Ojha	0			
8	R.K.Mohanty	c Shinde b Ojha	5			
9	D.S.Mohanty	b A.D.Yadav	9			
10	S.V.Sehgal	c Ravi Teja b A.D.Yadav	1			
11	P.Das	not out	1			
	Extras	b 4, lb 5, nb 10	19	b 2, lb 6, nb 3		11
			298	(1 wicket)		103

FoW (1): 1-29 (1), 2-99 (2), 3-189 (4), 4-248 (5), 5-256 (3), 6-256 (7), 7-275 (8), 8-292 (9), 9-294 (10), 10-298 (6)
FoW (2): 1-102 (1)

Orissa Bowling

	O	M	R	W				O	M	R	W	
D.S.Mohanty	32	9	63	5				16	6	25	5	
P.Das	16	5	42	0				8	4	17	0	1w,1nb
Jayachandra	9	1	39	1				8	0	25	1	
R.K.Mohanty	6	1	18	0	1nb	(5)		6	1	18	1	2nb
Behera	3	2	9	0		(6)		3	2	1	1	
Sehgal	30	6	61	4	1w,2nb	(4)		20.4	3	73	2	1nb

Hyderabad Bowling

	O	M	R	W				O	M	R	W	
Arjun	20	5	55	0	5nb	(2)		3	0	13	0	1nb
A.D.Yadav	19	2	75	4	1nb	(1)		6.4	0	23	0	2nb
Lalith Mohan	10	0	40	0		(4)		4	0	12	0	
Manohar	1	0	4	0								
Ojha	33.3	16	58	6		(3)		11	3	28	0	
Shinde	14	1	30	0		(5)		2	0	14	0	
B.S.K.Yadav	3	0	11	0								
Ravi Teja	2	0	10	0		(6)		1	0	5	0	
A.S.Yadav	1	0	6	0								

Umpires: A.Y.Dandekar and C.R.Mohite. Referee: C.Sharma.   Toss: Hyderabad

Close of Play: 1st day: Hyderabad (1) 201-8 (Ojha 19*, A.D.Yadav 13*, 81 overs); 2nd day: Orissa (1) 248-3 (Behera 102*, Jayachandra 29*, 77 overs); 3rd day: Hyderabad (2) 143-5 (Pai 48*, Arjun 1*, 52 overs).
N.J.Behera's 103 took 252 balls in 304 minutes and included 14 fours.

JAMMU AND KASHMIR v HARYANA

Played at Gandhi Memorial Science College Ground, Jammu, December 1, 2, 3, 2007.
Ranji Trophy 2007/08 - Plate Group B
Haryana won by an innings and 123 runs.   (Points: Jammu and Kashmir 0, Haryana 6)

HARYANA

1	V.Sahni	b Sharma	23
2	M.R.Beerala	c Dev Singh b Sharma	0
3	Sunny Singh	c Bali b Sharma	14
4	S.Sharma	b Beigh	50
5	S.Rana	c Bali b Sharma	132
6	S.S.Viswanathan	run out (Khajuria)	65
7	J.Sharma	b Beigh	0
8	*A.Mishra	c Sharma b Beigh	54
9	†Sandeep Singh	lbw b Sameer Ali	0
10	G.Vashisht	c Dev Singh b Beigh	16
11	J.Billa	not out	8
	Extras	b 14, lb 6, w 1, nb 21	42
			404

FoW (1): 1-5 (2), 2-34 (3), 3-54 (1), 4-156 (4), 5-280 (5), 6-281 (7), 7-359 (6), 8-360 (9), 9-379 (8), 10-404 (10)

JAMMU AND KASHMIR

1	Parminder Singh	c Sunny Singh b Billa	0	lbw b Vashisht	5
2	I.DevSingh	b J.Sharma	0	b Billa	2
3	†A.Bhatt	b Mishra	52	lbw b Vashisht	16
4	Kavaljit Singh	c Sunny Singh b Billa	15	c Rana b Billa	6
5	Majid Dar	b Billa	3	b Vashisht	14
6	Irshad Hassan	lbw b Mishra	51	c Vashisht b Mishra	1
7	P.Bali	c S.Sharma b Rana	12	c Sunny Singh b Mishra	2
8	*V.Sharma	b Rana	1	c Sandeep Singh b Billa	3
9	S.Beigh	c Rana b Mishra	11	b Vashisht	22
10	S.Khajuria	c Sunny Singh b Mishra	0	not out	0
11	Sameer Ali	not out	4	c S.Sharma b Vashisht	6
	Extras	b 7, lb 4, nb 14	25	b 13, lb 3, w 5, nb 9	30
			174		107

FoW (1): 1-1 (1), 2-6 (2), 3-39 (4), 4-79 (3), 5-86 (5), 6-119 (7), 7-129 (8), 8-163 (6), 9-168 (10), 10-174 (9)
FoW (2): 1-5 (2), 2-34 (1), 3-41 (3), 4-47 (4), 5-51 (6), 6-57 (7), 7-60 (8), 8-100 (9), 9-101 (5), 10-107 (11)

Jammu and Kashmir Bowling

	O	M	R	W	
Sharma	31	4	107	4	10nb
Beigh	30.3	6	99	4	7nb
Sameer Ali	17	2	59	1	1w,3nb
Majid Dar	3	0	10	0	
Khajuria	10	0	65	0	1nb
Bali	9	1	44	0	

Haryana Bowling

	O	M	R	W			O	M	R	W	
J.Sharma	11	2	63	1	7nb		4	1	6	0	
Billa	15	3	44	3	2nb		10	1	26	3	5w,5nb
Rana	13	4	26	2	2nb						
Sunny Singh	3	0	8	0	1nb	(5)	1	0	2	0	
Mishra	6.2	2	12	4	2nb	(3)	19	5	35	2	4nb
Vashisht	3	1	10	0		(4)	12.5	4	22	5	

Umpires: N.R.S.Prabhu and G.A.Pratapkumar.   Referee: K.D.Mokashi.   Toss: Jammu and Kashmir

Close of Play: 1st day: Haryana (1) 247-4 (Rana 108*, Viswanathan 28*, 57 overs); 2nd day: Jammu and Kashmir (1) 92-5 (Irshad Hassan 7*, Bali 3*, 31 overs).

The match was scheduled for four days but completed in three. S.Rana's 132 took 201 balls in 239 minutes and included 17 fours and 2 sixes.

JHARKHAND v GOA

Played at Keenan Stadium, Jamshedpur, December 1, 2, 3, 4, 2007.
Ranji Trophy 2007/08 - Plate Group B
Match drawn.   (Points: Jharkhand 3, Goa 1)

GOA

1	S.K.Kamat	c Nadeem b Roy	41	c and b Gupta	28
2	S.A.Asnodkar	c Ghosh b Rao	21	not out	103
3	S.S.Dhuri	c Ghosh b Roy	43	run out	36
4	*J.Arunkumar	c Ghosh b Roy	6		
5	M.V.Joglekar	c Nadeem b Roy	47		
6	†A.Ratra	c Gupta b Sharma	40		
7	S.B.Jakati	c Vidyarthi b Santosh Lal	38	(4) not out	2
8	R.R.D'Souza	c Nadeem b Roy	1		
9	S.S.Bandekar	c Ghosh b Rao	15		
10	A.R.Angle	c Hashmi b Gupta	45		
11	H.H.Gadekar	not out	11		
	Extras	b 14, lb 12, nb 2	28	b 10, lb 1, w 1	12
			336	**(2 wickets)**	**181**

FoW (1): 1-49 (2), 2-95 (1), 3-103 (4), 4-142 (3), 5-215 (5), 6-217 (6), 7-218 (8), 8-252 (9), 9-286 (7), 10-336 (10)
FoW (2): 1-62 (1), 2-167 (3)

JHARKHAND

1	†S.Ghosh	st Ratra b Jakati	57
2	*M.S.Vardhan	c D'Souza b Angle	179
3	A.K.Vidyarthi	c Arunkumar b Jakati	72
4	S.S.Tiwary	c Angle b Jakati	74
5	Santosh Lal	c Ratra b Bandekar	0
6	A.Hashmi	c Joglekar b Jakati	10
7	S.Gupta	not out	22
8	S.Nadeem	st Ratra b Jakati	6
9	S.S.Rao	c and b Jakati	2
10	K.Sharma	c Ratra b Gadekar	9
11	S.R.Roy	not out	7
	Extras	b 6, lb 8, w 2, nb 3	19
		(9 wickets, declared)	**457**

FoW (1): 1-103 (1), 2-375 (2), 3-394 (4), 4-394 (5), 5-406 (3), 6-411 (6), 7-421 (8), 8-427 (9), 9-441 (10)

Jharkhand Bowling	O	M	R	W			O	M	R	W	
Sharma	29	8	81	1	2nb	(2)	5	2	15	0	
Rao	29	5	67	2		(1)	7	3	20	0	
Santosh Lal	10	2	35	1		(4)	2	0	3	0	1w
Roy	26	4	77	5		(3)	10	1	50	0	
Nadeem	14	5	32	0		(6)	19	9	18	0	
Gupta	7.1	1	15	1		(5)	11	3	18	1	
Vardhan	2	0	3	0		(8)	1	0	8	0	
Vidyarthi						(7)	12	3	38	0	

Goa Bowling	O	M	R	W	
Bandekar	23	5	72	1	3nb
Gadekar	26	6	85	1	
D'Souza	13	2	43	0	
Jakati	67	17	149	6	2w
Angle	15	1	46	1	
Dhuri	17	5	38	0	
Asnodkar	2	0	7	0	
Arunkumar	1	0	3	0	

Umpires: P.S.Godbole and S.J.Phadkar.   Referee: A.Kaypee.   Toss: Goa

Close of Play: 1st day: Goa (1) 251-7 (Jakati 19*, Bandekar 14*, 90 overs); 2nd day: Jharkhand (1) 213-1 (Vardhan 113*, Vidyarthi 38*, 60 overs); 3rd day: Jharkhand (1) 405-4 (Vidyarthi 72*, Hashmi 9*, 150 overs).
M.S.Vardhan's 179 took 371 balls in 556 minutes and included 21 fours. S.A.Asnodkar's 103 took 212 balls in 256 minutes and included 14 fours. A.K.Vidyarthi retired hurt in the Jharkhand first innings having scored 59 (team score 278-1) - he returned when the score was 375-2.

KARNATAKA v RAJASTHAN

Played at Gangothri Glades Cricket Ground, Mysore, December 1, 2, 3, 4, 2007.
Ranji Trophy 2007/08 - Elite Group A
Match drawn.   **(Points: Karnataka 1, Rajasthan 3)**

RAJASTHAN

1	M.D.Sharma	lbw b Joshi	68	c Uthappa b Joshi	14
2	V.A.Saxena	c Uthappa b Aiyappa	42	lbw b Vinay Kumar	37
3	N.S.Doru	b Joshi	4	c Uthappa b Raghu	29
4	R.D.Bist	c Appanna b Vinay Kumar	99	run out	8
5	R.K.Bishnoi	c Shinde b Raghu	11	c Akhil b Appanna	0
6	†R.B.Jhalani	c Akhil b Aiyappa	62	c Vinay Kumar b Appanna	20
7	Afroz Khan	lbw b Joshi	5	c Uthappa b Joshi	4
8	Shamsher Singh	b Joshi	0	c Pawan b Raghu	0
9	Pankaj Singh	b Joshi	40	c Uthappa b Joshi	6
10	*Mohammad Aslam	c Akhil b Joshi	32	not out	0
11	S.O.Mathur	not out	0	c Pawan b Joshi	0
	Extras	b 9, lb 21	30	b 4, lb 4, pen 5	13
			393		131

FoW (1): 1-120 (1), 2-126 (3), 3-126 (2), 4-159 (5), 5-274 (6), 6-288 (7), 7-288 (8), 8-334 (4), 9-386 (9), 10-393 (10)
FoW (2): 1-18 (1), 2-61 (2), 3-69 (4), 4-74 (5), 5-110 (6), 6-117 (3), 7-117 (8), 8-126 (9), 9-131 (7), 10-131 (11)

KARNATAKA

1	K.B.Pawan	c Jhalani b Mathur	24	run out	5
2	R.V.Uthappa	lbw b Mohammad Aslam	55	c Bist b Mohammad Aslam	54
3	S.P.Shinde	c Mohammad Aslam b Shamsher Singh	25	not out	50
4	C.Raghu	c Doru b Shamsher Singh	41		
5	K.P.Appanna	c Saxena b Mohammad Aslam	2		
6	†V.S.T.Naidu	c Saxena b Mathur	21		
7	*Y.K.T.Goud	not out	110		
8	S.B.Joshi	c Mathur b Shamsher Singh	0		
9	B.Akhil	b Mohammad Aslam	3	(4) not out	42
10	R.Vinay Kumar	lbw b Shamsher Singh	14		
11	N.C.Aiyappa	b Mohammad Aslam	24		
	Extras	b 1, lb 4, nb 5	10	lb 1, nb 1	2
			329	(2 wickets)	153

FoW (1): 1-78 (2), 2-85 (1), 3-114 (3), 4-119 (5), 5-155 (6), 6-188 (4), 7-188 (8), 8-191 (9), 9-208 (10), 10-329 (11)
FoW (2): 1-32 (1), 2-84 (2)

Karnataka Bowling

	O	M	R	W		O	M	R	W
Vinay Kumar	30	11	100	1	(2)	9	3	16	1
Aiyappa	24	6	61	2	(3)	6	3	10	0
Akhil	10	5	18	0					
Joshi	42.2	11	83	6	(1)	28	18	25	4
Appanna	24	5	76	0		23	9	46	2
Raghu	7	3	25	1	(4)	9	4	21	2

Rajasthan Bowling

	O	M	R	W			O	M	R	W	
Pankaj Singh	17	3	57	0			5	0	30	0	1nb
Mathur	21	5	51	2	1nb		2	0	20	0	
Mohammad Aslam	43.2	14	91	4		(4)	8	0	53	1	
Afroz Khan	16	3	38	0	4nb	(3)	7	0	49	0	
Shamsher Singh	30	7	79	4							
Saxena	1	0	8	0							

Umpires: R.Y.Deshmukh and A.Y.Gokhale.   Referee: Balbir Singh.   Toss: Rajasthan

Close of Play: 1st day: Rajasthan (1) 266-4 (Bist 62*, Jhalani 60*, 94 overs); 2nd day: Karnataka (1) 118-3 (Raghu 9*, Appanna 2*, 44 overs); 3rd day: Rajasthan (2) 0-0 (Sharma 0*, Saxena 0*, 4 overs).

Y.K.T.Goud's 110 took 234 balls in 249 minutes and included 15 fours.

MADHYA PRADESH v RAILWAYS

Played at Maharani Usharaje Trust Cricket Ground, Indore, December 1, 2, 3, 4, 2007.
Ranji Trophy 2007/08 - Plate Group B
Match drawn.   (Points: Madhya Pradesh 1, Railways 3)

RAILWAYS

1	S.S.Joshi	b Jalaj S.Saxena	33
2	A.A.Pagnis	c and b Jalaj S.Saxena	66
3	*S.B.Bangar	lbw b Golwalkar	13
4	H.D.Rawle	c Ojha b Jalaj S.Saxena	17
5	S.C.Sanyal	lbw b Jalaj S.Saxena	46
6	†M.Rawat	c Tomar b Pandey	75
7	K.V.Sharma	lbw b Golwalkar	61
8	A.Raja Ali	b Golwalkar	88
9	K.S.Parida	b Pandey	15
10	Harvinder Singh	c Jatin S.Saxena b Pandey	0
11	M.S.Yadav	not out	17
	Extras	b 5, lb 10, w 1, nb 17	33
			464

FoW (1): 1-90 (1), 2-122 (2), 3-141 (4), 4-153 (3), 5-238 (5), 6-308 (6), 7-357 (7), 8-391 (9), 9-391 (10), 10-464 (8)

MADHYA PRADESH

1	†N.V.Ojha	b Bangar	44	not out	81
2	Jalaj S.Saxena	lbw b Bangar	37	b Bangar	3
3	Jatin S.Saxena	b Yadav	8	lbw b Sanyal	31
4	D.Bundela	lbw b Harvinder Singh	23	b Sanyal	4
5	R.N.Bakshi	b Harvinder Singh	17	not out	58
6	*B.R.Tomar	c Rawat b Harvinder Singh	10		
7	Murtuza Ali	b Sharma	36		
8	Y.A.Golwalkar	c Pagnis b Parida	15		
9	S.K.Pitre	c Pagnis b Sharma	5		
10	S.P.Pandey	c Pagnis b Sharma	0		
11	A.Rajan	not out	2		
	Extras	b 5, lb 2, nb 17	24	b 10, lb 1, nb 8	19
			221	(3 wickets)	196

FoW (1): 1-83 (1), 2-100 (2), 3-100 (3), 4-131 (5), 5-154 (4), 6-160 (6), 7-201 (8), 8-214 (9), 9-214 (10), 10-221 (7)
FoW (2): 1-6 (2), 2-72 (3), 3-82 (4)

Madhya Pradesh Bowling

	O	M	R	W	
Pandey	33.2	5	94	3	3nb
Rajan	21.4	3	107	0	1w,9nb
Pitre	18	3	44	0	2nb
Murtuza Ali	3	0	12	0	
Jalaj S.Saxena	48	17	89	4	
Golwalkar	31.2	3	98	3	3nb
Jatin S.Saxena	3	0	5	0	

Railways Bowling

	O	M	R	W			O	M	R	W	
Bangar	16	3	46	2	4nb	(3)	9	5	12	1	2nb
Harvinder Singh	27	5	54	3	6nb		12	3	28	0	3nb
Parida	22	6	43	1		(6)	10	4	25	0	
Sharma	5.1	1	9	3	1nb	(1)	17	4	43	0	
Sanyal	13	1	31	0	6nb		10	4	15	2	
Yadav	20	4	31	1		(4)	19	7	44	0	
Pagnis						(7)	5	1	18	0	3nb

Umpires: V.D.Nerurkar and M.S.Pathak. Referee: R.R.Jadeja.   Toss: Railways

Close of Play: 1st day: Railways (1) 256-5 (Rawat 50*, Sharma 5*, 90 overs); 2nd day: Madhya Pradesh (1) 50-0 (Ojha 31*, Jalaj S.Saxena 13*, 21 overs); 3rd day: Madhya Pradesh (2) 6-0 (Ojha 3*, Jalaj S.Saxena 3*, 5 overs).

MUMBAI v MAHARASHTRA

Played at Wankhede Stadium, Mumbai, December 1, 2, 3, 4, 2007.
Ranji Trophy 2007/08 - Elite Group A
Match drawn.   (Points: Mumbai 1, Maharashtra 3)

MAHARASHTRA

1	†V.V.More	b Murtuza Hussain	24	c Rahane b Powar	21
2	H.H.Khadiwale	c Kukreja b Murtuza Hussain	42	c sub (B.P.Patel) b Powar	37
3	H.H.Kanitkar	lbw b Nayar	18	not out	50
4	*Y.Venugopal Rao	lbw b Salvi	27	c Nayar b Muzumdar	15
5	Y.V.Takawale	lbw b Agarkar	126		
6	V.R.Bhilare	c Sharma b Agarkar	78		
7	K.M.Jadhav	c Kukreja b Nayar	81	(5) not out	8
8	S.V.Bahutule	c Rahane b Nayar	17		
9	S.A.Agharkar	lbw b Nayar	2		
10	S.M.Fallah	b Nayar	0		
11	W.S.Sayyed	not out	5		
	Extras	b 15, lb 7, w 5, nb 4	31	b 2, lb 2, nb 4	8
			451	(3 wickets)	139

FoW (1): 1-34 (1), 2-85 (3), 3-95 (2), 4-142 (4), 5-272 (6), 6-418 (7), 7-425 (5), 8-428 (9), 9-428 (10), 10-451 (8)
FoW (2): 1-54 (1), 2-81 (2), 3-123 (4)

MUMBAI

1	S.O.Kukreja	c More b Sayyed	18
2	A.M.Rahane	c Agharkar b Fallah	72
3	P.T.Naik	c More b Fallah	0
4	*A.A.Muzumdar	c More b Khadiwale	50
5	R.G.Sharma	lbw b Khadiwale	31
6	A.M.Nayar	c More b Khadiwale	6
7	A.B.Agarkar	c Fallah b Agharkar	95
8	R.R.Powar	c More b Sayyed	106
9	†V.R.Samant	c More b Fallah	22
10	Murtuza Hussain	c Khadiwale b Fallah	16
11	A.M.Salvi	not out	1
	Extras	b 3, lb 5, nb 11	19
			436

FoW (1): 1-71 (1), 2-77 (3), 3-132 (2), 4-165 (4), 5-183 (6), 6-197 (5), 7-382 (7), 8-394 (8), 9-433 (9), 10-436 (10)

Mumbai Bowling

	O	M	R	W			O	M	R	W	
Agarkar	31	6	86	2	2w,2nb						
Salvi	16	3	52	1							
Murtuza Hussain	31	4	89	2		(1)	12	5	29	0	2nb
Nayar	33.3	8	100	5	3w	(2)	9	4	29	0	
Powar	25	4	89	0	2nb	(3)	12	3	28	2	2nb
Sharma	2	0	13	0		(4)	4	0	16	0	
Naik						(5)	2	0	12	0	
Muzumdar						(6)	5	1	14	1	
Kukreja						(7)	4	1	7	0	

Maharashtra Bowling

	O	M	R	W	
Sayyed	35	5	94	2	3nb
Fallah	31.4	4	114	4	5nb
Bahutule	40	8	116	0	3nb
Agharkar	22	4	44	1	
Khadiwale	22	4	46	3	
Venugopal Rao	2	0	14	0	

Umpires: H.S.Sekhon and R.Subramanyam. Referee: A.K.Patel.   Toss: Mumbai

Close of Play: 1st day: Maharashtra (1) 308-5 (Takawale 83*, Jadhav 21*, 89 overs); 2nd day: Mumbai (1) 113-2 (Rahane 65*, Muzumdar 23*, 38 overs); 3rd day: Mumbai (1) 390-7 (Powar 102*, Samant 0*, 128 overs).
Y.V.Takawale's 126 took 279 balls in 459 minutes and included 13 fours and 1 six. R.R.Powar's 106 took 235 balls in 282 minutes and included 9 fours and 3 sixes.

TAMIL NADU v SAURASHTRA

Played at M.A.Chidambaram Stadium, Chepauk, Chennai, December 1, 2, 3, 4, 2007.
Ranji Trophy 2007/08 - Elite Group A
Match drawn.   (Points: Tamil Nadu 3, Saurashtra 1)

TAMIL NADU

1	A.Mukund	c Makwana b Maniar	120	
2	M.Vijay Krishna	not out	230	
3	*S.Badrinath	c Jobanputra b Dhruve	61	
4	K.Vasudevadas	not out	103	
5	R.Srinivasan			
6	†H.Gopinath			
7	R.Ramkumar			
8	V.Y.Mahesh			
9	P.Amarnath			
10	C.Suresh			
11	S.Suresh Kumar			
	Extras	b 7, lb 4, w 2, nb 4	17	
		(2 wickets, declared)	531	

FoW (1): 1-256 (1), 2-363 (3)

SAURASHTRA

1	K.M.Vaghela	c and b Ramkumar	1	b Suresh Kumar	3
2	†S.D.Jogiyani	c Gopinath b Amarnath	0	not out	46
3	S.H.Kotak	b Mahesh	12		
4	C.A.Pujara	c Badrinath b Ramkumar	62	not out	47
5	P.S.Mehta	c Gopinath b Ramkumar	21	(3) c Srinivasan b Vasudevadas	2
6	*J.N.Shah	c sub (R.Prasanna) b Ramkumar	24		
7	R.A.Jadeja	c Vasudevadas b Badrinath	33		
8	R.V.Dhruve	lbw b C.Suresh	46		
9	K.R.Makwana	c Srinivasan b C.Suresh	0		
10	S.P.Jobanputra	c and b C.Suresh	0		
11	S.M.Maniar	not out	0		
	Extras	b 1, lb 1, w 2, nb 8	12	lb 2, w 5	7
			211	(2 wickets)	105

FoW (1): 1-0 (2), 2-16 (3), 3-21 (1), 4-97 (4), 5-112 (5), 6-139 (6), 7-211 (8), 8-211 (9), 9-211 (7), 10-211 (10)
FoW (2): 1-23 (1), 2-30 (3)

Saurashtra Bowling	O	M	R	W	
Jobanputra	23	3	59	0	2w
Maniar	18	3	67	1	4nb
Dhruve	34	3	121	1	
Jadeja	45	7	136	0	
Makwana	20	3	77	0	
Pujara	2	0	8	0	
Kotak	3	0	10	0	
Shah	4	0	22	0	
Mehta	2	0	20	0	

Tamil Nadu Bowling	O	M	R	W			O	M	R	W	
Mahesh	11	2	53	1	2w,7nb						
Amarnath	13	5	38	1		(1)	5	2	16	0	1w
Ramkumar	26	5	68	4			15	12	14	0	
C.Suresh	6.2	1	19	3		(2)	18	13	21	0	
Suresh Kumar	9	0	23	0		(4)	17	8	23	1	
Vasudevadas	2	0	7	0			5	2	26	1	
Badrinath	2	1	1	1		(5)	4	2	3	0	

Umpires: K.Hariharan and S.Rao. Referee: S.Paul.   Toss: Tamil Nadu

Close of Play: 1st day: Tamil Nadu (1) 262-1 (Vijay Krishna 129*, Badrinath 4*, 90 overs); 2nd day: Saurashtra (1) 28-3 (Pujara 9*, Mehta 0*, 13 overs); 3rd day: Saurashtra (1) 120-5 (Shah 11*, Jadeja 2*, 41 overs).

A.Mukund's 120 took 271 balls in 362 minutes and included 13 fours and 1 six. M.Vijay Krishna's 230 took 443 balls in 632 minutes and included 22 fours and 7 sixes. K.Vasudevadas's 103 took 114 balls in 147 minutes and included 13 fours and 1 six.

TRIPURA v KERALA

Played at Maharaja Bir Bikram College Stadium, Agartala, December 1, 2, 3, 4, 2007.
Ranji Trophy 2007/08 - Plate Group A
Tripura won by four wickets.   (Points: Tripura 5, Kerala 0)

KERALA

1	*S.K.Cheruvathur	c Banik b T.S.Saha	22	(7) run out	14
2	M.Sebastian Antony	c Dutta b Jain	25	b Jain	64
3	V.A.Jagadeesh	lbw b Jain	22	(5) b Debnath	0
4	S.R.Nair	c R.H.Saha b Debnath	30	c Manoj Singh b T.S.Saha	53
5	P.Rohan Prem	c Chanda b Debnath	22	(6) b Manoj Singh	13
6	R.V.Gomez	c Dutta b Jain	12	(1) b Jain	108
7	P.Prasanth	c R.H.Saha b Debnath	0	(3) c Manoj Singh b Debnath	0
8	†C.M.Tejas	c and b Jain	19	not out	6
9	S.Anish	c Banik b Chanda	8	not out	3
10	T.Yohannan	b Chanda	0		
11	P.Chandran	not out	0		
	Extras	b 4, lb 6, nb 9	19	lb 3, w 2, nb 9	14
			179	(7 wickets, declared)	275

FoW (1): 1-39 (1), 2-72 (2), 3-77 (3), 4-133 (5), 5-136 (4), 6-136 (7), 7-165 (6), 8-167 (8), 9-172 (10), 10-179 (9)
FoW (2): 1-172 (1), 2-183 (2), 3-184 (3), 4-184 (5), 5-219 (6), 6-262 (7), 7-271 (4)

TRIPURA

1	Manoj Singh	lbw b Cheruvathur	22	b Yohannan	24
2	B.S.Das	c Tejas b Chandran	16	lbw b Cheruvathur	14
3	R.H.Saha	lbw b Chandran	0	lbw b Cheruvathur	48
4	S.D.Chowdhury	b Yohannan	2	(6) lbw b Cheruvathur	0
5	N.S.Shetty	c and b Chandran	21	not out	62
6	T.K.Chanda	lbw b Cheruvathur	4	(7) run out	16
7	*R.D.Banik	lbw b Cheruvathur	0	(4) c Tejas b Anish	76
8	†R.K.Dutta	c Jagadeesh b Anish	48	not out	6
9	T.S.Saha	st Tejas b Anish	47		
10	V.Jain	lbw b Anish	1		
11	J.S.Debnath	not out	3		
	Extras	b 8, lb 2, w 1, nb 10	21	b 3, lb 4, w 1, nb 16	24
			185	(6 wickets)	270

FoW (1): 1-29 (2), 2-30 (3), 3-37 (4), 4-54 (1), 5-71 (6), 6-71 (7), 7-85 (5), 8-176 (8), 9-181 (9), 10-185 (10)
FoW (2): 1-44 (1), 2-44 (2), 3-168 (4), 4-217 (3), 5-221 (6), 6-256 (7)

Tripura Bowling	O	M	R	W			O	M	R	W	
Jain	22	7	42	4	2nb		14	1	53	2	1w,3nb
Chanda	10.1	0	23	2	7nb		16	1	53	0	1w,6nb
T.S.Saha	18	3	47	1			19	1	77	0	
Das	6	3	16	0							
Debnath	15	4	24	3			28	6	63	2	
Manoj Singh	4	1	14	0	(4)		5	1	9	1	
Chowdhury	1	0	3	0							
Shetty					(6)		5	0	12	0	
Banik					(7)		1	0	5	0	

Kerala Bowling	O	M	R	W			O	M	R	W	
Yohannan	18	5	52	1	1w,9nb		13	4	32	1	4nb
Chandran	13	5	28	3			17	1	57	0	
Cheruvathur	15	2	36	3	1nb	(5)	14.5	4	33	3	
Anish	14.5	4	32	3			14	0	65	1	
Prasanth	7	2	14	0		(3)	9	2	34	0	7nb
Jagadeesh	2	0	2	0							
Nair	2	0	11	0			4	0	19	0	1nb
Gomez						(6)	7	3	23	0	1w

Umpires: A.K.Chowdhury and S.Dua.   Referee: S.S.Patil.   Toss: Tripura

Close of Play: 1st day: Tripura (1) 27-0 (Manoj Singh 8*, Das 14*, 7 overs); 2nd day: Kerala (2) 57-0 (Gomez 37*, Sebastian Antony 14*, 16 overs); 3rd day: Tripura (2) 25-0 (Manoj Singh 14*, Das 7*, 9 overs).
R.V.Gomez's 108 took 180 balls in 239 minutes and included 15 fours and 1 six.

UTTAR PRADESH v BARODA

Played at Dr Akhilesh Das Stadium, Lucknow, December 1, 2, 3, 4, 2007.
Ranji Trophy 2007/08 - Elite Group B
Baroda won by 48 runs.　(Points: Uttar Pradesh 0, Baroda 5)

BARODA

1	*C.C.Williams	c T.M.Srivastava b Kumar	1	lbw b Gupta	24
2	S.S.Parab	c Amir Khan b Chawla	71	st Amir Khan b Chawla	32
3	A.A.Bilakhia	c Shukla b Kumar	48	c T.M.Srivastava b Kaif	39
4	R.K.Solanki	c Kaif b Raina	57	c Chawla b Gupta	2
5	†P.R.Shah	b Kumar	3	c Shukla b Chawla	7
6	Y.K.Pathan	c Kaif b Chawla	37	(7) c R.P.Srivastava b Chawla	4
7	I.K.Pathan	b Raina	57	(6) lbw b Chawla	7
8	A.R.Chauhan	c Shukla b Chawla	12	(9) not out	18
9	K.N.Panchal	c Kaif b Raina	0	(8) lbw b Gupta	6
10	R.V.Pawar	c Amir Khan b Kumar	23	c Tahir Abbas b Gupta	0
11	S.M.Singh	not out	11	c Tahir Abbas b Gupta	0
	Extras	b 3, lb 8, w 3	14	b 8, lb 1	9
			334		148

FoW (1): 1-4 (1), 2-123 (3), 3-139 (2), 4-142 (5), 5-208 (6), 6-259 (4), 7-292 (7), 8-298 (9), 9-300 (8), 10-334 (10)
FoW (2): 1-59 (2), 2-77 (1), 3-81 (4), 4-89 (5), 5-103 (6), 6-107 (7), 7-118 (8), 8-142 (3), 9-145 (10), 10-148 (11)

UTTAR PRADESH

1	P.Kumar	c Bilakhia b Singh	25	(9) c Pawar b Y.K.Pathan	10
2	R.P.Srivastava	c Parab b Y.K.Pathan	27	(1) lbw b I.K.Pathan	44
3	T.M.Srivastava	c Chauhan b Y.K.Pathan	19	(2) run out	28
4	Tahir Abbas	lbw b I.K.Pathan	17	(3) c Shah b I.K.Pathan	3
5	*M.Kaif	lbw b I.K.Pathan	0	(4) c Solanki b Pawar	37
6	S.K.Raina	c I.K.Pathan b Pawar	55	(5) c Solanki b Pawar	20
7	R.U.Shukla	c Shah b I.K.Pathan	4	(6) c Bilakhia b Y.K.Pathan	12
8	†Amir Khan	b Y.K.Pathan	34	(7) lbw b Y.K.Pathan	17
9	P.P.Chawla	c Parab b Y.K.Pathan	22	(8) c Shah b Pawar	0
10	P.P.Gupta	not out	0	not out	50
11	S.Tyagi	b Y.K.Pathan	0	b Y.K.Pathan	2
	Extras	b 1, lb 4, w 1	6	b 2	2
			209		225

FoW (1): 1-41 (1), 2-65 (2), 3-82 (3), 4-90 (5), 5-95 (4), 6-99 (7), 7-185 (6), 8-204 (8), 9-209 (9), 10-209 (11)
FoW (2): 1-66 (2), 2-75 (3), 3-78 (1), 4-114 (5), 5-135 (6), 6-151 (4), 7-151 (8), 8-164 (9), 9-185 (7), 10-225 (11)

Uttar Pradesh Bowling

	O	M	R	W		O	M	R	W
Kumar	27.3	6	83	4		11	4	28	0
Tyagi	11	5	29	0	1w	7	2	7	0
R.P.Srivastava	5	0	21	0	2w				
Chawla	26	5	101	3		(3) 26	7	49	4
Gupta	12	0	49	0		(4) 20.3	7	35	5
Raina	16	1	40	3					
Kaif						(5) 8	1	20	1

Baroda Bowling

	O	M	R	W		O	M	R	W
I.K.Pathan	18	2	63	3	1w	16	3	61	2
Singh	12	2	45	1		3	0	8	0
Y.K.Pathan	21.3	7	31	5		(5) 33.1	9	68	4
Pawar	14	0	65	1		25	5	83	3
Panchal						(3) 2	1	1	0
Solanki						(6) 2	0	2	0

Umpires: V.N.Kulkarni and I.Shivram. Referee: S.K.Singh.　　Toss: Baroda

Close of Play: 1st day: Baroda (1) 318-9 (Pawar 13*, Singh 7*, 91 overs); 2nd day: Baroda (2) 17-0 (Williams 5*, Parab 4*, 4 overs); 3rd day: Uttar Pradesh (2) 58-0 (R.P.Srivastava 30*, T.M.Srivastava 28*, 28 overs).

INDIA v PAKISTAN

Played at M.Chinnaswamy Stadium, Bangalore, December 8, 9, 10, 11, 12, 2007.
Pakistan in India 2007/08 - 3rd Test
Match drawn.

INDIA

1	W.Jaffer	lbw b Yasir Arafat	17	lbw b Yasir Arafat	18
2	G.Gambhir	c Kamran Akmal b Mohammad Sami	5	b Shoaib Akhtar	3
3	R.S.Dravid	c Misbah-ul-Haq b Yasir Arafat	19	lbw b Danish Kaneria	42
4	S.C.Ganguly	b Danish Kaneria	239	c Faisal Iqbal b Mohammad Sami	91
5	V.V.S.Laxman	b Yasir Arafat	5	retired hurt	14
6	Yuvraj Singh	c Faisal Iqbal b Mohammad Sami	169	c Kamran Akmal b Mohammad Sami	2
7	†K.D.Karthik	c Kamran Akmal b Yasir Arafat	24	c Kamran Akmal b Yasir Arafat	52
8	I.K.Pathan	c Kamran Akmal b Danish Kaneria	102	not out	21
9	*A.Kumble	lbw b Danish Kaneria	4		
10	Harbhajan Singh	b Yasir Arafat	4		
11	I.Sharma	not out	0		
	Extras	b 13, lb 19, nb 6	38	b 9, lb 24, w 1, nb 7	41
			626	(6 wickets, declared)	284

FoW (1): 1-8 (2), 2-44 (3), 3-51 (1), 4-61 (5), 5-361 (6), 6-427 (7), 7-605 (4), 8-615 (9), 9-620 (10), 10-626 (8)
FoW (2): 1-17 (2), 2-26 (1), 3-178 (3), 4-178 (4), 5-184 (6), 6-284 (7)

PAKISTAN

1	Salman Butt	c Karthik b Ganguly	68	c Karthik b Kumble	8
2	Yasir Hameed	lbw b Kumble	19	b Kumble	39
3	*Younis Khan	b Harbhajan Singh	80	c and b Kumble	0
4	Mohammad Yousuf	c Yuvraj Singh b Pathan	24	(7) not out	10
5	Misbah-ul-Haq	not out	133	b Yuvraj Singh	37
6	Faisal Iqbal	c Gambhir b Sharma	22	(4) c Sharma b Kumble	51
7	†Kamran Akmal	st Karthik b Harbhajan Singh	65	(6) b Kumble	0
8	Yasir Arafat	b Sharma	44	b Yuvraj Singh	0
9	Mohammad Sami	b Sharma	1	not out	4
10	Shoaib Akhtar	c Gambhir b Sharma	1		
11	Danish Kaneria	c and b Sharma	4		
	Extras	b 35, lb 26, nb 15	76	b 12, lb 1	13
			537	(7 wickets)	162

FoW (1): 1-59 (2), 2-149 (1), 3-221 (3), 4-227 (4), 5-288 (6), 6-432 (7), 7-525 (8), 8-527 (9), 9-529 (10), 10-537 (11)
FoW (2): 1-44 (2), 2-44 (3), 3-73 (1), 4-144 (4), 5-144 (6), 6-148 (5), 7-154 (8)

Pakistan Bowling	O	M	R	W		O	M	R	W	
Shoaib Akhtar	10	3	23	0		17	6	43	1	
Mohammad Sami	36	5	149	2	4nb	20	2	63	2	1w,2nb
Yasir Arafat	39	5	161	5		13.3	3	49	2	1nb
Danish Kaneria	46.2	8	168	3		26	2	96	1	
Younis Khan	2	0	14	0						
Salman Butt	10	1	36	0	1nb					
Yasir Hameed	7	0	43	0	1nb					

India Bowling	O	M	R	W			O	M	R	W	
Pathan	37	14	80	1			7	4	30	0	
Sharma	33.1	10	118	5	9nb		6	3	22	0	
Kumble	44	12	116	1			14	2	60	5	
Ganguly	10	2	20	1	1nb						
Harbhajan Singh	38	7	131	2		(4)	6	1	28	0	
Yuvraj Singh	6	2	11	0	1nb	(5)	3	0	9	2	

Umpires: R.E.Koertzen and S.J.A.Taufel. Third umpire: G.A.Pratapkumar. Referee: R.S.Madugalle. Toss: India
Close of Play: 1st day: India (1) 365-5 (Ganguly 125*, Karthik 3*, 90 overs); 2nd day: Pakistan (1) 86-1 (Salman Butt 50*, Younis Khan 7*, 27 overs); 3rd day: Pakistan (1) 369-5 (Misbah-ul-Haq 54*, Kamran Akmal 32*, 117 overs); 4th day: India (2) 131-2 (Dravid 35*, Ganguly 63*, 37 overs).
Man of the Match: S.C.Ganguly.
S.C.Ganguly's 239 took 361 balls in 518 minutes and included 30 fours and 2 sixes. Yuvraj Singh's 169 took 203 balls in 250 minutes and included 28 fours and 1 six. I.K.Pathan's 102 took 133 balls in 173 minutes and included 10 fours and 4 sixes. Misbah-ul-Haq's 133 took 322 balls in 407 minutes and included 17 fours. V.V.S.Laxman retired hurt in the India second innings having scored 14 (team score 225-5).

ASSAM v TRIPURA

Played at Nehru Stadium, Guwahati, December 9, 10, 11, 12, 2007.
Ranji Trophy 2007/08 - Plate Group A
Match drawn.   (Points: Assam 1, Tripura 3)

TRIPURA

1	Manoj Singh	lbw b Goswami	0
2	B.S.Das	b K.S.Das	5
3	R.H.Saha	b K.S.Das	66
4	*R.D.Banik	lbw b Goswami	4
5	N.S.Shetty	b K.S.Das	165
6	T.K.Chanda	b Talukdar	72
7	A.A.Dey	b K.S.Das	4
8	†R.K.Dutta	c K.S.Das b Konwar	22
9	T.S.Saha	not out	73
10	V.Jain	c Amzad Ali b Konwar	1
11	J.S.Debnath	lbw b K.S.Das	36
	Extras	b 6, lb 6	12
			460

FoW (1): 1-1 (1), 2-17 (2), 3-32 (4), 4-138 (3), 5-286 (5), 6-290 (7), 7-337 (8), 8-377 (6), 9-378 (10), 10-460 (11)

ASSAM

1	P.M.Das	c R.H.Saha b T.S.Saha	114
2	G.K.Sharma	c R.H.Saha b Debnath	13
3	Tarjinder Singh	b Jain	10
4	N.H.Bordoloi	b T.S.Saha	16
5	M.D.Talukdar	c Dey b T.S.Saha	29
6	*S.Sharath	lbw b T.S.Saha	71
7	S.Ramesh	not out	101
8	D.S.Goswami	lbw b Banik	16
9	†Amzad Ali	c Das b Dey	0
10	A.Konwar	c R.H.Saha b Dey	10
11	K.S.Das	c Dutta b Debnath	1
	Extras	b 10, lb 6, nb 13	29
			410

FoW (1): 1-42 (2), 2-68 (3), 3-104 (4), 4-154 (5), 5-270 (1), 6-285 (6), 7-376 (8), 8-379 (9), 9-407 (10), 10-410 (11)

Assam Bowling

	O	M	R	W	
K.S.Das	37.1	7	140	5	
Goswami	26	1	76	2	
Talukdar	11	3	39	1	
Konwar	46	8	112	2	
Sharma	19	2	51	0	
Tarjinder Singh	6	0	30	0	

Tripura Bowling

	O	M	R	W	
Jain	26	9	62	1	5nb
Chanda	6	2	8	0	6nb
T.S.Saha	69	30	114	4	1nb
Manoj Singh	7	2	19	0	
Debnath	46.2	15	115	2	1nb
Dey	28	6	57	2	
Shetty	3	0	3	0	
R.H.Saha	1	0	2	0	
Banik	6	0	14	1	

Umpires: A.S.Datar and R.M.Deshpande. Referee: B.Raghunath.   Toss: Tripura

Close of Play: 1st day: Tripura (1) 285-4 (Shetty 164*, Chanda 36*, 92 overs); 2nd day: Assam (1) 68-1 (P.M.Das 35*, Tarjinder Singh 10*, 30 overs); 3rd day: Assam (1) 245-4 (P.M.Das 104*, Sharath 52*, 120 overs).

N.S.Shetty's 165 took 236 balls in 314 minutes and included 26 fours. P.M.Das's 114 took 424 balls in 532 minutes and included 14 fours. S.Ramesh's 101 took 161 balls in 198 minutes and included 12 fours.

BENGAL v ORISSA

Played at Kanchanjungwa Krirangan, Siliguri, December 9, 10, 11, 2007.
Ranji Trophy 2007/08 - Elite Group B
Orissa won by six wickets.   **(Points: Bengal 0, Orissa 5)**

BENGAL

1	A.P.Majumdar	c Behera b P.Das	15	c H.M.Das b D.S.Mohanty	1
2	A.S.Das	lbw b P.Das	0	c Parida b P.Das	47
3	S.M.Ghosh	b D.S.Mohanty	13	b P.Das	1
4	M.K.Tiwary	c H.M.Das b B.C.Mohanty	17	c S.S.Das b D.S.Mohanty	0
5	†W.P.Saha	lbw b B.C.Mohanty	9	c H.M.Das b D.S.Mohanty	8
6	*L.R.Shukla	c Jayachandra b B.C.Mohanty	36	c H.M.Das b D.S.Mohanty	4
7	K.H.Mondal	c Pati b B.C.Mohanty	0	run out	6
8	S.S.Sarkar	b B.C.Mohanty	5	not out	31
9	R.R.Bose	b D.S.Mohanty	0	c Pati b B.C.Mohanty	2
10	A.B.Dinda	b B.C.Mohanty	0	(11) c Parida b P.Das	18
11	S.S.Paul	not out	1	(10) b B.C.Mohanty	0
	Extras	lb 1, nb 10	11	lb 1, nb 5	6
			107		124

FoW (1): 1-2 (2), 2-27 (3), 3-52 (4), 4-59 (1), 5-63 (5), 6-78 (7), 7-100 (8), 8-101 (9), 9-102 (10), 10-107 (6)
FoW (2): 1-2 (1), 2-11 (3), 3-16 (4), 4-57 (5), 5-61 (2), 6-72 (6), 7-80 (7), 8-91 (9), 9-91 (10), 10-124 (11)

ORISSA

1	B.S.Pati	c Majumdar b Bose	7	c Dinda b Bose	30
2	*S.S.Das	c Majumdar b Paul	5	c Saha b Bose	0
3	N.J.Behera	c Saha b Bose	7	b Dinda	19
4	R.R.Parida	b Dinda	15	c Saha b Dinda	28
5	P.Jayachandra	c Saha b Sarkar	22	(6) not out	29
6	R.R.Das	c Tiwary b Sarkar	5	(5) not out	21
7	†H.M.Das	c Mondal b Sarkar	8		
8	D.S.Mohanty	c Majumdar b Sarkar	8		
9	S.V.Sehgal	b Paul	0		
10	B.C.Mohanty	not out	14		
11	P.Das	c Mondal b Sarkar	4		
	Extras	lb 2, nb 2	4	b 2, lb 5, w 2, nb 1	10
			99	(4 wickets)	137

FoW (1): 1-15 (1), 2-15 (2), 3-27 (3), 4-53 (4), 5-59 (5), 6-72 (6), 7-73 (7), 8-76 (9), 9-93 (8), 10-99 (11)
FoW (2): 1-30 (2), 2-33 (1), 3-72 (3), 4-83 (4)

Orissa Bowling

	O	M	R	W			O	M	R	W	
D.S.Mohanty	11	3	24	2	1nb		17	6	38	4	
P.Das	11	2	52	2	7nb		11.3	0	40	3	3nb
Jayachandra	4.3	2	2	0	1nb	(4)	7	3	16	0	1nb
B.C.Mohanty	8.3	2	28	6	1nb	(3)	15	8	29	2	1nb

Bengal Bowling

	O	M	R	W			O	M	R	W	
Bose	9	3	19	2			16	4	32	2	
Paul	12	3	36	2	2nb		11	4	34	0	1nb
Sarkar	11.4	2	31	5		(4)	7	0	25	0	1w
Dinda	6	2	11	1		(3)	14	4	33	2	1w
Tiwary						(5)	0.4	0	6	0	

Umpires: S.Asnani and P.S.Godbole. Referee: C.R.Vijayaraghavan.   Toss: Orissa

Close of Play: 1st day: Bengal (2) 0-0 (Majumdar 0*, Das 0*, 1.2 overs); 2nd day: Orissa (2) 82-3 (Parida 27*, R.R.Das 1*, 29 overs).

The match was scheduled for four days but completed in three.

GUJARAT v KERALA

Played at Lalabhai Contractor Stadium, Surat, December 9, 10, 11, 12, 2007.
Ranji Trophy 2007/08 - Plate Group A
Kerala won by nine wickets.   (Points: Gujarat 0, Kerala 5)

GUJARAT

1	*†P.A.Patel	c V.G.Nair b Yohannan	50	c Rohan Prem b Yohannan	74
2	R.K.Tabiyar	c V.G.Nair b Cheruvathur	19	b Cheruvathur	12
3	N.K.Patel	c Rohan Prem b Yohannan	32	c Gomez b Chandran	2
4	B.D.Thaker	lbw b Cheruvathur	0	lbw b Cheruvathur	15
5	D.M.Popat	c Jagadeesh b Chandran	7	not out	59
6	J.D.Desai	lbw b Cheruvathur	1	lbw b Cheruvathur	8
7	T.K.Patel	lbw b Cheruvathur	0	c V.G.Nair b Yohannan	15
8	M.B.Parmar	not out	28	c Jagadeesh b Cheruvathur	6
9	Amit Singh	lbw b Cheruvathur	6	c Rohan Prem b Cheruvathur	13
10	S.K.Trivedi	b Cheruvathur	0	c Yohannan b Anish	8
11	H.A.Majmudar	lbw b Cheruvathur	0	c Prasanth b Chandran	26
	Extras	lb 4, w 1, nb 6	11	b 4, lb 9, w 3, nb 5	21
			154		259

FoW (1): 1-72 (2), 2-72 (1), 3-73 (4), 4-96 (5), 5-99 (6), 6-100 (7), 7-129 (3), 8-154 (9), 9-154 (10), 10-154 (11)
FoW (2): 1-67 (2), 2-70 (3), 3-102 (4), 4-106 (1), 5-122 (6), 6-163 (7), 7-183 (8), 8-210 (9), 9-219 (10), 10-259 (11)

KERALA

1	R.V.Gomez	lbw b Trivedi	0	not out	31
2	M.Sebastian Antony	lbw b Parmar	12	b Parmar	15
3	V.A.Jagadeesh	lbw b Parmar	24	not out	21
4	S.R.Nair	lbw b Parmar	32		
5	P.Rohan Prem	c Tabiyar b T.K.Patel	124		
6	†V.G.Nair	c Parmar b Amit Singh	61		
7	P.Prasanth	st P.A.Patel b Parmar	0		
8	*S.K.Cheruvathur	lbw b Parmar	0		
9	S.Anish	c P.A.Patel b Majmudar	1		
10	T.Yohannan	c Tabiyar b T.K.Patel	11		
11	P.Chandran	not out	61		
	Extras	lb 4, w 1, nb 9	14	lb 5, nb 2	7
			340	(1 wicket)	74

FoW (1): 1-0 (1), 2-35 (3), 3-48 (2), 4-91 (4), 5-173 (6), 6-174 (7), 7-174 (8), 8-183 (9), 9-206 (10), 10-340 (5)
FoW (2): 1-39 (2)

Kerala Bowling

	O	M	R	W			O	M	R	W	
Yohannan	16	3	28	2	4nb		16	3	42	2	2nb
Chandran	15	2	44	1	1nb		15	1	58	2	3w
Cheruvathur	15.3	4	30	7	1w,1nb		25	6	95	5	
Anish	7	3	9	0	(6)		11	2	34	1	
Gomez	6	1	22	0			2	0	5	0	
S.R.Nair	6	2	17	0	(7)		1	0	2	0	
Prasanth					(4)		9	1	10	0	3nb

Gujarat Bowling

	O	M	R	W			O	M	R	W	
Trivedi	26	4	93	1	1w		3	2	14	0	
Majmudar	15	1	56	1	6nb	(3)	6	2	11	0	2nb
Amit Singh	21	7	68	1	1nb	(2)	6	3	9	0	
Parmar	36	8	77	5	1nb		5	1	17	1	
T.K.Patel	7.3	0	32	2	1nb		1.3	0	18	0	
N.K.Patel	1	0	1	0							
Desai	2	0	9	0							

Umpires: A.K.Chowdhury and K.Hariharan.   Referee: A.Patel.   Toss: Gujarat

Close of Play: 1st day: Kerala (1) 58-3 (S.R.Nair 20*, Rohan Prem 0*, 22 overs); 2nd day: Gujarat (2) 2-0 (P.A.Patel 1*, Tabiyar 0*, 1 over); 3rd day: Kerala (2) 27-0 (Gomez 17*, Sebastian Antony 9*, 10 overs).
P.Rohan Prem's 124 took 282 balls in 363 minutes and included 15 fours and 1 six. S.K.Cheruvathur took a hat-trick in the Gujarat first innings (Amit Singh, Trivedi, Majmudar).

HARYANA v MADHYA PRADESH

Played at Chaudhary Bansi Lal Cricket Stadium, Lahli, Rohtak, December 9, 10, 11, 12, 2007.
Ranji Trophy 2007/08 - Plate Group B
Match drawn.   **(Points: Haryana 3, Madhya Pradesh 1)**

HARYANA

1	M.R.Beerala	c Jatin S.Saxena b Pandey	5	lbw b Pandey	16
2	*A.Mishra	lbw b Pandey	17	c Ojha b Pandey	13
3	S.Sharma	lbw b Murtuza Ali	25	c Tomar b Dholpure	2
4	A.Lavasa	c Ojha b Jadhav	76	lbw b Dholpure	22
5	S.Rana	lbw b Jadhav	40	b Pandey	1
6	S.S.Viswanathan	c Ojha b Pandey	63	b Dholpure	6
7	J.Sharma	lbw b Jalaj S.Saxena	30	c Dholpure b Jalaj S.Saxena	5
8	P.P.Singh	c Golwalkar b Dholpure	0	(10) c Ojha b Golwalkar	19
9	†Sandeep Singh	lbw b Dholpure	5	(11) not out	0
10	G.Vashisht	lbw b Murtuza Ali	7	(8) lbw b Pandey	4
11	J.Billa	not out	11	(9) lbw b Pandey	20
	Extras	b 10, lb 9, nb 4	23	lb 2, nb 4	6
			302		**114**

FoW (1): 1-12 (1), 2-25 (2), 3-79 (3), 4-171 (5), 5-190 (6), 6-254 (7), 7-257 (8), 8-268 (9), 9-288 (10), 10-302 (6)
FoW (2): 1-28 (2), 2-34 (3), 3-34 (1), 4-36 (5), 5-49 (6), 6-68 (4), 7-68 (7), 8-86 (8), 9-108 (9), 10-114 (10)

MADHYA PRADESH

1	†N.V.Ojha	b Vashisht	45	b Billa	5
2	Jalaj S.Saxena	lbw b Rana	0	b Rana	8
3	Jatin S.Saxena	lbw b Mishra	15	lbw b J.Sharma	12
4	D.Bundela	b Mishra	19	c Rana b Billa	18
5	R.N.Bakshi	c Rana b J.Sharma	15	b Mishra	27
6	*B.R.Tomar	c Sandeep Singh b Billa	29	c Sandeep Singh b Billa	24
7	Murtuza Ali	c Viswanathan b P.P.Singh	10	lbw b Mishra	17
8	S.M.Dholpure	c S.Sharma b Vashisht	11	(9) lbw b J.Sharma	1
9	A.C.Jadhav	not out	25	(8) not out	26
10	Y.A.Golwalkar	b Mishra	1	c Rana b Billa	0
11	S.P.Pandey	lbw b Mishra	21	not out	6
	Extras	b 5, lb 7, nb 12	24	b 4, lb 13, nb 8	25
			215	**(9 wickets)**	**169**

FoW (1): 1-4 (2), 2-54 (3), 3-90 (4), 4-97 (1), 5-112 (5), 6-143 (7), 7-162 (8), 8-164 (6), 9-169 (10), 10-215 (11)
FoW (2): 1-17 (2), 2-21 (1), 3-48 (4), 4-61 (3), 5-98 (5), 6-126 (7), 7-136 (6), 8-146 (9), 9-154 (10)

Madhya Pradesh Bowling

	O	M	R	W			O	M	R	W	
Pandey	23.1	4	58	3	1nb		17	3	38	5	
Dholpure	21	5	44	2	2nb		20	3	49	3	4nb
Murtuza Ali	9	2	38	2		(5)	2	0	7	0	
Bundela	5	1	16	0	1nb						
Golwalkar	10	0	39	0		(3)	2.3	0	9	1	
Jalaj S.Saxena	26	5	53	1		(4)	4	0	9	1	
Jadhav	10	1	35	2							

Haryana Bowling

	O	M	R	W				O	M	R	W	
J.Sharma	11	3	23	1	1nb	(2)		16	8	22	2	5nb
Rana	16	2	41	1	2nb	(1)		14	4	21	1	1nb
Billa	13	4	26	1	1nb			20.3	3	52	4	2nb
Mishra	31.1	10	61	4	8nb			14	7	27	2	
P.P.Singh	13	2	30	1								
Vashisht	19	9	22	2		(5)		9	3	30	0	

Umpires: V.N.Kulkarni and R.Radhakrishnan.   Referee: S.S.Patil.   Toss: Haryana

Close of Play: 1st day: Haryana (1) 268-7 (Viswanathan 47*, Sandeep Singh 5*, 86.2 overs); 2nd day: Madhya Pradesh (1) 109-4 (Bakshi 13*, Tomar 4*, 51.5 overs); 3rd day: Haryana (2) 75-7 (Vashisht 1*, Billa 6*, 35 overs).

HYDERABAD v ANDHRA

Played at Rajiv Gandhi International Stadium, Uppal, Hyderabad, December 9, 10, 11, 12, 2007.
Ranji Trophy 2007/08 - Elite Group B
Hyderabad won by three wickets.   (Points: Hyderabad 5, Andhra 0)

ANDHRA

1	H.H.Watekar	b Shoaib Ahmed	38	lbw b Arjun	4
2	L.N.P.Reddy	lbw b Shoaib Ahmed	0	b Arjun	9
3	A.S.Verma	c A.S.Yadav b Arjun	1	b Arjun	0
4	*†M.S.K.Prasad	b Arjun	6	(6) b Arjun	9
5	Y.Gnaneswara Rao	st Habeeb Ahmed b Ojha	42	(7) c Prince b A.D.Yadav	61
6	A.G.Pradeep	c Habeeb Ahmed b A.D.Yadav	22	(4) b Arjun	0
7	G.Shankar Rao	b Ojha	0	(5) c Habeeb Ahmed b Arjun	0
8	B.A.Sumanth	c A.D.Yadav b Shinde	25	lbw b Shoaib Ahmed	28
9	Mohammad Faiq	lbw b A.D.Yadav	0	c Habeeb Ahmed b Shoaib Ahmed	5
10	D.Kalyankrishna	c Manohar b Ojha	11	lbw b Arjun	1
11	P.D.Vijaykumar	not out	1	not out	2
	Extras	lb 4, nb 9	13	b 1, lb 4, nb 3	8
			159		127

FoW (1): 1-1 (2), 2-7 (3), 3-21 (4), 4-96 (1), 5-102 (5), 6-104 (7), 7-147 (6), 8-147 (9), 9-147 (8), 10-159 (10)
FoW (2): 1-8 (1), 2-8 (3), 3-8 (4), 4-8 (5), 5-24 (2), 6-29 (6), 7-91 (8), 8-97 (9), 9-104 (10), 10-127 (7)

HYDERABAD

1	D.D.Prince	lbw b Kalyankrishna	8	(3) lbw b Kalyankrishna	0
2	D.B.Ravi Teja	c Prasad b Vijaykumar	0	c Prasad b Gnaneswara Rao	23
3	D.S.Manohar	c Pradeep b Vijaykumar	7	(1) lbw b Kalyankrishna	4
4	S.A.Pai	c Prasad b Vijaykumar	0	(6) b Vijaykumar	53
5	*A.S.Yadav	b Kalyankrishna	49	c Sumanth b Shankar Rao	43
6	M.P.Arjun	c Sumanth b Kalyankrishna	9	(9) not out	10
7	A.J.Shinde	c Prasad b Kalyankrishna	21	c Prasad b Kalyankrishna	1
8	†Habeeb Ahmed	b Shankar Rao	2		
9	P.P.Ojha	lbw b Watekar	16	(8) not out	7
10	Shoaib Ahmed	lbw b Shankar Rao	10	(4) c Prasad b Vijaykumar	7
11	A.D.Yadav	not out	4		
	Extras	w 1, nb 5	6	b 1, lb 2, w 2, nb 2	7
			132	(7 wickets)	155

FoW (1): 1-8 (1), 2-8 (2), 3-8 (4), 4-18 (3), 5-29 (6), 6-87 (7), 7-94 (8), 8-117 (9), 9-117 (5), 10-132 (10)
FoW (2): 1-5 (1), 2-13 (3), 3-35 (2), 4-35 (4), 5-128 (5), 6-136 (6), 7-138 (7)

Hyderabad Bowling

	O	M	R	W			O	M	R	W	
Shoaib Ahmed	11	5	19	2			15	7	23	2	
Arjun	12	2	40	2	8nb		17	5	56	7	3nb
A.D.Yadav	13	3	49	2	1nb	(4)	5.5	0	21	1	
Ojha	13.4	1	43	3		(5)	4	0	13	0	
Shinde	5	3	4	1		(6)	1	0	1	0	
Manohar						(3)	5	1	8	0	

Andhra Bowling

	O	M	R	W			O	M	R	W	
Kalyankrishna	25	8	42	4	1w,3nb		18.1	4	41	3	1nb
Vijaykumar	23	9	35	3			20	5	48	2	
Gnaneswara Rao	10	2	20	0		(4)	9	4	17	1	1w,1nb
Shankar Rao	12.3	5	13	2		(3)	10	3	15	1	
Watekar	7	2	10	1	2nb		5	0	18	0	
Mohammad Faiq	1	0	12	0		(7)	3	0	12	0	
Verma						(6)	2	1	1	0	1w

Umpires: S.D.Ranade and R.D.Risodkar.   Referee: Balbir Singh.   Toss: Andhra

Close of Play: 1st day: Hyderabad (1) 52-5 (A.S.Yadav 15*, Shinde 12*, 25 overs); 2nd day: Andhra (2) 72-6 (Gnaneswara Rao 22*, Sumanth 24*, 29 overs); 3rd day: Hyderabad (2) 137-6 (Shinde 1*, Ojha 1*, 59 overs).

JAMMU AND KASHMIR v GOA

Played at Gandhi Memorial Science College Ground, Jammu, December 9, 10, 11, 12, 2007.
Ranji Trophy 2007/08 - Plate Group B
Match drawn.   **(Points: Jammu and Kashmir 3, Goa 1)**

JAMMU AND KASHMIR
1	I.Dev Singh	c Jakati b Bandekar	20	c Ratra b Bandekar		25
2	Vivek Singh	c Ratra b D'Souza	28	c Ratra b D'Souza		5
3	†A.Bhatt	lbw b D'Souza	31	not out		21
4	Majid Dar	b Bandekar	7	b Bandekar		0
5	Gurupartap Singh	c Ratra b Bandekar	5	not out		0
6	Huwaid Ronga	b Bandekar	7			
7	*V.Sharma	c Arunkumar b Jakati	3			
8	S.Beigh	st Ratra b Jakati	4			
9	Manzoor Dar	not out	10			
10	P.Mahajan	b Bandekar	14			
11	R.Dutta	c Naik b D'Souza	4			
	Extras	b 2, lb 10, w 1, nb 1	14	lb 1, w 5, nb 2		8
			147	(3 wickets)		59

FoW (1): 1-43 (1), 2-82 (3), 3-83 (2), 4-97 (4), 5-108 (5), 6-111 (6), 7-115 (7), 8-118 (8), 9-135 (10), 10-147 (11)
FoW (2): 1-10 (2), 2-56 (1), 3-56 (4)

GOA
1	S.K.Kamat	c Dutta b Sharma	14
2	S.A.Asnodkar	c Bhatt b Sharma	22
3	S.S.Dhuri	c Majid Dar b Sharma	0
4	*J.Arunkumar	c Majid Dar b Beigh	1
5	M.V.Joglekar	lbw b Beigh	28
6	†A.Ratra	c Bhatt b Beigh	42
7	S.B.Jakati	lbw b Beigh	0
8	R.R.D'Souza	lbw b Beigh	0
9	S.S.Bandekar	c Bhatt b Sharma	7
10	A.R.Angle	c Sharma b Beigh	8
11	A.P.Naik	not out	0
	Extras	b 2, lb 5, nb 12	19
			141

FoW (1): 1-32 (1), 2-37 (3), 3-38 (4), 4-42 (2), 5-115 (5), 6-119 (7), 7-119 (8), 8-128 (9), 9-134 (6), 10-141 (10)

Goa Bowling
	O	M	R	W		O	M	R	W	
Bandekar	16	5	49	5	1nb	8	3	8	2	2nb
Naik	4	0	17	0	1w	(3)	2	1	12	0	1w
D'Souza	17.5	6	32	3		(4)	6	1	21	1	
Dhuri	9	3	13	0		(5)	2	1	4	0	
Jakati	8	2	10	2		(2)	9	2	13	0	
Angle	5	2	14	0						

Jammu and Kashmir Bowling
	O	M	R	W	
Sharma	18	4	47	4	4nb
Beigh	22.5	7	50	6	6nb
Mahajan	11	3	20	0	2nb
Majid Dar	3	1	10	0	
Dutta	1	0	7	0	

Umpires: M.S.Pathak and M.S.S.Ranawat.   Referee: K.V.S.D.Kamaraju.   Toss: Goa

Close of Play: 1st day: Jammu and Kashmir (1) 133-8 (Manzoor Dar 3*, Mahajan 13*, 53 overs); 2nd day: Goa (1) 104-4 (Joglekar 24*, Ratra 29*, 42.1 overs); 3rd day: No play.

KARNATAKA v SAURASHTRA

Played at Infosys Ground, Mysore, December 9, 10, 11, 12, 2007.
Ranji Trophy 2007/08 - Elite Group A
Saurashtra won by 3 runs.   (Points: Karnataka 0, Saurashtra 5)

SAURASHTRA

1	K.M.Vaghela	c Naidu b Vinay Kumar	37	c Naidu b Vinay Kumar	34
2	†S.D.Jogiyani	c Naidu b Vinay Kumar	0	c Naidu b Vinay Kumar	7
3	S.H.Kotak	lbw b Vinay Kumar	18	c Uthappa b Aiyappa	26
4	C.A.Pujara	c Uthappa b Vinay Kumar	48	b Joshi	22
5	F.U.Bambhaniya	c Naidu b Aiyappa	13	c Uthappa b Appanna	46
6	R.A.Jadeja	c Naidu b Aiyappa	9	c Naidu b Aiyappa	0
7	*J.N.Shah	c Appanna b Joshi	34	c Naidu b Appanna	12
8	R.V.Dhruve	c Naidu b Vinay Kumar	34	c Raghu b Joshi	19
9	K.R.Makwana	c Chipli b Aiyappa	16	c Naidu b Aiyappa	7
10	S.P.Jobanputra	c Shinde b Aiyappa	26	c Shinde b Aiyappa	54
11	S.M.Maniar	not out	0	not out	1
	Extras	lb 8, nb 2	10	b 7, lb 5, w 5	17
			245		**245**

FoW (1): 1-7 (2), 2-50 (3), 3-112 (4), 4-114 (1), 5-135 (6), 6-136 (5), 7-191 (8), 8-206 (7), 9-245 (10), 10-245 (9)
FoW (2): 1-14 (2), 2-59 (3), 3-81 (4), 4-95 (6), 5-110 (7), 6-116 (1), 7-141 (8), 8-167 (9), 9-241 (5), 10-245 (10)

KARNATAKA

1	K.B.Pawan	c Kotak b Maniar	120	c Makwana b Jobanputra	4
2	R.V.Uthappa	c Makwana b Jobanputra	5	c Jogiyani b Maniar	14
3	S.P.Shinde	c Dhruve b Jobanputra	11	(4) c Dhruve b Vaghela	21
4	B.Chipli	c Makwana b Jobanputra	5	(3) c Jogiyani b Vaghela	28
5	C.Raghu	c Jogiyani b Jobanputra	5	(6) c Jogiyani b Maniar	77
6	†V.S.T.Naidu	c Jogiyani b Dhruve	30	(8) run out	9
7	*Y.K.T.Goud	c Kotak b Dhruve	33	(9) not out	24
8	S.B.Joshi	run out (Jadeja/Jogiyani)	12	(5) c Jogiyani b Jobanputra	42
9	R.Vinay Kumar	c Jogiyani b Jobanputra	0	(7) c Jadeja b Maniar	24
10	N.C.Aiyappa	c Kotak b Jobanputra	0	c Jadeja b Maniar	0
11	K.P.Appanna	not out	0	c and b Jobanputra	3
	Extras	b 4, lb 5, nb 1	10	b 2, lb 8, w 4, nb 1	15
			226		**261**

FoW (1): 1-7 (2), 2-30 (3), 3-44 (4), 4-44 (5), 5-88 (6), 6-161 (7), 7-195 (8), 8-200 (9), 9-206 (10), 10-226 (1)
FoW (2): 1-6 (1), 2-34 (2), 3-64 (4), 4-71 (3), 5-152 (5), 6-199 (7), 7-218 (8), 8-249 (6), 9-249 (10), 10-261 (11)

Karnataka Bowling

	O	M	R	W		O	M	R	W	
Vinay Kumar	22.3	4	70	5	2nb	31	10	64	2	
Aiyappa	20.5	6	57	4		19.1	3	87	4	1w
Chipli	10	4	13	0						
Joshi	25.2	11	44	1		(3) 32	11	46	2	
Raghu	5	0	13	0						
Appanna	10.1	2	40	0		(4) 27	10	36	2	

Saurashtra Bowling

	O	M	R	W		O	M	R	W	
Jobanputra	27	2	70	6		19.4	3	74	3	1w
Maniar	12.4	3	39	1	1nb	15	2	54	4	2w,1nb
Jadeja	21	4	38	0		13	1	60	0	
Dhruve	14	1	40	2		(5) 6	0	21	0	
Vaghela	6	1	13	0		(4) 6	0	23	2	
Makwana	5	0	17	0						
Kotak						(6) 3	0	19	0	1w

Umpires: H.S.Sekhon and B.Sharma. Referee: S.K.Singh.   Toss: Karnataka

Close of Play: 1st day: Saurashtra (1) 229-8 (Makwana 9*, Jobanputra 17*, 90 overs); 2nd day: Karnataka (1) 216-9 (Pawan 110*, Appanna 0*, 83 overs); 3rd day: Saurashtra (2) 183-8 (Bambhaniya 28*, Jobanputra 16*, 85 overs).

K.B.Pawan's 120 took 282 balls in 380 minutes and included 10 fours and 1 six. F.U.Bambhaniya retired hurt in the Saurashtra second innings having scored 0 (team score 92-3) - he returned when the score was 116-6.

MAHARASHTRA v DELHI

Played at Indian Petrochemicals Corporation Limited Ground, Nagothane, December 9, 10, 11, 12, 2007.
Ranji Trophy 2007/08 - Elite Group A
Delhi won by seven wickets.　　(Points: Maharashtra 0, Delhi 5)

MAHARASHTRA

1	†V.V.More	c Chopra b Bhatia	35	b Awana	27
2	H.H.Khadiwale	c Bisht b Awana	0	lbw b Sangwan	0
3	H.H.Kanitkar	c Dhawan b Bhatia	67	st Bisht b Nanda	50
4	*Y.Venugopal Rao	c Bisht b Bhatia	5	lbw b Sangwan	13
5	Y.V.Takawale	c Bisht b Bhatia	8	lbw b Nanda	75
6	V.R.Bhilare	c Chopra b Nanda	31	lbw b Awana	34
7	K.M.Jadhav	b Nanda	33	lbw b Awana	0
8	S.V.Bahutule	c Manhas b Bhatia	0	b Awana	0
9	S.A.Agharkar	c Chopra b Nanda	17	b Nanda	17
10	S.M.Fallah	not out	6	not out	4
11	W.S.Sayyed	b Narender Singh	0	b Nanda	1
	Extras	b 3, lb 1, w 9, nb 4	17	b 7, lb 7, w 3, nb 2	19
			219		240

FoW (1): 1-8 (2), 2-54 (1), 3-63 (4), 4-74 (5), 5-144 (6), 6-167 (3), 7-170 (8), 8-198 (9), 9-218 (7), 10-219 (11)
FoW (2): 1-7 (2), 2-63 (1), 3-98 (3), 4-102 (4), 5-202 (6), 6-202 (7), 7-202 (8), 8-224 (5), 9-237 (9), 10-240 (11)

DELHI

1	A.S.Chopra	lbw b Bahutule	73	st More b Agharkar	2
2	S.Dhawan	c Takawale b Sayyed	7	lbw b Fallah	7
3	C.Nanda	c sub (D.Mohan) b Fallah	10		
4	*V.Sehwag	b Fallah	9		
5	M.Manhas	c More b Agharkar	74	not out	13
6	R.Bhatia	c Venugopal Rao b Agharkar	107	(3) c sub (D.K.Waghmare) b Agharkar	3
7	M.Tehlan	c sub (D.K.Waghmare) b Agharkar	53	(4) not out	13
8	†P.Bisht	c More b Fallah	4		
9	Narender Singh	c More b Agharkar	5		
10	P.Sangwan	not out	18		
11	P.Awana	lbw b Agharkar	4		
	Extras	b 15, lb 12, w 5, nb 13	45	b 4, w 1, nb 8	13
			409	(3 wickets)	51

FoW (1): 1-23 (2), 2-61 (3), 3-78 (4), 4-153 (1), 5-244 (5), 6-367 (7), 7-377 (8), 8-384 (6), 9-391 (9), 10-409 (11)
FoW (2): 1-5 (1), 2-12 (2), 3-20 (3)

Delhi Bowling

	O	M	R	W		O	M	R	W	
Sangwan	15	2	44	0	9w	17	5	46	2	2w
Awana	9	2	40	1		16	2	62	4	1w
Nanda	22	9	40	3		23.3	4	70	4	2nb
Bhatia	16	6	29	5	4nb	3	2	1	0	
Sehwag	6	0	29	0		1	0	5	0	
Narender Singh	9.4	0	33	1		14	2	42	0	

Maharashtra Bowling

	O	M	R	W			O	M	R	W	
Sayyed	27	11	56	1	2w	(4)	1	0	5	0	
Fallah	35	9	106	3	2w,12nb		4	0	16	1	1w,4nb
Khadiwale	15	3	30	0	1w						
Bahutule	17	0	68	1	1nb	(3)	2	0	12	0	2nb
Agharkar	37.5	6	85	5		(1)	7.5	4	14	2	
Venugopal Rao	18	1	37	0							

Umpires: S.Lakshmanan and S.Rao.　Referee: S.Paul.　　　　　Toss: Maharashtra

Close of Play: 1st day: Delhi (1) 23-1 (Chopra 12*, 6.2 overs); 2nd day: Delhi (1) 278-5 (Bhatia 66*, Tehlan 14*, 100 overs); 3rd day: Maharashtra (2) 129-4 (Takawale 18*, Bhilare 11*, 38 overs).

R.Bhatia's 107 took 314 balls in 371 minutes and included 5 fours and 2 sixes. P.Awana took a hat-trick in the Maharashtra second innings (Bhilare, Jadhav, Bahutule).

PUNJAB v BARODA

Played at Gandhi Sports Complex Ground, Amritsar, December 9, 10, 11, 12, 2007.
Ranji Trophy 2007/08 - Elite Group B
Match drawn.   (Points: Punjab 1, Baroda 3)

PUNJAB
1	R.S.Ricky	lbw b Vora	4
2	K.Goel	lbw b Singh	127
3	R.InderSingh	c Shah b Singh	142
4	*P.Dharmani	lbw b Chauhan	13
5	†U.Kaul	c Gaekwad b Vora	29
6	S.Sohal	c Vora b Pathan	55
7	A.Kakkar	not out	56
8	Charanjeet Singh	lbw b Pathan	0
9	Gagandeep Singh	c Bilakhia b Vora	27
10	M.S.Gony	not out	27
11	V.R.Singh		
	Extras	b 6, lb 9, w 1	16
		(8 wickets, declared)	496

FoW (1): 1-13 (1), 2-226 (2), 3-257 (4), 4-317 (3), 5-338 (5), 6-391 (6), 7-391 (8), 8-460 (9)

BARODA
1	S.S.Parab	lbw b Gony	80
2	*C.C.Williams	b Charanjeet Singh	185
3	A.A.Bilakhia	lbw b V.R.Singh	47
4	R.K.Solanki	b Charanjeet Singh	111
5	Y.K.Pathan	c V.R.Singh b Kakkar	20
6	†P.R.Shah	not out	53
7	S.A.Gaekwad	not out	54
8	R.V.Pawar		
9	S.M.Singh		
10	A.R.Chauhan		
11	S.D.Vora		
	Extras	b 10, lb 8, w 4, nb 11	33
		(5 wickets)	583

FoW (1): 1-124 (1), 2-251 (3), 3-435 (2), 4-468 (5), 5-484 (4)

Baroda Bowling
	O	M	R	W	
Singh	42	10	125	2	1w
Vora	36	6	128	3	
Chauhan	18	5	38	1	
Pathan	42	8	111	2	
Pawar	30	9	79	0	

Punjab Bowling
	O	M	R	W	
Gagandeep Singh	27	5	94	0	1nb
V.R.Singh	28	0	115	1	3w,6nb
Gony	27	4	93	1	1w,4nb
Charanjeet Singh	36	4	133	2	
Inder Singh	5	2	12	0	
Kakkar	21	5	76	1	
Goel	12	1	42	0	

Umpires: C.K.Nandan and R.Subramanyam.   Referee: R.Shamshad.   Toss: Baroda

Close of Play: 1st day: Punjab (1) 214-1 (Goel 121*, Inder Singh 84*, 84.2 overs); 2nd day: Punjab (1) 496-8 (Kakkar 56*, Gony 27*, 168 overs); 3rd day: Baroda (1) 251-1 (Williams 106*, Bilakhia 47*, 73 overs).

K.Goel's 127 took 281 balls in 364 minutes and included 17 fours. R.InderSingh's 142 took 324 balls in 470 minutes and included 22 fours. C.C.Williams's 185 took 361 balls in 516 minutes and included 29 fours. R.K.Solanki's 111 took 192 balls in 264 minutes and included 14 fours and 1 six.

RAILWAYS v JHARKHAND

Played at Karnail Singh Stadium, Delhi, December 9, 10, 11, 2007.
Ranji Trophy 2007/08 - Plate Group B
Railways won by an innings and 47 runs.   (Points: Railways 6, Jharkhand 0)

JHARKHAND

#	Batsman	Dismissal 1	R	Dismissal 2	R
1	†S.Ghosh	b Harvinder Singh	25	c sub (K.S.Parida) b Harvinder Singh	4
2	*M.S.Vardhan	c Sharma b Bangar	5	b Saxena	11
3	A.K.Vidyarthi	c Pagnis b Saxena	4	b Sanyal	19
4	S.S.Tiwary	run out (Harvinder Singh)	9	b Yadav	3
5	Ratan Kumar	c Rawat b Saxena	51	(4) lbw b Harvinder Singh	10
6	A.Hashmi	not out	66	(5) b Yadav	9
7	S.Gupta	c Pagnis b Harvinder Singh	0	(6) b Bangar	33
8	S.Nadeem	b Bangar	8	c Bangar b Saxena	15
9	S.S.Rao	lbw b Bangar	0	c Rawat b Saxena	4
10	K.Sharma	c Rawat b Bangar	0	b Bangar	8
11	S.R.Roy	c Sanyal b Yadav	0	not out	4
	Extras	b 1, lb 1, nb 13	15	b 4, lb 2, nb 5	11
			183		131

FoW (1): 1-18 (2), 2-29 (3), 3-49 (4), 4-50 (1), 5-52 (7), 6-160 (5), 7-170 (8), 8-170 (9), 9-170 (10), 10-183 (11)
FoW (2): 1-4 (1), 2-28 (2), 3-37 (3), 4-60 (5), 5-62 (4), 6-80 (7), 7-105 (8), 8-119 (6), 9-123 (9), 10-131 (10)

RAILWAYS

#	Batsman	Dismissal	R
1	S.S.Joshi	c Ghosh b Sharma	2
2	A.A.Pagnis	c Ghosh b Nadeem	33
3	*S.B.Bangar	c Vidyarthi b Rao	121
4	H.D.Rawle	c Vidyarthi b Rao	98
5	S.C.Sanyal	not out	51
6	†M.Rawat	not out	14
7	Harvinder Singh		
8	K.V.Sharma		
9	A.RajaAli		
10	M.S.Yadav		
11	S.R.Saxena		
	Extras	b 18, lb 8, w 4, nb 12	42
		(4 wickets, declared)	361

FoW (1): 1-12 (1), 2-61 (2), 3-269 (4), 4-306 (3)

Railways Bowling

	O	M	R	W			O	M	R	W	
Saxena	17	8	37	2	4nb	(3)	12	2	29	3	1nb
Bangar	17	6	36	4	3nb		7.4	2	26	2	
Harvinder Singh	13	2	41	2	5nb	(1)	12	2	31	2	3nb
Sanyal	8	0	15	0			5	2	16	1	1nb
Yadav	14.5	2	40	1	1nb		10	4	23	2	
Sharma	2	0	6	0							
Rawle	1	0	6	0							

Jharkhand Bowling

	O	M	R	W	
Sharma	34	4	138	1	1w,4nb
Rao	30	3	71	2	3nb
Nadeem	19	2	62	1	4nb
Roy	5	1	23	0	
Gupta	14	2	41	0	1w,1nb

Umpires: K.G.Lakshminarayan and C.R.Mohite.   Referee: Umesh Kumar.   Toss: Railways

Close of Play: 1st day: Railways (1) 12-1 (Pagnis 6*, Bangar 0*, 3 overs); 2nd day: Railways (1) 217-2 (Bangar 77*, Rawle 73*, 66.4 overs).

The match was scheduled for four days but completed in three. S.B.Bangar's 121 took 260 balls in 368 minutes and included 22 fours. Ratan Kumar retired hurt in the Jharkhand first innings having scored 0 (team score 49-3) - he returned when the score was 52-5.

144

RAJASTHAN v MUMBAI

Played at Sports Complex, Jhalwar, December 9, 10, 11, 12, 2007.
Ranji Trophy 2007/08 - Elite Group A
Mumbai won by 2 runs.   (Points: Rajasthan 0, Mumbai 5)

MUMBAI

#	Batsman	Dismissal 1	R	Dismissal 2	R
1	S.O.Kukreja	b Pankaj Singh	3	c Jhalani b Pankaj Singh	73
2	A.M.Rahane	b Shamsher Singh	90	c Sharma b Shamsher Singh	39
3	H.N.Shah	lbw b Afroz Khan	8	(6) not out	25
4	*A.A.Muzumdar	c Saxena b Pankaj Singh	20	not out	68
5	R.G.Sharma	b Shamsher Singh	62	(3) b Bist	34
6	A.M.Nayar	st Jhalani b Bishnoi	20	(5) c Mohammad Aslam b Shamsher Singh	12
7	R.R.Powar	lbw b Pankaj Singh	54		
8	†V.R.Samant	b Pankaj Singh	0		
9	Iqbal Abdulla	c Jhalani b Pankaj Singh	5		
10	U.R.Malvi	not out	6		
11	Murtuza Hussain	c Bist b Mohammad Aslam	9		
	Extras	b 3, lb 6, w 6, nb 3	18	lb 2, w 10, nb 4	16
			295	(4 wickets, declared)	**267**

FoW (1): 1-29 (1), 2-42 (3), 3-95 (4), 4-188 (2), 5-189 (5), 6-254 (6), 7-263 (8), 8-275 (7), 9-280 (9), 10-295 (11)
FoW (2): 1-119 (2), 2-126 (1), 3-190 (3), 4-213 (5)

RAJASTHAN

#	Batsman	Dismissal 1	R	Dismissal 2	R
1	M.D.Sharma	c Samant b Malvi	8	lbw b Malvi	6
2	G.K.Khoda	lbw b Murtuza Hussain	0	(7) run out	18
3	R.K.Bishnoi	b Powar	52	c Rahane b Nayar	44
4	V.A.Saxena	lbw b Nayar	6	(2) c Muzumdar b Iqbal Abdulla	122
5	N.S.Doru	not out	52	(4) run out	82
6	R.D.Bist	c Kukreja b Muzumdar	30	(5) run out	64
7	†R.B.Jhalani	lbw b Powar	7	(6) run out	14
8	Afroz Khan	b Powar	0	(9) b Murtuza Hussain	0
9	Pankaj Singh	c and b Iqbal Abdulla	9	(8) not out	10
10	Shamsher Singh	lbw b Powar	7	run out	1
11	*Mohammad Aslam	c Powar b Malvi	1	b Murtuza Hussain	0
	Extras	lb 4, nb 3	7	b 1, lb 9, w 4, nb 1, pen 5	20
			179		**381**

FoW (1): 1-0 (2), 2-28 (1), 3-44 (4), 4-76 (3), 5-129 (6), 6-137 (7), 7-141 (8), 8-152 (9), 9-171 (10), 10-179 (11)
FoW (2): 1-18 (1), 2-85 (3), 3-244 (2), 4-306 (4), 5-338 (6), 6-366 (7), 7-375 (5), 8-380 (9), 9-381 (10), 10-381 (11)

Rajasthan Bowling

	O	M	R	W		O	M	R	W	
Pankaj Singh	23	7	72	5		13	3	36	1	
Afroz Khan	23	3	81	1	1w,3nb	13	0	49	0	1w,3nb
Mohammad Aslam	18.4	4	56	1	(4)	14	1	55	0	3w
Bishnoi	11	1	27	1	1w (3)	7	0	27	0	2w
Shamsher Singh	16	1	50	2		17	2	85	2	
Bist					(6)	2	0	13	0	1nb

Mumbai Bowling

	O	M	R	W		O	M	R	W	
Malvi	17.5	4	48	2		20	6	61	1	1nb
Murtuza Hussain	17	1	36	1		15	1	58	2	
Nayar	9	5	11	1		16	4	60	1	
Powar	28	7	53	4	3nb	26	4	99	0	
Iqbal Abdulla	17	9	22	1		25	3	80	1	4w
Muzumdar	1	0	5	1		2	0	4	0	
Sharma					(7)	2	0	4	0	

Umpires: A.Bhattacharjee and M.S.Mahal. Referee: G.J.J.Raju.   Toss: Mumbai

Close of Play: 1st day: Mumbai (1) 290-9 (Malvi 6*, Murtuza Hussain 4*, 90 overs); 2nd day: Rajasthan (1) 175-9 (Doru 50*, Mohammad Aslam 1*, 86 overs); 3rd day: Rajasthan (2) 48-1 (Saxena 21*, Bishnoi 21*, 16 overs).

V.A.Saxena's 122 took 234 balls in 317 minutes and included 20 fours and 1 six.

TAMIL NADU v HIMACHAL PRADESH

Played at M.A.Chidambaram Stadium, Chepauk, Chennai, December 9, 10, 11, 12, 2007.
Ranji Trophy 2007/08 - Elite Group A
Tamil Nadu won by 180 runs. (Points: Tamil Nadu 5, Himachal Pradesh 0)

TAMIL NADU

1	A.Mukund	b Thakur	0	c Bisla b Thakur	96
2	M.Vijay Krishna	b Malik	35	c Bisla b Sarandeep Singh	9
3	*S.Badrinath	c Bisla b Thakur	111	(4) lbw b Sarandeep Singh	36
4	K.Vasudevadas	lbw b Thakur	39	(5) c Dogra b Sarandeep Singh	12
5	R.Srinivasan	c Bisla b Thakur	0	(6) c Dogra b Bhatia	34
6	S.Suresh Kumar	c S.Sharma b Sarandeep Singh	12	(7) not out	66
7	†H.Gopinath	st Bisla b Sarandeep Singh	21	(3) c Bisla b Malik	2
8	R.Ramkumar	c S.Sharma b Thakur	6	not out	9
9	V.Y.Mahesh	c Bisla b Thakur	2		
10	C.Suresh	c Mannu b Sarandeep Singh	0		
11	P.Amarnath	not out	0		
	Extras	b 6, nb 2	8	b 19, lb 11, nb 2	32
			234	(6 wickets, declared)	296

FoW (1): 1-5 (1), 2-48 (2), 3-145 (4), 4-147 (5), 5-166 (6), 6-206 (7), 7-221 (8), 8-225 (9), 9-226 (10), 10-234 (3)
FoW (2): 1-17 (2), 2-32 (3), 3-86 (4), 4-112 (5), 5-184 (6), 6-280 (1)

HIMACHAL PRADESH

1	M.Gupta	c C.Suresh b Amarnath	9	c Vijay Krishna b Ramkumar	23
2	*S.Sharma	c Badrinath b Ramkumar	7	lbw b Mahesh	6
3	P.Dogra	st Gopinath b C.Suresh	49	c Mahesh b Ramkumar	19
4	B.Sharma	c Vijay Krishna b C.Suresh	5	(6) b Ramkumar	7
5	†M.S.Bisla	c Vasudevadas b Badrinath	61	(4) c Vijay Krishna b Suresh Kumar	7
6	A.Mannu	c Gopinath b Mahesh	16	(5) lbw b Suresh Kumar	24
7	Sarandeep Singh	c Srinivasan b Mahesh	39	b Suresh Kumar	19
8	V.Bhatia	c Gopinath b Amarnath	28	c C.Suresh b Suresh Kumar	9
9	A.K.Thakur	c Srinivasan b Mahesh	2	run out	1
10	V.Malik	lbw b Mahesh	4	c Mukund b Amarnath	2
11	J.Mehta	not out	0	not out	0
	Extras	b 1, lb 4	5	b 7, lb 3	10
			223		127

FoW (1): 1-10 (2), 2-25 (1), 3-58 (4), 4-85 (3), 5-127 (6), 6-179 (5), 7-195 (7), 8-197 (9), 9-215 (10), 10-223 (8)
FoW (2): 1-17 (2), 2-46 (3), 3-58 (1), 4-64 (4), 5-73 (6), 6-115 (7), 7-124 (5), 8-125 (8), 9-127 (9), 10-127 (10)

Himachal Pradesh Bowling

	O	M	R	W		O	M	R	W	
Thakur	20	10	34	6		18	4	49	1	
Malik	14	4	29	1	2nb	11	2	45	1	
Mehta	7	0	43	0	(6)	8	1	26	0	
Sarandeep Singh	24	4	77	3		27	3	78	3	
Bhatia	11	1	37	0	(3)	23	4	54	1	2nb
S.Sharma	1	0	8	0	(5)	4	1	14	0	

Tamil Nadu Bowling

	O	M	R	W		O	M	R	W	
Mahesh	20	5	40	4		9	4	30	1	
Amarnath	18	4	45	2		7.3	3	19	1	
Ramkumar	20	3	50	1		21	12	26	3	
C.Suresh	17	4	39	2		10	4	11	0	
Suresh Kumar	10	1	33	0		11	1	31	4	
Vasudevadas	2	0	5	0						
Badrinath	3	0	6	1						

Umpires: M.G.Mandale and A.M.Saheba. Referee: S.Chaturvedi. Toss: Tamil Nadu

Close of Play: 1st day: Himachal Pradesh (1) 10-1 (Gupta 3*, 9.4 overs); 2nd day: Tamil Nadu (2) 19-1 (Mukund 5*, Gopinath 1*, 8 overs); 3rd day: Himachal Pradesh (2) 5-0 (Gupta 4*, S.Sharma 0*, 1.3 overs).

S.Badrinath's 111 took 206 balls in 322 minutes and included 13 fours.

VIDARBHA v SERVICES

Played at Vidarbha Cricket Association Ground, Nagpur, December 9, 10, 11, 12, 2007.
Ranji Trophy 2007/08 - Plate Group A
Vidarbha won by 309 runs.   (Points: Vidarbha 5, Services 0)

VIDARBHA

1	F.Y.Fazal	b Narender Kumar	24	lbw b Rakesh Kumar		80
2	A.G.Paunikar	c Israni b Mohanty	32	c Jasvir Singh b Rakesh Kumar		102
3	A.S.Naidu	b Narender Kumar	9	lbw b Pankaj Kumar		102
4	A.G.Mohod	c Israni b Pankaj Kumar	18	lbw b Rakesh Kumar		0
5	R.L.Jangid	b Sharma	3	b Rakesh Kumar		3
6	S.U.Shrivastava	c Tahir Khan b Mohanty	40	not out		61
7	†V.P.Gonnade	c Chatarjee b Rakesh Kumar	10	b Pankaj Kumar		0
8	*P.V.Gandhe	c Mumtaz Qadir b Rakesh Kumar	20			
9	A.B.Waghmare	b Sharma	0	(8) c Yashpal Singh b Rakesh Kumar		0
10	S.R.Singh	c Israni b Rakesh Kumar	0	(9) c sub (S.Upadhyay)		
					b Narender Kumar	29
11	Mohammad Hashim	not out	0			
	Extras	b 2, lb 3, w 1, nb 1	7	b 7, lb 9, w 3, nb 4		23
			163	(8 wickets, declared)		400

FoW (1): 1-56 (2), 2-58 (1), 3-71 (3), 4-74 (5), 5-100 (4), 6-116 (7), 7-160 (6), 8-163 (8), 9-163 (10), 10-163 (9)
FoW (2): 1-168 (1), 2-203 (2), 3-203 (4), 4-223 (5), 5-341 (3), 6-341 (7), 7-347 (8), 8-400 (9)

SERVICES

1	S.Chatarjee	b Mohammad Hashim	5	(7) c and b Mohammad Hashim		21
2	Tahir Khan	b Singh	0	c Fazal b Mohammad Hashim		10
3	†D.S.Israni	c Gonnade b Mohammad Hashim	9	(1) c Gandhe b Mohammad Hashim		0
4	Jasvir Singh	c Gonnade b Mohammad Hashim	30	(3) lbw b Naidu		24
5	*Yashpal Singh	lbw b Mohammad Hashim	0	(4) c sub (S.N.Binkar) b Singh		46
6	Mumtaz Qadir	c Gonnade b Singh	8	absent hurt		0
7	Narender Kumar	lbw b Mohammad Hashim	2	(5) c Jangid b Naidu		11
8	A.K.Mohanty	c Gandhe b Mohammad Hashim	27	(6) lbw b Singh		32
9	A.Sharma	b Mohammad Hashim	0	(8) c Mohod b Naidu		1
10	Pankaj Kumar	not out	3	(9) not out		7
11	Rakesh Kumar	b Singh	2	(10) c Waghmare b Mohammad Hashim		0
	Extras	lb 1, nb 4	5	lb 5, nb 6		11
			91			163

FoW (1): 1-5 (2), 2-13 (1), 3-20 (3), 4-20 (5), 5-32 (6), 6-39 (7), 7-83 (4), 8-83 (9), 9-87 (8), 10-91 (11)
FoW (2): 1-0 (1), 2-15 (2), 3-49 (3), 4-63 (5), 5-129 (6), 6-149 (4), 7-150 (8), 8-163 (7), 9-163 (10)

Services Bowling

	O	M	R	W			O	M	R	W	
Pankaj Kumar	13	2	26	1	1nb		16	3	55	2	1w
Rakesh Kumar	15	6	40	3			29	5	122	5	1w,1nb
Narender Kumar	14	1	48	2	1w		19.5	0	69	1	1w
Mohanty	8	2	20	2			20	2	73	0	3nb
Sharma	16.2	6	24	2			27	4	64	0	
Yashpal Singh					(6)		2	1	1	0	

Vidarbha Bowling

	O	M	R	W				O	M	R	W	
Singh	17.3	3	45	3	2nb		(2)	22	5	53	2	2nb
Mohammad Hashim	17	8	26	7	2nb		(1)	20	5	52	4	4nb
Naidu	7	1	19	0				15	8	31	3	
Waghmare	1	1	0	0				5	1	8	0	
Gandhe							(5)	4	0	14	0	
Jangid							(6)	2	2	0	0	

Umpires: A.Y.Gokhale and S.K.Tarapore. Referee: Shakti Singh.   Toss: Vidarbha

Close of Play: 1st day: Services (1) 38-5 (Jasvir Singh 14*, Narender Kumar 1*, 21 overs); 2nd day: Vidarbha (2) 237-4 (Naidu 38*, Shrivastava 5*, 66 overs); 3rd day: Services (2) 100-4 (Yashpal Singh 34*, Mohanty 16*, 40 overs).

A.G.Paunikar's 102 took 170 balls in 234 minutes and included 17 fours and 2 sixes. A.S.Naidu's 102 took 181 balls in 226 minutes and included 14 fours.

ANDHRA v BARODA

Played at Andhra Cricket Association-Visakhapatnam District Cricket Association Stadium, Visakhapatnam, December 17, 18, 19, 20, 2007.
Ranji Trophy 2007/08 - Elite Group B
Match drawn.   (Points: Andhra 3, Baroda 1)

ANDHRA

1	H.H.Watekar	c Pathan b Hamid Ali	24
2	L.N.P.Reddy	run out (Gaekwad)	67
3	A.S.Verma	c Parab b Pawar	29
4	Y.Gnaneswara Rao	c Shah b Hamid Ali	57
5	A.G.Pradeep	c Shah b Singh	30
6	*†M.S.K.Prasad	not out	121
7	B.A.Sumanth	st Shah b Pawar	72
8	M.Suresh	c Solanki b Singh	19
9	G.Shankar Rao	lbw b Pathan	13
10	D.Kalyankrishna	c Solanki b Pawar	27
11	P.D.Vijaykumar	not out	1
	Extras	b 5, lb 3, nb 1	9

(9 wickets, declared) 469

FoW (1): 1-45 (1), 2-95 (3), 3-116 (2), 4-212 (5), 5-214 (4), 6-329 (7), 7-364 (8), 8-394 (9), 9-455 (10)

BARODA

1	S.S.Parab	c Watekar b Kalyankrishna	0	(2) c Prasad b Kalyankrishna	3
2	*C.C.Williams	c Pradeep b Kalyankrishna	77	(1) not out	53
3	A.A.Bilakhia	c Suresh b Kalyankrishna	0	lbw b Suresh	12
4	R.K.Solanki	c Sumanth b Kalyankrishna	55	not out	52
5	S.A.Gaekwad	c Pradeep b Shankar Rao	91		
6	†P.R.Shah	c Kalyankrishna b Shankar Rao	30		
7	Y.K.Pathan	b Suresh	3		
8	R.V.Pawar	c Watekar b Shankar Rao	0		
9	S.D.Vora	b Shankar Rao	0		
10	S.A.HamidAli	lbw b Shankar Rao	2		
11	S.M.Singh	not out	0		
	Extras	lb 3, w 4, nb 5	12	b 1, lb 4, nb 1	6

270   (2 wickets)   126

FoW (1): 1-1 (1), 2-3 (3), 3-142 (2), 4-169 (4), 5-244 (6), 6-251 (7), 7-252 (8), 8-252 (9), 9-269 (5), 10-270 (10)
FoW (2): 1-7 (2), 2-30 (3)

Baroda Bowling	O	M	R	W	
Singh	27	7	70	2	
Vora	27	5	78	0	
Hamid Ali	32	10	67	2	1nb
Pawar	58	16	144	3	
Pathan	41	7	102	1	

Andhra Bowling	O	M	R	W			O	M	R	W	
Kalyankrishna	28	8	69	4	2w,1nb		5	2	6	1	
Shankar Rao	19.2	4	50	5	1w	(7)	4	1	16	0	
Vijaykumar	18	11	31	0		(2)	11	3	22	0	
Watekar	31	7	72	0	4nb						
Suresh	9	2	20	1		(3)	11	1	33	1	
Verma	6	1	16	0		(8)	4	1	9	0	
Gnaneswara Rao	4	1	9	0	1w						
Reddy						(4)	1	0	1	0	1nb
Sumanth						(5)	3	0	14	0	
Pradeep						(6)	2	1	6	0	
Prasad						(9)	2	0	14	0	

Umpires: S.Dua and B.Sharma. Referee: C.R.Vijayaraghavan.   Toss: Andhra

Close of Play: 1st day: Andhra (1) 214-4 (Gnaneswara Rao 57*, Prasad 2*, 90 overs); 2nd day: Andhra (1) 434-8 (Prasad 95*, Kalyankrishna 20*, 175 overs); 3rd day: Baroda (1) 136-2 (Williams 75*, Solanki 51*, 77 overs).

M.S.K.Prasad's 121 took 277 balls in 405 minutes and included 10 fours and 2 sixes.

BENGAL v UTTAR PRADESH

Played at Eden Gardens, Kolkata, December 17, 18, 19, 2007.
Ranji Trophy 2007/08 - Elite Group B
Uttar Pradesh won by an innings and 152 runs.   (Points: Bengal 0, Uttar Pradesh 6)

BENGAL

1	A.P.Majumdar	c Amir Khan b Bhuvneshwar Singh	19	c Kaif b Tyagi	60
2	A.S.Das	c Chawla b Bhuvneshwar Singh	19	c Kaif b Tyagi	31
3	S.M.Ghosh	lbw b Kumar	1	c T.M.Srivastava b Tyagi	0
4	M.K.Tiwary	lbw b Kumar	2	c Kaif b Gupta	24
5	†W.P.Saha	b Tyagi	14	c Amir Khan b Tyagi	8
6	*L.R.Shukla	c T.M.Srivastava b Chawla	22	c T.M.Srivastava b Gupta	41
7	K.H.Mondal	c Amir Khan b Bhuvneshwar Singh	8	lbw b Gupta	0
8	S.S.Lahiri	not out	40	b Gupta	4
9	S.S.Sarkar	c Raina b Chawla	0	b Chawla	11
10	R.R.Bose	c Amir Khan b Kumar	12	b Gupta	0
11	S.S.Paul	lbw b Chawla	9	not out	0
	Extras	b 2, lb 1	3	lb 10, w 3, nb 1	14
			149		**193**

FoW (1): 1-40 (1), 2-41 (3), 3-43 (4), 4-49 (2), 5-72 (5), 6-87 (7), 7-91 (6), 8-91 (9), 9-130 (10), 10-149 (11)
FoW (2): 1-100 (1), 2-100 (3), 3-107 (2), 4-123 (5), 5-160 (4), 6-160 (7), 7-172 (8), 8-185 (6), 9-193 (9), 10-193 (10)

UTTAR PRADESH

1	R.P.Srivastava	c Ghosh b Paul	58
2	T.M.Srivastava	lbw b Paul	13
3	S.K.Raina	c Mondal b Paul	63
4	P.P.Gupta	c Tiwary b Paul	35
5	*M.Kaif	c and b Sarkar	91
6	R.U.Shukla	c Saha b Paul	31
7	P.P.Chawla	c sub (P.I.Mukherjee) b Sarkar	53
8	†Amir Khan	c Das b Paul	46
9	P.Kumar	b Paul	67
10	Bhuvneshwar Singh	not out	22
11	S.Tyagi	b Lahiri	1
	Extras	lb 8, w 1, nb 5	14
			494

FoW (1): 1-30 (2), 2-121 (1), 3-158 (3), 4-171 (4), 5-263 (6), 6-349 (7), 7-360 (5), 8-464 (9), 9-483 (8), 10-494 (11)

Uttar Pradesh Bowling

	O	M	R	W		O	M	R	W	
Kumar	20	5	51	3		14	5	29	0	1nb
Tyagi	15	3	41	1		12	2	38	4	3w
Bhuvneshwar Singh	10	4	25	3		9	0	42	0	
Chawla	13.4	5	29	3		20	6	63	1	
Gupta					(5)	9.3	6	11	5	

Bengal Bowling

	O	M	R	W	
Bose	27	6	80	0	
Paul	38	8	113	7	
Shukla	4	0	14	0	
Sarkar	27	3	110	2	
Lahiri	34.3	4	135	1	5nb
Tiwary	2	0	20	0	
Majumdar	6	0	14	0	1w

Umpires: S.D.Ranade and R.Subramanyam.   Referee: M.InderSingh.   Toss: Bengal

Close of Play: 1st day: Uttar Pradesh (1) 128-2 (Raina 55*, Gupta 1*, 31 overs); 2nd day: Uttar Pradesh (1) 437-7 (Amir Khan 30*, Kumar 50*, 121 overs).

The match was scheduled for four days but completed in three.

HIMACHAL PRADESH v MUMBAI

Played at Himachal Pradesh Cricket Association Stadium, Dharmasala, December 17, 18, 19, 20, 2007.
Ranji Trophy 2007/08 - Elite Group A
Match drawn.   (Points: Himachal Pradesh 1, Mumbai 3)

MUMBAI

1	S.O.Kukreja	lbw b Malik	1	c P.Dogra b Malik		1
2	A.M.Rahane	lbw b Sarandeep Singh	37	not out		18
3	V.A.Indulkar	b Thakur	37	not out		39
4	*A.A.Muzumdar	lbw b Thakur	90			
5	R.G.Sharma	c Bisla b Thakur	13			
6	A.M.Nayar	c Malik b Sarandeep Singh	21			
7	A.B.Agarkar	lbw b Thakur	27			
8	R.R.Powar	c Mannu b Bhatia	9			
9	†V.R.Samant	not out	60			
10	Iqbal Abdulla	run out (Sangram Singh)	32			
11	Murtuza Hussain	b Malik	16			
	Extras	b 12, lb 10, w 3, nb 2	27	b 4, lb 1, nb 2		7
			370	(1 wicket)		65

FoW (1): 1-5 (1), 2-82 (3), 3-82 (2), 4-113 (5), 5-178 (6), 6-241 (7), 7-254 (4), 8-258 (8), 9-313 (10), 10-370 (11)
FoW (2): 1-5 (1)

HIMACHAL PRADESH

1	M.Gupta	lbw b Murtuza Hussain	29	lbw b Iqbal Abdulla	53
2	H.Dogra	c Samant b Murtuza Hussain	38	c and b Powar	47
3	Sangram Singh	c Kukreja b Murtuza Hussain	0	b Powar	0
4	*S.Sharma	c Samant b Murtuza Hussain	6	lbw b Iqbal Abdulla	8
5	P.Dogra	run out (Indulkar)	42	b Murtuza Hussain	51
6	†M.S.Bisla	c Samant b Iqbal Abdulla	37	lbw b Murtuza Hussain	19
7	A.Mannu	c Muzumdar b Powar	0	b Nayar	103
8	Sarandeep Singh	not out	22	lbw b Nayar	26
9	V.Bhatia	b Agarkar	15	c Samant b Nayar	0
10	A.K.Thakur	b Murtuza Hussain	7	not out	46
11	V.Malik	b Murtuza Hussain	2	c sub (B.P.Patel) b Kukreja	48
	Extras	b 8, lb 6, nb 2	16	b 8, lb 9, w 6, nb 6	29
			214		430

FoW (1): 1-56 (2), 2-67 (3), 3-70 (1), 4-78 (4), 5-156 (6), 6-161 (7), 7-164 (5), 8-191 (9), 9-206 (10), 10-214 (11)
FoW (2): 1-76 (2), 2-78 (3), 3-107 (4), 4-126 (1), 5-155 (6), 6-239 (5), 7-330 (8), 8-330 (9), 9-351 (7), 10-430 (11)

Himachal Pradesh Bowling	O	M	R	W		O	M	R	W	
Thakur	35	10	116	4	3w,1nb	7	2	19	0	
Malik	22.4	7	54	2	1nb	5	2	12	1	2nb
P.Dogra	2	1	12	0						
Bhatia	22	4	74	1						
Sarandeep Singh	23	3	79	2						
Sharma	2	0	13	0		1	0	3	0	
Bisla					(3)	2	0	12	0	
Gupta					(4)	1	0	5	0	
H.Dogra					(5)	1	0	9	0	

Mumbai Bowling	O	M	R	W		O	M	R	W	
Agarkar	14	3	65	1		5.2	1	12	0	1nb
Murtuza Hussain	18.5	1	58	6		25.4	3	93	2	
Nayar	11	1	35	0		43	11	79	3	6w
Iqbal Abdulla	11	4	16	1	(5)	38	18	81	2	1nb
Powar	13	3	26	1	2nb (4)	41	8	105	2	4nb
Sharma					(6)	6	0	24	0	
Muzumdar					(7)	5	1	19	0	
Kukreja					(8)	0.2	0	0	1	

Umpires: K.G.Lakshminarayan and I.Shivram.   Referee: H.R.Wasu.   Toss: Mumbai

Close of Play: 1st day: Mumbai (1) 324-9 (Samant 31*, Murtuza Hussain 1*, 90 overs); 2nd day: Himachal Pradesh (1) 180-7 (Sarandeep Singh 8*, Bhatia 4*, 59 overs); 3rd day: Himachal Pradesh (2) 236-5 (P.Dogra 50*, Mannu 42*, 87 overs).
A.Mannu's 103 took 217 balls in 293 minutes and included 15 fours and 2 sixes.

KARNATAKA v DELHI

Played at M.Chinnaswamy Stadium, Bangalore, December 17, 18, 19, 20, 2007.
Ranji Trophy 2007/08 - Elite Group A
Match drawn.   (Points: Karnataka 1, Delhi 1)

DELHI

1	S.Dhawan	c Uthappa b Joshi	148
2	A.S.Chopra	lbw b Dhananjaya	6
3	V.Kohli	c Naidu b Vinay Kumar	169
4	*M.Manhas	b Vinay Kumar	124
5	R.Bhatia	b Vinay Kumar	8
6	M.Tehlan	c Naidu b Vinay Kumar	41
7	†P.Bisht	c Raghu b Joshi	1
8	Narender Singh	run out (Patil)	9
9	C.Nanda	lbw b Joshi	0
10	P.Sangwan	not out	22
11	P.Awana	lbw b Vinay Kumar	1
	Extras	b 4, lb 1, nb 4	9

538

FoW (1): 1-22 (2), 2-288 (1), 3-363 (3), 4-401 (5), 5-497 (6), 6-504 (4), 7-504 (7), 8-504 (9), 9-533 (8), 10-538 (11)

KARNATAKA

1	K.B.Pawan	not out	0
2	R.V.Uthappa	not out	0
3	*Y.K.T.Goud		
4	†V.S.T.Naidu		
5	S.B.Joshi		
6	R.Vinay Kumar		
7	K.P.Appanna		
8	D.T.Patil		
9	C.Raghu		
10	S.Dhananjaya		
11	A.A.Verma		

(no wicket)   0

Karnataka Bowling

	O	M	R	W	
Vinay Kumar	40.5	10	121	5	
Dhananjaya	24	5	121	1	4nb
Joshi	42	10	124	3	
Appanna	29	5	93	0	
Raghu	7	1	31	0	
Verma	11	0	31	0	
Uthappa	1	0	12	0	

Delhi Bowling

	O	M	R	W
Sangwan	0.1	0	0	0

Umpires: A.Bhattacharjee and S.J.Phadkar. Referee: M.Y.Ranade.   Toss: Delhi

Close of Play: 1st day: Delhi (1) 337-2 (Kohli 154*, Manhas 26*, 92 overs); 2nd day: Karnataka (1) 0-0 (Pawan 0*, Uthappa 0*, 0.1 overs); 3rd day: No play.

There was no play on the final day. S.Dhawan's 148 took 211 balls in 307 minutes and included 24 fours. V.Kohli's 169 took 311 balls in 370 minutes and included 25 fours and 1 six. M.Manhas's 124 took 188 balls in 286 minutes and included 20 fours and 1 six.

MAHARASHTRA v SAURASHTRA

Played at Indian Petrochemicals Corporation Limited Ground, Nagothane, December 17, 18, 19, 2007.
Ranji Trophy 2007/08 - Elite Group A
Saurashtra won by eight wickets.　(Points: Maharashtra 0, Saurashtra 5)

MAHARASHTRA

1	†V.V.More	b Jobanputra	4	c Jogiyani b Jobanputra	7
2	H.H.Khadiwale	c Kotak b Jadeja	29	c Kotak b Maniar	23
3	H.H.Kanitkar	b Jobanputra	4	c Jadeja b Dhruve	62
4	*Y.Venugopal Rao	run out (Jadeja)	1	lbw b Jadeja	4
5	Y.V.Takawale	c Jogiyani b Jadeja	18	c Jogiyani b Jadeja	3
6	V.R.Bhilare	c Maniar b Jadeja	0	c sub (N.R.Rathod) b Jadeja	31
7	K.M.Jadhav	c Jobanputra b Makwana	9	(8) not out	27
8	S.V.Bahutule	c Dhruve b Jobanputra	46	(7) b Dhruve	0
9	S.A.Agharkar	b Jadeja	12	c Kotak b Dhruve	9
10	S.M.Fallah	b Jobanputra	7	lbw b Dhruve	4
11	W.S.Sayyed	not out	0	st Jogiyani b Dhruve	0
	Extras	lb 4, w 1, nb 1	6	b 6, nb 6	12
			136		182

FoW (1): 1-8 (1), 2-12 (3), 3-14 (4), 4-53 (5), 5-53 (6), 6-68 (7), 7-68 (2), 8-92 (9), 9-129 (10), 10-136 (8)
FoW (2): 1-13 (1), 2-54 (2), 3-66 (4), 4-101 (5), 5-115 (3), 6-115 (7), 7-152 (6), 8-172 (9), 9-182 (10), 10-182 (11)

SAURASHTRA

1	K.M.Vaghela	lbw b Fallah	5	not out	29
2	†S.D.Jogiyani	c Takawale b Fallah	1	c Khadiwale b Bahutule	25
3	S.H.Kotak	lbw b Sayyed	108	c Kanitkar b Bahutule	3
4	C.A.Pujara	c More b Fallah	35	not out	4
5	F.U.Bambhaniya	c Kanitkar b Sayyed	2		
6	*J.N.Shah	c More b Bahutule	6		
7	R.A.Jadeja	run out (Jadhav)	34		
8	R.V.Dhruve	lbw b Bahutule	10		
9	K.R.Makwana	c Venugopal Rao b Agharkar	5		
10	S.P.Jobanputra	b Bahutule	24		
11	S.M.Maniar	not out	0		
	Extras	b 9, lb 2, nb 12	23	b 4, nb 3	7
			253	(2 wickets)	68

FoW (1): 1-2 (2), 2-16 (1), 3-87 (4), 4-90 (5), 5-100 (6), 6-159 (7), 7-178 (8), 8-198 (9), 9-253 (3), 10-253 (10)
FoW (2): 1-42 (2), 2-64 (3)

Saurashtra Bowling

	O	M	R	W			O	M	R	W	
Jobanputra	11.4	3	27	4			13	1	44	1	
Maniar	8	3	12	0	1nb		11	2	24	1	4nb
Vaghela	4	1	12	0	1w	(5)	1	0	3	0	1nb
Jadeja	18	7	49	4		(3)	30	12	45	3	1nb
Dhruve	5	3	3	0		(6)	13.4	2	37	5	
Makwana	8	1	29	1		(4)	6	0	21	0	
Pujara						(7)	1	0	2	0	

Maharashtra Bowling

	O	M	R	W			O	M	R	W	
Fallah	24	7	52	3	5nb		3	1	4	0	
Sayyed	16	3	35	2		(4)	2	1	1	0	
Venugopal Rao	8	1	21	0							
Bahutule	30.1	8	72	3	6nb	(2)	13.5	3	35	2	3nb
Agharkar	15	4	39	1		(3)	12	5	21	0	
Khadiwale	13	3	23	0	1nb	(5)	1	0	3	0	

Umpires: S.Lakshmanan and S.M.Raju.　Referee: A.Kaypee.　　　　Toss: Maharashtra

Close of Play: 1st day: Saurashtra (1) 73-2 (Kotak 27*, Pujara 31*, 33 overs); 2nd day: Maharashtra (2) 34-1 (Khadiwale 8*, Kanitkar 11*, 14 overs).

The match was scheduled for four days but completed in three. S.H.Kotak's 108 took 277 balls in 432 minutes and included 6 fours.

PUNJAB v ORISSA

Played at Punjab Cricket Association Ground, Mohali, December 17, 18, 19, 20, 2007.
Ranji Trophy 2007/08 - Elite Group B
Punjab won by seven wickets.   (Points: Punjab 5, Orissa 0)

ORISSA

1	B.S.Pati	b Gagandeep Singh	13	c U.Kaul b Gagandeep Singh		15
2	*S.S.Das	b S.Kaul	19	b Gagandeep Singh		45
3	N.J.Behera	lbw b Gagandeep Singh	13	c U.Kaul b Gagandeep Singh		1
4	R.R.Parida	c Sohal b Goel	52	lbw b V.R.Singh		0
5	R.R.Das	c U.Kaul b S.Kaul	0	lbw b V.R.Singh		0
6	P.Jayachandra	b S.Kaul	36	(7) b V.R.Singh		0
7	†H.M.Das	c U.Kaul b S.Kaul	100	(8) c Dharmani b V.R.Singh		4
8	D.S.Mohanty	lbw b Gagandeep Singh	12	(9) lbw b Kakkar		6
9	S.V.Sehgal	c Sohal b S.Kaul	5	(6) b V.R.Singh		0
10	B.C.Mohanty	not out	18	lbw b Kakkar		0
11	P.Das	c U.Kaul b Gagandeep Singh	27	not out		0
	Extras	b 10, lb 6, nb 12	28	b 1, lb 1, nb 3		5
			323			**76**

FoW (1): 1-20 (1), 2-48 (3), 3-50 (2), 4-50 (5), 5-121 (6), 6-189 (4), 7-267 (8), 8-273 (7), 9-278 (9), 10-323 (11)
FoW (2): 1-24 (1), 2-26 (3), 3-27 (4), 4-27 (5), 5-27 (6), 6-28 (7), 7-33 (8), 8-74 (9), 9-74 (10), 10-76 (2)

PUNJAB

1	S.Sohal	c H.M.Das b B.C.Mohanty	22	c B.C.Mohanty b D.S.Mohanty	44
2	K.Goel	run out (Pati)	20	c Sehgal b P.Das	6
3	R.Inder Singh	c H.M.Das b B.C.Mohanty	0	lbw b Behera	74
4	*P.Dharmani	lbw b D.S.Mohanty	22	retired hurt	8
5	†U.Kaul	lbw b D.S.Mohanty	10	not out	21
6	R.S.Ricky	b P.Das	21	not out	3
7	A.Kakkar	c Parida b B.C.Mohanty	53		
8	Gagandeep Singh	not out	29		
9	Charanjeet Singh	c Behera b B.C.Mohanty	0		
10	S.Kaul	lbw b B.C.Mohanty	6		
11	V.R.Singh	c H.M.Das b D.S.Mohanty	5		
	Extras	b 4, lb 9, w 2, nb 22	37	lb 8, nb 11	19
			225	**(3 wickets)**	**175**

FoW (1): 1-46 (1), 2-46 (3), 3-59 (2), 4-84 (5), 5-91 (4), 6-146 (6), 7-188 (7), 8-193 (9), 9-218 (10), 10-225 (11)
FoW (2): 1-17 (2), 2-84 (1), 3-168 (3)

Punjab Bowling

	O	M	R	W			O	M	R	W	
Gagandeep Singh	22	3	65	4	1nb		14.4	5	25	3	
V.R.Singh	15	1	68	0	6nb	(3)	10	1	25	5	3nb
S.Kaul	23	6	79	5	3nb	(2)	7	1	18	0	
Inder Singh	5	1	11	0							
Kakkar	13	2	40	0	2nb	(4)	3	1	6	2	
Charanjeet Singh	12	2	28	0							
Goel	3	0	16	1							

Orissa Bowling

	O	M	R	W			O	M	R	W	
D.S.Mohanty	25	4	74	3	3nb		15	8	17	1	
P.Das	16	6	40	1	7nb		14	1	50	1	2nb
B.C.Mohanty	17	4	48	5	9nb		16	2	45	0	8nb
Jayachandra	15	6	35	0	2w,3nb	(5)	3	1	3	0	
Sehgal	3	0	15	0		(4)	13.2	2	42	0	1nb
Behera						(6)	8	1	10	1	

Umpires: P.Bhanu Prakash and S.K.Sharma. Referee: G.J.J.Raju.   Toss: Punjab

Close of Play: 1st day: Orissa (1) 273-8 (Sehgal 1*, 86 overs); 2nd day: Punjab (1) 207-8 (Gagandeep Singh 20*, S.Kaul 3*, 71 overs); 3rd day: Punjab (2) 117-2 (Inder Singh 47*, Dharmani 8*, 38 overs).
H.M.Das's 100 took 151 balls in 211 minutes and included 9 fours and 2 sixes. V.R.Singh took a hat-trick in the Orissa second innings (Parida, RR Das, Sehgal). P.Dharmani retired hurt in the Punjab second innings having scored 8 (team score 117-2, 37.6 overs).

TAMIL NADU v RAJASTHAN

Played at M.A.Chidambaram Stadium, Chepauk, Chennai, December 17, 18, 19, 20, 2007.
Ranji Trophy 2007/08 - Elite Group A
Match drawn.   (Points: Tamil Nadu 1, Rajasthan 1)

TAMIL NADU

1	A.Mukund	c Jhalani b Nishan Singh	7
2	M.Vijay Krishna	c and b Gajendra Singh	123
3	*S.Badrinath	c Jhalani b Mathur	138
4	K.Vasudevadas	c Jhalani b Mathur	1
5	R.Srinivasan	not out	30
6	S.Suresh Kumar	not out	4
7	†H.Gopinath		
8	R.Ramkumar		
9	V.Y.Mahesh		
10	C.Suresh		
11	P.Amarnath		
	Extras	b 4, lb 6, w 3, nb 8	21
		(4 wickets, declared)	324

FoW (1): 1-8 (1), 2-242 (3), 3-244 (4), 4-318 (2)

RAJASTHAN

1	V.A.Saxena	c Mukund b Badrinath	71
2	A.P.Sharma	b Suresh Kumar	6
3	R.K.Bishnoi	c Vasudevadas b Suresh Kumar	16
4	N.S.Doru	run out (C.Suresh)	11
5	R.D.Bist	not out	79
6	N.G.Gehlot	c Vasudevadas b Mahesh	18
7	*†R.B.Jhalani	b C.Suresh	18
8	Shamsher Singh	not out	0
9	Nishan Singh		
10	Gajendra Singh		
11	S.O.Mathur		
	Extras	b 6, lb 3, w 1	10
		(6 wickets)	229

FoW (1): 1-26 (2), 2-48 (3), 3-86 (4), 4-141 (1), 5-172 (6), 6-224 (7)

Rajasthan Bowling

	O	M	R	W	
Mathur	22	1	79	2	3w
Nishan Singh	11	0	45	1	6nb
Shamsher Singh	25	3	97	0	
Bishnoi	2	0	15	0	
Gajendra Singh	23	4	54	1	
Gehlot	7	1	24	0	2nb

Tamil Nadu Bowling

	O	M	R	W	
Mahesh	14	3	50	1	1w
Amarnath	13	7	25	0	
C.Suresh	19	6	22	1	
Ramkumar	28	10	48	0	
Suresh Kumar	17	3	50	2	
Badrinath	6	0	20	1	
Vasudevadas	4	1	5	0	

Umpires: A.Y.Dandekar and M.S.Mahal. Referee: V.D.Dhamasker.   Toss: Tamil Nadu

Close of Play: 1st day: Tamil Nadu (1) 302-3 (Vijay Krishna 112*, Srinivasan 25*, 81.4 overs); 2nd day: No play; 3rd day: Tamil Nadu (1) 324-4 (Srinivasan 30*, Suresh Kumar 4*, 90 overs).

M.Vijay Krishna's 123 took 255 balls in 375 minutes and included 11 fours and 2 sixes. S.Badrinath's 138 took 181 balls in 251 minutes and included 16 fours and 2 sixes.

BARODA v ORISSA

Played at Moti Bagh Stadium, Vadodara, December 25, 26, 27, 28, 2007.
Ranji Trophy 2007/08 - Elite Group B
Match drawn. (Points: Baroda 1, Orissa 3)

BARODA

1	*C.C.Williams	c Pati b R.K.Mohanty	15	c H.M.Das b B.C.Mohanty	10
2	S.S.Parab	c H.M.Das b B.C.Mohanty	9	b D.S.Mohanty	1
3	A.A.Bilakhia	lbw b D.S.Mohanty	35	c H.M.Das b B.C.Mohanty	49
4	R.K.Solanki	lbw b B.C.Mohanty	6	c Jayachandra b B.C.Mohanty	0
5	S.A.Gaekwad	b B.C.Mohanty	0	lbw b D.S.Mohanty	61
6	†P.R.Shah	c sub (P.Das) b B.C.Mohanty	44	c sub (R.R.Das) b R.K.Mohanty	148
7	Y.K.Pathan	c H.M.Das b D.S.Mohanty	9	c Pati b Sehgal	30
8	A.R.Chauhan	c Pati b Sehgal	35	c Pati b Behera	2
9	R.V.Pawar	c Pati b Sehgal	1	st H.M.Das b R.K.Mohanty	91
10	S.D.Vora	not out	56	not out	5
11	S.M.Singh	c Parida b D.S.Mohanty	32	not out	7
	Extras	b 3, lb 4, nb 6	13	b 4, lb 4, w 2, nb 10	20
			255	(9 wickets)	424

FoW (1): 1-11 (2), 2-43 (1), 3-71 (4), 4-71 (3), 5-71 (5), 6-86 (7), 7-141 (8), 8-143 (9), 9-170 (6), 10-255 (11)
FoW (2): 1-7 (2), 2-11 (1), 3-11 (4), 4-126 (5), 5-126 (3), 6-182 (7), 7-187 (8), 8-403 (6), 9-417 (9)

ORISSA

1	B.S.Pati	c Parab b Singh	24
2	*S.S.Das	c Chauhan b Pawar	114
3	N.J.Behera	lbw b Pawar	31
4	R.R.Parida	c Shah b Singh	1
5	P.R.Sinha	lbw b Vora	44
6	P.Jayachandra	b Pawar	44
7	†H.M.Das	c Gaekwad b Pawar	4
8	R.K.Mohanty	lbw b Singh	0
9	D.S.Mohanty	not out	14
10	B.C.Mohanty	c Gaekwad b Pawar	0
11	S.V.Sehgal	c Vora b Pawar	7
	Extras	b 1, lb 5, w 5	11
			294

FoW (1): 1-38 (1), 2-103 (3), 3-122 (4), 4-213 (5), 5-253 (2), 6-269 (6), 7-270 (8), 8-272 (7), 9-272 (10), 10-294 (11)

Orissa Bowling

	O	M	R	W			O	M	R	W	
D.S.Mohanty	24	7	36	3			24	11	46	2	1w
B.C.Mohanty	24	6	62	4	2nb		21	5	49	3	2nb
Sinha	2	0	13	0	1nb	(8)	4	0	26	0	1w,2nb
Jayachandra	3	0	14	0	2nb	(3)	8	3	29	0	4nb
R.K.Mohanty	12	1	38	1			14	1	61	2	1nb
Sehgal	22	4	68	2	1nb	(4)	19	0	95	1	1nb
Behera	6	2	17	0		(6)	26	2	98	1	
Pati						(7)	3	0	12	0	

Baroda Bowling

	O	M	R	W	
Singh	32	11	58	3	3w
Vora	21	6	53	1	1w
Pawar	40.2	17	66	6	
Pathan	23	4	66	0	
Chauhan	10	1	32	0	
Bilakhia	2	0	13	0	

Umpires: N.R.S.Prabhu and R.D.Risodkar. Referee: V.NarayananKutty.   Toss: Baroda

Close of Play: 1st day: Baroda (1) 241-9 (Vora 45*, Singh 29*, 90 overs); 2nd day: Orissa (1) 204-3 (S.S.Das 100*, Sinha 43*, 85 overs); 3rd day: Baroda (2) 120-3 (Bilakhia 46*, Gaekwad 58*, 44 overs).

S.S.Das's 114 took 338 balls in 447 minutes and included 11 fours and 1 six. P.R.Shah's 148 took 191 balls in 268 minutes and included 14 fours and 2 sixes.

BENGAL v ANDHRA

Played at Eden Gardens, Kolkata, December 25, 26, 27, 2007.
Ranji Trophy 2007/08 - Elite Group B
Andhra won by 101 runs.   (Points: Bengal 0, Andhra 5)

ANDHRA

1	H.H.Watekar	b Paul	7	c Saha b Mukherjee	67
2	L.N.P.Reddy	b Chowdhary	21	c Saha b Paul	12
3	A.S.Verma	lbw b Bose	0	(5) c Saha b Bose	6
4	Y.Gnaneswara Rao	c Saha b Bose	20	c Dinda b Bose	6
5	*†M.S.K.Prasad	b Chowdhary	1	(7) c Saha b Bose	54
6	A.G.Pradeep	c Saha b Bose	16	(8) c Mondal b Paul	22
7	B.A.Sumanth	b Dinda	30	(6) lbw b Bose	1
8	G.Shankar Rao	c Tiwary b Paul	0	(9) c Saha b Bose	2
9	D.Kalyankrishna	b Chowdhary	16	(3) lbw b Bose	12
10	I.Raju	not out	1	c Majumdar b Bose	0
11	P.D.Vijaykumar	b Chowdhary	0	not out	6
	Extras	lb 8, w 1	9	lb 1, w 1	2
			121		**190**

FoW (1): 1-21 (1), 2-24 (3), 3-45 (2), 4-47 (5), 5-73 (6), 6-80 (4), 7-81 (8), 8-120 (9), 9-120 (7), 10-121 (11)
FoW (2): 1-47 (2), 2-88 (3), 3-98 (1), 4-104 (4), 5-104 (5), 6-109 (6), 7-154 (8), 8-159 (9), 9-159 (10), 10-190 (7)

BENGAL

1	A.P.Majumdar	c Vijaykumar b Raju	10	c Prasad b Vijaykumar	8
2	A.S.Das	lbw b Kalyankrishna	17	c Shankar Rao b Vijaykumar	9
3	†W.P.Saha	lbw b Vijaykumar	19	c Watekar b Vijaykumar	0
4	P.I.Mukherjee	c Prasad b Vijaykumar	0	(8) lbw b Gnaneswara Rao	0
5	M.K.Tiwary	b Vijaykumar	0	(4) b Gnaneswara Rao	35
6	*L.R.Shukla	b Vijaykumar	4	lbw b Vijaykumar	39
7	K.H.Mondal	b Gnaneswara Rao	11	(5) lbw b Vijaykumar	0
8	R.P.Chowdhary	b Gnaneswara Rao	0	(7) c Prasad b Gnaneswara Rao	1
9	R.R.Bose	c Verma b Vijaykumar	1	(10) lbw b Gnaneswara Rao	8
10	A.B.Dinda	c Reddy b Raju	27	(9) c Watekar b Gnaneswara Rao	0
11	S.S.Paul	not out	7	not out	6
	Extras	lb 1, nb 1	2	lb 5, nb 1	6
			98		**112**

FoW (1): 1-15 (1), 2-46 (3), 3-46 (4), 4-48 (2), 5-48 (5), 6-61 (7), 7-63 (8), 8-63 (6), 9-72 (9), 10-98 (10)
FoW (2): 1-9 (1), 2-9 (3), 3-27 (2), 4-35 (5), 5-65 (4), 6-70 (7), 7-70 (8), 8-88 (9), 9-98 (6), 10-112 (10)

Bengal Bowling

	O	M	R	W		O	M	R	W	
Bose	16	3	47	3		26.1	6	74	7	1w
Paul	14	5	20	2		20	7	41	2	
Dinda	13	4	33	1	1w	9	2	38	0	
Chowdhary	6.2	1	13	4		3	1	19	0	
Mukherjee						(5) 6	2	17	1	

Andhra Bowling

	O	M	R	W		O	M	R	W	
Kalyankrishna	12	3	27	1		6	1	18	0	
Vijaykumar	16	5	31	5	1nb	13	3	56	5	1nb
Raju	6.2	3	13	2		4	0	15	0	
Shankar Rao	2	0	9	0		1	0	2	0	
Gnaneswara Rao	9	1	17	2		5.5	3	16	5	

Umpires: M.S.Pathak and S.L.Shastri. Referee: B.Raghunath.   Toss: Bengal

Close of Play: 1st day: Bengal (1) 46-1 (Das 15*, Saha 19*, 24 overs); 2nd day: Andhra (2) 147-6 (Prasad 26*, Pradeep 16*, 50 overs).

The match was scheduled for four days but completed in three.

GUJARAT v MADHYA PRADESH

Played at Karnail Singh Stadium, Delhi, December 25, 26, 27, 28, 2007.
Ranji Trophy 2007/08 - Plate Group Semi-Final
Gujarat won by 159 runs.

GUJARAT

1	N.D.Modi	c Ojha b Pandey	0	c Murtuza Ali b Pandey	49
2	R.K.Tabiyar	c Ojha b Rajan	12	c Ojha b Rajan	19
3	*†P.A.Patel	c Ojha b Dholpure	20	b Rajan	84
4	N.K.Patel	b Dholpure	5	lbw b Dholpure	21
5	B.D.Thaker	b Rajan	4	lbw b Dholpure	0
6	D.M.Popat	c Ojha b Dholpure	5	c Ojha b Dholpure	0
7	T.K.Patel	not out	71	not out	30
8	M.B.Parmar	lbw b Pandey	0	lbw b Pandey	19
9	Amit Singh	c Ojha b Pandey	5	b Pandey	10
10	A.M.Makda	c Ojha b Jalaj S.Saxena	40	b Dholpure	0
11	S.K.Trivedi	b Jalaj S.Saxena	6	b Dholpure	0
	Extras	b 7, lb 7, nb 10	24	b 8, lb 5, w 1, nb 19	33
			192		265

FoW (1): 1-0 (1), 2-32 (3), 3-39 (4), 4-46 (2), 5-51 (5), 6-75 (6), 7-76 (8), 8-92 (9), 9-178 (10), 10-192 (11)
FoW (2): 1-71 (2), 2-98 (1), 3-183 (4), 4-184 (5), 5-190 (6), 6-196 (3), 7-231 (8), 8-261 (9), 9-265 (10), 10-265 (11)

MADHYA PRADESH

1	†N.V.Ojha	c P.A.Patel b Makda	0	lbw b Trivedi	1
2	M.A.Pasha	c Thaker b Amit Singh	17	lbw b Makda	30
3	Jalaj S.Saxena	b Trivedi	3	(8) c Amit Singh b Trivedi	29
4	Jatin S.Saxena	c P.A.Patel b Amit Singh	8	(3) c Modi b Amit Singh	66
5	D.Bundela	run out (Parmar)	34	(4) c P.A.Patel b Trivedi	0
6	R.N.Bakshi	c Thaker b Makda	10	(5) lbw b Trivedi	0
7	*B.R.Tomar	c P.A.Patel b Trivedi	3	(6) b Trivedi	0
8	Murtuza Ali	c P.A.Patel b Amit Singh	0	(7) c Amit Singh b T.K.Patel	21
9	S.M.Dholpure	c P.A.Patel b Trivedi	3	c P.A.Patel b Makda	19
10	S.P.Pandey	c Modi b Amit Singh	1	c P.A.Patel b Trivedi	16
11	A.Rajan	not out	8	not out	5
	Extras	b 1, lb 5	6	b 8, lb 8, nb 2	18
			93		205

FoW (1): 1-1 (1), 2-14 (3), 3-28 (2), 4-33 (4), 5-52 (6), 6-65 (7), 7-66 (8), 8-71 (9), 9-78 (10), 10-93 (5)
FoW (2): 1-20 (1), 2-65 (2), 3-70 (4), 4-70 (5), 5-82 (6), 6-127 (7), 7-141 (3), 8-184 (9), 9-192 (8), 10-205 (10)

Madhya Pradesh Bowling

	O	M	R	W		O	M	R	W	
Pandey	24	8	56	3	2nb	23	6	47	3	1nb
Rajan	17	5	54	2	5nb	34	6	82	2	6nb
Bundela	6	4	8	0	2nb	(4) 10	2	23	0	1nb
Dholpure	20	8	28	3	1nb	(3) 24.3	1	64	5	1w,5nb
Jalaj S.Saxena	8.4	1	19	2		(6) 12	3	28	0	1nb
Murtuza Ali	2	0	13	0		(5) 2	0	8	0	

Gujarat Bowling

	O	M	R	W		O	M	R	W	
Trivedi	18.2	11	25	3		20.4	5	61	6	
Makda	11	1	31	2		15	4	64	2	
Amit Singh	10	3	31	4		11	4	33	1	2nb
Parmar						(4) 1	0	4	0	
T.K.Patel						(5) 8	2	27	0	

Umpires: H.S.Sekhon and I.Shivram.   Referee: T.B.Arothe.   Toss: Madhya Pradesh

Close of Play: 1st day: Madhya Pradesh (1) 3-1 (Pasha 1*, Jalaj S.Saxena 2*, 5.1 overs); 2nd day: Gujarat (2) 98-2 (P.A.Patel 15*, 43 overs); 3rd day: Madhya Pradesh (2) 63-1 (Pasha 30*, Jatin S.Saxena 27*, 17 overs).

The match was scheduled for five days but completed in four.

HYDERABAD v UTTAR PRADESH

Played at Rajiv Gandhi International Stadium, Uppal, Hyderabad, December 25, 26, 27, 28, 2007.
Ranji Trophy 2007/08 - Elite Group B
Uttar Pradesh won by 132 runs.   (Points: Hyderabad 0, Uttar Pradesh 5)

UTTAR PRADESH

1	R.P.Srivastava	c Abhinav Kumar b Shoaib Ahmed	0	lbw b Ojha	56	
2	T.M.Srivastava	c Abhinav Kumar b Sharma	81	lbw b Shinde	54	
3	S.K.Raina	b Sharma	35	lbw b Ojha	10	
4	*M.Kaif	lbw b Arjun	37	not out	100	
5	R.U.Shukla	lbw b Ojha	0	not out	70	
6	P.P.Chawla	c Arjun b Shoaib Ahmed	82			
7	†Amir Khan	c Abhinav Kumar b Mohammad Shakeer	50			
8	P.Kumar	b Ojha	36			
9	P.P.Gupta	c Pai b Sharma	6			
10	Bhuvneshwar Singh	not out	1			
11	S.Tyagi	c Manohar b Sharma	1			
	Extras	b 2, lb 1, w 1, nb 3	7	b 2, lb 2	4	
			336	(3 wickets, declared)	294	

FoW (1): 1-0 (1), 2-61 (3), 3-141 (4), 4-148 (5), 5-168 (2), 6-280 (6), 7-324 (7), 8-333 (9), 9-335 (8), 10-336 (11)
FoW (2): 1-100 (1), 2-116 (3), 3-124 (2)

HYDERABAD

1	D.S.Manohar	c T.M.Srivastava b Gupta	32	c Amir Khan b P.Kumar	33	
2	D.B.Ravi Teja	b P.Kumar	1	(7) not out	133	
3	S.A.Pai	lbw b Tyagi	18	c Bhuvneshwar Singh b Gupta	24	
4	*A.S.Yadav	c T.M.Srivastava b Gupta	22	(5) c Shukla b Tyagi	42	
5	A.J.Shinde	lbw b Gupta	0	(6) c Amir Khan b P.Kumar	43	
6	Mohammad Shakeer	b Chawla	49	(8) b Gupta	0	
7	†Abhinav Kumar	st Amir Khan b Chawla	8	(2) lbw b P.Kumar	2	
8	M.P.Arjun	b Chawla	25	(9) c Raina b P.Kumar	7	
9	P.P.Ojha	c R.P.Srivastava b Gupta	23	(10) c Raina b P.Kumar	1	
10	Shoaib Ahmed	not out	5	(4) c Chawla b P.Kumar	1	
11	V.G.Sharma	b Chawla	4	lbw b Tyagi	12	
	Extras	b 1, lb 3, w 1, nb 1	6	b 3, lb 1, w 1, nb 3	8	
			193		305	

FoW (1): 1-4 (2), 2-35 (3), 3-69 (4), 4-69 (5), 5-98 (1), 6-129 (7), 7-134 (6), 8-180 (9), 9-185 (8), 10-193 (11)
FoW (2): 1-6 (2), 2-55 (3), 3-61 (1), 4-81 (4), 5-121 (5), 6-199 (6), 7-202 (8), 8-221 (9), 9-221 (10), 10-305 (11)

Hyderabad Bowling	O	M	R	W			O	M	R	W	
Shoaib Ahmed	19	2	54	2	1w	(5)	1	0	6	0	
Arjun	22	3	80	1	3nb	(1)	12	3	48	0	
Sharma	24.3	5	73	4			10	0	62	0	
Ojha	28	3	86	2		(2)	35.4	9	109	2	
Shinde	6	0	24	0		(4)	25	7	65	1	
Mohammad Shakeer	5	0	7	1							
Ravi Teja	2	0	9	0							

Uttar Pradesh Bowling	O	M	R	W			O	M	R	W	
Tyagi	12	3	33	1	1w	(3)	14.2	3	76	2	1w
P.Kumar	10	2	37	1		(1)	23	3	65	6	3nb
Bhuvneshwar Singh	5	1	14	0		(2)	3	1	13	0	
Chawla	19.2	5	50	4		(5)	17	4	62	0	
Gupta	16	5	55	4	1nb	(4)	20	4	66	2	
Raina						(6)	2	0	12	0	
Kaif						(7)	3	0	7	0	

Umpires: R.Y.Deshmukh and M.G.Mandale. Referee: C.R.Vijayaraghavan.   Toss: Uttar Pradesh

Close of Play: 1st day: Uttar Pradesh (1) 293-6 (Amir Khan 44*, P.Kumar 7*, 90 overs); 2nd day: Uttar Pradesh (2) 28-0 (R.P.Srivastava 16*, T.M.Srivastava 12*, 8 overs); 3rd day: Hyderabad (2) 55-2 (Manohar 28*, Shoaib Ahmed 0*, 16 overs).

M.Kaif's 100 took 150 balls in 170 minutes and included 8 fours and 3 sixes. D.B.Ravi Teja's 133 took 118 balls in 155 minutes and included 21 fours and 3 sixes.

KERALA v RAILWAYS

Played at Vidarbha Cricket Association Ground, Nagpur, December 25, 26, 27, 28, 29, 2007.
Ranji Trophy 2007/08 - Plate Group Semi-Final
Match drawn.

KERALA

#	Batsman	Dismissal 1	Score 1	Dismissal 2	Score 2
1	M.Sebastian Antony	c Rawat b Bangar	52	(2) b Bangar	70
2	R.V.Gomez	c Sanyal b Saxena	13	(1) st Rawat b Bangar	101
3	*S.K.Cheruvathur	c Rawat b Harvinder Singh	26	(7) b Bangar	1
4	S.R.Nair	c Sanyal b Bangar	44	(3) c and b Kartik	24
5	P.Rohan Prem	b Kartik	28	(6) lbw b Kartik	2
6	V.A.Jagadeesh	c Pagnis b Kartik	17	(5) not out	52
7	P.Prasanth	b Harvinder Singh	17	(8) lbw b Bangar	2
8	†V.G.Nair	c Pagnis b Saxena	70	(4) c sub (K.S.Parida) b Bangar	1
9	T.Yohannan	c Rawat b Harvinder Singh	4	(10) run out	7
10	S.Anish	not out	55	(9) c Rawat b Kartik	4
11	P.Chandran	c Rawat b Bangar	8	not out	13
	Extras	b 2, lb 5, w 5, nb 11	23	lb 5, w 1, nb 7	13
			357	(9 wickets, declared)	290

FoW (1): 1-31 (2), 2-92 (3), 3-107 (1), 4-161 (5), 5-184 (6), 6-207 (4), 7-222 (7), 8-240 (9), 9-303 (8), 10-357 (11)
FoW (2): 1-165 (1), 2-198 (3), 3-201 (4), 4-223 (2), 5-238 (6), 6-243 (7), 7-249 (8), 8-255 (9), 9-262 (10)

RAILWAYS

#	Batsman	Dismissal 1	Score 1	Dismissal 2	Score 2
1	S.S.Joshi	lbw b Chandran	9	not out	41
2	A.A.Pagnis	c Gomez b Chandran	2	c and b Cheruvathur	23
3	*S.B.Bangar	lbw b Anish	13	c V.G.Nair b Cheruvathur	0
4	H.D.Rawle	b Anish	66	not out	59
5	S.C.Sanyal	lbw b Cheruvathur	115		
6	†M.Rawat	c and b Yohannan	77		
7	K.V.Sharma	c and b Yohannan	10		
8	A.Raja Ali	lbw b Yohannan	31		
9	M.Kartik	c Cheruvathur b S.R.Nair	39		
10	Harvinder Singh	c Prasanth b Anish	10		
11	S.R.Saxena	not out	1		
	Extras	b 10, lb 15, w 1, nb 3	29	lb 2, nb 3	5
			402	(2 wickets)	128

FoW (1): 1-17 (2), 2-20 (1), 3-41 (3), 4-160 (4), 5-276 (5), 6-303 (7), 7-310 (6), 8-373 (8), 9-401 (10), 10-402 (9)
FoW (2): 1-34 (2), 2-34 (3)

Railways Bowling	O	M	R	W		O	M	R	W	
Harvinder Singh	27	7	99	3	7nb	5	0	48	0	5nb
Saxena	18	8	43	2	1w	(4) 8	1	30	0	1w
Bangar	29.3	12	60	3	3w	(2) 30	2	118	5	
Sanyal	8	2	35	0	1w	(5) 4	0	19	0	
Kartik	32	11	81	2	4nb	(3) 24	3	70	3	1nb
Sharma	4	1	15	0						
Rawle	4	0	17	0						

Kerala Bowling	O	M	R	W		O	M	R	W	
Yohannan	37	11	87	3	1w,1nb	7	1	13	0	1nb
Chandran	29	8	60	2		6	1	21	0	
Cheruvathur	36	9	88	1	2nb	11	5	16	2	1nb
Gomez	8	2	20	0						
Anish	37	12	67	3		(4) 16	8	30	0	
Prasanth	12	2	37	0		8	6	8	0	
S.R.Nair	10.5	5	13	1		(5) 13	5	26	0	
Sebastian Antony	1	0	5	0						
Rohan Prem						(7) 2	0	10	0	
Jagadeesh						(8) 1	0	2	0	

Umpires: S.Asnani and S.J.Phadkar. Referee: A.Patel.   Toss: Railways
Close of Play: 1st day: Kerala (1) 207-6 (Prasanth 12*, 91 overs); 2nd day: Railways (1) 123-3 (Rawle 44*, Sanyal 40*, 56 overs); 3rd day: Railways (1) 348-7 (Raja Ali 22*, Kartik 7*, 146 overs); 4th day: Kerala (2) 249-7 (Jagadeesh 36*, 60.5 overs).
S.C.Sanyal's 115 took 300 balls in 366 minutes and included 17 fours. R.V.Gomez's 101 took 124 balls in 172 minutes and included 10 fours and 3 sixes.

MAHARASHTRA v KARNATAKA

Played at Chatrapati Shivaji Stadium, Ratnagiri, December 25, 26, 27, 28, 2007.
Ranji Trophy 2007/08 - Elite Group A
Karnataka won by an innings and 129 runs.   (Points: Maharashtra 0, Karnataka 6)

MAHARASHTRA

1	H.H.Khadiwale	c Naidu b Vinay Kumar	96	c Joshi b Vinay Kumar	12
2	A.R.Bawne	c Naidu b Vinay Kumar	27	b Vinay Kumar	0
3	A.J.Shrikhande	c Naidu b Aiyappa	16	(4) lbw b Vinay Kumar	0
4	*Y.Venugopal Rao	b Aiyappa	47	(5) c Raghu b Vinay Kumar	56
5	Y.V.Takawale	c Chipli b Joshi	15	(6) c Pawan b Joshi	39
6	D.Mohan	c Verma b Aiyappa	51	(7) c Vinay Kumar b Joshi	0
7	A.S.Joshi	b Vinay Kumar	0	(3) b Vinay Kumar	0
8	†S.G.Jadhav	c Raghu b Vinay Kumar	4	lbw b Joshi	4
9	A.P.Dole	c Raghu b Joshi	0	c Verma b Vinay Kumar	12
10	S.M.Fallah	run out (Patil)	2	(11) not out	0
11	W.S.Sayyed	not out	4	(10) c Chipli b Joshi	3
	Extras	b 4, lb 1, w 3, nb 6	14	b 5, lb 6, nb 3	14
			276		**140**

FoW (1): 1-42 (2), 2-74 (3), 3-165 (4), 4-210 (5), 5-214 (1), 6-214 (7), 7-226 (8), 8-241 (9), 9-258 (10), 10-276 (6)
FoW (2): 1-9 (2), 2-9 (3), 3-13 (4), 4-39 (1), 5-107 (6), 6-107 (7), 7-125 (8), 8-125 (5), 9-140 (9), 10-140 (10)

KARNATAKA

1	R.V.Uthappa	c Takawale b Sayyed	15
2	K.B.Pawan	b Joshi	102
3	D.T.Patil	c Mohan b Fallah	7
4	C.Raghu	c Mohan b Joshi	67
5	A.A.Verma	lbw b Venugopal Rao	1
6	†V.S.T.Naidu	c and b Venugopal Rao	58
7	*Y.K.T.Goud	lbw b Takawale	122
8	B.Chipli	not out	135
9	S.B.Joshi	lbw b Joshi	1
10	R.Vinay Kumar	c Fallah b Joshi	0
11	N.C.Aiyappa	not out	6
	Extras	b 14, lb 2, w 7, nb 8	31
		(9 wickets, declared)	**545**

FoW (1): 1-27 (1), 2-38 (3), 3-194 (4), 4-208 (5), 5-212 (2), 6-332 (6), 7-467 (7), 8-470 (9), 9-472 (10)

Karnataka Bowling	O	M	R	W		O	M	R	W	
Vinay Kumar	23	6	66	4	1w,1nb	13	3	38	6	1nb
Aiyappa	21.1	4	70	3	2w,4nb	10	2	40	0	2nb
Chipli	5	1	14	0	1nb	(5) 3	0	13	0	
Joshi	27	4	88	2		(3) 10.1	5	18	4	
Raghu	5	0	22	0		(4) 4	0	20	0	
Verma	5	1	11	0						

Maharashtra Bowling	O	M	R	W	
Fallah	30	4	103	1	4w,1nb
Dole	27	7	80	0	4nb
Sayyed	24	6	58	1	2w
Khadiwale	11	1	36	0	1w
Joshi	44	10	133	4	
Mohan	2	0	5	0	
Venugopal Rao	13	5	36	0	
Bawne	9	0	43	0	3nb
Takawale	12	0	35	1	

Umpires: S.Das and A.K.Mitra.   Referee: G.J.J.Raju.   Toss: Karnataka

Close of Play: 1st day: Karnataka (1) 2-0 (Uthappa 0*, Pawan 0*, 1 over); 2nd day: Karnataka (1) 239-5 (Naidu 25*, Goud 4*, 91 overs); 3rd day: Maharashtra (2) 18-3 (Khadiwale 5*, Venugopal Rao 3*, 7 overs).

K.B.Pawan's 102 took 230 balls in 347 minutes and included 12 fours. Y.K.T.Goud's 122 took 236 balls in 309 minutes and included 20 fours. B.Chipli's 135 took 184 balls in 215 minutes and included 16 fours and 4 sixes. R.Vinay Kumar took a hat-trick in the Maharashtra second innings (Bawne, Joshi, Shrikande).

MUMBAI v SAURASHTRA

Played at Wankhede Stadium, Mumbai, December 25, 26, 27, 28, 2007.
Ranji Trophy 2007/08 - Elite Group A
Match drawn.   (Points: Mumbai 1, Saurashtra 3)

SAURASHTRA

1	K.M.Vaghela	c Samant b Murtuza Hussain	35
2	†S.D.Jogiyani	b Murtuza Hussain	5
3	S.H.Kotak	not out	168
4	C.A.Pujara	b Mangela	63
5	N.R.Rathod	c Samant b Mangela	13
6	*J.N.Shah	c Sharma b Mangela	10
7	R.A.Jadeja	c Rahane b Kulkarni	87
8	R.V.Dhruve	c Muzumdar b Mangela	27
9	K.R.Makwana	c Kukreja b Murtuza Hussain	0
10	S.P.Jobanputra	c sub (H.N.Shah) b Murtuza Hussain	0
11	S.M.Maniar	c Kukreja b Mangela	26
	Extras	b 9, lb 18, w 7, nb 16	50
			484

FoW (1): 1-11 (2), 2-92 (1), 3-212 (4), 4-230 (5), 5-245 (6), 6-399 (7), 7-441 (8), 8-444 (9), 9-444 (10), 10-484 (11)

MUMBAI

1	S.O.Kukreja	lbw b Vaghela	10
2	A.M.Rahane	c Rathod b Maniar	149
3	V.A.Indulkar	c Jogiyani b Jobanputra	0
4	*A.A.Muzumdar	lbw b Maniar	187
5	R.G.Sharma	c Pujara b Jobanputra	41
6	A.M.Nayar	c Jogiyani b Makwana	41
7	R.R.Powar	c Pujara b Jobanputra	0
8	†V.R.Samant	c Pujara b Jobanputra	8
9	N.M.Kulkarni	run out (Vaghela)	3
10	M.G.Mangela	c Shah b Jobanputra	4
11	Murtuza Hussain	not out	0
	Extras	b 1, lb 9, w 4, nb 6	20
			463

FoW (1): 1-38 (1), 2-39 (3), 3-338 (2), 4-378 (4), 5-426 (5), 6-426 (7), 7-442 (8), 8-453 (9), 9-459 (6), 10-463 (10)

Mumbai Bowling

	O	M	R	W	
Murtuza Hussain	41	8	103	4	2w,3nb
Mangela	46.2	16	105	5	5w,8nb
Nayar	28	10	43	0	
Powar	31	10	75	0	1nb
Kulkarni	33	7	96	1	
Muzumdar	5	1	14	0	
Sharma	7	0	21	0	

Saurashtra Bowling

	O	M	R	W	
Jobanputra	37.5	4	116	5	2w,1nb
Maniar	28.4	8	100	2	4nb
Vaghela	22	10	51	1	2w
Jadeja	35	5	99	0	1nb
Dhruve	15	3	53	0	
Makwana	10	1	34	1	

Umpires: S.Dendapani and G.A.Pratapkumar.   Referee: Vidya Bhaskar.   Toss: Mumbai

Close of Play: 1st day: Saurashtra (1) 202-2 (Kotak 73*, Pujara 61*, 90 overs); 2nd day: Saurashtra (1) 465-9 (Kotak 162*, Maniar 15*, 180 overs); 3rd day: Mumbai (1) 187-2 (Rahane 83*, Muzumdar 86*, 76 overs).

S.H.Kotak's 168 took 543 balls in 796 minutes and included 20 fours. A.M.Rahane's 149 took 355 balls in 499 minutes and included 18 fours and 2 sixes. A.A.Muzumdar's 187 took 305 balls in 438 minutes and included 22 fours.

RAJASTHAN v HIMACHAL PRADESH

Played at Himachal Pradesh Cricket Association Stadium, Dharmasala, December 25, 26, 27, 2007.
Ranji Trophy 2007/08 - Elite Group A
Rajasthan won by nine wickets.   (Points: Rajasthan 5, Himachal Pradesh 0)

HIMACHAL PRADESH

1	M.Gupta	c Doru b Mathur	19	b Mathur		29
2	H.Dogra	c and b Shamsher Singh	71	(6) lbw b Mohammad Aslam		5
3	M.Sharma	c Jhalani b Shamsher Singh	101	lbw b Mathur		0
4	*S.Sharma	b S.G.Gehlot	13	(2) c Jhalani b S.G.Gehlot		43
5	P.Dogra	b S.G.Gehlot	0	(4) b Mathur		0
6	†M.S.Bisla	lbw b Mohammad Aslam	6	(5) c Jhalani b S.G.Gehlot		4
7	A.Mannu	c Jhalani b Mathur	1	c Jhalani b Mathur		26
8	Sarandeep Singh	lbw b Mathur	4	c and b Mathur		3
9	V.Bhatia	lbw b Mohammad Aslam	13	c Jhalani b Mathur		9
10	A.K.Thakur	not out	22	not out		1
11	V.Malik	c N.G.Gehlot b Mohammad Aslam	13	b Mathur		0
	Extras	b 8, lb 5, w 4	17	nb 2		2
			280			**122**

FoW (1): 1-32 (1), 2-159 (2), 3-176 (4), 4-176 (5), 5-183 (6), 6-186 (7), 7-190 (8), 8-219 (9), 9-257 (3), 10-280 (11)
FoW (2): 1-56 (1), 2-64 (3), 3-64 (4), 4-77 (5), 5-82 (6), 6-84 (2), 7-87 (8), 8-109 (9), 9-122 (7), 10-122 (11)

RAJASTHAN

1	V.A.Saxena	lbw b Malik	5	not out	101
2	S.S.Vijay	c Bisla b Bhatia	88	lbw b Thakur	14
3	R.K.Bishnoi	st Bisla b Sarandeep Singh	34	not out	63
4	N.S.Doru	c Bisla b Malik	25		
5	R.D.Bist	b Malik	0		
6	N.G.Gehlot	c Bisla b Thakur	16		
7	*†R.B.Jhalani	c S.Sharma b Bhatia	20		
8	Shamsher Singh	not out	5		
9	S.G.Gehlot	lbw b Thakur	12		
10	Mohammad Aslam	run out (Bhatia)	1		
11	S.O.Mathur	c Sarandeep Singh b Malik	4		
	Extras	lb 1, nb 7	8	lb 1, nb 6	7
			218	**(1 wicket)**	**185**

FoW (1): 1-5 (1), 2-72 (3), 3-120 (4), 4-120 (5), 5-157 (6), 6-190 (2), 7-195 (7), 8-209 (9), 9-211 (10), 10-218 (11)
FoW (2): 1-23 (2)

Rajasthan Bowling

	O	M	R	W		O	M	R	W	
Mathur	18	1	79	3		19	6	49	7	1nb
S.G.Gehlot	20	6	56	2	1w	13	3	44	2	1nb
Mohammad Aslam	26.2	7	64	3		15	7	29	1	
Shamsher Singh	18	4	48	2						
Bishnoi	2	0	13	0						
N.G.Gehlot	2	0	7	0						

Himachal Pradesh Bowling

	O	M	R	W			O	M	R	W	
Thakur	25	4	83	2			14	3	51	1	2nb
Malik	18.2	3	51	4	7nb		10	2	38	0	4nb
Bhatia	11	4	24	2			8	0	54	0	
Sarandeep Singh	27	4	59	1			8	0	28	0	
M.Sharma						(5)	1	0	1	0	
S.Sharma						(6)	0.5	0	12	0	

Umpires: R.M.Deshpande and C.K.Nandan.   Referee: V.D.Dhamasker.   Toss: Himachal Pradesh

Close of Play: 1st day: Rajasthan (1) 5-0 (Saxena 5*, Vijay 0*, 1 over); 2nd day: Himachal Pradesh (2) 19-0 (Gupta 8*, S.Sharma 10*, 7 overs).

The match was scheduled for four days but completed in three. M.Sharma's 101 took 214 balls in 309 minutes and included 13 fours. V.A.Saxena's 101 took 136 balls in 174 minutes and included 17 fours and 1 six. Shamsher Singh retired hurt in the Rajasthan first innings having scored 1 (team score 209-8) - he returned when the score was 211-9.

TAMIL NADU v DELHI

Played at M.A.Chidambaram Stadium, Chepauk, Chennai, December 25, 26, 27, 28, 2007.
Ranji Trophy 2007/08 - Elite Group A
Delhi won by eight wickets.　　(Points: Tamil Nadu 0, Delhi 5)

TAMIL NADU
1	A.Mukund	c Chopra b Nanda	51	c Bisht b Sangwan	21
2	M.Vijay Krishna	lbw b Bhatia	77	b Bhatia	6
3	*S.Badrinath	lbw b Nanda	9	c Bisht b Awana	11
4	K.Vasudevadas	b Nanda	0	c Bisht b Nanda	4
5	R.Srinivasan	c Bisht b Bhatia	23	c Bisht b Sangwan	11
6	S.Suresh Kumar	c Bisht b Sangwan	20	lbw b Nanda	1
7	†H.Gopinath	c Nanda b Narender Singh	13	b Nanda	37
8	R.Ramkumar	c Bisht b Sangwan	32	c Dhawan b Nanda	57
9	V.Y.Mahesh	c Bisht b Awana	8	b Awana	6
10	C.Suresh	lbw b Bhatia	14	b Nanda	0
11	P.Amarnath	not out	7	not out	0
	Extras	b 4, lb 5, nb 5	14	b 4, lb 9, nb 7	20
			268		174

FoW (1): 1-127 (1), 2-143 (3), 3-143 (4), 4-157 (2), 5-173 (5), 6-201 (7), 7-219 (6), 8-238 (9), 9-250 (8), 10-268 (10)
FoW (2): 1-19 (2), 2-39 (3), 3-45 (4), 4-56 (1), 5-61 (6), 6-61 (5), 7-143 (8), 8-156 (7), 9-174 (9), 10-174 (10)

DELHI
1	A.S.Chopra	c Vasudevadas b C.Suresh	55	c Srinivasan b Suresh Kumar	16
2	*G.Gambhir	c Mukund b C.Suresh	84	c Mahesh b C.Suresh	40
3	S.Dhawan	c Badrinath b C.Suresh	59	not out	14
4	M.Manhas	c Gopinath b Ramkumar	12	not out	32
5	V.Kohli	c Mukund b Ramkumar	19		
6	R.Bhatia	c Vijay Krishna b C.Suresh	10		
7	†P.Bisht	c Srinivasan b Mahesh	14		
8	P.Sangwan	c C.Suresh b Suresh Kumar	31		
9	Narender Singh	c Mukund b Suresh Kumar	34		
10	C.Nanda	c Srinivasan b Suresh Kumar	2		
11	P.Awana	not out	0		
	Extras	b 6, lb 7, w 1, nb 4	18	nb 3	3
			338	(2 wickets)	105

FoW (1): 1-141 (1), 2-146 (2), 3-169 (4), 4-224 (5), 5-237 (6), 6-252 (3), 7-267 (7), 8-322 (8), 9-336 (10), 10-338 (9)
FoW (2): 1-42 (1), 2-64 (2)

Delhi Bowling
	O	M	R	W			O	M	R	W	
Sangwan	22	8	48	2	3nb		8	3	18	2	1nb
Awana	16	2	58	1			11	2	35	2	
Narender Singh	21	4	72	1		(5)	10	1	43	0	
Bhatia	14.2	5	16	3	2nb	(3)	11	4	18	1	1nb
Nanda	22	5	65	3		(4)	15.1	4	47	5	1nb
Manhas	1	1	0	0							

Tamil Nadu Bowling
	O	M	R	W			O	M	R	W	
Mahesh	18	4	72	1	1w,3nb		7	1	23	0	3nb
Amarnath	15	2	46	0			6	2	14	0	
Ramkumar	30	3	94	2							
Suresh Kumar	10	1	30	3	1nb	(3)	6.5	0	38	1	
C.Suresh	31	6	83	4		(4)	6	1	30	1	

Umpires: V.D.Nerurkar and A.M.Saheba.　Referee: N.R.Yadav.　　　　Toss: Tamil Nadu

Close of Play: 1st day: Tamil Nadu (1) 250-9 (C.Suresh 3*, 89.3 overs); 2nd day: Delhi (1) 265-6 (Bisht 14*, Sangwan 2*, 81 overs); 3rd day: Delhi (2) 10-0 (Chopra 2*, Gambhir 6*, 5 overs).

BARODA v DELHI

Played at Maharani Usharaje Trust Cricket Ground, Indore, January 5, 6, 7, 8, 2008.
Ranji Trophy 2007/08 - Elite Group Semi-Final
Delhi won by seven wickets.

BARODA

1	S.S.Parab	c Narwal b Bhandari	5	b Awana	11
2	*C.C.Williams	b Bhandari	14	c Bisht b Awana	0
3	A.A.Bilakhia	c Dhawan b Narwal	26	b Bhatia	17
4	R.K.Solanki	c Dhawan b Bhandari	2	lbw b Bhatia	96
5	S.A.Gaekwad	c Bisht b Narwal	43	c and b Awana	46
6	†P.R.Shah	c Jain b Bhandari	46	b Nanda	15
7	Y.K.Pathan	c Awana b Narwal	14	c Jain b Bhandari	113
8	R.V.Pawar	lbw b Manhas	6	run out	11
9	S.D.Vora	c Chopra b Narwal	27	not out	24
10	S.M.Singh	lbw b Bhatia	0	lbw b Bhatia	0
11	S.Y.Veragi	not out	10	c and b Nanda	1
	Extras	lb 1, w 1, nb 4	6	b 6, lb 1, nb 1	8
			199		**342**

FoW (1): 1-12 (1), 2-25 (2), 3-35 (4), 4-62 (3), 5-110 (5), 6-152 (6), 7-152 (7), 8-171 (8), 9-177 (10), 10-199 (9)
FoW (2): 1-11 (2), 2-12 (1), 3-56 (3), 4-135 (5), 5-160 (6), 6-278 (4), 7-303 (8), 8-325 (7), 9-326 (10), 10-342 (11)

DELHI

1	A.S.Chopra	c Shah b Veragi	3		
2	*G.Gambhir	lbw b Singh	2	c Williams b Pathan	132
3	S.Dhawan	c Williams b Singh	0	(1) run out	48
4	M.Manhas	c Pathan b Pawar	97	c Williams b Veragi	36
5	A.Jain	run out (Shah)	48	(3) not out	39
6	R.Bhatia	c Pathan b Vora	38	(5) not out	6
7	†P.Bisht	lbw b Pawar	24		
8	S.Narwal	c Pathan b Vora	34		
9	C.Nanda	not out	5		
10	A.Bhandari	c Pawar b Vora	0		
11	P.Awana	c Pathan b Vora	12		
	Extras	b 2, lb 5, nb 1	8	lb 8, nb 3	11
			271	**(3 wickets)**	**272**

FoW (1): 1-3 (2), 2-5 (1), 3-5 (3), 4-136 (5), 5-163 (4), 6-203 (7), 7-237 (6), 8-253 (8), 9-253 (10), 10-271 (11)
FoW (2): 1-136 (1), 2-211 (2), 3-266 (4)

Delhi Bowling	O	M	R	W		O	M	R	W	
Bhandari	16	4	52	4	1nb	19	6	56	1	
Narwal	20.4	5	56	4		25	7	78	0	
Awana	10	0	47	0	1w	16	0	74	3	
Bhatia	12	3	26	1	2nb	11	1	42	3	
Nanda	3	0	14	0		18.2	4	53	2	
Manhas	3	2	3	1		7	0	13	0	
Jain					(7)	2	0	19	0	1nb

Baroda Bowling	O	M	R	W		O	M	R	W	
Singh	20	6	60	2		16	1	59	0	
Veragi	23	5	69	1	1nb	11.4	2	43	1	3nb
Vora	21.3	6	39	4		16	5	34	0	
Pawar	27	8	68	2	(5)	11	3	45	2	
Pathan	11	4	28	0	(4)	25	3	83	1	

Umpires: A.Y.Gokhale and I.Shivram. Third umpire: S.Asnani. Referee: R.R.Jadeja. Toss: Baroda

Close of Play: 1st day: Delhi (1) 49-3 (Manhas 26*, Jain 18*, 19 overs); 2nd day: Baroda (2) 8-0 (Parab 8*, Williams 0*, 4 overs); 3rd day: Baroda (2) 281-6 (Pathan 86*, Pawar 2*, 86 overs).

The match was scheduled for five days but completed in four. Y.K.Pathan's 113 took 81 balls in 155 minutes and included 16 fours and 3 sixes. G.Gambhir's 132 took 179 balls in 236 minutes and included 23 fours.

GUJARAT v RAILWAYS

Played at Brabourne Stadium, Mumbai, January 5, 6, 7, 8, 9, 2008.
Ranji Trophy 2007/08 - Plate Group Final
Gujarat won by one wicket.

RAILWAYS

1	S.B.Bangar	c P.A.Patel b Makda	26	(2) c N.K.Patel b Trivedi	0
2	S.S.Joshi	c T.K.Patel b Trivedi	0	(1) c P.A.Patel b Makda	1
3	K.V.Sharma	c T.K.Patel b Trivedi	8	(7) lbw b Amit Singh	7
4	H.D.Rawle	c P.A.Patel b Amit Singh	110	c and b T.K.Patel	45
5	S.C.Sanyal	lbw b Parmar	16	c N.K.Patel b Amit Singh	18
6	†M.Rawat	c P.A.Patel b Amit Singh	24	c Joshipura b Amit Singh	0
7	A.Raja Ali	c P.A.Patel b Parmar	17	(8) lbw b T.K.Patel	46
8	*M.Kartik	st P.A.Patel b Parmar	1	(3) lbw b Makda	18
9	Harvinder Singh	b Parmar	14	c P.A.Patel b Parmar	8
10	S.R.Saxena	c P.A.Patel b T.K.Patel	30	not out	13
11	K.S.Parida	not out	0	lbw b Parmar	2
	Extras	b 2, lb 6, w 3, nb 3	14	b 5, lb 4, nb 2	11
			260		169

FoW (1): 1-10 (2), 2-18 (3), 3-67 (1), 4-106 (5), 5-142 (6), 6-180 (7), 7-182 (8), 8-210 (9), 9-254 (4), 10-260 (10)
FoW (2): 1-5 (1), 2-23 (2), 3-23 (3), 4-60 (5), 5-63 (6), 6-79 (7), 7-137 (4), 8-154 (9), 9-154 (8), 10-169 (11)

GUJARAT

1	N.D.Modi	c Bangar b Harvinder Singh	107	c Rawat b Bangar	18
2	R.K.Tabiyar	c Rawat b Bangar	14	lbw b Bangar	13
3	*†P.A.Patel	b Saxena	52	c Joshi b Bangar	0
4	M.B.Parmar	lbw b Bangar	4	(5) c Parida b Kartik	41
5	N.K.Patel	c Bangar b Parida	14	(4) c Rawat b Saxena	27
6	H.R.Joshipura	c Rawat b Parida	36	c and b Kartik	7
7	J.D.Desai	lbw b Bangar	1	(8) not out	17
8	T.K.Patel	c Rawle b Bangar	17	(7) c Rawat b Bangar	0
9	Amit Singh	c and b Bangar	21	(10) lbw b Bangar	0
10	A.M.Makda	c Parida b Kartik	1	(9) b Bangar	1
11	S.K.Trivedi	not out	0	not out	2
	Extras	nb 13	13	lb 8, w 2, nb 16	26
			280	(9 wickets)	152

FoW (1): 1-53 (2), 2-140 (3), 3-148 (4), 4-193 (5), 5-218 (1), 6-219 (7), 7-255 (6), 8-267 (8), 9-280 (9), 10-280 (10)
FoW (2): 1-34 (1), 2-34 (3), 3-51 (2), 4-78 (4), 5-124 (5), 6-127 (6), 7-131 (7), 8-143 (9), 9-143 (10)

Gujarat Bowling

	O	M	R	W			O	M	R	W	
Trivedi	28	13	60	2			16	5	41	1	
Makda	23	7	59	1	1w,1nb		17	7	30	2	
Amit Singh	19	6	34	2	2nb	(4)	11	3	22	3	2nb
T.K.Patel	13.3	5	36	1		(5)	10	3	17	2	
Parmar	28	7	63	4	1w	(3)	22	4	50	2	

Railways Bowling

	O	M	R	W			O	M	R	W	
Harvinder Singh	22	9	38	1	2nb	(2)	10	5	28	0	3nb
Bangar	42	19	54	5	6nb	(1)	22	9	53	6	6nb
Sanyal	5	1	15	0							
Saxena	26	11	45	1	2nb	(3)	7	5	11	1	1w
Kartik	29.2	12	59	1	3nb	(4)	17	5	48	2	7nb
Parida	20	6	67	2		(5)	1	0	4	0	
Sharma	1	0	2	0							

Umpires: C.R.Mohite and G.A.Pratapkumar. Referee: D.Vasu.   Toss: Railways

Close of Play: 1st day: Railways (1) 202-7 (Rawle 89*, Harvinder Singh 11*, 90 overs); 2nd day: Gujarat (1) 140-2 (Modi 66*, Parmar 0*, 66 overs); 3rd day: Railways (2) 14-1 (Bangar 0*, Kartik 9*, 8 overs); 4th day: Gujarat (2) 30-0 (Modi 15*, Tabiyar 13*, 20 overs).

H.D.Rawle's 110 took 281 balls in 407 minutes and included 17 fours. N.D.Modi's 107 took 317 balls in 432 minutes and included 18 fours.

SAURASHTRA v UTTAR PRADESH

Played at Moti Bagh Stadium, Vadodara, January 5, 6, 7, 2008.
Ranji Trophy 2007/08 - Elite Group Semi-Final
Uttar Pradesh won by 48 runs.

UTTAR PRADESH

1	R.P.Srivastava	c Jogiyani b Maniar	3	lbw b Maniar	14
2	†Amir Khan	c Jogiyani b Maniar	4	b Dhruve	22
3	S.K.Raina	c Jogiyani b Maniar	2	lbw b Makwana	25
4	*M.Kaif	c Shah b Maniar	80	c Jogiyani b Makwana	8
5	R.U.Shukla	b Jobanputra	29	c Kotak b Dhruve	0
6	P.P.Chawla	lbw b Jobanputra	0	c Dhruve b Jobanputra	10
7	R.B.Elahi	c Jogiyani b Maniar	0	(9) b Dhruve	5
8	P.Kumar	b Vaghela	11	b Dhruve	2
9	Bhuvneshwar Singh	not out	33	(7) b Dhruve	5
10	P.P.Gupta	c Pujara b Maniar	6	c Jogiyani b Maniar	1
11	S.Tyagi	lbw b Jobanputra	0	not out	0
	Extras	b 4, lb 9, w 1, nb 6	20	b 4, lb 2, nb 2	8
			188		100

FoW (1): 1-3 (1), 2-5 (3), 3-15 (2), 4-69 (5), 5-69 (6), 6-79 (7), 7-110 (8), 8-159 (4), 9-173 (10), 10-188 (11)
FoW (2): 1-23 (1), 2-59 (3), 3-67 (2), 4-69 (5), 5-79 (4), 6-82 (6), 7-86 (8), 8-99 (7), 9-100 (9), 10-100 (10)

SAURASHTRA

1	K.M.Vaghela	c Kaif b Kumar	0	(3) c Amir Khan b Tyagi	0
2	*J.N.Shah	lbw b Tyagi	57	c Amir Khan b Tyagi	0
3	S.H.Kotak	lbw b Kumar	0	(5) b Tyagi	52
4	C.A.Pujara	b Tyagi	2	c Amir Khan b Tyagi	9
5	†S.D.Jogiyani	b Kumar	14	(1) lbw b Bhuvneshwar Singh	13
6	N.R.Rathod	c Shukla b Bhuvneshwar Singh	4	c Raina b Kumar	13
7	F.U.Bambhaniya	lbw b Bhuvneshwar Singh	0	(8) lbw b Kumar	0
8	R.V.Dhruve	lbw b Kumar	26	(7) c and b Gupta	1
9	K.R.Makwana	b Tyagi	0	c Amir Khan b Kumar	13
10	S.P.Jobanputra	b Tyagi	17	b Kumar	0
11	S.M.Maniar	not out	4	not out	1
	Extras	b 1, lb 2	3	b 2, lb 5, w 4	11
			127		113

FoW (1): 1-4 (1), 2-4 (3), 3-7 (4), 4-38 (5), 5-61 (6), 6-61 (7), 7-87 (2), 8-87 (9), 9-121 (10), 10-127 (8)
FoW (2): 1-2 (2), 2-2 (3), 3-25 (4), 4-25 (1), 5-49 (6), 6-50 (7), 7-63 (8), 8-103 (9), 9-105 (10), 10-113 (5)

Saurashtra Bowling

	O	M	R	W			O	M	R	W	
Jobanputra	18.5	1	60	3	1w		12	5	20	1	1nb
Maniar	23	2	88	6	6nb		10.1	5	20	2	1nb
Vaghela	6	2	17	1			3	0	20	0	
Dhruve	4	0	10	0			14	7	20	5	
Makwana						(5)	5	1	14	2	

Uttar Pradesh Bowling

	O	M	R	W			O	M	R	W	
Kumar	12.3	4	40	4			22	7	39	4	
Tyagi	13	2	49	4			20.5	5	42	4	3w
Bhuvneshwar Singh	6	0	23	2			8	2	12	1	
Chawla	6	2	12	0		(5)	2	0	3	0	
Gupta						(4)	5	2	10	2	

Umpires: S.L.Shastri and S.K.Tarapore. Referee: S.S.Patil.   Toss: Saurashtra

Close of Play: 1st day: Saurashtra (1) 116-8 (Dhruve 21*, Jobanputra 15*, 34 overs); 2nd day: Saurashtra (2) 93-7 (Kotak 41*, Makwana 9*, 45 overs).

The match was scheduled for five days but completed in three.

DELHI v UTTAR PRADESH

Played at Wankhede Stadium, Mumbai, January 16, 17, 18, 19, 2008.
Ranji Trophy 2007/08 - Elite Group Final
Delhi won by nine wickets.

UTTAR PRADESH

1	R.P.Srivastava	lbw b Narwal	6	c Bisht b Bhatia	18
2	T.M.Srivastava	c Dhawan b Sangwan	105	run out	1
3	S.K.Raina	lbw b Sangwan	16	c Bisht b Sangwan	85
4	*M.Kaif	c Chopra b Nanda	16	c Bisht b Sangwan	21
5	R.U.Shukla	c Manhas b Bhatia	96	c Jain b Bhandari	0
6	P.P.Chawla	c Jain b Narwal	20	c Dhawan b Narwal	4
7	†Amir Khan	c Chopra b Sangwan	15	(8) c Bisht b Sangwan	12
8	P.Kumar	c Manhas b Narwal	8	(9) b Sangwan	1
9	Bhuvneshwar Singh	c Jain b Narwal	10	(7) b Sangwan	19
10	P.P.Gupta	c Bhatia b Sangwan	27	c Bhatia b Bhandari	13
11	S.Tyagi	not out	0	not out	0
	Extras	b 1, lb 13, w 4, nb 5	23	lb 1, nb 2	3
			342		177

FoW (1): 1-21 (1), 2-60 (3), 3-99 (4), 4-200 (2), 5-231 (6), 6-274 (7), 7-285 (8), 8-297 (9), 9-341 (5), 10-342 (10)
FoW (2): 1-1 (2), 2-63 (1), 3-123 (4), 4-126 (3), 5-130 (5), 6-130 (6), 7-154 (7), 8-160 (9), 9-169 (8), 10-177 (10)

DELHI

1	A.S.Chopra	lbw b P.Kumar	102	c Kaif b Gupta	33
2	*G.Gambhir	c Raina b P.Kumar	0	not out	130
3	S.Dhawan	b P.Kumar	14	not out	54
4	M.Manhas	lbw b P.Kumar	0		
5	A.Jain	c Raina b Tyagi	8		
6	R.Bhatia	not out	139		
7	†P.Bisht	lbw b P.Kumar	0		
8	S.Narwal	b P.Kumar	5		
9	C.Nanda	c Raina b Tyagi	0		
10	P.Sangwan	lbw b P.Kumar	9		
11	A.Bhandari	lbw b P.Kumar	0		
	Extras	lb 7, w 2, nb 4	13	b 5, lb 3, w 3, nb 2	13
			290	(1 wicket)	230

FoW (1): 1-1 (2), 2-15 (3), 3-15 (4), 4-36 (5), 5-232 (1), 6-232 (7), 7-244 (8), 8-247 (9), 9-270 (10), 10-290 (11)
FoW (2): 1-91 (1)

Delhi Bowling

	O	M	R	W			O	M	R	W	
Sangwan	27.1	7	80	4	2nb		20	6	46	5	
Bhandari	21	3	79	0	2w	(3)	11.2	2	28	2	
Narwal	26	5	81	4	2w	(2)	16	6	65	1	
Bhatia	19	3	41	1	1nb		9	4	14	1	
Nanda	16	2	39	1	2nb		7	1	23	0	2nb
Manhas	1	0	8	0							

Uttar Pradesh Bowling

	O	M	R	W			O	M	R	W	
P.Kumar	32.1	8	68	8	1w,2nb		18	4	48	0	1nb
Tyagi	24	5	63	2	2nb		11	2	50	0	1w
Bhuvneshwar Singh	15	5	54	0	1w		4.1	1	17	0	2w
Chawla	13	2	57	0		(5)	8	0	30	0	
Gupta	10	2	29	0		(4)	14	0	77	1	1nb
Shukla	2	0	7	0							
R.P.Srivastava	2	0	5	0							

Umpires: A.V.Jayaprakash and A.M.Saheba. Third umpire: S.D.Ranade. Referee: S.Mukherjee.　　　　Toss: Delhi

Close of Play: 1st day: Uttar Pradesh (1) 292-7 (Shukla 80*, Bhuvneshwar Singh 6*, 90 overs); 2nd day: Delhi (1) 196-4 (Chopra 85*, Bhatia 81*, 67 overs); 3rd day: Uttar Pradesh (2) 154-6 (Bhuvneshwar Singh 19*, Amir Khan 4*, 53 overs).
The match was scheduled for five days but completed in four. T.M.Srivastava's 105 took 174 balls in 261 minutes and included 13 fours and 1 six. A.S.Chopra's 102 took 260 balls in 319 minutes and included 17 fours. R.Bhatia's 139 took 218 balls in 323 minutes and included 18 fours and 4 sixes. G.Gambhir's 130 took 154 balls in 213 minutes and included 17 fours.

NORTH ZONE v SOUTH ZONE

Played at Sardar Patel Stadium, Motera, Ahmedabad, January 26, 27, 28, 2008.
Duleep Trophy 2007/08 - Group A
North Zone won by eight wickets.   (Points: North Zone 5, South Zone 0)

SOUTH ZONE

1	S.A.Asnodkar	b Malik	16	(2) c Thakur b Rana		37
2	D.B.Ravi Teja	c Kaul b Thakur	41	(1) c Rana b Malik		15
3	M.Vijay Krishna	lbw b Malik	0	c Kaul b Mishra		39
4	*S.Badrinath	b Malik	0	lbw b Malik		22
5	A.S.Yadav	b Malik	8	c Kaul b Bhatia		0
6	†V.S.T.Naidu	c Kaul b Malik	0	absent hurt		0
7	R.Ashwin	c Goel b Bhatia	0	(6) c Kaul b Mishra		16
8	R.Vinay Kumar	not out	41	(7) c and b Mishra		6
9	P.P.Ojha	c Chopra b Bhatia	4	c Manhas b Mishra		6
10	D.Kalyankrishna	c Kaul b Bhatia	31	(8) not out		31
11	N.C.Aiyappa	b Bhatia	1	(10) c and b Bhatia		24
	Extras	lb 4, nb 11	15	lb 3, w 1, nb 11		15
			157			**211**

FoW (1): 1-37 (1), 2-37 (3), 3-43 (4), 4-63 (5), 5-69 (6), 6-72 (2), 7-76 (7), 8-84 (9), 9-152 (10), 10-157 (11)
FoW (2): 1-24 (1), 2-78 (2), 3-121 (4), 4-123 (3), 5-123 (5), 6-143 (7), 7-150 (6), 8-156 (9), 9-211 (10)

NORTH ZONE

1	A.S.Chopra	lbw b Vinay Kumar	37	lbw b Aiyappa		11
2	S.Dhawan	c Ravi Teja b Aiyappa	23			
3	K.Goel	c Vijay Krishna b Aiyappa	0	(2) not out		23
4	*M.Manhas	b Vinay Kumar	3			
5	Yashpal Singh	c Ravi Teja b Vinay Kumar	97	(4) not out		13
6	R.Bhatia	c Yadav b Ojha	8			
7	†U.Kaul	c Vijay Krishna b Vinay Kumar	33			
8	S.Rana	c Asnodkar b Ashwin	28	(3) c Yadav b Kalyankrishna		8
9	A.Mishra	b Kalyankrishna	47			
10	V.Malik	b Aiyappa	5			
11	A.K.Thakur	not out	6			
	Extras	b 9, lb 3	12	b 12, lb 4, w 1		17
			299	(2 wickets)		**72**

FoW (1): 1-58 (2), 2-58 (3), 3-60 (1), 4-65 (4), 5-94 (6), 6-165 (7), 7-211 (8), 8-258 (5), 9-263 (10), 10-299 (9)
FoW (2): 1-26 (1), 2-47 (3)

North Zone Bowling

	O	M	R	W		O	M	R	W	
Malik	16	2	44	5	8nb	20	4	67	2	1w,7nb
Thakur	16	3	58	1	1nb	7	2	10	0	
Bhatia	10.5	5	13	4		16	5	39	2	1nb
Rana	7	4	6	0		9	0	37	1	
Mishra	6	2	32	0	2nb	14	2	51	4	3nb
Manhas					(6)	1	0	4	0	

South Zone Bowling

	O	M	R	W		O	M	R	W	
Vinay Kumar	24	4	87	4		5	0	12	0	
Kalyankrishna	15.5	4	40	1	(3)	4.3	0	11	1	
Aiyappa	20	1	54	3	(2)	7	4	14	1	1w
Ojha	19	2	79	1		2	0	19	0	
Ashwin	10	2	27	1						

Umpires: A.Y.Dandekar and S.Das. Referee: T.B.Arothe.   Toss: North Zone

Close of Play: 1st day: North Zone (1) 104-5 (Yashpal Singh 24*, Kaul 4*, 31 overs); 2nd day: South Zone (2) 95-2 (Vijay Krishna 24*, Badrinath 10*, 29 overs).

The match was scheduled for four days but completed in three.

S.A.Asnodkar kept wicket in the North Zone second innings.

WEST ZONE v CENTRAL ZONE

Played at Madhavrao Scindia Cricket Ground, Rajkot, January 26, 27, 28, 29, 2008.
Duleep Trophy 2007/08 - Group B
Match drawn.   (Points: West Zone 3, Central Zone 1)

WEST ZONE

1	S.O.Kukreja	c Rawat b Sanyal	72	c Kaif b Mathur	40
2	A.M.Rahane	c Kaif b Sanyal	50	lbw b Sanyal	89
3	*†P.A.Patel	c Sanyal b Bangar	3	c Sanyal b Mathur	74
4	C.A.Pujara	b Bangar	44	c Jatin S.Saxena b Mathur	11
5	R.K.Solanki	c Rawle b Tyagi	25	c Rawat b Mathur	6
6	Y.K.Pathan	c Rawle b Sanyal	107	run out	9
7	R.R.Powar	c sub (P.P.Gupta) b Bangar	9	not out	47
8	R.V.Dhruve	lbw b Bangar	21	lbw b Mathur	1
9	S.P.Jobanputra	c Kaif b Sanyal	45	not out	40
10	M.M.Patel	not out	14		
11	S.K.Trivedi	lbw b Kartik	5		
	Extras	b 4, lb 1, w 1, nb 10	16	b 5, lb 3, w 2, nb 8	18
			411	(7 wickets, declared)	335

FoW (1): 1-124 (1), 2-129 (2), 3-129 (3), 4-174 (5), 5-310 (6), 6-310 (4), 7-320 (7), 8-349 (8), 9-405 (9), 10-411 (11)
FoW (2): 1-99 (1), 2-197 (2), 3-218 (3), 4-231 (4), 5-241 (6), 6-242 (5), 7-248 (8)

CENTRAL ZONE

1	V.A.Saxena	c P.A.Patel b M.M.Patel	2
2	T.M.Srivastava	c Rahane b Trivedi	12
3	Jatin S.Saxena	lbw b Dhruve	46
4	*M.Kaif	c Dhruve b Trivedi	160
5	H.D.Rawle	c P.A.Patel b M.M.Patel	3
6	S.B.Bangar	c P.A.Patel b Dhruve	26
7	†M.Rawat	c Pathan b Jobanputra	48
8	S.C.Sanyal	st P.A.Patel b Dhruve	31
9	M.Kartik	lbw b Dhruve	19
10	S.O.Mathur	not out	10
11	S.Tyagi	b M.M.Patel	12
	Extras	b 4, lb 3, w 1, nb 7	15
			384

FoW (1): 1-6 (1), 2-49 (2), 3-73 (3), 4-91 (5), 5-134 (6), 6-268 (7), 7-319 (8), 8-357 (9), 9-362 (4), 10-384 (11)

Central Zone Bowling

	O	M	R	W			O	M	R	W	
Bangar	29	9	72	4	1nb		28	6	89	0	2w,1nb
Tyagi	13	1	64	1	1w						
Kartik	22.1	4	78	1	4nb		26	7	62	0	3nb
Mathur	15	2	67	0			21	2	63	5	
Sanyal	22	2	113	4	5nb	(2)	22	2	68	1	2nb
Jatin S.Saxena	2	0	12	0		(5)	10	0	40	0	2nb
Rawle						(6)	2	0	5	0	

West Zone Bowling

	O	M	R	W	
M.M.Patel	29	6	90	3	4nb
Jobanputra	24	6	69	1	2nb
Trivedi	27	5	88	2	1nb
Dhruve	33	12	84	4	1w
Powar	12	2	40	0	
Pathan	1	0	6	0	

Umpires: G.A.Pratapkumar and S.K.Tarapore. Third umpire: R.D.Risodkar. Referee: S.Banerjee.   Toss: West Zone

Close of Play: 1st day: West Zone (1) 349-7 (Dhruve 21*, Jobanputra 4*, 90 overs); 2nd day: Central Zone (1) 237-5 (Kaif 96*, Rawat 40*, 74 overs); 3rd day: West Zone (2) 99-0 (Kukreja 40*, Rahane 53*, 36 overs).

Y.K.Pathan's 107 took 66 balls in 88 minutes and included 13 fours and 5 sixes. M.Kaif's 160 took 316 balls in 461 minutes and included 19 fours.

CENTRAL ZONE v ENGLAND LIONS

Played at Moti Bagh Stadium, Vadodara, February 3, 4, 5, 6, 2008.
Duleep Trophy 2007/08 - Group B
England Lions won by five wickets.   (Points: Central Zone 0, England Lions 5)

CENTRAL ZONE

1	F.Y.Fazal	lbw b Kirby	37	b Onions	4
2	V.A.Saxena	c Foster b Richardson	34	c Foster b Onions	29
3	Jatin S.Saxena	c Foster b Onions	9	(7) c Panesar b Richardson	27
4	*M.Kaif	b Rashid	64	(5) b Panesar	42
5	S.B.Bangar	c Foster b Panesar	29	(4) lbw b Onions	2
6	H.D.Rawle	b Onions	27	lbw b Kirby	25
7	†M.Rawat	c Joyce b Richardson	13	(8) lbw b Kirby	1
8	S.C.Sanyal	b Richardson	18	(9) lbw b Rashid	37
9	P.P.Gupta	c Foster b Onions	8	(3) c Foster b Richardson	0
10	Pankaj Singh	c sub (J.C.Hildreth) b Richardson	11	b Rashid	0
11	S.O.Mathur	not out	7	not out	3
	Extras	lb 5, nb 8	13	b 1, lb 9	10
			270		**180**

FoW (1): 1-54 (1), 2-70 (3), 3-124 (2), 4-179 (4), 5-201 (5), 6-223 (6), 7-227 (7), 8-252 (8), 9-256 (9), 10-270 (10)
FoW (2): 1-12 (1), 2-17 (3), 3-30 (4), 4-39 (2), 5-97 (6), 6-111 (5), 7-112 (8), 8-172 (7), 9-173 (10), 10-180 (9)

ENGLAND LIONS

1	M.A.Carberry	c Gupta b Jatin S.Saxena	35	lbw b Mathur	112
2	J.L.Denly	c Rawat b Pankaj Singh	0	lbw b Gupta	15
3	*M.H.Yardy	c Bangar b Pankaj Singh	5	c Kaif b Pankaj Singh	57
4	E.C.Joyce	lbw b Gupta	24	c Rawat b Mathur	54
5	I.J.L.Trott	lbw b Gupta	14	not out	28
6	†J.S.Foster	lbw b Pankaj Singh	18	c Rawat b Mathur	0
7	A.U.Rashid	c Rawat b Sanyal	40	not out	24
8	G.Onions	c Rawat b Gupta	1		
9	M.S.Panesar	c Rawat b Pankaj Singh	0		
10	S.P.Kirby	not out	11		
11	A.Richardson	c Kaif b Sanyal	0		
	Extras	lb 7	7	lb 4, nb 3	7
			155	**(5 wickets)**	**297**

FoW (1): 1-0 (2), 2-22 (3), 3-66 (4), 4-66 (1), 5-94 (5), 6-110 (6), 7-115 (8), 8-120 (9), 9-155 (7), 10-155 (11)
FoW (2): 1-30 (2), 2-146 (3), 3-244 (4), 4-245 (1), 5-249 (6)

England Lions Bowling

	O	M	R	W			O	M	R	W	
Onions	26	7	85	3	3nb		14	6	40	3	
Richardson	25.4	12	50	4			16	4	50	2	
Kirby	11	3	34	1			9	1	38	2	
Trott	11	2	30	0	4nb						
Panesar	18	5	49	1		(4)	8	0	39	1	
Rashid	10	3	17	1		(5)	1.5	1	3	2	

Central Zone Bowling

	O	M	R	W			O	M	R	W	
Bangar	5	3	9	0			8	5	12	0	
Pankaj Singh	16	9	35	4			20.4	4	85	1	
Mathur	6	1	25	0	(6)	8	2	25	3	
Gupta	23	13	32	3	(3)	24	4	88	1	
Jatin S.Saxena	12	2	40	1	(4)	10	2	32	0	
Sanyal	7	2	7	2	(5)	19	3	51	0	3nb

Umpires: S.N.Bandekar and S.L.Shastri.   Referee: B.Raghunath.   Toss: England Lions

Close of Play: 1st day: Central Zone (1) 238-7 (Sanyal 8*, Gupta 4*, 91 overs); 2nd day: Central Zone (2) 23-2 (V.A.Saxena 19*, Bangar 0*, 7 overs); 3rd day: England Lions (2) 146-1 (Carberry 71*, Yardy 57*, 46 overs).

M.A.Carberry's 112 took 239 balls in 316 minutes and included 15 fours and 1 six.

EAST ZONE v SOUTH ZONE

Played at Wankhede Stadium, Mumbai, February 3, 4, 5, 6, 2008.
Duleep Trophy 2007/08 - Group A
East Zone won by 68 runs.   (Points: East Zone 5, South Zone 0)

EAST ZONE

1	*S.S.Das	c Vijay Krishna b Ashwin	82	b Aiyappa	10
2	A.S.Das	lbw b Vinay Kumar	0	c sub (R.V.Gomez) b Vijaykumar	5
3	A.P.Majumdar	c Vijay Krishna b Aiyappa	19	b Ashwin	44
4	N.J.Behera	c Reddy b Aiyappa	8	c Badrinath b Ojha	8
5	M.S.Vardhan	c Vijay Krishna b Vinay Kumar	20	c Vinay Kumar b Ojha	4
6	P.M.Das	c Asnodkar b Ashwin	14	c Ravi Teja b Ashwin	5
7	†H.M.Das	c Vinay Kumar b Aiyappa	93	not out	52
8	T.S.Saha	c Ojha b Vijaykumar	29	c Vijay Krishna b Aiyappa	28
9	D.S.Mohanty	lbw b Aiyappa	16	c Reddy b Vijaykumar	3
10	R.R.Bose	not out	6	lbw b Ashwin	0
11	S.S.Paul	c Asnodkar b Aiyappa	17	b Vinay Kumar	0
	Extras	lb 4, nb 5	9	lb 2, nb 2	4
			313		163

FoW (1): 1-6 (2), 2-46 (3), 3-54 (4), 4-102 (5), 5-134 (6), 6-170 (1), 7-241 (8), 8-285 (9), 9-290 (7), 10-313 (11)
FoW (2): 1-18 (2), 2-18 (1), 3-37 (4), 4-55 (5), 5-78 (6), 6-79 (3), 7-126 (8), 8-141 (9), 9-158 (10), 10-163 (11)

SOUTH ZONE

1	D.B.Ravi Teja	c H.M.Das b Mohanty	13	(2) lbw b Saha	54
2	S.A.Asnodkar	c A.S.Das b Bose	4	(7) c S.S.Das b Bose	15
3	M.Vijay Krishna	c Mohanty b Saha	46	(1) c H.M.Das b Mohanty	0
4	*S.Badrinath	b Paul	23	(3) c S.S.Das b Bose	57
5	A.S.Yadav	lbw b P.M.Das	41	(4) lbw b Saha	12
6	†L.N.P.Reddy	c Behera b Saha	20	(5) c H.M.Das b Paul	39
7	R.Ashwin	hit wkt b Saha	13	(6) c H.M.Das b Bose	0
8	R.Vinay Kumar	c A.S.Das b Saha	24	c S.S.Das b Saha	1
9	N.C.Aiyappa	c H.M.Das b Bose	6	c Mohanty b P.M.Das	14
10	P.P.Ojha	run out (P.M.Das)	0	c Bose b P.M.Das	6
11	P.D.Vijaykumar	not out	0	not out	0
	Extras	b 10, lb 2, w 1, nb 1	14	lb 5, nb 1	6
			204		204

FoW (1): 1-4 (2), 2-26 (1), 3-68 (4), 4-127 (3), 5-147 (5), 6-169 (7), 7-180 (6), 8-197 (9), 9-202 (10), 10-204 (8)
FoW (2): 1-4 (1), 2-85 (2), 3-113 (4), 4-143 (3), 5-143 (6), 6-171 (7), 7-184 (5), 8-184 (8), 9-200 (10), 10-204 (9)

South Zone Bowling

	O	M	R	W		O	M	R	W	
Vinay Kumar	20	4	88	2	1nb	10.5	5	26	1	
Aiyappa	21.3	2	84	5	2nb	11	3	20	2	1nb
Vijaykumar	16	5	38	1	2nb	11	4	28	2	1nb
Ojha	19	4	48	0		19	5	54	2	
Ashwin	13	1	48	2		13	3	33	3	
Badrinath	2	1	3	0						

East Zone Bowling

	O	M	R	W			O	M	R	W	
Mohanty	17	6	24	1	1nb		14	3	36	1	
Bose	19	7	60	2			14	2	67	3	
Paul	12	2	33	1	1w		14	3	34	1	1nb
Behera	4	1	14	0		(5)	2	0	2	0	
Saha	22.2	6	47	4		(4)	17	4	56	3	
P.M.Das	5	0	14	1			0.4	0	4	2	

Umpires: K.Hariharan and A.M.Saheba. Third umpire: R.Y.Deshmukh. Referee: R.R.Jadeja.   Toss: East Zone

Close of Play: 1st day: East Zone (1) 265-7 (H.M.Das 78*, Mohanty 6*, 79 overs); 2nd day: East Zone (2) 5-0 (S.S.Das 4*,
A.S.Das 0*, 1 over); 3rd day: South Zone (2) 113-3 (Badrinath 42*, Reddy 0*, 29 overs).

NORTH ZONE v EAST ZONE

Played at Madhavrao Scindia Cricket Ground, Rajkot, February 11, 12, 13, 14, 2008.
Duleep Trophy 2007/08 - Group A
North Zone won by 433 runs. (Points: North Zone 5, East Zone 0)

NORTH ZONE

1	A.S.Chopra	b Paul	10	(2) not out	205
2	S.Dhawan	c H.M.Das b Mohanty	18	(1) lbw b Mohanty	4
3	†K.Goel	b Paul	0	c H.M.Das b Bose	34
4	*M.Manhas	c sub (S.S.Sarkar) b Behera	88	not out	205
5	Yashpal Singh	c H.M.Das b Paul	25		
6	R.Bhatia	c S.S.Das b Mohanty	24		
7	U.Kaul	c A.S.Das b Paul	48		
8	A.Mishra	c W.P.Saha b Paul	52		
9	C.Nanda	b T.S.Saha	58		
10	V.Malik	b T.S.Saha	13		
11	V.R.Singh	not out	20		
	Extras	nb 4	4	b 5, lb 1, w 1, nb 4	11
			360	(2 wickets, declared)	459

FoW (1): 1-20 (1), 2-28 (3), 3-28 (2), 4-82 (5), 5-161 (6), 6-183 (4), 7-260 (8), 8-289 (7), 9-314 (10), 10-360 (9)
FoW (2): 1-4 (1), 2-91 (3)

EAST ZONE

1	*S.S.Das	c Kaul b V.R.Singh	23	lbw b Nanda	33
2	A.S.Das	lbw b V.R.Singh	7	(3) c Kaul b Malik	15
3	A.P.Majumdar	b V.R.Singh	8	(4) run out	82
4	W.P.Saha	not out	56	(2) b Bhatia	2
5	M.S.Vardhan	lbw b V.R.Singh	0	c and b Mishra	83
6	†H.M.Das	b V.R.Singh	8	c sub (R.InderSingh) b V.R.Singh	4
7	T.S.Saha	c Nanda b Mishra	4	b V.R.Singh	0
8	D.S.Mohanty	b Mishra	8	c and b Mishra	0
9	R.R.Bose	lbw b Nanda	4	not out	0
10	S.S.Paul	c Dhawan b Nanda	0	b V.R.Singh	0
11	N.J.Behera	absent hurt	0	absent hurt	0
	Extras	b 6, lb 2, nb 17	25	lb 4, nb 20	24
			143		243

FoW (1): 1-17 (2), 2-34 (3), 3-69 (1), 4-69 (5), 5-93 (6), 6-105 (7), 7-114 (8), 8-143 (9), 9-143 (10)
FoW (2): 1-15 (2), 2-51 (3), 3-70 (1), 4-238 (4), 5-242 (6), 6-242 (5), 7-242 (8), 8-243 (7), 9-243 (10)

East Zone Bowling

	O	M	R	W				O	M	R	W	
Mohanty	18	9	39	2				12	1	41	1	1nb
Bose	21	2	65	0				15	3	57	1	
Paul	28	6	106	5	2nb	(4)	17	5	71	0	
T.S.Saha	21	1	102	2	2nb	(3)	43.5	2	192	0	1w,3nb
Behera	17	1	38	1							
Majumdar	3	0	10	0		(5)	14	0	74	0	
Vardhan						(6)	2	0	18	0	

North Zone Bowling

	O	M	R	W				O	M	R	W	
V.R.Singh	12	2	59	5	9nb	(6)	11.3	3	46	3	6nb
Malik	10	1	50	0	5nb	(1)	16	3	63	1	6nb
Mishra	11	2	26	2	3nb	(4)	13	4	37	2	2nb
Nanda	0.3	0	0	2		(3)	12	1	52	1	6nb
Bhatia						(2)	5	4	2	1	
Manhas						(5)	9	1	39	0	

Umpires: S.S.Hazare and C.R.Mohite. Referee: S.Rao.   Toss: North Zone

Close of Play: 1st day: North Zone (1) 260-7 (Kaul 40*, Nanda 0*, 90 overs); 2nd day: North Zone (2) 109-2 (Chopra 56*, Manhas 12*, 28 overs); 3rd day: East Zone (2) 28-1 (S.S.Das 18*, A.S.Das 2*, 12 overs).

A.S.Chopra's 205 took 301 balls in 441 minutes and included 21 fours. M.Manhas's 205 took 255 balls in 335 minutes and included 27 fours and 2 sixes.

WEST ZONE v ENGLAND LIONS

Played at Moti Bagh Stadium, Vadodara, February 11, 12, 13, 14, 2008.
Duleep Trophy 2007/08 - Group B
West Zone won by nine wickets.   **(Points: West Zone 5, England Lions 0)**

ENGLAND LIONS

1	M.A.Carberry	lbw b Makda	1	lbw b Pathan	17
2	J.L.Denly	run out (Trivedi)	32	(7) b Trivedi	3
3	*M.H.Yardy	b Jobanputra	169	(2) lbw b Trivedi	2
4	E.C.Joyce	lbw b Makda	32	(3) lbw b Pathan	66
5	I.J.L.Trott	lbw b Makda	44	(4) c Kukreja b Dhruve	6
6	G.Onions	c Kukreja b Jobanputra	31	(9) lbw b Trivedi	0
7	†J.S.Foster	lbw b Dhruve	0	(5) c Rahane b Pathan	3
8	A.U.Rashid	not out	9	(6) c Makda b Pathan	39
9	L.E.Plunkett	c Kukreja b Powar	19	(8) lbw b Trivedi	5
10	S.P.Kirby	lbw b Dhruve	3	c Pujara b Pathan	5
11	M.S.Panesar	c Pujara b Dhruve	1	not out	4
	Extras	b 4, lb 8, nb 2	14	b 7, lb 8	15
			355		165

FoW (1): 1-1 (1), 2-51 (2), 3-126 (4), 4-267 (5), 5-322 (3), 6-323 (6), 7-323 (7), 8-342 (9), 9-353 (10), 10-355 (11)
FoW (2): 1-3 (2), 2-39 (1), 3-59 (4), 4-72 (5), 5-103 (3), 6-115 (7), 7-135 (8), 8-135 (9), 9-158 (10), 10-165 (6)

WEST ZONE

1	S.O.Kukreja	c Foster b Onions	0	not out	12
2	W.Jaffer	c Foster b Kirby	151		
3	A.M.Rahane	lbw b Kirby	172	(2) c Plunkett b Onions	6
4	Y.K.Pathan	c and b Plunkett	29		
5	*†P.A.Patel	b Panesar	59		
6	C.A.Pujara	lbw b Rashid	28	(3) not out	9
7	R.R.Powar	lbw b Panesar	5		
8	R.V.Dhruve	b Panesar	2		
9	S.P.Jobanputra	b Rashid	19		
10	A.M.Makda	b Rashid	1		
11	S.K.Trivedi	not out	0		
	Extras	b 6, lb 7, w 5, nb 10	28	lb 1	1
			494	(1 wicket)	28

FoW (1): 1-0 (1), 2-342 (3), 3-365 (2), 4-391 (4), 5-450 (6), 6-461 (7), 7-465 (8), 8-492 (5), 9-493 (10), 10-494 (9)
FoW (2): 1-13 (2)

West Zone Bowling

	O	M	R	W		O	M	R	W
Trivedi	22	0	73	0	2nb	16	7	28	4
Makda	18	4	61	3		5	3	4	0
Jobanputra	13	4	44	2	(6)	3	0	7	0
Powar	26	5	62	1		12	1	33	0
Dhruve	24	8	53	3	(3)	25	11	43	1
Pathan	21	7	39	0	(5)	21	8	35	5
Rahane	2	0	11	0					

England Lions Bowling

	O	M	R	W		O	M	R	W
Onions	20	2	81	1	2nb	7.2	2	19	1
Kirby	27	1	83	2	1nb	7	3	8	0
Panesar	32	5	106	3	3w				
Plunkett	21	2	87	1	2w,3nb				
Trott	9	2	24	0	1nb				
Rashid	18.5	1	88	3	3nb				
Yardy	3	0	12	0					

Umpires: S.Asnani and V.N.Kulkarni. Referee: S.Chaturvedi.   Toss: England Lions

Close of Play: 1st day: England Lions (1) 273-4 (Yardy 151*, Onions 0*, 92 overs); 2nd day: West Zone (1) 187-1 (Jaffer 82*, Rahane 93*, 55 overs); 3rd day: England Lions (2) 14-1 (Carberry 5*, Joyce 5*, 12 overs).
M.H.Yardy's 169 took 325 balls in 403 minutes and included 23 fours. W.Jaffer's 151 took 310 balls in 425 minutes and included 22 fours and 1 six. A.M.Rahane's 172 took 293 balls in 400 minutes and included 26 fours.

WEST ZONE v NORTH ZONE

Played at Wankhede Stadium, Mumbai, February 19, 20, 21, 22, 2008.
Duleep Trophy 2007/08 - Final
North Zone won by six wickets.

WEST ZONE

1	S.O.Kukreja	b Mishra	28	c Kaul b V.R.Singh	4
2	W.Jaffer	c Kaul b V.R.Singh	23	b Thakur	23
3	A.M.Rahane	lbw b Malik	91	lbw b V.R.Singh	43
4	*†P.A.Patel	c Kaul b V.R.Singh	1	c Goel b Malik	3
5	C.A.Pujara	b V.R.Singh	0	b Malik	0
6	R.K.Solanki	c Manhas b V.R.Singh	38	(7) c Dhawan b V.R.Singh	33
7	Y.K.Pathan	c V.R.Singh b Mishra	27	(6) c sub (P.Dogra) b Mishra	61
8	R.V.Dhruve	not out	20	c Mishra b V.R.Singh	41
9	S.P.Jobanputra	c Chopra b V.R.Singh	6	c Goel b V.R.Singh	0
10	A.M.Makda	run out (Malik)	14	c Goel b Bhatia	0
11	S.K.Trivedi	c Manhas b Mishra	0	not out	0
	Extras	lb 11, w 1, nb 14	26	b 2, lb 8, nb 13	23
			274		231

FoW (1): 1-34 (2), 2-122 (1), 3-139 (4), 4-139 (5), 5-170 (3), 6-217 (7), 7-238 (6), 8-247 (9), 9-270 (10), 10-274 (11)
FoW (2): 1-7 (1), 2-56 (2), 3-66 (4), 4-70 (5), 5-108 (3), 6-167 (6), 7-222 (7), 8-222 (9), 9-227 (10), 10-231 (8)

NORTH ZONE

1	A.S.Chopra	c Pujara b Trivedi	35	lbw b Trivedi	12
2	S.Dhawan	b Trivedi	30	not out	94
3	K.Goel	c Patel b Trivedi	0	c Patel b Makda	1
4	*M.Manhas	c Patel b Trivedi	26	c Jaffer b Trivedi	1
5	Yashpal Singh	c Jobanputra b Dhruve	59	c Rahane b Makda	15
6	R.Bhatia	c Makda b Trivedi	84	not out	33
7	†U.Kaul	c Patel b Dhruve	15		
8	A.Mishra	c Patel b Trivedi	15		
9	V.Malik	c Patel b Jobanputra	3		
10	A.K.Thakur	not out	33		
11	V.R.Singh	st Patel b Dhruve	33		
	Extras	lb 4, w 3	7	lb 1, w 5, nb 4	10
			340	(4 wickets)	166

FoW (1): 1-53 (1), 2-53 (3), 3-88 (2), 4-97 (4), 5-225 (5), 6-249 (7), 7-268 (8), 8-271 (6), 9-274 (9), 10-340 (11)
FoW (2): 1-28 (1), 2-39 (3), 3-40 (4), 4-103 (5)

North Zone Bowling

	O	M	R	W			O	M	R	W	
V.R.Singh	20	4	91	5	1w,8nb		18	0	86	5	4nb
Malik	13	3	32	1	4nb		14	3	62	2	5nb
Thakur	12	1	49	0			11	3	21	1	3nb
Bhatia	6	1	34	0	1nb	(5)	2	0	7	1	
Mishra	17.2	6	57	3	1nb	(4)	15	2	45	1	1nb

West Zone Bowling

	O	M	R	W			O	M	R	W	
Trivedi	27	6	67	6	1w		20	11	42	2	
Makda	17	6	55	0		(3)	18.1	4	59	2	1nb
Pathan	12	0	54	0							
Dhruve	24	3	87	3			2	0	13	0	1w
Jobanputra	20	4	73	1	2w	(2)	18	5	51	0	3nb

Umpires: A.V.Jayaprakash and S.J.Phadkar. Third umpire: V.D.Nerurkar. Referee: D.Vasu. Toss: North Zone

Close of Play: 1st day: North Zone (1) 53-0 (Chopra 35*, Dhawan 17*, 16 overs); 2nd day: West Zone (2) 2-0 (Kukreja 0*, Jaffer 0*, 2 overs); 3rd day: North Zone (2) 74-3 (Dhawan 44*, Yashpal Singh 15*, 26 overs).

INDIA v SOUTH AFRICA

Played at M.A.Chidambaram Stadium, Chepauk, Chennai, March 26, 27, 28, 29, 30, 2008.
South Africa in India 2007/08 - 1st Test
Match drawn.

SOUTH AFRICA

1	*G.C.Smith	c Laxman b Kumble	73	(2) lbw b Harbhajan Singh	35
2	N.D.McKenzie	c Dravid b Harbhajan Singh	94	(1) not out	155
3	H.M.Amla	run out (Sreesanth/Dhoni/Kumble)	159	c Dravid b Kumble	81
4	J.H.Kallis	c Jaffer b Harbhajan Singh	13	c R.P.Singh b Harbhajan Singh	19
5	A.G.Prince	c and b Kumble	23	c Jaffer b Harbhajan Singh	5
6	A.B.de Villiers	c Dhoni b Sreesanth	44	c Ganguly b Sehwag	11
7	†M.V.Boucher	c Dravid b Sehwag	70	not out	11
8	M.Morkel	c and b Harbhajan Singh	35		
9	P.L.Harris	c Dhoni b Harbhajan Singh	5		
10	D.W.Steyn	c R.P.Singh b Harbhajan Singh	15		
11	M.Ntini	not out	1		
	Extras	b 1, lb 5, w 1, nb 1	8	b 8, lb 5, nb 1	14
			540	(5 wickets, declared)	331

FoW (1): 1-132 (1), 2-196 (2), 3-244 (4), 4-291 (5), 5-357 (6), 6-456 (3), 7-510 (7), 8-520 (8), 9-529 (9), 10-540 (10)
FoW (2): 1-53 (2), 2-210 (3), 3-264 (4), 4-272 (5), 5-306 (6)

INDIA

1	W.Jaffer	c Kallis b Harris	73
2	V.Sehwag	c McKenzie b Ntini	319
3	R.S.Dravid	c Kallis b Ntini	111
4	S.R.Tendulkar	c Kallis b Ntini	0
5	S.C.Ganguly	c Boucher b Harris	24
6	V.V.S.Laxman	c and b Harris	39
7	†M.S.Dhoni	c Boucher b Steyn	16
8	*A.Kumble	b Steyn	3
9	Harbhajan Singh	b Steyn	0
10	R.P.Singh	b Steyn	0
11	S.Sreesanth	not out	4
	Extras	b 20, lb 10, w 4, nb 4	38
			627

FoW (1): 1-213 (1), 2-481 (2), 3-481 (4), 4-526 (5), 5-573 (3), 6-598 (7), 7-610 (8), 8-610 (9), 9-612 (10), 10-627 (6)

India Bowling	O	M	R	W		O	M	R	W	
R.P.Singh	23	1	111	0	(2)	9	1	43	0	
Sreesanth	26	5	104	1	1w,1nb (1)	12	0	42	0	1nb
Kumble	45	11	106	2	(5)	20	2	57	1	
Harbhajan Singh	44.5	4	164	5	(3)	34	1	101	3	
Sehwag	11	1	37	1	(6)	22	2	55	1	
Ganguly	3	0	12	0	(4)	2	1	1	0	
Laxman					(7)	10	2	19	0	

South Africa Bowling	O	M	R	W	
Steyn	32	3	103	4	
Ntini	28	3	128	3	
Morkel	25	4	76	0	1w,2nb
Harris	53.1	6	203	3	1w,2nb
Kallis	14	0	71	0	
Prince	3	0	16	0	1w

Umpires: Asad Rauf and A.L.Hill.   Third umpire: A.M.Saheba.   Referee: R.S.Mahanama.   Toss: South Africa

Close of Play: 1st day: South Africa (1) 304-4 (Amla 85*, de Villiers 10*, 90 overs); 2nd day: India (1) 82-0 (Jaffer 25*, Sehwag 52*, 21 overs); 3rd day: India (1) 468-1 (Sehwag 309*, Dravid 65*, 106 overs); 4th day: South Africa (2) 131-1 (McKenzie 59*, Amla 35*, 33 overs).

Man of the Match: V.Sehwag.
H.M.Amla's 159 took 262 balls in 406 minutes and included 20 fours. V.Sehwag's 319 took 304 balls in 530 minutes and included 42 fours and 5 sixes. R.S.Dravid's 111 took 291 balls in 396 minutes and included 15 fours. N.D.McKenzie's 155 took 339 balls in 445 minutes and included 13 fours and 1 six.

INDIA v SOUTH AFRICA

Played at Sardar Patel Stadium, Motera, Ahmedabad, April 3, 4, 5, 2008.
South Africa in India 2007/08 - 2nd Test
South Africa won by an innings and 90 runs.

INDIA

1	W.Jaffer	c Smith b Ntini	9	(2) c de Villiers b Kallis	19	
2	V.Sehwag	b Steyn	6	(1) lbw b Ntini	17	
3	R.S.Dravid	b Steyn	3	c de Villiers b Morkel	17	
4	V.V.S.Laxman	b Ntini	3	c Boucher b Morkel	35	
5	S.C.Ganguly	b Ntini	0	c Boucher b Steyn	87	
6	†M.S.Dhoni	c Boucher b Morkel	14	c Smith b Ntini	52	
7	I.K.Pathan	not out	21	not out	43	
8	*A.Kumble	b Morkel	0	b Harris	5	
9	Harbhajan Singh	lbw b Steyn	1	lbw b Steyn	4	
10	R.P.Singh	c Smith b Steyn	0	c Kallis b Steyn	8	
11	S.Sreesanth	b Steyn	0	b Ntini	17	
	Extras	b 4, lb 11, w 2, nb 2	19	b 5, lb 7, w 7, nb 5	24	
			76		**328**	

FoW (1): 1-16 (1), 2-24 (2), 3-30 (4), 4-30 (5), 5-53 (3), 6-55 (6), 7-55 (8), 8-56 (9), 9-76 (10), 10-76 (11)
FoW (2): 1-31 (1), 2-64 (3), 3-70 (2), 4-125 (4), 5-235 (5), 6-268 (6), 7-273 (8), 8-292 (9), 9-306 (10), 10-328 (11)

SOUTH AFRICA

1	*G.C.Smith	lbw b Sreesanth	34
2	N.D.McKenzie	c Dravid b Harbhajan Singh	42
3	H.M.Amla	c Jaffer b Harbhajan Singh	16
4	J.H.Kallis	b Sreesanth	132
5	A.G.Prince	lbw b Harbhajan Singh	2
6	A.B.de Villiers	not out	217
7	†M.V.Boucher	lbw b Kumble	21
8	M.Morkel	lbw b Harbhajan Singh	1
9	P.L.Harris	not out	9
10	D.W.Steyn		
11	M.Ntini		
	Extras	b 2, lb 14, w 4	20
		(7 wickets, declared)	494

FoW (1): 1-78 (1), 2-100 (2), 3-101 (3), 4-117 (5), 5-373 (4), 6-439 (7), 7-452 (8)

South Africa Bowling

	O	M	R	W		O	M	R	W	
Steyn	8	2	23	5	2w,1nb	23	1	91	3	2w
Ntini	6	1	18	3		16.2	3	44	3	
Morkel	6	1	20	2	1nb	20	0	87	2	1w,5nb
Kallis					(4)	10	3	26	1	
Harris					(5)	25	4	68	1	

India Bowling

	O	M	R	W	
Sreesanth	23	4	87	2	1w
R.P.Singh	21	2	81	0	
Pathan	21.2	3	85	0	3w
Harbhajan Singh	40	5	135	4	
Kumble	33	2	78	1	
Ganguly	3	0	12	0	

Umpires: B.R.Doctrove and A.L.Hill. Third umpire: S.L.Shastri. Referee: R.S.Mahanama.   Toss: India

Close of Play: 1st day: South Africa (1) 223-4 (Kallis 60*, de Villiers 59*, 64 overs); 2nd day: South Africa (1) 494-7 (de Villiers 217*, Harris 9*, 141.2 overs).

Man of the Match: A.B.de Villiers.

The match was scheduled for five days but completed in three. J.H.Kallis's 132 took 275 balls in 359 minutes and included 14 fours and 1 six. A.B.de Villiers's 217 took 333 balls in 480 minutes and included 17 fours and 2 sixes.

INDIA v SOUTH AFRICA

Played at Modi Stadium, Kanpur, April 11, 12, 13, 2008.
South Africa in India 2007/08 - 3rd Test
India won by eight wickets.

SOUTH AFRICA

1	N.D.McKenzie	st Dhoni b Chawla	36	lbw b Sreesanth	14
2	*G.C.Smith	c Jaffer b Yuvraj Singh	69	b Sehwag	35
3	H.M.Amla	b Sharma	51	c Jaffer b Harbhajan Singh	0
4	J.H.Kallis	b Harbhajan Singh	1	c Jaffer b Sehwag	15
5	A.G.Prince	lbw b Sehwag	16	not out	22
6	A.B.de Villiers	c Ganguly b Chawla	25	c Laxman b Harbhajan Singh	7
7	†M.V.Boucher	b Sharma	29	c Dhoni b Sharma	5
8	M.Morkel	c Dravid b Harbhajan Singh	17	b Sharma	0
9	P.L.Harris	b Sharma	12	c Dravid b Harbhajan Singh	0
10	D.W.Steyn	c sub (M.Kaif) b Harbhajan Singh	0	b Harbhajan Singh	7
11	M.Ntini	not out	0	c Ganguly b Sehwag	0
	Extras	lb 3, w 2, nb 4	9	b 12, lb 1, w 1, nb 2	16
			265		**121**

FoW (1): 1-61 (1), 2-152 (2), 3-160 (3), 4-161 (4), 5-199 (6), 6-215 (5), 7-241 (8), 8-264 (7), 9-265 (10), 10-265 (9)
FoW (2): 1-26 (1), 2-27 (3), 3-65 (4), 4-72 (2), 5-90 (6), 6-101 (7), 7-101 (8), 8-102 (9), 9-114 (10), 10-121 (11)

INDIA

1	W.Jaffer	lbw b Morkel	15	lbw b Morkel	10
2	V.Sehwag	lbw b Steyn	8	c Prince b Harris	22
3	R.S.Dravid	c de Villiers b Morkel	29	(4) not out	18
4	V.V.S.Laxman	b Morkel	50		
5	S.C.Ganguly	c Amla b Steyn	87	(3) not out	13
6	Yuvraj Singh	c de Villiers b Harris	32		
7	*†M.S.Dhoni	st Boucher b Harris	32		
8	Harbhajan Singh	lbw b Steyn	6		
9	P.P.Chawla	c Smith b Ntini	4		
10	S.Sreesanth	c Prince b Harris	29		
11	I.Sharma	not out	14		
	Extras	b 8, lb 6, w 1, nb 4	19	nb 1	1
			325	**(2 wickets)**	**64**

FoW (1): 1-18 (2), 2-35 (1), 3-113 (3), 4-123 (4), 5-188 (6), 6-248 (7), 7-268 (8), 8-279 (9), 9-279 (5), 10-325 (10)
FoW (2): 1-32 (2), 2-32 (1)

India Bowling

	O	M	R	W			O	M	R	W	
Sreesanth	11	0	32	0	1w,2nb	(3)	9	4	9	1	2nb
Sharma	12.3	1	55	3	1w,2nb		10	2	18	2	1w
Harbhajan Singh	31	9	52	3		(1)	23	7	44	4	
Chawla	16	3	66	2			4	0	18	0	
Yuvraj Singh	11	1	39	1		(6)	1	0	7	0	
Sehwag	6	2	18	1		(5)	8.5	2	12	3	

South Africa Bowling

	O	M	R	W			O	M	R	W	
Steyn	20	1	71	3	1w		2	0	15	0	
Ntini	21	7	47	1			1	0	5	0	
Morkel	15	2	63	3	3nb	(4)	5	1	8	1	1nb
Harris	32.4	8	101	3	1nb	(3)	5.1	0	36	1	
Kallis	9	1	23	0							
Amla	2	0	6	0							

Umpires: Asad Rauf and B.R.Doctrove.   Third umpire: G.A.Pratapkumar.   Referee: R.S.Mahanama.   Toss: South Africa

Close of Play: 1st day: South Africa (1) 265 all out; 2nd day: India (1) 288-9 (Sreesanth 9*, Sharma 0*, 88 overs).

Man of the Match: S.C.Ganguly.

The match was scheduled for five days but completed in three.

KENYA v INDIA A

Played at Mombasa Sports Club Ground, August 5, 6, 7, 2007.
India A in Kenya and Zimbabwe 2007/08
India A won by an innings and 98 runs.

KENYA

1	†M.A.Ouma	b Pathan	0	c Kaif b Ojha	35
2	D.O.Obuya	c Kaif b Chawla	24	c Chawla b Pathan	19
3	A.Obanda	lbw b Mahesh	0	lbw b Pankaj Singh	0
4	*S.O.Tikolo	c Sharma b Pankaj Singh	28	(7) b Chawla	13
5	C.O.Obuya	c Uthappa b Ojha	3	c Pankaj Singh b Mahesh	51
6	T.Mishra	b Mahesh	27	(4) lbw b Chawla	32
7	J.K.Kamande	lbw b Chawla	10	(6) c Ojha b Chawla	1
8	R.L.Bhudia	b Pankaj Singh	0	c Badrinath b Chawla	25
9	P.J.Ongondo	b Mahesh	1	lbw b Pankaj Singh	16
10	H.A.Varaiya	not out	1	not out	1
11	E.Otieno	lbw b Mahesh	0	lbw b Pankaj Singh	0
	Extras	lb 1, nb 2	3	b 4, lb 9, w 1, nb 4	18
			97		**211**

FoW (1): 1-0 (1), 2-1 (3), 3-39 (4), 4-55 (2), 5-60 (5), 6-93 (7), 7-93 (8), 8-96 (9), 9-97 (6), 10-97 (11)
FoW (2): 1-40 (2), 2-41 (3), 3-61 (1), 4-120 (4), 5-124 (6), 6-154 (7), 7-160 (5), 8-192 (8), 9-211 (9), 10-211 (11)

INDIA A

1	C.A.Pujara	c Ouma b Ongondo	9
2	R.V.Uthappa	c Varaiya b Bhudia	1
3	†P.A.Patel	c Kamande b Varaiya	124
4	*M.Kaif	c C.O.Obuya b Varaiya	25
5	R.G.Sharma	lbw b Ongondo	35
6	S.Badrinath	not out	133
7	I.K.Pathan	c Ongondo b C.O.Obuya	32
8	P.P.Chawla	c sub (N.Odhiambo) b Kamande	0
9	V.Y.Mahesh	run out (C.O.Obuya)	0
10	Pankaj Singh	not out	40
11	P.P.Ojha		
	Extras	b 4, lb 2, w 1	7
		(8 wickets, declared)	**406**

FoW (1): 1-6 (2), 2-14 (1), 3-82 (4), 4-158 (5), 5-261 (3), 6-326 (7), 7-329 (8), 8-330 (9)

India A Bowling

	O	M	R	W			O	M	R	W	
Pathan	7	2	18	1			12	2	44	1	
Mahesh	7.4	1	21	4			8	1	62	1	1w
Pankaj Singh	8	2	15	2			5.2	1	19	3	
Chawla	7	1	13	2		(5)	15	7	32	4	
Ojha	8	1	29	1	2nb	(4)	12	3	41	1	4nb

Kenya Bowling

	O	M	R	W	
Ongondo	16	4	74	2	
Bhudia	15	2	53	1	
Otieno	10	3	35	0	
Varaiya	19	0	119	2	
Kamande	24	4	62	1	
C.O.Obuya	11	0	57	1	1w

Umpires: R.D'Mello and K.Gulamabbas.   Referee: S.R.Modi.   Toss: Kenya

Close of Play: 1st day: India A (1) 205-4 (Patel 100*, Badrinath 29*, 51 overs); 2nd day: Kenya (2) 192-8 (Ongondo 6*, Varaiya 0*, 44 overs).

Man of the Match: P.A.Patel.

P.A.Patel's 124 took 159 balls and included 18 fours. S.Badrinath's 133 took 180 balls and included 18 fours and 2 sixes.

KENYA v INDIA A

Played at Mombasa Sports Club Ground, August 10, 11, 12, 2007.
India A in Kenya and Zimbabwe 2007/08
India A won by an innings and 87 runs.

KENYA

1	†M.A.Ouma	lbw b Pathan	2	c sub (C.A.Pujara) b Pathan	4
2	D.O.Obuya	c Rawat b Pathan	30	lbw b Pathan	0
3	A.O.Suji	lbw b Pankaj Singh	0	(4) lbw b Ojha	11
4	A.Obanda	lbw b Ojha	21	(5) c Rawat b Mahesh	0
5	T.Mishra	c Rawat b Pawar	20	(6) st Rawat b Ojha	24
6	*T.M.Odoyo	c Rawat b Pathan	51	(7) c Kaif b Ojha	16
7	J.K.Kamande	c Kaif b Ojha	24	(8) c Rawat b Pathan	30
8	N.Odhiambo	c Pathan b Pankaj Singh	41	(9) c and b Ojha	6
9	H.A.Varaiya	not out	15	(3) lbw b Ojha	18
10	L.N.Onyango	b Pankaj Singh	0	c Mahesh b Ojha	2
11	P.J.Ongondo	lbw b Ojha	5	not out	0
	Extras	b 4, lb 3, w 1, nb 1	9	lb 7, w 3, nb 3	13
			218		**124**

FoW (1): 1-21 (1), 2-22 (3), 3-44 (2), 4-67 (4), 5-84 (5), 6-127 (7), 7-183 (6), 8-207 (8), 9-207 (10), 10-218 (11)
FoW (2): 1-4 (1), 2-4 (2), 3-36 (4), 4-41 (5), 5-51 (3), 6-73 (7), 7-88 (6), 8-100 (9), 9-122 (8), 10-124 (10)

INDIA A

1	P.A.Patel	lbw b Odhiambo	164
2	N.K.Patel	c Suji b Odhiambo	1
3	*M.Kaif	c Ouma b Odhiambo	4
4	I.K.Pathan	c Odoyo b Onyango	16
5	S.Badrinath	not out	160
6	A.S.Yadav	c Kamande b Suji	60
7	Pankaj Singh	not out	0
8	R.V.Pawar		
9	V.Y.Mahesh		
10	†M.Rawat		
11	P.P.Ojha		
	Extras	b 16, w 2, nb 6	24
		(5 wickets, declared)	429

FoW (1): 1-14 (2), 2-18 (3), 3-75 (4), 4-267 (1), 5-422 (6)

India A Bowling

	O	M	R	W		O	M	R	W	
Pathan	18	3	57	3	1w	10	2	26	3	2w,3nb
Pankaj Singh	17	7	35	3		(3) 10	2	14	0	
Ojha	20.3	6	54	3	1nb	(2) 18.1	9	31	6	
Mahesh	9	1	31	0		(5) 7	1	18	1	1w
Pawar	15	5	34	1		(4) 11	3	28	0	

Kenya Bowling

	O	M	R	W	
Odoyo	2	1	4	0	
Ongondo	17	0	74	0	6nb
Odhiambo	17	2	64	3	
Onyango	18	3	69	1	2w
Kamande	22	0	99	0	
Varaiya	10	0	66	0	
Suji	6	0	37	1	

Umpires: R.D'Mello and K.Gulamabbas. Referee: S.R.Modi.   Toss: India A

Close of Play: 1st day: India A (1) 30-2 (P.A.Patel 19*, Pathan 4*, 9 overs); 2nd day: Kenya (2) 4-2 (Varaiya 0*, Suji 0*, 3 overs).

Man of the Match: S.Badrinath.

P.A.Patel's 164 took 188 balls and included 22 fours and 1 six. S.Badrinath's 160 took 231 balls and included 19 fours and 1 six.

NAMIBIA v NORTH WEST

Played at Wanderers Cricket Ground, Windhoek, October 18, 19, 20, 2007.
South African Airways Provincial Three-Day Challenge 2007/08 - Pool B
Match drawn.   (Points: Namibia 8.8, North West 9.74)

NORTH WEST

1	J.F.Mostert	lbw b Klazinga	18	c Rudolph b Klazinga		18
2	C.Jonker	c Silver b Snyman	15	retired hurt		64
3	M.Lazenby	b Klazinga	17	(8) not out		25
4	N.Bredenkamp	c Williams b Scholtz	125	c Scholtz b K.B.Burger		125
5	L.J.Kgamadi	not out	125	c sub (W.Slabber) b Scholtz		41
6	R.Bhayat	run out (Rudolph)	7	(3) c K.B.Burger b Scholtz		105
7	*W.A.Deacon	c Rudolph b Scholtz	12	not out		60
8	†T.A. Bula	c Silver b Scholtz	1	(6) c Williams b K.B.Burger		7
9	G.J.de Bruin	not out	0			
10	K.M.Naicker					
11	P.S.Letsoalo					
	Extras	b 5, lb 5, w 4, nb 3	17	b 10, lb 7, w 4, nb 2		23
		(7 wickets)	337	(5 wickets, declared)		468

FoW (1): 1-32 (2), 2-55 (3), 3-60 (1), 4-274 (4), 5-297 (6), 6-312 (7), 7-316 (8)
FoW (2): 1-31 (1), 2-314 (4), 3-340 (3), 4-355 (6), 5-400 (5)

NAMIBIA

1	A.J.Burger	c Naicker b Deacon	1	c Deacon b Naicker	12
2	S.Silver	c Bhayat b Naicker	43	lbw b Letsoalo	22
3	G.J.Rudolph	c Bula b Deacon	49	not out	46
4	G.Snyman	c Jonker b Naicker	90	c sub (M.P.Siboto) b Naicker	9
5	C.Williams	c Letsoalo b Naicker	55	not out	57
6	*L.P.Vorster	run out (Bula)	21		
7	N.R.P.Scholtz	not out	24		
8	†T.Verwey	c Naicker b Mostert	15		
9	K.B.Burger	c Letsoalo b Naicker	14		
10	M.C.van Zyl	st Bula b Naicker	13		
11	L.Klazinga				
	Extras	b 2, lb 4, w 1, nb 8	15	w 1	1
		(9 wickets)	340	(3 wickets)	147

FoW (1): 1-6 (1), 2-100 (2), 3-112 (3), 4-238 (4), 5-261 (5), 6-280 (6), 7-306 (8), 8-321 (9), 9-340 (10)
FoW (2): 1-14 (1), 2-44 (2), 3-57 (4)

Namibia Bowling	O	M	R	W		O	M	R	W	
Snyman	13	2	47	1	1w,2nb	6	2	30	0	1nb
K.B.Burger	12	2	30	0	2w	15	0	70	2	2w
Klazinga	12	4	36	2	1nb	11	0	85	1	1w,1nb
Scholtz	17	1	74	3		(6) 24	1	109	2	
van Zyl	6	1	29	0		(4) 15	3	54	0	1w
A.J.Burger	21	3	88	0		(5) 16	1	81	0	
Williams	4	0	23	0		6	0	22	0	

North West Bowling	O	M	R	W		O	M	R	W	
de Bruin	11	2	44	0	4nb					
Deacon	14	3	47	2	3nb	(6) 0.2	0	0	0	
Letsoalo	12	3	49	0	1w	6	0	25	1	
Naicker	37	7	120	5		(2) 26	6	57	2	
Bhayat	1	0	14	0		(1) 7	0	21	0	1w
Mostert	10	0	60	1	1nb	(5) 1	0	8	0	
Kgamadi						(4) 14	3	36	0	

Umpires: A.W.Louw and G.H.Pienaar.   Toss: North West

Close of Play: 1st day: Namibia (1) 73-1 (Silver 34*, Rudolph 33*, 25 overs); 2nd day: North West (2) 239-1 (Bhayat 60*, Bredenkamp 78*, 56 overs).
N.Bredenkamp's 125 took 166 balls in 207 minutes and included 15 fours and 7 sixes. L.J.Kgamadi's 125 took 199 balls in 240 minutes and included 10 fours and 2 sixes. R.Bhayat's 105 took 192 balls in 269 minutes and included 8 fours. N.Bredenkamp's 125 took 154 balls in 192 minutes and included 14 fours and 2 sixes. C.Jonker retired hurt in the North West second innings having scored 64 (team score 101-1).

NAMIBIA v GRIQUALAND WEST

Played at Wanderers Cricket Ground, Windhoek, November 8, 9, 10, 2007.
South African Airways Provincial Three-Day Challenge 2007/08 - Pool B
Griqualand West won by 148 runs.   (Points: Namibia 5.52, Griqualand West 16.96)

GRIQUALAND WEST
1	A.K.Kruger	run out (Klazinga/Snyman)	1	lbw b Snyman		4
2	M.Akoojee	b Snyman	11	b Snyman		13
3	A.P.McLaren	b K.B.Burger	27	c K.B.Burger b Williams		118
4	R.R.Hendricks	c van Schoor b Snyman	0	c van Schoor b K.B.Burger		22
5	*†W.Bossenger	c Rudolph b Williams	30	c van Schoor b Williams		25
6	H.G.de Kock	c Slabber b Klazinga	18	lbw b Snyman		18
7	F.S.Holtzhausen	c and b Williams	10	c and b Williams		27
8	J.Coetzee	not out	37	c Snyman b Klazinga		51
9	R.A.Adams	c van Schoor b Klazinga	0	b Scholtz		37
10	A.P.T.Mabuya	b Scholtz	26	b Klazinga		8
11	D.D.Carolus	c Klazinga b Williams	16	not out		0
	Extras	lb 7, w 1, nb 14	22	b 2, lb 13, w 6, nb 5		26
			198			**349**

FoW (1): 1-8 (1), 2-38 (2), 3-38 (4), 4-77 (3), 5-81 (5), 6-104 (7), 7-112 (6), 8-112 (9), 9-170 (10), 10-198 (11)
FoW (2): 1-4 (1), 2-45 (2), 3-91 (4), 4-147 (5), 5-179 (6), 6-248 (3), 7-253 (7), 8-335 (9), 9-341 (8), 10-349 (10)

NAMIBIA
1	G.W.Cloete	b Coetzee	6	lbw b Coetzee		0
2	†R.van Schoor	c de Kock b Coetzee	23	c Coetzee b Kruger		41
3	G.J.Rudolph	b Holtzhausen	1	(7) c Bossenger b Kruger		3
4	G.Snyman	c Mabuya b Coetzee	17	c Holtzhausen b Coetzee		121
5	*A.J.Burger	c Bossenger b Mabuya	32	c Adams b Mabuya		28
6	C.Williams	c McLaren b Holtzhausen	1	(3) c Holtzhausen b Carolus		61
7	N.R.P.Scholtz	c de Kock b Kruger	0	(6) c Bossenger b Kruger		0
8	E.Steenkamp	c Bossenger b Kruger	4	lbw b Kruger		0
9	W.Slabber	not out	20	run out		9
10	K.B.Burger	c McLaren b Holtzhausen	4	c Bossenger b Kruger		9
11	L.Klazinga	lbw b Coetzee	0	not out		1
	Extras	b 4, lb 12, w 1, nb 1	18	lb 5, w 2, nb 2		9
			126			**273**

FoW (1): 1-22 (1), 2-29 (3), 3-50 (4), 4-50 (2), 5-52 (6), 6-67 (7), 7-78 (8), 8-107 (5), 9-121 (10), 10-126 (11)
FoW (2): 1-4 (1), 2-100 (3), 3-115 (2), 4-189 (5), 5-197 (6), 6-229 (7), 7-229 (8), 8-229 (9), 9-244 (10), 10-273 (4)

Namibia Bowling	O	M	R	W			O	M	R	W	
Snyman	14	1	56	2	6nb		16	0	74	3	3w,3nb
Klazinga	11	0	53	2	8nb		14.1	0	63	2	2w,2nb
Williams	13.4	0	54	3	1w	(5)	11	3	46	3	
K.B.Burger	8	3	18	1		(3)	10	1	35	1	1w
Scholtz	4	0	10	1		(4)	23	1	77	1	
A.J.Burger						(6)	3	0	15	0	
Slabber						(7)	5	1	24	0	

Griqualand West Bowling	O	M	R	W			O	M	R	W	
Coetzee	14.2	5	31	4			19.5	8	68	2	2w,1nb
Carolus	5	0	19	0	1nb	(7)	11	3	46	1	
Holtzhausen	15	7	26	3		(2)	15	3	37	0	1nb
Kruger	8	2	9	2			19	6	53	5	
Adams	5	0	20	0	1w	(3)	2	0	6	0	
Mabuya	3	1	5	1		(8)	10	3	49	1	
de Kock						(5)	2	0	9	0	
McLaren						(6)	1	0	1	0	

Umpires: J.J.Luck and J.E.P.Ostrom.   Toss: Griqualand West

Close of Play: 1st day: Namibia (1) 126 all out; 2nd day: Namibia (2) 64-1 (van Schoor 26*, Williams 35*, 22 overs).
A.P.McLaren's 118 took 169 balls in 192 minutes and included 12 fours. G.Snyman's 121 took 161 balls in 203 minutes and included 14 fours and 8 sixes.

NAMIBIA v ZIMBABWE PROVINCES

Played at Wanderers Cricket Ground, Windhoek, January 10, 11, 12, 2008.
South African Airways Provincial Three-Day Challenge 2007/08 - Pool B
Zimbabwe Provinces won by eight wickets.　　(Points: Namibia 4.14, Zimbabwe Provinces 19.78)

ZIMBABWE PROVINCES

1	T.M.K.Mawoyo	c Verwey b S.F.Burger	15	c Verwey b Klazinga	33
2	F.Kasteni	b Klazinga	50	run out	21
3	A.G.Cremer	c Klazinga b S.F.Burger	32	not out	35
4	B.Mujuru	c Rudolph b Klazinga	59		
5	†R.W.Chakabva	not out	118		
6	S.K.Nyamuzinga	c Rudolph b Williams	32	(4) not out	2
7	K.O.Meth	lbw b Williams	8		
8	A.M.Manyumwa	not out	2		
9	*N.B.Mahwire				
10	P.M.Tsvanhu				
11	E.C.Rainsford				
	Extras	b 2, lb 9, w 5, nb 7	23	b 2, lb 1, w 2, nb 6	11
		(6 wickets)	339	(2 wickets)	102

FoW (1): 1-53 (1), 2-92 (2), 3-134 (3), 4-251 (4), 5-313 (6), 6-331 (7)
FoW (2): 1-44 (2), 2-89 (1)

NAMIBIA

1	A.J.Burger	b Mahwire	23	c Kasteni b Mahwire	3
2	D.H.Botha	b Mahwire	18	c Rainsford b Mahwire	120
3	†T.Verwey	b Mahwire	0	(9) not out	18
4	G.J.Rudolph	c Nyamuzinga b Tsvanhu	11	(3) c Mawoyo b Cremer	33
5	G.Snyman	c Kasteni b Mahwire	2	(4) c Mawoyo b Cremer	27
6	*L.J.Burger	c Chakabva b Manyumwa	21	(5) c Nyamuzinga b Meth	43
7	C.Williams	c Nyamuzinga b Manyumwa	10	(6) lbw b Manyumwa	30
8	S.F.Burger	lbw b Cremer	6	(7) lbw b Mahwire	1
9	L.P.van der Westhuizen	c Tsvanhu b Manyumwa	6	(8) c Mawoyo b Cremer	11
10	K.B.Burger	c Cremer b Mahwire	4	c Chakabva b Manyumwa	0
11	L.Klazinga	not out	5	lbw b Meth	18
	Extras	b 1, w 2, nb 4	7	b 8, lb 9, w 5, nb 5	27
			107		331

FoW (1): 1-23 (2), 2-37 (3), 3-43 (1), 4-45 (5), 5-80 (6), 6-84 (4), 7-97 (7), 8-97 (8), 9-97 (9), 10-107 (10)
FoW (2): 1-13 (1), 2-86 (3), 3-137 (4), 4-252 (2), 5-252 (5), 6-253 (7), 7-295 (8), 8-295 (6), 9-295 (10), 10-331 (11)

Namibia Bowling	O	M	R	W			O	M	R	W	
Snyman	12	2	40	0	1w,4nb		5	0	34	0	5nb
Klazinga	14	3	46	2	3nb		5	1	20	1	2w,1nb
S.F.Burger	17	8	52	2	1w	(4)	2	0	15	0	
K.B.Burger	15	2	55	0	2w	(3)	4	0	22	0	
van der Westhuizen	7	2	25	0							
A.J.Burger	4	0	21	0		(5)	1	0	8	0	
Williams	8	0	48	2							
L.J.Burger	8	1	41	0							

Zimbabwe Provinces Bowling	O	M	R	W			O	M	R	W	
Rainsford	10	3	29	0	1w		18	6	40	0	2w
Tsvanhu	7	0	35	1	3nb	(3)	6	0	34	0	1w,5nb
Mahwire	9.3	4	11	5	1nb	(2)	19	12	23	3	
Manyumwa	8	3	30	3	1w	(5)	13	4	49	2	
Cremer	4	3	1	1		(4)	41	10	96	3	
Meth						(6)	22	4	62	2	2w
Kasteni						(7)	1	0	10	0	
Nyamuzinga						(8)	1	1	0	0	

Umpires: J.J.Luck and L.J.Willemse.　　　　　　　　Toss: Zimbabwe Provinces

Close of Play: 1st day: Namibia (1) 30-1 (A.J.Burger 11*, Verwey 0*, 9 overs); 2nd day: Namibia (2) 218-3 (Botha 104*, L.J.Burger 27*, 80 overs).
R.W.Chakabva's 118 took 119 balls in 161 minutes and included 17 fours. D.H.Botha's 120 took 279 balls in 376 minutes and included 17 fours.

NAMIBIA v FREE STATE

Played at Wanderers Cricket Ground, Windhoek, February 7, 8, 9, 2008.
South African Airways Provincial Three-Day Challenge 2007/08 - Pool B
Match drawn.   (Points: Namibia 4, Free State 4.54)

FREE STATE
1	†L.N.Mosena	c Rudolph b S.F.Burger	27
2	M.P.Fick	c Klazinga b S.F.Burger	24
3	E.H.Weirich	c Rudolph b Geldenhuys	53
4	*H.O.von Rauenstein	c Rudolph b S.F.Burger	0
5	G.N.Nieuwoudt	c Klazinga b Durant	83
6	M.N.Erlank	c Verwey b A.J.Burger	27
7	R.K.Terblanche	not out	24
8	G.D.Perry	c Slabber b Durant	0
9	W.J.van Zyl	c S.F.Burger b A.J.Burger	7
10	B.B.Kops	b A.J.Burger	2
11	M.N.Saliwa	not out	19
	Extras	lb 2, w 6, nb 3	11

(9 wickets)   277

FoW (1): 1-45 (1), 2-69 (2), 3-69 (4), 4-144 (3), 5-211 (6), 6-229 (5), 7-229 (8), 8-241 (9), 9-246 (10)

NAMIBIA
1	A.J.Burger	not out	32
2	G.J.Rudolph	c Terblanche b Saliwa	17
3	C.Williams	not out	0
4	G.Snyman		
5	*L.J.Burger		
6	S.F.Burger		
7	†T.Verwey		
8	M.Durant		
9	W.Slabber		
10	H.W.Geldenhuys		
11	L.Klazinga		
	Extras	w 4, nb 1	5

(1 wicket)   54

FoW (1): 1-52 (2)

Namibia Bowling
	O	M	R	W	
Klazinga	8	0	23	0	1w,3nb
Geldenhuys	9	2	31	1	2w
Williams	14	1	41	0	1w
S.F.Burger	17	4	38	3	1w
A.J.Burger	15	0	58	3	1w
L.J.Burger	4	1	10	0	
Durant	13	2	51	2	
Slabber	5	0	23	0	

Free State Bowling
	O	M	R	W	
Kops	3.3	0	28	0	4w
Saliwa	3	0	26	1	1nb

Umpires: L.M.Engelbrecht and A.W.Louw.   Toss: Namibia

Close of Play: 1st day: Namibia (1) 54-1 (A.J.Burger 32*, Williams 0*, 6.3 overs); 2nd day: No play.

There was no play on the final day.

CANTERBURY v AUCKLAND

Played at Village Green, Christchurch, November 12, 13, 14, 15, 2007.
State Championship 2007/08
Match drawn.   (Points: Canterbury 0, Auckland 2)

AUCKLAND
1	T.G.McIntosh	b Robertson	76	run out		23
2	*R.A.Jones	c Rae b Ellis	80	c Anderson b Astle		43
3	M.J.Guptill	c Myburgh b Astle	40	(4) c van Wyk b Astle		3
4	R.J.Nicol	st van Wyk b Robertson	47	(5) run out		1
5	G.J.Hopkins	b Ellis	0	(3) c Astle b Bennett		8
6	C.de Grandhomme	c Bennett b Astle	62	not out		3
7	†R.A.Young	not out	56	not out		5
8	A.R.Adams	c Astle b Hiini	30			
9	L.J.Shaw	lbw b Hiini	8			
10	G.P.Hayne	not out	4			
11	A.J.McKay					
	Extras	lb 5, w 3, nb 6	14	b 4, lb 3		7
		(8 wickets, declared)	417	(5 wickets, declared)		93

FoW (1): 1-135 (2), 2-176 (1), 3-222 (3), 4-228 (5), 5-304 (4), 6-326 (6), 7-393 (8), 8-412 (9)
FoW (2): 1-66 (1), 2-70 (2), 3-84 (4), 4-85 (5), 5-85 (3)

CANTERBURY
1	T.D.Astle	lbw b Adams	4	not out		75
2	S.L.Stewart	lbw b Adams	9	c Young b McKay		0
3	B.J.Rae	lbw b Adams	2	b McKay		0
4	J.G.Myburgh	c Hopkins b Adams	0	b Shaw		60
5	A.M.Ellis	lbw b Shaw	58	c and b Hayne		0
6	C.J.Anderson	b Shaw	0	b de Grandhomme		31
7	*†C.F.K.van Wyk	b Adams	21	not out		4
8	I.A.Robertson	not out	0			
9	B.C.Hiini	lbw b Adams	71			
10	L.M.Burtt	not out	0			
11	H.K.Bennett					
	Extras	b 5, lb 4, w 3, nb 3	15	b 1, lb 8		9
		(8 wickets, declared)	180	(5 wickets)		179

FoW (1): 1-8 (1), 2-17 (2), 3-17 (4), 4-24 (3), 5-27 (6), 6-60 (7), 7-171 (5), 8-179 (9)
FoW (2): 1-0 (2), 2-0 (3), 3-104 (4), 4-105 (5), 5-161 (6)

Canterbury Bowling
	O	M	R	W			O	M	R	W
Burtt	12.5	5	26	0	1w					
Bennett	19	4	68	0	1w,6nb	(1)	9	0	35	1
Hiini	34	8	89	2		(2)	6	0	15	0
Anderson	14	1	44	0	1w	(3)	5	0	26	0
Ellis	11	5	13	2						
Robertson	40.1	9	100	2						
Astle	23	2	72	2		(4)	6	0	10	2

Auckland Bowling
	O	M	R	W			O	M	R	W
Adams	29	10	42	6	3nb		12	5	21	0
McKay	20	6	39	0	3w		9	1	24	2
Shaw	17	7	27	2			14	6	33	1
Hayne	19	6	49	0		(5)	19	6	32	1
Nicol	9	2	14	0		(4)	8	1	38	0
Young						(6)	2	0	3	0
de Grandhomme			.			(7)	5	1	19	1

Umpires: G.A.V.Baxter and E.A.Watkin.   Toss: Auckland

Close of Play: 1st day: Auckland (1) 259-4 (Nicol 41*, de Grandhomme 13*, 100 overs); 2nd day: Canterbury (1) 85-6 (Ellis 30*, Hiini 12*, 38 overs); 3rd day: Canterbury (1) 177-7 (Hiini 68*, Burtt 0*, 90 overs).
I.A.Robertson retired hurt in the Canterbury first innings having scored 0 (team score 60-6) - he returned when the score was 179-8.

CENTRAL DISTRICTS v OTAGO

Played at Nelson Park, Napier, November 12, 13, 14, 15, 2007.
State Championship 2007/08
Match drawn.   (Points: Central Districts 2, Otago 0)

CENTRAL DISTRICTS

1	G.E.F.Barnett	b Scott	0	c Wells b McCullum	4
2	P.J.Ingram	c de Boorder b McMillan	0	not out	140
3	M.S.Sinclair	not out	243	c McSkimming b Redmond	47
4	T.I.Weston	lbw b McSkimming	0	st de Boorder b Redmond	70
5	G.R.Hay	b McMillan	10	c de Boorder b Scott	6
6	*†B.B.J.Griggs	c McCullum b Redmond	69		
7	T.I.Lythe	not out	69		
8	B.E.Hefford				
9	B.J.Diamanti			(6) not out	29
10	R.J.Schaw				
11	M.J.McClenaghan				
	Extras	b 4, lb 7, w 1, nb 2	14	b 1, lb 4, w 3, nb 1	9
		(5 wickets, declared)	405	(4 wickets, declared)	305

FoW (1): 1-1 (2), 2-30 (1), 3-39 (4), 4-57 (5), 5-221 (6)
FoW (2): 1-18 (1), 2-124 (3), 3-227 (4), 4-246 (5)

OTAGO

1	L.J.Morgan	c Weston b McClenaghan	40	c and b Schaw	81
2	A.J.Redmond	c Barnett b Lythe	73	c Barnett b Schaw	102
3	G.R.Todd	c and b Schaw	69	c Griggs b Schaw	49
4	N.T.Broom	c Weston b Schaw	1	st Griggs b Schaw	51
5	M.N.McKenzie	c Barnett b Diamanti	10	(7) not out	4
6	†D.C.de Boorder	c Griggs b Lythe	4		
7	*N.L.McCullum	c Barnett b Hefford	56	(6) c Griggs b Diamanti	2
8	S.R.Wells	c Lythe b Schaw	15	not out	5
9	W.C.McSkimming	c Hay b Schaw	60	(5) st Griggs b Schaw	6
10	B.E.Scott	c Ingram b Lythe	5		
11	J.M.McMillan	not out	15		
	Extras	b 2, lb 2, w 5	9	b 3, lb 7, w 4	14
			357	(6 wickets)	314

FoW (1): 1-59 (1), 2-181 (2), 3-184 (4), 4-189 (3), 5-200 (6), 6-200 (5), 7-241 (8), 8-301 (7), 9-316 (10), 10-357 (9)
FoW (2): 1-161 (1), 2-210 (2), 3-291 (3), 4-299 (4), 5-305 (6), 6-305 (5)

Otago Bowling

	O	M	R	W			O	M	R	W	
McSkimming	25	5	91	1	1nb	(2)	6	1	24	0	
McMillan	20	2	78	2	1w	(1)	4	2	9	0	
Scott	25	11	41	1		(4)	10	2	39	1	2w,1nb
Wells	18	2	59	0							
McCullum	31	6	77	0		(3)	24	3	96	1	1w
Redmond	10	1	30	1		(5)	20	2	69	2	
Broom	1	0	3	0		(6)	6	0	42	0	
Todd	6	1	15	0	1nb	(7)	3	0	21	0	

Central Districts Bowling

	O	M	R	W			O	M	R	W	
Hefford	25	2	76	1	1w						
McClenaghan	16	3	66	1	1w	(1)	8	1	46	0	
Diamanti	22	6	48	1		(2)	12	4	33	1	1w
Lythe	39	9	106	3	3w	(3)	22	2	85	0	
Schaw	17.5	2	57	4		(4)	25	0	130	5	1w
Sinclair						(5)	1	0	10	0	

Umpires: D.M.Quested and D.J.Walker.   Toss: Central Districts

Close of Play: 1st day: Central Districts (1) 304-5 (Sinclair 189*, Lythe 24*, 101 overs); 2nd day: Otago (1) 195-4 (McKenzie 8*, de Boorder 1*, 65 overs); 3rd day: Central Districts (2) 139-2 (Ingram 74*, Weston 10*, 43 overs).
M.S.Sinclair's 243 took 385 balls in 524 minutes and included 23 fours. P.J.Ingram's 140 took 203 balls in 278 minutes and included 9 fours and 3 sixes. A.J.Redmond's 102 took 148 balls in 199 minutes and included 9 fours and 1 six.

NORTHERN DISTRICTS v WELLINGTON

Played at Seddon Park, Hamilton, November 12, 13, 14, 15, 2007.
State Championship 2007/08
Wellington won by nine wickets.   (Points: Northern Districts 0, Wellington 8)

NORTHERN DISTRICTS

1	B.J.Watling	c Edwards b Ryder	56	c N.R.Parlane b Shreck	13	
2	G.G.Robinson	lbw b Bowden	18	c Shreck b Ryder	28	
3	M.G.Orchard	c M.E.Parlane b Ryder	33	c Edwards b Houghton	68	
4	*J.A.H.Marshall	c Nevin b Shreck	7	lbw b Elliott	15	
5	N.K.W.Horsley	c Nevin b Bowden	11	c Nevin b Houghton	21	
6	D.R.Flynn	c Shreck b Houghton	22	c Nevin b Shreck	16	
7	†P.D.McGlashan	c Nevin b Shreck	5	b Shreck	18	
8	B.P.Martin	b Woodcock	1	c Elliott b Shreck	0	
9	T.G.Southee	b Houghton	0	b Shreck	11	
10	G.W.Aldridge	not out	36	b Houghton	9	
11	B.J.Arnel	run out (Bell)	8	not out	2	
	Extras	b 2, lb 17, w 4, nb 4	27	lb 9, nb 7	16	
			224		217	

FoW (1): 1-42 (2), 2-80 (3), 3-99 (4), 4-131 (5), 5-151 (1), 6-167 (7), 7-170 (8), 8-171 (9), 9-174 (6), 10-224 (11)
FoW (2): 1-37 (1), 2-83 (2), 3-127 (3), 4-160 (5), 5-160 (4), 6-185 (6), 7-185 (8), 8-201 (9), 9-212 (7), 10-217 (10)

WELLINGTON

1	M.D.Bell	lbw b Orchard	81	b Southee	22	
2	L.J.Woodcock	c McGlashan b Arnel	17	not out	29	
3	*M.E.Parlane	c Flynn b Arnel	11	not out	27	
4	J.D.Ryder	b Arnel	4			
5	N.R.Parlane	lbw b Aldridge	18			
6	G.D.Elliott	b Orchard	6			
7	†C.J.Nevin	c Robinson b Southee	72			
8	D.J.Bowden	not out	106			
9	M.V.Houghton	b Aldridge	4			
10	L.J.Edwards	lbw b Orchard	27			
11	C.E.Shreck	not out	1			
	Extras	lb 2, w 1, nb 10	13	b 4, lb 1, nb 1	6	
		(9 wickets, declared)	360	(1 wicket)	84	

FoW (1): 1-35 (2), 2-79 (3), 3-118 (1), 4-124 (4), 5-142 (6), 6-150 (5), 7-266 (7), 8-284 (9), 9-350 (10)
FoW (2): 1-41 (1)

Wellington Bowling

	O	M	R	W			O	M	R	W	
Shreck	23.3	9	50	2	1w,1nb		30	10	66	5	5nb
Edwards	17	8	52	0	2w	(4)	8	1	22	0	
Bowden	15	4	37	2	2nb	(2)	15	6	37	0	1nb
Ryder	13	7	27	2	1w,1nb	(3)	10	2	23	1	1nb
Elliott	6	3	6	0		(6)	12	7	24	1	
Woodcock	11	3	18	1		(5)	5	2	16	0	
Houghton	6	0	15	2			19.2	7	20	3	

Northern Districts Bowling

	O	M	R	W			O	M	R	W	
Aldridge	20	3	72	2	3nb		4	0	13	0	1nb
Southee	21	4	90	1	4nb	(3)	5	0	25	1	
Arnel	24	5	72	3	1w	(2)	5	1	14	0	
Orchard	16	9	43	3	2nb		5	1	16	0	
Martin	22	5	55	0	1nb		1.2	0	11	0	
Flynn	5	0	26	0							

Umpires: B.G.Frost and P.D.Jones.   Toss: Wellington

Close of Play: 1st day: Northern Districts (1) 219-9 (Aldridge 32*, Arnel 7*, 89 overs); 2nd day: Wellington (1) 302-8 (Bowden 69*, Edwards 9*, 93 overs); 3rd day: Northern Districts (2) 120-2 (Orchard 64*, Marshall 5*, 49 overs).

D.J.Bowden's 106 took 177 balls in 210 minutes and included 15 fours.

AUCKLAND v CENTRAL DISTRICTS

Played at Eden Park Outer Oval, Auckland, November 19, 20, 21, 2007.
State Championship 2007/08
Auckland won by an innings and 195 runs. (Points: Auckland 8, Central Districts 0)

CENTRAL DISTRICTS

1	G.E.F.Barnett	c Young b Adams	2	c Young b Adams	14
2	P.J.Ingram	b McKay	2	lbw b Shaw	39
3	*†B.B.J.Griggs	lbw b McKay	14	b Adams	0
4	T.I.Weston	b Adams	6	run out	62
5	G.R.Hay	c Young b Bates	0	lbw b Shaw	28
6	T.I.Lythe	c Young b Bates	9	c Young b Shaw	6
7	R.J.Schaw	lbw b Adams	10	b McKay	0
8	B.J.Diamanti	b McKay	5	b McKay	0
9	K.D.Richards	b Adams	0	c Young b Shaw	0
10	B.E.Hefford	not out	2	c Jones b McKay	0
11	M.J.McClenaghan	lbw b Adams	0	not out	0
	Extras	b 4, lb 5, w 2	11	b 1, lb 1, w 1	3
			61		**152**

FoW (1): 1-4 (2), 2-4 (1), 3-15 (4), 4-16 (5), 5-39 (3), 6-40 (6), 7-56 (8), 8-58 (9), 9-61 (7), 10-61 (11)
FoW (2): 1-29 (1), 2-29 (3), 3-84 (2), 4-144 (4), 5-146 (5), 6-147 (7), 7-147 (8), 8-148 (9), 9-152 (6), 10-152 (10)

AUCKLAND

1	T.G.McIntosh	lbw b Lythe	71
2	*R.A.Jones	c Schaw b Hefford	1
3	M.J.Guptill	c McClenaghan b Lythe	83
4	R.J.Nicol	c Griggs b Richards	42
5	C.de Grandhomme	b McClenaghan	5
6	K.W.M.Todd	c Griggs b Hefford	21
7	†R.A.Young	c Lythe b Diamanti	34
8	A.R.Adams	c sub (J.A.Raval) b Hefford	38
9	M.D.Bates	b Lythe	11
10	L.J.Shaw	not out	52
11	A.J.McKay	not out	36
	Extras	b 2, lb 11, w 1	14
		(9 wickets, declared)	**408**

FoW (1): 1-1 (2), 2-135 (1), 3-204 (4), 4-204 (3), 5-212 (5), 6-267 (6), 7-281 (7), 8-313 (8), 9-322 (9)

Auckland Bowling

	O	M	R	W			O	M	R	W	
Adams	15.5	11	12	5	1w	(2)	17	6	39	2	
McKay	13	5	31	3		(1)	15.1	4	35	3	1w
Bates	9	5	7	2	1w	(4)	9	0	33	0	
Shaw	5	4	2	0		(3)	14	4	32	4	
Nicol						(5)	6	3	11	0	

Central Districts Bowling

	O	M	R	W	
Hefford	34	11	87	3	
McClenaghan	28	6	74	1	
Richards	17	2	75	1	
Diamanti	35.5	12	79	1	1w
Lythe	18	5	73	3	
Schaw	4	1	7	0	

Umpires: A.L.Hill and D.G.Paterson.   Toss: Auckland

Close of Play: 1st day: Auckland (1) 162-2 (Guptill 66*, Nicol 18*, 55 overs); 2nd day: Central Districts (2) 25-0 (Barnett 10*, Ingram 14*, 16 overs).

The match was scheduled for four days but completed in three.

CANTERBURY v NORTHERN DISTRICTS

Played at MainPower Oval, Rangiora, November 19, 20, 21, 22, 2007.
State Championship 2007/08
Canterbury won by five wickets.   **(Points: Canterbury 6, Northern Districts 2)**

NORTHERN DISTRICTS

#	Batsman	Dismissal (1st)	R	Dismissal (2nd)	R
1	B.J.Watling	b Bennett	17	c van Wyk b Hiini	45
2	G.G.Robinson	c van Wyk b Hiini	16	b Hiini	4
3	M.G.Orchard	lbw b Hiini	8	(5) lbw b Ellis	32
4	*J.A.H.Marshall	c van Wyk b Hiini	117	c Myburgh b Robertson	0
5	N.K.W.Horsley	lbw b Hiini	5	(3) c and b Robertson	41
6	D.R.Flynn	c Myburgh b Robertson	70	run out	14
7	J.A.F.Yovich	c van Wyk b Lonsdale	2	c Astle b Robertson	3
8	†P.D.McGlashan	c and b Astle	0	c van Wyk b Bennett	27
9	B.P.Martin	c van Wyk b Ellis	50	c Robertson b Astle	11
10	T.G.Southee	not out	2	c Anderson b Bennett	19
11	B.J.Arnel	lbw b Astle	4	not out	1
	Extras	lb 10, w 6, nb 11	27	b 5, lb 3, w 3	11
			318		**208**

FoW (1): 1-39 (1), 2-47 (2), 3-61 (3), 4-67 (5), 5-180 (6), 6-187 (8), 7-191 (8), 8-311 (4), 9-311 (9), 10-318 (11)
FoW (2): 1-22 (2), 2-79 (3), 3-79 (4), 4-101 (1), 5-139 (6), 6-142 (5), 7-149 (7), 8-175 (9), 9-191 (8), 10-208 (10)

CANTERBURY

#	Batsman	Dismissal (1st)	R	Dismissal (2nd)	R
1	T.D.Astle	c Marshall b Yovich	14	c Robinson b Arnel	9
2	S.L.Stewart	c McGlashan b Southee	23	c McGlashan b Southee	55
3	P.G.Fulton	b Martin	22	lbw b Martin	72
4	J.G.Myburgh	b Southee	0	run out	1
5	A.M.Ellis	run out (Marshall)	39	(6) not out	36
6	C.J.Anderson	c Yovich b Martin	79	(7) not out	22
7	*†C.F.K.van Wyk	b Orchard	63	(5) lbw b Southee	13
8	I.A.Robertson	lbw b Martin	28		
9	B.C.Hiini	lbw b Southee	16		
10	W.M.Lonsdale	lbw b Southee	5		
11	H.K.Bennett	not out	1		
	Extras	b 2, lb 11, nb 7	20	b 5, lb 4	9
			310	**(5 wickets)**	**217**

FoW (1): 1-32 (1), 2-59 (2), 3-59 (4), 4-73 (3), 5-159 (5), 6-250 (7), 7-273 (6), 8-289 (8), 9-309 (9), 10-310 (10)
FoW (2): 1-25 (1), 2-127 (2), 3-128 (4), 4-150 (5), 5-162 (3)

Canterbury Bowling

	O	M	R	W		O	M	R	W	
Bennett	17	1	62	1	1w,6nb	14.4	6	25	2	1w
Lonsdale	20	3	69	1	4w	8	3	15	0	1w
Hiini	17	5	46	4	1w	19	8	31	2	
Ellis	13	4	32	1	5nb	(6) 15	6	17	1	1w
Robertson	11	3	29	1		(4) 40	15	58	3	
Anderson	10	3	25	0						
Astle	11.4	1	45	2		(5) 12	1	54	1	

Northern Districts Bowling

	O	M	R	W		O	M	R	W	
Southee	30.2	11	61	4		13	2	51	2	
Arnel	24	10	37	0		7	1	34	1	
Orchard	27	8	61	1		9	0	48	0	
Yovich	18	4	43	1	7nb					
Martin	44	14	91	3		(4) 16.4	0	75	3	
Marshall	3	0	4	0						

Umpires: G.A.V.Baxter, E.J.Gray and G.C.Holdem.   Toss: Canterbury

Close of Play: 1st day: Northern Districts (1) 318 all out; 2nd day: Canterbury (1) 243-5 (Anderson 69*, van Wyk 59*, 101 overs); 3rd day: Northern Districts (2) 125-4 (Orchard 19*, Flynn 11*, 59 overs).

J.A.H.Marshall's 117 took 215 balls in 310 minutes and included 12 fours.

WELLINGTON v OTAGO

Played at Basin Reserve, Wellington, November 19, 20, 21, 22, 2007.
State Championship 2007/08
Match drawn.   (Points: Wellington 2, Otago 0)

OTAGO

1	L.J.Morgan	lbw b Bowden	28	c Nevin b Ryder	25
2	A.J.Redmond	b Ryder	23	c Bell b Woodcock	58
3	G.R.Todd	c Woodcock b Shreck	110	c Edwards b Houghton	165
4	N.T.Broom	c Woodcock b Bowden	10	b Ryder	0
5	M.N.McKenzie	lbw b Bowden	0	b Edwards	74
6	*N.L.McCullum	b Edwards	23	(7) c Elliott b Woodcock	55
7	†D.C.de Boorder	b Ryder	18	(6) c Bowden b Woodcock	11
8	W.C.McSkimming	lbw b Bowden	6	c Ryder b Shreck	29
9	B.E.Scott	c Woodcock b Houghton	26	c Shreck b Woodcock	2
10	A.D.Bullick	b Houghton	0	not out	3
11	J.M.McMillan	not out	0	c Elliott b Shreck	10
	Extras	lb 17, w 9, nb 2	28	b 4, lb 6, w 3, nb 4	17
			272		**449**

FoW (1): 1-45 (2), 2-57 (1), 3-68 (4), 4-68 (5), 5-104 (6), 6-133 (7), 7-140 (8), 8-234 (9), 9-238 (10), 10-272 (3)
FoW (2): 1-38 (1), 2-154 (2), 3-162 (4), 4-330 (3), 5-347 (5), 6-402 (7), 7-422 (6), 8-425 (9), 9-439 (8), 10-449 (11)

WELLINGTON

1	M.D.Bell	c Redmond b McSkimming	83	(2) run out	18
2	L.J.Woodcock	b Scott	6		
3	*M.E.Parlane	c McKenzie b McCullum	104	b McMillan	2
4	J.D.Ryder	c de Boorder b Scott	52	(1) c Todd b McMillan	17
5	N.R.Parlane	b Scott	46	(4) not out	59
6	G.D.Elliott	lbw b McMillan	17	c Morgan b Scott	3
7	†C.J.Nevin	not out	70	(5) c Redmond b Broom	10
8	M.V.Houghton	b McCullum	5		
9	L.J.Edwards	b Bullick	5		
10	D.J.Bowden	c Redmond b McCullum	25	(7) not out	25
11	C.E.Shreck	c Redmond b McCullum	4		
	Extras	b 6, lb 13, w 3, nb 9	31	lb 7, nb 8	15
			448	**(5 wickets)**	**149**

FoW (1): 1-21 (2), 2-205 (1), 3-209 (3), 4-292 (4), 5-321 (5), 6-344 (6), 7-368 (8), 8-378 (9), 9-440 (10), 10-448 (11)
FoW (2): 1-20 (1), 2-27 (3), 3-56 (2), 4-77 (5), 5-85 (6)

Wellington Bowling	O	M	R	W			O	M	R	W	
Shreck	17.1	3	43	1	1w		31.1	8	72	2	
Edwards	9	1	35	1	1w		25	6	71	1	
Ryder	15	6	42	2	2w,1nb		20	6	62	2	1w,4nb
Bowden	14	4	57	4	2w,1nb		15	5	35	0	
Elliott	7	1	27	0	1w	(7)	15	2	48	0	1w
Woodcock	6	0	26	0			26	4	70	4	
Houghton	14	3	25	2		(5)	27	10	62	1	
N.R.Parlane						(8)	3	0	19	0	

Otago Bowling	O	M	R	W			O	M	R	W	
McSkimming	23	7	62	1	1nb	(2)	4	0	30	0	
McMillan	22	3	104	1	3w,5nb	(1)	5	0	36	2	5nb
Scott	24	9	56	3		(4)	6	1	18	1	3nb
Bullick	22	4	77	1	1nb	(6)	2	0	12	0	
Redmond	8	1	36	0							
Todd	3	0	23	0	2nb						
McCullum	29.4	11	71	4		(5)	10	5	22	0	
Broom						(3)	2	0	9	1	
McKenzie						(7)	3	0	15	0	

Umpires: P.D.Jones and D.M.Quested.   Toss: Wellington
Close of Play: 1st day: Wellington (1) 49-1 (Bell 30*, M.E.Parlane 8*, 18 overs); 2nd day: Wellington (1) 391-8 (Nevin 43*, Bowden 2*, 118 overs); 3rd day: Otago (2) 252-3 (Todd 122*, McKenzie 38*, 91 overs).
G.R.Todd's 110 took 204 balls in 268 minutes and included 15 fours. M.E.Parlane's 104 took 160 balls in 212 minutes and included 14 fours and 2 sixes. G.R.Todd's 165 took 290 balls in 347 minutes and included 21 fours and 2 sixes.

WELLINGTON v CANTERBURY

Played at Basin Reserve, Wellington, November 28, 29, 30, December 1, 2007.
State Championship 2007/08
Wellington won by 90 runs.   (Points: Wellington 6, Canterbury 2)

WELLINGTON

1	M.D.Bell	c van Wyk b Lonsdale	33	not out	188
2	L.J.Woodcock	b Lonsdale	2	b Lonsdale	0
3	*M.E.Parlane	lbw b Bennett	0	lbw b Hiini	12
4	J.D.Ryder	c Myburgh b Hiini	22	c van Wyk b Lonsdale	10
5	N.R.Parlane	c van Wyk b Lonsdale	54	c Stewart b Anderson	78
6	G.D.Elliott	c van Wyk b Anderson	38	c Papps b Ellis	64
7	†C.J.Nevin	lbw b Hiini	63	c Stewart b Myburgh	5
8	D.J.Bowden	b Hiini	5	b Myburgh	2
9	M.V.Houghton	c van Wyk b Hiini	20	run out	24
10	F.J.Quarterman	c Fulton b Hiini	3	not out	0
11	C.E.Shreck	not out	0		
	Extras	b 1, lb 6, w 5, nb 4	16	b 9, lb 17, w 3, nb 2	31
			256	(8 wickets, declared)	414

FoW (1): 1-5 (2), 2-16 (3), 3-62 (1), 4-62 (4), 5-163 (5), 6-182 (6), 7-191 (8), 8-247 (7), 9-255 (10), 10-256 (9)
FoW (2): 1-4 (2), 2-25 (3), 3-39 (4), 4-207 (5), 5-338 (6), 6-353 (7), 7-360 (8), 8-412 (9)

CANTERBURY

1	S.L.Stewart	c N.R.Parlane b Shreck	2	lbw b Quarterman	3
2	M.H.W.Papps	c Nevin b Quarterman	29	b Bowden	28
3	P.G.Fulton	b Bowden	22	c N.R.Parlane b Elliott	92
4	W.M.Lonsdale	b Elliott	0	(10) c Bowden b Ryder	7
5	J.G.Myburgh	c Nevin b Shreck	51	(4) lbw b Bowden	0
6	A.M.Ellis	c Elliott b Houghton	38	(5) c Ryder b Houghton	13
7	C.J.Anderson	b Ryder	10	(6) lbw b Shreck	32
8	*†C.F.K.van Wyk	b Shreck	111	(7) b Shreck	42
9	T.D.Astle	b Shreck	12	(8) b Woodcock	15
10	B.C.Hiini	c N.R.Parlane b Shreck	8	(9) c N.R.Parlane b Bowden	20
11	H.K.Bennett	not out	0	not out	0
	Extras	b 10, lb 13, w 5, nb 2	30	b 7, lb 2, w 4, nb 2	15
			313		267

FoW (1): 1-4 (1), 2-53 (3), 3-53 (4), 4-73 (2), 5-161 (6), 6-161 (5), 7-205 (7), 8-256 (9), 9-283 (10), 10-313 (8)
FoW (2): 1-16 (1), 2-70 (2), 3-70 (4), 4-119 (5), 5-139 (3), 6-213 (7), 7-224 (6), 8-243 (8), 9-263 (10), 10-267 (9)

Canterbury Bowling	O	M	R	W			O	M	R	W	
Bennett	11	0	48	1	1w,2nb		24	6	79	0	1w,1nb
Lonsdale	12	0	57	3			15	5	44	2	2w
Ellis	15	1	42	0	2nb	(4)	22	8	50	1	1nb
Hiini	15.3	3	32	5		(3)	23	3	73	1	
Anderson	11	2	36	1		(6)	13	3	33	1	
Astle	3	0	21	0		(5)	14	2	50	0	
Myburgh	9	2	13	0			15	1	59	2	

Wellington Bowling	O	M	R	W			O	M	R	W	
Shreck	26.1	8	77	5	1w		30	12	55	2	
Quarterman	15	3	39	1	3w	(3)	9	2	26	1	
Bowden	13	2	48	1	1w	(5)	7.4	2	24	3	
Elliott	15	3	42	1		(7)	11	8	10	1	
Woodcock	4	0	21	0		(2)	18	6	65	1	2w
Houghton	9	0	32	1			29	13	49	0	
Ryder	10	1	31	1	2nb	(4)	10	3	29	1	2nb

Umpires: E.J.Gray and D.J.Walker.   Toss: Wellington

Close of Play: 1st day: Canterbury (1) 58-3 (Papps 20*, Myburgh 0*, 23 overs); 2nd day: Wellington (2) 91-3 (Bell 43*, N.R.Parlane 16*, 33 overs); 3rd day: Canterbury (2) 6-0 (Stewart 1*, Papps 5*, 5 overs).

C.F.K.van Wyk's 111 took 105 balls in 139 minutes and included 19 fours. M.D.Bell's 188 took 383 balls in 517 minutes and included 24 fours.

NORTHERN DISTRICTS v CENTRAL DISTRICTS

Played at Seddon Park, Hamilton, December 3, 4, 5, 6, 2007.
State Championship 2007/08
Match drawn.   (Points: Northern Districts 2, Central Districts 0)

NORTHERN DISTRICTS

1	B.S.Wilson	c Lythe b Hefford	0	lbw b Thompson		3
2	B.J.Watling	c Griggs b Hefford	32	c Griggs b Thompson		14
3	N.K.W.Horsley	c Griggs b Thompson	8	c Weston b Thompson		28
4	*J.A.H.Marshall	c Diamanti b Lythe	99	not out		52
5	M.G.Orchard	c Griggs b McInnis	11	not out		62
6	D.R.Flynn	c Griggs b Hefford	110			
7	J.A.F.Yovich	c Griggs b Lythe	18			
8	†P.D.McGlashan	c Griggs b McInnis	8			
9	G.W.Aldridge	c Lythe b McInnis	21			
10	T.G.Southee	c Griggs b Hefford	2			
11	B.J.Arnel	not out	2			
	Extras	b 4, lb 15, w 2, nb 9	30	lb 6, nb 3		9
			341	(3 wickets, declared)		168

FoW (1): 1-11 (1), 2-40 (3), 3-71 (2), 4-93 (5), 5-194 (4), 6-251 (7), 7-271 (8), 8-334 (9), 9-336 (6), 10-341 (10)
FoW (2): 1-10 (1), 2-39 (2), 3-48 (3)

CENTRAL DISTRICTS

1	G.E.F.Barnett	b Aldridge	13	c Marshall b Aldridge	3
2	P.J.Ingram	lbw b Aldridge	35	b Arnel	17
3	*†B.B.J.Griggs	b Arnel	74	b Aldridge	0
4	T.I.Weston	c Flynn b Yovich	4	lbw b Yovich	28
5	G.R.Hay	c Orchard b Southee	99	not out	95
6	E.P.Thompson	b Aldridge	2	c Marshall b Orchard	0
7	T.I.Lythe	run out (Horsley)	6	not out	43
8	R.J.Schaw	c Marshall b Aldridge	14		
9	B.J.Diamanti	c Horsley b Aldridge	1		
10	E.J.McInnis	c Yovich b Arnel	0		
11	B.E.Hefford	not out	0		
	Extras	b 3, lb 16, w 2	21	lb 2, w 3, nb 2	7
			269	(5 wickets)	193

FoW (1): 1-47 (1), 2-58 (2), 3-69 (4), 4-197 (3), 5-235 (5), 6-235 (6), 7-257 (8), 8-263 (9), 9-264 (10), 10-269 (7)
FoW (2): 1-17 (1), 2-17 (3), 3-29 (2), 4-70 (4), 5-71 (6)

Central Districts Bowling

	O	M	R	W			O	M	R	W	
Hefford	29.2	8	56	4			10	0	31	0	
McInnis	25	2	77	3	3nb		13	5	29	0	3nb
Thompson	18	2	62	1	6nb		10	1	28	3	
Diamanti	15	4	42	0			7	0	29	0	
Schaw	11	1	37	0		(6)	8	0	26	0	
Lythe	10	0	48	2	2w	(5)	7	0	19	2	

Northern Districts Bowling

	O	M	R	W			O	M	R	W	
Southee	20	10	36	1	1w		12	1	42	0	
Arnel	17	2	52	2	1w	(3)	10	3	28	1	
Orchard	16	1	64	0		(5)	11.3	4	25	1	
Aldridge	21.2	10	27	5		(2)	13	1	47	2	
Yovich	12	1	44	1		(4)	9	1	32	1	3w,2nb
Marshall	2	0	7	0							
Flynn	11	2	20	0		(6)	5	0	17	0	

Umpires: B.G.Frost and T.J.Parlane.   Toss: Central Districts

Close of Play: 1st day: Northern Districts (1) 318-7 (Flynn 104*, Aldridge 10*, 100 overs); 2nd day: Central Districts (1) 255-6 (Lythe 3*, Schaw 12*, 90 overs); 3rd day: Northern Districts (2) 168-3 (Marshall 52*, Orchard 62*, 55 overs).

D.R.Flynn's 110 took 178 balls in 254 minutes and included 14 fours.

OTAGO v AUCKLAND

Played at University Oval, Dunedin, December 3, 4, 2007.
State Championship 2007/08
Otago won by six wickets.   (Points: Otago 8, Auckland 0)

AUCKLAND

1	*R.A.Jones	c Broom b Scott	11	(2) c de Boorder b McSkimming	0
2	T.G.McIntosh	b McSkimming	14	(1) c Broom b Scott	47
3	M.J.Guptill	c McSkimming b Scott	2	(4) c McSkimming b Scott	6
4	R.J.Nicol	lbw b Scott	0	(5) run out	0
5	C.de Grandhomme	b Scott	1	(6) run out	22
6	K.W.M.Todd	b McSkimming	2	(7) b Wells	0
7	†R.A.Young	c Wells b Scott	1	(8) not out	33
8	A.R.Adams	c de Boorder b Scott	29	(9) b McSkimming	8
9	M.D.Bates	c Redmond b McSkimming	15	(10) c McCullum b Redmond	2
10	L.J.Shaw	c and b McCullum	0	(3) lbw b McSkimming	0
11	A.J.McKay	not out	3	c de Boorder b McSkimming	0
	Extras	b 1, lb 2, w 4, nb 9	16	b 4, lb 2, w 3, nb 1	10
			94		128

FoW (1): 1-23 (1), 2-29 (3), 3-29 (4), 4-32 (2), 5-34 (5), 6-36 (6), 7-36 (7), 8-76 (8), 9-90 (10), 10-94 (9)
FoW (2): 1-7 (2), 2-9 (3), 3-24 (4), 4-24 (5), 5-72 (6), 6-73 (7), 7-103 (1), 8-116 (9), 9-127 (10), 10-128 (11)

OTAGO

1	L.J.Morgan	c Guptill b Adams	0	b Adams	0
2	A.J.Redmond	c Todd b Bates	8	not out	30
3	G.R.Todd	c Jones b McKay	4	c Young b Adams	0
4	N.T.Broom	c Young b Adams	31	b Bates	8
5	M.N.McKenzie	b McKay	31	c Guptill b Adams	12
6	*N.L.McCullum	b Adams	22	not out	3
7	S.R.Wells	c Jones b Bates	22		
8	†D.C.de Boorder	not out	29		
9	W.C.McSkimming	c Young b Bates	2		
10	B.E.Scott	c Young b Bates	4		
11	A.D.Bullick	b McKay	8		
	Extras	lb 7, w 1, nb 1	9	nb 2	2
			170	(4 wickets)	55

FoW (1): 1-0 (1), 2-5 (3), 3-18 (2), 4-60 (4), 5-89 (5), 6-98 (6), 7-136 (7), 8-144 (9), 9-148 (10), 10-170 (11)
FoW (2): 1-0 (1), 2-0 (3), 3-13 (4), 4-44 (5)

Otago Bowling

	O	M	R	W			O	M	R	W	
McSkimming	10.4	2	23	3	1w,1nb		17.5	9	32	4	
Bullick	5	1	20	0	3w,1nb	(3)	6	1	27	0	
Scott	9	1	20	6	1nb	(2)	16	4	32	2	3w,1nb
Wells	3	1	28	0	2nb	(5)	6	1	9	1	
McCullum	1	1	0	1		(4)	11	5	17	0	
Redmond						(6)	1	0	5	1	

Auckland Bowling

	O	M	R	W			O	M	R	W	
Adams	19	1	52	3			11.2	6	16	3	
McKay	9.4	2	25	3		(4)	1	1	0	0	
Bates	16	3	47	4	1nb		6	0	22	1	2nb
Shaw	14	4	31	0		(2)	6	1	17	0	
Nicol	3	1	8	0	1w						

Umpires: G.A.V.Baxter and D.M.Quested.   Toss: Otago

Close of Play: 1st day: Auckland (2) 22-2 (McIntosh 12*, Guptill 6*, 7 overs).

The match was scheduled for four days but completed in two.

AUCKLAND v NORTHERN DISTRICTS

Played at Eden Park Outer Oval, Auckland, December 10, 11, 12, 2007.
State Championship 2007/08
Auckland won by an innings and 16 runs.   (Points: Auckland 8, Northern Districts 0)

NORTHERN DISTRICTS

1	B.J.Watling	c Young b Adams	6	lbw b McKay		8
2	B.S.Wilson	c McIntosh b Morgan	16	lbw b Adams		1
3	K.S.Williamson	lbw b Adams	2	lbw b Adams		0
4	*J.A.H.Marshall	c Jones b Adams	30	(5) c Todd b Shaw		12
5	M.G.Orchard	c de Grandhomme b McKay	9	(6) c Young b Adams		0
6	D.R.Flynn	not out	60	(7) c and b Adams		23
7	J.A.F.Yovich	lbw b Shaw	4	(8) not out		30
8	†P.D.McGlashan	b de Grandhomme	18	(9) c de Grandhomme b Adams		12
9	B.P.Martin	lbw b Adams	6	(4) lbw b McKay		0
10	G.W.Aldridge	c Young b de Grandhomme	2	lbw b Adams		1
11	T.G.Southee	lbw b Shaw	1	c Adams b McKay		0
	Extras	b 1, lb 9, w 1, nb 4	15	b 4, lb 4, w 1, nb 5		14
			169			101

FoW (1): 1-15 (1), 2-21 (3), 3-31 (2), 4-43 (5), 5-78 (4), 6-95 (7), 7-150 (8), 8-162 (9), 9-166 (10), 10-169 (11)
FoW (2): 1-9 (2), 2-9 (1), 3-10 (3), 4-20 (4), 5-29 (6), 6-30 (5), 7-82 (7), 8-98 (9), 9-100 (10), 10-101 (11)

AUCKLAND

1	T.G.McIntosh	lbw b Southee	12
2	*R.A.Jones	c Watling b Southee	4
3	M.J.Guptill	c Wilson b Southee	11
4	R.J.Nicol	run out (Flynn)	5
5	C.de Grandhomme	run out (McGlashan/Southee)	13
6	K.W.M.Todd	c Watling b Aldridge	8
7	†R.A.Young	b Southee	114
8	A.R.Adams	c Aldridge b Southee	0
9	L.J.Shaw	c Flynn b Southee	9
10	G.J.Morgan	not out	83
11	A.J.McKay	b Yovich	18
	Extras	lb 2, w 2, nb 5	9
			286

FoW (1): 1-9 (2), 2-16 (1), 3-22 (4), 4-36 (3), 5-45 (5), 6-65 (6), 7-65 (8), 8-85 (9), 9-236 (7), 10-286 (11)

Auckland Bowling

	O	M	R	W		O	M	R	W	
Adams	21	7	30	4		15	7	28	6	
McKay	16	4	35	1	3nb	11.4	5	18	3	1w
Shaw	15.2	4	45	2	1w	(4) 6	1	22	1	
Morgan	11	4	21	1	1nb	(3) 2	1	1	0	
Nicol	10	3	24	0		(6) 5	3	3	0	
de Grandhomme	3	0	4	2		(5) 2	0	21	0	5nb

Northern Districts Bowling

	O	M	R	W	
Southee	24	7	68	6	1nb
Aldridge	23	5	68	1	1nb
Orchard	18	4	43	0	
Yovich	12.2	2	50	1	3nb
Martin	13	1	42	0	
Marshall	3	0	13	0	1w

Umpires: B.F.Bowden and D.J.Walker.   Toss: Auckland

Close of Play: 1st day: Auckland (1) 18-2 (Guptill 1*, Nicol 1*, 8.3 overs); 2nd day: Northern Districts (2) 10-3 (Martin 0*, Marshall 0*, 7 overs).

The match was scheduled for four days but completed in three. R.A.Young's 114 took 176 balls in 232 minutes and included 10 fours and 2 sixes.

CANTERBURY v OTAGO

Played at Village Green, Christchurch, December 10, 11, 12, 13, 2007.
State Championship 2007/08
Match drawn.   (Points: Canterbury 2, Otago 0)

CANTERBURY

1	T.D.Astle	c Broom b McSkimming	0	c Broom b Smith		0
2	M.H.W.Papps	c Smith b McSkimming	17	not out		35
3	S.L.Stewart	lbw b Smith	3	not out		14
4	P.G.Fulton	lbw b Scott	126			
5	J.G.Myburgh	c McSkimming b Todd	105			
6	A.M.Ellis	st de Boorder b McCullum	66			
7	*†C.F.K.van Wyk	st de Boorder b McCullum	10			
8	I.A.Robertson	lbw b Smith	33			
9	B.C.Hiini	c Morgan b Wells	7			
10	H.K.Bennett	c Cumming b Smith	0			
11	Amandeep Singh	not out	4			
	Extras	b 8, lb 2, w 4, nb 12	26	b 1, lb 4		5
			397	**(1 wicket)**		**54**

FoW (1): 1-0 (1), 2-13 (3), 3-47 (2), 4-234 (5), 5-282 (4), 6-337 (8), 7-358 (9), 8-359 (10), 9-371 (7), 10-397 (6)
FoW (2): 1-7 (1)

OTAGO

1	*C.D.Cumming	lbw b Ellis	21
2	A.J.Redmond	c Papps b Ellis	40
3	G.R.Todd	c Ellis b Hiini	56
4	L.J.Morgan	c sub (C.Frauenstein) b Bennett	29
5	N.T.Broom	c Myburgh b Amandeep Singh	42
6	N.L.McCullum	c Robertson b Bennett	2
7	S.R.Wells	lbw b Astle	10
8	†D.C.de Boorder	not out	71
9	W.C.McSkimming	c Papps b Hiini	14
10	B.E.Scott	c Fulton b Amandeep Singh	18
11	C.M.Smith	c Papps b Hiini	24
	Extras	b 5, lb 6, w 7, nb 20	38
			365

FoW (1): 1-56 (1), 2-94 (2), 3-157 (3), 4-192 (4), 5-196 (6), 6-213 (7), 7-235 (5), 8-260 (9), 9-293 (10), 10-365 (11)

Otago Bowling

	O	M	R	W		O	M	R	W
McSkimming	16.2	5	50	2	2nb				
Scott	31	3	93	1	2w,4nb (1)	8	2	27	0
Smith	27	8	74	3	3nb (2)	6	3	13	1
Wells	17.4	4	61	1	2w,3nb				
McCullum	19.2	3	75	2					
Redmond	4	0	15	0					
Todd	8	2	19	1	(3)	4	0	9	0

Canterbury Bowling

	O	M	R	W	
Bennett	24	3	95	2	1w,9nb
Amandeep Singh	27	7	65	2	5w
Hiini	24.5	6	63	3	1w
Ellis	25	5	61	2	7nb
Robertson	14	3	27	0	
Stewart	3	0	20	0	4nb
Astle	7	0	23	1	

Umpires: P.D.Jones and E.A.Watkin.   Toss: Otago

Close of Play: 1st day: Canterbury (1) 322-5 (Ellis 20*, Robertson 27*, 100 overs); 2nd day: Otago (1) 213-6 (Broom 30*, 73.4 overs); 3rd day: Canterbury (2) 54-1 (Papps 35*, Stewart 14*, 18 overs).
There was no play on the final day. P.G.Fulton's 126 took 242 balls in 289 minutes and included 13 fours and 2 sixes.
J.G.Myburgh's 105 took 141 balls in 184 minutes and included 13 fours and 1 six. C.F.K.van Wyk retired hurt in the Canterbury first innings having scored 0 (team score 282-5) - he returned when the score was 359-8 (retired at 86.2 ov).

CENTRAL DISTRICTS v WELLINGTON

Played at McLean Park, Napier, December 10, 11, 12, 13, 2007.
State Championship 2007/08
Match drawn.   (Points: Central Districts 2, Wellington 0)

WELLINGTON

1	M.D.Bell	b Thompson	32	c Worker b Lythe	265
2	L.J.Woodcock	c Barnett b McInnis	0	b Worker	104
3	*M.E.Parlane	c Hay b Thompson	8	c sub (M.J.McClenaghan) b Lythe	25
4	N.R.Parlane	b McInnis	134	(5) c Weston b Lythe	8
5	G.D.Elliott	c Griggs b Diamanti	16	(4) c sub (M.J.McClenaghan) b Worker	20
6	†C.J.Nevin	b McInnis	31	not out	44
7	D.J.Bowden	c McInnis b Hefford	7		
8	M.V.Houghton	c Lythe b Hefford	81		
9	I.E.O'Brien	c Worker b McInnis	2		
10	F.J.Quarterman	c Thompson b Lythe	47		
11	C.E.Shreck	not out	1		
	Extras	lb 7, w 2, nb 5	14	nb 2	2
			373	(5 wickets, declared)	468

FoW (1): 1-11 (2), 2-23 (3), 3-66 (1), 4-104 (5), 5-168 (6), 6-188 (7), 7-295 (4), 8-303 (9), 9-357 (8), 10-373 (10)
FoW (2): 1-253 (2), 2-311 (3), 3-356 (4), 4-367 (5), 5-468 (1)

CENTRAL DISTRICTS

1	G.H.Worker	c N.R.Parlane b Elliott	71
2	G.E.F.Barnett	c Bell b Quarterman	17
3	*†B.B.J.Griggs	st Nevin b Woodcock	22
4	T.I.Weston	lbw b Shreck	75
5	G.R.Hay	not out	164
6	T.I.Lythe	b O'Brien	31
7	P.J.Ingram	c sub (L.J.Edwards) b Houghton	9
8	E.P.Thompson	b Woodcock	17
9	B.J.Diamanti	c Houghton b Woodcock	4
10	E.J.McInnis	c Quarterman b Elliott	47
11	B.E.Hefford	c and b Woodcock	3
	Extras	b 5, lb 17, w 1, nb 3	26
			486

FoW (1): 1-72 (2), 2-125 (1), 3-125 (3), 4-268 (4), 5-360 (6), 6-373 (7), 7-400 (8), 8-404 (9), 9-477 (10), 10-486 (11)

Central Districts Bowling

	O	M	R	W			O	M	R	W	
Hefford	27	6	81	2			12	5	44	0	
McInnis	28	7	71	4	3nb		5	1	17	0	
Thompson	28	5	88	2	2nb		18	3	84	0	2nb
Diamanti	20	3	68	1	2w	(6)	10	4	28	0	
Lythe	17.5	3	58	1		(4)	38.3	6	185	3	
Worker						(5)	25	4	110	2	

Wellington Bowling

	O	M	R	W	
Shreck	24	7	87	1	
O'Brien	28	4	96	1	2nb
Bowden	19	6	48	0	1nb
Quarterman	12	4	37	1	
Houghton	32	9	80	1	
Woodcock	29.5	8	81	4	
Elliott	9	1	35	2	1w

Umpires: B.G.Frost and A.L.Hill.   Toss: Central Districts

Close of Play: 1st day: Wellington (1) 293-6 (N.R.Parlane 131*, Houghton 52*, 100 overs); 2nd day: Central Districts (1) 245-3 (Weston 68*, Hay 50*, 77 overs); 3rd day: Wellington (2) 116-0 (Bell 75*, Woodcock 40*, 22 overs).

N.R.Parlane's 134 took 271 balls in 402 minutes and included 8 fours and 4 sixes. G.R.Hay's 164 took 328 balls and included 21 fours. M.D.Bell's 265 took 327 balls in 425 minutes and included 37 fours and 1 six. L.J.Woodcock's 104 took 194 balls in 262 minutes and included 14 fours.

NEW ZEALAND v BANGLADESH

Played at University Oval, Dunedin, January 4, 5, 6, 2008.
Bangladesh in New Zealand 2007/08 - 1st Test
New Zealand won by nine wickets.

BANGLADESH

1	Tamim Iqbal	c Fulton b Martin	53	b Mills	84
2	Junaid Siddique	c Fleming b Martin	1	c Fleming b Martin	74
3	Habibul Bashar	c McCullum b Martin	23	c Sinclair b Oram	11
4	*Mohammad Ashraful	lbw b Martin	0	c Cumming b O'Brien	23
5	Shahriar Nafees	b Vettori	16	lbw b Vettori	28
6	Aftab Ahmed	b Oram	0	c Bell b O'Brien	0
7	†Mushfiqur Rahim	c Bell b Mills	7	lbw b Vettori	6
8	Mashrafe Mortaza	b Oram	22	c McCullum b Vettori	10
9	Shahadat Hossain	c McCullum b Oram	0	(10) lbw b Vettori	0
10	Enamul Haque	not out	2	(9) not out	6
11	Sajidul Islam	c McCullum b Mills	4	c McCullum b Martin	1
	Extras	b 1, lb 2, w 3, nb 3	9	lb 4, nb 7	11
			137		254

FoW (1): 1-5 (2), 2-43 (3), 3-47 (4), 4-82 (5), 5-98 (6), 6-100 (1), 7-129 (8), 8-129 (9), 9-133 (7), 10-137 (11)
FoW (2): 1-161 (1), 2-167 (2), 3-179 (3), 4-205 (4), 5-205 (6), 6-222 (7), 7-232 (8), 8-252 (5), 9-252 (10), 10-254 (11)

NEW ZEALAND

1	C.D.Cumming	lbw b Sajidul Islam	1	(2) lbw b Mashrafe Mortaza	4
2	M.D.Bell	lbw b Mohammad Ashraful	107	(1) not out	20
3	P.G.Fulton	b Shahadat Hossain	14	not out	15
4	S.P.Fleming	c Mushfiqur Rahim b Sajidul Islam	14		
5	M.S.Sinclair	lbw b Mashrafe Mortaza	29		
6	J.D.P.Oram	b Mashrafe Mortaza	117		
7	†B.B.McCullum	c Junaid Siddique b Mohammad Ashraful	7		
8	*D.L.Vettori	c Enamul Haque b Shahadat Hossain	32		
9	K.D.Mills	c Mushfiqur Rahim b Mashrafe Mortaza	0		
10	I.E.O'Brien	c Mushfiqur Rahim b Mashrafe Mortaza	5		
11	C.S.Martin	not out	12		
	Extras	b 4, lb 10, w 2, nb 3	19		
			357	(1 wicket)	39

FoW (1): 1-5 (1), 2-31 (3), 3-58 (4), 4-121 (5), 5-260 (2), 6-270 (7), 7-320 (6), 8-320 (9), 9-340 (8), 10-357 (10)
FoW (2): 1-13 (2)

New Zealand Bowling

	O	M	R	W			O	M	R	W	
Martin	13	1	64	4			20.1	6	56	2	2nb
Mills	7.1	1	29	2			12	1	54	1	
Oram	13	4	23	3	2w,1nb	(5)	12	5	21	1	
O'Brien	7	2	10	0	1w,1nb	(3)	15	2	49	2	2nb
Vettori	6	2	8	1	1nb	(4)	24	6	70	4	3nb

Bangladesh Bowling

	O	M	R	W			O	M	R	W
Shahadat Hossain	18	0	95	2	1nb	(3)	1	0	6	0
Sajidul Islam	19	2	71	2	2w,1nb		3	1	13	0
Mashrafe Mortaza	23	3	74	4		(1)	4	0	14	1
Enamul Haque	22	4	57	0	1nb					
Mohammad Ashraful	9	0	46	2		(4)	0.1	0	6	0

Umpires: N.J.Llong and P.D.Parker. Third umpire: A.L.Hill. Referee: B.C.Broad. Toss: New Zealand

Close of Play: 1st day: New Zealand (1) 156-4 (Bell 74*, Oram 17*, 41 overs); 2nd day: Bangladesh (2) 148-0 (Tamim Iqbal 72*, Junaid Siddique 69*, 39 overs).

Man of the Match: J.D.P.Oram.

The match was scheduled for five days but completed in three. M.D.Bell's 107 took 184 balls in 273 minutes and included 18 fours. J.D.P.Oram's 117 took 166 balls in 189 minutes and included 17 fours and 1 six.

New Zealand in 2007/08

NEW ZEALAND v BANGLADESH

Played at Basin Reserve, Wellington, January 12, 13, 14, 2008.
Bangladesh in New Zealand 2007/08 - 2nd Test
New Zealand won by an innings and 137 runs.

BANGLADESH

1	Tamim Iqbal	c Sinclair b Mills	15	absent ill		0
2	Junaid Siddique	c Bell b Martin	13	c McCullum b Mills		2
3	Habibul Bashar	c McCullum b Martin	1	lbw b Martin		25
4	*Mohammad Ashraful	c McCullum b O'Brien	35	c Fleming b Mills		1
5	Shahriar Nafees	c Fulton b O'Brien	6	(1) c Bell b Martin		12
6	Aftab Ahmed	not out	25	(5) c Fleming b O'Brien		5
7	†Mushfiqur Rahim	lbw b Martin	8	(6) c Bell b Oram		0
8	Shakib Al Hasan	c Fulton b Martin	5	(7) not out		41
9	Shahadat Hossain	c McCullum b O'Brien	1	(8) c McCullum b O'Brien		5
10	Sajidul Islam	c Fleming b Martin	6	(9) run out		3
11	Mashrafe Mortaza	c Bell b Vettori	15	(10) c Mills b Oram		6
	Extras	b 2, lb 11	13	lb 2, w 5, nb 6		13
			143			**113**

FoW (1): 1-17 (1), 2-18 (3), 3-49 (2), 4-68 (5), 5-71 (4), 6-86 (7), 7-110 (8), 8-111 (9), 9-122 (10), 10-143 (11)
FoW (2): 1-10 (2), 2-14 (1), 3-30 (4), 4-44 (5), 5-45 (6), 6-56 (3), 7-79 (8), 8-83 (9), 9-113 (10)

NEW ZEALAND

1	C.D.Cumming	lbw b Shakib Al Hasan	42
2	M.D.Bell	c Mushfiqur Rahim b Sajidul Islam	1
3	P.G.Fulton	lbw b Mashrafe Mortaza	22
4	S.P.Fleming	c Aftab Ahmed b Shakib Al Hasan	87
5	M.S.Sinclair	c Mushfiqur Rahim b Shahadat Hossain	47
6	J.D.P.Oram	c Mushfiqur Rahim b Shahadat Hossain	1
7	†B.B.McCullum	c Shakib Al Hasan b Shahadat Hossain	40
8	*D.L.Vettori	c and b Aftab Ahmed	94
9	K.D.Mills	b Mashrafe Mortaza	4
10	I.E.O'Brien	b Aftab Ahmed	4
11	C.S.Martin	not out	0
	Extras	b 5, lb 23, w 10, nb 13	51
			393

FoW (1): 1-2 (2), 2-35 (3), 3-118 (1), 4-214 (5), 5-216 (6), 6-242 (4), 7-323 (7), 8-362 (9), 9-390 (8), 10-393 (10)

New Zealand Bowling

	O	M	R	W		O	M	R	W	
Martin	16	3	65	5		13	1	35	2	1nb
Mills	9	3	19	1		11	4	29	2	
O'Brien	15	7	34	3	(4)	11	2	23	2	1nb
Oram	3	2	2	0	(3)	11	3	21	2	1w
Vettori	2.3	0	10	1		1	0	3	0	

Bangladesh Bowling

	O	M	R	W	
Mashrafe Mortaza	29	5	100	2	1w
Sajidul Islam	14	1	91	1	4w,5nb
Shahadat Hossain	27	4	83	3	1w,6nb
Aftab Ahmed	12.2	4	31	2	
Shakib Al Hasan	19	7	44	2	
Mohammad Ashraful	2	0	16	0	

Umpires: N.J.Llong and P.D.Parker. Third umpire: G.A.V.Baxter. Referee: B.C.Broad.   Toss: New Zealand

Close of Play: 1st day: New Zealand (1) 134-3 (Fleming 39*, Sinclair 9*, 42 overs); 2nd day: Bangladesh (2) 51-5 (Habibul Bashar 21*, Shakib Al Hasan 4*, 22 overs).

Man of the Match: D.L.Vettori.

The match was scheduled for five days but completed in three.

197

MAJOR ASSOCIATION XI v ENGLAND XI

Played at University Oval, Dunedin, February 28, 29, March 1, 2008.
England in New Zealand 2007/08
Match drawn.

ENGLAND XI

#	Batsman	Dismissal	Runs	Dismissal (2)	Runs (2)
1	A.N.Cook	c Patel b Gillespie	19	c sub (S.B.Haig) b Gillespie	12
2	*M.P.Vaughan	c Griggs b O'Brien	0	c Griggs b Gillespie	13
3	A.J.Strauss	c How b O'Brien	5	retired out	104
4	K.P.Pietersen	c Griggs b Orchard	50	c Griggs b Orchard	53
5	I.R.Bell	c Griggs b Elliott	10	not out	104
6	P.D.Collingwood	c Griggs b Elliott	2	c Orchard b Patel	0
7	†T.R.Ambrose	lbw b O'Brien	12	b O'Brien	33
8	C.T.Tremlett	not out	17		
9	M.J.Hoggard	b O'Brien	2	(8) c Taylor b O'Brien	0
10	S.J.Harmison	c Taylor b Gillespie	0		
11	M.S.Panesar	b Gillespie	4	(9) not out	3
	Extras	lb 6, w 2, nb 2	10	lb 2, nb 1	3
			131	(7 wickets)	325

FoW (1): 1-2 (2), 2-17 (3), 3-38 (1), 4-64 (5), 5-91 (6), 6-95 (4), 7-122 (7), 8-124 (9), 9-125 (10), 10-131 (11)
FoW (2): 1-25 (2), 2-27 (1), 3-117 (4), 4-242 (3), 5-242 (6), 6-302 (7), 7-306 (8)

MAJOR ASSOCIATION XI

#	Batsman	Dismissal	Runs
1	M.D.Bell	c Ambrose b Hoggard	40
2	*J.M.How	c Cook b Tremlett	65
3	P.G.Fulton	lbw b Collingwood	23
4	L.R.P.L.Taylor	c Strauss b Harmison	8
5	M.S.Sinclair	c Strauss b Panesar	47
6	G.D.Elliott	c Ambrose b Harmison	28
7	M.G.Orchard	b Harmison	0
8	†B.B.J.Griggs	c Ambrose b Harmison	11
9	J.S.Patel	c Ambrose b Harmison	24
10	M.R.Gillespie	c Hoggard b Panesar	4
11	I.E.O'Brien	not out	4
	Extras	lb 12, w 1, nb 4	17
			271

FoW (1): 1-98 (1), 2-127 (2), 3-144 (4), 4-148 (3), 5-219 (6), 6-219 (7), 7-232 (5), 8-258 (8), 9-267 (9), 10-271 (10)

Major Association XI Bowling

	O	M	R	W		O	M	R	W	
Gillespie	14.1	0	62	3	2w	17	1	74	2	1nb
O'Brien	12	2	34	4	1nb	22	3	98	2	
Elliott	8	3	12	2	(4)	13	2	28	0	
Orchard	6	2	17	1	(3)	11	2	35	1	
Patel					(5)	24	4	84	1	
Taylor					(6)	2	0	4	0	

England XI Bowling

	O	M	R	W	
Hoggard	20	7	51	1	
Tremlett	18	4	62	1	2nb
Harmison	22	2	100	5	1w,2nb
Collingwood	5	0	19	1	
Panesar	11.2	2	27	2	

Umpires: B.G.Frost and P.D.Jones.   Toss: Major Association XI

Close of Play: 1st day: Major Association XI (1) 177-4 (Sinclair 14*, Elliott 13*, 47 overs); 2nd day: England XI (2) 155-3 (Strauss 55*, Bell 21*, 44 overs).

A.J.Strauss's 104 took 186 balls in 241 minutes and included 15 fours. I.R.Bell's 104 took 151 balls in 240 minutes and included 15 fours and 1 six.

NEW ZEALAND v ENGLAND

Played at Seddon Park, Hamilton, March 5, 6, 7, 8, 9, 2008.
England in New Zealand 2007/08 - 1st Test
New Zealand won by 189 runs.

NEW ZEALAND

1	J.M.How	c Collingwood b Panesar	92	c Hoggard b Sidebottom	39	
2	M.D.Bell	c Cook b Harmison	19	c Ambrose b Sidebottom	0	
3	S.P.Fleming	c Cook b Sidebottom	41	c Cook b Sidebottom	66	
4	M.S.Sinclair	c and b Collingwood	8	c Cook b Sidebottom	2	
5	L.R.P.L.Taylor	c and b Pietersen	120	(6) c and b Panesar	6	
6	J.D.P.Oram	c Cook b Hoggard	10	(7) lbw b Sidebottom	0	
7	†B.B.McCullum	c Ambrose b Sidebottom	51	(5) c Strauss b Panesar	0	
8	*D.L.Vettori	c Strauss b Collingwood	88	c Cook b Sidebottom	35	
9	K.D.Mills	not out	25	lbw b Panesar	11	
10	J.S.Patel	c Strauss b Sidebottom	5	not out	13	
11	C.S.Martin	b Sidebottom	0	not out	0	
	Extras	b 1, lb 6, w 1, nb 3	11	lb 5	5	
			470	**(9 wickets, declared)**	**177**	

FoW (1): 1-44 (2), 2-108 (3), 3-129 (4), 4-176 (1), 5-191 (6), 6-277 (7), 7-425 (5), 8-451 (8), 9-470 (10), 10-470 (11)
FoW (2): 1-1 (2), 2-99 (1), 3-109 (3), 4-110 (5), 5-115 (4), 6-115 (7), 7-119 (6), 8-141 (9), 9-173 (8)

ENGLAND

1	A.N.Cook	c sub (N.K.W.Horsley) b Martin	38	c McCullum b Mills	13	
2	*M.P.Vaughan	c McCullum b Patel	63	lbw b Mills	9	
3	M.J.Hoggard	c Fleming b Martin	2	(9) c McCullum b Martin	4	
4	A.J.Strauss	b Vettori	43	(3) c McCullum b Mills	2	
5	K.P.Pietersen	c and b Vettori	42	(4) lbw b Mills	6	
6	I.R.Bell	b Mills	25	(5) not out	54	
7	P.D.Collingwood	lbw b Oram	66	(6) b Vettori	2	
8	†T.R.Ambrose	c Fleming b Patel	55	(7) b Martin	0	
9	R.J.Sidebottom	not out	3	(8) c McCullum b Martin	0	
10	S.J.Harmison	c Fleming b Patel	0	c Fleming b Patel	1	
11	M.S.Panesar	lbw b Mills	0	c McCullum b Oram	8	
	Extras	b 4, lb 1, nb 6	11	b 4, nb 7	11	
			348		**110**	

FoW (1): 1-84 (1), 2-86 (3), 3-130 (2), 4-159 (4), 5-203 (6), 6-245 (5), 7-335 (7), 8-347 (8), 9-347 (10), 10-348 (11)
FoW (2): 1-19 (1), 2-24 (2), 3-25 (3), 4-30 (4), 5-59 (6), 6-60 (7), 7-60 (8), 8-67 (9), 9-77 (10), 10-110 (11)

England Bowling

	O	M	R	W			O	M	R	W	
Sidebottom	34.3	8	90	4	3nb		17	4	49	6	
Hoggard	26	2	122	1			12	3	29	0	
Harmison	23	3	97	1	1w	(4)	4	0	24	0	
Panesar	37	10	101	1		(5)	16	2	50	3	
Collingwood	15	2	42	2		(3)	6	1	20	0	
Pietersen	3	1	11	1							

New Zealand Bowling

	O	M	R	W			O	M	R	W	
Martin	32	15	60	2			13	4	33	3	
Mills	21.1	6	61	2			13	4	16	4	3nb
Patel	43	14	107	3	1nb	(5)	11	2	39	1	
Oram	21	9	27	1		(3)	4	2	2	1	
Vettori	56	17	88	2	5nb	(4)	14	6	16	1	4nb

Umpires: S.J.Davis and D.J.Harper. Third umpire: B.F.Bowden. Referee: J.Srinath.   Toss: New Zealand

Close of Play: 1st day: New Zealand (1) 282-6 (Taylor 54*, Vettori 4*, 90 overs); 2nd day: England (1) 87-2 (Vaughan 44*, Strauss 1*, 41 overs); 3rd day: England (1) 286-6 (Collingwood 41*, Ambrose 23*, 134 overs); 4th day: New Zealand (2) 147-8 (Vettori 13*, Patel 6*, 48 overs).

Man of the Match: D.L.Vettori.
L.R.P.L.Taylor's 120 took 235 balls in 322 minutes and included 18 fours. R.J.Sidebottom took a hat-trick in the New Zealand second innings (Fleming, Sinclair, Oram).

199

AUCKLAND v WELLINGTON

Played at Eden Park Outer Oval, Auckland, March 6, 7, 8, 9, 2008.
State Championship 2007/08
Wellington won by an innings and 95 runs.　　(Points: Auckland 0, Wellington 8)

AUCKLAND

1	T.G.McIntosh	c Nevin b Gillespie	0	lbw b Shreck		5
2	M.J.Guptill	c N.R.Parlane b Bowden	21	c M.E.Parlane b Woodcock		44
3	*R.A.Jones	c Nevin b Elliott	22	c Woodcock b Shreck		4
4	R.J.Nicol	c Gellatly b Gillespie	34	c M.E.Parlane b Gillespie		0
5	C.de Grandhomme	b Bowden	9	c N.R.Parlane b Gillespie		22
6	†G.J.Hopkins	c M.E.Parlane b Houghton	66	c M.E.Parlane b Woodcock		0
7	A.P.de Boorder	c Woodcock b Shreck	88	run out		0
8	M.D.Bates	b Shreck	28	not out		14
9	J.M.Anderson	b Shreck	0	c Nevin b Gillespie		5
10	G.P.Hayne	not out	4	c and b Woodcock		12
11	A.J.McKay	b Shreck	0	c Shreck b Woodcock		13
	Extras	b 8, lb 10, w 2, nb 5	25	lb 7, w 5, nb 1		13
			297			132

FoW (1): 1-4 (1), 2-41 (3), 3-71 (2), 4-91 (5), 5-104 (4), 6-210 (6), 7-289 (8), 8-289 (9), 9-297 (7), 10-297 (11)
FoW (2): 1-10 (1), 2-14 (3), 3-16 (4), 4-83 (2), 5-83 (6), 6-85 (7), 7-89 (5), 8-97 (9), 9-112 (10), 10-132 (11)

WELLINGTON

1	*M.E.Parlane	b Hayne	61
2	L.J.Woodcock	c Hopkins b Anderson	13
3	N.R.Parlane	c Hopkins b Anderson	165
4	G.D.Elliott	b Hayne	108
5	S.J.Gellatly	not out	67
6	B.J.Crook	run out (Guptill/Nicol)	31
7	†C.J.Nevin	run out (Guptill/Hopkins)	0
8	D.J.Bowden	not out	59
9	M.V.Houghton		
10	M.R.Gillespie		
11	C.E.Shreck		
	Extras	b 8, lb 10, w 2	20
		(6 wickets, declared)	524

FoW (1): 1-30 (2), 2-109 (1), 3-355 (4), 4-363 (3), 5-436 (6), 6-442 (7)

Wellington Bowling

	O	M	R	W			O	M	R	W	
Gillespie	24	9	57	2	2nb		15	8	41	3	1w
Shreck	26.2	8	68	4			16	4	35	2	
Elliott	18	4	48	1	2w	(5)	4	1	4	0	
Bowden	15	2	53	2	3nb	(3)	3	0	21	0	1nb
Woodcock	17	4	36	0		(4)	11.1	4	24	4	
Houghton	8	2	17	1							

Auckland Bowling

	O	M	R	W	
McKay	25	5	79	0	
Anderson	38	13	95	2	1w
Bates	18	1	74	0	
de Grandhomme	14	2	27	0	1w
Nicol	23	1	120	0	
Hayne	37	7	111	2	

Umpires: E.J.Gray and D.M.Quested.　　　　　　　　　　Toss: Auckland

Close of Play: 1st day: Auckland (1) 289-6 (de Boorder 85*, Bates 28*, 100 overs); 2nd day: Wellington (1) 169-2 (N.R.Parlane 54*, Elliott 32*, 56.1 overs); 3rd day: Auckland (2) 16-2 (Guptill 2*, Nicol 0*, 8 overs).

N.R.Parlane's 165 took 314 balls in 387 minutes and included 23 fours and 1 six. G.D.Elliott's 108 took 202 balls in 247 minutes and included 12 fours and 2 sixes.

CENTRAL DISTRICTS v CANTERBURY

Played at McLean Park, Napier, March 6, 7, 8, 9, 2008.
State Championship 2007/08
Canterbury won by nine wickets.   (Points: Central Districts 0, Canterbury 8)

CENTRAL DISTRICTS

#	Batsman	Dismissal	Runs	Dismissal 2	Runs 2
1	G.E.F.Barnett	c van Wyk b Burtt	0	lbw b Hiini	19
2	G.H.Worker	lbw b Burtt	1	lbw b Hiini	25
3	P.J.Ingram	lbw b Hiini	38	c Stewart b Myburgh	79
4	G.R.Hay	c Papps b Bennett	1	c Ellis b Burtt	127
5	T.I.Weston	c van Wyk b Hiini	75	c Stewart b Robertson	25
6	*†B.B.J.Griggs	c Papps b Burtt	3	(7) not out	6
7	R.J.Schaw	c van Wyk b Davidson	6	(8) not out	5
8	B.J.Diamanti	c van Wyk b Astle	136	(6) c Robertson b Burtt	35
9	R.R.Sherlock	c Hiini b Astle	64		
10	B.E.Hefford	not out	32		
11	M.J.McClenaghan	lbw b Astle	6		
	Extras	lb 7, w 1, nb 6	14	b 15, lb 10, w 1	26
			376	(6 wickets, declared)	347

FoW (1): 1-0 (1), 2-1 (2), 3-3 (4), 4-115 (5), 5-122 (6), 6-122 (3), 7-158 (7), 8-317 (9), 9-358 (8), 10-376 (11)
FoW (2): 1-42 (1), 2-57 (2), 3-206 (3), 4-249 (5), 5-320 (6), 6-338 (4)

CANTERBURY

#	Batsman	Dismissal	Runs	Dismissal 2	Runs 2
1	T.D.Astle	lbw b Schaw	48	c sub (M.P.Taiaroa) b Schaw	41
2	M.H.W.Papps	b Sherlock	2	not out	134
3	J.G.Myburgh	c Worker b Hefford	62	not out	148
4	S.L.Stewart	c Griggs b Worker	87		
5	A.M.Ellis	c Griggs b McClenaghan	18		
6	I.A.Robertson	c Griggs b Diamanti	85		
7	*†C.F.K.van Wyk	lbw b Sherlock	9		
8	B.C.Hiini	not out	28		
9	M.P.F.Davidson	c Barnett b Sherlock	2		
10	L.M.Burtt	not out	28		
11	H.K.Bennett				
	Extras	b 1, lb 5, w 4, nb 1	11	b 7, lb 8, w 5, nb 1	21
					<@151>—
		(8 wickets, declared)	380	(1 wicket)	344

FoW (1): 1-17 (2), 2-116 (1), 3-116 (3), 4-177 (5), 5-308 (6), 6-314 (4), 7-320 (7), 8-326 (9)
FoW (2): 1-90 (1)

Canterbury Bowling

	O	M	R	W		O	M	R	W	
Burtt	25	4	90	3	1w,4nb	15	4	63	2	
Bennett	8	0	31	1		12	0	55	0	1w
Hiini	25	8	57	2	1nb	16	6	35	2	
Davidson	24	9	66	1	(5)	8	1	33	0	
Stewart	8	4	26	0	1nb					
Astle	25	3	67	3		11	1	35	0	
Robertson	17	2	32	0	(4)	17	1	77	1	
Myburgh					(7)	7	1	24	1	

Central Districts Bowling

	O	M	R	W			O	M	R	W	
Sherlock	21	1	98	3	1w		10	0	60	0	3w
McClenaghan	15	1	65	1	1w	(3)	5	0	24	0	1w
Hefford	22	5	57	1	1w	(2)	9	2	25	0	1nb
Schaw	19	1	105	1	1nb	(5)	28	0	146	1	1w
Diamanti	16.1	3	35	1	1w	(4)	7	3	15	0	
Worker	4	0	14	1			17	1	59	0	

Umpires: B.G.Frost and E.A.Watkin.   Toss: Canterbury
Close of Play: 1st day: Central Districts (1) 228-7 (Diamanti 67*, Sherlock 28*, 72 overs); 2nd day: Canterbury (1) 225-4 (Stewart 60*, Robertson 30*, 59 overs); 3rd day: Central Districts (2) 218-3 (Hay 66*, Weston 6*, 66 overs).
B.J.Diamanti's 136 took 267 balls in 334 minutes and included 16 fours and 1 six. G.R.Hay's 127 took 212 balls in 265 minutes and included 13 fours. M.H.W.Papps's 134 took 224 balls in 224 minutes and included 14 fours. J.G.Myburgh's 148 took 154 balls in 134 minutes and included 16 fours and 4 sixes.

OTAGO v NORTHERN DISTRICTS

Played at Queen's Park, Invercargill, March 6, 7, 8, 9, 2008.
State Championship 2007/08
Match drawn.   (Points: Otago 0, Northern Districts 2)

OTAGO

1	*C.D.Cumming	b Aldridge	62			
2	A.J.Redmond	b Arnel	0	(1) not out		41
3	G.R.Todd	b Arnel	0	(2) b Southee		18
4	N.T.Broom	b Arnel	5	not out		12
5	J.W.Sheed	c Orchard b Martin	22	(3) c Merchant b Southee		34
6	N.L.McCullum	b Orchard	57			
7	†D.C.de Boorder	b Arnel	74			
8	W.C.McSkimming	c Marshall b Aldridge	7			
9	B.E.Scott	not out	58			
10	C.M.Smith	c McGlashan b Southee	1			
11	J.M.McMillan	c McGlashan b Arnel	4			
	Extras	b 3, lb 10, nb 2	15	lb 4, nb 6		10
			305	(2 wickets)		115

FoW (1): 1-2 (2), 2-4 (3), 3-18 (4), 4-58 (5), 5-118 (1), 6-183 (6), 7-197 (8), 8-289 (7), 9-296 (10), 10-305 (11)
FoW (2): 1-32 (2), 2-91 (3)

NORTHERN DISTRICTS

1	B.S.Wilson	c Redmond b Smith	100
2	B.J.Watling	c de Boorder b McSkimming	9
3	C.J.Merchant	c Smith b McSkimming	18
4	*J.A.H.Marshall	c Redmond b McCullum	67
5	D.R.Flynn	lbw b Smith	46
6	†P.D.McGlashan	st de Boorder b Redmond	69
7	M.G.Orchard	c Redmond b McCullum	2
8	B.P.Martin	run out (McMillan)	10
9	T.G.Southee	c McCullum b Broom	12
10	G.W.Aldridge	not out	33
11	B.J.Arnel		
	Extras	b 11, lb 23, w 8, nb 2	44
		(9 wickets, declared)	410

FoW (1): 1-25 (2), 2-57 (3), 3-183 (4), 4-271 (1), 5-278 (5), 6-281 (7), 7-308 (8), 8-352 (9), 9-410 (6)

Northern Districts Bowling

	O	M	R	W		O	M	R	W	
Southee	27	13	42	1		16	7	24	2	
Arnel	27.1	10	80	5		11	5	20	0	
Aldridge	20	5	51	2		9	4	15	0	
Orchard	20	5	58	1		9	5	15	0	
Martin	15	2	57	1	2nb	15	6	30	0	6nb
Flynn	4	1	4	0						
Wilson					(6)	2	0	7	0	

Otago Bowling

	O	M	R	W	
McSkimming	21	5	79	2	2w
McMillan	20	3	76	0	1w
Scott	25	9	43	0	
Smith	19	4	42	2	2nb
Cumming	7	1	15	0	
McCullum	22	9	55	2	
Broom	6	0	35	1	1w
Redmond	5.1	0	31	1	

Umpires: P.D.Jones and D.J.Walker.   Toss: Northern Districts

Close of Play: 1st day: Otago (1) 276-7 (de Boorder 71*, Scott 39*, 101 overs); 2nd day: Northern Districts (1) 77-2 (Wilson 30*, Marshall 4*, 25.1 overs); 3rd day: Otago (2) 7-0 (Redmond 0*, Todd 6*, 5.4 overs).

B.S.Wilson's 100 took 289 balls in 370 minutes and included 12 fours.

NEW ZEALAND v ENGLAND

Played at Basin Reserve, Wellington, March 13, 14, 15, 16, 17, 2008.
England in New Zealand 2007/08 - 2nd Test
England won by 126 runs.

ENGLAND

1	A.N.Cook	c McCullum b Oram	44	c Fleming b Mills	60
2	*M.P.Vaughan	b Oram	32	c McCullum b Mills	13
3	A.J.Strauss	c Sinclair b Mills	8	lbw b Oram	44
4	K.P.Pietersen	b Gillespie	31	run out	17
5	I.R.Bell	c McCullum b Martin	11	c Sinclair b Oram	41
6	P.D.Collingwood	lbw b Gillespie	65	lbw b Gillespie	59
7	†T.R.Ambrose	c Taylor b Mills	102	b Oram	5
8	S.C.J.Broad	b Oram	1	c McCullum b Martin	16
9	R.J.Sidebottom	c Bell b Gillespie	14	c How b Gillespie	0
10	M.S.Panesar	c McCullum b Gillespie	6	c Taylor b Martin	10
11	J.M.Anderson	not out	0	not out	12
	Extras	b 5, lb 15, nb 8	28	b 6, lb 5, nb 5	16
			342		**293**

FoW (1): 1-79 (2), 2-82 (1), 3-94 (3), 4-126 (5), 5-136 (4), 6-300 (7), 7-305 (8), 8-335 (6), 9-342 (9), 10-342 (10)
FoW (2): 1-21 (2), 2-127 (1), 3-129 (3), 4-160 (4), 5-219 (5), 6-231 (7), 7-259 (8), 8-260 (9), 9-277 (6), 10-293 (10)

NEW ZEALAND

1	J.M.How	c Strauss b Anderson	7	c Bell b Sidebottom	8
2	M.D.Bell	b Anderson	0	c Ambrose b Broad	29
3	S.P.Fleming	c Pietersen b Anderson	34	b Broad	31
4	M.S.Sinclair	c Ambrose b Anderson	9	c Bell b Anderson	39
5	L.R.P.L.Taylor	c Ambrose b Anderson	53	lbw b Sidebottom	55
6	J.D.P.Oram	lbw b Sidebottom	8	c Pietersen b Sidebottom	30
7	†B.B.McCullum	c Strauss b Broad	25	c Sidebottom b Panesar	85
8	*D.L.Vettori	not out	50	c Cook b Sidebottom	0
9	K.D.Mills	c Bell b Collingwood	1	lbw b Sidebottom	13
10	M.R.Gillespie	b Collingwood	0	c Ambrose b Anderson	9
11	C.S.Martin	b Collingwood	1	not out	0
	Extras	lb 8, w 1, nb 1	10	lb 11, w 1	12
			198		**311**

FoW (1): 1-4 (2), 2-9 (1), 3-31 (4), 4-102 (3), 5-113 (6), 6-113 (5), 7-165 (7), 8-176 (9), 9-180 (10), 10-198 (11)
FoW (2): 1-18 (1), 2-69 (2), 3-70 (3), 4-151 (4), 5-173 (5), 6-242 (6), 7-246 (8), 8-270 (9), 9-311 (10), 10-311 (7)

New Zealand Bowling

	O	M	R	W			O	M	R	W	
Martin	20	1	80	1			24.4	4	77	2	1nb
Mills	30	4	86	2	1nb		23	5	59	2	1nb
Gillespie	20	2	79	4	1nb	(4)	15	1	63	2	1nb
Oram	29	11	46	3	2nb	(3)	20	9	44	3	
Vettori	8	0	31	0			15	2	39	0	2nb

England Bowling

	O	M	R	W			O	M	R	W	
Sidebottom	17	3	36	1			31	10	105	5	
Anderson	20	4	73	5	1w		15	2	57	2	1w
Broad	12	0	56	1	1nb		23	6	62	2	
Collingwood	7.5	1	23	3			9	2	20	0	
Panesar	1	0	2	0			21.3	1	53	1	
Pietersen						(6)	1	0	3	0	

Umpires: S.J.Davis and R.E.Koertzen. Third umpire: E.A.Watkin. Referee: J.Srinath.   Toss: New Zealand

Close of Play: 1st day: England (1) 291-5 (Collingwood 48*, Ambrose 97*, 90 overs); 2nd day: England (2) 4-0 (Cook 2*, Vaughan 0*, 5 overs); 3rd day: England (2) 277-9 (Panesar 6*, 94.1 overs); 4th day: New Zealand (2) 242-6 (McCullum 43*, Vettori 0*, 81 overs).

Man of the Match: T.R.Ambrose.
T.R.Ambrose's 102 took 149 balls in 176 minutes and included 16 fours and 2 sixes.

CANTERBURY v CENTRAL DISTRICTS

Played at Village Green, Christchurch, March 14, 15, 16, 2008.
State Championship 2007/08
Canterbury won by eight wickets.   (Points: Canterbury 8, Central Districts 0)

CENTRAL DISTRICTS

1	G.H.Worker	b Davidson	1	b Davidson	6
2	*T.I.Lythe	b Burson	52	c van Wyk b Davidson	13
3	P.J.Ingram	lbw b Hiini	83	c Burson b Davidson	2
4	T.I.Weston	b Hiini	0	lbw b Davidson	16
5	†B.B.J.Griggs	c Papps b Burtt	55	c Fulton b Hiini	0
6	M.P.Taiaroa	c Myburgh b Davidson	1	absent hurt	0
7	J.W.de Terte	lbw b Davidson	1	(6) lbw b Burtt	17
8	B.J.Diamanti	b Davidson	0	(7) b Hiini	6
9	R.J.Schaw	c Hiini b Robertson	16	(8) c van Wyk b Burson	23
10	M.J.Mason	c Astle b Robertson	0	(9) not out	39
11	G.J.T.Hegglun	not out	10	(10) c Hiini b Davidson	10
	Extras	lb 4, w 1, nb 2	7	b 4, lb 10, w 2	16
			226		148

FoW (1): 1-3 (1), 2-114 (3), 3-114 (4), 4-148 (2), 5-149 (6), 6-151 (7), 7-151 (8), 8-198 (9), 9-202 (10), 10-226 (5)
FoW (2): 1-15 (1), 2-21 (3), 3-38 (2), 4-43 (4), 5-43 (5), 6-53 (7), 7-83 (6), 8-114 (8), 9-148 (10)

CANTERBURY

1	T.D.Astle	b Diamanti	22	c Griggs b Mason	1
2	M.H.W.Papps	c Griggs b Mason	4	not out	40
3	J.G.Myburgh	lbw b Mason	30	c Hegglun b Mason	11
4	P.G.Fulton	c sub (R.R.Sherlock) b Diamanti	42	not out	35
5	S.L.Stewart	lbw b Lythe	33		
6	I.A.Robertson	c Griggs b Diamanti	1		
7	*†C.F.K.van Wyk	not out	82		
8	B.C.Hiini	b Diamanti	1		
9	M.P.F.Davidson	c Worker b Schaw	56		
10	L.M.Burtt	c Ingram b Hegglun	4		
11	R.D.Burson	run out (Diamanti)	0		
	Extras	b 4, lb 6, w 1	11	b 1, lb 1	2
			286	(2 wickets)	89

FoW (1): 1-11 (2), 2-53 (1), 3-63 (3), 4-120 (4), 5-127 (6), 6-184 (5), 7-185 (8), 8-273 (9), 9-281 (10), 10-286 (11)
FoW (2): 1-8 (1), 2-31 (3)

Canterbury Bowling

	O	M	R	W			O	M	R	W	
Burtt	18.1	2	61	1	1w,1nb		15	4	49	1	2w
Davidson	23	11	55	4			12.2	4	39	5	
Hiini	21	7	53	2			7	0	22	2	
Burson	18	6	46	1	1nb	(5)	1	1	0	1	
Astle	1	0	5	0							
Robertson	4	3	2	2		(4)	4	0	24	0	

Central Districts Bowling

	O	M	R	W			O	M	R	W	
Mason	18	1	62	2	1w		11	3	22	2	
Diamanti	25	7	57	4			12	4	20	0	
Hegglun	15.5	4	47	1			9.1	2	37	0	
Lythe	11	1	63	1							
Schaw	8	1	47	1		(4)	3	0	8	0	

Umpires: D.M.Quested and D.J.Smith.   Toss: Canterbury

Close of Play: 1st day: Canterbury (1) 48-1 (Astle 18*, Myburgh 21*, 12 overs); 2nd day: Central Districts (2) 114-8 (Mason 15*, 33.3 overs).

The match was scheduled for four days but completed in three.

NORTHERN DISTRICTS v AUCKLAND

Played at Harry Barker Reserve, Gisborne, March 14, 15, 16, 17, 2008.
State Championship 2007/08
Northern Districts won by seven wickets.   (Points: Northern Districts 8, Auckland 0)

AUCKLAND

1	T.G.McIntosh	c McGlashan b Arnel	9	st McGlashan b Aldridge	13
2	M.J.Guptill	c Wilson b Arnel	5	c Wilson b Arnel	18
3	*R.A.Jones	b Arnel	6	c Merchant b Orchard	6
4	R.J.Nicol	c McGlashan b Aldridge	3	lbw b Orchard	17
5	C.de Grandhomme	c McGlashan b Arnel	10	lbw b Southee	0
6	†G.J.Hopkins	c McGlashan b Southee	99	lbw b Southee	52
7	A.P.de Boorder	c Watling b Southee	10	c Marshall b Arnel	9
8	G.J.Morgan	c Marshall b Southee	0	c McGlashan b Orchard	8
9	R.M.Hira	st McGlashan b Martin	37	not out	45
10	Azhar Abbas	c Watling b Southee	1	c Martin b Southee	3
11	A.J.McKay	not out	0	c Wilson b Aldridge	10
	Extras	lb 4, w 1, nb 1	6	b 4, lb 6, w 1, nb 5	16
			186		**197**

FoW (1): 1-15 (1), 2-18 (2), 3-23 (3), 4-33 (5), 5-37 (4), 6-64 (7), 7-70 (8), 8-163 (9), 9-169 (10), 10-186 (6)
FoW (2): 1-32 (1), 2-32 (2), 3-43 (3), 4-46 (5), 5-71 (4), 6-102 (7), 7-132 (6), 8-138 (8), 9-157 (10), 10-197 (11)

NORTHERN DISTRICTS

1	B.S.Wilson	c de Grandhomme b McKay	5	(2) c Morgan b Azhar Abbas	5
2	B.J.Watling	c Hopkins b Azhar Abbas	6	(1) c Hopkins b Azhar Abbas	11
3	B.P.Martin	c Morgan b de Grandhomme	46		
4	C.J.Merchant	c Nicol b McKay	17	(3) lbw b Morgan	5
5	*J.A.H.Marshall	c Hopkins b Morgan	33	(4) not out	32
6	D.R.Flynn	c Hira b de Grandhomme	38	(5) not out	37
7	†P.D.McGlashan	lbw b Morgan	51		
8	M.G.Orchard	b de Grandhomme	8		
9	T.G.Southee	c McIntosh b Hira	25		
10	G.W.Aldridge	c Azhar Abbas b de Grandhomme	32		
11	B.J.Arnel	not out	1		
	Extras	b 8, lb 4, w 5, nb 4	21	b 3, lb 8	11
			283	**(3 wickets)**	**101**

FoW (1): 1-11 (1), 2-11 (2), 3-32 (4), 4-109 (5), 5-125 (3), 6-186 (6), 7-212 (8), 8-228 (7), 9-266 (9), 10-283 (10)
FoW (2): 1-7 (2), 2-25 (3), 3-25 (1)

Northern Districts Bowling

	O	M	R	W		O	M	R	W	
Southee	17.1	4	34	4	1w	18	6	43	3	
Arnel	19	6	38	4		18	9	42	2	
Aldridge	16	2	49	1		14	4	30	2	1nb
Orchard	17	5	38	0		20	4	52	3	1w
Martin	11	5	23	1	1nb	5	1	20	0	

Auckland Bowling

	O	M	R	W			O	M	R	W	
Azhar Abbas	27	8	59	1		(2)	11	4	16	2	
McKay	25	9	51	2		(1)	11	2	48	0	
de Grandhomme	21.4	3	65	4	2w	(4)	3	0	13	0	
Morgan	18	5	46	2	3nb	(3)	6.4	2	13	1	
Hira	11	2	27	1	1w,1nb						
Nicol	3	0	9	0							
McIntosh	5	1	14	0	1w						

Umpires: G.A.V.Baxter and C.B.Gaffaney.   Toss: Northern Districts

Close of Play: 1st day: Northern Districts (1) 15-2 (Martin 0*, Merchant 4*, 11 overs); 2nd day: Northern Districts (1) 283 all out; 3rd day: Northern Districts (2) 44-3 (Marshall 16*, Flynn 3*, 21.2 overs).

OTAGO v WELLINGTON

Played at University Oval, Dunedin, March 14, 15, 2008.
State Championship 2007/08
Otago won by an innings and 116 runs. (Points: Otago 8, Wellington 0)

WELLINGTON

1	*M.E.Parlane	c de Boorder b Scott	7	c de Boorder b Scott		44
2	L.J.Woodcock	c McCullum b McMillan	17	lbw b Scott		5
3	N.R.Parlane	c de Boorder b McMillan	4	b Smith		1
4	G.D.Elliott	c Redmond b Wells	6	c Broom b McMillan		1
5	S.J.Gellatly	c McCullum b McMillan	0	b Scott		1
6	B.J.Crook	c de Boorder b Smith	6	lbw b Wells		21
7	†C.J.Nevin	c de Boorder b Wells	4	c McCullum b Scott		1
8	D.J.Bowden	b Smith	4	lbw b McCullum		49
9	F.J.Quarterman	c McCullum b Scott	8	c and b McCullum		12
10	C.E.Shreck	c Broom b McMillan	8	c McMillan b McCullum		0
11	M.Burns	not out	2	not out		3
	Extras	lb 9, nb 1	10	b 2, lb 6, w 2, nb 2		12
			76			150

FoW (1): 1-29 (2), 2-33 (1), 3-33 (3), 4-33 (5), 5-45 (4), 6-49 (6), 7-50 (7), 8-54 (8), 9-62 (10), 10-76 (9)
FoW (2): 1-26 (2), 2-36 (3), 3-49 (4), 4-53 (1), 5-55 (5), 6-61 (7), 7-130 (6), 8-132 (8), 9-132 (10), 10-150 (9)

OTAGO

1	*C.D.Cumming	c Burns b Shreck	93
2	A.J.Redmond	c M.E.Parlane b Burns	56
3	G.R.Todd	c N.R.Parlane b Burns	48
4	N.T.Broom	b Burns	8
5	J.W.Sheed	c Nevin b Elliott	38
6	N.L.McCullum	c and b Elliott	3
7	†D.C.de Boorder	lbw b Shreck	24
8	S.R.Wells	b Bowden	29
9	B.E.Scott	lbw b Shreck	12
10	C.M.Smith	c N.R.Parlane b Bowden	0
11	J.M.McMillan	not out	4
	Extras	lb 11, w 7, nb 9	27
			342

FoW (1): 1-134 (1), 2-211 (2), 3-221 (3), 4-236 (4), 5-258 (6), 6-272 (5), 7-325 (7), 8-329 (8), 9-337 (9), 10-342 (10)

Otago Bowling

	O	M	R	W		O	M	R	W	
McMillan	11	4	29	4		12	3	43	1	2w,2nb
Smith	8	4	17	2	(3)	9	2	19	1	
Scott	8.1	4	14	2	(2)	14	6	36	4	
Wells	4	2	7	2	1nb	10	3	24	1	
McCullum					(5)	10.4	2	20	3	

Wellington Bowling

	O	M	R	W	
Shreck	30	8	105	3	1nb
Bowden	18.2	3	61	2	6nb
Quarterman	10	2	38	0	6w
Elliott	22	7	55	2	
Burns	14	0	57	3	1w,1nb
Woodcock	10	2	15	0	1nb

Umpires: B.G.Frost and D.J.Walker.   Toss: Otago

Close of Play: 1st day: Otago (1) 201-1 (Redmond 50*, Todd 40*, 68 overs).

The match was scheduled for four days but completed in two.

NEW ZEALAND v ENGLAND

Played at McLean Park, Napier, March 22, 23, 24, 25, 26, 2008.
England in New Zealand 2007/08 - 3rd Test
England won by 121 runs.

ENGLAND

1	A.N.Cook	b Martin	2	c McCullum b Patel		37
2	*M.P.Vaughan	lbw b Southee	2	c McCullum b Martin		4
3	A.J.Strauss	c How b Southee	0	c Bell b Patel		177
4	K.P.Pietersen	c How b Southee	129	c Taylor b Vettori		34
5	I.R.Bell	c and b Elliott	9	c Sinclair b Vettori		110
6	P.D.Collingwood	c Elliott b Patel	30	c and b Vettori		22
7	†T.R.Ambrose	c Taylor b Patel	11	c and b Vettori		31
8	S.C.J.Broad	c McCullum b Southee	42	not out		31
9	R.J.Sidebottom	c Bell b Southee	14	not out		12
10	M.S.Panesar	b Martin	1			
11	J.M.Anderson	not out	0			
	Extras	lb 9, w 3, nb 1	13	lb 3, w 1, nb 5		9
			253	(7 wickets, declared)		467

FoW (1): 1-4 (2), 2-4 (3), 3-4 (1), 4-36 (5), 5-125 (6), 6-147 (7), 7-208 (4), 8-240 (8), 9-253 (10), 10-253 (9)
FoW (2): 1-5 (2), 2-77 (1), 3-140 (4), 4-327 (5), 5-361 (6), 6-424 (3), 7-425 (7)

NEW ZEALAND

1	J.M.How	c Strauss b Sidebottom	44	lbw b Panesar	11
2	M.D.Bell	lbw b Sidebottom	0	c Broad b Panesar	69
3	S.P.Fleming	c Collingwood b Sidebottom	59	c Ambrose b Panesar	66
4	M.S.Sinclair	c Broad b Sidebottom	7	c Ambrose b Broad	6
5	L.R.P.L.Taylor	c Ambrose b Broad	2	c Collingwood b Panesar	74
6	G.D.Elliott	c Ambrose b Sidebottom	6	c Bell b Broad	4
7	†B.B.McCullum	b Sidebottom	9	b Panesar	42
8	*D.L.Vettori	c Cook b Sidebottom	14	c Ambrose b Anderson	43
9	T.G.Southee	c Pietersen b Broad	5	(10) not out	77
10	J.S.Patel	c Panesar b Broad	4	(9) c Broad b Panesar	18
11	C.S.Martin	not out	4	b Sidebottom	5
	Extras	lb 13, w 1	14	b 6, lb 5, w 4, nb 1	16
			168		431

FoW (1): 1-1 (2), 2-103 (3), 3-116 (1), 4-119 (5), 5-119 (4), 6-137 (7), 7-138 (6), 8-152 (9), 9-164 (10), 10-168 (8)
FoW (2): 1-48 (1), 2-147 (2), 3-156 (3), 4-160 (4), 5-172 (6), 6-276 (5), 7-281 (7), 8-329 (9), 9-347 (8), 10-431 (11)

New Zealand Bowling

	O	M	R	W		O	M	R	W	
Martin	26	6	74	2	2w	18	2	60	1	1w
Southee	23.1	8	55	5	1w	24	5	84	0	
Elliott	10	2	27	1		14	1	58	0	
Vettori	19	6	51	0	(5)	45	6	158	4	4nb
Patel	18	3	37	2	1nb (4)	30.5	4	104	2	1nb

England Bowling

	O	M	R	W		O	M	R	W	
Sidebottom	21.4	6	47	7		19.5	3	83	1	1w
Anderson	7	1	54	0		17	2	99	1	
Broad	17	3	54	3	1w	32	10	78	2	3w,1nb
Panesar	1	1	0	0		46	17	126	6	
Collingwood	2	2	0	0		2	0	20	0	
Pietersen					(6)	2	0	14	0	

Umpires: D.J.Harper and R.E.Koertzen. Third umpire: G.A.V.Baxter. Referee: J.Srinath. Toss: England

Close of Play: 1st day: England (1) 240-7 (Broad 42*, Sidebottom 3*, 92 overs); 2nd day: England (2) 91-2 (Strauss 42*, Pietersen 7*, 32 overs); 3rd day: England (2) 416-5 (Strauss 173*, Ambrose 28*, 122 overs); 4th day: New Zealand (2) 222-5 (Taylor 34*, McCullum 24*, 82 overs).

Man of the Match: R.J.Sidebottom.
K.P.Pietersen's 129 took 208 balls in 292 minutes and included 12 fours and 1 six. A.J.Strauss's 177 took 343 balls in 481 minutes and included 25 fours. I.R.Bell's 110 took 167 balls in 186 minutes and included 17 fours and 2 sixes.

NORTHERN DISTRICTS v OTAGO

Played at Seddon Park, Hamilton, March 22, 23, 24, 25, 2008.
State Championship 2007/08
Match drawn. (Points: Northern Districts 2, Otago 0)

OTAGO

1	*C.D.Cumming	lbw b Arnel	4	c Watling b Arnel		0
2	A.J.Redmond	c McGlashan b Yovich	0	b Yovich		14
3	G.R.Todd	c McGlashan b Orchard	15	c Orchard b Martin		29
4	N.T.Broom	c Flynn b Yovich	150	c Flynn b Yovich		36
5	J.W.Sheed	c Marshall b Aldridge	6	run out		42
6	N.L.McCullum	c Wilson b Aldridge	18	not out		106
7	†D.C.de Boorder	c Wilson b Arnel	3	lbw b Aldridge		7
8	W.C.McSkimming	c Wilson b Yovich	71	not out		81
9	B.E.Scott	c Marshall b Arnel	30			
10	W.E.R.Somerville	c McGlashan b Arnel	5			
11	J.M.McMillan	not out	6			
	Extras	lb 11, w 2, nb 6	19	b 6, lb 6, w 2, nb 3		17
			327	(6 wickets, declared)		332

FoW (1): 1-4 (2), 2-8 (1), 3-39 (3), 4-52 (5), 5-101 (6), 6-108 (7), 7-220 (8), 8-297 (9), 9-319 (10), 10-327 (4)
FoW (2): 1-0 (1), 2-21 (2), 3-65 (4), 4-115 (3), 5-155 (5), 6-180 (7)

NORTHERN DISTRICTS

1	B.S.Wilson	c Broom b Scott	12	c Redmond b McMillan	4
2	B.J.Watling	c Redmond b Scott	32	c de Boorder b McSkimming	118
3	C.J.Merchant	c de Boorder b Scott	89	c Broom b McCullum	27
4	*J.A.H.Marshall	c McSkimming b Scott	0	b Scott	117
5	D.R.Flynn	c de Boorder b McSkimming	109	c de Boorder b Scott	9
6	†P.D.McGlashan	lbw b Somerville	43	b Scott	1
7	J.A.F.Yovich	lbw b Somerville	18	(8) not out	6
8	M.G.Orchard	c de Boorder b McCullum	3	(7) c McMillan b McSkimming	4
9	B.P.Martin	not out	7	b McSkimming	0
10	G.W.Aldridge	not out	4	not out	3
11	B.J.Arnel				
	Extras	lb 8, w 2, nb 1	11	b 1, lb 6, w 3, nb 1	11
		(8 wickets, declared)	328	(8 wickets)	300

FoW (1): 1-18 (1), 2-82 (2), 3-82 (4), 4-209 (3), 5-281 (5), 6-314 (7), 7-317 (8), 8-317 (6)
FoW (2): 1-8 (1), 2-58 (3), 3-248 (4), 4-282 (5), 5-284 (6), 6-284 (2), 7-293 (7), 8-295 (9)

Northern Districts Bowling

	O	M	R	W			O	M	R	W	
Arnel	28	9	85	4			12	1	42	1	
Yovich	17.5	4	76	3			13	2	39	2	1w
Orchard	17	4	53	1	2w	(4)	19	3	61	0	1w
Aldridge	27	8	60	2		(3)	20	1	77	1	
Martin	19	8	25	0	6nb		35.4	10	101	1	3nb
Flynn	7	2	17	0							

Otago Bowling

	O	M	R	W			O	M	R	W	
McSkimming	20	5	67	1		(4)	14	1	65	3	2w
McMillan	15	4	63	0	2w,1nb	(1)	15	2	48	1	
Scott	25	7	59	4		(2)	18	3	62	3	1w
McCullum	31	7	79	1		(3)	16	2	74	1	
Somerville	17.4	4	52	2			5	1	22	0	
Redmond						(6)	4	0	22	0	1nb

Umpires: T.J.Parlane and D.M.Quested.   Toss: Otago

Close of Play: 1st day: Otago (1) 271-7 (Broom 116*, Scott 19*, 103 overs); 2nd day: Northern Districts (1) 260-4 (Flynn 101*, McGlashan 21*, 85 overs); 3rd day: Otago (2) 211-6 (McCullum 59*, McSkimming 13*, 74 overs).

N.T.Broom's 150 took 309 balls in 413 minutes and included 20 fours. D.R.Flynn's 109 took 175 balls in 229 minutes and included 16 fours and 1 six. N.L.McCullum's 106 took 183 balls in 230 minutes and included 13 fours and 1 six. B.J.Watling's 118 took 183 balls in 267 minutes and included 14 fours. J.A.H.Marshall's 117 took 132 balls in 158 minutes and included 13 fours and 4 sixes.

AUCKLAND v CANTERBURY

Played at Eden Park Outer Oval, Auckland, March 23, 24, 25, 26, 2008.
State Championship 2007/08
Match drawn. (Points: Auckland 2, Canterbury 0)

AUCKLAND

1	T.G.McIntosh	c Davidson b Burtt	268	b Burtt	2
2	*R.A.Jones	c Myburgh b Davidson	25	b Burtt	20
3	M.J.Guptill	b Hiini	17	c Hiini b Burtt	9
4	R.J.Nicol	lbw b Burtt	12	c Stewart b Astle	73
5	†G.J.Hopkins	c Papps b Robertson	42	run out	86
6	A.P.de Boorder	c van Wyk b Burtt	32	c Fulton b Davidson	22
7	C.de Grandhomme	c van Wyk b Burtt	10	not out	28
8	R.M.Hira	run out (Stewart)	14	c van Wyk b Burtt	6
9	C.Munro	c Hiini b Burtt	37		
10	Azhar Abbas	not out	0		
11	A.J.McKay	c van Wyk b Burtt	0		
	Extras	lb 3, w 2, nb 7	12	b 2, lb 12, w 1	15
			469	(7 wickets, declared)	261

FoW (1): 1-47 (2), 2-85 (3), 3-140 (4), 4-229 (5), 5-311 (6), 6-342 (7), 7-390 (8), 8-463 (9), 9-469 (1), 10-469 (11)
FoW (2): 1-18 (1), 2-30 (3), 3-35 (2), 4-202 (5), 5-204 (4), 6-236 (6), 7-261 (8)

CANTERBURY

1	T.D.Astle	c McIntosh b Azhar Abbas	1	b McKay	12
2	M.H.W.Papps	c Hopkins b McKay	0	not out	18
3	J.G.Myburgh	c Hopkins b Azhar Abbas	89	retired hurt	0
4	P.G.Fulton	lbw b Munro	28	lbw b McKay	0
5	S.L.Stewart	lbw b McKay	118	not out	3
6	I.A.Robertson	c McIntosh b de Grandhomme	96		
7	*†C.F.K.van Wyk	c Jones b McKay	46		
8	B.C.Hiini	c Nicol b de Grandhomme	0		
9	M.P.F.Davidson	c McIntosh b McKay	34		
10	L.M.Burtt	c Jones b Munro	6		
11	R.D.Burson	not out	6		
	Extras	b 4, lb 3, w 1, nb 3	11	lb 5	5
			435	(2 wickets)	38

FoW (1): 1-1 (2), 2-7 (1), 3-40 (4), 4-178 (3), 5-312 (5), 6-370 (6), 7-380 (8), 8-396 (7), 9-414 (10), 10-435 (9)
FoW (2): 1-29 (1), 2-29 (4)

Canterbury Bowling	O	M	R	W			O	M	R	W	
Burtt	30	5	108	6	1w,6nb		22.4	4	76	4	
Davidson	36	13	77	1	1w		25	9	56	1	1w
Burson	28	4	99	0	1nb	(4)	13	1	50	0	
Hiini	30	10	79	1		(3)	15	8	26	0	
Robertson	18	3	59	1							
Stewart	2	0	17	0							
Astle	3	0	26	0		(5)	10	0	39	1	
Myburgh	1	0	1	0							

Auckland Bowling	O	M	R	W			O	M	R	W	
McKay	23.1	4	78	4		(2)	5	1	20	2	
Azhar Abbas	32	7	91	2		(1)	5	2	12	0	
Munro	22	5	79	2	3nb	(4)	1	1	0	0	
de Grandhomme	19	3	54	2		(3)	1.1	0	1	0	
Hira	12	0	63	0							
Nicol	12	2	63	0	1w						

Umpires: P.D.Jones and D.J.Smith.   Toss: Canterbury

Close of Play: 1st day: Auckland (1) 342-5 (McIntosh 196*, de Grandhomme 10*, 100 overs); 2nd day: Canterbury (1) 176-3 (Myburgh 87*, Stewart 58*, 50 overs); 3rd day: Auckland (2) 35-3 (Nicol 0*, Hopkins 0*, 14 overs).

T.G.McIntosh's 268 took 419 balls in 589 minutes and included 40 fours and 3 sixes. S.L.Stewart's 118 took 198 balls in 254 minutes and included 18 fours and 2 sixes. J.G.Myburgh retired hurt in the Canterbury second innings having scored 0 (team score 29-1, 7.5 overs).

CENTRAL DISTRICTS v WELLINGTON

Played at Fitzherbert Park, Palmerston North, March 23, 24, 25, 2008.
State Championship 2007/08
Wellington won by two wickets.   (Points: Central Districts 0, Wellington 8)

CENTRAL DISTRICTS

1	G.H.Worker	c Gellatly b Burns	38	c Crook b Gillespie	34	
2	*T.I.Lythe	lbw b Bowden	12	c Gellatly b Bowden	75	
3	P.J.Ingram	c Bowden b Shreck	11	c sub (I.E.O'Brien) b Gillespie	60	
4	G.R.Hay	c Nevin b Bowden	4	(5) b Gillespie	38	
5	T.I.Weston	c N.R.Parlane b Shreck	9	(6) c Bowden b Gillespie	43	
6	†B.B.J.Griggs	c N.R.Parlane b Shreck	4	(7) lbw b Gillespie	0	
7	B.J.Diamanti	hit wkt b Gillespie	16	(8) b Gillespie	0	
8	M.J.Mason	b Burns	10	(9) not out	39	
9	R.J.Schaw	c Crook b Burns	7	(4) c Brodie b Woodcock	16	
10	R.R.Sherlock	c N.R.Parlane b Gillespie	6	c N.R.Parlane b Bowden	5	
11	G.J.T.Hegglun	not out	0	run out	1	
	Extras	b 7, lb 12, w 7, nb 7	33	b 13, lb 18, w 6, nb 5	42	
			150		**353**	

FoW (1): 1-38 (2), 2-58 (3), 3-62 (4), 4-85 (5), 5-94 (6), 6-114 (1), 7-137 (7), 8-137 (8), 9-150 (10), 10-150 (9)
FoW (2): 1-68 (1), 2-163 (3), 3-200 (4), 4-234 (2), 5-269 (5), 6-269 (7), 7-269 (8), 8-334 (6), 9-349 (10), 10-353 (11)

WELLINGTON

1	L.J.Woodcock	c Griggs b Diamanti	6	(2) c Griggs b Sherlock	0	
2	J.M.Brodie	c Lythe b Mason	4	(1) c Lythe b Schaw	34	
3	N.R.Parlane	lbw b Mason	14	c Lythe b Sherlock	5	
4	*M.E.Parlane	lbw b Mason	54	c Griggs b Diamanti	4	
5	S.J.Gellatly	b Diamanti	35	not out	53	
6	B.J.Crook	c Weston b Schaw	70	b Schaw	0	
7	D.J.Bowden	c Griggs b Hegglun	64	(8) c Weston b Sherlock	22	
8	†C.J.Nevin	c Ingram b Sherlock	54	(7) c Weston b Sherlock	10	
9	M.R.Gillespie	lbw b Diamanti	0	b Schaw	29	
10	M.Burns	c Worker b Sherlock	8			
11	C.E.Shreck	not out	1	(10) not out	0	
	Extras	b 5, lb 14, w 17	36	nb 1	1	
			346	**(8 wickets)**	**158**	

FoW (1): 1-7 (2), 2-25 (1), 3-45 (3), 4-127 (5), 5-156 (4), 6-249 (6), 7-287 (7), 8-288 (9), 9-337 (8), 10-346 (10)
FoW (2): 1-0 (2), 2-10 (3), 3-30 (4), 4-61 (1), 5-61 (6), 6-94 (7), 7-126 (8), 8-156 (9)

Wellington Bowling

	O	M	R	W			O	M	R	W	
Gillespie	12	3	37	2		(2)	30	9	114	6	1w,2nb
Shreck	13	2	40	3	1nb	(1)	28	9	86	0	1w
Bowden	6	0	24	2	2w,4nb		16.2	3	53	2	3nb
Burns	8.4	2	30	3	1w,1nb						
Woodcock						(4)	26	8	69	1	

Central Districts Bowling

	O	M	R	W			O	M	R	W	
Mason	26	5	78	3			13	5	21	0	1nb
Sherlock	22.1	6	96	2	4w		11	3	36	4	
Diamanti	23	8	50	3	1w		5	3	5	1	
Hegglun	16	4	55	1		(5)	5	1	27	0	
Schaw	18	5	38	1		(4)	9	2	65	3	
Lythe	4	0	10	0			1.3	0	4	0	

Umpires: D.J.Walker and E.A.Watkin.   Toss: Wellington

Close of Play: 1st day: Wellington (1) 163-5 (Crook 25*, Bowden 6*, 58 overs); 2nd day: Central Districts (2) 164-2 (Lythe 35*, Schaw 1*, 46 overs).

The match was scheduled for four days but completed in three.

CENTRAL DISTRICTS v NORTHERN DISTRICTS

Played at McLean Park, Napier, March 30, 31, April 1, 2, 2008.
State Championship 2007/08
Match drawn.   **(Points: Central Districts 2, Northern Districts 0)**

CENTRAL DISTRICTS

1	*J.M.How	c Flynn b Orchard	53	c Watling b Arnel	68
2	P.J.Ingram	c and b Martin	112	c Watling b Arnel	24
3	M.S.Sinclair	c McGlashan b Arnel	90	b Southee	57
4	L.R.P.L.Taylor	c McGlashan b Southee	69	c Watling b Aldridge	152
5	G.R.Hay	b Arnel	12	c Watling b Southee	7
6	†B.B.J.Griggs	c Marshall b Arnel	6	c Watling b Arnel	23
7	T.I.Lythe	b Arnel	4	lbw b Orchard	19
8	M.J.Mason	b Arnel	3	c Wilson b Aldridge	0
9	R.R.Sherlock	c Orchard b Aldridge	13	not out	6
10	G.J.T.Hegglun	b Arnel	0	b Arnel	18
11	B.E.Hefford	not out	1		
	Extras	b 9, lb 10, w 6, nb 2	27	b 8, lb 7, w 1, nb 2	18
			390	(9 wickets, declared)	392

FoW (1): 1-115 (1), 2-236 (2), 3-342 (4), 4-354 (3), 5-364 (6), 6-373 (5), 7-375 (7), 8-378 (8), 9-378 (10), 10-390 (9)
FoW (2): 1-79 (2), 2-108 (1), 3-306 (4), 4-326 (5), 5-327 (3), 6-365 (7), 7-366 (8), 8-368 (6), 9-392 (10)

NORTHERN DISTRICTS

1	B.S.Wilson	c Griggs b Sherlock	5
2	B.J.Watling	c Griggs b Sherlock	57
3	C.J.Merchant	b Lythe	67
4	*J.A.H.Marshall	c How b Mason	35
5	D.R.Flynn	c Sinclair b Lythe	109
6	†P.D.McGlashan	lbw b Lythe	42
7	M.G.Orchard	lbw b Mason	0
8	B.P.Martin	c Griggs b Sherlock	8
9	T.G.Southee	c Taylor b Sinclair	0
10	G.W.Aldridge	c and b Lythe	11
11	B.J.Arnel	not out	0
	Extras	b 17, lb 3, w 10, nb 1	31
			365

FoW (1): 1-11 (1), 2-120 (3), 3-154 (2), 4-213 (4), 5-293 (6), 6-297 (7), 7-329 (8), 8-331 (9), 9-362 (10), 10-365 (5)

Northern Districts Bowling

	O	M	R	W		O	M	R	W	
Southee	23	3	68	1		16	3	41	2	
Arnel	27	9	82	6	1w	25.5	6	65	4	
Aldridge	16.5	2	65	1		19	4	51	2	
Orchard	19	3	83	1	1w	26	5	112	1	1w,1nb
Martin	24	6	73	1	2nb	14	3	83	0	1nb
Wilson						(6) 1	0	19	0	
Merchant						(7) 2	0	6	0	

Central Districts Bowling

	O	M	R	W	
Mason	27	7	76	2	2w
Sherlock	21	5	78	3	2w
Hefford	5	0	22	0	1w,1nb
Lythe	26.1	3	89	4	
Hegglun	18	3	51	0	
Taylor	8	2	14	0	
Sinclair	4	0	15	1	1w

Umpires: P.D.Jones and D.J.Walker.   Toss: Northern Districts

Close of Play: 1st day: Central Districts (1) 357-4 (Hay 6*, Griggs 1*, 89.2 overs); 2nd day: Northern Districts (1) 182-3 (Marshall 28*, Flynn 14*, 56.4 overs); 3rd day: Central Districts (2) 97-1 (How 60*, Sinclair 11*, 34 overs).

P.J.Ingram's 112 took 173 balls in 227 minutes and included 21 fours. D.R.Flynn's 109 took 194 balls in 273 minutes and included 5 fours and 1 six. L.R.P.L.Taylor's 152 took 111 balls in 148 minutes and included 20 fours and 8 sixes.

OTAGO v CANTERBURY

Played at Carisbrook, Dunedin, March 30, 31, April 1, 2, 2008.
State Championship 2007/08
Match drawn.   (Points: Otago 2, Canterbury 0)

CANTERBURY

1	T.D.Astle	lbw b Scott	6	(2) not out	79
2	M.H.W.Papps	lbw b McSkimming	10	(1) c McCullum b Scott	11
3	J.G.Myburgh	b McSkimming	60	st de Boorder b Cumming	55
4	P.G.Fulton	c de Boorder b McSkimming	0	c Sheed b Cumming	3
5	S.L.Stewart	c Redmond b Scott	1	not out	55
6	I.A.Robertson	c Cumming b McSkimming	4		
7	*†C.F.K.van Wyk	c Scott b McMillan	59		
8	B.C.Hiini	c Cumming b McSkimming	33		
9	M.P.F.Davidson	c Todd b McCullum	45		
10	L.M.Burtt	c de Boorder b McCullum	10		
11	H.K.Bennett	not out	2		
	Extras	b 1, lb 9, w 1, nb 6	17	b 2, lb 6, w 3, nb 1	12
			247	(3 wickets)	215

FoW (1): 1-19 (2), 2-21 (1), 3-47 (4), 4-48 (5), 5-54 (6), 6-136 (3), 7-157 (7), 8-194 (8), 9-223 (10), 10-247 (9)
FoW (2): 1-27 (1), 2-117 (3), 3-121 (4)

OTAGO

1	*C.D.Cumming	b Davidson	61
2	A.J.Redmond	c Fulton b Burtt	2
3	G.R.Todd	lbw b Davidson	13
4	N.T.Broom	lbw b Bennett	17
5	J.W.Sheed	lbw b Hiini	9
6	N.L.McCullum	c van Wyk b Burtt	14
7	†D.C.de Boorder	c Myburgh b Bennett	42
8	W.C.McSkimming	c Robertson b Hiini	71
9	B.E.Scott	not out	59
10	C.M.Smith	c Myburgh b Hiini	13
11	J.M.McMillan	not out	21
	Extras	lb 18, w 2, nb 4	24
		(9 wickets, declared)	346

FoW (1): 1-4 (2), 2-33 (3), 3-75 (4), 4-94 (5), 5-120 (6), 6-134 (1), 7-223 (7), 8-263 (8), 9-321 (10)

Otago Bowling

	O	M	R	W		O	M	R	W	
McSkimming	21	5	56	5		11	3	27	0	
McMillan	15	4	49	1	2nb	8	0	34	0	2w,1nb
Scott	13	2	58	2	1w	4	1	15	1	
Smith	9	1	47	0		11	1	29	0	
Cumming	1	0	1	0	(7)	5	1	8	2	
McCullum	3.3	0	26	2		6	1	23	0	
Redmond					(5)	14	1	49	0	1w
Todd					(8)	6	2	12	0	
Broom					(9)	6	2	10	0	
Sheed					(10)	1	1	0	0	

Canterbury Bowling

	O	M	R	W	
Burtt	31	6	105	2	2nb
Davidson	22	6	67	2	1w
Hiini	20	2	80	3	
Bennett	26	7	67	2	1w,2nb
Stewart	3	1	9	0	

Umpires: G.A.V.Baxter and E.A.Watkin.   Toss: Otago

Close of Play: 1st day: Otago (1) 26-1 (Cumming 11*, Todd 11*, 13 overs); 2nd day: Otago (1) 287-8 (Scott 32*, Smith 4*, 83 overs); 3rd day: Otago (1) 346-9 (Scott 59*, McMillan 21*, 102 overs).

WELLINGTON v AUCKLAND

Played at Basin Reserve, Wellington, March 30, 31, April 1, 2, 2008.
State Championship 2007/08
Match drawn.   (Points: Wellington 1, Auckland 1)

WELLINGTON

1	M.D.Bell	b Azhar Abbas	5
2	*M.E.Parlane	b de Grandhomme	20
3	N.R.Parlane	c de Grandhomme b Munro	110
4	G.D.Elliott	not out	196
5	S.J.Gellatly	c Hopkins b Azhar Abbas	44
6	B.J.Crook	c Hopkins b Morgan	4
7	†C.J.Nevin	c Morgan b de Grandhomme	27
8	J.S.Patel	c Jones b Guptill	0
9	M.R.Gillespie	c de Grandhomme b Munro	5
10	I.E.O'Brien	lbw b McKay	10
11	C.E.Shreck	lbw b Munro	6
	Extras	b 2, lb 6, w 6, nb 3	17
			444

FoW (1): 1-18 (1), 2-33 (2), 3-205 (3), 4-312 (5), 5-325 (6), 6-401 (7), 7-406 (8), 8-411 (9), 9-427 (10), 10-444 (11)

AUCKLAND

1	T.G.McIntosh	b Gillespie	9
2	*R.A.Jones	not out	9
3	M.J.Guptill	not out	0
4	R.J.Nicol		
5	†G.J.Hopkins		
6	A.P.de Boorder		
7	C.de Grandhomme		
8	C.Munro		
9	G.J.Morgan		
10	Azhar Abbas		
11	A.J.McKay		
	Extras	b 4, nb 1	5
		(1 wicket)	23

FoW (1): 1-19 (1)

Auckland Bowling

	O	M	R	W	
Azhar Abbas	32	8	84	2	1nb
McKay	29	7	71	1	1w,1nb
Munro	33	4	106	3	1nb
de Grandhomme	25	6	85	2	
Morgan	21	2	82	1	1w
Guptill	2	0	8	1	

Wellington Bowling

	O	M	R	W	
Gillespie	5	1	10	1	1nb
O'Brien	5	2	9	0	

Umpires: B.G.Frost and D.M.Quested.   Toss: Auckland

Close of Play: 1st day: No play; 2nd day: No play; 3rd day: Wellington (1) 167-2 (N.R.Parlane 92*, Elliott 45*, 57 overs).

N.R.Parlane's 110 took 183 balls in 255 minutes and included 15 fours. G.D.Elliott's 196 took 365 balls in 518 minutes and included 23 fours and 2 sixes.

WELLINGTON v CANTERBURY

Played at Basin Reserve, Wellington, April 7, 8, 9, 10, 11, 2008.
State Championship 2007/08 - Final
Canterbury won by 49 runs.

CANTERBURY

1	T.D.Astle	c N.R.Parlane b O'Brien	25	lbw b Gillespie	14
2	M.H.W.Papps	lbw b Patel	46	c Nevin b Gillespie	11
3	J.G.Myburgh	c M.E.Parlane b O'Brien	2	b Gillespie	1
4	P.G.Fulton	c Nevin b Elliott	11	c N.R.Parlane b Woodcock	16
5	S.L.Stewart	lbw b Patel	25	not out	84
6	I.A.Robertson	c Bowden b O'Brien	20	c M.E.Parlane b O'Brien	27
7	*†C.F.K.van Wyk	lbw b Gillespie	16	lbw b Gillespie	6
8	B.C.Hiini	not out	31	c Gellatly b Gillespie	37
9	M.P.F.Davidson	run out (Patel)	8	c Bowden b Gillespie	8
10	L.M.Burtt	b O'Brien	0	not out	6
11	H.K.Bennett	b O'Brien	0		
	Extras	b 6, lb 11, w 10, nb 4	31	b 1, lb 9, w 1	11
			215	(8 wickets, declared)	221

FoW (1): 1-47 (1), 2-50 (3), 3-76 (4), 4-107 (2), 5-146 (6), 6-146 (5), 7-182 (7), 8-195 (9), 9-207 (10), 10-215 (11)
FoW (2): 1-19 (2), 2-26 (1), 3-29 (3), 4-61 (4), 5-99 (6), 6-117 (7), 7-196 (8), 8-214 (9)

WELLINGTON

1	M.D.Bell	lbw b Bennett	3	b Davidson	1
2	*M.E.Parlane	c van Wyk b Davidson	11	c Fulton b Davidson	0
3	N.R.Parlane	c van Wyk b Bennett	39	c Papps b Astle	74
4	G.D.Elliott	b Burtt	52	lbw b Davidson	0
5	S.J.Gellatly	c van Wyk b Bennett	0	b Davidson	0
6	†C.J.Nevin	lbw b Bennett	15	lbw b Hiini	25
7	L.J.Woodcock	not out	35	c Bennett b Astle	65
8	D.J.Bowden	c van Wyk b Hiini	22	c Robertson b Astle	0
9	J.S.Patel	b Bennett	0	c van Wyk b Astle	0
10	M.R.Gillespie	c van Wyk b Bennett	0	b Bennett	14
11	I.E.O'Brien	c Burtt b Bennett	1	not out	4
	Extras	b 7, w 3	10	b 5, lb 9, w 1, nb 1	16
			188		199

FoW (1): 1-14 (1), 2-18 (2), 3-90 (3), 4-90 (5), 5-125 (4), 6-126 (6), 7-174 (8), 8-177 (9), 9-179 (10), 10-188 (11)
FoW (2): 1-1 (1), 2-2 (2), 3-2 (4), 4-6 (5), 5-71 (6), 6-154 (3), 7-154 (8), 8-154 (9), 9-173 (10), 10-199 (7)

Wellington Bowling

	O	M	R	W		O	M	R	W	
Gillespie	23	4	63	1	1w	21	9	42	6	
O'Brien	22.5	6	70	5	4w,1nb	18	2	62	1	
Bowden	7	1	21	0	3nb	4	1	21	0	
Elliott	8	2	14	1	1w	14	4	38	0	1w
Patel	9	2	30	2	(6)	8	1	26	0	
Woodcock					(5)	13	6	22	1	

Canterbury Bowling

	O	M	R	W		O	M	R	W	
Burtt	17	4	39	1		14	2	61	0	
Davidson	17	7	34	1		15	6	28	4	
Bennett	16.3	3	50	7	3w	12	1	39	1	1w,1nb
Hiini	17	4	53	1		11	5	25	1	
Robertson	6	4	5	0		2	0	6	0	
Astle					(6)	10.1	3	26	4	

Umpires: B.G.Frost and P.D.Jones.   Toss: Wellington

Close of Play: 1st day: Canterbury (1) 165-6 (van Wyk 7*, Hiini 11*, 55.3 overs); 2nd day: Wellington (1) 163-6 (Woodcock 19*, Bowden 18*, 62 overs); 3rd day: Canterbury (2) 10-0 (Astle 3*, Papps 6*, 7 overs); 4th day: Wellington (2) 14-4 (N.R.Parlane 5*, Nevin 0*, 9 overs).

KARACHI URBAN v MUMBAI

Played at National Stadium, Karachi, September 8, 9, 10, 11, 2007.
Mohammad Nissar Trophy 2007/08
Match drawn.

MUMBAI

1	S.O.Kukreja	c Amin-ur-Rehman b Anwar Ali	110
2	A.M.Rahane	c Amin-ur-Rehman b Uzair-ul-Haq	143
3	*V.R.Mane	run out (Khurram Manzoor)	19
4	H.N.Shah	lbw b Uzair-ul-Haq	47
5	P.T.Naik	c Saeed Bin Nasir b Hasan Raza	118
6	A.M.Nayar	c Asim Kamal b Anwar Ali	152
7	†O.D.Gurav	not out	10
8	Iqbal Abdulla	not out	6
9	M.G.Mangela		
10	V.S.Yeligati		
11	A.M.Salvi		
	Extras	b 7, lb 6, w 2, nb 3	18
		(6 wickets, declared)	623

FoW (1): 1-247 (1), 2-259 (2), 3-285 (3), 4-350 (4), 5-585 (5), 6-615 (6)

KARACHI URBAN

1	Agha Sabir	b Iqbal Abdulla	14	c Gurav b Salvi		9
2	Khurram Manzoor	c Mane b Iqbal Abdulla	200	c sub (B.J.Thakkar) b Mangela		9
3	†Amin-ur-Rehman	lbw b Salvi	9			
4	Asif Zakir	c Gurav b Nayar	11	(3) c Shah b Yeligati		21
5	*Hasan Raza	run out (Yeligati)	12	(4) lbw b Iqbal Abdulla		25
6	Asim Kamal	c Mangela b Yeligati	25	not out		38
7	Saeed Bin Nasir	lbw b Salvi	92	(5) not out		47
8	Anwar Ali	c Gurav b Nayar	1			
9	Azam Hussain	b Yeligati	14			
10	Uzair-ul-Haq	c Kukreja b Yeligati	1			
11	Malik Aftab	not out	0			
	Extras	b 4, lb 1, w 3, nb 2	10	b 17, lb 1, w 5		23
			389	(4 wickets)		172

FoW (1): 1-29 (1), 2-57 (3), 3-77 (4), 4-97 (5), 5-163 (6), 6-338 (7), 7-339 (8), 8-385 (9), 9-389 (10), 10-389 (2)
FoW (2): 1-24 (2), 2-24 (1), 3-80 (4), 4-82 (3)

Karachi Urban Bowling

	O	M	R	W	
Anwar Ali	37	3	148	2	1w,1nb
Malik Aftab	24	7	80	0	
Uzair-ul-Haq	29	3	135	2	2nb
Azam Hussain	42	7	152	0	
Asif Zakir	16	1	62	0	
Hasan Raza	10	1	33	1	1w

Mumbai Bowling

	O	M	R	W		O	M	R	W	
Salvi	35	10	88	2	2w,1nb	8	3	20	1	
Mangela	19	7	58	0		15	4	48	1	1w
Nayar	26	4	82	2	1w,1nb					
Iqbal Abdulla	34.5	9	86	2		11	5	18	1	
Yeligati	14	4	56	3	(3)	19	3	68	1	
Naik	3	0	14	0						

Umpires: Nadeem Ghauri and Saleem Badar. Third umpire: Shakeel Khan. Referee: Anis Sheikh.   Toss: Karachi Urban

Close of Play: 1st day: Mumbai (1) 325-3 (Shah 38*, Naik 6*, 90 overs); 2nd day: Karachi Urban (1) 30-1 (Khurram Manzoor 14*, Amin-ur-Rehman 0*, 20 overs); 3rd day: Karachi Urban (1) 339-7 (Khurram Manzoor 167*, 109.3 overs).

S.O.Kukreja's 110 took 196 balls and included 16 fours. A.M.Rahane's 143 took 207 balls and included 28 fours. P.T.Naik's 118 took 227 balls and included 11 fours and 1 six. A.M.Nayar's 152 took 162 balls and included 16 fours and 3 sixes. Khurram Manzoor's 200 took 427 balls and included 28 fours and 2 sixes.

PAKISTAN A v AUSTRALIA A

Played at Iqbal Stadium, Faisalabad, September 12, 13, 14, 15, 2007.
Australia A in Pakistan 2007/08
Australia A won by an innings and 203 runs.

PAKISTAN A

1	Khalid Latif	c Ronchi b Hopes	16	c Bollinger b Cullen	3
2	Taufeeq Umar	b Bollinger	0	lbw b MacGill	29
3	Yasir Hameed	c Hussey b Bollinger	11	c Ronchi b Hopes	47
4	Hasan Raza	c Voges b Bollinger	0	c Ronchi b Noffke	3
5	*Faisal Iqbal	lbw b Hopes	33	(6) lbw b MacGill	24
6	Mansoor Amjad	c Voges b Cullen	25	(7) c and b Hussey	40
7	†Sarfraz Ahmed	c Ronchi b Noffke	9	(8) c Hussey b Bollinger	48
8	Abdur Rauf	c Voges b White	73	(9) c White b MacGill	12
9	Atif Maqbool	c Voges b White	12	(10) c Voges b Cullen	2
10	Mohammad Irshad	b Cullen	5	(5) c Hussey b Cullen	27
11	Najaf Shah	not out	2	not out	0
	Extras	b 2, lb 3, w 3, nb 5	13	b 4, lb 13, nb 3	20
			199		255

FoW (1): 1-2, 2-18, 3-18, 4-57, 5-67, 6-92, 7-128, 8-155, 9-175, 10-199
FoW (2): 1-17, 2-63, 3-74, 4-99, 5-129, 6-148, 7-236, 8-255, 9-255, 10-255

AUSTRALIA A

1	P.A.Jaques	c Khalid Latif b Mansoor Amjad	152
2	C.J.L.Rogers	c Sarfraz Ahmed b Abdur Rauf	56
3	D.J.Hussey	c Sarfraz Ahmed b Atif Maqbool	185
4	*A.C.Voges	st Sarfraz Ahmed b Atif Maqbool	7
5	C.L.White	lbw b Abdur Rauf	35
6	J.R.Hopes	b Mansoor Amjad	144
7	†L.Ronchi	lbw b Atif Maqbool	22
8	A.A.Noffke	c sub b Mansoor Amjad	39
9	D.J.Cullen	not out	4
10	S.C.G.MacGill		
11	D.E.Bollinger		
	Extras	b 4, lb 5, w 1, nb 3	13
		(8 wickets, declared)	657

FoW (1): 1-125, 2-256, 3-277, 4-363, 5-525, 6-561, 7-641, 8-657

Australia A Bowling

	O	M	R	W			O	M	R	W	
Bollinger	13	3	34	3	1w,2nb		19	5	45	1	3nb
Noffke	13	2	43	1	2nb		14	4	24	1	
Hopes	10	5	20	2	1nb	(5)	9	3	15	1	
MacGill	4	0	26	0			40	14	81	3	
Cullen	8	2	26	2	1w	(3)	37.2	11	65	3	
White	8	0	45	2	1w		5	2	4	0	
Voges						(7)	1	1	0	0	
Hussey						(8)	3	1	4	1	

Pakistan A Bowling

	O	M	R	W	
Najaf Shah	29	5	79	0	2nb
Mohammad Irshad	17	1	80	0	
Atif Maqbool	51	2	187	3	
Abdur Rauf	17	1	71	2	
Mansoor Amjad	40.5	1	178	3	1nb
Taufeeq Umar	5	2	14	0	
Hasan Raza	11	1	39	0	1w

Umpires: Iftikhar Malik and Riazuddin.   Referee: Arshad Pervez.   Toss: Pakistan A

Close of Play: 1st day: Australia A (1) 109-0 (Jaques 56*, Rogers 50*, 34 overs); 2nd day: Australia A (1) 438-4 (Hussey 143*, Hopes 34*, 116 overs); 3rd day: Pakistan A (2) 86-3 (Yasir Hameed 36*, Mohammad Irshad 5*, 41 overs).
P.A.Jaques's 152 took 218 balls in 311 minutes and included 10 fours and 3 sixes. D.J.Hussey's 185 took 278 balls in 444 minutes and included 21 fours. J.R.Hopes's 144 took 236 balls in 258 minutes and included 7 fours and 2 sixes.

PAKISTAN A v AUSTRALIA A

Played at Gaddafi Stadium, Lahore, September 19, 20, 21, 22, 2007.
Australia A in Pakistan 2007/08
Match drawn.

AUSTRALIA A

1	P.A.Jaques	b Mohammad Sami	82	(2) c Naved Latif b Tahir Khan		136
2	C.J.L.Rogers	run out (Mohammad Sami)	0	(1) lbw b Mohammad Khalil		54
3	D.J.Hussey	c Sarfraz Ahmed b Mohammad Sami	3	b Mansoor Amjad		112
4	*A.C.Voges	c Sarfraz Ahmed b Anwar Ali	12	not out		34
5	C.L.White	c Sarfraz Ahmed b Mohammad Khalil	1	not out		4
6	J.R.Hopes	c Naved Latif b Tahir Khan	34			
7	†L.Ronchi	c Faisal Iqbal b Mansoor Amjad	107			
8	C.B.Bailey	lbw b Anwar Ali	31			
9	J.N.Gillespie	c Faisal Iqbal b Mansoor Amjad	5			
10	D.E.Bollinger	b Mohammad Khalil	10			
11	S.C.G.MacGill	not out	4			
	Extras	lb 2, nb 2	4	b 8, lb 5, w 1, nb 7		21
			293	(3 wickets, declared)		361

FoW (1): 1-12, 2-17, 3-54, 4-59, 5-128, 6-144, 7-250, 8-276, 9-289, 10-293
FoW (2): 1-101, 2-269, 3-354

PAKISTAN A

1	Khalid Latif	c Ronchi b Bollinger	0	retired hurt		21
2	Khurram Manzoor	c Ronchi b Bollinger	19	not out		17
3	Yasir Hameed	c Ronchi b Hopes	1	not out		6
4	Anwar Ali	c Ronchi b Hopes	0			
5	Naved Latif	run out (Rogers)	41			
6	*Faisal Iqbal	c White b MacGill	74			
7	Mansoor Amjad	c White b Gillespie	10			
8	†Sarfraz Ahmed	c Bailey b Bollinger	61			
9	Mohammad Sami	b Bollinger	32			
10	Tahir Khan	lbw b Bollinger	6			
11	Mohammad Khalil	not out	1			
	Extras	b 4, lb 1, nb 4	9	nb 1		1
			254	(no wicket)		45

FoW (1): 1-14, 2-16, 3-16, 4-25, 5-111, 6-138, 7-166, 8-237, 9-245, 10-254

Pakistan A Bowling

	O	M	R	W		O	M	R	W	
Mohammad Sami	12	0	51	2		10	0	64	0	
Anwar Ali	18	2	64	2	1nb	15	2	67	0	1nb
Mohammad Khalil	11.1	1	40	2	1nb	17	0	83	1	1w,3nb
Tahir Khan	15	3	68	1		22	2	66	1	1nb
Mansoor Amjad	12	1	68	2		13	0	68	1	2nb

Australia A Bowling

	O	M	R	W		O	M	R	W	
Bollinger	14.5	8	15	5	2nb	5	0	27	0	1nb
Gillespie	16	5	38	1		5	1	12	0	
Hopes	12	4	21	2	1nb	1	0	6	0	
MacGill	14	2	68	1						
White	9	1	41	0						
Bailey	16	2	51	0						
Hussey	3	0	15	0						

Umpires: Afzaal Ahmed and Shakeel Khan.   Referee: Ishtiaq Ahmed.   Toss: Pakistan A

Close of Play: 1st day: Pakistan A (1) 22-3 (Khurram Manzoor 19*, Naved Latif 0*, 11 overs); 2nd day: Pakistan A (1) 238-8 (Sarfraz Ahmed 56*, Tahir Khan 0*, 81.1 overs); 3rd day: Australia A (2) 288-2 (Hussey 69*, Voges 11*; 60 overs).

L.Ronchi's 107 took 109 balls in 159 minutes and included 16 fours and 2 sixes. P.A.Jaques's 136 took 176 balls in 248 minutes and included 12 fours and 2 sixes. D.J.Hussey's 112 took 141 balls in 265 minutes and included 13 fours. Khalid Latif retired hurt in the Pakistan A second innings having scored 21 (team had lost 0 wickets).

PAKISTAN v SOUTH AFRICA

Played at National Stadium, Karachi, October 1, 2, 3, 4, 5, 2007.
South Africa in Pakistan 2007/08 - 1st Test
South Africa won by 160 runs.

SOUTH AFRICA

1	H.H.Gibbs	c Mohammad Hafeez b Umar Gul	54	(2) c Faisal Iqbal b Danish Kaneria	18
2	*G.C.Smith	lbw b Mohammad Hafeez	42	(1) c Kamran Akmal b Abdur Rehman	25
3	H.M.Amla	b Mohammad Asif	71	st Kamran Akmal b Abdur Rehman	0
4	J.H.Kallis	c Kamran Akmal b Danish Kaneria	155	not out	100
5	A.G.Prince	c and b Danish Kaneria	36	b Danish Kaneria	45
6	A.B.de Villiers	b Umar Gul	77	b Abdur Rehman	1
7	†M.V.Boucher	c Kamran Akmal b Abdur Rehman	1	c Misbah-ul-Haq b Danish Kaneria	29
8	A.Nel	c Misbah-ul-Haq b Abdur Rehman	2	c Misbah-ul-Haq b Abdur Rehman	33
9	P.L.Harris	c Kamran Akmal b Abdur Rehman	1	not out	0
10	D.W.Steyn	b Abdur Rehman	0		
11	M.Ntini	not out	0		
	Extras	b 1, lb 6, nb 4	11	b 10, lb 2	12
			450	**(7 wickets, declared)**	**264**

FoW (1): 1-87 (2), 2-109 (1), 3-279 (3), 4-352 (4), 5-373 (5), 6-392 (7), 7-408 (8), 8-412 (9), 9-448 (10), 10-450 (6)
FoW (2): 1-41 (1), 2-43 (2), 3-43 (2), 4-131 (5), 5-132 (6), 6-188 (7), 7-251 (8)

PAKISTAN

1	Mohammad Hafeez	c Kallis b Harris	34	b Steyn	1
2	†Kamran Akmal	lbw b Harris	42	(8) c Boucher b Harris	9
3	Younis Khan	b Nel	6	b Steyn	126
4	Faisal Iqbal	b Kallis	7	c Kallis b Harris	44
5	Misbah-ul-Haq	c Boucher b Steyn	23	(6) lbw b Nel	23
6	*Shoaib Malik	st Boucher b Harris	73	(7) c Nel b Ntini	30
7	Abdur Rehman	c Boucher b Nel	9	(9) lbw b Steyn	0
8	Salman Butt	lbw b Harris	24	(2) c Amla b Steyn	3
9	Umar Gul	st Boucher b Harris	12	(10) c Nel b Steyn	8
10	Danish Kaneria	not out	26	(11) not out	0
11	Mohammad Asif	b Steyn	10˙	(5) c Amla b Nel	6
	Extras	b 15, lb 7, w 1, nb 2	25	b 8, lb 4, nb 1	13
			291		**263**

FoW (1): 1-71 (2), 2-82 (1), 3-84 (3), 4-97 (4), 5-120 (5), 6-149 (7), 7-233 (8), 8-238 (6), 9-259 (9), 10-291 (11)
FoW (2): 1-1 (1), 2-20 (2), 3-134 (4), 4-161 (5), 5-197 (3), 6-230 (6), 7-239 (8), 8-249 (9), 9-257 (10), 10-263 (7)

Pakistan Bowling	O	M	R	W		O	M	R	W	
Mohammad Asif	26	6	83	1		6	1	14	0	
Umar Gul	21.3	6	60	2	2nb	12	1	35	0	
Danish Kaneria	36	3	124	2	(4)	28	3	85	3	
Abdur Rehman	31	3	105	4	(3)	38	6	105	4	
Shoaib Malik	8	2	31	0	2nb					
Mohammad Hafeez	14	0	40	1	(5)	5	0	13	0	

South Africa Bowling	O	M	R	W		O	M	R	W	
Steyn	13.3	2	50	2	2nb	(2) 15	3	56	5	
Ntini	11	2	48	0	(1)	12.5	4	34	1	
Harris	36	13	73	5	(4)	30	8	58	2	
Nel	20	4	59	2	(3)	19	5	59	2	1nb
Kallis	11	3	21	1	1w	(6) 4	3	4	0	
Smith	6	1	18	0	(5)	3	0	33	0	
Amla					(7)	1	0	7	0	

Umpires: M.R.Benson and S.J.A.Taufel. Third umpire: Riazuddin. Referee: A.G.Hurst.   Toss: South Africa

Close of Play: 1st day: South Africa (1) 294-3 (Kallis 118*, Prince 3*, 90 overs); 2nd day: Pakistan (1) 127-5 (Shoaib Malik 9*, Abdur Rehman 1*, 40 overs); 3rd day: South Africa (2) 76-3 (Kallis 18*, Prince 11*, 32 overs); 4th day: Pakistan (2) 146-3 (Younis Khan 93*, Mohammad Asif 1*, 33 overs).

Man of the Match: J.H.Kallis.
J.H.Kallis's 155 took 249 balls in 304 minutes and included 19 fours. J.H.Kallis's 100 took 201 balls in 291 minutes and included 4 fours and 1 six. Younis Khan's 126 took 160 balls in 233 minutes and included 18 fours and 1 six.

PAKISTAN v SOUTH AFRICA

Played at Gaddafi Stadium, Lahore, October 8, 9, 10, 11, 12, 2007.
South Africa in Pakistan 2007/08 - 2nd Test
Match drawn.

SOUTH AFRICA

1	H.H.Gibbs	c Misbah-ul-Haq b Umar Gul	13	(2) c Kamran Akmal b Umar Gul	16
2	*G.C.Smith	b Danish Kaneria	46	(1) c sub (Yasir Hameed)	
				b Danish Kaneria	133
3	H.M.Amla	b Mohammad Asif	10	b Abdur Rehman	17
4	J.H.Kallis	lbw b Danish Kaneria	59	not out	107
5	A.G.Prince	b Abdur Rehman	63	b Abdur Rehman	11
6	A.B.de Villiers	run out (Mohammad Asif)	45	not out	8
7	†M.V.Boucher	c Abdur Rehman b Danish Kaneria	54		
8	A.Nel	c Misbah-ul-Haq b Umar Gul	0		
9	P.L.Harris	c Shoaib Malik b Umar Gul	46		
10	D.W.Steyn	b Danish Kaneria	0		
11	M.Ntini	not out	0		
	Extras	lb 2, w 7, nb 7, pen 5	21	b 12, nb 1	13
			357	**(4 wickets, declared)**	**305**

FoW (1): 1-24 (1), 2-47 (3), 3-100 (2), 4-160 (4), 5-243 (5), 6-259 (6), 7-259 (8), 8-347 (9), 9-350 (10), 10-357 (7)
FoW (2): 1-34 (2), 2-66 (3), 3-273 (1), 4-290 (5)

PAKISTAN

1	Salman Butt	c Smith b Harris	40	c sub (S.M.Pollock) b Ntini	6
2	†Kamran Akmal	c Smith b Harris	52	b Harris	71
3	Younis Khan	b Nel	3	c Boucher b Kallis	130
4	Mohammad Yousuf	lbw b Steyn	25	not out	63
5	Inzamam-ul-Haq	c Boucher b Kallis	14	st Boucher b Harris	3
6	Misbah-ul-Haq	c Boucher b Ntini	41		
7	*Shoaib Malik	c Amla b Steyn	1	(6) not out	20
8	Abdur Rehman	not out	25		
9	Umar Gul	lbw b Ntini	0		
10	Danish Kaneria	c Boucher b Ntini	0		
11	Mohammad Asif	c Amla b Harris	4		
	Extras	lb 1	1	b 3, lb 14, w 5, nb 1	23
			206	**(4 wickets)**	**316**

FoW (1): 1-90 (1), 2-93 (3), 3-99 (2), 4-123 (4), 5-149 (5), 6-150 (7), 7-189 (6), 8-189 (9), 9-189 (10), 10-206 (11)
FoW (2): 1-15 (1), 2-176 (2), 3-265 (3), 4-272 (5)

Pakistan Bowling

	O	M	R	W		O	M	R	W	
Mohammad Asif	34	9	83	1		4	1	14	0	
Umar Gul	29	4	103	3	3w,6nb	16	3	48	1	1nb
Danish Kaneria	43.1	5	114	4		44.3	11	99	1	
Abdur Rehman	14	5	30	1		42	7	112	2	
Shoaib Malik	5	0	20	0	1nb					
Younis Khan						(5) 4	0	20	0	

South Africa Bowling

	O	M	R	W		O	M	R	W	
Ntini	8	1	42	3		(2) 17	3	60	1	
Steyn	12	3	60	2		(1) 15	2	56	0	1nb
Nel	16	3	39	1		(4) 20	1	75	0	1w
Harris	20	5	57	3		(5) 40	14	60	2	
Kallis	7	3	7	1		(3) 15	0	48	1	

Umpires: M.R.Benson and S.J.A.Taufel. Third umpire: Nadeem Ghauri. Referee: A.G.Hurst.   Toss: South Africa

Close of Play: 1st day: South Africa (1) 259-6 (Boucher 9*, Nel 0*, 83 overs); 2nd day: Pakistan (1) 140-4 (Inzamam-ul-Haq 10*, Misbah-ul-Haq 10*, 37 overs); 3rd day: South Africa (2) 154-2 (Smith 75*, Kallis 37*, 55 overs); 4th day: Pakistan (2) 108-1 (Kamran Akmal 49*, Younis Khan 48*, 31 overs).
Man of the Match: J.H.Kallis.
G.C.Smith's 133 took 296 balls in 407 minutes and included 17 fours. J.H.Kallis's 107 took 242 balls in 358 minutes and included 8 fours. Younis Khan's 130 took 246 balls in 350 minutes and included 16 fours.

FAISALABAD v MULTAN

Played at Sports Stadium, Sargodha, October 20, 21, 22, 23, 2007.
Quaid-e-Azam Trophy 2007/08 - Group A
Match drawn.   (Points: Faisalabad 3, Multan 0)

FAISALABAD

1	Imran Ali	b Imranullah Aslam	20	b Imranullah Aslam	22
2	Abdul Mannan	c Mohammad Sarwar			
		b Mohammad Hafeez	51	c Abdur Rauf b Zulfiqar Babar	18
3	Asif Hussain	c Abdur Rauf b Zulfiqar Babar	109		
4	Mohammad Sami	b Imranullah Aslam	5	(3) c Gulraiz Sadaf b Imranullah Aslam	5
5	Usman Arshad	c Mohammad Hafeez			
		b Imranullah Aslam	17	(4) not out	50
6	*Ijaz Ahmed	lbw b Ansar Javed	47		
7	†Mohammad Salman	b Ansar Javed	0	(5) not out	53
8	Ahmed Hayat	c Mohammad Sarwar b Zulfiqar Babar	71		
9	Asad Zarar	b Imranullah Aslam	40		
10	Shafqat Hussain	not out	2		
11	Mohammad Talha	c Ansar Javed b Imranullah Aslam	4		
	Extras	b 6, lb 10, nb 20	36	lb 2, nb 11	13
			402	(3 wickets)	161

FoW (1): 1-44, 2-115, 3-136, 4-183, 5-268, 6-268, 7-295, 8-387, 9-398, 10-402
FoW (2): 1-51, 2-52, 3-55

MULTAN

1	Usman Tariq	b Ahmed Hayat	0
2	Hammad Tariq	run out (Mohammad Talha)	2
3	Mohammad Hafeez	lbw b Ahmed Hayat	70
4	Kashif Naved	c Asad Zarar b Ijaz Ahmed	15
5	Mohammad Sarwar	b Ahmed Hayat	66
6	†Gulraiz Sadaf	c Mohammad Salman b Ahmed Hayat	50
7	*Abdur Rauf	c Ijaz Ahmed b Shafqat Hussain	56
8	Imranullah Aslam	c Usman Arshad b Ahmed Hayat	17
9	Ansar Javed	not out	7
10	Zulfiqar Babar	b Ahmed Hayat	0
11	Mohammad Tanvir	lbw b Shafqat Hussain	2
	Extras	b 4, lb 7, w 5, nb 7	23
			308

FoW (1): 1-0, 2-8, 3-30, 4-160, 5-163, 6-271, 7-291, 8-301, 9-301, 10-308

Multan Bowling

	O	M	R	W		O	M	R	W	
Abdur Rauf	24	5	53	0	7nb	12	2	27	0	4nb
Ansar Javed	16	1	54	2	9nb	3	0	7	0	3nb
Mohammad Tanvir	13	2	59	0	3nb	3	0	7	0	4nb
Imranullah Aslam	31.1	3	82	5	1nb	22	1	63	2	
Zulfiqar Babar	38	3	100	2		15	2	43	1	
Mohammad Hafeez	3	1	3	1						
Usman Tariq	8	0	35	0	(6)	3	0	12	0	

Faisalabad Bowling

	O	M	R	W	
Ahmed Hayat	25	6	48	6	2nb
Mohammad Talha	31	7	69	0	5w,5nb
Asad Zarar	8	2	21	0	
Ijaz Ahmed	23	7	47	1	
Shafqat Hussain	41.5	10	95	2	
Usman Arshad	4	2	10	0	
Imran Ali	1	0	7	0	

Umpires: Rasheed Bhatti and Raweed Khan.   Referee: Arshad Pervez.   Toss: Faisalabad

Close of Play: 1st day: Faisalabad (1) 205-4 (Asif Hussain 89*, Ijaz Ahmed 11*, 83 overs); 2nd day: Multan (1) 46-2 (Mohammad Hafeez 20*, Mohammad Sarwar 6*, 32 overs); 3rd day: Multan (1) 271-6 (Gulraiz Sadaf 42*, 117.3 overs).
Asif Hussain's 109 took 255 balls in 359 minutes and included 9 fours and 1 six.

ISLAMABAD v ABBOTTABAD

Played at Diamond Club Ground, Islamabad, October 20, 21, 22, 23, 2007.
Quaid-e-Azam Trophy 2007/08 - Group B
Islamabad won by four wickets.　(Points: Islamabad 9, Abbottabad 0)

ABBOTTABAD

1	Mohammad Naeem	c Naeem Anjum b Saad Altaf	10	c Naeem Anjum b Saad Altaf	0
2	†Fawad Khan	c Naeem Anjum b Saad Altaf	22	c Raheel Majeed b Atif Maqbool	10
3	Usman Khan	c Naeem Anjum b Saad Altaf	0	c Naeem Anjum b Saad Altaf	50
4	*Adnan Raees	b Rauf Akbar	13	c Rauf Akbar b Atif Maqbool	52
5	Riaz Kail	b Saad Altaf	9	run out	94
6	Mohammad Kashif	c Naeem Anjum b Saad Altaf	2	b Rauf Akbar	19
7	Khalid Usman	b Atif Maqbool	50	b Rauf Akbar	1
8	Iftikhar Mahmood	c Naeem Anjum b Saad Altaf	36	c Naeem Anjum b Saad Altaf	20
9	Rahimbaz Khan	c Fayyaz Ahmed b Atif Maqbool	12	c Naeem Anjum b Saad Altaf	1
10	Noor-ul-Amin	c Naeem Anjum b Rauf Akbar	12	c sub (Asadullah Sumari) b Atif Maqbool	0
11	Junaid Khan	not out	4	not out	16
	Extras	b 6, lb 3, w 2, nb 31	42	b 4, lb 2, w 6, nb 24	36
			212		**299**

FoW (1): 1-28, 2-29, 3-55, 4-74, 5-79, 6-79, 7-156, 8-185, 9-199, 10-212
FoW (2): 1-0, 2-35, 3-100, 4-160, 5-187, 6-189, 7-253, 8-258, 9-268, 10-299

ISLAMABAD

1	Raheel Majeed	st Fawad Khan b Noor-ul-Amin	54	c Fawad Khan b Rahimbaz Khan	32
2	Umair Khan	run out (Khalid Usman)	41	c Fawad Khan b Noor-ul-Amin	51
3	Farrukh Hayat	c Mohammad Kashif b Noor-ul-Amin	5	c Fawad Khan b Rahimbaz Khan	0
4	*Ashar Zaidi	c Khalid Usman b Rahimbaz Khan	7	c Mohammad Naeem b Noor-ul-Amin	47
5	Fayyaz Ahmed	lbw b Rahimbaz Khan	0	c Riaz Kail b Junaid Khan	26
6	Zeeshan Mushtaq	b Noor-ul-Amin	9	c sub (Wajid Ali) b Noor-ul-Amin	2
7	†Naeem Anjum	run out (Junaid Khan)	21	not out	37
8	Zohaib Ahmed	c Adnan Raees b Noor-ul-Amin	10		
9	Rauf Akbar	c Usman Khan b Iftikhar Mahmood	80	(8) not out	48
10	Atif Maqbool	c Adnan Raees b Noor-ul-Amin	11		
11	Saad Altaf	not out	6		
	Extras	b 5, lb 5	10	b 8, lb 5, w 3	16
			254	**(6 wickets)**	**259**

FoW (1): 1-88, 2-100, 3-107, 4-107, 5-116, 6-126, 7-140, 8-180, 9-198, 10-254
FoW (2): 1-47, 2-47, 3-127, 4-166, 5-166, 6-170

Islamabad Bowling

	O	M	R	W			O	M	R	W	
Saad Altaf	24w,18nb	5	73	6	1w,19nb		27	5	94	4	
Zohaib Ahmed	12	1	59	0	9nb	(6)	4	1	11	0	1nb
Rauf Akbar	14	5	35	2	1w,2nb	(2)	19	5	44	2	2w,3nb
Zeeshan Mushtaq	1	0	5	0	1nb						
Atif Maqbool	15	9	26	2		(4)	30.3	3	77	3	1nb
Ashar Zaidi	2	0	5	0		(3)	14	3	37	0	
Raheel Majeed						(5)	11	2	30	0	1nb

Abbottabad Bowling

	O	M	R	W			O	M	R	W	
Junaid Khan	21	3	82	0			14	2	57	1	1w
Rahimbaz Khan	15	2	42	2			20	4	70	2	2w
Noor-ul-Amin	28	8	81	5			32	7	97	3	
Iftikhar Mahmood	7.3	1	22	1		(5)	4	2	5	0	
Riaz Kail	3	1	10	0		(4)	3	0	17	0	
Khalid Usman	1	0	7	0							

Umpires: Afzaal Ahmed and Hakeem Shah.　Referee: Anis Sheikh.　　　Toss: Abbottabad

Close of Play: 1st day: Islamabad (1) 77-0 (Raheel Majeed 47*, Umair Khan 29*, 16 overs); 2nd day: Abbottabad (2) 66-2 (Fawad Khan 36*, Usman Khan 13*, 23 overs); 3rd day: Abbottabad (2) 299 all out.

KHAN RESEARCH LABORATORIES v ZARAI TARAQIATI BANK LIMITED

Played at Khan Research Laboratories Ground, Rawalpindi, October 20, 21, 22, 23, 2007.
Quaid-e-Azam Trophy 2007/08 - Group B
Match drawn.   (Points: Khan Research Laboratories 3, Zarai Taraqiati Bank Limited 0)

KHAN RESEARCH LABORATORIES

1	Saeed Anwar	lbw b Imran Sabir	6	c sub (Inam-ul-Haq) b Junaid Nadir	19
2	Azhar Ali	c Shakeel Ansar b Imran Sabir	6	not out	100
3	Bilal Asad	lbw b Mohammad Khalil	0	b Junaid Nadir	8
4	Bazid Khan	c Afaq Raheem b Mohammad Khalil	122	c Wajahatullah Wasti b Zohaib Khan	5
5	*Mohammad Wasim	run out (Aamer Bashir)	92	(6) b Junaid Nadir	20
6	Shehzad Malik	b Mohammad Khalil	0	(5) c Mohammad Khalil b Imran Sabir	7
7	Yasir Arafat	lbw b Mohammad Khalil	23	b Junaid Nadir	0
8	†Zulfiqar Jan	not out	29	lbw b Mohammad Khalil	8
9	Shoaib Akhtar	b Imran Sabir	0	not out	11
10	Jaffar Nazir	c Wajahatullah Wasti b Mohammad Khalil	18		
11	Saeed Ajmal	lbw b Mohammad Khalil	0		
	Extras	lb 5, w 1, nb 3	9	b 22, lb 6, w 1, nb 12	41
			305	(7 wickets, declared)	219

FoW (1): 1-11, 2-12, 3-12, 4-204, 5-206, 6-256, 7-257, 8-258, 9-305, 10-305
FoW (2): 1-55, 2-75, 3-88, 4-108, 5-165, 6-170, 7-187

ZARAI TARAQIATI BANK LIMITED

1	Afaq Raheem	st Zulfiqar Jan b Saeed Ajmal	43	not out	22
2	Atif Ashraf	c Zulfiqar Jan b Yasir Arafat	1	lbw b Yasir Arafat	7
3	Umar Javed	lbw b Jaffar Nazir	12	lbw b Mohammad Wasim	9
4	Aamer Bashir	c Zulfiqar Jan b Jaffar Nazir	10		
5	*Wajahatullah Wasti	c Bazid Khan b Yasir Arafat	76		
6	Adnan Raza	c Zulfiqar Jan b Yasir Arafat	44		
7	†Shakeel Ansar	b Jaffar Nazir	11	(4) not out	1
8	Imran Sabir	b Shoaib Akhtar	26		
9	Zohaib Khan	not out	21		
10	Junaid Nadir	b Yasir Arafat	0		
11	Mohammad Khalil	c Zulfiqar Jan b Jaffar Nazir	14		
	Extras	b 3, lb 4, w 5, nb 5	17	b 1	1
			275	(2 wickets)	40

FoW (1): 1-4, 2-30, 3-56, 4-80, 5-157, 6-188, 7-235, 8-241, 9-243, 10-275
FoW (2): 1-12, 2-39

ZTBl Bowling	O	M	R	W			O	M	R	W	
Mohammad Khalil	24.5	6	62	6			15	6	22	1	
Imran Sabir	19	1	71	3			16	7	37	1	1w
Junaid Nadir	13	1	59	0	1w,1nb	(4)	13	1	59	4	5nb
Zohaib Khan	36	3	90	0		(5)	22.3	4	48	1	4nb
Umar Javed	4	0	11	0	2nb	(3)	11	4	23	0	3nb
Adnan Raza	3	0	7	0							
Wajahatullah Wasti						(6)	1	0	2	0	

KRL Bowling	O	M	R	W			O	M	R	W	
Shoaib Akhtar	17	2	49	1	3nb		5	0	21	0	
Yasir Arafat	25	4	69	4	5w		5	1	8	1	
Jaffar Nazir	18.5	2	51	4	2nb		2	0	6	0	
Bilal Asad	16	6	29	0							
Saeed Ajmal	28	8	67	1		(4)	5	5	0	0	
Saeed Anwar	2	0	3	0							
Mohammad Wasim						(5)	4	1	4	1	
Shehzad Malik						(6)	1	1	0	0	

Umpires: Iftikhar Malik and Ijaz Ahmed. Referee: Aziz-ur-Rehman.   Toss: Zarai Taraqiati Bank Limited
Close of Play: 1st day: Khan Research Laboratories (1) 253-5 (Bazid Khan 120*, Yasir Arafat 22*, 83 overs); 2nd day: Zarai Taraqiati Bank Limited (1) 155-4 (Wajahatullah Wasti 39*, Adnan Raza 44*, 59 overs); 3rd day: Khan Research Laboratories (2) 75-2 (Azhar Ali 36*, 26 overs).
Bazid Khan's 122 took 250 balls in 316 minutes and included 15 fours. Azhar Ali's 100 took 250 balls in 363 minutes and included 11 fours and 1 six.

LAHORE RAVI v WATER AND POWER DEVELOPMENT AUTHORITY

Played at Lahore City Cricket Association Ground, October 20, 21, 22, 23, 2007.
Quaid-e-Azam Trophy 2007/08 - Group A
Water and Power Development Authority won by nine wickets.   (Points: Lahore Ravi 0, Water and Power Development Authority 9)

LAHORE RAVI

1	Kashif Siddiq	c Sarfraz Ahmed b Shabbir Ahmed	53	(6) not out	52
2	Rizwan Ahmed	c Zulqarnain Haider b Shabbir Ahmed	8	(1) c Zulqarnain Haider b Sarfraz Ahmed	5
3	Rizwan Aamer	c Aqeel Ahmed b Bilal Khilji	11	(2) lbw b Aqeel Ahmed	32
4	Ashraf Ali	c Atiq-ur-Rehman b Aqeel Ahmed	2	(3) c Atiq-ur-Rehman b Kashif Raza	10
5	Arsalan Mir	lbw b Shabbir Ahmed	5	(4) c and b Aqeel Ahmed	56
6	†Shahbaz Butt	c Tariq Aziz b Aqeel Ahmed	22	(5) lbw b Aqeel Ahmed	16
7	*Junaid Zia	c Zulqarnain Haider b Sarfraz Ahmed	50	b Aqeel Ahmed	1
8	Waqas Ahmed	c sub b Aqeel Ahmed	45	b Shabbir Ahmed	2
9	Kashif Shafi	c Zulqarnain Haider b Kashif Raza	13	c Atiq-ur-Rehman b Aqeel Ahmed	1
10	Usama Aftab	not out	11	c Zulqarnain Haider b Shabbir Ahmed	6
11	Salman Rahat	c Kashif Raza b Aqeel Ahmed	7	lbw b Aqeel Ahmed	9
	Extras	b 4, lb 4, nb 16	24	lb 1, nb 24	25
			251		**215**

FoW (1): 1-40, 2-64, 3-82, 4-89, 5-116, 6-124, 7-206, 8-218, 9-228, 10-251
FoW (2): 1-5, 2-32, 3-59, 4-79, 5-158, 6-163, 7-172, 8-175, 9-193, 10-215

WATER AND POWER DEVELOPMENT AUTHORITY

1	Masood Asim	c Waqas Ahmed b Salman Rahat	12	c Waqas Ahmed b Junaid Zia	1
2	Atiq-ur-Rehman	c Shahbaz Butt b Salman Rahat	19	not out	8
3	†Zulqarnain Haider	c Arsalan Mir b Waqas Ahmed	37		
4	Tariq Aziz	c Shahbaz Butt b Junaid Zia	53	(3) not out	12
5	Aamer Sajjad	lbw b Salman Rahat	88		
6	Bilal Khilji	not out	127		
7	Ali Azmat	c Ashraf Ali b Junaid Zia	14		
8	Aqeel Ahmed	c Rizwan Ahmed b Junaid Zia	5		
9	*Shabbir Ahmed	lbw b Waqas Ahmed	32		
10	Kashif Raza	st Shahbaz Butt b Usama Aftab	22		
11	Sarfraz Ahmed	c Ashraf Ali b Usama Aftab	0		
	Extras	b 12, lb 10, w 3, nb 12	37		
			446	(1 wicket)	**21**

FoW (1): 1-21, 2-67, 3-77, 4-176, 5-288, 6-305, 7-323, 8-379, 9-446, 10-446
FoW (2): 1-2

Water and Power Development Authority Bowling

	O	M	R	W			O	M	R	W	
Shabbir Ahmed	16	4	60	3	10nb		17	3	53	2	10nb
Kashif Raza	16	2	69	1	5nb	(3)	14	2	52	1	6nb
Sarfraz Ahmed	17	8	25	1		(2)	14	5	34	1	1nb
Bilal Khilji	4	2	4	1							
Aqeel Ahmed	17.2	3	80	4	1nb	(4)	20.3	1	75	6	3nb
Ali Azmat	1	0	5	0							

Lahore Ravi Bowling

	O	M	R	W			O	M	R	W
Junaid Zia	35	5	107	3	1nb		1.4	0	11	1
Salman Rahat	29	2	112	3	3w,4nb		1	0	10	0
Waqas Ahmed	20	5	64	2	5nb					
Arsalan Mir	8	2	27	0	2nb					
Kashif Shafi	26	9	53	0						
Usama Aftab	11	3	47	2						
Kashif Siddiq	4	0	14	0						

Umpires: Ehtesham-ul-Haq and Mohammad Arif.   Referee: Abdus Sami.   Toss: Water and Power Development Authority

Close of Play: 1st day: Water and Power Development Authority (1) 33-1 (Atiq-ur-Rehman 9*, Zulqarnain Haider 8*, 9 overs); 2nd day: Water and Power Development Authority (1) 276-4 (Aamer Sajjad 86*, Bilal Khilji 47*, 92 overs); 3rd day: Lahore Ravi (2) 101-4 (Arsalan Mir 20*, Kashif Siddiq 8*, 34 overs).
Bilal Khilji's 127 took 233 balls in 330 minutes and included 19 fours.

PAKISTAN INTERNATIONAL AIRLINES v SUI NORTHERN GAS PIPELINES LIMITED

Played at Sheikhupura Stadium, October 20, 21, 22, 23, 2007.
Quaid-e-Azam Trophy 2007/08 - Group B
Pakistan International Airlines won by six wickets. (Points: Pakistan International Airlines 9, Sui Northern Gas Pipelines Limited 0)

SUI NORTHERN GAS PIPELINES LIMITED

1	Yasir Arafat	b Najaf Shah	24	run out	74
2	Majid Jahangir	b Fazl-e-Akbar	4	lbw b Fazl-e-Akbar	0
3	Bilal Azmat	lbw b Fazl-e-Akbar	1	lbw b Fazl-e-Akbar	14
4	*Azhar Shafiq	c Agha Sabir b Tahir Khan	15	(6) b Fazl-e-Akbar	55
5	Khurram Shehzad	c Sarfraz Ahmed b Najaf Shah	0	(4) lbw b Anwar Ali	0
6	Saleem Mughal	c Sarfraz Ahmed b Najaf Shah	29	(7) run out	6
7	†Adnan Akmal	c Sarfraz Ahmed b Fazl-e-Akbar	9	(8) st Sarfraz Ahmed b Tahir Khan	31
8	Imran Khalid	not out	39	(5) b Fazl-e-Akbar	1
9	Samiullah Khan	c and b Tahir Khan	1	(11) c and b Tahir Khan	1
10	Adil Raza	st Sarfraz Ahmed b Tahir Khan	8	(9) c Agha Sabir b Anwar Ali	1
11	Imran Ali	c Faisal Iqbal b Najaf Shah	5	(10) not out	1
	Extras	lb 13, w 3, nb 1	17	b 5, lb 4, w 2	11
			152		**195**

FoW (1): 1-17, 2-22, 3-46, 4-46, 5-60, 6-75, 7-116, 8-119, 9-137, 10-152
FoW (2): 1-1, 2-37, 3-38, 4-45, 5-141, 6-147, 7-186, 8-189, 9-193, 10-195

PAKISTAN INTERNATIONAL AIRLINES

1	Khurram Manzoor	b Samiullah Khan	21	c Majid Jahangir b Imran Ali	47
2	Kamran Sajid	c Majid Jahangir b Adil Raza	22	lbw b Samiullah Khan	31
3	Agha Sabir	c Majid Jahangir b Adil Raza	42	c Majid Jahangir b Imran Ali	11
4	*Faisal Iqbal	b Adil Raza	2	c Adil Raza b Samiullah Khan	18
5	Shoaib Khan	b Adil Raza	8	not out	20
6	Fahad Iqbal	c Bilal Azmat b Adil Raza	0	not out	4
7	†Sarfraz Ahmed	c and b Imran Ali	59		
8	Tahir Khan	c Imran Ali b Imran Khalid	22		
9	Anwar Ali	c Adil Raza b Imran Ali	8		
10	Najaf Shah	c Bilal Azmat b Imran Khalid	10		
11	Fazl-e-Akbar	not out	1		
	Extras	lb 16, w 1, nb 2	19	b 1, lb 1, nb 1	3
			214	(4 wickets)	**134**

FoW (1): 1-51, 2-51, 3-53, 4-76, 5-76, 6-143, 7-193, 8-193, 9-209, 10-214
FoW (2): 1-62, 2-74, 3-109, 4-

Pakistan International Airlines Bowling

	O	M	R	W		O	M	R	W	
Fazl-e-Akbar	12	2	31	3	1nb	17	3	41	4	
Najaf Shah	14.4	6	42	4		15	1	57	0	
Anwar Ali	14	3	42	0	3w	13	6	22	2	2w
Tahir Khan	11	5	20	3		24	7	50	2	
Kamran Sajid	3	0	4	0		4	0	7	0	
Agha Sabir					(6)	3	0	9	0	

Sui Northern Gas Pipelines Limited Bowling

	O	M	R	W			O	M	R	W	
Samiullah Khan	16	3	42	1	1nb		17	3	73	2	
Imran Ali	25	7	63	2	1w	(3)	12	5	27	2	
Adil Raza	20	6	42	5	1nb	(2)	12	6	25	0	1nb
Imran Khalid	19	4	51	2			5	2	4	0	
Yasir Arafat						(5)	0.5	0	3	0	

Umpires: Ahmed Shahab and Javed Ashraf. Referee: Saadat Ali. Toss: Pakistan International Airlines

Close of Play: 1st day: Pakistan International Airlines (1) 46-0 (Khurram Manzoor 21*, Kamran Sajid 17*, 19 overs); 2nd day: Sui Northern Gas Pipelines Limited (2) 43-3 (Yasir Arafat 23*, Imran Khalid 0*, 11 overs); 3rd day: Pakistan International Airlines (2) 30-0 (Khurram Manzoor 24*, Kamran Sajid 5*, 11 overs).

PESHAWAR v LAHORE SHALIMAR

Played at Arbab Niaz Stadium, Peshawar, October 20, 21, 22, 23, 2007.
Quaid-e-Azam Trophy 2007/08 - Group B
Match drawn.   (Points: Peshawar 3, Lahore Shalimar 0)

LAHORE SHALIMAR

1	Junaid Malik	lbw b Nauman Habib	10	c Sajjad Ahmed b Akbar Badshah	59	
2	Salman Akbar	c Shehzad Khan b Imran Khan	15	c Mohammad Fayyaz b Akbar Badshah	79	
3	Haroon Rasheed	b Nauman Habib	35	lbw b Nauman Habib	6	
4	Shahnawaz Malik	lbw b Nauman Habib	0	not out	51	
5	Suleman Khan	c Shehzad Khan b Mohammad Fayyaz	26	c Fawad Ali b Mohammad Fayyaz	84	
6	Ahmed Butt	c Nawaz Ahmed b Imran Khan	29	not out	1	
7	Mohammad Hussain	c Mahfooz Sabri b Mohammad Fayyaz	1			
8	*†Ali Raza	not out	56			
9	Mohammad Saeed	b Riaz Afridi	55			
10	Asif Raza	b Nauman Habib	4			
11	Usman Malik	c Sajjad Ahmed b Nauman Habib	0			
	Extras	b 4, lb 7, w 1, nb 3	15	b 5, lb 2, w 1, nb 13	21	
			246	(4 wickets)	301	

FoW (1): 1-23, 2-33, 3-33, 4-93, 5-105, 6-110, 7-138, 8-225, 9-236, 10-246
FoW (2): 1-146, 2-156, 3-156, 4-291

PESHAWAR

1	Naved Khan	c Ahmed Butt b Mohammad Saeed	40
2	Fawad Ali	c Ali Raza b Asif Raza	2
3	Mohammad Fayyaz	c Ali Raza b Asif Raza	71
4	Nawaz Ahmed	lbw b Mohammad Saeed	109
5	*Akbar Badshah	lbw b Mohammad Saeed	38
6	Sajjad Ahmed	b Asif Raza	0
7	Mahfooz Sabri	not out	58
8	†Shehzad Khan	c Mohammad Saeed b Mohammad Hussain	57
9	Riaz Afridi		
10	Nauman Habib		
11	Imran Khan		
	Extras	b 1, lb 14, w 8, nb 13	36
		(7 wickets, declared)	411

FoW (1): 1-8, 2-129, 3-151, 4-253, 5-259, 6-318, 7-410

Peshawar Bowling

	O	M	R	W		O	M	R	W	
Riaz Afridi	23	6	59	1		7.2	3	17	0	
Nauman Habib	19.5	6	46	5	1w,2nb	19	4	60	1	
Imran Khan	20	7	53	2	1nb	22.4	7	63	0	2nb
Mohammad Fayyaz	22	4	61	2		24	6	69	1	
Akbar Badshah	3	1	3	0		16	7	27	2	7nb
Mahfooz Sabri	1	0	13	0		4	1	25	0	
Nawaz Ahmed					(7)	3	0	19	0	1w,4nb
Sajjad Ahmed					(8)	10	2	14	0	

Lahore Shalimar Bowling

	O	M	R	W	
Asif Raza	36	9	110	3	4nb
Mohammad Saeed	24	3	117	3	8w,9nb
Mohammad Hussain	48	17	107	1	
Usman Malik	22	6	54	0	
Ahmed Butt	2	0	8	0	

Umpires: Islam Khan and Saleem Badar. Referee: Ishtiaq Ahmed.   Toss: Lahore Shalimar

Close of Play: 1st day: Lahore Shalimar (1) 230-8 (Ali Raza 44*, Asif Raza 1*, 83 overs); 2nd day: Peshawar (1) 228-3 (Nawaz Ahmed 58*, Akbar Badshah 28*, 81 overs); 3rd day: Lahore Shalimar (2) 108-0 (Junaid Malik 42*, Salman Akbar 59*, 30 overs).

Nawaz Ahmed's 109 took 199 balls in 243 minutes and included 15 fours and 1 six.

SIALKOT v NATIONAL BANK OF PAKISTAN

Played at Jinnah Stadium, Sialkot, October 20, 21, 2007.
Quaid-e-Azam Trophy 2007/08 - Group A (replayed)
Match drawn.

SIALKOT

1	Mohammad Boota	c Amin-ur-Rehman b Wasim Khan	1
2	Qamar Shahzad	c Nasir Jamshed b Tahir Mughal	2
3	Shahid Siddiq	not out	27
4	Faisal Khan	run out (Wahab Riaz)	0
5	Bilal Hussain	c Nasir Jamshed b Wasim Khan	48
6	Imran Malik	run out (Uzair-ul-Haq)	0
7	*Mohammad Ayub	retired hurt	2
8	†Khalid Mahmood	not out	4
9	Mohammad Wasim		
10	Mohammad Ali		
11	Naeem Anjum		
	Extras	b 19, lb 4, w 1, nb 6	30
		(5 wickets)	114

FoW (1): 1-4, 2-4, 3-4, 4-97, 5-97

NATIONAL BANK OF PAKISTAN

1   Nasir Jamshed
2   †Amin-ur-Rehman
3   Shahid Yousuf
4   Naumanullah
5   Naved Latif
6   *Mansoor Amjad
7   Tahir Mughal
8   Fawad Alam
9   Wahab Riaz
10   Wasim Khan
11   Uzair-ul-Haq

National Bank of Pakistan Bowling

	O	M	R	W	
Tahir Mughal	11	4	20	1	1nb
Wasim Khan	10	4	27	2	1w
Wahab Riaz	5	0	21	0	5nb
Uzair-ul-Haq	5.2	0	23	0	
Mansoor Amjad	1	1	0	0	

Umpires: Atiq Khan and Masood Khan.   Referee: Mohammad Javed.   Toss: National Bank of Pakistan

Close of Play: 1st day: Sialkot (1) 106-5 (Shahid Siddiq 23*, Mohammad Ayub 2*, 30 overs).

Mohammad Ayub retired hurt in the Sialkot first innings having scored 2 (team had lost 5 wickets).

The match, originally scheduled for four days, was called off owing to poor pitch conditions early on the second day. It was not counted in the Quaid-e-Azam Group A table but is still regarded as first-class. After a fresh pitch had been prepared, a new match was started on what would have been day 4, but only one day was available for it and it is not regarded as first-class. The match was eventually replayed on 24-27 December (see page 320).

HABIB BANK LIMITED v PAKISTAN CUSTOMS

Played at National Bank of Pakistan Sports Complex, Karachi, October 21, 22, 23, 24, 2007.
Quaid-e-Azam Trophy 2007/08 - Group A
Habib Bank Limited won by 262 runs.   (Points: Habib Bank Limited 9, Pakistan Customs 0)

HABIB BANK LIMITED

1	Imran Farhat	c Yasir Shah b Rehan Riaz	60	c Yasir Shah b Yasir Hussain	61
2	Taufeeq Umar	lbw b Raees Amjad	9	c Rehan Riaz b Yasir Hussain	73
3	Rafatullah Mohmand	lbw b Sajjad Hussain	8	run out	32
4	*Hasan Raza	b Rehan Riaz	1	lbw b Yasir Shah	47
5	Khaqan Arsal	c Khan b Raees Amjad	1	(8) not out	9
6	Aftab Alam	run out	65	(5) b Raees Amjad	17
7	†Humayun Farhat	lbw b Rehan Rafiq	75	(6) lbw b Rehan Riaz	7
8	Danish Kaneria	c Raees Amjad b Sajjad Hussain	14	(9) b Yasir Hussain	19
9	Kamran Hussain	b Yasir Hussain	29	(7) c Sajjad Hussain b Yasir Shah	13
10	Fahad Masood	not out	1		
11	Irfan Fazil	lbw b Yasir Hussain	0	(10) c Hasnain Abbas b Yasir Shah	0
	Extras	b 10, lb 7, w 2, nb 7	26	b 3, lb 3, w 2, nb 5	13
			289	(9 wickets, declared)	291

FoW (1): 1-19, 2-42, 3-45, 4-52, 5-90, 6-200, 7-231, 8-286, 9-289, 10-289
FoW (2): 1-135, 2-160, 3-216, 4-233, 5-246, 6-263, 7-263, 8-290, 9-291

PAKISTAN CUSTOMS

1	Hasnain Abbas	lbw b Danish Kaneria	7	st Humayun Farhat b Danish Kaneria	25
2	R.M.Khan	lbw b Fahad Masood	46	c Humayun Farhat b Kamran Hussain	6
3	B.M.Shafayat	b Irfan Fazil	38	b Fahad Masood	0
4	Asif Iqbal	c Humayun Farhat b Fahad Masood	9	lbw b Fahad Masood	0
5	*Rehan Rafiq	lbw b Kamran Hussain	9	not out	45
6	Yasir Hussain	c Humayun Farhat b Kamran Hussain	0	b Danish Kaneria	0
7	†Mohammad Hasan	b Danish Kaneria	19	c Taufeeq Umar b Fahad Masood	23
8	Yasir Shah	lbw b Kamran Hussain	17	c Imran Farhat b Kamran Hussain	6
9	Raees Amjad	b Kamran Hussain	38	lbw b Danish Kaneria	8
10	Sajjad Hussain	b Kamran Hussain	0	lbw b Irfan Fazil	2
11	Rehan Riaz	not out	3	c and b Irfan Fazil	1
	Extras	b 3, lb 3, nb 4	10	lb 1, nb 5	6
			196		122

FoW (1): 1-27, 2-69, 3-81, 4-114, 5-114, 6-114, 7-148, 8-174, 9-174, 10-196
FoW (2): 1-15, 2-16, 3-16, 4-47, 5-56, 6-86, 7-95, 8-111, 9-114, 10-122

Pakistan Customs Bowling

	O	M	R	W		O	M	R	W	
Raees Amjad	12	0	54	2	3nb	11	1	55	1	
Sajjad Hussain	18	3	78	2	1nb	9	0	54	0	2nb
Rehan Riaz	9	2	30	2	1w	10	0	35	1	2w
Yasir Shah	18	2	53	0		25.3	1	74	3	1nb
Asif Iqbal	4	1	13	0	1w					
Rehan Rafiq	10	1	32	1	2nb					
Yasir Hussain	3.5	0	12	2		(5) 16	3	67	3	2nb

Habib Bank Limited Bowling

	O	M	R	W		O	M	R	W	
Fahad Masood	17	7	37	2		12	1	30	3	
Kamran Hussain	16.1	5	30	5		11	2	38	2	
Danish Kaneria	26	11	77	3	(4)	11	4	21	3	
Irfan Fazil	6	2	21	1	4nb	(3) 7.3	1	28	2	5nb
Imran Farhat	4	0	21	0						
Taufeeq Umar	1	0	4	0						
Aftab Alam						(5) 4	3	4	0	

Umpires: Khalid Mahmood and Shakeel Khan. Referee: Ilyas Khan.   Toss: Pakistan Customs

Close of Play: 1st day: Pakistan Customs (1) 9-0 (Hasnain Abbas 2*, Khan 7*, 6 overs); 2nd day: Habib Bank Limited (2) 65-0 (Imran Farhat 16*, Taufeeq Umar 41*, 16 overs); 3rd day: Pakistan Customs (2) 77-5 (Rehan Rafiq 26*, Mohammad Hasan 17*, 27 overs).

HYDERABAD v KARACHI WHITES

Played at Niaz Stadium, Hyderabad, October 21, 22, 23, 24, 2007.
Quaid-e-Azam Trophy 2007/08 - Group A
Match drawn.   (Points: Hyderabad 0, Karachi Whites 3)

HYDERABAD

1	Akram Khan	c and b Mohammad Sami	72	c Tanvir Ahmed b Tabish Nawab	29
2	Faisal Athar	lbw b Tanvir Ahmed	4	c Afsar Nawaz b Tanvir Ahmed	16
3	Hanif-ur-Rehman	b Mohammad Sami	25		
4	Rizwan Ahmed	c Asim Kamal b Mohammad Sami	101		
5	Zahid Khan	lbw b Tabish Nawab	37	(3) lbw b Tabish Nawab	80
6	Shahid Qambrani	c Fahad Khan b Afsar Nawaz	98	(7) not out	7
7	*†Hanif Malik	c Afsar Nawaz b Tabish Nawab	24	(4) c Asim Kamal b Afsar Nawaz	64
8	Nasir Awais	c Afsar Nawaz b Tabish Nawab	0	(5) c and b Afsar Nawaz	7
9	Farhan Ayub	c Asim Kamal b Tabish Nawab	9	(8) not out	1
10	Naeem-ur-Rehman	c Wajihuddin b Tabish Nawab	14	(6) c Asad Shafiq b Afsar Nawaz	8
11	Sufyan Ali	not out	1		
	Extras	b 5, lb 4, w 6, nb 9	24	b 4, lb 2, nb 11	17
			409	**(6 wickets)**	**229**

FoW (1): 1-6, 2-50, 3-194, 4-234, 5-289, 6-375, 7-375, 8-393, 9-395, 10-409
FoW (2): 1-26, 2-74, 3-196, 4-211, 5-212, 6-221

KARACHI WHITES

1	Shan Masood	lbw b Rizwan Ahmed	54
2	Asad Shafiq	lbw b Nasir Awais	113
3	Wajihuddin	lbw b Rizwan Ahmed	7
4	Zeeshan Pervez	b Naeem-ur-Rehman	23
5	Asim Kamal	c Akram Khan b Rizwan Ahmed	26
6	Afsar Nawaz	c Zahid Khan b Nasir Awais	108
7	†Owais Rehmani	c Hanif Malik b Naeem-ur-Rehman	12
8	*Mohammad Sami	lbw b Farhan Ayub	17
9	Tanvir Ahmed	lbw b Rizwan Ahmed	50
10	Tabish Nawab	run out (Akram Khan)	10
11	Fahad Khan	not out	0
	Extras	b 2, lb 2, w 9, nb 26	39
			459

FoW (1): 1-154, 2-162, 3-215, 4-220, 5-257, 6-296, 7-335, 8-408, 9-459, 10-459

Karachi Whites Bowling	O	M	R	W		O	M	R	W	
Mohammad Sami	28.3	6	82	3		5	0	28	0	2nb
Tanvir Ahmed	27.3	3	73	1	2nb	6	2	26	1	3nb
Fahad Khan	25	7	69	0	1w	3	0	14	0	
Tabish Nawab	44.1	6	124	5	7nb	16	0	81	2	6nb
Afsar Nawaz	10	1	29	1		10	3	19	3	
Wajihuddin	6	2	23	0						
Asim Kamal						(6) 3	0	15	0	
Zeeshan Pervez						(7) 2	0	18	0	
Asad Shafiq						(8) 3	0	22	0	

Hyderabad Bowling	O	M	R	W	
Farhan Ayub	23.4	3	99	1	2w,10nb
Sufyan Ali	9	1	32	0	
Naeem-ur-Rehman	18	1	71	2	3w,2nb
Nasir Awais	33.3	8	88	2	
Rizwan Ahmed	42	6	147	4	14nb
Hanif-ur-Rehman	3.2	1	6	0	
Faisal Athar	3	0	12	0	

Umpires: Ahsan Raza and Zaheer Ahmed. Referee: Naeem Ahmed.   Toss: Hyderabad

Close of Play: 1st day: Hyderabad (1) 227-3 (Rizwan Ahmed 100*, Zahid Khan 11*, 83 overs); 2nd day: Karachi Whites (1) 101-0 (Shan Masood 32*, Asad Shafiq 63*, 24 overs); 3rd day: Karachi Whites (1) 386-7 (Afsar Nawaz 64*, Tanvir Ahmed 35*, 107 overs).
Rizwan Ahmed's 101 took 234 balls in 295 minutes and included 7 fours and 2 sixes. Asad Shafiq's 113 took 183 balls in 257 minutes and included 14 fours. Afsar Nawaz's 108 took 211 balls in 294 minutes and included 12 fours.

KARACHI BLUES v RAWALPINDI

Played at United Bank Limited Sports Complex, Karachi, October 21, 22, 23, 24, 2007.
Quaid-e-Azam Trophy 2007/08 - Group B
Rawalpindi won by 152 runs.   (Points: Karachi Blues 0, Rawalpindi 9)

RAWALPINDI

1	Mohammad Ibrahim	run out (Malik Aftab)	51	run out (Malik Aftab)		0
2	Babar Naeem	c Shadab Kabir b Azam Hussain	41	c Sajid Hanif b Tariq Haroon		28
3	Adnan Mufti	run out (Fahadullah Khan)	11	(6) lbw b Tariq Haroon		1
4	Zahid Mansoor	c Fahadullah Khan b Faraz Ahmed	11	(3) b Malik Aftab		17
5	*Naved Ashraf	c Mansoor Baig b Azam Hussain	76	lbw b Faraz Ahmed		47
6	Usman Saeed	c Faraz Ahmed b Azam Hussain	0	(4) lbw b Tariq Haroon		1
7	Yasim Murtaza	c Sajid Hanif b Tariq Haroon	5	c Mansoor Baig b Azam Hussain		54
8	†Sajid Mahmood	c Shadab Kabir b Azam Hussain	5	(11) b Azam Hussain		0
9	Yasir Ali	c Fahadullah Khan b Azam Hussain	18	(8) st Sajid Hanif b Azam Hussain		19
10	Rizwan Akbar	c Shadab Kabir b Azam Hussain	5	(9) lbw b Azam Hussain		0
11	Mohammad Ayaz	not out	2	(10) not out		0
	Extras	b 3, lb 4, w 1, nb 1	9	lb 4, w 5		9
			234			**176**

FoW (1): 1-98, 2-98, 3-118, 4-127, 5-138, 6-157, 7-172, 8-223, 9-227, 10-234
FoW (2): 1-0, 2-42, 3-48, 4-52, 5-53, 6-134, 7-167, 8-171, 9-176, 10-176

KARACHI BLUES

1	Shadab Kabir	c Sajid Mahmood b Mohammad Ayaz	47	c Babar Naeem b Rizwan Akbar	17
2	Ali Asad	c Sajid Mahmood b Rizwan Akbar	2	run out	4
3	†Sajid Hanif	b Yasir Ali	8	(9) c Adnan Mufti b Mohammad Ibrahim	5
4	Faraz Patel	c Sajid Mahmood b Rizwan Akbar	63	(5) c Zahid Mansoor b Mohammad Ayaz	19
5	Fahadullah Khan	lbw b Mohammad Ayaz	0	(6) b Rizwan Akbar	0
6	*Mansoor Khan	lbw b Rizwan Akbar	3	(7) c Mohammad Ibrahim b Rizwan Akbar	3
7	Tariq Haroon	c Sajid Mahmood b Rizwan Akbar	18	(8) lbw b Mohammad Ayaz	16
8	Mansoor Baig	lbw b Babar Naeem	1	(3) c Yasim Murtaza b Rizwan Akbar	1
9	Azam Hussain	c Sajid Mahmood b Babar Naeem	0	(10) not out	0
10	Faraz Ahmed	lbw b Rizwan Akbar	1	(4) c Mohammad Ibrahim b Yasir Ali	4
11	Malik Aftab	not out	21	run out	0
	Extras	lb 2, w 1, nb 14	17	lb 2, nb 5	7
			181		**77**

FoW (1): 1-21, 2-46, 3-75, 4-81, 5-101, 6-127, 7-128, 8-130, 9-131, 10-181
FoW (2): 1-6, 2-11, 3-22, 4-32, 5-33, 6-39, 7-59, 8-75, 9-75, 10-77

Karachi Blues Bowling

	O	M	R	W			O	M	R	W	
Malik Aftab	17	3	41	0		(2)	23	3	63	1	4w
Faraz Ahmed	14	3	42	1	1w,1nb	(1)	10	3	39	1	1w
Tariq Haroon	17	6	54	1			13	7	17	3	
Azam Hussain	24.2	5	70	6			12.2	2	40	4	
Mansoor Khan	10	2	20	0			5	2	13	0	

Rawalpindi Bowling

	O	M	R	W			O	M	R	W	
Yasir Ali	18	4	42	1	3nb		13	5	21	1	
Rizwan Akbar	26	10	47	5	3nb		17	7	37	4	2nb
Mohammad Ayaz	13	0	38	2	1w,8nb		6.4	2	10	2	2nb
Yasim Murtaza	13	7	29	0							
Babar Naeem	16	7	23	2							
Mohammad Ibrahim						(4)	2	0	7	1	

Umpires: Akbar Khan and Mian Mohammad Aslam. Referee: Mahmood Rasheed.   Toss: Karachi Blues

Close of Play: 1st day: Rawalpindi (1) 234 all out; 2nd day: Karachi Blues (1) 174-9 (Faraz Patel 62*, Malik Aftab 15*, 83 overs);
3rd day: Karachi Blues (2) 22-3 (Faraz Ahmed 0*, 11.4 overs).

FAISALABAD v NATIONAL BANK OF PAKISTAN

Played at Iqbal Stadium, Faisalabad, October 26, 27, 28, 29, 2007.
Quaid-e-Azam Trophy 2007/08 - Group A
National Bank of Pakistan won by eight wickets.   (Points: Faisalabad 0, National Bank of Pakistan 9)

FAISALABAD

1	Imran Ali	b Wahab Riaz	2	c Amin-ur-Rehman b Tahir Mughal	10
2	Abdul Mannan	c Amin-ur-Rehman b Uzair-ul-Haq	24	c Rashid Riaz b Wahab Riaz	1
3	Asif Hussain	lbw b Tahir Mughal	14	c Nasir Jamshed b Uzair-ul-Haq	1
4	Ammar Mahmood	c Irfanuddin b Uzair-ul-Haq	0	c Amin-ur-Rehman b Wahab Riaz	36
5	Usman Arshad	lbw b Irfanuddin	62	(6) c Fawad Alam b Irfanuddin	10
6	*Ijaz Ahmed	lbw b Tahir Mughal	5	(7) c Amin-ur-Rehman b Uzair-ul-Haq	23
7	†Mohammad Salman	lbw b Wasim Khan	61	(8) c Amin-ur-Rehman b Wahab Riaz	2
8	Ahmed Hayat	c Nasir Jamshed b Wahab Riaz	22	(9) b Wasim Khan	47
9	Asad Zarar	c Rashid Riaz b Irfanuddin	7	(5) c Rashid Riaz b Tahir Mughal	11
10	Shafqat Hussain	not out	10	c Amin-ur-Rehman b Tahir Mughal	3
11	Mohammad Talha	c Irfanuddin b Uzair-ul-Haq	20	not out	4
	Extras	b 2, lb 5, nb 11	18	b 4, lb 6, w 1, nb 5	16
			245		164

FoW (1): 1-13, 2-46, 3-46, 4-46, 5-62, 6-172, 7-207, 8-211, 9-216, 10-245
FoW (2): 1-6, 2-12, 3-22, 4-38, 5-70, 6-82, 7-90, 8-118, 9-137, 10-164

NATIONAL BANK OF PAKISTAN

1	Nasir Jamshed	c Asad Zarar b Ijaz Ahmed	126	not out	63
2	Rashid Riaz	run out (Shafqat Hussain)	51	run out (Shafqat Hussain)	20
3	Naumanullah	lbw b Ahmed Hayat	25	lbw b Shafqat Hussain	5
4	Qaiser Abbas	c and b Ijaz Ahmed	0	not out	14
5	*Fawad Alam	c Usman Arshad b Ahmed Hayat	9		
6	Tahir Mughal	lbw b Ahmed Hayat	33		
7	†Amin-ur-Rehman	run out (Usman Arshad)	4		
8	Wasim Khan	lbw b Shafqat Hussain	15		
9	Wahab Riaz	not out	6		
10	Irfanuddin	b Mohammad Talha	4		
11	Uzair-ul-Haq	b Mohammad Talha	0		
	Extras	b 2, lb 6, w 7, nb 3	18	b 4, lb 6, w 2, nb 5	17
			291	(2 wickets)	119

FoW (1): 1-160, 2-207, 3-207, 4-220, 5-221, 6-229, 7-247, 8-285, 9-291, 10-291
FoW (2): 1-67, 2-78

National Bank of Pakistan Bowling

	O	M	R	W			O	M	R	W	
Wasim Khan	19	5	55	1		(2)	9.3	3	16	1	
Wahab Riaz	16	1	51	2	7nb	(1)	12	2	32	3	4nb
Uzair-ul-Haq	11.5	2	31	3	3nb		12	3	42	2	1w
Tahir Mughal	12	3	43	2	1nb		15	4	35	3	1nb
Irfanuddin	20	5	40	2			8	0	15	1	
Qaiser Abbas	2	0	5	0			5	1	8	0	
Fawad Alam	3	0	13	0			1	0	5	0	
Naumanullah						(8)	1	0	1	0	

Faisalabad Bowling

	O	M	R	W			O	M	R	W	
Ahmed Hayat	16	0	67	3							
Mohammad Talha	20.4	3	75	2	7w,3nb	(1)	10	3	28	0	1w,5nb
Asad Zarar	14	6	34	0		(2)	11	0	28	0	1w
Shafqat Hussain	20	1	74	1			5.3	2	25	1	
Ijaz Ahmed	15	3	24	2		(3)	7	1	28	0	
Ammar Mahmood	1	0	9	0		(5)	1	1	0	0	

Umpires: Haider Lehri and Kaukab Butt.   Referee: Arshad Pervez.   Toss: National Bank of Pakistan

Close of Play: 1st day: Faisalabad (1) 243-9 (Shafqat Hussain 9*, Mohammad Talha 18*, 83 overs); 2nd day: National Bank of Pakistan (1) 269-7 (Tahir Mughal 26*, Wahab Riaz 3*, 80 overs); 3rd day: National Bank of Pakistan (2) 19-0 (Nasir Jamshed 6*, Rashid Riaz 6*, 8 overs).
Nasir Jamshed's 126 took 187 balls in 250 minutes and included 18 fours and a six.

HYDERABAD v HABIB BANK LIMITED

Played at Niaz Stadium, Hyderabad, October 26, 27, 28, 2007.
Quaid-e-Azam Trophy 2007/08 - Group A
Habib Bank Limited won by an innings and 122 runs.   (Points: Hyderabad 0, Habib Bank Limited 9)

HYDERABAD
1	Akram Khan	lbw b Mohammad Aslam	97	lbw b Kamran Hussain		0
2	Faisal Athar	c Humayun Farhat b Fahad Masood	6	lbw b Mohammad Aslam		30
3	Hanif-ur-Rehman	c Taufeeq Umar b Fahad Masood	9	b Mohammad Aslam		7
4	Zahid Khan	c Aftab Alam b Danish Kaneria	5	absent		0
5	Shahid Qambrani	c Khaqan Arsal b Mohammad Aslam	41	(4) lbw b Mohammad Aslam		5
6	*†Hanif Malik	c Hasan Raza b Mohammad Aslam	17	(5) run out		10
7	Nasir Awais	c Hasan Raza b Danish Kaneria	4	c Hasan Raza b Mohammad Aslam		42
8	Kashif Bhatti	lbw b Danish Kaneria	6	b Danish Kaneria		3
9	Farhan Ayub	lbw b Danish Kaneria	0	c Khaqan Arsal b Danish Kaneria		0
10	Naeem-ur-Rehman	not out	0	(6) c Taufeeq Umar b Mohammad Aslam		13
11	Kashif Pervez	lbw b Mohammad Aslam	4	(10) not out		0
	Extras	b 4, lb 3, w 1	8	b 3, nb 1		4
			197			114

FoW (1): 1-9, 2-25, 3-34, 4-114, 5-167, 6-174, 7-189, 8-189, 9-193, 10-197
FoW (2): 1-0, 2-34, 3-40, 4-47, 5-55, 6-79, 7-86, 8-114, 9-114

HABIB BANK LIMITED
1	Imran Farhat	c Hanif Malik b Kashif Pervez	9
2	Taufeeq Umar	b Farhan Ayub	71
3	Rafatullah Mohmand	c Naeem-ur-Rehman b Kashif Bhatti	51
4	*Hasan Raza	c Hanif Malik b Naeem-ur-Rehman	69
5	Aftab Alam	c Nasir Awais b Farhan Ayub	102
6	Khaqan Arsal	run out (Akram Khan)	13
7	†Humayun Farhat	lbw b Farhan Ayub	27
8	Kamran Hussain	lbw b Naeem-ur-Rehman	0
9	Danish Kaneria	b Nasir Awais	42
10	Fahad Masood	c Nasir Awais b Kashif Bhatti	26
11	Mohammad Aslam	not out	0
	Extras	b 7, lb 3, w 5, nb 8	23
			433

FoW (1): 1-28, 2-120, 3-165, 4-277, 5-315, 6-358, 7-359, 8-375, 9-429, 10-433

Habib Bank Limited Bowling	O	M	R	W		O	M	R	W	
Fahad Masood	12	3	18	2	(2)	2	1	7	0	
Kamran Hussain	7	1	26	0	(1)	7	1	25	1	1nb
Danish Kaneria	27	10	64	4		17.4	5	49	2	
Mohammad Aslam	23	10	33	4		15	8	28	5	
Imran Farhat	9	0	34	0						
Khaqan Arsal	1	0	2	0						
Aftab Alam	2	0	3	0						
Hasan Raza	3	0	10	0	1w					
Taufeeq Umar					(5)	1	0	2	0	

Hyderabad Bowling	O	M	R	W	
Farhan Ayub	21	1	84	3	4nb
Kashif Pervez	15	1	65	1	
Shahid Qambrani	5	0	12	0	
Naeem-ur-Rehman	8	1	48	2	4w,4nb
Nasir Awais	31.5	4	115	1	1w
Kashif Bhatti	26	3	78	2	
Hanif-ur-Rehman	6	1	21	0	

Umpires: Khalid Mahmood and Shakeel Khan.   Referee: Ilyas Khan.   Toss: Hyderabad

Close of Play: 1st day: Hyderabad (1) 193-4 (Naeem-ur-Rehman 14*, Kashif Pervez 14*, 82 overs); 2nd day: Habib Bank Limited (1) 299-4 (Aftab Alam 75*, Khaqan Arsal 6*, 80 overs).

The match was scheduled for four days but completed in three. Aftab Alam's 102 took 136 balls in 205 minutes and included 17 fours.

ISLAMABAD v LAHORE SHALIMAR

Played at Diamond Club Ground, Islamabad, October 26, 27, 28, 29, 2007.
Quaid-e-Azam Trophy 2007/08 - Group B
Islamabad won by two wickets. (Points: Islamabad 9, Lahore Shalimar 0)

LAHORE SHALIMAR

1	Junaid Malik	c Naeem Anjum b Rauf Akbar	10	b Shehzad Azam	2
2	Salman Akbar	c Fayyaz Ahmed b Saad Altaf	5	c Naeem Anjum b Saad Altaf	2
3	Haroon Rasheed	b Saad Altaf	4	(4) lbw b Saad Altaf	17
4	Sibtain Raza	c Naeem Anjum b Rauf Akbar	10	(3) b Saad Altaf	12
5	Suleman Khan	b Ameer Khan	88	lbw b Saad Altaf	4
6	Shahnawaz Malik	lbw b Rauf Akbar	0	(7) c Naeem Anjum b Saad Altaf	32
7	*†Ali Raza	c Naeem Anjum b Shehzad Azam	1	(9) not out	34
8	Mohammad Hussain	b Saad Altaf	34	b Ashar Zaidi	59
9	Mohammad Saeed	b Shehzad Azam	31	(6) c Fakhar Hussain b Shehzad Azam	4
10	Asif Raza	c Ashar Zaidi b Saad Altaf	16	c Raheel Majeed b Ashar Zaidi	0
11	Shahzad Ali	not out	0	c Naeem Anjum b Raheel Majeed	5
	Extras	b 9, lb 10, w 11, nb 20	50	b 6, lb 9, w 7, nb 22	44
			249		**215**

FoW (1): 1-13, 2-18, 3-22, 4-38, 5-43, 6-49, 7-148, 8-212, 9-235, 10-249
FoW (2): 1-5, 2-6, 3-33, 4-41, 5-51, 6-55, 7-127, 8-200, 9-200, 10-215

ISLAMABAD

1	Raheel Majeed	lbw b Asif Raza	4	c Sibtain Raza b Shahzad Ali	8
2	Umair Khan	c Ali Raza b Asif Raza	1	lbw b Mohammad Saeed	44
3	Farrukh Hayat	lbw b Asif Raza	2	c Mohammad Hussain b Mohammad Saeed	9
4	†Naeem Anjum	c Salman Akbar b Shahzad Ali	2	(7) c Ali Raza b Shahzad Ali	10
5	Fayyaz Ahmed	lbw b Shahzad Ali	58	b Shahzad Ali	32
6	Ameer Khan	c Salman Akbar b Asif Raza	5	c and b Mohammad Saeed	8
7	*Ashar Zaidi	c Suleman Khan b Mohammad Saeed	3	(4) c Junaid Malik b Mohammad Saeed	12
8	Rauf Akbar	lbw b Shahzad Ali	98	not out	39
9	Fakhar Hussain	c Ali Raza b Mohammad Saeed	36	c Shahnawaz Malik b Mohammad Hussain	24
10	Shehzad Azam	b Asif Raza	0	not out	4
11	Saad Altaf	not out	15		
	Extras	b 8, lb 8, w 11, nb 4	31	b 6, lb 11, w 5, nb 1	23
			255	(8 wickets)	**213**

FoW (1): 1-2, 2-4, 3-9, 4-9, 5-36, 6-50, 7-127, 8-213, 9-216, 10-255
FoW (2): 1-18, 2-51, 3-77, 4-91, 5-112, 6-130, 7-147, 8-184

Islamabad Bowling

	O	M	R	W			O	M	R	W	
Saad Altaf	20.4,10nb	3	81	4	7w,10nb		18	5	65	5	
Rauf Akbar	16	3	49	3	1nb	(3)	14	2	29	0	2nb
Shehzad Azam	13	2	65	2	1w,9nb	(2)	12	1	46	2	6w,2nb
Fakhar Hussain	3	0	16	0			1	0	5	0	4nb
Raheel Majeed	4	0	19	0		(7)	7	0	31	1	
Ameer Khan	2	2	0	1		(5)	3	0	11	0	
Ashar Zaidi						(6)	7	3	13	2	

Lahore Shalimar Bowling

	O	M	R	W			O	M	R	W	
Shahzad Ali	15.5	1	63	3	9w	(2)	17	6	53	3	
Asif Raza	24	1	104	5	2w,3nb	(1)	29.5	10	89	0	2w
Mohammad Saeed	14	2	57	2	1nb		16	2	47	4	3w,1nb
Mohammad Hussain	4	0	15	0			8	4	7	1	

Umpires: Afzaal Ahmed and Raweed Khan. Referee: Saadat Ali. Toss: Islamabad

Close of Play: 1st day: Islamabad (1) 34-4 (Fayyaz Ahmed 15*, Ameer Khan 5*, 11 overs); 2nd day: Lahore Shalimar (2) 115-6 (Shahnawaz Malik 25*, Mohammad Hussain 17*, 29 overs); 3rd day: Islamabad (2) 140-6 (Naeem Anjum 4*, Rauf Akbar 10*, 44.5 overs).

KARACHI WHITES v LAHORE RAVI

Played at Asghar Ali Shah Stadium, Karachi, October 26, 27, 28, 29, 2007.
Quaid-e-Azam Trophy 2007/08 - Group A
Lahore Ravi won by an innings and 118 runs.   (Points: Karachi Whites 0, Lahore Ravi 9)

KARACHI WHITES

1	Shan Masood	c Kashif Siddiq b Junaid Zia	11	c Shahbaz Butt b Junaid Zia	4
2	Asad Shafiq	c Arsalan Mir b Kashif Shafi	45	lbw b Junaid Zia	19
3	Wajihuddin	lbw b Junaid Zia	7	lbw b Azam Khan	4
4	Zeeshan Pervez	c Shahbaz Butt b Waqas Ahmed	16	b Azam Khan	0
5	Asim Kamal	b Saad Nasim	15	(7) c Kashif Siddiq b Saad Nasim	1
6	Afsar Nawaz	c Shahbaz Butt b Saad Nasim	52	(5) c and b Kashif Shafi	36
7	*Mohammad Sami	c Shahbaz Butt b Arsalan Mir	31	(8) c Azam Khan b Saad Nasim	4
8	Tanvir Ahmed	b Kashif Shafi	15	(9) c and b Kashif Shafi	0
9	†Owais Rehmani	lbw b Junaid Zia	2	(6) c Kashif Siddiq b Kashif Shafi	56
10	Tabish Nawab	c Rizwan Ahmed b Kashif Shafi	8	not out	0
11	Adnan Kaleem	not out	5	run out	8
	Extras	w 1, nb 10	11	b 4, lb 5, w 2, nb 2	13
			218		145

FoW (1): 1-15, 2-27, 3-48, 4-94, 5-98, 6-152, 7-188, 8-197, 9-208, 10-218
FoW (2): 1-6, 2-15, 3-17, 4-36, 5-124, 6-131, 7-133, 8-137, 9-137, 10-145

LAHORE RAVI

1	Kashif Siddiq	c sub (Babar Rehman) b Adnan Kaleem	21
2	Rizwan Aamer	b Mohammad Sami	0
3	Rizwan Ahmed	b Adnan Kaleem	54
4	Ashraf Ali	c Owais Rehmani b Tanvir Ahmed	25
5	Arsalan Mir	b Tabish Nawab	112
6	Saad Nasim	c Shan Masood b Tanvir Ahmed	95
7	†Shahbaz Butt	c Zeeshan Pervez b Adnan Kaleem	14
8	*Junaid Zia	c Owais Rehmani b Afsar Nawaz	21
9	Waqas Ahmed	c Shan Masood b Tabish Nawab	98
10	Kashif Shafi	c Shan Masood b Afsar Nawaz	14
11	Azam Khan	not out	0
	Extras	b 8, w 4, nb 15	27
			481

FoW (1): 1-0, 2-38, 3-91, 4-124, 5-324, 6-342, 7-344, 8-436, 9- , 10-481

Lahore Ravi Bowling

	O	M	R	W			O	M	R	W	
Junaid Zia	17	0	52	3	1w		15	4	40	2	2w
Azam Khan	12	2	34	0	4nb		11	2	39	2	
Arsalan Mir	7	1	28	1	3nb		2	0	2	0	2nb
Waqas Ahmed	9	2	34	1	3nb						
Saad Nasim	16	5	38	2		(4)	13	3	24	2	
Kashif Shafi	18.1	4	32	3		(5)	15.4	4	25	3	
Rizwan Aamer						(6)	3	0	6	0	

Karachi Whites Bowling

	O	M	R	W	
Tanvir Ahmed	27	5	92	2	2w,5nb
Mohammad Sami	18	3	68	1	1w
Tabish Nawab	37.4	4	122	2	10nb
Adnan Kaleem	50	13	133	3	
Afsar Nawaz	8	0	48	2	1w
Asad Shafiq	3	0	10	0	

Umpires: Akbar Khan and Iqbal Butt.   Referee: Naeem Ahmed.   Toss: Karachi Whites

Close of Play: 1st day: Lahore Ravi (1) 0-0 (Kashif Siddiq 0*, Rizwan Aamer 0*, 1 over); 2nd day: Lahore Ravi (1) 226-4 (Arsalan Mir 67*, Saad Nasim 41*, 86 overs); 3rd day: Karachi Whites (2) 74-4 (Afsar Nawaz 17*, Owais Rehmani 27*, 25 overs).

Arsalan Mir's 112 took 232 balls in 297 minutes and included 14 fours.

233

KHAN RESEARCH LABORATORIES v PAKISTAN INTERNATIONAL AIRLINES

Played at Khan Research Laboratories Ground, Rawalpindi, October 26, 27, 28, 29, 2007.
Quaid-e-Azam Trophy 2007/08 - Group B
Match drawn.   (Points: Khan Research Laboratories 3, Pakistan International Airlines 0)

PAKISTAN INTERNATIONAL AIRLINES

1	Khurram Manzoor	c Bilal Asad b Jaffar Nazir	10	c Zulfiqar Jan b Akhtar Ayub	9
2	Kamran Sajid	not out	64	c Azhar Ali b Saeed Ajmal	52
3	Agha Sabir	c Saeed Ajmal b Akhtar Ayub	11	c Zulfiqar Jan b Saeed Ajmal	46
4	*Faisal Iqbal	c Bazid Khan b Jaffar Nazir	39	c Zulfiqar Jan b Ali Naqvi	68
5	Shoaib Khan	lbw b Bilal Asad	8	(6) c Azhar Ali b Saeed Ajmal	24
6	Fahad Iqbal	c Zulfiqar Jan b Bilal Asad	2	(7) not out	64
7	†Anop Santosh	c Mohammad Wasim b Bilal Asad	13	(8) c Saeed Anwar b Saeed Ajmal	3
8	Nauman Alavi	b Bilal Asad	0	(9) c and b Mohammad Wasim	23
9	Anwar Ali	c Azhar Ali b Saeed Ajmal	26	(10) not out	0
10	Najaf Shah	c Zulfiqar Jan b Ali Naqvi	0	(5) lbw b Saeed Ajmal	7
11	Fazl-e-Akbar	b Saeed Ajmal	2		
	Extras	b 2, lb 9, w 8, nb 17	36	b 9, lb 5, w 2, nb 7	23
			211	(8 wickets)	319

FoW (1): 1-16, 2-47, 3-126, 4-144, 5-148, 6-167, 7-169, 8-207, 9-208, 10-211
FoW (2): 1-31, 2-112, 3-133, 4-158, 5-203, 6-245, 7-250, 8-319

KHAN RESEARCH LABORATORIES

1	Saeed Anwar	c Shoaib Khan b Fazl-e-Akbar	6
2	Azhar Ali	c Kamran Sajid b Najaf Shah	0
3	Saeed Ajmal	lbw b Fazl-e-Akbar	7
4	Ali Naqvi	b Najaf Shah	120
5	Bazid Khan	c and b Nauman Alavi	97
6	*Mohammad Wasim	run out (sub [Jamshed Ahmed])	17
7	Bilal Asad	lbw b Najaf Shah	4
8	†Zulfiqar Jan	lbw b Kamran Sajid	20
9	Jaffar Nazir	c Najaf Shah b Nauman Alavi	0
10	Akhtar Ayub	c Faisal Iqbal b Nauman Alavi	4
11	Mohammad Irshad	not out	4
	Extras	b 4, lb 4, nb 7	15
			292

FoW (1): 1-2, 2-9, 3-16, 4-209, 5-246, 6-250, 7-281, 8-282, 9-285, 10-292

Khan Research Laboratories Bowling

	O	M	R	W			O	M	R	W	
Jaffar Nazir	17	5	52	2	8w,3nb		14	4	25	0	1nb
Mohammad Irshad	8	1	21	0	8nb		12	2	32	0	1w
Akhtar Ayub	10	0	39	1	4nb		14	3	33	1	2nb
Ali Naqvi	10	3	24	1	2nb	(5)	16	7	29	1	3nb
Saeed Ajmal	9.4	2	27	2		(6)	33	10	89	5	
Bilal Asad	14	1	37	4		(4)	14	2	41	0	1nb
Mohammad Wasim						(7)	11	2	32	1	
Saeed Anwar						(8)	5	0	11	0	
Azhar Ali						(9)	4	0	13	0	1w

Pakistan International Airlines Bowling

	O	M	R	W	
Fazl-e-Akbar	23	6	62	2	2nb
Najaf Shah	25	4	73	3	1nb
Anwar Ali	1	0	9	0	
Kamran Sajid	18	6	38	1	
Nauman Alavi	36.3	7	93	3	4nb
Khurram Manzoor	3	1	7	0	
Agha Sabir	2	1	2	0	

Umpires: Iftikhar Malik and Jamil Kamran.   Referee: Mohammad Javed.   Toss: Khan Research Laboratories
Close of Play: 1st day: Khan Research Laboratories (1) 4-1 (Saeed Anwar 2*, Saeed Ajmal 1*, 1.3 overs); 2nd day: Khan Research Laboratories (1) 232-4 (Ali Naqvi 108*, Mohammad Wasim 4*, 81 overs); 3rd day: Pakistan International Airlines (2) 134-3 (Faisal Iqbal 13*, Najaf Shah 0*, 47 overs).
Ali Naqvi's 120 took 242 balls in 357 minutes and included 12 fours and a six.

PAKISTAN CUSTOMS v SUI SOUTHERN GAS CORPORATION

Played at National Bank of Pakistan Sports Complex, Karachi, October 26, 27, 28, 29, 2007.
Quaid-e-Azam Trophy 2007/08 - Group A
Sui Southern Gas Corporation won by 126 runs.   (Points: Pakistan Customs 0, Sui Southern Gas Corporation 9)

SUI SOUTHERN GAS CORPORATION

1	Asif Zakir	run out	41	not out	136
2	Mohtashim Ali	c Mohammad Hasan b Sajjad Hussain	5	not out	121
3	Imran Abbas	c Asif Iqbal b Raees Amjad	0		
4	*Saeed Bin Nasir	c Rehan Rafiq b Raees Amjad	10		
5	Ali Hussain	c Asif Iqbal b Raees Amjad	83		
6	Ashraf Ali	lbw b Yasir Shah	49		
7	†Ahmed Zeeshan	c Shafayat b Sajjad Hussain	67		
8	Adnan Malik	c Zahoor Elahi b Raees Amjad	0		
9	Rajesh Ramesh	c Mohammad Hasan b Yasir Shah	36		
10	Sohail Khan	lbw b Yasir Shah	6		
11	Waqar Ahmed	not out	0		
	Extras	b 14, lb 6, w 2, nb 9	31	b 1, lb 2, w 2	5
			328	(no wicket, declared)	262

FoW (1): 1-6, 2-7, 3-19, 4-91, 5-174, 6-233, 7-239, 8-301, 9-327, 10-328

PAKISTAN CUSTOMS

1	Hasnain Abbas	c Ahmed Zeeshan b Sohail Khan	53	run out	16
2	R.M.Khan	c Ahmed Zeeshan b Waqar Ahmed	7	c Ahmed Zeeshan b Sohail Khan	49
3	B.M.Shafayat	c Asif Zakir b Sohail Khan	24	b Sohail Khan	13
4	*Zahoor Elahi	c Ahmed Zeeshan b Rajesh Ramesh	32	(5) c Waqar Ahmed b Rajesh Ramesh	15
5	Asif Iqbal	c Asif Zakir b Adnan Malik	6	(6) c Ashraf Ali b Rajesh Ramesh	29
6	Rehan Rafiq	run out	36	(4) lbw b Sohail Khan	5
7	†Mohammad Hasan	c Mohtashim Ali b Rajesh Ramesh	38	c Mohtashim Ali b Rajesh Ramesh	22
8	Yasir Shah	c Ahmed Zeeshan b Sohail Khan	3	c Mohtashim Ali b Sohail Khan	37
9	Raees Amjad	lbw b Sohail Khan	0	c Imran Abbas b Sohail Khan	7
10	Sajjad Hussain	b Sohail Khan	0	lbw b Waqar Ahmed	4
11	Ahsan Jamil	not out	0	not out	8
	Extras	b 14, nb 5	19	b 24, lb 8, w 2, nb 7	41
			218		246

FoW (1): 1-11, 2-83, 3-96, 4-133, 5-133, 6-194, 7-203, 8-203, 9-216, 10-218
FoW (2): 1-63, 2-68, 3-80, 4-91, 5-132, 6-165, 7-167, 8-194, 9-233, 10-246

Pakistan Customs Bowling

	O	M	R	W			O	M	R	W	
Raees Amjad	28	6	68	4	2nb		10	0	41	0	
Sajjad Hussain	28	8	77	2	1nb		12	3	35	0	1w
Ahsan Jamil	18	1	59	0	2w,6nb		9	2	30	0	1w
Asif Iqbal	3	1	6	0							
Yasir Shah	32.1	7	89	3		(4)	18	1	99	0	
Rehan Rafiq	3	1	6	0			8	0	48	0	
Zahoor Elahi	1	0	3	0		(5)	1	0	6	0	

Sui Southern Gas Corporation Bowling

	O	M	R	W			O	M	R	W	
Rajesh Ramesh	20	5	43	2			29	8	67	3	1w
Waqar Ahmed	13	3	60	1	3nb		14.1	2	46	1	1w,5nb
Sohail Khan	25	8	59	5	1nb		23	5	74	5	1nb
Adnan Malik	17	6	42	1	1nb		14	7	27	0	1nb

Umpires: Ijaz Ahmed and Mian Mohammad Aslam.   Referee: Mahmood Rasheed.   Toss: Pakistan Customs

Close of Play: 1st day: Sui Southern Gas Corporation (1) 239-7 (Ahmed Zeeshan 24*, Adnan Malik 0*, 82.4 overs); 2nd day: Pakistan Customs (1) 180-5 (Rehan Rafiq 16*, Mohammad Hasan 28*, 50 overs); 3rd day: Sui Southern Gas Corporation (2) 262-0 (Asif Zakir 136*, Mohtashim Ali 121*, 58 overs).

Asif Zakir's 136 took 188 balls in 255 minutes and included 10 fours and 3 sixes. Mohtashim Ali's 121 took 160 balls in 255 minutes and included 15 fours.

QUETTA v KARACHI BLUES

Played at Bugti Stadium, Quetta, October 26, 27, 28, 29, 2007.
Quaid-e-Azam Trophy 2007/08 - Group B
Match drawn.   (Points: Quetta 0, Karachi Blues 3)

KARACHI BLUES

1	Shadab Kabir	lbw b Naseer Khan	136
2	Ali Asad	c Sanaullah Khan b Naseer Khan	66
3	Faraz Patel	c Sanaullah Khan b Naseer Khan	48
4	Sharjeel Ashraf	c Sanaullah Khan b Arun Lal	33
5	*Mansoor Khan	c Shoaib Khan b Naseer Khan	11
6	Mansoor Baig	lbw b Arun Lal	30
7	Tariq Haroon	lbw b Arun Lal	17
8	†Sajid Hanif	c Taimur Ali b Nazar Hussain	31
9	Azam Hussain	not out	18
10	Malik Aftab	c Mohammad Alam b Naseer Khan	21
11	Shahzaib Ahmed	lbw b Arun Lal	0
	Extras	b 5, lb 10, w 8, nb 10	33
			444

FoW (1): 1-146, 2-265, 3-270, 4-290, 5-346, 6-371, 7-382, 8-408, 9-440, 10-444

QUETTA

1	Shoaib Khan	c Azam Hussain b Malik Aftab	17	c Tariq Haroon b Mansoor Baig	113
2	Samiullah Agha	c Ali Asad b Malik Aftab	0	(3) c Shadab Kabir b Azam Hussain	41
3	Taimur Ali	b Tariq Haroon	110	(4) lbw b Shahzaib Ahmed	33
4	*Nasim Khan	c Faraz Patel b Azam Hussain	21	(5) c Sajid Hanif b Tariq Haroon	63
5	Arun Lal	c sub b Azam Hussain	11	(7) b Shahzaib Ahmed	9
6	Naseer Khan	c Tariq Haroon b Shahzaib Ahmed	0	st Sajid Hanif b Shahzaib Ahmed	27
7	†Sanaullah Khan	lbw b Malik Aftab	14	(8) lbw b Tariq Haroon	21
8	Mohammad Alam	c Ali Asad b Azam Hussain	7	(9) not out	71
9	Faisal Irfan	not out	60	(2) c and b Azam Hussain	43
10	Nazar Hussain	b Malik Aftab	8		
11	Sher Hasan	lbw b Malik Aftab	0	(10) not out	12
	Extras	b 2, lb 2	4	b 4, lb 6, w 1	11
			252	(8 wickets)	444

FoW (1): 1-1, 2-20, 3-59, 4-88, 5-89, 6-142, 7-155, 8-223, 9-246, 10-252
FoW (2): 1-93, 2-183, 3-227, 4-236, 5-282, 6-303, 7-344, 8-378

Quetta Bowling

	O	M	R	W	
Faisal Irfan	23	7	71	0	2w,5nb
Nazar Hussain	25.5	6	97	1	
Sher Hasan	12	1	39	0	2w,1nb
Arun Lal	26.5	4	84	4	4w,4nb
Naseer Khan	28	4	101	5	
Mohammad Alam	5	0	37	0	
Nasim Khan	0.1	0	0	0	

Karachi Blues Bowling

	O	M	R	W	O	M	R	W	
Malik Aftab	23	6	70	5	17	5	70	0	
Tariq Haroon	10	1	50	1	17	3	58	2	1w
Azam Hussain	31	7	57	3	41	6	142	2	
Mansoor Baig	2	0	10	0	17	2	50	1	
Shahzaib Ahmed	21	3	61	1	26	2	94	3	
Faraz Patel					(6) 3	0	20	0	

Umpires: Ahsan Raza and Atiq Khan. Referee: Farooq Shera.   Toss: Quetta

Close of Play: 1st day: Karachi Blues (1) 308-4 (Sharjeel Ashraf 20*, Mansoor Baig 3*, 83 overs); 2nd day: Quetta (1) 128-5 (Taimur Ali 64*, Sanaullah Khan 13*, 43 overs); 3rd day: Quetta (2) 152-1 (Shoaib Khan 77*, Samiullah Agha 30*, 43 overs).

Shadab Kabir's 136 took 206 balls in 281 minutes and included 22 fours and 4 sixes. Taimur Ali's 110 took 234 balls in 280 minutes and included 15 fours. Shoaib Khan's 113 took 205 balls in 226 minutes and included 13 fours and 2 sixes.

SIALKOT v MULTAN

Played at Sheikhupura Stadium, October 26, 27, 28, 29, 2007.
Quaid-e-Azam Trophy 2007/08 - Group A
Multan won by an innings and 139 runs.   (Points: Sialkot 0, Multan 9)

SIALKOT

1	Mohammad Boota	b Ansar Javed	0	(2) c Usman Tariq b Mohammad Kashif		21
2	Qamar Shahzad	b Mohammad Kashif	25	(1) b Mohammad Kashif		0
3	Shahid Siddiq	lbw b Mohammad Kashif	0	lbw b Mohammad Tanvir		12
4	Faisal Khan	b Mohammad Kashif	0	c Mohammad Hafeez		
					b Mohammad Kashif	4
5	Bilal Hussain	lbw b Ansar Javed	0	b Zulfiqar Babar		46
6	*Mohammad Ayub	c Imranullah Aslam		not out		87
		b Mohammad Kashif	23			
7	†Khalid Mahmood	c Mohammad Kashif		c Mohammad Hafeez		
		b Imranullah Aslam	19		b Mohammad Kashif	40
8	Aamer Jaffery	c Kashif Naved b Zulfiqar Babar	13	lbw b Imranullah Aslam		7
9	Imran Malik	c Usman Tariq b Imranullah Aslam	9	lbw b Imranullah Aslam		7
10	Mohammad Wasim	c Mohammad Kashif b Imranullah Aslam	0	c Mohammad Hafeez b Imranullah Aslam		0
11	Mohammad Ali	not out	0	b Mohammad Kashif		0
	Extras	b 5, lb 4, nb 2	11	b 11, lb 1, nb 7		19
			100			**243**

FoW (1): 1-0, 2-3, 3-7, 4-10, 5-45, 6-58, 7-84, 8-100, 9-100, 10-100
FoW (2): 1-9, 2-32, 3-38, 4-58, 5-117, 6-140, 7-205, 8-218, 9-238, 10-243

MULTAN

1	Hammad Tariq	c and b Aamer Jaffery	116
2	*Usman Tariq	b Mohammad Ali	91
3	Mohammad Hafeez	lbw b Mohammad Ali	14
4	Kashif Naved	c Mohammad Boota b Aamer Jaffery	1
5	Mohammad Sarwar	c Khalid Mahmood b Qamar Shahzad	51
6	†Gulraiz Sadaf	c Shahid Siddiq b Mohammad Ali	4
7	Imranullah Aslam	b Mohammad Ali	115
8	Ansar Javed	lbw b Bilal Hussain	1
9	Zulfiqar Babar	c Mohammad Boota b Mohammad Ali	50
10	Mohammad Kashif	not out	8
11	Mohammad Tanvir		
	Extras	b 6, lb 2, w 9, nb 9, pen 5	31
		(9 wickets, declared)	**482**

FoW (1): 1-211, 2-219, 3-233, 4-248, 5-268, 6-368, 7-371, 8-458, 9-482

Multan Bowling	O	M	R	W		O	M	R	W	
Ansar Javed	8	2	22	2	1nb	10	1	29	0	2nb
Mohammad Kashif	12	4	30	4		20.5	4	54	5	
Mohammad Tanvir	6	2	14	0	1nb	8	2	19	1	5nh
Imranullah Aslam	8	3	18	3		27	5	101	3	
Zulfiqar Babar	2.4	0	7	1		15	3	27	1	
Usman Tariq					(6)	1	0	1	0	

Sialkot Bowling	O	M	R	W	
Imran Malik	21	3	70	0	2w
Mohammad Wasim	35	6	105	0	1w,5nb
Mohammad Ali	29.3	9	102	5	1nb
Aamer Jaffery	22	2	116	2	1w,2nb
Mohammad Boota	3	0	12	0	
Qamar Shahzad	15	2	47	1	
Bilal Hussain	5	1	17	1	5w

Umpires: Ahmed Shahab and Akmal Hayat.   Referee: Abdus Sami.   Toss: Multan

Close of Play: 1st day: Multan (1) 116-0 (Usman Tariq 56*, Hammad Tariq 52*, 44 overs); 2nd day: Multan (1) 458-8 (Zulfiqar Babar 34*, 126.1 overs); 3rd day: Sialkot (2) 238-8 (Mohammad Ayub 23*, Mohammad Wasim 0*, 77 overs).

Hammad Tariq's 116 took 211 balls in 265 minutes and included 13 fours and 3 sixes. Imranullah Aslam's 115 took 99 balls in 132 minutes and included 16 fours and 2 sixes.

SUI NORTHERN GAS PIPELINES LIMITED v ZARAI TARAQIATI BANK LIMITED

Played at Arbab Niaz Stadium, Peshawar, October 26, 27, 28, 2007.
Quaid-e-Azam Trophy 2007/08 - Group B
Sui Northern Gas Pipelines Limited won by nine wickets.   (Points: Sui Northern Gas Pipelines Limited 9, Zarai Taraqiati Bank Limited 0)

SUI NORTHERN GAS PIPELINES LIMITED

1	*Mohammad Hafeez	c Adnan Raza b Zohaib Khan	27	c Afaq Raheem b Imran Sabir	18
2	Yasir Arafat	c Zohaib Khan b Mohammad Khalil	11	not out	23
3	Umar Akmal	c Wajahatullah Wasti b Imran Sabir	0	not out	29
4	Azhar Shafiq	c Shakeel Ansar b Junaid Nadir	95		
5	Saleem Mughal	lbw b Junaid Nadir	4		
6	Khurram Shehzad	c sub (Kamran Naeem) b Zohaib Khan	75		
7	†Adnan Akmal	lbw b Zohaib Khan	27		
8	Imran Khalid	c Adnan Raza b Junaid Nadir	8		
9	Imran Ali	not out	22		
10	Adil Raza	lbw b Mohammad Khalil	1		
11	Samiullah Khan	b Junaid Nadir	0		
	Extras	lb 16, w 3, nb 14	33		
			303	(1 wicket)	70

FoW (1): 1-23, 2-28, 3-58, 4-63, 5-227, 6-267, 7-267, 8-292, 9-302, 10-303
FoW (2): 1-26

ZARAI TARAQIATI BANK LIMITED

1	Afaq Raheem	c Saleem Mughal b Samiullah Khan	9	c and b Imran Khalid	14
2	†Shakeel Ansar	b Samiullah Khan	9	(3) b Samiullah Khan	3
3	Umar Javed	lbw b Samiullah Khan	1	(4) lbw b Samiullah Khan	4
4	Aamer Bashir	c Adnan Akmal b Samiullah Khan	4	(5) c Adnan Akmal b Adil Raza	23
5	*Wajahatullah Wasti	c Mohammad Hafeez b Adil Raza	16	(6) b Imran Ali	10
6	Adnan Raza	c Khurram Shehzad b Imran Ali	19	(7) c Imran Ali b Adil Raza	67
7	Zohaib Khan	b Adil Raza	0	(8) c Mohammad Hafeez	
				b Samiullah Khan	30
8	Junaid Nadir	b Adil Raza	10	(2) c Adnan Akmal b Imran Khalid	90
9	Imran Sabir	not out	5	c Mohammad Hafeez b Samiullah Khan	29
10	Mohammad Khalil	c Adnan Akmal b Imran Ali	2	not out	0
11	Atif Ashraf	absent hurt		absent hurt	0
	Extras	b 1, w 1, nb 8	10	lb 5, nb 10	15
			85		285

FoW (1): 1-21, 2-23, 3-24, 4-30, 5-60, 6-60, 7-73, 8-83, 9-85
FoW (2): 1-44, 2-59, 3-102, 4-140, 5-157, 6-160, 7-249, 8-283, 9-285

Zarai Taraqiati Bank Limited Bowling

	O	M	R	W		O	M	R	W	
Mohammad Khalil	25	11	61	2	1nb	5.1	1	39	0	
Imran Sabir	16	4	60	1	1nb	4	0	28	1	
Zohaib Khan	22	3	80	3	1nb					
Junaid Nadir	16.2	4	54	4	3w,2nb					
Umar Javed	6	0	32	0	9nb					
Adnan Raza						(3) 1	0	3	0	

Sui Northern Gas Pipelines Limited Bowling

	O	M	R	W		O	M	R	W	
Samiullah Khan	13	1	28	4	6nb	19	3	81	4	2nb
Imran Ali	7.4	1	22	2	1w	14	6	54	1	1nb
Adil Raza	10	3	34	3	2nb	24.5	6	71	2	7nb
Imran Khalid						(4) 20	9	47	2	
Mohammad Hafeez						(5) 6	3	17	0	
Azhar Shafiq						(6) 2	0	10	0	

Umpires: Islam Khan and Mohammad Arif. Referee: Ishtiaq Ahmed.   Toss: Zarai Taraqiati Bank Limited

Close of Play: 1st day: Sui Northern Gas Pipelines Limited (1) 287-7 (Imran Khalid 6*, Imran Ali 8*, 78 overs); 2nd day: Zarai Taraqiati Bank Limited (2) 100-2 (Junaid Nadir 72*, Aamer Bashir 4*, 37 overs).

The match was scheduled for four days but completed in three.

ABBOTTABAD v RAWALPINDI

Played at Abbottabad Cricket Stadium, October 27, 28, 29, 30, 2007.
Quaid-e-Azam Trophy 2007/08 - Group B
Match drawn.   (Points: Abbottabad 0, Rawalpindi 3)

ABBOTTABAD

1	Wajid Ali	c Mohammad Ibrahim b Rizwan Akbar	75
2	Mohammad Naeem	lbw b Mohammad Ayaz	34
3	Usman Khan	c Zahid Mansoor b Mohammad Ayaz	1
4	*Adnan Raees	b Alamgir Khan	8
5	Riaz Kail	c Babar Naeem b Mohammad Ayaz	37
6	Khalid Usman	c Zahid Mansoor b Mohammad Ayaz	6
7	†Fawad Khan	run out (Rizwan Akbar)	73
8	Iftikhar Mahmood	c Adnan Mufti b Yasir Ali	35
9	Noor-ul-Amin	b Yasir Ali	0
10	Junaid Khan	c and b Babar Naeem	71
11	Armaghan Elahi	not out	21
	Extras	b 2, lb 6, w 1, nb 6	15
			376

FoW (1): 1-68, 2-71, 3-89, 4-156, 5-165, 6-174, 7-257, 8-257, 9-308, 10-376

RAWALPINDI

1	Mohammad Ibrahim	lbw b Noor-ul-Amin	45
2	Babar Naeem	c Fawad Khan b Armaghan Elahi	4
3	Adnan Mufti	c Fawad Khan b Junaid Khan	31
4	Yasim Murtaza	b Riaz Kail	17
5	Usman Saeed	b Khalid Usman	243
6	Yasir Ali	lbw b Noor-ul-Amin	129
7	*Naved Ashraf	c Fawad Khan b Adnan Raees	23
8	†Zahid Mansoor	lbw b Khalid Usman	47
9	Alamgir Khan	not out	35
10	Rizwan Akbar	b Noor-ul-Amin	14
11	Mohammad Ayaz	st Fawad Khan b Iftikhar Mahmood	2
	Extras	b 1, lb 6, w 1, nb 3	11
			601

FoW (1): 1-5, 2-70, 3-98, 4-104, 5-360, 6-414, 7-546, 8-547, 9-579, 10-601

Rawalpindi Bowling	O	M	R	W	
Yasir Ali	22	5	66	2	1nb
Rizwan Akbar	27	5	72	1	
Mohammad Ayaz	26	6	99	4	1w,3nb
Alamgir Khan	20	5	55	1	2nb
Yasim Murtaza	14	4	42	0	
Babar Naeem	8.4	2	25	1	
Naved Ashraf	2	0	3	0	
Mohammad Ibrahim	1	0	6	0	

Abbottabad Bowling	O	M	R	W	
Junaid Khan	50	17	113	1	2nb
Armaghan Elahi	23	6	74	1	1w,1nb
Noor-ul-Amin	61	11	200	3	
Adnan Raees	17	4	40	1	
Iftikhar Mahmood	31.4	10	82	1	
Riaz Kail	10	2	33	1	
Mohammad Naeem	5	2	7	0	
Khalid Usman	9	2	16	2	
Wajid Ali	7	1	29	0	

Umpires: Hakeem Shah and Zaheer Ahmed. Referee: Khalid Niazi.   Toss: Abbottabad

Close of Play: 1st day: Abbottabad (1) 225-6 (Fawad Khan 24*, Iftikhar Mahmood 28*, 83 overs); 2nd day: Rawalpindi (1) 106-4 (Usman Saeed 6*, Yasir Ali 2*, 45 overs); 3rd day: Rawalpindi (1) 352-4 (Usman Saeed 103*, Yasir Ali 127*, 137 overs).

Usman Saeed's 243 took 471 balls in 602 minutes and included 30 fours and 2 sixes. Yasir Ali's 129 took 285 balls in 355 minutes and included 14 fours and 3 sixes.

FAISALABAD v PAKISTAN CUSTOMS

Played at Iqbal Stadium, Faisalabad, November 1, 2, 3, 4, 2007.
Quaid-e-Azam Trophy 2007/08 - Group A
Faisalabad won by eight wickets.   (Points: Faisalabad 9, Pakistan Customs 0)

PAKISTAN CUSTOMS

1	Hasnain Abbas	c Ammar Mahmood b Ahmed Hayat	6	c Usman Arshad b Mohammad Talha	98
2	R.M.Khan	c Mohammad Salman b Ahmed Hayat	25	(4) c Ali Rafiq b Mohammad Talha	29
3	B.M.Shafayat	lbw b Ahmed Hayat	1	(6) lbw b Ali Raza	12
4	Asif Iqbal	c Mohammad Salman b Mohammad Talha	28	(3) run out	51
5	*Zahoor Elahi	lbw b Saadat Munir	60	c Ali Rafiq b Mohammad Talha	1
6	Rehan Rafiq	c Mohammad Salman b Mohammad Talha	0	(2) c Mohammad Salman b Ahmed Hayat	37
7	†Mohammad Hasan	c Ali Rafiq b Ahmed Hayat	8		
	Adnan Naved			lbw b Mohammad Talha	4
8	Majid Majeed	c Mohammad Salman b Ahmed Hayat	3	(9) c Ali Rafiq b Ahmed Hayat	8
9	Yasir Shah	c Imran Ali b Mohammad Talha	24	(8) not out	8
10	Raees Amjad	c Mohammad Salman b Mohammad Talha	2	c Mohammad Salman b Mohammad Talha	4
11	Sajjad Hussain	not out	1	c Mohammad Salman b Ali Raza	1
	Extras	lb 2, w 3, nb 19	24	b 4, lb 1, w 4, nb 17	26
			182		**279**

FoW (1): 1-14, 2-16, 3-63, 4-84, 5-115, 6-124, 7-128, 8-164, 9-168, 10-182
FoW (2): 1-77, 2-206, 3-207, 4-208, 5-233, 6-256, 7-258, 8-267, 9-272, 10-279

FAISALABAD

1	Imran Ali	c Asif Iqbal b Sajjad Hussain	0	(2) lbw b Sajjad Hussain	3
2	Ali Rafiq	c Asif Iqbal b Raees Amjad	5	(1) c Majid Majeed b Raees Amjad	3
3	Ammar Mahmood	b Yasir Shah	52	not out	8
4	Usman Arshad	b Majid Majeed	52		
5	Asif Hussain	c Rehan Rafiq b Yasir Shah	95		
6	*Ijaz Ahmed	c Shafayat b Yasir Shah	93		
7	†Mohammad Salman	c Hasnain Abbas b Raees Amjad	4	(4) not out	20
8	Ahmed Hayat	st Mohammad Hasan b Yasir Shah	46		
9	Ali Raza	c Mohammad Hasan b Yasir Shah	31		
10	Saadat Munir	c Shafayat b Yasir Shah	19		
11	Mohammad Talha	not out	0		
	Extras	b 2, lb 8, w 6, nb 7	23	lb 7, w 2, nb 2	11
			420	**(2 wickets)**	**45**

FoW (1): 1-6, 2-6, 3-99, 4-137, 5-278, 6-289, 7-359, 8-372, 9-420, 10-420
FoW (2): 1-8, 2-9

Faisalabad Bowling

	O	M	R	W		O	M	R	W	
Ahmed Hayat	12	0	48	5	2nb	21	1	71	2	3nb
Mohammad Talha	18.4,12nb	1	56	4	1w,13nb	22	3	57	5	
Ali Raza	10	1	45	0	2w,4nb	11.1	2	51	2	2nb
Saadat Munir	15	4	28	1		21	6	66	0	
Ijaz Ahmed	1	0	3	0		11	4	22	0	
Usman Arshad					(6)	1	0	7	0	

Pakistan Customs Bowling

	O	M	R	W		O	M	R	W	
Raees Amjad	25	0	75	2	1w,2nb	6	0	12	1	2nb
Sajjad Hussain	32	3	128	1	5w,4nb	4	1	13	1	2w
Majid Majeed	32	6	101	1						
Yasir Shah	33	8	89	6	(3)	1.5	0	13	0	
Rehan Rafiq	5	0	17	0	1nb					

Umpires: Hakeem Shah and Rasheed Bhatti.   Referee: Arshad Pervez.   Toss: Pakistan Customs

Close of Play: 1st day: Faisalabad (1) 50-2 (Ammar Mahmood 25*, Usman Arshad 16*, 14.4 overs); 2nd day: Faisalabad (1) 278-5 (Ijaz Ahmed 54*, 97.3 overs); 3rd day: Pakistan Customs (2) 178-1 (Hasnain Abbas 81*, Asif Iqbal 40*, 48.2 overs).
Adnan Naved was a full substitute for Customs, replacing Mohammad Hasan (he was called up for Pakistan Under-19s on day 4).

ISLAMABAD v RAWALPINDI

Played at Diamond Club Ground, Islamabad, November 1, 2, 3, 4, 2007.
Quaid-e-Azam Trophy 2007/08 - Group B
Islamabad won by six wickets.   (Points: Islamabad 9, Rawalpindi 0)

RAWALPINDI

1	Mohammad Ibrahim	lbw b Rauf Akbar	10	lbw b Saad Altaf		0
2	Babar Naeem	b Saad Altaf	0	c Fayyaz Ahmed b Rauf Akbar		16
3	Najam-ul-Hasan	c Naeem Anjum b Shehzad Azam	29	c Asadullah Sumari b Saad Altaf		9
4	Adnan Mufti	b Imad Wasim	83	lbw b Saad Altaf		19
5	Usman Saeed	c Imad Wasim b Rauf Akbar	42	(6) lbw b Saad Altaf		1
6	*Naved Ashraf	c Ashar Zaidi b Shehzad Azam	35	(5) lbw b Raheel Majeed		40
7	†Zahid Mansoor	c Raheel Majeed b Saad Altaf	18	c Naeem Anjum b Saad Altaf		48
8	Yasir Ali	c Naeem Anjum b Shehzad Azam	11	(9) c Fakhar Hussain b Imad Wasim		5
9	Alamgir Khan	c Naeem Anjum b Saad Altaf	0	(8) b Saad Altaf		34
10	Rizwan Akbar	not out	4	c Ashar Zaidi b Saad Altaf		3
11	Mohammad Ayaz	b Shehzad Azam	0	not out		2
	Extras	b 4, lb 2, w 2, nb 6	14	b 10, lb 5, w 2, nb 9		26
			246			203

FoW (1): 1-3, 2-13, 3-83, 4-155, 5-196, 6-214, 7-238, 8-238, 9-242, 10-246
FoW (2): 1-0, 2-27, 3-39, 4-69, 5-80, 6-138, 7-178, 8-190, 9-200, 10-203

ISLAMABAD

1	Raheel Majeed	c Babar Naeem b Rizwan Akbar	34	not out	67
2	Umair Khan	c Mohammad Ibrahim			
		b Mohammad Ayaz	53	lbw b Rizwan Akbar	16
3	Fakhar Hussain	b Alamgir Khan	29	b Mohammad Ayaz	5
4	Asadullah Sumari	c Zahid Mansoor b Rizwan Akbar	48	lbw b Yasir Ali	34
5	Fayyaz Ahmed	c Mohammad Ibrahim			
		b Mohammad Ayaz	3	c sub (Yasim Murtaza) b Yasir Ali	5
6	†Naeem Anjum	c Mohammad Ibrahim b Rizwan Akbar	8		
7	*Ashar Zaidi	c Babar Naeem b Yasir Ali	20	(6) not out	11
8	Rauf Akbar	b Yasir Ali	54		
9	Imad Wasim	c Zahid Mansoor b Rizwan Akbar	4		
10	Shehzad Azam	c Rizwan Akbar b Alamgir Khan	9		
11	Saad Altaf	not out	24		
	Extras	b 8, lb 2, w 7, nb 3	20	b 4, lb 1, nb 1	6
			306	(4 wickets)	144

FoW (1): 1-73, 2-122, 3-131, 4-138, 5-153, 6-258, 7-258, 8-272, 9-273, 10-306
FoW (2): 1-33, 2-38, 3-98, 4-119

Islamabad Bowling

	O	M	R	W			O	M	R	W	
Saad Altaf	22	6	55	3			26.1	9	63	7	2w,4nb
Rauf Akbar	15	3	51	2	1nb		10	1	28	1	3nb
Shehzad Azam	19.3	3	94	4	1w,5nb						
Fakhar Hussain	2	0	12	0	1w	(3)	13	3	51	0	
Imad Wasim	7	1	28	1		(4)	15	2	38	1	2nb
Raheel Majeed						(5)	4	2	8	1	

Rawalpindi Bowling

	O	M	R	W			O	M	R	W	
Yasir Ali	25	5	91	2			9	1	24	2	
Rizwan Akbar	30	8	112	4	7w,2nb		18.3	4	64	1	1nb
Mohammad Ayaz	18	6	38	2	1nb		9	1	27	1	
Alamgir Khan	12.5	2	37	2			3	0	16	0	
Mohammad Ibrahim	2	1	2	0							
Babar Naeem	4	0	16	0		(5)	3	0	8	0	

Umpires: Afzaal Ahmed and Riazuddin.   Referee: Khalid Niazi.   Toss: Islamabad

Close of Play: 1st day: Islamabad (1) 34-0 (Raheel Majeed 14*, Umair Khan 16*, 9 overs); 2nd day: Islamabad (1) 267-7 (Asadullah Sumari 47*, Imad Wasim 4*, 85 overs); 3rd day: Rawalpindi (2) 190-8 (Alamgir Khan 26*, Rizwan Akbar 0*, 60 overs).

KARACHI BLUES v PESHAWAR

Played at National Bank of Pakistan Sports Complex, Karachi, November 1, 2, 3, 2007.
Quaid-e-Azam Trophy 2007/08 - Group B
Karachi Blues won by an innings and 188 runs.   (Points: Karachi Blues 9, Peshawar 0)

KARACHI BLUES

1	Shadab Kabir	b Jibran Khan	70
2	Ali Asad	c Usman Zeb b Jibran Khan	117
3	Aariz Kamal	c Usman Zeb b Nauman Habib	76
4	Sharjeel Ashraf	lbw b Bilal Khan	48
5	Tariq Haroon	b Jibran Khan	13
6	*Mansoor Khan	c sub (Mahfooz Sabri)	
		b Mohammad Fayyaz	4
7	Faraz Patel	not out	18
8	†Sajid Hanif	c Usman Zeb b Bilal Khan	9
9	Azam Hussain	c Akbar Badshah b Bilal Khan	8
10	Malik Aftab	c Usman Zeb b Bilal Khan	0
11	Shahzaib Ahmed		
	Extras	b 26, lb 2, w 3, nb 10	41
		(9 wickets, declared)	404

FoW (1): 1-151, 2-239, 3-313, 4-362, 5-369, 6-369, 7-389, 8-403, 9-404

PESHAWAR

1	Naved Khan	lbw b Malik Aftab	0	(3) c Sajid Hanif b Tariq Haroon	0
2	Usman Zeb	b Malik Aftab	1	(1) b Shahzaib Ahmed	36
3	Mohammad Fayyaz	lbw b Tariq Haroon	0	(4) b Tariq Haroon	0
4	Nawaz Ahmed	not out	60	(5) lbw b Malik Aftab	5
5	Sajjad Ahmed	b Malik Aftab	4	(6) b Azam Hussain	20
6	*Akbar Badshah	b Shahzaib Ahmed	17	(7) b Tariq Haroon	4
7	†Shehzad Khan	c Aariz Kamal b Azam Hussain	13	(2) lbw b Tariq Haroon	0
8	Jibran Khan	c Sajid Hanif b Malik Aftab	0	not out	0
9	Nauman Habib	c Faraz Patel b Azam Hussain	4	st Sajid Hanif b Azam Hussain	11
10	Imran Khan	b Malik Aftab	0	(11) st Sajid Hanif b Azam Hussain	0
11	Bilal Khan	b Azam Hussain	13	(10) b Azam Hussain	4
	Extras	b 6	6	b 12, lb 5, nb 1	18
			118		98

FoW (1): 1-0, 2-1, 3-1, 4-5, 5-53, 6-72, 7-77, 8-90, 9-97, 10-118
FoW (2): 1-8, 2-10, 3-16, 4-31, 5-64, 6-83, 7-83, 8-94, 9-98, 10-98

Peshawar Bowling

	O	M	R	W	
Nauman Habib	26	6	80	1	1nb
Imran Khan	27	12	60	0	1w,5nb
Bilal Khan	21	5	63	4	1nb
Akbar Badshah	19	7	44	0	2nb
Jibran Khan	24	5	67	3	1nb
Mohammad Fayyaz	8	2	29	1	
Usman Zeb	9	3	21	0	
Nawaz Ahmed	6	1	12	0	2w

Karachi Blues Bowling

	O	M	R	W		O	M	R	W	
Malik Aftab	21	7	58	5		5	0	16	1	
Tariq Haroon	11	5	15	1		12	4	32	4	
Azam Hussain	11.4	4	30	3		11.4	4	24	4	1nb
Shahzaib Ahmed	3	0	9	1		5	3	9	4	

Umpires: Akbar Khan and Ijaz Ahmed. Referee: Anwar Khan.   Toss: Peshawar

Close of Play: 1st day: Karachi Blues (1) 265-2 (Aariz Kamal 49*, Sharjeel Ashraf 27*, 83 overs); 2nd day: Peshawar (1) 59-5 (Nawaz Ahmed 29*, Shehzad Khan 4*, 24 overs).

The match was scheduled for four days but completed in three. Ali Asad's 117 took 238 balls in 277 minutes and included 18 fours.

KARACHI WHITES v SUI SOUTHERN GAS CORPORATION

Played at National Stadium, Karachi, November 1, 2, 3, 2007.
Quaid-e-Azam Trophy 2007/08 - Group A
Karachi Whites won by seven wickets.   (Points: Karachi Whites 9, Sui Southern Gas Corporation 0)

SUI SOUTHERN GAS CORPORATION

1	Asif Zakir	lbw b Mohammad Sami	4	c Khalid Latif b Fahad Khan	31
2	Mohtashim Ali	c and b Tabish Nawab	69	c Owais Rehmani b Mohammad Sami	5
3	Imran Abbas	lbw b Fahad Khan	39	lbw b Tanvir Ahmed	4
4	*Saeed Bin Nasir	c Owais Rehmani b Tabish Nawab	0	(5) c Afsar Nawaz b Fahad Khan	4
5	Ali Hussain	c Fahad Khan b Tanvir Ahmed	36	(4) b Tanvir Ahmed	17
6	Ashraf Ali	c Zeeshan Pervez b Tanvir Ahmed	7	c Owais Rehmani b Tanvir Ahmed	16
7	†Ahmed Zeeshan	run out	13	c Khalid Latif b Tanvir Ahmed	32
8	Rajesh Ramesh	c Asad Shafiq b Mohammad Sami	7	(9) c Mohammad Sami b Fahad Khan	20
9	Sohail Khan	c and b Mohammad Sami	21	(10) c Tanvir Ahmed b Fahad Khan	8
10	Adnan Malik	not out	8	(8) b Tanvir Ahmed	12
11	Waqar Ahmed	b Tanvir Ahmed	4	not out	0
	Extras	lb 2, nb 11	13	lb 2, w 1, nb 3	6
			221		155

FoW (1): 1-13, 2-122, 3-122, 4-122, 5-141, 6-157, 7-165, 8-209, 9-209, 10-221
FoW (2): 1-23, 2-33, 3-46, 4-52, 5-72, 6-91, 7-120, 8-146, 9-150, 10-155

KARACHI WHITES

1	Khalid Latif	c Ahmed Zeeshan b Sohail Khan	23	b Sohail Khan	14
2	Shan Masood	c Ahmed Zeeshan b Rajesh Ramesh	32	b Waqar Ahmed	12
3	Asad Shafiq	c Ashraf Ali b Sohail Khan	69	not out	39
4	Zeeshan Pervez	c Ahmed Zeeshan b Sohail Khan	13	c Ahmed Zeeshan b Rajesh Ramesh	14
5	Asim Kamal	b Sohail Khan	35	not out	1
6	Afsar Nawaz	not out	65		
7	†Owais Rehmani	c Ahmed Zeeshan b Sohail Khan	4		
8	*Mohammad Sami	c sub (Asim Zaidi) b Rajesh Ramesh	16		
9	Tanvir Ahmed	c Ahmed Zeeshan b Rajesh Ramesh	10		
10	Fahad Khan	b Waqar Ahmed	3		
11	Tabish Nawab	lbw b Waqar Ahmed	0		
	Extras	b 12, lb 7, w 5, nb 3	27		
			297	(3 wickets)	80

FoW (1): 1-44, 2-74, 3-89, 4-178, 5-184, 6-202, 7-227, 8-242, 9-294, 10-297
FoW (2): 1-26, 2-26, 3-68

Karachi Whites Bowling

	O	M	R	W		O	M	R	W	
Mohammad Sami	24	6	49	3		19	7	36	1	1nb
Tanvir Ahmed	24.1	6	57	3	6nb	23	2	80	5	1nb
Fahad Khan	18	5	42	1	5nb	14	2	37	4	1w,1nb
Khalid Latif	2	0	7	0						
Tabish Nawab	21	2	60	2						
Afsar Nawaz	2	1	4	0						

Sui Southern Gas Corporation Bowling

	O	M	R	W			O	M	R	W
Rajesh Ramesh	22	3	104	3	1w	(3)	2	1	5	1
Waqar Ahmed	19	6	40	2	1nb		5	0	25	1
Sohail Khan	18	2	68	5		(1)	7.5	0	50	1
Adnan Malik	17	2	54	0	2nb					
Asif Zakir	2	0	12	0						

Umpires: Iqbal Butt and Mian Mohammad Aslam.   Referee: Naeem Ahmed.   Toss: Karachi Whites

Close of Play: 1st day: Sui Southern Gas Corporation (1) 193-7 (Ali Hussain 27*, Sohail Khan 14*, 83 overs); 2nd day: Karachi Whites (1) 280-8 (Afsar Nawaz 50*, Fahad Khan 3*, 72 overs).

The match was scheduled for four days but completed in three.

KHAN RESEARCH LABORATORIES v SUI NORTHERN GAS PIPELINES LIMITED

Played at Khan Research Laboratories Ground, Rawalpindi, November 1, 2, 3, 4, 2007.
Quaid-e-Azam Trophy 2007/08 - Group B
Sui Northern Gas Pipelines Limited won by 53 runs.   (Points: Khan Research Laboratories 0, Sui Northern Gas Pipelines Limited 9)

SUI NORTHERN GAS PIPELINES LIMITED

1	*Mohammad Hafeez	c Zulfiqar Jan b Jaffar Nazir	12	b Jaffar Nazir	33
2	Yasir Arafat	lbw b Akhtar Ayub	30	c Mohammad Wasim b Jaffar Nazir	12
3	Umar Akmal	c Zulfiqar Jan b Bilal Asad	32	c Mohammad Wasim b Saeed Ajmal	43
4	Azhar Shafiq	c Mohammad Wasim b Akhtar Ayub	35	c Zulfiqar Jan b Yasir Arafat	1
5	Saleem Mughal	c Yasir Arafat b Akhtar Ayub	54	c Azhar Ali b Yasir Arafat	2
6	Khurram Shehzad	c Zulfiqar Jan b Yasir Arafat	27	c Zulfiqar Jan b Jaffar Nazir	28
7	†Adnan Akmal	c Saeed Ajmal b Akhtar Ayub	18	b Yasir Arafat	9
8	Imran Khalid	c Zulfiqar Jan b Yasir Arafat	8	lbw b Yasir Arafat	7
9	Asad Ali	c Zulfiqar Jan b Yasir Arafat	0	(10) b Saeed Ajmal	6
10	Samiullah Khan	not out	7	(9) not out	18
11	Adil Raza	lbw b Mohammad Wasim	13	lbw b Yasir Arafat	0
	Extras	b 4, lb 6, w 5, nb 3	18	b 2, lb 10, w 2, nb 2	16
			254		**175**

FoW (1): 1-22, 2-79, 3-85, 4-167, 5-194, 6-216, 7-228, 8-228, 9-235, 10-254
FoW (2): 1-46, 2-47, 3-48, 4-50, 5-98, 6-126, 7-142, 8-161, 9-175, 10-175

KHAN RESEARCH LABORATORIES

1	Ali Naqvi	c Adnan Akmal b Samiullah Khan	46	c Mohammad Hafeez b Samiullah Khan	13
2	Azhar Ali	c Adil Raza b Asad Ali	18	lbw b Samiullah Khan	13
3	Saeed Anwar	lbw b Asad Ali	0	(6) lbw b Adil Raza	16
4	Bazid Khan	c Adnan Akmal b Adil Raza	14	c Adnan Akmal b Asad Ali	10
5	*Mohammad Wasim	lbw b Asad Ali	8	c Mohammad Hafeez b Asad Ali	54
6	Bilal Asad	c Mohammad Hafeez b Imran Khalid	12	(7) c Samiullah Khan b Asad Ali	26
7	Yasir Arafat	not out	45	(8) c Mohammad Hafeez b Asad Ali	9
8	†Zulfiqar Jan	c Mohammad Hafeez b Asad Ali	4	(3) b Adil Raza	16
9	Jaffar Nazir	b Samiullah Khan	2	c Azhar Shafiq b Asad Ali	4
10	Akhtar Ayub	c Azhar Shafiq b Asad Ali	0	not out	10
11	Saeed Ajmal	b Adil Raza	17	b Adil Raza	7
	Extras	b 6, lb 3, nb 15	24	b 1, lb 3, w 1, nb 3	8
			190		**186**

FoW (1): 1-47, 2-47, 3-64, 4-84, 5-111, 6-111, 7-122, 8-126, 9-127, 10-190
FoW (2): 1-25, 2-32, 3-50, 4-60, 5-92, 6-154, 7-163, 8-167, 9-171, 10-186

Khan Research Laboratories Bowling

	O	M	R	W		O	M	R	W	
Yasir Arafat	17	3	49	3	1nb	22	10	43	5	1nb
Jaffar Nazir	15	6	43	1	1w,1nb	18	6	37	3	1w,1nb
Akhtar Ayub	18	3	72	4	4w,1nb	10	5	19	0	1w
Bilal Asad	18	5	48	1						
Ali Naqvi	2	0	10	0	(4)	12	2	34	0	
Saeed Ajmal	10	4	21	0		14	5	25	2	
Mohammad Wasim	1.1	0	1	1	(5)	1	0	5	0	

Sui Northern Gas Pipelines Limited Bowling

	O	M	R	W		O	M	R	W	
Samiullah Khan	19	7	43	2	2nb	21	3	56	2	1nb
Asad Ali	22	6	57	5	7nb	22	4	51	5	1w
Adil Raza	13.3	3	47	2	6nb	22.1	4	67	3	2nb
Imran Khalid	7	1	34	1	1nb	1	0	8	0	

Umpires: Islam Khan and Zameer Haider. Referee: Ishtiaq Ahmed.   Toss: Khan Research Laboratories

Close of Play: 1st day: Sui Northern Gas Pipelines Limited (1) 254 all out; 2nd day: Sui Northern Gas Pipelines Limited (2) 36-0 (Mohammad Hafeez 28*, Yasir Arafat 7*, 10.2 overs); 3rd day: Sui Northern Gas Pipelines Limited (2) 175-9 (Samiullah Khan 18*, Adil Raza 0*, 75.4 overs).

LAHORE RAVI v NATIONAL BANK OF PAKISTAN

Played at Gaddafi Stadium, Lahore, November 1, 2, 3, 4, 2007.
Quaid-e-Azam Trophy 2007/08 - Group A
National Bank of Pakistan won by seven wickets.   **(Points: Lahore Ravi 0, National Bank of Pakistan 9)**

LAHORE RAVI

1	Kashif Siddiq	lbw b Wahab Riaz	62	b Wasim Khan	30
2	Ahmed Shehzad	c Amin-ur-Rehman b Tahir Mughal	34	c and b Wasim Khan	25
3	Rizwan Ahmed	c Shahid Yousuf b Tahir Mughal	30	lbw b Wahab Riaz	1
4	Ashraf Ali	c Rashid Riaz b Wasim Khan	53	lbw b Mansoor Amjad	19
5	Arsalan Mir	c Naumanullah b Uzair-ul-Haq	22	run out	4
6	Saad Nasim	c Amin-ur-Rehman b Wahab Riaz	20	c Amin-ur-Rehman b Wahab Riaz	94
7	Waqas Ahmed	lbw b Wahab Riaz	1	(8) b Mansoor Amjad	0
8	*Junaid Zia	lbw b Tahir Mughal	9	(9) c Wasim Khan b Tahir Mughal	67
9	†Shahbaz Butt	lbw b Mansoor Amjad	0	(7) c Amin-ur-Rehman b Uzair-ul-Haq	13
10	Kashif Shafi	c Rashid Riaz b Wahab Riaz	23	not out	22
11	Azam Khan	not out	7	absent hurt	0
	Extras	b 4, lb 8, w 3, nb 7	22	lb 5, nb 9	14
			283		**289**

FoW (1): 1-53, 2-119, 3-168, 4-195, 5-211, 6-212, 7-237, 8-244, 9-260, 10-283
FoW (2): 1-27, 2-30, 3-63, 4-71, 5-103, 6-132, 7-133, 8-234, 9-289

NATIONAL BANK OF PAKISTAN

1	Nasir Jamshed	lbw b Azam Khan	27	run out	15
2	Rashid Riaz	c Shahbaz Butt b Arsalan Mir	33	not out	63
3	Naumanullah	c Ahmed Shehzad b Arsalan Mir	44	st Shahbaz Butt b Kashif Shafi	58
4	Shahid Yousuf	lbw b Junaid Zia	21	c Junaid Zia b Arsalan Mir	11
5	Naved Latif	b Arsalan Mir	176		
6	*Mansoor Amjad	c Ashraf Ali b Saad Nasim	31	(5) not out	1
7	Tahir Mughal	c sub (Usama Aftab) b Saad Nasim	0		
8	†Amin-ur-Rehman	run out	69		
9	Wasim Khan	c Shahbaz Butt b Arsalan Mir	5		
10	Wahab Riaz	c Shahbaz Butt b Junaid Zia	1		
11	Uzair-ul-Haq	not out	3		
	Extras	w 1, nb 7	8	b 1, lb 2, w 1, nb 5	9
			418	**(3 wickets)**	**157**

FoW (1): 1-31, 2-97, 3-110, 4-137, 5-211, 6-211, 7-378, 8-391, 9-414, 10-418
FoW (2): 1-18, 2-123, 3-151

National Bank of Pakistan Bowling

	O	M	R	W		O	M	R	W	
Wasim Khan	19	4	46	1	1w	16	3	68	2	1nb
Wahab Riaz	22.2	5	75	4	1nb	14	3	45	2	
Tahir Mughal	20	7	44	3	2nb	12.3	8	20	1	1nb
Uzair-ul-Haq	12	1	68	1	2w,1nb	15	5	75	1	3nb
Mansoor Amjad	9	0	33	1	3nb	15	0	76	2	4nb
Shahid Yousuf	1	0	5	0						

Lahore Ravi Bowling

	O	M	R	W			O	M	R	W	
Junaid Zia	27.5	6	141	2	1w,1nb		7	0	42	0	1w,3nb
Azam Khan	20.4	1	97	1							
Waqas Ahmed	15	1	43	0	2nb	(2)	6	1	21	0	
Arsalan Mir	19	3	65	4	3nb	(3)	9.3	1	53	1	2nb
Kashif Shafi	11	3	43	0		(4)	9	1	32	1	
Saad Nasim	9	3	29	2	1nb						
Kashif Siddiq						(5)	1	0	6	0	

Umpires: Jamil Kamran and Saleem Badar.   Referee: Mahmood Rasheed.   Toss: National Bank of Pakistan

Close of Play: 1st day: Lahore Ravi (1) 250-8 (Saad Nasim 20*, Kashif Shafi 0*, 76.5 overs); 2nd day: National Bank of Pakistan (1) 275-6 (Naved Latif 97*, Amin-ur-Rehman 18*, 69 overs); 3rd day: Lahore Ravi (2) 108-5 (Saad Nasim 21*, Shahbaz Butt 5*, 34.3 overs).

Naved Latif's 176 took 247 balls in 341 minutes and included 27 fours and 4 sixes.

MULTAN v WATER AND POWER DEVELOPMENT AUTHORITY

Played at Multan Cricket Stadium, November 1, 2, 3, 4, 2007.
Quaid-e-Azam Trophy 2007/08 - Group A
Water and Power Development Authority won by an innings and 34 runs.   (Points: Multan 0, Water and Power
Development Authority 9)

MULTAN

1	Hammad Tariq	lbw b Nawaz Sardar	8	b Sarfraz Ahmed		0
2	Usman Tariq	b Sarfraz Ahmed	34	c Sarfraz Ahmed b Azharullah		26
3	Naved Yasin	c Jahangir Mirza b Sarfraz Ahmed	1	(4) lbw b Bilal Khilji		10
4	Mohammad Hafeez	c Zulqarnain Haider b Nawaz Sardar	2	(3) lbw b Nawaz Sardar		4
5	Kashif Naved	c Sarfraz Ahmed b Azharullah	89	c Zulqarnain Haider b Azharullah		11
6	Mohammad Sarwar	b Azharullah	21	not out		54
7	Ansar Javed	c Zulqarnain Haider b Azharullah	0	(8) b Aqeel Ahmed		14
8	†Gulraiz Sadaf	c Zulqarnain Haider b Azharullah	0	(7) c Zulqarnain Haider b Azharullah		2
9	*Abdur Rauf	c Jahangir Mirza b Aqeel Ahmed	47	c Zulqarnain Haider b Sarfraz Ahmed		43
10	Mohammad Kashif	b Azharullah	16	lbw b Sarfraz Ahmed		10
11	Ahmed Raza	not out	0	b Aqeel Ahmed		23
	Extras	lb 5, w 2, nb 13	20	lb 6, nb 5		11
			238			**208**

FoW (1): 1-35, 2-43, 3-46, 4-53, 5-87, 6-87, 7-87, 8-191, 9-237, 10-238
FoW (2): 1-5, 2-14, 3-37, 4-37, 5-58, 6-67, 7-85, 8-142, 9-160, 10-208

WATER AND POWER DEVELOPMENT AUTHORITY

1	†Zulqarnain Haider	lbw b Ansar Javed	11
2	Masood Asim	c Gulraiz Sadaf b Ahmed Raza	37
3	Nawaz Sardar	st Gulraiz Sadaf b Ahmed Raza	38
4	Tariq Aziz	c Hammad Tariq b Abdur Rauf	6
5	*Aamer Sajjad	c and b Abdur Rauf	41
6	Bilal Khilji	c Kashif Naved b Mohammad Kashif	147
7	Jahangir Mirza	lbw b Ansar Javed	32
8	Ali Azmat	c Gulraiz Sadaf b Ahmed Raza	29
9	Aqeel Ahmed	c Abdur Rauf b Ahmed Raza	61
10	Sarfraz Ahmed	b Ahmed Raza	55
11	Azharullah	not out	0
	Extras	b 4, lb 10, nb 9	23
			480

FoW (1): 1-11, 2-78, 3-87, 4-113, 5-187, 6-277, 7-331, 8-389, 9-467, 10-480

Water and Power Development Authority Bowling

	O	M	R	W			O	M	R	W	
Sarfraz Ahmed	23	6	52	2			20	10	29	3	
Azharullah	17.5	2	64	5	1w	(3)	16	0	80	3	
Nawaz Sardar	15	3	65	2	1w,9nb	(2)	6	0	20	1	2nb
Bilal Khilji	2	1	4	0			2	1	1	1	
Aqeel Ahmed	16	1	48	1	4nb		13.3	3	72	2	3nb

Multan Bowling

	O	M	R	W	
Abdur Rauf	39	1	155	2	3nb
Ansar Javed	21	1	66	2	6nb
Mohammad Kashif	22	1	91	1	
Ahmed Raza	42.2	8	111	5	
Mohammad Hafeez	11	2	26	0	
Usman Tariq	5	1	17	0	

Umpires: Ahsan Raza and Nadeem Ghauri. Referee: Mohammad Javed.   Toss: Water and Power Development Authority

Close of Play: 1st day: Water and Power Development Authority (1) 20-1 (Masood Asim 5*, Nawaz Sardar 4*, 7 overs); 2nd day: Water and Power Development Authority (1) 223-5 (Bilal Khilji 68*, Jahangir Mirza 12*, 90 overs); 3rd day: Multan (2) 71-6 (Mohammad Sarwar 8*, Ansar Javed 3*, 28.1 overs).

Bilal Khilji's 147 took 219 balls in 337 minutes and included 17 fours.

PAKISTAN INTERNATIONAL AIRLINES v ZARAI TARAQIATI BANK LIMITED

Played at Sheikhupura Stadium, November 1, 2, 3, 4, 2007.
Quaid-e-Azam Trophy 2007/08 - Group B
Pakistan International Airlines won by eight wickets.   (Points: Pakistan International Airlines 9, Zarai Taraqiati Bank Limited 0)

ZARAI TARAQIATI BANK LIMITED

1	Afaq Raheem	c Shoaib Khan b Aizaz Cheema	74	lbw b Tahir Khan	9
2	Inam-ul-Haq	c Sarfraz Ahmed b Jamshed Ahmed	4	lbw b Ali Imran	6
3	Faisal Naved	c Sarfraz Ahmed b Aizaz Cheema	1	(4) b Aizaz Cheema	3
4	Aamer Bashir	lbw b Ali Imran	26	(6) lbw b Aizaz Cheema	14
5	Wajahatullah Wasti	b Aizaz Cheema	93	(8) run out	5
6	Adnan Raza	c Agha Sabir b Tahir Khan	5	(5) b Tahir Khan	31
7	*Abdul Razzaq	c Sarfraz Ahmed b Aizaz Cheema	30	c Faisal Iqbal b Tahir Khan	51
8	Junaid Nadir	c Fahad Iqbal b Ali Imran	15	(10) c Sarfraz Ahmed b Ali Imran	5
9	†Shakeel Ansar	c Sarfraz Ahmed b Ali Imran	5	c Shoaib Khan b Tahir Khan	9
10	Zohaib Khan	not out	0	(3) c Khurram Manzoor b Ali Imran	28
11	Mohammad Khalil	c Sarfraz Ahmed b Ali Imran	0	not out	0
	Extras	b 7, lb 7, w 1, nb 7	22	b 5, lb 3, w 1, nb 3	12
			275		173

FoW (1): 1-23, 2-24, 3-90, 4-132, 5-151, 6-254, 7-255, 8-275, 9-275, 10-275
FoW (2): 1-12, 2-24, 3-33, 4-57, 5-96, 6-129, 7-136, 8-168, 9-173, 10-173

PAKISTAN INTERNATIONAL AIRLINES

1	Khurram Manzoor	c Aamer Bashir b Junaid Nadir	74	b Adnan Raza	34
2	Kamran Sajid	c Afaq Raheem b Mohammad Khalil	4	lbw b Inam-ul-Haq	2
3	Agha Sabir	b Zohaib Khan	55	not out	4
4	*Faisal Iqbal	c and b Zohaib Khan	55		
5	Shoaib Khan	c Shakeel Ansar b Abdul Razzaq	13	(4) not out	0
6	Fahad Iqbal	c Inam-ul-Haq b Junaid Nadir	63		
7	†Sarfraz Ahmed	lbw b Inam-ul-Haq	73		
8	Tahir Khan	c Afaq Raheem b Junaid Nadir	18		
9	Jamshed Ahmed	c Adnan Raza b Junaid Nadir	0		
10	Ali Imran	not out	4		
11	Aizaz Cheema	b Junaid Nadir	17		
	Extras	b 25, lb 3, w 2, nb 1	31	b 2, lb 1	3
			407	(2 wickets)	43

FoW (1): 1-25, 2-128, 3-142, 4-193, 5-214, 6-349, 7-373, 8-378, 9-383, 10-407
FoW (2): 1-35, 2-39

Pakistan International Airlines Bowling

	O	M	R	W			O	M	R	W	
Ali Imran	22.3	4	61	4	3nb		12.1	0	50	3	
Jamshed Ahmed	22	2	62	1	1w,4nb	(4)	5	2	4	0	1w
Aizaz Cheema	24	6	56	4		(2)	20	7	55	2	
Kamran Sajid	6	2	14	0		(5)	1	0	2	0	
Tahir Khan	28	5	68	1		(3)	13	1	54	4	3nb

Zarai Taraqiati Bank Limited Bowling

	O	M	R	W			O	M	R	W	
Mohammad Khalil	22	5	61	1	1w,1nb	(2)	3	0	10	0	
Junaid Nadir	26.3	3	89	5	1w	(3)	2	1	1	0	
Abdul Razzaq	25	11	51	1		(1)	2	0	8	0	
Zohaib Khan	48	13	152	2			2	1	1	0	
Faisal Naved	1	0	2	0							
Inam-ul-Haq	7	0	24	1		(5)	2.1	0	15	1	
Aamer Bashir	1	1	0	0							
Adnan Raza						(6)	1	0	5	1	

Umpires: Iftikhar Malik and Zaheer Ahmed. Referee: Ilyas Khan.   Toss: Zarai Taraqiati Bank Limited

Close of Play: 1st day: Zarai Taraqiati Bank Limited (1) 210-5 (Wajahatullah Wasti 61*, Abdul Razzaq 19*, 83 overs); 2nd day: Pakistan International Airlines (1) 193-3 (Faisal Iqbal 44*, Shoaib Khan 13*, 61 overs); 3rd day: Zarai Taraqiati Bank Limited (2) 24-2 (Zohaib Khan 9*, 10.3 overs).

QUETTA v LAHORE SHALIMAR

Played at Bugti Stadium, Quetta, November 1, 2, 3, 2007.
Quaid-e-Azam Trophy 2007/08 - Group B
Lahore Shalimar won by five wickets.　　(Points: Quetta 0, Lahore Shalimar 9)

QUETTA

1	Shoaib Khan	c Suleman Khan b Mohammad Shahzad	12	lbw b Asif Raza	15
2	Samiullah Agha	run out (Mohammad Saeed)	23	b Mohammad Hussain	21
3	Taimur Ali	c Junaid Malik b Mohammad Shahzad	0	c Ali Raza b Asif Raza	5
4	Sabir Hussain	c Suleman Khan b Mohammad Shahzad	0	lbw b Asif Raza	49
5	Jalat Khan	c Ali Raza b Usman Malik	5	(6) c Ali Raza b Mohammad Saeed	25
6	*Nasim Khan	not out	43	(5) b Mohammad Shahzad	10
7	Naseer Khan	c Mohammad Hussain		(8) c Salman Akbar	
		b Mohammad Shahzad	12	b Mohammad Shahzad	30
8	Faisal Irfan	c Usman Malik b Mohammad Shahzad	3	(9) not out	37
9	†Sanaullah Khan	c Salman Akbar b Mohammad Saeed	1	(10) c Haseeb Rasheed b Asif Raza	30
10	Arun Lal	c Junaid Malik b Mohammad Saeed	10	(7) c Ali Raza b Mohammad Saeed	6
11	Nazar Hussain	c Salman Akbar b Mohammad Saeed	0	c Usman Malik b Mohammad Hussain	1
	Extras	b 8, lb 3, nb 10	21	b 4, lb 2, nb 12	18
			130		247

FoW (1): 1-19, 2-20, 3-20, 4-29, 5-62, 6-90, 7-98, 8-109, 9-130, 10-130
FoW (2): 1-36, 2-45, 3-48, 4-63, 5-101, 6-116, 7-165, 8-182, 9-246, 10-247

LAHORE SHALIMAR

1	Junaid Malik	c Sanaullah Khan b Nazar Hussain	3	c and b Nazar Hussain	1
2	Salman Akbar	b Nazar Hussain	8	c Sanaullah Khan b Arun Lal	12
3	Ahmed Butt	lbw b Nazar Hussain	0		
4	Suleman Khan	lbw b Faisal Irfan	15	c Arun Lal b Naseer Khan	38
5	Haseeb Rasheed	c Sanaullah Khan b Nazar Hussain	12	lbw b Faisal Irfan	15
6	Mohammad Hussain	c Sanaullah Khan b Nazar Hussain	33	not out	26
7	*†Ali Raza	c Jalat Khan b Arun Lal	3	(3) c Sanaullah Khan b Nazar Hussain	8
8	Mohammad Saeed	c Nasim Khan b Nazar Hussain	59	(7) not out	7
9	Asif Raza	lbw b Naseer Khan	24		
10	Usman Malik	c Taimur Ali b Naseer Khan	67		
11	Mohammad Shahzad	not out	20		
	Extras	b 1, lb 6, w 1, nb 9	17	b 1, lb 1, w 5, nb 3	10
			261	(5 wickets)	117

FoW (1): 1-3, 2-7, 3-19, 4-32, 5-48, 6-55, 7-115, 8-168, 9-174, 10-261
FoW (2): 1-3, 2-20, 3-25, 4-61, 5-110

Lahore Shalimar Bowling

	O	M	R	W			O	M	R	W	
Asif Raza	7	5	8	0		(4)	14	3	36	4	3nb
Mohammad Shahzad	16	4	47	5	10nb	(1)	14	2	60	2	2nb
Usman Malik	17	6	44	1		(5)	13	0	29	0	
Mohammad Hussain	4	0	10	0		(3)	21.4	9	54	2	
Mohammad Saeed	3.5	1	10	3		(2)	13	1	62	2	7nb

Quetta Bowling

	O	M	R	W			O	M	R	W	
Faisal Irfan	14	2	44	1	3nb		11	2	30	1	1w,2nb
Nazar Hussain	23	6	83	6	1w		16	6	45	2	
Arun Lal	8	1	73	1	6nb		9	2	25	1	4w,1nb
Naseer Khan	14.4	7	22	2			3	1	9	1	
Jalat Khan	5	0	32	0							
Shoaib Khan						(5)	0.1	0	6	0	

Umpires: Raweed Khan and Shakeel Khan.　Referee: Saadat Ali.　　　　Toss: Quetta

Close of Play: 1st day: Lahore Shalimar (1) 118-7 (Mohammad Saeed 37*, Asif Raza 0*, 33 overs); 2nd day: Quetta (2) 170-7 (Naseer Khan 26*, Faisal Irfan 4*, 49 overs).

The match was scheduled for four days but completed in three.

SIALKOT v HABIB BANK LIMITED

Played at Lahore Country Club, Muridke, November 1, 2, 3, 2007.
Quaid-e-Azam Trophy 2007/08 - Group A
Habib Bank Limited won by an innings and 75 runs.   (Points: Sialkot 0, Habib Bank Limited 9)

HABIB BANK LIMITED

1	Imran Farhat	c Mohammad Ayub	
		b Mohammad Wasim	41
2	Taufeeq Umar	lbw b Mohammad Ayub	131
3	Rafatullah Mohmand	c Khalid Mahmood	
		b Mohammad Wasim	85
4	*Hasan Raza	b Mohammad Wasim	3
5	Aftab Alam	c Faisal Khan b Mohammad Ali	23
6	Khaqan Arsal	run out	0
7	†Humayun Farhat	c Bilal Hussain b Mohammad Ali	6
8	Kamran Hussain	not out	44
9	Danish Kaneria	c Arsalan Anwar b Mohammad Wasim	0
10	Fahad Masood	b Mohammad Ali	12
11	Mohammad Aslam	c Naeem Anjum b Mohammad Wasim	7
	Extras	b 1, lb 10, w 3, nb 3	17
			369

FoW (1): 1-84, 2-260, 3-269, 4-274, 5-274, 6-293, 7-332, 8-332, 9-358, 10-369

SIALKOT

1	Naeemuddin	b Fahad Masood	12	(2) b Kamran Hussain	31
2	Shahid Siddiq	b Mohammad Aslam	15	(1) c Imran Farhat b Fahad Masood	8
3	Arsalan Anwar	c and b Danish Kaneria	11	c Taufeeq Umar b Mohammad Aslam	17
4	Faisal Khan	c Rafatullah Mohmand b Danish Kaneria	0	c Taufeeq Umar b Mohammad Aslam	0
5	Bilal Hussain	c Taufeeq Umar b Mohammad Aslam	33	lbw b Kamran Hussain	0
6	*Mohammad Ayub	c and b Imran Farhat	28	c Humayun Farhat b Mohammad Aslam	23
7	Adeel Malik	lbw b Mohammad Aslam	0	c Hasan Raza b Mohammad Aslam	39
8	†Khalid Mahmood	lbw b Danish Kaneria	49	c Kamran Hussain b Danish Kaneria	0
9	Mohammad Wasim	c sub (Irfan Fazil) b Imran Farhat	8	c sub (Sulaman Qadir)	
				b Mohammad Aslam	0
10	Naeem Anjum	not out	0	c Taufeeq Umar b Danish Kaneria	4
11	Mohammad Ali	lbw b Danish Kaneria	0	not out	0
	Extras	b 2, lb 7	9	lb 7	7
			165		129

FoW (1): 1-18, 2-39, 3-40, 4-49, 5-93, 6-93, 7-149, 8-165, 9-165, 10-165
FoW (2): 1-27, 2-57, 3-57, 4-57, 5-61, 6-114, 7-121, 8-125, 9-127, 10-129

Sialkot Bowling

	O	M	R	W	
Mohammad Wasim	27.5	1	110	5	2nb
Mohammad Ali	29	5	123	3	3w,1nb
Naeem Anjum	19	3	60	0	
Adeel Malik	10	0	50	0	
Mohammad Ayub	5	0	15	1	

Habib Bank Limited Bowling

	O	M	R	W		O	M	R	W
Fahad Masood	12	3	28	1	(2)	10	2	29	1
Kamran Hussain	5	2	4	0	(1)	11	3	23	2
Danish Kaneria	17.3	1	82	4	(4)	17.2	5	39	2
Mohammad Aslam	16	9	32	3	(3)	18	8	31	5
Imran Farhat	4	2	10	2					

Umpires: Ahmed Shahab and Kaukab Butt. Referee: Abdus Sami.   Toss: Habib Bank Limited

Close of Play: 1st day: Habib Bank Limited (1) 340-8 (Kamran Hussain 28*, Fahad Masood 7*, 83 overs); 2nd day: Sialkot (2) 30-1 (Naeem Anjum 21*, Arsalan Anwar 0*, 13 overs).

The match was scheduled for four days but completed in three. Taufeeq Umar's 131 took 174 balls in 238 minutes and included 12 fours and 1 six.

FAISALABAD v WATER AND POWER DEVELOPMENT AUTHORITY

Played at Iqbal Stadium, Faisalabad, November 7, 8, 9, 10, 2007.
Quaid-e-Azam Trophy 2007/08 - Group A
Match drawn.   (Points: Faisalabad 0, Water and Power Development Authority 3)

FAISALABAD

1	Imran Ali	c Zulqarnain Haider b Bilal Khilji	30	c Aqeel Ahmed b Azharullah		23
2	Abdul Mannan	c Zulqarnain Haider b Kashif Raza	19	c Sarfraz Ahmed b Azharullah		24
3	Ammar Mahmood	lbw b Azharullah	87	c Jahangir Mirza b Sarfraz Ahmed		106
4	Usman Arshad	c Zulqarnain Haider b Kashif Raza	13	b Farooq Iqbal		50
5	Imran Ahmed	c Masood Asim b Azharullah	42	not out		32
6	*Ijaz Ahmed	c Jahangir Mirza b Aqeel Ahmed	13			
7	†Mohammad Salman	b Kashif Raza	22	(6) not out		19
8	Ahmed Hayat	c and b Aqeel Ahmed	0			
9	Shafqat Hussain	c Zulqarnain Haider b Kashif Raza	6			
10	Ali Raza	c Aqeel Ahmed b Sarfraz Ahmed	23			
11	Mohammad Talha	not out	0			
	Extras	lb 6, nb 7	13	lb 7, w 4, nb 4		15
			268	(4 wickets)		269

FoW (1): 1-35, 2-60, 3-89, 4-176, 5-211, 6-211, 7-211, 8-236, 9-267, 10-268
FoW (2): 1-51, 2-54, 3-158, 4-236

WATER AND POWER DEVELOPMENT AUTHORITY

1	†Zulqarnain Haider	run out (Imran Ahmed)	5
2	Masood Asim	c Mohammad Salman b Ahmed Hayat	9
3	Tariq Aziz	c Mohammad Salman b Ali Raza	167
4	*Aamer Sajjad	lbw b Ali Raza	99
5	Bilal Khilji	not out	84
6	Jahangir Mirza	c Imran Ali b Ali Raza	0
7	Farooq Iqbal	b Ijaz Ahmed	5
8	Aqeel Ahmed	b Ijaz Ahmed	12
9	Kashif Raza	lbw b Ijaz Ahmed	0
10	Sarfraz Ahmed	c Usman Arshad b Shafqat Hussain	11
11	Azharullah	c Ahmed Hayat b Ali Raza	0
	Extras	b 8, lb 14, w 6, nb 27	55
			447

FoW (1): 1-15, 2-23, 3-309, 4-342, 5-343, 6-367, 7-389, 8-389, 9-416, 10-447

Water and Power Development Authority Bowling

	O	M	R	W			O	M	R	W	
Sarfraz Ahmed	22	8	59	1		(2)	23	8	35	1	4w
Kashif Raza	20.1	4	61	4	5nb	(1)	12	2	32	0	1nb
Azharullah	16	0	61	2			23	4	75	2	
Bilal Khilji	2	0	8	1							
Aqeel Ahmed	18	1	49	2	2nb	(4)	21	1	62	0	3nb
Farooq Iqbal	14	6	24	0		(5)	26	9	45	1	
Jahangir Mirza						(6)	3	0	13	0	

Faisalabad Bowling

	O	M	R	W	
Ahmed Hayat	24	2	97	1	8nb
Mohammad Talha	17	1	77	0	7nb
Ali Raza	24.3	1	83	4	3w,11nb
Shafqat Hussain	24	1	86	1	
Ijaz Ahmed	26	4	59	3	
Imran Ahmed	1	0	7	0	
Ammar Mahmood	5	1	16	0	3w,1nb

Umpires: Kaukab Butt and Nadeem Ghauri.   Referee: Arshad Pervez.   Toss: Water and Power Development Authority

Close of Play: 1st day: Faisalabad (1) 243-8 (Mohammad Salman 16*, Ali Raza 6*, 85 overs); 2nd day: Water and Power Development Authority (1) 307-2 (Tariq Aziz 155*, Aamer Sajjad 99*, 73 overs); 3rd day: Faisalabad (2) 75-2 (Ammar Mahmood 10*, Usman Arshad 12*, 32 overs).
Tariq Aziz's 167 took 239 balls in 323 minutes and included 18 fours. Ammar Mahmood's 106 took 226 balls in 304 minutes and included 9 fours and 3 sixes.

HYDERABAD v SUI SOUTHERN GAS CORPORATION

Played at Niaz Stadium, Hyderabad, November 7, 8, 9, 10, 2007.
Quaid-e-Azam Trophy 2007/08 - Group A
Sui Southern Gas Corporation won by nine wickets.   (Points: Hyderabad 0, Sui Southern Gas Corporation 9)

HYDERABAD

1	Akram Khan	b Sohail Khan	0	b Sohail Khan	0
2	Zahid Khan	c Ahmed Zeeshan b Shehzad Butt	25	c Ahmed Zeeshan b Sohail Khan	24
3	Faisal Athar	c Ashraf Ali b Haaris Ayaz	25	(5) b Sohail Khan	53
4	Rizwan Ahmed	b Sohail Khan	5	(6) b Mansoor Ahmed	40
5	Shahid Qambrani	c Asif Zakir b Mansoor Ahmed	20	(4) c Asif Zakir b Haaris Ayaz	134
6	Hanif-ur-Rehman	c and b Mansoor Ahmed	18	(7) c Ali Hussain b Shehzad Butt	14
7	*†Hanif Malik	lbw b Shehzad Butt	23	(8) c Asif Zakir b Haaris Ayaz	1
8	Pir Zulfiqar	c Sohail Khan b Haaris Ayaz	49	(3) b Sohail Khan	0
9	Kashif Bhatti	lbw b Sohail Khan	37	c Mohtashim Ali b Shehzad Butt	33
10	Farhan Ayub	b Sohail Khan	0	(11) c Ali Hussain b Sohail Khan	10
11	Naeem-ur-Rehman	not out	4	(10) not out	16
	Extras	b 4, lb 6, w 1, nb 10	21	b 6, lb 2, w 3, nb 8	19
			227		344

FoW (1): 1-0, 2-38, 3-46, 4-77, 5-104, 6-118, 7-134, 8-215, 9-215, 10-227
FoW (2): 1-0, 2-0, 3-55, 4-164, 5-264, 6-264, 7-270, 8-299, 9-321, 10-344

SUI SOUTHERN GAS CORPORATION

1	Asif Zakir	lbw b Farhan Ayub	1	not out	87
2	Mohtashim Ali	c Akram Khan b Rizwan Ahmed	50	c Shahid Qambrani b Pir Zulfiqar	34
3	Imran Abbas	lbw b Rizwan Ahmed	37	not out	25
4	Ali Hussain	c Shahid Qambrani b Pir Zulfiqar	4		
5	*Saeed Bin Nasir	st Hanif Malik b Pir Zulfiqar	163		
6	Ashraf Ali	lbw b Pir Zulfiqar	44		
7	†Ahmed Zeeshan	c Hanif Malik b Farhan Ayub	28		
8	Shehzad Butt	b Kashif Bhatti	50		
9	Haaris Ayaz	st Hanif Malik b Pir Zulfiqar	0		
10	Sohail Khan	not out	0		
11	Mansoor Ahmed	c Shahid Qambrani b Kashif Bhatti	7		
	Extras	b 8, lb 2, w 1, nb 21	32	lb 3, w 2, nb 5	10
			416	(1 wicket)	156

FoW (1): 1-13, 2-75, 3-84, 4-137, 5-249, 6-328, 7-407, 8-409, 9-409, 10-416
FoW (2): 1-81

Sui Southern Gas Corporation Bowling

	O	M	R	W			O	M	R	W	
Sohail Khan	23	5	68	4			23.5	5	90	5	1w,1nb
Shehzad Butt	14	2	38	2	1w,5nb		18	3	77	2	2w
Mansoor Ahmed	23	3	70	2	5nb		27	3	97	1	3nb
Haaris Ayaz	9.5	0	37	2			22	4	60	2	4nb
Mohtashim Ali	1	0	4	0			6	1	12	0	

Hyderabad Bowling

	O	M	R	W				O	M	R	W	
Farhan Ayub	21	2	83	2	4nb			4	0	31	0	
Naeem-ur-Rehman	19	4	83	0	7nb			4	0	23	0	2w,3nb
Pir Zulfiqar	33	9	72	4	2nb			13	2	45	1	
Hanif-ur-Rehman	6	1	22	0								
Rizwan Ahmed	17	0	88	2	8nb	(4)		5	0	27	0	1nb
Kashif Bhatti	12.4	3	48	2		(5)		6.4	0	27	0	
Akram Khan	1	0	5	0								
Zahid Khan	1	0	5	0								

Umpires: Jamil Kamran and Mohammad Arif.   Referee: Mahmood Rasheed.   Toss: Hyderabad

Close of Play: 1st day: Sui Southern Gas Corporation (1) 34-1 (Mohtashim Ali 17*, Saeed Bin Nasir 9*, 10 overs); 2nd day: Sui Southern Gas Corporation (1) 336-6 (Saeed Bin Nasir 140*, Shehzad Butt 0*, 93 overs); 3rd day: Hyderabad (2) 214-4 (Shahid Qambrani 103*, Rizwan Ahmed 22*, 63 overs).
Saeed Bin Nasir's 163 took 231 balls in 335 minutes and included 23 fours and 1 six. Shahid Qambrani's 134 took 258 balls in 311 minutes and included 14 fours.

ISLAMABAD v ZARAI TARAQIATI BANK LIMITED

Played at Diamond Club Ground, Islamabad, November 7, 8, 9, 2007.
Quaid-e-Azam Trophy 2007/08 - Group B
Zarai Taraqiati Bank Limited won by six wickets.   (Points: Islamabad 0, Zarai Taraqiati Bank Limited 9)

ISLAMABAD

1	Raheel Majeed	b Abdul Razzaq	0	c Adnan Raza b Zohaib Khan	44
2	Umair Khan	c Kamran Naeem b Mohammad Khalil	0	b Abdul Razzaq	15
3	Ameer Khan	b Abdul Razzaq	21	c Aamer Bashir b Mohammad Khalil	2
4	Fayyaz Ahmed	c Wajahatullah Wasti		(5) c Wajahatullah Wasti	
		b Mohammad Khalil	25	b Mohammad Khalil	73
5	*Ashar Zaidi	c Kamran Naeem b Mohammad Khalil	0	(8) b Mohammad Khalil	7
6	Asadullah Sumari	lbw b Mohammad Khalil	4	(4) c Kamran Naeem b Azhar Attari	18
7	Rauf Akbar	lbw b Abdul Razzaq	2	c Aamer Bashir b Mohammad Khalil	36
8	Sajid Ali	b Mohammad Khalil	6	(6) c Abdul Razzaq b Azhar Attari	6
9	†Mohammad Kashif	c Abdul Razzaq b Mohammad Khalil	7	c Aamer Bashir b Azhar Attari	4
10	Shehzad Azam	c Wajahatullah Wasti b Abdul Razzaq	15	not out	16
11	Saad Altaf	not out	0	run out	5
	Extras	b 1, lb 11, w 2, nb 1	15	b 5, lb 7, w 6, nb 13	31
			95		**257**

FoW (1): 1-0, 2-0, 3-53, 4-55, 5-59, 6-61, 7-65, 8-72, 9-83, 10-95
FoW (2): 1-33, 2-36, 3-90, 4-90, 5-108, 6-169, 7-182, 8-210, 9-236, 10-257

ZARAI TARAQIATI BANK LIMITED

1	Afaq Raheem	b Raheel Majeed	26	lbw b Rauf Akbar	18
2	Atif Ashraf	lbw b Rauf Akbar	32	lbw b Sajid Ali	18
3	Faisal Naved	lbw b Rauf Akbar	5	c Fayyaz Ahmed b Sajid Ali	6
4	Adnan Raza	lbw b Shehzad Azam	14	b Rauf Akbar	15
5	Wajahatullah Wasti	c Shehzad Azam b Rauf Akbar	31	not out	28
6	Aamer Bashir	c Asadullah Sumari b Shehzad Azam	6		
7	*Abdul Razzaq	c Mohammad Kashif b Rauf Akbar	52	(6) not out	36
8	†Kamran Naeem	b Rauf Akbar	1		
9	Zohaib Khan	run out	13		
10	Mohammad Khalil	run out	4		
11	Azhar Attari	not out	0		
	Extras	b 5, lb 6, w 6, nb 16	33	b 4, w 1, nb 12	17
			217	(4 wickets)	**138**

FoW (1): 1-65, 2-67, 3-87, 4-87, 5-103, 6-170, 7-200, 8-201, 9-206, 10-217
FoW (2): 1-39, 2-39, 3-68, 4-78

Zarai Taraqiati Bank Limited Bowling

	O	M	R	W		O	M	R	W	
Abdul Razzaq	14.3	4	38	4	1w	18	1	71	1	
Mohammad Khalil	14	3	45	6	2w,1nb	22.5	4	81	4	4w,4nb
Azhar Attari				(3)		25	5	82	3	2w,7nb
Faisal Naved				(4)	2	0	4	0		1nb
Zohaib Khan				(5)	6	1	7	0		1nb

Islamabad Bowling

	O	M	R	W			O	M	R	W	
Saad Altaf	16	6	36	0							
Rauf Akbar	22.1	6	55	5	6w,7nb	(1)	12	2	49	2	1w,6nb
Shehzad Azam	19	3	84	2	9nb	(2)	8	1	43	0	4nb
Raheel Majeed	8	1	31	1		(3)	4.3	1	21	0	
Sajid Ali	1	1	0	0		(4)	4	0	21	2	

Umpires: Mian Mohammad Aslam and Zameer Haider. Referee: Anwar Khan. Toss: Zarai Taraqiati Bank Limited

Close of Play: 1st day: Zarai Taraqiati Bank Limited (1) 118-5 (Wajahatullah Wasti 9*, Abdul Razzaq 6*, 41 overs); 2nd day: Islamabad (2) 158-5 (Fayyaz Ahmed 22*, Rauf Akbar 32*, 45 overs).

The match was scheduled for four days but completed in three.

KARACHI WHITES v SIALKOT

Played at United Bank Limited Sports Complex, Karachi, November 7, 8, 9, 10, 2007.
Quaid-e-Azam Trophy 2007/08 - Group A
Karachi Whites won by 209 runs.   (Points: Karachi Whites 9, Sialkot 0)

KARACHI WHITES

1	Khalid Latif	c Nayyer Abbas b Imran Malik	1	c Mohammad Wasim b Mohammad Ali	104
2	Asad Shafiq	lbw b Imran Malik	17	lbw b Imran Malik	16
3	Daniyal Ahsan	c Faisal Khan b Mohammad Wasim	15	lbw b Imran Malik	0
4	Atif Ali	c Faisal Khan b Mohammad Wasim	8	lbw b Mohammad Ayub	30
5	Asim Kamal	c Faisal Khan b Mohammad Wasim	62	b Mohammad Ayub	8
6	Afsar Nawaz	c Faisal Khan b Mohammad Ali	12	c Qamar Shahzad b Nayyer Abbas	38
7	†Javed Mansoor	not out	77	(8) b Nayyer Abbas	19
8	*Mohammad Sami	c Mohammad Ali b Mohammad Wasim	16	(7) c Qamar Shahzad b Imran Malik	12
9	Tanvir Ahmed	lbw b Mohammad Wasim	0	not out	8
10	Misbah Khan	c Nayyer Abbas b Mohammad Ali	47	not out	0
11	Fahad Khan	c Khalid Mahmood b Mohammad Ali	0		
	Extras	b 2, lb 7, w 2, nb 6	17	b 3, lb 6, nb 1	10
			272	**(8 wickets, declared)**	**245**

FoW (1): 1-1, 2-27, 3-46, 4-47, 5-78, 6-145, 7-167, 8-168, 9-272, 10-272
FoW (2): 1-35, 2-37, 3-134, 4-150, 5-190, 6-206, 7-225, 8-237

SIALKOT

1	Naeemuddin	lbw b Misbah Khan	35	b Mohammad Sami	6
2	Qamar Shahzad	c Asad Shafiq b Tanvir Ahmed	4	b Tanvir Ahmed	2
3	Haris Sohail	c Asad Shafiq b Fahad Khan	7	b Mohammad Sami	0
4	Faisal Khan	c Javed Mansoor b Fahad Khan	2	c Javed Mansoor b Mohammad Sami	70
5	Bilal Hussain	c Misbah Khan b Mohammad Sami	14	lbw b Mohammad Sami	3
6	*Mohammad Ayub	b Tanvir Ahmed	16	c Tanvir Ahmed b Mohammad Sami	12
7	Nayyer Abbas	c Javed Mansoor b Tanvir Ahmed	19	c Afsar Nawaz b Fahad Khan	3
8	†Khalid Mahmood	c Mohammad Sami b Tanvir Ahmed	51	c Javed Mansoor b Mohammad Sami	30
9	Mohammad Wasim	c Javed Mansoor b Tanvir Ahmed	5	c Javed Mansoor b Mohammad Sami	3
10	Imran Malik	lbw b Tanvir Ahmed	5	not out	2
11	Mohammad Ali	not out	0	b Mohammad Sami	9
	Extras	lb 5, w 1, nb 2	8	w 2	2
			166		**142**

FoW (1): 1-10, 2-32, 3-42, 4-56, 5-70, 6-90, 7-128, 8-144, 9-165, 10-166
FoW (2): 1-6, 2-9, 3-9, 4-13, 5-33, 6-54, 7-108, 8-132, 9-142, 10-142

Sialkot Bowling

	O	M	R	W			O	M	R	W	
Mohammad Wasim	27	3	82	5	6nb		12	2	29	0	1nb
Imran Malik	23	3	51	2	2w	(3)	11	1	36	3	
Mohammad Ali	35	12	76	3		(2)	21	2	95	1	
Nayyer Abbas	12	0	42	0			11	0	51	2	
Qamar Shahzad	4	1	12	0							
Mohammad Ayub						(5)	7	0	25	2	

Karachi Whites Bowling

	O	M	R	W			O	M	R	W	
Mohammad Sami	21	3	54	1	1nb		16.3	3	39	8	1w
Tanvir Ahmed	25.4	9	43	6			18	3	54	1	1w
Fahad Khan	12	4	33	2	1w,1nb		7	2	15	1	
Misbah Khan	14	5	31	1			4	0	34	0	

Umpires: Akbar Khan and Ijaz Ahmed. Referee: Ilyas Khan.   Toss: Karachi Whites

Close of Play: 1st day: Karachi Whites (1) 242-8 (Javed Mansoor 72*, Misbah Khan 24*, 93 overs); 2nd day: Sialkot (1) 144-8 (Khalid Mahmood 32*, 62.5 overs); 3rd day: Sialkot (2) 9-3 (Faisal Khan 0*, 6.3 overs).

Khalid Latif's 104 took 155 balls in 234 minutes and included 10 fours and 1 six.

LAHORE RAVI v PAKISTAN CUSTOMS

Played at Lahore City Cricket Association Ground, November 7, 8, 9, 2007.
Quaid-e-Azam Trophy 2007/08 - Group A
Lahore Ravi won by nine wickets.   (Points: Lahore Ravi 9, Pakistan Customs 0)

PAKISTAN CUSTOMS

1	Hasnain Abbas	c Shahbaz Butt b Junaid Zia	2	b Waqas Ahmed	4
2	R.M.Khan	lbw b Waqas Ahmed	25	lbw b Waqas Ahmed	7
3	Asif Iqbal	c Saad Nasim b Waqas Ahmed	27	c Shahbaz Butt b Waqas Ahmed	0
4	Mohammad Nabi	c Ashraf Ali b Arsalan Mir	5	c Shahbaz Butt b Junaid Zia	9
5	*Zahoor Elahi	c Shahbaz Butt b Junaid Zia	7	(6) not out	59
6	Rehan Rafiq	c Shahbaz Butt b Salman Rahat	0	(7) c Shahbaz Butt b Salman Rahat	16
7	†Adnan Naved	c Saad Nasim b Junaid Zia	16	(5) lbw b Junaid Zia	1
8	Yasir Shah	c Ashraf Ali b Junaid Zia	12	c Saad Nasim b Salman Rahat	16
9	Raees Amjad	c Waqas Ahmed b Junaid Zia	4	c Shahbaz Butt b Salman Rahat	4
10	Hameed Hasan	b Junaid Zia	1	(11) run out	0
11	Sajjad Hussain	not out	0	(10) b Waqas Ahmed	0
	Extras	lb 5, w 3, nb 5	13	b 4, lb 4, w 3, nb 6	17
			112		**133**

FoW (1): 1-3, 2-47, 3-57, 4-66, 5-74, 6-82, 7-107, 8-111, 9-111, 10-112
FoW (2): 1-10, 2-10, 3-27, 4-27, 5-39, 6-76, 7-111, 8-121, 9-122, 10-133

LAHORE RAVI

1	Kashif Siddiq	lbw b Raees Amjad	0	not out	19
2	Sohail Ahmed	lbw b Yasir Shah	42	c Asif Iqbal b Raees Amjad	0
3	Rizwan Ahmed	c Hasnain Abbas b Sajjad Hussain	24	not out	12
4	Ashraf Ali	c Rehan Rafiq b Sajjad Hussain	1		
5	Arsalan Mir	lbw b Hameed Hasan	66		
6	Saad Nasim	b Raees Amjad	7		
7	†Shahbaz Butt	lbw b Raees Amjad	30		
8	*Junaid Zia	lbw b Yasir Shah	8		
9	Waqas Ahmed	c Yasir Shah b Sajjad Hussain	8		
10	Salman Rahat	c Adnan Naved b Raees Amjad	0		
11	Tehseen Mirza	not out	0		
	Extras	b 6, lb 6, w 3, nb 11	26	b 3, lb 1, nb 1	5
			212	**(1 wicket)**	**36**

FoW (1): 1-1, 2-53, 3-60, 4-137, 5-158, 6-158, 7-197, 8-211, 9-212, 10-212
FoW (2): 1-6

Lahore Ravi Bowling

	O	M	R	W			O	M	R	W	
Junaid Zia	14.1	5	34	6	1nb		17	2	46	2	3w,5nb
Salman Rahat	12	1	42	1	3w	(3)	7	1	28	3	
Waqas Ahmed	9	1	21	2	1nb	(2)	16.3	3	51	4	1nb
Arsalan Mir	7	1	10	1	3nb						

Pakistan Customs Bowling

	O	M	R	W			O	M	R	W	
Raees Amjad	19	4	55	4	3w,6nb		4	1	14	1	1nb
Hameed Hasan	19	6	48	1	1nb						
Sajjad Hussain	22.2	9	63	3	4nb	(2)	4	1	18	0	
Asif Iqbal	12	8	14	0							
Yasir Shah	11	4	20	2	2nb						

Umpires: Iqbal Butt and Saleem Badar. Referee: Abdus Sami.   Toss: Lahore Ravi

Close of Play: 1st day: Lahore Ravi (1) 61-3 (Sohail Ahmed 29*, Arsalan Mir 0*, 24.2 overs); 2nd day: Pakistan Customs (2) 28-4 (Adnan Naved 1*, Zahoor Elahi 0*, 13 overs).

The match was scheduled for four days but completed in three.

LAHORE SHALIMAR v KHAN RESEARCH LABORATORIES

Played at Gaddafi Stadium, Lahore, November 7, 8, 9, 10, 2007.
Quaid-e-Azam Trophy 2007/08 - Group B
Match drawn.   (Points: Lahore Shalimar 0, Khan Research Laboratories 3)

LAHORE SHALIMAR

1	Asif Khan	lbw b Yasir Arafat	11	(2) c Zulfiqar Jan b Yasir Arafat	22	
2	Salman Akbar	c Bazid Khan b Jaffar Nazir	9	(1) lbw b Azhar Ali	26	
3	Junaid Malik	b Yasir Arafat	0	c Saeed Anwar b Akhtar Ayub	4	
4	Asif Raza	c Zulfiqar Jan b Jaffar Nazir	1	(5) c and b Azhar Ali	16	
5	Suleman Khan	c Bazid Khan b Akhtar Ayub	29	(4) not out	129	
6	Shahnawaz Malik	c Zulfiqar Jan b Bilal Asad	18	c Saeed Anwar b Jaffar Nazir	19	
7	Mohammad Hussain	c Zulfiqar Jan b Yasir Arafat	62	b Akhtar Ayub	32	
8	*†Ali Raza	c Bazid Khan b Jaffar Nazir	67	b Akhtar Ayub	16	
9	Mohammad Saeed	c Shehzad Malik b Jaffar Nazir	2	c Shehzad Malik b Yasir Arafat	12	
10	Mohammad Shahzad	not out	1	c Yasir Arafat b Akhtar Ayub	6	
11	Usman Malik	c Shehzad Malik b Yasir Arafat	5	not out	0	
	Extras	b 5, lb 11, w 2, nb 4	22	lb 4, w 1, nb 2	7	
			227	**(9 wickets)**	**289**	

FoW (1): 1-21, 2-25, 3-25, 4-37, 5-61, 6-92, 7-209, 8-217, 9-221, 10-227
FoW (2): 1-35, 2-52, 3-62, 4-96, 5-136, 6-222, 7-263, 8-276, 9-288

KHAN RESEARCH LABORATORIES

1	Ali Naqvi	b Asif Raza	12
2	*Mohammad Wasim	c sub (Ahmed Butt) b Mohammad Shahzad	125
3	Azhar Ali	run out (Mohammad Shahzad)	110
4	Bazid Khan	c sub (Ahmed Butt) b Mohammad Shahzad	1
5	Saeed Anwar	c Suleman Khan b Mohammad Hussain	106
6	Bilal Asad	c Junaid Malik b Asif Raza	48
7	Shehzad Malik	not out	48
8	Yasir Arafat	not out	8
9	†Zulfiqar Jan		
10	Jaffar Nazir		
11	Akhtar Ayub		
	Extras	b 6, lb 5, w 4, nb 18	33
		(6 wickets, declared)	**491**

FoW (1): 1-25, 2-204, 3-207, 4-384, 5-387, 6-464

KRL Bowling	O	M	R	W		O	M	R	W	
Yasir Arafat	20.2	6	56	4	1w,1nb	30	7	73	2	1nb
Jaffar Nazir	18	5	25	4	1w,3nb	6.2	1	20	1	1nb
Akhtar Ayub	14	2	49	1		26.3	5	72	4	1w
Bilal Asad	20	7	28	1	(7)	7	4	8	0	
Ali Naqvi	4	1	11	0	(4)	10	1	34	0	
Saeed Anwar	4	0	11	0	(8)	5	4	4	0	
Mohammad Wasim	5	0	22	0	(5)	5	1	11	0	
Azhar Ali	3	0	9	0	(6)	19	4	63	2	

Lahore Shalimar Bowling	O	M	R	W	
Mohammad Shahzad	19	0	87	2	1w,10nb
Asif Raza	28	7	102	2	1w,3nb
Mohammad Saeed	23	1	97	0	1w,5nb
Mohammad Hussain	17	2	80	1	
Usman Malik	31	4	114	0	

Umpires: Afzaal Ahmed and Zaheer Ahmed. Referee: Khalid Niazi.   Toss: Khan Research Laboratories

Close of Play: 1st day: Lahore Shalimar (1) 201-6 (Mohammad Hussain 50*, Ali Raza 62*, 78.4 overs); 2nd day: Khan Research Laboratories (1) 236-3 (Azhar Ali 64*, Saeed Anwar 20*, 68 overs); 3rd day: Lahore Shalimar (2) 73-3 (Suleman Khan 2*, Asif Raza 17*, 24 overs).
Mohammad Wasim's 125 took 192 balls and included 21 fours. Azhar Ali's 110 took 271 balls and included 8 fours. Saeed Anwar's 106 took 110 balls and included 16 fours. Suleman Khan's 129 took 294 balls and included 18 fours.

MULTAN v NATIONAL BANK OF PAKISTAN

Played at Gymkhana Ground, Okara, November 7, 8, 9, 10, 2007.
Quaid-e-Azam Trophy 2007/08 - Group A
National Bank of Pakistan won by an innings and 53 runs.   (Points: Multan 0, National Bank of Pakistan 9)

NATIONAL BANK OF PAKISTAN

1	Nasir Jamshed	c Kashif Naved b Mohammad Kashif	37
2	Rashid Riaz	c Gulraiz Sadaf b Abdur Rauf	128
3	Naumanullah	c Gulraiz Sadaf b Abdur Rauf	161
4	Shahid Yousuf	c Gulraiz Sadaf b Mohammad Kashif	73
5	Naved Latif	c Gulraiz Sadaf b Abdur Rauf	1
6	*Mansoor Amjad	c Ahmed Raza b Hammad Tariq	7
7	†Amin-ur-Rehman	c and b Hammad Tariq	22
8	Wasim Khan	c Mohammad Hafeez b Kashif Naved	61
9	Wahab Riaz	b Kashif Naved	2
10	Irfanuddin	not out	1
11	Uzair-ul-Haq		
	Extras	b 3, lb 8, w 2, nb 8	21
		(9 wickets, declared)	514

FoW (1): 1-60, 2-339, 3-352, 4-364, 5-374, 6-412, 7-490, 8-503, 9-514

MULTAN

1	Hammad Tariq	c Naved Latif b Irfanuddin	101	c Irfanuddin b Wahab Riaz		0
2	Usman Tariq	b Wasim Khan	7	c Nasir Jamshed b Wahab Riaz		32
3	Mohammad Hafeez	lbw b Wasim Khan	12	lbw b Irfanuddin		49
4	Kashif Naved	c Naved Latif b Wahab Riaz	29	(5) lbw b Irfanuddin		22
5	Itmad-ul-Haq	c Naved Latif b Irfanuddin	16	(6) lbw b Mansoor Amjad		15
6	Mohammad Sarwar	c and b Irfanuddin	1	absent hurt		0
7	†Gulraiz Sadaf	c Shahid Yousuf b Wahab Riaz	9	(4) c sub (Imran Javed) b Uzair-ul-Haq		35
8	*Abdur Rauf	c Amin-ur-Rehman b Wahab Riaz	38	(7) c Rashid Riaz b Irfanuddin		19
9	Ansar Javed	c Naved Latif b Mansoor Amjad	1	(8) not out		19
10	Ahmed Raza	not out	6	(9) c Rashid Riaz b Mansoor Amjad		8
11	Mohammad Kashif	b Mansoor Amjad	4	(10) run out		1
	Extras	b 10, w 2, nb 10	22	b 9, lb 1, w 1, nb 4		15
			246			215

FoW (1): 1-22, 2-52, 3-143, 4-161, 5-173, 6-179, 7-226, 8-231, 9-231, 10-246
FoW (2): 1-0, 2-62, 3-128, 4-130, 5-165, 6-171, 7-191, 8-204, 9-215

Multan Bowling

	O	M	R	W	
Abdur Rauf	31	3	123	3	
Ansar Javed	18	0	72	0	8nb
Mohammad Kashif	23	3	118	2	2w
Ahmed Raza	23	2	95	0	
Mohammad Hafeez	1	0	1	0	
Itmad-ul-Haq	3	0	12	0	
Hammad Tariq	17	3	46	2	
Kashif Naved	6.1	1	36	2	

National Bank of Pakistan Bowling

	O	M	R	W			O	M	R	W	
Wasim Khan	17	6	58	2	1w,1nb						
Wahab Riaz	20	6	51	3	6nb	(1)	19	14	14	2	
Uzair-ul-Haq	15	5	44	0	1w	(2)	15	3	46	1	
Irfanuddin	11	2	54	3		(3)	24	5	72	3	
Mansoor Amjad	9.5	4	29	2	3nb	(4)	16.1	1	67	2	4nb
Shahid Yousuf						(5)	3	1	6	0	1w

Umpires: Ahsan Raza and Iftikhar Malik. Referee: Mohammad Javed.   Toss: Multan

Close of Play: 1st day: National Bank of Pakistan (1) 307-1 (Rashid Riaz 126*, Naumanullah 131*, 81.1 overs); 2nd day: Multan (1) 115-2 (Hammad Tariq 68*, Kashif Naved 19*, 32 overs); 3rd day: Multan (2) 113-2 (Mohammad Hafeez 48*, Gulraiz Sadaf 21*, 40 overs).

Rashid Riaz's 128 took 277 balls in 360 minutes and included 18 fours. Naumanullah's 161 took 230 balls in 320 minutes and included 23 fours and 2 sixes. Hammad Tariq's 101 took 158 balls in 213 minutes and included 19 fours and 1 six.

PESHAWAR v PAKISTAN INTERNATIONAL AIRLINES

Played at Arbab Niaz Stadium, Peshawar, November 7, 8, 9, 2007.
Quaid-e-Azam Trophy 2007/08 - Group B
Pakistan International Airlines won by 262 runs.   (Points: Peshawar 0, Pakistan International Airlines 9)

PAKISTAN INTERNATIONAL AIRLINES

1	Khurram Manzoor	c Sajjad Ahmed b Imran Khan	44	c Shehzad Khan b Riaz Afridi	143
2	Kamran Sajid	c Sajjad Ahmed b Nauman Habib	12	c Mohammad Fayyaz b Nauman Habib	0
3	Agha Sabir	lbw b Nauman Habib	0	b Nauman Habib	16
4	*Faisal Iqbal	b Imran Khan	9	c Shehzad Khan b Imran Khan	0
5	Shoaib Khan	c Sajjad Ahmed b Inamullah	68	c Sajjad Ahmed b Nauman Habib	0
6	Fahad Iqbal	b Riaz Afridi	54	c and b Riaz Afridi	69
7	†Sarfraz Ahmed	c Shehzad Khan b Inamullah	0	not out	32
8	Tahir Khan	not out	20	run out	4
9	Ali Imran	c Shehzad Khan b Inamullah	5	(10) not out	2
10	Aizaz Cheema	c Shehzad Khan b Nauman Habib	9	(9) lbw b Riaz Afridi	0
11	Fazl-e-Akbar	st Shehzad Khan b Inamullah	0		
	Extras	lb 2, nb 6	8	b 5, lb 7, w 1, nb 4	17
			229	(8 wickets, declared)	283

FoW (1): 1-36, 2-36, 3-64, 4-72, 5-194, 6-194, 7-194, 8-209, 9-228, 10-229
FoW (2): 1-12, 2-40, 3-45, 4-46, 5-216, 6-266, 7-275, 8-275

PESHAWAR

1	Naved Khan	lbw b Fazl-e-Akbar	4	lbw b Aizaz Cheema	6
2	Usman Zeb	lbw b Fazl-e-Akbar	11	b Fazl-e-Akbar	0
3	Mohammad Fayyaz	c Sarfraz Ahmed b Aizaz Cheema	4	lbw b Aizaz Cheema	21
4	Nawaz Ahmed	lbw b Fazl-e-Akbar	0	lbw b Aizaz Cheema	11
5	*Akbar Badshah	lbw b Aizaz Cheema	9	b Fazl-e-Akbar	0
6	Sajjad Ahmed	lbw b Aizaz Cheema	13	c Ali Imran b Tahir Khan	25
7	†Shehzad Khan	c Tahir Khan b Aizaz Cheema	6	c Sarfraz Ahmed b Fazl-e-Akbar	7
8	Riaz Afridi	not out	40	c sub (Jannisar Khan) b Ali Imran	40
9	Nauman Habib	c Faisal Iqbal b Tahir Khan	0	c Sarfraz Ahmed b Tahir Khan	0
10	Inamullah	lbw b Aizaz Cheema	8	not out	19
11	Imran Khan	c and b Aizaz Cheema	0	st Sarfraz Ahmed b Tahir Khan	4
	Extras	lb 4, w 3, nb 9	16	b 1, lb 2, nb 3	6
			111		139

FoW (1): 1-19, 2-25, 3-31, 4-32, 5-51, 6-58, 7-93, 8-100, 9-111, 10-111
FoW (2): 1-3, 2-9, 3-36, 4-37, 5-45, 6-60, 7-110, 8-110, 9-123, 10-139

Peshawar Bowling

	O	M	R	W			O	M	R	W	
Riaz Afridi	26	5	82	1			14	2	63	3	
Nauman Habib	22	5	67	3	2nb		16	2	83	3	1w
Imran Khan	10	5	30	2	1nb		10	0	49	1	2nb
Nawaz Ahmed	1	0	15	0	1nb						
Inamullah	13.5	4	31	4	2nb	(4)	3	0	23	0	1nb
Mohammad Fayyaz	1	0	2	0		(5)	6	1	20	0	
Akbar Badshah						(6)	6	1	33	0	1nb

Pakistan International Airlines Bowling

	O	M	R	W			O	M	R	W	
Fazl-e-Akbar	9	1	20	3	6nb		13	2	56	5	3nb
Ali Imran	8	2	19	0	3nb	(4)	2	0	3	1	
Aizaz Cheema	10.4	0	38	6	2w	(2)	16	1	53	3	
Tahir Khan	4	0	30	1		(3)	6.3	1	24	3	

Umpires: Islam Khan and Rasheed Bhatti. Referee: Ishtiaq Ahmed.   Toss: Peshawar

Close of Play: 1st day: Peshawar (1) 2-0 (Naved Khan 1*, Usman Zeb 0*, 1.1 overs); 2nd day: Pakistan International Airlines (2) 184-4 (Khurram Manzoor 106*, Fahad Iqbal 50*, 34.3 overs).

The match was scheduled for four days but completed in three. Khurram Manzoor's 143 took 164 balls and included 21 fours and 1 six.

QUETTA v ABBOTTABAD

Played at Bugti Stadium, Quetta, November 7, 8, 9, 10, 2007.
Quaid-e-Azam Trophy 2007/08 - Group B
Match drawn.   (Points: Quetta 3, Abbottabad 0)

QUETTA

1	Shoaib Khan	c Waqar Ali b Amjad Waqas	185
2	Hameedullah Khan	lbw b Nabeeullah	10
3	†Shahzad Tareen	b Rahimbaz Khan	5
4	Taimur Ali	c Fawad Khan b Noor-ul-Amin	11
5	Sabir Hussain	c Nabeeullah b Amjad Waqas	2
6	*Nasim Khan	b Amjad Waqas	151
7	Jalat Khan	c Fawad Khan b Amjad Waqas	12
8	Naseer Khan	c Fawad Khan b Nabeeullah	33
9	Faisal Irfan	not out	17
10	Gauhar Faiz	lbw b Amjad Waqas	1
11	Nazar Hussain	c sub b Amjad Waqas	0
	Extras	b 8, lb 19, w 3, nb 4	34
			461

FoW (1): 1-36, 2-53, 3-91, 4-100, 5-289, 6-396, 7-433, 8-442, 9-461, 10-461

ABBOTTABAD

1	Wajid Ali	c Shahzad Tareen b Jalat Khan	114	c Shahzad Tareen b Gauhar Faiz	1
2	†Fawad Khan	lbw b Gauhar Faiz	10	(3) c Naseer Khan b Jalat Khan	76
3	Usman Khan	c Taimur Ali b Gauhar Faiz	4	(2) st Shahzad Tareen b Jalat Khan	15
4	*Adnan Raees	b Naseer Khan	28	(5) lbw b Nazar Hussain	75
5	Riaz Kail	c Gauhar Faiz b Faisal Irfan	26	(6) not out	20
6	Iftikhar Mahmood	c Hameedullah Khan b Jalat Khan	37	(7) not out	7
7	Rahimbaz Khan	run out	0	(4) lbw b Nazar Hussain	76
8	Amjad Waqas	b Nazar Hussain	22		
9	Noor-ul-Amin	not out	17		
10	Waqar Ali	c Shoaib Khan b Nazar Hussain	9		
11	Nabeeullah	c Shoaib Khan b Gauhar Faiz	0		
	Extras	b 1, lb 4, w 2, nb 8	15	b 2, lb 11, w 2, nb 2	17
			282	(5 wickets)	287

FoW (1): 1-31, 2-40, 3-87, 4-143, 5-222, 6-227, 7-237, 8-263, 9-281, 10-282
FoW (2): 1-6, 2-56, 3-116, 4-252, 5-259

Abbottabad Bowling

	O	M	R	W	
Rahimbaz Khan	23	4	73	1	2w,1nb
Nabeeullah	22	2	84	2	1w,3nb
Adnan Raees	7	2	15	0	
Riaz Kail	7	0	19	0	
Noor-ul-Amin	21	4	62	1	
Waqar Ali	9	0	61	0	
Amjad Waqas	23.4	3	92	6	
Iftikhar Mahmood	7	0	28	0	

Quetta Bowling

	O	M	R	W		O	M	R	W	
Faisal Irfan	22	4	45	1	1nb	13	4	37	0	
Nazar Hussain	26	8	67	2	1nb	14	1	47	2	
Gauhar Faiz	16	1	67	3	2w,6nb	13	2	43	1	2w,2nb
Naseer Khan	22	8	66	1		19	6	37	0	
Jalat Khan	21	10	32	2		29	7	75	2	
Shoaib Khan					(6)	8	1	16	0	
Sabir Hussain					(7)	2	0	19	0	

Umpires: Raweed Khan and Shakeel Khan. Referee: Naeem Ahmed.   Toss: Abbottabad

Close of Play: 1st day: Quetta (1) 355-4 (Shoaib Khan 165*, Nasim Khan 135*, 85 overs); 2nd day: Abbottabad (1) 143-3 (Wajid Ali 68*, Riaz Kail 26*, 46 overs); 3rd day: Abbottabad (2) 78-2 (Fawad Khan 54*, Rahimbaz Khan 8*, 46 overs).
Shoaib Khan's 185 took 275 balls and included 24 fours and 1 six. Nasim Khan's 151 took 197 balls and included 14 fours and 2 sixes. Wajid Ali's 114 took 234 balls and included 14 fours.

RAWALPINDI v SUI NORTHERN GAS PIPELINES LIMITED

Played at Khan Research Laboratories Ground, Rawalpindi, November 7, 8, 9, 10, 2007.
Quaid-e-Azam Trophy 2007/08 - Group B
Sui Northern Gas Pipelines Limited won by 94 runs.   (Points: Rawalpindi 0, Sui Northern Gas Pipelines Limited 9)

SUI NORTHERN GAS PIPELINES LIMITED

1	*Mohammad Hafeez	c Babar Naeem b Rizwan Akbar	25	c Zahid Mansoor b Yasir Ali	47
2	Yasir Arafat	c Zahid Mansoor b Yasir Ali	6	c Yasim Murtaza b Rizwan Akbar	17
3	Umar Akmal	c and b Yasir Ali	61	c Najam-ul-Hasan b Yasir Ali	69
4	Azhar Shafiq	lbw b Yasir Ali	25	c Babar Naeem b Yasim Murtaza	0
5	Saleem Mughal	c Zahid Mansoor b Yasir Ali	73	c Rizwan Akbar b Yasir Ali	20
6	Khurram Shehzad	lbw b Yasir Ali	60	c Yasim Murtaza b Babar Naeem	24
7	†Adnan Akmal	lbw b Yasim Murtaza	18	not out	17
8	Adnan Rasool	lbw b Mohammad Ayaz	7	c Mohammad Ayaz b Yasim Murtaza	5
9	Samiullah Khan	lbw b Mohammad Ayaz	0	not out	0
10	Imran Ali	not out	3		
11	Asad Ali	lbw b Mohammad Ayaz	0		
	Extras	b 8, lb 5, nb 15	28	b 7, lb 2, w 2, nb 4	15
			306	(7 wickets, declared)	214

FoW (1): 1-17, 2-53, 3-119, 4-131, 5-270, 6-277, 7-299, 8-303, 9-306, 10-306
FoW (2): 1-30, 2-137, 3-137, 4-154, 5-190, 6-193, 7-206

RAWALPINDI

1	Mohammad Ibrahim	lbw b Imran Ali	19	c Adnan Akmal b Samiullah Khan	42
2	Babar Naeem	c Adnan Akmal b Asad Ali	32	c Khurram Shehzad b Samiullah Khan	14
3	Najam-ul-Hasan	c Adnan Akmal b Asad Ali	6	c Adnan Akmal b Imran Ali	8
4	Adnan Mufti	lbw b Samiullah Khan	38	lbw b Imran Ali	45
5	*Naved Ashraf	c and b Imran Ali	6	b Adnan Rasool	35
6	Usman Saeed	lbw b Samiullah Khan	2	c Adnan Akmal b Samiullah Khan	50
7	†Zahid Mansoor	c Mohammad Hafeez b Samiullah Khan	4	c Khurram Shehzad b Imran Ali	1
8	Yasim Murtaza	c Mohammad Hafeez b Imran Ali	16	c Adnan Akmal b Imran Ali	1
9	Yasir Ali	c sub (Tauqeer Hussain) b Mohammad Hafeez	36	not out	4
10	Rizwan Akbar	c Imran Ali b Adnan Rasool	19	lbw b Imran Ali	2
11	Mohammad Ayaz	not out	0	b Imran Ali	0
	Extras	b 3, lb 5, nb 20	28	b 2, lb 6, nb 11	19
			206		220

FoW (1): 1-42, 2-61, 3-76, 4-88, 5-126, 6-127, 7-140, 8-154, 9-206, 10-206
FoW (2): 1-23, 2-38, 3-121, 4-121, 5-212, 6-213, 7-213, 8-213, 9-220, 10-220

Rawalpindi Bowling

	O	M	R	W			O	M	R	W	
Rizwan Akbar	31	7	94	1	5nb		10	1	76	1	4nb
Yasir Ali	35	12	81	5	4nb		16	3	60	3	1w
Mohammad Ayaz	13.5	4	56	3	4nb						
Babar Naeem	6	1	20	0		(3)	9	0	46	1	1w
Yasim Murtaza	16	6	42	1	2nb	(4)	3	0	23	2	

Sui Northern Gas Pipelines Limited Bowling

	O	M	R	W			O	M	R	W	
Samiullah Khan	22	5	57	3	4nb		22	8	43	3	4nb
Asad Ali	17	2	46	2	6nb	(4)	5	0	35	0	4nb
Imran Ali	26	5	63	3	10nb	(2)	24.2	10	41	6	
Adnan Rasool	9.3	2	27	1		(3)	25	9	69	1	1nb
Mohammad Hafeez	3	2	5	1			6	2	16	0	
Yasir Arafat						(6)	1	0	8	0	2nb

Umpires: Ahmed Shahab and Riazuddin.   Referee: Saadat Ali.   Toss: Sui Northern Gas Pipelines Limited

Close of Play: 1st day: Sui Northern Gas Pipelines Limited (1) 249-4 (Saleem Mughal 56*, Khurram Shehzad 52*, 76 overs); 2nd day: Rawalpindi (1) 135-6 (Zahid Mansoor 0*, Yasim Murtaza 8*, 52 overs); 3rd day: Rawalpindi (2) 7-0 (Mohammad Ibrahim 5*, Babar Naeem 2*, 6 overs).

FAISALABAD v HABIB BANK LIMITED

Played at Sports Stadium, Sargodha, November 13, 14, 15, 2007.
Quaid-e-Azam Trophy 2007/08 - Group A
Habib Bank Limited won by ten wickets.   (Points: Faisalabad 0, Habib Bank Limited 9)

FAISALABAD

1	†Mohammad Salman	b Shahid Nazir	14	(2) b Fahad Masood	3
2	Abdul Mannan	b Shahid Nazir	19	(1) c Kamran Hussain b Dilawar Khan	18
3	Ammar Mahmood	c Humayun Farhat b Fahad Masood	8	lbw b Mohammad Aslam	34
4	Usman Arshad	lbw b Shahid Nazir	15	c Hasan Raza b Dilawar Khan	0
5	Asif Hussain	c Dilawar Khan b Mohammad Aslam	22	c Khaqan Arsal b Dilawar Khan	23
6	*Ijaz Ahmed	c Shahid Nazir b Dilawar Khan	33	lbw b Dilawar Khan	25
7	Ahmed Hayat	c Sulaman Qadir b Dilawar Khan	8	c Khaqan Arsal b Dilawar Khan	0
8	Asad Zarar	lbw b Fahad Masood	3	run out	0
9	Saadat Munir	b Fahad Masood	0	(10) not out	0
10	Ali Raza	not out	5	(9) c Aftab Alam b Dilawar Khan	13
11	Mohammad Maqsood	b Dilawar Khan	0	c Sulaman Qadir b Dilawar Khan	0
	Extras	b 3, nb 14	17	lb 3, nb 5	8
			144		**124**

FoW (1): 1-26, 2-41, 3-51, 4-86, 5-91, 6-105, 7-116, 8-118, 9-144, 10-144
FoW (2): 1-8, 2-59, 3-59, 4-61, 5-99, 6-104, 7-104, 8-121, 9-124, 10-124

HABIB BANK LIMITED

1	Rafatullah Mohmand	c Ijaz Ahmed b Ahmed Hayat	0		
2	Khaqan Arsal	c Asif Hussain b Ali Raza	0		
3	Mohammad Aslam	c Mohammad Salman b Saadat Munir	36		
4	Aftab Alam	c Asad Zarar b Ahmed Hayat	10		
5	*Hasan Raza	b Saadat Munir	149		
6	Sulaman Qadir	lbw b Ijaz Ahmed	6	(1) not out	2
7	†Humayun Farhat	lbw b Saadat Munir	24		
8	Kamran Hussain	run out (Ammar Mahmood)	19		
9	Fahad Masood	lbw b Saadat Munir	0	(2) not out	5
10	Shahid Nazir	b Saadat Munir	0		
11	Dilawar Khan	not out	0		
	Extras	b 5, lb 2, nb 8	15	nb 3	3
			259	(no wicket)	**10**

FoW (1): 1-0, 2-0, 3-19, 4-158, 5-190, 6-236, 7-243, 8-249, 9-251, 10-259

Habib Bank Limited Bowling

	O	M	R	W		O	M	R	W	
Shahid Nazir	12	1	48	3	6nb	4	0	22	0	3nb
Fahad Masood	17	5	47	3	3nb	11	2	29	1	2nb
Mohammad Aslam	7	1	17	1	3nb	15	7	22	1	
Kamran Hussain	12	3	23	0	2nb	4	1	12	0	
Dilawar Khan	7.5	3	6	3		16.2	3	33	7	
Sulaman Qadir					(6)	1	0	3	0	

Faisalabad Bowling

	O	M	R	W		O	M	R	W	
Ahmed Hayat	9	2	35	2	3nb	1	0	7	0	3nb
Ali Raza	10	0	50	1	1nb					
Asad Zarar	8	0	51	0	1nb	(2) 1	0	3	0	
Saadat Munir	21	4	49	5						
Mohammad Maqsood	12	0	42	0	4nb					
Ijaz Ahmed	10	1	25	1						

Umpires: Iftikhar Malik and Mohammad Arif.   Referee: Arshad Pervez.   Toss: Faisalabad

Close of Play: 1st day: Habib Bank Limited (1) 0-2 (Mohammad Aslam 0*, Aftab Alam 0*, 1.1 overs); 2nd day: Habib Bank Limited (1) 259-9 (Kamran Hussain 19*, Dilawar Khan 0*, 69 overs).

The match was scheduled for four days but completed in three. Hasan Raza's 149 took 192 balls and included 14 fours and 1 six.

ISLAMABAD v KARACHI BLUES

Played at Diamond Club Ground, Islamabad, November 13, 14, 15, 16, 2007.
Quaid-e-Azam Trophy 2007/08 - Group B
Islamabad won by nine wickets. (Points: Islamabad 9, Karachi Blues 0)

ISLAMABAD

1	Raheel Majeed	b Tariq Haroon	75	b Faraz Ahmed	5
2	Umair Khan	lbw b Tariq Haroon	45	not out	68
3	Farrukh Hayat	c Shadab Kabir b Azam Hussain	14	not out	51
4	Asadullah Sumari	b Malik Aftab	9		
5	Fayyaz Ahmed	c Ali Asad b Mansoor Khan	21		
6	Ameer Khan	lbw b Azam Hussain	41		
7	*Rauf Akbar	c Aariz Kamal b Mansoor Khan	13		
8	Atif Maqbool	c Mansoor Khan b Azam Hussain	1		
9	†Mohammad Kashif	b Tariq Haroon	8		
10	Shehzad Azam	b Tariq Haroon	28		
11	Mir Usman	not out	21		
	Extras	b 13, lb 10, w 1, nb 2	26	b 13, lb 9, w 1, nb 2	25
			302	(1 wicket)	149

FoW (1): 1-122, 2-146, 3-161, 4-179, 5-194, 6-232, 7-243, 8-244, 9-255, 10-302
FoW (2): 1-9

KARACHI BLUES

1	Shadab Kabir	lbw b Rauf Akbar	7	c Mohammad Kashif b Rauf Akbar	95
2	Aariz Kamal	c Umair Khan b Rauf Akbar	3	(3) lbw b Mir Usman	0
3	Ali Asad	b Shehzad Azam	17	(2) lbw b Mir Usman	32
4	Faraz Patel	b Rauf Akbar	9	c Ameer Khan b Rauf Akbar	7
5	Sharjeel Ashraf	c Mohammad Kashif b Shehzad Azam	4	(6) c Mohammad Kashif b Rauf Akbar	8
6	*Mansoor Khan	c Rauf Akbar b Shehzad Azam	0	(8) lbw b Rauf Akbar	30
7	Tariq Haroon	c Rauf Akbar b Shehzad Azam	19	(5) not out	142
8	†Sajid Hanif	lbw b Rauf Akbar	0	(7) st Mohammad Kashif b Shehzad Azam	5
9	Azam Hussain	b Rauf Akbar	0	c Atif Maqbool b Shehzad Azam	1
10	Malik Aftab	lbw b Shehzad Azam	0	c Mohammad Kashif b Shehzad Azam	12
11	Faraz Ahmed	not out	0	lbw b Ameer Khan	3
	Extras	lb 4, w 6, nb 6	16	b 18, lb 5, w 4, nb 10	37
			75		372

FoW (1): 1-13, 2-14, 3-47, 4-51, 5-52, 6-60, 7-60, 8-75, 9-75, 10-75
FoW (2): 1-81, 2-81, 3-185, 4-201, 5-206, 6-230, 7-307, 8-320, 9-336, 10-372

Karachi Blues Bowling

	O	M	R	W			O	M	R	W	
Faraz Ahmed	12	5	44	0	1w,2nb	(2)	14	3	43	1	1nb
Malik Aftab	19	3	67	1		(1)	7	0	26	0	1w,1nb
Tariq Haroon	30.2	5	111	4			7	0	39	0	
Mansoor Khan	6	0	24	2		(5)	1	0	3	0	
Azam Hussain	18	6	33	3		(4)	4	2	16	0	
Aariz Kamal						(6)	1	1	0	0	

Islamabad Bowling

	O	M	R	W			O	M	R	W	
Rauf Akbar	12	2	35	5	1w,4nb		28	4	107	4	6nb
Shehzad Azam	11.3	5	36	5	1w,2nb		23	2	128	3	2w,3nb
Mir Usman						(3)	7	1	32	2	2w,1nb
Atif Maqbool						(4)	8	1	40	0	
Raheel Majeed						(5)	10	1	38	0	
Ameer Khan						(6)	2	0	4	1	

Umpires: Ahsan Raza and Ijaz Ahmed. Referee: Saadat Ali.   Toss: Karachi Blues

Close of Play: 1st day: Islamabad (1) 295-9 (Shehzad Azam 27*, Mir Usman 15*, 83 overs); 2nd day: Karachi Blues (2) 210-5 (Tariq Haroon 50*, Faraz Patel 2*, 32.5 overs); 3rd day: Islamabad (2) 87-1 (Umair Khan 35*, Farrukh Hayat 46*, 23 overs).

Tariq Haroon's 142 took 223 balls and included 18 fours and 2 sixes. Faraz Patel retired hurt in the Karachi Blues second innings having scored 2 (team score 83-2) - he returned when the score was 206-5.

KARACHI WHITES v NATIONAL BANK OF PAKISTAN

Played at National Bank of Pakistan Sports Complex, Karachi, November 13, 14, 15, 16, 2007.
Quaid-e-Azam Trophy 2007/08 - Group A
National Bank of Pakistan won by eight wickets.   (Points: Karachi Whites 0, National Bank of Pakistan 9)

KARACHI WHITES

1	Khalid Latif	lbw b Wahab Riaz	14	c Amin-ur-Rehman b Wasim Khan	7
2	Asad Shafiq	lbw b Uzair-ul-Haq	51	c Amin-ur-Rehman b Wahab Riaz	34
3	Daniyal Ahsan	c Amin-ur-Rehman b Uzair-ul-Haq	6	b Wahab Riaz	63
4	Atif Ali	c Naumanullah b Wahab Riaz	4	lbw b Wasim Khan	18
5	Asim Kamal	lbw b Wahab Riaz	9	(6) c sub (Naeem Ahmed) b Irfanuddin	1
6	Afsar Nawaz	c Amin-ur-Rehman b Wahab Riaz	68	(7) lbw b Wasim Khan	10
7	†Javed Mansoor	b Uzair-ul-Haq	46	(8) c Rashid Riaz b Wasim Khan	0
8	*Mohammad Sami	c Wahab Riaz b Wasim Khan	13	(9) b Wasim Khan	0
9	Tanvir Ahmed	c Amin-ur-Rehman b Wasim Khan	6	(10) lbw b Irfanuddin	27
10	Misbah Khan	lbw b Mansoor Amjad	27	(5) b Irfanuddin	21
11	Fahad Khan	not out	2	not out	2
	Extras	lb 18, w 13, nb 9	40	lb 13, nb 6	19
			286		202

FoW (1): 1-26, 2-46, 3-61, 4-92, 5-97, 6-223, 7-237, 8-244, 9-254, 10-286
FoW (2): 1-27, 2-41, 3-88, 4-138, 5-140, 6-156, 7-164, 8-164, 9-192, 10-202

NATIONAL BANK OF PAKISTAN

1	Nasir Jamshed	c Javed Mansoor b Misbah Khan	127	not out	40
2	Rashid Riaz	c Javed Mansoor b Tanvir Ahmed	16	c Javed Mansoor b Tanvir Ahmed	14
3	Naumanullah	c Javed Mansoor b Tanvir Ahmed	66		
4	Shahid Yousuf	c Javed Mansoor b Tanvir Ahmed	46	(3) c Javed Mansoor b Tanvir Ahmed	8
5	Naved Latif	lbw b Mohammad Sami	23		
6	*Mansoor Amjad	b Misbah Khan	47	(4) not out	15
7	†Amin-ur-Rehman	b Misbah Khan	5		
8	Wasim Khan	c Asim Kamal b Misbah Khan	34		
9	Wahab Riaz	lbw b Mohammad Sami	30		
10	Irfanuddin	b Tanvir Ahmed	6		
11	Uzair-ul-Haq	not out	0		
	Extras	lb 2, w 4, nb 6	12	nb 2	2
			412	(2 wickets)	79

FoW (1): 1-21, 2-135, 3-233, 4-269, 5-306, 6-316, 7-359, 8-376, 9-412, 10-412
FoW (2): 1-18, 2-26

National Bank of Pakistan Bowling

	O	M	R	W			O	M	R	W	
Wasim Khan	27	6	83	2	2w	(2)	23	9	64	5	4nb
Wahab Riaz	27	9	68	4	1w,4nb	(1)	13	3	49	2	
Uzair-ul-Haq	25	10	41	3	2w,3nb		14	4	37	0	2nb
Shahid Yousuf	1	1	0	0							
Irfanuddin	12	2	34	0		(4)	9.4	1	39	3	
Mansoor Amjad	8.1	2	39	1	2nb						
Naumanullah	3	1	3	0							

Karachi Whites Bowling

	O	M	R	W			O	M	R	W	
Mohammad Sami	25	8	61	2	2w		7	3	17	0	1nb
Tanvir Ahmed	30.5	6	121	4	3nb		7	0	41	2	1nb
Fahad Khan	25	5	105	0	2w,3nb	(4)	1	0	3	0	
Misbah Khan	24	3	81	4		(3)	2	0	14	0	
Asad Shafiq	1	0	9	0							
Afsar Nawaz	7	0	33	0							
Asim Kamal						(5)	0.3	0	4	0	

Umpires: Akbar Khan and Rasheed Bhatti. Referee: Naeem Ahmed.   Toss: National Bank of Pakistan

Close of Play: 1st day: Karachi Whites (1) 218-5 (Afsar Nawaz 68*, Javed Mansoor 40*, 83 overs); 2nd day: National Bank of Pakistan (1) 229-2 (Nasir Jamshed 100*, Shahid Yousuf 44*, 60 overs); 3rd day: Karachi Whites (2) 97-3 (Daniyal Ahsan 26*, Misbah Khan 6*, 27.5 overs).
Nasir Jamshed's 127 took 255 balls and included 19 fours and 1 six.

LAHORE RAVI v HYDERABAD

Played at Lahore City Cricket Association Ground, November 13, 14, 15, 2007.
Quaid-e-Azam Trophy 2007/08 - Group A
Lahore Ravi won by 173 runs.   (Points: Lahore Ravi 9, Hyderabad 0)

LAHORE RAVI

1	Kashif Siddiq	b Naeem-ur-Rehman	26	b Sufyan Ali	8
2	Sohail Ahmed	c Shahid Qambrani b Sufyan Ali	1	c Hanif Malik b Pir Zulfiqar	46
3	Ashraf Ali	lbw b Sufyan Ali	4	(6) c Hanif Malik b Naeem-ur-Rehman	10
4	Ali Haider	b Naeem-ur-Rehman	10	c Rizwan Ahmed b Faisal Athar	5
5	Arsalan Mir	c Hanif Malik b Naeem-ur-Rehman	17	run out (Akram Khan)	9
6	Saad Nasim	c Faisal Athar b Naeem-ur-Rehman	2	(7) lbw b Naeem-ur-Rehman	32
7	*Junaid Zia	not out	52	(8) c Farhan Ayub b Naeem-ur-Rehman	58
8	Waqas Ahmed	c Akram Khan b Farhan Ayub	35	(9) c Hanif Malik b Farhan Ayub	27
9	†Shahbaz Butt	c Sufyan Ali b Farhan Ayub	5	(3) c sub (Jamshed Baig) b Naeem-ur-Rehman	39
10	Salman Rahat	lbw b Naeem-ur-Rehman	2	c Zahid Khan b Naeem-ur-Rehman	3
11	Tehseen Mirza	b Naeem-ur-Rehman	4	not out	0
	Extras	b 2, lb 5, w 6, nb 16	29	b 9, lb 7, w 4, nb 8	28
			187		**265**

FoW (1): 1-2, 2-8, 3-42, 4-53, 5-71, 6-81, 7-144, 8-152, 9-159, 10-187
FoW (2): 1-15, 2-87, 3-117, 4-129, 5-133, 6-145, 7-219, 8-260, 9-264, 10-265

HYDERABAD

1	Zahid Khan	b Junaid Zia	0	(3) lbw b Waqas Ahmed	2
2	Akram Khan	b Waqas Ahmed	2	lbw b Waqas Ahmed	55
3	Faisal Athar	lbw b Waqas Ahmed	21	(1) lbw b Waqas Ahmed	4
4	Rizwan Ahmed	lbw b Junaid Zia	16	c and b Waqas Ahmed	5
5	Khadim Hussain	c Shahbaz Butt b Junaid Zia	1	c Ali Haider b Salman Rahat	13
6	Pir Zulfiqar	c Junaid Zia b Waqas Ahmed	15	c Shahbaz Butt b Junaid Zia	14
7	Shahid Qambrani	c Saad Nasim b Junaid Zia	0	absent hurt	0
8	*†Hanif Malik	b Waqas Ahmed	0	(7) c Shahbaz Butt b Waqas Ahmed	22
9	Naeem-ur-Rehman	b Junaid Zia	0	(8) c Ashraf Ali b Saad Nasim	38
10	Farhan Ayub	b Waqas Ahmed	2	(9) run out	21
11	Sufyan Ali	not out	0	(10) not out	1
	Extras	b 4, lb 1, w 7, nb 9	21	b 8, lb 4, w 2, nb 10	24
			80		**199**

FoW (1): 1-6, 2-13, 3-45, 4-46, 5-63, 6-63, 7-74, 8-76, 9-79, 10-80
FoW (2): 1-15, 2-19, 3-25, 4-54, 5-98, 6-133, 7-135, 8-194, 9-199

Hyderabad Bowling

	O	M	R	W		O	M	R	W	
Farhan Ayub	18	1	59	2	3w,4nb	20	0	73	1	4w,6nb
Sufyan Ali	11	2	37	2	1w	10	0	37	1	
Naeem-ur-Rehman	14.4	1	68	6	1w,12nb	18.2	2	80	5	2nb
Pir Zulfiqar	2	1	5	0	1w	10	3	32	1	
Shahid Qambrani	1	0	11	0						
Faisal Athar						(5) 9	0	27	1	

Lahore Ravi Bowling

	O	M	R	W		O	M	R	W	
Junaid Zia	14.3	1	46	5	6w,9nb	16	2	58	1	6nb
Waqas Ahmed	14	4	29	5	1w	13	0	42	5	2w,2nb
Tehseen Mirza					(3)	6	1	12	0	
Salman Rahat					(4)	6	0	29	1	2nb
Saad Nasim					(5)	6	0	36	1	
Kashif Siddiq					(6)	3	0	10	0	

Umpires: Raweed Khan and Saleem Badar. Referee: Aziz-ur-Rehman.   Toss: Hyderabad

Close of Play: 1st day: Hyderabad (1) 57-4 (Rizwan Ahmed 12*, Pir Zulfiqar 6*, 14 overs); 2nd day: Lahore Ravi (2) 179-6 (Saad Nasim 19*, Junaid Zia 17*, 48 overs).

The match was scheduled for four days but completed in three.

LAHORE SHALIMAR v ZARAI TARAQIATI BANK LIMITED

Played at Gaddafi Stadium, Lahore, November 13, 14, 15, 2007.
Quaid-e-Azam Trophy 2007/08 - Group B
Zarai Taraqiati Bank Limited won by ten wickets.   (Points: Lahore Shalimar 0, Zarai Taraqiati Bank Limited 9)

LAHORE SHALIMAR

1	Asif Khan	c Wajahatullah Wasti b Junaid Nadir	19	(2) c Kamran Naeem b Azhar Attari	0
2	Kashif Ali	lbw b Mohammad Khalil	41	(1) c Kamran Naeem b Azhar Attari	5
3	Salman Akbar	c Kamran Naeem b Mohammad Khalil	15	(4) c Kamran Naeem b Junaid Nadir	20
4	Haseeb Rasheed	c Wajahatullah Wasti b Zohaib Khan	28	(5) c and b Mohammad Khalil	1
5	Suleman Khan	lbw b Mohammad Khalil	2	(6) c and b Azhar Attari	9
6	Mohammad Hussain	c Kamran Naeem b Mohammad Khalil	0	(7) c Adnan Raza b Mohammad Khalil	11
7	*†Ali Raza	b Azhar Attari	25	(8) not out	14
8	Sibtain Raza	c Aamer Bashir b Zohaib Khan	10	(10) c Mohammad Khalil b Junaid Nadir	25
9	Mohammad Saeed	c Mohammad Khalil b Azhar Attari	11	c Kamran Naeem b Junaid Nadir	0
10	Asif Raza	c Afaq Raheem b Mohammad Khalil	0	(3) lbw b Azhar Attari	6
11	Shahzad Ali	not out	0	c Adnan Raza b Junaid Nadir	0
	Extras	b 1, lb 6, w 3, nb 11	21	b 17, lb 7, nb 13	37
			172		128

FoW (1): 1-53, 2-82, 3-88, 4-100, 5-102, 6-131, 7-149, 8-165, 9-171, 10-172
FoW (2): 1-4, 2-21, 3-22, 4-24, 5-49, 6-68, 7-79, 8-85, 9-128, 10-128

ZARAI TARAQIATI BANK LIMITED

1	Afaq Raheem	b Asif Raza	11	not out	21
2	Atif Ashraf	c Salman Akbar b Shahzad Ali	13	not out	24
3	Umar Javed	c Ali Raza b Asif Raza	0		
4	Adnan Raza	c Ali Raza b Mohammad Saeed	50		
5	*Wajahatullah Wasti	c Ali Raza b Asif Raza	0		
6	Aamer Bashir	c Ali Raza b Mohammad Saeed	89		
7	Junaid Nadir	b Asif Raza	13		
8	Zohaib Khan	c Salman Akbar b Shahzad Ali	26		
9	†Kamran Naeem	c Suleman Khan b Shahzad Ali	14		
10	Mohammad Khalil	b Asif Raza	5		
11	Azhar Attari	not out	2		
	Extras	b 1, lb 16, w 1, nb 14	32	lb 2	2
			255	(no wicket)	47

FoW (1): 1-29, 2-29, 3-30, 4-30, 5-111, 6-138, 7-184, 8-235, 9-247, 10-255

Zarai Taraqiati Bank Limited Bowling

	O	M	R	W		O	M	R	W	
Mohammad Khalil	21	7	48	5	3nb	13	5	24	2	1nb
Azhar Attari	20.2	4	53	2	8nb	15	1	64	4	12nb
Junaid Nadir	11	0	41	1	3w	7.5	2	16	4	
Umar Javed	3	2	4	0						
Zohaib Khan	5	1	19	2						

Lahore Shalimar Bowling

	O	M	R	W			O	M	R	W	
Shahzad Ali	14.1	3	60	3		(2)	2	0	23	0	
Asif Raza	24	5	82	5	10nb	(1)	2	0	13	0	
Mohammad Saeed	18	2	77	2	1w,4nb						
Mohammad Hussain	3	0	13	0							
Sibtain Raza	2	0	6	0		(3)	1	0	9	0	

Umpires: Iqbal Butt and Riazuddin. Referee: Abdus Sami.   Toss: Zarai Taraqiati Bank Limited

Close of Play: 1st day: Zarai Taraqiati Bank Limited (1) 1-0 (Afaq Raheem 1*, Atif Ashraf 0*, 1 over); 2nd day: Lahore Shalimar (2) 8-1 (Kashif Ali 0*, Asif Raza 4*, 1.2 overs).

The match was scheduled for four days but completed in three.

MULTAN v SUI SOUTHERN GAS CORPORATION

Played at Multan Cricket Stadium, November 13, 14, 15, 16, 2007.
Quaid-e-Azam Trophy 2007/08 - Group A
Multan won by three wickets.   (Points: Multan 9, Sui Southern Gas Corporation 0)

SUI SOUTHERN GAS CORPORATION

1	Asif Zakir	c Gulraiz Sadaf b Abdur Rauf	0	(4) c Kashif Naved b Zulfiqar Babar	9
2	Mohtashim Ali	c Gulraiz Sadaf b Zulfiqar Babar	59	lbw b Abdur Rauf	52
3	Imran Abbas	lbw b Mohammad Tanvir	37	lbw b Abdur Rauf	14
4	Mohammad Zafar	b Mohammad Kashif	28	(1) b Mohammad Kashif	3
5	*Saeed Bin Nasir	lbw b Zulfiqar Babar	6	c Zulfiqar Babar b Mohammad Kashif	21
6	Ali Hussain	c Kashif Naved b Mohammad Kashif	13	c and b Abdur Rauf	18
7	†Ahmed Zeeshan	c Hammad Tariq b Abdur Rauf	5	c Naved Yasin b Mohammad Kashif	0
8	Shehzad Butt	not out	77	lbw b Abdur Rauf	16
9	Sohail Khan	b Abdur Rauf	29	(10) lbw b Zulfiqar Babar	0
10	Adnan Malik	c Gulraiz Sadaf b Mohammad Tanvir	10	(9) b Abdur Rauf	10
11	Shakeel-ur-Rehman	c Sohaib Maqsood b Mohammad Tanvir	4	not out	0
	Extras	b 4, lb 6, w 7, nb 14	31	lb 4, w 2, nb 3	9
			299		152

FoW (1): 1-6, 2-100, 3-121, 4-135, 5-163, 6-166, 7-186, 8-257, 9-268, 10-299
FoW (2): 1-7, 2-42, 3-59, 4-105, 5-109, 6-114, 7-134, 8-149, 9-150, 10-152

MULTAN

1	Hammad Tariq	lbw b Sohail Khan	0	c Ahmed Zeeshan b Shakeel-ur-Rehman	10
2	Usman Tariq	lbw b Sohail Khan	63	lbw b Shehzad Butt	0
3	†Gulraiz Sadaf	lbw b Sohail Khan	70	c Ahmed Zeeshan b Shakeel-ur-Rehman	8
4	Mohammad Kashif	c Asif Zakir b Shakeel-ur-Rehman	17	(7) c Ahmed Zeeshan b Shakeel-ur-Rehman	17
5	Sohaib Maqsood	b Shakeel-ur-Rehman	3	(6) lbw b Shakeel-ur-Rehman	25
6	Naved Yasin	c Ahmed Zeeshan b Shehzad Butt	59	(4) not out	27
7	Kashif Naved	c Ahmed Zeeshan b Shakeel-ur-Rehman	6	(5) c Ali Hussain b Sohail Khan	0
8	Itmad-ul-Haq	c Ahmed Zeeshan b Sohail Khan	6		
9	*Abdur Rauf	c Ahmed Zeeshan b Shakeel-ur-Rehman	21	not out	20
10	Zulfiqar Babar	c Mohammad Zafar b Shakeel-ur-Rehman	47	(8) lbw b Shakeel-ur-Rehman	4
11	Mohammad Tanvir	not out	1		
	Extras	b 17, lb 11, w 4, nb 11	43	b 4, lb 2, w 1	7
			336	(7 wickets)	118

FoW (1): 1-0, 2-163, 3-170, 4-189, 5-194, 6-200, 7-223, 8-252, 9-316, 10-336
FoW (2): 1-2, 2-21, 3-22, 4-23, 5-60, 6-84, 7-94

Multan Bowling

	O	M	R	W			O	M	R	W	
Abdur Rauf	36	13	74	3	5w	(3)	25.4	6	66	5	2w
Mohammad Kashif	23	4	69	2	1nb		18	4	46	3	2nb
Mohammad Tanvir	24.4	4	74	3	1w,11nb (1)		5	0	23	0	1nb
Kashif Naved	4	1	8	0	1w						
Hammad Tariq	5	1	20	0							
Zulfiqar Babar	12	1	23	2		(4)	8	2	13	2	
Sohaib Maqsood	3	0	21	0	1nb						

Sui Southern Gas Corporation Bowling

	O	M	R	W			O	M	R	W	
Sohail Khan	34	9	102	4			18	4	39	1	
Shakeel-ur-Rehman	28.5	3	98	5	4w,6nb	(3)	14.5	0	64	5	1w
Shehzad Butt	19	3	63	1	3nb	(2)	3	1	9	1	
Saeed Bin Nasir	4	0	10	0							
Adnan Malik	7	0	35	0	2nb						

Umpires: Hakeem Shah and Khalid Mahmood. Referee: Mohammad Javed.   Toss: Multan

Close of Play: 1st day: Sui Southern Gas Corporation (1) 206-7 (Shehzad Butt 26*, Sohail Khan 8*, 82 overs); 2nd day: Multan (1) 169-2 (Usman Tariq 63*, Mohammad Kashif 1*, 49 overs); 3rd day: Sui Southern Gas Corporation (2) 103-3 (Mohtashim Ali 51*, Saeed Bin Nasir 9*, 34 overs).

PAKISTAN CUSTOMS v WATER AND POWER DEVELOPMENT AUTHORITY

Played at Jinnah Stadium, Gujranwala, November 13, 14, 15, 2007.
Quaid-e-Azam Trophy 2007/08 - Group A
Water and Power Development Authority won by an innings and 45 runs.   (Points: Pakistan Customs 0, Water and Power Development Authority 9)

PAKISTAN CUSTOMS

1	Hasnain Abbas	c Zulqarnain Haider b Kashif Raza	0	c Zulqarnain Haider b Kashif Raza	4
2	R.M.Khan	c Zulqarnain Haider b Kashif Raza	1	c Zulqarnain Haider b Kashif Raza	32
3	B.M.Shafayat	c Aamer Sajjad b Azharullah	20	c Aamer Sajjad b Azharullah	6
4	Mohammad Nabi	c Aqeel Ahmed b Sarfraz Ahmed	2	(6) c Aqeel Ahmed b Sarfraz Ahmed	5
5	*Zahoor Elahi	b Azharullah	1	c Atiq-ur-Rehman b Kashif Raza	49
6	†Adnan Naved	b Azharullah	8	(4) c Masood Asim b Sarfraz Ahmed	7
7	Yasir Hussain	c and b Azharullah	7	c Bilal Khilji b Sarfraz Ahmed	0
8	Yasir Shah	c Kashif Raza b Azharullah	5	c Aqeel Ahmed b Sarfraz Ahmed	9
9	Ali Hussain	b Azharullah	6	(10) b Kashif Raza	0
10	Raees Amjad	c Azharullah b Kashif Raza	17	(9) c Aqeel Ahmed b Sarfraz Ahmed	12
11	Sajjad Hussain	not out	2	not out	0
	Extras	lb 3, w 1	4	b 1, lb 3, nb 1	5
			73		129

FoW (1): 1-0, 2-5, 3-22, 4-25, 5-29, 6-34, 7-42, 8-48, 9-71, 10-73
FoW (2): 1-27, 2-38, 3-48, 4-72, 5-96, 6-96, 7-109, 8-126, 9-129, 10-129

WATER AND POWER DEVELOPMENT AUTHORITY

1	Masood Asim	c Adnan Naved b Sajjad Hussain	19
2	Kashif Rasheed	c Adnan Naved b Raees Amjad	4
3	Atiq-ur-Rehman	c Adnan Naved b Yasir Shah	9
4	*Aamer Sajjad	b Yasir Shah	52
5	Bilal Khilji	b Yasir Hussain	73
6	Sunny Irshad	c Raees Amjad b Sajjad Hussain	3
7	†Zulqarnain Haider	lbw b Sajjad Hussain	0
8	Aqeel Ahmed	st Adnan Naved b Yasir Shah	18
9	Kashif Raza	lbw b Yasir Shah	35
10	Sarfraz Ahmed	c Mohammad Nabi b Yasir Hussain	8
11	Azharullah	not out	4
	Extras	b 11, lb 1, nb 10	22
			247

FoW (1): 1-30, 2-30, 3-42, 4-120, 5-140, 6-140, 7-176, 8-230, 9-236, 10-247

Water and Power Development Authority Bowling

	O	M	R	W			O	M	R	W
Kashif Raza	14	4	17	3		(2)	15.2	6	32	4
Sarfraz Ahmed	10	5	18	1		(1)	20	7	46	5
Azharullah	10.1	3	35	6	1w	(4)	14	4	46	1
Bilal Khilji						(3)	1	0	1	0
Aqeel Ahmed						(5)	1	1	0	0

Pakistan Customs Bowling

	O	M	R	W	
Raees Amjad	18	2	65	1	9nb
Sajjad Hussain	21	10	40	3	1nb
Yasir Shah	23	5	72	4	
Ali Hussain	15	1	48	0	
Yasir Hussain	4	1	10	2	

Umpires: Jamil Kamran and Kaukab Butt. Referee: Anis Sheikh.   Toss: Water and Power Development Authority

Close of Play: 1st day: Water and Power Development Authority (1) 123-4 (Bilal Khilji 19*, Sunny Irshad 2*, 38 overs); 2nd day: Pakistan Customs (2) 71-3 (Adnan Naved 7*, Zahoor Elahi 20*, 33.2 overs).

The match was scheduled for four days but completed in three.

PESHAWAR v ABBOTTABAD

Played at Arbab Niaz Stadium, Peshawar, November 13, 14, 15, 2007.
Quaid-e-Azam Trophy 2007/08 - Group B
Peshawar won by 43 runs.   (Points: Peshawar 9, Abbottabad 0)

PESHAWAR

#	Batsman	Dismissal 1	R1	Dismissal 2	R2
1	Sajjad Ahmed	c Wajid Ali b Junaid Khan	0	c Fawad Khan b Noor-ul-Amin	34
2	Fawad Ali	run out (Rahimbaz Khan)	37	lbw b Armaghan Elahi	2
3	†Shehzad Khan	c Wajid Ali b Junaid Khan	0	(7) c Wajid Ali b Junaid Khan	6
4	Riaz Afridi	b Armaghan Elahi	0	(8) c sub (Ghulam Mohammad) b Junaid Khan	0
5	Nawaz Ahmed	c Fawad Khan b Junaid Khan	3	(4) c and b Junaid Khan	2
6	Mohammad Fayyaz	c Wajid Ali b Armaghan Elahi	4	(5) c Wajid Ali b Junaid Khan	35
7	*Akbar Badshah	c Armaghan Elahi b Junaid Khan	3	(3) c Fawad Khan b Armaghan Elahi	6
8	Mahfooz Sabri	not out	47	(6) c Wajid Ali b Junaid Khan	2
9	Nauman Habib	b Armaghan Elahi	0	(10) c Noor-ul-Amin b Junaid Khan	26
10	Bilal Khan	b Junaid Khan	16	(9) b Junaid Khan	11
11	Imran Khan	b Junaid Khan	2	not out	8
	Extras	lb 2, nb 3	5	b 2, lb 4, nb 2	8
			117		140

FoW (1): 1-0, 2-2, 3-6, 4-13, 5-25, 6-40, 7-51, 8-52, 9-88, 10-117
FoW (2): 1-16, 2-23, 3-26, 4-80, 5-83, 6-90, 7-90, 8-94, 9-113, 10-140

ABBOTTABAD

#	Batsman	Dismissal 1	R1	Dismissal 2	R2
1	Wajid Ali	c Fawad Ali b Nauman Habib	25	c Akbar Badshah b Nauman Habib	20
2	Mohammad Naeem	b Riaz Afridi	0	lbw b Riaz Afridi	2
3	†Fawad Khan	lbw b Nauman Habib	1	(6) b Nauman Habib	17
4	*Adnan Raees	b Riaz Afridi	8	lbw b Nauman Habib	10
5	Riaz Kail	c Mahfooz Sabri b Riaz Afridi	2	c Shehzad Khan b Bilal Khan	23
6	Iftikhar Mahmood	c Mohammad Fayyaz b Nauman Habib	30	(7) not out	16
7	Junaid Khan	b Nauman Habib	0	(10) c Bilal Khan b Nauman Habib	0
8	Rahimbaz Khan	c Mohammad Fayyaz b Riaz Afridi	6	(3) c Mahfooz Sabri b Riaz Afridi	0
9	Amjad Waqas	not out	3	(8) c Nawaz Ahmed b Nauman Habib	16
10	Noor-ul-Amin	run out (Mahfooz Sabri)	5	(9) c Shehzad Khan b Nauman Habib	0
11	Armaghan Elahi	c Fawad Ali b Riaz Afridi	5	c Nawaz Ahmed b Nauman Habib	0
	Extras	b 1, lb 5, w 2	8	b 3, lb 12, w 1, nb 1	17
			93		121

FoW (1): 1-1, 2-14, 3-28, 4-30, 5-66, 6-66, 7-80, 8-80, 9-85, 10-93
FoW (2): 1-19, 2-21, 3-40, 4-47, 5-67, 6-88, 7-114, 8-114, 9-116, 10-121

Abbottabad Bowling

	O	M	R	W		O	M	R	W	
Junaid Khan	13.1	4	31	6	1nb	20.1	4	46	7	
Armaghan Elahi	8	0	32	3	1nb	9	1	27	2	2nb
Rahimbaz Khan	7	2	35	0	1nb	6	0	22	0	
Noor-ul-Amin	5	2	17	0		12	2	39	1	

Peshawar Bowling

	O	M	R	W		O	M	R	W	
Riaz Afridi	15.2	5	49	5		9	2	13	2	1nb
Nauman Habib	15	3	38	4	2w	18.3	3	63	7	1w
Imran Khan						(3) 6	1	17	0	
Bilal Khan						(4) 4	1	13	1	

Umpires: Ahmed Shahab and Islam Khan. Referee: Ilyas Khan.   Toss: Abbottabad

Close of Play: 1st day: Peshawar (2) 2-0 (Sajjad Ahmed 2*, Fawad Ali 0*); 2nd day: Abbottabad (2) 78-5 (Riaz Kail 14*, Iftikhar Mahmood 3*, 23 overs).

The match was scheduled for four days but completed in three.

QUETTA v KHAN RESEARCH LABORATORIES

Played at Bugti Stadium, Quetta, November 13, 14, 15, 16, 2007.
Quaid-e-Azam Trophy 2007/08 - Group B
Khan Research Laboratories won by five wickets.   (Points: Quetta 0, Khan Research Laboratories 6)

QUETTA

1	Shoaib Khan	c Zulfiqar Jan b Bilal Asad	98	c Bilal Asad b Faisal Afridi		4
2	Hameedullah Khan	lbw b Saeed Ajmal	31	(7) c Zulfiqar Jan b Mohammad Irshad		0
3	†Shahzad Tareen	b Saeed Ajmal	10	(2) c Zulfiqar Jan b Akhtar Ayub		4
4	Taimur Ali	c Azhar Ali b Saeed Ajmal	0	(3) b Mohammad Irshad		42
5	Sabir Hussain	run out	22	(4) c Bazid Khan b Mohammad Irshad		19
6	Jalat Khan	c Azhar Ali b Bilal Asad	5	(8) c Zulfiqar Jan b Faisal Afridi		11
7	*Nasim Khan	b Faisal Afridi	109	(5) not out		33
8	Faisal Irfan	b Saeed Ajmal	28	(6) c Zulfiqar Jan b Mohammad Irshad		4
9	Naseer Khan	b Akhtar Ayub	19	c Zulfiqar Jan b Saeed Ajmal		2
10	Gauhar Faiz	c Zulfiqar Jan b Akhtar Ayub	0	b Saeed Ajmal		0
11	Nazar Hussain	not out	13	b Mohammad Irshad		0
	Extras	b 5, lb 2, w 1, nb 3, pen 5	16	b 5, lb 5, w 2, nb 3		15
			351			134

FoW (1): 1-110, 2-144, 3-144, 4-144, 5-156, 6-217, 7-295, 8-331, 9-335, 10-351
FoW (2): 1-6, 2-33, 3-77, 4-89, 5-95, 6-95, 7-124, 8-133, 9-133, 10-134

KHAN RESEARCH LABORATORIES

1	Azhar Ali	c Shahzad Tareen b Faisal Irfan	0	c Shahzad Tareen b Jalat Khan		50
2	*Mohammad Wasim	c Shoaib Khan b Faisal Irfan	9	c Shoaib Khan b Naseer Khan		27
3	Bazid Khan	b Jalat Khan	35			
4	Bilal Asad	c Sabir Hussain b Nazar Hussain	17	(7) not out		4
5	Ali Naqvi	c Shahzad Tareen b Faisal Irfan	110			
6	Shehzad Malik	b Jalat Khan	9			
7	†Zulfiqar Jan	c Shahzad Tareen b Jalat Khan	6	(3) c Shoaib Khan b Gauhar Faiz		16
8	Faisal Afridi	c Naseer Khan b Jalat Khan	37	(4) c Naseer Khan b Jalat Khan		36
9	Mohammad Irshad	lbw b Faisal Irfan	54	(5) lbw b Gauhar Faiz		1
10	Akhtar Ayub	c and b Jalat Khan	33	(6) not out		0
11	Saeed Ajmal	not out	18			
	Extras	b 4, lb 2, w 3, nb 5	14	b 6, lb 1, w 1, nb 3		11
			342	(5 wickets)		145

FoW (1): 1-0, 2-13, 3-42, 4-98, 5-116, 6-124, 7-182, 8-288, 9-289, 10-342
FoW (2): 1-58, 2-91, 3-116, 4-117, 5-141

Khan Research Laboratories Bowling

	O	M	R	W		O	M	R	W	
Mohammad Irshad	14	1	43	0	1nb	9.4	1	44	5	3nb
Akhtar Ayub	19	3	46	2	1w	7	1	19	1	2w
Faisal Afridi	12.3	1	61	1	2nb	10	3	19	2	
Saeed Ajmal	31	5	115	4		12	2	42	2	
Ali Naqvi	1	0	6	0						
Bilal Asad	18	3	52	2						
Azhar Ali	3	0	16	0						

Quetta Bowling

	O	M	R	W		O	M	R	W	
Faisal Irfan	21	8	40	4		9	2	28	0	
Nazar Hussain	35	4	134	1	2w	8	3	28	0	
Gauhar Faiz	7	0	54	0	1w,2nb	8	2	42	2	1w,3nb
Jalat Khan	25.4	4	101	5	2nb	4.2	0	38	2	
Naseer Khan	5	2	7	0	1nb	2	0	2	1	

Umpires: Shakeel Khan and Zaheer Ahmed. Referee: Khalid Niazi.   Toss: Quetta

Close of Play: 1st day: Quetta (1) 311-7 (Nasim Khan 96*, Naseer Khan 7*, 83 overs); 2nd day: Khan Research Laboratories (1) 246-7 (Ali Naqvi 83*, Mohammad Irshad 39*, 65 overs); 3rd day: Khan Research Laboratories (2) 62-1 (Azhar Ali 31*, Zulfiqar Jan 0*, 13 overs).

Nasim Khan's 109 took 138 balls and included 12 fours and 1 six. Ali Naqvi's 110 took 195 balls and included 12 fours.

RAWALPINDI v PAKISTAN INTERNATIONAL AIRLINES

Played at Khan Research Laboratories Ground, Rawalpindi, November 13, 14, 15, 16, 2007.
Quaid-e-Azam Trophy 2007/08 - Group B
Match drawn.　(Points: Rawalpindi 3, Pakistan International Airlines 0)

RAWALPINDI

1	Mohammad Ibrahim	lbw b Fazl-e-Akbar	4	(3) c Anwar Ali b Kamran Sajid	43
2	Umar Amin	c Anop Santosh b Aizaz Cheema	89	(1) run out	56
3	Yasir Ali	run out (Khurram Manzoor)	1	(9) not out	17
4	Babar Naeem	c Anop Santosh b Anwar Ali	18	(2) c Anwar Ali b Nauman Alavi	59
5	*Naved Ashraf	lbw b Aizaz Cheema	28	c Aizaz Cheema b Nauman Alavi	23
6	Adnan Mufti	b Aizaz Cheema	7	lbw b Fahad Iqbal	11
7	Usman Saeed	c Anop Santosh b Nauman Alavi	19	(4) c Anwar Ali b Shoaib Khan	50
8	†Sajid Mahmood	lbw b Nauman Alavi	17	(7) lbw b Shoaib Khan	40
9	Yasim Murtaza	c Anop Santosh b Aizaz Cheema	14	(8) lbw b Agha Sabir	10
10	Mohammad Rameez	lbw b Anwar Ali	11	not out	7
11	Rizwan Akbar	not out	0		
	Extras	b 10, w 4, nb 3	17	b 9, lb 1, nb 10	20
			225	(8 wickets)	336

FoW (1): 1-4, 2-21, 3-43, 4-80, 5-97, 6-142, 7-191, 8-203, 9-225, 10-225
FoW (2): 1-120, 2-130, 3-200, 4-235, 5-253, 6-271, 7-312, 8-312

PAKISTAN INTERNATIONAL AIRLINES

1	*Khurram Manzoor	c Babar Naeem b Rizwan Akbar	35
2	Kamran Sajid	c Mohammad Ibrahim b Yasir Ali	8
3	Agha Sabir	c Yasim Murtaza b Mohammad Rameez	19
4	Shoaib Khan	lbw b Rizwan Akbar	5
5	Fahad Iqbal	c Sajid Mahmood b Yasir Ali	6
6	Jannisar Khan	b Rizwan Akbar	33
7	Anwar Ali	c Adnan Mufti b Rizwan Akbar	17
8	†Anop Santosh	c Sajid Mahmood b Rizwan Akbar	4
9	Nauman Alavi	b Yasim Murtaza	20
10	Aizaz Cheema	c Rizwan Akbar b Babar Naeem	20
11	Fazl-e-Akbar	not out	0
	Extras	lb 1, w 1, nb 13	15
			182

FoW (1): 1-26, 2-66, 3-73, 4-73, 5-81, 6-110, 7-128, 8-140, 9-182, 10-182

Pakistan International Airlines Bowling

	O	M	R	W			O	M	R	W	
Fazl-e-Akbar	12	3	46	1	2nb		13	7	20	0	3nb
Anwar Ali	14.4	3	37	2	2w		15	6	26	0	
Aizaz Cheema	19	5	44	4	1w		14	4	40	0	
Nauman Alavi	22	5	68	2	1w,1nb	(6)	32	5	90	2	3nb
Jannisar Khan	4	0	15	0			10	2	37	0	4nb
Kamran Sajid	5	3	5	0		(4)	20	7	56	1	
Shoaib Khan						(7)	10	5	18	2	
Agha Sabir						(8)	13	8	18	1	
Fahad Iqbal						(9)	6	0	21	0	
Khurram Manzoor						(10)	1	1	0	0	

Rawalpindi Bowling

	O	M	R	W	
Mohammad Rameez	22	6	60	1	2nb
Yasir Ali	21	5	61	2	4nb
Rizwan Akbar	30	13	52	5	1w,7nb
Yasim Murtaza	5	1	8	1	
Babar Naeem	0.4	0	0	1	

Umpires: Mian Mohammad Aslam and Zameer Haider. Referee: Anwar Khan. Toss: Pakistan International Airlines

Close of Play: 1st day: Rawalpindi (1) 215-8 (Yasim Murtaza 14*, Mohammad Rameez 1*, 71.3 overs); 2nd day: Pakistan International Airlines (1) 128-7 (Jannisar Khan 22*, Nauman Alavi 0*, 63 overs); 3rd day: Rawalpindi (2) 152-2 (Mohammad Ibrahim 19*, Usman Saeed 7*, 58 overs).

ABBOTTABAD v KARACHI BLUES

Played at Abbottabad Cricket Stadium, November 19, 20, 21, 22, 2007.
Quaid-e-Azam Trophy 2007/08 - Group B
Match drawn.   (Points: Abbottabad 3, Karachi Blues 0)

KARACHI BLUES

1	Shadab Kabir	c Adnan Raees b Noor-ul-Amin	167	c and b Noor-ul-Amin	84
2	Aariz Kamal	lbw b Armaghan Elahi	1	not out	100
3	Fahadullah Khan	lbw b Noor-ul-Amin	27	(5) not out	5
4	Mohammad Masroor	lbw b Amjad Waqas	26	(3) lbw b Noor-ul-Amin	1
5	*Mansoor Khan	lbw b Amjad Waqas	69		
6	†Nadeem Shad	c Adnan Raees b Armaghan Elahi	2		
7	Tariq Haroon	lbw b Noor-ul-Amin	24	(4) c sub (Khalid Usman) b Adnan Raees	46
8	Rizwan Saeed	b Noor-ul-Amin	4		
9	Ijaz Ahmed	c Fawad Khan b Noor-ul-Amin	1		
10	Azam Hussain	c Ghulam Mohammad b Armaghan Elahi	8		
11	Malik Aftab	not out	9		
	Extras	b 6, lb 10, w 3, nb 6	25	b 1, lb 14	15
			363	(3 wickets)	251

FoW (1): 1-6, 2-72, 3-125, 4-272, 5-278, 6-319, 7-327, 8-346, 9-347, 10-363
FoW (2): 1-132, 2-145, 3-227

ABBOTTABAD

1	Wajid Ali	c Mohammad Masroor b Rizwan Saeed	19
2	Sajjad Ali	lbw b Malik Aftab	4
3	†Ghulam Mohammad	c Tariq Haroon b Malik Aftab	21
4	*Adnan Raees	c Shadab Kabir b Azam Hussain	42
5	Riaz Kail	b Azam Hussain	112
6	Mohammad Kashif	b Tariq Haroon	72
7	Iftikhar Mahmood	not out	88
8	Fawad Khan	c Tariq Haroon b Azam Hussain	16
9	Armaghan Elahi	c and b Tariq Haroon	12
10	Noor-ul-Amin	c Tariq Haroon b Azam Hussain	8
11	Amjad Waqas	c Mohammad Masroor b Tariq Haroon	13
	Extras	b 10, lb 10, w 5	25
			432

FoW (1): 1-24, 2-38, 3-67, 4-161, 5-265, 6-287, 7-319, 8-338, 9-369, 10-432

Abbottabad Bowling

	O	M	R	W		O	M	R	W
Armaghan Elahi	24.2	2	88	3	1w,6nb	9	2	36	0
Adnan Raees	12	2	22	0	2w	14	5	30	1
Noor-ul-Amin	40	9	131	5		33	6	101	2
Amjad Waqas	40	8	90	2					
Iftikhar Mahmood	3	1	9	0		15	2	42	0
Riaz Kail	2	0	7	0	(4)	9	2	27	0

Karachi Blues Bowling

	O	M	R	W	
Malik Aftab	13	2	56	2	5w
Rizwan Saeed	11	0	30	1	
Tariq Haroon	23	4	65	3	
Mansoor Khan	27	6	67	0	
Azam Hussain	61	15	128	4	
Ijaz Ahmed	11	1	52	0	
Aariz Kamal	5	0	14	0	

Umpires: Ijaz Ahmed and Nadeem Ghauri.   Referee: Khalid Niazi.   Toss: Karachi Blues

Close of Play: 1st day: Karachi Blues (1) 272-4 (Shadab Kabir 126*, Nadeem Shad 0*, 87 overs); 2nd day: Abbottabad (1) 198-4 (Riaz Kail 78*, Mohammad Kashif 22*, 53 overs); 3rd day: Abbottabad (1) 432-9 (Iftikhar Mahmood 88*, Amjad Waqas 13*, 149 overs).

Shadab Kabir's 167 took 312 balls in 434 minutes and included 18 fours and 3 sixes. Riaz Kail's 112 took 201 balls in 278 minutes and included 20 fours. Aariz Kamal's 100 took 281 balls in 271 minutes and included 12 fours.

FAISALABAD v HYDERABAD

Played at Iqbal Stadium, Faisalabad, November 19, 20, 21, 22, 2007.
Quaid-e-Azam Trophy 2007/08 - Group A
Faisalabad won by seven wickets.　(Points: Faisalabad 9, Hyderabad 0)

HYDERABAD

1	Akram Khan	c Mohammad Salman b Ahmed Hayat	0	b Asad Zarar	11
2	Zahid Khan	c Imran Ali b Ijaz Ahmed	95	c Mohammad Salman b Mohammad Talha	8
3	Faisal Athar	c Asad Zarar b Ahmed Hayat	18	lbw b Saadat Munir	65
4	Rizwan Ahmed	lbw b Asad Zarar	33	b Asad Zarar	0
5	*Shahid Qambrani	c Mohammad Salman b Asad Zarar	11	c Asif Hussain b Asad Zarar	4
6	Khadim Hussain	c Imran Ali b Mohammad Talha	23	c and b Saadat Munir	5
7	†Hanif Malik	c and b Asad Zarar	26	c Ahmed Hayat b Asad Zarar	4
8	Pir Zulfiqar	lbw b Ijaz Ahmed	3	not out	23
9	Naeem-ur-Rehman	c Mohammad Salman b Asad Zarar	1	(10) st Mohammad Salman b Saadat Munir	18
10	Farhan Ayub	not out	3	(9) b Asad Zarar	1
11	Sufyan Ali	c Usman Arshad b Asad Zarar	0	c Usman Arshad b Saadat Munir	0
	Extras	lb 3, w 3, nb 26	32	b 5, lb 5, w 2, nb 9	21
			245		**160**

FoW (1): 1-0, 2-36, 3-100, 4-119, 5-203, 6-212, 7-218, 8-219, 9-244, 10-245
FoW (2): 1-8, 2-55, 3-55, 4-98, 5-105, 6-110, 7-116, 8-124, 9-160, 10-160

FAISALABAD

1	Imran Ali	lbw b Farhan Ayub	6	(2) lbw b Farhan Ayub	40
2	Usman Arshad	c Hanif Malik b Naeem-ur-Rehman	31	(1) lbw b Pir Zulfiqar	24
3	Ammar Mahmood	c Hanif Malik b Naeem-ur-Rehman	16	c Naeem-ur-Rehman b Pir Zulfiqar	45
4	*Ijaz Ahmed	c Akram Khan b Pir Zulfiqar	72	not out	20
5	Asif Hussain	c Shahid Qambrani b Pir Zulfiqar	24		
6	Imran Ahmed	c Akram Khan b Pir Zulfiqar	10		
7	†Mohammad Salman	c Naeem-ur-Rehman b Pir Zulfiqar	10		
8	Ahmed Hayat	c Hanif Malik b Sufyan Ali	21		
9	Asad Zarar	c Hanif Malik b Naeem-ur-Rehman	19	(5) not out	0
10	Saadat Munir	b Pir Zulfiqar	18		
11	Mohammad Talha	not out	15		
	Extras	lb 5, w 9, nb 14	28	b 4, w 1, nb 3	8
			270	**(3 wickets)**	**137**

FoW (1): 1-16, 2-49, 3-88, 4-141, 5-172, 6-188, 7-192, 8-215, 9-248, 10-270
FoW (2): 1-47, 2-89, 3-135

Faisalabad Bowling

	O	M	R	W		O	M	R	W	
Ahmed Hayat	16	2	46	2		10	2	33	0	2nb
Mohammad Talha	14	0	72	1	1w,24nb	15	2	49	1	2w,7nb
Asad Zarar	19.5	4	67	5		12	3	47	5	
Saadat Munir	8	0	28	0	(5)	6.5	1	12	4	
Ammar Mahmood	2	0	8	0	2nb					
Ijaz Ahmed	8	2	21	2	(4)	3	0	9	0	

Hyderabad Bowling

	O	M	R	W		O	M	R	W	
Farhan Ayub	28	4	66	1	1w,10nb	7	1	26	1	1nb
Sufyan Ali	16	1	59	1	2w	4	0	33	0	
Naeem-ur-Rehman	23	2	74	3	2w,4nb	3	0	7	0	
Pir Zulfiqar	25.3	6	53	5		7	2	23	2	
Shahid Qambrani	2	0	3	0						
Rizwan Ahmed	3	1	10	0	(5)	6	0	41	0	2nb
Faisal Athar					(6)	1	0	1	0	
Akram Khan					(7)	0.1	0	2	0	

Umpires: Hakeem Shah and Saleem Badar.　Referee: Arshad Pervez.　　Toss: Faisalabad

Close of Play: 1st day: Faisalabad (1) 6-0 (Imran Ali 2*, Usman Arshad 1*, 5 overs); 2nd day: Faisalabad (1) 227-8 (Ahmed Hayat 14*, Saadat Munir 3*, 83 overs); 3rd day: Faisalabad (2) 18-0 (Usman Arshad 1*, Imran Ali 13*, 4 overs).

HABIB BANK LIMITED v WATER AND POWER DEVELOPMENT AUTHORITY

Played at Sheikhupura Stadium, November 19, 20, 21, 22, 2007.
Quaid-e-Azam Trophy 2007/08 - Group A
Water and Power Development Authority won by 138 runs. (Points: Habib Bank Limited 0, Water and Power Development Authority 9)

WATER AND POWER DEVELOPMENT AUTHORITY

1	†Zulqarnain Haider	c Hasan Raza b Shahid Nazir	0	(2) b Mohammad Aslam		11
2	Atiq-ur-Rehman	c Humayun Farhat b Kamran Hussain	32	(1) lbw b Kamran Hussain		5
3	Tariq Aziz	lbw b Mohammad Aslam	74	c Aftab Alam b Dilawar Khan		68
4	*Aamer Sajjad	b Mohammad Aslam	0	c Humayun Farhat b Mohammad Aslam		0
5	Bilal Khilji	c Kamran Hussain b Dilawar Khan	17	c Khaqan Arsal b Mohammad Aslam		5
6	Jahangir Mirza	c Humayun Farhat b Dilawar Khan	24	lbw b Mohammad Aslam		0
7	Nawaz Sardar	lbw b Mohammad Aslam	7	(8) lbw b Mohammad Aslam		42
8	Farooq Iqbal	lbw b Mohammad Aslam	7	(9) lbw b Dilawar Khan		51
9	Kashif Raza	c Sulaman Qadir b Mohammad Aslam	2	(10) c Humayun Farhat b Dilawar Khan		23
10	Sarfraz Ahmed	b Kamran Hussain	15	(7) c Humayun Farhat b Dilawar Khan		52
11	Azharullah	not out	2	not out		15
	Extras	lb 13, nb 1	14	b 1, lb 1		2
			194			**274**

FoW (1): 1-0, 2-70, 3-73, 4-125, 5-138, 6-166, 7-170, 8-175, 9-190, 10-194
FoW (2): 1-13, 2-28, 3-36, 4-46, 5-48, 6-143, 7-143, 8-218, 9-244, 10-274

HABIB BANK LIMITED

1	Rafatullah Mohmand	b Kashif Raza	52	b Azharullah		21
2	Khaqan Arsal	lbw b Kashif Raza	3	(5) b Farooq Iqbal		9
3	Aftab Alam	b Kashif Raza	0	(4) b Azharullah		2
4	Sulaman Qadir	c Jahangir Mirza b Kashif Raza	0	(7) st Zulqarnain Haider b Farooq Iqbal		0
5	*Hasan Raza	c Sarfraz Ahmed b Kashif Raza	32	(6) st Zulqarnain Haider b Farooq Iqbal		37
6	Kamran Hussain	c Aamer Sajjad b Azharullah	0	(3) c Atiq-ur-Rehman b Farooq Iqbal		81
7	†Humayun Farhat	c Zulqarnain Haider b Azharullah	23	(8) c and b Farooq Iqbal		28
8	Mohammad Aslam	not out	10	(2) c Zulqarnain Haider b Kashif Raza		0
9	Shahid Nazir	run out (Nawaz Sardar)	4	c Zulqarnain Haider b Sarfraz Ahmed		6
10	Fahad Masood	c Zulqarnain Haider b Sarfraz Ahmed	5	b Sarfraz Ahmed		0
11	Dilawar Khan	b Azharullah	1	not out		0
	Extras	b 2, lb 3, nb 3	8	lb 5, nb 3		8
			138			**192**

FoW (1): 1-5, 2-5, 3-5, 4-59, 5-59, 6-90, 7-119, 8-125, 9-135, 10-138
FoW (2): 1-1, 2-42, 3-48, 4-81, 5-141, 6-145, 7-169, 8-183, 9-185, 10-192

Habib Bank Limited Bowling

	O	M	R	W			O	M	R	W	
Shahid Nazir	9	3	22	1			7	2	27	0	
Fahad Masood	15	1	53	0	1nb	(3)	8	2	25	0	
Khaqan Arsal	1	1	0	0							
Kamran Hussain	18.1	6	28	2		(2)	11	4	25	2	
Dilawar Khan	19	3	49	2			27.5	3	125	4	
Mohammad Aslam	24	11	29	5		(4)	33	15	57	5	
Aftab Alam						(6)	4	0	13	0	

Water and Power Development Authority Bowling

	O	M	R	W			O	M	R	W	
Sarfraz Ahmed	12	2	50	1		(2)	29	13	51	2	
Kashif Raza	12	3	35	5	3nb	(1)	7	2	13	1	
Azharullah	12.3	2	30	3			23	9	54	2	
Farooq Iqbal	7	1	18	0			25.3	8	37	5	
Nawaz Sardar						(5)	10	1	30	0	3nb
Jahangir Mirza						(6)	1	0	2	0	

Umpires: Ahmed Shahab and Riazuddin. Referee: Aziz-ur-Rehman.   Toss: Habib Bank Limited

Close of Play: 1st day: Water and Power Development Authority (1) 190-8 (Farooq Iqbal 7*, Sarfraz Ahmed 13*, 83 overs); 2nd day: Water and Power Development Authority (2) 46-3 (Tariq Aziz 24*, Bilal Khilji 5*, 24 overs); 3rd day: Habib Bank Limited (2) 48-3 (Kamran Hussain 24*, 24.5 overs).

ISLAMABAD v PAKISTAN INTERNATIONAL AIRLINES

Played at Diamond Club Ground, Islamabad, November 19, 20, 21, 2007.
Quaid-e-Azam Trophy 2007/08 - Group B
Pakistan International Airlines won by an innings and 169 runs.   (Points: Islamabad 0, Pakistan International Airlines 9)

PAKISTAN INTERNATIONAL AIRLINES

1	Agha Sabir	c Mohammad Kashif b Fakhar Hussain	45
2	*Khurram Manzoor	c Mohammad Kashif b Shehzad Azam	38
3	Kamran Sajid	c Mohammad Kashif b Shehzad Azam	57
4	Shoaib Khan	b Rauf Akbar	76
5	Fahad Iqbal	c Mohammad Kashif b Rauf Akbar	41
6	Jannisar Khan	c Mohammad Kashif b Fakhar Hussain	34
7	Anwar Ali	c Fakhar Hussain b Shehzad Azam	74
8	†Anop Santosh	b Fakhar Hussain	2
9	Aizaz Cheema	not out	2
10	Ali Imran		
11	Fazl-e-Akbar		
	Extras	b 6, lb 9, w 1, nb 19	35
		(8 wickets, declared)	404

FoW (1): 1-52, 2-119, 3-210, 4-266, 5-289, 6-394, 7-397, 8-404

ISLAMABAD

1	Raheel Majeed	lbw b Fazl-e-Akbar	5	c Anop Santosh b Aizaz Cheema	30
2	Umair Khan	c Anop Santosh b Aizaz Cheema	35	b Anwar Ali	19
3	Farrukh Hayat	lbw b Fazl-e-Akbar	3	lbw b Aizaz Cheema	1
4	Asadullah Sumari	lbw b Aizaz Cheema	15	lbw b Anwar Ali	10
5	Fayyaz Ahmed	c Jannisar Khan b Aizaz Cheema	9	(7) c Fazl-e-Akbar b Anwar Ali	0
6	Fakhar Hussain	c Agha Sabir b Aizaz Cheema	0	(8) b Anwar Ali	10
7	Ameer Khan	c Agha Sabir b Fazl-e-Akbar	9	(6) c Kamran Sajid b Aizaz Cheema	9
8	*Rauf Akbar	b Aizaz Cheema	7	absent hurt	0
9	Shehzad Azam	not out	20	(5) c Khurram Manzoor b Anwar Ali	0
10	†Mohammad Kashif	b Aizaz Cheema	0	(9) b Aizaz Cheema	1
11	Yasin Bari	c Fahad Iqbal b Aizaz Cheema	4	(10) not out	14
	Extras	b 10, lb 6, nb 3	19	b 10, lb 3, w 1, nb 1	15
			126		109

FoW (1): 1-10, 2-26, 3-74, 4-81, 5-81, 6-88, 7-98, 8-104, 9-112, 10-126
FoW (2): 1-42, 2-44, 3-65, 4-70, 5-75, 6-75, 7-89, 8-94, 9-109

Islamabad Bowling

	O	M	R	W	
Rauf Akbar	27	4	90	2	8nb
Yasin Bari	25	7	62	0	1w,2nb
Shehzad Azam	25	1	112	3	5nb
Raheel Majeed	19	4	60	0	
Fakhar Hussain	9	1	34	3	4nb
Ameer Khan	2	0	9	0	
Fayyaz Ahmed	4	0	22	0	

Pakistan International Airlines Bowling

	O	M	R	W			O	M	R	W	
Fazl-e-Akbar	16	1	54	3			3	0	23	0	1nb
Anwar Ali	5	2	9	0		(3)	8	1	25	5	1w
Ali Imran	3	0	23	0	3nb						
Aizaz Cheema	11.5	5	24	7		(2)	10.5	1	48	4	
Kamran Sajid	1	1	0	0							

Umpires: Ahsan Raza and Mian Mohammad Aslam. Referee: Naeem Ahmed. Toss: Islamabad

Close of Play: 1st day: Pakistan International Airlines (1) 214-3 (Shoaib Khan 46*, Fahad Iqbal 2*, 71 overs); 2nd day: Islamabad (1) 88-6 (Ameer Khan 2*, Rauf Akbar 0*, 25 overs).

The match was scheduled for four days but completed in three.

KARACHI WHITES v MULTAN

Played at United Bank Limited Sports Complex, Karachi, November 19, 20, 21, 22, 2007.
Quaid-e-Azam Trophy 2007/08 - Group A
Match drawn.   (Points: Karachi Whites 0, Multan 3)

KARACHI WHITES

1	Khalid Latif	c and b Zulfiqar Babar	153	c Gulraiz Sadaf b Ansar Javed	34
2	Asad Shafiq	lbw b Mohammad Tanvir	7	b Zulfiqar Babar	28
3	Daniyal Ahsan	b Mohammad Kashif	5	not out	7
4	Atif Ali	c Usman Tariq b Zulfiqar Babar	73	not out	12
5	*Asim Kamal	c Sohaib Maqsood b Abdur Rauf	11		
6	Afsar Nawaz	lbw b Mohammad Kashif	19		
7	†Javed Mansoor	c Gulraiz Sadaf b Hammad Tariq	40		
8	Tanvir Ahmed	c and b Zulfiqar Babar	32		
9	Misbah Khan	c Gulraiz Sadaf b Abdur Rauf	4		
10	Babar Rehman	c Ansar Javed b Abdur Rauf	19		
11	Fahad Khan	not out	0		
	Extras	b 2, lb 11, w 1, nb 14	28	b 1, lb 5, nb 2	8
			391	(2 wickets)	89

FoW (1): 1-20, 2-34, 3-143, 4-183, 5-215, 6-307, 7-355, 8-368, 9-370, 10-391
FoW (2): 1-51, 2-75

MULTAN

1	Hammad Tariq	b Tanvir Ahmed	6
2	Usman Tariq	c Afsar Nawaz b Babar Rehman	2
3	Rameez Alam	c Javed Mansoor b Tanvir Ahmed	60
4	Ansar Javed	c Afsar Nawaz b Fahad Khan	24
5	Naved Yasin	c Misbah Khan b Tanvir Ahmed	49
6	Sohaib Maqsood	c Khalid Latif b Fahad Khan	123
7	†Gulraiz Sadaf	c Javed Mansoor b Fahad Khan	47
8	*Abdur Rauf	c Asad Shafiq b Fahad Khan	0
9	Zulfiqar Babar	c Babar Rehman b Fahad Khan	8
10	Mohammad Kashif	c sub (Ahmed Iqbal) b Misbah Khan	48
11	Mohammad Tanvir	not out	9
	Extras	b 6, lb 3, w 4, nb 6	19
			395

FoW (1): 1-9, 2-9, 3-65, 4-144, 5-159, 6-303, 7-307, 8-331, 9-338, 10-395

Multan Bowling

	O	M	R	W			O	M	R	W	
Abdur Rauf	36.4	14	92	3	3nb		12	3	38	0	1nb
Ansar Javed	16	2	42	0	6nb	(3)	3	0	10	1	1nb
Mohammad Tanvir	13	7	22	1	1nb	(2)	4	0	23	0	
Mohammad Kashif	27	5	51	2	1w,2nb						
Zulfiqar Babar	40	9	113	3		(4)	5	2	12	1	
Hammad Tariq	18	2	43	1							
Sohaib Maqsood	3	1	13	0	2nb						
Usman Tariq	1	0	2	0							

Karachi Whites Bowling

	O	M	R	W	
Tanvir Ahmed	39	10	105	3	4nb
Babar Rehman	27	5	81	1	4w
Fahad Khan	34	6	78	5	2nb
Misbah Khan	24.3	4	94	1	
Afsar Nawaz	4	0	19	0	
Asad Shafiq	1	0	9	0	

Umpires: Kaukab Butt and Shakeel Khan.   Referee: Ilyas Khan.   Toss: Multan

Close of Play: 1st day: Karachi Whites (1) 178-3 (Khalid Latif 70*, Asim Kamal 10*, 85 overs); 2nd day: Multan (1) 29-2 (Rameez Alam 16*, Ansar Javed 3*, 11 overs); 3rd day: Multan (1) 274-5 (Sohaib Maqsood 85*, Gulraiz Sadaf 32*, 94 overs).

Khalid Latif's 153 took 449 balls in 565 minutes and included 11 fours and 3 sixes. Sohaib Maqsood's 123 took 157 balls in 221 minutes and included 12 fours and 3 sixes.

LAHORE RAVI v SUI SOUTHERN GAS CORPORATION

Played at Lahore Country Club, Muridke, November 19, 20, 21, 22, 2007.
Quaid-e-Azam Trophy 2007/08 - Group A
Match drawn.   (Points: Lahore Ravi 0, Sui Southern Gas Corporation 3)

LAHORE RAVI

1	Kashif Siddiq	c and b Mansoor Ahmed	62	c Asif Zakir b Rajesh Ramesh		14
2	Sohail Ahmed	c Ahmed Zeeshan b Sohail Khan	48	c Asif Zakir b Mansoor Ahmed		35
3	Ali Haider	c Ali Hussain b Mansoor Ahmed	0	(4) b Sohail Khan		45
4	Afzal Shah	lbw b Sohail Khan	6	(3) lbw b Rajesh Ramesh		0
5	Arsalan Mir	c Ahmed Zeeshan b Shehzad Butt	42	c Ahmed Zeeshan b Shakeel-ur-Rehman		15
6	Saad Nasim	c Shehzad Butt b Sohail Khan	7	(7) c Rajesh Ramesh b Sohail Khan		39
7	*Junaid Zia	lbw b Rajesh Ramesh	46	(6) c Ali Hussain b Shehzad Butt		9
8	†Shahbaz Butt	c Mohtashim Ali b Shakeel-ur-Rehman	2	(9) c sub (Mansoor Ali) b Sohail Khan		1
9	Waqas Ahmed	c Shakeel-ur-Rehman b Mansoor Ahmed	114	(8) st Ahmed Zeeshan b Mansoor Ahmed		42
10	Salman Rahat	not out	17	not out		0
11	Imran Haider	c Asif Zakir b Rajesh Ramesh	2	not out		1
	Extras	b 12, lb 2, w 7, nb 4	25	b 4, lb 3, nb 1		8
			371	**(9 wickets)**		**209**

FoW (1): 1-116, 2-116, 3-122, 4-129, 5-150, 6-204, 7-206, 8-236, 9-352, 10-371
FoW (2): 1-17, 2-17, 3-75, 4-100, 5-113, 6-142, 7-190, 8-206, 9-208

SUI SOUTHERN GAS CORPORATION

1	Asif Zakir	lbw b Salman Rahat	168
2	Mohtashim Ali	lbw b Salman Rahat	4
3	Imran Abbas	lbw b Kashif Siddiq	49
4	*Saeed Bin Nasir	c Shahbaz Butt b Saad Nasim	34
5	Ali Hussain	c Waqas Ahmed b Saad Nasim	4
6	†Ahmed Zeeshan	c Kashif Siddiq b Saad Nasim	33
7	Shehzad Butt	c Shahbaz Butt b Imran Haider	82
8	Rajesh Ramesh	c Shahbaz Butt b Junaid Zia	2
9	Sohail Khan	not out	28
10	Mansoor Ahmed	c Arsalan Mir b Imran Haider	41
11	Shakeel-ur-Rehman		
	Extras	lb 12, w 4, nb 15	31
		(9 wickets, declared)	**476**

FoW (1): 1-39, 2-140, 3-154, 4-228, 5-335, 6-399, 7-399, 8-401, 9-476

Sui Southern Gas Corporation Bowling

	O	M	R	W			O	M	R	W	
Rajesh Ramesh	12.4	4	48	2	7w	(2)	10	2	33	2	
Sohail Khan	25	1	93	3		(1)	15	3	48	3	
Shakeel-ur-Rehman	18	3	107	1		(4)	13	6	49	1	1nb
Mansoor Ahmed	25	4	85	3	4nb	(3)	15	3	55	2	
Asif Zakir	1	0	4	0							
Shehzad Butt	8	2	20	1		(5)	5	1	17	1	

Lahore Ravi Bowling

	O	M	R	W	
Junaid Zia	43	10	140	1	7nb
Waqas Ahmed	22	3	80	0	1w,1nb
Salman Rahat	25	4	93	2	3w,5nb
Arsalan Mir	5.2	1	17	0	2nb
Imran Haider	20.2	4	52	2	
Saad Nasim	29	9	79	3	
Kashif Siddiq	2	0	3	1	

Umpires: Iqbal Butt and Mohammad Arif. Referee: Abdus Sami.   Toss: Sui Southern Gas Corporation

Close of Play: 1st day: Lahore Ravi (1) 285-8 (Waqas Ahmed 54*, Salman Rahat 2*, 75.1 overs); 2nd day: Sui Southern Gas Corporation (1) 169-3 (Asif Zakir 90*, Ahmed Zeeshan 9*, 54.1 overs); 3rd day: Sui Southern Gas Corporation (1) 404-8 (Sohail Khan 1*, Mansoor Ahmed 2*, 133 overs).
Waqas Ahmed's 114 took 79 balls in 115 minutes and included 13 fours and 4 sixes. Asif Zakir's 168 took 338 balls in 465 minutes and included 21 fours.

LAHORE SHALIMAR v RAWALPINDI

Played at Mirpur Cricket Stadium, November 19, 20, 21, 22, 2007.
Quaid-e-Azam Trophy 2007/08 - Group B
Match drawn.   (Points: Lahore Shalimar 0, Rawalpindi 3)

RAWALPINDI

1	Mohammad Ibrahim	c Ali Raza b Mohammad Naved	4	(2) c Junaid Malik b Mohammad Saeed	19
2	Babar Naeem	c Ali Raza b Mohammad Naved	8	(1) c Ali Raza b Mohammad Naved	4
3	Adnan Mufti	lbw b Mohammad Saeed	69	lbw b Mohammad Saeed	1
4	*Naved Ashraf	c Ali Raza b Mohammad Saeed	3	(5) c Ali Raza b Mohammad Naved	30
5	†Zahid Mansoor	c Suleman Khan b Mohammad Naved	18	(7) c sub (Usman Malik)	
				b Mohammad Hussain	1
6	Usman Saeed	c Asif Raza b Mohammad Naved	7	c Ali Raza b Mohammad Hussain	17
7	Awais Zia	b Mohammad Naved	64	(4) c Asif Raza b Mohammad Saeed	30
8	Yasir Ali	c Asif Khan b Mohammad Saeed	39	(9) run out (sub [Usman Malik])	10
9	Yasim Murtaza	c Shahnawaz Malik			
		b Mohammad Naved	19	(8) c Ali Raza b Mohammad Naved	56
10	Rizwan Akbar	c Suleman Khan b Mohammad Saeed	4	not out	9
11	Mohammad Ayaz	not out	1		
	Extras	b 6, lb 17, w 1, nb 24	48	b 2, lb 3, w 6, nb 4	15
			284	**(9 wickets, declared)**	**192**

FoW (1): 1-4, 2-34, 3-38, 4-80, 5-107, 6-161, 7-251, 8-255, 9-280, 10-284
FoW (2): 1-4, 2-8, 3-62, 4-64, 5-113, 6-114, 7-115, 8-160, 9-192

LAHORE SHALIMAR

1	Asif Khan	lbw b Mohammad Ayaz	15	c Mohammad Ibrahim b Rizwan Akbar	24
2	Kashif Ali	run out (Mohammad Ayaz)	0	lbw b Rizwan Akbar	18
3	Junaid Malik	c Zahid Mansoor b Yasir Ali	31	c Awais Zia b Yasir Ali	85
4	Suleman Khan	c Awais Zia b Rizwan Akbar	7	(7) not out	0
5	Mohammad Hussain	c Mohammad Ibrahim			
		b Mohammad Ayaz	3		
6	Ahmed Butt	lbw b Yasim Murtaza	22	(8) not out	0
7	Shahnawaz Malik	c Awais Zia b Yasir Ali	4	(4) c Naved Ashraf b Yasim Murtaza	46
8	*†Ali Raza	b Yasim Murtaza	19		
9	Mohammad Saeed	b Yasim Murtaza	23	(5) c Awais Zia b Rizwan Akbar	32
10	Asif Raza	c Zahid Mansoor b Rizwan Akbar	4	(6) c Adnan Mufti b Rizwan Akbar	6
11	Mohammad Naved	not out	0		
	Extras	b 10, lb 3, w 1, nb 5	19	b 6, lb 2, w 4, nb 3	15
			147	**(6 wickets)**	**226**

FoW (1): 1-4, 2-31, 3-42, 4-45, 5-88, 6-94, 7-107, 8-136, 9-147, 10-147
FoW (2): 1-36, 2-62, 3-170, 4-216, 5-226, 6-226

Lahore Shalimar Bowling

	O	M	R	W		O	M	R	W	
Mohammad Naved	40	14	91	6	4nb	23.1	4	90	3	
Asif Raza	26	10	55	0	7nb (3)	5	1	15	0	
Mohammad Saeed	28	4	73	4	1w,13nb (2)	17	3	50	3	6w,4nb
Mohammad Hussain	14	2	34	0		12	3	32	2	
Ahmed Butt	3	0	8	0						

Rawalpindi Bowling

	O	M	R	W		O	M	R	W	
Rizwan Akbar	19.3	6	30	2	2nb	26	6	73	4	2w,1nb
Yasir Ali	18	7	46	2	1w,3nb	15.3	2	59	1	2w,2nb
Mohammad Ayaz	16	6	36	2		10	3	23	0	
Yasim Murtaza	6	2	21	3		13	0	56	1	
Babar Naeem	2	1	1	0		4	1	7	0	

Umpires: Akbar Khan and Zaheer Ahmed. Referee: Mahmood Rasheed.   Toss: Lahore Shalimar

Close of Play: 1st day: Rawalpindi (1) 213-6 (Awais Zia 49*, Yasir Ali 17*, 80.1 overs); 2nd day: Lahore Shalimar (1) 92-5 (Junaid Malik 27*, Shahnawaz Malik 4*, 43.2 overs); 3rd day: Rawalpindi (2) 175-8 (Yasim Murtaza 48*, Rizwan Akbar 2*, 55.1 overs).

PESHAWAR v SUI NORTHERN GAS PIPELINES LIMITED

Played at Arbab Niaz Stadium, Peshawar, November 19, 20, 21, 2007.
Quaid-e-Azam Trophy 2007/08 - Group B
Sui Northern Gas Pipelines Limited won by ten wickets.   (Points: Peshawar 0, Sui Northern Gas Pipelines Limited 9)

PESHAWAR

1	Sajjad Ahmed	b Imran Ali	2	(3) b Imran Ali	0
2	Fawad Ali	c Saleem Mughal b Tauqeer Hussain	24	c Adnan Akmal b Imran Ali	23
3	Mohammad Fayyaz	c Mohammad Hafeez b Asad Ali	11	(1) c Adnan Akmal b Imran Ali	53
4	Nawaz Ahmed	run out (Saleem Mughal)	50	lbw b Faisal Rasheed	5
5	*Akbar Badshah	b Tauqeer Hussain	2	(7) c Azhar Shafiq b Mohammad Hafeez	26
6	Mahfooz Sabri	c sub (Farhan Asghar) b Asad Ali	6	(5) c Mohammad Hafeez b Faisal Rasheed	0
7	Jamaluddin	c Adnan Akmal b Imran Ali	5	(6) b Imran Ali	9
8	†Gauhar Ali	c Faisal Rasheed b Tauqeer Hussain	37	c Adnan Akmal b Imran Ali	0
9	Bilal Khan	lbw b Mohammad Hafeez	4	run out (Umar Akmal/Adnan Akmal)	20
10	Nauman Habib	c Asad Ali b Tauqeer Hussain	2	(11) st Adnan Akmal b Mohammad Hafeez	0
11	Imran Khan	not out	0	(10) not out	6
	Extras	b 2, lb 2, nb 11	15	lb 2, w 1, nb 9	12
			158		**154**

FoW (1): 1-2, 2-28, 3-46, 4-49, 5-84, 6-102, 7-135, 8-155, 9-158, 10-158
FoW (2): 1-44, 2-44, 3-62, 4-62, 5-85, 6-102, 7-102, 8-128, 9-154, 10-154

SUI NORTHERN GAS PIPELINES LIMITED

1	*Mohammad Hafeez	c Bilal Khan b Imran Khan	9		
2	Yasir Arafat	lbw b Nauman Habib	10	(1) not out	4
3	Umar Akmal	c Gauhar Ali b Imran Khan	6	(2) not out	13
4	Azhar Shafiq	c Gauhar Ali b Imran Khan	6		
5	Saleem Mughal	c Gauhar Ali b Nauman Habib	7		
6	Tauqeer Hussain	c Gauhar Ali b Nauman Habib	2		
7	Khurram Shehzad	c Akbar Badshah b Mohammad Fayyaz	166		
8	†Adnan Akmal	c Nawaz Ahmed b Bilal Khan	23		
9	Faisal Rasheed	c and b Mohammad Fayyaz	39		
10	Imran Ali	c Akbar Badshah b Mohammad Fayyaz	6		
11	Asad Ali	not out	1		
	Extras	b 7, lb 7, nb 9	23		
			298	(no wicket)	**17**

FoW (1): 1-15, 2-25, 3-26, 4-31, 5-37, 6-53, 7-129, 8-277, 9-289, 10-298

Sui Northern Gas Pipelines Limited Bowling

	O	M	R	W			O	M	R	W	
Imran Ali	19	5	70	2	2nb		18	3	78	5	1w,3nb
Asad Ali	14	3	41	2	3nb		15	2	59	0	
Tauqeer Hussain	10.4	1	27	4	6nb	(5)	3	1	6	0	
Faisal Rasheed	3	0	5	0		(3)	2	0	3	2	1nb
Mohammad Hafeez	2	0	11	1		(4)	2.2	0	6	2	

Peshawar Bowling

	O	M	R	W			O	M	R	W
Nauman Habib	23	5	99	3	4nb		2.5	1	12	0
Imran Khan	21	3	67	3	5nb		2	0	5	0
Bilal Khan	17	4	47	1						
Akbar Badshah	6	1	31	0						
Mohammad Fayyaz	8.5	0	40	3						

Umpires: Islam Khan and Zameer Haider. Referee: Anwar Khan.   Toss: Sui Northern Gas Pipelines Limited

Close of Play: 1st day: Sui Northern Gas Pipelines Limited (1) 52-5 (Saleem Mughal 7*, Khurram Shehzad 9*, 20 overs); 2nd day: Peshawar (2) 64-4 (Mohammad Fayyaz 28*, Jamaluddin 2*, 16.2 overs).

The match was scheduled for four days but completed in three. Khurram Shehzad's 166 took 192 balls in 288 minutes and included 24 fours and 2 sixes.

SIALKOT v PAKISTAN CUSTOMS

Played at Jinnah Stadium, Sialkot, November 19, 20, 21, 22, 2007.
Quaid-e-Azam Trophy 2007/08 - Group A
Sialkot won by two wickets.   (Points: Sialkot 9, Pakistan Customs 0)

PAKISTAN CUSTOMS

1	Hasnain Abbas	lbw b Mohammad Wasim	0	b Mohammad Ali	117
2	†Adnan Naved	b Imran Malik	6		
3	Rehan Rafiq	lbw b Mohammad Wasim	25	c Khalid Mahmood b Nayyer Abbas	55
4	B.M.Shafayat	lbw b Imran Malik	10	lbw b Mohammad Ali	63
5	*Zahoor Elahi	b Mohammad Ali	5	c Khalid Mahmood b Nayyer Abbas	4
6	Asif Iqbal	lbw b Mohammad Ali	0	lbw b Mohammad Ayub	25
7	Mohammad Nabi	b Mohammad Ali	6	c Shahid Siddiq b Nayyer Abbas	37
8	Murtaza Hussain	c Khalid Mahmood b Imran Malik	20	(2) lbw b Bilal Hussain	56
9	Yasir Shah	c Faisal Khan b Imran Malik	51	not out	8
10	Raees Amjad	lbw b Mohammad Ali	5	(8) not out	6
11	Sajjad Hussain	not out	0		
	Extras	lb 7, nb 10	17	b 6, lb 4, nb 1	11
			145	**(7 wickets, declared)**	**382**

FoW (1): 1-8, 2-8, 3-24, 4-33, 5-33, 6-40, 7-61, 8-124, 9-145, 10-145
FoW (2): 1-164, 2-186, 3-279, 4-286, 5-323, 6-353, 7-371

SIALKOT

1	Naeemuddin	lbw b Sajjad Hussain	31	lbw b Raees Amjad	12
2	Bilal Hussain	lbw b Sajjad Hussain	2	lbw b Sajjad Hussain	5
3	Arsalan Anwar	lbw b Sajjad Hussain	4	(6) lbw b Sajjad Hussain	9
4	Faisal Khan	c Adnan Naved b Yasir Shah	66	b Yasir Shah	69
5	*Mohammad Ayub	lbw b Sajjad Hussain	10	c Adnan Naved b Raees Amjad	93
6	Shahid Siddiq	b Sajjad Hussain	0	(8) c Yasir Shah b Raees Amjad	22
7	Nayyer Abbas	c Zahoor Elahi b Yasir Shah	14	(3) c Rehan Rafiq b Sajjad Hussain	5
8	†Khalid Mahmood	b Raees Amjad	55	(7) not out	56
9	Imran Malik	c Mohammad Nabi b Yasir Shah	8	(10) not out	1
10	Mohammad Wasim	c Hasnain Abbas b Yasir Shah	26	(9) run out	7
11	Mohammad Ali	not out	0		
	Extras	b 2, lb 3, nb 4	9	b 15, lb 2, w 1, nb 6	24
			225	**(8 wickets)**	**303**

FoW (1): 1-3, 2-12, 3-69, 4-84, 5-84, 6-111, 7-188, 8-190, 9-208, 10-225
FoW (2): 1-12, 2-19, 3-25, 4-161, 5-182, 6-240, 7-291, 8-301

Sialkot Bowling

	O	M	R	W		O	M	R	W	
Mohammad Wasim	14	3	43	2	2nb	20	3	87	0	1nb
Imran Malik	13.1	2	48	4		15	3	79	0	
Mohammad Ali	12	2	36	4	8nb	21	6	78	2	
Nayyer Abbas	4	0	11	0		30	8	69	3	
Bilal Hussain					(5)	6	0	21	1	
Mohammad Ayub					(6)	5	0	38	1	

Pakistan Customs Bowling

	O	M	R	W		O	M	R	W	
Raees Amjad	18	5	38	1	3nb	15	1	73	3	1w,5nb
Sajjad Hussain	25	5	75	5	1nb	17.5	3	99	3	
Murtaza Hussain	14	4	54	0	(4)	20	3	38	0	1nb
Yasir Shah	22.3	5	53	4	(3)	25	7	74	1	
Rehan Rafiq					(5)	4	3	2	0	

Umpires: Iftikhar Malik and Khalid Mahmood.   Referee: Saadat Ali.   Toss: Sialkot

Close of Play: 1st day: Sialkot (1) 69-2 (Naeemuddin 31*, Faisal Khan 29*, 26 overs); 2nd day: Pakistan Customs (2) 80-0 (Hasnain Abbas 63*, Murtaza Hussain 16*, 28 overs); 3rd day: Sialkot (2) 19-1 (Naeemuddin 8*, Nayyer Abbas 5*, 3 overs).

Hasnain Abbas's 117 took 176 balls in 257 minutes and included 21 fours and 1 six.

ZARAI TARAQIATI BANK LIMITED v QUETTA

Played at Khan Research Laboratories Ground, Rawalpindi, November 19, 20, 21, 22, 2007.
Quaid-e-Azam Trophy 2007/08 - Group B
Match drawn.   (Points: Zarai Taraqiati Bank Limited 3, Quetta 0)

QUETTA
1	Shoaib Khan	c Adnan Raza b Jawad Hameed	81
2	Samiullah Agha	b Mohammad Khalil	5
3	Taimur Ali	c Adnan Raza b Jawad Hameed	21
4	Sabir Hussain	c Zohaib Khan b Mohammad Khalil	8
5	*Nasim Khan	lbw b Azhar Attari	4
6	Jalat Khan	c Atif Ashraf b Mohammad Khalil	75
7	Faisal Irfan	c and b Zohaib Khan	34
8	Arun Lal	run out (Mohammad Khalil)	68
9	Naseer Khan	c Zohaib Khan b Azhar Attari	52
10	†Sanaullah Khan	not out	50
11	Nazar Hussain	not out	25
	Extras	b 1, lb 10, w 2, nb 24	37

(9 wickets, declared)   460

FoW (1): 1-10, 2-69, 3-86, 4-97, 5-158, 6-245, 7-264, 8-337, 9-420

ZARAI TARAQIATI BANK LIMITED
1	Afaq Raheem	c Shoaib Khan b Naseer Khan	275
2	Umar Javed	c Shoaib Khan b Nazar Hussain	134
3	Atif Ashraf	c Jalat Khan b Naseer Khan	37
4	Adnan Raza	b Naseer Khan	34
5	†Shakeel Ansar	not out	0
6	Jawad Hameed	not out	0
7	Aamer Bashir		
8	*Wajahatullah Wasti		
9	Zohaib Khan		
10	Mohammad Khalil		
11	Azhar Attari		
	Extras	b 8, lb 4, w 4, nb 19	35

(4 wickets)   515

FoW (1): 1-332, 2-440, 3-511, 4-515

Zarai Taraqiati Bank Limited Bowling
	O	M	R	W	
Mohammad Khalil	40	6	126	3	1w,2nb
Azhar Attari	36	3	118	2	20nb
Umar Javed	3	0	11	0	1nb
Zohaib Khan	35	7	115	1	
Jawad Hameed	31.2	7	61	2	
Adnan Raza	5	0	18	0	2nb

Quetta Bowling
	O	M	R	W	
Faisal Irfan	28	4	86	0	
Nazar Hussain	29	6	72	1	3w
Arun Lal	22	3	78	0	1w,11nb
Naseer Khan	44	7	121	3	
Jalat Khan	37	3	130	0	8nb
Shoaib Khan	1	0	8	0	
Nasim Khan	4	1	8	0	

Umpires: Rasheed Bhatti and Raweed Khan. Referee: Mohammad Javed.   Toss: Zarai Taraqiati Bank Limited

Close of Play: 1st day: Quetta (1) 200-5 (Jalat Khan 52*, Faisal Irfan 14*, 78 overs); 2nd day: Zarai Taraqiati Bank Limited (1) 8-0 (Afaq Raheem 4*, Umar Javed 4*, 5.2 overs); 3rd day: Zarai Taraqiati Bank Limited (1) 265-0 (Afaq Raheem 151*, Umar Javed 101*, 88 overs).

Afaq Raheem's 275 took 472 balls in 644 minutes and included 31 fours. Umar Javed's 134 took 302 balls in 443 minutes and included 17 fours and 1 six.

ABBOTTABAD v ZARAI TARAQIATI BANK LIMITED

Played at Abbottabad Cricket Stadium, November 25, 26, 27, 28, 2007.
Quaid-e-Azam Trophy 2007/08 - Group B
Match drawn.   (Points: Abbottabad 3, Zarai Taraqiati Bank Limited 0)

ZARAI TARAQIATI BANK LIMITED

1	Afaq Raheem	st Ghulam Mohammad b Noor-ul-Amin	21	c Ghulam Mohammad b Rashid Mansoor	1
2	Umar Javed	b Khalid Usman	16		
3	Atif Ashraf	st Ghulam Mohammad b Noor-ul-Amin	54	(2) c Iftikhar Mahmood	
				b Armaghan Elahi	28
4	Adnan Raza	c Ghulam Mohammad b Noor-ul-Amin	91	not out	103
5	Wajahatullah Wasti	c Sajjad Ali b Rashid Mansoor	8		
6	Faisal Naved	c Riaz Kail b Rashid Mansoor	32		
7	†Shakeel Ansar	lbw b Armaghan Elahi	11		
8	*Iftikhar Anjum	c Ghulam Mohammad b Rashid Mansoor	4		
9	Zohaib Khan	c Adnan Raees b Armaghan Elahi	1	(3) not out	68
10	Jawad Hameed	b Noor-ul-Amin	10		
11	Mohammad Khalil	not out	15		
	Extras	b 7, lb 8, w 3, nb 5	23	b 8, nb 4	12
			286	(2 wickets)	212

FoW (1): 1-40, 2-62, 3-142, 4-182, 5-220, 6-246, 7-259, 8-260, 9-260, 10-286
FoW (2): 1-1, 2-41

ABBOTTABAD

1	Fawad Khan	b Zohaib Khan	15
2	†Ghulam Mohammad	c Shakeel Ansar b Zohaib Khan	72
3	Khalid Usman	c Faisal Naved b Zohaib Khan	25
4	*Adnan Raees	lbw b Jawad Hameed	25
5	Riaz Kail	b Iftikhar Anjum	153
6	Rashid Mansoor	c Shakeel Ansar b Iftikhar Anjum	41
7	Sajjad Ali	b Iftikhar Anjum	16
8	Iftikhar Mahmood	b Mohammad Khalil	43
9	Mohammad Kashif	lbw b Adnan Raza	37
10	Noor-ul-Amin	not out	3
11	Armaghan Elahi	b Iftikhar Anjum	4
	Extras	b 2, lb 7, w 1, nb 2	12
			446

FoW (1): 1-41, 2-101, 3-124, 4-161, 5-243, 6-271, 7-369, 8-437, 9-440, 10-446

Abbottabad Bowling	O	M	R	W			O	M	R	W	
Armaghan Elahi	18	9	39	2	1w,2nb		8	1	19	1	3nb
Rashid Mansoor	17	5	44	3	1w,1nb		10	3	34	1	1nb
Noor-ul-Amin	34.3	8	104	4	1w		24	6	50	0	
Khalid Usman	23	4	66	1	1nb		11	1	21	0	
Adnan Raees	2	0	10	0			2	0	13	0	
Riaz Kail	1	0	5	0		(7)	11.2	3	32	0	
Iftikhar Mahmood	2	0	3	0	1nb	(6)	15	2	35	0	

ZTBL Bowling	O	M	R	W	
Iftikhar Anjum	20	4	64	4	
Mohammad Khalil	31	7	111	1	1w,1nb
Zohaib Khan	45	19	101	3	
Jawad Hameed	42	12	112	1	
Atif Ashraf	1	0	6	0	
Adnan Raza	6	0	20	1	
Wajahatullah Wasti	2	0	10	0	
Faisal Naved	4	1	13	0	1nb

Umpires: Ahsan Raza and Rasheed Bhatti. Referee: Mohammad Javed.   Toss: Zarai Taraqiati Bank Limited

Close of Play: 1st day: Zarai Taraqiati Bank Limited (1) 247-6 (Faisal Naved 28*, Iftikhar Anjum 0*, 84.1 overs); 2nd day: Abbottabad (1) 184-4 (Riaz Kail 35*, Rashid Mansoor 6*, 63.3 overs); 3rd day: Abbottabad (1) 441-9 (Noor-ul-Amin 3*, Armaghan Elahi 0*, 150 overs).

Riaz Kail's 153 took 331 balls in 432 minutes and included 17 fours and 3 sixes. Adnan Raza's 103 took 229 balls in 319 minutes and included 8 fours and 1 six.

FAISALABAD v SUI SOUTHERN GAS CORPORATION

Played at Sports Stadium, Sargodha, November 25, 26, 27, 28, 2007.
Quaid-e-Azam Trophy 2007/08 - Group A
Match drawn.   (Points: Faisalabad 3, Sui Southern Gas Corporation 0)

FAISALABAD

1	Usman Arshad	c Ahmed Zeeshan b Sohail Khan	82	c and b Waqar Ahmed	105
2	Imran Ali	c sub (Mansoor Ali) b Mansoor Ahmed	86	c Asif Zakir b Haaris Ayaz	29
3	Ammar Mahmood	c Ahmed Zeeshan b Shehzad Butt	62	c Mansoor Ahmed b Asif Zakir	2
4	*Ijaz Ahmed	lbw b Sohail Khan	53		
5	Asif Hussain	c Ahmed Zeeshan b Shehzad Butt	6	(4) run out (Saeed Bin Nasir)	80
6	Imran Ahmed	c Ahmed Zeeshan b Shehzad Butt	84	(5) not out	12
7	†Mohammad Salman	run out (Saeed Bin Nasir)	58		
8	Ahmed Hayat	not out	54	(6) c Waqar Ahmed b Shehzad Butt	2
9	Asad Zarar	not out	10		
10	Mohammad Talha				
11	Saadat Munir				
	Extras	b 2, lb 14, w 1, nb 9	26	b 17, lb 5, nb 2	24
		(7 wickets, declared)	521	(5 wickets)	254

FoW (1): 1-146, 2-190, 3-280, 4-288, 5-311, 6-437, 7-500
FoW (2): 1-99, 2-108, 3-206, 4-213, 5-254

SUI SOUTHERN GAS CORPORATION

1	Asif Zakir	c Usman Arshad b Ahmed Hayat	16
2	Mohtashim Ali	lbw b Mohammad Talha	0
3	Ali Hussain	c Asif Hussain b Saadat Munir	33
4	*Saeed Bin Nasir	b Mohammad Talha	73
5	Mohammad Zafar	c Ammar Mahmood b Usman Arshad	81
6	†Ahmed Zeeshan	lbw b Asad Zarar	99
7	Shehzad Butt	lbw b Ahmed Hayat	1
8	Haaris Ayaz	lbw b Ahmed Hayat	0
9	Sohail Khan	c Imran Ahmed b Mohammad Talha	12
10	Mansoor Ahmed	b Ahmed Hayat	26
11	Waqar Ahmed	not out	9
	Extras	b 11, lb 1, nb 12	24
			374

FoW (1): 1-6, 2-25, 3-88, 4-174, 5-281, 6-286, 7-286, 8-318, 9-346, 10-374

Sui Southern Gas Corporation Bowling

	O	M	R	W				O	M	R	W	
Waqar Ahmed	30	4	147	0	6nb	(2)		7	0	31	1	
Sohail Khan	36	6	103	2	1nb	(1)		8	2	26	0	
Shehzad Butt	21	2	86	3				10	3	31	1	
Mansoor Ahmed	15	1	89	1	2nb	(5)		6	0	27	0	1nb
Haaris Ayaz	19	4	65	0		(4)		21	5	59	1	1nb
Mohtashim Ali	2	0	15	0								
Asif Zakir						(6)		11	1	28	1	
Saeed Bin Nasir						(7)		3	0	12	0	
Ali Hussain						(8)		4	0	18	0	

Faisalabad Bowling

	O	M	R	W	
Ahmed Hayat	25.1	3	130	4	1nb
Mohammad Talha	27.2	5	68	3	10nb
Asad Zarar	16.4	4	65	1	1nb
Ijaz Ahmed	10	2	23	0	
Saadat Munir	16	4	61	1	
Usman Arshad	4	0	15	1	

Umpires: Iftikhar Malik and Mohammad Arif. Referee: Arshad Pervez.   Toss: Sui Southern Gas Corporation

Close of Play: 1st day: Faisalabad (1) 264-2 (Ammar Mahmood 42*, Ijaz Ahmed 43*, 89 overs); 2nd day: Sui Southern Gas Corporation (1) 52-2 (Ali Hussain 17*, Saeed Bin Nasir 17*, 22 overs); 3rd day: Sui Southern Gas Corporation (1) 346-9 (Mansoor Ahmed 8*, Waqar Ahmed 0*, 93.3 overs).
Usman Arshad's 105 took 195 balls in 221 minutes and included 13 fours.

ISLAMABAD v SUI NORTHERN GAS PIPELINES LIMITED

Played at Diamond Club Ground, Islamabad, November 25, 26, 27, 2007.
Quaid-e-Azam Trophy 2007/08 - Group B
Sui Northern Gas Pipelines Limited won by an innings and 54 runs.   (Points: Islamabad 0, Sui Northern Gas Pipelines Limited 9)

ISLAMABAD

1	*Raheel Majeed	lbw b Samiullah Khan	7	c Farhan Asghar b Samiullah Khan	11
2	Umair Khan	c Bilal Azmat b Asad Ali	42	lbw b Asad Ali	0
3	Farrukh Hayat	c Mohammad Farrukh b Asad Ali	31	c Farhan Asghar b Asad Ali	20
4	Zeeshan Mushtaq	c Khurram Shehzad b Asad Ali	0	(7) c Khurram Shehzad b Tauqeer Hussain	1
5	Fayyaz Ahmed	lbw b Asad Ali	0	c Bilal Azmat b Tauqeer Hussain	28
6	Zohaib Ahmed	lbw b Mohammad Hafeez	0	b Asad Ali	1
7	Sajid Ali	c Mohammad Hafeez b Imran Ali	12	(8) lbw b Asad Ali	2
8	Shehzad Azam	lbw b Asad Ali	0	(9) c Samiullah Khan b Asad Ali	15
9	Fakhar Hussain	c Mohammad Farrukh b Samiullah Khan	56	(4) c Farhan Asghar b Samiullah Khan	0
10	†Mohammad Kashif	c Mohammad Farrukh b Mohammad Hafeez	14	c Farhan Asghar b Samiullah Khan	53
11	Yasin Bari	not out	3	not out	22
	Extras	b 4, lb 6, nb 3	13	b 6, lb 2, nb 7	15
			178		**168**

FoW (1): 1-14, 2-73, 3-73, 4-73, 5-74, 6-94, 7-94, 8-106, 9-158, 10-178
FoW (2): 1-8, 2-31, 3-36, 4-44, 5-50, 6-63, 7-72, 8-85, 9-102, 10-168

SUI NORTHERN GAS PIPELINES LIMITED

1	*Mohammad Hafeez	b Shehzad Azam	36
2	Yasir Arafat	c Raheel Majeed b Yasin Bari	69
3	Mohammad Farrukh	lbw b Fakhar Hussain	5
4	Azhar Shafiq	c Fayyaz Ahmed b Shehzad Azam	0
5	Bilal Azmat	c Mohammad Kashif b Fakhar Hussain	7
6	Khurram Shehzad	not out	145
7	Tauqeer Hussain	c Mohammad Kashif b Fayyaz Ahmed	58
8	†Farhan Asghar	c sub (Asad) b Fayyaz Ahmed	16
9	Samiullah Khan	c Farrukh Hayat b Fayyaz Ahmed	14
10	Imran Ali	lbw b Raheel Majeed	0
11	Asad Ali	b Fayyaz Ahmed	0
	Extras	lb 2, w 8, nb 40	50
			400

FoW (1): 1-81, 2-99, 3-100, 4-141, 5-165, 6-300, 7-332, 8-387, 9-388, 10-400

Sui Northern Gas Pipelines Limited Bowling

	O	M	R	W		O	M	R	W	
Samiullah Khan	10.4	0	39	2	3nb	15.1	2	35	3	1nb
Imran Ali	9	2	33	1						
Asad Ali	11	1	52	5	(2)	19	3	72	5	5nb
Mohammad Hafeez	9	0	44	2	(3)	4	1	8	0	
Tauqeer Hussain					(4)	10	2	45	2	1nb

Islamabad Bowling

	O	M	R	W	
Shehzad Azam	21	2	113	2	1w,27nb
Yasin Bari	13	2	41	1	2w,1nb
Fakhar Hussain	11	0	57	2	5w,12nb
Raheel Majeed	14	0	68	1	
Sajid Ali	13	0	56	0	
Fayyaz Ahmed	10.3	0	63	4	

Umpires: Islam Khan and Saleem Badar.   Referee: Anwar Khan.   Toss: Sui Northern Gas Pipelines Limited

Close of Play: 1st day: Sui Northern Gas Pipelines Limited (1) 114-3 (Yasir Arafat 54*, Bilal Azmat 0*, 22.2 overs); 2nd day: Islamabad (2) 25-1 (Raheel Majeed 11*, Farrukh Hayat 9*, 8.3 overs).
The match was scheduled for four days but completed in three. Khurram Shehzad's 145 took 134 balls in 205 minutes and included 18 fours and 1 six. Asad Ali took a hat-trick in the Islamabad first innings (victims: Farrukh Hayat, Zeeshan Mushtaq, Fayyaz Ahmed).

KARACHI BLUES v LAHORE SHALIMAR

Played at Sheikhupura Stadium, November 25, 26, 27, 28, 2007.
Quaid-e-Azam Trophy 2007/08 - Group B
Lahore Shalimar won by 197 runs.   (Points: Karachi Blues 0, Lahore Shalimar 9)

LAHORE SHALIMAR

1	Junaid Malik	b Malik Aftab	0	b Malik Aftab	0
2	Asif Khan	b Tariq Haroon	14	c Mohammad Masroor b Tariq Haroon	39
3	Haroon Rasheed	b Faraz Ahmed	35	c Mohammad Masroor b Faraz Ahmed	21
4	Ahmed Butt	c Sharjeel Ashraf b Tariq Haroon	26	c sub (Faraz Patel) b Mansoor Khan	75
5	Suleman Khan	c Mohammad Masroor b Faraz Ahmed	15	lbw b Tariq Haroon	0
6	Mohammad Hussain	b Malik Aftab	2	c Mohammad Masroor b Faraz Ahmed	12
7	*†Ali Raza	lbw b Faraz Ahmed	7	b Tariq Haroon	60
8	Mohammad Saeed	c Faraz Ahmed b Tariq Haroon	22	c Sharjeel Ashraf b Mansoor Baig	42
9	Mohammad Shahzad	c Mohammad Masroor b Tariq Haroon	12	c sub (Faraz Patel) b Mansoor Baig	55
10	Usman Malik	lbw b Malik Aftab	12	not out	1
11	Mohammad Naved	not out	0	c sub (Faraz Patel) b Mansoor Baig	6
	Extras	b 1, lb 5, w 6	12	b 6, lb 4, w 2, nb 6	18
			157		329

FoW (1): 1-0, 2-36, 3-78, 4-96, 5-96, 6-105, 7-113, 8-132, 9-157, 10-157
FoW (2): 1-5, 2-35, 3-94, 4-94, 5-112, 6-192, 7-246, 8-310, 9-323, 10-329

KARACHI BLUES

1	Shadab Kabir	b Mohammad Naved	0	c Haroon Rasheed b Mohammad Shahzad	20
2	Aariz Kamal	c Junaid Malik b Mohammad Shahzad	9	b Mohammad Naved	5
3	Fahadullah Khan	b Mohammad Naved	0	b Mohammad Naved	16
4	Mansoor Baig	b Mohammad Shahzad	5	b Mohammad Hussain	7
5	Sharjeel Ashraf	c Ali Raza b Mohammad Saeed	37	c Asif Khan b Mohammad Naved	8
6	†Mohammad Masroor	c Ali Raza b Mohammad Naved	4	c Ali Raza b Mohammad Saeed	4
7	Tariq Haroon	b Mohammad Shahzad	12	(8) c sub (Shahzad Ali) b Mohammad Naved	46
8	*Mansoor Khan	c Junaid Malik b Mohammad Naved	19	(7) c Usman Malik b Mohammad Naved	41
9	Faraz Ahmed	c Ali Raza b Mohammad Naved	25	c Mohammad Naved b Mohammad Hussain	1
10	Azam Hussain	c Ali Raza b Mohammad Naved	0	not out	0
11	Malik Aftab	not out	0	absent hurt	0
	Extras	b 10, lb 5, nb 9	24	lb 3, w 1, nb 2	6
			135		154

FoW (1): 1-2, 2-2, 3-22, 4-24, 5-29, 6-55, 7-90, 8-135, 9-135, 10-135
FoW (2): 1-25, 2-27, 3-41, 4-53, 5-60, 6-77, 7-135, 8-154, 9-154

Karachi Blues Bowling

	O	M	R	W			O	M	R	W	
Malik Aftab	16.3	2	59	3		(2)	8	1	29	1	
Faraz Ahmed	9	1	22	3	1w	(1)	27	5	88	2	2w,6nb
Tariq Haroon	21	4	70	4	5w		25	7	63	3	
Azam Hussain						(4)	8	1	57	0	
Mansoor Khan						(5)	17	1	54	1	
Sharjeel Ashraf						(6)	2	1	1	0	
Mansoor Baig						(7)	4	0	27	3	

Lahore Shalimar Bowling

	O	M	R	W			O	M	R	W	
Mohammad Naved	17	5	51	6			18	3	74	5	
Mohammad Shahzad	10	0	43	3	8nb		4	0	14	1	
Mohammad Saeed	8.1	2	26	1	1nb	(5)	8	0	54	1	1w,2nb
Mohammad Hussain						(3)	7.2	3	7	2	
Usman Malik						(4)	2	1	2	0	

Umpires: Jamil Kamran and Kaukab Butt. Referee: Khalid Niazi.   Toss: Karachi Blues

Close of Play: 1st day: Lahore Shalimar (1) 143-8 (Mohammad Saeed 11*, Usman Malik 9*, 41 overs); 2nd day: Lahore Shalimar (2) 83-2 (Asif Khan 39*, Ahmed Butt 17*, 29 overs); 3rd day: Karachi Blues (2) 41-3 (Fahadullah Khan 5*, Sharjeel Ashraf 0*, 13 overs).

LAHORE RAVI v HABIB BANK LIMITED

Played at Lahore Country Club, Muridke, November 25, 26, 27, 28, 2007.
Quaid-e-Azam Trophy 2007/08 - Group A
Habib Bank Limited won by 138 runs.   (Points: Lahore Ravi 0, Habib Bank Limited 9)

HABIB BANK LIMITED

1	Rafatullah Mohmand	c Sohail Ahmed b Junaid Zia	0	(2) c Shahbaz Butt b Junaid Zia	50
2	Sajid Shah	b Junaid Zia	1	(8) lbw b Waqas Ahmed	0
3	Kamran Hussain	b Kashif Siddiq	84	c Shahbaz Butt b Junaid Zia	20
4	Aftab Alam	c Afzal Shah b Salman Rahat	86	b Salman Rahat	12
5	*Hasan Raza	c Arsalan Mir b Salman Rahat	10	(6) not out	25
6	Khaqan Arsal	run out (Waqas Ahmed/Salman Rahat)	6	(5) lbw b Junaid Zia	8
7	†Humayun Farhat	not out	19	c Shahbaz Butt b Junaid Zia	52
8	Farhan Iqbal	lbw b Salman Rahat	4	(1) c Shahbaz Butt b Junaid Zia	2
9	Mohammad Aslam	lbw b Salman Rahat	6		
10	Irfan Fazil	c Shahbaz Butt b Salman Rahat	1		
11	Fahad Masood	run out (Arsalan Mir)	0	(9) not out	20
	Extras	lb 7, w 1, nb 8	16	b 12, lb 5, w 1, nb 5	23
			233	(7 wickets, declared)	212

FoW (1): 1-0, 2-13, 3-136, 4-175, 5-186, 6-204, 7-214, 8-223, 9-226, 10-233
FoW (2): 1-10, 2-61, 3-90, 4-94, 5-109, 6-188, 7-189

LAHORE RAVI

1	Kashif Siddiq	not out	61	lbw b Fahad Masood	2
2	Sohail Ahmed	c Humayun Farhat b Sajid Shah	7	c Humayun Farhat b Fahad Masood	1
3	Ali Haider	b Sajid Shah	0	(4) c Irfan Fazil b Sajid Shah	66
4	Afzal Shah	lbw b Fahad Masood	7	(3) lbw b Fahad Masood	1
5	Arsalan Mir	lbw b Fahad Masood	12	c Aftab Alam b Fahad Masood	0
6	Saad Nasim	c Rafatullah Mohmand b Kamran Hussain	3	c Humayun Farhat b Sajid Shah	14
7	Rizwan Ahmed	b Kamran Hussain	2	b Sajid Shah	0
8	*Junaid Zia	c Sajid Shah b Fahad Masood	11	c Kamran Hussain b Sajid Shah	9
9	Waqas Ahmed	c Irfan Fazil b Sajid Shah	4	c Humayun Farhat b Sajid Shah	37
10	†Shahbaz Butt	c Irfan Fazil b Sajid Shah	8	not out	32
11	Salman Rahat	c Rafatullah Mohmand b Kamran Hussain	0	lbw b Sajid Shah	5
	Extras	lb 4, w 1, nb 8	13	b 4, lb 1, nb 7	12
			128		179

FoW (1): 1-20, 2-20, 3-41, 4-64, 5-73, 6-81, 7-98, 8-106, 9-124, 10-128
FoW (2): 1-1, 2-3, 3-14, 4-14, 5-59, 6-63, 7-73, 8-129, 9-165, 10-179

Lahore Ravi Bowling

	O	M	R	W		O	M	R	W	
Junaid Zia	19	4	62	2		24	6	86	5	1w
Waqas Ahmed	10	0	57	0		9	3	39	1	
Salman Rahat	16.2	2	62	5	2w,7nb	18	4	70	1	5nb
Arsalan Mir	4	1	17	0						
Kashif Siddiq	4	1	11	1	1nb					
Saad Nasim	5	1	17	0						

Habib Bank Limited Bowling

	O	M	R	W			O	M	R	W	
Irfan Fazil	2	0	16	0	4nb	(4)	1	0	14	0	3nb
Kamran Hussain	14	5	20	3	1nb	(5)	4	0	18	0	
Sajid Shah	12	0	50	4	3nb	(2)	21.1	2	67	6	4nb
Fahad Masood	18	4	38	3	1w	(1)	14	4	59	4	
Mohammad Aslam						(3)	5	0	16	0	

Umpires: Ehtesham-ul-Haq and Zaheer Ahmed. Referee: Abdus Sami.   Toss: Lahore Ravi

Close of Play: 1st day: Lahore Ravi (1) 30-2 (Kashif Siddiq 13*, Afzal Shah 5*, 9 overs); 2nd day: Habib Bank Limited (2) 57-1 (Rafatullah Mohmand 32*, Kamran Hussain 17*, 21 overs); 3rd day: Lahore Ravi (2) 58-4 (Ali Haider 35*, Saad Nasim 14*, 19.2 overs).

MULTAN v PAKISTAN CUSTOMS

Played at Gymkhana Ground, Okara, November 25, 26, 27, 28, 2007.
Quaid-e-Azam Trophy 2007/08 - Group A
Match drawn.   (Points: Multan 0, Pakistan Customs 3)

MULTAN

1	†Gulraiz Sadaf	b Raees Amjad	57	st Shafayat b Majid Majeed	90
2	Usman Tariq	lbw b Sajjad Hussain	91	c and b Sajjad Hussain	4
3	*Abdur Rauf	c Hasnain Abbas b Raees Amjad	98		
4	Rameez Alam	not out	155	(3) not out	31
5	Naved Yasin	c Khan b Majid Majeed	36	(4) not out	0
6	Sohaib Maqsood	c Asif Iqbal b Yasir Hussain	96		
7	Mohammad Hafeez				
8	Mohammad Tanvir				
9	Zulfiqar Babar				
10	Mohammad Kashif				
11	Ahmed Raza				
	Extras	b 9, lb 6, w 8, nb 11	34	b 9, nb 4	13
		(5 wickets, declared)	567	(2 wickets)	138

FoW (1): 1-130, 2-183, 3-308, 4-391, 5-567
FoW (2): 1-5, 2-137

PAKISTAN CUSTOMS

1	Hasnain Abbas	c Usman Tariq b Mohammad Tanvir	36
2	R.M.Khan	lbw b Ahmed Raza	62
3	Mubashar Ijaz	lbw b Ahmed Raza	20
4	Majid Majeed	b Abdur Rauf	3
5	*Zahoor Elahi	run out (Naved Yasin)	132
6	†B.M.Shafayat	c Gulraiz Sadaf b Mohammad Tanvir	99
7	Asif Iqbal	c Usman Tariq b Ahmed Raza	93
8	Yasir Hussain	lbw b Mohammad Hafeez	77
9	Raees Amjad	c Ahmed Raza b Abdur Rauf	3
10	Tahir Maqsood	not out	22
11	Sajjad Hussain	c Naved Yasin b Mohammad Tanvir	17
	Extras	b 1, lb 6, nb 9	16
			580

FoW (1): 1-109, 2-122, 3-124, 4-131, 5-293, 6-382, 7-531, 8-538, 9-545, 10-580

Pakistan Customs Bowling

	O	M	R	W		O	M	R	W	
Raees Amjad	24	7	68	2	3nb	3	1	7	0	1nb
Tahir Maqsood	25	1	137	0	2w,6nb	4	1	24	0	2nb
Sajjad Hussain	28	6	97	1	5w	3	0	20	1	
Majid Majeed	20	3	113	1		7	0	43	1	
Yasir Hussain	14.1	1	82	1	2nb	2	0	12	0	1nb
Asif Iqbal	6	0	37	0	1w					
Zahoor Elahi	2	0	18	0	(6)	2	0	23	0	

Multan Bowling

	O	M	R	W	
Abdur Rauf	52	7	144	2	
Mohammad Kashif	29	8	107	0	5nb
Mohammad Tanvir	20.3	1	91	3	4nb
Zulfiqar Babar	29	5	77	0	
Ahmed Raza	32	4	115	3	
Mohammad Hafeez	4	1	15	1	
Usman Tariq	2	0	12	0	
Sohaib Maqsood	4	0	12	0	

Umpires: Ahmed Shahab and Riazuddin.   Referee: Aziz-ur-Rehman.   Toss: Pakistan Customs

Close of Play: 1st day: Multan (1) 286-2 (Abdur Rauf 83*, Rameez Alam 33*, 75.2 overs); 2nd day: Pakistan Customs (1) 122-2 (Majid Majeed 1*, 35 overs); 3rd day: Pakistan Customs (1) 446-6 (Asif Iqbal 55*, Yasir Hussain 26*, 118 overs).
Rameez Alam's 155 took 216 balls in 300 minutes and included 25 fours and 2 sixes. Zahoor Elahi's 132 took 191 balls in 259 minutes and included 23 fours.

285

NATIONAL BANK OF PAKISTAN v WATER AND POWER DEVELOPMENT AUTHORITY

Played at National Bank of Pakistan Sports Complex, Karachi, November 25, 26, 27, 28, 2007.
Quaid-e-Azam Trophy 2007/08 - Group A
Match drawn.　(Points: National Bank of Pakistan 3, Water and Power Development Authority 0)

NATIONAL BANK OF PAKISTAN

1	Nasir Jamshed	c Zulqarnain Haider b Sarfraz Ahmed	134	c Sarfraz Ahmed b Farooq Iqbal	32
2	*Imran Nazir	c Masood Asim b Nawaz Sardar	0		
3	Naumanullah	c Zulqarnain Haider b Sarfraz Ahmed	176	not out	101
4	Shahid Yousuf	c Bilal Khilji b Farooq Iqbal	1	(2) c Bilal Khilji b Zeeshan Nadir	28
5	Fawad Alam	c Zulqarnain Haider b Sarfraz Ahmed	7		
6	Naved Latif	c Zulqarnain Haider b Zeeshan Nadir	12		
7	Mansoor Amjad	c Masood Asim b Azharullah	28	(4) not out	101
8	†Rashid Riaz	c Nawaz Sardar b Farooq Iqbal	52		
9	Tahir Mughal	c Zulqarnain Haider b Sarfraz Ahmed	0		
10	Wasim Khan	c Azharullah b Farooq Iqbal	0		
11	Wahab Riaz	not out	14		
	Extras	b 1, lb 2, w 3, nb 13	19	b 4, lb 3, w 1, nb 2	10
			443	(2 wickets, declared)	272

FoW (1): 1-7, 2-238, 3-255, 4-288, 5-305, 6-354, 7-412, 8-412, 9-413, 10-443
FoW (2): 1-59, 2-68

WATER AND POWER DEVELOPMENT AUTHORITY

1	Masood Asim	c Shahid Yousuf b Wahab Riaz	12	(2) lbw b Tahir Mughal	12
2	Atiq-ur-Rehman	b Wasim Khan	0	(1) not out	8
3	Tariq Aziz	lbw b Wahab Riaz	28		
4	Nawaz Sardar	lbw b Wasim Khan	35		
5	*Aamer Sajjad	c Rashid Riaz b Wahab Riaz	88		
6	Bilal Khilji	c Tahir Mughal b Wahab Riaz	58		
7	†Zulqarnain Haider	c Rashid Riaz b Tahir Mughal	33	(3) not out	8
8	Farooq Iqbal	lbw b Wahab Riaz	0		
9	Sarfraz Ahmed	c Naved Latif b Tahir Mughal	18		
10	Azharullah	c Shahid Yousuf b Tahir Mughal	2		
11	Zeeshan Nadir	not out	0		
	Extras	b 3, lb 9, w 5, nb 21	38	b 5, w 1	6
			312	(1 wicket)	34

FoW (1): 1-10, 2-25, 3-56, 4-133, 5-217, 6-267, 7-269, 8-297, 9-303, 10-312
FoW (2): 1-25

WAPDA Bowling	O	M	R	W			O	M	R	W	
Sarfraz Ahmed	26.2	7	70	4			16	4	44	0	
Nawaz Sardar	15	2	56	1	11nb	(3)	4	0	31	0	1nb
Azharullah	19	3	72	1		(2)	9	0	38	0	
Bilal Khilji	12	3	25	0		(6)	7	1	24	0	
Zeeshan Nadir	21.4	1	101	1	1w,1nb		13	1	53	1	1w
Farooq Iqbal	27.1	3	83	3	1nb	(4)	22	8	38	1	
Aamer Sajjad	11	1	33	0			5	0	19	0	1nb
Masood Asim						(8)	4.5	0	18	0	

NBP Bowling	O	M	R	W			O	M	R	W	
Wahab Riaz	29	5	93	5	1w,9nb		1	0	4	0	
Wasim Khan	20.5	3	79	2	3nb						
Tahir Mughal	22.2	2	71	3	3w,4nb	(2)	5	0	15	1	
Naved Latif	3	0	10	0	1w						
Mansoor Amjad	19	3	43	0		(3)	4	1	10	0	
Naumanullah	2	0	4	0							

Umpires: Akbar Khan and Khalid Mahmood.　Referee: Mahmood Rasheed.　Toss: Water and Power Development Authority
Close of Play: 1st day: National Bank of Pakistan (1) 278-3 (Naumanullah 126*, Fawad Alam 6*, 83 overs); 2nd day: Water and Power Development Authority (1) 121-3 (Nawaz Sardar 32*, Aamer Sajjad 31*, 33 overs); 3rd day: National Bank of Pakistan (2) 59-0 (Nasir Jamshed 32*, Shahid Yousuf 22*, 17 overs).
Nasir Jamshed's 134 took 210 balls in 279 minutes and included 19 fours and 1 six. Naumanullah's 176 took 330 balls in 551 minutes and included 24 fours. Naumanullah's 101 took 169 balls in 253 minutes and included 9 fours and 1 six. Mansoor Amjad's 101 took 203 balls in 239 minutes and included 12 fours.

PAKISTAN INTERNATIONAL AIRLINES v QUETTA

Played at Khan Research Laboratories Ground, Rawalpindi, November 25, 26, 27, 28, 2007.
Quaid-e-Azam Trophy 2007/08 - Group B
Pakistan International Airlines won by eight wickets. (Points: Pakistan International Airlines 9, Quetta 0)

QUETTA

1	Shoaib Khan	c Anop Santosh b Anwar Ali	16	c Anop Santosh b Aizaz Cheema	16	
2	Hameedullah Khan	lbw b Anwar Ali	27	c Anop Santosh b Anwar Ali	56	
3	Taimur Ali	c sub (Jannisar Khan) b Kamran Sajid	42	c Tahir Khan b Aizaz Cheema	13	
4	Sabir Hussain	c Shoaib Khan b Ali Imran	13	c Fahad Iqbal b Tahir Khan	19	
5	*Nasim Khan	c Fahad Iqbal b Tahir Khan	15	(7) c Imran Ali b Tahir Khan	32	
6	Arun Lal	b Tahir Khan	3	(5) c Fahad Iqbal b Tahir Khan	0	
7	Jalat Khan	st Anop Santosh b Tahir Khan	0	(6) c Anop Santosh b Ali Imran	36	
8	Faisal Irfan	c Khurram Manzoor b Anwar Ali	8	(9) c Fahad Iqbal b Tahir Khan	6	
9	Naseer Khan	run out (Aizaz Cheema)	13	(8) c Shoaib Khan b Ali Imran	4	
10	†Sanaullah Khan	lbw b Anwar Ali	8	not out	2	
11	Nazar Hussain	not out	4	b Tahir Khan	0	
	Extras	b 5, lb 7, w 3, nb 7	22	b 4, lb 7, w 1, nb 6	18	
			171		**202**	

FoW (1): 1-32, 2-72, 3-102, 4-128, 5-131, 6-131, 7-134, 8-155, 9-160, 10-171
FoW (2): 1-36, 2-54, 3-98, 4-98, 5-130, 6-166, 7-172, 8-191, 9-202, 10-202

PAKISTAN INTERNATIONAL AIRLINES

1	Agha Sabir	lbw b Naseer Khan	95			
2	*Khurram Manzoor	b Faisal Irfan	71	(1) run out (Arun Lal)	23	
3	Kamran Sajid	lbw b Arun Lal	44	(4) not out	4	
4	Imran Ali	run out (Jalat Khan)	4	(2) not out	9	
5	Shoaib Khan	lbw b Jalat Khan	31			
6	Fahad Iqbal	c Sanaullah Khan b Nazar Hussain	28			
7	Tahir Khan	c Sanaullah Khan b Faisal Irfan	5			
8	Anwar Ali	c Sanaullah Khan b Faisal Irfan	18			
9	Ali Imran	c Sanaullah Khan b Faisal Irfan	4			
10	†Anop Santosh	c Sanaullah Khan b Nazar Hussain	4	(3) b Arun Lal	1	
11	Aizaz Cheema	not out	6			
	Extras	b 3, lb 2, w 1, nb 8	14	lb 2, w 6, nb 5	13	
			324	**(2 wickets)**	**50**	

FoW (1): 1-138, 2-182, 3-195, 4-248, 5-259, 6-292, 7-292, 8-311, 9-316, 10-324
FoW (2): 1-32, 2-38

Pakistan International Airlines Bowling

	O	M	R	W		O	M	R	W	
Anwar Ali	18	7	46	4	2w	14	4	41	1	
Aizaz Cheema	14	2	33	0	1w	15	1	59	2	1w
Ali Imran	9	1	34	1	7nb	11	3	32	2	6nb
Tahir Khan	9	0	25	3		11.5	4	44	5	
Kamran Sajid	8	2	21	1		4	1	15	0	

Quetta Bowling

	O	M	R	W			O	M	R	W	
Faisal Irfan	25	6	73	4							
Nazar Hussain	25.5	5	88	2	1w	(1)	5.5	2	22	0	4w
Arun Lal	18	5	44	1	5nb	(2)	5	0	26	1	2w,5nb
Naseer Khan	17	1	73	1							
Jalat Khan	14	4	41	1	3nb						

Umpires: Raweed Khan and Zameer Haider. Referee: Saadat Ali.   Toss: Quetta

Close of Play: 1st day: Pakistan International Airlines (1) 15-0 (Agha Sabir 4*, Khurram Manzoor 11*, 4 overs); 2nd day: Pakistan International Airlines (1) 276-5 (Fahad Iqbal 13*, Tahir Khan 5*, 77 overs); 3rd day: Quetta (2) 166-6 (Nasim Khan 10*, Naseer Khan 0*, 40.3 overs).

PESHAWAR v KHAN RESEARCH LABORATORIES

Played at Arbab Niaz Stadium, Peshawar, November 25, 26, 27, 28, 2007.
Quaid-e-Azam Trophy 2007/08 - Group B
Khan Research Laboratories won by an innings and 70 runs.   (Points: Peshawar 0, Khan Research Laboratories 9)

KHAN RESEARCH LABORATORIES
1	Azhar Ali	c Gauhar Ali b Imran Khan	8
2	*Mohammad Wasim	c and b Nauman Habib	14
3	Saeed Anwar	c Gauhar Ali b Akbar Badshah	130
4	Bazid Khan	c Mohammad Fayyaz b Nauman Habib	2
5	Ali Naqvi	lbw b Imran Khan	64
6	Saeed Ajmal	b Imran Khan	5
7	Bilal Asad	not out	105
8	Yasir Arafat	not out	100
9	†Zulfiqar Jan		
10	Mohammad Irshad		
11	Faisal Afridi		
	Extras	b 6, lb 5, w 1, nb 12	24
		(6 wickets, declared)	452

FoW (1): 1-25, 2-25, 3-38, 4-182, 5-188, 6-280

PESHAWAR
1	Mohammad Fayyaz	b Yasir Arafat	0	c Bilal Asad b Ali Naqvi	19
2	Fawad Ali	c Zulfiqar Jan b Yasir Arafat	26	b Ali Naqvi	30
3	Naved Khan	c Zulfiqar Jan b Mohammad Irshad	11	c Azhar Ali b Saeed Ajmal	10
4	Nawaz Ahmed	c Mohammad Wasim b Yasir Arafat	2	(5) c Zulfiqar Jan b Mohammad Irshad	51
5	Mahfooz Sabri	c Zulfiqar Jan b Faisal Afridi	27	(4) lbw b Bilal Asad	82
6	*Akbar Badshah	lbw b Yasir Arafat	2	c Bilal Asad b Mohammad Irshad	0
7	†Gauhar Ali	c sub (Shehzad Malik) b Faisal Afridi	42	(8) c Zulfiqar Jan b Yasir Arafat	1
8	Azam Jan	c Zulfiqar Jan b Faisal Afridi	0	(7) retired hurt	27
9	Hidayatullah Khan	b Yasir Arafat	4	not out	12
10	Nauman Habib	b Yasir Arafat	0	(11) c Azhar Ali b Yasir Arafat	4
11	Imran Khan	not out	0	(10) c Zulfiqar Jan b Yasir Arafat	4
	Extras	b 4, lb 3, nb 10	17	lb 1, w 1, nb 9	11
			131		251

FoW (1): 1-0, 2-39, 3-41, 4-42, 5-49, 6-114, 7-114, 8-125, 9-125, 10-131
FoW (2): 1-42, 2-57, 3-73, 4-192, 5-193, 6-205, 7-221, 8-247, 9-251

Peshawar Bowling
	O	M	R	W	
Nauman Habib	18	3	45	2	
Imran Khan	28	8	106	3	2nb
Hidayatullah Khan	17	0	96	0	
Akbar Badshah	35.1	6	106	1	4nb
Mohammad Fayyaz	3	0	9	0	
Nawaz Ahmed	17	1	79	0	1w,6nb

Khan Research Laboratories Bowling
	O	M	R	W			O	M	R	W	
Yasir Arafat	13	5	59	6	1nb		12.3	1	71	3	1w,1nb
Faisal Afridi	8.4	3	31	3		(6)	5	1	7	0	
Mohammad Irshad	5	0	31	1	5nb	(2)	17	2	51	2	6nb
Ali Naqvi	1	0	3	0			10	5	18	2	1nb
Bilal Asad						(3)	10	2	24	1	
Mohammad Wasim						(5)	3	0	18	0	
Saeed Ajmal						(7)	16	2	61	1	1nb

Umpires: Ijaz Ahmed and Nadeem Ghauri.   Referee: Naeem Ahmed.   Toss: Peshawar

Close of Play: 1st day: Khan Research Laboratories (1) 192-5 (Saeed Anwar 86*, Bilal Asad 9*, 56.5 overs); 2nd day: Peshawar (1) 94-5 (Mahfooz Sabri 6*, Gauhar Ali 30*, 17 overs); 3rd day: Peshawar (2) 205-5 (Nawaz Ahmed 51*, Azam Jan 3*, 65 overs).

Saeed Anwar's 130 took 253 balls in 312 minutes and included 16 fours and 2 sixes. Bilal Asad's 105 took 176 balls in 244 minutes and included 13 fours. Yasir Arafat's 100 took 94 balls in 112 minutes and included 8 fours and 3 sixes. Azam Jan retired hurt at ?/7.

SIALKOT v HYDERABAD

Played at Jinnah Stadium, Sialkot, November 25, 26, 27, 28, 2007.
Quaid-e-Azam Trophy 2007/08 - Group A
Match drawn.   (Points: Sialkot 3, Hyderabad 0)

HYDERABAD

1	Zahid Khan	c Imran Malik b Mohammad Imran	14
2	Aqeel Anjum	c Khalid Mahmood	
		b Mohammad Imran	204
3	Faisal Athar	c Kamran Younis b Imran Malik	33
4	†Hanif Malik	run out (Naeemuddin)	33
5	Rizwan Ahmed	c Khalid Mahmood b Mohammad Ali	0
6	*Shahid Qambrani	lbw b Mohammad Ali	24
7	Jamshed Baig	c Khalid Mahmood b Mohammad Ali	4
8	Pir Zulfiqar	c Khalid Mahmood b Nayyer Abbas	17
9	Nasir Awais	c Nayyer Abbas b Mohammad Imran	25
10	Naeem-ur-Rehman	c Mohammad Ayub b Nayyer Abbas	34
11	Farhan Ayub	not out	13
	Extras	b 4, lb 6, w 2, nb 2	14
			415

FoW (1): 1-15, 2-74, 3-193, 4-201, 5-257, 6-261, 7-322, 8-354, 9-383, 10-415

SIALKOT

1	Kamran Younis	c Hanif Malik b Pir Zulfiqar	90
2	Naeemuddin	not out	216
3	*Mohammad Ayub	c Shahid Qambrani b Pir Zulfiqar	4
4	Faisal Khan	run out (Rizwan Ahmed)	64
5	Ayaz Tasawwar	st Hanif Malik b Rizwan Ahmed	70
6	Shahid Siddiq	c Naeem-ur-Rehman b Rizwan Ahmed	0
7	Nayyer Abbas	c sub (Sufyan Ali) b Shahid Qambrani	83
8	†Khalid Mahmood	c Zahid Khan b Rizwan Ahmed	83
9	Imran Malik	not out	5
10	Mohammad Imran		
11	Mohammad Ali		
	Extras	b 14, lb 11, w 1, nb 25	51
		(7 wickets)	**666**

FoW (1): 1-158, 2-164, 3-290, 4-433, 5-433, 6-554, 7-658

Sialkot Bowling

	O	M	R	W	
Mohammad Imran	38	10	108	3	1w,1nb
Imran Malik	26	7	68	1	1w
Mohammad Ali	33	6	111	3	1nb
Nayyer Abbas	24.5	3	85	2	
Kamran Younis	8	2	15	0	
Mohammad Ayub	7	2	18	0	

Hyderabad Bowling

	O	M	R	W	
Farhan Ayub	25	2	94	0	13nb
Naeem-ur-Rehman	15	2	68	0	9nb
Nasir Awais	34	4	157	0	
Pir Zulfiqar	39	4	136	2	1nb
Rizwan Ahmed	37	7	118	3	1w,2nb
Shahid Qambrani	6	1	24	1	
Jamshed Baig	9	1	33	0	
Faisal Athar	2	0	11	0	

Umpires: Hakeem Shah and Mian Mohammad Aslam. Referee: Anis Sheikh. Toss: Sialkot

Close of Play: 1st day: Hyderabad (1) 208-4 (Aqeel Anjum 113*, Shahid Qambrani 3*, 73.4 overs); 2nd day: Sialkot (1) 48-0 (Kamran Younis 17*, Naeemuddin 16*, 7 overs); 3rd day: Sialkot (1) 346-3 (Naeemuddin 122*, Ayaz Tasawwar 27*, 83.2 overs).

Aqeel Anjum's 204 took 375 balls in 509 minutes and included 33 fours. Naeemuddin's 216 took 414 balls in 642 minutes and included 19 fours and 3 sixes.

ABBOTTABAD v SUI NORTHERN GAS PIPELINES LIMITED

Played at Abbottabad Cricket Stadium, December 1, 2, 3, 4, 2007.
Quaid-e-Azam Trophy 2007/08 - Group B
Match drawn. (Points: Abbottabad 3, Sui Northern Gas Pipelines Limited 0)

SUI NORTHERN GAS PIPELINES LIMITED

1	*Mohammad Hafeez	c Rashid Mansoor b Noor-ul-Amin	11
2	Yasir Arafat	not out	100
3	Umar Akmal	c Riaz Kail b Noor-ul-Amin	97
4	Azhar Shafiq	c and b Noor-ul-Amin	44
5	Imran Khalid	c Khalid Usman b Noor-ul-Amin	21
6	Mohammad Farrukh	b Iftikhar Mahmood	24
7	†Farhan Asghar	not out	3
8	Khurram Shehzad		
9	Adnan Rasool		
10	Asad Ali		
11	Samiullah Khan		
	Extras	b 5, lb 5, w 4, nb 3	17
		(5 wickets, declared)	317

FoW (1): 1-15, 2-145, 3-234, 4-268, 5-306

ABBOTTABAD

1	Fawad Khan	c Khurram Shehzad b Mohammad Hafeez	90
2	†Ghulam Mohammad	c Mohammad Farrukh b Asad Ali	7
3	Wajid Ali	not out	115
4	*Adnan Raees	not out	115
5	Armaghan Elahi		
6	Rashid Mansoor		
7	Noor-ul-Amin		
8	Khalid Usman		
9	Iftikhar Mahmood		
10	Riaz Kail		
11	Mohammad Kashif		
	Extras	b 10, lb 5, w 3, nb 10	28
		(2 wickets)	355

FoW (1): 1-16, 2-152

Abbottabad Bowling

	O	M	R	W	
Armaghan Elahi	11	6	31	0	1nb
Rashid Mansoor	10	1	42	0	1w,2nb
Noor-ul-Amin	31.5	6	124	4	3w
Khalid Usman	4	0	33	0	
Adnan Raees	2	0	11	0	
Iftikhar Mahmood	11	1	47	1	
Riaz Kail	4	1	19	0	

Sui Northern Gas Pipelines Limited Bowling

	O	M	R	W	
Samiullah Khan	14	3	66	0	1w
Asad Ali	11	3	62	1	2w,4nb
Adnan Rasool	18	1	92	0	6nb
Imran Khalid	17	2	72	0	
Mohammad Hafeez	9	1	48	1	

Umpires: Mian Mohammad Aslam and Raweed Khan. Referee: Naeem Ahmed. Toss: Abbottabad

Close of Play: 1st day: No play; 2nd day: No play; 3rd day: Sui Northern Gas Pipelines Limited (1) 286-4 (Yasir Arafat 88*, Mohammad Farrukh 12*, 69 overs).

Yasir Arafat's 100 took 196 balls in 296 minutes and included 10 fours. Wajid Ali's 115 took 194 balls in 272 minutes and included 9 fours and 2 sixes. Adnan Raees's 115 took 95 balls in 132 minutes and included 7 fours and 8 sixes.

FAISALABAD v KARACHI WHITES

Played at Iqbal Stadium, Faisalabad, December 1, 2, 3, 4, 2007.
Quaid-e-Azam Trophy 2007/08 - Group A
Match drawn.   (Points: Faisalabad 3, Karachi Whites 0)

FAISALABAD

1	Usman Arshad	c sub (Daniyal Ahsan)				
		b Mohammad Hasnain	4	(2) c Javed Mansoor b Fahad Khan		0
2	Imran Ali	c Asad Shafiq b Tanvir Ahmed	6	(1) not out		37
3	Ammar Mahmood	c Afsar Nawaz b Tabish Nawab	38			
4	*Ijaz Ahmed	c Afsar Nawaz b Fahad Khan	18			
5	Asif Hussain	lbw b Tanvir Ahmed	116	(4) c Mohammad Hasnain b Fahad Khan		5
6	Imran Ahmed	b Tanvir Ahmed	66	(3) c sub (Daniyal Ahsan)		
				b Mohammad Hasnain		1
7	†Mohammad Salman	not out	126	(5) not out		49
8	Ahmed Hayat	c Khalid Latif b Mohammad Hasnain	55			
9	Asad Zarar	c Wasim Naeem b Fahad Khan	24			
10	Zulqarnain	st Javed Mansoor b Wasim Naeem	19			
11	Mohammad Talha	c Khalid Latif b Wasim Naeem	0			
	Extras	lb 9, w 1, nb 17	27	b 2, lb 4, nb 2		8
			499	(3 wickets)		100

FoW (1): 1-8, 2-27, 3-56, 4-98, 5-265, 6-278, 7-366, 8-422, 9-499, 10-499
FoW (2): 1-3, 2-6, 3-17

KARACHI WHITES

1	Khalid Latif	b Mohammad Talha	55
2	Asad Shafiq	b Mohammad Talha	223
3	Wasim Naeem	lbw b Ahmed Hayat	1
4	Atif Ali	c Asif Hussain b Ijaz Ahmed	24
5	*Asim Kamal	c Mohammad Salman b Asad Zarar	15
6	Afsar Nawaz	b Ahmed Hayat	4
7	†Javed Mansoor	c Usman Arshad b Ijaz Ahmed	50
8	Tanvir Ahmed	c Ijaz Ahmed b Ahmed Hayat	42
9	Mohammad Hasnain	c Imran Ali b Ijaz Ahmed	8
10	Tabish Nawab	not out	1
11	Fahad Khan	c Usman Arshad b Ahmed Hayat	0
	Extras	lb 10, nb 18	28
			451

FoW (1): 1-108, 2-118, 3-203, 4-234, 5-262, 6-380, 7-406, 8-443, 9-451, 10-451

Karachi Whites Bowling

	O	M	R	W			O	M	R	W	
Tanvir Ahmed	33	4	108	3	9nb						
Mohammad Hasnain	30	6	102	2	3nb	(1)	10	3	21	1	
Fahad Khan	23	2	91	2	1w,1nb	(2)	8	1	27	2	2nb
Tabish Nawab	38	6	147	1	4nb						
Wasim Naeem	10	0	42	2		(3)	5	0	22	0	
Khalid Latif						(4)	4	0	24	0	

Faisalabad Bowling

	O	M	R	W	
Ahmed Hayat	25.5	4	102	4	4nb
Mohammad Talha	41	6	144	2	14nb
Zulqarnain	16	2	55	0	
Ijaz Ahmed	38	11	67	3	
Asad Zarar	27	5	60	1	
Usman Arshad	2	0	13	0	

Umpires: Kaukab Butt and Nadeem Ghauri.   Referee: Khalid Niazi.   Toss: Karachi Whites

Close of Play: 1st day: Faisalabad (1) 260-4 (Asif Hussain 108*, Imran Ahmed 65*, 80 overs); 2nd day: Karachi Whites (1) 106-0 (Khalid Latif 54*, Asad Shafiq 49*, 21.4 overs); 3rd day: Karachi Whites (1) 330-5 (Asad Shafiq 197*, Javed Mansoor 17*, 102.1 overs).
Asif Hussain's 116 took 232 balls in 291 minutes and included 10 fours and 1 six. Mohammad Salman's 126 took 162 balls in 219 minutes and included 15 fours and 2 sixes. Asad Shafiq's 223 took 350 balls in 512 minutes and included 25 fours and 2 sixes.

HYDERABAD v WATER AND POWER DEVELOPMENT AUTHORITY

Played at Niaz Stadium, Hyderabad, December 1, 2, 3, 4, 2007.
Quaid-e-Azam Trophy 2007/08 - Group A
Match drawn.   (Points: Hyderabad 3, Water and Power Development Authority 0)

HYDERABAD

1	Aqeel Anjum	b Azharullah	46	c Zulqarnain Haider b Kashif Raza	36
2	Azeem Ghumman	b Aqeel Ahmed	46	c Kashif Rasheed b Farooq Iqbal	24
3	Faisal Athar	c Aqeel Ahmed b Zeeshan Nadir	25	c Aamer Sajjad b Azharullah	92
4	†Hanif Malik	b Aqeel Ahmed	32	(7) not out	24
5	Rizwan Ahmed	b Azharullah	67	(4) c Aqeel Ahmed b Azharullah	41
6	*Shahid Qambrani	b Aqeel Ahmed	4	(5) not out	28
7	Jamshed Baig	lbw b Azharullah	51	(6) c Aqeel Ahmed b Farooq Iqbal	19
8	Pir Zulfiqar	c Ahmed Said b Azharullah	11		
9	Kashif Bhatti	c Aamer Sajjad b Azharullah	22		
10	Naeem-ur-Rehman	not out	19		
11	Sufyan Ali	lbw b Aqeel Ahmed	0		
	Extras	b 1, lb 2, w 8, nb 5	16	b 18, lb 1, w 3, nb 4	26
			339	(5 wickets, declared)	290

FoW (1): 1-79, 2-97, 3-143, 4-177, 5-186, 6-280, 7-294, 8-301, 9-334, 10-339
FoW (2): 1-56, 2-84, 3-205, 4-226, 5-257

WATER AND POWER DEVELOPMENT AUTHORITY

1	Ahmed Said	lbw b Sufyan Ali	8	run out (Kashif Bhatti)	80
2	Kashif Rasheed	c Azeem Ghumman b Kashif Bhatti	23	c Aqeel Anjum b Jamshed Baig	71
3	Tariq Aziz	c Azeem Ghumman b Pir Zulfiqar	25	c sub (Zahid Mahmood) b Jamshed Baig	17
4	*Aamer Sajjad	c Faisal Athar b Kashif Bhatti	1	c Jamshed Baig b Sufyan Ali	41
5	Bilal Khilji	c Azeem Ghumman b Kashif Bhatti	3	lbw b Naeem-ur-Rehman	30
6	†Zulqarnain Haider	st Hanif Malik b Kashif Bhatti	0	not out	51
7	Farooq Iqbal	c Azeem Ghumman b Pir Zulfiqar	28	(8) not out	2
8	Aqeel Ahmed	c Azeem Ghumman b Kashif Bhatti	0		
9	Kashif Raza	not out	64	(7) c Hanif Malik b Kashif Bhatti	38
10	Azharullah	c Aqeel Anjum b Rizwan Ahmed	5		
11	Zeeshan Nadir	c Jamshed Baig b Rizwan Ahmed	1		
	Extras	b 8, lb 1, w 1, nb 4	14	b 7, lb 5, w 9, nb 4, pen 5	30
			172	(6 wickets)	360

FoW (1): 1-13, 2-61, 3-61, 4-65, 5-65, 6-68, 7-68, 8-147, 9-169, 10-172
FoW (2): 1-128, 2-157, 3-181, 4-245, 5-255, 6-351

Water and Power Development Authority Bowling

	O	M	R	W			O	M	R	W	
Kashif Raza	17	3	43	0			6	1	18	1	1nb
Zeeshan Nadir	13	3	45	1	2w		14	2	54	0	1w
Aqeel Ahmed	35	0	126	4	5nb		17	0	63	0	2nb
Azharullah	22	1	86	5	2w		19	4	51	2	
Farooq Iqbal	15	6	36	0			23	4	66	2	1w,1nb
Aamer Sajjad						(6)	6	1	19	0	

Hyderabad Bowling

	O	M	R	W			O	M	R	W	
Naeem-ur-Rehman	6	0	23	0			15	1	68	1	1w,1nb
Sufyan Ali	9	2	25	1			11	0	49	1	3w,1nb
Kashif Bhatti	14	2	35	5			19	5	67	1	
Aqeel Anjum	1	0	10	0	1w,2nb		1	1	0	0	
Pir Zulfiqar	10	3	26	2			15	6	63	0	
Rizwan Ahmed	9	0	39	2	2nb		13	1	29	0	5w
Shahid Qambrani	4	1	5	0			2	0	10	0	
Jamshed Baig						(8)	14	0	53	2	
Azeem Ghumman						(9)	3	1	4	0	2nb

Umpires: Islam Khan and Khalid Mahmood. Referee: Ilyas Khan.   Toss: Hyderabad

Close of Play: 1st day: Hyderabad (1) 277-5 (Rizwan Ahmed 60*, Jamshed Baig 51*, 83 overs); 2nd day: Hyderabad (2) 29-0 (Aqeel Anjum 18*, Azeem Ghumman 7*, 7 overs); 3rd day: Water and Power Development Authority (2) 6-0 (Ahmed Said 4*, Kashif Rasheed 2*, 3 overs).

KHAN RESEARCH LABORATORIES v KARACHI BLUES

Played at Khan Research Laboratories Ground, Rawalpindi, December 1, 2, 3, 4, 2007.
Quaid-e-Azam Trophy 2007/08 - Group B
Match drawn.   (Points: Khan Research Laboratories 3, Karachi Blues 0)

KHAN RESEARCH LABORATORIES

1	Azhar Ali	c Azam Hussain b Mansoor Baig	113
2	*Mohammad Wasim	b Abdul Ameer	138
3	Saeed Anwar	c Mohammad Masroor b Abdul Ameer	19
4	Bazid Khan	c Mohammad Masroor b Azam Hussain	44
5	Ali Naqvi	run out (Tariq Haroon)	8
6	Faisal Afridi	c Tariq Haroon b Azam Hussain	1
7	Bilal Asad	not out	51
8	†Zulfiqar Jan	c Mohammad Masroor b Azam Hussain	0
9	Mohammad Irshad	not out	10
10	Akhtar Ayub		
11	Saeed Ajmal		
	Extras	b 4, lb 3, w 4, nb 8	19
		(7 wickets, declared)	403

FoW (1): 1-253, 2-273, 3-287, 4-299, 5-304, 6-376, 7-376

KARACHI BLUES

1	*Shadab Kabir	lbw b Akhtar Ayub	54	(7) not out	64
2	Aariz Kamal	c Saeed Anwar b Faisal Afridi	2	(1) lbw b Faisal Afridi	10
3	Mubashir Ahmed	b Faisal Afridi	10	(2) lbw b Saeed Ajmal	42
4	Faraz Patel	c Mohammad Wasim b Saeed Ajmal	28	not out	69
5	Sharjeel Ashraf	c Zulfiqar Jan b Bilal Asad	27	(3) lbw b Akhtar Ayub	29
6	†Mohammad Masroor	c Bilal Asad b Mohammad Irshad	56	lbw b Faisal Afridi	5
7	Mansoor Baig	b Saeed Ajmal	9		
8	Tariq Haroon	c Zulfiqar Jan b Mohammad Irshad	9	(5) b Azhar Ali	2
9	Faraz Ahmed	lbw b Faisal Afridi	0		
10	Abdul Ameer	not out	0		
11	Azam Hussain	absent	0		
	Extras	b 5, lb 8, w 7, nb 3	23	b 7, lb 10, w 4, nb 2	23
			218	(5 wickets)	244

FoW (1): 1-40, 2-72, 3-92, 4-134, 5-162, 6-200, 7-217, 8-218, 9-218
FoW (2): 1-20, 2-83, 3-123, 4-126, 5-147

Karachi Blues Bowling

	O	M	R	W	
Faraz Ahmed	25	4	86	0	7nb
Tariq Haroon	16	2	41	0	1w
Abdul Ameer	23	1	119	2	3w,1nb
Azam Hussain	26.1	3	88	3	
Aariz Kamal	9	0	35	0	
Mansoor Baig	9	0	27	1	

Khan Research Laboratories Bowling

	O	M	R	W			O	M	R	W	
Mohammad Irshad	14.2	4	44	2	1nb		11	4	32	0	1nb
Faisal Afridi	13	1	37	3	2nb		14	4	33	2	
Akhtar Ayub	9	0	36	1	7w		10	4	22	1	3w
Saeed Ajmal	15	1	56	2			17	3	74	1	1nb
Bilal Asad	8	1	25	1			7	0	26	0	1w
Saeed Anwar	2	0	7	0			2	1	8	0	
Azhar Ali						(7)	8	1	25	1	
Mohammad Wasim						(8)	3	0	7	0	

Umpires: Ahsan Raza and Zaheer Ahmed. Referee: Arshad Pervez.   Toss: Karachi Blues

Close of Play: 1st day: Khan Research Laboratories (1) 66-0 (Azhar Ali 25*, Mohammad Wasim 37*, 23.1 overs); 2nd day: Khan Research Laboratories (1) 347-5 (Bazid Khan 30*, Bilal Asad 24*, 97.2 overs); 3rd day: Karachi Blues (1) 217-7 (Tariq Haroon 8*, Faraz Ahmed 0*, 59.3 overs).
Azhar Ali's 113 took 339 balls in 319 minutes and included 9 fours and 1 six. Mohammad Wasim's 138 took 236 balls in 355 minutes and included 14 fours and 1 six.

LAHORE SHALIMAR v PAKISTAN INTERNATIONAL AIRLINES

Played at Gaddafi Stadium, Lahore, December 1, 2, 3, 4, 2007.
Quaid-e-Azam Trophy 2007/08 - Group B
Match drawn.   (Points: Lahore Shalimar 0, Pakistan International Airlines 3)

PAKISTAN INTERNATIONAL AIRLINES

1	Agha Sabir	lbw b Mohammad Naved	105	b Mohammad Saeed		20
2	*Khurram Manzoor	c Kashif Mahmood b Mohammad Saeed	56	c Kashif Mahmood b Mohammad Saeed		108
3	Kamran Sajid	c Shahzad Ali b Mohammad Naved	64	not out		103
4	Shoaib Khan	b Mohammad Naved	42			
5	Fahad Iqbal	not out	156			
6	Tahir Khan	run out (Haroon Rasheed)	11			
7	Anwar Ali	not out	100			
8	Ali Imran					
9	†Anop Santosh					
10	Aizaz Cheema					
11	Fazl-e-Akbar					
	Extras	b 3, lb 12, w 4, nb 11	30	lb 3, w 5, nb 6		14
		(5 wickets, declared)	564	(2 wickets, declared)		245

FoW (1): 1-116, 2-214, 3-282, 4-310, 5-340
FoW (2): 1-23, 2-245

LAHORE SHALIMAR

1	Junaid Malik	c Anop Santosh b Fazl-e-Akbar	20
2	Asif Khan	lbw b Fazl-e-Akbar	35
3	Haroon Rasheed	c Khurram Manzoor b Tahir Khan	38
4	Ahmed Butt	c Fahad Iqbal b Tahir Khan	45
5	Suleman Khan	c Anop Santosh b Anwar Ali	82
6	*Ali Raza	c Anop Santosh b Fazl-e-Akbar	65
7	Mohammad Saeed	b Fazl-e-Akbar	14
8	†Kashif Mahmood	c Anop Santosh b Fazl-e-Akbar	19
9	Sibtain Raza	not out	85
10	Mohammad Naved	lbw b Fazl-e-Akbar	0
11	Shahzad Ali	lbw b Fazl-e-Akbar	0
	Extras	b 1, lb 7, nb 25	33
			436

FoW (1): 1-53, 2-57, 3-129, 4-181, 5-282, 6-308, 7-326, 8-436, 9-436, 10-436

Lahore Shalimar Bowling

	O	M	R	W			O	M	R	W	
Mohammad Naved	48.2	12	184	3			8	0	32	0	
Shahzad Ali	24	2	117	0	1w,2nb	(3)	3	0	29	0	
Mohammad Saeed	25	3	99	1	3w,9nb	(2)	15	1	115	2	5w,6nb
Sibtain Raza	13	1	74	0		(5)	4	0	27	0	
Ahmed Butt	10	2	41	0		(4)	6	0	39	0	
Suleman Khan	6	0	34	0							

Pakistan International Airlines Bowling

	O	M	R	W	
Fazl-e-Akbar	27	6	103	7	9nb
Aizaz Cheema	25	6	71	0	1nb
Anwar Ali	15	2	64	1	
Ali Imran	13	0	70	0	10nb
Tahir Khan	27	4	81	2	3nb
Kamran Sajid	11	4	24	0	1nb
Agha Sabir	1	0	5	0	
Fahad Iqbal	1	0	10	0	1nb

Umpires: Akmal Hayat and Mohammad Arif. Referee: Saadat Ali.   Toss: Lahore Shalimar
Close of Play: 1st day: Pakistan International Airlines (1) 257-2 (Kamran Sajid 51*, Shoaib Khan 25*, 67 overs); 2nd day: Lahore Shalimar (1) 52-0 (Junaid Malik 20*, Asif Khan 28*, 14 overs); 3rd day: Lahore Shalimar (1) 315-6 (Ali Raza 60*, Kashif Mahmood 0*, 89 overs).
Agha Sabir's 105 took 164 balls in 232 minutes and included 20 fours and 1 six. Fahad Iqbal's 156 took 170 balls in 211 minutes and included 18 fours and 4 sixes. Anwar Ali's 100 took 107 balls in 140 minutes and included 14 fours and 1 six. Khurram Manzoor's 108 took 89 balls in 160 minutes and included 15 fours. Kamran Sajid's 103 took 118 balls in 143 minutes and included 20 fours.

MULTAN v HABIB BANK LIMITED

Played at Multan Cricket Stadium, December 1, 2, 3, 4, 2007.
Quaid-e-Azam Trophy 2007/08 - Group A
Habib Bank Limited won by two wickets.   (Points: Multan 0, Habib Bank Limited 9)

MULTAN

1	†Gulraiz Sadaf	lbw b Fahad Masood	12	lbw b Sajid Shah	1
2	*Usman Tariq	c Mohammad Aslam b Kamran Hussain	39	(5) c Rafatullah Mohmand	
				b Mohammad Aslam	20
3	Hammad Tariq	lbw b Kamran Hussain	21	(2) b Kamran Hussain	34
4	Rameez Alam	c Humayun Farhat b Mohammad Aslam	4	b Sajid Shah	4
5	Naved Yasin	c Rafatullah Mohmand b Sajid Shah	29	(6) c Humayun Farhat	
				b Mohammad Aslam	42
6	Sohaib Maqsood	c Humayun Farhat b Fahad Masood	22	(7) c Humayun Farhat b Dilawar Khan	66
7	Imranullah Aslam	c Farhan Iqbal b Kamran Hussain	24	(8) c Farhan Iqbal b Fahad Masood	12
8	Ansar Javed	b Fahad Masood	27	(9) c Humayun Farhat b Dilawar Khan	9
9	Mohammad Kashif	c Aftab Alam b Kamran Hussain	0	(3) b Sajid Shah	0
10	Ahmed Raza	b Sajid Shah	15	st Humayun Farhat b Mohammad Aslam	0
11	Rahat Ali	not out	6	not out	1
	Extras	b 8, lb 2, w 5, nb 6	21	b 1, lb 4, w 1, nb 1	7
			220		196

FoW (1): 1-30, 2-74, 3-79, 4-89, 5-124, 6-145, 7-170, 8-176, 9-198, 10-220
FoW (2): 1-1, 2-1, 3-10, 4-65, 5-65, 6-153, 7-184, 8-188, 9-188, 10-196

HABIB BANK LIMITED

1	Rafatullah Mohmand	b Ansar Javed	90	b Rahat Ali	4
2	Fahad Masood	lbw b Ahmed Raza	20	c Naved Yasin b Rahat Ali	13
3	Kamran Hussain	c Usman Tariq b Imranullah Aslam	43	lbw b Rahat Ali	4
4	Aftab Alam	c Rahat Ali b Imranullah Aslam	2	c Usman Tariq b Ansar Javed	5
5	*Hasan Raza	c Imranullah Aslam b Ansar Javed	38	not out	55
6	†Humayun Farhat	b Ahmed Raza	55	lbw b Ansar Javed	12
7	Farhan Iqbal	c Ahmed Raza b Rahat Ali	14	b Ansar Javed	
8	Sulaman Qadir	c Ansar Javed b Ahmed Raza	2	(9) c Ansar Javed b Rahat Ali	6
9	Sajid Shah	not out	8	(10) not out	7
10	Mohammad Aslam	b Imranullah Aslam	7	(8) lbw b Ansar Javed	10
11	Dilawar Khan	c Gulraiz Sadaf b Imranullah Aslam	1		
	Extras	b 1, lb 6, nb 5	12	lb 2, w 1, nb 13	16
			285	(8 wickets)	132

FoW (1): 1-50, 2-122, 3-134, 4-199, 5-201, 6-268, 7-276, 8-276, 9-281, 10-285
FoW (2): 1-8, 2-21, 3-26, 4-26, 5-63, 6-63, 7-88, 8-104

Habib Bank Limited Bowling

	O	M	R	W			O	M	R	W	
Sajid Shah	14.4	2	43	2	2nb	(2)	14	7	30	3	1nb
Fahad Masood	14	2	38	3	5w,4nb	(1)	17	3	44	1	
Dilawar Khan	10	0	43	0		(4)	5.4	0	47	2	
Kamran Hussain	18	5	35	4		(3)	12	5	21	1	
Mohammad Aslam	27	7	51	1			18	2	49	3	

Multan Bowling

	O	M	R	W			O	M	R	W	
Mohammad Kashif	16	2	73	0	2nb	(3)	8	0	39	0	6nb
Ansar Javed	16	3	48	2	3nb	(1)	14	0	49	4	1w,7nb
Rahat Ali	22	7	52	1		(2)	13	1	31	4	
Ahmed Raza	17	7	36	3			3	0	4	0	
Hammad Tariq	1	0	7	0							
Imranullah Aslam	11.3	2	62	0		(5)	3.5	2	7	0	

Umpires: Rasheed Bhatti and Riazuddin.   Referee: Mohammad Javed.   Toss: Habib Bank Limited

Close of Play: 1st day: Multan (1) 218-9 (Ahmed Raza 15*, Rahat Ali 6*, 83 overs); 2nd day: Habib Bank Limited (1) 276-8 (Sajid Shah 0*, Mohammad Aslam 0*, 80 overs); 3rd day: Habib Bank Limited (2) 7-0 (Rafatullah Mohmand 3*, Fahad Masood 4*, 3 overs).

NATIONAL BANK OF PAKISTAN v PAKISTAN CUSTOMS

Played at National Bank of Pakistan Sports Complex, Karachi, December 1, 2, 3, 4, 2007.
Quaid-e-Azam Trophy 2007/08 - Group A
National Bank of Pakistan won by 214 runs.   (Points: National Bank of Pakistan 9, Pakistan Customs 0)

NATIONAL BANK OF PAKISTAN

1	Nasir Jamshed	run out (Tahir Maqsood)	32	c Yasir Hussain b Tahir Maqsood	0
2	*Imran Nazir	c Yasir Hussain b Tahir Maqsood	20	c Khan b Tahir Maqsood	74
3	Naumanullah	lbw b Tahir Maqsood	0	run out (Yasir Shah)	136
4	Shahid Yousuf	lbw b Hameed Hasan	1	not out	125
5	Fawad Alam	c Zahoor Elahi b Yasir Shah	69	not out	17
6	Mansoor Amjad	b Tahir Maqsood	0		
7	Qaiser Abbas	c Zahoor Elahi b Yasir Shah	69		
8	†Rashid Riaz	lbw b Tahir Maqsood	0		
9	Tahir Mughal	c Shafayat b Tahir Maqsood	32		
10	Wahab Riaz	st Shafayat b Yasir Shah	4		
11	Uzair-ul-Haq	not out	1		
	Extras	lb 4, w 1, nb 32	37	b 12, lb 2, w 2, nb 18	34
			265	(3 wickets, declared)	386

FoW (1): 1-45, 2-53, 3-56, 4-68, 5-72, 6-211, 7-212, 8-222, 9-256, 10-265
FoW (2): 1-0, 2-134, 3-329

PAKISTAN CUSTOMS

1	Mubashar Ijaz	lbw b Wahab Riaz	3	(6) c Rashid Riaz b Tahir Mughal	9
2	R.M.Khan	lbw b Wahab Riaz	8	lbw b Tahir Mughal	2
3	Asif Iqbal	c Shahid Yousuf b Wahab Riaz	73	c Naumanullah b Tahir Mughal	36
4	Yasir Shah	lbw b Tahir Mughal	5	(8) c Fawad Alam b Tahir Mughal	31
5	†B.M.Shafayat	c Tahir Mughal b Wahab Riaz	5	(4) c and b Tahir Mughal	63
6	*Zahoor Elahi	b Mansoor Amjad	91	(5) c Qaiser Abbas b Tahir Mughal	17
7	Mohammad Nabi	c Nasir Jamshed b Tahir Mughal	21	c Fawad Alam b Tahir Mughal	15
8	Yasir Hussain	not out	8	(1) c Naumanullah b Wahab Riaz	8
9	Tahir Maqsood	c Rashid Riaz b Wahab Riaz	4	(10) lbw b Mansoor Amjad	4
10	Ali Hussain	lbw b Wahab Riaz	0	(9) b Mansoor Amjad	0
11	Hameed Hasan	lbw b Mansoor Amjad	2	not out	7
	Extras	b 1, lb 14, nb 7	22	lb 1, nb 2	3
			242		195

FoW (1): 1-4, 2-18, 3-36, 4-43, 5-170, 6-225, 7-227, 8-235, 9-235, 10-242
FoW (2): 1-10, 2-10, 3-110, 4-111, 5-135, 6-150, 7-163, 8-169, 9-177, 10-195

Pakistan Customs Bowling

	O	M	R	W		O	M	R	W	
Tahir Maqsood	26	8	92	5	1w,14nb	13	4	45	2	1w,2nb
Hameed Hasan	15	1	62	1	12nb	17	0	99	0	13nb
Asif Iqbal	5	1	21	0						
Yasir Shah	18.4	3	72	3		(3) 23	5	65	0	
Yasir Hussain	5	2	13	0	2nb	14	0	93	0	3nb
Mohammad Nabi	1	0	1	0						
Ali Hussain						(4) 20	1	70	0	1w

National Bank of Pakistan Bowling

	O	M	R	W		O	M	R	W	
Wahab Riaz	20	5	64	6	5nb	9	1	28	1	2nb
Uzair-ul-Haq	11	1	56	0	1nb	(3) 9	0	39	0	
Tahir Mughal	16	4	66	2	1nb	(2) 26	8	59	7	
Qaiser Abbas	9	4	11	0						
Mansoor Amjad	9.2	1	30	2		(4) 16	1	68	2	

Umpires: Akbar Khan and Saleem Badar.   Referee: Mahmood Rasheed.   Toss: Pakistan Customs

Close of Play: 1st day: Pakistan Customs (1) 23-2 (Asif Iqbal 4*, Yasir Shah 4*, 7 overs); 2nd day: National Bank of Pakistan (2) 130-1 (Imran Nazir 71*, Naumanullah 48*, 22 overs); 3rd day: Pakistan Customs (2) 52-2 (Asif Iqbal 20*, Shafayat 21*, 16 overs).

Naumanullah's 136 took 223 balls in 305 minutes and included 12 fours and 1 six. Shahid Yousuf's 125 took 212 balls in 252 minutes and included 7 fours and 4 sixes.

PESHAWAR v QUETTA

Played at Arbab Niaz Stadium, Peshawar, December 1, 2, 3, 4, 2007.
Quaid-e-Azam Trophy 2007/08 - Group B
Match drawn.   (Points: Peshawar 3, Quetta 0)

PESHAWAR

1	Usman Zeb	c Arun Lal b Faisal Irfan	5
2	Fawad Ali	c Samiullah Agha b Nazar Hussain	53
3	†Gauhar Ali	c Jalat Khan b Faisal Irfan	10
4	Nawaz Ahmed	c Sanaullah Khan b Nazar Hussain	5
5	Mahfooz Sabri	c and b Mohammad Alam	89
6	*Akbar Badshah	c Sanaullah Khan b Nazar Hussain	12
7	Sajjad Ahmed	st Sanaullah Khan b Nazar Hussain	80
8	Azam Jan	c Shoaib Khan b Nazar Hussain	15
9	Nauman Habib	c Hameedullah Khan b Arun Lal	19
10	Rahatullah	c Arun Lal b Nazar Hussain	5
11	Imran Khan	not out	0
	Extras	b 1, lb 1, w 1, nb 11	14
			307

FoW (1): 1-21, 2-55, 3-69, 4-75, 5-117, 6-230, 7-269, 8-293, 9-302, 10-307

QUETTA

1	Shoaib Khan	c Imran Khan b Nauman Habib	18	c Akbar Badshah b Rahatullah	14
2	Hameedullah Khan	b Imran Khan	5	(4) c Gauhar Ali b Mahfooz Sabri	79
3	Samiullah Agha	lbw b Imran Khan	4	b Mahfooz Sabri	99
4	Taimur Ali	lbw b Nauman Habib	10	(5) st Gauhar Ali b Mahfooz Sabri	17
5	*Nasim Khan	b Nauman Habib	39	(9) b Rahatullah	12
6	Mohammad Alam	c Gauhar Ali b Nauman Habib	14	(7) c Azam Jan b Mahfooz Sabri	22
7	Arun Lal	c Gauhar Ali b Rahatullah	4	(8) c Nawaz Ahmed b Rahatullah	15
8	Jalat Khan	b Nauman Habib	15	(6) b Rahatullah	28
9	Faisal Irfan	b Rahatullah	18	(10) not out	21
10	†Sanaullah Khan	not out	3	(2) c sub (Naved Khan) b Nauman Habib	1
11	Nazar Hussain	c Usman Zeb b Rahatullah	1	not out	38
	Extras	lb 6, nb 6	12	b 4, lb 2, w 1, nb 7	14
			143	(9 wickets)	360

FoW (1): 1-15, 2-27, 3-29, 4-62, 5-97, 6-99, 7-107, 8-129, 9-139, 10-143
FoW (2): 1-5, 2-30, 3-185, 4-206, 5-225, 6-253, 7-284, 8-297, 9-299

Quetta Bowling

	O	M	R	W	
Faisal Irfan	28	4	94	2	
Nazar Hussain	37.1	13	80	6	1w,5nb
Arun Lal	26	7	71	1	5nb
Jalat Khan	11	2	33	0	1nb
Samiullah Agha	2	1	10	0	
Mohammad Alam	5	1	17	1	

Peshawar Bowling

	O	M	R	W			O	M	R	W	
Nauman Habib	19	4	62	5	5nb		6	1	19	1	
Imran Khan	10	3	34	2							
Rahatullah	9	0	41	3	1nb	(2)	32	5	104	4	
Akbar Badshah						(3)	34	5	82	0	1nb
Nawaz Ahmed						(4)	15	3	62	0	1w,6nb
Usman Zeb						(5)	11	1	25	0	
Mahfooz Sabri						(6)	16	1	56	4	
Sajjad Ahmed						(7)	1	0	6	0	

Umpires: Iftikhar Malik and Ijaz Ahmed. Referee: Ishtiaq Ahmed.   Toss: Quetta

Close of Play: 1st day: Peshawar (1) 121-5 (Mahfooz Sabri 27*, Sajjad Ahmed 1*, 48 overs); 2nd day: Quetta (1) 47-3 (Taimur Ali 9*, Nasim Khan 6*, 11.3 overs); 3rd day: Quetta (2) 118-2 (Samiullah Agha 61*, Hameedullah Khan 40*, 38.3 overs).

SIALKOT v SUI SOUTHERN GAS CORPORATION

Played at Jinnah Stadium, Gujranwala, December 1, 2, 3, 4, 2007.
Quaid-e-Azam Trophy 2007/08 - Group A
Match drawn.   (Points: Sialkot 3, Sui Southern Gas Corporation 0)

SUI SOUTHERN GAS CORPORATION

1	Asif Zakir	lbw b Mohammad Ali	98	c Ayaz Tasawwar b Kamran Younis	170	
2	Mohtashim Ali	b Mohammad Wasim	16	c Khalid Mahmood b Mohammad Wasim	28	
3	Imran Abbas	c Ayaz Tasawwar b Mohammad Imran	6	(4) c Faisal Khan b Kamran Younis	32	
4	Saeed Bin Nasir	c Kamran Younis b Mohammad Ali	0			
5	Mohammad Zafar	c Khalid Mahmood b Mohammad Ali	0	(3) b Nayyer Abbas	39	
6	*Atiq-uz-Zaman	c Nayyer Abbas b Mohammad Imran	48	(5) not out	22	
7	†Ahmed Zeeshan	not out	60	(6) not out	4	
8	Shehzad Butt	lbw b Mohammad Ali	0			
9	Rajesh Ramesh	lbw b Mohammad Ali	6			
10	Adnan Malik	run out (Naeemuddin/Khalid Mahmood)	0			
11	Sohail Khan	b Mohammad Wasim	4			
	Extras	b 1, lb 4, w 3, nb 23	31	b 7, lb 3, w 2, nb 13	25	
			269	**(4 wickets)**	**320**	

FoW (1): 1-36, 2-54, 3-58, 4-62, 5-144, 6-216, 7-216, 8-224, 9-237, 10-269
FoW (2): 1-72, 2-181, 3-259, 4-315

SIALKOT

1	Kamran Younis	c Saeed Bin Nasir b Shehzad Butt	50
2	Naeemuddin	run out	39
3	Faisal Khan	b Shehzad Butt	23
4	Nayyer Abbas	not out	93
5	*Mohammad Ayub	b Sohail Khan	19
6	Bilal Hussain	lbw b Sohail Khan	4
7	Ayaz Tasawwar	lbw b Rajesh Ramesh	45
8	†Khalid Mahmood	c Sohail Khan b Shehzad Butt	2
9	Mohammad Wasim	lbw b Sohail Khan	2
10	Mohammad Imran	b Sohail Khan	0
11	Mohammad Ali	b Sohail Khan	0
	Extras	b 6, lb 2, w 1, nb 1	10
			287

FoW (1): 1-87, 2-97, 3-129, 4-167, 5-175, 6-258, 7-265, 8-287, 9-287, 10-287

Sialkot Bowling

	O	M	R	W		O	M	R	W	
Mohammad Wasim	19.4	3	56	2	2w,3nb	23	2	100	1	1w,8nb
Mohammad Imran	28	7	106	2	1w,15nb	17	4	58	0	3nb
Mohammad Ali	22	6	76	5	4nb	11	2	26	0	
Nayyer Abbas	11	2	26	0	1nb	9	4	19	1	
Mohammad Ayub					(5)	12	3	25	0	
Ayaz Tasawwar					(6)	17	1	60	0	1w,1nb
Bilal Hussain					(7)	1	0	1	0	
Kamran Younis					(8)	5	0	21	2	1nb

Sui Southern Gas Corporation Bowling

	O	M	R	W	
Rajesh Ramesh	18	2	90	1	1w
Sohail Khan	24	2	86	5	
Shehzad Butt	20	4	72	3	1nb
Adnan Malik	12	5	31	0	

Umpires: Ahmed Shahab and Zameer Haider. Referee: Aziz-ur-Rehman.   Toss: Sialkot

Close of Play: 1st day: Sui Southern Gas Corporation (1) 92-4 (Asif Zakir 38*, Atiq-uz-Zaman 20*, 34 overs); 2nd day: Sialkot (1) 99-2 (Faisal Khan 5*, Nayyer Abbas 2*, 22 overs); 3rd day: Sui Southern Gas Corporation (2) 74-1 (Asif Zakir 41*, Mohammad Zafar 0*, 18.2 overs).

Asif Zakir's 170 took 258 balls in 374 minutes and included 20 fours.

ZARAI TARAQIATI BANK LIMITED v RAWALPINDI

Played at Mirpur Cricket Stadium, December 1, 2, 3, 4, 2007.
Quaid-e-Azam Trophy 2007/08 - Group B
Match drawn.　(Points: Zarai Taraqiati Bank Limited 3, Rawalpindi 0)

ZARAI TARAQIATI BANK LIMITED

1	Afaq Raheem	c Ali Sarfraz b Rizwan Akbar	23	not out	0
2	Inam-ul-Haq	lbw b Yasir Ali	35	not out	3
3	Wajahatullah Wasti	c Usama Shahroon b Yasir Ali	19		
4	Adnan Raza	c Ali Sarfraz b Rizwan Akbar	10		
5	Faisal Naved	b Rizwan Akbar	80		
6	Atif Ashraf	c Adnan Mufti b Yasir Ali	22		
7	†Shakeel Ansar	b Rizwan Akbar	3		
8	Zohaib Khan	not out	53		
9	*Iftikhar Anjum	c Ali Sarfraz b Adnan Mufti	18		
10	Mohammad Khalil	lbw b Babar Naeem	23		
11	Azhar Attari	not out	5		
	Extras	b 5, lb 8, w 1, nb 21	35		
		(9 wickets, declared)	326	(no wicket)	3

FoW (1): 1-33, 2-85, 3-98, 4-105, 5-145, 6-154, 7-247, 8-274, 9-313

RAWALPINDI

1	Usama Shahroon	c Afaq Raheem b Iftikhar Anjum	55
2	Babar Naeem	b Iftikhar Anjum	0
3	Adnan Mufti	c Shakeel Ansar b Mohammad Khalil	13
4	Awais Zia	c Shakeel Ansar b Mohammad Khalil	14
5	*Naved Ashraf	c Shakeel Ansar b Mohammad Khalil	0
6	Usman Saeed	b Mohammad Khalil	73
7	†Ali Sarfraz	lbw b Inam-ul-Haq	24
8	Yasir Ali	run out (Iftikhar Anjum)	11
9	Rizwan Akbar	b Inam-ul-Haq	6
10	Alamgir Khan	not out	4
11	Mohammad Haroon	c Faisal Naved b Inam-ul-Haq	19
	Extras	b 4, lb 7, nb 12	23
			242

FoW (1): 1-1, 2-33, 3-74, 4-74, 5-118, 6-196, 7-205, 8-215, 9-217, 10-242

Rawalpindi Bowling

	O	M	R	W		O	M	R	W
Yasir Ali	39	13	105	3	1w,4nb	2	1	2	0
Rizwan Akbar	45.4	11	109	4	17nb				
Mohammad Haroon	17	4	52	0					
Alamgir Khan	1.2	1	0	0					
Adnan Mufti	4	0	19	1					
Babar Naeem	6	0	23	1	(2)	1.1	0	1	0
Awais Zia	1	0	5	0					

Zarai Taraqiati Bank Limited Bowling

	O	M	R	W	
Iftikhar Anjum	23	5	79	2	
Mohammad Khalil	24	6	76	4	9nb
Azhar Attari	10	0	56	0	2nb
Faisal Naved	5	1	8	0	1nb
Inam-ul-Haq	11.5	7	12	3	

Umpires: Hakeem Shah and Jamil Kamran. Referee: Anwar Khan.　　Toss: Rawalpindi

Close of Play: 1st day: No play; 2nd day: Zarai Taraqiati Bank Limited (1) 132-4 (Faisal Naved 12*, Atif Ashraf 17*, 53.2 overs); 3rd day: Rawalpindi (1) 22-1 (Usama Shahroon 10*, Adnan Mufti 9*, 5.4 overs).

ABBOTTABAD v PAKISTAN INTERNATIONAL AIRLINES

Played at Abbottabad Cricket Stadium, December 7, 8, 9, 10, 2007.
Quaid-e-Azam Trophy 2007/08 - Group B
Match drawn.   (Points: Abbottabad 0, Pakistan International Airlines 0)

PAKISTAN INTERNATIONAL AIRLINES

1	Agha Sabir	b Noor-ul-Amin	89
2	*Khurram Manzoor	c Adnan Raees b Rashid Mansoor	52
3	Kamran Sajid	c Mohammad Kashif b Noor-ul-Amin	50
4	Imran Ali	lbw b Noor-ul-Amin	5
5	Fahad Iqbal	run out (Noor-ul-Amin)	20
6	†Sarfraz Ahmed	c and b Amjad Waqas	117
7	Anwar Ali	run out (Mohammad Naeem)	48
8	Tahir Khan	run out (Mohammad Naeem)	26
9	Nauman Alavi	lbw b Noor-ul-Amin	4
10	Aizaz Cheema	b Amjad Waqas	0
11	Fazl-e-Akbar	not out	0
	Extras	b 4, lb 10, w 8, nb 3	25
			436

FoW (1): 1-109, 2-178, 3-196, 4-223, 5-242, 6-342, 7-407, 8-430, 9-431, 10-436

ABBOTTABAD

1	Mohammad Naeem	lbw b Anwar Ali	1
2	Fawad Khan	b Aizaz Cheema	47
3	Wajid Ali	b Fazl-e-Akbar	0
4	†Ghulam Mohammad	lbw b Tahir Khan	125
5	*Adnan Raees	c Anwar Ali b Kamran Sajid	44
6	Riaz Kail	c and b Tahir Khan	65
7	Rashid Mansoor	lbw b Tahir Khan	0
8	Iftikhar Mahmood	b Aizaz Cheema	0
9	Mohammad Kashif	b Aizaz Cheema	2
10	Amjad Waqas	not out	23
11	Noor-ul-Amin	not out	1
	Extras	b 6, lb 7, w 2, nb 2	17
		(9 wickets)	325

FoW (1): 1-16, 2-17, 3-107, 4-212, 5-252, 6-252, 7-253, 8-257, 9-321

Abbottabad Bowling

	O	M	R	W	
Rashid Mansoor	20	4	58	1	3nb
Adnan Raees	4	1	24	0	6w
Noor-ul-Amin	58	8	170	4	1w
Amjad Waqas	36.3	3	135	2	1w
Riaz Kail	13	2	35	0	

Pakistan International Airlines Bowling

	O	M	R	W	
Fazl-e-Akbar	11	2	45	1	
Anwar Ali	15	1	79	1	1w
Aizaz Cheema	17	3	77	3	1w,1nb
Tahir Khan	18	5	52	3	1nb
Nauman Alavi	8	3	33	0	
Kamran Sajid	6	2	26	1	

Umpires: Ahmed Shahab and Hakeem Shah. Referee: Mohammad Javed.   Toss: Pakistan International Airlines

Close of Play: 1st day: Pakistan International Airlines (1) 223-4 (Fahad Iqbal 16*, 81 overs); 2nd day: Abbottabad (1) 151-3 (Ghulam Mohammad 74*, Adnan Raees 14*, 25 overs); 3rd day: Abbottabad (1) 325-9 (Amjad Waqas 23*, Noor-ul-Amin 1*, 75 overs).

There was no play on the final day. Sarfraz Ahmed's 117 took 153 balls in 179 minutes and included 8 fours and 2 sixes. Ghulam Mohammad's 125 took 117 balls in 184 minutes and included 25 fours and 1 six.

HABIB BANK LIMITED v SUI SOUTHERN GAS CORPORATION

Played at United Bank Limited Sports Complex, Karachi, December 7, 8, 9, 2007.
Quaid-e-Azam Trophy 2007/08 - Group A
Habib Bank Limited won by an innings and 9 runs.   (Points: Habib Bank Limited 9, Sui Southern Gas Corporation 0)

HABIB BANK LIMITED
1	Rafatullah Mohmand	b Sohail Khan	0
2	Aftab Alam	lbw b Sohail Khan	7
3	Khaqan Arsal	b Sohail Khan	13
4	Hasan Raza	c Saeed Bin Nasir b Sohail Khan	204
5	*Shahid Afridi	c Sohail Khan b Mansoor Ahmed	33
6	Kamran Hussain	c sub (Haaris Ayaz) b Mansoor Ahmed	14
7	†Humayun Farhat	c Asif Zakir b Shehzad Butt	19
8	Sajid Shah	lbw b Mansoor Ahmed	34
9	Mohammad Aslam	lbw b Sohail Khan	21
10	Fahad Masood	not out	40
11	Dilawar Khan	c Ahmed Zeeshan b Sohail Khan	0
	Extras	b 10, lb 6, w 7, nb 11	34
			419

FoW (1): 1-4, 2-18, 3-23, 4-87, 5-110, 6-139, 7-208, 8-287, 9-419, 10-419

SUI SOUTHERN GAS CORPORATION
1	Asif Zakir	c Hasan Raza b Fahad Masood	5	c Aftab Alam b Fahad Masood	11
2	Mohtashim Ali	c Hasan Raza b Fahad Masood	11	c Humayun Farhat b Sajid Shah	8
3	Ali Hussain	b Fahad Masood	3	b Fahad Masood	25
4	Saeed Bin Nasir	not out	128	c Humayun Farhat b Kamran Hussain	15
5	*Atiq-uz-Zaman	lbw b Kamran Hussain	5	(6) lbw b Fahad Masood	38
6	†Ahmed Zeeshan	lbw b Dilawar Khan	24	(7) c Hasan Raza b Dilawar Khan	18
7	Mohammad Zafar	lbw b Shahid Afridi	21	(5) lbw b Dilawar Khan	4
8	Shehzad Butt	c Aftab Alam b Dilawar Khan	14	c Fahad Masood b Mohammad Aslam	25
9	Mansoor Ahmed	c Humayun Farhat b Mohammad Aslam	0	c Hasan Raza b Dilawar Khan	13
10	Sohail Khan	c Mohammad Aslam b Dilawar Khan	7	not out	8
11	Shakeel-ur-Rehman	b Dilawar Khan	0	c and b Dilawar Khan	0
	Extras	b 4, lb 3, nb 15	22	nb 5	5
			240		170

FoW (1): 1-14, 2-22, 3-31, 4-38, 5-91, 6-139, 7-172, 8-178, 9-236, 10-240
FoW (2): 1-17, 2-42, 3-53, 4-61, 5-83, 6-116, 7-146, 8-154, 9-170, 10-170

Sui Southern Gas Corporation Bowling
	O	M	R	W	
Sohail Khan	24	3	102	6	
Shakeel-ur-Rehman	19	5	93	0	2w,3nb
Shehzad Butt	22	0	93	1	1w,1nb
Mansoor Ahmed	27	1	110	3	7nb
Asif Zakir	3	1	5	0	

Habib Bank Limited Bowling
	O	M	R	W			O	M	R	W	
Kamran Hussain	9	2	26	1	3nb	(2)	14	5	29	1	
Sajid Shah	7	0	18	0		(1)	11	2	35	1	
Shahid Afridi	15.3	5	24	1							
Fahad Masood	12	1	34	3	9nb		11	1	38	3	5nb
Mohammad Aslam	24	5	71	1	2nb		16	5	24	1	
Dilawar Khan	14.4	4	56	4		(3)	12	2	44	4	
Aftab Alam	1	0	4	0							

Umpires: Iftikhar Malik and Islam Khan. Referee: Mahmood Rasheed.   Toss: Sui Southern Gas Corporation

Close of Play: 1st day: Habib Bank Limited (1) 334-8 (Hasan Raza 158*, Fahad Masood 9*, 83 overs); 2nd day: Sui Southern Gas Corporation (1) 194-8 (Saeed Bin Nasir 88*, Sohail Khan 2*, 72 overs).

The match was scheduled for four days but completed in three. Hasan Raza's 204 took 253 balls in 394 minutes and included 20 fours and 1 six. Saeed Bin Nasir's 128 took 228 balls in 241 minutes and included 16 fours and 3 sixes.

HYDERABAD v NATIONAL BANK OF PAKISTAN

Played at Niaz Stadium, Hyderabad, December 7, 8, 9, 10, 2007.
Quaid-e-Azam Trophy 2007/08 - Group A
Match drawn.   (Points: Hyderabad 0, National Bank of Pakistan 3)

NATIONAL BANK OF PAKISTAN

1	Nasir Jamshed	c Azeem Ghumman b Kashif Pervez	0	c Faisal Athar b Farhan Ayub	0
2	*Imran Nazir	c Kashif Bhatti b Farhan Ayub	30	(6) st Hanif Malik b Rizwan Ahmed	14
3	Naumanullah	b Kashif Bhatti	89	c Rizwan Ahmed b Kashif Pervez	12
4	†Shahid Yousuf	c Rizwan Ahmed b Farhan Ayub	1	(7) not out	5
5	Fawad Alam	b Kashif Bhatti	151		
6	Qaiser Abbas	run out	70	(9) not out	5
7	Mansoor Amjad	c Shahid Qambrani b Faisal Athar	45	(2) c Mohammad Sharif b Farhan Ayub	2
8	Tahir Mughal	not out	51	(4) c Jamshed Baig b Rizwan Ahmed	45
9	Wasim Khan	lbw b Rizwan Ahmed	16	(8) c Farhan Ayub b Rizwan Ahmed	2
10	Wahab Riaz	c and b Mohammad Sharif	0	(5) b Kashif Bhatti	62
11	Irfanuddin	lbw b Mohammad Sharif	9		
	Extras	b 5, lb 2, w 4, nb 4	15	b 1, lb 2, w 2, nb 2, pen 5	12
			477	(7 wickets, declared)	**159**

FoW (1): 1-1, 2-51, 3-66, 4-166, 5-292, 6-368, 7-424, 8-452, 9-453, 10-477
FoW (2): 1-1, 2-19, 3-19, 4-115, 5-146, 6-146, 7-148

HYDERABAD

1	Aqeel Anjum	lbw b Wahab Riaz	50	b Wahab Riaz	3
2	Azeem Ghumman	c and b Fawad Alam	109	c sub (Naeem Ahmed) b Irfanuddin	35
3	Faisal Athar	c sub (Rashid Riaz) b Wahab Riaz	94	c Naumanullah b Wasim Khan	3
4	Rizwan Ahmed	lbw b Qaiser Abbas	1	c Nasir Jamshed b Qaiser Abbas	90
5	*Shahid Qambrani	c Nasir Jamshed b Mansoor Amjad	15	(6) c Shahid Yousuf b Qaiser Abbas	2
6	Jamshed Baig	lbw b Mansoor Amjad	0	(7) not out	22
7	†Hanif Malik	lbw b Qaiser Abbas	12	(5) c Wahab Riaz b Fawad Alam	26
8	Kashif Bhatti	c Nasir Jamshed b Wahab Riaz	6	not out	29
9	Mohammad Sharif	c and b Wahab Riaz	12		
10	Farhan Ayub	not out	2		
11	Kashif Pervez	not out	1		
	Extras	b 13, lb 9, w 2, nb 8	32	b 8, lb 3	11
		(9 wickets, declared)	**334**	(6 wickets)	**221**

FoW (1): 1-125, 2-229, 3-230, 4-277, 5-277, 6-290, 7-315, 8-324, 9-333
FoW (2): 1-9, 2-12, 3-91, 4-146, 5-155, 6-178

Hyderabad Bowling	O	M	R	W			O	M	R	W	
Farhan Ayub	21	4	78	2	1w,4nb		11	2	40	2	1w,2nb
Kashif Pervez	13	1	76	1	1w		7	4	12	1	1w
Kashif Bhatti	35	3	99	2			13	5	36	1	
Shahid Qambrani	4	0	14	0							
Jamshed Baig	12	0	45	0							
Mohammad Sharif	10.5	3	47	2		(5)	4	0	18	0	
Rizwan Ahmed	18	4	80	1		(4)	14	0	45	3	
Faisal Athar	6	0	31	1	2w						

NBP Bowling	O	M	R	W			O	M	R	W	
Wahab Riaz	25	3	60	4	5nb	(2)	4	1	13	1	
Wasim Khan	18	1	73	0	1w,2nb	(1)	5	1	13	1	
Irfanuddin	21	5	60	0		(5)	5	1	20	1	
Tahir Mughal	14	3	34	0			2	0	8	0	
Mansoor Amjad	14	1	41	2		(3)	9	1	66	0	
Qaiser Abbas	16	5	26	2	1w		9	1	50	2	
Fawad Alam	8	2	18	1	1nb		7	0	40	1	

Umpires: Khalid Mahmood and Zaheer Ahmed. Referee: Naeem Ahmed.   Toss: National Bank of Pakistan

Close of Play: 1st day: National Bank of Pakistan (1) 328-5 (Fawad Alam 104*, Mansoor Amjad 21*, 85 overs); 2nd day: Hyderabad (1) 115-0 (Aqeel Anjum 49*, Azeem Ghumman 61*, 46 overs); 3rd day: National Bank of Pakistan (2) 33-3 (Tahir Mughal 12*, Wahab Riaz 2*, 11 overs).
Fawad Alam's 151 took 253 balls in 353 minutes and included 18 fours. Azeem Ghumman's 109 took 259 balls in 348 minutes and included 11 fours.

ISLAMABAD v KHAN RESEARCH LABORATORIES

Played at Diamond Club Ground, Islamabad, December 7, 8, 9, 10, 2007.
Quaid-e-Azam Trophy 2007/08 - Group B
Match drawn.   (Points: Islamabad 0, Khan Research Laboratories 3)

KHAN RESEARCH LABORATORIES

1	Azhar Ali	c Naeem Anjum b Shehzad Azam	150
2	*Mohammad Wasim	c Naeem Anjum b Shehzad Azam	17
3	Saeed Anwar	lbw b Ashar Zaidi	144
4	Bazid Khan	c Ashar Zaidi b Raheel Majeed	11
5	Bilal Asad	c Naeem Anjum b Rauf Akbar	23
6	Ali Khan	c Fayyaz Ahmed b Shehzad Azam	10
7	†Zulfiqar Jan	not out	37
8	Faisal Afridi	lbw b Rauf Akbar	8
9	Jaffar Nazir	c Umair Khan b Raheel Majeed	14
10	Khaleeq Ahmed	b Raheel Majeed	4
11	Saeed Ajmal		
	Extras	b 2, lb 10, w 10, nb 25	47
		(9 wickets, declared)	465

FoW (1): 1-34, 2-293, 3-307, 4-367, 5-391, 6-396, 7-406, 8-436, 9-465

ISLAMABAD

1	Raheel Majeed	c Zulfiqar Jan b Khaleeq Ahmed	107	c Zulfiqar Jan b Faisal Afridi	27
2	Umair Khan	lbw b Jaffar Nazir	10	b Khaleeq Ahmed	14
3	*Ashar Zaidi	c Zulfiqar Jan b Khaleeq Ahmed	7	lbw b Bilal Asad	34
4	Fakhar Hussain	lbw b Jaffar Nazir	3	(9) not out	0
5	Fayyaz Ahmed	c Ali Khan b Saeed Ajmal	16	c Azhar Ali b Saeed Ajmal	13
6	Asadullah Sumari	lbw b Saeed Ajmal	19	retired hurt	54
7	†Naeem Anjum	not out	27	c Bilal Asad b Faisal Afridi	16
8	Rauf Akbar	b Saeed Ajmal	3	not out	80
9	Farrukh Hayat	c Azhar Ali b Saeed Ajmal	29	(4) c Azhar Ali b Bilal Asad	27
10	Shehzad Azam	b Saeed Ajmal	9		
11	Saad Altaf	run out (Khaleeq Ahmed)	0		
	Extras	lb 18, nb 6	24	lb 5, nb 6	11
			254	(6 wickets)	276

FoW (1): 1-49, 2-68, 3-86, 4-133, 5-183, 6-204, 7-206, 8-244, 9-254, 10-254
FoW (2): 1-31, 2-52, 3-94, 4-117, 5-123, 6-147

Islamabad Bowling	O	M	R	W	
Saad Altaf	22	1	80	0	2nb
Rauf Akbar	23	1	84	2	2nb
Shehzad Azam	19	0	108	3	2w,19nb
Ashar Zaidi	19	0	60	1	1w
Fakhar Hussain	2	0	24	0	7w,1nb
Raheel Majeed	20.5	0	92	3	1nb
Fayyaz Ahmed	1	0	5	0	

KRL Bowling

	O	M	R	W			O	M	R	W	
Jaffar Nazir	19	3	75	2	3nb		2.5	0	22	0	
Faisal Afridi	13	0	48	0		(3)	21.3	3	70	2	2nb
Khaleeq Ahmed	15	3	65	2	3nb	(2)	19	3	74	1	3nb
Saeed Ajmal	20	6	40	5			25	6	66	1	
Bilal Asad	3	1	7	0			13	6	28	2	
Saeed Anwar	5	4	1	0		(8)	2	1	2	0	
Azhar Ali						(6)	2	0	6	0	
Ali Khan						(7)	3	0	3	0	

Umpires: Ahsan Raza and Ijaz Ahmed. Referee: Khalid Niazi.   Toss: Islamabad
Close of Play: 1st day: Khan Research Laboratories (1) 345-3 (Azhar Ali 124*, Bilal Asad 15*, 77.2 overs); 2nd day: Islamabad (1) 164-4 (Raheel Majeed 101*, Asadullah Sumari 7*, 40.2 overs); 3rd day: Islamabad (2) 52-1 (Raheel Majeed 27*, Ashar Zaidi 7*, 17 overs).

Asadullah Sumari retired hurt in the Islamabad second innings on 54* with the score at ?/6. Azhar Ali's 150 took 285 balls in 397 minutes and included 18 fours. Saeed Anwar's 144 took 173 balls in 230 minutes and included 15 fours and 2 sixes. Raheel Majeed's 107 took 161 balls in 187 minutes and included 15 fours and 2 sixes.

KARACHI BLUES v SUI NORTHERN GAS PIPELINES LIMITED

Played at Asghar Ali Shah Stadium, Karachi, December 7, 8, 9, 10, 2007.
Quaid-e-Azam Trophy 2007/08 - Group B
Sui Northern Gas Pipelines Limited won by an innings and 186 runs.   (Points: Karachi Blues 0, Sui Northern Gas Pipelines Limited 9)

SUI NORTHERN GAS PIPELINES LIMITED

1	*Mohammad Hafeez	c sub (Fahad Khan) b Faraz Patel	145
2	Yasir Arafat	c Mohammad Waqas b Tariq Haroon	46
3	Umar Akmal	run out	248
4	Azhar Shafiq	b Faraz Patel	100
5	Khurram Shehzad	lbw b Faraz Patel	5
6	Mohammad Farrukh	not out	51
7	†Adnan Akmal	not out	9
8	Samiullah Khan		
9	Imran Ali		
10	Adnan Rasool		
11	Imran Khalid		
	Extras	b 5, lb 4, w 8, nb 3	20
		(5 wickets, declared)	624

FoW (1): 1-93, 2-406, 3-489, 4-512, 5-585

KARACHI BLUES

1	Shadab Kabir	b Imran Ali	13	c Mohammad Hafeez b Imran Ali	0
2	Mubashir Ahmed	c Umar Akmal b Imran Ali	0	c Mohammad Farrukh b Mohammad Hafeez	10
3	Faraz Patel	b Samiullah Khan	3	(4) lbw b Mohammad Hafeez	0
4	Sharjeel Ashraf	c Adnan Akmal b Mohammad Hafeez	44	(3) c Yasir Arafat b Mohammad Hafeez	27
5	Mohammad Masroor	c Imran Ali b Mohammad Hafeez	26	lbw b Samiullah Khan	3
6	*Mansoor Khan	c Umar Akmal b Adnan Rasool	35	c Mohammad Farrukh b Samiullah Khan	101
7	Tariq Haroon	c Umar Akmal b Imran Ali	63	c Mohammad Hafeez b Samiullah Khan	46
8	†Mohammad Waqas	b Mohammad Hafeez	18	c Adnan Akmal b Imran Ali	0
9	Faraz Ahmed	lbw b Samiullah Khan	4	(10) c Mohammad Hafeez b Samiullah Khan	7
10	Ijaz Ahmed	not out	19	(9) c Umar Akmal b Samiullah Khan	1
11	Malik Aftab	c Imran Khalid b Imran Ali	0	not out	1
	Extras	lb 1, w 1, nb 1	3	b 8, lb 5, nb 1	14
			228		210

FoW (1): 1-13, 2-15, 3-25, 4-54, 5-117, 6-141, 7-172, 8-181, 9-228, 10-228
FoW (2): 1-0, 2-18, 3-18, 4-21, 5-99, 6-180, 7-185, 8-190, 9-209, 10-210

Karachi Blues Bowling	O	M	R	W	
Faraz Ahmed	16	1	61	0	3nb
Malik Aftab	21	3	113	0	1w
Tariq Haroon	29	4	132	1	3w
Ijaz Ahmed	17	1	117	0	
Mansoor Khan	9	0	64	0	
Faraz Patel	16	2	96	3	
Shadab Kabir	3	0	32	0	

Sui Northern Gas Bowling	O	M	R	W			O	M	R	W	
Samiullah Khan	19	6	51	2	1w		18	11	23	5	
Imran Ali	18.5	6	37	4	1nb	(1)	21	8	41	2	
Mohammad Hafeez	18	4	62	3			26	2	70	3	
Imran Khalid	7	0	35	0			8	0	38	0	
Adnan Rasool	12	1	42	1			8	1	25	0	1nb

Umpires: Kaukab Butt and Zameer Haider. Referee: Ilyas Khan.   Toss: Sui Northern Gas Pipelines Limited
Close of Play: 1st day: Sui Northern Gas Pipelines Limited (1) 427-2 (Umar Akmal 215*, Azhar Shafiq 10*, 83 overs); 2nd day: Karachi Blues (1) 172-6 (Tariq Haroon 31*, Mohammad Waqas 18*, 53 overs); 3rd day: Karachi Blues (2) 172-5 (Mansoor Khan 101*, Tariq Haroon 29*, 61 overs).

Mohammad Hafeez's 145 took 215 balls in 311 minutes. Umar Akmal's 248 took 225 balls in 291 minutes and included 26 fours and 4 sixes. Azhar Shafiq's 100 took 104 balls in 154 minutes and included 8 fours and 2 sixes. Mansoor Khan's 101 took 168 balls in 209 minutes and included 14 fours and 1 six.

KARACHI WHITES v WATER AND POWER DEVELOPMENT AUTHORITY

Played at National Stadium, Karachi, December 7, 8, 9, 10, 2007.
Quaid-e-Azam Trophy 2007/08 - Group A
Match drawn.   (Points: Karachi Whites 0, Water and Power Development Authority 3)

KARACHI WHITES

1	Khalid Latif	c Ahmed Said b Kashif Raza	2	lbw b Kashif Raza	124
2	Asad Shafiq	b Bilal Khilji	22	lbw b Azharullah	8
3	Wajihuddin	lbw b Zeeshan Nadir	73	lbw b Zeeshan Nadir	7
4	Daniyal Ahsan	st Ahmed Said b Bilal Khilji	8	c Ahmed Said b Azharullah	15
5	*Asim Kamal	b Zeeshan Nadir	22	(6) b Azharullah	61
6	Afsar Nawaz	c Farooq Iqbal b Zeeshan Nadir	105	(5) c Bilal Khilji b Kashif Raza	6
7	†Javed Mansoor	c Aamer Sajjad b Kashif Raza	16	not out	19
8	Tanvir Ahmed	c Aamer Sajjad b Azharullah	38	lbw b Azharullah	0
9	Mohammad Hasnain	c Ahmed Said b Azharullah	14	(10) not out	13
10	Tabish Nawab	lbw b Azharullah	0	(9) c Kashif Rasheed b Azharullah	0
11	Fahad Khan	not out	0		
	Extras	b 1, lb 7, w 2, nb 5	15	b 1, w 11, nb 2	14
			315	(8 wickets)	267

FoW (1): 1-10, 2-61, 3-80, 4-135, 5-138, 6-177, 7-264, 8-315, 9-315, 10-315
FoW (2): 1-22, 2-44, 3-95, 4-102, 5-224, 6-228, 7-229, 8-229

WATER AND POWER DEVELOPMENT AUTHORITY

1	†Ahmed Said	c Javed Mansoor b Mohammad Hasnain	69
2	Kashif Rasheed	lbw b Tanvir Ahmed	2
3	Tariq Aziz	c Khalid Latif b Tabish Nawab	70
4	Nawaz Sardar	c Javed Mansoor b Tabish Nawab	75
5	*Aamer Sajjad	c Wajihuddin b Tanvir Ahmed	25
6	Bilal Khilji	b Fahad Khan	24
7	Jahangir Mirza	c Asad Shafiq b Tabish Nawab	7
8	Farooq Iqbal	b Tanvir Ahmed	34
9	Kashif Raza	c Asad Shafiq b Fahad Khan	31
10	Azharullah	c sub (Atif Ali) b Mohammad Hasnain	41
11	Zeeshan Nadir	not out	6
	Extras	b 4, lb 4, w 2, nb 31	41
			425

FoW (1): 1-26, 2-137, 3-197, 4-205, 5-224, 6-239, 7-295, 8-351, 9-414, 10-425

Water and Power Development Authority Bowling

	O	M	R	W			O	M	R	W	
Kashif Raza	25	7	74	2			19	8	33	2	1w,1nb
Azharullah	19	3	52	3	1w		26	8	59	5	1nb
Zeeshan Nadir	18.2	5	60	3	1w,1nb	(5)	22	14	18	1	3w
Bilal Khilji	11	3	27	2		(3)	4	3	4	0	
Nawaz Sardar	7	2	35	0	4nb	(6)	7	1	18	0	
Farooq Iqbal	15	4	50	0		(4)	18	1	87	0	
Jahangir Mirza	1	0	6	0		(8)	3	0	24	0	
Aamer Sajjad	1	0	3	0		(7)	3	1	10	0	
Ahmed Said						(9)	2	0	13	0	2w

Karachi Whites Bowling

	O	M	R	W	
Tanvir Ahmed	23	3	112	3	9nb
Mohammad Hasnain	20	4	76	2	12nb
Fahad Khan	22	2	99	2	2w,4nb
Tabish Nawab	40	1	127	3	6nb
Afsar Nawaz	1	0	3	0	

Umpires: Akbar Khan and Jamil Kamran.   Referee: Anwar Khan.   Toss: Karachi Whites

Close of Play: 1st day: Karachi Whites (1) 279-7 (Afsar Nawaz 85*, Mohammad Hasnain 2*, 83 overs); 2nd day: Water and Power Development Authority (1) 277-6 (Ahmed Said 18*, Farooq Iqbal 23*, 66 overs); 3rd day: Karachi Whites (2) 94-2 (Khalid Latif 63*, Daniyal Ahsan 14*, 41 overs).
Afsar Nawaz's 105 took 180 balls in 254 minutes and included 16 fours. Khalid Latif's 124 took 246 balls in 294 minutes and included 15 fours and 4 sixes.

LAHORE RAVI v MULTAN

Played at Gaddafi Stadium, Lahore, December 7, 8, 9, 10, 2007.
Quaid-e-Azam Trophy 2007/08 - Group A
Match drawn.   (Points: Lahore Ravi 3, Multan 0)

LAHORE RAVI

1	Kashif Siddiq	c Sohaib Maqsood b Ansar Javed	17	b Rahat Ali		50
2	Sohail Ahmed	c Usman Tariq b Rahat Ali	19	lbw b Ansar Javed		32
3	Rizwan Aamer	c Gulraiz Sadaf b Abdur Rauf	21	c Rahat Ali b Abdur Rauf		13
4	Ali Haider	c Gulraiz Sadaf b Abdur Rauf	122	b Abdur Rauf		0
5	Arsalan Mir	c Usman Tariq b Ansar Javed	1	b Abdur Rauf		31
6	Ashraf Ali	b Abdur Rauf	132	c Gulraiz Sadaf b Abdur Rauf		23
7	Saad Nasim	b Abdur Rauf	9	b Qaiser Shehzad		44
8	*Junaid Zia	lbw b Ansar Javed	19	b Qaiser Shehzad		54
9	Waqas Ahmed	c Ansar Javed b Abdur Rauf	46	c Mohammad Sarwar b Abdur Rauf		4
10	†Mohammad Zohaib	c Gulraiz Sadaf b Rahat Ali	5	c Gulraiz Sadaf b Qaiser Shehzad		0
11	Azam Khan	not out	0	not out		4
	Extras	b 1, lb 4, w 1	6	b 6, lb 4, w 5, nb 4		19
			397			**274**

FoW (1): 1-27, 2-38, 3-58, 4-60, 5-297, 6-311, 7-340, 8-362, 9-373, 10-397
FoW (2): 1-79, 2-105, 3-106, 4-111, 5-153, 6-176, 7-251, 8-258, 9-259, 10-274

MULTAN

1	†Gulraiz Sadaf	b Waqas Ahmed	9	b Waqas Ahmed		21
2	Usman Tariq	c Mohammad Zohaib b Waqas Ahmed	69	not out		16
3	Rameez Alam	c Arsalan Mir b Saad Nasim	131	lbw b Waqas Ahmed		5
4	Naved Yasin	c Mohammad Zohaib b Azam Khan	55			
5	Sohaib Maqsood	c and b Junaid Zia	37	not out		2
6	Mohammad Sarwar	c Arsalan Mir b Azam Khan	7			
7	*Abdur Rauf	c Mohammad Zohaib b Azam Khan	0			
8	Imranullah Aslam	c Junaid Zia b Azam Khan	5			
9	Ansar Javed	not out	13	(4) lbw b Waqas Ahmed		0
10	Rahat Ali	b Junaid Zia	1			
11	Qaiser Shehzad	c Ali Haider b Junaid Zia	1			
	Extras	b 3, lb 3, w 2, nb 9	17	b 4, nb 1		5
			345	(3 wickets)		**49**

FoW (1): 1-15, 2-167, 3-275, 4-309, 5-321, 6-325, 7-325, 8-332, 9-343, 10-345
FoW (2): 1-31, 2-37, 3-37

Multan Bowling

	O	M	R	W		O	M	R	W	
Abdur Rauf	28.5	2	134	5	1w	22	5	80	5	5w
Ansar Javed	16	2	68	3	(3)	15	4	47	1	4nb
Rahat Ali	21	2	91	2	(2)	14	4	48	1	
Imranullah Aslam	14	2	51	0	(5)	2	0	20	0	
Qaiser Shehzad	16	4	40	0	(4)	10.1	1	69	3	
Sohaib Maqsood	3	0	8	0						

Lahore Ravi Bowling

	O	M	R	W		O	M	R	W	
Junaid Zia	29.1	6	78	3	1w,4nb	5	1	27	0	
Waqas Ahmed	25	5	70	2	2nb	4	1	18	3	1nb
Saad Nasim	27	3	95	1						
Azam Khan	16	1	58	4	1w					
Arsalan Mir	3	0	21	0	3nb					
Kashif Siddiq	4	1	12	0						
Sohail Ahmed	5	2	5	0						

Umpires: Raweed Khan and Riazuddin.   Referee: Aziz-ur-Rehman.   Toss: Multan

Close of Play: 1st day: Lahore Ravi (1) 295-4 (Ali Haider 121*, Ashraf Ali 111*, 79 overs); 2nd day: Multan (1) 184-2 (Rameez Alam 88*, Naved Yasin 9*, 54 overs); 3rd day: Lahore Ravi (2) 52-0 (Kashif Siddiq 31*, Sohail Ahmed 18*, 14.4 overs).

Ali Haider's 122 took 199 balls in 299 minutes and included 16 fours. Ashraf Ali's 132 took 243 balls in 346 minutes and included 17 fours. Rameez Alam's 131 took 268 balls in 329 minutes and included 11 fours.

PESHAWAR v ZARAI TARAQIATI BANK LIMITED

Played at Arbab Niaz Stadium, Peshawar, December 7, 8, 9, 10, 2007.
Quaid-e-Azam Trophy 2007/08 - Group B
Match drawn.   (Points: Peshawar 0, Zarai Taraqiati Bank Limited 3)

ZARAI TARAQIATI BANK LIMITED

1	Afaq Raheem	lbw b Nauman Habib	29
2	Inam-ul-Haq	lbw b Jamaluddin	106
3	Atif Ashraf	b Bilal Khan	17
4	Adnan Raza	c Gauhar Ali b Inamullah	64
5	†Kamran Naeem	c sub (Mohammad Fayyaz) b Rahatullah	2
6	*Wajahatullah Wasti	c Mahfooz Sabri b Rahatullah	50
7	Faisal Naved	c Gauhar Ali b Bilal Khan	29
8	Zohaib Khan	b Rahatullah	15
9	Kashif Daud	c Gauhar Ali b Rahatullah	24
10	Mohammad Khalil	c Azam Jan b Bilal Khan	24
11	Azhar Attari	not out	1
	Extras	b 5, lb 4, w 9, nb 19	37
			398

FoW (1): 1-64, 2-97, 3-212, 4-241, 5-298, 6-327, 7-329, 8-357, 9-395, 10-398

PESHAWAR

1	Fawad Ali	c Atif Ashraf b Kashif Daud	20	c sub (Shakeel Ansar) b Kashif Daud	1
2	Naved Khan	b Mohammad Khalil	11	c Afaq Raheem b Mohammad Khalil	0
3	Jamaluddin	b Mohammad Khalil	8	(4) c Wajahatullah Wasti b Mohammad Khalil	2
4	Mahfooz Sabri	c sub (Shakeel Ansar) b Mohammad Khalil	13		
5	Sajjad Ahmed	c Kamran Naeem b Azhar Attari	36	(6) not out	39
6	Azam Jan	c Wajahatullah Wasti b Zohaib Khan	2	(3) not out	51
7	†Gauhar Ali	c Afaq Raheem b Azhar Attari	5	(5) b Azhar Attari	8
8	Bilal Khan	not out	16		
9	Inamullah	lbw b Zohaib Khan	0		
10	*Nauman Habib	c Kamran Naeem b Zohaib Khan	1		
11	Rahatullah	b Zohaib Khan	0		
	Extras	b 8, lb 3, nb 18	29	lb 5, nb 7	12
			141	(4 wickets)	113

FoW (1): 1-36, 2-44, 3-49, 4-78, 5-92, 6-105, 7-124, 8-134, 9-141, 10-141
FoW (2): 1-1, 2-3, 3-34, 4-48

Peshawar Bowling

	O	M	R	W	
Nauman Habib	15	4	38	1	2nb
Bilal Khan	34	3	134	3	1w,15nb
Rahatullah	28.1	5	88	4	8w,2nb
Inamullah	32	7	92	1	
Mahfooz Sabri	2	0	9	0	
Jamaluddin	14	5	20	1	
Naved Khan	1	0	8	0	

Zarai Taraqiati Bank Limited Bowling

	O	M	R	W		O	M	R	W	
Mohammad Khalil	19	5	36	3	3nb	7	1	25	2	4nb
Kashif Daud	15	3	42	1	5nb	10	0	47	1	1nb
Zohaib Khan	11.4	3	16	4	(4)	9	3	20	0	
Azhar Attari	8	0	36	2	10nb (3)	6	3	12	1	2nb
Wajahatullah Wasti					(5)	1	0	4	0	

Umpires: Javed Ashraf and Mohammad Arif. Referee: Ishtiaq Ahmed.   Toss: Peshawar

Close of Play: 1st day: Zarai Taraqiati Bank Limited (1) 205-2 (Inam-ul-Haq 87*, Kamran Naeem 0*, 59.4 overs); 2nd day: Peshawar (1) 25-0 (Fawad Ali 10*, Naved Khan 7*, 12 overs); 3rd day: Peshawar (1) 44-2 (Jamaluddin 4*, 18.3 overs).

Inam-ul-Haq's 106 took 226 balls in 354 minutes and included 13 fours.

RAWALPINDI v QUETTA

Played at Khan Research Laboratories Ground, Rawalpindi, December 7, 8, 9, 10, 2007.
Quaid-e-Azam Trophy 2007/08 - Group B
Match drawn.   (Points: Rawalpindi 3, Quetta 0)

QUETTA

1	Shoaib Khan	c Sajid Mahmood b Yasir Ali	60	c Sajid Mahmood b Yasir Ali		15
2	Hameedullah Khan	lbw b Rizwan Akbar	0	c Babar Naeem b Naved Ashraf		67
3	Samiullah Agha	b Rizwan Akbar	14	c Sajid Mahmood b Rizwan Akbar		13
4	Taimur Ali	lbw b Yasir Ali	0	c Sajid Mahmood b Yasir Ali		0
5	*Nasim Khan	run out (Yasir Ali)	13	c Usama Shahroon b Yasir Ali		1
6	Mohammad Alam	c Babar Naeem b Haseeb Azam	0	lbw b Rizwan Akbar		2
7	Jalat Khan	not out	59	not out		50
8	Faisal Irfan	lbw b Rizwan Akbar	13	not out		10
9	†Sanaullah Khan	b Haseeb Azam	0			
10	Nazar Hussain	c Yasir Ali b Haseeb Azam	9			
11	Sanaullah Baloch	run out (Yasir Ali)	0			
	Extras	lb 1, nb 4	5	lb 4, w 2, nb 11		17
			173	**(6 wickets)**		**175**

FoW (1): 1-0, 2-28, 3-29, 4-55, 5-55, 6-112, 7-142, 8-147, 9-159, 10-173
FoW (2): 1-26, 2-44, 3-51, 4-55, 5-62, 6-145

RAWALPINDI

1	Usama Shahroon	c Sanaullah Khan b Faisal Irfan	4
2	Babar Naeem	c Hameedullah Khan b Sanaullah Baloch	42
3	Adnan Mufti	st Sanaullah Khan b Sanaullah Baloch	28
4	Mohammad Ibrahim	c Faisal Irfan b Sanaullah Baloch	29
5	*Naved Ashraf	lbw b Jalat Khan	98
6	Usman Saeed	c Sanaullah Khan b Jalat Khan	31
7	Awais Zia	b Faisal Irfan	60
8	†Sajid Mahmood	c Hameedullah Khan b Faisal Irfan	22
9	Yasir Ali	not out	51
10	Rizwan Akbar		
11	Haseeb Azam		
	Extras	b 5, lb 8, w 3, nb 9	25
		(8 wickets, declared)	**390**

FoW (1): 1-9, 2-84, 3-96, 4-165, 5-243, 6-257, 7-292, 8-390

Rawalpindi Bowling

	O	M	R	W		O	M	R	W
Yasir Ali	15	5	36	2		21	8	39	3
Rizwan Akbar	20w,11nb	2	79	3	4nb	23	3	58	2
Haseeb Azam	14	5	47	3		5	2	6	0
Babar Naeem	2	0	10	0		21	6	41	0
Naved Ashraf					(5)	8	2	16	1
Mohammad Ibrahim					(6)	3	1	5	0
Adnan Mufti					(7)	2	0	4	0
Usman Saeed					(8)	1	0	2	0

Quetta Bowling

	O	M	R	W	
Faisal Irfan	26.2	6	92	3	3w,1nb
Nazar Hussain	24	3	82	0	2nb
Sanaullah Baloch	26	3	101	3	
Jalat Khan	30	4	91	2	6nb
Mohammad Alam	4	0	11	0	

Umpires: Mian Mohammad Aslam and Saleem Badar.   Referee: Abdus Sami.   Toss: Rawalpindi

Close of Play: 1st day: Rawalpindi (1) 41-1 (Babar Naeem 17*, Adnan Mufti 13*, 15.4 overs); 2nd day: Rawalpindi (1) 328-7 (Awais Zia 27*, Yasir Ali 23*, 104 overs); 3rd day: Quetta (2) 25-0 (Shoaib Khan 15*, Hameedullah Khan 8*, 8 overs).

SIALKOT v FAISALABAD

Played at Sheikhupura Stadium, December 7, 8, 9, 10, 2007.
Quaid-e-Azam Trophy 2007/08 - Group A
Match drawn.   (Points: Sialkot 0, Faisalabad 3)

FAISALABAD

1	Ali Rafiq	c Ayaz Tasawwar b Mohammad Imran	7	c Mohammad Ayub b Nayyer Abbas	21
2	Usman Arshad	b Mohammad Imran	0	c Khalid Mahmood b Mohammad Imran	4
3	Ammar Mahmood	c Kamran Younis b Mohammad Wasim	3	b Nayyer Abbas	38
4	*Ijaz Ahmed	c Kamran Younis b Mohammad Ali	44	b Nayyer Abbas	91
5	Asif Hussain	c Khalid Mahmood b Mohammad Ali	8	c Faisal Khan b Nayyer Abbas	3
6	Imran Ahmed	c Khalid Mahmood b Mohammad Imran	8	c Naeemuddin b Nayyer Abbas	0
7	†Mohammad Salman	c Naeemuddin b Mohammad Imran	63	c Kamran Younis b Mohammad Wasim	10
8	Ahmed Hayat	c Khalid Mahmood b Mohammad Imran	38	c Mohammad Ayub b Mohammad Imran	5
9	Asad Zarar	c Ayaz Tasawwar b Mohammad Imran	1	b Mohammad Imran	12
10	Saadat Munir	b Nayyer Abbas	0	lbw b Mohammad Wasim	4
11	Mohammad Talha	not out	0	not out	2
	Extras	lb 7, nb 14	21	b 13, lb 7, w 2, nb 3	25
			193		**215**

FoW (1): 1-6, 2-8, 3-16, 4-63, 5-70, 6-91, 7-190, 8-192, 9-193, 10-193
FoW (2): 1-9, 2-58, 3-95, 4-121, 5-127, 6-147, 7-156, 8-173, 9-193, 10-215

SIALKOT

1	Kamran Younis	c Usman Arshad b Asad Zarar	29	not out	29
2	Naeemuddin	lbw b Asad Zarar	8	not out	16
3	Faisal Khan	c Ijaz Ahmed b Asad Zarar	0		
4	Ayaz Tasawwar	c Mohammad Salman b Ahmed Hayat	12		
5	Nayyer Abbas	c Ijaz Ahmed b Saadat Munir	23		
6	*Mohammad Ayub	c Mohammad Salman b Ahmed Hayat	9		
7	Adeel Malik	c Ali Rafiq b Saadat Munir	29		
8	†Khalid Mahmood	c Mohammad Salman b Asad Zarar	28		
9	Mohammad Wasim	lbw b Saadat Munir	1		
10	Mohammad Imran	not out	1		
11	Mohammad Ali	c Ali Rafiq b Saadat Munir	0		
	Extras	b 9, lb 9, w 1, nb 2	21		
			161	(no wicket)	**45**

FoW (1): 1-32, 2-32, 3-59, 4-64, 5-99, 6-99, 7-142, 8-155, 9-160, 10-161

Sialkot Bowling

	O	M	R	W		O	M	R	W	
Mohammad Wasim	17	0	80	1	9nb	21	5	70	2	1w
Mohammad Imran	16.5	3	42	6	4nb	21	5	62	3	1w,3nb
Mohammad Ali	16	0	59	2	1nb	6	0	19	0	
Nayyer Abbas	4	0	5	1		26.5	10	44	5	

Faisalabad Bowling

	O	M	R	W			O	M	R	W
Ahmed Hayat	12	4	34	2	2nb		4	1	16	0
Mohammad Talha	9	0	45	0			3	1	11	0
Asad Zarar	17	6	32	4	1w		1	0	4	0
Saadat Munir	13.4	3	32	4		(5)	1	0	10	0
Ijaz Ahmed	1	1	0	0		(4)	2	1	4	0

Umpires: Nadeem Ghauri and Rasheed Bhatti. Referee: Saadat Ali.   Toss: Sialkot

Close of Play: 1st day: Sialkot (1) 63-3 (Ayaz Tasawwar 12*, Nayyer Abbas 0*, 18.5 overs); 2nd day: Faisalabad (2) 127-5 (Ijaz Ahmed 49*, 47 overs); 3rd day: Sialkot (2) 45-0 (Kamran Younis 29*, Naeemuddin 16*, 11 overs).

There was no play on the final day.

ABBOTTABAD v KHAN RESEARCH LABORATORIES

Played at Abbottabad Cricket Stadium, December 13, 14, 15, 16, 2007.
Quaid-e-Azam Trophy 2007/08 - Group B
Khan Research Laboratories won by 246 runs.   (Points: Abbottabad 0, Khan Research Laboratories 6)

KHAN RESEARCH LABORATORIES

1	Azhar Ali	first innings forfeited	b Noor-ul-Amin	33
2	*Mohammad Wasim		lbw b Noor-ul-Amin	23
3	Saeed Anwar		c Rashid Mansoor b Noor-ul-Amin	107
4	Bazid Khan		b Adnan Raees	78
5	Bilal Asad		c Rashid Mansoor b Noor-ul-Amin	23
6	Ali Naqvi		lbw b Sajjad Ali	5
7	Faisal Afridi		c Fawad Khan b Junaid Khan	26
8	†Zulfiqar Jan		b Junaid Khan	25
9	Mohammad Irshad		not out	16
10	Khaleeq Ahmed			
11	Saeed Ajmal			
	Extras		b 1, lb 8, w 4, nb 8	21
			(8 wickets, declared)	357

FoW (2): 1-49, 2-76, 3-227, 4-272, 5-283, 6-285, 7-335, 8-357

ABBOTTABAD

1	†Fawad Khan	first innings forfeited	b Saeed Ajmal	40
2	Sajjad Ali		c Zulfiqar Jan b Faisal Afridi	5
3	Ghulam Mohammad		c Azhar Ali b Faisal Afridi	22
4	Wajid Ali		c sub (Ali Khan) b Khaleeq Ahmed	9
5	*Adnan Raees		c Mohammad Wasim	
			b Mohammad Irshad	16
6	Riaz Kail		b Saeed Ajmal	3
7	Rashid Mansoor		c Zulfiqar Jan b Mohammad Irshad	3
8	Khalid Usman		not out	7
9	Amjad Waqas		b Mohammad Irshad	0
10	Junaid Khan		b Mohammad Irshad	0
11	Noor-ul-Amin		absent	0
	Extras		lb 2, nb 4	6
				111

FoW (2): 1-6, 2-38, 3-48, 4-92, 5-97, 6-100, 7-105, 8-110, 9-111

Abbotobad Bowling

	O	M	R	W	
Junaid Khan	16.2	2	55	2	1nb
Rashid Mansoor	11	1	31	0	1w,2nb
Noor-ul-Amin	50	13	132	4	
Amjad Waqas	15	1	68	0	3w
Khalid Usman	2	0	9	0	
Adnan Raees	4	1	18	1	
Sajjad Ali	6	0	35	1	5nb

Khan Research Laboratories Bowling

	O	M	R	W	
Mohammad Irshad	11.3	1	37	4	2nb
Faisal Afridi	6	0	23	2	
Khaleeq Ahmed	5	0	7	1	2nb
Saeed Ajmal	10	2	42	2	

Umpires: Ahmed Shahab and Naushad Khan.   Referee: Ishtiaq Ahmed.   Toss: Abbottabad

Close of Play: 1st day: No play; 2nd day: Khan Research Laboratories (2) 26-0 (Azhar Ali 9*, Mohammad Wasim 13*, 13.5 overs); 3rd day: Khan Research Laboratories (2) 356-7 (Zulfiqar Jan 25*, Mohammad Irshad 15*, 104 overs).

Saeed Anwar's 107 took 198 balls in 206 minutes and included 10 fours.

ISLAMABAD v QUETTA

Played at Diamond Club Ground, Islamabad, December 13, 14, 15, 16, 2007.
Quaid-e-Azam Trophy 2007/08 - Group B
Match drawn. (Points: Islamabad 3, Quetta 0)

QUETTA

1	Shoaib Khan	c Kamran Hussain b Rauf Akbar	45	(3) b Ashar Zaidi	154
2	Hameedullah Khan	c Umair Mir b Saad Altaf	1	(1) c Ashar Zaidi b Rauf Akbar	25
3	*Samiullah Agha	c Saad Altaf b Rauf Akbar	13	(4) b Imad Wasim	30
4	Shahzad Tareen	b Shehzad Azam	13	(2) c Umair Mir b Rauf Akbar	4
5	Nasim Khan	c Raheel Majeed b Rauf Akbar	6	b Rauf Akbar	8
6	Jalat Khan	b Rauf Akbar	18	c Raheel Majeed b Rauf Akbar	46
7	Faisal Irfan	c Ameer Khan b Rauf Akbar	50	(8) c sub (Mohammad Kashif) b Rauf Akbar	13
8	†Sanaullah Khan	lbw b Shehzad Azam	9	(7) c Umair Khan b Rauf Akbar	0
9	Sher Hasan	st Umair Mir b Raheel Majeed	18	c sub (Yasin Bari) b Rauf Akbar	0
10	Gauhar Faiz	lbw b Rauf Akbar	19	not out	4
11	Nazar Hussain	not out	30	not out	0
	Extras	b 11, lb 1, w 1, nb 9	22	b 16, lb 2, w 2, nb 17	37
			244	(9 wickets, declared)	321

FoW (1): 1-5, 2-65, 3-65, 4-88, 5-107, 6-118, 7-138, 8-182, 9-197, 10-244
FoW (2): 1-20, 2-58, 3-132, 4-141, 5-238, 6-244, 7-272, 8-272, 9-319

ISLAMABAD

1	Raheel Majeed	c Sanaullah Khan b Faisal Irfan	20	c Shoaib Khan b Faisal Irfan	12
2	Umair Khan	c Faisal Irfan b Sher Hasan	6	c Sanaullah Khan b Sher Hasan	13
3	†Umair Mir	c Sanaullah Khan b Nazar Hussain	9	c Shoaib Khan b Faisal Irfan	13
4	*Ashar Zaidi	c Samiullah Agha b Faisal Irfan	60	lbw b Faisal Irfan	99
5	Asadullah Sumari	lbw b Sher Hasan	16	c Faisal Irfan b Sher Hasan	38
6	Ameer Khan	c Sanaullah Khan b Faisal Irfan	92	not out	6
7	Imad Wasim	run out (Sanaullah Khan)	41		
8	Kamran Hussain	c Faisal Irfan b Gauhar Faiz	1		
9	Rauf Akbar	c Shahzad Tareen b Nazar Hussain	17	(7) not out	3
10	Shehzad Azam	b Faisal Irfan	0		
11	Saad Altaf	not out	0		
	Extras	b 5, lb 3, w 2, nb 10	20	b 2, lb 3, w 2, nb 8	15
			282	(5 wickets)	199

FoW (1): 1-22, 2-31, 3-47, 4-110, 5-118, 6-219, 7-220, 8-244, 9-274, 10-282
FoW (2): 1-12, 2-27, 3-63, 4-181, 5-194

Islamabad Bowling

	O	M	R	W			O	M	R	W	
Saad Altaf	15	5	43	1							
Rauf Akbar	19.3	4	66	6		(1)	30	4	95	7	1w
Shehzad Azam	21	3	68	2	1w,8nb	(2)	15	2	62	0	1w,11nb
Imad Wasim	8.2	1	21	0	1nb		25	0	88	1	6nb
Ashar Zaidi	0.4	0	1	0		(3)	6	2	17	1	
Raheel Majeed	13	3	33	1		(6)	2	0	11	0	
Kamran Hussain						(5)	7	0	30	0	

Quetta Bowling

	O	M	R	W			O	M	R	W	
Faisal Irfan	21.1	9	35	4	1nb		11	2	53	3	1w,1nb
Sher Hasan	17	1	72	2	1w,4nb		8	0	43	2	3nb
Nazar Hussain	22	6	50	2			8	3	30	0	
Gauhar Faiz	15	2	87	1	1w,4nb		7	0	32	0	1w
Jalat Khan	10	0	30	0	1nb		11	3	35	0	4nb
Shoaib Khan						(6)	2	1	1	0	

Umpires: Hakeem Shah and Iftikhar Malik. Referee: Abdus Sami.   Toss: Islamabad

Close of Play: 1st day: Quetta (1) 243-9 (Gauhar Faiz 19*, Nazar Hussain 29*, 75 overs); 2nd day: Islamabad (1) 229-7 (Ameer Khan 58*, Rauf Akbar 4*, 69 overs); 3rd day: Quetta (2) 237-4 (Shoaib Khan 95*, Jalat Khan 46*, 56 overs).

Shoaib Khan's 154 took 240 balls in 330 minutes and included 16 fours and 2 sixes.

KARACHI BLUES v ZARAI TARAQIATI BANK LIMITED

Played at United Bank Limited Sports Complex, Karachi, December 13, 14, 15, 16, 2007.
Quaid-e-Azam Trophy 2007/08 - Group B
Zarai Taraqiati Bank Limited won by an innings and 181 runs.   (Points: Karachi Blues 0, Zarai Taraqiati Bank Limited 9)

KARACHI BLUES

1	Shadab Kabir	b Kashif Daud	1	b Kashif Daud	12
2	†Ali Asad	c Shakeel Ansar b Kashif Daud	65	b Kashif Daud	0
3	Faraz Patel	c Inam-ul-Haq b Kashif Daud	0	c Shakeel Ansar b Kashif Daud	18
4	Sharjeel Ashraf	c Shakeel Ansar b Inam-ul-Haq	8	c Faisal Naved b Zohaib Khan	37
5	Fahadullah Khan	c Kashif Daud b Zohaib Khan	17	lbw b Imran Sabir	23
6	Tariq Haroon	lbw b Zohaib Khan	0	c Faisal Naved b Zohaib Khan	25
7	*Mansoor Khan	c Wajahatullah Wasti b Zohaib Khan	38	c Atif Ashraf b Zohaib Khan	11
8	Faisal Hussain	lbw b Kashif Daud	0	lbw b Zohaib Khan	1
9	Azam Hussain	c Shakeel Ansar b Kashif Daud	39	run out	0
10	Malik Aftab	c and b Zohaib Khan	0	(11) c Junaid Nadir b Zohaib Khan	3
11	Tabish Khan	not out	8	(10) not out	2
	Extras	lb 4, w 1, nb 7	12	b 4, lb 4, w 6	14
			188		**146**

FoW (1): 1-4, 2-4, 3-41, 4-81, 5-81, 6-95, 7-95, 8-158, 9-158, 10-188
FoW (2): 1-1, 2-12, 3-57, 4-84, 5-123, 6-129, 7-131, 8-141, 9-141, 10-146

ZARAI TARAQIATI BANK LIMITED

1	Afaq Raheem	not out	205
2	Inam-ul-Haq	c Faraz Patel b Tabish Khan	45
3	Atif Ashraf	c Fahadullah Khan b Tabish Khan	12
4	Adnan Raza	c Faraz Patel b Tariq Haroon	62
5	*Wajahatullah Wasti	c Sharjeel Ashraf b Faraz Patel	123
6	Imran Sabir	run out (Tabish Khan)	42
7	Kashif Daud		
8	Junaid Nadir		
9	Zohaib Khan		
10	Faisal Naved		
11	†Shakeel Ansar		
	Extras	b 17, lb 4, w 4, nb 1	26
		(5 wickets, declared)	515

FoW (1): 1-118, 2-136, 3-239, 4-471, 5-515

Zarai Taraqiati Bank Limited Bowling

	O	M	R	W		O	M	R	W	
Kashif Daud	17.4	5	37	5		12	2	28	3	
Imran Sabir	14	3	44	0	2nb	13	2	33	1	
Junaid Nadir	13	4	23	0	1w,1nb	(4) 13	5	27	0	2w
Inam-ul-Haq	6	1	22	1		(5) 1	0	1	0	
Zohaib Khan	23	3	58	4		(3) 23.5	6	49	5	

Karachi Blues Bowling

	O	M	R	W	
Malik Aftab	18	1	59	0	
Tabish Khan	35.1	7	127	2	3w,1nb
Azam Hussain	46	11	113	0	
Tariq Haroon	37	8	132	1	1w
Mansoor Khan	13	0	39	0	
Shadab Kabir	2	0	9	0	
Faraz Patel	2	0	15	0	

Umpires: Kaukab Butt and Zameer Haider.   Referee: Mahmood Rasheed.   Toss: Karachi Blues

Close of Play: 1st day: Zarai Taraqiati Bank Limited (1) 15-0 (Afaq Raheem 13*, Inam-ul-Haq 1*, 7 overs); 2nd day: Zarai Taraqiati Bank Limited (1) 251-3 (Afaq Raheem 107*, Wajahatullah Wasti 11*, 94 overs); 3rd day: Karachi Blues (2) 51-2 (Faraz Patel 14*, Sharjeel Ashraf 21*, 23 overs).

Afaq Raheem's 205 took 480 balls in 601 minutes and included 24 fours. Wajahatullah Wasti's 123 took 175 balls in 257 minutes and included 13 fours and 3 sixes.

KARACHI WHITES v PAKISTAN CUSTOMS

Played at National Stadium, Karachi, December 13, 14, 15, 16, 2007.
Quaid-e-Azam Trophy 2007/08 - Group A
Match drawn.   (Points: Karachi Whites 0, Pakistan Customs 3)

PAKISTAN CUSTOMS

1	Hasnain Abbas	lbw b Tanvir Ahmed	12	c Khalid Latif b Mohammad Hasnain	4
2	Murtaza Hussain	c Javed Mansoor b Mohammad Hasnain	30	lbw b Mohammad Hasnain	12
3	Asif Iqbal	lbw b Fahad Khan	106	b Fahad Khan	9
4	Rehan Rafiq	c Asad Shafiq b Tabish Nawab	0	lbw b Fahad Khan	64
5	*Zahoor Elahi	b Fahad Khan	101	c Khalid Latif b Mohammad Hasnain	1
6	Yasir Hussain	c Mohammad Hasnain b Fahad Khan	1	c Javed Mansoor b Fahad Khan	39
7	†Mohammad Hasan	c and b Tabish Nawab	43	c Afsar Nawaz b Tabish Nawab	76
8	Yasir Shah	c sub (Atif Ali) b Tanvir Ahmed	3	c Mohammad Hasnain b Fahad Khan	3
9	Raees Amjad	c Mohammad Hasnain b Tabish Nawab	17	c Tanvir Ahmed b Mohammad Hasnain	34
10	Tahir Maqsood	lbw b Fahad Khan	0	(11) not out	5
11	Sajjad Hussain	not out	7	(10) b Tabish Nawab	7
	Extras	lb 4, w 1, nb 13	18	b 4, lb 3, nb 10	17
			338		**271**

FoW (1): 1-18, 2-96, 3-102, 4-261, 5-265, 6-272, 7-277, 8-319, 9-320, 10-338
FoW (2): 1-4, 2-23, 3-37, 4-39, 5-136, 6-137, 7-145, 8-236, 9-248, 10-271

KARACHI WHITES

1	Khalid Latif	c Hasnain Abbas b Murtaza Hussain	42	lbw b Sajjad Hussain	15
2	Asad Shafiq	run out (sub [Mohammad Nabi])	12	not out	25
3	Wajihuddin	lbw b Raees Amjad	1		
4	Afsar Nawaz	c Asif Iqbal b Tahir Maqsood	33	(3) c Asif Iqbal b Sajjad Hussain	8
5	*Asim Kamal	c Tahir Maqsood b Sajjad Hussain	50		
6	Ahmed Iqbal	lbw b Raees Amjad	13	(4) b Tahir Maqsood	7
7	†Javed Mansoor	lbw b Sajjad Hussain	42	(5) b Murtaza Hussain	1
8	Tanvir Ahmed	c Yasir Hussain b Raees Amjad	50	(6) not out	2
9	Mohammad Hasnain	not out	0		
10	Tabish Nawab	lbw b Sajjad Hussain	0		
11	Fahad Khan	b Sajjad Hussain	0		
	Extras	b 10, lb 5, nb 22	37	lb 1, nb 1	2
			280	**(4 wickets)**	**60**

FoW (1): 1-22, 2-43, 3-67, 4-134, 5-165, 6-172, 7-279, 8-280, 9-280, 10-280
FoW (2): 1-19, 2-39, 3-46, 4-57

Karachi Whites Bowling

	O	M	R	W		O	M	R	W	
Tanvir Ahmed	28	10	79	2	7nb	18	3	62	0	3nb
Mohammad Hasnain	17	4	57	1	1nb	22	4	72	4	6nb
Fahad Khan	28	7	87	4	1w,1nb	24	6	54	4	
Tabish Nawab	29	4	88	3	4nb	26.3	7	57	2	1nb
Ahmed Iqbal	6	0	23	0		4	0	13	0	
Asad Shafiq					(6)	1	0	6	0	

Pakistan Customs Bowling

	O	M	R	W		O	M	R	W	
Raees Amjad	18	4	51	3	10nb	7	1	28	0	1nb
Sajjad Hussain	20	6	50	4		6	2	14	2	
Tahir Maqsood	14	4	52	1	12nb	6	3	7	1	
Murtaza Hussain	24	8	56	1		6	3	10	1	
Yasir Shah	16	4	56	0						

Umpires: Jamil Kamran and Rasheed Bhatti. Referee: Ilyas Khan.   Toss: Karachi Whites

Close of Play: 1st day: Pakistan Customs (1) 223-3 (Asif Iqbal 94*, Zahoor Elahi 74*, 77 overs); 2nd day: Karachi Whites (1) 154-4 (Asim Kamal 47*, Ahmed Iqbal 9*, 56 overs); 3rd day: Pakistan Customs (2) 116-4 (Rehan Rafiq 60*, Yasir Hussain 26*, 45 overs).

Asif Iqbal's 106 took 239 balls in 334 minutes and included 18 fours. Zahoor Elahi's 101 took 127 balls in 172 minutes and included 17 fours.

313

LAHORE RAVI v SIALKOT

Played at Lahore City Cricket Association Ground, December 13, 14, 15, 16, 2007.
Quaid-e-Azam Trophy 2007/08 - Group A
Lahore Ravi won by three wickets.   (Points: Lahore Ravi 9, Sialkot 0)

SIALKOT

1	Kamran Younis	c Saad Nasim b Junaid Zia	0	c Kashif Siddiq b Waqas Ahmed	18
2	Naeemuddin	lbw b Junaid Zia	1	c Kashif Siddiq b Junaid Zia	1
3	Faisal Khan	c Kashif Siddiq b Junaid Zia	35	c Ahmed Shehzad b Arsalan Mir	32
4	Ayaz Tasawwar	c Shahbaz Butt b Waqas Ahmed	1	(5) c Shahbaz Butt b Kashif Shafi	25
5	*Mohammad Ayub	lbw b Waqas Ahmed	5	(4) c Usama Aftab b Waqas Ahmed	124
6	Adeel Malik	c Saad Nasim b Junaid Zia	0	c Shahbaz Butt b Waqas Ahmed	39
7	Nayyer Abbas	lbw b Junaid Zia	0	lbw b Waqas Ahmed	17
8	†Khalid Mahmood	c Shahbaz Butt b Waqas Ahmed	1	c Usama Aftab b Waqas Ahmed	0
9	Mohammad Wasim	b Junaid Zia	14	lbw b Junaid Zia	4
10	Mohammad Imran	c sub (Rizwan Ahmed) b Waqas Ahmed	17	not out	8
11	Mohammad Ali	not out	1	lbw b Waqas Ahmed	7
	Extras	b 4, lb 6, nb 3	13	b 6, w 1, nb 6	13
			88		**288**

FoW (1): 1-0, 2-9, 3-16, 4-52, 5-52, 6-52, 7-53, 8-53, 9-86, 10-88
FoW (2): 1-7, 2-32, 3-68, 4-135, 5-200, 6-250, 7-254, 8-273, 9-275, 10-288

LAHORE RAVI

1	Ahmed Shehzad	c Khalid Mahmood b Mohammad Imran	6	(2) c Khalid Mahmood b Mohammad Ali	0
2	Kashif Siddiq	c Adeel Malik b Mohammad Imran	0	(1) c Faisal Khan b Mohammad Imran	26
3	Ali Haider	c Mohammad Imran b Mohammad Wasim	3	lbw b Mohammad Ali	12
4	Ashraf Ali	lbw b Mohammad Ali	31	b Nayyer Abbas	64
5	Arsalan Mir	lbw b Mohammad Ali	18	(6) lbw b Mohammad Ali	14
6	Saad Nasim	c Ayaz Tasawwar b Mohammad Ali	15	(7) c Faisal Khan b Mohammad Ali	8
7	*Junaid Zia	c Naeemuddin b Mohammad Wasim	5	(5) c Adeel Malik b Mohammad Imran	0
8	†Shahbaz Butt	c Kamran Younis b Mohammad Imran	26	not out	45
9	Waqas Ahmed	c Khalid Mahmood b Mohammad Ali	45	not out	30
10	Kashif Shafi	c Mohammad Imran b Mohammad Ali	6		
11	Usama Aftab	not out	0		
	Extras	b 4, lb 1, w 2, nb 3	10	b 4, lb 7, w 1, nb 3	15
			165	(7 wickets)	**214**

FoW (1): 1-0, 2-9, 3-11, 4-60, 5-74, 6-87, 7-87, 8-154, 9-161, 10-165
FoW (2): 1-4, 2-27, 3-53, 4-59, 5-85, 6-101, 7-149

Lahore Ravi Bowling

	O	M	R	W			O	M	R	W	
Junaid Zia	13	2	30	6			27	1	74	2	1w
Waqas Ahmed	13	1	48	4	3nb		21.2	5	70	6	
Arsalan Mir						(3)	17	5	43	1	6nb
Kashif Shafi						(4)	17	1	54	1	
Saad Nasim						(5)	4	0	17	0	
Kashif Siddiq						(6)	4	2	17	0	
Usama Aftab						(7)	4	1	7	0	

Sialkot Bowling

	O	M	R	W			O	M	R	W	
Mohammad Wasim	16	3	65	2	1nb	(3)	5	0	18	0	
Mohammad Imran	14	4	48	3	2w	(1)	23.1	4	94	2	1w,3nb
Mohammad Ali	10	1	38	5	2nb	(2)	19	2	75	4	
Nayyer Abbas	2	0	9	0			7	1	16	1	

Umpires: Akbar Khan and Zaheer Ahmed. Referee: Saadat Ali.   Toss: Lahore Ravi

Close of Play: 1st day: Lahore Ravi (1) 146-7 (Shahbaz Butt 18*, Waqas Ahmed 41*, 36.1 overs); 2nd day: Sialkot (2) 211-5 (Mohammad Ayub 81*, Nayyer Abbas 5*, 73.1 overs); 3rd day: Lahore Ravi (2) 177-7 (Shahbaz Butt 26*, Waqas Ahmed 14*, 49 overs).

Mohammad Ayub's 124 took 240 balls in 348 minutes and included 15 fours and 2 sixes.

LAHORE SHALIMAR v SUI NORTHERN GAS PIPELINES LIMITED

Played at Gaddafi Stadium, Lahore, December 13, 14, 15, 2007.
Quaid-e-Azam Trophy 2007/08 - Group B
Sui Northern Gas Pipelines Limited won by ten wickets.   (Points: Lahore Shalimar 0, Sui Northern Gas Pipelines Limited 9)

LAHORE SHALIMAR

1	Salman Akbar	lbw b Samiullah Khan	9	lbw b Asad Ali	32
2	Haroon Rasheed	c Saleem Mughal b Samiullah Khan	26	c Adnan Akmal b Asad Ali	4
3	Sibtain Raza	c Tauqeer Hussain b Samiullah Khan	14	(9) c sub (Adnan Rosool)	
				b Samiullah Khan	16
4	Ahmed Butt	c Yasir Arafat b Samiullah Khan	0	(3) run out	5
5	Suleman Khan	c Adnan Akmal b Samiullah Khan	8	(4) c Imran Ali b Asad Ali	74
6	*†Ali Raza	c Saleem Mughal b Imran Ali	3	b Imran Ali	39
7	Mohammad Hussain	not out	52	c Khurram Shehzad b Imran Ali	0
8	Asif Raza	lbw b Samiullah Khan	25	lbw b Samiullah Khan	8
9	Mohammad Shahzad	c Asad Ali b Samiullah Khan	10	(10) c Mohammad Hafeez	
				b Samiullah Khan	0
10	Mohammad Naved	c Adnan Akmal b Imran Ali	3	(11) not out	12
11	Zaheer Maqsood	c Adnan Akmal b Asad Ali	0	(5) b Asad Ali	0
	Extras	lb 6, w 1, nb 5	12	b 5, lb 4, nb 7	16
			162		206

FoW (1): 1-32, 2-48, 3-48, 4-66, 5-69, 6-71, 7-116, 8-126, 9-149, 10-162
FoW (2): 1-10, 2-40, 3-46, 4-58, 5-122, 6-122, 7-161, 8-181, 9-181, 10-206

SUI NORTHERN GAS PIPELINES LIMITED

1	*Mohammad Hafeez	c Ali Raza b Mohammad Hussain	113		
2	Yasir Arafat	c Ali Raza b Asif Raza	6	(1) not out	47
3	Tauqeer Hussain	c Ali Raza b Mohammad Naved	3	(2) not out	19
4	Umar Akmal	c Ali Raza b Mohammad Naved	65		
5	Azhar Shafiq	c Ali Raza b Mohammad Naved	1		
6	Khurram Shehzad	c and b Mohammad Hussain	64		
7	Saleem Mughal	lbw b Zaheer Maqsood	2		
8	†Adnan Akmal	c Mohammad Shahzad			
		b Mohammad Naved	15		
9	Samiullah Khan	c Ali Raza b Mohammad Naved	1		
10	Imran Ali	not out	0		
11	Asad Ali	b Mohammad Naved	12		
	Extras	lb 5, w 2, nb 8	15	lb 1, w 6	7
			297	(no wicket)	73

FoW (1): 1-16, 2-20, 3-184, 4-188, 5-227, 6-238, 7-273, 8-280, 9-285, 10-297

Sui Northern Gas Pipelines Limited Bowling

	O	M	R	W		O	M	R	W	
Samiullah Khan	24	4	82	7	1w,1nb	17	4	54	3	
Asad Ali	11.5	0	31	1	4nb	18.2	0	80	4	7nb
Imran Ali	16	6	43	2		13	1	37	2	
Tauqeer Hussain					(4)	6	1	26	0	

Lahore Shalimar Bowling

	O	M	R	W		O	M	R	W	
Mohammad Naved	30.4	13	91	6	1w	2	0	20	0	
Asif Raza	18	1	81	1	1w,5nb	2	0	29	0	
Mohammad Shahzad	7	0	34	0						
Zaheer Maqsood	10	1	60	1	(3)	2	0	4	0	
Mohammad Hussain	14	4	26	2						
Sibtain Raza					(4)	1.1	0	19	0	6w

Umpires: Raweed Khan and Saleem Badar. Referee: Anis Sheikh.   Toss: Sui Northern Gas Pipelines Limited

Close of Play: 1st day: Sui Northern Gas Pipelines Limited (1) 78-2 (Mohammad Hafeez 30*, Umar Akmal 27*, 18.5 overs); 2nd day: Lahore Shalimar (2) 52-3 (Suleman Khan 6*, Zaheer Maqsood 0*, 15 overs).

The match was scheduled for four days but completed in three. Mohammad Hafeez's 113 took 184 balls in 255 minutes and included 21 fours.

MULTAN v HYDERABAD

Played at Multan Cricket Stadium, December 13, 14, 15, 16, 2007.
Quaid-e-Azam Trophy 2007/08 - Group A
Multan won by nine wickets.   (Points: Multan 9, Hyderabad 0)

HYDERABAD

1	Aqeel Anjum	c Atiq Ahmed b Ansar Javed	2	lbw b Ansar Javed	32
2	Azeem Ghumman	b Ansar Javed	96	c Atiq Ahmed b Abdur Rauf	36
3	Faisal Athar	b Abdur Rauf	65	b Rahat Ali	2
4	Rizwan Ahmed	st Atiq Ahmed b Sohaib Maqsood	58	lbw b Abdur Rauf	38
5	*Shahid Qambrani	c Atiq Ahmed b Rahat Ali	55	(6) c Atiq Ahmed b Abdur Rauf	24
6	Naeem-ur-Rehman	b Ahmed Raza	21	(9) c Itmad-ul-Haq b Abdur Rauf	1
7	Khadim Hussain	b Ansar Javed	12	(5) c Atiq Ahmed b Abdur Rauf	2
8	†Hanif Malik	lbw b Rahat Ali	0	(7) c Atiq Ahmed b Rahat Ali	4
9	Pir Zulfiqar	c Naved Yasin b Rahat Ali	0	(8) c Rameez Alam b Abdur Rauf	20
10	Farhan Ayub	not out	0	run out (Itmad-ul-Haq)	0
11	Mohammad Sharif	b Rahat Ali	0	not out	0
	Extras	b 10, lb 3, nb 13	26	b 8, lb 6, nb 7	21
			335		**180**

FoW (1): 1-9, 2-109, 3-212, 4-252, 5-310, 6-334, 7-334, 8-334, 9-335, 10-335
FoW (2): 1-56, 2-59, 3-99, 4-101, 5-131, 6-140, 7-175, 8-177, 9-180, 10-180

MULTAN

1	Hammad Tariq	c Hanif Malik b Naeem-ur-Rehman	22	c Khadim Hussain b Mohammad Sharif	19
2	Usman Tariq	c sub (Jamshed Baig)			
		b Naeem-ur-Rehman	218	not out	29
3	Rameez Alam	c Hanif Malik b Naeem-ur-Rehman	3		
4	Naved Yasin	c Pir Zulfiqar b Mohammad Sharif	28		
5	†Atiq Ahmed	lbw b Naeem-ur-Rehman	10		
6	Itmad-ul-Haq	lbw b Naeem-ur-Rehman	88		
7	Sohaib Maqsood	c Hanif Malik b Farhan Ayub	18	(3) not out	15
8	*Abdur Rauf	b Naeem-ur-Rehman	0		
9	Ansar Javed	not out	27		
10	Ahmed Raza	c sub (Jamshed Baig) b Pir Zulfiqar	10		
11	Rahat Ali	b Pir Zulfiqar	0		
	Extras	b 3, lb 4, w 2, nb 13	22	b 4, lb 1, nb 2	7
			446	**(1 wicket)**	**70**

FoW (1): 1-44, 2-62, 3-135, 4-162, 5-386, 6-393, 7-393, 8-424, 9-446, 10-446
FoW (2): 1-37

Multan Bowling	O	M	R	W		O	M	R	W	
Abdur Rauf	29	6	76	1		25.1	7	72	6	3nb
Ansar Javed	23	4	76	3	9nb	14	3	50	1	4nb
Rahat Ali	14.4	4	35	4		12	1	40	2	
Ahmed Raza	17	2	68	1						
Hammad Tariq	8	2	20	0						
Sohaib Maqsood	7	0	32	1	4nb					
Usman Tariq	6	0	15	0	(4)	7	6	4	0	

Hyderabad Bowling	O	M	R	W			O	M	R	W	
Farhan Ayub	25	3	113	1	6nb		6	1	26	0	1nb
Naeem-ur-Rehman	32	8	101	6	2w,5nb		5	2	8	0	
Khadim Hussain	2	0	15	0							
Pir Zulfiqar	23.4	2	75	2							
Rizwan Ahmed	17	1	83	0	2nb	(5)	0.2	0	6	0	1nb
Mohammad Sharif	12	2	36	1		(3)	3	0	11	1	
Shahid Qambrani	3	0	16	0							
Azeem Ghumman						(4)	2	0	14	0	

Umpires: Ijaz Ahmed and Nadeem Ghauri.   Referee: Mohammad Javed.   Toss: Multan
Close of Play: 1st day: Hyderabad (1) 260-4 (Shahid Qambrani 25*, Naeem-ur-Rehman 1*, 84 overs); 2nd day: Multan (1) 229-4 (Usman Tariq 118*, Itmad-ul-Haq 32*, 60 overs); 3rd day: Hyderabad (2) 98-2 (Azeem Ghumman 36*, Rizwan Ahmed 24*, 25.4 overs).
Usman Tariq's 218 took 348 balls in 400 minutes and included 20 fours and 5 sixes.

NATIONAL BANK OF PAKISTAN v HABIB BANK LIMITED

Played at National Bank of Pakistan Sports Complex, Karachi, December 13, 14, 15, 16, 2007.
Quaid-e-Azam Trophy 2007/08 - Group A
Match drawn.   (Points: National Bank of Pakistan 0, Habib Bank Limited 3)

NATIONAL BANK OF PAKISTAN

1	Nasir Jamshed	c Humayun Farhat b Mohammad Aslam	31	run out (Rafatullah Mohmand)	75
2	*Imran Nazir	c Humayun Farhat b Sajid Shah	7	(4) c Humayun Farhat b Dilawar Khan	30
3	Naumanullah	c Humayun Farhat b Mohammad Aslam	15	lbw b Dilawar Khan	23
4	†Rashid Riaz	c Humayun Farhat b Fahad Masood	73	(2) c Humayun Farhat b Sajid Shah	9
5	Fawad Alam	c and b Fahad Masood	5	not out	66
6	Naved Latif	c Hasan Raza b Mohammad Aslam	5	lbw b Rafatullah Mohmand	11
7	Qaiser Abbas	c Humayun Farhat b Fahad Masood	74	c Rafatullah Mohmand b Sulaman Qadir	3
8	Mansoor Amjad	c Hasan Raza b Sajid Shah	35	not out	21
9	Tahir Mughal	b Mohammad Aslam	13		
10	Wahab Riaz	lbw b Mohammad Aslam	17		
11	Uzair-ul-Haq	not out	1		
	Extras	lb 3, w 1, nb 17	21	b 5, nb 8	13
			297	(6 wickets)	251

FoW (1): 1-7, 2-28, 3-87, 4-93, 5-98, 6-206, 7-236, 8-268, 9-288, 10-297
FoW (2): 1-41, 2-119, 3-128, 4-152, 5-189, 6-200

HABIB BANK LIMITED

1	Rafatullah Mohmand	c Naved Latif b Wahab Riaz	36
2	Fahad Masood	c Rashid Riaz b Wahab Riaz	38
3	Kamran Hussain	c Mansoor Amjad b Uzair-ul-Haq	31
4	Aftab Alam	c Naved Latif b Fawad Alam	80
5	Khaqan Arsal	not out	109
6	*Hasan Raza	c Rashid Riaz b Fawad Alam	0
7	Sulaman Qadir	c sub (Imran Javed) b Fawad Alam	0
8	†Humayun Farhat	c sub (Irfanuddin) b Mansoor Amjad	33
9	Sajid Shah	run out (Wahab Riaz)	1
10	Mohammad Aslam	lbw b Mansoor Amjad	1
11	Dilawar Khan	lbw b Fawad Alam	0
	Extras	b 2, lb 4, w 3, nb 3	12
			341

FoW (1): 1-66, 2-83, 3-130, 4-287, 5-287, 6-289, 7-331, 8-334, 9-340, 10-341

Habib Bank Limited Bowling

	O	M	R	W			O	M	R	W	
Sajid Shah	14	4	29	2			19	10	37	1	4nb
Fahad Masood	22	3	62	3	1w,16nb	(4)	5	0	23	0	4nb
Kamran Hussain	18	4	64	0		(2)	5	2	24	0	
Mohammad Aslam	37.1	13	81	5	1nb	(3)	31	17	46	0	
Dilawar Khan	16	3	58	0		(6)	16	4	49	2	
Aftab Alam						(5)	9	3	21	0	
Hasan Raza						(7)	2	0	9	0	
Sulaman Qadir						(8)	15	6	27	1	
Rafatullah Mohmand						(9)	3	1	10	1	

National Bank of Pakistan Bowling

	O	M	R	W	
Wahab Riaz	23	7	68	2	1w,2nb
Uzair-ul-Haq	16	3	69	1	1nb
Tahir Mughal	12	2	47	0	
Qaiser Abbas	9	1	27	0	
Fawad Alam	21.1	6	51	4	
Mansoor Amjad	27	5	73	2	1w

Umpires: Khalid Mahmood and Riazuddin.   Referee: Aziz-ur-Rehman.   Toss: Habib Bank Limited

Close of Play: 1st day: National Bank of Pakistan (1) 207-6 (Qaiser Abbas 54*, Mansoor Amjad 1*, 83 overs); 2nd day: Habib Bank Limited (1) 195-3 (Aftab Alam 55*, Khaqan Arsal 28*, 56 overs); 3rd day: National Bank of Pakistan (2) 86-1 (Nasir Jamshed 58*, Naumanullah 9*, 28 overs).
Khaqan Arsal's 109 took 221 balls in 289 minutes and included 16 fours.

PESHAWAR v RAWALPINDI

Played at Arbab Niaz Stadium, Peshawar, December 13, 14, 15, 16, 2007.
Quaid-e-Azam Trophy 2007/08 - Group B
Match drawn.   (Points: Peshawar 0, Rawalpindi 3)

PESHAWAR

1	Usman Zeb	c Babar Naeem b Rizwan Akbar	13	b Mohammad Rameez	70
2	Shahid Iqbal	lbw b Yasir Ali	4	c Sajid Mahmood b Rizwan Akbar	22
3	Azam Jan	b Rizwan Akbar	13	c Yasim Murtaza b Yasir Ali	12
4	Nawaz Ahmed	c Sajid Mahmood b Yasir Ali	16	c Babar Naeem b Yasir Ali	4
5	Mahfooz Sabri	c Sajid Mahmood b Yasir Ali	36	(8) not out	17
6	*Akbar Badshah	c Yasim Murtaza b Babar Naeem	18	c Sajid Mahmood b Mohammad Rameez	0
7	Sajjad Ahmed	not out	83	(5) c Sajid Mahmood b Yasim Murtaza	40
8	†Shehzad Khan	lbw b Yasim Murtaza	23	(7) c Mohammad Ibrahim b Yasim Murtaza	53
9	Nauman Habib	lbw b Yasim Murtaza	31	b Babar Naeem	17
10	Rahatullah	c Awais Zia b Yasim Murtaza	0	lbw b Babar Naeem	0
11	Imran Khan	b Rizwan Akbar	8	lbw b Babar Naeem	0
	Extras	b 4, lb 1, w 1, nb 5	11	b 8, lb 5, nb 10	23
			256		**258**

FoW (1): 1-5, 2-23, 3-34, 4-61, 5-103, 6-108, 7-150, 8-208, 9-232, 10-256
FoW (2): 1-41, 2-57, 3-74, 4-134, 5-134, 6-214, 7-229, 8-251, 9-258, 10-258

RAWALPINDI

1	Umar Amin	c Shehzad Khan b Imran Khan	9	not out	22
2	Babar Naeem	c Mahfooz Sabri b Nauman Habib	28	c Shehzad Khan b Rahatullah	0
3	Mohammad Ibrahim	lbw b Rahatullah	37	not out	20
4	Awais Zia	c Shehzad Khan b Nauman Habib	27		
5	*Naved Ashraf	c Shehzad Khan b Imran Khan	34		
6	Usman Saeed	c Shehzad Khan b Nauman Habib	94		
7	Yasim Murtaza	b Rahatullah	46		
8	†Sajid Mahmood	lbw b Rahatullah	0		
9	Yasir Ali	c Imran Khan b Nauman Habib	4		
10	Mohammad Rameez	c Akbar Badshah b Rahatullah	18		
11	Rizwan Akbar	not out	5		
	Extras	lb 2, w 2, nb 10	14	lb 2, nb 2	4
			316	(1 wicket)	**46**

FoW (1): 1-9, 2-69, 3-83, 4-140, 5-144, 6-252, 7-252, 8-266, 9-300, 10-316
FoW (2): 1-4

Rawalpindi Bowling

	O	M	R	W		O	M	R	W	
Yasir Ali	29	12	52	3	1w	21	8	57	2	
Rizwan Akbar	34.5	12	77	3	3nb	17	5	59	1	6nb
Mohammad Rameez	20	6	44	0	(4)	10	3	42	2	1nb
Yasim Murtaza	24	5	51	3	2nb (3)	18	6	57	2	
Babar Naeem	6	0	27	1		8.3	4	14	3	
Usman Saeed					(6)	3	0	16	0	3nb

Peshawar Bowling

	O	M	R	W		O	M	R	W	
Nauman Habib	22	6	79	4	2w,1nb	4	0	22	0	2nb
Imran Khan	22	3	92	2	8nb					
Rahatullah	19.2	7	57	4	(2)	4	1	14	1	
Akbar Badshah	19	7	40	0						
Usman Zeb	4	0	15	0	1nb					
Mahfooz Sabri	4	0	21	0						
Nawaz Ahmed	2	0	10	0	(4)	1	0	1	0	
Sajjad Ahmed					(3)	1	0	7	0	

Umpires: Mian Mohammad Aslam and Mohammad Arif.   Referee: Khalid Niazi.   Toss: Peshawar

Close of Play: 1st day: Peshawar (1) 134-6 (Sajjad Ahmed 12*, Shehzad Khan 17*, 72 overs); 2nd day: Rawalpindi (1) 140-3 (Awais Zia 27*, Naved Ashraf 34*, 37 overs); 3rd day: Peshawar (2) 45-1 (Usman Zeb 18*, Azam Jan 2*, 14 overs).

SUI SOUTHERN GAS CORPORATION v WATER AND POWER DEVELOPMENT AUTHORITY

Played at Asghar Ali Shah Stadium, Karachi, December 13, 14, 15, 16, 2007.
Quaid-e-Azam Trophy 2007/08 - Group A
Match drawn.   (Points: Sui Southern Gas Corporation 3, Water and Power Development Authority 0)

WATER AND POWER DEVELOPMENT AUTHORITY

1	†Ahmed Said	b Sohail Khan	6	c Ahmed Zeeshan b Sohail Khan		8
2	Kashif Rasheed	lbw b Rajesh Ramesh	28	lbw b Sohail Khan		4
3	Atiq-ur-Rehman	c Rajesh Ramesh b Sohail Khan	4	(9) c Ahmed Zeeshan b Sohail Khan		6
4	*Aamer Sajjad	c Ahmed Zeeshan b Sohail Khan	22	(5) b Sohail Khan		40
5	Bilal Khilji	lbw b Sohail Khan	39	(6) c Saeed Bin Nasir b Sohail Khan		80
6	Nawaz Sardar	c Ahmed Zeeshan b Sohail Khan	53	(3) lbw b Sohail Khan		98
7	Sunny Irshad	b Sohail Khan	2	c Mansoor Ali b Sohail Khan		75
8	Aqeel Ahmed	c Ashraf Ali b Haaris Ayaz	0	(4) c Ashraf Ali b Rajesh Ramesh		6
9	Farooq Iqbal	c Mansoor Ali b Haaris Ayaz	4	(10) lbw b Sohail Khan		0
10	Sarfraz Ahmed	b Sohail Khan	26	(8) b Sohail Khan		2
11	Azharullah	not out	1	not out		2
	Extras	b 4, lb 5, nb 6	15	b 17, lb 9, w 3, nb 3		32
			200			**353**

FoW (1): 1-18, 2-33, 3-45, 4-68, 5-115, 6-167, 7-168, 8-168, 9-179, 10-200
FoW (2): 1-5, 2-42, 3-57, 4-157, 5-188, 6-334, 7-334, 8-347, 9-350, 10-353

SUI SOUTHERN GAS CORPORATION

1	Asif Zakir	lbw b Sarfraz Ahmed	0	lbw b Azharullah		4
2	Mohammad Zafar	c Ahmed Said b Sarfraz Ahmed	11	c Ahmed Said b Sarfraz Ahmed		0
3	Ashraf Ali	c Ahmed Said b Sarfraz Ahmed	35	lbw b Farooq Iqbal		21
4	Saeed Bin Nasir	c Sunny Irshad b Sarfraz Ahmed	1	b Azharullah		104
5	*Atiq-uz-Zaman	c Ahmed Said b Azharullah	18	lbw b Azharullah		91
6	Mansoor Ali	c Bilal Khilji b Sarfraz Ahmed	24			
7	†Ahmed Zeeshan	b Aqeel Ahmed	51	(6) not out		16
8	Rajesh Ramesh	c Ahmed Said b Sarfraz Ahmed	0			
9	Haaris Ayaz	run out	64	(7) c Bilal Khilji b Aqeel Ahmed		7
10	Mansoor Ahmed	b Azharullah	1			
11	Sohail Khan	not out	8	(8) not out		0
	Extras	b 6, lb 5, w 1, nb 1	13	b 6, lb 7, w 1, nb 7		21
			226	(6 wickets)		**264**

FoW (1): 1-0, 2-23, 3-29, 4-63, 5-75, 6-117, 7-120, 8-197, 9-198, 10-226
FoW (2): 1-1, 2-13, 3-68, 4-227, 5-248, 6-261

Sui Southern Gas Corporation Bowling

	O	M	R	W		O	M	R	W	
Sohail Khan	19	2	80	7		33.5	7	109	9	1w
Rajesh Ramesh	10	2	32	1		21	5	69	1	2w
Mansoor Ahmed	15	2	45	0	5nb	17	4	52	0	3nb
Haaris Ayaz	17	3	34	2	1nb	24	2	65	0	
Mansoor Ali						(5) 4	0	18	0	
Asif Zakir						(6) 4	1	14	0	

Water and Power Development Authority Bowling

	O	M	R	W		O	M	R	W	
Sarfraz Ahmed	28	9	48	6	1w	24	8	62	1	
Azharullah	27	2	89	2		21	4	76	3	
Nawaz Sardar	10	2	25	0	1nb	2	0	9	0	
Aqeel Ahmed	11	1	40	1		(6) 10	1	47	1	
Bilal Khilji	1	1	0	0						
Farooq Iqbal	6	0	13	0		(5) 18	6	46	1	1w
Sunny Irshad						(4) 1	0	11	0	7nb

Umpires: Ahsan Raza and Rashid Khan.   Referee: Anwar Khan.   Toss: Water and Power Development Authority
Close of Play: 1st day: Sui Southern Gas Corporation (1) 63-3 (Ashraf Ali 29*, Atiq-uz-Zaman 18*, 23 overs); 2nd day: Water and Power Development Authority (2) 43-2 (Nawaz Sardar 30*, Aqeel Ahmed 0*, 21 overs); 3rd day: Water and Power Development Authority (2) 353 all out.
Saeed Bin Nasir's 104 took 208 balls in 266 minutes and included 11 fours.

NATIONAL BANK OF PAKISTAN v SIALKOT

Played at Multan Cricket Stadium, December 24, 25, 26, 27, 2007.
Quaid-e-Azam Trophy 2007/08 - Group A
National Bank of Pakistan won by 107 runs.   (Points: National Bank of Pakistan 9, Sialkot 0)

NATIONAL BANK OF PAKISTAN

1	Nasir Jamshed	c Mohammad Ayub b Mohammad Ali	13	c Kamran Younis b Mohammad Imran	48
2	†Rashid Riaz	lbw b Tariq Mahmood	48	c Mohammad Ayub b Mohammad Imran	20
3	Naumanullah	c Ahmed Butt b Mohammad Imran	34	st Ahmed Butt b Tariq Mahmood	4
4	Shahid Yousuf	c Ahmed Butt b Mohammad Ali	13	lbw b Mohammad Imran	46
5	Fawad Alam	b Nayyer Abbas	33	c Nayyer Abbas b Mohammad Imran	46
6	Qaiser Abbas	c Naeemuddin b Mohammad Ali	9	not out	23
7	Naved Latif	c Adeel Malik b Mohammad Ali	100		
8	*Mansoor Amjad	c Mohammad Ayub b Mohammad Imran	32	(7) not out	29
9	Imran Javed	not out	26		
10	Wahab Riaz	lbw b Nayyer Abbas	2		
11	Uzair-ul-Haq	c Adeel Malik b Tariq Mahmood	9		
	Extras	lb 8, w 3, nb 14	25	lb 1, w 3, nb 5	9
			344	(5 wickets, declared)	**225**

FoW (1): 1-27, 2-90, 3-116, 4-116, 5-152, 6-181, 7-288, 8-307, 9-317, 10-344
FoW (2): 1-69, 2-75, 3-75, 4-154, 5-182

SIALKOT

1	Naeemuddin	c Uzair-ul-Haq b Wahab Riaz	24	c Imran Javed b Wahab Riaz	25
2	Kamran Younis	c Qaiser Abbas b Wahab Riaz	43	c Rashid Riaz b Imran Javed	42
3	Haris Sohail	c Mansoor Amjad b Imran Javed	64	b Wahab Riaz	58
4	Faisal Khan	c Naved Latif b Wahab Riaz	0	c Shahid Yousuf b Uzair-ul-Haq	41
5	*Mohammad Ayub	b Uzair-ul-Haq	13	b Uzair-ul-Haq	10
6	Adeel Malik	c Rashid Riaz b Uzair-ul-Haq	0	c Uzair-ul-Haq b Mansoor Amjad	49
7	†Ahmed Butt	c Rashid Riaz b Uzair-ul-Haq	9	not out	2
8	Nayyer Abbas	c and b Wahab Riaz	17	c Uzair-ul-Haq b Wahab Riaz	8
9	Tariq Mahmood	not out	11	b Mansoor Amjad	3
10	Mohammad Imran	b Wahab Riaz	0	c Rashid Riaz b Wahab Riaz	3
11	Mohammad Ali	lbw b Mansoor Amjad	2	c Rashid Riaz b Wahab Riaz	0
	Extras	b 1, lb 6, w 2, nb 11	20	b 4, lb 5, w 2, nb 7	18
			203		**259**

FoW (1): 1-39, 2-87, 3-90, 4-135, 5-135, 6-155, 7-189, 8-189, 9-189, 10-203
FoW (2): 1-64, 2-76, 3-112, 4-126, 5-218, 6-230, 7-252, 8-255, 9-259, 10-259

Sialkot Bowling

	O	M	R	W		O	M	R	W	
Mohammad Imran	27	7	84	2	8nb	19	3	66	4	3w,3nb
Mohammad Ali	28	4	96	4	2w,4nb	4	0	34	0	2nb
Nayyer Abbas	29	7	83	2	1w,2nb	8	0	47	0	
Tariq Mahmood	23.5	4	65	2		7	0	58	1	
Mohammad Ayub	2	0	8	0		3	0	19	0	

National Bank of Pakistan Bowling

	O	M	R	W		O	M	R	W	
Wahab Riaz	23	6	64	5	1w,4nb	20.2	2	85	5	1w,3nb
Uzair-ul-Haq	17	6	62	3	1w,7nb	11	2	45	0	1w,4nb
Imran Javed	16	7	31	1		16	3	49	1	
Fawad Alam	4	0	11	0						
Mansoor Amjad	5.2	0	28	1	(4)	17	4	66	2	
Qaiser Abbas	1	1	0	0	(5)	3	3	0	0	
Naumanullah					(6)	3	1	5	0	

Umpires: Aftab Gillani and Jamil Kamran.   Referee: Mohammad Javed.   Toss: Sialkot

Close of Play: 1st day: National Bank of Pakistan (1) 256-6 (Naved Latif 62*, Mansoor Amjad 27*, 83 overs); 2nd day: Sialkot (1) 163-6 (Haris Sohail 56*, Nayyer Abbas 3*, 49 overs); 3rd day: Sialkot (2) 33-0 (Naeemuddin 7*, Kamran Younis 25*, 8 overs).

This match is the replay of the match started on October 20th. Naved Latif's 100 took 159 balls in 191 minutes and included 15 fours and 2 sixes.

FAISALABAD v LAHORE RAVI

Played at Iqbal Stadium, Faisalabad, December 26, 27, 28, 29, 2007.
Quaid-e-Azam Trophy 2007/08 - Group A
Match drawn. (Points: Faisalabad 0, Lahore Ravi 0)

FAISALABAD

1	Usman Arshad	b Waqas Ahmed	23
2	Asif Hussain	b Waqas Ahmed	3
3	Ammar Mahmood	c sub (Saad Nasim) b Imran Haider	76
4	*Ijaz Ahmed	c Shahbaz Butt b Junaid Zia	174
5	Hamza Zaheer	c Abid Ali b Imran Haider	8
6	†Mohammad Salman	c Shahbaz Butt b Imran Haider	10
7	Ahmed Hayat	c Junaid Zia b Imran Haider	20
8	Asad Zarar	c Abid Ali b Imran Haider	80
9	Ali Raza	c Kashif Shafi b Junaid Zia	1
10	Saadat Munir	c Abid Ali b Imran Haider	24
11	Hasan Mahmood	not out	8
	Extras	b 1, lb 1, w 11, nb 9	22
			449

FoW (1): 1-26, 2-27, 3-214, 4-248, 5-272, 6-310, 7-359, 8-363, 9-429, 10-449

LAHORE RAVI

1	Ahmed Shehzad	b Saadat Munir	37
2	Ashfaq Ahmed	lbw b Saadat Munir	25
3	Abid Ali	not out	28
4	Kashif Siddiq	c Asif Hussain b Ahmed Hayat	44
5	†Shahbaz Butt	not out	13
6	*Junaid Zia		
7	Waqas Ahmed		
8	Kashif Shafi		
9	Shahab Basharat		
10	Usama Aftab		
11	Imran Haider		
	Extras	lb 2, nb 6	8
		(3 wickets)	155

FoW (1): 1-54, 2-76, 3-131

Lahore Ravi Bowling

	O	M	R	W	
Junaid Zia	39	8	157	2	11w,5nb
Waqas Ahmed	23	3	68	2	1nb
Kashif Shafi	12	4	31	0	
Shahab Basharat	3	1	20	0	
Usama Aftab	9	1	39	0	
Imran Haider	27.5	2	132	6	3nb

Faisalabad Bowling

	O	M	R	W	
Ahmed Hayat	11	1	44	1	
Ali Raza	9	1	29	0	4nb
Asad Zarar	2	0	16	0	
Saadat Munir	18	7	34	2	1nb
Hasan Mahmood	7	3	10	0	1nb
Ijaz Ahmed	5	0	20	0	

Umpires: Hakeem Shah and Mian Mohammad Aslam. Referee: Abdus Sami. Toss: Faisalabad

Close of Play: 1st day: Faisalabad (1) 330-6 (Ijaz Ahmed 167*, Asad Zarar 6*, 85 overs); 2nd day: Lahore Ravi (1) 155-3 (Abid Ali 28*, Shahbaz Butt 13*, 52 overs); 3rd day: No play.

Ijaz Ahmed's 174 took 265 balls in 316 minutes and included 23 fours and 2 sixes. The last two days were called off following the assassination of Benazir Bhutto. PCB first announced the match would be replayed but then later reversed this decision.

HYDERABAD v PAKISTAN CUSTOMS

Played at Niaz Stadium, Hyderabad, December 26, 27, 28, 29, 2007.
Quaid-e-Azam Trophy 2007/08 - Group A
Match drawn.   (Points: Hyderabad 0, Pakistan Customs 0)

HYDERABAD

1	Aqeel Anjum	not out	73
2	Azeem Ghumman	c Mohammad Hasan b Sajjad Hussain	9
3	Faisal Athar	not out	114
4	Rizwan Ahmed		
5	*Shahid Qambrani		
6	Shabih Haider		
7	Nauman Ali		
8	Shoaib Laghari		
9	†Hanif Malik		
10	Mir Ali		
11	Naeem-ur-Rehman		
	Extras	b 3, lb 1, nb 7	11
		(1 wicket)	207

FoW (1): 1-25

PAKISTAN CUSTOMS

1   *Zahoor Elahi
2   Murtaza Hussain
3   Asif Iqbal
4   Rehan Rafiq
5   Yasir Hussain
6   Mohammad Nabi
7   †Mohammad Hasan
8   Yasir Shah
9   Raees Amjad
10 Tahir Maqsood
11 Sajjad Hussain

Pakistan Customs Bowling

	O	M	R	W	
Raees Amjad	15	3	54	0	5nb
Sajjad Hussain	13	2	39	1	
Tahir Maqsood	6	0	16	0	1nb
Murtaza Hussain	13	3	34	0	
Yasir Shah	10	0	42	0	
Yasir Hussain	8	0	18	0	1nb

Umpires: Riazuddin and Saleem Badar.   Referee: Mahmood Rasheed.   Toss: Pakistan Customs

Close of Play: 1st day: No play; 2nd day: Hyderabad (1) 207-1 (Aqeel Anjum 73*, Faisal Athar 114*, 65 overs); 3rd day: No play.

Faisal Athar's 114 took 170 balls in 219 minutes and included 11 fours and 3 sixes. The last two days were called off following the assassination of Benazir Bhutto. PCB first announced the match would be replayed but then later reversed this decision.

ISLAMABAD v PESHAWAR

Played at Diamond Club Ground, Islamabad, December 26, 27, 28, 29, 2007.
Quaid-e-Azam Trophy 2007/08 - Group B
Match drawn.   (Points: Islamabad 3, Peshawar 0)

PESHAWAR

1	Usman Zeb	c Shehzad Azam b Rauf Akbar	26
2	Gauhar Ali	c Naeem Anjum b Rauf Akbar	6
3	Nawaz Ahmed	c Naeem Anjum b Rauf Akbar	10
4	Mahfooz Sabri	c Naeem Anjum b Rauf Akbar	0
5	*Akbar Badshah	c Fayyaz Ahmed b Rauf Akbar	11
6	Sajjad Ahmed	not out	62
7	Azam Jan	b Ashar Zaidi	16
8	†Shehzad Khan	run out (Fayyaz Ahmed/Imad Wasim)	0
9	Riaz Afridi	c Imad Wasim b Ameer Khan	44
10	Nauman Habib	c Ashar Zaidi b Ameer Khan	1
11	Hidayatullah Khan	c Naeem Anjum b Ameer Khan	10
	Extras	lb 2, w 3, nb 11	16
			202

FoW (1): 1-20, 2-37, 3-42, 4-54, 5-70, 6-102, 7-105, 8-170, 9-185, 10-202

ISLAMABAD

1	Fakhar Hussain	b Nauman Habib	8
2	Umair Khan	lbw b Riaz Afridi	5
3	*Ashar Zaidi	c Mahfooz Sabri b Riaz Afridi	4
4	Fayyaz Ahmed	c Usman Zeb b Akbar Badshah	118
5	Asadullah Sumari	c sub (Inamullah) b Nawaz Ahmed	137
6	Ameer Khan	lbw b Usman Zeb	12
7	†Naeem Anjum	c Gauhar Ali b Usman Zeb	70
8	Imad Wasim	not out	27
9	Rauf Akbar	b Usman Zeb	1
10	Shehzad Azam	lbw b Riaz Afridi	5
11	Yasin Bari	not out	0
	Extras	b 4, lb 3, w 4, nb 8	19
		(9 wickets)	406

FoW (1): 1-9, 2-13, 3-19, 4-225, 5-239, 6-348, 7-388, 8-390, 9-395

Islamabad Bowling

	O	M	R	W	
Rauf Akbar	13	1	48	5	3nb
Shehzad Azam	6	0	31	0	2w,3nb
Yasin Bari	11	2	44	0	1w
Imad Wasim	11	1	53	0	5nb
Ashar Zaidi	5	1	10	1	
Ameer Khan	6.2	0	14	3	

Peshawar Bowling

	O	M	R	W	
Riaz Afridi	31	5	112	3	4nb
Nauman Habib	14	5	38	1	1nb
Akbar Badshah	28	8	87	1	2w,1nb
Hidayatullah Khan	9	0	52	0	
Usman Zeb	17	3	72	3	2nb
Nawaz Ahmed	7	0	24	1	2w
Mahfooz Sabri	2	0	14	0	

Umpires: Akmal Hayat and Mohammad Arif. Referee: Ishtiaq Ahmed.   Toss: Peshawar

Close of Play: 1st day: Islamabad (1) 86-3 (Fayyaz Ahmed 44*, Asadullah Sumari 20*, 24.4 overs); 2nd day: Islamabad (1) 406-9 (Imad Wasim 27*, Yasin Bari 0*, 108 overs); 3rd day: No play.

Fayyaz Ahmed's 118 took 167 balls in 248 minutes and included 21 fours. Asadullah Sumari's 137 took 271 balls in 342 minutes and included 16 fours and 2 sixes. The last two days were called off following the assassination of Benazir Bhutto. PCB first announced the match would be replayed but then later reversed this decision.

Pakistan in 2007/08

KARACHI BLUES v PAKISTAN INTERNATIONAL AIRLINES

Played at Gaddafi Stadium, Lahore, December 26, 27, 28, 29, 2007.
Quaid-e-Azam Trophy 2007/08 - Group B
Match drawn.   (Points: Karachi Blues 0, Pakistan International Airlines 0)

KARACHI BLUES
1	Shadab Kabir	lbw b Anwar Ali	4
2	Ali Asad	c Sarfraz Ahmed b Anwar Ali	18
3	†Naved Khan	c Faisal Iqbal b Anwar Ali	0
4	Sheharyar Ghani	c Kamran Sajid b Tahir Khan	122
5	Fazal Subhan	b Aizaz Cheema	6
6	Tariq Haroon	c Agha Sabir b Tahir Khan	34
7	*Mansoor Khan	b Aizaz Cheema	1
8	Azam Hussain	b Anwar Ali	3
9	Tabish Khan	run out	52
10	Faraz Ahmed	not out	11
11	Abdul Ameer	c Agha Sabir b Aizaz Cheema	0
	Extras	b 9, lb 9, nb 1	19
			270

FoW (1): 1-10, 2-10, 3-31, 4-62, 5-131, 6-132, 7-165, 8-232, 9-270, 10-270

PAKISTAN INTERNATIONAL AIRLINES
1	Yasir Hameed	c Mansoor Khan b Faraz Ahmed	14
2	Khurram Manzoor	c Ali Asad b Abdul Ameer	15
3	Agha Sabir	b Azam Hussain	19
4	*Faisal Iqbal	c Naved Khan b Faraz Ahmed	11
5	Fahad Iqbal	c Naved Khan b Faraz Ahmed	4
6	Kamran Sajid	c sub (Faraz Patel) b Azam Hussain	41
7	†Sarfraz Ahmed	c Sheharyar Ghani b Azam Hussain	76
8	Anwar Ali	not out	4
9	Tahir Khan	not out	6
10	Aizaz Cheema		
11	Najaf Shah		
	Extras	nb 11	11
		(7 wickets)	201

FoW (1): 1-29, 2-35, 3-56, 4-60, 5-93, 6-186, 7-191

Pakistan International Airlines Bowling
	O	M	R	W	
Najaf Shah	11	2	37	0	1nb
Anwar Ali	25	7	70	4	
Aizaz Cheema	19.5	7	56	3	
Kamran Sajid	6	1	14	0	
Tahir Khan	21	3	63	2	
Yasir Hameed	4	0	12	0	

Karachi Blues Bowling
	O	M	R	W	
Tabish Khan	6	2	14	0	
Abdul Ameer	12	1	50	1	5nb
Faraz Ahmed	15	4	36	3	6nb
Tariq Haroon	16	6	20	0	
Azam Hussain	21	6	57	3	
Mansoor Khan	7	0	24	0	

Umpires: Ahsan Raza and Zameer Haider. Referee: Saadat Ali.   Toss: Pakistan International Airlines

Close of Play: 1st day: Karachi Blues (1) 260-8 (Tabish Khan 48*, Faraz Ahmed 9*, 83 overs); 2nd day: Pakistan International Airlines (1) 201-7 (Anwar Ali 4*, Tahir Khan 6*, 77 overs); 3rd day: No play.

Sheharyar Ghani's 122 took 274 balls in 301 minutes and included 22 fours. The last two days were called off following the assassination of Benazir Bhutto. PCB first announced the match would be replayed but then later reversed this decision.

KARACHI WHITES v HABIB BANK LIMITED

Played at United Bank Limited Sports Complex, Karachi, December 26, 27, 28, 29, 2007.
Quaid-e-Azam Trophy 2007/08 - Group A
Match drawn.   (Points: Karachi Whites 0, Habib Bank Limited 0)

HABIB BANK LIMITED

1	Fahad Masood	c Faraz Ahmed b Fahad Khan	33
2	Rafatullah Mohmand	b Mohammad Hasnain	1
3	Abdur Rehman	c Mohammad Hasnain b Tanvir Ahmed	47
4	Hasan Raza	b Fahad Khan	65
5	*Shahid Afridi	run out (sub [Atif Ali])	70
6	Khaqan Arsal	c Mohammad Hasnain b Fahad Khan	0
7	Aftab Alam	b Tabish Nawab	63
8	†Humayun Farhat	b Fahad Khan	9
9	Kamran Hussain	c Javed Mansoor b Tanvir Ahmed	59
10	Sajid Shah	b Tabish Nawab	25
11	Mohammad Aslam	not out	0
	Extras	b 1, lb 2, w 1, nb 28	32
			404

FoW (1): 1-4, 2-58, 3-111, 4-233, 5-233, 6-237, 7-257, 8-360, 9-383, 10-404

KARACHI WHITES

1	*Khalid Latif	c Fahad Masood b Kamran Hussain	5
2	Asad Shafiq	c Humayun Farhat b Fahad Masood	17
3	Shan Masood	c Humayun Farhat b Kamran Hussain	10
4	Wajihuddin	c Rafatullah Mohmand b Fahad Masood	0
5	Afsar Nawaz	c Hasan Raza b Fahad Masood	66
6	†Javed Mansoor	b Fahad Masood	1
7	Tanvir Ahmed	b Fahad Masood	1
8	Faraz Ahmed	c Rafatullah Mohmand b Kamran Hussain	44
9	Mohammad Hasnain	not out	16
10	Tabish Nawab	b Kamran Hussain	0
11	Fahad Khan	not out	1
	Extras	lb 1, nb 2	3
		(9 wickets)	164

FoW (1): 1-10, 2-26, 3-26, 4-32, 5-33, 6-37, 7-141, 8-145, 9-145

Karachi Whites Bowling

	O	M	R	W	
Tanvir Ahmed	20	1	76	2	18nb
Mohammad Hasnain	15	2	48	1	4nb
Fahad Khan	21	5	85	4	1w
Faraz Ahmed	27	3	92	0	4nb
Tabish Nawab	24.1	5	100	2	2nb

Habib Bank Limited Bowling

	O	M	R	W	
Kamran Hussain	15	3	37	4	
Sajid Shah	3	0	7	0	
Fahad Masood	11	1	42	5	2nb
Abdur Rehman	17	1	39	0	
Mohammad Aslam	11	2	29	0	
Rafatullah Mohmand	1	0	9	0	

Umpires: Ahmed Shahab and Iftikhar Malik. Referee: Ilyas Khan.   Toss: Karachi Whites

Close of Play: 1st day: Habib Bank Limited (1) 329-7 (Aftab Alam 40*, Kamran Hussain 39*, 83 overs); 2nd day: Karachi Whites (1) 164-9 (Mohammad Hasnain 16*, Fahad Khan 1*, 58 overs); 3rd day: No play.

The last two days were called off following the assassination of Benazir Bhutto. PCB first announced the match would be replayed but then later reversed this decision.

KHAN RESEARCH LABORATORIES v RAWALPINDI

Played at Khan Research Laboratories Ground, Rawalpindi, December 26, 27, 28, 29, 2007.
Quaid-e-Azam Trophy 2007/08 - Group B
Match drawn.   (Points: Khan Research Laboratories 0, Rawalpindi 0)

RAWALPINDI

1	Umar Amin	c Zulfiqar Jan b Sohail Tanvir	22
2	Usman Ashraf	b Sohail Tanvir	0
3	Hamid Riaz	lbw b Bilal Asad	30
4	*Babar Naeem	c Zulfiqar Jan b Akhtar Ayub	13
5	Fawad Hussain	not out	103
6	Usman Saeed	c and b Bilal Asad	0
7	Yasim Murtaza	lbw b Yasir Arafat	23
8	†Sajid Mahmood	c and b Saeed Ajmal	19
9	Yasir Ali	c Zulfiqar Jan b Saeed Ajmal	0
10	Rizwan Akbar	c Zulfiqar Jan b Saeed Ajmal	4
11	Yasir Aamer	lbw b Akhtar Ayub	11
	Extras	b 8, lb 19, w 5, nb 11	43

268

FoW (1): 1-4, 2-43, 3-72, 4-88, 5-88, 6-173, 7-234, 8-240, 9-249, 10-268

KHAN RESEARCH LABORATORIES

1	Azhar Ali	c Babar Naeem b Yasir Ali	2
2	Fahad-ul-Haq	c Sajid Mahmood b Yasir Ali	7
3	Saeed Anwar	c Yasim Murtaza b Rizwan Akbar	2
4	Bazid Khan	c Yasim Murtaza b Rizwan Akbar	0
5	Ali Naqvi	c Yasim Murtaza b Yasir Ali	7
6	Bilal Asad	b Babar Naeem	43
7	Yasir Arafat	not out	65
8	Sohail Tanvir	not out	11
9	*†Zulfiqar Jan		
10	Akhtar Ayub		
11	Saeed Ajmal		
	Extras	b 1, w 2, nb 8	11

(6 wickets)   148

FoW (1): 1-4, 2-7, 3-12, 4-19, 5-29, 6-111

Khan Research Laboratories Bowling

	O	M	R	W	
Yasir Arafat	16	5	56	1	1w,1nb
Sohail Tanvir	18	1	76	2	2w,10nb
Akhtar Ayub	16.2	2	51	2	2w
Bilal Asad	10	5	17	2	
Saeed Ajmal	18	8	26	3	
Ali Naqvi	2	0	9	0	
Saeed Anwar	7	2	6	0	

Rawalpindi Bowling

	O	M	R	W	
Yasir Ali	19	5	38	3	1w,4nb
Rizwan Akbar	21	9	39	2	1w,1nb
Yasim Murtaza	5	1	26	0	
Yasir Aamer	4	0	22	0	3nb
Babar Naeem	6	2	22	1	

Umpires: Akbar Khan and Nadeem Ghauri. Referee: Arshad Pervez.   Toss: Khan Research Laboratories

Close of Play: 1st day: Rawalpindi (1) 255-9 (Fawad Hussain 102*, Yasir Aamer 0*, 82 overs); 2nd day: Khan Research Laboratories (1) 148-6 (Yasir Arafat 65*, Sohail Tanvir 11*, 55 overs); 3rd day: No play.

Fawad Hussain's 103 took 213 balls in 285 minutes and included 14 fours. The last two days were called off following the assassination of Benazir Bhutto. PCB first announced the match would be replayed but then later reversed this decision.

LAHORE SHALIMAR v ABBOTTABAD

Played at Lahore City Cricket Association Ground, December 26, 27, 2007.
Quaid-e-Azam Trophy 2007/08 - Group B
Abbottabad won by an innings and 79 runs.   (Points: Lahore Shalimar 0, Abbottabad 9)

ABBOTTABAD

1	*Fawad Khan	c Ali Raza b Asif Raza	17
2	†Ghulam Mohammad	c Ali Raza b Mohammad Saeed	32
3	Wajid Ali	lbw b Mohammad Naved	3
4	Adnan Raees	run out (Asif Raza)	39
5	Riaz Kail	c Mohammad Hussain b Mohammad Saeed	28
6	Iftikhar Mahmood	b Mohammad Saeed	14
7	Khalid Usman	c Ali Raza b Mohammad Naved	66
8	Rashid Mansoor	c Ali Raza b Mohammad Naved	0
9	Junaid Khan	c Ali Raza b Mohammad Saeed	7
10	Noor-ul-Amin	not out	17
11	Armaghan Elahi	c Mohammad Hussain b Mohammad Naved	0
	Extras	lb 6, w 4, nb 3	13
			236

FoW (1): 1-33, 2-43, 3-77, 4-111, 5-135, 6-147, 7-148, 8-161, 9-236, 10-236

LAHORE SHALIMAR

1	Junaid Malik	c Adnan Raees b Armaghan Elahi	3	c Wajid Ali b Armaghan Elahi	1
2	Haroon Rasheed	b Armaghan Elahi	1	(3) lbw b Armaghan Elahi	4
3	Ahmed Butt	c Fawad Khan b Junaid Khan	6	(6) lbw b Rashid Mansoor	17
4	Usman Salahuddin	b Armaghan Elahi	0	c Wajid Ali b Rashid Mansoor	26
5	Suleman Khan	lbw b Junaid Khan	1	lbw b Junaid Khan	0
6	Usman Malik	c Riaz Kail b Armaghan Elahi	6	(10) not out	4
7	Mohammad Hussain	b Junaid Khan	0	c Fawad Khan b Rashid Mansoor	0
8	*†Ali Raza	c Junaid Khan b Rashid Mansoor	7	(2) c Fawad Khan b Armaghan Elahi	8
9	Mohammad Saeed	b Armaghan Elahi	9	(8) c Khalid Usman b Rashid Mansoor	15
10	Asif Raza	c Iftikhar Mahmood b Armaghan Elahi	3	(9) c Khalid Usman b Armaghan Elahi	14
11	Mohammad Naved	not out	0	c sub (Sajjad Ahmed) b Rashid Mansoor	0
	Extras	lb 6, w 2, nb 4	12	b 2, lb 6, w 10, nb 2	20
			48		109

FoW (1): 1-3, 2-8, 3-9, 4-12, 5-14, 6-14, 7-35, 8-39, 9-48, 10-48
FoW (2): 1-8, 2-14, 3-24, 4-29, 5-70, 6-71, 7-71, 8-95, 9-109, 10-109

Lahore Shalimar Bowling

	O	M	R	W	
Mohammad Naved	30.3	6	77	4	1w
Asif Raza	13	2	47	1	ˆ3nb
Mohammad Saeed	13	2	54	4	3w
Usman Malik	8	2	30	0	
Mohammad Hussain	3	0	22	0	

Abbottabad Bowling

	O	M	R	W		O	M	R	W	
Junaid Khan	11	6	22	3	1w	12	6	23	1	
Armaghan Elahi	11.4	5	16	6	1w,4nb	17	4	58	4	7w,2nb
Rashid Mansoor	1	0	4	1		8.3	3	19	5	2w
Adnan Raees					(4)	3	2	1	0	1w

Umpires: Khalid Mahmood and Zaheer Ahmed.   Referee: Pervez Akhtar.   Toss: Lahore Shalimar

Close of Play: 1st day: Lahore Shalimar (1) 19-6 (Usman Malik 0*, Ali Raza 4*, 9 overs).

The match was scheduled for four days but completed in two.

SUI NORTHERN GAS PIPELINES LIMITED v QUETTA

Played at Gaddafi Stadium, Lahore, December 26, 27, 28, 29, 2007.
Quaid-e-Azam Trophy 2007/08 - Group B
Match drawn. (Points: Sui Northern Gas Pipelines Limited 3, Quetta 0)

QUETTA

1	Shoaib Khan	c Adnan Rasool b Adil Raza	21
2	†Hameedullah Khan	c Mohammad Hafeez b Adil Raza	0
3	Taimur Ali	b Faisal Rasheed	23
4	Sabir Hussain	c Farhan Asghar b Faisal Rasheed	37
5	*Nasim Khan	c Misbah-ul-Haq b Adnan Rasool	26
6	Jalat Khan	c Faisal Rasheed b Adnan Rasool	21
7	Arun Lal	c Farhan Asghar b Adil Raza	13
8	Naseer Khan	c Samiullah Khan b Adnan Rasool	0
9	Faisal Irfan	run out (Majid Jahangir)	3
10	Sher Hasan	not out	14
11	Nazar Hussain	c Misbah-ul-Haq b Mohammad Hafeez	19
	Extras	lb 4, w 1, nb 13	18
			195

FoW (1): 1-11, 2-49, 3-49, 4-109, 5-137, 6-143, 7-147, 8-152, 9-168, 10-195

SUI NORTHERN GAS PIPELINES LIMITED

1	*Mohammad Hafeez	c Hameedullah Khan b Jalat Khan	163
2	Yasir Arafat	c Hameedullah Khan b Arun Lal	45
3	Umar Akmal	not out	186
4	Majid Jahangir	c Hameedullah Khan b Jalat Khan	4
5	Misbah-ul-Haq	not out	32
6	Khurram Shehzad		
7	†Farhan Asghar		
8	Samiullah Khan		
9	Adil Raza		
10	Adnan Rasool		
11	Faisal Rasheed		
	Extras	lb 4, w 2, nb 15	21
		(3 wickets)	451

FoW (1): 1-128, 2-356, 3-370

Sui Northern Gas Pipelines Limited Bowling

	O	M	R	W	
Samiullah Khan	13	2	44	0	
Adil Raza	20	3	79	3	1w,10nb
Faisal Rasheed	9	2	45	2	2nb
Adnan Rasool	9	0	23	3	1nb
Mohammad Hafeez	0.2	0	0	1	

Quetta Bowling

	O	M	R	W	
Faisal Irfan	16	2	41	0	1nb
Sher Hasan	20	1	99	0	1w,9nb
Nazar Hussain	14	3	51	0	1w
Arun Lal	11	2	44	1	1nb
Jalat Khan	17.1	1	98	2	3nb
Naseer Khan	20	0	98	0	1nb
Shoaib Khan	1.5	0	16	0	

Umpires: Ehtesham-ul-Haq and Raweed Khan. Referee: Khalid Niazi. Toss: Quetta

Close of Play: 1st day: Sui Northern Gas Pipelines Limited (1) 75-0 (Mohammad Hafeez 45*, Yasir Arafat 23*, 18.2 overs); 2nd day: Sui Northern Gas Pipelines Limited (1) 451-3 (Umar Akmal 186*, Misbah-ul-Haq 32*, 100 overs); 3rd day: No play.

Mohammad Hafeez's 163 took 265 balls in 355 minutes and included 23 fours. Umar Akmal's 186 took 170 balls in 240 minutes and included 20 fours and 4 sixes. The last two days were called off following the assassination of Benazir Bhutto. PCB first announced the match would be replayed but then later reversed this decision.

NATIONAL BANK OF PAKISTAN v SUI SOUTHERN GAS CORPORATION

Played at National Bank of Pakistan Sports Complex, Karachi, December 29, 30, 31, 2007, January 1, 2008.
Quaid-e-Azam Trophy 2007/08 - Group A
Match abandoned. **(Points: National Bank of Pakistan 0, Sui Southern Gas Corporation 0)**

Umpires: Nadeem Ghauri and Rasheed Bhatti. Referee: Anwar Khan.

This match was not played following the assassination of Benazir Bhutto.

SIALKOT v WATER AND POWER DEVELOPMENT AUTHORITY

Played at Jinnah Stadium, Sialkot, December 29, 30, 31, 2007, January 1, 2008.
Quaid-e-Azam Trophy 2007/08 - Group A
Match abandoned. **(Points: Sialkot 0, Water and Power Development Authority 0)**

Umpires: Atiq Khan and Ijaz Ahmed. Referee: Aziz-ur-Rehman.

This match was not played following the assassination of Benazir Bhutto.

HABIB BANK LIMITED v SUI NORTHERN GAS PIPELINES LIMITED

Played at National Stadium, Karachi, January 7, 8, 9, 10, 11, 2008.
Quaid-e-Azam Trophy 2007/08 - Final
Match drawn.

SUI NORTHERN GAS PIPELINES LIMITED

1	*Mohammad Hafeez	c Younis Khan b Fahad Masood	69	lbw b Kamran Hussain		0
2	Yasir Arafat	c Younis Khan b Kamran Hussain	12	c Fahad Masood b Danish Kaneria		31
3	Umar Akmal	c Humayun Farhat b Kamran Hussain	2	c Danish Kaneria b Kamran Hussain		4
4	Azhar Shafiq	c Younis Khan b Kamran Hussain	29	lbw b Kamran Hussain		0
5	Misbah-ul-Haq	lbw b Fahad Masood	64	c Humayun Farhat b Kamran Hussain		161
6	Khurram Shehzad	b Fahad Masood	27	lbw b Abdur Rehman		40
7	†Adnan Akmal	lbw b Danish Kaneria	54	c Humayun Farhat b Danish Kaneria		2
8	Imran Ali	b Danish Kaneria	17	not out		18
9	Samiullah Khan	c Fahad Masood b Danish Kaneria	17	b Fahad Masood		0
10	Asad Ali	not out	4	c Shahid Afridi b Danish Kaneria		24
11	Adil Raza	c Humayun Farhat b Kamran Hussain	5			
	Extras	b 7, lb 12, w 2, nb 30	51	lb 8, nb 16		24
			351	(9 wickets, declared)		**304**

FoW (1): 1-31, 2-35, 3-119, 4-149, 5-227, 6-245, 7-276, 8-330, 9-341, 10-351
FoW (2): 1-0, 2-14, 3-14, 4-72, 5-179, 6-194, 7-257, 8-263, 9-304

HABIB BANK LIMITED

1	Rafatullah Mohmand	c Adnan Akmal b Asad Ali	8	not out	65
2	†Humayun Farhat	lbw b Samiullah Khan	7		
3	Younis Khan	lbw b Samiullah Khan	5		
4	Hasan Raza	lbw b Samiullah Khan	50		
5	*Shahid Afridi	b Asad Ali	9		
6	Aftab Alam	b Asad Ali	4		
7	Kamran Hussain	c Khurram Shehzad b Imran Ali	38	(2) c Umar Akmal b Mohammad Hafeez	89
8	Abdur Rehman	lbw b Imran Ali	3		
9	Sajid Shah	lbw b Asad Ali	23		
10	Fahad Masood	c Adnan Akmal b Asad Ali	3		
11	Danish Kaneria	not out	9		
	Extras	b 5, lb 1, w 1, nb 26	33	b 3, lb 4, nb 5	12
			192	(1 wicket)	**166**

FoW (1): 1-11, 2-24, 3-27, 4-41, 5-48, 6-129, 7-134, 8-162, 9-165, 10-192
FoW (2): 1-166

Habib Bank Limited Bowling

	O	M	R	W			O	M	R	W	
Kamran Hussain	26.5	4	99	4	10nb		13	5	41	4	1nb
Sajid Shah	13	4	41	0	7nb	(5)	6	1	22	0	3nb
Danish Kaneria	25	6	79	3			32.4	8	84	3	
Fahad Masood	20	2	71	3	1w,13nb	(2)	14	1	72	1	12nb
Abdur Rehman	12	1	35	0		(6)	12	2	32	1	
Shahid Afridi	1	0	5	0		(7)	8	1	20	0	
Younis Khan	1	0	2	0		(4)	6	2	25	0	

Sui Northern Gas Pipelines Limited Bowling

	O	M	R	W			O	M	R	W	
Samiullah Khan	20	2	48	3	6nb		7	1	19	0	1nb
Asad Ali	22.1	9	67	5	1w,8nb		6	2	39	0	
Adil Raza	4	0	24	0	4nb		8	0	52	0	4nb
Imran Ali	14	2	46	2	4nb						
Mohammad Hafeez	1	0	1	0		(4)	8.4	0	49	1	

Umpires: Saleem Badar and Zameer Haider. Referee: Anwar Khan.　　　　Toss: Habib Bank Limited

Close of Play: 1st day: Sui Northern Gas Pipelines Limited (1) 203-4 (Misbah-ul-Haq 42*, Khurram Shehzad 14*, 58 overs); 2nd day: No play; 3rd day: Habib Bank Limited (1) 106-5 (Hasan Raza 37*, Kamran Hussain 16*, 27 overs); 4th day: Sui Northern Gas Pipelines Limited (2) 145-4 (Misbah-ul-Haq 71*, Khurram Shehzad 29*, 46 overs).

Sui Northern Gas Pipelines Limited won the Trophy on first innings. Misbah-ul-Haq's 161 took 272 balls in 287 minutes and included 23 fours and 2 sixes.

PAKISTAN CRICKET BOARD PATRON'S XI v ZIMBABWEANS

Played at Defence Housing Authority Stadium, Karachi, January 14, 15, 16, 17, 2008.
Zimbabwe in Pakistan 2007/08
Pakistan Cricket Board Patron's XI won by an innings and 34 runs.

ZIMBABWEANS

1	V.Sibanda	c Sarfraz Ahmed b Kamran Hussain	29	lbw b Samiullah Khan	23
2	*H.Masakadza	b Samiullah Khan	0	lbw b Sohail Khan	44
3	B.R.M.Taylor	c Shahid Afridi b Yasir Shah	64	lbw b Samiullah Khan	4
4	†T.Taibu	c Naumanullah b Shahid Afridi	46	c Afaq Raheem b Samiullah Khan	30
5	S.C.Williams	c and b Fawad Alam	32	c Naumanullah b Sohail Khan	4
6	K.M.Dabengwa	c Nasir Jamshed b Shahid Afridi	12	(7) lbw b Sohail Khan	0
7	E.Chigumbura	c Sarfraz Ahmed b Shahid Afridi	21	(6) lbw b Samiullah Khan	2
8	G.B.Brent	c Yasir Shah b Shahid Afridi	1	b Shahid Afridi	31
9	T.Maruma	b Yasir Shah	3	c Sarfraz Ahmed b Shahid Afridi	71
10	R.W.Price	lbw b Yasir Shah	0	not out	12
11	C.B.Mpofu	not out	0	lbw b Samiullah Khan	4
	Extras	lb 1	1	lb 10, nb 1	11
			209		**236**

FoW (1): 1-4, 2-56, 3-118, 4-156, 5-182, 6-184, 7-198, 8-209, 9-209, 10-209
FoW (2): 1-28, 2-36, 3-99, 4-103, 5-109, 6-109, 7-115, 8-211, 9-218, 10-236

PAKISTAN CRICKET BOARD PATRON'S XI

1	Nasir Jamshed	c Brent b Chigumbura	182
2	Khalid Latif	c Taibu b Chigumbura	18
3	Afaq Raheem	c Mpofu b Price	77
4	Naumanullah	c and b Price	86
5	Fawad Alam	not out	82
6	*Shahid Afridi	c Mpofu b Price	13
7	Kamran Hussain	c Maruma b Price	2
8	†Sarfraz Ahmed	not out	8
9	Sohail Khan		
10	Yasir Shah		
11	Samiullah Khan		
	Extras	lb 1, w 4, nb 6	11
		(6 wickets, declared)	**479**

FoW (1): 1-78, 2-283, 3-293, 4-420, 5-452, 6-456

Pakistan Cricket Board Patron's XI Bowling

	O	M	R	W		O	M	R	W	
Sohail Khan	12	1	46	0		24	3	76	3	
Samiullah Khan	12	2	43	1		24	13	42	5	1nb
Kamran Hussain	10	3	26	1		13	4	35	0	
Yasir Shah	14.1	1	42	3		23	13	36	0	
Shahid Afridi	16	4	37	4		23	11	31	2	
Fawad Alam	5	2	14	1		2	1	6	0	

Zimbabweans Bowling

	O	M	R	W	
Mpofu	24	8	61	0	
Chigumbura	26	6	80	2	1w
Brent	27	4	85	0	1w
Price	35	5	130	4	
Maruma	13	0	69	0	6nb
Masakadza	4	1	14	0	2w
Dabengwa	7	0	39	0	

Umpires: Ahmed Shahab and Riazuddin. Referee: Abdus Sami. Toss: Zimbabweans

Close of Play: 1st day: Pakistan Cricket Board Patron's XI 65-0 (Nasir Jamshed 48*, Khalid Latif 17*, 21 overs); 2nd day: Pakistan Cricket Board Patron's XI (1) 361-3 (Naumanullah 46*, Fawad Alam 28*, 111 overs); 3rd day: Zimbabweans (2) 111-6 (Chigumbura 2*, Brent 0*, 65 overs).

Nasir Jamshed's 182 took 240 balls in 341 minutes and included 16 fours and 7 sixes.

PUNJAB v FEDERAL AREAS

Played at Gaddafi Stadium, Lahore, February 10, 11, 12, 13, 2008.
ABN-AMRO Pentangular Cup 2007/08
Match drawn. (Points: Punjab 3, Federal Areas 0)

FEDERAL AREAS

1	Raheel Majeed	c Nasir Jamshed b Mohammad Khalil	107	lbw b Aizaz Cheema	11
2	Afaq Raheem	b Abdur Rehman	40	c Kamran Akmal b Aizaz Cheema	7
3	Babar Naeem	c Mohammad Hafeez b Wahab Riaz	17	c Misbah-ul-Haq b Abdur Rehman	0
4	Bazid Khan	c Kamran Akmal b Wahab Riaz	25	lbw b Mansoor Amjad	172
5	Usman Saeed	c Aizaz Cheema b Wahab Riaz	69	b Mohammad Hafeez	65
6	Naved Ashraf	c Kamran Akmal b Aizaz Cheema	58	lbw b Mansoor Amjad	39
7	Yasir Arafat	c Wahab Riaz b Abdur Rehman	31	not out	56
8	†Naeem Anjum	lbw b Abdur Rehman	4		
9	Sohail Tanvir	c Misbah-ul-Haq b Abdur Rehman	3	(8) not out	21
10	*Shoaib Akhtar	c Mohammad Yousuf b Wahab Riaz	0		
11	Shehzad Azam	not out	0		
	Extras	b 1, lb 8, w 2, nb 18	29	lb 6, nb 8	14
			383	(6 wickets)	385

FoW (1): 1-80, 2-136, 3-160, 4-222, 5-327, 6-354, 7-375, 8-375, 9-382, 10-383
FoW (2): 1-18, 2-19, 3-19, 4-170, 5-252, 6-347

PUNJAB

1	Salman Butt	c Babar Naeem b Shehzad Azam	290
2	Mohammad Hafeez	lbw b Sohail Tanvir	77
3	Nasir Jamshed	c sub (Atif Maqbool) b Shehzad Azam	108
4	Mohammad Yousuf	c Naved Ashraf b Babar Naeem	56
5	*Misbah-ul-Haq	b Shehzad Azam	9
6	†Kamran Akmal	c Usman Saeed b Babar Naeem	23
7	Mansoor Amjad	not out	16
8	Wahab Riaz	c sub (Fayyaz Ahmed) b Afaq Raheem	0
9	Abdur Rehman		
10	Mohammad Khalil		
11	Aizaz Cheema		
	Extras	b 1, lb 7, w 1, nb 11	20
		(7 wickets, declared)	599

FoW (1): 1-191, 2-481, 3-499, 4-511, 5-567, 6-598, 7-599

Punjab Bowling

	O	M	R	W		O	M	R	W	
Wahab Riaz	29.4	5	112	4	16nb	18	2	89	0	7nb
Mohammad Khalil	17	1	67	1	1w,2nb					
Aizaz Cheema	19	1	62	1	1w	(2) 18	5	66	2	
Abdur Rehman	40	13	86	4		(3) 18	2	57	1	
Mohammad Hafeez	4	1	18	0		(4) 13	1	59	1	
Mansoor Amjad	17	3	29	0		(5) 31	4	108	2	1nb

Federal Areas Bowling

	O	M	R	W	
Shoaib Akhtar	18	2	72	0	1w,1nb
Sohail Tanvir	25	4	107	1	1nb
Yasir Arafat	18	3	76	0	1nb
Raheel Majeed	1	0	16	0	
Shehzad Azam	20	0	133	3	8nb
Babar Naeem	22	1	115	2	
Naved Ashraf	3	0	20	0	
Afaq Raheem	8.2	0	47	1	
Bazid Khan	3	1	5	0	

Umpires: Aleem Dar and Nadeem Ghauri. Referee: Anis Sheikh.   Toss: Federal Areas
Close of Play: 1st day: Federal Areas (1) 301-4 (Usman Saeed 52*, Naved Ashraf 41*, 90 overs); 2nd day: Punjab (1) 219-1 (Salman Butt 135*, Nasir Jamshed 6*, 48 overs); 3rd day: Federal Areas (2) 37-3 (Bazid Khan 14*, Usman Saeed 4*, 14 overs).
Raheel Majeed's 107 took 130 balls in 196 minutes and included 12 fours and 3 sixes. Salman Butt's 290 took 318 balls in 424 minutes and included 50 fours and 1 six. Nasir Jamshed's 108 took 184 balls in 263 minutes and included 14 fours and 1 six. Bazid Khan's 172 took 255 balls in 324 minutes and included 22 fours and 1 six.

SIND v NORTH WEST FRONTIER PROVINCE

Played at National Stadium, Karachi, February 10, 11, 12, 13, 2008.
ABN-AMRO Pentangular Cup 2007/08
Sind won by five wickets.   (Points: Sind 6, North West Frontier Province 0)

NORTH WEST FRONTIER PROVINCE

1	Yasir Hameed	b Sohail Khan	5	(2) lbw b Anwar Ali	26
2	Rafatullah Mohmand	c Shahid Afridi b Uzair-ul-Haq	23	(1) c Khalid Latif b Uzair-ul-Haq	25
3	Riaz Kail	b Sohail Khan	0	lbw b Anwar Ali	4
4	*Younis Khan	lbw b Anwar Ali	12	lbw b Shahid Afridi	111
5	Wajahatullah Wasti	c Uzair-ul-Haq b Danish Kaneria	16	c Sarfraz Ahmed b Anwar Ali	17
6	Adnan Raees	c Shahid Afridi b Danish Kaneria	30	c Khurram Manzoor b Danish Kaneria	16
7	†Zulfiqar Jan	b Sohail Khan	2	lbw b Danish Kaneria	18
8	Mohammad Aslam	lbw b Shahid Afridi	29	c Sarfraz Ahmed b Danish Kaneria	6
9	Samiullah Khan	c Faisal Iqbal b Sohail Khan	0	(10) lbw b Danish Kaneria	2
10	Shakeel-ur-Rehman	b Shahid Afridi	45	(9) c Khurram Manzoor b Danish Kaneria	11
11	Fazl-e-Akbar	not out	16	not out	0
	Extras	b 4, lb 3, w 8, nb 10	25	b 2, lb 13, nb 3	18
			203		**254**

FoW (1): 1-7, 2-11, 3-42, 4-56, 5-97, 6-105, 7-105, 8-105, 9-174, 10-203
FoW (2): 1-41, 2-51, 3-71, 4-150, 5-150, 6-188, 7-226, 8-236, 9-251, 10-254

SIND

1	Khurram Manzoor	c Wajahatullah Wasti b Samiullah Khan	5	b Samiullah Khan	118
2	Khalid Latif	c Rafatullah Mohmand b Shakeel-ur-Rehman	17	lbw b Mohammad Aslam	72
3	Naumanullah	b Shakeel-ur-Rehman	47	lbw b Samiullah Khan	35
4	Faisal Iqbal	c Yasir Hameed b Shakeel-ur-Rehman	1	lbw b Shakeel-ur-Rehman	0
5	Fawad Alam	lbw b Fazl-e-Akbar	9	not out	51
6	*Shahid Afridi	c Rafatullah Mohmand b Shakeel-ur-Rehman	17	c Rafatullah Mohmand b Fazl-e-Akbar	29
7	†Sarfraz Ahmed	not out	34	not out	3
8	Anwar Ali	c Yasir Hameed b Shakeel-ur-Rehman	1		
9	Danish Kaneria	c Zulfiqar Jan b Shakeel-ur-Rehman	0		
10	Sohail Khan	c Zulfiqar Jan b Samiullah Khan	0		
11	Uzair-ul-Haq	run out (Mohammad Aslam)	2		
	Extras	b 1, lb 2, nb 13	16	nb 1	1
			149	(5 wickets)	**309**

FoW (1): 1-9, 2-79, 3-80, 4-85, 5-110, 6-110, 7-119, 8-119, 9-126, 10-149
FoW (2): 1-161, 2-223, 3-224, 4-226, 5-288

Sind Bowling

	O	M	R	W		O	M	R	W	
Sohail Khan	18.5	3	65	4		17	3	58	0	
Anwar Ali	14.1	2	32	1	6nb	23	5	66	3	1nb
Uzair-ul-Haq	6	0	19	1	4w,4nb	(4) 7	2	20	1	2nb
Danish Kaneria	18	5	39	2		(3) 25.4	7	62	5	
Shahid Afridi	15.1	2	41	2		14	5	28	1	
Fawad Alam						(6) 1	0	5	0	

North West Frontier Province Bowling

	O	M	R	W		O	M	R	W	
Fazl-e-Akbar	18	5	62	1	12nb	20	3	90	1	1nb
Samiullah Khan	21.1	3	49	2	1nb	24	7	92	2	
Shakeel-ur-Rehman	14	6	28	6		(4) 19	6	56	1	
Mohammad Aslam	2	0	7	0		(5) 28	12	57	1	
Wajahatullah Wasti						(3) 5	3	9	0	
Rafatullah Mohmand						(6) 0.2	0	5	0	

Umpires: Riazuddin and Saleem Badar. Referee: Anwar Khan.   Toss: Sind
Close of Play: 1st day: Sind (1) 60-1 (Khalid Latif 12*, Naumanullah 33*, 15 overs); 2nd day: North West Frontier Province (2) 146-3 (Younis Khan 68*, Wajahatullah Wasti 14*, 47 overs); 3rd day: Sind (2) 130-0 (Khurram Manzoor 74*, Khalid Latif 56*, 47 overs).
Younis Khan's 111 took 168 balls in 259 minutes and included 19 fours. Khurram Manzoor's 118 took 263 balls in 343 minutes and included 18 fours and 1 six.

BALUCHISTAN v FEDERAL AREAS

Played at National Stadium, Karachi, February 22, 23, 24, 2008.
ABN-AMRO Pentangular Cup 2007/08
Federal Areas won by an innings and 212 runs.   (Points: Baluchistan 0, Federal Areas 9)

BALUCHISTAN

1	Shoaib Khan	lbw b Yasir Arafat	25	c Bazid Khan b Sohail Tanvir		2
2	Usman Tariq	lbw b Sohail Tanvir	68	run out (Usman Saeed)		19
3	Saeed Anwar	c Raheel Majeed b Sohail Tanvir	8	lbw b Yasir Arafat		2
4	Bilal Khilji	b Sohail Tanvir	4	(5) lbw b Yasir Arafat		0
5	Saeed Bin Nasir	c Naeem Anjum b Sohail Tanvir	1	(4) c Naeem Anjum b Shehzad Azam		19
6	*Nasim Khan	c Fayyaz Ahmed b Yasir Arafat	31	lbw b Sohail Tanvir		26
7	Kamran Hussain	c Naeem Anjum b Yasir Arafat	7	absent hurt		0
8	†Gulraiz Sadaf	c Bazid Khan b Sohail Tanvir	0	(7) c Sohail Tanvir b Shehzad Azam		13
9	Abdur Rauf	c Raheel Majeed b Yasir Arafat	7	absent hurt		0
10	Imranullah Aslam	not out	51	(8) c Usman Saeed b Sohail Tanvir		26
11	Azharullah	lbw b Saeed Ajmal	20	(9) not out		13
	Extras	b 14, lb 4, w 1, nb 12	31	b 2, lb 1, w 2, nb 7		12
			253			**132**

FoW (1): 1-41, 2-78, 3-82, 4-92, 5-165, 6-170, 7-170, 8-172, 9-200, 10-253
FoW (2): 1-2, 2-6, 3-47, 4-48, 5-49, 6-88, 7-104, 8-132

FEDERAL AREAS

1	Raheel Majeed	c Kamran Hussain b Bilal Khilji	98
2	Afaq Raheem	c Gulraiz Sadaf b Kamran Hussain	2
3	Fayyaz Ahmed	c Gulraiz Sadaf b Azharullah	16
4	Bazid Khan	c Bilal Khilji b Azharullah	0
5	Usman Saeed	lbw b Kamran Hussain	109
6	*Naved Ashraf	c Gulraiz Sadaf b Saeed Anwar	141
7	Yasir Arafat	c Gulraiz Sadaf b Kamran Hussain	0
8	Sohail Tanvir	c Azharullah b Imranullah Aslam	132
9	†Naeem Anjum	not out	56
10	Saeed Ajmal	not out	1
11	Shehzad Azam		
	Extras	b 15, lb 11, nb 16	42
		(8 wickets, declared)	**597**

FoW (1): 1-6, 2-52, 3-52, 4-173, 5-360, 6-360, 7-428, 8-583

Federal Areas Bowling

	O	M	R	W		O	M	R	W	
Sohail Tanvir	23	9	66	5	1w,1nb	11.3	3	42	3	
Yasir Arafat	20	2	83	4	6nb	12	2	39	2	1w,1nb
Shehzad Azam	9	2	35	0	4nb	9	0	48	2	1w,6nb
Saeed Ajmal	8.2	1	36	1	1nb					
Raheel Majeed	1	0	15	0						

Baluchistan Bowling

	O	M	R	W	
Abdur Rauf	21	5	90	0	4nb
Kamran Hussain	17	2	71	3	12nb
Azharullah	30	3	148	2	
Bilal Khilji	27	6	98	1	
Imranullah Aslam	27	1	103	1	
Saeed Anwar	18	2	61	1	

Umpires: Ahsan Raza and Nadeem Ghauri. Referee: Naeem Ahmed.   Toss: Federal Areas

Close of Play: 1st day: Federal Areas (1) 79-3 (Raheel Majeed 42*, Usman Saeed 13*, 17 overs); 2nd day: Federal Areas (1) 441-7 (Sohail Tanvir 38*, Naeem Anjum 2*, 107 overs).

The match was scheduled for four days but completed in three. Usman Saeed's 109 took 196 balls in 316 minutes and included 16 fours. Naved Ashraf's 141 took 200 balls in 272 minutes and included 24 fours and 2 sixes. Sohail Tanvir's 132 took 174 balls in 195 minutes and included 19 fours and 1 six.

PUNJAB v NORTH WEST FRONTIER PROVINCE

Played at Gaddafi Stadium, Lahore, February 22, 23, 24, 25, 2008.
ABN-AMRO Pentangular Cup 2007/08
Match drawn.   (Points: Punjab 0, North West Frontier Province 3)

PUNJAB

1	Salman Butt	run out (Khurram Shehzad)	72	lbw b Mohammad Aslam	117
2	Mohammad Hafeez	c Zulfiqar Jan b Fazl-e-Akbar	3	c Zulfiqar Jan b Samiullah Khan	16
3	Nasir Jamshed	lbw b Fazl-e-Akbar	16	b Wajahatullah Wasti	59
4	Misbah-ul-Haq	c Rafatullah Mohmand			
		b Samiullah Khan	53	not out	100
5	*Shoaib Malik	c Zulfiqar Jan b Shakeel-ur-Rehman	41		
6	†Kamran Akmal	lbw b Mohammad Aslam	40		
7	Abdur Rehman	b Samiullah Khan	16		
8	Waqas Ahmed	lbw b Fazl-e-Akbar	13		
9	Junaid Zia	c Zulfiqar Jan b Fazl-e-Akbar	11	(5) st Zulfiqar Jan b Mohammad Aslam	36
10	Wahab Riaz	c Khurram Shehzad			
		b Shakeel-ur-Rehman	44	(6) not out	2
11	Aizaz Cheema	not out	10		
	Extras	b 3, lb 7, nb 25	35	lb 6, nb 4	10
			354	**(4 wickets)**	**340**

FoW (1): 1-10, 2-70, 3-112, 4-188, 5-230, 6-266, 7-270, 8-296, 9-315, 10-354
FoW (2): 1-31, 2-167, 3-227, 4-332

NORTH WEST FRONTIER PROVINCE

1	Rafatullah Mohmand	b Abdur Rehman	54
2	Yasir Hameed	c Kamran Akmal b Waqas Ahmed	37
3	Wajahatullah Wasti	lbw b Junaid Zia	39
4	*Younis Khan	c Nasir Jamshed b Abdur Rehman	117
5	Khurram Shehzad	c Kamran Akmal b Wahab Riaz	41
6	Adnan Raees	lbw b Wahab Riaz	21
7	†Zulfiqar Jan	not out	73
8	Mohammad Aslam	b Wahab Riaz	0
9	Shakeel-ur-Rehman	c Kamran Akmal b Wahab Riaz	22
10	Fazl-e-Akbar	c Junaid Zia b Wahab Riaz	13
11	Samiullah Khan	b Aizaz Cheema	0
	Extras	lb 16, w 3, nb 10	29
			446

FoW (1): 1-82, 2-114, 3-180, 4-253, 5-319, 6-333, 7-337, 8-412, 9-431, 10-446

NWFP Bowling	O	M	R	W		O	M	R	W	
Fazl-e-Akbar	23	2	74	4	14nb	5	1	13	0	
Samiullah Khan	26	5	85	2	6nb	10	1	62	1	3nb
Shakeel-ur-Rehman	16.2	2	72	2	5nb	(5) 10	0	45	0	1nb
Mohammad Aslam	29	5	91	1		22	2	111	2	
Wajahatullah Wasti	5	0	22	0		(3) 15	2	57	1	
Rafatullah Mohmand						(6) 5	0	28	0	
Yasir Hameed						(7) 2	0	18	0	

Punjab Bowling	O	M	R	W	
Waqas Ahmed	13	1	52	1	1w,3nb
Junaid Zia	18	7	50	1	3nb
Aizaz Cheema	28.1	4	92	1	1w
Wahab Riaz	35	6	113	5	1w,4nb
Abdur Rehman	42	9	96	2	
Mohammad Hafeez	12	5	20	0	
Shoaib Malik	6	3	7	0	

Umpires: Riazuddin and Saleem Badar. Referee: Abdus Sami.   Toss: North West Frontier Province

Close of Play: 1st day: Punjab (1) 295-7 (Waqas Ahmed 12*, Junaid Zia 10*, 83.5 overs); 2nd day: North West Frontier Province (1) 181-3 (Younis Khan 36*, Khurram Shehzad 0*, 53 overs); 3rd day: North West Frontier Province (1) 392-7 (Zulfiqar Jan 35*, Shakeel-ur-Rehman 21*, 143 overs).
Younis Khan's 117 took 211 balls in 337 minutes and included 16 fours. Salman Butt's 117 took 157 balls in 218 minutes and included 18 fours. Misbah-ul-Haq's 100 took 108 balls in 120 minutes and included 9 fours and 2 sixes.

NORTH WEST FRONTIER PROVINCE v FEDERAL AREAS

Played at Arbab Niaz Stadium, Peshawar, February 28, 29, March 1, 2, 2008.
ABN-AMRO Pentangular Cup 2007/08
Match drawn.   (Points: North West Frontier Province 3, Federal Areas 0)

NORTH WEST FRONTIER PROVINCE

1	Rafatullah Mohmand	c Bazid Khan b Saeed Ajmal	100
2	Yasir Hameed	b Saeed Ajmal	107
3	Wajahatullah Wasti	c Naeem Anjum b Sohail Tanvir	8
4	Khurram Shehzad	c Naeem Anjum b Yasir Ali	53
5	Aftab Alam	not out	178
6	*Younis Khan	c Yasir Ali b Saeed Ajmal	59
7	†Zulfiqar Jan	c Naeem Anjum b Sohail Tanvir	1
8	Yasir Shah	c Naeem Anjum b Sohail Tanvir	4
9	Nauman Habib	c Bazid Khan b Sohail Tanvir	40
10	Fazl-e-Akbar	st Naeem Anjum b Raheel Majeed	1
11	Waqar Ahmed	b Raheel Majeed	5
	Extras	b 11, lb 2, w 2, nb 2	17
			573

FoW (1): 1-196, 2-211, 3-219, 4-348, 5-445, 6-451, 7-455, 8-543, 9-560, 10-573

FEDERAL AREAS

1	Raheel Majeed	c Zulfiqar Jan b Waqar Ahmed	16	c Khurram Shehzad b Waqar Ahmed	31
2	Afaq Raheem	b Yasir Shah	31	c Zulfiqar Jan b Waqar Ahmed	22
3	Ashar Zaidi	c Yasir Shah b Fazl-e-Akbar	4	c Aftab Alam b Yasir Shah	75
4	Bazid Khan	c Khurram Shehzad b Nauman Habib	170	c Khurram Shehzad b Yasir Shah	100
5	Usman Saeed	lbw b Nauman Habib	1	(6) not out	7
6	*Naved Ashraf	lbw b Yasir Shah	78		
7	Yasir Arafat	b Yasir Shah	58		
8	Sohail Tanvir	c Zulfiqar Jan b Nauman Habib	0	(5) c Khurram Shehzad b Yasir Hameed	50
9	†Naeem Anjum	b Waqar Ahmed	9	(7) not out	0
10	Yasir Ali	not out	4		
11	Saeed Ajmal	c Zulfiqar Jan b Nauman Habib	1		
	Extras	b 5, lb 8, w 1, nb 4	18	b 2, lb 8, nb 1	11
			390	(5 wickets)	**296**

FoW (1): 1-33, 2-37, 3-102, 4-107, 5-276, 6-358, 7-358, 8-371, 9-389, 10-390
FoW (2): 1-53, 2-62, 3-231, 4-249, 5-291

Federal Areas Bowling	O	M	R	W	
Sohail Tanvir	41	6	132	4	2w
Yasir Arafat	28	5	106	0	
Yasir Ali	27	8	83	1	
Saeed Ajmal	52	9	186	3	2nb
Ashar Zaidi	9	0	24	0	
Raheel Majeed	4.5	0	29	2	

NWFP Bowling	O	M	R	W			O	M	R	W	
Fazl-e-Akbar	25	4	70	1		(2)	8	1	27	0	
Waqar Ahmed	18	3	73	2	1nb	(3)	7	1	21	2	
Yasir Shah	33	8	97	3	1w	(4)	29	9	79	2	
Nauman Habib	18.1	1	76	4	2nb	(1)	8	0	44	0	1nb
Wajahatullah Wasti	17	0	58	0							
Aftab Alam	1	0	3	0		(7)	1	0	5	0	
Khurram Shehzad						(5)	12	1	61	0	
Rafatullah Mohmand						(6)	4	1	8	0	
Zulfiqar Jan						(8)	2	0	13	0	
Yasir Hameed						(9)	2	0	24	1	
Younis Khan						(10)	1	0	4	0	

Umpires: Ahmed Shahab and Nadeem Ghauri.   Referee: Abdus Sami.   Toss: Federal Areas
Close of Play: 1st day: North West Frontier Province (1) 342-3 (Khurram Shehzad 53*, Aftab Alam 64*, 90 overs); 2nd day: Federal Areas (1) 57-2 (Afaq Raheem 19*, Bazid Khan 16*, 16 overs); 3rd day: Federal Areas (1) 381-8 (Yasir Arafat 53*, Yasir Ali 1*, 106 overs).
Rafatullah Mohmand's 100 took 160 balls in 197 minutes and included 16 fours. Yasir Hameed's 107 took 116 balls in 168 minutes and included 14 fours and 2 sixes. Aftab Alam's 178 took 346 balls in 434 minutes and included 22 fours and 2 sixes. Bazid Khan's 170 took 272 balls in 316 minutes and included 24 fours. Bazid Khan's 100 took 164 balls in 184 minutes and included 13 fours.

SIND v BALUCHISTAN

Played at National Stadium, Karachi, February 28, 29, 2008.
ABN-AMRO Pentangular Cup 2007/08
Sind won by six wickets.   (Points: Sind 6, Baluchistan 0)

BALUCHISTAN

1	Shoaib Khan	c Danish Kaneria b Fahad Khan	40	lbw b Sohail Khan	3
2	Usman Tariq	c Sarfraz Ahmed b Sohail Khan	1	b Sohail Khan	2
3	Saeed Anwar	b Shahid Afridi	9	lbw b Sohail Khan	1
4	Saeed Bin Nasir	c Sarfraz Ahmed b Anwar Ali	45	(5) b Anwar Ali	0
5	Bilal Khilji	b Shahid Afridi	29	(6) c Faisal Iqbal b Sohail Khan	0
6	*Nasim Khan	lbw b Anwar Ali	1	(7) c Khurram Manzoor b Anwar Ali	4
7	†Gulraiz Sadaf	lbw b Anwar Ali	0	(4) b Sohail Khan	0
8	Faisal Irfan	b Anwar Ali	7	lbw b Anwar Ali	3
9	Tanvir Ahmed	c Fawad Alam b Danish Kaneria	20	st Sarfraz Ahmed b Danish Kaneria	13
10	Azharullah	not out	7	c Khurram Manzoor b Sohail Khan	7
11	Nazar Hussain	c Fahad Khan b Danish Kaneria	5	not out	2
	Extras	b 5, lb 5, w 2, nb 11	23	b 1, lb 6	7
			187		**42**

FoW (1): 1-23, 2-62, 3-64, 4-132, 5-133, 6-133, 7-152, 8-154, 9-178, 10-187
FoW (2): 1-6, 2-7, 3-7, 4-12, 5-12, 6-17, 7-17, 8-25, 9-40, 10-42

SIND

1	Khurram Manzoor	b Tanvir Ahmed	5	b Tanvir Ahmed	6
2	Khalid Latif	lbw b Tanvir Ahmed	2	lbw b Azharullah	19
3	Naumanullah	b Faisal Irfan	9	c Shoaib Khan b Azharullah	7
4	Faisal Iqbal	c Nazar Hussain b Azharullah	52	(5) not out	22
5	Fawad Alam	c Usman Tariq b Tanvir Ahmed	6	(4) run out	14
6	*Shahid Afridi	c Gulraiz Sadaf b Faisal Irfan	5		
7	†Sarfraz Ahmed	b Azharullah	6	(6) not out	16
8	Anwar Ali	b Azharullah	9		
9	Danish Kaneria	c Shoaib Khan b Faisal Irfan	24		
10	Sohail Khan	c Gulraiz Sadaf b Tanvir Ahmed	5		
11	Fahad Khan	not out	0		
	Extras	b 4, lb 5, w 1, nb 6	16	lb 4, nb 4	8
			139	**(4 wickets)**	**92**

FoW (1): 1-4, 2-10, 3-20, 4-39, 5-44, 6-50, 7-67, 8-126, 9-139, 10-139
FoW (2): 1-6, 2-31, 3-49, 4-54

Sind Bowling

	O	M	R	W			O	M	R	W	
Sohail Khan	10	2	38	1			9.2	4	21	6	
Anwar Ali	18	6	41	4	2w,9nb		8	5	12	3	
Shahid Afridi	14	4	35	2							
Fahad Khan	5	0	28	1	2nb						
Danish Kaneria	5.4	0	35	2		(3)	1	0	2	1	

Baluchistan Bowling

	O	M	R	W			O	M	R	W	
Tanvir Ahmed	13	2	43	4	1w,3nb		6	2	21	1	3nb
Faisal Irfan	10	0	35	3			6	0	25	0	
Azharullah	13.3	2	31	3			9	1	32	2	
Nazar Hussain	6	3	10	0	1nb		2	0	4	0	1nb
Bilal Khilji	2	0	11	0			0.2	0	6	0	

Umpires: Ahsan Raza and Saleem Badar.   Referee: Naeem Ahmed.   Toss: Sind

Close of Play: 1st day: Sind (1) 131-8 (Faisal Iqbal 46*, Sohail Khan 4*, 37 overs).

The match was scheduled for four days but completed in two.

FEDERAL AREAS v SIND

Played at Diamond Club Ground, Islamabad, March 5, 6, 7, 8, 2008.
ABN-AMRO Pentangular Cup 2007/08
Federal Areas won by one wicket.   (Points: Federal Areas 9, Sind 0)

SIND

1	Khurram Manzoor	c Naeem Anjum b Yasir Arafat	15	c Umair Khan b Shehzad Azam	73
2	Khalid Latif	c Bazid Khan b Sohail Tanvir	11	lbw b Saeed Ajmal	74
3	Naumanullah	c Usman Saeed b Shehzad Azam	53	c Usman Saeed b Shehzad Azam	43
4	Faisal Iqbal	c Raheel Majeed b Sohail Tanvir	10	not out	105
5	Rizwan Ahmed	run out (Yasir Arafat)	27	c Usman Saeed b Sohail Tanvir	71
6	*Shahid Afridi	c and b Saeed Ajmal	70		
7	†Sarfraz Ahmed	c Naeem Anjum b Sohail Tanvir	7	(6) not out	18
8	Anwar Ali	b Saeed Ajmal	1		
9	Danish Kaneria	c Naeem Anjum b Sohail Tanvir	10		
10	Sohail Khan	lbw b Sohail Tanvir	2		
11	Abdul Ameer	not out	0		
	Extras	b 8, lb 2, w 2, nb 4	16	b 1, lb 2, w 7	10
			222	(4 wickets, declared)	394

FoW (1): 1-26, 2-42, 3-77, 4-108, 5-158, 6-194, 7-209, 8-212, 9-215, 10-222
FoW (2): 1-119, 2-191, 3-203, 4-347

FEDERAL AREAS

1	Raheel Majeed	c Sarfraz Ahmed b Sohail Khan	72	c sub (Tahir Khan) b Shahid Afridi	52
2	Umair Khan	lbw b Shahid Afridi	19	c and b Shahid Afridi	106
3	Ashar Zaidi	not out	87	(5) c Sarfraz Ahmed b Naumanullah	20
4	Usman Saeed	b Sohail Khan	0	(7) not out	41
5	*Naved Ashraf	c Naumanullah b Sohail Khan	34	(6) c Rizwan Ahmed b Sohail Khan	14
6	Bazid Khan	b Shahid Afridi	10	(4) b Danish Kaneria	45
7	Yasir Arafat	c Khalid Latif b Rizwan Ahmed	27	(8) c Anwar Ali b Shahid Afridi	0
8	Sohail Tanvir	c Sarfraz Ahmed b Sohail Khan	4	(3) b Danish Kaneria	1
9	†Naeem Anjum	c Sarfraz Ahmed b Sohail Khan	7	lbw b Shahid Afridi	25
10	Saeed Ajmal	lbw b Danish Kaneria	15	lbw b Shahid Afridi	0
11	Shehzad Azam	b Danish Kaneria	0	not out	12
	Extras	b 4, lb 5, w 1, nb 10	20	b 1, lb 4, nb 1	6
			295	(9 wickets)	322

FoW (1): 1-82, 2-114, 3-114, 4-186, 5-188, 6-192, 7-210, 8-246, 9-283, 10-295
FoW (2): 1-84, 2-85, 3-174, 4-203, 5-224, 6-262, 7-262, 8-309, 9-309

Federal Areas Bowling

	O	M	R	W			O	M	R	W	
Sohail Tanvir	20.3	4	58	5	1w		27.1	3	127	1	5w
Yasir Arafat	16	4	53	1	1nb		23	2	103	0	1w
Shehzad Azam	11	1	47	1	1w,2nb		15	2	72	2	1w
Saeed Ajmal	6	0	54	2	1nb		22	3	61	1	
Raheel Majeed						(5)	7	1	28	0	

Sind Bowling

	O	M	R	W				O	M	R	W	
Sohail Khan	20	5	56	5				11	0	47	1	
Anwar Ali	10	0	54	0	2nb	(3)		3	0	15	0	1nb
Danish Kaneria	16.1	4	42	2		(2)		36.5	1	157	2	
Abdul Ameer	10	2	41	0	1w,8nb							
Shahid Afridi	19	6	58	2		(4)		21	5	55	5	
Rizwan Ahmed	4	0	35	1		(5)		7	0	24	0	
Naumanullah						(6)		5	1	19	1	

Umpires: Ahmed Shahab and Ahsan Raza. Referee: Ishtiaq Ahmed.   Toss: Federal Areas

Close of Play: 1st day: Federal Areas (1) 119-3 (Ashar Zaidi 24*, Naved Ashraf 0*, 30.2 overs); 2nd day: Sind (2) 128-1 (Khalid Latif 47*, Naumanullah 5*, 28 overs); 3rd day: Sind (2) 345-3 (Faisal Iqbal 77*, Rizwan Ahmed 70*, 87 overs).

Faisal Iqbal's 105 took 160 balls in 211 minutes and included 13 fours and 1 six. Umair Khan's 106 took 190 balls in 278 minutes and included 13 fours.

PUNJAB v BALUCHISTAN

Played at Jinnah Stadium, Sialkot, March 5, 6, 7, 8, 2008.
ABN-AMRO Pentangular Cup 2007/08
Punjab won by an innings and 128 runs.   (Points: Punjab 9, Baluchistan 0)

BALUCHISTAN

1	Yasir Arafat	b Wahab Riaz	62	lbw b Aizaz Cheema		3
2	Usman Tariq	run out (Junaid Zia)	8	b Wahab Riaz		2
3	Rameez Alam	b Mohammad Hafeez	84	c Kamran Akmal b Wahab Riaz		48
4	Saeed Bin Nasir	lbw b Abdur Rehman	46	lbw b Abdur Rehman		16
5	*Nasim Khan	c Kamran Akmal b Wahab Riaz	5	lbw b Mohammad Hafeez		1
6	†Gulraiz Sadaf	c and b Mohammad Hafeez	55	c Ammar Mahmood b Mohammad Hafeez		0
7	Abdur Rauf	b Junaid Zia	15	(8) b Abdur Rehman		24
8	Tanvir Ahmed	c sub (Waqas Ahmed) b Aizaz Cheema	0	(10) not out		47
9	Jalat Khan	lbw b Mohammad Hafeez	15	c Kamran Akmal b Abdur Rehman		11
10	Imranullah Aslam	st Kamran Akmal b Abdur Rehman	31	(7) c Kamran Akmal b Junaid Zia		51
11	Azharullah	not out	5	c Kamran Akmal b Junaid Zia		0
	Extras	b 13, lb 13, w 1, nb 22	49	b 4, nb 13		17
			375			**220**

FoW (1): 1-21, 2-146, 3-208, 4-228, 5-241, 6-295, 7-298, 8-330, 9-349, 10-375
FoW (2): 1-3, 2-19, 3-66, 4-67, 5-67, 6-98, 7-129, 8-149, 9-220, 10-220

PUNJAB

1	Salman Butt	c Yasir Arafat b Jalat Khan	160
2	Mohammad Hafeez	lbw b Abdur Rauf	0
3	Nasir Jamshed	retired hurt	140
4	Misbah-ul-Haq	not out	208
5	Ammar Mahmood	c Saeed Bin Nasir b Jalat Khan	94
6	*Shoaib Malik	c sub (Faisal Irfan) b Abdur Rauf	60
7	†Kamran Akmal		
8	Abdur Rehman		
9	Junaid Zia		
10	Wahab Riaz		
11	Aizaz Cheema		
	Extras	b 4, lb 11, w 13, nb 33	61
		(4 wickets, declared)	723

FoW (1): 1-26, 2-277, 3-593, 4-723

Punjab Bowling

	O	M	R	W		O	M	R	W	
Wahab Riaz	19	2	54	2	8nb	10	1	45	2	7nb
Aizaz Cheema	18	2	70	1		6	0	34	1	
Abdur Rehman	25.1	6	74	2	(5) 14	1	65	3		
Junaid Zia	15	2	65	1	1w,11nb	3.4	0	25	2	6nb
Shoaib Malik	9	1	26	0						
Mohammad Hafeez	15	1	60	3	(3) 15	0	47	2		

Baluchistan Bowling

	O	M	R	W	
Abdur Rauf	13.2	0	102	2	1w,8nb
Tanvir Ahmed	10	0	88	0	11nb
Azharullah	8	1	38	0	
Jalat Khan	36.3	2	189	2	5w,8nb
Imranullah Aslam	40	0	239	0	5w
Usman Tariq	1	0	8	0	
Saeed Bin Nasir	1.3	0	12	0	
Yasir Arafat	4	0	32	0	2w,2nb

Umpires: Riazuddin and Saleem Badar.   Referee: Abdus Sami.   Toss: Baluchistan

Close of Play: 1st day: Baluchistan (1) 298-7 (Gulraiz Sadaf 36*, 90 overs); 2nd day: Punjab (1) 425-2 (Misbah-ul-Haq 82*, Ammar Mahmood 10*, 76 overs); 3rd day: Baluchistan (2) 207-8 (Imranullah Aslam 49*, Tanvir Ahmed 36*, 46.1 overs). Salman Butt's 160 took 164 balls in 212 minutes and included 25 fours and a six. Nasir Jamshed's 140 took 176 balls in 249 minutes and included 14 fours and 3 sixes. Misbah-ul-Haq's 208 took 218 balls in 272 minutes and included 17 fours and 6 sixes. Nasir Jamshed retired hurt in the Punjab first innings having scored 140 (team score 364-2).

NORTH WEST FRONTIER PROVINCE v BALUCHISTAN

Played at Arbab Niaz Stadium, Peshawar, March 11, 12, 13, 14, 2008.
ABN-AMRO Pentangular Cup 2007/08
North West Frontier Province won by an innings and 11 runs.   (Points: North West Frontier Province 9, Baluchistan 0)

BALUCHISTAN

1	Agha Sabir	c Fawad Khan b Waqar Ahmed	0	(8) b Yasir Shah	6
2	Yasir Arafat	c Aftab Alam b Shakeel-ur-Rehman	20	(1) c Shakeel-ur-Rehman b Waqar Ahmed	3
3	Rameez Alam	b Waqar Ahmed	28	lbw b Waqar Ahmed	0
4	Saeed Bin Nasir	not out	149	c Fawad Khan b Waqar Ahmed	133
5	*Nasim Khan	c Younis Khan b Nauman Habib	4	(6) st Fawad Khan b Yasir Shah	38
6	Sohaib Maqsood	c Rafatullah Mohmand b Shakeel-ur-Rehman	60	(5) c sub (Wajid Ali) b Yasir Shah	70
7	†Gulraiz Sadaf	c Yasir Hameed b Yasir Shah	10	(2) c Younis Khan b Yasir Shah	20
8	Abdur Rauf	c Younis Khan b Yasir Shah	5	(11) not out	9
9	Jalat Khan	c Khurram Shehzad b Nauman Habib	9	(7) c Fawad Khan b Waqar Ahmed	10
10	Faisal Irfan	b Waqar Ahmed	16	(9) c Shakeel-ur-Rehman b Yasir Shah	40
11	Mohammad Irshad	lbw b Waqar Ahmed	0	(10) c sub (Wajid Ali) b Rafatullah Mohmand	5
	Extras	nb 7	7	b 5, lb 4, nb 2	11
			308		**345**

FoW (1): 1-0, 2-43, 3-60, 4-73, 5-161, 6-211, 7-227, 8-239, 9-308, 10-308
FoW (2): 1-14, 2-14, 3-53, 4-174, 5-264, 6-272, 7-285, 8-291, 9-311, 10-345

NORTH WEST FRONTIER PROVINCE

1	Rafatullah Mohmand	c Sohaib Maqsood b Abdur Rauf	11
2	Yasir Hameed	c Gulraiz Sadaf b Abdur Rauf	300
3	Asad Shafiq	c sub (Imranullah Aslam) b Abdur Rauf	181
4	Khurram Shehzad	lbw b Abdur Rauf	13
5	Aftab Alam	c Gulraiz Sadaf b Abdur Rauf	3
6	*Younis Khan	not out	44
7	†Fawad Khan	c sub (Imranullah Aslam) b Abdur Rauf	8
8	Yasir Shah	not out	51
9	Shakeel-ur-Rehman		
10	Nauman Habib		
11	Waqar Ahmed		
	Extras	b 8, lb 5, w 7, nb 33	53
	(6 wickets, declared)		664

FoW (1): 1-42, 2-473, 3-508, 4-528, 5-548, 6-556

NWFP Bowling	O	M	R	W			O	M	R	W	
Waqar Ahmed	16.4	5	47	4			22	7	71	4	
Shakeel-ur-Rehman	15	4	59	2	6nb	(3)	16	1	76	0	
Nauman Habib	18	4	62	2	1nb	(2)	9	1	37	0	2nb
Yasir Shah	27	2	122	2			27.1	5	106	5	
Younis Khan	1	0	9	0			2	0	6	0	
Khurram Shehzad	3	1	9	0							
Aftab Alam						(6)	5	1	20	0	
Rafatullah Mohmand						(7)	4	0	20	1	

Baluchistan Bowling	O	M	R	W	
Abdur Rauf	33.1	2	193	6	16nb
Mohammad Irshad	0.1	0	4	0	
Faisal Irfan	23.5	3	95	0	
Jalat Khan	32	1	132	0	6w,9nb
Yasir Arafat	13	0	51	0	1w,1nb
Sohaib Maqsood	16	0	108	0	7nb
Saeed Bin Nasir	10	0	68	0	

Umpires: Ahmed Shahab and Ahsan Raza. Referee: Anis Sheikh.   Toss: North West Frontier Province
Close of Play: 1st day: North West Frontier Province (1) 36-0 (Rafatullah Mohmand 11*, Yasir Hameed 19*, 7 overs); 2nd day: North West Frontier Province (1) 503-2 (Yasir Hameed 265*, Khurram Shehzad 9*, 97 overs); 3rd day: Baluchistan (2) 243-4 (Saeed Bin Nasir 118*, Nasim Khan 27*, 56 overs).
Saeed Bin Nasir's 149 took 193 balls in 299 minutes and included 17 fours and 8 sixes. Yasir Hameed's 300 took 367 balls in 472 minutes and included 49 fours. Asad Shafiq's 181 took 251 balls in 325 minutes and included 33 fours and 1 six. Saeed Bin Nasir's 133 took 203 balls in 203 minutes and included 20 fours and 3 sixes.

SIND v PUNJAB

Played at National Stadium, Karachi, March 11, 12, 13, 2008.
ABN-AMRO Pentangular Cup 2007/08
Sind won by an innings and 31 runs. (Points: Sind 9, Punjab 0)

PUNJAB

1	Salman Butt	c Sarfraz Ahmed b Sohail Khan	20	(6) not out	29
2	Mohammad Hafeez	c Khalid Latif b Abdul Ameer	17	(1) c Naumanullah b Shahid Afridi	17
3	Nasir Jamshed	c Rizwan Ahmed b Anwar Ali	21	(2) lbw b Shahid Afridi	27
4	*Misbah-ul-Haq	c Sarfraz Ahmed b Sohail Khan	4	c Naumanullah b Sohail Khan	51
5	Ammar Mahmood	c Sarfraz Ahmed b Sohail Khan	15	(3) lbw b Shahid Afridi	40
6	Adnan Raza	c Shahid Afridi b Rizwan Ahmed	45	(5) run out	0
7	†Kamran Akmal	c Sarfraz Ahmed b Sohail Khan	6	c Fawad Alam b Anwar Ali	0
8	Abdur Rehman	c Rizwan Ahmed b Shahid Afridi	21	lbw b Anwar Ali	6
9	Junaid Zia	not out	8	b Anwar Ali	9
10	Fahad Masood	lbw b Rizwan Ahmed	2	(11) lbw b Sohail Khan	9
11	Wahab Riaz	c Naumanullah b Shahid Afridi	4	(10) c Khurram Manzoor b Anwar Ali	0
	Extras	b 4, lb 7, nb 10	21	b 2, lb 4, nb 8	14
			184		**202**

FoW (1): 1-39, 2-68, 3-72, 4-93, 5-94, 6-113, 7-158, 8-167, 9-171, 10-184
FoW (2): 1-43, 2-54, 3-141, 4-145, 5-157, 6-162, 7-178, 8-188, 9-188, 10-202

SIND

1	Khurram Manzoor	c Mohammad Hafeez b Fahad Masood	36
2	Khalid Latif	c Salman Butt b Wahab Riaz	21
3	Naumanullah	c Kamran Akmal b Wahab Riaz	6
4	Rizwan Ahmed	c Misbah-ul-Haq b Wahab Riaz	79
5	Faisal Iqbal	c Kamran Akmal b Wahab Riaz	65
6	Fawad Alam	c Kamran Akmal b Junaid Zia	43
7	*Shahid Afridi	c Fahad Masood b Mohammad Hafeez	14
8	†Sarfraz Ahmed	not out	82
9	Anwar Ali	not out	33
10	Sohail Khan		
11	Abdul Ameer		
	Extras	b 15, lb 9, w 1, nb 13	38
		(7 wickets, declared)	**417**

FoW (1): 1-47, 2-59, 3-86, 4-224, 5-227, 6-248, 7-336

Sind Bowling

	O	M	R	W			O	M	R	W	
Sohail Khan	23	6	58	4			13	4	41	2	
Anwar Ali	16	4	59	1	3nb	(3)	16	5	45	4	
Abdul Ameer	13	5	29	1	5nb	(2)	9	2	31	0	3nb
Shahid Afridi	9.5	3	25	2	2nb		16	4	60	3	1nb
Rizwan Ahmed	2	0	2	2			1	0	19	0	4nb

Punjab Bowling

	O	M	R	W	
Wahab Riaz	28	2	99	4	1w,9nb
Junaid Zia	22	2	92	1	3nb
Fahad Masood	29	3	78	1	
Abdur Rehman	20	2	78	0	1nb
Mohammad Hafeez	12	1	46	1	

Umpires: Nadeem Ghauri and Riazuddin. Referee: Anwar Khan.   Toss: Sind

Close of Play: 1st day: Punjab (1) 173-9 (Junaid Zia 2*, Wahab Riaz 0*, 61 overs); 2nd day: Sind (1) 303-6 (Fawad Alam 29*, Sarfraz Ahmed 25*, 35 overs).

The match was scheduled for four days but completed in three.

BORDER v KWAZULU-NATAL

Played at Mercedes Benz Park, East London, October 11, 12, 13, 2007.
South African Airways Provincial Three-Day Challenge 2007/08 - Pool A
Match drawn.   (Points: Border 6.36, KwaZulu-Natal 6.6)

KWAZULU-NATAL

1	K.Smit	c Bennett b Pangabantu	8	lbw b Pangabantu	8
2	*R.Gobind	b Fojela	4	c Dyili b Brown	4
3	F.B.Lazarus	c Fojela b Mgijima	34	run out	19
4	M.Bekker	c Dyili b Brown	31	lbw b Pangabantu	0
5	S.C.Mabuya	c Kreusch b Voke	22	(6) b de Kock	16
6	†C.Hauptfleisch	c Dyili b Pangabantu	9	(5) lbw b Pangabantu	12
7	C.A.Flowers	b Pangabantu	31	not out	57
8	A.N.W.Tweedie	b Voke	9	(11) not out	26
9	V.Gobind	not out	14	(8) c Mgijima b de Kock	4
10	T.D.Pillay	st Dyili b de Kock	1	(9) c Kreusch b Pangabantu	24
11	D.N.Horsfall	lbw b Pangabantu	3	(10) b Brown	0
	Extras	b 2, lb 7, w 3, nb 2	14	lb 7, w 1, nb 2	10

	180	
	(9 wickets, declared)	**180**

FoW (1): 1-14 (1), 2-16 (2), 3-76 (4), 4-88 (3), 5-106 (6), 6-141 (5), 7-159 (8), 8-161 (7), 9-165 (10), 10-180 (11)
FoW (2): 1-12 (1), 2-27 (2), 3-32 (4), 4-32 (3), 5-61 (6), 6-73 (5), 7-77 (8), 8-139 (9), 9-140 (10)

BORDER

1	K.D.Bennett	c Horsfall b Tweedie	0
2	*J.P.Kreusch	c Hauptfleisch b V.Gobind	10
3	L.Masingatha	c Lazarus b Bekker	6
4	†A.Z.M.Dyili	lbw b Tweedie	8
5	D.L.Brown	lbw b Bekker	0
6	S.Booi	c R.Gobind b Bekker	32
7	A.Mgijima	c Horsfall b Tweedie	1
8	S.de Kock	c Hauptfleisch b Tweedie	5
9	B.M.Voke	c and b Pillay	68
10	P.Fojela	c R.Gobind b Pillay	28
11	Y.Pangabantu	not out	0
	Extras	lb 6, w 1, nb 3	10

	168

FoW (1): 1-0 (1), 2-16 (2), 3-27 (3), 4-27 (4), 5-27 (5), 6-28 (7), 7-34 (8), 8-105 (6), 9-143 (10), 10-168 (9)

Border Bowling

	O	M	R	W		O	M	R	W	
Pangabantu	20.1	7	35	4	1w,1nb	19	7	45	4	1nb
Fojela	14	2	26	1	1w,1nb	3	0	19	0	1nb
Voke	12	1	50	2		(5) 8	1	26	0	
Brown	12	1	42	1		(3) 17	4	43	2	1w
Mgijima	2	1	9	1		(6) 1.4	1	1	0	
de Kock	4	2	9	1		(4) 11	0	39	2	

KwaZulu-Natal Bowling

	O	M	R	W	
Tweedie	21	5	55	4	1w
V.Gobind	13	4	38	1	3nb
Bekker	10	3	25	3	
Pillay	7.1	1	21	2	
Horsfall	5	1	23	0	

Umpires: E.C.Hendrikse and A.T.Holdstock.   Toss: KwaZulu-Natal

Close of Play: 1st day: No play; 2nd day: Border (1) 60-7 (Booi 15*, Voke 10*, 27.4 overs).

DOLPHINS v EAGLES

Played at Sahara Stadium, Kingsmead, Durban, October 11, 12, 13, 14, 2007.
SuperSport Series 2007/08
Eagles won by 43 runs.   (Points: Dolphins 4, Eagles 17.46)

EAGLES

#					
1	D.Elgar	c Watson b Friend	13	c Smit b Mlongo	34
2	A.P.McLaren	lbw b Abdulla	11	b Friend	0
3	J.A.Rudolph	c Smit b Kent	29	c Kent b Abdulla	66
4	*H.H.Dippenaar	lbw b Mlongo	115	c van Vuuren b Kent	17
5	†M.N.van Wyk	c Smit b Kent	0	c Khan b Kent	8
6	R.T.Bailey	c Smit b Kent	0	not out	27
7	R.McLaren	c Smit b Friend	46	c Khan b Abdulla	0
8	D.du Preez	c Khan b Mlongo	12	not out	12
9	T.Tshabalala	c Watson b Abdulla	19		
10	B.B.Kops	not out	17		
11	P.V.Mpitsang				
	Extras	lb 5, w 3, nb 3	11	b 1, lb 1, w 1, nb 2	5
		(9 wickets, declared)	273	(6 wickets, declared)	169

FoW (1): 1-19 (1), 2-34 (2), 3-89 (3), 4-89 (5), 5-89 (6), 6-160 (7), 7-175 (8), 8-223 (9), 9-273 (4)
FoW (2): 1-4 (2), 2-75 (1), 3-103 (4), 4-115 (5), 5-141 (3), 6-149 (7)

DOLPHINS

#					
1	D.J.Watson	c Rudolph b Mpitsang	24	lbw b Kops	0
2	I.Khan	c van Wyk b Kops	0	c Rudolph b Tshabalala	28
3	J.C.Kent	c Dippenaar b Kops	11	b Kops	0
4	*A.M.Amla	c Dippenaar b R.McLaren	1	c Dippenaar b Rudolph	112
5	W.L.Madsen	c Dippenaar b Kops	8	lbw b Rudolph	39
6	M.S.van Vuuren	c du Preez b Kops	27	c A.P.McLaren b du Preez	48
7	†D.Smit	c A.P.McLaren b du Preez	2	(8) b du Preez	10
8	J.Louw	c Dippenaar b du Preez	0	(7) c and b Rudolph	32
9	Q.Friend	b du Preez	7	c van Wyk b du Preez	0
10	Y.A.Abdulla	c van Wyk b du Preez	4	c Dippenaar b Rudolph	10
11	S.Mlongo	not out	1	not out	7
	Extras	b 2, lb 2, w 3, nb 12	19	b 4, lb 1, w 1, nb 3	9
			104		295

FoW (1): 1-10 (2), 2-34 (3), 3-35 (4), 4-52 (5), 5-63 (1), 6-66 (7), 7-66 (8), 8-80 (9), 9-91 (10), 10-104 (6)
FoW (2): 1-0 (1), 2-0 (3), 3-48 (2), 4-182 (4), 5-191 (5), 6-255 (7), 7-276 (6), 8-276 (9), 9-277 (8), 10-295 (10)

Dolphins Bowling

	O	M	R	W		O	M	R	W	
Abdulla	21	5	68	2	1nb	14	0	46	2	1nb
Friend	21	5	54	2	1w	7	1	38	1	1w
Louw	19	3	63	0	2w,1nb	8	1	20	0	
Mlongo	16.2	4	40	2	1nb	6	0	34	1	1nb
Kent	14	4	24	3		5	0	29	2	
van Vuuren	3	1	19	0						

Eagles Bowling

	O	M	R	W			O	M	R	W	
R.McLaren	7	0	26	1	1w,1nb	(2)	14	0	51	0	
Kops	10.2	2	39	4	2w,3nb	(1)	19	5	52	2	2nb
Mpitsang	8	4	23	1	4nb	(4)	15	4	33	0	1w,1nb
du Preez	7	1	12	4		(3)	18	6	39	3	
Tshabalala						(5)	9	0	46	1	
Rudolph						(6)	16.2	1	69	4	

Umpires: K.H.Hurter and D.J.Smith. Referee: S.B.Lambson.   Toss: Dolphins

Close of Play: 1st day: No play; 2nd day: Dolphins (1) 15-1 (Watson 8*, Kent 3*, 3.5 overs); 3rd day: Dolphins (2) 4-2 (Khan 0*, Amla 4*, 0.5 overs).

Man of the Match: H.H.Dippenaar.
H.H.Dippenaar's 115 took 242 balls in 349 minutes and included 18 fours. A.M.Amla's 112 took 149 balls in 224 minutes and included 15 fours and 2 sixes.

FREE STATE v GRIQUALAND WEST

Played at OUTsurance Oval, Bloemfontein, October 11, 12, 13, 2007.
South African Airways Provincial Three-Day Challenge 2007/08 - Pool B
Match drawn. (Points: Free State 6.52, Griqualand West 9.2)

GRIQUALAND WEST

1	A.K.Kruger	c Puchert b van Zyl	134	c Moreeng b Motsamai	26
2	C.N.Bennett	c Moreeng b Saliwa	30	c Moreeng b Saliwa	4
3	M.Akoojee	c de Lange b Vries	7	lbw b Saliwa	6
4	P.J.Koortzen	lbw b Saliwa	23	lbw b Saliwa	1
5	*†W.Bossenger	c Moreeng b Saliwa	52	not out	73
6	A.G.Doherty	c von Rauenstein b van Zyl	11	lbw b Saliwa	0
7	C.Pietersen	c von Rauenstein b Saliwa	7	b Puchert	25
8	F.S.Holtzhausen	c Brooker b van Zyl	16	c Moreeng b Motsamai	8
9	J.Coetzee	c Brooker b Vries	12	c O'Neill b Saliwa	1
10	K.B.Sekonyela	c von Rauenstein b Vries	4	b Motsamai	14
11	N.O.Arthur	not out	1	not out	13
	Extras	lb 6, w 1, nb 6	13	lb 7, w 2	9
			310	(9 wickets, declared)	180

FoW (1): 1-66 (2), 2-99 (3), 3-161 (4), 4-231 (1), 5-261 (6), 6-271 (7), 7-280 (5), 8-304 (8), 9-309 (10), 10-310 (9)
FoW (2): 1-15 (2), 2-32 (3), 3-40 (1), 4-40 (4), 5-46 (6), 6-87 (7), 7-105 (8), 8-110 (9), 9-141 (10)

FREE STATE

1	I.D.J.O'Neill	lbw b Holtzhausen	31	c Bossenger b Coetzee	4
2	A.D.de Lange	c Bossenger b Coetzee	12	lbw b Pietersen	8
3	J.Brooker	c Koortzen b Holtzhausen	13	b Arthur	56
4	*H.O.von Rauenstein	c Bossenger b Holtzhausen	11	c Kruger b Pietersen	14
5	G.N.Nieuwoudt	b Arthur	29	not out	50
6	†H.K.Moreeng	c Bossenger b Kruger	6	c Pietersen b Arthur	2
7	H.Puchert	c Bossenger b Pietersen	24	not out	0
8	W.J.van Zyl	c Coetzee b Arthur	23		
9	G.A.Vries	not out	8		
10	M.N.Saliwa	c Bossenger b Arthur	6		
11	T.S.Motsamai	lbw b Coetzee	3		
	Extras	lb 4, w 4, nb 2	10	lb 2, w 1, nb 7	10
			176	(5 wickets)	144

FoW (1): 1-19 (2), 2-56 (3), 3-70 (4), 4-71 (1), 5-88 (6), 6-118 (5), 7-151 (8), 8-160 (7), 9-166 (10), 10-176 (11)
FoW (2): 1-12 (2), 2-12 (1), 3-52 (4), 4-130 (3), 5-132 (6)

Free State Bowling

	O	M	R	W		O	M	R	W	
Saliwa	21	0	108	4	4nb	15	1	56	5	
Motsamai	21	5	53	0	1w	17	3	59	3	1w
Puchert	9	1	60	0		10	2	18	1	
Vries	12.4	2	36	3	2nb	13	2	40	0	
van Zyl	19	1	47	3						

Griqualand West Bowling

	O	M	R	W		O	M	R	W	
Coetzee	14	7	9	2		8	2	23	1	
Pietersen	14	6	27	1	1nb	9	2	37	2	3nb
Holtzhausen	14	3	62	3	1w	6	0	24	0	
Sekonyela	7	1	20	0	1nb	3	0	21	0	1w,4nb
Kruger	8	3	9	1	1w	6	1	13	0	
Arthur	22	6	45	3		8	3	24	3	

Umpires: L.M.Engelbrecht and I.H.van Kerwel.   Toss: Free State

Close of Play: 1st day: Griqualand West (1) 310 all out; 2nd day: Griqualand West (2) 82-5 (Bossenger 18*, Pietersen 23*, 25 overs).

A.K.Kruger's 134 took 183 balls in 251 minutes and included 20 fours.

KWAZULU-NATAL INLAND v BOLAND

Played at City Oval, Pietermaritzburg, October 11, 12, 13, 2007.
South African Airways Provincial Three-Day Challenge 2007/08 - Pool A
Match drawn.   (Points: KwaZulu-Natal Inland 6.08, Boland 6.96)

BOLAND

1	J.L.C.Lotz	b Qasim Khurshid	12	b Qasim Khurshid		7
2	A.W.Olivier	c Moses b G.M.Hampson	0	st Gqadushe b Bowyer		48
3	B.C.Adams	lbw b Qasim Khurshid	57	c Gqadushe b Qasim Khurshid		0
4	*P.C.Laing	lbw b van Vuuren	6	b Qasim Khurshid		9
5	D.L.Campbell	lbw b van Vuuren	10	lbw b van Vuuren		0
6	Q.K.Kannemeyer	b G.M.Hampson	21	lbw b van Vuuren		18
7	†L.R.Walters	b G.M.Hampson	36	c Gqadushe b Brown		28
8	S.F.Grobler	b Bowyer	10	c Gqadushe b G.M.Hampson		33
9	J.M.van Wyk	lbw b Bowyer	18	b G.M.Hampson		26
10	J.P.Bothma	not out	13	run out		7
11	H.H.Paulse	not out	2	not out		0
	Extras	b 3, lb 8, nb 2	13	b 1, lb 12, w 7		20
		(9 wickets)	198			196

FoW (1): 1-4 (2), 2-35 (1), 3-61 (4), 4-91 (3), 5-91 (5), 6-141 (6), 7-162 (7), 8-162 (8), 9-187 (9)
FoW (2): 1-9 (1), 2-9 (3), 3-37 (4), 4-38 (5), 5-67 (6), 6-97 (2), 7-132 (7), 8-186 (8), 9-196 (10), 10-196 (9)

KWAZULU-NATAL INLAND

1	R.D.McMillan	c Walters b Paulse	9	c Walters b Paulse	8
2	C.S.Bowyer	run out (Olivier)	17	lbw b Laing	66
3	K.Padayachee	lbw b Paulse	1	c Adams b Laing	3
4	M.B.Hampson	lbw b Bothma	8	c sub (T.D.Groenewald) b Kannemeyer	22
5	B.Moses	c and b Paulse	80	b Kannemeyer	9
6	L.Brown	b van Wyk	6	lbw b Laing	5
7	*A.van Vuuren	c Grobler b van Wyk	4	c Laing b Kannemeyer	6
8	G.M.Hampson	b van Wyk	0	b Laing	19
9	S.Dorasamy	c Grobler b Laing	12	c Laing b Grobler	9
10	†M.Gqadushe	not out	7	not out	8
11	Qasim Khurshid	c Walters b Paulse	0	not out	1
	Extras	b 2, lb 4, nb 4	10	b 1, lb 4, w 2, nb 1	8
			154	(9 wickets)	164

FoW (1): 1-12 (1), 2-25 (3), 3-37 (4), 4-47 (2), 5-72 (6), 6-94 (7), 7-94 (8), 8-130 (9), 9-146 (5), 10-154 (11)
FoW (2): 1-42 (1), 2-76 (3), 3-86 (2), 4-103 (5), 5-116 (6), 6-120 (4), 7-137 (7), 8-150 (8), 9-154 (9)

KwaZulu-Natal Inland Bowling

	O	M	R	W			O	M	R	W	
Qasim Khurshid	14	3	34	2	1nb		20	5	50	3	1w
G.M.Hampson	22	4	74	3			16.5	5	40	2	
McMillan	13	5	21	0	1nb	(4)	3	1	8	0	
van Vuuren	23	10	33	2		(3)	12	3	18	2	1w
Dorasamy	3	1	6	0							
Bowyer	10	4	19	2		(5)	10	3	19	1	
M.B.Hampson						(6)	3	1	4	0	
Brown						(7)	12	2	27	1	1w
Moses						(8)	3	0	17	0	

Boland Bowling

	O	M	R	W			O	M	R	W	
Paulse	14.3	2	46	4	3nb		6.2	1	27	1	
Bothma	14	2	38	1			5	0	27	0	2w
Grobler	10	4	28	0		(6)	5	0	21	1	
van Wyk	9	4	24	3		(3)	7	2	26	0	
Kannemeyer	5	3	5	0			12	2	39	3	1nb
Laing	4	3	7	1		(4)	14	8	19	4	

Umpires: B.N.Harrison and C.L.Joubert.   Toss: KwaZulu-Natal Inland

Close of Play: 1st day: KwaZulu-Natal Inland (1) 29-2 (Bowyer 15*, M.B.Hampson 0*, 9.2 overs); 2nd day: Boland (2) 156-7 (Grobler 18*, van Wyk 11*, 65 overs).

345

LIONS v WARRIORS

Played at New Wanderers Stadium, Johannesburg, October 11, 12, 13, 14, 2007.
SuperSport Series 2007/08
Match drawn.   (Points: Lions 5.66, Warriors 7.56)

LIONS

1	B.D.Snijman	c D.J.Jacobs b Meyer	44	c Ackerman b Meyer	38
2	S.C.Cook	lbw b Tsotsobe	12	run out	41
3	A.N.Petersen	c A.Jacobs b Tsotsobe	0	b Peterson	27
4	*N.D.McKenzie	lbw b Tsotsobe	0	c D.J.Jacobs b Hayward	33
5	J.L.Ontong	c de Bruyn b Tsotsobe	69	c A.Jacobs b Meyer	108
6	H.W.le Roux	c Olivier b de Bruyn	1	c Tsotsobe b Olivier	37
7	†M.J.Harris	c Ackerman b Hayward	16	not out	33
8	C.W.Henderson	lbw b Tsotsobe	0	c Meyer b Olivier	1
9	F.de Wet	c Olivier b Tsotsobe	14	c D.J.Jacobs b Meyer	10
10	G.J.P.Kruger	not out	0	not out	9
11	C.J.Alexander	c Ingram b Tsotsobe	0		
	Extras	lb 9, w 7, nb 11	27	lb 12, w 9, nb 20	41
			183	**(8 wickets, declared)**	**378**

FoW (1): 1-35 (2), 2-36 (3), 3-36 (4), 4-109 (1), 5-141 (6), 6-148 (5), 7-148 (8), 8-183 (7), 9-183 (9), 10-183 (11)
FoW (2): 1-85 (1), 2-95 (2), 3-129 (3), 4-208 (4), 5-312 (5), 6-312 (6), 7-318 (8), 8-360 (9)

WARRIORS

1	C.A.Ingram	c Petersen b de Wet	22	c Ontong b Kruger	6
2	C.A.Thyssen	c Cook b Alexander	16	c Cook b Kruger	0
3	*Z.de Bruyn	lbw b Alexander	25	st Harris b Henderson	38
4	H.D.Ackerman	b le Roux	31	not out	22
5	A.Jacobs	c Petersen b Alexander	19	not out	5
6	†D.J.Jacobs	c Harris b Kruger	58		
7	R.J.Peterson	c Harris b Kruger	16		
8	L.Meyer	c Harris b de Wet	21		
9	M.W.Olivier	c Harris b Alexander	17		
10	M.Hayward	c Henderson b de Wet	4		
11	L.L.Tsotsobe	not out	27		
	Extras	lb 8, w 4, nb 10	22	lb 6	6
			278	**(3 wickets)**	**77**

FoW (1): 1-33 (2), 2-41 (1), 3-94 (3), 4-111 (4), 5-115 (5), 6-157 (7), 7-220 (6), 8-220 (8), 9-237 (10), 10-278 (9)
FoW (2): 1-1 (2), 2-22 (1), 3-64 (3)

Warriors Bowling

	O	M	R	W			O	M	R	W	
Hayward	17	2	57	1	5w,3nb	(2)	20	1	74	1	1nb
Tsotsobe	21	8	39	7	1nb	(1)	26	2	102	0	4nb
Olivier	8	2	33	0			17	1	72	2	3nb
de Bruyn	11	4	29	1			14	4	43	0	1w,1nb
Meyer	8w,11nb	0	16	1	2w,7nb		12.4	0	47	3	
Peterson						(6)	17	6	28	1	

Lions Bowling

	O	M	R	W		O	M	R	W	
Kruger	29	10	79	2	5nb	8	3	19	2	
de Wet	25	6	67	3		9.3	5	10	1	
Alexander	21.1	4	68	4		7	1	23	0	
le Roux	17	8	32	1	1nb	7	3	10	1	
Henderson	7	2	24	0	1w	3	1	9	1	

Umpires: M.W.Brown and J.D.Cloete.   Referee: D.Govindjee.   Toss: Warriors

Close of Play: 1st day: Lions (1) 125-4 (Ontong 53*, le Roux 1*, 31 overs); 2nd day: Warriors (1) 189-6 (D.J.Jacobs 46*, Meyer 8*, 68 overs); 3rd day: Lions (2) 204-3 (McKenzie 31*, Ontong 49*, 65 overs).

Man of the Match: J.L.Ontong.

J.L.Ontong's 108 took 164 balls in 224 minutes and included 12 fours and 1 six.

NORTH WEST v NORTHERNS

Played at Sedgars Park, Potchefstroom, October 11, 12, 13, 2007.
South African Airways Provincial Three-Day Challenge 2007/08 - Pool B
Match drawn.   (Points: North West 7.78, Northerns 6.98)

NORTHERNS

1	A.F.Viljoen	c Mostert b Deacon	67	c Bredenkamp b Coetsee	9	
2	R.Jappie	c Bula b Coetsee	7	c Bula b de Bruin	20	
3	P.J.van Biljon	c Coetsee b Bhayat	3	lbw b Deacon	7	
4	F.Behardien	c de Bruin b Coetsee	47	c de Bruin b Letsoalo	82	
5	S.A.Engelbrecht	c Naicker b Bhayat	45	lbw b de Bruin	0	
6	*A.M.Phangiso	c Bula b Deacon	14	lbw b Bhayat	35	
7	†A.L.Ndlovu	c Bula b Bhayat	8	c sub (M.P.Siboto) b Letsoalo	39	
8	R.E.van der Merwe	not out	23	not out	54	
9	M.A.Mashimbyi	c Mostert b Bhayat	12	not out	34	
10	N.Wagner	c Bula b Bredenkamp	0			
11	M.Arnold	run out (Lazenby)	7			
	Extras	lb 5, w 1, nb 10	16	lb 7, nb 11	18	
			249	(7 wickets, declared)	298	

FoW (1): 1-30 (3), 2-101 (4), 3-109 (2), 4-144 (1), 5-179 (6), 6-205 (5), 7-206 (7), 8-222 (9), 9-222 (10), 10-249 (11)
FoW (2): 1-23 (1), 2-41 (3), 3-43 (2), 4-43 (5), 5-136 (6), 6-175 (4), 7-234 (7)

NORTH WEST

1	J.F.Mostert	b Engelbrecht	80	(2) b Mashimbyi	24	
2	W.L.Coetsee	lbw b Wagner	0	(1) b Engelbrecht	41	
3	M.Lazenby	c Ndlovu b Arnold	3	c Arnold b Engelbrecht	2	
4	N.Bredenkamp	lbw b Behardien	23	c Mashimbyi b Engelbrecht	13	
5	L.J.Kgamadi	b van der Merwe	56	c Ndlovu b Phangiso	0	
6	R.Bhayat	b Arnold	4	not out	29	
7	*W.A.Deacon	c Ndlovu b Arnold	39	not out	15	
8	†T.A.Bula	b Phangiso	9			
9	G.J.de Bruin	b Mashimbyi	21			
10	K.M.Naicker	not out	0			
11	P.S.Letsoalo	not out	8			
	Extras	lb 3, w 1, nb 8	12	lb 2, w 1, nb 5	8	
		(9 wickets)	255	(5 wickets)	132	

FoW (1): 1-4 (2), 2-7 (3), 3-77 (4), 4-141 (1), 5-161 (6), 6-192 (5), 7-211 (8), 8-247 (7), 9-247 (9)
FoW (2): 1-37 (2), 2-46 (3), 3-81 (1), 4-86 (5), 5-96 (4)

North West Bowling

	O	M	R	W		O	M	R	W	
de Bruin	14	6	20	0	2nb	15	4	42	2	4nb
Deacon	16	4	40	2	4nb	18	2	56	1	4nb
Bhayat	12.4	1	73	4	3nb (4)	9	0	38	1	
Letsoalo	12.3	8	21	0	(5)	11	2	46	2	3nb
Coetsee	22	4	69	2	1w (3)	27	8	96	1	
Naicker	4	0	20	0		3	0	13	0	
Bredenkamp	0.3	0	1	1	1nb					

Northerns Bowling

	O	M	R	W		O	M	R	W	
Arnold	16	3	44	3	1nb	7	1	27	0	3nb
Wagner	14	0	48	1	4nb	6	2	24	0	1nb
Mashimbyi	11	4	45	1	2nb	2	0	4	1	1w
Behardien	8	3	15	1	1w,1nb					
Phangiso	18	4	41	1		8	3	21	1	1nb
Engelbrecht	7	2	22	1	(4)	9.5	1	47	3	
van der Merwe	14	0	37	1	(6)	3	1	7	0	

Umpires: C.J.Conradie and Z.T.A.Ndamane.   Toss: North West

Close of Play: 1st day: North West (1) 4-0 (Mostert 4*, Coetsee 0*, 1 over); 2nd day: Northerns (2) 31-1 (Jappie 15*, van Biljon 3*, 20 overs).

R.Jappie retired hurt in the Northerns first innings having scored 1 (team score 23-0) - he returned when the score was 101-2.

TITANS v CAPE COBRAS

Played at Willowmoore Park Main Oval, Benoni, October 11, 12, 13, 14, 2007.
SuperSport Series 2007/08
Match drawn.   (Points: Titans 7.68, Cape Cobras 7.54)

CAPE COBRAS

1	A.J.A.Gray	c Reddy b Joubert	38	c Kuhn b Mbhalati	1
2	A.G.Puttick	c Aronstam b Mbhalati	33	b Mbhalati	23
3	H.Davids	c Kuhn b Mbhalati	0	not out	123
4	J.G.Strydom	lbw b Imran Tahir	82	c du Plessis b Joubert	4
5	*B.Hector	c van Jaarsveld b Imran Tahir	64	lbw b Joubert	0
6	S.van Zyl	c Aronstam b Thomas	74	run out	67
7	†T.L.Tsolekile	c van Jaarsveld b Joubert	13	c van Jaarsveld b Imran Tahir	2
8	R.K.Kleinveldt	c Kuhn b Imran Tahir	0		
9	C.D.de Lange	not out	47	(8) not out	18
10	T.Henderson	c du Plessis b Mbhalati	0		
11	M.Zondeki	c Mbhalati b Thomas	5		
	Extras	b 1, lb 13, nb 8	22	b 2, lb 4, w 7, nb 8	21
			378	**(6 wickets)**	**259**

FoW (1): 1-63 (2), 2-63 (3), 3-97 (1), 4-208 (4), 5-273 (5), 6-311 (7), 7-312 (8), 8-372 (6), 9-373 (10), 10-378 (11)
FoW (2): 1-1 (1), 2-40 (2), 3-49 (4), 4-49 (5), 5-209 (6), 6-211 (7)

TITANS

1	M.A.Aronstam	c Davids b Henderson	52
2	†H.G.Kuhn	c Strydom b Zondeki	51
3	*M.van Jaarsveld	b Henderson	89
4	F.du Plessis	lbw b Kleinveldt	13
5	G.H.Bodi	c Kleinveldt b de Lange	11
6	P.de Bruyn	c and b Zondeki	25
7	P.Joubert	c Davids b Zondeki	85
8	A.C.Thomas	b Kleinveldt	14
9	B.L.Reddy	not out	11
10	Imran Tahir	c Henderson b Zondeki	4
11	N.E.Mbhalati	c Gray b Zondeki	7
	Extras	b 2, lb 4, w 4, nb 24	34
			396

FoW (1): 1-109 (1), 2-109 (2), 3-144 (4), 4-172 (5), 5-216 (6), 6-331 (3), 7-366 (8), 8-376 (7), 9-384 (10), 10-396 (11)

Titans Bowling

	O	M	R	W			O	M	R	W	
Thomas	30.4	11	73	2			10.3	1	56	0	3w,2nb
Mbhalati	32	8	84	3	2nb		14	5	44	2	2nb
Reddy	14	3	31	0	6nb	(5)	9	4	21	0	4nb
Joubert	22	11	36	2		(3)	13	5	33	2	
Imran Tahir	30	3	107	3		(4)	15	2	54	1	
van Jaarsveld	8	1	22	0		(7)	3	0	14	0	
du Plessis	2	0	11	0							
Aronstam						(6)	5	0	31	0	

Cape Cobras Bowling

	O	M	R	W	
Zondeki	25.4	5	101	5	3nb
Henderson	22	5	70	2	1w,2nb
Kleinveldt	24	5	81	2	13nb
de Lange	17	0	89	1	3nb
van Zyl	9	1	31	0	3w,3nb
Gray	3.5	0	17	0	
Davids	0.1	0	1	0	

Umpires: I.L.Howell and B.G.Jerling.   Referee: C.J.Mitchley.   Toss: Titans

Close of Play: 1st day: Cape Cobras (1) 41-0 (Gray 16*, Puttick 19*, 25.3 overs); 2nd day: Cape Cobras (1) 356-7 (van Zyl 66*, de Lange 38*, 132 overs); 3rd day: Titans (1) 366-6 (Joubert 77*, Thomas 14*, 93.1 overs).
Man of the Match: S.van Zyl.
H.Davids's 123 took 198 balls in 290 minutes and included 11 fours and 2 sixes.

DOLPHINS v TITANS

Played at Sahara Stadium, Kingsmead, Durban, October 18, 19, 20, 21, 2007.
SuperSport Series 2007/08
Dolphins won by seven wickets.   **(Points: Dolphins 17.54, Titans 4)**

TITANS

1	M.A.Aronstam	c Smit b Friend	20	run out		26
2	†H.G.Kuhn	c van Vuuren b Louw	18	c Smit b Kent		31
3	*M.van Jaarsveld	c Khan b Friend	12	(7) c Louw b van Vuuren		18
4	F.du Plessis	lbw b Friend	0	(3) c Smit b Louw		17
5	G.H.Bodi	c Watson b Friend	40	c Watson b Louw		1
6	P.de Bruyn	c Watson b Abdulla	15	c Benkenstein b van Vuuren		28
7	P.Joubert	c Smit b Kent	19	(8) lbw b Louw		23
8	A.C.Thomas	c Smit b Kent	0	(9) b Louw		33
9	B.L.Reddy	not out	4	(4) c Watson b Louw		38
10	Imran Tahir	c van Vuuren b Abdulla	2	b Louw		11
11	N.E.Mbhalati	b Friend	0	not out		0
	Extras	lb 12, w 2, nb 3	17	lb 5, w 7, nb 2		14
			147			**240**

FoW (1): 1-37 (2), 2-41 (1), 3-41 (4), 4-63 (3), 5-102 (5), 6-138 (7), 7-138 (8), 8-138 (6), 9-145 (10), 10-147 (11)
FoW (2): 1-59 (2), 2-70 (1), 3-86 (3), 4-88 (5), 5-123 (4), 6-156 (7), 7-177 (6), 8-207 (8), 9-231 (10), 10-240 (9)

DOLPHINS

1	D.J.Watson	lbw b Thomas	24	c van Jaarsveld b Joubert		28
2	I.Khan	lbw b Reddy	80	not out		45
3	H.M.Amla	b Imran Tahir	59	c Mbhalati b Aronstam		12
4	*A.M.Amla	lbw b Imran Tahir	20			
5	D.M.Benkenstein	b Imran Tahir	14	(4) st Kuhn b Aronstam		5
6	J.C.Kent	c Joubert b Reddy	11	(5) not out		12
7	M.S.van Vuuren	b Imran Tahir	1			
8	J.Louw	c van Jaarsveld b Reddy	0			
9	†D.Smit	b Mbhalati	32			
10	Q.Friend	c sub (F.Behardien) b Mbhalati	13			
11	Y.A.Abdulla	not out	0			
	Extras	lb 9, w 3, nb 11	23	b 1, lb 4, w 1, nb 3		9
			277	(3 wickets)		**111**

FoW (1): 1-52 (1), 2-160 (3), 3-194 (4), 4-214 (2), 5-215 (5), 6-227 (6), 7-227 (8), 8-240 (7), 9-277 (10), 10-277 (9)
FoW (2): 1-39 (1), 2-73 (3), 3-83 (4)

Dolphins Bowling

	O	M	R	W			O	M	R	W	
Abdulla	12	1	46	2	2nb	(2)	21	7	60	0	
Louw	15	6	36	1	1w	(3)	28	6	88	6	2w
Friend	15	6	30	5	1w	(1)	23	10	52	0	1w,2nb
Kent	10	2	23	2	1nb		13	4	21	1	
van Vuuren						(5)	7	3	10	2	
Smit						(6)	4	1	4	0	

Titans Bowling

	O	M	R	W			O	M	R	W	
Thomas	21	5	67	1			6	1	28	0	1w,1nb
Mbhalati	20.3	4	50	2	2w,4nb		4	0	19	0	
Joubert	10	2	29	0			9	3	18	1	
Reddy	13	3	37	3	1w,7nb		5	0	23	0	2nb
Imran Tahir	16	3	75	4							
Aronstam	4	1	10	0		(5)	5.3	0	18	2	

Umpires: S.George and B.G.Jerling. Referee: A.Barnes.   Toss: Dolphins

Close of Play: 1st day: No play; 2nd day: Dolphins (1) 51-0 (Watson 23*, Khan 21*, 16.2 overs); 3rd day: Titans (2) 75-2 (du Plessis 10*, Reddy 4*, 35 overs).

Man of the Match: J.Louw.

EAGLES v LIONS

Played at De Beers Diamond Oval, Kimberley, October 18, 19, 20, 21, 2007.
SuperSport Series 2007/08
Eagles won by 113 runs. (Points: Eagles 15.98, Lions 4)

EAGLES

1	D.Elgar	c Petersen b de Wet	6	c Harris b de Wet	20
2	A.P.McLaren	c Petersen b Alexander	27	b Kruger	6
3	J.A.Rudolph	b Snijman	34	c Snijman b Kruger	15
4	*H.H.Dippenaar	c McKenzie b Alexander	5	c Harris b McKenzie	153
5	†M.N.van Wyk	c Cook b Alexander	18	c Snijman b Cook	41
6	R.T.Bailey	c McKenzie b Henderson	41	c Harris b Kruger	9
7	R.McLaren	b Kruger	10	b de Wet	36
8	D.du Preez	b Alexander	16	b Alexander	25
9	T.Tshabalala	st Harris b Henderson	13	c de Wet b Alexander	18
10	B.B.Kops	b Alexander	19	c Kruger b McKenzie	0
11	P.V.Mpitsang	not out	0	not out	0
	Extras	lb 6, w 1, nb 3	10	b 10, lb 10, nb 8	28
			199		**351**

FoW (1): 1-14 (1), 2-36 (2), 3-42 (4), 4-84 (5), 5-110 (3), 6-130 (7), 7-155 (6), 8-176 (9), 9-198 (8), 10-199 (10)
FoW (2): 1-10 (2), 2-33 (3), 3-70 (1), 4-136 (5), 5-180 (6), 6-282 (7), 7-328 (8), 8-342 (4), 9-342 (10), 10-351 (9)

LIONS

1	B.D.Snijman	lbw b du Preez	2	(2) c Dippenaar b du Preez	6
2	S.C.Cook	b du Preez	0	(1) lbw b du Preez	8
3	A.N.Petersen	c Dippenaar b du Preez	0	(4) c van Wyk b R.McLaren	21
4	*N.D.McKenzie	c van Wyk b du Preez	32	(5) run out	54
5	†M.J.Harris	b R.McLaren	1	(7) c Dippenaar b R.McLaren	41
6	H.W.le Roux	c Dippenaar b Mpitsang	6	(8) c Dippenaar b du Preez	32
7	C.W.Henderson				
	W.L.Coetsee	lbw b Mpitsang	3	(3) c van Wyk b Kops	60
8	J.L.Ontong	c Rudolph b R.McLaren	31	(6) b Mpitsang	21
9	F.de Wet	c van Wyk b du Preez	16	c Rudolph b du Preez	26
10	G.J.P.Kruger	b du Preez	4	not out	25
11	C.J.Alexander	not out	1	lbw b Rudolph	4
	Extras	lb 4, w 5, nb 5	14	b 5, lb 11, w 8, nb 5	29
			110		**327**

FoW (1): 1-6 (2), 2-6 (3), 3-11 (1), 4-12 (5), 5-40 (6), 6-48 (7), 7-48 (4), 8-104 (9), 9-104 (8), 10-110 (10)
FoW (2): 1-12 (1), 2-21 (2), 3-68 (4), 4-117 (3), 5-158 (6), 6-210 (5), 7-243 (7), 8-289 (8), 9-312 (9), 10-327 (11)

Lions Bowling	O	M	R	W			O	M	R	W	
Kruger	12	3	35	1	1w,1nb	(2)	21	4	75	3	8nb
de Wet	19	6	39	1		(1)	26	6	54	2	
Alexander	17.2	3	73	5			17.4	2	91	2	
le Roux	13	8	19	0	2nb		23	5	58	0	
Snijman	1	0	8	1							
Henderson	14	7	19	2							
Cook						(5)	8	2	15	1	
Coetsee						(6)	11	3	25	0	
McKenzie						(7)	6	2	13	2	

Eagles Bowling	O	M	R	W			O	M	R	W	
Kops	8	2	26	0	3w,3nb	(2)	15	3	50	1	4w,3nb
du Preez	15.2	6	40	6		(1)	33	11	72	4	
R.McLaren	9	1	26	2			25	4	68	2	
Mpitsang	7	4	14	2	1w,1nb		24	7	52	1	2nb
Tshabalala						(5)	22	6	47	0	
Rudolph						(6)	12.2	3	22	1	

Umpires: M.W.Brown and E.C.Hendrikse. Referee: S.Wadvalla. Toss: Lions
Close of Play: 1st day: Lions (1) 40-4 (McKenzie 27*, le Roux 6*, 17 overs); 2nd day: Eagles (2) 210-5 (Dippenaar 85*, R.McLaren 13*, 71 overs); 3rd day: Lions (2) 147-4 (McKenzie 20*, Ontong 17*, 52 overs).
Man of the Match: D.du Preez, H.H.Dippenaar.
W.L.Coetsee was a full substitute for Lions, replacing C.W.Henderson because of illness in Henderson's family. H.H.Dippenaar's 153 took 289 balls in 403 minutes and included 23 fours.

WARRIORS v CAPE COBRAS

Played at Sahara Oval, St George's Park, Port Elizabeth, October 18, 19, 20, 2007.
SuperSport Series 2007/08
Warriors won by six wickets.   (Points: Warriors 17.66, Cape Cobras 4)

CAPE COBRAS

1	A.G.Puttick	c D.J.Jacobs b Hayward	5	(2) c D.J.Jacobs b Hayward	92
2	H.Davids	c D.J.Jacobs b Hayward	0	(1) lbw b Tsotsobe	10
3	J.G.Strydom	c A.Jacobs b Tsotsobe	5	c Thyssen b Peterson	65
4	A.G.Prince	c Thyssen b Tsotsobe	48	c D.J.Jacobs b Hayward	5
5	*B.Hector	c D.J.Jacobs b Tsotsobe	0	c de Bruyn b Peterson	8
6	S.van Zyl	lbw b Olivier	13	c D.J.Jacobs b Hayward	38
7	†T.L.Tsolekile	c Ackerman b Hayward	3	c D.J.Jacobs b Mjekula	0
8	C.D.de Lange	run out (Thyssen)	8	c Thyssen b Olivier	8
9	R.K.Kleinveldt	c D.J.Jacobs b Mjekula	13	c A.Jacobs b Mjekula	3
10	T.Henderson	c sub (L.Meyer) b Tsotsobe	0	c Peterson b Tsotsobe	13
11	M.Zondeki	not out	6	not out	0
	Extras	lb 4, w 1, nb 4	9	b 4, lb 14, w 1, nb 6	25
			110		**267**

FoW (1): 1-1 (2), 2-6 (1), 3-14 (3), 4-14 (5), 5-34 (6), 6-43 (7), 7-63 (8), 8-76 (9), 9-79 (10), 10-110 (4)
FoW (2): 1-11 (1), 2-134 (3), 3-159 (4), 4-186 (5), 5-204 (2), 6-208 (7), 7-237 (8), 8-243 (9), 9-267 (6), 10-267 (10)

WARRIORS

1	J.P.Kreusch	b Henderson	14	(2) c Prince b Zondeki	2
2	C.A.Thyssen	st Tsolekile b de Lange	87	(1) b Zondeki	5
3	*Z.de Bruyn	c Tsolekile b Kleinveldt	19	c Tsolekile b Zondeki	11
4	H.D.Ackerman	c Tsolekile b Kleinveldt	32	c Tsolekile b Zondeki	0
5	A.Jacobs	c Kleinveldt b Zondeki	93	not out	31
6	†D.J.Jacobs	lbw b Kleinveldt	5	not out	45
7	R.J.Peterson	c Puttick b Henderson	14		
8	M.W.Olivier	lbw b Zondeki	0		
9	L.L.Tsotsobe	c and b Zondeki	3		
10	M.Hayward	not out	5		
11	S.Mjekula	c Tsolekile b Kleinveldt	0		
	Extras	lb 6, w 1, nb 4	11	w 1, nb 3	4
			283	(4 wickets)	**98**

FoW (1): 1-27 (1), 2-76 (3), 3-144 (4), 4-202 (2), 5-227 (6), 6-262 (7), 7-263 (8), 8-278 (5), 9-278 (9), 10-283 (11)
FoW (2): 1-7 (2), 2-9 (1), 3-9 (4), 4-26 (3)

Warriors Bowling

	O	M	R	W			O	M	R	W	
Hayward	16	5	31	3	1nb		27	11	43	3	1w
Tsotsobe	11.2	3	34	4	2nb		15.2	4	43	2	
Mjekula	13	4	28	1	1nb		14	4	38	2	1nb
Olivier	9	3	13	1	1w		8	1	30	1	1nb
Peterson						(5)	24	5	70	2	
A.Jacobs						(6)	1	0	7	0	
de Bruyn						(7)	6	2	18	0	4nb

Cape Cobras Bowling

	O	M	R	W			O	M	R	W	
Zondeki	28	7	70	3	1w,1nb	(2)	8.2	2	32	4	1w
Henderson	25	6	71	2		(3)	5	2	18	0	
Kleinveldt	26.3	7	77	4		(1)	8	1	24	0	3nb
de Lange	14	4	50	1	3nb		3	0	24	0	
van Zyl	3	1	9	0							

Umpires: I.L.Howell and K.H.Hurter. Referee: E.H.Mall.   Toss: Warriors

Close of Play: 1st day: Warriors (1) 72-1 (Thyssen 41*, de Bruyn 15*, 30 overs); 2nd day: Cape Cobras (2) 81-1 (Puttick 33*, Strydom 36*, 33 overs).

Man of the Match: A.Jacobs.

The match was scheduled for four days but completed in three.

WESTERN PROVINCE v KWAZULU-NATAL

Played at Sahara Park Newlands, Cape Town, October 18, 19, 20, 2007.
South African Airways Provincial Three-Day Challenge 2007/08 - Pool A
Western Province won by 91 runs.   (Points: Western Province 19.08, KwaZulu-Natal 7.46)

WESTERN PROVINCE

1	M.Williamson	c Miller b Africa	28	b Frylinck	0
2	C.D.Williams	run out (Lazarus/Pillay)	66	b Africa	17
3	T.J.Mdodana	lbw b Africa	0	lbw b Pillay	5
4	J.M.Kuiper	c Bekker b Frylinck	49	c Miller b Africa	102
5	F.D.Telo	c Frylinck b Africa	35	lbw b Pillay	5
6	*†R.C.C.Canning	not out	53	c Hauptfleisch b V.Gobind	23
7	W.C.Hantam	b Flowers	36	run out	25
8	C.W.S.Birch	not out	27	c Africa b Pillay	82
9	P.R.Adams			c Pillay b Africa	35
10	M.de Stadler			b Frylinck	14
11	L.F.Simpson			not out	4
	Extras	b 2, lb 5, w 3	10	b 8, lb 13	21
		(6 wickets)	304		333

FoW (1): 1-36 (1), 2-36 (3), 3-111 (4), 4-167 (5), 5-215 (2), 6-257 (7)
FoW (2): 1-0 (1), 2-21 (3), 3-35 (2), 4-52 (5), 5-111 (6), 6-151 (7), 7-222 (4), 8-272 (9), 9-329 (8), 10-333 (10)

KWAZULU-NATAL

1	W.Hauptfleisch	b Simpson	14	lbw b de Stadler	62
2	*R.Gobind	lbw b Simpson	17	lbw b Simpson	23
3	F.B.Lazarus	lbw b Simpson	4	c Canning b Simpson	0
4	K.Smit	lbw b Birch	62	c Adams b de Stadler	14
5	M.Bekker	c Mdodana b de Stadler	56	c Hantam b de Stadler	114
6	C.A.Flowers	run out (Mdodana/Canning)	31	b Adams	9
7	†D.R.Miller	lbw b de Stadler	0	(8) b Adams	9
8	R.Frylinck	c Canning b Simpson	52	(7) c Canning b Birch	1
9	K.C.Africa	lbw b Simpson	15	c Birch b de Stadler	21
10	T.D.Pillay	not out	13	not out	6
11	V.Gobind	c Hantam b Simpson	0	c and b Adams	6
	Extras	lb 7, w 1, nb 1	9	b 2, lb 4, w 2	8
			273		273

FoW (1): 1-32 (1), 2-37 (2), 3-39 (3), 4-116 (5), 5-183 (4), 6-186 (7), 7-201 (6), 8-244 (9), 9-273 (8), 10-273 (11)
FoW (2): 1-58 (2), 2-58 (3), 3-83 (4), 4-108 (1), 5-127 (6), 6-158 (7), 7-205 (8), 8-254 (9), 9-265 (5), 10-273 (11)

KwaZulu-Natal Bowling

	O	M	R	W			O	M	R	W	
V.Gobind	14	3	38	0		(2)	7.5	3	18	1	
Frylinck	17	6	47	1	1w	(1)	25.3	6	86	2	
Africa	18	6	55	3	1w	(4)	13	0	69	3	
Bekker	5	1	33	0		(8)	1	0	11	0	
Pillay	20	4	71	0		(3)	13	2	56	3	
Hauptfleisch	7	1	25	0	1w	(9)	2	0	13	0	
Flowers	4	0	28	1		(6)	4	0	20	0	
Smit						(5)	6	0	35	0	
R.Gobind						(7)	0.1	0	4	0	

Western Province Bowling

	O	M	R	W			O	M	R	W	
Simpson	17	3	58	6			10	1	52	2	1w
Hantam	8	2	42	0		(3)	5	0	31	0	
Birch	18	5	64	1	1w,1nb	(2)	8	0	34	1	1w
de Stadler	18	7	56	2			17	3	78	4	
Adams	12	1	46	0			16	3	72	3	

Umpires: D.J.Smith and B.M.White.   Toss: Western Province

Close of Play: 1st day: KwaZulu-Natal (1) 70-3 (Smit 10*, Bekker 21*, 18.3 overs); 2nd day: Western Province (2) 209-6 (Kuiper 93*, Birch 28*, 50 overs).
J.M.Kuiper's 102 took 101 balls in 155 minutes and included 17 fours. M.Bekker's 114 took 99 balls in 139 minutes and included 11 fours and 5 sixes.

BORDER v SOUTH WESTERN DISTRICTS

Played at Mercedes Benz Park, East London, October 25, 26, 27, 2007.
South African Airways Provincial Three-Day Challenge 2007/08 - Pool A
Border won by eight wickets.   (Points: Border 17.56, South Western Districts 3)

SOUTH WESTERN DISTRICTS

1	*J.A.Beukes	lbw b Olivier	8	c Dyili b Fojela	120
2	S.E.Avontuur	b Pangabantu	8	b Fojela	8
3	B.C.de Wett	lbw b Brown	9	c de Kock b Olivier	13
4	N.G.Brouwers	c Dyili b Brown	27	c Dyili b Olivier	61
5	P.A.Stuurman	b Fojela	4	c Masingatha b Pangabantu	24
6	M.Masimela	c Brown b Fojela	12	b Pangabantu	6
7	†R.P.Hugo	c Dyili b Fojela	13	c Dyili b Pangabantu	5
8	W.Hartslief	lbw b Fojela	0	lbw b Pangabantu	0
9	N.M.Murray	c Ranger b Brown	0	run out	13
10	B.L.Fransman	c Booi b Brown	1	c Masingatha b Pangabantu	8
11	N.Nobebe	not out	4	not out	6
	Extras	lb 6, w 1, nb 2	9	lb 3, w 2, nb 5	10
			95		**274**

FoW (1): 1-12 (2), 2-20 (1), 3-34 (3), 4-60 (5), 5-64 (4), 6-87 (7), 7-87 (8), 8-90 (6), 9-90 (9), 10-95 (10)
FoW (2): 1-17 (2), 2-41 (3), 3-173 (4), 4-232 (5), 5-241 (1), 6-245 (6), 7-245 (8), 8-248 (7), 9-266 (9), 10-274 (10)

BORDER

1	S.de Kock	c Hugo b Nobebe	10	lbw b Nobebe	0
2	S.Booi	c Hugo b Nobebe	24	not out	16
3	L.Masingatha	lbw b Masimela	75	c Hugo b Hartslief	37
4	†A.Z.M.Dyili	c Hugo b Nobebe	4	not out	45
5	K.D.Bennett	c Beukes b Masimela	14		
6	*M.N.Ranger	c Hugo b Murray	90		
7	D.L.Brown	c Hartslief b Masimela	1		
8	M.W.Olivier	lbw b Masimela	10		
9	B.M.Voke	b Masimela	8		
10	P.Fojela	not out	19		
11	Y.Pangabantu	c de Wett b Nobebe	2		
	Extras	lb 4, w 2, nb 2	8	b 4, w 5	9
			265	**(2 wickets)**	**107**

FoW (1): 1-36 (2), 2-39 (1), 3-45 (4), 4-68 (5), 5-214 (6), 6-222 (7), 7-223 (3), 8-236 (8), 9-249 (9), 10-265 (11)
FoW (2): 1-5 (1), 2-53 (3)

Border Bowling

	O	M	R	W		O	M	R	W	
Olivier	8	2	24	1	2nb	23	3	103	2	2nb
Pangabantu	6	2	19	1	1w	14.4	3	48	5	2w,1nb
Brown	7.4	1	34	4	(4)	5	0	25	0	
Fojela	6	2	12	4	(3)	20	6	68	2	2nb
Ranger					(5)	7	0	24	0	
de Kock					(6)	3	1	3	0	

South Western Districts Bowling

	O	M	R	W			O	M	R	W	
Fransman	13	5	27	0	1w						
Nobebe	13	1	46	4	1w	(1)	5	1	17	1	1w
Hartslief	15	3	52	0		(2)	6	2	17	1	
Murray	15	4	36	1		(3)	5	1	21	0	
Masimela	11	5	17	5	2nb						
Brouwers	11	1	32	0		(4)	3	1	40	0	
de Wett	17	2	51	0		(5)	2	1	8	0	

Umpires: S.George and C.D.Isaacs.   Toss: Border

Close of Play: 1st day: Border (1) 196-4 (Masingatha 63*, Ranger 76*, 69.1 overs); 2nd day: South Western Districts (2) 216-3 (Beukes 109*, Stuurman 18*, 54 overs).

J.A.Beukes's 120 took 181 balls in 276 minutes and included 22 fours.

EASTERN PROVINCE v WESTERN PROVINCE

Played at Sahara Oval, St George's Park, Port Elizabeth, October 25, 26, 27, 2007.
South African Airways Provincial Three-Day Challenge 2007/08 - Pool A
Eastern Province won by 214 runs.   (Points: Eastern Province 17.48, Western Province 6.46)

EASTERN PROVINCE

1	J.T.Smuts	c Sodumo b Simpson	4	c Canning b Simpson	45
2	C.Baxter	b van Wyk	22	lbw b Mahlombe	27
3	U.Abrahams	c Telo b Mahlombe	1	not out	115
4	*M.B.A.Smith	c Simpson b de Stadler	70	b Mahlombe	2
5	†S.R.Adair	lbw b van Wyk	3	c Williams b Simpson	17
6	R.R.Jeggels	c Canning b Simpson	10	b van Wyk	11
7	L.Meyer	lbw b de Stadler	24	c Mahlombe b de Stadler	30
8	J.Theron	lbw b van Wyk	2	c Bennett b Adams	1
9	C.R.Dolley	c Canning b de Stadler	0		
10	A.C.R.Birch	c Telo b Mahlombe	41		
11	B.D.Walters	not out	25		
	Extras	lb 12, w 5, nb 5	22	lb 7, w 3, nb 1	11
			224	(7 wickets, declared)	**259**

FoW (1): 1-22 (1), 2-30 (3), 3-54 (2), 4-58 (5), 5-74 (6), 6-133 (7), 7-138 (8), 8-143 (9), 9-162 (4), 10-224 (10)
FoW (2): 1-33 (2), 2-138 (1), 3-153 (4), 4-182 (5), 5-197 (6), 6-256 (7), 7-259 (8)

WESTERN PROVINCE

1	C.D.Williams	c Meyer b Walters	5	b Theron	5
2	M.Williamson	c Smith b Birch	43	c Adair b Meyer	19
3	B.L.Bennett	c Smith b Walters	10	lbw b Theron	0
4	F.D.Telo	run out (Dolley)	2	b Theron	0
5	A.M.Sodumo	c Adair b Birch	1	c Smith b Theron	0
6	*†R.C.C.Canning	c Abrahams b Theron	25	b Birch	14
7	E.P.van Wyk	c Adair b Birch	8	run out	26
8	M.de Stadler	c Adair b Meyer	7	b Theron	14
9	P.R.Adams	c Baxter b Walters	18	c Walters b Meyer	0
10	M.Mahlombe	not out	13	b Theron	0
11	L.F.Simpson	b Theron	13	not out	4
	Extras	lb 6, w 4, nb 18	28	b 3, lb 2, nb 9	14
			173		**96**

FoW (1): 1-11 (1), 2-29 (3), 3-60 (4), 4-65 (5), 5-83 (2), 6-104 (7), 7-116 (8), 8-145 (9), 9-154 (6), 10-173 (11)
FoW (2): 1-13 (1), 2-13 (3), 3-13 (4), 4-17 (5), 5-39 (2), 6-52 (6), 7-87 (7), 8-92 (8), 9-92 (10), 10-96 (9)

Western Province Bowling

	O	M	R	W		O	M	R	W	
Simpson	13	2	36	2	4w,5nb	12	2	50	2	1w
Mahlombe	11.4	2	50	2	1w	14	3	45	2	2w,1nb
de Stadler	26	4	66	3		21	6	50	1	
van Wyk	17	7	29	3		12	0	60	1	
Adams	6	0	31	0		9	1	47	1	

Eastern Province Bowling

	O	M	R	W		O	M	R	W	
Theron	18.5	6	56	2	1w,2nb	11	3	22	6	4nb
Walters	16	4	31	3		10	0	36	0	1nb
Birch	20	8	44	3	3w,1nb (4)	9	3	16	1	
Meyer	7	0	36	1	15nb (3)	9.5	4	17	2	4nb

Umpires: Z.T.A.Ndamane and B.M.White.   Toss: Western Province

Close of Play: 1st day: Western Province (1) 66-4 (Williamson 33*, Canning 1*, 25 overs); 2nd day: Eastern Province (2) 155-3 (Abrahams 72*, Adair 1*, 44.5 overs).

U.Abrahams's 115 took 168 balls in 245 minutes and included 14 fours and 1 six.

GAUTENG v FREE STATE

Played at Braam Fisherville, Dobsonville, Johannesburg, October 25, 26, 27, 2007.
South African Airways Provincial Three-Day Challenge 2007/08 - Pool B
Match drawn.   (Points: Gauteng 3, Free State 9.04)

FREE STATE

1	I.D.J.O'Neill	c Vilas b Cameron	16
2	D.Elgar	c Motaung b Cameron	41
3	†L.N.Mosena	c Vilas b Cameron	0
4	R.T.Bailey	not out	186
5	*H.O.von Rauenstein	run out (Motaung)	112
6	G.N.Nieuwoudt	lbw b Cameron	5
7	C.J.D.de Villiers	run out (Symes)	14
8	W.J.van Zyl	c Das Neves b Burger	4
9	G.A.Vries	not out	1
10	M.N.Saliwa		
11	T.S.Motsamai		
	Extras	b 3, lb 7, w 7, nb 6	23
		(7 wickets)	402

FoW (1): 1-60 (1), 2-60 (3), 3-65 (2), 4-285 (5), 5-308 (6), 6-343 (7), 7-371 (8)

GAUTENG

1	J.Symes	c O'Neill b Saliwa	28
2	W.B.Motaung	b de Villiers	7
3	O.A.Ramela	c Mosena b Saliwa	1
4	W.C.Swan	lbw b Saliwa	0
5	D.L.Makalima	not out	16
6	*S.Burger	not out	8
7	†D.J.Vilas		
8	R.Cameron		
9	R.Das Neves		
10	B.M.Mathebula		
11	J.T.Mafa		
	Extras	w 2	2
		(4 wickets)	62

FoW (1): 1-20 (2), 2-29 (3), 3-33 (4), 4-45 (1)

Gauteng Bowling

	O	M	R	W	
Mathebula	12	0	66	0	2w,3nb
Burger	22	3	91	1	
Cameron	23	7	70	4	1w
Mafa	14	0	92	0	3nb
Das Neves	6	0	39	0	
Swan	4	0	10	0	
Symes	3	0	15	0	
Motaung	1	0	9	0	

Free State Bowling

	O	M	R	W	
de Villiers	9	2	20	1	1w
Saliwa	8.4	1	42	3	1w

Umpires: C.J.Conradie and L.B.Gcuma.   Toss: Gauteng

Close of Play: 1st day: Free State (1) 281-3 (Bailey 98*, von Rauenstein 110*, 67 overs); 2nd day: Gauteng (1) 62-4 (Makalima 16*, Burger 8*, 17.4 overs).

There was no play on the final day. R.T.Bailey's 186 took 186 balls in 282 minutes and included 20 fours and 6 sixes. H.O.von Rauenstein's 112 took 155 balls in 206 minutes and included 16 fours.

NORTH WEST v EASTERNS

Played at Sedgars Park, Potchefstroom, October 25, 26, 27, 2007.
South African Airways Provincial Three-Day Challenge 2007/08 - Pool B
Match drawn.　(Points: North West 10.34, Easterns 4.94)

NORTH WEST

1	C.Jonker	c Reddy b Pienaar	143
2	B.J.Pelser	lbw b Plaatjie	2
3	M.Lazenby	c Bodibe b Wiese	47
4	N.Bredenkamp	c sub (P.T.Mofokeng) b Hlengani	44
5	L.J.Kgamadi	b Reddy	63
6	†T.A.Bula	not out	51
7	*W.A.Deacon		
8	J.P.Campher		
9	C.J.Alexander		
10	K.M.Naicker		
11	P.S.Letsoalo		
	Extras	b 2, lb 8, w 1, nb 6	17
		(5 wickets)	367

FoW (1): 1-6 (2), 2-154 (3), 3-235 (4), 4-271 (1), 5-367 (5)

EASTERNS

1	I.C.Hlengani	b Alexander	23	c Deacon b Naicker	24
2	†T.M.Bodibe	lbw b Alexander	0	b Campher	0
3	A.J.Seymore	b Alexander	18		
4	J.Booysen	c Bula b Alexander	0	(3) c Bredenkamp b Letsoalo	25
5	G.Toyana	b Deacon	4	(4) lbw b Naicker	86
6	D.Wiese	lbw b Deacon	16	(5) not out	115
7	J.J.Pienaar	lbw b Alexander	65	(6) c Bula b Kgamadi	37
8	*S.P.O'Connor	c Bula b Letsoalo	6		
9	P.P.van den Berg	c Bula b Campher	8		
10	B.L.Reddy	c Bula b Campher	25		
11	T.R.Plaatjie	not out	1		
	Extras	b 7, lb 4, w 6, nb 14	31	b 4, lb 7, w 1, nb 20	32
			197	(5 wickets)	319

FoW (1): 1-6 (2), 2-39 (3), 3-39 (4), 4-44 (5), 5-68 (1), 6-86 (6), 7-103 (8), 8-131 (9), 9-187 (7), 10-197 (10)
FoW (2): 1-4 (2), 2-46 (3), 3-98 (1), 4-215 (4), 5-319 (6)

Easterns Bowling

	O	M	R	W	
Reddy	15	2	62	1	1nb
Plaatjie	4	0	23	1	2nb
Wiese	16	2	61	1	1w
Pienaar	13	0	83	1	2nb
van den Berg	14	1	56	0	
O'Connor	3	1	17	0	
Hlengani	20	4	55	1	1nb

North West Bowling

	O	M	R	W			O	M	R	W	
Campher	10.5	1	62	2	1w,12nb	(2)	10	0	74	1	16nb
Alexander	16	6	59	5		(1)	15	7	37	0	1w
Deacon	11	5	32	2	2nb		13	3	43	0	
Letsoalo	5	1	14	1	1w		12	4	33	1	
Naicker	2	0	19	0			15	0	98	2	
Bredenkamp						(6)	5	1	21	0	
Kgamadi						(7)	1.1	0	2	1	

Umpires: B.N.Harrison and B.D.A.Westraadt.　　　　　　Toss: Easterns

Close of Play: 1st day: Easterns (1) 61-4 (Hlengani 23*, Wiese 4*, 16.1 overs); 2nd day: Easterns (1) 171-8 (Pienaar 61*, Reddy 14*, 41 overs).
C.Jonker's 143 took 195 balls in 264 minutes and included 24 fours and 1 six. D.Wiese's 115 took 126 balls in 167 minutes and included 21 fours. I.C.Hlengani retired hurt in the Easterns second innings having scored 0 (team score 0-0) - he returned when the score was 46-2.

SOUTH AFRICAN INVITATION XI v NEW ZEALANDERS

Played at OUTsurance Oval, Bloemfontein, October 25, 26, 27, 2007.
New Zealand in South Africa 2007/08
New Zealanders won by 216 runs.

NEW ZEALANDERS

1	C.D.Cumming	c Khan b Abdulla	12	lbw b Mbhalati	67
2	M.H.W.Papps	c Jacobs b Mbhalati	2	c Amla b Tsotsobe	4
3	S.P.Fleming	c Tsolekile b Mbhalati	33	lbw b Kent	5
4	S.B.Styris	c Jacobs b Mbhalati	29	c Jacobs b Mbhalati	5
5	L.R.P.L.Taylor	c de Bruyn b Tsotsobe	12	b Mbhalati	0
6	J.D.P.Oram	lbw b Kent	23	st Tsolekile b Tshabalala	12
7	†B.B.McCullum	c and b Tsotsobe	46	c Tsolekile b Kent	18
8	*D.L.Vettori	c van Wyk b Abdulla	99	b Kent	10
9	S.E.Bond	lbw b Abdulla	28	b Kent	8
10	M.J.Mason	not out	8	not out	8
11	C.S.Martin	lbw b Abdulla	0	c Jacobs b Tsotsobe	4
	Extras	b 1, lb 15, w 7, nb 3	26	lb 4	4
			318		**145**

FoW (1): 1-19 (2), 2-21 (1), 3-76 (3), 4-91 (5), 5-126 (4), 6-126 (6), 7-236 (7), 8-293 (9), 9-318 (8), 10-318 (11)
FoW (2): 1-19 (2), 2-63 (3), 3-76 (4), 4-76 (5), 5-81 (1), 6-108 (7), 7-115 (6), 8-129 (8), 9-138 (9), 10-145 (11)

SOUTH AFRICAN INVITATION XI

1	I.Khan	c McCullum b Martin	6	(2) b Oram	11
2	*M.N.van Wyk	c McCullum b Bond	2	(1) c Styris b Bond	21
3	Z.de Bruyn	b Martin	4	c McCullum b Oram	1
4	A.M.Amla	c and b Vettori	67	c Fleming b Bond	0
5	D.J.Jacobs	c McCullum b Oram	9	c Styris b Bond	4
6	J.C.Kent	lbw b Oram	8	c McCullum b Mason	13
7	†T.L.Tsolekile	c Papps b Oram	25	c Martin b Vettori	30
8	T.Tshabalala	c McCullum b Oram	0	c McCullum b Martin	2
9	L.L.Tsotsobe	b Vettori	9	c McCullum b Martin	0
10	Y.A.Abdulla	not out	8	c McCullum b Vettori	4
11	N.E.Mbhalati	st McCullum b Vettori	0	not out	0
	Extras	lb 16, w 2	18	b 1, lb 2, w 2	5
			156		**91**

FoW (1): 1-21 (2), 2-22 (1), 3-33 (3), 4-46 (5), 5-58 (6), 6-133 (7), 7-135 (8), 8-147 (4), 9-156 (9), 10-156 (11)
FoW (2): 1-25 (1), 2-31 (3), 3-34 (4), 4-38 (2), 5-44 (5), 6-68 (6), 7-83 (8), 8-83 (9), 9-91 (7), 10-91 (10)

South African Invitation XI Bowling

	O	M	R	W			O	M	R	W	
Mbhalati	20	8	50	3	1nb		18	6	53	3	
Tsotsobe	18	3	62	2	2nb		9.2	4	27	2	
Abdulla	19.5	4	81	4	3w						
Kent	16	6	43	1		(3)	18	7	45	4	
Tshabalala	14	1	66	0		(4)	9	3	16	1	

New Zealanders Bowling

	O	M	R	W			O	M	R	W	
Bond	14	5	23	1	2w		7	0	26	3	2w
Martin	13	6	25	2			8	1	27	2	
Mason	13	5	31	0		(4)	2	0	4	1	
Oram	14	5	17	4		(3)	6	0	14	2	
Vettori	11.5	1	44	3			2.5	0	17	2	

Umpires: K.H.Hurter and R.E.Koertzen. Referee: A.Barnes.   Toss: South African Invitation XI

Close of Play: 1st day: New Zealanders (1) 318 all out; 2nd day: South African Invitation XI (1) 156 all out.

The match was scheduled for four days but completed in three.

GRIQUALAND WEST v NORTH WEST

Played at De Beers Diamond Oval, Kimberley, November 1, 2, 3, 2007.
South African Airways Provincial Three-Day Challenge 2007/08 - Pool B
Match drawn.   (Points: Griqualand West 8.36, North West 5.28)

GRIQUALAND WEST

1	A.K.Kruger	c Bula b Deacon	24	lbw b Coetsee	15
2	M.Akoojee	c Kgamadi b Deacon	11	run out	28
3	A.P.McLaren	c Gerber b Letsoalo	94	c Bula b Letsoalo	5
4	L.L.Bosman	c Coetsee b Gerber	17	c Kgamadi b Letsoalo	2
5	P.J.Koortzen	b Letsoalo	42	b Coetsee	39
6	*†W.Bossenger	lbw b Deacon	24	b Coetsee	2
7	R.R.Hendricks	b Coetsee	8	(8) run out	19
8	J.Coetzee	c Bula b Coetsee	14	(7) not out	16
9	A.R.Swanepoel	lbw b Coetsee	17	b Letsoalo	1
10	R.A.Adams	not out	5		
11	D.D.Carolus	b Coetsee	0		
	Extras	lb 6, w 1, nb 5	12	lb 8, w 3, nb 1	12
			268	(8 wickets)	139

FoW (1): 1-24 (2), 2-47 (1), 3-94 (4), 4-191 (3), 5-201 (5), 6-232 (6), 7-236 (7), 8-259 (8), 9-264 (9), 10-268 (11)
FoW (2): 1-31 (1), 2-42 (3), 3-48 (4), 4-76 (2), 5-83 (6), 6-113 (5), 7-138 (8), 8-139 (9)

NORTH WEST

1	J.F.Mostert	c Coetzee b Kruger	11	b Carolus	64
2	B.J.Pelser	run out (Kruger)	13	c McLaren b Kruger	6
3	W.L.Coetsee	b Kruger	1	c Bossenger b Adams	59
4	N.Bredenkamp	lbw b Swanepoel	48	c Bossenger b Carolus	9
5	L.J.Kgamadi	c Bossenger b Carolus	11	c McLaren b Carolus	10
6	†T.A.Bula	c Bossenger b Carolus	5	c Bossenger b Kruger	29
7	*W.A.Deacon	run out (Hendricks/Bossenger)	0	run out (Hendricks/Bossenger)	70
8	E.Gerber	c and b Carolus	9	c Swanepoel b Kruger	8
9	K.M.Naicker	c Hendricks b Carolus	0	(10) lbw b Coetzee	0
10	P.S.Letsoalo	c McLaren b Carolus	5	(11) not out	5
11	C.J.Alexander	not out	3	(9) c Swanepoel b Carolus	25
	Extras	b 4, w 1, nb 3	8	b 7, lb 9, w 4, pen 5	25
			114		310

FoW (1): 1-26 (1), 2-26 (2), 3-30 (3), 4-91 (4), 5-97 (6), 6-97 (7), 7-97 (5), 8-99 (9), 9-105 (10), 10-114 (8)
FoW (2): 1-6 (2), 2-134 (1), 3-140 (3), 4-156 (4), 5-157 (5), 6-206 (6), 7-232 (8), 8-289 (9), 9-295 (10), 10-310 (7)

North West Bowling

	O	M	R	W			O	M	R	W	
Alexander	3	1	19	0							
Deacon	17	2	43	3	5nb	(1)	2	0	19	0	1nb
Letsoalo	16	2	74	2	1w	(2)	11.1	0	67	0	1w
Gerber	7	1	26	1							
Coetsee	16.3	3	69	4		(3)	10	1	45	3	
Naicker	5	0	31	0							

Griqualand West Bowling

	O	M	R	W			O	M	R	W	
Coetzee	7	2	22	0	1w		17	5	33	1	3w
Carolus	15	3	37	5	3nb	(4)	20	6	66	4	
Kruger	8	4	6	2		(2)	22	3	88	3	1w
Adams	3	0	13	0		(3)	20	7	67	1	
Swanepoel	10	1	32	1			10	1	35	0	

Umpires: J.E.P.Ostrom and B.M.White.   Toss: North West

Close of Play: 1st day: Griqualand West (1) 41-1 (Kruger 22*, McLaren 4*, 7.4 overs); 2nd day: North West (2) 4-0 (Mostert 0*, Pelser 4*, 2.2 overs).

NORTHERNS v FREE STATE

Played at L.C.de Villiers Oval, Pretoria, November 1, 2, 3, 2007.
South African Airways Provincial Three-Day Challenge 2007/08 - Pool B
Northerns won by an innings and 91 runs.   (Points: Northerns 18.36, Free State 3)

FREE STATE

1	I.D.J.O'Neill	c van der Merwe b Wagner	8	c Ndlovu b Wagner	0
2	A.D.de Lange	c Engelbrecht b Wagner	20	lbw b Wagner	76
3	†L.N.Mosena	run out (Wagner/Liebisch)	0	c Ndlovu b Mashimbyi	7
4	*H.O.von Rauenstein	c Mashimbyi b Liebisch	41	c Viljoen b Wagner	29
5	G.N.Nieuwoudt	c van der Merwe b Mashimbyi	7	c Behardien b Mashimbyi	39
6	C.J.D.de Villiers	c Ndlovu b Mashimbyi	2	c Mashimbyi b Liebisch	4
7	W.J.van Zyl	c Ndlovu b Mashimbyi	4	c Ndlovu b Liebisch	1
8	T.S.Motsamai	not out	10	run out	1
9	B.B.Kops	c Engelbrecht b Liebisch	2	c Viljoen b Wagner	14
10	G.A.Vries	c Behardien b Liebisch	0	not out	2
11	M.N.Saliwa	c Ndlovu b Liebisch	0	c Behardien b Wagner	1
	Extras	lb 3, w 1	4	lb 2, nb 3	5
			98		**179**

FoW (1): 1-29 (2), 2-30 (1), 3-34 (3), 4-44 (5), 5-46 (6), 6-54 (7), 7-92 (4), 8-94 (9), 9-94 (10), 10-98 (11)
FoW (2): 1-0 (1), 2-15 (3), 3-61 (4), 4-141 (5), 5-152 (6), 6-158 (7), 7-159 (8), 8-175 (2), 9-178 (9), 10-179 (11)

NORTHERNS

1	A.F.Viljoen	c Mosena b de Villiers	39
2	R.Jappie	lbw b de Villiers	19
3	P.J.van Biljon	c Mosena b de Villiers	16
4	F.Behardien	c Mosena b Kops	86
5	S.A.Engelbrecht	c O'Neill b Kops	31
6	S.W.Liebisch	st Mosena b van Zyl	91
7	*A.M.Phangiso	c Mosena b Saliwa	7
8	†A.L.Ndlovu	b Kops	37
9	R.E.van der Merwe	not out	10
10	M.A.Mashimbyi	run out (von Rauenstein/Mosena)	0
11	N.Wagner	b van Zyl	0
	Extras	b 3, lb 5, w 8, nb 16	32
			368

FoW (1): 1-41 (2), 2-72 (3), 3-106 (1), 4-195 (5), 5-213 (4), 6-239 (7), 7-354 (6), 8-362 (8), 9-368 (10), 10-368 (11)

Northerns Bowling

	O	M	R	W		O	M	R	W	
Wagner	11	2	37	2	1w	15.1	3	59	5	2nb
Mashimbyi	13	4	34	3		15	6	31	2	1nb
Liebisch	12	8	7	4		16	6	38	2	
Phangiso	4	2	7	0		8	1	13	0	
Engelbrecht	2	0	10	0	(7)	2	0	13	0	
van der Merwe					(5)	3	0	16	0	
Behardien					(6)	4	2	7	0	

Free State Bowling

	O	M	R	W	
Saliwa	17	5	66	1	2w,2nb
Kops	30	4	80	3	2w,8nb
de Villiers	24	5	71	3	3w,5nb
Vries	8	5	7	0	1w
Motsamai	17	5	55	0	1nb
van Zyl	16	2	52	2	
O'Neill	5	0	29	0	

Umpires: R.Ellis and A.T.Holdstock.   Toss: Northerns

Close of Play: 1st day: Northerns (1) 207-4 (Behardien 81*, Liebisch 3*, 60 overs); 2nd day: Free State (2) 127-3 (de Lange 50*, Nieuwoudt 39*, 43 overs).

SOUTH AFRICA A v NEW ZEALANDERS

Played at Sedgars Park, Potchefstroom, November 1, 2, 3, 4, 2007.
New Zealand in South Africa 2007/08
South Africa A won by 85 runs.

SOUTH AFRICA A

1	A.N.Petersen	c Papps b O'Brien	23	(2) c Papps b Martin	0
2	G.H.Bodi	c Styris b Bond	20	(1) c Taylor b Martin	5
3	N.D.McKenzie	c McCullum b Oram	182	lbw b Oram	34
4	*H.H.Dippenaar	c Styris b Oram	99	(5) lbw b Oram	5
5	J.P.Duminy	c McCullum b Bond	12	(6) lbw b Vettori	0
6	†M.N.van Wyk	lbw b Vettori	34	(7) lbw b Vettori	9
7	R.K.Kleinveldt	lbw b Vettori	28	(8) c McCullum b Oram	5
8	T.Tshabalala	b Martin	6	(4) b Martin	3
9	F.de Wet	lbw b Vettori	2	c Vincent b Oram	0
10	C.K.Langeveldt	c Vettori b Oram	9	c Vincent b Oram	21
11	L.L.Tsotsobe	not out	0	not out	16
	Extras	b 4, lb 19, nb 5	28	lb 2, w 6	8
			443		**106**

FoW (1): 1-39 (2), 2-49 (1), 3-273 (4), 4-309 (5), 5-378 (6), 6-416 (7), 7-432 (3), 8-432 (8), 9-443 (10), 10-443 (9)
FoW (2): 1-11 (2), 2-16 (1), 3-20 (4), 4-54 (5), 5-55 (6), 6-57 (3), 7-63 (8), 8-69 (7), 9-73 (9), 10-106 (10)

NEW ZEALANDERS

1	C.D.Cumming	c Bodi b de Wet	11	b Langeveldt	14
2	M.H.W.Papps	b Langeveldt	1	lbw b Tsotsobe	22
3	L.Vincent	c Petersen b Tsotsobe	21	lbw b Kleinveldt	8
4	S.B.Styris	b de Wet	10	c van Wyk b Tsotsobe	0
5	L.R.P.L.Taylor	c and b de Wet	36	c Dippenaar b de Wet	86
6	J.D.P.Oram	b Tsotsobe	2	lbw b Tsotsobe	9
7	†B.B.McCullum	c Dippenaar b Tsotsobe	8	b de Wet	77
8	*D.L.Vettori	c Tsotsobe b de Wet	83	b Bodi	30
9	S.E.Bond	lbw b de Wet	4	c Dippenaar b de Wet	6
10	I.E.O'Brien	b de Wet	0	b Duminy	6
11	C.S.Martin	not out	4	not out	1
	Extras	b 6, lb 2, nb 4	12	b 2, lb 3, w 2, nb 6	13
			192		**272**

FoW (1): 1-8 (2), 2-37 (3), 3-37 (1), 4-52 (4), 5-55 (6), 6-63 (7), 7-132 (5), 8-164 (9), 9-164 (10), 10-192 (8)
FoW (2): 1-24 (1), 2-46 (3), 3-46 (2), 4-51 (4), 5-67 (6), 6-206 (7), 7-239 (5), 8-255 (9), 9-268 (10), 10-272 (8)

New Zealanders Bowling

	O	M	R	W		O	M	R	W	
Bond	24	2	112	2	2nb	8	1	32	0	1w
Martin	22	3	99	1	2nb	8	4	20	3	1w
O'Brien	21	3	74	1	1nb					
Oram	20	6	39	3		(3) 6.5	3	16	5	
Vettori	27.2	2	80	3		(4) 6	0	36	2	
Styris	3	0	16	0						

South Africa A Bowling

	O	M	R	W		O	M	R	W	
de Wet	16	3	50	6		23	3	76	3	1nb
Langeveldt	10	2	45	1	1nb	20	10	58	1	1nb
Tsotsobe	14	2	67	3	3nb	14	1	53	3	1w,1nb
Tshabalala	4	0	22	0		(5) 5	0	27	0	
Kleinveldt						(4) 9	2	40	1	1w,1nb
McKenzie						(6) 5	1	6	0	
Duminy						(7) 2	0	3	1	
Bodi						(8) 1	0	4	1	2nb

Umpires: M.Erasmus and B.G.Jerling. Referee: D.Govindjee.   Toss: New Zealanders

Close of Play: 1st day: South Africa A (1) 350-4 (McKenzie 156*, van Wyk 18*, 90 overs); 2nd day: South Africa A (2) 20-2 (McKenzie 5*, Tshabalala 3*, 7.1 overs); 3rd day: New Zealanders (2) 230-6 (Taylor 79*, Vettori 14*, 59 overs).

N.D.McKenzie's 182 took 301 balls in 432 minutes and included 25 fours.

SOUTH WESTERN DISTRICTS v WESTERN PROVINCE

Played at Recreation Ground, Oudtshoorn, November 1, 2, 3, 2007.
South African Airways Provincial Three-Day Challenge 2007/08 - Pool A
Western Province won by eight wickets.   (Points: South Western Districts 4.64, Western Province 17.9)

SOUTH WESTERN DISTRICTS

1	*J.A.Beukes	c Hantam b van Wyk	71	lbw b Hantam	9
2	S.E.Avontuur	lbw b Hantam	6	c Canning b Hantam	80
3	B.C.de Wett	c Canning b van Wyk	15	c Canning b van Wyk	3
4	N.G.Brouwers	c Simpson b van Wyk	0	b P.R.Adams	9
5	P.A.Stuurman	c Bennett b van Wyk	0	lbw b van Wyk	5
6	M.Masimela	c van Wyk b Simpson	15	lbw b van Wyk	0
7	†R.P.Hugo	c Canning b Hantam	12	b P.R.Adams	7
8	W.Hartslief	c Hantam b de Stadler	2	st Canning b Hantam	7
9	N.M.Murray	lbw b P.R.Adams	1	c Canning b P.R.Adams	51
10	B.L.Fransman	not out	1	c Hantam b van Wyk	9
11	N.Nobebe	b van Wyk	0	not out	13
	Extras	lb 6, w 1, nb 2	9	lb 7, w 3, nb 2	12
			132		205

FoW (1): 1-11 (2), 2-38 (3), 3-38 (4), 4-38 (5), 5-63 (6), 6-103 (7), 7-114 (8), 8-130 (9), 9-132 (1), 10-132 (11)
FoW (2): 1-16 (1), 2-51 (3), 3-61 (4), 4-72 (5), 5-72 (6), 6-83 (7), 7-106 (8), 8-155 (2), 9-164 (10), 10-205 (9)

WESTERN PROVINCE

1	M.Williamson	lbw b Fransman	6	lbw b Fransman	8
2	C.D.Williams	c Masimela b Murray	69	b Nobebe	1
3	B.L.Bennett	b Fransman	0	not out	44
4	F.D.Telo	lbw b Nobebe	34	not out	29
5	M.Q.Adams	lbw b Nobebe	4		
6	*†R.C.C.Canning	st Hugo b Brouwers	42		
7	E.P.van Wyk	c Beukes b Fransman	41		
8	W.C.Hantam	lbw b Masimela	28		
9	M.de Stadler	b Fransman	0		
10	P.R.Adams	not out	2		
11	L.F.Simpson	b Fransman	0		
	Extras	b 1, lb 15, w 1, nb 8	25	b 1, lb 2, w 2	5
			251	(2 wickets)	87

FoW (1): 1-14 (1), 2-14 (3), 3-57 (4), 4-61 (5), 5-162 (6), 6-180 (2), 7-239 (8), 8-244 (9), 9-251 (7), 10-251 (11)
FoW (2): 1-11 (2), 2-11 (1)

Western Province Bowling

	O	M	R	W			O	M	R	W	
Simpson	10	1	38	1	1nb		10	2	25	0	2w
Hantam	18	4	43	2	1w		20	6	58	3	
van Wyk	16	7	20	5	1nb	(4)	20	7	47	4	1w,2nb
de Stadler	13	5	20	1		(3)	10	5	24	0	
P.R.Adams	4	2	5	1			21.4	7	38	3	
Telo						(6)	1	0	6	0	

South Western Districts Bowling

	O	M	R	W			O	M	R	W	
Fransman	18.4	7	36	5			7	1	18	1	
Nobebe	11	3	32	2			7	1	37	1	1w
Hartslief	2	1	16	0							
Murray	17	5	38	1		(3)	3.5	0	25	0	1w
Masimela	12	2	43	1	7nb						
Brouwers	16	3	51	1	1nb						
de Wett	12	3	19	0	1w	(4)	1	0	4	0	

Umpires: C.L.Joubert and L.J.Willemse.   Toss: South Western Districts

Close of Play: 1st day: Western Province (1) 117-4 (Williams 39*, Canning 21*, 41 overs); 2nd day: South Western Districts (2) 147-7 (Avontuur 79*, Murray 19*, 60 overs).

CAPE COBRAS v LIONS

Played at Boland Bank Park, Paarl, November 8, 9, 10, 11, 2007.
SuperSport Series 2007/08
Match drawn.   (Points: Cape Cobras 7.64, Lions 6.2)

CAPE COBRAS

1	A.G.Puttick	lbw b Harmison	15	c Snijman b Harmison		45
2	J.G.Strydom	c Coetsee b de Wet	1	lbw b Harmison		0
3	H.Davids	c and b Coetsee	74	c Snijman b de Wet		50
4	J.P.Duminy	c Harris b Harmison	42	(5) not out		71
5	*J.M.Kemp	c Ontong b de Wet	26	(6) lbw b de Wet		0
6	S.van Zyl	c Snijman b Harmison	30	(7) not out		46
7	†T.L.Tsolekile	c Coetsee b Harmison	0			
8	C.D.de Lange	c Snijman b Harmison	30			
9	T.Henderson	c Harris b de Wet	15	(4) c Ontong b Harmison		2
10	M.Zondeki	not out	10			
11	C.K.Langeveldt	c Henderson b Harmison	2			
	Extras	b 2, lb 13, w 20, nb 14	49	b 4, lb 4, w 3, nb 6		17
			294	**(5 wickets, declared)**		**231**

FoW (1): 1-7 (2), 2-33 (1), 3-155 (4), 4-159 (3), 5-200 (5), 6-203 (7), 7-261 (8), 8-282 (9), 9-282 (6), 10-294 (11)
FoW (2): 1-9 (2), 2-95 (1), 3-98 (4), 4-127 (3), 5-127 (6)

LIONS

1	A.N.Petersen	c and b de Lange	102	(2) c Kemp b Henderson		95
2	B.D.Snijman	b Langeveldt	2	(1) lbw b Zondeki		18
3	W.L.Coetsee	c Puttick b Henderson	9	b Zondeki		13
4	*N.D.McKenzie	c Tsolekile b Langeveldt	44	c de Lange b Zondeki		0
5	J.L.Ontong	lbw b Henderson	59	c Kemp b Henderson		32
6	D.L.Makalima	c Henderson b Zondeki	24	(7) not out		10
7	†M.J.Harris	c Puttick b Zondeki	11			
8	C.W.Henderson	c de Lange b Henderson	0	(6) not out		11
9	F.de Wet	lbw b Zondeki	0			
10	S.J.Harmison	b Zondeki	0			
11	B.M.Mathebula	not out	0			
	Extras	lb 1, w 3, nb 5	9	b 4, lb 5, w 3, nb 3		15
			260	**(5 wickets)**		**194**

FoW (1): 1-5 (2), 2-25 (3), 3-123 (4), 4-202 (5), 5-243 (1), 6-251 (6), 7-260 (7), 8-260 (9), 9-260 (10), 10-260 (8)
FoW (2): 1-56 (1), 2-73 (3), 3-88 (4), 4-169 (2), 5-170 (5)

Lions Bowling

	O	M	R	W		O	M	R	W	
de Wet	32	13	70	3	4nb	20	5	54	2	2nb
Harmison	27.3	4	91	6	14w,9nb	28	2	78	3	2w,3nb
Mathebula	14	3	35	0	1w,1nb	6	0	25	0	1w,1nb
Henderson	17	3	62	0		18	7	31	0	
Snijman	1	0	8	0						
Coetsee	11	8	13	1		(5) 12	3	35	0	

Cape Cobras Bowling

	O	M	R	W			O	M	R	W	
Zondeki	25	6	70	4	1w,1nb	(4)	18	2	63	3	3w
Langeveldt	23	5	92	2	4nb	(1)	16	4	53	0	3nb
Henderson	24.3	8	50	3		(2)	9	3	18	2	
de Lange	21	4	47	1	2w	(3)	13.1	4	51	0	

Umpires: J.D.Cloete and S.George.   Referee: E.H.Mall.   Toss: Cape Cobras

Close of Play: 1st day: Cape Cobras (1) 195-4 (Kemp 22*, van Zyl 15*, 63 overs); 2nd day: Lions (1) 123-2 (Petersen 66*, McKenzie 44*, 38 overs); 3rd day: Cape Cobras (2) 103-3 (Davids 43*, Duminy 3*, 39 overs).

Man of the Match: A.N.Petersen.

A.N.Petersen's 102 took 246 balls in 345 minutes and included 11 fours and 1 six.

EASTERN PROVINCE v BORDER

Played at ABSA Oval, Nelson Mandela Metropole University, Port Elizabeth, November 8, 9, 10, 2007.
South African Airways Provincial Three-Day Challenge 2007/08 - Pool A
Eastern Province won by six wickets.　　(Points: Eastern Province 19.26, Border 6.84)

BORDER

#	Batsman	Dismissal	R	Dismissal	R
1	S.de Kock	c Dolley b Luscombe	40	c Adair b Fynn	76
2	S.Booi	c Adair b Walters	13	lbw b Theron	0
3	L.Masingatha	c Dolley b Walters	0	c Smith b Walters	9
4	†A.Z.M.Dyili	lbw b Luscombe	0	lbw b Fynn	62
5	K.D.Bennett	b Luscombe	6	(6) lbw b Theron	2
6	*M.N.Ranger	c Adair b Walters	33	(7) c Meyer b Fynn	8
7	D.L.Brown	lbw b Theron	30	(8) lbw b Fynn	2
8	L.Mbane	c Jeggels b Meyer	6	(9) b Theron	3
9	M.W.Olivier	b Bell	43	(5) c Theron b Fynn	9
10	P.Fojela	not out	8	c Adair b Fynn	21
11	Y.Pangabantu	not out	2	not out	4
	Extras	b 2, lb 7, w 1, nb 1	11	b 13, lb 5, w 5	23
		(9 wickets)	192		219

FoW (1): 1-26 (2), 2-30 (3), 3-30 (4), 4-36 (5), 5-90 (1), 6-97 (6), 7-107 (8), 8-166 (9), 9-190 (7)
FoW (2): 1-3 (2), 2-26 (3), 3-143 (4), 4-157 (5), 5-164 (6), 6-173 (1), 7-179 (8), 8-186 (7), 9-200 (9), 10-219 (10)

EASTERN PROVINCE

#	Batsman	Dismissal	R	Dismissal	R
1	C.A.Ingram	c Dyili b Fojela	37	c Olivier b de Kock	37
2	W.F.S.Fynn	c Mbane b de Kock	104	c Ranger b Olivier	1
3	C.R.Dolley	run out (de Kock/Brown)	31		
4	*M.B.A.Smith	lbw b Ranger	30	lbw b de Kock	10
5	W.E.Bell	b de Kock	52	(3) lbw b Fojela	33
6	†S.R.Adair	b de Kock	11	(5) not out	5
7	R.R.Jeggels	st Dyili b de Kock	5	(6) not out	4
8	L.Meyer	not out	19		
9	J.Theron	c Pangabantu b Mbane	3		
10	B.D.Walters	not out	9		
11	M.J.Luscombe				
	Extras	b 1, lb 8, nb 3	12	b 4, lb 4, w 2	10
		(8 wickets)	313	(4 wickets)	100

FoW (1): 1-65 (1), 2-135 (3), 3-186 (4), 4-252 (2), 5-275 (5), 6-283 (7), 7-286 (6), 8-292 (9)
FoW (2): 1-4 (2), 2-81 (3), 3-81 (1), 4-96 (4)

Eastern Province Bowling

	O	M	R	W		O	M	R	W	
Theron	21	8	40	1	1w,1nb	20	3	48	3	3w
Walters	11	5	20	3		7	5	11	1	
Meyer	16	12	17	1		6	2	15	0	
Luscombe	11.3	5	19	3		5	1	13	0	
Bell	7.3	0	30	1						
Dolley	3	2	6	0		7	0	34	0	1w
Fynn	15	5	51	0	(5)	23.1	6	59	6	
Smith					(7)	3	0	21	0	

Border Bowling

	O	M	R	W		O	M	R	W	
Olivier	14	3	61	0	3nb	7	3	28	1	2w
Pangabantu	9	2	49	0		5	0	19	0	
Fojela	17	6	32	1	(4)	4	0	12	1	
Brown	14	4	46	0						
de Kock	17	6	52	4	(3)	6	0	33	2	
Ranger	7	2	22	1						
Mbane	7	0	42	1						

Umpires: A.T.Holdstock and B.M.White.　　　　　　　　Toss: Border

Close of Play: 1st day: Eastern Province (1) 75-1 (Fynn 32*, Dolley 5*, 19 overs); 2nd day: Border (2) 148-3 (de Kock 63*, Olivier 4*, 42 overs).
W.F.S.Fynn's 104 took 190 balls in 279 minutes and included 19 fours.

FREE STATE v EASTERNS

Played at OUTsurance Oval, Bloemfontein, November 8, 9, 10, 2007.
South African Airways Provincial Three-Day Challenge 2007/08 - Pool B
Match drawn.   (Points: Free State 7.4, Easterns 8.28)

FREE STATE

1	I.D.J.O'Neill	st Bodibe b Hlengani	56	c Bodibe b van den Berg		45
2	A.D.de Lange	c Bodibe b Plaatjie	0	c Bodibe b Reddy		1
3	R.R.Rossouw	c Reddy b van den Berg	83	lbw b Wiese		34
4	*H.O.von Rauenstein	c Bodibe b Wiese	9	c Pienaar b Wiese		72
5	G.N.Nieuwoudt	st Bodibe b Hlengani	47	run out		15
6	†H.K.Moreeng	lbw b Wiese	0	lbw b Wiese		12
7	T.Tshabalala	c Hlengani b Wiese	12	c Toyana b Wiese		1
8	H.Puchert	not out	6	b O'Connor		33
9	G.A.Vries	run out (Wiese/Hlengani)	0	b Wiese		4
10	M.N.Saliwa	run out (Hlengani)	1	c Bodibe b Fourie		26
11	L.J.Volkwyn	lbw b O'Connor	0	not out		0
	Extras	b 2, lb 3, nb 1	6	b 6, lb 13, w 2, nb 1		22
			220			**265**

FoW (1): 1-0 (2), 2-129 (3), 3-144 (1), 4-154 (4), 5-166 (6), 6-190 (7), 7-217 (5), 8-218 (9), 9-219 (10), 10-220 (11)
FoW (2): 1-1 (2), 2-46 (3), 3-134 (1), 4-156 (5), 5-189 (4), 6-191 (7), 7-198 (6), 8-208 (9), 9-265 (10), 10-265 (8)

EASTERNS

1	I.C.Hlengani	c de Lange b Saliwa	13	c O'Neill b Tshabalala		18
2	A.J.Seymore	c Moreeng b Saliwa	21	not out		8
3	†T.M.Bodibe	c O'Neill b Puchert	30			
4	G.Toyana	c Tshabalala b Vries	7			
5	D.Wiese	c O'Neill b Saliwa	50			
6	J.J.Pienaar	c Moreeng b Tshabalala	21			
7	*S.P.O'Connor	b Vries	34			
8	P.P.van den Berg	run out (O'Neill/Vries)	14			
9	J.C.Fourie	not out	49	(3) not out		8
10	B.L.Reddy	c Moreeng b von Rauenstein	1			
11	T.R.Plaatjie	c Moreeng b von Rauenstein	18			
	Extras	lb 7, nb 11	18	nb 2		2
			276	(1 wicket)		**36**

FoW (1): 1-30 (1), 2-48 (2), 3-57 (4), 4-112 (3), 5-156 (6), 6-156 (5), 7-206 (7), 8-208 (8), 9-214 (10), 10-276 (11)
FoW (2): 1-27 (1)

Easterns Bowling

	O	M	R	W		O	M	R	W	
Reddy	15	10	20	0	1nb	20	8	37	1	
Plaatjie	5	1	26	1		21	7	41	0	1w,1nb
Wiese	20	4	63	3	(4)	25	5	58	5	
van den Berg	13	6	20	1	(3)	22	7	38	1	
O'Connor	8.5	1	37	1	(8)	4.1	0	25	1	
Hlengani	14	2	38	2	(5)	20	8	34	0	
Fourie	4	0	11	0	(9)	3	2	7	0	
Toyana					(6)	1	0	1	0	
Pienaar					(7)	3	1	5	0	

Free State Bowling

	O	M	R	W		O	M	R	W	
Saliwa	24	8	65	3	2nb	4	2	9	0	
Vries	19	3	63	2	7nb	4	0	7	0	2nb
von Rauenstein	10.4	3	31	2						
Tshabalala	23	6	75	1		2	0	2	0	
Puchert	8	1	28	1						
Volkwyn	2	0	7	0	(3)	3	0	18	0	

Umpires: C.D.Isaacs and I.H.van Kerwel.   Toss: Free State

Close of Play: 1st day: Easterns (1) 48-1 (Seymore 21*, Bodibe 10*, 23 overs); 2nd day: Free State (2) 64-2 (O'Neill 26*, von Rauenstein 1*, 34 overs).

KWAZULU-NATAL v BOLAND

Played at Sahara Stadium, Kingsmead, Durban, November 8, 9, 10, 2007.
South African Airways Provincial Three-Day Challenge 2007/08 - Pool A
KwaZulu-Natal won by five wickets.   (Points: KwaZulu-Natal 19.14, Boland 9.4)

BOLAND

1	W.S.Groeneveld	c Pillay b Africa	23	c Madsen b Shezi		10
2	A.W.Olivier	c Mabuya b Pillay	69	c Madsen b Bekker		18
3	B.Hector	b Africa	0	c Madsen b Shezi		0
4	B.C.Adams	c Bekker b Shezi	92	c Pillay b Smit		18
5	R.G.Arendse	c Madsen b Govender	66	c Lombard b Pillay		33
6	*P.C.Laing	lbw b Pillay	36	c Madsen b Shezi		6
7	†L.R.Walters	not out	20	lbw b Smit		59
8	S.F.Grobler	not out	1	b Pillay		2
9	J.P.Bothma			c Bekker b Horsfall		57
10	H.H.Paulse			not out		7
11	D.B.Childs			b Africa		1
	Extras	b 4, lb 5, w 1, nb 3	13	lb 6, w 3		9
		(6 wickets)	320			220

FoW (1): 1-50 (1), 2-50 (3), 3-150 (2), 4-242 (4), 5-279 (5), 6-313 (6)
FoW (2): 1-16 (1), 2-17 (3), 3-49 (2), 4-49 (4), 5-70 (6), 6-104 (5), 7-110 (8), 8-206 (7), 9-213 (9), 10-220 (11)

KWAZULU-NATAL

1	W.P.Lombard	c Hector b Bothma	31	c Walters b Paulse		21
2	K.Smit	c Walters b Grobler	113	b Childs		9
3	*†W.L.Madsen	b Childs	65	lbw b Grobler		79
4	M.Bekker	c Bothma b Paulse	30	b Paulse		4
5	S.C.Mabuya	c Walters b Laing	53	lbw b Bothma		24
6	K.Zondo	c Adams b Bothma	10	not out		39
7	K.C.Africa	run out (Walters)	21	not out		0
8	T.D.Pillay	lbw b Grobler	5			
9	M.Shezi	c Laing b Grobler	1			
10	D.N.Horsfall	not out	2			
11	U.Govender	not out	9			
	Extras	b 8, lb 5, w 1, nb 3	17	b 9, lb 1		10
		(9 wickets)	357	(5 wickets)		186

FoW (1): 1-84 (1), 2-163 (2), 3-214 (4), 4-265 (3), 5-290 (6), 6-323 (7), 7-330 (8), 8-338 (5), 9-340 (9)
FoW (2): 1-11 (2), 2-57 (1), 3-65 (4), 4-117 (5), 5-177 (3)

KwaZulu-Natal Bowling

	O	M	R	W			O	M	R	W	
Govender	20	4	49	1	1w		9	1	46	0	1w
Shezi	18	2	75	1	3nb		13	2	37	3	1w
Africa	21	1	101	2		(7)	1.4	0	7	1	
Bekker	3	1	2	0		(3)	3	1	15	1	
Horsfall	7	1	30	0			17	5	47	1	1w
Pillay	16	1	54	2			14	5	25	2	
Smit						(4)	11	3	37	2	

Boland Bowling

	O	M	R	W			O	M	R	W	
Paulse	11	1	51	1		(3)	3	0	19	2	
Childs	12	2	46	1	2nb	(1)	6	0	31	1	
Bothma	17	1	77	2	1w,1nb	(2)	12	1	56	1	
Laing	14	2	63	1		(5)	3	0	18	0	
Grobler	31	3	107	3		(4)	13	0	52	0	

Umpires: C.J.Conradie and R.Ellis.   Toss: Boland

Close of Play: 1st day: Boland (1) 236-3 (Adams 90*, Arendse 44*, 64 overs); 2nd day: Boland (2) 3-0 (Groeneveld 1*, Olivier 0*, 2 overs).

K.Smit's 113 took 108 balls in 131 minutes and included 19 fours and 1 six.

SOUTH AFRICA v NEW ZEALAND

Played at New Wanderers Stadium, Johannesburg, November 8, 9, 10, 11, 2007.
New Zealand in South Africa 2007/08 - 1st Test
South Africa won by 358 runs.

SOUTH AFRICA

1	*G.C.Smith	b Martin	1	(2) b Martin		9
2	H.H.Gibbs	c Fleming b Martin	63	(1) c Papps b Bond		8
3	H.M.Amla	c McCullum b Bond	12	not out		176
4	J.H.Kallis	c McCullum b O'Brien	29	c McCullum b Oram		186
5	A.G.Prince	c Fleming b Bond	1	not out		25
6	A.B.de Villiers	c Oram b Bond	33			
7	†M.V.Boucher	c Papps b Vettori	43			
8	A.Nel	c McCullum b Bond	15			
9	P.L.Harris	lbw b Vettori	3			
10	D.W.Steyn	c McCullum b Martin	13			
11	M.Ntini	not out	0			
	Extras	lb 6, w 1, nb 6	13	b 9, lb 7, w 1, nb 1		18
			226	(3 wickets, declared)		**422**

FoW (1): 1-1 (1), 2-20 (3), 3-73 (4), 4-92 (5), 5-141 (2), 6-162 (6), 7-182 (8), 8-195 (9), 9-219 (7), 10-226 (10)
FoW (2): 1-8 (1), 2-20 (2), 3-350 (4)

NEW ZEALAND

1	C.D.Cumming	lbw b Steyn	12	c Smith b Steyn		7
2	M.H.W.Papps	c de Villiers b Ntini	2	(7) c de Villiers b Kallis		5
3	S.P.Fleming	c de Villiers b Ntini	40	(2) c Smith b Nel		17
4	S.E.Bond	b Steyn	1	absent hurt		0
5	S.B.Styris	c Smith b Kallis	11	(3) c Boucher b Steyn		16
6	L.R.P.L.Taylor	c Gibbs b Kallis	15	(4) c Kallis b Nel		4
7	J.D.P.Oram	c Kallis b Steyn	1	(6) c Nel b Harris		40
8	†B.B.McCullum	lbw b Steyn	9	(5) c Gibbs b Steyn		26
9	*D.L.Vettori	c Harris b Ntini	7	(8) not out		46
10	I.E.O'Brien	not out	14	(9) c Amla b Steyn		0
11	C.S.Martin	c Harris b Steyn	0	(10) b Steyn		0
	Extras	lb 5, nb 1	6	b 7, lb 1, w 2, nb 1		11
			118			**172**

FoW (1): 1-16 (2), 2-40 (1), 3-54 (4), 4-64 (3), 5-83 (5), 6-84 (7), 7-88 (6), 8-102 (9), 9-118 (8), 10-118 (11)
FoW (2): 1-12 (1), 2-34 (4), 3-39 (4), 4-60 (3), 5-90 (5), 6-109 (7), 7-154 (6), 8-170 (9), 9-172 (10)

New Zealand Bowling

	O	M	R	W		O	M	R	W	
Bond	17	1	73	4	1w,3nb	16	1	60	1	
Martin	17.3	3	67	3		24	6	55	1	
Oram	12	3	31	0		16.4	2	49	1	1w
O'Brien	10	4	23	1		23	5	91	0	
Vettori	18	6	26	2	3nb	37	3	116	0	1nb
Styris					(6)	6	2	25	0	
Taylor					(7)	3.2	0	10	0	

South Africa Bowling

	O	M	R	W		O	M	R	W	
Steyn	14.3	3	34	5	1nb	17	1	59	5	1nb
Ntini	14	3	47	3		13	0	42	0	
Nel	9	1	21	0		12	1	37	2	2w
Kallis	4	0	11	2		3	0	15	1	
Harris					˜(5)	6	2	11	1	

Umpires: M.R.Benson and D.J.Harper. Third umpire: M.Erasmus. Referee: J.Srinath.   Toss: South Africa

Close of Play: 1st day: New Zealand (1) 41-2 (Fleming 22*, Bond 0*, 13 overs); 2nd day: South Africa (2) 179-2 (Amla 85*, Kallis 76*, 55 overs); 3rd day: New Zealand (2) 57-3 (Styris 16*, McCullum 11*, 17 overs).

Man of the Match: D.W.Steyn.
The match was scheduled for five days but completed in four. H.M.Amla's 176 took 378 balls in 511 minutes and included 24 fours. J.H.Kallis's 186 took 262 balls in 383 minutes and included 25 fours and 3 sixes.

TITANS v EAGLES

Played at Willowmoore Park Main Oval, Benoni, November 8, 9, 10, 11, 2007.
SuperSport Series 2007/08
Match drawn.   (Points: Titans 5.3, Eagles 8.6)

TITANS

1	M.A.Aronstam	c Elgar b Mpitsang	1	c Dippenaar b du Preez	86
2	†H.G.Kuhn	c Koortzen b Mpitsang	9	c Dippenaar b du Preez	0
3	F.du Plessis	c Elgar b Kops	36	c van Wyk b du Preez	74
4	G.H.Bodi	c van Wyk b de Villiers	0	lbw b du Preez	15
5	P.de Bruyn	b de Villiers	4	c Dippenaar b du Preez	0
6	F.Behardien	c Bailey b Kops	30	(7) b du Preez	6
7	J.A.Morkel	b de Villiers	44	(8) c Kops b Koortzen	151
8	P.Joubert	c van Wyk b de Villiers	43	(9) b de Villiers	27
9	*A.C.Thomas	c and b Rudolph	8	(10) c van Wyk b du Preez	21
10	R.E.van der Merwe	c de Villiers b Rudolph	8	(6) b Mpitsang	27
11	N.E.Mbhalati	not out	0	not out	0
	Extras	b 4, lb 6, w 1, nb 20	31	b 16, lb 11, w 13, nb 15	55
			214		**462**

FoW (1): 1-1 (1), 2-36 (2), 3-41 (4), 4-65 (3), 5-66 (5), 6-141 (7), 7-152 (6), 8-199 (9), 9-213 (10), 10-214 (8)
FoW (2): 1-6 (2), 2-164 (3), 3-198 (1), 4-204 (5), 5-220 (4), 6-233 (7), 7-286 (6), 8-342 (9), 9-411 (10), 10-462 (8)

EAGLES

1	D.Elgar	c de Bruyn b Mbhalati	1	c Kuhn b de Bruyn	13
2	L.L.Bosman	b Joubert	55	b Mbhalati	3
3	J.A.Rudolph	c Kuhn b Joubert	53	not out	6
4	*H.H.Dippenaar	c Morkel b Mbhalati	4	not out	0
5	†M.N.van Wyk	c Kuhn b Mbhalati	2		
6	R.T.Bailey	lbw b Morkel	47		
7	P.J.Koortzen	run out (de Bruyn/Kuhn)	158		
8	D.du Preez	lbw b Joubert	29		
9	C.J.D.de Villiers	b Joubert	58		
10	B.B.Kops	c Kuhn b Joubert	8		
11	P.V.Mpitsang	not out	10		
	Extras	lb 6, w 4, nb 15	25	b 3, lb 1, w 1, nb 1	6
			450	**(2 wickets)**	**28**

FoW (1): 1-3 (1), 2-105 (2), 3-126 (4), 4-128 (3), 5-129 (5), 6-249 (6), 7-309 (8), 8-406 (9), 9-420 (10), 10-450 (7)
FoW (2): 1-8 (2), 2-28 (1)

Eagles Bowling	O	M	R	W		O	M	R	W	
du Preez	15	6	30	0		37	7	108	7	1w
Mpitsang	17	5	40	2	4nb	30.5	6	84	1	8nb
de Villiers	16.2	3	53	4	1w	30.1	4	98	1	1w,5nb
Kops	10	0	53	2	12nb	20	4	71	0	5w,2nb
Bailey	3	0	11	0	(6)	7	0	27	0	2w
Rudolph	11	2	17	2	(5)	13	1	44	0	
Koortzen					(7)	1.1	0	3	0	

Titans Bowling	O	M	R	W		O	M	R	W	
Morkel	31	5	116	1	2w,12nb					
Mbhalati	21	5	93	3	1w,3nb	(1) 7	2	12	1	1nb
Thomas	20	6	58	0		(2) 6	1	11	0	1w
Joubert	28	10	74	5						
van der Merwe	13.4	1	39	0		(3) 1	1	0	0	
Aronstam	6	1	24	0						
Behardien	9	3	20	0	1w					
Bodi	2	0	20	0						
de Bruyn						(4) 1	0	1	0	

Umpires: M.W.Brown and D.J.Smith. Referee: A.Barnes.   Toss: Titans
Close of Play: 1st day: Eagles (1) 52-1 (Bosman 18*, Rudolph 26*, 14.2 overs); 2nd day: Eagles (1) 387-7 (Koortzen 123*, de Villiers 49*, 116 overs); 3rd day: Titans (2) 209-4 (Bodi 14*, van der Merwe 2*, 79 overs).
Man of the Match: J.A.Morkel.
P.J.Koortzen's 158 took 253 balls in 377 minutes and included 28 fours and 1 six. J.A.Morkel's 151 took 159 balls in 223 minutes and included 17 fours and 6 sixes.

WARRIORS v DOLPHINS

Played at Mercedes Benz Park, East London, November 8, 9, 10, 11, 2007.
SuperSport Series 2007/08
Dolphins won by ten wickets.   **(Points: Warriors 5.06, Dolphins 19.46)**

WARRIORS

1	J.P.Kreusch	lbw b Pollock	0	(2) c Pollock b Louw	0
2	C.A.Thyssen	c Vandiar b Louw	5	(1) c Louw b Plunkett	25
3	*Z.de Bruyn	c Pollock b Louw	4	lbw b Louw	122
4	H.D.Ackerman	c Smit b Louw	8	c Gobind b Louw	46
5	A.Jacobs	c Smit b Plunkett	26	c Gobind b Louw	0
6	†D.J.Jacobs	c Gobind b van Vuuren	90	c Watson b Pollock	29
7	R.J.Peterson	b Louw	16	lbw b Smit	25
8	J.Botha	not out	44	c Pollock b Smit	25
9	L.L.Tsotsobe	c Smit b van Vuuren	1	b Pollock	1
10	M.Hayward	b Louw	0	not out	16
11	S.Mjekula	c Gobind b Louw	0	c Khan b Louw	4
	Extras	lb 7, nb 2	9	b 14, lb 8, w 2, nb 3	27
			203		**320**

FoW (1): 1-4 (1), 2-9 (3), 3-17 (4), 4-18 (2), 5-78 (5), 6-119 (7), 7-196 (6), 8-202 (9), 9-203 (10), 10-203 (11)
FoW (2): 1-12 (2), 2-53 (1), 3-176 (4), 4-178 (5), 5-237 (6), 6-237 (3), 7-289 (8), 8-294 (7), 9-300 (9), 10-320 (11)

DOLPHINS

1	D.J.Watson	c D.J.Jacobs b Tsotsobe	97	not out	23
2	I.Khan	c Kreusch b Mjekula	24	not out	33
3	R.Gobind	c Thyssen b Peterson	5		
4	*A.M.Amla	c Kreusch b Peterson	62		
5	J.C.Kent	b Botha	10		
6	S.M.Pollock	c and b Botha	63		
7	J.D.Vandiar	c D.J.Jacobs b Kreusch	61		
8	M.S.van Vuuren	lbw b Hayward	3		
9	J.Louw	c Ackerman b Tsotsobe	76		
10	L.E.Plunkett	b Mjekula	32		
11	†D.Smit	not out	10		
	Extras	b 4, lb 1, w 1, nb 13	19	b 4, lb 2	6
			462	**(no wicket)**	**62**

FoW (1): 1-32 (2), 2-62 (3), 3-147 (4), 4-177 (5), 5-238 (1), 6-281 (6), 7-286 (8), 8-397 (7), 9-428 (9), 10-462 (10)

Dolphins Bowling

	O	M	R	W			O	M	R	W	
Pollock	13	5	22	1			28	10	42	2	1w
Louw	21.5	8	45	6			28.4	13	47	5	1nb
Kent	13	1	44	0	1nb	(6)	12	1	36	0	1nb
Plunkett	14	2	62	1	1nb		14	2	43	1	1w,1nb
van Vuuren	11	3	23	2		(3)	17	2	51	0	
Smit						(5)	23	4	72	2	
Khan						(7)	2	0	7	0	

Warriors Bowling

	O	M	R	W			O	M	R	W	
Hayward	25	3	87	1	1w,3nb	(2)	5	2	10	0	
Tsotsobe	28	6	92	2	2nb						
Mjekula	16.2	2	56	2		(1)	3	1	12	0	
Peterson	23	4	94	2	3nb		2.2	0	9	0	
Botha	17	3	71	2	1nb	(3)	5	0	25	0	
de Bruyn	11	1	36	0	4nb						
Kreusch	5	1	21	1							

Umpires: I.L.Howell and G.H.Pienaar.   Referee: S.B.Lambson.   Toss: Dolphins

Close of Play: 1st day: Dolphins (1) 68-2 (Watson 32*, Amla 4*, 21 overs); 2nd day: Dolphins (1) 409-8 (Louw 62*, Plunkett 4*, 108 overs); 3rd day: Warriors (2) 215-4 (de Bruyn 118*, D.J.Jacobs 15*, 81 overs).

Man of the Match: J.Louw.
Z.de Bruyn's 122 took 253 balls in 330 minutes and included 17 fours.

BOLAND v WESTERN PROVINCE

Played at Boland Bank Park, Paarl, November 15, 16, 17, 2007.
South African Airways Provincial Three-Day Challenge 2007/08 - Pool A
Boland won by nine wickets.   (Points: Boland 20.2, Western Province 5.2)

WESTERN PROVINCE

1	G.G.Fearon	c Walters b Henderson	0	b Grobler	42
2	C.D.Williams	lbw b Sandri	10	c Laing b Adams	31
3	R.E.Levi	c Walters b Henderson	1	run out	63
4	F.D.Telo	not out	134	c Laing b Henderson	132
5	T.J.Mdodana	b Henderson	7	b Grobler	1
6	*†R.C.C.Canning	lbw b Henderson	1	st Walters b Grobler	36
7	E.P.van Wyk	c Hector b Sandri	28	c Walters b Henderson	0
8	C.W.S.Birch	b Sandri	0	b Grobler	2
9	M.Mahlombe	c Olivier b Henderson	8	b Henderson	0
10	A.A.Temoor	b Henderson	0	not out	0
11	L.F.Simpson	c Hector b Henderson	12	c Adams b Grobler	0
	Extras	lb 1, w 2, nb 6	9	b 17, lb 9, nb 4	30
			210		**337**

FoW (1): 1-1 (1), 2-13 (3), 3-18 (2), 4-48 (5), 5-58 (6), 6-130 (7), 7-130 (8), 8-165 (9), 9-182 (10), 10-210 (11)
FoW (2): 1-68 (2), 2-84 (1), 3-270 (3), 4-272 (5), 5-316 (4), 6-324 (7), 7-336 (8), 8-337 (9), 9-337 (6), 10-337 (11)

BOLAND

1	J.G.Strydom	b Simpson	0	(2) b Simpson	13
2	A.W.Olivier	c Birch b Simpson	5	(1) not out	12
3	B.Hector	c Canning b Birch	183	not out	22
4	B.C.Adams	b Temoor	42		
5	R.G.Arendse	c Canning b Mahlombe	6		
6	*P.C.Laing	c Simpson b Temoor	154		
7	†L.R.Walters	b Mahlombe	32		
8	T.Henderson	c Levi b Temoor	0		
9	S.F.Grobler	not out	29		
10	P.S.E.Sandri	not out	26		
11	H.H.Paulse				
	Extras	b 1, lb 17, w 2, nb 2	22	w 1, nb 1	2
		(8 wickets)	**499**	(1 wicket)	**49**

FoW (1): 1-0 (1), 2-10 (2), 3-100 (4), 4-120 (5), 5-360 (3), 6-438 (6), 7-438 (7), 8-448 (8)
FoW (2): 1-16 (2)

Boland Bowling

	O	M	R	W			O	M	R	W	
Sandri	14	5	26	3	1w	(2)	19	2	66	0	1nb
Henderson	21	4	67	7	1w,5nb	(1)	20	9	48	3	1nb
Laing	10	1	44	0		(6)	9	2	23	0	
Paulse	4	1	30	0	1nb		11	1	36	0	2nb
Grobler	6	2	21	0		(3)	40.5	10	113	5	
Adams	7	0	21	0		(5)	6	1	25	1	

Western Province Bowling

	O	M	R	W			O	M	R	W	
Simpson	15	2	64	2			3	0	20	1	1w
Birch	21	1	78	1	1nb		2	0	13	0	1nb
Mahlombe	18	2	82	2	1w						
van Wyk	22	1	114	0	1w,1nb						
Temoor	32	4	143	3		(3)	2	0	10	0	
Telo						(4)	1.5	0	6	0	

Umpires: Z.T.A.Ndamane and J.E.P.Ostrom.   Toss: Boland

Close of Play: 1st day: Boland (1) 151-4 (Hector 75*, Laing 19*, 39 overs); 2nd day: Western Province (2) 107-2 (Levi 8*, Telo 18*, 35 overs).

F.D.Telo's 134 took 156 balls in 217 minutes and included 19 fours. B.Hector's 183 took 263 balls in 325 minutes and included 21 fours and 1 six. P.C.Laing's 154 took 203 balls in 274 minutes and included 20 fours and 2 sixes. F.D.Telo's 132 took 188 balls in 270 minutes and included 20 fours.

CAPE COBRAS v EAGLES

Played at Sahara Park Newlands, Cape Town, November 15, 16, 17, 18, 2007.
SuperSport Series 2007/08
Match drawn.   (Points: Cape Cobras 5.42, Eagles 7.12)

EAGLES

1	D.Elgar	c Kemp b Kleinveldt	166	
2	L.L.Bosman	c Tsolekile b Kleinveldt	24	
3	J.A.Rudolph	c van Zyl b de Lange	94	
4	*H.H.Dippenaar	c Tsolekile b Langeveldt	32	
5	†M.N.van Wyk	c Kemp b Langeveldt	4	
6	R.T.Bailey	c Tsolekile b Philander	15	
7	P.J.Koortzen	c Kemp b Zondeki	3	
8	D.du Preez	c van Zyl b Zondeki	122	
9	C.J.D.de Villiers	c and b de Lange	16	
10	M.N.Saliwa	b Philander	14	
11	P.V.Mpitsang	not out	0	
	Extras	b 6, lb 3, w 2, nb 10	21	
			511	

FoW (1): 1-44 (2), 2-193 (3), 3-256 (4), 4-264 (5), 5-304 (6), 6-313 (7), 7-400 (1), 8-443 (9), 9-507 (10), 10-511 (8)

CAPE COBRAS

1	A.G.Puttick	lbw b du Preez	52	(2) not out	152
2	C.D.de Lange	lbw b Rudolph	39	(1) lbw b de Villiers	46
3	†T.L.Tsolekile	lbw b Saliwa	1		
4	H.Davids	lbw b Mpitsang	67	(3) not out	108
5	J.P.Duminy	lbw b Rudolph	29		
6	*J.M.Kemp	c van Wyk b du Preez	7		
7	S.van Zyl	c Elgar b Rudolph	6		
8	V.D.Philander	c Saliwa b Rudolph	83		
9	R.K.Kleinveldt	c van Wyk b Mpitsang	5		
10	M.Zondeki	c Elgar b Rudolph	34		
11	C.K.Langeveldt	not out	2		
	Extras	b 2, lb 5, w 2, nb 6	15	b 1, lb 2, nb 2	5
			340	(1 wicket)	**311**

FoW (1): 1-72 (2), 2-96 (1), 3-97 (3), 4-150 (5), 5-157 (6), 6-180 (7), 7-254 (4), 8-260 (9), 9-325 (10), 10-340 (8)
FoW (2): 1-87 (1)

Cape Cobras Bowling	O	M	R	W	
Langeveldt	40	9	127	2	1w,1nb
Zondeki	28.4	6	81	2	1w
Kleinveldt	31	12	89	2	2nb
Philander	26	6	80	2	4nb
de Lange	34	6	108	2	2nb
Duminy	2	0	12	0	1nb
Kemp	1	0	5	0	

Eagles Bowling	O	M	R	W			O	M	R	W	
du Preez	26	5	70	2		(2)	6	0	29	0	
Mpitsang	23	8	59	2	4nb	(3)	6	2	16	0	1nb
de Villiers	18	5	54	0	1nb	(5)	11	1	33	1	1nb
Rudolph	29.3	3	80	5	1w	(1)	18	4	67	0	
Saliwa	18	1	59	1	1w,1nb	(4)	10	2	36	0	
Bailey	3	0	11	0		(7)	17	1	60	0	
Koortzen						(6)	14	0	63	0	
Dippenaar						(8)	2	0	4	0	

Umpires: B.G.Jerling and D.J.Smith.   Referee: D.Govindjee.   Toss: Cape Cobras

Close of Play: 1st day: Eagles (1) 295-4 (Elgar 123*, Bailey 10*, 96 overs); 2nd day: Cape Cobras (1) 77-1 (Puttick 36*, Tsolekile 0*, 27 overs); 3rd day: Cape Cobras (2) 1-0 (de Lange 0*, Puttick 1*, 3 overs).
Man of the Match: J.A.Rudolph.
D.Elgar's 166 took 424 balls in 564 minutes and included 15 fours and 1 six. D.du Preez's 122 took 164 balls in 239 minutes and included 11 fours and 5 sixes. A.G.Puttick's 152 took 264 balls in 327 minutes and included 16 fours and 2 sixes. H.Davids's 108 took 178 balls in 230 minutes and included 10 fours.

EASTERNS v NAMIBIA

Played at Willowmoore Park Main Oval, Benoni, November 15, 16, 17, 2007.
South African Airways Provincial Three-Day Challenge 2007/08 - Pool B
Match drawn.   (Points: Easterns 9.72, Namibia 8.3)

EASTERNS

1	I.C.Hlengani	c van Schoor b Williams	30	c van Schoor b van Zyl		6
2	†T.M.Bodibe	c Rudolph b van Zyl	3	b van Zyl		17
3	A.J.Seymore	c van Schoor b Klazinga	89	(4) c Rudolph b van der Westhuizen		87
4	D.Wiese	c Snyman b van Zyl	90			
5	J.Booysen	c and b Williams	0	(3) not out		129
6	G.Toyana	st van Schoor b Durant	44			
7	J.J.Pienaar	b Rudolph	3			
8	*S.P.O'Connor	lbw b Snyman	12			
9	P.P.van den Berg	not out	21			
10	T.R.Plaatjie	run out (Snyman/van Schoor)	1	(5) not out		8
11	P.T.Mofokeng	c van Schoor b Burger	7			
	Extras	b 7, lb 7, w 7, nb 15	36	b 10, lb 3, w 1, nb 6		20
			336	(3 wickets, declared)		267

FoW (1): 1-28 (2), 2-59 (1), 3-215 (4), 4-221 (5), 5-244 (3), 6-255 (7), 7-295 (8), 8-315 (6), 9-324 (10), 10-336 (11)
FoW (2): 1-8 (1), 2-40 (2), 3-256 (4)

NAMIBIA

1	†R.van Schoor	run out (Pienaar)	13	c sub (E.Nyawo) b Wiese	1
2	C.Williams	c Bodibe b van den Berg	9	not out	31
3	G.J.Rudolph	c Bodibe b Plaatjie	6	c Bodibe b van den Berg	2
4	*G.Snyman	c Booysen b Wiese	58	not out	13
5	M.Durant	b Wiese	18		
6	N.R.P.Scholtz	b Hlengani	23		
7	L.P.van der Westhuizen	c van den Berg b Toyana	29		
8	E.Steenkamp	lbw b Wiese	15		
9	K.B.Burger	c Seymore b Pienaar	41		
10	M.C.van Zyl	not out	22		
11	L.Klazinga	c Bodibe b van den Berg	6		
	Extras	b 3, lb 12, w 6, nb 4	25	b 8, lb 1, w 1, nb 1	11
			265	(2 wickets)	58

FoW (1): 1-19 (2), 2-34 (1), 3-37 (3), 4-107 (5), 5-124 (4), 6-146 (6), 7-193 (8), 8-199 (7), 9-244 (9), 10-265 (11)
FoW (2): 1-11 (1), 2-35 (3)

Namibia Bowling	O	M	R	W		O	M	R	W	
Snyman	15	5	39	1	2w,6nb	14	2	47	0	6nb
van Zyl	17	2	51	2	1w	12	4	38	2	
Burger	11.2	2	43	1	1w	(4) 9	1	44	0	1w
Williams	10	3	48	2	2nb	(7) 2	0	23	0	
Klazinga	7	1	28	1	2w,7nb	5	0	23	0	
Durant	10	1	35	1	1w					
Scholtz	6	0	26	0		(3) 17	1	68	0	
van der Westhuizen	3	0	19	0		1	0	1	1	
Rudolph	5	0	33	0		(6) 2	0	10	0	

Easterns Bowling	O	M	R	W		O	M	R	W	
Plaatjie	11	3	42	1	2w,2nb	4	2	2	0	
Wiese	21	5	60	3		4	2	6	1	
van den Berg	16.5	3	28	2		(4) 5	0	16	1	1nb
Hlengani	11	2	39	1						
Pienaar	12	2	32	1	2nb	1	0	4	0	
O'Connor	5	0	29	0						
Toyana	5	1	20	1						
Mofokeng						(3) 7	1	21	0	1w

Umpires: C.L.Joubert and L.J.Willemse.   Toss: Namibia

Close of Play: 1st day: Namibia (1) 20-1 (van Schoor 5*, Rudolph 0*, 8 overs); 2nd day: Easterns (2) 40-2 (Booysen 11*, 11.3 overs).
J.Booysen's 129 took 180 balls in 226 minutes and included 11 fours and 2 sixes.

GRIQUALAND WEST v GAUTENG

Played at De Beers Diamond Oval, Kimberley, November 15, 16, 17, 2007.
South African Airways Provincial Three-Day Challenge 2007/08 - Pool B
Griqualand West won by ten wickets.   (Points: Griqualand West 19.16, Gauteng 7.22)

GAUTENG

1	S.C.Cook	c Bossenger b Coetzee	36	lbw b Coetzee	0
2	O.A.Ramela	c Mabuya b Holtzhausen	26	b Kruger	23
3	W.B.Motaung	c Hendricks b Kruger	0	c Holtzhausen b Coetzee	89
4	J.Symes	lbw b Holtzhausen	12	lbw b Coetzee	18
5	†D.J.Vilas	lbw b Kruger	69	c Kruger b Holtzhausen	1
6	*S.Burger	c Bossenger b Kruger	40	c Bossenger b Holtzhausen	2
7	H.W.le Roux	c McLaren b Coetzee	2	c Bossenger b Mabuya	10
8	R.Das Neves	c Akoojee b Holtzhausen	9	c Bossenger b Carolus	9
9	Y.Keiller	not out	8	c Hendricks b Coetzee	18
10	B.M.Mathebula	c Adams b Holtzhausen	2	c Bossenger b Coetzee	2
11	J.T.Mafa	c Carolus b Coetzee	0	not out	1
	Extras	lb 3, w 1, nb 3	7	b 1, lb 2, w 2, nb 1	6
			211		**179**

FoW (1): 1-47 (2), 2-52 (3), 3-70 (4), 4-92 (1), 5-185 (6), 6-192 (5), 7-197 (7), 8-201 (8), 9-203 (10), 10-211 (11)
FoW (2): 1-0 (1), 2-47 (2), 3-69 (4), 4-72 (5), 5-74 (6), 6-92 (7), 7-133 (8), 8-169 (9), 9-176 (3), 10-179 (10)

GRIQUALAND WEST

1	A.K.Kruger	b le Roux	31	not out	49
2	M.Akoojee	c Symes b Mathebula	53	not out	34
3	A.P.McLaren	c le Roux b Mafa	11		
4	R.R.Hendricks	c Vilas b Das Neves	50		
5	*†W.Bossenger	lbw b le Roux	59		
6	H.G.de Kock	c Ramela b le Roux	0		
7	F.S.Holtzhausen	c Ramela b Symes	18		
8	J.Coetzee	c Vilas b Keiller	22		
9	R.A.Adams	c Motaung b Mathebula	44		
10	A.P.T.Mabuya	c Cook b Symes	0		
11	D.D.Carolus	not out	4		
	Extras	b 1, lb 1, w 6, nb 8	16	nb 1	1
			308	**(no wicket)**	**84**

FoW (1): 1-78 (1), 2-101 (3), 3-119 (2), 4-206 (4), 5-211 (6), 6-236 (5), 7-236 (7), 8-288 (8), 9-289 (10), 10-308 (9)

Griqualand West Bowling	O	M	R	W		O	M	R	W	
Coetzee	21.5	7	48	3	1nb	17.4	6	24	5	1w
Carolus	7	1	33	0	1nb	8	1	30	1	1nb
Kruger	15	2	56	3	1w	14	5	36	1	
Holtzhausen	16	1	60	4	1nb	19	3	51	2	
Adams	2	0	11	0						
Mabuya						(5) 12	3	33	1	
de Kock						(6) 1	0	2	0	1w

Gauteng Bowling	O	M	R	W		O	M	R	W	
Burger	8	0	38	0		(4) 2	0	13	0	
Mafa	14	2	51	1	1w,3nb	1	0	8	0	
Mathebula	8.4	0	44	2	3nb	3	0	13	0	1nb
Keiller	12	5	31	1	5w,2nb	(5) 1	0	14	0	
le Roux	17	3	48	3		(1) 4	1	14	0	
Das Neves	10	0	55	1						
Symes	11	2	39	2		1	0	3	0	
Cook						(6) 1.5	0	19	0	

Umpires: A.T.Holdstock and G.H.Pienaar.   Toss: Griqualand West

Close of Play: 1st day: Gauteng (1) 197-6 (le Roux 2*, Das Neves 5*, 57 overs); 2nd day: Gauteng (2) 66-2 (Motaung 25*, Symes 15*, 22 overs).

KWAZULU-NATAL INLAND v EASTERN PROVINCE

Played at City Oval, Pietermaritzburg, November 15, 16, 17, 2007.
South African Airways Provincial Three-Day Challenge 2007/08 - Pool A
Match drawn.   (Points: KwaZulu-Natal Inland 5.98, Eastern Province 6.38)

EASTERN PROVINCE

1	W.F.S.Fynn	c Hampson b McMillan	29	b Hampson	8
2	†G.E.von Hoesslin	c Moses b Hampson	12	b Qasim Khurshid	8
3	W.E.Bell	c Gqadushe b McMillan	28	c Gqadushe b Qasim Khurshid	54
4	*M.B.A.Smith	c Gqadushe b McMillan	0	lbw b McMillan	23
5	S.R.Adair	c Matika b Qasim Khurshid	16	c Gqadushe b van Vuuren	3
6	R.R.Jeggels	c Qasim Khurshid b Hampson	54	not out	25
7	J.Theron	c Gqadushe b Qasim Khurshid	2	not out	31
8	C.R.Dolley	c Gqadushe b Hampson	8		
9	B.D.Walters	b McMillan	3		
10	M.J.Luscombe	b McMillan	0		
11	S.Mjekula	not out	0		
	Extras	b 3, lb 7, nb 7	17	b 4, lb 4, nb 1	9
			169	(5 wickets, declared)	161

FoW (1): 1-21 (2), 2-70 (1), 3-70 (4), 4-87 (3), 5-113 (5), 6-125 (7), 7-161 (6), 8-164 (9), 9-164 (10), 10-169 (8)
FoW (2): 1-13 (1), 2-25 (2), 3-58 (4), 4-81 (5), 5-100 (3)

KWAZULU-NATAL INLAND

1	R.D.McMillan	c Dolley b Theron	8	c Smith b Walters	8
2	C.S.Bowyer	c Dolley b Walters	0	lbw b Theron	10
3	G.N.Addicott	c Jeggels b Mjekula	36	b Theron	6
4	B.Moses	c Smith b Mjekula	12	lbw b Walters	7
5	L.Brown	b Mjekula	15	not out	8
6	M.M.Matika	c Smith b Luscombe	20	not out	0
7	*A.van Vuuren	c von Hoesslin b Mjekula	0		
8	G.M.Hampson	c Smith b Theron	30		
9	†M.Gqadushe	c Adair b Mjekula	11		
10	L.L.Lwana	b Walters	8		
11	Qasim Khurshid	not out	5		
	Extras	b 1, lb 1, nb 2	4	b 2, lb 1	3
			149	(4 wickets)	42

FoW (1): 1-2 (2), 2-12 (1), 3-41 (4), 4-68 (5), 5-78 (3), 6-88 (7), 7-98 (6), 8-119 (9), 9-143 (8), 10-149 (10)
FoW (2): 1-19 (1), 2-19 (2), 3-28 (3), 4-42 (4)

KwaZulu-Natal Inland Bowling

	O	M	R	W			O	M	R	W	
Qasim Khurshid	13	2	55	2			9	3	33	2	
Hampson	19	4	36	3	5nb		8	1	26	1	1nb
Brown	4	0	16	0							
Lwana	7	4	18	0	1nb						
McMillan	9	3	30	5	1nb	(3)	11	3	50	1	
van Vuuren	1	0	4	0		(4)	6	0	44	1	

Eastern Province Bowling

	O	M	R	W			O	M	R	W	
Theron	13	1	37	2	2nb		7	3	23	2	
Walters	8	3	29	2			7	3	16	2	
Luscombe	8	0	38	1							
Mjekula	15	7	33	5							
Bell	2	0	10	0							

Umpires: C.D.Isaacs and B.D.A.Westraadt.   Toss: KwaZulu-Natal Inland

Close of Play: 1st day: Eastern Province (1) 122-5 (Jeggels 25*, Theron 0*, 34 overs); 2nd day: KwaZulu-Natal Inland (1) 148-9 (Lwana 8*, Qasim Khurshid 5*, 45.2 overs).

LIONS v DOLPHINS

Played at Sedgars Park, Potchefstroom, November 15, 16, 17, 18, 2007.
SuperSport Series 2007/08
Match drawn.   (Points: Lions 8.74, Dolphins 6.6)

LIONS

1	B.D.Snijman	c and b Friend	8
2	A.N.Petersen	b Plunkett	64
3	W.L.Coetsee	c Gobind b Plunkett	131
4	*N.D.McKenzie	b Smit	164
5	J.L.Ontong	c sub (S.Mlongo) b Plunkett	77
6	D.L.Makalima	c Smit b Kent	0
7	†M.J.Harris	not out	63
8	C.W.Henderson	c Plunkett b Smit	12
9	G.J.P.Kruger	b Smit	3
10	F.de Wet	not out	20
11	S.J.Harmison		
	Extras	lb 2, w 1, nb 8	11
		(8 wickets, declared)	553

FoW (1): 1-23 (1), 2-91 (2), 3-361 (3), 4-380 (6), 5-474 (5), 6-485 (4), 7-509 (8), 8-517 (9)

DOLPHINS

1	I.Khan	c McKenzie b Henderson	64	(2) c Harris b Kruger	1
2	D.J.Watson	c Harris b Harmison	24	(1) c Petersen b de Wet	11
3	W.L.Madsen	c Makalima b Harmison	39	(6) lbw b Harmison	38
4	*A.M.Amla	b Kruger	123	lbw b Henderson	1
5	J.C.Kent	c Harris b de Wet	0	lbw b de Wet	8
6	J.D.Vandiar	c Coetsee b Henderson	18	(7) c Harris b Harmison	36
7	R.Gobind	c McKenzie b Henderson	1	(3) lbw b Coetsee	43
8	J.Louw	c Ontong b Henderson	33	b Kruger	6
9	L.E.Plunkett	b Kruger	45	b Kruger	0
10	†D.Smit	not out	13	not out	20
11	Q.Friend	c Coetsee b de Wet	0	not out	0
	Extras	b 2, lb 6, w 1, nb 18	27	b 12, lb 10, w 1, nb 5	28
			387	(9 wickets)	192

FoW (1): 1-39 (1), 2-112 (2), 3-167 (3), 4-179 (5), 5-220 (6), 6-222 (7), 7-303 (8), 8-359 (4), 9-386 (9), 10-387 (11)
FoW (2): 1-1 (1), 2-30 (2), 3-39 (4), 4-62 (5), 5-92 (3), 6-152 (7), 7-167 (6), 8-168 (9), 9-177 (8)

Dolphins Bowling	O	M	R	W	
Louw	34	7	86	0	
Friend	22	0	91	1	5nb
Kent	21	6	65	1	
Plunkett	23	2	100	3	3nb
Smit	22.3	4	121	3	
Vandiar	7	1	31	0	
Khan	13	0	49	0	1w
Watson	2	0	8	0	

Lions Bowling	O	M	R	W		O	M	R	W	
de Wet	22.1	5	80	2	1nb	21	7	35	2	
Kruger	21	3	70	2	7nb	19.2	9	33	3	3nb
Harmison	14	2	67	2	1w,8nb	13	6	26	2	1w,1nb
Henderson	33	8	115	4	1nb	27	11	48	1	
Coetsee	12	1	47	0		9	3	16	1	
Ontong						(6) 2	0	12	0	1nb

Umpires: J.D.Cloete and S.George.   Referee: C.J.Mitchley.   Toss: Dolphins

Close of Play: 1st day: Lions (1) 380-3 (McKenzie 157*, Ontong 9*, 96 overs); 2nd day: Lions (1) 553-8 (Harris 63*, de Wet 20*, 144.3 overs); 3rd day: Dolphins (1) 357-7 (Amla 122*, Plunkett 33*, 92.4 overs).
Man of the Match: N.D.McKenzie.
W.L.Coetsee's 131 took 249 balls in 350 minutes and included 12 fours. N.D.McKenzie's 164 took 239 balls in 307 minutes and included 21 fours and 1 six. A.M.Amla's 123 took 179 balls in 242 minutes and included 18 fours and 2 sixes. N.D.McKenzie retired not out in the Lions first innings having scored 157 (team score 380-3) - he returned when the score was 474-5. He was called up to the national squad as cover for A.B.de Villiers but was released before the toss.

WARRIORS v TITANS

Played at Sahara Oval, St George's Park, Port Elizabeth, November 15, 16, 17, 18, 2007.
SuperSport Series 2007/08
Match drawn.   (Points: Warriors 6.18, Titans 5.42)

TITANS

1	R.Jappie	c and b de Bruyn	5	(2) lbw b de Bruyn	16
2	†H.G.Kuhn	lbw b de Bruyn	45	(1) lbw b Tsotsobe	137
3	F.du Plessis	lbw b de Bruyn	44	c D.J.Jacobs b de Bruyn	123
4	G.H.Bodi	c D.J.Jacobs b Tsotsobe	4	c Thyssen b Tsotsobe	3
5	P.de Bruyn	c Botha b de Bruyn	3	not out	37
6	F.Behardien	c Botha b de Bruyn	0		
7	J.A.Morkel	c Ackerman b de Bruyn	13	(6) not out	38
8	P.Joubert	not out	22		
9	*A.C.Thomas	c A.Jacobs b de Bruyn	0		
10	R.E.van der Merwe	c D.J.Jacobs b Olivier	19		
11	N.E.Mbhalati	c A.Jacobs b Olivier	0		
	Extras	lb 3, w 5, nb 8	16	b 6, lb 5, w 8, nb 7	26
			171	(4 wickets, declared)	380

FoW (1): 1-22 (1), 2-84 (2), 3-104 (4), 4-106 (3), 5-106 (6), 6-115 (5), 7-120 (7), 8-120 (9), 9-162 (10), 10-171 (11)
FoW (2): 1-62 (2), 2-281 (1), 3-292 (4), 4-310 (3)

WARRIORS

1	C.A.Thyssen	c Kuhn b Mbhalati	5	(2) b Thomas	18
2	C.A.Ingram	lbw b Morkel	30	(1) c du Plessis b Morkel	16
3	*Z.de Bruyn	b Thomas	2	c du Plessis b Joubert	52
4	A.Jacobs	c Kuhn b Thomas	4	lbw b van der Merwe	13
5	H.D.Ackerman	c Kuhn b Thomas	58	not out	36
6	†D.J.Jacobs	c Kuhn b Joubert	0	not out	6
7	R.J.Peterson	c Joubert b Thomas	14		
8	J.Botha	c Kuhn b Morkel	54		
9	L.Meyer	c du Plessis b van der Merwe	30		
10	M.W.Olivier	not out	4		
11	L.L.Tsotsobe	b van der Merwe	1		
	Extras	b 4, lb 2, nb 1	7	b 4, lb 4, w 5, nb 5	18
			209	(4 wickets)	159

FoW (1): 1-13 (1), 2-16 (3), 3-20 (4), 4-72 (2), 5-77 (6), 6-118 (7), 7-119 (5), 8-200 (9), 9-208 (8), 10-209 (11)
FoW (2): 1-37 (1), 2-41 (2), 3-84 (4), 4-145 (3)

Warriors Bowling	O	M	R	W			O	M	R	W	
Tsotsobe	17	6	38	1	1nb		20	4	73	2	2nb
Olivier	9.2	2	37	2	1nb		11	1	39	0	2w
de Bruyn	21	4	67	7	1w,2nb	(6)	25	3	93	2	1w,3nb
Meyer	9	0	26	0	4w,4nb		9	1	41	0	4w,2nb
Botha						(3)	9	0	40	0	
Peterson						(5)	22	5	47	0	1w
A.Jacobs						(7)	5	0	24	0	
Thyssen						(8)	2	0	12	0	

Titans Bowling	O	M	R	W			O	M	R	W	
Thomas	25	7	65	4			13	4	39	1	1w,2nb
Mbhalati	13	2	39	1			6	3	19	0	1nb
Morkel	15	4	47	2	1nb	(4)	12	5	21	1	2nb
Joubert	20	8	46	1		(5)	10	5	15	1	
van der Merwe	5	2	6	2		(3)	10	1	31	1	
du Plessis						(6)	7	0	26	0	

Umpires: E.C.Hendrikse and I.L.Howell. Referee: S.Wadvalla.   Toss: Titans

Close of Play: 1st day: Titans (1) 101-2 (du Plessis 42*, Bodi 4*, 27 overs); 2nd day: Warriors (1) 169-7 (Botha 36*, Meyer 13*, 57 overs); 3rd day: Titans (2) 277-1 (Kuhn 137*, du Plessis 100*, 81 overs).

Man of the Match: Z.de Bruyn.
H.G.Kuhn's 137 took 250 balls in 330 minutes and included 13 fours and 2 sixes. F.du Plessis's 123 took 201 balls in 273 minutes and included 15 fours.

SOUTH AFRICA v NEW ZEALAND

Played at Centurion Park, November 16, 17, 18, 2007.
New Zealand in South Africa 2007/08 - 2nd Test
South Africa won by an innings and 59 runs.

NEW ZEALAND

1	C.D.Cumming	retired hurt	48	absent hurt		0
2	M.H.W.Papps	c Gibbs b Ntini	9	lbw b Steyn		1
3	L.Vincent	c Harris b Steyn	33	(1) lbw b Steyn		4
4	S.P.Fleming	c Prince b Kallis	43	(3) lbw b Steyn		54
5	S.B.Styris	lbw b Steyn	3	(4) c de Villiers b Kallis		29
6	L.R.P.L.Taylor	c Prince b Nel	17	(5) run out		8
7	†B.B.McCullum	c de Villiers b Nel	13	(6) c Smith b Steyn		21
8	*D.L.Vettori	not out	17	(7) c de Villiers b Ntini		8
9	M.R.Gillespie	lbw b Steyn	0	(8) c Kallis b Steyn		0
10	I.E.O'Brien	c Gibbs b Steyn	0	(9) b Steyn		0
11	C.S.Martin	c Kallis b Ntini	0	(10) not out		0
	Extras	lb 2, nb 3	5	b 1, lb 9, nb 1		11
			188			**136**

FoW (1): 1-26 (2), 2-88 (3), 3-105 (5), 4-147 (6), 5-165 (4), 6-184 (7), 7-187 (9), 8-187 (10), 9-188 (11)
FoW (2): 1-4 (1), 2-9 (2), 3-69 (4), 4-78 (5), 5-117 (3), 6-128 (6), 7-128 (8), 8-136 (7), 9-136 (9)

SOUTH AFRICA

1	*G.C.Smith	b Martin	2
2	H.H.Gibbs	b Martin	25
3	H.M.Amla	c Papps b O'Brien	103
4	J.H.Kallis	lbw b Gillespie	131
5	A.G.Prince	c sub (J.M.How) b Gillespie	13
6	A.B.de Villiers	c McCullum b Gillespie	33
7	†M.V.Boucher	b Gillespie	1
8	P.L.Harris	c McCullum b Gillespie	0
9	A.Nel	lbw b Vettori	25
10	D.W.Steyn	c Papps b O'Brien	25
11	M.Ntini	not out	0
	Extras	b 6, lb 4, w 2, nb 13	25
			383

FoW (1): 1-2 (1), 2-31 (2), 3-251 (4), 4-282 (5), 5-312 (3), 6-325 (7), 7-332 (6), 8-332 (8), 9-383 (9), 10-383 (10)

South Africa Bowling

	O	M	R	W			O	M	R	W	
Steyn	14	5	42	4	1nb		10.3	1	49	6	1nb
Ntini	15.4	4	52	2			12	4	39	1	
Kallis	11	2	35	1	2nb	(4)	5	2	18	1	
Nel	13	3	42	2		(3)	7	2	20	0	
Harris	3	0	15	0							

New Zealand Bowling

	O	M	R	W	
Martin	22	6	81	2	2w,3nb
Gillespie	30	7	136	5	5nb
O'Brien	21.3	6	78	2	1nb
Vettori	20	2	61	1	3nb
Styris	4	0	17	0	1nb

Umpires: M.R.Benson and D.J.Harper. Third umpire: K.H.Hurter. Referee: J.Srinath.　　　　Toss: New Zealand

Close of Play: 1st day: New Zealand (1) 187-8 (Vettori 16*, Martin 0*, 56 overs); 2nd day: South Africa (1) 272-3 (Amla 89*, Prince 8*, 66 overs).

Man of the Match: D.W.Steyn.

The match was scheduled for five days but completed in three. H.M.Amla's 103 took 216 balls in 350 minutes and included 15 fours. J.H.Kallis's 131 took 177 balls in 221 minutes and included 17 fours and 2 sixes. C.D.Cumming retired hurt in the New Zealand first innings having scored 48 (team score 101-2).

SOUTH AFRICAN COMPOSITE XI v ZIMBABWE

Played at Sedgars Park, Potchefstroom, November 22, 23, 24, 25, 2007.
SuperSport Challenge 2007/08
Zimbabwe won by ten wickets.

SOUTH AFRICAN COMPOSITE XI

1	S.C.Cook	c Matsikenyeri b Maruma	45	c Masakadza b Chigumbura		3
2	B.D.Snijman	b Chigumbura	7	b Brent		70
3	*B.Hector	b Utseya	79	lbw b Utseya		96
4	P.J.Koortzen	c Masakadza b Chigumbura	39	(5) c Sibanda b Maruma		3
5	S.van Zyl	c Mawoyo b Chigumbura	12	(6) c Maruma b Utseya		35
6	D.L.Makalima	c Sibanda b Maruma	17	(7) c Sibanda b Utseya		8
7	J.Symes	c Matsikenyeri b Chibhabha	24	(8) not out		15
8	†A.Z.M.Dyili	lbw b Utseya	6	(9) b Maruma		0
9	W.A.Deacon	b Maruma	13	absent hurt		0
10	P.S.E.Sandri	not out	19	(4) lbw b Maruma		8
11	S.Mjekula	lbw b Maruma	11	(10) run out		0
	Extras	lb 5, nb 11	16	b 9, lb 3, nb 11		23
			288			**261**

FoW (1): 1-12 (2), 2-94 (1), 3-178 (4), 4-184 (3), 5-193 (5), 6-222 (6), 7-244 (7), 8-244 (8), 9-274 (9), 10-288 (11)
FoW (2): 1-12 (1), 2-125 (2), 3-175 (4), 4-187 (5), 5-207 (3), 6-234 (7), 7-260 (6), 8-261 (9), 9-261 (10)

ZIMBABWE

1	V.Sibanda	c Snijman b Mjekula	33	not out	19
2	B.R.M.Taylor	c and b Symes	41	not out	35
3	C.J.Chibhabha	c Dyili b Symes	9		
4	†T.Taibu	c Hector b Symes	49		
5	S.Matsikenyeri	b Sandri	2		
6	H.Masakadza	c Hector b Sandri	88		
7	T.M.K.Mawoyo	c Koortzen b Sandri	34		
8	E.Chigumbura	b van Zyl	47		
9	*P.Utseya	not out	115		
10	G.B.Brent	b Symes	20		
11	T.Maruma	lbw b Mjekula	35		
	Extras	b 2, lb 4, w 8, nb 6	20	b 2, lb 1	3
			493	(no wicket)	**57**

FoW (1): 1-56 (1), 2-69 (3), 3-98 (2), 4-106 (5), 5-161 (4), 6-261 (7), 7-262 (6), 8-354 (8), 9-408 (10), 10-493 (11)

Zimbabwe Bowling

	O	M	R	W			O	M	R	W	
Chigumbura	16	4	54	3	3nb		8	0	20	1	1nb
Brent	12	3	40	0			8	4	11	1	
Chibhabha	12	3	42	1	1nb		5	0	23	0	
Maruma	20.5	5	68	4	6nb	(6)	29	3	91	3	10nb
Utseya	28	6	75	2	1nb		24.1	1	92	3	
Matsikenyeri	1	0	4	0							
Masakadza						(4)	4	1	12	0	

South African Composite XI Bowling

	O	M	R	W			O	M	R	W	
Deacon	2.2	1	5	0	1nb						
Sandri	27	2	108	3	1w,4nb		3.3	0	16	0	
Mjekula	25.2	6	77	2	1w						
Symes	62	11	191	4		(1)	4.4	0	38	0	
Koortzen	9	1	53	0							
van Zyl	25	9	41	0	1w,1nb						
Cook	5	0	12	0	1w	(3)	0.3	0	0	0	

Umpires: M.W.Brown and G.H.Pienaar.   Referee: C.J.Mitchley.   Toss: South African Composite XI

Close of Play: 1st day: South African Composite XI (1) 236-6 (Symes 20*, Dyili 2*, 71 overs); 2nd day: Zimbabwe (1) 262-7 (Chigumbura 1*, 86.3 overs); 3rd day: South African Composite XI (2) 137-2 (Hector 53*, Sandri 1*, 38 overs).

Man of the Match: P.Utseya.
P.Utseya's 115 took 214 balls in 282 minutes and included 10 fours.

DOLPHINS v CAPE COBRAS

Played at City Oval, Pietermaritzburg, November 29, 30, December 1, 2, 2007.
SuperSport Series 2007/08
Dolphins won by 47 runs.   (Points: Dolphins 15.28, Cape Cobras 4)

DOLPHINS

1	I.Khan	c Tsolekile b Kleinveldt	37	c Tsolekile b Zondeki	30
2	D.J.Watson	b Henderson	26	c Puttick b Kleinveldt	5
3	H.M.Amla	lbw b Zondeki	1	c Puttick b Zondeki	53
4	*A.M.Amla	lbw b Kleinveldt	24	c de Lange b Zondeki	6
5	W.L.Madsen	lbw b Zondeki	0	c Davids b de Lange	17
6	J.D.Vandiar	c Kemp b Zondeki	0	c van Zyl b de Lange	5
7	J.Louw	b Zondeki	50	c Puttick b Sandri	1
8	L.E.Plunkett	c van Zyl b Sandri	7	c Prince b Kleinveldt	17
9	†D.Smit	c van Zyl b Sandri	0	c Tsolekile b Zondeki	7
10	Q.Friend	c Tsolekile b Zondeki	15	b Zondeki	0
11	S.Mlongo	not out	3	not out	0
	Extras	nb 1	1	lb 1, nb 5	6
			164		**147**

FoW (1): 1-58 (2), 2-59 (3), 3-81 (1), 4-88 (5), 5-88 (6), 6-88 (4), 7-117 (8), 8-121 (9), 9-155 (7), 10-164 (10)
FoW (2): 1-20 (2), 2-87 (1), 3-92 (3), 4-102 (4), 5-118 (6), 6-121 (7), 7-121 (5), 8-145 (9), 9-147 (10), 10-147 (8)

CAPE COBRAS

1	A.G.Puttick	c Smit b Louw	2	(2) b Louw	10
2	C.D.de Lange	c Plunkett b Louw	9	(1) c H.M.Amla b Smit	48
3	H.Davids	c Plunkett b Mlongo	14	c H.M.Amla b Louw	0
4	A.G.Prince	c H.M.Amla b Mlongo	24	c Smit b Friend	35
5	*J.M.Kemp	c Plunkett b Friend	6	lbw b Friend	17
6	S.van Zyl	lbw b Friend	6	not out	26
7	†T.L.Tsolekile	b Louw	6	b Friend	0
8	R.K.Kleinveldt	c and b Mlongo	0	c Louw b Mlongo	1
9	T.Henderson	c Friend b Louw	0	lbw b Plunkett	0
10	M.Zondeki	b Mlongo	8	b Smit	6
11	P.S.E.Sandri	not out	4	c H.M.Amla b Smit	14
	Extras	b 4, lb 1, w 3, nb 1	9	b 3, lb 11, w 6, nb 5	25
			82		**182**

FoW (1): 1-14 (1), 2-19 (2), 3-45 (3), 4-52 (5), 5-52 (6), 6-70 (4), 7-70 (7), 8-70 (8), 9-70 (9), 10-82 (10)
FoW (2): 1-25 (2), 2-25 (1), 3-88 (3), 4-112 (4), 5-125 (5), 6-130 (7), 7-133 (8), 8-137 (9), 9-155 (10), 10-182 (11)

Cape Cobras Bowling

	O	M	R	W			O	M	R	W	
Zondeki	22.2	6	51	5			17	4	42	5	
Henderson	14	4	44	1		(3)	3	0	11	0	1nb
Kleinveldt	13	4	19	2		(2)	14.2	4	25	2	3nb
Sandri	8	1	34	2			8	3	31	1	
de Lange	5	0	16	0	1nb		7	1	16	2	
Kemp						(6)	7	2	21	0	1nb

Dolphins Bowling

	O	M	R	W			O	M	R	W	
Louw	12	4	34	4	1w		17	6	34	2	2w
Friend	6	1	17	2	1w		18	4	51	3	1w,3nb
Mlongo	10	3	18	4	1nb		18	8	19	1	
Plunkett	2	1	6	0	1w		10	1	36	1	3w,2nb
Smit	2	0	2	0			12.1	4	28	3	

Umpires: J.D.Cloete and B.M.White. Referee: D.Govindjee.   Toss: Dolphins

Close of Play: 1st day: Cape Cobras (1) 68-5 (Prince 23*, Tsolekile 6*, 24 overs); 2nd day: Dolphins (2) 133-7 (Plunkett 7*, Smit 4*, 48 overs); 3rd day: Cape Cobras (2) 166-9 (van Zyl 21*, Sandri 5*, 66 overs).

Man of the Match: J.Louw.

Madsen kept wicket when Smit bowled in both Cape Cobras innings.

EAGLES v WARRIORS

Played at OUTsurance Oval, Bloemfontein, November 29, 30, December 1, 2, 2007.
SuperSport Series 2007/08
Eagles won by ten wickets.   (Points: Eagles 18, Warriors 4)

WARRIORS

1	C.A.Ingram	c Elgar b Mpitsang	10	(2) c Dippenaar b du Preez	0
2	C.A.Thyssen	b Coetzee	8	(1) c Rudolph b de Villiers	18
3	*Z.de Bruyn	c van Wyk b Mpitsang	0	lbw b du Preez	1
4	A.Jacobs	b Mpitsang	1	c Tshabalala b du Preez	78
5	H.D.Ackerman	c Dippenaar b du Preez	21	b de Villiers	6
6	†D.J.Jacobs	c Rudolph b du Preez	9	lbw b de Villiers	0
7	R.J.Peterson	not out	30	b du Preez	24
8	L.Meyer	c Bailey b Mpitsang	10	c Rudolph b Mpitsang	48
9	J.Theron	lbw b Coetzee	1	c Bailey b de Villiers	19
10	M.W.Olivier	b Coetzee	5	c McLaren b de Villiers	5
11	L.L.Tsotsobe	run out (Elgar/Coetzee)	2	not out	0
	Extras	lb 3, w 3, nb 5	11	b 4, lb 3, w 5, nb 4	16
			108		215

FoW (1): 1-18 (1), 2-18 (3), 3-18 (2), 4-36 (4), 5-53 (5), 6-60 (6), 7-80 (8), 8-83 (9), 9-103 (10), 10-108 (11)
FoW (2): 1-9 (2), 2-11 (3), 3-34 (1), 4-65 (5), 5-67 (6), 6-125 (7), 7-144 (4), 8-203 (8), 9-205 (9), 10-215 (10)

EAGLES

1	D.Elgar	lbw b Olivier	43	(2) not out	17
2	L.L.Bosman	b Olivier	46	(1) not out	7
3	J.A.Rudolph	lbw b Olivier	41		
4	*H.H.Dippenaar	c Ackerman b Olivier	112		
5	†M.N.van Wyk	c Ingram b Olivier	0		
	A.P.McLaren				
6	R.T.Bailey	c Ackerman b Olivier	2		
7	D.du Preez	lbw b Olivier	2		
8	C.J.D.de Villiers	lbw b Olivier	3		
9	T.Tshabalala	lbw b Olivier	1		
10	J.Coetzee	not out	23		
11	P.V.Mpitsang	c D.J.Jacobs b Olivier	0		
	Extras	lb 7, w 10, nb 10	27		
			300	(no wicket)	24

FoW (1): 1-102 (2), 2-115 (1), 3-182 (3), 4-182 (5), 5-188 (6), 6-204 (7), 7-210 (8), 8-224 (9), 9-297 (4), 10-300 (11)

Eagles Bowling

	O	M	R	W			O	M	R	W	
du Preez	12	3	26	2			23	8	41	4	
Coetzee	16.4	8	20	3	1w		13	5	31	0	
Mpitsang	12	1	40	4	2w,4nb	(4)	13	6	13	1	1nb
de Villiers	7	3	19	0		(3)	19.4	3	65	5	1w,1nb
Tshabalala						(5)	13	1	35	0	2nb
Rudolph						(6)	5	0	23	0	

Warriors Bowling

	O	M	R	W			O	M	R	W	
Tsotsobe	16	2	62	0	2w,2nb						
Olivier	26.3	4	65	10	2w,3nb						
Theron	20	3	59	0	3w,1nb						
de Bruyn	18	4	52	0	2w,2nb						
Meyer	3	0	18	0	1w,2nb						
Peterson	4	0	23	0		(2)	2	0	8	0	
A.Jacobs	5	0	14	0		(1)	3	0	16	0	

Umpires: G.H.Pienaar and D.J.Smith. Referee: C.J.Mitchley.   Toss: Eagles

Close of Play: 1st day: Eagles (1) 103-1 (Elgar 38*, Rudolph 0*, 29.3 overs); 2nd day: Eagles (1) 177-2 (Rudolph 37*, Dippenaar 27*, 50 overs); 3rd day: Warriors (2) 138-6 (A.Jacobs 73*, Meyer 8*, 58 overs).
Man of the Match: M.W.Olivier.
A.P.McLaren was a full substitute for Eagles, replacing M.N.van Wyk (called up for international duty). H.H.Dippenaar's 112 took 191 balls in 253 minutes and included 15 fours.

TITANS v LIONS

Played at Centurion Park, November 29, 30, December 1, 2, 2007.
SuperSport Series 2007/08
Match drawn.   **(Points: Titans 6.58, Lions 4.32)**

LIONS

1	B.D.Snijman	c du Plessis b Harris	41	c Kuhn b Joubert	46
2	A.N.Petersen	c Behardien b Mbhalati	22	b Mbhalati	1
3	W.L.Coetsee	c van Jaarsveld b Harris	16	c Mbhalati b Harris	39
4	*N.D.McKenzie	b Thomas	3	b Behardien	88
5	J.L.Ontong	lbw b Thomas	4	c Harris b Mbhalati	45
6	H.W.le Roux	c van Jaarsveld b Aronstam	80	b Aronstam	4
7	†M.J.Harris	c van Jaarsveld b Joubert	8	not out	50
8	C.W.Henderson	c Kuhn b Mbhalati	36		
9	F.de Wet	c du Plessis b Aronstam	56		
10	G.J.P.Kruger	c Kuhn b Aronstam	0		
11	C.J.Alexander	not out	0		
	Extras	b 4, lb 1, nb 5	10	lb 2	2
			276	**(6 wickets, declared)**	**275**

FoW (1): 1-35 (2), 2-84 (3), 3-87 (1), 4-87 (4), 5-92 (5), 6-104 (7), 7-185 (8), 8-255 (6), 9-265 (10), 10-276 (9)
FoW (2): 1-8 (2), 2-78 (1), 3-98 (3), 4-173 (5), 5-182 (6), 6-275 (4)

TITANS

1	M.A.Aronstam	lbw b Alexander	15
2	†H.G.Kuhn	c Harris b Henderson	50
3	*M.van Jaarsveld	lbw b Alexander	56
4	F.du Plessis	b Henderson	17
5	G.H.Bodi	b Henderson	2
6	F.Behardien	b le Roux	44
7	P.Joubert	c McKenzie b Kruger	87
8	A.C.Thomas	c McKenzie b Kruger	16
9	B.L.Reddy	not out	3
10	P.L.Harris	c Snijman b Henderson	0
11	N.E.Mbhalati	c Petersen b Kruger	0
	Extras	b 1, lb 8, w 2, nb 17	28
			318

FoW (1): 1-43 (1), 2-127 (2), 3-153 (4), 4-157 (5), 5-161 (3), 6-269 (6), 7-301 (8), 8-317 (7), 9-318 (10), 10-318 (11)

Titans Bowling

	O	M	R	W			O	M	R	W
Thomas	30	11	61	2			16	4	55	0
Mbhalati	24	5	83	2	5nb		11	3	39	2
Reddy	12	5	21	0		(4)	11	6	34	0
Joubert	15	3	42	1		(5)	15	6	33	1
Harris	36	17	60	2		(3)	31	11	71	1
Aronstam	2.1	1	4	3			9	2	31	1
van Jaarsveld						(7)	2	1	2	0
Behardien						(8)	2	0	8	1

Lions Bowling

	O	M	R	W	
Kruger	23.1	3	74	3	1w,10nb
de Wet	24	4	66	0	7nb
Alexander	18	2	82	2	1w
le Roux	12	5	19	1	
Henderson	36	7	59	4	
Coetsee	5	1	9	0	

Umpires: M.W.Brown and E.C.Hendrikse.   Referee: E.H.Mall.   Toss: Lions

Close of Play: 1st day: Lions (1) 169-6 (le Roux 43*, Henderson 27*, 83.1 overs); 2nd day: Titans (1) 73-1 (Kuhn 34*, van Jaarsveld 12*, 22.2 overs); 3rd day: Lions (2) 18-1 (Snijman 13*, Coetsee 4*, 9 overs).

Man of the Match: C.W.Henderson.

CAPE COBRAS v WARRIORS

Played at Boland Bank Park, Paarl, December 6, 7, 8, 9, 2007.
SuperSport Series 2007/08
Match drawn.   (Points: Cape Cobras 6.58, Warriors 6.44)

WARRIORS

1	†D.J.Jacobs	c Kleinveldt b Zondeki	8	(9) c Canning b Philander	6
2	C.A.Thyssen	lbw b Langeveldt	5	(3) b Philander	26
3	*Z.de Bruyn	lbw b Philander	10	(1) b Zondeki	44
4	A.Jacobs	c Kemp b Langeveldt	30	c Kemp b Zondeki	4
5	H.D.Ackerman	b Philander	97	(6) b de Lange	16
6	J.T.Smuts	c Canning b Kemp	15	(2) lbw b Zondeki	53
7	J.Botha	not out	91	c Duminy b Zondeki	69
8	R.J.Peterson	b Langeveldt	55	c de Lange b Philander	48
9	M.W.Olivier	c Canning b Philander	1	(5) b Philander	13
10	L.L.Tsotsobe	lbw b de Lange	3	lbw b de Lange	2
11	S.Mjekula	lbw b de Lange	0	not out	0
	Extras	b 2, lb 15, w 2, nb 12	31	lb 5, w 9, nb 7	21
			346		302

FoW (1): 1-15 (2), 2-19 (1), 3-51 (3), 4-125 (4), 5-156 (6), 6-187 (5), 7-290 (8), 8-303 (9), 9-326 (10), 10-346 (11)
FoW (2): 1-107 (1), 2-110 (2), 3-114 (4), 4-153 (5), 5-168 (3), 6-180 (6), 7-242 (8), 8-263 (9), 9-298 (10), 10-302 (7)

CAPE COBRAS

1	A.G.Puttick	c D.J.Jacobs b Botha	104	(2) c A.Jacobs b Tsotsobe	24
2	C.D.de Lange	lbw b Olivier	6	(1) c A.Jacobs b Tsotsobe	3
3	H.Davids	lbw b Olivier	2	lbw b Botha	14
4	J.P.Duminy	c D.J.Jacobs b Peterson	71	not out	36
5	A.G.Prince	b Olivier	50	not out	10
6	*J.M.Kemp	c A.Jacobs b Tsotsobe	6		
7	V.D.Philander	c Thyssen b Peterson	54		
8	†R.C.C.Canning	lbw b Peterson	41		
9	R.K.Kleinveldt	c Tsotsobe b Peterson	17		
10	M.Zondeki	c de Bruyn b Botha	12		
11	C.K.Langeveldt	not out	6		
	Extras	b 12, lb 2, nb 2	16	b 10, nb 1	11
			385	(3 wickets)	98

FoW (1): 1-11 (2), 2-21 (3), 3-137 (4), 4-236 (1), 5-249 (5), 6-257 (6), 7-324 (7), 8-356 (9), 9-373 (10), 10-385 (8)
FoW (2): 1-7 (1), 2-34 (2), 3-62 (3)

Cape Cobras Bowling

	O	M	R	W			O	M	R	W	
Langeveldt	29	7	94	3	8nb	(2)	15	4	55	0	2w,3nb
Zondeki	17	4	54	1	1w	(1)	21.4	4	65	4	2w
Philander	26	7	74	3	1w,2nb	(4)	23	4	61	4	1nb
Kleinveldt	14	2	46	0	1nb	(3)	13	2	38	0	1w,3nb
Kemp	12	3	42	1							
de Lange	10.5	6	15	2	1nb	(5)	29	8	78	2	
Duminy	1	0	4	0							

Warriors Bowling

	O	M	R	W			O	M	R	W	
Olivier	22	4	53	3			2	0	11	0	
Tsotsobe	22	6	79	1			6	0	14	2	
Botha	31	5	85	2	1nb	(4)	7	0	26	1	
Mjekula	11	4	32	0		(3)	2	0	13	0	
de Bruyn	13	2	37	0	1nb						
Peterson	34.4	7	85	4		(5)	4.2	2	24	0	1nb

Umpires: I.L.Howell and G.H.Pienaar. Referee: S.B.Lambson.   Toss: Cape Cobras

Close of Play: 1st day: Warriors (1) 303-8 (Botha 54*, 94.3 overs); 2nd day: Cape Cobras (1) 228-3 (Puttick 100*, Prince 37*, 79 overs); 3rd day: Warriors (2) 115-3 (Thyssen 1*, Olivier 1*, 39 overs).

Man of the Match: R.J.Peterson, J.Botha.
A.G.Puttick's 104 took 236 balls in 343 minutes and included 12 fours.

DOLPHINS v LIONS

Played at Sahara Stadium, Kingsmead, Durban, December 6, 7, 8, 9, 2007.
SuperSport Series 2007/08
Match drawn.   (Points: Dolphins 4, Lions 6.2)

LIONS

1	B.D.Snijman	c Plunkett b Pollock	28
2	A.N.Petersen	c Plunkett b Pollock	0
3	W.L.Coetsee	lbw b Pollock	0
4	*N.D.McKenzie	c Smit b Louw	46
5	J.L.Ontong	b Louw	20
6	H.W.le Roux	b Plunkett	41
7	†M.J.Harris	c Smit b Louw	39
8	C.W.Henderson	c Gobind b Plunkett	18
9	F.deWet	not out	0
10	G.J.P.Kruger	c sub (S.Mlongo) b Plunkett	6
11	C.J.Alexander		
	Extras	b 2, lb 8, nb 2	12
		(9 wickets, declared)	210

FoW (1): 1-7 (2), 2-7 (3), 3-77 (1), 4-87 (4), 5-104 (5), 6-177 (7), 7-201 (8), 8-202 (6), 9-210 (10)

DOLPHINS

1	*I.Khan	c le Roux b Henderson	34
2	W.L.Madsen	b Kruger	34
3	H.M.Amla	lbw b Kruger	30
4	S.M.Pollock	c McKenzie b Henderson	8
5	J.Louw	b Kruger	0
6	L.E.Plunkett	c Harris b Kruger	11
7	R.Gobind	c McKenzie b Henderson	0
8	†D.Smit	b Kruger	0
9	J.D.Vandiar	c Petersen b Alexander	20
10	Q.Friend	b Kruger	0
11	D.J.Watson	not out	4
	Extras	nb 6	6
			147

FoW (1): 1-55 (1), 2-89 (2), 3-108 (3), 4-108 (4), 5-108 (5), 6-113 (7), 7-119 (6), 8-120 (8), 9-127 (10), 10-147 (9)

Dolphins Bowling

	O	M	R	W	
Pollock	22	10	41	3	
Louw	15.1	6	24	3	
Friend	14.5	1	79	0	2nb
Plunkett	17.5	3	56	3	

Lions Bowling

	O	M	R	W	
de Wet	8	2	16	0	
Kruger	14	3	49	6	6nb
le Roux	3	0	17	0	
Alexander	8	2	26	1	
Henderson	16	4	39	3	

Umpires: S.George and K.H.Hurter. Referee: C.J.Mitchley.   Toss: Dolphins

Close of Play: 1st day: Lions (1) 77-3 (McKenzie 44*, Ontong 0*, 29 overs); 2nd day: No play; 3rd day: No play.

Man of the Match: G.J.P.Kruger.

EAGLES v TITANS

Played at OUTsurance Oval, Bloemfontein, December 6, 7, 8, 2007.
SuperSport Series 2007/08
Titans won by 231 runs.   (Points: Eagles 4, Titans 14)

TITANS

1	†H.G.Kuhn	c Rudolph b McLaren	24	lbw b Mpitsang	6
2	R.Jappie	c Dippenaar b de Villiers	14	c Elgar b Tshabalala	43
3	F.du Plessis	c van Wyk b de Villiers	0	c Dippenaar b Mpitsang	50
4	*M.van Jaarsveld	lbw b McLaren	0	c van Wyk b du Preez	65
5	F.Behardien	c van Wyk b du Preez	7	c Dippenaar b Mpitsang	0
6	J.A.Morkel	c van Wyk b de Villiers	7	c Rudolph b Tshabalala	20
7	P.Joubert	lbw b du Preez	10	lbw b Tshabalala	16
8	B.L.Reddy	b Mpitsang	18	c and b de Villiers	55
9	P.L.Harris	not out	15	lbw b de Villiers	30
10	D.W.Steyn	c Elgar b Mpitsang	4	c Dippenaar b Mpitsang	39
11	N.E.Mbhalati	b Mpitsang	3	not out	2
	Extras	b 4, lb 3, w 2, nb 7	16	b 11, lb 4, w 6, nb 9	30
			118		356

FoW (1): 1-46 (1), 2-47 (3), 3-48 (4), 4-49 (2), 5-59 (6), 6-73 (5), 7-76 (7), 8-100 (8), 9-104 (10), 10-118 (11)
FoW (2): 1-19 (1), 2-99 (3), 3-116 (2), 4-117 (5), 5-141 (6), 6-164 (7), 7-253 (8), 8-290 (4), 9-333 (9), 10-356 (10)

EAGLES

1	D.Elgar	c Jappie b Steyn	0	(2) c Kuhn b Steyn	14
2	L.L.Bosman	c Mbhalati b Steyn	16	(1) lbw b Steyn	35
3	J.A.Rudolph	c Kuhn b Steyn	17	retired hurt	0
4	*H.H.Dippenaar	b Steyn	6	lbw b Harris	16
5	†M.N.van Wyk	c van Jaarsveld b Steyn	4	c van Jaarsveld b Steyn	0
6	R.T.Bailey	b Joubert	18	b Steyn	0
7	R.McLaren	c Kuhn b Steyn	10	b Harris	53
8	D.du Preez	lbw b Steyn	0	b Steyn	0
9	C.J.D.de Villiers	not out	9	b Steyn	2
10	T.Tshabalala	c Kuhn b Steyn	0	b Harris	5
11	P.V.Mpitsang	c Reddy b Joubert	2	not out	16
	Extras	lb 4, nb 3	7	b 4, nb 9	13
			89		154

FoW (1): 1-0 (1), 2-33 (3), 3-41 (4), 4-46 (2), 5-46 (5), 6-66 (6), 7-67 (8), 8-82 (7), 9-82 (10), 10-89 (11)
FoW (2): 1-46 (1), 2-53 (2), 3-53 (5), 4-53 (6), 5-103 (4), 6-104 (8), 7-106 (9), 8-113 (10), 9-154 (7)

Eagles Bowling

	O	M	R	W			O	M	R	W	
du Preez	12	3	38	2			20	7	46	1	
Mpitsang	14	2	31	3	1w,5nb	(3)	21.5	2	64	4	8nb
de Villiers	12	2	23	3		(4)	19	5	52	2	2w
McLaren	10	1	19	2	1w,2nb	(2)	16	2	65	0	
Tshabalala						(5)	31	3	97	3	1nb
Rudolph						(6)	2	0	17	0	

Titans Bowling

	O	M	R	W			O	M	R	W	
Steyn	13	3	41	8	1nb		16	3	69	6	6nb
Mbhalati	2	0	19	0	2nb	(3)	4	1	8	0	1nb
Joubert	11	2	25	2							
Reddy						(2)	3	0	18	0	1nb
Harris						(4)	10.5	0	40	3	
du Plessis						(5)	1	0	10	0	
van Jaarsveld						(6)	1	0	5	0	

Umpires: M.Erasmus and B.M.White. Referee: A.Barnes.   Toss: Eagles

Close of Play: 1st day: Titans (2) 13-0 (Kuhn 1*, Jappie 12*, 4.3 overs); 2nd day: Titans (2) 330-8 (Harris 30*, Steyn 17*, 103 overs).
Man of the Match: D.W.Steyn.
The match was scheduled for four days but completed in three. D.W.Steyn took a hat-trick in the Eagles second innings (Elgar, van Wyk, Bailey). J.A.Rudolph retired hurt in the Eagles second innings having scored 0 (team score 47-1).

CAPE COBRAS v DOLPHINS

Played at Sahara Park Newlands, Cape Town, December 13, 14, 15, 2007.
SuperSport Series 2007/08
Cape Cobras won by an innings and 44 runs. **(Points: Cape Cobras 17.82, Dolphins 5.2)**

DOLPHINS

1	I.Khan	c Canning b Kemp	23	c Canning b Zondeki	3
2	W.L.Madsen	c Kemp b Zondeki	10	c Canning b Zondeki	12
3	H.M.Amla	c Prince b Langeveldt	7	c Kemp b Zondeki	21
4	*A.M.Amla	b Kemp	15	(7) lbw b Kemp	6
5	D.J.Watson	c Canning b Zondeki	47	c Kemp b Zondeki	1
6	J.D.Vandiar	c Canning b Langeveldt	21	(4) b Langeveldt	4
7	J.Louw	c Canning b Kleinveldt	0	(6) b Zondeki	1
8	L.E.Plunkett	c Canning b Langeveldt	1	c Zondeki b Kemp	9
9	†D.Smit	b Kleinveldt	65	b Kleinveldt	0
10	Y.A.Abdulla	lbw b Zondeki	0	c Canning b Kleinveldt	0
11	Q.Friend	not out	13	not out	4
	Extras	lb 3, w 1, nb 4	8	w 1, nb 1	2
			210		**63**

FoW (1): 1-12 (2), 2-25 (3), 3-56 (4), 4-63 (1), 5-113 (6), 6-114 (7), 7-115 (8), 8-161 (5), 9-161 (10), 10-210 (9)
FoW (2): 1-15 (2), 2-16 (1), 3-21 (4), 4-34 (5), 5-40 (6), 6-45 (3), 7-54 (7), 8-55 (9), 9-55 (10), 10-63 (8)

CAPE COBRAS

1	A.G.Puttick	c H.M.Amla b Plunkett	55
2	C.D.de Lange	c Khan b Louw	0
3	H.Davids	c H.M.Amla b Smit	74
4	A.G.Prince	c Plunkett b Louw	51
5	R.K.Kleinveldt	c Watson b Smit	6
6	S.van Zyl	c Smit b Plunkett	24
7	*J.M.Kemp	c Vandiar b Abdulla	47
8	F.D.Telo	c H.M.Amla b Plunkett	0
9	†R.C.C.Canning	not out	25
10	M.Zondeki	lbw b Smit	0
11	C.K.Langeveldt	c H.M.Amla b Smit	6
	Extras	b 8, lb 13, w 5, nb 3	29
			317

FoW (1): 1-5 (2), 2-134 (1), 3-165 (3), 4-171 (5), 5-228 (4), 6-236 (6), 7-236 (8), 8-307 (7), 9-307 (10), 10-317 (11)

Cape Cobras Bowling

	O	M	R	W			O	M	R	W	
Langeveldt	18	6	34	3	1nb		8	1	23	1	1nb
Zondeki	22	6	69	3	1nb		10	2	26	5	1w
Kleinveldt	19.3	3	61	2	2nb	(4)	1	0	5	2	
Kemp	17	3	40	2	1w	(3)	3.2	0	9	2	
de Lange	1	0	3	0							

Dolphins Bowling

	O	M	R	W	
Louw	29	8	56	2	1w
Abdulla	18	2	65	1	2w
Plunkett	25	5	66	3	1w,1nb
Friend	14	2	41	0	2nb
Smit	21.5	4	68	4	1w

Umpires: S.George and D.J.Smith. Referee: S.B.Lambson.   Toss: Dolphins

Close of Play: 1st day: Cape Cobras (1) 34-1 (Puttick 18*, Davids 5*, 14.5 overs); 2nd day: Dolphins (2) 3-0 (Khan 1*, Madsen 1*, 1 over).

Man of the Match: M.Zondeki.

The match was scheduled for four days but completed in three.

LIONS v EAGLES

Played at New Wanderers Stadium, Johannesburg, December 13, 14, 15, 2007.
SuperSport Series 2007/08
Eagles won by 63 runs. (Points: Lions 5.48, Eagles 15.54)

EAGLES

1	D.Elgar	c Harris b de Wet	10	(2) lbw b Mafa	11
2	L.L.Bosman	run out (le Roux)	23	(1) c le Roux b Alexander	5
3	R.T.Bailey	c Harris b le Roux	19	c Coetsee b Alexander	0
4	*H.H.Dippenaar	c McKenzie b le Roux	66	c Ontong b le Roux	44
5	†A.P.McLaren	c le Roux b Alexander	8	b Mafa	15
6	P.J.Koortzen	c McKenzie b le Roux	6	lbw b Alexander	0
7	R.McLaren	c Coetsee b le Roux	22	c Harris b Alexander	51
8	D.du Preez	c Harris b le Roux	3	b Alexander	12
9	C.J.D.de Villiers	lbw b Henderson	0	c Harris b Mafa	8
10	T.Tshabalala	not out	6	c Harris b le Roux	2
11	P.V.Mpitsang	c Petersen b le Roux	3	not out	0
	Extras	lb 6, w 2, nb 3	11	b 4, lb 9, w 1, nb 1	15
			177		**163**

FoW (1): 1-31 (1), 2-41 (2), 3-70 (3), 4-79 (5), 5-94 (6), 6-157 (4), 7-166 (7), 8-167 (9), 9-169 (8), 10-177 (11)
FoW (2): 1-5 (1), 2-5 (3), 3-30 (2), 4-54 (5), 5-55 (6), 6-105 (4), 7-118 (8), 8-139 (9), 9-163 (10), 10-163 (7)

LIONS

1	B.D.Snijman	b du Preez	21	(2) c Koortzen b du Preez	18
2	A.N.Petersen	lbw b de Villiers	10	(1) b du Preez	5
3	W.L.Coetsee	c A.P.McLaren b R.McLaren	40	c A.P.McLaren b Mpitsang	1
4	*N.D.McKenzie	lbw b du Preez	22	c A.P.McLaren b R.McLaren	15
5	J.L.Ontong	c Elgar b R.McLaren	13	c A.P.McLaren b Mpitsang	17
6	H.W.le Roux	lbw b Mpitsang	0	c A.P.McLaren b du Preez	11
7	†M.J.Harris	not out	30	c Dippenaar b du Preez	8
8	C.W.Henderson	c A.P.McLaren b du Preez	8	not out	17
9	F.de Wet	c R.McLaren b Mpitsang	7	c A.P.McLaren b de Villiers	0
10	C.J.Alexander	c Koortzen b de Villiers	0	c A.P.McLaren b de Villiers	2
11	J.T.Mafa	run out (Elgar/A.P.McLaren)	5	c R.McLaren b de Villiers	0
	Extras	lb 15, w 1, nb 2	18	lb 5, w 1, nb 3	9
			174		**103**

FoW (1): 1-24 (2), 2-34 (1), 3-85 (4), 4-109 (3), 5-115 (6), 6-125 (5), 7-146 (8), 8-160 (9), 9-161 (10), 10-174 (11)
FoW (2): 1-21 (1), 2-22 (3), 3-28 (2), 4-62 (4), 5-66 (5), 6-81 (6), 7-84 (7), 8-85 (9), 9-87 (10), 10-103 (11)

Lions Bowling

	O	M	R	W		O	M	R	W	
de Wet	23	10	45	1		16	5	22	0	
Alexander	14	1	40	1	1w	18.3	4	61	5	
Mafa	15	3	39	0	1w,2nb	14	5	22	3	1w,1nb
le Roux	16.4	4	29	6	1nb	16	1	45	1	
Henderson	9	0	18	1						

Eagles Bowling

	O	M	R	W			O	M	R	W	
du Preez	20	3	45	3		(2)	13	5	29	4	
Mpitsang	18	3	46	2	2nb	(1)	11	2	28	2	3nb
de Villiers	16.2	3	47	2			11.1	3	18	3	1w
R.McLaren	14	5	21	2	1w		9	2	23	1	

Umpires: M.W.Brown and K.H.Hurter. Referee: E.H.Mall.   Toss: Eagles

Close of Play: 1st day: Lions (1) 2-0 (Snijman 1*, Petersen 0*, 2.3 overs); 2nd day: Eagles (2) 80-5 (Dippenaar 29*, R.McLaren 13*, 31 overs).

Man of the Match: R.McLaren.

The match was scheduled for four days but completed in three.

TITANS v WARRIORS

Played at Centurion Park, December 13, 14, 15, 2007.
SuperSport Series 2007/08
Warriors won by one wicket.   **(Points: Titans 4, Warriors 16.88)**

TITANS

1	M.A.Aronstam	b Olivier	2	c Smith b Tsotsobe	3
2	†H.G.Kuhn	c Ackerman b Mjekula	10	c Peterson b Olivier	5
3	R.Jappie	lbw b Tsotsobe	1	(4) c Jacobs b Tsotsobe	8
4	F.du Plessis	c Jacobs b Mjekula	9	(3) lbw b Theron	27
5	*M.van Jaarsveld	c de Bruyn b Tsotsobe	84	b Mjekula	111
6	P.Joubert	c Jacobs b Mjekula	0	c Jacobs b Peterson	24
7	B.L.Reddy	c Thyssen b Mjekula	4	c Mjekula b Peterson	13
8	A.C.Thomas	c Jacobs b Tsotsobe	15	c Jacobs b Tsotsobe	3
9	P.L.Harris	c Ackerman b Theron	3	c Jacobs b Theron	1
10	Imran Tahir	c Theron b Tsotsobe	3	c Smuts b Mjekula	24
11	N.E.Mbhalati	not out	2	not out	4
	Extras	nb 3	3	b 7, lb 4, w 2, nb 10	23
			136		**246**

FoW (1): 1-2 (1), 2-7 (3), 3-21 (2), 4-26 (4), 5-26 (6), 6-34 (7), 7-69 (8), 8-74 (9), 9-117 (10), 10-136 (5)
FoW (2): 1-12 (1), 2-12 (2), 3-39 (4), 4-56 (3), 5-144 (6), 6-171 (7), 7-175 (8), 8-178 (9), 9-235 (5), 10-246 (10)

WARRIORS

1	C.A.Thyssen	c du Plessis b Thomas	4	(2) c van Jaarsveld b Imran Tahir	17
2	M.B.A.Smith	c and b Imran Tahir	19	(1) b Harris	7
3	*Z.de Bruyn	lbw b Imran Tahir	33	c Aronstam b Harris	50
4	†A.Jacobs	c Aronstam b Imran Tahir	104	run out	13
5	H.D.Ackerman	c du Plessis b Harris	2	c and b Imran Tahir	8
6	J.T.Smuts	lbw b Imran Tahir	0	b Imran Tahir	0
7	R.J.Peterson	c du Plessis b van Jaarsveld	47	lbw b Imran Tahir	8
8	J.Theron	lbw b Imran Tahir	6	not out	25
9	M.W.Olivier	c van Jaarsveld b Imran Tahir	1	st Kuhn b Harris	0
10	L.L.Tsotsobe	b Imran Tahir	18	c van Jaarsveld b Imran Tahir	1
11	S.Mjekula	not out	5	not out	0
	Extras	b 1, lb 2, nb 2	5	b 10	10
			244	**(9 wickets)**	**139**

FoW (1): 1-4 (1), 2-59 (2), 3-60 (3), 4-73 (5), 5-74 (6), 6-158 (7), 7-188 (8), 8-221 (4), 9-221 (9), 10-244 (10)
FoW (2): 1-29 (1), 2-29 (2), 3-64 (4), 4-80 (5), 5-90 (6), 6-108 (7), 7-108 (3), 8-110 (9), 9-117 (10)

Warriors Bowling	O	M	R	W			O	M	R	W	
Olivier	6	3	19	1	2nb		9	3	11	1	1nb
Tsotsobe	17.5	5	48	4			22	4	52	3	
Theron	10	2	30	1		(6)	9	0	34	2	4nb
Mjekula	8	1	29	4			15.3	6	40	2	2w
de Bruyn	3	1	10	0	1nb	(7)	5	0	21	0	5nb
Peterson						(3)	30	8	63	2	
Smuts						(5)	4	2	14	0	

Titans Bowling	O	M	R	W			O	M	R	W	
Thomas	10	3	24	1		(2)	2	0	2	0	
Mbhalati	2	0	6	0	2nb						
Harris	40	14	100	1		(1)	23	8	66	3	
Imran Tahir	35	9	93	7		(3)	20.3	4	61	5	
van Jaarsveld	3	0	14	1							
Aronstam	1	0	4	0							

Umpires: G.H.Pienaar and B.M.White. Referee: S.Wadvalla.   Toss: Titans

Close of Play: 1st day: Warriors (1) 94-5 (Jacobs 14*, Peterson 17*, 49 overs); 2nd day: Titans (2) 107-4 (van Jaarsveld 42*, Joubert 12*, 58 overs).

Man of the Match: A.Jacobs.

The match was scheduled for four days but completed in three. A.Jacobs's 104 took 160 balls in 184 minutes and included 14 fours and 2 sixes. M.van Jaarsveld's 111 took 197 balls in 286 minutes and included 13 fours and 2 sixes.

SOUTH AFRICA A v WEST INDIANS

Played at Mercedes Benz Park, East London, December 19, 20, 21, 2007.
West Indies in South Africa 2007/08
South Africa A won by ten wickets.

WEST INDIANS

1	D.S.Smith	c van Wyk b Zondeki	10	lbw b Langeveldt	5
2	D.Ganga	c Ontong b Philander	10	lbw b Zondeki	0
3	R.S.Morton	c Philander b Langeveldt	54	c McKenzie b Philander	16
4	M.N.Samuels	lbw b Zondeki	14	c van Wyk b Zondeki	21
5	S.Chanderpaul	c Botha b Zondeki	0	c van Wyk b Zondeki	9
6	*D.J.Bravo	c Ontong b Zondeki	4	c Bodi b Botha	67
7	†D.Ramdin	b Philander	10	b Philander	35
8	D.J.G.Sammy	c van Wyk b Langeveldt	40	lbw b Botha	57
9	R.N.Lewis	c Bodi b Zondeki	40	c de Wet b Botha	3
10	F.H.Edwards	not out	2	not out	0
11	P.T.Collins	c McKenzie b Botha	1	c Langeveldt b Botha	0
	Extras	b 4, lb 1, nb 3	8	w 1	1
			193		**214**

FoW (1): 1-12 (1), 2-48 (2), 3-83 (4), 4-83 (5), 5-91 (6), 6-95 (3), 7-112 (7), 8-169 (8), 9-192 (9), 10-193 (11)
FoW (2): 1-5 (2), 2-5 (1), 3-29 (3), 4-50 (4), 5-53 (5), 6-118 (7), 7-205 (6), 8-213 (8), 9-214 (9), 10-214 (11)

SOUTH AFRICA A

1	A.N.Petersen	b Sammy	8	(2) not out	15
2	†M.N.van Wyk	b Edwards	89	(1) not out	23
3	*N.D.McKenzie	lbw b Bravo	54		
4	J.P.Duminy	c Bravo b Lewis	62		
5	J.L.Ontong	not out	114		
6	G.H.Bodi	c Ramdin b Edwards	6		
7	V.D.Philander	c Ramdin b Bravo	9		
8	J.Botha	lbw b Bravo	7		
9	F.de Wet	c Ramdin b Bravo	1		
10	M.Zondeki	b Bravo	11		
11	C.K.Langeveldt	b Bravo	4		
	Extras	lb 3, w 2, nb 1	6	w 1	1
			371	(no wicket)	**39**

FoW (1): 1-15 (1), 2-106 (3), 3-187 (2), 4-291 (4), 5-316 (6), 6-329 (7), 7-349 (8), 8-351 (9), 9-365 (10), 10-371 (11)

South Africa A Bowling

	O	M	R	W			O	M	R	W	
Zondeki	16	2	39	5			17	3	61	3	1w
Langeveldt	15	3	55	2			20	5	59	1	
de Wet	12	3	27	0	2nb	(5)	12	3	38	0	
Philander	12	5	40	2		(3)	16	4	36	2	
Botha	9.1	1	23	1		(4)	13.3	5	20	4	
Ontong	1	0	4	0	1nb						

West Indians Bowling

	O	M	R	W			O	M	R	W	
Edwards	19	5	39	2	1w	(2)	3	0	13	0	
Collins	20	3	72	0	1nb	(1)	5	1	24	0	1w
Sammy	18	3	71	1	1w						
Samuels	16	1	58	0		(3)	1	0	2	0	
Lewis	17	1	71	1							
Bravo	15.5	4	51	6							
Ganga	1	0	6	0							

Umpires: I.L.Howell and B.G.Jerling. Referee: D.Govindjee.   Toss: West Indians

Close of Play: 1st day: South Africa A (1) 78-1 (van Wyk 25*, McKenzie 43*, 22 overs); 2nd day: South Africa A (1) 351-7 (Ontong 109*, de Wet 1*, 100.1 overs).

Man of the Match: M.Zondeki.
The match was scheduled for four days but completed in three. J.L.Ontong's 114 took 145 balls in 231 minutes and included 11 fours and 2 sixes.

SOUTH AFRICAN COMPOSITE XI v ZIMBABWE

Played at Boland Bank Park, Paarl, December 20, 21, 22, 2007.
SuperSport Challenge 2007/08
Zimbabwe won by 51 runs.

ZIMBABWE

1	H.Masakadza	c Reddy b Coetzee	4	c Snijman b Kruger	9
2	V.Sibanda	c Adams b Burger	0	lbw b Burger	5
3	C.J.Chibhabha	c Dyili b Burger	1	c Dyili b Burger	35
4	†T.Taibu	c Burger b Kruger	20	c Snijman b Burger	100
5	B.R.M.Taylor	lbw b Coetzee	2	c Kruger b Burger	0
6	S.Matsikenyeri	c Madsen b Coetzee	7	c Madsen b Liebisch	0
7	K.M.Dabengwa	c Madsen b Kruger	5	c Dyili b Kruger	17
8	E.Chigumbura	c Liebisch b Kruger	35	c Madsen b Adams	49
9	*P.Utseya	lbw b Coetzee	0	c Hector b Liebisch	7
10	R.W.Price	c Hector b Burger	2	b Burger	10
11	C.B.Mpofu	not out	0	not out	4
	Extras	lb 11, w 1, nb 1	13	b 4, lb 2, w 2, nb 2	10
			89		**246**

FoW (1): 1-0 (2), 2-1 (3), 3-9 (1), 4-27 (5), 5-35 (4), 6-48 (7), 7-51 (6), 8-51 (9), 9-83 (10), 10-89 (8)
FoW (2): 1-14 (2), 2-20 (1), 3-83 (3), 4-83 (5), 5-84 (6), 6-116 (7), 7-202 (8), 8-225 (9), 9-237 (4), 10-246 (10)

SOUTH AFRICAN COMPOSITE XI

1	B.D.Snijman	b Chigumbura	9	b Chigumbura	5
2	R.Jappie	run out (Chibhabha)	2	c Masakadza b Chigumbura	3
3	*B.Hector	c Dabengwa b Chigumbura	5	b Mpofu	4
4	W.L.Madsen	not out	70	lbw b Chibhabha	9
5	S.W.Liebisch	c Utseya b Mpofu	19	b Chigumbura	10
6	S.Burger	b Masakadza	19	lbw b Mpofu	13
7	A.K.Kruger	b Utseya	37	c Taibu b Chigumbura	1
8	†A.Z.M.Dyili	c Dabengwa b Utseya	2	st Taibu b Price	9
9	J.Coetzee	b Utseya	11	(10) not out	17
10	P.R.Adams	c Chibhabha b Utseya	4	(11) c Utseya b Mpofu	12
11	B.L.Reddy	c Chibhabha b Utseya	0	(9) c Dabengwa b Chigumbura	8
	Extras	lb 6, w 2	8	b 1, lb 5, w 1	7
			186		**98**

FoW (1): 1-11 (2), 2-14 (1), 3-19 (3), 4-49 (5), 5-73 (6), 6-153 (7), 7-157 (8), 8-175 (9), 9-181 (10), 10-186 (11)
FoW (2): 1-7 (1), 2-8 (2), 3-12 (3), 4-25 (4), 5-48 (5), 6-50 (6), 7-56 (7), 8-60 (8), 9-70 (9), 10-98 (11)

South African Composite XI Bowling

	O	M	R	W		O	M	R	W	
Coetzee	15	9	19	4		2.2	0	7	0	
Burger	8	4	13	3		13.4	0	59	5	
Reddy	11	5	26	0	1nb	6.4	1	20	0	
Kruger	7.3	3	15	3	1w	11	0	61	2	1w
Liebisch	2	1	5	0		14	1	54	2	2nb
Adams					(6)	8	2	39	1	1w

Zimbabwe Bowling

	O	M	R	W		O	M	R	W	
Mpofu	16	3	45	1	1w	12.1	4	22	3	1w
Chigumbura	11	1	49	2	1w	13	5	33	5	
Chibhabha	7	2	14	0	(4)	5	2	10	1	
Masakadza	3	1	6	1	(3)	4	1	8	0	
Price	13	3	26	0		6	1	18	1	
Utseya	11.3	3	40	5		1	0	1	0	

Umpires: M.W.Brown and M.Erasmus. Referee: S.Wadvalla.   Toss: Zimbabwe

Close of Play: 1st day: South African Composite XI (1) 157-7 (Madsen 56*, 49.2 overs); 2nd day: South African Composite XI (2) 42-4 (Liebisch 4*, Burger 11*, 22 overs).

Man of the Match: T.Taibu.
The match was scheduled for four days but completed in three. T.Taibu's 100 took 112 balls in 198 minutes and included 11 fours and 1 six.

SOUTH AFRICA v WEST INDIES

Played at Sahara Oval, St George's Park, Port Elizabeth, December 26, 27, 28, 29, 2007.
West Indies in South Africa 2007/08 - 1st Test
West Indies won by 128 runs.

WEST INDIES

1	*C.H.Gayle	c Kallis b Harris	66	c Boucher b Ntini	29
2	D.Ganga	c Boucher b Nel	33	run out	45
3	R.S.Morton	c Prince b Ntini	33	lbw b Kallis	5
4	M.N.Samuels	c Kallis b Steyn	94	b Steyn	40
5	S.Chanderpaul	b Nel	104	c Kallis b Steyn	8
6	D.J.Bravo	c and b Ntini	12	c Gibbs b Harris	10
7	†D.Ramdin	c Boucher b Ntini	1	c Gibbs b Steyn	0
8	D.J.G.Sammy	run out (de Villiers)	38	lbw b Harris	3
9	J.E.Taylor	b Steyn	9	c Nel b Harris	22
10	D.B.L.Powell	not out	1	b Harris	6
11	F.H.Edwards	c Prince b Nel	0	not out	0
	Extras	b 2, lb 8, w 3, nb 4	17	b 1, w 1, nb 5	7
			408		**175**

FoW (1): 1-98 (2), 2-102 (1), 3-166 (3), 4-277 (4), 5-296 (6), 6-304 (7), 7-361 (8), 8-385 (9), 9-407 (5), 10-408 (11)
FoW (2): 1-32 (1), 2-57 (3), 3-122 (2), 4-123 (4), 5-141 (6), 6-141 (5), 7-144 (8), 8-144 (7), 9-160 (10), 10-175 (9)

SOUTH AFRICA

1	*G.C.Smith	lbw b Taylor	28	(2) c Ganga b Edwards	11
2	H.H.Gibbs	c Ramdin b Powell	0	(1) lbw b Powell	0
3	H.M.Amla	b Powell	29	c Ramdin b Edwards	8
4	J.H.Kallis	c Bravo b Taylor	0	c Ramdin b Edwards	85
5	A.G.Prince	c Morton b Powell	20	c Gayle b Taylor	10
6	A.B.de Villiers	b Bravo	59	c Samuels b Taylor	60
7	†M.V.Boucher	c Powell b Taylor	20	b Taylor	13
8	P.L.Harris	c Taylor b Bravo	9	b Bravo	0
9	A.Nel	c Ganga b Bravo	16	c Ramdin b Sammy	34
10	D.W.Steyn	c Powell b Bravo	7	not out	33
11	M.Ntini	not out	0	c Powell b Samuels	1
	Extras	b 4, lb 1, w 1, nb 1	7	lb 4, w 1	5
			195		**260**

FoW (1): 1-1 (2), 2-45 (1), 3-53 (4), 4-63 (3), 5-96 (5), 6-129 (7), 7-172 (6), 8-181 (8), 9-194 (9), 10-195 (10)
FoW (2): 1-4 (1), 2-17 (3), 3-20 (2), 4-45 (5), 5-157 (4), 6-183 (7), 7-190 (8), 8-192 (6), 9-259 (9), 10-260 (11)

South Africa Bowling

	O	M	R	W			O	M	R	W	
Steyn	31	4	121	2	2w,3nb		17	3	67	3	1w,5nb
Ntini	30	6	100	3			11	3	35	1	
Nel	25.4	7	85	3	1nb		7	1	21	0	
Harris	30	9	69	1		(5)	15.4	5	35	4	
Kallis	17	8	23	0	1w	(4)	7	1	16	1	

West Indies Bowling

	O	M	R	W			O	M	R	W	
Powell	17	4	58	3	1w		14	2	47	1	1w
Edwards	15	3	56	0	1nb		13	3	37	3	
Taylor	13	4	46	3			18	1	66	3	
Bravo	13.1	3	24	4			16	2	63	1	
Sammy	4	2	6	0			7	0	29	1	
Samuels						(6)	6.5	1	14	1	

Umpires: Aleem Dar and R.B.Tiffin. Third umpire: R.E.Koertzen. Referee: R.S.Mahanama.   Toss: South Africa

Close of Play: 1st day: West Indies (1) 281-4 (Chanderpaul 43*, Bravo 0*, 84 overs); 2nd day: South Africa (1) 122-5 (de Villiers 22*, Boucher 18*, 34 overs); 3rd day: West Indies (2) 146-8 (Taylor 2*, Powell 0*, 52 overs).

Man of the Match: M.N.Samuels.
The match was scheduled for five days but completed in four. S.Chanderpaul's 104 took 254 balls in 394 minutes and included 12 fours.

389

SOUTH AFRICA v WEST INDIES

Played at Sahara Park Newlands, Cape Town, January 2, 3, 4, 5, 2008.
West Indies in South Africa 2007/08 - 2nd Test
South Africa won by seven wickets.

WEST INDIES

1	*C.H.Gayle	c McKenzie b Nel	46	(6) c Harris b Steyn		38
2	D.Ganga	c Boucher b Steyn	3	(1) b Ntini		22
3	R.S.Morton	c Ntini b Kallis	23	c Boucher b Steyn		1
4	M.N.Samuels	c Boucher b Ntini	51	lbw b Nel		18
5	S.Chanderpaul	not out	65	not out		70
6	D.J.Bravo	c Kallis b Ntini	0	(7) c Smith b Nel		12
7	†D.Ramdin	lbw b Steyn	21	(2) c Boucher b Kallis		32
8	R.N.Lewis	b Steyn	0	c Amla b Harris		1
9	J.E.Taylor	c and b Steyn	8	c Kallis b Steyn		21
10	D.B.L.Powell	c Kallis b Nel	0	c Smith b Steyn		1
11	F.H.Edwards	c de Villiers b Nel	2	c Harris b Nel		21
	Extras	b 5, lb 10, w 1, nb 8	24	b 4, lb 20, w 1		25
			243			**262**

FoW (1): 1-12 (2), 2-71 (3), 3-77 (1), 4-183 (4), 5-185 (6), 6-220 (7), 7-220 (8), 8-237 (9), 9-241 (10), 10-243 (11)
FoW (2): 1-59 (2), 2-60 (3), 3-81 (1), 4-93 (4), 5-126 (7), 6-133 (8), 7-163 (9), 8-167 (10), 9-192 (11), 10-262 (6)

SOUTH AFRICA

1	*G.C.Smith	c Ramdin b Taylor	28	c Gayle b Lewis		85
2	N.D.McKenzie	c Gayle b Taylor	23			
3	H.M.Amla	lbw b Bravo	32	c Gayle b Lewis		37
4	J.H.Kallis	c Ramdin b Bravo	36	not out		22
5	A.G.Prince	run out (Taylor/Ramdin)	98	not out		12
6	A.B.de Villiers	c Ramdin b Bravo	2	(2) c sub (D.J.G.Sammy) b Bravo		23
7	†M.V.Boucher	b Bravo	59			
8	P.L.Harris	c Morton b Powell	4			
9	A.Nel	c Ramdin b Powell	5			
10	D.W.Steyn	c Morton b Lewis	19			
11	M.Ntini	not out	3			
	Extras	b 4, lb 5, w 3	12	lb 5, w 1, nb 1		7
			321	**(3 wickets)**		**186**

FoW (1): 1-46 (2), 2-61 (1), 3-120 (4), 4-123 (3), 5-131 (6), 6-260 (7), 7-265 (8), 8-284 (9), 9-301 (5), 10-321 (10)
FoW (2): 1-57 (2), 2-140 (3), 3-152 (1)

South Africa Bowling

	O	M	R	W			O	M	R	W	
Steyn	20	5	60	4	8nb	(3)	19.5	7	44	4	
Ntini	22	7	63	2			26	8	62	1	1w
Nel	22	5	61	3	1w	(1)	27	12	62	3	
Kallis	9	1	11	1			19	6	34	1	
Harris	19	5	33	0			10	0	36	1	

West Indies Bowling

	O	M	R	W			O	M	R	W	
Powell	35	4	123	2	2w		11	0	57	0	1w
Edwards	4.5	1	12	0							
Samuels	8.1	3	18	0		(4)	3	0	17	0	
Taylor	21	6	51	2		(2)	6	0	31	0	
Bravo	37	9	82	4	1w	(3)	7	0	34	1	
Lewis	12.2	3	26	1		(5)	8.2	0	42	2	1nb

Umpires: S.J.A.Taufel and R.B.Tiffin. Third umpire: M.Erasmus. Referee: R.S.Mahanama.   Toss: West Indies

Close of Play: 1st day: West Indies (1) 240-8 (Chanderpaul 64*, Powell 0*, 89 overs); 2nd day: South Africa (1) 218-5 (Prince 55*, Boucher 35*, 85 overs); 3rd day: West Indies (2) 96-4 (Chanderpaul 8*, Gayle 1*, 50 overs).

Man of the Match: A.G.Prince.
The match was scheduled for five days but completed in four. C.H.Gayle retired hurt in the West Indies second innings having scored 1 (team score 97-4) - he returned when the score was 192-9.

SOUTH AFRICAN COMPOSITE XI v ZIMBABWE

Played at De Beers Diamond Oval, Kimberley, January 3, 4, 5, 6, 2008.
SuperSport Challenge 2007/08
Zimbabwe won by 134 runs.

ZIMBABWE

1	H.Masakadza	c Bossenger b Walters	1	c Bossenger b Mjekula	27	
2	V.Sibanda	c Bossenger b Walters	25	c Walters b Mjekula	0	
3	C.J.Chibhabha	c Bossenger b Kreusch	45	c Tshabalala b Walters	17	
4	†T.Taibu	c Bossenger b Kruger	0	c Symes b Kruger	78	
5	S.C.Williams	c Koortzen b Tshabalala	28	c Akoojee b Tshabalala	107	
6	K.M.Dabengwa	c Bossenger b Kreusch	79	run out	18	
7	E.Chigumbura	c McLaren b Kruger	5	c Kreusch b Walters	71	
8	*P.Utseya	lbw b Walters	38	b Tshabalala	57	
9	R.W.Price	c Bossenger b Kruger	7	(10) b Walters	11	
10	T.Maruma	c and b Kreusch	23	(9) c Tshabalala b Walters	0	
11	C.B.Mpofu	not out	0	not out	2	
	Extras	lb 3, nb 2	5	b 2, lb 17, w 8, nb 2	29	
			256		417	

FoW (1): 1-9 (1), 2-46 (2), 3-51 (4), 4-88 (3), 5-104 (5), 6-111 (7), 7-187 (8), 8-217 (9), 9-255 (6), 10-256 (10)
FoW (2): 1-0 (2), 2-42 (3), 3-56 (1), 4-240 (4), 5-258 (5), 6-270 (6), 7-364 (7), 8-364 (9), 9-412 (8), 10-417 (10)

SOUTH AFRICAN COMPOSITE XI

1	J.P.Kreusch	c Taibu b Chibhabha	29	(2) c Chibhabha b Mpofu	0	
2	M.Akoojee	st Taibu b Price	29	(1) c Masakadza b Mpofu	8	
3	A.P.McLaren	c Dabengwa b Utseya	80	(4) c Masakadza b Chigumbura	14	
4	P.J.Koortzen	c Masakadza b Utseya	80	(3) lbw b Chibhabha	16	
5	J.Symes	c Masakadza b Utseya	17	c Maruma b Utseya	16	
6	R.R.Jeggels	lbw b Chigumbura	53	lbw b Maruma	46	
7	*†W.Bossenger	c Dabengwa b Maruma	30	c Dabengwa b Utseya	46	
8	A.K.Kruger	c Williams b Utseya	27	c and b Maruma	4	
9	T.Tshabalala	c Masakadza b Price	1	b Chibhabha	28	
10	B.D.Walters	c Chibhabha b Utseya	0	not out	1	
11	S.Mjekula	not out	0	c Maruma b Utseya	0	
	Extras	lb 6, w 1	7	b 4, lb 3	7	
			353		186	

FoW (1): 1-54 (2), 2-84 (1), 3-195 (3), 4-235 (5), 5-248 (4), 6-294 (7), 7-348 (6), 8-353 (9), 9-353 (8), 10-353 (10)
FoW (2): 1-1 (2), 2-14 (1), 3-34 (3), 4-55 (5), 5-69 (4), 6-131 (6), 7-137 (8), 8-185 (7), 9-185 (9), 10-186 (11)

South African Composite XI Bowling

	O	M	R	W			O	M	R	W	
Mjekula	13	1	30	0		(2)	22	4	86	2	1w
Walters	13	3	38	3	1nb	(1)	32	6	114	4	2w
Kruger	19	4	59	3		(4)	15	2	71	1	1w
Kreusch	8.1	2	28	3		(5)	9	1	23	0	
Tshabalala	19	3	63	1	1nb	(3)	27	5	82	2	2nb
Symes	6	0	35	0			6	1	22	0	

Zimbabwe Bowling

	O	M	R	W			O	M	R	W	
Mpofu	13	3	41	0			8	1	19	2	
Chigumbura	18	4	60	1			7	0	37	1	
Price	29	5	86	2		(6)	12	0	38	0	
Masakadza	4	0	14	0							
Chibhabha	6	0	34	1		(3)	9	2	34	2	
Maruma	10	0	42	1		(5)	14	3	41	2	
Utseya	19	3	70	5	1w	(4)	3.4	1	10	3	

Umpires: B.G.Jerling and R.E.Koertzen. Referee: C.J.Mitchley.   Toss: South African Composite XI

Close of Play: 1st day: South African Composite XI (1) 47-0 (Kreusch 22*, Akoojee 24*, 15 overs); 2nd day: Zimbabwe (2) 42-2 (Masakadza 22*, 14 overs); 3rd day: Zimbabwe (2) 412-9 (Price 8*, Mpofu 0*, 107.3 overs).

Man of the Match: P.Utseya.
S.C.Williams's 107 took 137 balls in 182 minutes and included 16 fours.

LIONS v CAPE COBRAS

Played at Sedgars Park, Potchefstroom, January 10, 11, 12, 13, 2008.
SuperSport Series 2007/08
Cape Cobras won by five wickets.   (Points: Lions 5.62, Cape Cobras 14)

LIONS

1	B.D.Snijman	c Canning b Zondeki	31	c Canning b Kleinveldt	67
2	A.N.Petersen	c Canning b Sandri	35	lbw b Philander	8
3	S.C.Cook	c Canning b Philander	17	c Canning b Philander	2
4	*J.L.Ontong	c Duminy b Kemp	22	b Philander	0
5	W.L.Coetsee	c Duminy b Kemp	6	lbw b Philander	33
6	H.W.le Roux	b Philander	2	c Canning b Philander	49
7	†M.J.Harris	lbw b Zondeki	17	c Canning b de Lange	24
8	C.W.Henderson	not out	34	c Kemp b Philander	6
9	F.deWet	c Canning b Zondeki	0	lbw b Philander	32
10	G.J.P.Kruger	lbw b Zondeki	0	c Kemp b Kleinveldt	8
11	C.J.Alexander	b Zondeki	4	not out	0
	Extras	lb 4, w 2, nb 7	13	b 9, lb 11, nb 4	24
			181		253

FoW (1): 1-51 (1), 2-79 (2), 3-111 (4), 4-116 (3), 5-118 (5), 6-128 (6), 7-156 (7), 8-156 (9), 9-156 (10), 10-181 (11)
FoW (2): 1-18 (2), 2-20 (3), 3-20 (4), 4-88 (5), 5-141 (1), 6-188 (7), 7-201 (8), 8-224 (6), 9-253 (9), 10-253 (10)

CAPE COBRAS

1	A.G.Puttick	b de Wet	6	(2) lbw b le Roux	15
2	C.D.de Lange	c Harris b de Wet	2	(1) lbw b Kruger	59
3	H.Davids	b Kruger	4	c Alexander b Coetsee	96
4	J.P.Duminy	c Harris b de Wet	9	not out	115
5	S.van Zyl	c Snijman b Kruger	0	c Alexander b Kruger	15
6	*J.M.Kemp	c Snijman b Kruger	4	c Ontong b Snijman	16
7	V.D.Philander	not out	23	not out	1
8	†R.C.C.Canning	c Harris b le Roux	16		
9	R.K.Kleinveldt	c Harris b le Roux	4		
10	M.Zondeki	c Coetsee b Kruger	2		
11	P.S.E.Sandri	c Coetsee b le Roux	0		
	Extras	lb 3, w 2, nb 5	10	b 6, lb 16, w 1, nb 18	41
			80	(5 wickets)	358

FoW (1): 1-6 (1), 2-9 (2), 3-19 (3), 4-24 (4), 5-24 (5), 6-30 (6), 7-71 (8), 8-75 (9), 9-79 (10), 10-80 (11)
FoW (2): 1-40 (2), 2-116 (1), 3-242 (3), 4-275 (5), 5-351 (6)

Cape Cobras Bowling	O	M	R	W		O	M	R	W	
Zondeki	17.3	3	55	5	2w	26	8	70	0	1nb
Philander	16	5	42	2	3nb	30	10	64	7	
Kleinveldt	8	1	38	0	3nb	(6) 10.1	2	24	2	2nb
Sandri	6	0	21	1	1nb	7	0	25	0	1nb
Kemp	10	3	21	2		(3) 15	3	38	0	
van Zyl						(5) 3	1	8	0	
de Lange						(7) 5	4	4	1	

Lions Bowling	O	M	R	W		O	M	R	W	
de Wet	7	2	23	3	2nb	23	4	61	0	8nb
Kruger	8	2	27	4	3nb	18	2	85	2	9nb
Alexander	3	0	20	0	2w	(4) 12	1	51	0	
le Roux	4.5	3	7	3		(3) 14	2	41	1	1w
Henderson						(5) 12	2	61	0	1nb
Snijman						(6) 7	3	12	1	
Coetsee						(7) 8	2	11	1	
Ontong						(8) 1	0	4	0	
Cook						(9) 1.5		10	0	

Umpires: M.Erasmus and I.L.Howell. Referee: S.B.Lambson.   Toss: Cape Cobras

Close of Play: 1st day: Lions (1) 175-9 (Henderson 29*, Alexander 4*, 55.1 overs); 2nd day: Lions (2) 130-4 (Snijman 62*, le Roux 10*, 48.1 overs); 3rd day: Cape Cobras (2) 192-2 (Davids 73*, Duminy 26*, 54 overs).
Man of the Match: V.D.Philander, J.P.Duminy.
J.P.Duminy's 115 took 218 balls in 265 minutes and included 17 fours.

SOUTH AFRICA v WEST INDIES

Played at Sahara Stadium, Kingsmead, Durban, January 10, 11, 12, 2008.
West Indies in South Africa 2007/08 - 3rd Test
South Africa won by an innings and 100 runs.

WEST INDIES

1	D.Ganga	c Smith b Steyn	3	c Kallis b Ntini		11
2	B.A.Parchment	c Gibbs b Pollock	11	lbw b Steyn		20
3	R.S.Morton	lbw b Pollock	1	lbw b Pollock		37
4	M.N.Samuels	c Boucher b Ntini	6	b Steyn		105
5	S.Chanderpaul	c Kallis b Ntini	0	absent ill		0
6	*D.J.Bravo	c Gibbs b Pollock	13	(5) lbw b Steyn		75
7	†D.Ramdin	c Gibbs b Nel	30	(6) c Boucher b Nel		25
8	D.J.G.Sammy	c Smith b Nel	28	(7) c and b Steyn		17
9	J.E.Taylor	c Steyn b Pollock	25	(8) not out		17
10	D.B.L.Powell	not out	15	(9) b Steyn		0
11	F.H.Edwards	c Boucher b Nel	0	(10) b Steyn		0
	Extras	b 1, lb 6	7	lb 8, w 1, nb 1		10
			139			**317**

FoW (1): 1-10 (1), 2-11 (3), 3-22 (2), 4-26 (4), 5-33 (5), 6-57 (6), 7-74 (7), 8-116 (9), 9-139 (8), 10-139 (11)
FoW (2): 1-33 (2), 2-49 (1), 3-88 (3), 4-232 (5), 5-273 (6), 6-292 (4), 7-305 (7), 8-305 (9), 9-317 (10)

SOUTH AFRICA

1	*G.C.Smith	c Ramdin b Taylor	147
2	H.H.Gibbs	b Powell	27
3	H.M.Amla	c Bravo b Sammy	69
4	J.H.Kallis	c Morton b Samuels	74
5	A.G.Prince	not out	123
6	A.B.de Villiers	not out	103
7	†M.V.Boucher		
8	S.M.Pollock		
9	A.Nel		
10	D.W.Steyn		
11	M.Ntini		
	Extras	b 6, lb 7	13
		(4 wickets, declared)	556

FoW (1): 1-53 (2), 2-252 (3), 3-252 (1), 4-374 (4)

South Africa Bowling

	O	M	R	W		O	M	R	W	
Steyn	8	2	18	1		21.5	6	72	6	
Ntini	7	1	30	2		20	4	95	1	
Pollock	11	2	35	4		17	4	50	1	1nb
Nel	6.3	0	45	3		17	2	67	1	
Kallis	2	1	4	0		8	2	14	0	1w
Amla					(6)	3	0	11	0	

West Indies Bowling

	O	M	R	W
Powell	26	1	128	1
Edwards	23	0	129	0
Taylor	25	3	92	1
Sammy	25	4	104	1
Samuels	21	0	90	1

Umpires: Aleem Dar and S.J.A.Taufel. Third umpire: B.G.Jerling. Referee: R.S.Mahanama.   Toss: South Africa

Close of Play: 1st day: South Africa (1) 213-1 (Smith 122*, Amla 55*, 43 overs); 2nd day: West Indies (2) 23-0 (Ganga 6*, Parchment 17*, 11 overs).

Man of the Match: A.G.Prince.
The match was scheduled for five days but completed in three. G.C.Smith's 147 took 165 balls in 236 minutes and included 27 fours. A.G.Prince's 123 took 196 balls in 280 minutes and included 15 fours. A.B.de Villiers's 103 took 109 balls in 160 minutes and included 15 fours and a six. M.N.Samuels's 105 took 190 balls in 283 minutes and included 18 fours.

TITANS v DOLPHINS

Played at Willowmoore Park Main Oval, Benoni, January 10, 11, 12, 13, 2008.
SuperSport Series 2007/08
Match drawn.   (Points: Titans 6.34, Dolphins 3.8)

DOLPHINS

1	I.Khan	c Behardien b Joubert	25
2	D.J.Watson	lbw b M.Morkel	0
3	W.L.Madsen	c du Plessis b M.Morkel	2
4	*A.M.Amla	c Jappie b Mbhalati	0
5	K.Smit	lbw b Mbhalati	0
6	K.Zondo	c du Plessis b Joubert	25
7	J.Louw	c Jappie b Imran Tahir	6
8	†D.Smit	not out	89
9	R.D.McMillan	c J.A.Morkel b Joubert	8
10	Q.Friend	b Mbhalati	23
11	S.Mlongo	c Joubert b Behardien	3
	Extras	lb 2, nb 7	9
			190

FoW (1): 1-3 (2), 2-6 (3), 3-24 (4), 4-26 (5), 5-30 (1), 6-45 (7), 7-109 (6), 8-126 (9), 9-170 (10), 10-190 (11)

TITANS

1	†H.G.Kuhn	c Khan b Friend	17
2	R.Jappie	lbw b Louw	43
3	M.Morkel	c Louw b McMillan	29
4	F.du Plessis	lbw b Louw	49
5	*M.van Jaarsveld	lbw b Friend	7
6	G.H.Bodi	c Mlongo b Louw	29
7	F.Behardien	not out	56
8	J.A.Morkel	not out	61
9	P.Joubert		
10	Imran Tahir		
11	N.E.Mbhalati		
	Extras	lb 2, w 2, nb 4	8
		(6 wickets)	299

FoW (1): 1-34 (1), 2-89 (3), 3-97 (2), 4-114 (5), 5-177 (4), 6-182 (6)

Titans Bowling

	O	M	R	W	
M.Morkel	16	3	48	2	7nb
Mbhalati	17	6	26	3	
Joubert	12	3	26	3	
Imran Tahir	17	3	56	1	
J.A.Morkel	12	2	32	0	
Behardien	0.4	0	0	1	

Dolphins Bowling

	O	M	R	W	
Louw	24	8	59	3	1w,1nb
Friend	23	10	34	2	
Mlongo	21	5	61	0	3nb
McMillan	21	10	26	1	
D.Smit	15	2	76	0	
Amla	10	1	34	0	
Watson	2	0	7	0	

Umpires: R.E.Koertzen and G.H.Pienaar.   Referee: D.Govindjee.   Toss: Titans

Close of Play: 1st day: No play; 2nd day: No play; 3rd day: Titans (1) 44-1 (Jappie 22*, M.Morkel 3*, 29 overs).

Man of the Match: D.Smit.

W.L.Madsen kept wicket when D.Smit bowled in the Titans first innings.

WARRIORS v EAGLES

Played at Sahara Oval, St George's Park, Port Elizabeth, January 10, 11, 12, 13, 2008.
SuperSport Series 2007/08
Match drawn.   (Points: Warriors 7.58, Eagles 6.9)

WARRIORS

1	C.A.Thyssen	c van Wyk b Mpitsang	1	c Dippenaar b du Preez	4
2	J.Botha	c Dippenaar b de Villiers	24	c van Wyk b Tshabalala	51
3	*Z.de Bruyn	lbw b Tshabalala	111	c van Wyk b du Preez	0
4	A.Jacobs	c Bosman b de Villiers	27	c van Wyk b Mpitsang	21
5	H.D.Ackerman	b Tshabalala	12	c R.McLaren b de Villiers	0
6	†D.J.Jacobs	c Bailey b Mpitsang	61	b de Villiers	0
7	R.J.Peterson	c Dippenaar b du Preez	1	c Dippenaar b Mpitsang	22
8	J.Theron	lbw b Tshabalala	11	c de Villiers b Tshabalala	16
9	M.W.Olivier	c van Wyk b Mpitsang	1	c van Wyk b de Villiers	51
10	L.L.Tsotsobe	c A.P.McLaren b Tshabalala	3	not out	6
11	S.Mjekula	not out	4	lbw b R.McLaren	0
	Extras	lb 4, w 1, nb 18	23	b 5, lb 7, nb 12	24
			279		195

FoW (1): 1-1 (1), 2-67 (2), 3-141 (4), 4-176 (5), 5-213 (3), 6-214 (7), 7-267 (8), 8-269 (6), 9-269 (9), 10-279 (10)
FoW (2): 1-5 (1), 2-5 (3), 3-51 (4), 4-58 (5), 5-58 (6), 6-102 (7), 7-120 (2), 8-141 (8), 9-195 (9), 10-195 (11)

EAGLES

1	L.L.Bosman	c D.J.Jacobs b Olivier	0	not out	29
2	A.P.McLaren	lbw b Tsotsobe	39		
3	D.Elgar	c Botha b Mjekula	63		
4	*H.H.Dippenaar	c D.J.Jacobs b Mjekula	48		
5	†M.N.van Wyk	c D.J.Jacobs b Theron	4	(2) not out	12
6	R.T.Bailey	c Thyssen b Botha	43		
7	R.McLaren	c Ackerman b Botha	6		
8	D.du Preez	lbw b Tsotsobe	24		
9	C.J.D.de Villiers	lbw b Theron	6		
10	T.Tshabalala	not out	0		
11	P.V.Mpitsang	c Ackerman b Theron	0		
	Extras	lb 2, w 5, nb 5	12	lb 1	1
			245	(no wicket)	42

FoW (1): 1-8 (1), 2-76 (2), 3-132 (3), 4-139 (5), 5-180 (4), 6-198 (7), 7-229 (6), 8-245 (8), 9-245 (9), 10-245 (11)

Eagles Bowling

	O	M	R	W			O	M	R	W	
du Preez	18	3	53	1		(2)	24	8	37	2	
Mpitsang	15	3	55	3	6nb	(1)	15	4	34	2	5nb
de Villiers	17	3	61	2	1w,4nb	(4)	19	7	27	3	1nb
R.McLaren	13	2	44	0	8nb	(3)	20.1	2	49	1	5nb
Tshabalala	15.5	3	57	4			10	2	32	2	1nb
Elgar	2	0	5	0			2	0	4	0	

Warriors Bowling

	O	M	R	W			O	M	R	W	
Olivier	11	2	37	1	1w,3nb	(2)	3	0	18	0	
Tsotsobe	21	3	57	2	1w,2nb	(1)	4.3	0	19	0	
Mjekula	17	3	51	2							
Botha	13	3	33	2							
Peterson	7	3	18	0							
A.Jacobs	1	0	6	0							
Theron	17.4	3	41	3	3w	(3)	1	0	4	0	

Umpires: M.W.Brown and P.D.Jones. Referee: S.Wadvalla.   Toss: Warriors

Close of Play: 1st day: Eagles (1) 61-1 (A.P.McLaren 31*, Elgar 28*, 13 overs); 2nd day: Warriors (2) 21-2 (Botha 5*, A.Jacobs 9*, 19 overs); 3rd day: Eagles (2) 1-0 (Bosman 1*, van Wyk 0*, 1.1 overs).

Man of the Match: Z.de Bruyn.

Z.de Bruyn's 111 took 173 balls in 275 minutes and included 16 fours.

CAPE COBRAS v TITANS

Played at Boland Bank Park, Paarl, January 17, 18, 19, 20, 2008.
SuperSport Series 2007/08
Cape Cobras won by six wickets.   (Points: Cape Cobras 17.98, Titans 6.96)

TITANS

1	M.A.Aronstam	c Puttick b Zondeki	0	c Canning b Philander	9
2	†H.G.Kuhn	c Canning b de Lange	68	c Kemp b Philander	22
3	F.du Plessis	c Puttick b Kemp	88	(6) c Kemp b Philander	43
4	*M.van Jaarsveld	lbw b Philander	7	(3) c Kemp b Zondeki	13
5	G.H.Bodi	lbw b Philander	70	(7) lbw b Philander	13
6	F.Behardien	lbw b de Lange	3	(4) c Kemp b Philander	11
7	P.Joubert	c Zondeki b de Lange	4	(5) c Hector b de Lange	0
8	B.L.Reddy	b Philander	8	b Kleinveldt	17
9	N.Wagner	c Canning b de Lange	11	run out	2
10	Imran Tahir	not out	14	c Davids b Kleinveldt	1
11	N.E.Mbhalati	c Kemp b Philander	10	not out	9
	Extras	lb 5, w 2, nb 8	15	b 1, lb 4, w 1, nb 2	8
			298		**148**

FoW (1): 1-0 (1), 2-120 (2), 3-127 (4), 4-190 (3), 5-197 (6), 6-218 (7), 7-233 (8), 8-273 (5), 9-275 (9), 10-298 (11)
FoW (2): 1-31 (2), 2-34 (1), 3-53 (3), 4-56 (5), 5-62 (4), 6-80 (7), 7-135 (8), 8-135 (6), 9-136 (10), 10-148 (9)

CAPE COBRAS

1	A.G.Puttick	run out (Aronstam/Reddy)	66	(2) c and b Imran Tahir	46
2	C.D.de Lange	lbw b Imran Tahir	59	(1) c Aronstam b Joubert	0
3	H.Davids	st Kuhn b van Jaarsveld	21	c Kuhn b Imran Tahir	37
4	B.Hector	c sub (R.Jappie) b Imran Tahir	39	c Aronstam b Wagner	2
5	S.van Zyl	c van Jaarsveld b Imran Tahir	2	not out	3
6	*J.M.Kemp	lbw b Imran Tahir	63	not out	7
7	V.D.Philander	c du Plessis b Imran Tahir	6		
8	F.D.Telo	b Joubert	20		
9	†R.C.C.Canning	c Kuhn b Wagner	22		
10	R.K.Kleinveldt	st Kuhn b Imran Tahir	30		
11	M.Zondeki	not out	0		
	Extras	b 5, lb 10, nb 5	20	b 1, nb 3	4
			348	**(4 wickets)**	**99**

FoW (1): 1-89 (2), 2-135 (3), 3-172 (1), 4-178 (5), 5-209 (4), 6-221 (7), 7-264 (8), 8-303 (6), 9-340 (9), 10-348 (10)
FoW (2): 1-4 (1), 2-63 (3), 3-74 (4), 4-89 (2)

Cape Cobras Bowling

	O	M	R	W		O	M	R	W	
Zondeki	22	5	83	1		19	5	41	1	1w,1nb
Kleinveldt	16	4	51	0	1w,3nb	18	4	42	2	1nb
Philander	21.3	2	50	4	1nb	15.1	7	13	5	
Kemp	14	1	37	1	1w					
de Lange	27	7	72	4	4nb	(4) 22	6	47	1	

Titans Bowling

	O	M	R	W			O	M	R	W	
Mbhalati	16	5	34	0		(3)	4	1	16	0	
Wagner	14	4	48	1		(4)	6	1	20	1	
Joubert	19	5	34	1		(1)	5	2	9	1	
Reddy	15	2	58	0	5nb	(6)	1	0	4	0	1nb
Imran Tahir	30.5	3	122	6		(2)	16.4	4	41	2	2nb
Aronstam	12	5	26	0							
van Jaarsveld	6	3	11	1		(5)	1	0	8	0	

Umpires: M.Erasmus and P.D.Jones.   Referee: C.J.Mitchley.   Toss: Cape Cobras

Close of Play: 1st day: Titans (1) 283-9 (Imran Tahir 7*, Mbhalati 2*, 96 overs); 2nd day: Cape Cobras (1) 286-7 (Kemp 53*, Canning 2*, 90 overs); 3rd day: Titans (2) 144-9 (Wagner 1*, Mbhalati 6*, 71 overs).

Man of the Match: V.D.Philander.

EAGLES v DOLPHINS

Played at OUTsurance Oval, Bloemfontein, January 17, 18, 19, 2008.
SuperSport Series 2007/08
Eagles won by 82 runs.   (Points: Eagles 18.2, Dolphins 5.16)

EAGLES

1	L.L.Bosman	c D.Smit b Mlongo	31	lbw b Louw	12
2	†M.N.van Wyk	c Khan b Friend	0	b Friend	36
3	D.Elgar	lbw b Friend	39	c Khan b Louw	12
4	*H.H.Dippenaar	c D.Smit b Mlongo	13	lbw b Louw	7
5	A.P.McLaren	c H.M.Amla b Mlongo	64	run out	3
6	R.T.Bailey	lbw b Mlongo	81	c Khan b Louw	3
7	R.McLaren	c Khan b Louw	18	b Louw	0
8	D.du Preez	c H.M.Amla b Friend	36	(9) c D.Smit b Friend	2
9	C.J.D.de Villiers	lbw b Louw	5	(10) lbw b Louw	5
10	T.Tshabalala	c Mlongo b Hewer	4	(8) c Khan b Friend	0
11	P.V.Mpitsang	not out	0	not out	0
	Extras	b 1, lb 11, w 2, nb 5	19	lb 6, nb 2	8
			310		88

FoW (1): 1-3 (2), 2-54 (1), 3-83 (3), 4-94 (4), 5-175 (5), 6-226 (7), 7-288 (6), 8-294 (9), 9-310 (8), 10-310 (10)
FoW (2): 1-13 (1), 2-39 (3), 3-59 (4), 4-69 (5), 5-77 (6), 6-77 (7), 7-79 (2), 8-81 (9), 9-86 (8), 10-88 (10)

DOLPHINS

1	I.Khan	c A.P.McLaren b du Preez	17	c van Wyk b du Preez	5
2	D.J.Watson	c Elgar b R.McLaren	10	c van Wyk b du Preez	4
3	H.M.Amla	b Tshabalala	34	c van Wyk b R.McLaren	10
4	*A.M.Amla	c A.P.McLaren b R.McLaren	22	lbw b du Preez	23
5	K.Smit	lbw b Elgar	5	b R.McLaren	34
6	K.Zondo	c van Wyk b R.McLaren	3	(7) lbw b R.McLaren	4
7	J.Louw	lbw b Tshabalala	0	(8) b du Preez	1
8	†D.Smit	lbw b de Villiers	27	(6) lbw b R.McLaren	45
9	Q.Friend	c A.P.McLaren b Tshabalala	1	c Mpitsang b R.McLaren	13
10	S.Mlongo	not out	15	not out	0
11	N.D.Hewer	c Bailey b du Preez	7	c van Wyk b R.McLaren	0
	Extras	lb 10, nb 7	17	b 4, lb 15	19
			158		158

FoW (1): 1-28 (1), 2-41 (2), 3-76 (3), 4-88 (5), 5-100 (4), 6-101 (7), 7-101 (6), 8-102 (9), 9-147 (8), 10-158 (11)
FoW (2): 1-9 (2), 2-14 (1), 3-42 (3), 4-46 (4), 5-116 (5), 6-128 (7), 7-145 (8), 8-151 (6), 9-158 (9), 10-158 (11)

Dolphins Bowling

	O	M	R	W		O	M	R	W	
Louw	21	7	52	2	1nb	18.4	7	39	6	2nb
Friend	18	4	70	3	1nb	13	3	30	3	
Hewer	17.1	3	47	1	1w					
Mlongo	19	8	53	4	1w,3nb (3)	5	2	13	0	
Khan	4	0	21	0						
D.Smit	12	1	55	0						

Eagles Bowling

	O	M	R	W		O	M	R	W	
du Preez	14.2	3	47	2		12	2	37	4	
R.McLaren	14	7	19	3	1nb	13.5	5	43	6	
Mpitsang	6	1	17	0	1nb	6	2	8	0	
de Villiers	9	2	17	1	2nb	6	2	18	0	
Tshabalala	14	1	39	3	3nb	8	0	33	0	
Elgar	1	0	9	1						

Umpires: K.H.Hurter and G.H.Pienaar. Referee: S.Wadvalla.   Toss: Eagles

Close of Play: 1st day: Dolphins (1) 8-0 (Khan 5*, Watson 3*, 2 overs); 2nd day: Eagles (2) 40-2 (van Wyk 15*, Dippenaar 0*, 15.4 overs).

Man of the Match: R.McLaren.

The match was scheduled for four days but completed in three.

WARRIORS v LIONS

Played at Mercedes Benz Park, East London, January 17, 18, 19, 20, 2008.
SuperSport Series 2007/08
Warriors won by nine wickets.   (Points: Warriors 18.52, Lions 5.4)

LIONS

1	B.D.Snijman	c D.J.Jacobs b Tsotsobe	8	b Tsotsobe	6
2	*A.N.Petersen	c Ackerman b Theron	28	c D.J.Jacobs b Mjekula	22
3	S.C.Cook	c D.J.Jacobs b Theron	152	lbw b Peterson	35
4	V.B.van Jaarsveld	c D.J.Jacobs b Tsotsobe	38	b Peterson	4
5	L.J.Kgamadi	c D.J.Jacobs b Olivier	60	c D.J.Jacobs b Tsotsobe	1
6	W.L.Coetsee	lbw b Peterson	1	c and b Peterson	50
7	†M.J.Harris	c Smith b Theron	13	lbw b Tsotsobe	15
8	H.W.le Roux	lbw b Tsotsobe	0	c Smith b Tsotsobe	0
9	W.A.Deacon	c D.J.Jacobs b Theron	43	lbw b Peterson	3
10	G.J.P.Kruger	lbw b Theron	0	c Jeggels b Mjekula	3
11	C.J.Alexander	not out	1	not out	0
	Extras	lb 4, w 3, nb 10	17	b 1, lb 1, w 1, nb 1	4
			361		**143**

FoW (1): 1-20 (1), 2-49 (2), 3-123 (4), 4-217 (5), 5-221 (6), 6-261 (7), 7-262 (8), 8-358 (9), 9-358 (10), 10-361 (3)
FoW (2): 1-6 (1), 2-47 (2), 3-71 (4), 4-72 (5), 5-72 (3), 6-99 (7), 7-121 (8), 8-128 (9), 9-136 (10), 10-143 (6)

WARRIORS

1	M.B.A.Smith	lbw b Deacon	41	not out	49
2	R.R.Jeggels	lbw b le Roux	35	run out	6
3	*Z.de Bruyn	run out (Kgamadi/Coetsee)	90	not out	53
4	A.Jacobs	c Deacon b Coetsee	32		
5	H.D.Ackerman	c Coetsee b Alexander	25		
6	†D.J.Jacobs	b Kruger	46		
7	R.J.Peterson	c Snijman b Kruger	30		
8	J.Theron	c le Roux b Coetsee	47		
9	M.W.Olivier	not out	6		
10	S.Mjekula	c Snijman b Coetsee	2		
11	L.L.Tsotsobe				
	Extras	b 4, lb 2, w 4, nb 28	38	b 1, lb 1, w 1, nb 2	5
		(9 wickets, declared)	**392**	(1 wicket)	**113**

FoW (1): 1-62 (2), 2-95 (1), 3-161 (4), 4-214 (5), 5-280 (6), 6-324 (7), 7-384 (8), 8-385 (3), 9-392 (10)
FoW (2): 1-11 (2)

Warriors Bowling

	O	M	R	W		O	M	R	W	
Tsotsobe	23	4	56	3		21	7	38	4	
Olivier	17	1	65	1	1w,5nb (4)	3	0	12	0	1w,1nb
Theron	27.1	2	78	5	2w,4nb (2)	15	5	35	0	
Mjekula	17	6	39	0	(3)	11	1	33	2	
de Bruyn	18	3	57	0	1nb					
Peterson	28	9	62	1	(5)	10.4	2	23	4	

Lions Bowling

	O	M	R	W		O	M	R	W	
Kruger	26	7	81	2	10nb	1	0	8	0	
Deacon	18	2	95	1	2w,14nb (4)	6	0	33	0	1w,2nb
le Roux	24	5	62	1	3nb (2)	5	1	7	0	
Alexander	21	3	105	1	1w,1nb (3)	8	4	21	0	
Coetsee	17.1	2	43	3	1w	6	1	39	0	
Snijman					(6)	0.3	0	3	0	

Umpires: M.W.Brown and D.J.Smith. Referee: D.Govindjee.   Toss: Lions

Close of Play: 1st day: Lions (1) 265-7 (Cook 102*, Deacon 2*, 96 overs); 2nd day: Warriors (1) 202-3 (de Bruyn 50*, Ackerman 19*, 59 overs); 3rd day: Lions (2) 99-5 (Coetsee 12*, Harris 15*, 45 overs).

Man of the Match: L.L.Tsotsobe.

S.C.Cook's 152 took 349 balls in 540 minutes and included 15 fours.

BOLAND v BORDER

Played at Boland Bank Park, Paarl, January 24, 25, 26, 2008.
South African Airways Provincial Three-Day Challenge 2007/08 - Pool A
Match drawn.   (Points: Boland 7.68, Border 10.94)

BORDER

1	S.de Kock	c Walters b Bothma	16	lbw b J.M.van Wyk	8
2	C.A.Thyssen	run out (sub [C.J.August])	119	c Bothma b J.M.van Wyk	1
3	M.F.Richardson	c Walters b de Wet	37	b Grobler	37
4	*M.N.Ranger	run out (L.van Wyk/Walters)	4	lbw b Bothma	59
5	†A.Z.M.Dyili	c Walters b J.M.van Wyk	98	c Walters b Bothma	58
6	L.Masingatha	c Walters b L.van Wyk	52	c and b Bothma	0
7	S.Makongolo	c Walters b de Wet	1	not out	19
8	D.L.Brown	not out	34	not out	30
9	L.Mbane	not out	25		
10	P.Fojela				
11	Y.Pangabantu				
	Extras	b 3, lb 6, w 2	11	b 1, lb 5, w 6, nb 1	13
		(7 wickets)	397	(6 wickets, declared)	225

FoW (1): 1-68 (1), 2-178 (2), 3-179 (3), 4-183 (4), 5-323 (6), 6-324 (7), 7-355 (5)
FoW (2): 1-10 (2), 2-14 (1), 3-93 (3), 4-155 (4), 5-161 (6), 6-174 (5)

BOLAND

1	H.W.de Wet	run out (de Kock/Dyili)	12	c Dyili b Brown	34
2	W.D.Hayward	c Brown b Pangabantu	13	c Brown b de Kock	75
3	*B.C.Adams	not out	164	run out	19
4	L.van Wyk	b Brown	45	c Fojela b Brown	26
5	R.G.Arendse	c Dyili b Brown	0	not out	22
6	R.F.Jacobs	b Ranger	0	not out	13
7	†L.R.Walters	c Dyili b Brown	17		
8	S.F.Grobler	c Dyili b Brown	0		
9	J.P.Bothma	lbw b de Kock	4		
10	J.M.van Wyk	st Dyili b de Kock	8		
11	H.H.Paulse	not out	10		
	Extras	b 2, lb 2, w 4, nb 3	11	b 6, lb 8, w 2	16
		(9 wickets)	284	(4 wickets)	205

FoW (1): 1-13 (2), 2-62 (1), 3-143 (4), 4-143 (5), 5-151 (6), 6-193 (7), 7-195 (8), 8-220 (9), 9-234 (10)
FoW (2): 1-64 (1), 2-106 (3), 3-166 (2), 4-166 (4)

Boland Bowling	O	M	R	W		O	M	R	W	
J.M.van Wyk	13	2	64	1		12	3	56	2	1w,1nb
Paulse	8	1	47	0	1w	11	1	36	0	1w
Bothma	13	3	53	1	1w	15	2	49	3	
de Wet	18	4	50	2		11	2	34	0	
Grobler	13	0	63	0	(6)	7	3	20	1	
Adams	7	0	38	0						
L.van Wyk	12	1	67	1	(5)	7	1	24	0	
Jacobs	1	0	6	0						

Border Bowling	O	M	R	W		O	M	R	W	
Pangabantu	17	3	54	1		9	2	42	0	
Fojela	18	3	71	0	3w,3nb	8	2	20	0	
Mbane	10	0	40	0		6	2	22	0	
Brown	15	2	49	4	1w	11	3	35	2	2w
de Kock	12	2	41	2		20	6	40	1	
Ranger	12	4	15	0		4	0	8	0	
Makongolo	1	0	10	0		9	3	24	0	

Umpires: C.D.Isaacs and L.J.Willemse.   Toss: Boland

Close of Play: 1st day: Boland (1) 62-1 (de Wet 12*, Adams 35*, 18 overs); 2nd day: Border (2) 105-3 (Ranger 45*, Dyili 4*, 36 overs).

C.A.Thyssen's 119 took 117 balls in 167 minutes and included 20 fours and 1 six. B.C.Adams's 164 took 251 balls in 363 minutes and included 21 fours and 1 six.

DOLPHINS v WARRIORS

Played at City Oval, Pietermaritzburg, January 24, 25, 26, 27, 2008.
SuperSport Series 2007/08
Match drawn.   (Points: Dolphins 4.26, Warriors 8.24)

WARRIORS

1	M.B.A.Smith	lbw b Louw	0
2	R.R.Jeggels	c D.Smit b McMillan	48
3	*Z.de Bruyn	c H.M.Amla b McMillan	47
4	A.Jacobs	not out	218
5	H.D.Ackerman	c D.Smit b McMillan	112
6	†D.J.Jacobs	not out	67
7	R.J.Peterson		
8	J.Theron		
9	M.W.Olivier		
10	L.L.Tsotsobe		
11	S.Mjekula		
	Extras	b 2, lb 5, w 1	8
		(4 wickets, declared)	500

FoW (1): 1-8 (1), 2-82 (2), 3-97 (3), 4-343 (5)

DOLPHINS

1	I.Khan	c de Bruyn b Peterson	69	c Theron b Peterson	37
2	D.J.Watson	c Ackerman b Peterson	78	lbw b de Bruyn	32
3	H.M.Amla	lbw b de Bruyn	24	c de Bruyn b Peterson	99
4	*A.M.Amla	c Ackerman b Peterson	4	not out	150
5	K.Smit	c D.J.Jacobs b Tsotsobe	4	c Mjekula b Peterson	16
6	†D.Smit	c de Bruyn b Tsotsobe	19	not out	26
7	D.A.Miller	not out	63		
8	J.Louw	c Jeggels b Peterson	16		
9	R.D.McMillan	lbw b Mjekula	25		
10	Q.Friend	c and b Peterson	1		
11	S.Mlongo	b Mjekula	2		
	Extras	b 3, lb 5, w 11, nb 3	22	b 4, lb 2, w 3, nb 3	12
			327	(4 wickets, declared)	372

FoW (1): 1-127 (2), 2-170 (3), 3-178 (1), 4-183 (4), 5-199 (5), 6-212 (6), 7-247 (8), 8-318 (9), 9-321 (10), 10-327 (11)
FoW (2): 1-76 (2), 2-76 (1), 3-295 (3), 4-322 (5)

Dolphins Bowling	O	M	R	W	
Louw	31	11	68	1	
Friend	28	4	128	0	1w
Mlongo	7	1	29	0	
McMillan	25	4	81	3	
Khan	4	2	6	0	
D.Smit	27	2	105	0	
A.M.Amla	6	0	32	0	
K.Smit	8	2	28	0	
H.M.Amla	2	0	16	0	

Warriors Bowling	O	M	R	W			O	M	R	W	
Tsotsobe	18	4	52	2	1w,2nb		11	1	48	0	2w,1nb
Theron	11	5	28	0	1nb		7	1	15	0	
Peterson	50	10	124	5	1w		39	7	136	3	1w
Mjekula	18.5	4	56	2	1w	(5)	2	0	9	0	
Olivier	9.1	2	24	0	1w	(6)	12	1	48	0	2nb
de Bruyn	13.5	4	22	1	3w	(4)	9	2	20	1	
A.Jacobs	5	0	13	0			18	0	90	0	

Umpires: M.W.Brown and E.C.Hendrikse.   Referee: S.B.Lambson.   Toss: Warriors
Close of Play: 1st day: Warriors (1) 293-3 (A.Jacobs 115*, Ackerman 81*, 80 overs); 2nd day: Dolphins (1) 108-0 (Khan 39*, Watson 64*, 44 overs); 3rd day: Dolphins (2) 28-0 (Khan 4*, Watson 21*, 11.1 overs).
Man of the Match: R.J.Peterson, A.Jacobs.
A.Jacobs's 218 took 388 balls in 485 minutes and included 29 fours. H.D.Ackerman's 112 took 193 balls in 270 minutes and included 11 fours. A.M.Amla's 150 took 203 balls in 286 minutes and included 15 fours and 3 sixes. H.M.Amla kept wicket when D.Smit bowled in the Warriors first innings

EAGLES v CAPE COBRAS

Played at OUTsurance Oval, Bloemfontein, January 24, 25, 26, 27, 2008.
SuperSport Series 2007/08
Match drawn.   (Points: Eagles 5.72, Cape Cobras 6.68)

CAPE COBRAS

1	A.G.Puttick	c and b R.McLaren	4	c van Wyk b du Preez	22
2	C.D.de Lange	lbw b du Preez	3		
3	H.Davids	lbw b de Villiers	15	c Hendricks b Elgar	108
4	F.D.Telo	c Mpitsang b de Villiers	104	c Dippenaar b Mpitsang	26
5	S.van Zyl	not out	152	not out	58
6	*J.M.Kemp	c van Wyk b R.McLaren	33	not out	2
7	B.Hector	c van Wyk b Mpitsang	3	(2) lbw b du Preez	1
8	V.D.Philander	c van Wyk b Mpitsang	6		
9	†R.C.C.Canning	c Bailey b du Preez	23		
10	R.K.Kleinveldt	c A.P.McLaren b Kruger	5		
11	M.Zondeki	c Bailey b Kruger	7		
	Extras	b 3, lb 15, w 3, nb 19	40	b 3, nb 7	10
			395	**(4 wickets, declared)**	**227**

FoW (1): 1-8 (1), 2-8 (2), 3-41 (3), 4-195 (4), 5-262 (6), 6-278 (7), 7-307 (8), 8-363 (9), 9-383 (10), 10-395 (11)
FoW (2): 1-8 (2), 2-38 (1), 3-102 (4), 4-221 (3)

EAGLES

1	†M.N.van Wyk	lbw b Kleinveldt	5	(2) c Canning b Zondeki	14
2	A.P.McLaren	lbw b Kleinveldt	1	(1) c de Lange b Zondeki	3
3	D.Elgar	c Puttick b Kleinveldt	122	not out	54
4	*H.H.Dippenaar	c Davids b Kleinveldt	1	c Canning b Philander	5
5	R.T.Bailey	c Canning b Kleinveldt	30	not out	30
6	R.R.Hendricks	lbw b Kemp	28		
7	R.McLaren	not out	121		
8	A.K.Kruger	c Philander b Zondeki	8		
9	D.du Preez	c Canning b Kemp	0		
10	C.J.D.de Villiers	c Canning b Philander	8		
11	P.V.Mpitsang	c Canning b Davids	10		
	Extras	lb 5, nb 14	19	b 4, lb 1, nb 3	8
			353	**(3 wickets)**	**114**

FoW (1): 1-2 (2), 2-14 (1), 3-21 (4), 4-100 (5), 5-147 (6), 6-255 (3), 7-277 (8), 8-280 (9), 9-328 (10), 10-353 (11)
FoW (2): 1-11 (1), 2-24 (2), 3-41 (4)

Eagles Bowling	O	M	R	W		O	M	R	W	
du Preez	30	8	91	2		14	4	40	2	
R.McLaren	26	7	67	2	7nb (4)	5	1	17	0	
Mpitsang	20	6	49	2	1w,6nb (2)	12	3	50	1	6nb
de Villiers	25	5	52	2	1w,6nb (3)	10	3	23	0	1nb
Elgar	7	0	17	0	(7)	4	0	18	1	
Kruger	18.5	3	63	2	(5)	7	3	22	0	
Bailey	13	0	38	0	1w (6)	11	0	39	0	
Hendricks					(8)	2	0	15	0	

Cape Cobras Bowling	O	M	R	W		O	M	R	W	
Zondeki	27	6	77	1	2nb	16	7	39	2	
Kleinveldt	26	8	92	5	7nb	9	1	33	0	3nb
Philander	25	5	75	1	2nb	5	2	9	1	
de Lange	7	1	34	0	1nb	14	7	28	0	
Kemp	17	2	36	2	2nb					
Davids	15.3	4	34	1						

Umpires: G.H.Pienaar and D.J.Smith.   Referee: A.Barnes.   Toss: Eagles

Close of Play: 1st day: Cape Cobras (1) 283-6 (van Zyl 90*, Philander 0*, 96 overs); 2nd day: Eagles (1) 170-5 (Elgar 78*, R.McLaren 16*, 50 overs); 3rd day: Cape Cobras (2) 40-2 (Davids 11*, Telo 2*, 15.4 overs).
Man of the Match: S.van Zyl.
F.D.Telo's 104 took 187 balls in 240 minutes and included 18 fours. S.van Zyl's 152 took 374 balls in 487 minutes and included 15 fours. D.Elgar's 122 took 260 balls in 336 minutes and included 18 fours. R.McLaren's 121 took 236 balls in 313 minutes and included 16 fours and a six. H.Davids's 108 took 179 balls in 252 minutes and included 15 fours and 1 six.

FREE STATE v ZIMBABWE PROVINCES

Played at University of Orange Free State Ground, Bloemfontein, January 24, 25, 26, 2008.
South African Airways Provincial Three-Day Challenge 2007/08 - Pool B
Zimbabwe Provinces won by five wickets. (Points: Free State 7.16, Zimbabwe Provinces 17.06)

FREE STATE

1	M.P.Fick	b Cremer	84	(2) c Kasteni b Cremer	30	
2	†L.N.Mosena	c Chakabva b Rainsford	0	(1) c Chakabva b Manyumwa	25	
3	R.R.Rossouw	lbw b Manyumwa	4	c Cremer b Manyumwa	24	
4	*H.O.von Rauenstein	st Chakabva b Cremer	39	c Manyumwa b Rainsford	4	
5	G.N.Nieuwoudt	b Cremer	6	lbw b Rainsford	2	
6	M.N.Erlank	lbw b Cremer	41	b Rainsford	0	
7	R.K.Terblanche	run out (Manyumwa/Chakabva)	1	lbw b Rainsford	1	
8	C.J.D.van der Schyff	c Chakabva b Rainsford	9	b Manyumwa	4	
9	W.J.van Zyl	c Chakabva b Rainsford	0	lbw b Rainsford	0	
10	B.B.Kops	b Rainsford	6	b Rainsford	0	
11	M.N.Saliwa	not out	3	not out	0	
	Extras	b 5, lb 3, w 1, nb 6	15	lb 7, w 2, nb 2	11	
			208		**101**	

FoW (1): 1-1 (2), 2-23 (3), 3-94 (4), 4-104 (5), 5-168 (1), 6-178 (7), 7-195 (8), 8-197 (9), 9-200 (6), 10-208 (10)
FoW (2): 1-56 (2), 2-82 (3), 3-85 (1), 4-91 (4), 5-91 (6), 6-94 (5), 7-95 (7), 8-95 (9), 9-100 (10), 10-101 (8)

ZIMBABWE PROVINCES

1	T.M.K.Mawoyo	c Fick b van der Schyff	37	b Kops	0	
2	F.Kasteni	lbw b Saliwa	1	c and b Saliwa	0	
3	T.Duffin	c Mosena b Kops	0	c Mosena b Kops	0	
4	B.Mujuru	run out (Saliwa/Mosena)	11	c von Rauenstein b van der Schyff	10	
5	*N.B.Mahwire	c Rossouw b Terblanche	0			
6	†R.W.Chakabva	c Mosena b Terblanche	25	(5) c von Rauenstein b Saliwa	25	
7	S.K.Nyamuzinga	c Mosena b Terblanche	44	not out	21	
8	A.G.Cremer	c and b Kops	42	(6) not out	31	
9	A.M.Manyumwa	b van Zyl	10			
10	T.Muzarabani	c Mosena b van Zyl	7			
11	E.C.Rainsford	not out	0			
	Extras	b 2, lb 5, w 8, nb 11	26	w 4, nb 16	20	
			203	(5 wickets)	**107**	

FoW (1): 1-8 (2), 2-9 (3), 3-47 (4), 4-47 (5), 5-83 (1), 6-120 (6), 7-149 (7), 8-182 (9), 9-190 (10), 10-203 (8)
FoW (2): 1-0 (1), 2-0 (2), 3-6 (3), 4-33 (5), 5-62 (4)

Zimbabwe Provinces Bowling

	O	M	R	W			O	M	R	W	
Rainsford	16.2	2	39	4	1nb		14	8	21	6	2w
Muzarabani	9	3	30	0	2nb	(3)	6	3	11	0	
Manyumwa	11	3	36	1	1w,2nb	(5)	8.2	2	13	3	2nb
Mahwire	13	3	24	0	1nb	(2)	5	0	19	0	
Cremer	28	6	71	4		(4)	6	1	30	1	

Free State Bowling

	O	M	R	W			O	M	R	W	
Kops	21.3	7	38	2	3w,2nb		12	3	34	2	2nb
Saliwa	7	1	28	1	4nb		9	3	26	2	1w,2nb
van der Schyff	9	0	25	1	3w,4nb	(4)	2	0	19	1	2w,4nb
Terblanche	11	2	40	3	2w,1nb	(3)	3	1	21	0	4nb
van Zyl	16	0	65	2			1	0	7	0	

Umpires: B.N.Harrison and C.L.Joubert.   Toss: Free State

Close of Play: 1st day: Zimbabwe Provinces (1) 66-4 (Mawoyo 33*, Chakabva 4*, 24 overs); 2nd day: Zimbabwe Provinces (2) 20-3 (Mujuru 5*, Chakabva 13*, 14 overs).

GAUTENG v NORTHERNS

Played at New Wanderers Stadium, Johannesburg, January 24, 25, 26, 2008.
South African Airways Provincial Three-Day Challenge 2007/08 - Pool B
Gauteng won by one wicket.   (Points: Gauteng 16.58, Northerns 6.6)

NORTHERNS

1	P.J.Malan	c Vilas b Burger	11	b Mafa		2
2	W.T.Dikgale	lbw b Mafa	0	c Vilas b Mafa		1
3	S.W.Liebisch	c Symes b Keiller	17	b Mafa		0
4	S.A.Engelbrecht	c Symes b Keiller	12	c Symes b Cameron		32
5	P.J.van Biljon	c Ramela b Deeb	57	c Swan b Cameron		7
6	*A.M.Phangiso	lbw b Mafa	11	c Burger b Symes		10
7	R.E.van der Merwe	lbw b Deeb	7	c Vilas b Mafa		33
8	†A.L.Ndlovu	c Swan b Deeb	16	c Vilas b Mafa		7
9	M.A.Mashimbyi	c Symes b Deeb	15	lbw b Cameron		11
10	C.R.Kellerman	not out	4	not out		21
11	L.M.G.Masekela	lbw b Keiller	2	lbw b Deeb		5
	Extras	b 4, lb 11, w 1, nb 12	28	b 4, w 6, nb 5		15
			180			144

FoW (1): 1-4 (2), 2-31 (1), 3-32 (3), 4-70 (4), 5-116 (6), 6-138 (7), 7-143 (5), 8-170 (8), 9-175 (9), 10-180 (11)
FoW (2): 1-4 (1), 2-5 (3), 3-10 (2), 4-35 (5), 5-54 (4), 6-68 (6), 7-92 (8), 8-101 (7), 9-127 (9), 10-144 (11)

GAUTENG

1	J.Symes	c Phangiso b Liebisch	18	b Mashimbyi	6
2	O.A.Ramela	c Dikgale b van der Merwe	48	c Ndlovu b Liebisch	8
3	W.B.Motaung	c Ndlovu b van der Merwe	41	b Liebisch	13
4	W.C.Swan	c Ndlovu b Phangiso	16	c Phangiso b Liebisch	0
5	†D.J.Vilas	c Phangiso b van der Merwe	27	(7) lbw b Phangiso	16
6	*S.Burger	lbw b Phangiso	1	c Phangiso b van der Merwe	23
7	R.Cameron	run out (Liebisch/Ndlovu)	1	(8) not out	33
8	D.L.Makalima	c van der Merwe b Kellerman	8	(5) c Ndlovu b Kellerman	19
9	D.R.Deeb	c van Biljon b Phangiso	9	run out	2
10	Y.Keiller	c and b Phangiso	0	c Ndlovu b Mashimbyi	9
11	J.T.Mafa	not out	0	not out	3
	Extras	lb 5, w 1, nb 4	10	lb 6, w 1, nb 8	15
			179	(9 wickets)	147

FoW (1): 1-33 (1), 2-116 (3), 3-117 (2), 4-151 (5), 5-152 (6), 6-153 (7), 7-166 (4), 8-179 (9), 9-179 (10), 10-179 (8)
FoW (2): 1-17 (1), 2-21 (2), 3-21 (4), 4-56 (5), 5-56 (3), 6-90 (7), 7-100 (6), 8-102 (9), 9-134 (10)

Gauteng Bowling

	O	M	R	W			O	M	R	W	
Burger	21	9	38	1			13	4	27	0	
Mafa	15	2	34	2	2nb		14	3	37	5	4w,3nb
Keiller	19.4	8	28	3	1w,1nb	(4)	3	0	18	0	2w
Cameron	7	0	32	0	8nb	(3)	10	3	22	3	2nb
Deeb	13	4	33	4		(6)	8.4	1	26	1	
Symes						(5)	6	2	10	1	

Northerns Bowling

	O	M	R	W			O	M	R	W	
Liebisch	12	1	32	1	1w	(2)	15.2	3	52	3	1nb
Masekela	9	2	23	0							
Kellerman	5.3	0	34	1	4nb		6	0	28	1	3nb
Mashimbyi	4	1	19	0		(1)	8	1	33	2	1w,4nb
van der Merwe	18	2	38	3			4	0	20	1	
Phangiso	13	8	14	4		(4)	4	0	8	1	
Engelbrecht	5	0	14	0							

Umpires: C.J.Conradie and A.T.Holdstock.   Toss: Gauteng

Close of Play: 1st day: Northerns (1) 77-4 (van Biljon 21*, Phangiso 0*, 31.1 overs); 2nd day: Gauteng (1) 179-9 (Makalima 8*, 65.3 overs).

KWAZULU-NATAL v KWAZULU-NATAL INLAND

Played at Chatsworth Stadium, January 24, 25, 26, 2008.
South African Airways Provincial Three-Day Challenge 2007/08 - Pool A
Match drawn.   (Points: KwaZulu-Natal 7.46, KwaZulu-Natal Inland 6.4)

KWAZULU-NATAL

1	*†W.L.Madsen	lbw b van Vuuren	3	(2) lbw b Bowyer	24
2	R.Gobind	c Gqadushe b Brown	33	(1) lbw b Qasim Khurshid	5
3	D.Govender	c and b van Vuuren	13	c Gqadushe b Bowyer	11
4	M.Bekker	c M.B.Hampson b van Vuuren	45	b van Vuuren	9
5	K.Zondo	lbw b van Vuuren	20	c and b Moses	34
6	J.D.Vandiar	b van Vuuren	42	st Gqadushe b Moses	52
7	J.C.Kent	c Gqadushe b van Vuuren	15		
8	C.A.Flowers	not out	18	(7) not out	9
9	M.Shezi	b Qasim Khurshid	4		
10	N.D.Hewer	run out (M.B.Hampson)	6		
11	U.Govender	c Penford b G.M.Hampson	5		
	Extras	b 4, lb 7, w 2, nb 6	19	b 4, w 5, nb 4	13
			223	**(6 wickets, declared)**	**157**

FoW (1): 1-8 (1), 2-36 (3), 3-74 (2), 4-106 (4), 5-158 (5), 6-184 (7), 7-191 (6), 8-198 (9), 9-210 (10), 10-223 (11)
FoW (2): 1-13 (1), 2-51 (3), 3-60 (2), 4-64 (4), 5-141 (5), 6-157 (6)

KWAZULU-NATAL INLAND

1	G.Penford	c Gobind b Kent	24	c Gobind b Hewer	1
2	C.S.Bowyer	c Madsen b Hewer	16	b Kent	7
3	*A.van Vuuren	c Madsen b Hewer	40	(5) not out	47
4	B.Moses	c Vandiar b Hewer	21	c Gobind b Hewer	12
5	M.B.Hampson	c Madsen b Flowers	3	(6) c Vandiar b Flowers	12
6	L.Brown	lbw b Hewer	2	(3) c and b Hewer	0
7	S.Duda	c Zondo b Flowers	8	c Vandiar b Flowers	0
8	G.M.Hampson	c Madsen b Hewer	0	c Madsen b Flowers	22
9	T.Chihota	lbw b U.Govender	24	c Bekker b Hewer	18
10	†M.Gqadushe	c Madsen b U.Govender	17	not out	5
11	Qasim Khurshid	not out	0		
	Extras	b 1, lb 4, w 7, nb 3	15	b 7, lb 2	9
			170	**(8 wickets)**	**133**

FoW (1): 1-33 (2), 2-45 (1), 3-103 (3), 4-112 (4), 5-114 (6), 6-120 (5), 7-127 (7), 8-127 (8), 9-169 (10), 10-170 (9)
FoW (2): 1-8 (1), 2-8 (2), 3-8 (3), 4-35 (4), 5-50 (6), 6-55 (7), 7-85 (8), 8-120 (9)

KwaZulu-Natal Inland Bowling

	O	M	R	W			O	M	R	W	
Qasim Khurshid	19	6	41	1		(2)	9	2	21	1	
G.M.Hampson	20.2	5	52	1	1w,4nb	(3)	12	3	39	0	1w,4nb
van Vuuren	30	5	78	6		(4)	11	4	27	1	
Brown	6	1	21	1	1nb	(1)	5	1	17	0	
Chihota	6	1	20	0	1w,1nb						
Moses						(5)	5.1	0	23	2	
Bowyer						(6)	8	2	26	2	

KwaZulu-Natal Bowling

	O	M	R	W			O	M	R	W	
U.Govender	10.3	2	29	2	2w	(3)	5	3	11	0	
Hewer	20	5	45	5	2nb	(1)	10	1	32	4	
Kent	13	5	24	1	1nb	(2)	7	2	21	1	
Flowers	18	8	41	2			12	4	41	3	
Shezi	6	0	26	0	1w						
Vandiar						(5)	4	0	19	0	

Umpires: L.M.Engelbrecht and B.D.A.Westraadt.   Toss: KwaZulu-Natal Inland

Close of Play: 1st day: KwaZulu-Natal (1) 223 all out; 2nd day: KwaZulu-Natal (2) 96-4 (Zondo not out, Vandiar not out, 36.3 overs).

Madsen kept wicket in the first innings, Gobind in the second innings.

LIONS v TITANS

Played at Sedgars Park, Potchefstroom, January 24, 25, 26, 27, 2008.
SuperSport Series 2007/08
Match drawn.　(Points: Lions 6.32, Titans 7.92)

TITANS

1	M.A.Aronstam	c Harris b Mathebula	38	c van Jaarsveld b le Roux	16
2	†H.G.Kuhn	run out (Petersen)	86	not out	176
3	R.Jappie	c Kgamadi b Mathebula	76	run out	39
4	*M.van Jaarsveld	c van Jaarsveld b Deacon	1	lbw b Deacon	0
5	J.Booysen	lbw b Deacon	0	c Harris b Deacon	3
6	F.Behardien	lbw b Mathebula	50	c Deacon b Alexander	25
7	P.Joubert	lbw b Alexander	17	not out	51
8	B.L.Reddy	c van Jaarsveld b Alexander	57		
9	P.L.Harris	c Deacon b Coetsee	4		
10	Imran Tahir	run out (Kgamadi)	12		
11	N.E.Mbhalati	not out	7		
	Extras	lb 5, w 3, nb 9	17	lb 3, w 2, nb 7	12
			365	(5 wickets, declared)	322

FoW (1): 1-127 (1), 2-144 (2), 3-149 (4), 4-149 (5), 5-234 (6), 6-275 (3), 7-287 (7), 8-319 (9), 9-349 (10), 10-365 (8)
FoW (2): 1-37 (1), 2-140 (3), 3-140 (4), 4-146 (5), 5-194 (6)

LIONS

1	*A.N.Petersen	c Kuhn b Mbhalati	8	lbw b Imran Tahir	26
2	B.D.Snijman	b Mbhalati	29	lbw b Imran Tahir	55
3	S.C.Cook	lbw b Joubert	90	not out	108
4	V.B.van Jaarsveld	c and b Harris	17	lbw b van Jaarsveld	34
5	L.J.Kgamadi	lbw b Harris	0		
6	W.L.Coetsee	c Kuhn b Mbhalati	30		
7	†M.J.Harris	c Kuhn b Joubert	8	(5) not out	53
8	H.W.le Roux	c Aronstam b Joubert	19		
9	W.A.Deacon	not out	45		
10	C.J.Alexander	c Reddy b Mbhalati	0		
11	B.M.Mathebula	b Harris	9		
	Extras	b 2, lb 1, nb 8	11	b 6, lb 1	7
			266	(3 wickets)	283

FoW (1): 1-10 (1), 2-50 (2), 3-90 (4), 4-114 (5), 5-177 (3), 6-186 (6), 7-190 (7), 8-235 (8), 9-250 (10), 10-266 (11)
FoW (2): 1-64 (1), 2-102 (2), 3-154 (4)

Lions Bowling	O	M	R	W			O	M	R	W	
Alexander	24.1	1	64	2	1nb		23	2	78	1	1w
Deacon	30	5	86	2			20	4	62	2	1w,1nb
le Roux	17	2	69	0	1nb		18	4	65	1	
Mathebula	21	1	70	3	2w,7nb		12.1	2	79	0	6nb
Snijman	5	0	14	0	1w	(6)	2	0	13	0	
Coetsee	21	6	57	1							
Kgamadi						(5)	2	0	21	0	
Cook						(7)	2	1	1	0	

Titans Bowling	O	M	R	W			O	M	R	W	
Mbhalati	17	2	63	4	5nb		17	4	42	0	
Joubert	21	4	57	3			18	7	50	0	
Reddy	10	2	27	0	3nb						
Harris	25.5	12	47	3		(3)	25	12	60	0	
Imran Tahir	13	1	51	0			16	1	78	2	
Aronstam	5	0	18	0		(4)	10	2	37	0	
van Jaarsveld						(6)	4	1	9	1	

Umpires: S.George and K.H.Hurter.　Referee: D.Govindjee.　　　　Toss: Titans

Close of Play: 1st day: Titans (1) 210-4 (Jappie 38*, Behardien 36*, 70 overs); 2nd day: Lions (1) 172-4 (Cook 90*, Coetsee 21*, 57 overs); 3rd day: Titans (2) 255-5 (Kuhn 147*, Joubert 13*, 69 overs).
Man of the Match: H.G.Kuhn.
H.G.Kuhn's 176 took 236 balls in 337 minutes and included 28 fours. S.C.Cook's 108 took 204 balls in 241 minutes and included 14 fours.

SOUTH WESTERN DISTRICTS v EASTERN PROVINCE

Played at Recreation Ground, Oudtshoorn, January 24, 25, 26, 2008.
South African Airways Provincial Three-Day Challenge 2007/08 - Pool A
South Western Districts won by 82 runs. (Points: South Western Districts 18.52, Eastern Province 7.8)

SOUTH WESTERN DISTRICTS

1	S.E.Avontuur	c Adair b Njoloza	48	lbw b Birch	11
2	*J.A.Beukes	c Adair b Meyer	19	c Dolley b Njoloza	26
3	B.C.de Wett	c Adair b Birch	37	c Ingram b Meyer	17
4	R.de Reuck	c Adair b Birch	25	b Bell	8
5	P.A.Stuurman	c dos Santos b Birch	70	b Ingram	17
6	N.G.Brouwers	lbw b Meyer	1	b Walters	30
7	†R.P.Hugo	c Baxter b Ingram	40	(8) lbw b Dolley	65
8	N.M.Murray	run out (Adair)	13	(7) c Adair b Bell	25
9	W.Hartslief	not out	2	b Dolley	6
10	N.Nobebe	not out	1	c dos Santos b Dolley	0
11	B.L.Fransman			not out	2
	Extras	b 6, lb 5, w 5, nb 4	20	b 13, lb 6, nb 1	20
		(8 wickets)	276		227

FoW (1): 1-47 (2), 2-95 (1), 3-142 (4), 4-145 (3), 5-157 (6), 6-224 (7), 7-267 (8), 8-274 (5)
FoW (2): 1-31 (1), 2-53 (2), 3-68 (3), 4-80 (4), 5-121 (6), 6-129 (5), 7-219 (8), 8-219 (7), 9-220 (10), 10-227 (9)

EASTERN PROVINCE

1	*C.A.Ingram	c Brouwers b Hartslief	44	c Fransman b Murray	41
2	C.Baxter	b Hartslief	15	run out	55
3	W.E.Bell	c Hugo b Hartslief	8	c Hugo b Murray	5
4	C.R.Dolley	c Brouwers b Murray	37	(9) not out	11
5	J.T.Smuts	c de Wett b Nobebe	15	(4) st Hugo b Brouwers	1
6	†S.R.Adair	b Fransman	19	(5) c and b Brouwers	7
7	A.dos Santos	lbw b de Wett	13	(6) c Hugo b Brouwers	4
8	L.Meyer	not out	61	(7) c and b de Wett	19
9	A.C.R.Birch	c Hugo b Hartslief	9	(8) c Hartslief b Brouwers	6
10	B.D.Walters	c de Wett b Brouwers	12	b Fransman	13
11	M.B.Njoloza	lbw b Fransman	0	st Hugo b Murray	6
	Extras	lb 5, w 1, nb 1	7	b 1, lb 1, w 7, nb 4	13
			240		181

FoW (1): 1-19 (2), 2-37 (3), 3-82 (1), 4-102 (5), 5-135 (6), 6-151 (7), 7-184 (4), 8-214 (9), 9-234 (10), 10-240 (11)
FoW (2): 1-67 (1), 2-83 (3), 3-84 (4), 4-103 (5), 5-111 (6), 6-138 (7), 7-148 (8), 8-149 (2), 9-169 (10), 10-181 (11)

Eastern Province Bowling

	O	M	R	W			O	M	R	W	
Walters	16	2	54	0	1w,1nb		14	2	57	1	1nb
Njoloza	10	1	29	1			5	1	18	1	
Birch	19	3	60	3			16	3	44	1	
Meyer	16	3	51	2			10	1	16	1	
Dolley	14	3	34	0	3nb		16.2	4	37	3	
Ingram	10	1	37	1			11	2	27	1	
Bell						(7)	8	3	9	2	

South Western Districts Bowling

	O	M	R	W			O	M	R	W	
Fransman	15.4	3	51	2			12	4	32	1	
Nobebe	10	2	40	1	1w		4	0	29	0	3w
Hartslief	19	4	41	4			5	1	20	0	
de Wett	5	0	17	1	1nb	(6)	9	1	33	1	2nb
Murray	11	3	36	1		(4)	9	1	24	3	
Brouwers	17	3	50	2		(5)	25	8	41	4	2nb

Umpires: A.Crafford and Z.T.A.Ndamane.   Toss: South Western Districts

Close of Play: 1st day: Eastern Province (1) 54-2 (Ingram 25*, Dolley 4*, 17 overs); 2nd day: South Western Districts (2) 130-6 (Murray 2*, Hugo 1*, 41 overs).

EASTERNS v NORTHERNS

Played at Willowmoore Park Main Oval, Benoni, January 31, February 1, 2, 2008.
South African Airways Provincial Three-Day Challenge 2007/08 - Pool B
Northerns won by 177 runs.　　(Points: Easterns 9.94, Northerns 15.92)

EASTERNS

#	Batsman	Dismissal 1	Score 1	Dismissal 2	Score 2
1	I.C.Hlengani	b Wagner	0	b Wagner	0
2	†T.M.Bodibe	lbw b Phangiso	33	(8) lbw b Phangiso	10
3	J.Booysen	not out	207	(7) lbw b Phangiso	12
4	D.Wiese	b Mashimbyi	41	(6) run out	8
5	A.J.Seymore	c Ndlovu b Phangiso	15	(2) c Kellerman b Liebisch	5
6	G.Toyana	c Liebisch b Phangiso	3	(5) b Liebisch	2
7	J.J.Pienaar	lbw b van der Merwe	31	(3) c van Biljon b Wagner	20
8	*S.P.O'Connor	run out (Mashimbyi)	9	(9) c Jappie b van der Merwe	4
9	P.P.van den Berg	not out	0	(10) lbw b van der Merwe	5
10	E.Nyawo			(4) lbw b Liebisch	1
11	T.R.Plaatjie			not out	2
	Extras	lb 6, w 1, nb 1	8	b 2	2
		(7 wickets)	347		71

FoW (1): 1-0 (1), 2-99 (2), 3-195 (4), 4-229 (5), 5-243 (6), 6-320 (7), 7-345 (8)
FoW (2): 1-0 (1), 2-12 (2), 3-16 (4), 4-20 (5), 5-29 (6), 6-40 (3), 7-56 (7), 8-63 (9), 9-67 (8), 10-71 (10)

NORTHERNS

#	Batsman	Dismissal 1	Score 1	Dismissal 2	Score 2
1	P.J.Malan	c Booysen b Hlengani	63	c Bodibe b van den Berg	62
2	W.T.Dikgale	b van den Berg	66	c Bodibe b Pienaar	15
3	R.Jappie	c Bodibe b Wiese	1	lbw b van den Berg	8
4	S.W.Liebisch	c Seymore b van den Berg	12	c Booysen b van den Berg	53
5	P.J.van Biljon	c Nyawo b van den Berg	0	c Toyana b Hlengani	69
6	*A.M.Phangiso	lbw b van den Berg	2	lbw b Pienaar	69
7	R.E.van der Merwe	not out	23	(8) c Bodibe b Pienaar	16
8	†A.L.Ndlovu	c Seymore b Pienaar	10	(7) b O'Connor	48
9	M.A.Mashimbyi	b Pienaar	0	c Nyawo b Hlengani	22
10	N.Wagner	c Hlengani b Wiese	0	not out	4
11	C.R.Kellerman	lbw b Wiese	8		
	Extras	b 2, lb 3, nb 4	9	b 16, lb 8, w 1, nb 8	33
			196	(9 wickets, declared)	399

FoW (1): 1-117 (1), 2-118 (3), 3-146 (4), 4-147 (2), 5-149 (6), 6-150 (5), 7-174 (8), 8-174 (9), 9-187 (10), 10-196 (11)
FoW (2): 1-30 (2), 2-46 (3), 3-139 (1), 4-148 (4), 5-286 (5), 6-326 (6), 7-352 (8), 8-394 (9), 9-399 (7)

Northerns Bowling

	O	M	R	W			O	M	R	W	
Wagner	15	1	75	1	1w		7	0	30	2	
Liebisch	7	1	25	0			7	1	20	3	
Mashimbyi	11	2	47	1							
Phangiso	26	1	95	3		(3)	6	1	6	2	
Kellerman	4	0	21	0	1nb						
van der Merwe	22	0	78	1		(4)	5.3	1	13	2	

Easterns Bowling

	O	M	R	W			O	M	R	W	
Wiese	21	5	61	3			18	1	75	0	
Plaatjie	5	0	34	0		(7)	3	0	13	0	1w
van den Berg	16	4	29	4			26	11	37	3	
Pienaar	11	3	30	2	3nb	(2)	27	8	90	3	1nb
Hlengani	16	4	37	1	1nb	(4)	48	11	112	2	7nb
O'Connor						(5)	5.2	3	23	1	
Toyana						(6)	6	0	25	0	

Umpires: L.M.Engelbrecht and B.D.A.Westraadt.　　　　Toss: Easterns

Close of Play: 1st day: Northerns (1) 79-0 (Malan 39*, Dikgale 37*, 32 overs); 2nd day: Northerns (2) 188-4 (van Biljon 26*, Phangiso 9*, 69 overs).

J.Booysen's 207 took 219 balls in 301 minutes and included 23 fours and 3 sixes.

GRIQUALAND WEST v ZIMBABWE PROVINCES

Played at De Beers Diamond Oval, Kimberley, January 31, February 1, 2, 2008.
South African Airways Provincial Three-Day Challenge 2007/08 - Pool B
Griqualand West won by 11 runs.   (Points: Griqualand West 18.86, Zimbabwe Provinces 6.88)

GRIQUALAND WEST

1	A.K.Kruger	c Cremer b Mahwire	25	run out	32
2	M.Akoojee	c Rainsford b Mahwire	8	lbw b Garwe	15
3	A.P.McLaren	c Mahwire b Rainsford	7	c Chakabva b Garwe	0
4	P.J.Koortzen	c Mawoyo b Cremer	78	c Cremer b Manyumwa	0
5	*†W.Bossenger	c Chakabva b Mahwire	88	b Cremer	5
6	R.R.Hendricks	lbw b Garwe	47	c Chakabva b Manyumwa	0
7	C.Pietersen	c Duffin b Garwe	24	c Chakabva b Mahwire	32
8	R.A.Adams	b Garwe	0	c Nyamuzinga b Cremer	2
9	A.P.T.Mabuya	c Chakabva b Garwe	4	c Chakabva b Cremer	0
10	R.Pietersen	lbw b Cremer	0	lbw b Manyumwa	0
11	D.D.Carolus	not out	0	not out	0
	Extras	lb 6, w 1, nb 5	12	b 4	4
			293		**90**

FoW (1): 1-31 (2), 2-46 (3), 3-46 (1), 4-194 (4), 5-242 (5), 6-281 (6), 7-283 (8), 8-290 (7), 9-292 (10), 10-293 (9)
FoW (2): 1-40 (2), 2-40 (3), 3-40 (4), 4-48 (1), 5-50 (6), 6-64 (5), 7-70 (8), 8-70 (9), 9-75 (10), 10-90 (7)

ZIMBABWE PROVINCES

1	T.M.K.Mawoyo	c Bossenger b C.Pietersen	7	b Adams	33
2	T.Duffin	c Koortzen b C.Pietersen	9	c Bossenger b C.Pietersen	0
3	B.Mujuru	c McLaren b Mabuya	14	c Kruger b C.Pietersen	28
4	F.Kasteni	c Hendricks b C.Pietersen	61	c Bossenger b Kruger	20
5	†R.W.Chakabva	c Mabuya b Carolus	46	b Kruger	35
6	A.G.Cremer	c McLaren b Adams	14	c Bossenger b C.Pietersen	2
7	S.K.Nyamuzinga	c Bossenger b Carolus	3	c Bossenger b C.Pietersen	0
8	A.M.Manyumwa	c McLaren b Carolus	4	lbw b C.Pietersen	0
9	*N.B.Mahwire	c Bossenger b R.Pietersen	13	b C.Pietersen	34
10	T.N.Garwe	c McLaren b Carolus	4	c Akoojee b Carolus	6
11	E.C.Rainsford	not out	4	not out	3
	Extras	lb 7, w 1, nb 7	15	lb 9, w 5, nb 3	17
			194		**178**

FoW (1): 1-14 (2), 2-25 (1), 3-59 (3), 4-134 (4), 5-158 (6), 6-163 (7), 7-172 (5), 8-184 (8), 9-188 (10), 10-194 (9)
FoW (2): 1-2 (2), 2-66 (1), 3-77 (3), 4-119 (4), 5-122 (6), 6-128 (7), 7-128 (8), 8-132 (5), 9-163 (10), 10-178 (9)

Zimbabwe Provinces Bowling

	O	M	R	W			O	M	R	W
Rainsford	9	1	33	1						
Garwe	16.2	3	49	4	1w		8	1	29	2
Mahwire	14	3	61	3	1nb	(1)	7.4	0	29	1
Manyumwa	11	3	37	0		(3)	11	5	18	3
Cremer	27	3	94	2	4nb	(4)	6	2	10	3
Kasteni	2	0	13	0						

Griqualand West Bowling

	O	M	R	W			O	M	R	W	
C.Pietersen	15	5	29	3	1nb		25.3	6	66	6	4w,1nb
Carolus	13	3	26	4	2nb	(4)	16	5	34	1	1nb
Kruger	11	1	39	0	1w,1nb	(2)	18	8	22	2	1w,1nb
Adams	9	3	26	1	2nb	(6)	11	5	19	1	
Mabuya	7	1	22	1			9	3	16	0	
Koortzen	1	0	5	0							
R.Pietersen	11.2	3	40	1	1nb	(3)	7	2	12	0	

Umpires: A.Crafford and B.M.White.   Toss: Zimbabwe Provinces

Close of Play: 1st day: Zimbabwe Provinces (1) 72-3 (Kasteni 24*, Chakabva 8*, 25 overs); 2nd day: Zimbabwe Provinces (2) 41-1 (Mawoyo 21*, Mujuru 15*, 24 overs).

NORTH WEST v GAUTENG

Played at Sedgars Park, Potchefstroom, January 31, February 1, 2, 2008.
South African Airways Provincial Three-Day Challenge 2007/08 - Pool B
North West won by eight wickets.   (Points: North West 19.28, Gauteng 6.82)

GAUTENG

#	Batsman	First innings		Second innings	
1	B.D.Snijman	b Letsoalo	20	c Kgamadi b Naicker	56
2	J.Symes	c Siboto b Gerber	24	c Letsoalo b Naicker	59
3	W.B.Motaung	b Gerber	1	c and b Naicker	35
4	V.B.van Jaarsveld	c Gerber b Naicker	54	c Bula b Letsoalo	64
5	D.L.Makalima	c Bula b Gerber	22	lbw b Deacon	65
6	*S.Burger	run out (Letsoalo)	8	b Gerber	37
7	†D.J.Vilas	b Naicker	19	c Kgamadi b Deacon	4
8	D.R.Deeb	c Deacon b Naicker	20	c Bula b Gerber	0
9	Y.Keiller	b Siboto	1	lbw b Gerber	0
10	B.M.Mathebula	b Siboto	4	not out	1
11	J.T.Mafa	not out	12	b Deacon	0
	Extras	lb 1, w 2, nb 3	6	w 1, nb 6	7
			191		**328**

FoW (1): 1-42 (2), 2-49 (1), 3-53 (3), 4-117 (5), 5-133 (6), 6-134 (4), 7-168 (7), 8-175 (9), 9-175 (8), 10-191 (10)
FoW (2): 1-88 (2), 2-144 (1), 3-173 (3), 4-247 (4), 5-310 (6), 6-319 (7), 7-320 (8), 8-320 (9), 9-328 (5), 10-328 (11)

NORTH WEST

#	Batsman	First innings		Second innings	
1	J.F.Mostert	b Burger	16	b Burger	23
2	C.Jonker	c Vilas b Mafa	15	st Vilas b Deeb	92
3	M.Lazenby	c Symes b Mafa	10	not out	65
4	N.Bredenkamp	lbw b Mathebula	1	not out	9
5	L.J.Kgamadi	b Mathebula	92		
6	*W.A.Deacon	c Vilas b Mafa	82		
7	†T.A.Bula	b Mafa	41		
8	M.P.Siboto	run out (Snijman/Vilas)	18		
9	E.Gerber	b Deeb	15		
10	K.M.Naicker	not out	1		
11	P.S.Letsoalo	b Mafa	5		
	Extras	b 5, lb 3, w 5, nb 11	24	lb 6, w 7, nb 1	14
			320	**(2 wickets)**	**203**

FoW (1): 1-28 (1), 2-32 (2), 3-41 (4), 4-51 (3), 5-217 (6), 6-250 (5), 7-282 (8), 8-310 (9), 9-314 (7), 10-320 (11)
FoW (2): 1-35 (1), 2-194 (2)

North West Bowling

	O	M	R	W			O	M	R	W	
Deacon	12	2	35	0	3nb		19.4	9	48	3	2nb
Gerber	14	5	46	3			23	9	52	3	
Letsoalo	15	4	39	1	1w		19	5	92	1	1nb
Siboto	12	1	40	2	1w	(5)	5	1	18	0	
Naicker	8	0	30	3		(4)	28	4	106	3	2nb
Mostert						(6)	4	2	6	0	1w
Jonker						(7)	4	2	6	0	1nb

Gauteng Bowling

	O	M	R	W			O	M	R	W	
Burger	13	1	54	1	1nb	(2)	6	1	25	1	1w
Mafa	16.2	5	51	5	1w	(1)	4.1	0	36	0	
Mathebula	15	0	82	2	2w,10nb		4	0	21	0	3w,1nb
Keiller	12	1	30	0	2w		3	0	14	0	3w
Deeb	18	2	56	1		(6)	7	0	43	1	
Symes	5	1	16	0		(7)	4	0	39	0	
Snijman	8	2	23	0		(5)	4	0	19	0	

Umpires: A.T.Holdstock and L.J.Willemse.   Toss: Gauteng

Close of Play: 1st day: North West (1) 170-4 (Kgamadi 54*, Deacon 61*, 43 overs); 2nd day: Gauteng (2) 184-3 (van Jaarsveld 23*, Makalima 6*, 44 overs).

SOUTH WESTERN DISTRICTS v BOLAND

Played at Recreation Ground, Oudtshoorn, January 31, February 1, 2, 2008.
South African Airways Provincial Three-Day Challenge 2007/08 - Pool A
Boland won by seven wickets.   **(Points: South Western Districts 5.5, Boland 16.86)**

SOUTH WESTERN DISTRICTS

1	S.E.Avontuur	lbw b Sandri	45	c Olivier b Sandri		0
2	*J.A.Beukes	lbw b Sandri	21	c Bothma b Grobler		84
3	B.C.de Wett	lbw b Sandri	0	st Olivier b Grobler		19
4	R.deReuck	lbw b Sandri	0	lbw b Sandri		41
5	P.A.Stuurman	b Paulse	27	lbw b Sandri		0
6	R.E.Hillermann	b Bothma	0	c and b Grobler		3
7	N.G.Brouwers	b de Wet	46	c Hayward b Grobler		1
8	†R.P.Hugo	b de Wet	14	c Olivier b Paulse		3
9	N.M.Murray	c and b de Wet	1	b Paulse		17
10	N.Nobebe	lbw b de Wet	2	lbw b Paulse		41
11	B.L.Fransman	not out	0	not out		9
	Extras	b 1, lb 8, w 6, nb 4	19	b 17, lb 4, w 1, nb 5		27
			175			245

FoW (1): 1-40 (2), 2-40 (3), 3-40 (4), 4-102 (5), 5-102 (1), 6-102 (6), 7-129 (8), 8-145 (9), 9-173 (10), 10-175 (7)
FoW (2): 1-5 (1), 2-43 (3), 3-122 (4), 4-126 (5), 5-143 (6), 6-155 (7), 7-162 (8), 8-179 (2), 9-229 (10), 10-245 (9)

BOLAND

1	A.W.Olivier	c Hugo b Nobebe	25	b de Wett		9
2	W.D.Hayward	run out (de Reuck)	32	b Fransman		4
3	B.Hector	not out	118	not out		54
4	*B.C.Adams	lbw b Brouwers	4	st Hugo b Brouwers		7
5	S.F.Grobler	run out (Brouwers)	13			
6	R.G.Arendse	lbw b Brouwers	5	(5) not out		34
7	H.W.de Wet	c de Wett b Brouwers	0			
8	†L.R.Walters	c Hillermann b Murray	75			
9	J.P.Bothma	b Murray	11			
10	P.S.E.Sandri	not out	4			
11	H.H.Paulse					
	Extras	b 6, lb 7, w 1, nb 2	16	b 3, lb 5, w 1, nb 1		10
		(8 wickets)	303	(3 wickets)		118

FoW (1): 1-30 (1), 2-82 (2), 3-88 (4), 4-113 (5), 5-142 (6), 6-142 (7), 7-277 (8), 8-299 (9)
FoW (2): 1-5 (2), 2-38 (1), 3-61 (4)

Boland Bowling

	O	M	R	W			O	M	R	W	
Sandri	20	8	47	4	1w,2nb		23	8	38	3	
Paulse	14	2	42	1	1w,1nb		13	2	43	3	4nb
de Wet	15.2	5	29	4		(5)	13	5	26	0	
Bothma	12	3	29	1	1nb	(3)	5	1	11	0	
Grobler	2	0	19	0		(4)	33	9	80	4	1w,1nb
Adams						(6)	7	2	26	0	

South Western Districts Bowling

	O	M	R	W			O	M	R	W	
Fransman	21	3	67	0	1nb		10	0	29	1	
Nobebe	13	2	33	1	1w	(3)	2	0	9	0	1w
Murray	18	3	52	2		(5)	3	1	15	1	
Hillermann	10	2	24	0							
Brouwers	40	9	103	3	1nb	(2)	14	3	28	1	
de Wett	4	0	11	0		(4)	11	1	29	1	1nb

Umpires: B.N.Harrison and C.L.Joubert.   Toss: South Western Districts

Close of Play: 1st day: Boland (1) 99-3 (Hector 31*, Grobler 1*, 35 overs); 2nd day: South Western Districts (2) 117-2 (Beukes 46*, de Reuck 38*, 39 overs).

B.Hector's 118 took 285 balls in 356 minutes and included 12 fours and 2 sixes. P.S.E.Sandri took a hat-trick in the South Western Districts first innings (Beukes, de Wett, de Reuck). Olivier kept wicket in the South Western Districts second innings.

WESTERN PROVINCE v KWAZULU-NATAL INLAND

Played at Sahara Park Newlands, Cape Town, January 31, February 1, 2, 2008.
South African Airways Provincial Three-Day Challenge 2007/08 - Pool A
Western Province won by 225 runs.   (Points: Western Province 18.68, KwaZulu-Natal Inland 4.8)

WESTERN PROVINCE

1	A.J.A.Gray	c Gqadushe b McMillan	68	c Penford b Qasim Khurshid	56
2	M.Williamson	b McMillan	30	lbw b Hampson	20
3	R.E.Levi	c Gqadushe b McMillan	4	lbw b Humphries	37
4	J.M.Kuiper	c Moses b McMillan	6	c Humphries b Qasim Khurshid	11
5	†T.L.Tsolekile	lbw b Humphries	1	not out	50
6	A.M.Sodumo	run out (van Vuuren/Gqadushe)	7	not out	56
7	E.P.van Wyk	not out	99		
8	C.W.S.Birch	b Hampson	35		
9	*P.R.Adams	not out	19		
10	M.deStadler				
11	L.F.Simpson				
	Extras	lb 7, nb 8	15	lb 6	6
		(7 wickets)	284	(4 wickets, declared)	236

FoW (1): 1-46 (2), 2-50 (3), 3-60 (4), 4-65 (5), 5-86 (6), 6-195 (1), 7-255 (8)
FoW (2): 1-40 (2), 2-105 (3), 3-120 (4), 4-125 (1)

KWAZULU-NATAL INLAND

1	G.Penford	c Adams b de Stadler	36	b Simpson	4
2	K.Padayachee	lbw b Birch	11	c de Stadler b Birch	2
3	*A.van Vuuren	c Adams b van Wyk	41	(5) b Adams	41
4	†M.Gqadushe	c Tsolekile b Simpson	3	(3) c Tsolekile b Simpson	11
5	B.Moses	c Williamson b van Wyk	7	(6) c Tsolekile b Simpson	40
6	R.D.McMillan	c Gray b de Stadler	13	(7) c Birch b Simpson	18
7	T.Chihota	b van Wyk	0	(8) c Tsolekile b Adams	8
8	G.M.Hampson	b van Wyk	0	(9) c Kuiper b Adams	16
9	K.Nipper	not out	15	(10) c Gray b Adams	4
10	O.E.Humphries	lbw b van Wyk	5	(4) b Simpson	1
11	Qasim Khurshid	b Adams	5	not out	3
	Extras	lb 2, w 2	4	lb 5, nb 2	7
			140		155

FoW (1): 1-21 (2), 2-59 (1), 3-75 (4), 4-93 (5), 5-108 (3), 6-108 (7), 7-112 (8), 8-123 (6), 9-128 (10), 10-140 (11)
FoW (2): 1-11 (2), 2-11 (1), 3-16 (4), 4-31 (3), 5-95 (5), 6-107 (6), 7-124 (7), 8-138 (8), 9-142 (10), 10-155 (9)

KwaZulu-Natal Inland Bowling

	O	M	R	W		O	M	R	W	
Qasim Khurshid	11	3	41	0		11	1	54	2	
Humphries	9	0	42	1	7nb	11	2	46	1	
Hampson	23	12	42	1		14	5	35	1	
McMillan	19	8	57	4	1nb	14	3	67	0	
van Vuuren	10	5	32	0						
Nipper	13	2	63	0	(5)	5	0	28	0	

Western Province Bowling

	O	M	R	W		O	M	R	W	
Simpson	11	4	21	1	1w	15	2	59	5	
Birch	6	1	20	1		7	1	20	1	2nb
de Stadler	23	8	49	2	(4)	8	2	17	0	
van Wyk	12	4	44	5	1w	(5) 9	2	28	0	
Adams	2.2	1	4	1	(3)	14.1	5	26	4	

Umpires: L.B.Gcuma and I.H.van Kerwel.   Toss: Western Province

Close of Play: 1st day: KwaZulu-Natal Inland (1) 66-2 (van Vuuren 14*, Gqadushe 3*, 20 overs); 2nd day: KwaZulu-Natal Inland (2) 30-3 (Gqadushe 11*, van Vuuren 6*, 12 overs).

Sodumo scored his fifty off 47 balls in Western Province's 2nd innings.

EASTERN PROVINCE v KWAZULU-NATAL

Played at Sahara Oval, St George's Park, Port Elizabeth, February 7, 8, 9, 2008.
South African Airways Provincial Three-Day Challenge 2007/08 - Pool A
Match drawn. (Points: Eastern Province 4.9, KwaZulu-Natal 8.46)

EASTERN PROVINCE

1	*C.A.Ingram	lbw b Tweedie	4	lbw b Madsen	75
2	C.Baxter	c Hauptfleisch b Mlongo	0	b Maharaj	14
3	†G.E.von Hoesslin	c Maharaj b U.Govender	22	c Hauptfleisch b Madsen	18
4	W.E.Bell	c Bekker b Mlongo	10	lbw b Maharaj	5
5	R.R.Jeggels	c Tweedie b Shezi	23	not out	35
6	S.R.Adair	c Bekker b U.Govender	0	lbw b Maharaj	0
7	M.M.Matika	c Hauptfleisch b Maharaj	36	b Madsen	0
8	A.C.R.Birch	c Bekker b Shezi	7	not out	24
9	C.R.Dolley	c Smit b Maharaj	18		
10	B.D.Walters	c Bekker b Maharaj	14		
11	M.J.Luscombe	not out	7		
	Extras	lb 1, nb 3	4	b 7, lb 1, nb 3	11
			145	**(6 wickets)**	**182**

FoW (1): 1-4 (1), 2-4 (2), 3-16 (4), 4-60 (3), 5-60 (6), 6-60 (5), 7-68 (8), 8-123 (7), 9-126 (9), 10-145 (10)
FoW (2): 1-59 (2), 2-90 (3), 3-103 (4), 4-134 (1), 5-135 (6), 6-138 (7)

KWAZULU-NATAL

1	†C.Hauptfleisch	c Walters b Dolley	53
2	*W.L.Madsen	b Birch	62
3	K.Smit	b Ingram	63
	R.M.Gouveia		
4	D.Govender	run out (Baxter/Luscombe)	10
5	M.Bekker	c and b Luscombe	10
6	K.Zondo	run out (Bell/von Hoesslin)	85
7	K.A.Maharaj	c Birch b Dolley	1
8	A.N.W.Tweedie	c Ingram b Dolley	12
9	S.Mlongo	lbw b Walters	10
10	U.Govender	b Birch	5
11	M.Shezi	not out	2
	Extras	lb 5, w 1, nb 5	11
			324

FoW (1): 1-108 (1), 2-128 (2), 3-155 (4), 4-182 (5), 5-224 (3), 6-227 (7), 7-245 (8), 8-274 (9), 9-303 (10), 10-324 (6)

KwaZulu-Natal Bowling

	O	M	R	W			O	M	R	W	
Tweedie	13	3	30	1			6	2	11	0	
Mlongo	10	2	22	2	2nb		5	2	18	0	1nb
U.Govender	7	2	35	2		(4)	7	3	18	0	
Shezi	6	2	18	2							
Maharaj	8.4	1	24	3	1nb	(3)	31	9	69	3	2nb
Madsen	6	2	15	0		(5)	23	6	45	3	
Gouveia						(6)	1	0	13	0	

Eastern Province Bowling

	O	M	R	W	
Birch	22	3	73	2	1w,3nb
Walters	17	2	43	1	2nb
Luscombe	14	2	61	1	
Bell	7	3	18	0	
Dolley	18	1	68	3	
Ingram	15.1	1	56	1	

Umpires: A.T.Holdstock and L.J.Willemse.   Toss: KwaZulu-Natal

Close of Play: 1st day: Eastern Province (1) 4-2 (von Hoesslin 0*, 2 overs); 2nd day: KwaZulu-Natal (1) 157-3 (Smit 23*, Bekker 0*, 49.1 overs).

R.M.Gouveia was a full substitute for KwaZulu-Natal, replacing K.Smit who was called up to the Dolphins squad at tea on the third day.

GRIQUALAND WEST v EASTERNS

Played at De Beers Diamond Oval, Kimberley, February 7, 8, 9, 2008.
South African Airways Provincial Three-Day Challenge 2007/08 - Pool B
Griqualand West won by 209 runs.   (Points: Griqualand West 17, Easterns 5.2)

GRIQUALAND WEST

1	C.N.Bennett	b Pienaar	0	lbw b Mofokeng	46
2	M.Akoojee	c Bodibe b Pienaar	0	(3) c Seymore b Picnaar	6
3	A.P.McLaren	c Bodibe b Wiese	3	(7) c Mofokeng b Pienaar	108
4	P.J.Koortzen	lbw b van den Berg	15	c Bodibe b Wiese	0
5	*†W.Bossenger	c Bodibe b Wiese	28	c Bodibe b Hlengani	43
6	A.K.Kruger	c Bodibe b Wiese	2	(2) c Bodibe b Pienaar	22
7	C.Pietersen	c Bodibe b Mofokeng	87	(6) b Hlengani	24
8	A.R.Swanepoel	c Hlengani b Pienaar	6	c Bodibe b Hlengani	3
9	N.O.Arthur	c Bodibe b van den Berg	16	c Seymore b Wiese	0
10	D.D.Carolus	c Fourie b Mofokeng	21	c Makua b Pienaar	33
11	R.Pietersen	not out	1	not out	1
	Extras	lb 12, w 1, nb 8	21	lb 9, w 7	16
			200		**302**

FoW (1): 1-1 (2), 2-7 (1), 3-53 (4), 4-55 (5), 5-56 (6), 6-62 (3), 7-79 (8), 8-146 (9), 9-197 (7), 10-200 (10)
FoW (2): 1-26 (2), 2-32 (3), 3-33 (4), 4-121 (1), 5-121 (5), 6-159 (6), 7-166 (8), 8-177 (9), 9-292 (10), 10-302 (7)

EASTERNS

1	†T.M.Bodibe	c Koortzen b C.Pietersen	40	b Swanepoel	18
2	A.J.Seymore	c Koortzen b Kruger	2	lbw b C.Pietersen	11
3	I.C.Hlengani	c C.Pietersen b Kruger	3	(7) b R.Pietersen	20
4	D.Wiese	lbw b R.Pietersen	14	(5) c and b Swanepoel	12
5	J.J.Pienaar	c Bossenger b R.Pietersen	30	(6) c C.Pietersen b Carolus	13
6	G.Toyana	lbw b Swanepoel	0	(4) c sub (C.R.Tiger) b Swanepoel	21
7	D.T.Makua	lbw b C.Pietersen	0	(10) lbw b Arthur	8
8	*S.P.O'Connor	b C.Pietersen	0	b Swanepoel	16
9	P.P.van den Berg	b C.Pietersen	0	not out	12
10	J.C.Fourie	c Bossenger b C.Pietersen	1	(3) c Koortzen b C.Pietersen	33
11	P.T.Mofokeng	not out	12	c Koortzen b R.Pietersen	1
	Extras	lb 1, w 3, nb 4	8	b 7, lb 9, w 2	18
			110		**183**

FoW (1): 1-14 (2), 2-25 (3), 3-46 (4), 4-84 (1), 5-85 (6), 6-90 (7), 7-90 (8), 8-90 (9), 9-92 (10), 10-110 (5)
FoW (2): 1-18 (2), 2-60 (3), 3-67 (1), 4-101 (5), 5-104 (4), 6-118 (6), 7-145 (8), 8-173 (7), 9-182 (10), 10-183 (11)

Easterns Bowling

	O	M	R	W		O	M	R	W	
Wiese	18	3	46	3	1nb	15	4	43	2	
Pienaar	18	3	64	3	7nb	18.1	5	72	4	
van den Berg	14	6	37	2	(4)	10	0	53	0	
O'Connor	6	1	30	0	(3)	5	0	30	0	
Mofokeng	3.1	1	11	2	1w	15	2	59	1	7w
Hlengani					(6)	12	3	36	3	

Griqualand West Bowling

	O	M	R	W		O	M	R	W	
C.Pietersen	13	5	29	5		14	2	41	2	2w
Kruger	9	1	17	2	2nb	6	1	37	0	
Carolus	6	0	24	0	1nb	(5) 5	0	15	1	
R.Pietersen	7.3	1	24	2	2w,1nb	(3) 11.3	4	30	2	
Swanepoel	5	0	15	1	1w	(4) 13	2	37	4	
Arthur					(6)	3	0	7	1	

Umpires: R.Ellis and B.M.White.   Toss: Griqualand West

Close of Play: 1st day: Easterns (1) 110 all out; 2nd day: Easterns (2) 69-3 (Toyana 2*, Wiese 0*, 17 overs).

A.P.McLaren's 108 took 157 balls in 178 minutes and included 10 fours and 3 sixes. A.P.McLaren retired hurt in the Griqualand West first innings having scored 0 (team score 6-1) - he returned when the score was 56-5.

KWAZULU-NATAL INLAND v SOUTH WESTERN DISTRICTS

Played at City Oval, Pietermaritzburg, February 7, 8, 9, 2008.
South African Airways Provincial Three-Day Challenge 2007/08 - Pool A
Match drawn.   (Points: KwaZulu-Natal Inland 3, South Western Districts 5.3)

SOUTH WESTERN DISTRICTS

1	S.E.Avontuur	c Brown b Hampson	105	(2) c Drummond b Qasim Khurshid	12
2	*J.A.Beukes	c Drummond b Hampson	92	(5) not out	7
3	B.C.de Wett	c Brown b Dorasamy	17		
4	R.de Reuck	c Drummond b Dorasamy	5		
5	P.A.Stuurman	not out	36	(4) c Padayachee b Hampson	0
6	R.E.Hillermann	c Padayachee b Qasim Khurshid	31		
7	†R.P.Hugo	b Qasim Khurshid	10	(3) not out	20
8	N.G.Brouwers	not out	7	(1) c Padayachee b Qasim Khurshid	4
9	N.M.Murray				
10	N.Nobebe				
11	B.L.Fransman				
	Extras	b 3, lb 2, w 1, nb 6	12	w 2	2

(6 wickets)	315	(3 wickets, declared)	45

FoW (1): 1-202 (1), 2-204 (2), 3-228 (4), 4-231 (3), 5-287 (6), 6-298 (7)
FoW (2): 1-7 (1), 2-18 (2), 3-20 (4)

KWAZULU-NATAL INLAND

1	G.Penford	not out	18	b Nobebe	0
2	K.Padayachee	not out	7	lbw b Fransman	43
3	†T.J.Drummond			lbw b Hillermann	21
4	M.S.van Vuuren			b Murray	0
5	B.Moses			c Stuurman b Brouwers	13
6	*G.M.Hampson			c de Wett b Brouwers	6
7	S.Dorasamy			c Nobebe b Murray	0
8	L.Brown			not out	46
9	K.Nipper			lbw b Hillermann	0
10	M.Gqadushe			b Fransman	7
11	Qasim Khurshid			not out	0
	Extras			b 4, lb 7, w 1	12

(no wicket, declared)	25	(9 wickets)	148

FoW (2): 1-1 (1), 2-35 (3), 3-36 (4), 4-55 (5), 5-65 (6), 6-66 (7), 7-125 (2), 8-132 (9), 9-139 (10)

KwaZulu-Natal Inland Bowling

	O	M	R	W		O	M	R	W	
Qasim Khurshid	15	4	60	2		6	1	23	2	2w
Hampson	22	2	86	2	6nb	5	0	22	1	
Brown	9	1	38	0	1w					
Nipper	19	3	57	0						
Dorasamy	8	2	25	2						
van Vuuren	12	3	44	0						

South Western Districts Bowling

	O	M	R	W			O	M	R	W	
Fransman	3	1	11	0			12.4	2	31	2	1w
Nobebe	3	0	14	0			4	1	13	1	
Hillermann						(3)	13	5	39	2	
Murray						(4)	11	4	22	2	
Brouwers						(5)	12	6	14	2	
de Wett						(6)	4	0	18	0	

Umpires: A.Crafford and B.N.Harrison.   Toss: South Western Districts

Close of Play: 1st day: KwaZulu-Natal Inland (1) 25-0 (Penford 18*, Padayachee 7*, 6 overs); 2nd day: No play.

S.E.Avontuur's 105 took 170 balls in 203 minutes and included 18 fours.

BOLAND v EASTERN PROVINCE

Played at Boland Bank Park, Paarl, February 14, 15, 16, 2008.
South African Airways Provincial Three-Day Challenge 2007/08 - Pool A
Boland won by an innings and 15 runs.　　(Points: Boland 17.06, Eastern Province 2)

EASTERN PROVINCE

1	*C.A.Ingram	c Ramela b Sandri	6	lbw b Grobler	42
2	C.Baxter	run out (Bothma)	3	c Walters b Bothma	13
3	†G.E.von Hoesslin	c Adams b Bothma	5	c Walters b Bothma	0
4	A.dos Santos	b Bothma	6	lbw b Sandri	10
5	W.E.Bell	b de Wet	35	b Sandri	6
6	S.R.Adair	not out	17	lbw b de Wet	9
7	M.M.Matika	b de Wet	0	not out	14
8	A.C.R.Birch	lbw b de Wet	0	(9) c Hector b Bothma	15
9	C.R.Dolley	b de Wet	4	(8) lbw b Grobler	0
10	B.D.Walters	b de Wet	12	b Sandri	2
11	M.B.Njoloza	b Paulse	0	c Walters b Sandri	0
	Extras	lb 1, nb 3	4	b 4, lb 10, w 3	17
			92		128

FoW (1): 1-6 (1), 2-10 (2), 3-19 (3), 4-28 (4), 5-65 (5), 6-65 (7), 7-65 (8), 8-71 (9), 9-89 (10), 10-92 (11)
FoW (2): 1-19 (2), 2-19 (3), 3-39 (4), 4-45 (5), 5-69 (6), 6-104 (1), 7-104 (8), 8-125 (9), 9-128 (10), 10-128 (11)

BOLAND

1	O.A.Ramela	c Baxter b Birch	85
2	W.D.Hayward	c Matika b Walters	6
3	B.Hector	run out (Birch)	6
4	*B.C.Adams	c Baxter b Dolley	79
5	R.G.Arendse	lbw b Walters	3
6	H.W.de Wet	c von Hoesslin b Dolley	1
7	†L.R.Walters	c von Hoesslin b Walters	22
8	S.F.Grobler	b Birch	0
9	P.S.E.Sandri	c von Hoesslin b Walters	2
10	J.P.Bothma	not out	0
11	H.H.Paulse	b Walters	0
	Extras	b 11, lb 16, w 3, nb 1	31
			235

FoW (1): 1-11 (2), 2-22 (3), 3-185 (4), 4-197 (5), 5-198 (6), 6-217 (1), 7-219 (8), 8-234 (9), 9-235 (7), 10-235 (11)

Boland Bowling

	O	M	R	W		O	M	R	W	
Sandri	9	2	31	1	2nb	14.5	5	21	4	
Paulse	8.4	4	19	1	1nb	10	4	27	0	1w
Bothma	9	3	24	2		16	5	32	3	2w
de Wet	6	0	17	5		7	2	17	1	
Grobler					(5)	8	3	17	2	

Eastern Province Bowling

	O	M	R	W	
Walters	28	14	38	5	1w
Njoloza	14	4	37	0	1w
Birch	24	4	61	2	1w,1nb
Bell	18	3	47	0	
Dolley	14	3	21	2	
Matika	1	0	4	0	

Umpires: R.Ellis and J.E.P.Ostrom.　　　　　　Toss: Boland

Close of Play: 1st day: Boland (1) 105-2 (Ramela 35*, Adams 41*, 39 overs); 2nd day: Eastern Province (2) 116-7 (Matika 12*, Birch 10*, 48 overs).

H.W.de Wet took a hat-trick in the Eastern Province first innings (Bell, Matika, Birch).

GAUTENG v NAMIBIA

Played at New Wanderers Stadium, Johannesburg, February 14, 15, 16, 2008.
South African Airways Provincial Three-Day Challenge 2007/08 - Pool B
Gauteng won by an innings and 103 runs. (Points: Gauteng 21.44, Namibia 6.66)

GAUTENG
1	J.Symes	c Snyman b Williams	61
2	W.B.Motaung	c Ludik b N.R.P.Scholtz	73
3	E.T.Nkwe	c Snyman b Durant	5
4	W.C.Swan	c R.Scholtz b Klazinga	61
5	D.L.Makalima	c Snyman b R.Scholtz	13
6	†D.J.Vilas	run out (Durant/Ludik)	71
7	H.W.le Roux	c Rudolph b Williams	82
8	*S.Burger	run out (Klazinga)	22
9	B.M.Mathebula	not out	14
10	D.R.Deeb	not out	5
11	Y.Keiller		
	Extras	lb 3, w 4, nb 8	15
		(8 wickets)	422

FoW (1): 1-115 (1), 2-128 (3), 3-155 (2), 4-195 (5), 5-269 (4), 6-331 (6), 7-401 (7), 8-415 (8)

NAMIBIA
1	P.J.Grove	c Makalima b le Roux	13	(2) lbw b le Roux	0
2	G.J.Rudolph	c Vilas b Nkwe	9	(1) b Burger	0
3	M.Durant	lbw b Burger	28	lbw b Burger	16
4	*G.Snyman	c Vilas b Mathebula	22	c Makalima b le Roux	1
5	C.Williams	c Vilas b Mathebula	0	c Symes b Keiller	32
6	N.R.P.Scholtz	b Symes	23	lbw b Mathebula	5
7	†H.Ludik	c Nkwe b Mathebula	4	c and b le Roux	39
8	M.C.van Zyl	c Swan b Symes	50	lbw b Symes	6
9	W.Slabber	c Motaung b Deeb	5	c Vilas b le Roux	6
10	L.Klazinga	c Makalima b Deeb	10	not out	10
11	R.Scholtz	not out	2	c Vilas b Symes	4
	Extras	lb 4, w 2, nb 11	17	b 4, lb 6, w 1, nb 6	17
			183		136

FoW (1): 1-26 (1), 2-38 (2), 3-87 (4), 4-87 (3), 5-87 (5), 6-91 (7), 7-131 (6), 8-140 (9), 9-167 (10), 10-183 (8)
FoW (2): 1-0 (2), 2-0 (1), 3-1 (4), 4-45 (5), 5-52 (6), 6-108 (3), 7-108 (7), 8-116 (9), 9-126 (8), 10-136 (11)

Namibia Bowling
	O	M	R	W	
Klazinga	10	1	53	1	5nb
R.Scholtz	12	1	50	1	1nb
van Zyl	11	1	97	0	2nb
Williams	21	0	81	2	3w
Durant	21	2	86	1	1w
N.R.P.Scholtz	7	1	35	1	
Slabber	3	0	17	0	

Gauteng Bowling
	O	M	R	W			O	M	R	W	
Keiller	10	6	13	0		(4)	5	1	23	1	1w,1nb
Burger	15	9	21	1		(1)	11	6	10	2	
Mathebula	10	2	32	3	1w,8nb		13	1	37	1	4nb
Nkwe	6	1	22	1	1w						
le Roux	5	1	18	1	3nb	(2)	12	5	35	4	1nb
Deeb	16	3	48	2			2	1	5	0	
Symes	10.2	3	25	2		(5)	5.5	1	16	2	

Umpires: C.L.Joubert and L.J.Willemse.   Toss: Gauteng

Close of Play: 1st day: Gauteng (1) 378-6 (le Roux 65*, Burger 15*, 80.1 overs); 2nd day: Namibia (2) 84-5 (Durant 13*, Ludik 19*, 25 overs).

NORTH WEST v ZIMBABWE PROVINCES

Played at Sedgars Park, Potchefstroom, February 14, 15, 16, 2008.
South African Airways Provincial Three-Day Challenge 2007/08 - Pool B
Match drawn.   (Points: North West 10.14, Zimbabwe Provinces 7.78)

NORTH WEST

1	J.F.Mostert	c Mawoyo b Garwe	60	c Maruma b Garwe		6
2	C.Jonker	c Nyamuzinga b Rainsford	0	lbw b Rainsford		0
3	A.P.Agathagelou	c Matsikenyeri b Maruma	84	lbw b Matsikenyeri		57
4	N.Bredenkamp	c Kasteni b Maruma	80	lbw b Rainsford		1
5	*†T.A.Bula	not out	88	c Nyamuzinga b Chibhabha		67
6	M.Lazenby	b Garwe	0	not out		10
7	V.C.M.Mazibuko	c and b Maruma	17	c Mujuru b Chibhabha		2
8	M.P.Siboto	not out	16	not out		2
9	E.Gerber					
10	K.M.Naicker					
11	P.S.Letsoalo					
	Extras	lb 8, nb 4	12	b 4, lb 10, nb 1		15

(6 wickets) 357	(6 wickets, declared) 160

FoW (1): 1-1 (2), 2-124 (1), 3-170 (3), 4-292 (4), 5-294 (6), 6-329 (7)
FoW (2): 1-5 (2), 2-9 (1), 3-10 (4), 4-119 (3), 5-146 (5), 6-156 (7)

ZIMBABWE PROVINCES

1	†T.M.K.Mawoyo	c Bula b Siboto	50	(8) not out	15
2	F.Kasteni	b Gerber	17	(1) st Bula b Mostert	38
3	B.Mujuru	lbw b Mostert	34		
4	C.J.Chibhabha	c Bredenkamp b Gerber	30	(3) b Mazibuko	4
5	*S.Matsikenyeri	c Jonker b Gerber	0	(2) c Siboto b Gerber	55
6	T.Maruma	not out	74	(5) c Lazenby b Mostert	3
7	S.K.Nyamuzinga	c Agathagelou b Naicker	31	(4) not out	59
8	N.B.Mahwire	c Mazibuko b Mostert	34	(6) c Gerber b Mostert	4
9	A.M.Manyumwa	b Mostert	4		
10	T.N.Garwe	not out	0	(7) st Bula b Mostert	0
11	E.C.Rainsford				
	Extras	b 8, nb 7	15	b 2, lb 2, nb 2	6

(8 wickets) 289	(6 wickets) 184

FoW (1): 1-39 (2), 2-80 (1), 3-132 (3), 4-136 (4), 5-137 (5), 6-187 (7), 7-266 (8), 8-289 (9)
FoW (2): 1-79 (2), 2-91 (3), 3-121 (1), 4-131 (5), 5-146 (6), 6-147 (7)

Zimbabwe Provinces Bowling

	O	M	R	W			O	M	R	W	
Rainsford	16	1	65	1			6	0	19	2	
Mahwire	12	2	41	0	1nb	(3)	4	0	18	0	
Garwe	17	1	71	2	1nb	(2)	5	0	14	1	
Manyumwa	12	2	53	0		(5)	5	0	23	0	
Maruma	26	5	105	3		(4)	17	3	43	0	1nb
Nyamuzinga	2	0	14	0	2nb						
Matsikenyeri						(6)	5	0	19	1	
Chibhabha						(7)	3	0	10	2	

North West Bowling

	O	M	R	W			O	M	R	W	
Gerber	19	8	40	3			7	0	41	1	
Letsoalo	18	7	47	0	1nb						
Siboto	9	2	30	1	2nb						
Naicker	25	2	96	1	4nb	(2)	7	0	83	0	
Mostert	14	2	68	3		(4)	6	0	16	4	
Mazibuko						(3)	5	0	40	1	2nb

Umpires: C.J.Conradie and B.D.A.Westraadt.   Toss: Zimbabwe Provinces

Close of Play: 1st day: North West (1) 102-1 (Mostert 40*, Agathagelou 61*, 31.1 overs); 2nd day: Zimbabwe Provinces (1) 133-3 (Chibhabha 27*, Matsikenyeri 0*, 43 overs).

NORTHERNS v GRIQUALAND WEST

Played at L.C.de Villiers Oval, Pretoria, February 14, 15, 16, 2008.
South African Airways Provincial Three-Day Challenge 2007/08 - Pool B
Griqualand West won by 52 runs.   (Points: Northerns 6.66, Griqualand West 15.8)

GRIQUALAND WEST

1	M.C.Arthur	c Nkuna b Wagner	13	c Roux b Liebisch	20
2	C.N.Bennett	c Wagner b Liebisch	3	lbw b Wagner	9
3	M.Akoojee	c Ndlovu b Liebisch	3	c Ndlovu b Nel	44
4	A.P.McLaren	c Wagner b Liebisch	18	c Ndlovu b Masekela	65
5	*†W.Bossenger	not out	66	c Ndlovu b Nel	2
6	G.M.Joseph	c Liebisch b Masekela	2	c Ndlovu b Masekela	3
7	C.Pietersen	c Roux b Nel	10	c Ndlovu b Liebisch	20
8	A.R.Swanepoel	c Ndlovu b Nel	0	not out	108
9	D.D.Carolus	b Wagner	16	b Wagner	0
10	R.C.Williams	b Wagner	0	c Ndlovu b Liebisch	20
11	R.Pietersen	c Liebisch b Wagner	0	b Liebisch	6
	Extras	b 1, lb 1, w 3, nb 4	9	b 1, lb 8, w 1, nb 1	11
			140		**308**

FoW (1): 1-8 (2), 2-19 (3), 3-22 (1), 4-48 (4), 5-74 (6), 6-107 (7), 7-109 (8), 8-138 (9), 9-140 (10), 10-140 (11)
FoW (2): 1-29 (1), 2-29 (2), 3-140 (3), 4-142 (4), 5-142 (5), 6-146 (6), 7-195 (8), 8-235 (9), 9-274 (10), 10-308 (11)

NORTHERNS

1	H.E.van der Dussen	c Bossenger b C.Pietersen	2	c McLaren b Carolus	34
2	R.Jappie	c Bossenger b R.Pietersen	32	st Bossenger b Swanepoel	23
3	M.J.Nkuna	c Bossenger b Williams	5	c Bossenger b R.Pietersen	1
4	S.W.Liebisch	c Arthur b R.Pietersen	45	(6) c McLaren b C.Pietersen	36
5	P.J.van Biljon	b R.Pietersen	7	c McLaren b Carolus	9
6	*A.M.Phangiso	not out	42	(7) c Bossenger b R.Pietersen	23
7	L.G.Nel	c Bossenger b Carolus	23	(8) b Carolus	11
8	†A.L.Ndlovu	c McLaren b Swanepoel	10	(4) lbw b Carolus	49
9	A.Roux	c C.Pietersen b Swanepoel	0	lbw b R.Pietersen	16
10	N.Wagner	c McLaren b R.Pietersen	2	c Bossenger b Carolus	1
11	L.M.G.Masekela	lbw b Swanepoel	0	not out	0
	Extras	lb 3, w 11, nb 1	15	lb 5, w 5	10
			183		**213**

FoW (1): 1-2 (1), 2-19 (3), 3-83 (2), 4-94 (4), 5-96 (5), 6-139 (7), 7-170 (8), 8-170 (9), 9-182 (10), 10-183 (11)
FoW (2): 1-41 (2), 2-43 (3), 3-78 (1), 4-88 (5), 5-149 (4), 6-180 (4), 7-192 (8), 8-194 (7), 9-205 (10), 10-213 (9)

Northerns Bowling

	O	M	R	W			O	M	R	W	
Wagner	12.4	0	48	4	2w,2nb	(4)	14	1	81	2	1w
Liebisch	14	4	47	3	1w,2nb	(1)	16.4	4	62	4	
Nel	6	0	20	2		(5)	8	1	40	2	
Masekela	4	0	23	1		(6)	6.1	1	16	2	
Roux						(2)	13.5	1	52	0	
Phangiso						(3)	12	1	48	0	1nb

Griqualand West Bowling

	O	M	R	W			O	M	R	W	
C.Pietersen	20	4	40	1	5w		21	8	48	1	3w
Williams	13	2	29	1		(4)	8	1	24	0	
R.Pietersen	14	1	52	4	4w		14.2	5	29	3	1w
Carolus	11	0	34	1	2w	(5)	16	5	25	5	1w
Swanepoel	10	2	25	3	1nb	(2)	28	5	82	5	

Umpires: A.T.Holdstock and B.M.White.   Toss: Northerns

Close of Play: 1st day: Northerns (1) 96-4 (van Biljon 7*, Phangiso 0*, 35 overs); 2nd day: Northerns (2) 12-0 (van der Dussen 8*, Jappie 4*, 4 overs).

A.R.Swanepoel's 108 took 95 balls in 126 minutes and included 9 fours and 5 sixes.

WESTERN PROVINCE v BORDER

Played at Sahara Park Newlands, Cape Town, February 14, 15, 2008.
South African Airways Provincial Three-Day Challenge 2007/08 - Pool A
Western Province won by an innings and 5 runs.   (Points: Western Province 18.4, Border 4)

BORDER

1	S.de Kock	c Sodumo b Birch	1	c Gray b Simpson	7
2	M.F.Richardson	b Simpson	5	lbw b Simpson	7
3	S.Makongolo	c Gray b de Stadler	24	c Levi b Temoor	28
4	*M.N.Ranger	c Sodumo b Simpson	0	c Levi b de Stadler	4
5	†A.Z.M.Dyili	b Birch	5	c Tsolekile b de Stadler	30
6	L.Masingatha	b van Wyk	15	lbw b de Stadler	7
7	S.Booi	c Temoor b de Stadler	2	c Sodumo b Temoor	1
8	D.L.Brown	lbw b Birch	3	c Temoor b de Stadler	69
9	L.Mbane	c Levi b de Stadler	8	c Gray b Temoor	20
10	M.W.Olivier	lbw b Simpson	3	st Tsolekile b Temoor	2
11	Y.Pangabantu	not out	5	not out	6
	Extras	lb 9, w 2, nb 1	12	lb 1	1
			83		**182**

FoW (1): 1-2 (1), 2-10 (2), 3-13 (4), 4-33 (5), 5-45 (3), 6-51 (7), 7-59 (6), 8-70 (9), 9-77 (10), 10-83 (8)
FoW (2): 1-7 (2), 2-30 (1), 3-42 (4), 4-68 (3), 5-84 (5), 6-85 (7), 7-85 (6), 8-106 (9), 9-114 (10), 10-182 (8)

WESTERN PROVINCE

1	A.J.A.Gray	b Pangabantu	60
2	M.Williamson	c Mbane b Pangabantu	8
3	R.E.Levi	b Pangabantu	6
4	A.M.Sodumo	c Booi b Brown	6
5	†T.L.Tsolekile	run out (Mbane)	55
6	*J.P.Geoghegan	c Pangabantu b Brown	19
7	E.P.van Wyk	c and b Brown	0
8	C.W.S.Birch	c Dyili b Mbane	36
9	M.de Stadler	c Dyili b Mbane	28
10	A.A.Temoor	c Ranger b de Kock	21
11	L.F.Simpson	not out	2
	Extras	lb 10, nb 19	29
			270

FoW (1): 1-24 (2), 2-32 (3), 3-70 (4), 4-134 (1), 5-165 (6), 6-165 (7), 7-194 (5), 8-218 (8), 9-268 (9), 10-270 (10)

Western Province Bowling

	O	M	R	W		O	M	R	W
Simpson	9	3	17	3	2w	8	2	16	2
Birch	9.3	4	17	3	1nb	7	1	19	0
de Stadler	12	6	17	3	(4)	13.1	3	42	4
van Wyk	10	4	23	1	(3)	5	2	16	0
Temoor					(5)	13	6	58	4
Gray					(6)	4	0	30	0

Border Bowling

	O	M	R	W	
Olivier	14	1	73	0	19nb
Pangabantu	18	7	60	3	
Brown	19	5	62	3	
Mbane	12	1	42	2	
Ranger	3	0	16	0	
de Kock	2	1	7	1	

Umpires: L.B.Gcuma and B.N.Harrison.   Toss: Western Province

Close of Play: 1st day: Western Province (1) 183-6 (Tsolekile 54*, Birch 10*, 44 overs).

The match was scheduled for three days but completed in two.

BORDER v KWAZULU-NATAL INLAND

Played at Mercedes Benz Park, East London, February 21, 22, 23, 2008.
South African Airways Provincial Three-Day Challenge 2007/08 - Pool A
Match drawn.   (Points: Border 8.16, KwaZulu-Natal Inland 7.02)

BORDER

1	S.de Kock	b Brown	17	c and b Bowyer	76
2	M.F.Richardson	c Brown b Humphries	6	c McMillan b Bowyer	44
3	S.Makongolo	b McMillan	23	(4) b McMillan	16
4	†A.Z.M.Dyili	c McMillan b Brown	16	(3) b Nipper	0
5	L.Masingatha	c Padayachee b Qasim Khurshid	48	b McMillan	37
6	S.Booi	b Qasim Khurshid	68	(7) c Bowyer b Nipper	14
7	*D.L.Brown	c Harridave b Humphries	27	(8) lbw b Bowyer	12
8	M.M.Joko	c Drummond b Qasim Khurshid	5	(9) not out	12
9	L.Mbane	lbw b Brown	15	(6) c Humphries b McMillan	0
10	M.W.Olivier	c Drummond b McMillan	17	not out	13
11	Y.Pangabantu	not out	3		
	Extras	b 5, lb 2, w 1, nb 5	13	b 1, lb 2, nb 4	7
			258	(8 wickets, declared)	231

FoW (1): 1-12 (2), 2-47 (1), 3-59 (3), 4-67 (4), 5-181 (5), 6-189 (6), 7-198 (8), 8-214 (9), 9-249 (7), 10-258 (10)
FoW (2): 1-120 (1), 2-121 (3), 3-125 (2), 4-156 (4), 5-156 (6), 6-185 (7), 7-198 (5), 8-213 (8)

KWAZULU-NATAL INLAND

1	K.Padayachee	c Brown b Olivier	2	run out	38
2	C.S.Bowyer	run out (de Kock)	11	run out (de Kock)	37
3	†T.J.Drummond	c Booi b Pangabantu	9	c and b de Kock	13
4	*R.D.McMillan	c Dyili b Makongolo	69	c Dyili b de Kock	37
5	L.Brown	b Olivier	8	(6) c Masingatha b Makongolo	14
6	M.Gqadushe	c and b de Kock	32	(5) b Makongolo	41
7	K.Nipper	c Booi b Brown	22	(8) not out	3
8	O.E.Humphries	lbw b Olivier	21	(7) not out	16
9	S.Dorasamy	c Booi b Olivier	8		
10	Qasim Khurshid	not out	4		
11	N.Harridave	c Dyili b Olivier	0		
	Extras	lb 4, w 2, nb 9	15	b 2, nb 8	10
			201	(6 wickets)	209

FoW (1): 1-13 (1), 2-18 (2), 3-29 (3), 4-66 (5), 5-114 (6), 6-165 (7), 7-169 (4), 8-190 (9), 9-200 (8), 10-201 (11)
FoW (2): 1-50 (2), 2-74 (3), 3-107 (1), 4-176 (5), 5-180 (4), 6-198 (6)

KwaZulu-Natal Inland Bowling

	O	M	R	W			O	M	R	W	
Qasim Khurshid	15	5	39	3	1nb		16	5	42	0	
Humphries	13	3	47	2	3nb		7	1	37	0	2nb
McMillan	10.1	5	34	2	1nb		15	4	24	3	1nb
Brown	9	1	45	3	1w		3	1	5	0	1nb
Nipper	9	1	36	0			26	4	80	2	
Harridave	8	0	23	0							
Dorasamy	2	0	6	0							
Bowyer	8	1	21	0		(6)	18	2	40	3	

Border Bowling

	O	M	R	W			O	M	R	W	
Olivier	12	0	53	5	1w,9nb		9.4	1	56	0	8nb
Pangabantu	14	4	37	1			4	0	25	0	
Mbane	9	1	38	0		(5)	7	3	19	0	
Brown	13	4	30	1	1w	(3)	7	3	13	0	
de Kock	9	4	20	1		(4)	26	9	57	2	
Makongolo	6	0	19	1			10	2	37	2	

Umpires: L.M.Engelbrecht and J.E.P.Ostrom.   Toss: KwaZulu-Natal Inland

Close of Play: 1st day: KwaZulu-Natal Inland (1) 46-3 (McMillan 21*, Brown 1*, 14 overs); 2nd day: Border (2) 149-3
(Makongolo 10*, Masingatha 16*, 58 overs).

EASTERNS v GAUTENG

Played at Willowmoore Park Main Oval, Benoni, February 21, 22, 23, 2008.
South African Airways Provincial Three-Day Challenge 2007/08 - Pool B
Match drawn.   (Points: Easterns 6.7, Gauteng 10.66)

GAUTENG

1	J.Symes	c Toyana b Mutch	5	c Bodibe b Mutch	23
2	W.B.Motaung	b Pienaar	0	lbw b van den Berg	27
3	E.T.Nkwe	run out (Fourie)	67	b Hlengani	35
4	W.C.Swan	c Seymore b van den Berg	13	c Pienaar b Mutch	25
5	*D.L.Makalima	lbw b van den Berg	10	c Pienaar b Hlengani	41
6	D.J.Vilas	c O'Connor b Mutch	120	c Fourie b Toyana	57
7	†M.J.Harris	not out	122	not out	1
8	H.W.le Roux	not out	38		
9	D.R.Deeb				
10	Y.Keiller				
11	B.M.Mathebula				
	Extras	lb 4, w 3, nb 1	8	b 3, lb 7	10
		(6 wickets)	383	(6 wickets, declared)	219

FoW (1): 1-5 (2), 2-5 (1), 3-27 (4), 4-61 (5), 5-179 (3), 6-277 (6)
FoW (2): 1-31 (1), 2-62 (2), 3-116 (3), 4-117 (4), 5-215 (6), 6-219 (5)

EASTERNS

1	I.C.Hlengani	c Makalima b Keiller	21	c le Roux b Mathebula	0
2	†T.M.Bodibe	c Vilas b Deeb	73	c Swan b Deeb	20
3	J.C.Fourie	c Makalima b Keiller	1	(6) c Nkwe b Swan	7
4	A.J.Seymore	lbw b Keiller	0	run out	35
5	J.J.Pienaar	c Makalima b Mathebula	31	lbw b Deeb	0
6	G.Toyana	b Deeb	25	(3) c Symes b le Roux	5
7	*S.P.O'Connor	c Keiller b Deeb	0	not out	29
8	P.P.van den Berg	c Makalima b Deeb	46	c sub (R.Cameron) b Keiller	0
9	D.T.Makua	c and b Deeb	4		
10	R.G.Mutch	not out	27		
11	P.T.Mofokeng	c Nkwe b Deeb	1		
	Extras	lb 5, nb 1	6	w 1, nb 3	4
			235	(7 wickets)	100

FoW (1): 1-29 (1), 2-31 (3), 3-31 (4), 4-86 (5), 5-139 (6), 6-139 (7), 7-176 (2), 8-186 (9), 9-233 (8), 10-235 (11)
FoW (2): 1-7 (1), 2-26 (3), 3-34 (2), 4-34 (5), 5-43 (6), 6-99 (4), 7-100 (8)

Easterns Bowling

	O	M	R	W		O	M	R	W	
Pienaar	19	1	86	1	1nb	11	2	47	0	
Mutch	18	5	73	2		13	4	43	2	
van den Berg	15	3	53	2	(4)	14	7	16	1	
O'Connor	6	1	30	0						
Hlengani	6	0	33	0	(3)	20.1	5	59	2	
Mofokeng	11	0	54	0	3w (5)	14	5	40	0	
Toyana	10	0	50	0	(6)	1	0	4	0	

Gauteng Bowling

	O	M	R	W		O	M	R	W	
Keiller	13	1	50	3	1nb	4	2	5	1	
le Roux	10	4	20	0	(4)	6	3	7	1	1w
Mathebula	9	2	37	1	(2)	7	0	14	1	3nb
Deeb	21.1	3	50	6	(3)	16	3	40	2	
Symes	15	3	36	0	(6)	10	3	19	0	
Nkwe	6	0	28	0	(7)	2	0	7	0	
Swan	2	0	9	0	(5)	3	1	8	1	

Umpires: A.T.Holdstock and I.H.van Kerwel.   Toss: Gauteng

Close of Play: 1st day: Easterns (1) 60-3 (Bodibe 18*, Pienaar 19*, 20 overs); 2nd day: Gauteng (2) 116-3 (Swan 25*, Makalima 0*, 52 overs).
D.J.Vilas's 120 took 143 balls in 171 minutes and included 16 fours. M.J.Harris's 122 took 106 balls in 125 minutes and included 16 fours and 2 sixes.

FREE STATE v NORTH WEST

Played at OUTsurance Oval, Bloemfontein, February 21, 22, 23, 2008.
South African Airways Provincial Three-Day Challenge 2007/08 - Pool B
Free State won by seven wickets.   (Points: Free State 19.48, North West 7.12)

NORTH WEST

1	J.F.Mostert	c von Rauenstein b Vries	38	c Mosena b de Villiers		15
2	C.Jonker	lbw b Vries	27	c Weirich b de Villiers		21
3	M.Lazenby	c Mosena b Saliwa	63	c Terblanche b Saliwa		12
4	N.Bredenkamp	c Mosena b de Villiers	12	(5) b Vries		5
5	*†T.A.Bula	b de Villiers	21	(4) c Mosena b Kops		8
6	V.C.M.Mazibuko	c Weirich b de Villiers	1	lbw b Kops		11
7	M.P.Siboto	c Mosena b Kops	27	lbw b de Villiers		22
8	E.Gerber	c von Rauenstein b Saliwa	23	c Mosena b Fick		0
9	D.Klein	not out	14	c de Villiers b Saliwa		10
10	C.J.Alexander	b Kops	0	c Kops b Saliwa		7
11	P.S.Letsoalo	c Weirich b de Villiers	4	not out		16
	Extras	lb 8, w 9, nb 9	26	lb 7, w 10, nb 1		18
			256			**145**

FoW (1): 1-69 (1), 2-81 (2), 3-103 (4), 4-164 (5), 5-166 (6), 6-187 (3), 7-233 (8), 8-245 (7), 9-245 (10), 10-256 (11)
FoW (2): 1-38 (2), 2-53 (3), 3-53 (1), 4-58 (5), 5-67 (4), 6-87 (6), 7-95 (8), 8-120 (7), 9-120 (9), 10-145 (10)

FREE STATE

1	†L.N.Mosena	c Alexander b Gerber	20	c Siboto b Gerber		9
2	M.P.Fick	run out (Mazibuko)	49	b Alexander		0
3	E.H.Weirich	b Gerber	5	not out		26
4	*H.O.von Rauenstein	c Bula b Alexander	18	c Bula b Alexander		8
5	G.N.Nieuwoudt	c Lazenby b Alexander	78	not out		0
6	R.Jordaan	lbw b Siboto	51			
7	C.J.D.de Villiers	c Lazenby b Mostert	72			
8	R.K.Terblanche	c Letsoalo b Mostert	18			
9	G.A.Vries	lbw b Mostert	0			
10	B.B.Kops	b Alexander	9			
11	M.N.Saliwa	not out	1			
	Extras	b 8, lb 8, w 12, nb 9	37	lb 1, nb 1		2
			358	**(3 wickets)**		**45**

FoW (1): 1-24 (3), 2-45 (4), 3-61 (1), 4-189 (6), 5-224 (5), 6-324 (7), 7-330 (2), 8-330 (9), 9-356 (10), 10-358 (8)
FoW (2): 1-9 (2), 2-11 (1), 3-25 (4)

Free State Bowling

	O	M	R	W		O	M	R	W	
de Villiers	22	5	69	4	2w,2nb	14	4	51	3	2w
Saliwa	12	1	46	2	1w,4nb	11.5	2	43	3	1w,1nb
Kops	17	4	52	2	1w,2nb	9	1	27	2	3w
Vries	8	2	19	2	4w,1nb	7	4	3	1	
Terblanche	4	0	24	0	1w					
Jordaan	8	0	38	0						
Fick					(5)	4	0	14	1	

North West Bowling

	O	M	R	W		O	M	R	W	
Alexander	23	2	88	3	4w	5	0	18	2	
Gerber	15	3	53	2	1w	4.2	1	26	1	1nb
Letsoalo	12	8	21	0						
Klein	6	1	27	0	2w,3nb					
Mazibuko	7	1	39	0	2w,6nb					
Siboto	10	1	46	1	2w					
Mostert	19.4	1	68	3						

Umpires: C.J.Conradie and C.L.Joubert.   Toss: Free State

Close of Play: 1st day: North West (1) 237-7 (Siboto 25*, Klein 4*, 63.5 overs); 2nd day: Free State (1) 358 all out.

M.P.Fick retired hurt in the Free State first innings having scored 1 (team score 10-0) - he returned when the score was 224-5.

KWAZULU-NATAL v SOUTH WESTERN DISTRICTS

Played at Sahara Stadium, Kingsmead, Durban, February 21, 22, 23, 2008.
South African Airways Provincial Three-Day Challenge 2007/08 - Pool A
South Western Districts won by four wickets.   (Points: KwaZulu-Natal 4, South Western Districts 17.42)

KWAZULU-NATAL

1	*†W.L.Madsen	b Fransman	2	c de Wett b Fransman	24
2	D.Govender	lbw b Hartslief	3	lbw b de Wett	85
3	K.Zondo	b Hartslief	6	b Fransman	67
4	M.Bekker	c Beukes b Murray	34	lbw b Hillermann	67
5	C.A.Flowers	c Stuurman b Murray	1	c de Wett b Fransman	5
6	R.Frylinck	lbw b Hillermann	0	c Hugo b Fransman	12
7	K.A.Maharaj	c Avontuur b Hartslief	30	c Hugo b Fransman	37
8	N.D.Hewer	b Fransman	5	b Hartslief	0
9	S.Mlongo	not out	6	b de Wett	0
10	V.Gobind	c Hugo b Hartslief	0	not out	17
11	M.Shezi	b Hartslief	0	b Hartslief	0
	Extras	lb 5	5	lb 5, w 4	9
			92		**323**

FoW (1): 1-10 (2), 2-10 (1), 3-34 (3), 4-37 (5), 5-47 (6), 6-51 (4), 7-77 (8), 8-92 (7), 9-92 (10), 10-92 (11)
FoW (2): 1-62 (1), 2-145 (2), 3-216 (3), 4-252 (4), 5-254 (5), 6-269 (6), 7-283 (8), 8-288 (9), 9-322 (7), 10-323 (11)

SOUTH WESTERN DISTRICTS

1	S.E.Avontuur	lbw b Mlongo	5	c Bekker b Hewer	8
2	*J.A.Beukes	c Madsen b Mlongo	25	c Govender b Flowers	44
3	B.C.de Wett	c Madsen b Mlongo	0	b Shezi	5
4	R.de Reuck	c Bekker b Shezi	18	c Madsen b Shezi	4
5	P.A.Stuurman	lbw b Frylinck	16	b Shezi	14
6	R.E.Hillermann	b Hewer	56	not out	50
7	N.G.Brouwers	c Madsen b Hewer	11	c Govender b Maharaj	16
8	†R.P.Hugo	c Mlongo b Frylinck	10	not out	47
9	N.M.Murray	not out	58		
10	W.Hartslief	c Madsen b Hewer	1		
11	B.L.Fransman	c Madsen b Flowers	6		
	Extras	b 1, lb 5, w 2, nb 7	15	b 3, lb 1, w 1, nb 2	7
			221	**(6 wickets)**	**195**

FoW (1): 1-5 (1), 2-5 (3), 3-36 (4), 4-66 (2), 5-83 (5), 6-100 (7), 7-127 (8), 8-172 (6), 9-187 (10), 10-221 (11)
FoW (2): 1-12 (1), 2-21 (3), 3-31 (4), 4-73 (2), 5-84 (5), 6-116 (7)

South Western Districts Bowling

	O	M	R	W		O	M	R	W	
Fransman	11	5	11	2		24	7	60	5	2w
Hartslief	8.1	0	26	5		20.3	7	65	2	
Murray	7	2	15	2		17	6	49	0	2w
Hillermann	6	1	26	1		12	1	67	1	
Brouwers	4	1	8	0		8	0	48	0	
de Wett	1	0	1	0		12	4	29	2	

KwaZulu-Natal Bowling

	O	M	R	W			O	M	R	W	
Hewer	15	3	63	3	1w,2nb	(2)	10	4	34	1	1w
Mlongo	16	8	33	3	1w,2nb	(1)	12	7	24	0	
Shezi	6	3	19	1			12	2	29	3	2nb
Gobind	10	3	34	0	3nb						
Frylinck	14	4	44	2		(4)	6.5	1	36	0	
Flowers	4.5	0	19	1		(5)	9	1	31	1	
Maharaj	2	0	3	0		(6)	9	0	37	1	

Umpires: B.N.Harrison and C.D.Isaacs.   Toss: South Western Districts

Close of Play: 1st day: South Western Districts (1) 127-7 (Hillermann 34*, Murray 0*, 43.5 overs); 2nd day: KwaZulu-Natal (2) 306-8 (Maharaj 31*, Gobind 7*, 85 overs).

423

NORTHERNS v NAMIBIA

Played at L.C.de Villiers Oval, Pretoria, February 21, 22, 2008.
South African Airways Provincial Three-Day Challenge 2007/08 - Pool B
Northerns won by ten wickets.   (Points: Northerns 18.16, Namibia 5.54)

NAMIBIA

1	P.J.Grove	lbw b Wagner	0	lbw b Wagner		0
2	W.Slabber	c Ndlovu b Liebisch	0	lbw b Wagner		0
3	M.Durant	lbw b Wagner	0	(7) b Roux		24
4	*G.Snyman	c Dikgale b Liebisch	19	(6) c Ndlovu b Masekela		18
5	C.Williams	c Ndlovu b Masekela	42	(4) lbw b Wagner		0
6	G.J.Rudolph	c Jappie b Masekela	18	(3) c Liebisch b Roux		43
7	N.R.P.Scholtz	c Liebisch b Masekela	7	(5) c Jappie b Wagner		5
8	†H.Ludik	c Ndlovu b Masekela	0	c Phangiso b Roux		11
9	K.B.Burger	c Roux b Masekela	31	c and b Phangiso		17
10	M.C.van Zyl	not out	1	not out		3
11	L.Klazinga	b Masekela	5	c van der Dussen b Wagner		6
	Extras	lb 3, nb 1	4	b 2, lb 6, nb 3		11
			127			138

FoW (1): 1-0 (1), 2-1 (2), 3-1 (3), 4-29 (4), 5-78 (5), 6-83 (6), 7-83 (8), 8-110 (7), 9-121 (9), 10-127 (11)
FoW (2): 1-0 (1), 2-2 (2), 3-3 (4), 4-18 (5), 5-60 (6), 6-84 (3), 7-102 (8), 8-129 (9), 9-129 (7), 10-138 (11)

NORTHERNS

1	H.E.van der Dussen	c Snyman b Burger	15	not out		1
2	R.Jappie	c Ludik b Burger	11	not out		2
3	W.T.Dikgale	c Rudolph b Durant	21			
4	L.G.Nel	b Scholtz	42			
5	P.J.van Biljon	c and b Burger	45			
6	S.W.Liebisch	c Rudolph b van Zyl	59			
7	†A.L.Ndlovu	c Ludik b Burger	19			
8	*A.M.Phangiso	lbw b Williams	7			
9	A.Roux	not out	18			
10	N.Wagner	c Ludik b van Zyl	5			
11	L.M.G.Masekela	c Ludik b van Zyl	0			
	Extras	b 1, lb 7, w 3, nb 5	16	lb 2, w 3		5
			258	(no wicket)		8

FoW (1): 1-27 (1), 2-42 (2), 3-99 (3), 4-99 (4), 5-180 (5), 6-216 (7), 7-231 (6), 8-231 (8), 9-248 (10), 10-258 (11)

Northerns Bowling

	O	M	R	W		O	M	R	W	
Wagner	12	6	31	2		18.4	3	48	5	2nb
Liebisch	10	5	23	2	1nb	4	1	14	0	1nb
Nel	5	1	29	0						
Roux	7	5	11	0	(5)	12	5	30	3	
Masekela	8.4	3	30	6	(4)	7	4	4	1	
Phangiso					(3)	17	8	34	1	

Namibia Bowling

	O	M	R	W		O	M	R	W	
Burger	21	2	78	4	1w	2	0	2	0	
Klazinga	11	3	14	0	4nb	1.2	0	4	0	3w
van Zyl	13	3	40	3	1w,1nb					
Scholtz	10	2	18	1						
Durant	10	0	45	1						
Williams	8	1	31	1	1w					
Slabber	8	0	24	0						

Umpires: R.Ellis and B.M.White.   Toss: Namibia

Close of Play: 1st day: Northerns (1) 209-5 (Liebisch 47*, Ndlovu 18*, 57 overs).

The match was scheduled for three days but completed in two.

GRIQUALAND WEST v WESTERN PROVINCE

Played at De Beers Diamond Oval, Kimberley, March 13, 14, 15, 2008.
South African Airways Provincial Three-Day Challenge 2007/08 - Final
Griqualand West won by 42 runs.

GRIQUALAND WEST

1	C.N.Bennett	lbw b Simpson	5	b Birch	17
2	A.K.Kruger	lbw b Simpson	1	c van Wyk b de Stadler	4
3	L.L.Bosman	c Tsolekile b Birch	8	run out	4
4	P.J.Koortzen	lbw b Birch	36	(5) b de Stadler	17
5	*†W.Bossenger	c Sodumo b Simpson	2	(6) c Gray b Birch	38
6	R.R.Hendricks	b Simpson	26	(7) c Telo b van Wyk	4
7	C.Pietersen	c Sodumo b Simpson	20	(8) c de Stadler b Birch	27
8	A.R.Swanepoel	c Tsolekile b de Stadler	0	(9) b Gray	59
9	F.S.Holtzhausen	c Gray b de Stadler	13	(10) c Sodumo b Gray	21
10	J.Coetzee	not out	13	(4) c Tsolekile b van Wyk	25
11	D.D.Carolus	b Birch	0	not out	1
	Extras	lb 14, w 3, nb 3	20	b 3, lb 2, w 2, nb 3	10
			144		**227**

FoW (1): 1-4 (2), 2-22 (3), 3-22 (1), 4-30 (5), 5-91 (4), 6-100 (6), 7-113 (8), 8-121 (7), 9-137 (9), 10-144 (11)
FoW (2): 1-23 (2), 2-27 (1), 3-35 (3), 4-68 (5), 5-92 (4), 6-96 (7), 7-136 (8), 8-160 (6), 9-214 (10), 10-227 (9)

WESTERN PROVINCE

1	A.J.A.Gray	c Bossenger b Coetzee	26	lbw b Coetzee	2
2	M.Williamson	c Swanepoel b Pietersen	4	lbw b Coetzee	3
3	R.E.Levi	b Carolus	49	c Hendricks b Pietersen	15
4	F.D.Telo	b Pietersen	28	not out	99
5	A.M.Sodumo	c Hendricks b Pietersen	9	c Hendricks b Pietersen	6
6	†T.L.Tsolekile	c Coetzee b Pietersen	0	c Bossenger b Holtzhausen	16
7	E.P.van Wyk	c Hendricks b Coetzee	21	c Bennett b Carolus	21
8	C.W.S.Birch	c Bossenger b Carolus	2	c Swanepoel b Coetzee	4
9	M.de Stadler	c Bossenger b Coetzee	6	lbw b Pietersen	1
10	*P.R.Adams	not out	1	lbw b Pietersen	0
11	L.F.Simpson	c Bosman b Coetzee	0	run out	0
	Extras	lb 4, w 2, nb 3	9	lb 3, w 3, nb 1	7
			155		**174**

FoW (1): 1-16 (2), 2-73 (1), 3-106 (3), 4-117 (4), 5-117 (6), 6-126 (5), 7-140 (8), 8-152 (7), 9-155 (9), 10-155 (11)
FoW (2): 1-4 (2), 2-11 (1), 3-30 (3), 4-53 (5), 5-124 (6), 6-162 (7), 7-167 (8), 8-170 (9), 9-170 (10), 10-174 (11)

Western Province Bowling

	O	M	R	W			O	M	R	W	
Simpson	13	3	27	5			2	1	6	0	1w
Birch	14	4	41	3	2w,3nb		17	3	65	3	1w,3nb
van Wyk	4	0	27	0	1w	(4)	7	0	45	2	
de Stadler	14	5	35	2		(3)	21	6	66	2	
Adams						(5)	6	0	34	0	
Gray						(6)	2.4	0	6	2	

Griqualand West Bowling

	O	M	R	W			O	M	R	W	
Pietersen	18	6	41	4			20.1	3	64	4	
Holtzhausen	11	2	37	0	1w,3nb	(3)	10	2	35	1	1nb
Kruger	5	0	32	0		(5)	2	0	14	0	1w
Coetzee	6.5	2	8	4	1w	(2)	13	3	29	3	1w
Carolus	9	3	16	2		(4)	9	4	13	1	1w
Swanepoel	8	2	17	0			4	1	16	0	

Umpires: B.M.White and L.J.Willemse. Referee: M.Gajjar. Toss: Western Province

Close of Play: 1st day: Western Province (1) 142-7 (van Wyk 15*, de Stadler 0*, 49 overs); 2nd day: Western Province (2) 43-3 (Telo 21*, Sodumo 0*, 19.5 overs).

The match was scheduled for four days but completed in three.

SRI LANKA CRICKET XI v TAMIL NADU

Played at Colts Cricket Club Ground, Colombo, September 26, 27, 28, 2007.
Gopalan Trophy 2007/08
Sri Lanka Cricket XI won by an innings and 96 runs.

TAMIL NADU

1	A.Mukund	c Paranavitana b Welagedara	11	c Suraj b Prasad	20
2	M.Vijay Krishna	c Jayawardene b Amerasinghe	1	c Vithana b Welagedara	9
3	E.Suresh	lbw b Welagedara	0	(5) lbw b Herath	7
4	K.Vasudevadas	c Paranavitana b Welagedara	4	b Welagedara	8
5	R.Srinivasan	c Jayawardene b Prasad	2	(3) c Warnapura b Prasad	73
6	S.Suresh Kumar	b Prasad	4	c Jayawardene b Welagedara	41
7	†H.Gopinath	run out	18	b Welagedara	0
8	*R.Ashwin	c Jayawardene b Prasad	4	lbw b Herath	12
9	C.Ganapathy	b Welagedara	14	(10) c Prasad b Welagedara	23
10	R.Naresh	not out	12	(9) c Nawela b Amerasinghe	0
11	P.Amarnath	b Welagedara	2	not out	0
	Extras	b 1, lb 1	2	b 1, lb 3, w 2, nb 3	9
			74		**202**

FoW (1): 1-12, 2-12, 3-13, 4-16, 5-21, 6-22, 7-31, 8-46, 9-60, 10-74
FoW (2): 1-27, 2-33, 3-44, 4-71, 5-162, 6-162, 7-164, 8-170, 9-190, 10-202

SRI LANKA CRICKET XI

1	M.G.Vandort	c Mukund b Ashwin	32
2	N.T.Paranavitana	c Gopinath b Ganapathy	166
3	H.E.Vithana	c Vijay Krishna b Ganapathy	29
4	*B.S.M.Warnapura	c Vijay Krishna b Naresh	31
5	†H.A.P.W.Jayawardene	c Ashwin b Naresh	4
6	N.M.N.P.Nawela	c Vasudevadas b Amarnath	13
7	K.T.G.D.Prasad	run out	57
8	H.M.R.K.B.Herath	not out	18
9	M.M.M.Suraj	c Gopinath b Ashwin	5
10	U.W.M.B.C.A.Welagedara	c Vijay Krishna b Ashwin	5
11	M.K.D.I.Amerasinghe		
	Extras	b 4, lb 5, w 2, nb 1	12
		(9 wickets, declared)	**372**

FoW (1): 1-70, 2-141, 3-207, 4-221, 5-245, 6-330, 7-355, 8-360, 9-372

Sri Lanka Cricket XI Bowling

	O	M	R	W		O	M	R	W	
Welagedara	12.4	2	34	5		17.3	3	61	5	1w,3nb
Amerasinghe	8	5	6	1		9	2	39	1	
Prasad	5	2	18	3		11	3	23	2	1w
Herath	9	2	12	0		15	3	33	2	
Suraj	2	1	2	0		7	1	28	0	
Warnapura					(6)	3	0	14	0	

Tamil Nadu Bowling

	O	M	R	W	
Ganapathy	21	1	84	2	1w,1nb
Amarnath	16	2	77	1	
Naresh	20	4	74	2	1w
Ashwin	27.4	3	100	3	
Suresh Kumar	5	1	21	0	
Vasudevadas	3	0	7	0	

Umpires: A.G.Dissanayake and M.G.Silva.　　　　　　　　　Toss: Sri Lanka Cricket XI

Close of Play: 1st day: Sri Lanka Cricket XI (1) 202-2 (Paranavitana 103*, Warnapura 26*); 2nd day: Tamil Nadu (2) 154-4 (Srinivasan 67*, Suresh Kumar 38*).

The match was scheduled for four days but completed in three. N.T.Paranavitana's 166 took 229 balls and included 20 fours and 1 six.

SRI LANKA BOARD PRESIDENT'S XI v ENGLAND XI

Played at Nondescripts Cricket Club Ground, Colombo, November 25, 26, 27, 2007.
England in Sri Lanka 2007/08
England XI won by five wickets.

SRI LANKA BOARD PRESIDENT'S XI

1	W.U.Tharanga	c Bell b Anderson	86	b Hoggard	5
2	M.L.Udawatte	c Vaughan b Hoggard	18	c Prior b Bopara	45
3	B.S.M.Warnapura	c Prior b Bopara	16	lbw b Bopara	4
4	*T.M.Dilshan	c Anderson b Harmison	23	c Shah b Hoggard	3
5	J.Mubarak	c Prior b Hoggard	68	lbw b Hoggard	0
6	C.K.Kapugedera	c Bopara b Hoggard	13	c sub (P.D.Collingwood) b Hoggard	0
7	†J.K.Silva	c Cook b Panesar	53	c Prior b Hoggard	2
8	K.S.Lokuarachchi	lbw b Panesar	0	absent hurt	0
9	W.R.S.de Silva	not out	1	(8) run out	4
10	U.W.M.B.C.A.Welagedara	c Cook b Panesar	1	(9) c Prior b Anderson	9
11	M.K.D.I.Amerasinghe	not out	0	(10) not out	0
	Extras	b 6, lb 7, nb 6	19	b 4, lb 2, nb 3	9
		(9 wickets, declared)	298		81

FoW (1): 1-55 (2), 2-79 (3), 3-116 (4), 4-158 (1), 5-182 (6), 6-287 (7), 7-287 (8), 8-297 (5), 9-298 (10)
FoW (2): 1-9 (1), 2-14 (3), 3-32 (4), 4-32 (5), 5-32 (6), 6-40 (7), 7-52 (8), 8-75 (2), 9-81 (9)

ENGLAND XI

1	A.N.Cook	lbw b Lokuarachchi	35	lbw b Mubarak	58
2	*M.P.Vaughan	b de Silva	0	c Dilshan b Mubarak	28
3	I.R.Bell	c J.K.Silva b de Silva	3	c Welagedara b Dilshan	6
4	K.P.Pietersen	c J.K.Silva b Welagedara	1	c J.K.Silva b Kapugedera	59
5	O.A.Shah	b Amerasinghe	26	not out	33
6	R.S.Bopara	c Kapugedera b de Silva	47	c and b Mubarak	21
7	†M.J.Prior	c Warnapura b Kapugedera	10	not out	27
8	M.J.Hoggard	b de Silva	0		
9	J.M.Anderson	b Welagedara	0		
10	M.S.Panesar	not out	0		
11	S.J.Harmison	absent hurt	0		
	Extras	lb 3, nb 9	12	lb 3, w 2, nb 10	15
			134	(5 wickets)	247

FoW (1): 1-6 (2), 2-20 (3), 3-21 (4), 4-44 (1), 5-98 (5), 6-123 (7), 7-125 (8), 8-134 (6), 9-134 (9)
FoW (2): 1-50 (2), 2-74 (3), 3-139 (1), 4-167 (4), 5-210 (6)

England XI Bowling

	O	M	R	W			O	M	R	W	
Hoggard	17	3	57	3	2nb		9	3	25	5	
Anderson	15.3	4	55	1	1nb	(5)	1	0	4	1	
Harmison	10.3	1	45	1	1nb						
Bopara	11	2	43	1	1nb	(2)	10	2	32	2	3nb
Panesar	22	4	67	3		(3)	9	4	14	0	
Pietersen	4	0	15	0		(4)	1	1	0	0	
Vaughan	1	0	3	0							

Sri Lanka Board President's XI Bowling

	O	M	R	W			O	M	R	W	
Welagedara	10.2	2	35	2	4nb		11	1	38	0	1w,4nb
de Silva	10	1	41	4	5nb		10	0	53	0	1w,3nb
Kapugedera	7	2	15	1		(6)	7	1	24	1	
Amerasinghe	11	4	16	1		(3)	9	0	38	0	
Lokuarachchi	7.2	3	9	1							
Dilshan	4.4	0	15	0		(5)	9	1	34	0	
Mubarak						(4)	15	0	57	3	3nb

Umpires: R.Martinesz and W.A.Senanayake.   Toss: Sri Lanka Board President's XI

Close of Play: 1st day: Sri Lanka Board President's XI (1) 298-9 (de Silva 1*, Amerasinghe 0*, 81 overs); 2nd day: Sri Lanka Board President's XI (2) 77-8 (Welagedara 5*, Amerasinghe 0*, 28.4 overs).

SRI LANKA v ENGLAND

Played at Asgiriya Stadium, Kandy, December 1, 2, 3, 4, 5, 2007.
England in Sri Lanka 2007/08 - 1st Test
Sri Lanka won by 88 runs.

SRI LANKA

1	M.G.Vandort	c Vaughan b Hoggard	8	c Bell b Anderson	49
2	S.T.Jayasuriya	c Pietersen b Sidebottom	10	lbw b Hoggard	78
3	K.C.Sangakkara	c Collingwood b Anderson	92	c Vaughan b Collingwood	152
4	*D.P.M.D.Jayawardene	c Prior b Hoggard	1	c Prior b Hoggard	65
5	L.P.C.Silva	c Prior b Hoggard	2	lbw b Panesar	37
6	J.Mubarak	c Prior b Hoggard	0	c sub (G.P.Swann) b Panesar	9
7	†H.A.P.W.Jayawardene	c Cook b Panesar	51	b Collingwood	20
8	W.P.U.J.C.Vaas	b Panesar	12	not out	6
9	C.R.D.Fernando	c Vaughan b Panesar	0	(10) not out	9
10	S.L.Malinga	not out	1	(9) b Panesar	2
11	M.Muralitharan	run out (Bopara/Anderson)	1		
	Extras	lb 8, nb 2	10	b 5, lb 10	15
			188	(8 wickets, declared)	442

FoW (1): 1-11 (2), 2-29 (1), 3-40 (4), 4-42 (5), 5-42 (6), 6-148 (7), 7-180 (8), 8-182 (9), 9-186 (3), 10-188 (11)
FoW (2): 1-113 (2), 2-166 (1), 3-288 (4), 4-359 (5), 5-387 (6), 6-423 (7), 7-426 (3), 8-429 (9)

ENGLAND

1	A.N.Cook	lbw b Vaas	0	c Silva b Vaas	4
2	*M.P.Vaughan	c Silva b Muralitharan	37	c H.A.P.W.Jayawardene b Vaas	5
3	I.R.Bell	c Silva b Muralitharan	83	(4) b Muralitharan	74
4	K.P.Pietersen	lbw b Muralitharan	31	(5) b Fernando	18
5	P.D.Collingwood	b Muralitharan	45	(6) c Sangakkara b Fernando	16
6	R.S.Bopara	c H.A.P.W.Jayawardene b Muralitharan	8	(7) lbw b Jayasuriya	34
7	†M.J.Prior	c Mubarak b Fernando	0	(8) b Muralitharan	63
8	R.J.Sidebottom	c H.A.P.W.Jayawardene b Malinga	31	(9) lbw b Muralitharan	1
9	M.J.Hoggard	st H.A.P.W.Jayawardene b Muralitharan	15	(10) b Malinga	8
10	J.M.Anderson	lbw b Vaas	9	(3) b Vaas	11
11	M.S.Panesar	not out	2	not out	2
	Extras	b 6, lb 1, w 2, nb 11	20	b 5, lb 9, nb 11	25
			281		261

FoW (1): 1-0 (1), 2-107 (2), 3-132 (3), 4-170 (4), 5-182 (6), 6-185 (7), 7-242 (8), 8-266 (5), 9-272 (9), 10-281 (10)
FoW (2): 1-4 (1), 2-22 (2), 3-27 (3), 4-55 (5), 5-90 (6), 6-139 (7), 7-248 (8), 8-249 (4), 9-253 (9), 10-261 (10)

England Bowling

	O	M	R	W			O	M	R	W	
Sidebottom	15	1	58	1		(2)	25	5	65	0	
Hoggard	14	3	29	4	1nb	(1)	18	5	55	2	
Anderson	15.4	3	39	1		(4)	23	4	128	1	
Bopara	1	0	8	0	1nb	(5)	8	3	16	0	
Panesar	14	4	46	3		(3)	45	5	132	3	
Vaughan						(6)	3	0	6	0	
Collingwood						(7)	8	0	25	2	

Sri Lanka Bowling

	O	M	R	W		O	M	R	W	
Vaas	18.1	3	76	2	2nb	17	3	56	3	5nb
Malinga	20	2	86	1	2w,8nb	15	3	39	1	4nb
Muralitharan	35	14	55	6		36	12	85	3	1nb
Jayasuriya	2	0	9	0		14	6	28	1	
Fernando	18	2	48	1		12	1	39	2	1nb

Umpires: Aleem Dar and Asad Rauf. Third umpire: T.H.Wijewardene. Referee: J.J.Crowe.   Toss: Sri Lanka

Close of Play: 1st day: England (1) 49-1 (Vaughan 13*, Bell 36*, 17 overs); 2nd day: England (1) 186-6 (Collingwood 14*, Sidebottom 1*, 63 overs); 3rd day: Sri Lanka (2) 167-2 (Sangakkara 30*, D.P.M.D.Jayawardene 0*, 52 overs); 4th day: England (2) 9-1 (Vaughan 1*, Anderson 4*, 5 overs).

Man of the Match: K.C.Sangakkara.
K.C.Sangakkara's 152 took 269 balls in 397 minutes and included 19 fours.

SRI LANKA v ENGLAND

Played at Sinhalese Sports Club Ground, Colombo, December 9, 10, 11, 12, 13, 2007.
England in Sri Lanka 2007/08 - 2nd Test
Match drawn.

ENGLAND

1	A.N.Cook	lbw b Malinga	81	c D.P.M.D.Jayawardene b Silva		62
2	*M.P.Vaughan	c Mubarak b Muralitharan	87	c and b Fernando		61
3	I.R.Bell	c Mubarak b Muralitharan	15	c Vandort b Muralitharan		54
4	K.P.Pietersen	c Sangakkara b Vaas	1	not out		45
5	P.D.Collingwood	lbw b Vaas	52	not out		23
6	R.S.Bopara	b Malinga	0			
7	†M.J.Prior	c and b Muralitharan	79			
8	S.C.J.Broad	lbw b Malinga	2			
9	R.J.Sidebottom	c D.P.M.D.Jayawardene b Muralitharan	17			
10	S.J.Harmison	c Silva b Muralitharan	0			
11	M.S.Panesar	not out	0			
	Extras	b 8, lb 2, nb 7	17	nb 5		5
			351	**(3 wickets)**		**250**

FoW (1): 1-133 (2), 2-168 (3), 3-171 (4), 4-237 (1), 5-237 (6), 6-269 (5), 7-272 (8), 8-346 (9), 9-350 (10), 10-351 (7)
FoW (2): 1-107 (2), 2-152 (1), 3-204 (3)

SRI LANKA

1	M.G.Vandort	lbw b Sidebottom	138
2	W.U.Tharanga	c Prior b Sidebottom	10
3	K.C.Sangakkara	c Prior b Sidebottom	1
4	*D.P.M.D.Jayawardene	c Collingwood b Panesar	195
5	L.P.C.Silva	c Bopara b Harmison	49
6	J.Mubarak	c Bell b Harmison	9
7	†H.A.P.W.Jayawardene	c Prior b Harmison	79
8	W.P.U.J.C.Vaas	c Bell b Broad	4
9	S.L.Malinga	lbw b Panesar	9
10	C.R.D.Fernando	not out	36
11	M.Muralitharan		
	Extras	b 7, lb 9, w 1, nb 1	18
		(9 wickets, declared)	**548**

FoW (1): 1-20 (2), 2-22 (3), 3-249 (1), 4-377 (5), 5-399 (6), 6-420 (4), 7-425 (8), 8-450 (9), 9-548 (7)

Sri Lanka Bowling	O	M	R	W			O	M	R	W	
Vaas	32	8	68	2	2nb		16	2	56	0	2nb
Malinga	24	3	78	3	4nb		8	1	37	0	1nb
Fernando	23	3	79	0	1nb		10	0	30	1	
Muralitharan	47.2	9	116	5		(5)	27	5	58	0	1nb
Mubarak						(4)	1	0	8	0	
D.P.M.D.Jayawardene						(6)	2	1	4	0	
Silva						(7)	13	1	57	1	1nb

England Bowling	O	M	R	W	
Sidebottom	36	4	100	3	1w
Broad	36	5	95	1	
Harmison	41.5	9	111	3	1nb
Panesar	50	7	151	2	
Pietersen	15	0	57	0	
Collingwood	1	1	0	0	
Bopara	7	2	18	0	

Umpires: Aleem Dar and D.J.Harper. Third umpire: M.G.Silva. Referee: J.J.Crowe.   Toss: England

Close of Play: 1st day: England (1) 258-5 (Collingwood 49*, Prior 10*, 87 overs); 2nd day: Sri Lanka (1) 105-2 (Vandort 50*, D.P.M.D.Jayawardene 43*, 38 overs); 3rd day: Sri Lanka (1) 379-4 (D.P.M.D.Jayawardene 167*, Mubarak 2*, 128 overs); 4th day: England (2) 48-0 (Cook 19*, Vaughan 28*, 13 overs).

Man of the Match: D.P.M.D.Jayawardene.
M.G.Vandort's 138 took 259 balls in 348 minutes and included 18 fours and 1 six. D.P.M.D.Jayawardene's 195 took 422 balls in 578 minutes and included 16 fours and 1 six.

SRI LANKA v ENGLAND

Played at Galle International Stadium, December 18, 19, 20, 21, 22, 2007.
England in Sri Lanka 2007/08 - 3rd Test
Match drawn.

SRI LANKA

1	M.G.Vandort	lbw b Sidebottom	18
2	W.U.Tharanga	lbw b Harmison	16
3	K.C.Sangakkara	c Panesar b Harmison	46
4	*D.P.M.D.Jayawardene	not out	213
5	L.P.C.Silva	c Bell b Harmison	1
6	T.M.Dilshan	run out (Cook)	84
7	†H.A.P.W.Jayawardene	c Prior b Bopara	0
8	W.P.U.J.C.Vaas	c Vaughan b Hoggard	90
9	S.L.Malinga	b Collingwood	5
10	U.W.M.B.C.A.Welagedara		
11	M.Muralitharan		
	Extras	b 1, lb 14, w 8, nb 3	26
		(8 wickets, declared)	499

FoW (1): 1-34 (1), 2-44 (2), 3-132 (3), 4-138 (5), 5-287 (6), 6-287 (7), 7-470 (8), 8-499 (9)

ENGLAND

1	A.N.Cook	c H.A.P.W.Jayawardene b Vaas	13	c H.A.P.W.Jayawardene b Welagedara	118
2	*M.P.Vaughan	lbw b Vaas	1	c D.P.M.D.Jayawardene b Welagedara	24
3	I.R.Bell	run out (Dilshan)	1	b Muralitharan	34
4	K.P.Pietersen	c H.A.P.W.Jayawardene b Malinga	1	c D.P.M.D.Jayawardene b Muralitharan	30
5	P.D.Collingwood	b Welagedara	29	st H.A.P.W.Jayawardene b Muralitharan	0
6	R.S.Bopara	c Welagedara b Vaas	0	run out	0
7	†M.J.Prior	b Vaas	4	not out	19
8	R.J.Sidebottom	c Dilshan b Muralitharan	11	not out	0
9	S.J.Harmison	not out	9		
10	M.J.Hoggard	c D.P.M.D.Jayawardene b Welagedara	0		
11	M.S.Panesar	run out			
		(Welagedara/H.A.P.W.Jayawardene)	0		
	Extras	b 4, nb 8	12	b 6, lb 5, w 1, nb 14	26
			81	(6 wickets)	251

FoW (1): 1-5 (2), 2-9 (3), 3-22 (1), 4-22 (4), 5-25 (6), 6-33 (7), 7-70 (8), 8-72 (5), 9-72 (10), 10-81 (11)
FoW (2): 1-67 (2), 2-128 (3), 3-200 (4), 4-200 (5), 5-200 (6), 6-250 (1)

England Bowling	O	M	R	W	
Sidebottom	34	8	95	1	1w
Hoggard	32	4	121	1	1w
Harmison	34	4	104	3	2w,3nb
Panesar	26	3	76	0	
Bopara	10	1	39	1	
Collingwood	9.5	2	38	1	1w
Pietersen	3	0	11	0	

Sri Lanka Bowling	O	M	R	W			O	M	R	W	
Vaas	9.5	2	28	4	4nb	(2)	18	7	37	0	2nb
Malinga	9	2	26	1	2nb	(3)	20	3	42	0	3nb
Welagedara	8	1	17	2	2nb	(4)	14	1	59	2	1w,1nb
Muralitharan	4	2	6	1		(1)	38	8	91	3	8nb
Dilshan						(5)	3	1	8	0	
Silva						(6)	2	1	3	0	

Umpires: Asad Rauf and D.J.Harper. Third umpire: E.A.R.de Silva. Referee: J.J.Crowe.   Toss: England

Close of Play: 1st day: Sri Lanka (1) 147-4 (D.P.M.D.Jayawardene 51*, Dilshan 7*, 55 overs); 2nd day: Sri Lanka (1) 384-6 (D.P.M.D.Jayawardene 149*, Vaas 46*, 129 overs); 3rd day: England (2) 2-0 (Cook 1*, Vaughan 1*, 1 over); 4th day: England (2) 102-1 (Cook 53*, Bell 17*, 33.5 overs).

Man of the Match: D.P.M.D.Jayawardene.
D.P.M.D.Jayawardene's 213 took 411 balls in 610 minutes and included 25 fours. A.N.Cook's 118 took 285 balls in 355 minutes and included 12 fours.

BADURELIYA SPORTS CLUB v CHILAW MARIANS CRICKET CLUB

Played at Colts Cricket Club Ground, Colombo, January 17, 18, 19, 20, 2008.
Premier Championship 2007/08 - Tier A
Badureliya Sports Club won by 19 runs.   (Points: Badureliya Sports Club 16.83, Chilaw Marians Cricket Club 4.735)

BADURELIYA SPORTS CLUB

#	Batsman	Dismissal (1)	R	Dismissal (2)	R
1	†D.W.A.N.D.Vitharana	c C.S.Fernando b Eranga	26	c G.A.C.R.Perera b Hettiarachchi	36
2	M.M.D.P.V.Perera	b G.A.C.R.Perera	1	c Eranga b Hettiarachchi	10
3	T.M.N.Sampath	lbw b Ramyakumara	3	b Hettiarachchi	13
4	*R.P.A.H.Wickramaratne	c C.S.Fernando b G.A.C.R.Perera	4	c C.S.Fernando b Eranga	25
5	W.J.S.D.Perera	b Ramyakumara	1	b G.A.C.R.Perera	76
6	K.A.D.M.Fernando	b Hettiarachchi	50	c Ramyakumara b K.H.R.K.Fernando	45
7	R.M.A.R.Ratnayake	c Gunaratne b Hettiarachchi	7	c K.H.R.K.Fernando b Cooray	47
8	P.S.Liyanage	not out	71	c C.S.Fernando b K.H.R.K.Fernando	3
9	M.R.C.N.Bandaratilleke	c C.S.Fernando b Eranga	26	c Udawatte b Cooray	24
10	K.L.S.L.Dias	c Jayasundera b Gunaratne	3	c sub (T.A.M.Siriwardene) b Cooray	11
11	S.D.C.Malinga	lbw b K.H.R.K.Fernando	27	not out	17
	Extras	lb 5, w 2, nb 5	12	b 9, lb 7, w 1, nb 11	28
			231		335

FoW (1): 1-2 (2), 2-5 (3), 3-10 (4), 4-23 (5), 5-60 (1), 6-67 (7), 7-101 (6), 8-152 (9), 9-165 (10), 10-231 (11)
FoW (2): 1-28 (2), 2-58 (3), 3-73 (1), 4-102 (4), 5-230 (6), 6-230 (5), 7-254 (8), 8-306 (9), 9-307 (7), 10-335 (10)

CHILAW MARIANS CRICKET CLUB

#	Batsman	Dismissal (1)	R	Dismissal (2)	R
1	M.L.Udawatte	c M.M.D.P.V.Perera b Fernando	2	c Wickramaratne b Fernando	13
2	N.H.G.Cooray	b Malinga	3	(3) lbw b Ratnayake	114
3	K.H.R.K.Fernando	lbw b Bandaratilleke	84	(5) run out	76
4	M.M.D.N.R.G.Perera	c Wickramaratne b Fernando	4	c Sampath b Fernando	1
5	W.M.G.Ramyakumara	lbw b Malinga	0	(6) c Sampath b Fernando	37
6	†C.S.Fernando	c Wickramaratne b Dias	46	(7) c Vitharana b Fernando	13
7	D.Hettiarachchi	c Sampath b Fernando	8	(11) not out	1
8	L.J.P.Gunaratne	lbw b Malinga	9	(2) lbw b Malinga	13
9	*J.M.P.C.Jayasundera	c W.J.S.D.Perera b Sampath	56	(8) c Sampath b Fernando	9
10	G.A.C.R.Perera	c Sampath b Malinga	6	(9) b Malinga	1
11	R.M.S.Eranga	not out	12	(10) lbw b Dias	10
	Extras	b 1, lb 6, w 4, nb 4	15	b 1, lb 6, w 4, nb 3	14
			245		302

FoW (1): 1-4 (1), 2-10 (2), 3-19 (4), 4-22 (5), 5-114 (6), 6-125 (7), 7-143 (8), 8-191 (3), 9-210 (10), 10-245 (9)
FoW (2): 1-17 (1), 2-34 (2), 3-36 (4), 4-155 (5), 5-219 (6), 6-242 (7), 7-265 (8), 8-266 (9), 9-286 (10), 10-302 (3)

Chilaw Marians Bowling	O	M	R	W		O	M	R	W	
Ramyakumara	8	3	23	2		3	0	19	0	1w
G.A.C.R.Perera	13	2	55	2	1nb	17	2	60	1	4nb
Eranga	14	0	64	2	2w,4nb	19	2	61	1	4nb
Hettiarachchi	14	0	61	2		25.5	5	75	3	2nb
Gunaratne	6	0	18	1		11.1	1	35	0	
Jayasundera	3	0	4	0						
K.H.R.K.Fernando	0.2	0	1	1		(6) 13	1	39	2	
M.M.D.N.R.G.Perera						(7) 3	0	13	0	1nb
Cooray						(8) 4	0	17	3	

Badureliya Bowling	O	M	R	W		O	M	R	W	
Malinga	12	0	49	4	3w	17	3	50	2	
Fernando	16	2	57	3	1nb	21	4	69	5	3w,3nb
Ratnayake	6	0	20	0	1nb	(7) 6.1	0	15	1	
Bandaratilleke	17	2	52	1		16	4	54	0	
Liyanage	7	1	21	0	1w,2nb	(3) 3	0	9	0	
Dias	15	1	36	1		(5) 14	2	44	1	
Sampath	1.1	0	3	1		(6) 7	2	19	0	
W.J.S.D.Perera						(8) 6	1	23	0	
M.M.D.P.V.Perera						(9) 2	0	12	0	

Umpires: B.P.J.Mendis and M.S.K.Nandiweera. Referee: C.T.M.Devaraj.   Toss: Chilaw Marians Cricket Club
Close of Play: 1st day: Chilaw Marians Cricket Club (1) 116-5 (K.H.R.K.Fernando 48*, Hettiarachchi 0*, 27 overs); 2nd day: Badureliya Sports Club (2) 150-4 (W.J.S.D.Perera 38*, Fernando 10*, 40 overs); 3rd day: Chilaw Marians Cricket Club (2) 104-3 (Cooray 25*, K.H.R.K.Fernando 44*, 34 overs).
N.H.G.Cooray's 114 took 259 balls and included 12 fours.

BLOOMFIELD CRICKET AND ATHLETIC CLUB v COLTS CRICKET CLUB

Played at Bloomfield Cricket and Athletic Club Ground, Colombo, January 17, 18, 19, 20, 2008.
Premier Championship 2007/08 - Tier A
Colts Cricket Club won by 29 runs.   (Points: Bloomfield Cricket and Athletic Club 4.19, Colts Cricket Club 16.335)

COLTS CRICKET CLUB

1	*B.S.M.Warnapura	c Gunaratne b Gamage	7	c and b Gamage	2
2	S.Kalavitigoda	lbw b Gamage	0	b Gamage	0
3	M.D.K.Perera	c Jayawardene b Gamage	0	lbw b Katipiarchchi	94
4	H.G.J.M.Kulatunga	c Jayawardene b Ranasinghe	1	c Ranasinghe b Dilshan	78
5	A.D.Mathews	c Jayawardene b Ranasinghe	56	not out	67
6	D.N.Pathirana	c Katipiarchchi b Gamage	5	c Masmulla b Gamage	21
7	†T.R.Peiris	lbw b Ranasinghe	9	lbw b Dissanayake	0
8	K.M.D.N.Kulasekara	c Dilshan b Gamage	11	lbw b Dissanayake	30
9	S.Weerakoon	c Jayawardene b Ranasinghe	23	c Jayawardene b Ranasinghe	17
10	P.D.R.L.Perera	c Silva b Gamage	9	run out	4
11	M.K.D.I.Amerasinghe	not out	0	lbw b Ranasinghe	1
	Extras	b 4, lb 5, w 5, nb 6	20	b 5, lb 2, w 1, nb 4	12
			141		326

FoW (1): 1-2 (2), 2-11 (3), 3-14 (1), 4-14 (4), 5-23 (6), 6-36 (7), 7-90 (8), 8-128 (9), 9-139 (10), 10-141 (5)
FoW (2): 1-0 (2), 2-11 (1), 3-142 (4), 4-198 (3), 5-244 (6), 6-245 (7), 7-284 (8), 8-308 (9), 9-325 (10), 10-326 (11)

BLOOMFIELD CRICKET AND ATHLETIC CLUB

1	T.S.Masmulla	lbw b Amerasinghe	6	c sub (T.P.Attanayake) b Weerakoon	52
2	S.T.Jayasuriya	c Peiris b P.D.R.L.Perera	4	c Pathirana b Kulasekara	8
3	M.T.Gunaratne	c Peiris b P.D.R.L.Perera	23	b Kulasekara	0
4	T.M.Dilshan	c M.D.K.Perera b Kulasekara	6	c Peiris b Kulasekara	2
5	L.P.C.Silva	c P.D.R.L.Perera b M.D.K.Perera	50	c Kulasekara b P.D.R.L.Perera	7
6	†H.A.P.W.Jayawardene	c Amerasinghe b M.D.K.Perera	53	c Peiris b Kulasekara	50
7	W.S.Jayantha	not out	38	c Kulasekara b Weerakoon	0
8	*D.M.G.S.Dissanayake	c Peiris b Kulasekara	6	c Kulatunga b Kulasekara	12
9	A.U.Katipiarachchi	b M.D.K.Perera	32	lbw b Kulasekara	5
10	M.P.Ranasinghe	c Warnapura b M.D.K.Perera	14	not out	6
11	T.P.Gamage	c Weerakoon b P.D.R.L.Perera	18	c Warnapura b Kulasekara	1
	Extras	b 5, lb 9, w 1, nb 16	31	lb 2, w 2, nb 10	14
			281		157

FoW (1): 1-9 (2), 2-29 (1), 3-40 (4), 4-62 (3), 5-127 (5), 6-196 (8), 7-214 (6), 8-235 (10), 9-260 (11), 10-281 (9)
FoW (2): 1-36 (2), 2-37 (3), 3-43 (4), 4-51 (5), 5-121 (1), 6-125 (7), 7-143 (6), 8-144 (8), 9-155 (9), 10-157 (11)

Bloomfield Cricket and Athletic Club Bowling

	O	M	R	W		O	M	R	W	
Ranasinghe	13.2	3	58	4	2w,5nb	19.1	2	84	2	4nb
Gamage	14	1	52	6	2w	22	5	94	3	1w
Katipiarchchi	3	0	12	0	1w,1nb	7	1	29	1	
Dissanayake	2	0	10	0		22	5	59	2	
Dilshan						(5) 9	1	30	1	
Silva						(6) 2	0	13	0	
Jayasuriya						(7) 5	1	10	0	

Colts Cricket Club Bowling

	O	M	R	W		O	M	R	W	
P.D.R.L.Perera	19	2	57	3	3nb	14	1	59	1	2w,4nb
Kulasekara	15	0	35	2	1w,5nb	12.1	3	27	7	6nb
Amerasinghe	12	3	51	1	4nb	5	1	18	0	
Weerakoon	15	1	71	0		(5) 11	1	29	2	
Mathews	8	0	34	0	4nb	(6) 4	0	9	0	
Kulatunga	3	1	3	0						
M.D.K.Perera	11.1	3	16	4		(4) 4	1	13	0	

Umpires: A.G.Dissanayake and B.B.J.Nandakumar.   Referee: V.B.John.   Toss: Bloomfield Cricket and Athletic Club
Close of Play: 1st day: Bloomfield Cricket and Athletic Club (1) 151-5 (Jayawardene 35*, Jayantha 12*, 46 overs); 2nd day: Colts Cricket Club (2) 204-4 (Mathews 24*, Pathirana 1*, 50 overs); 3rd day: Bloomfield Cricket and Athletic Club (2) 156-9 (Ranasinghe 6*, Gamage 0*, 48.2 overs).
W.S.Jayantha retired hurt in the Bloomfield Cricket and Athletic Club first innings having scored 32 (team score 186-5) - he returned when the score was 260-9.

MOORS SPORTS CLUB v COLOMBO CRICKET CLUB

Played at Moors Sports Club Ground, Colombo, January 17, 18, 2008.
Premier Championship 2007/08 - Tier A
Moors Sports Club won by four wickets.   (Points: Moors Sports Club 15.49, Colombo Cricket Club 3.08)

COLOMBO CRICKET CLUB

#	Batsman	Dismissal 1	R1	Dismissal 2	R2
1	M.G.Vandort	c Herath b Welagedara	0	lbw b Welagedara	4
2	†D.K.Ranaweera	lbw b Rideegammanagedera	22	lbw b Rideegammanagedera	16
3	K.G.N.Randika	c Randika b Ranjith	10	c Dilhara b Welagedara	4
4	J.Mubarak	c Rideegammanagedera b Ranjith	67	c Hewage b Rideegammanagedera	12
5	C.K.Kapugedera	c Randika b Rideegammanagedera	0	c and b Herath	25
6	*B.M.T.T.Mendis	c Dilhara b Rideegammanagedera	0	c Randika b Herath	24
7	P.D.G.Chandrakumara	lbw b Herath	10	not out	27
8	M.P.N.L.Perera	c Randika b Herath	20	c Randika b Welagedara	4
9	N.S.Rupasinghe	b Herath	11	lbw b Herath	0
10	W.R.S.de Silva	not out	1	c Hewage b Herath	12
11	M.I.Ratnayake	lbw b Herath	5	c Hewage b Herath	6
	Extras	nb 3	3	b 1, lb 1, nb 11	13
			149		147

FoW (1): 1-0 (1), 2-21 (3), 3-59 (2), 4-59 (5), 5-59 (6), 6-79 (7), 7-130 (4), 8-136 (8), 9-143 (9), 10-149 (11)
FoW (2): 1-9 (1), 2-24 (3), 3-42 (4), 4-44 (2), 5-94 (5), 6-103 (6), 7-122 (8), 8-123 (9), 9-137 (10), 10-147 (11)

MOORS SPORTS CLUB

#	Batsman	Dismissal 1	R1	Dismissal 2	R2
1	T.K.D.Sudarshana	lbw b de Silva	13	lbw b Rupasinghe	9
2	N.M.N.P.Nawela	lbw b Chandrakumara	42	lbw b Rupasinghe	6
3	†M.D.Randika	c Ranaweera b Rupasinghe	22	c Perera b Chandrakumara	0
4	W.M.B.Perera	c Perera b Rupasinghe	0	not out	32
5	A.Rideegammanagedera	b de Silva	24	b de Silva	15
6	A.S.A.Perera	lbw b Rupasinghe	0	b de Silva	7
7	*L.H.D.Dilhara	c Mendis b Chandrakumara	76	c Chandrakumara b de Silva	5
8	H.M.R.K.B.Herath	c Perera b de Silva	0	not out	8
9	P.C.Hewage	not out	17		
10	U.W.M.B.C.A.Welagedara	c Randika b Ratnayake	7		
11	P.N.Ranjith	c Mubarak b Ratnayake	0		
	Extras	b 4, lb 5, w 1, nb 2	12	b 1, lb 1, w 1	3
			213	(6 wickets)	85

FoW (1): 1-20 (1), 2-72 (3), 3-78 (4), 4-94 (2), 5-95 (6), 6-141 (5), 7-141 (8), 8-201 (7), 9-213 (10), 10-213 (11)
FoW (2): 1-17 (2), 2-18 (3), 3-20 (1), 4-43 (5), 5-55 (6), 6-61 (7)

Moors Sports Club Bowling

	O	M	R	W		O	M	R	W	
Welagedara	4.3	2	20	1	1nb	15	3	58	3	11nb
Ranjith	11	2	40	2		3	0	12	0	
Dilhara	8.3	1	30	0	2nb					
Rideegammanagedera	12	4	18	3		(3) 11	2	44	2	
Herath	10.3	4	26	4		(4) 9.1	1	31	5	
Hewage	2	1	15	0						

Colombo Cricket Club Bowling

	O	M	R	W		O	M	R	W	
de Silva	16	1	82	3	2nb	8	1	28	3	
Ratnayake	4.5	1	17	2	1w	2	0	6	0	1w
Randika	1	1	0	0						
Rupasinghe	13	1	57	3		(3) 7.4	2	39	2	
Chandrakumara	14	3	33	2		(4) 2	0	10	1	
Perera	4	1	15	0						

Umpires: S.S.K.Gallage and J.W.L.Nandana.   Referee: U.Warnapura.   Toss: Moors Sports Club

Close of Play: 1st day: Moors Sports Club (1) 171-7 (Dilhara 56*, Hewage 6*, 39 overs).

The match was scheduled for four days but completed in two.

433

SINHALESE SPORTS CLUB v RAGAMA CRICKET CLUB

Played at Sinhalese Sports Club Ground, Colombo, January 17, 18, 19, 20, 2008.
Premier Championship 2007/08 - Tier A
Sinhalese Sports Club won by 240 runs.   (Points: Sinhalese Sports Club 17.15, Ragama Cricket Club 3.55)

SINHALESE SPORTS CLUB

1	N.T.Paranavitana	lbw b Weeraratne	38	c Perera b Weeraratne		6
2	*D.A.Gunawardene	lbw b Weeraratne	31	c Ranatunga b Bandara		72
3	†J.K.Silva	c Perera b Weeraratne	6	c de Zoysa b Weeraratne		0
4	T.T.Samaraweera	c Perera b Darshanpriya	46	b Darshanpriya		96
5	S.H.T.Kandamby	c Ranatunga b Nayanakantha	47	lbw b Vithana		58
6	E.D.J.Sriyapala	c de Zoysa b Nayanakantha	4	not out		62
7	K.S.Lokuarachchi	run out (de Zoysa/Vithana)	61	(8) not out		8
8	K.P.S.P.Karunanayake	c de Saram b Darshanpriya	10	(7) b Bandara		9
9	M.T.T.Mirando	c Ranatunga b Bandara	41			
10	S.M.Senanayake	c Vithana b Weeraratne	5			
11	C.W.Vidanapathirana	not out	6			
	Extras	b 2, lb 1, w 4	7	b 9, lb 6, w 2		17
			302	(6 wickets, declared)		**328**

FoW (1): 1-52 (2), 2-72 (3), 3-81 (1), 4-160 (4), 5-168 (6), 6-186 (5), 7-212 (8), 8-267 (7), 9-290 (10), 10-302 (9)
FoW (2): 1-14 (1), 2-14 (3), 3-175 (5), 4-203 (4), 5-296 (2), 6-316 (7)

RAGAMA CRICKET CLUB

1	D.A.Ranatunga	not out	75	c Vidanapathirana b Senanayake	40
2	H.E.Vithana	c Silva b Vidanapathirana	0	c Karunanayake b Mirando	66
3	†R.S.S.S.de Zoysa	c Samaraweera b Karunanayake	30	c Sriyapala b Senanayake	0
4	P.K.J.R.N.Nonis	b Karunanayake	0	retired hurt	9
5	W.D.D.S.Perera	lbw b Mirando	4	c Lokuarachchi b Senanayake	24
6	*S.I.de Saram	c Paranavitana b Vidanapathirana	2	(7) st Silva b Lokuarachchi	17
7	K.Weeraratne	c Silva b Mirando	6	(8) not out	45
8	C.M.Bandara	c Kandamby b Lokuarachchi	15	(9) c Vidanapathirana b Mirando	6
9	R.D.Dissanayake	b Vidanapathirana	6	(6) b Senanayake	7
10	H.G.D.Nayanakantha	lbw b Lokuarachchi	0	lbw b Senanayake	7
11	T.D.D.Darshanpriya	c Silva b Vidanapathirana	0	c Silva b Mirando	0
	Extras	b 2, lb 2, w 3, nb 4	11	b 14, lb 4, w 2	20
			149		**241**

FoW (1): 1-10 (2), 2-67 (3), 3-75 (4), 4-80 (5), 5-83 (6), 6-98 (7), 7-122 (8), 8-143 (9), 9-144 (10), 10-149 (11)
FoW (2): 1-92 (1), 2-92 (3), 3-120 (2), 4-148 (6), 5-177 (7), 6-198 (5), 7-225 (9), 8-240 (10), 9-241 (11)

Ragama Cricket Club Bowling

	O	M	R	W			O	M	R	W	
Nayanakantha	14	1	78	2	3w	(2)	12	1	36	0	
Weeraratne	15	4	46	4		(1)	20	3	66	2	
Darshanpriya	18	3	73	2	1w		9	1	37	1	1w
Dissanayake	8	2	34	0		(5)	13	1	57	0	
Bandara	19.3	1	68	1		(6)	16	3	66	2	
Perera						(4)	2	0	10	0	
Vithana						(7)	15	4	39	0	
de Saram						(8)	1	0	2	0	

Sinhalese Sports Club Bowling

	O	M	R	W			O	M	R	W	
Vidanapathirana	11	2	36	4	1w		14	2	45	0	
Karunanayake	13	1	50	2	1w		8	1	29	0	1w
Lokuarachchi	12	2	20	2		(5)	17	4	50	1	
Senanayake	4	1	4	0			21	7	50	5	
Mirando	11	1	35	2	4nb	(3)	16	4	49	3	1w

Umpires: M.G.Silva and N.D.Withana.   Referee: M.C.Mendis.   Toss: Ragama Cricket Club

Close of Play: 1st day: Ragama Cricket Club (1) 36-1 (Ranatunga 17*, de Zoysa 13*, 13 overs); 2nd day: Sinhalese Sports Club (2) 181-3 (Samaraweera 82*, Sriyapala 0*, 43 overs); 3rd day: Ragama Cricket Club (2) 124-3 (Perera 2*, Dissanayake 1*, 43 overs).

D.A.Gunawardene retired hurt in the Sinhalese Sports Club second innings having scored 15 (team score 43-2) - he returned when the score was 203-4. P.K.J.R.N.Nonis retired hurt in the Ragama Cricket Club second innings having scored 9 (team score 115-2).

TAMIL UNION CRICKET AND ATHLETIC CLUB v NONDESCRIPTS CRICKET CLUB

Played at P.Saravanamuttu Stadium, Colombo, January 17, 18, 19, 20, 2008.
Premier Championship 2007/08 - Tier A
Match drawn.   (Points: Tamil Union Cricket and Athletic Club 12.23, Nondescripts Cricket Club 4.87)

NONDESCRIPTS CRICKET CLUB

1	W.U.Tharanga	c G.T.de Silva b Wijesiriwardene	4	c Rupasinghe b Maduwantha		31
2	†M.H.Wessels	c Daniel b Maduwantha	16	c K.M.Fernando b Wijesiriwardene		8
3	K.D.Gunawardene	lbw b Maduwantha	13	lbw b Pushpakumara		25
4	C.G.Wijesinghe	not out	61	(5) c G.T.de Silva b Wijesiriwardene		250
5	*M.K.Gajanayake	c and b Maduwantha	4	(6) c K.M.Fernando b Pushpakumara		56
6	M.S.R.Wijeratne	c Pushpakumara b Wijesiriwardene	15	(7) not out		28
7	C.K.B.Kulasekara	c G.T.de Silva b Lakmal	6	(8) not out		0
8	M.M.M.Suraj	b Maduwantha	7	(4) c and b Wijesiriwardene		33
9	H.W.U.Varuna	c G.T.de Silva b Maduwantha	24			
10	W.C.A.Ganegama	run out (G.T.de Silva)	33			
11	N.C.Komasaru	lbw b Rupasinghe	0			
	Extras	b 5, lb 4, nb 2	11	lb 3, w 6, nb 1		10
			194	(6 wickets, declared)		441

FoW (1): 1-15 (1), 2-31 (2), 3-38 (3), 4-44 (5), 5-82 (6), 6-92 (7), 7-99 (8), 8-135 (9), 9-192 (10), 10-194 (11)
FoW (2): 1-20 (2), 2-64 (1), 3-64 (3), 4-221 (4), 5-346 (6), 6-441 (5)

TAMIL UNION CRICKET AND ATHLETIC CLUB

1	G.I.Daniel	c Wessels b Kulasekara	14	c and b Komasaru		19
2	H.M.Maduwantha	lbw b Kulasekara	14	lbw b Kulasekara		6
3	S.I.Fernando	c Wessels b Kulasekara	57	not out		142
4	*S.K.L.de Silva	lbw b Komasaru	51	b Suraj		11
5	†G.T.de Silva	c Tharanga b Komasaru	33	(7) c Gunawardene b Suraj		29
6	M.Pushpakumara	c Tharanga b Komasaru	2	c Wijeratne b Gajanayake		29
7	K.M.Fernando	b Suraj	22	(8) c Suraj b Komasaru		3
8	R.J.M.G.M.Rupasinghe	run out (Tharanga)	15	(5) b Ganegama		47
9	O.L.A.Wijesiriwardene	lbw b Komasaru	1	b Komasaru		0
10	P.L.U.Irandika	lbw b Suraj	10	c Gunawardene b Gajanayake		0
11	R.A.S.Lakmal	not out	3	not out		0
	Extras	lb 2, nb 3	5	b 9, lb 3, nb 1		13
			227	(9 wickets)		299

FoW (1): 1-29 (1), 2-30 (2), 3-112 (3), 4-161 (4), 5-174 (5), 6-178 (6), 7-213 (8), 8-214 (9), 9-222 (7), 10-227 (10)
FoW (2): 1-26 (2), 2-28 (1), 3-56 (4), 4-155 (5), 5-222 (6), 6-290 (7), 7-295 (8), 8-295 (9), 9-295 (10)

Tamil Union Bowling	O	M	R	W			O	M	R	W	
Lakmal	12	1	75	1	1nb		10	2	51	0	2w
Wijesiriwardene	13	2	25	2			14	0	75	3	
Maduwantha	19	5	41	5			19	4	56	1	
Rupasinghe	5.3	1	16	1	1nb	(5)	10	0	44	0	1w,1nb
Irandika	6	1	28	0		(6)	27	0	110	0	3w
Pushpakumara						(4)	25	2	80	2	
Daniel						(7)	2	0	14	0	
K.M.Fernando						(8)	1	0	8	0	

Nondescripts Bowling	O	M	R	W			O	M	R	W	
Ganegama	14	5	49	0			12	1	28	1	
Kulasekara	17	3	54	3			19	3	52	1	
Varuna	7	1	31	0	3nb	(7)	1	0	5	0	
Suraj	20	5	48	2		(5)	39	12	85	2	
Komasaru	16	5	43	4		(3)	25	8	73	3	
Wijesinghe						(4)	4	0	15	0	1nb
Gajanayake						(6)	24	12	29	2	

Umpires: N.S.Bopage and W.A.Senanayake. Referee: S.Ranatunga.   Toss: Tamil Union Cricket and Athletic Club

Close of Play: 1st day: Tamil Union Cricket and Athletic Club (1) 116-3 (S.K.L.de Silva 27*, G.T.de Silva 0*, 34 overs); 2nd day: Nondescripts Cricket Club (2) 210-3 (Suraj 31*, Wijesinghe 113*, 48 overs); 3rd day: Tamil Union Cricket and Athletic Club (2) 116-3 (S.I.Fernando 48*, Rupasinghe 28*, 30 overs).
C.G.Wijesinghe's 250 took 307 balls and included 32 fours and 3 sixes. S.I.Fernando's 142 took 312 balls and included 14 fours and 4 sixes.

MORATUWA SPORTS CLUB v SINGHA SPORTS CLUB

Played at Tyronne Fernando Stadium, Moratuwa, January 18, 19, 20, 2008.
Premier Championship 2007/08 - Tier B
Match drawn.   (Points: Moratuwa Sports Club 12.3, Singha Sports Club 4.255)

SINGHA SPORTS CLUB

1	D.A.Faux	lbw b Deshapriya	29	b S.P.Rupasinghe	17
2	K.M.S.de Silva	b Deshapriya	0	c and b S.J.C.de Silva	36
3	T.J.Madanayake	c H.U.K.de Silva b P.C.M.Fernando	15	lbw b S.J.C.de Silva	115
4	H.W.M.Kumara	c M.D.S.Perera b S.P.Rupasinghe	66	run out	39
5	†H.H.R.Kavinga	b M.D.S.Perera	44	b M.D.S.Perera	27
6	H.S.M.Zoysa	c P.C.M.Fernando b S.J.C.de Silva	45	c Wijemanne b S.J.C.de Silva	33
7	*N.C.K.Liyanage	lbw b S.P.Rupasinghe	2		
8	S.I.Vithana	c and b M.D.S.Perera	1	(7) not out	19
9	S.K.C.Randunu	c R.C.Rupasinghe b S.J.C.de Silva	34	(8) c and b S.J.C.de Silva	25
10	K.S.H.de Silva	c R.A.A.I.Perera b S.J.C.de Silva	20		
11	P.L.S.Gamage	not out	2		
	Extras	b 1, lb 2, w 1, nb 2	6	lb 4, w 1, nb 11	16
			264	**(7 wickets, declared)**	**327**

FoW (1): 1-4 (2), 2-28 (3), 3-48 (1), 4-133 (5), 5-165 (4), 6-184 (7), 7-189 (8), 8-220 (6), 9-252 (9), 10-264 (10)
FoW (2): 1-44 (1), 2-69 (2), 3-151 (4), 4-215 (5), 5-278 (6), 6-291 (3), 7-327 (8)

MORATUWA SPORTS CLUB

1	R.C.Rupasinghe	b Gamage	65	b Gamage	65
2	R.A.A.I.Perera	run out (Vithana/Kavinga)	4	b K.S.H.de Silva	23
3	*W.S.T.Fernando	b Vithana	29	b Randunu	1
4	L.T.A.de Silva	b Vithana	57	not out	58
5	†D.S.Wijemanne	c Randunu b Vithana	88		
6	H.U.K.de Silva	b Gamage	25	(5) not out	13
7	A.L.D.M.Deshapriya	b Vithana	1		
8	M.D.S.Perera	lbw b Randunu	7		
9	S.J.C.de Silva	b Randunu	2		
10	S.P.Rupasinghe	b Randunu	57		
11	P.C.M.Fernando	not out	0		
	Extras	b 9, lb 3, w 4, nb 4	20	lb 2, nb 3	5
			355	**(3 wickets)**	**165**

FoW (1): 1-10 (2), 2-84 (3), 3-145 (1), 4-176 (4), 5-229 (6), 6-230 (7), 7-237 (8), 8-255 (9), 9-351 (5), 10-355 (10)
FoW (2): 1-26 (2), 2-55 (3), 3-133 (1)

Moratuwa Sports Club Bowling

	O	M	R	W			O	M	R	W	
P.C.M.Fernando	9	1	51	1	1w,1nb		10	1	36	0	
Deshapriya	7	0	36	2	1nb		6	1	29	0	1w,1nb
L.T.A.de Silva	2	1	13	0							
S.J.C.de Silva	11.2	1	46	3		(5)	20.3	4	55	4	1nb
S.P.Rupasinghe	16	0	68	2		(3)	24	1	117	1	6nb
M.D.S.Perera	9	1	47	2		(4)	18	0	80	1	2nb
W.S.T.Fernando						(6)	2	0	4	0	
R.A.A.I.Perera						(7)	1	0	2	0	

Singha Sports Club Bowling

	O	M	R	W			O	M	R	W	
K.S.H.de Silva	10	0	42	0	1w		4	1	14	1	
Liyanage	16	2	71	0	2w,1nb		2	0	15	0	1nb
Gamage	17	2	64	2	1w,3nb	(6)	5	1	34	1	1nb
Randunu	26.2	5	70	3		(3)	8	2	34	1	1nb
Zoysa	3	0	18	0							
Vithana	25	4	74	4		(4)	10	0	51	0	
Madanayake	1	0	4	0		(5)	2	0	10	0	
Kumara						(7)	1	0	5	0	

Umpires: D.Ekanayake and M.V.D.Zilva. Referee: N.S.H.M.R.Kodituwakku. Toss: Moratuwa Sports Club
Close of Play: 1st day: Moratuwa Sports Club (1) 145-2 (R.C.Rupasinghe 65*, L.T.A.de Silva 38*, 35 overs); 2nd day: Singha Sports Club (2) 88-2 (Madanayake 22*, Kumara 9*, 24 overs).
T.J.Madanayake's 115 took 194 balls and included 9 fours.

PANADURA SPORTS CLUB v BURGHER RECREATION CLUB

Played at Panadura Esplanade, January 18, 19, 20, 2008.
Premier Championship 2007/08 - Tier B
Panadura Sports Club won by six wickets. (Points: Panadura Sports Club 16.2, Burgher Recreation Club 3.695)

BURGHER RECREATION CLUB

1	D.H.Sandagirigoda	b Mendis	0	c M.T.T.Fernando b de Silva	10
2	L.S.D.Perera	c G.S.U.Fernando b Mendis	4	c M.T.T.Fernando b de Silva	5
3	I.C.D.Perera	b Mendis	0	lbw b Fonseka	97
4	D.F.Arnolda	b Mendis	62	lbw b de Silva	0
5	†P.H.M.G.Fernando	c G.Y.S.R.Perera b de Silva	5	(7) c M.T.T.Fernando b Mendis	7
6	*V.S.K.Waragoda	c G.S.U.Fernando b de Silva	0	(5) b Wanasinghe	24
7	I.C.Soysa	c Wanasinghe b de Silva	0	(6) lbw b Cooray	22
8	W.T.Abeyratne	c M.T.T.Fernando b Mendis	42	run out	67
9	G.D.R.Eranga	b Mendis	12	c Peiris b Cooray	9
10	C.A.M.Madusanka	not out	19	not out	24
11	A.N.P.R.Fernando	b G.A.S.Perera	8		
	Extras	b 2, lb 4, w 1	7	b 19, lb 12, nb 4	35
			159	(9 wickets, declared)	300

FoW (1): 1-0 (1), 2-0 (3), 3-7 (2), 4-12 (5), 5-12 (6), 6-12 (7), 7-107 (8), 8-127 (4), 9-138 (9), 10-159 (11)
FoW (2): 1-23 (1), 2-34 (2), 3-34 (4), 4-72 (5), 5-124 (6), 6-139 (7), 7-222 (3), 8-235 (9), 9-300 (8)

PANADURA SPORTS CLUB

1	†G.Y.S.R.Perera	c Sandagirigoda b Abeyratne	17	c Waragoda b Eranga	1
2	M.T.T.Fernando	c P.H.M.G.Fernando b Eranga	5	b Madusanka	51
3	G.S.U.Fernando	b Arnolda	8	not out	101
4	*J.S.K.Peiris	b Arnolda	37	(5) lbw b Madusanka	13
5	W.M.P.N.Wanasinghe	b Waragoda	84		
6	M.N.R.Cooray	c P.H.M.G.Fernando b Arnolda	8	(4) run out	6
7	G.A.S.Perera	c P.H.M.G.Fernando b Soysa	21	(6) not out	15
8	H.F.M.Fonseka	c Madusanka b Abeyratne	26		
9	S.R.Abeywardene	b Arnolda	16		
10	B.R.S.Mendis	c Arnolda b Eranga	1		
11	H.D.N.de Silva	not out	12		
	Extras	b 11, lb 9, w 3, nb 4	27	b 9, lb 2	11
			262	(4 wickets)	198

FoW (1): 1-19 (2), 2-29 (1), 3-46 (3), 4-105 (4), 5-115 (6), 6-147 (7), 7-218 (5), 8-225 (8), 9-236 (10), 10-262 (9)
FoW (2): 1-10 (1), 2-101 (2), 3-113 (4), 4-159 (5)

Panadura Sports Club Bowling

	O	M	R	W			O	M	R	W	
Mendis	15	4	48	6			14	2	42	1	1nb
de Silva	14	2	54	3	1w		9	1	35	3	
Abeywardene	4	0	27	0		(7)	4	0	14	0	
Wanasinghe	5	0	15	0		(3)	12	2	48	1	2nb
G.A.S.Perera	1.5	0	9	1			12	3	29	0	
Peiris						(4)	3	0	13	0	
Cooray						(6)	21	4	54	2	
Fonseka						(8)	12	3	29	1	
G.S.U.Fernando						(9)	0.4	0	5	0	1nb

Burgher Recreation Club Bowling

	O	M	R	W			O	M	R	W	
Eranga	18	6	36	2	1w,2nb		4	0	20	1	
Soysa	6	2	23	1			2	0	13	0	
Abeyratne	16	5	31	2			6.1	0	41	0	
A.N.P.R.Fernando	12	2	33	0	2w	(7)	4	0	38	0	
Arnolda	15	2	63	4	2nb	(4)	6	0	30	0	
Madusanka	20	3	55	0			12	2	35	2	
Waragoda	1	0	1	1		(5)	1	0	10	0	

Umpires: R.A.Kottahachchi and R.R.Wimalasiri. Referee: A.J.Samarasekera. Toss: Panadura Sports Club
Close of Play: 1st day: Panadura Sports Club (1) 147-5 (Wanasinghe 43*, G.A.S.Perera 21*, 41 overs); 2nd day: Burgher Recreation Club (2) 152-6 (I.C.D.Perera 63*, Abeyratne 6*, 41 overs).
G.S.U.Fernando's 101 took 122 balls and included 12 fours and 3 sixes.

437

POLICE SPORTS CLUB v LANKAN CRICKET CLUB

Played at Police Park Ground, Colombo, January 18, 19, 20, 2008.
Premier Championship 2007/08 - Tier B
Lankan Cricket Club won by ten wickets.   (Points: Police Sports Club 3.365, Lankan Cricket Club 16.13)

POLICE SPORTS CLUB

1	P.H.K.S.Nirmala	b Priyadarshana	0	c sub (D.G.N.de Silva) b Dhammika	52
2	S.A.Wijeratne	c E.F.M.U.Fernando b Dhammika	49	run out	4
3	J.P.M.Abeyratne	lbw b Perera	0	lbw b Silva	51
4	W.N.M.Soysa	lbw b Perera	13	(6) c Gunawardene b K.G.D.Fernando	23
5	P.R.Nirmal	lbw b Silva	19	b Dhammika	0
6	*R.G.D.Sanjeewa	b K.G.D.Fernando	15	(7) lbw b K.G.D.Fernando	24
7	H.P.A.Priyantha	b K.G.D.Fernando	41	(8) c Gunawardene b Priyadarshana	23
8	†K.A.D.M.C.Kuruppu	c Gunawardene b Silva	6	(4) c E.F.M.U.Fernando b Dhammika	47
9	M.M.Rasmijinan	c Tillakaratne b K.G.D.Fernando	21	c Gunawardene b K.G.D.Fernando	59
10	H.M.Jayawardene	c and b K.G.D.Fernando	0	c E.F.M.U.Fernando b K.G.D.Fernando	19
11	R.S.K.A.P.Dilantha	not out	4	not out	4
	Extras	lb 7, w 2, nb 12	21	b 4, lb 9, w 1, nb 24	38
			189		**344**

FoW (1): 1-1 (1), 2-9 (3), 3-69 (2), 4-77 (4), 5-99 (6), 6-126 (5), 7-132 (8), 8-175 (9), 9-175 (10), 10-189 (7)
FoW (2): 1-8 (2), 2-101 (3), 3-148 (1), 4-148 (5), 5-193 (6), 6-222 (7), 7-226 (4), 8-310 (8), 9-331 (9), 10-344 (10)

LANKAN CRICKET CLUB

1	C.M.Withanage	c Rasmijinan b Soysa	166	not out	14
2	D.V.Gunawardene	c Soysa b Rasmijinan	50		
3	K.N.S.Fernando	c Nirmala b Sanjeewa	41		
4	B.A.R.S.Priyadarshana	c Nirmala b Sanjeewa	3	(2) not out	10
5	†E.F.M.U.Fernando	not out	124		
6	Y.N.Tillakaratne	b Sanjeewa	11		
7	D.G.R.Dhammika	st Nirmala b Sanjeewa	73		
8	*S.H.S.M.K.Silva	run out (Abeyratne)	1		
9	K.G.D.Fernando	not out	19		
10	P.S.A.N.Shiroman				
11	L.D.I.Perera				
	Extras	lb 12, w 3, nb 5	20	w 1, nb 1	2
		(7 wickets, declared)	**508**	(no wicket)	**26**

FoW (1): 1-118 (2), 2-234 (3), 3-240 (4), 4-294 (1), 5-317 (6), 6-471 (7), 7-474 (8)

Lankan Cricket Club Bowling

	O	M	R	W			O	M	R	W	
Priyadarshana	5	1	36	1	2nb		14	0	48	1	6nb
Perera	14	3	59	2	1w		15	2	56	0	
Dhammika	6	0	25	1	6nb	(7)	26	8	72	3	1nb
K.G.D.Fernando	5.2,15nb	0	38	4	1w,4nb		14.2	1	49	4	
Silva	9	4	24	2			22	8	65	1	
Gunawardene						(3)	2	0	10	0	2nb
K.N.S.Fernando						(6)	4	0	25	0	
Tillakaratne						(8)	2	0	6	0	

Police Sports Club Bowling

	O	M	R	W			O	M	R	W	
Dilantha	15	0	88	0	1nb		2	0	20	0	1nb
Rasmijinan	26	3	113	1	3w		1	0	6	0	1w
Priyantha	8	1	30	0	1nb						
Wijeratne	4	0	24	0							
Jayawardene	16	0	80	0							
Sanjeewa	16	2	86	4							
Soysa	23	2	75	1	3nb						

Umpires: W.Jayasena and E.J.A.P.A.M.Jayasuriya.   Referee: K.T.Francis.   Toss: Lankan Cricket Club

Close of Play: 1st day: Lankan Cricket Club (1) 158-1 (Withanage 100*, K.N.S.Fernando 4*, 33 overs); 2nd day: Police Sports Club (2) 70-1 (Nirmala 22*, Abeyratne 33*, 18 overs).
C.M.Withanage's 166 took 206 balls and included 16 fours and 4 sixes. E.F.M.U.Fernando's 124 took 153 balls and included 10 fours and 3 sixes.

SARACENS SPORTS CLUB v SRI LANKA ARMY SPORTS CLUB

Played at Burgher Recreation Club Ground, Colombo, January 18, 19, 20, 2008.
Premier Championship 2007/08 - Tier B
Sri Lanka Army Sports Club won by an innings and 41 runs.   (Points: Saracens Sports Club 2.76, Sri Lanka Army Sports Club 17.965)

SRI LANKA ARMY SPORTS CLUB
1	S.Sanjeewa	b Alwis	69
2	P.N.Kalua rachchi	c Abeyratne b Nishantha	1
3	H.H.M.de Zoysa	c Serasinghe b Vishwaranga	18
4	S.Prasanna	c Alwis b Vishwaranga	4
5	K.C.Prasad	not out	153
6	B.A.W.Mendis	run out (Alwis)	8
7	T.R.D.Mendis	lbw b Pushpakumara	44
8	†T.D.T.Soysa	lbw b Pushpakumara	7
9	*P.K.N.M.K.Rathnayake	b Abdeen	24
10	P.P.M.Peiris	c Serasinghe b Abdeen	1
11	W.R.Palleguruge	c sub (M.L.R.Karunaratne) b Serasinghe	21
	Extras	b 14, lb 6, w 5, nb 18	43
			393

FoW (1): 1-9 (2), 2-59 (3), 3-70 (4), 4-151 (1), 5-159 (6), 6-237 (7), 7-257 (8), 8-296 (9), 9-311 (10), 10-393 (11)

SARACENS SPORTS CLUB
1	W.G.R.K.Alwis	run out (Soysa)	75	c Palleguruge b Peiris	15
2	*G.N.Abeyratne	c Soysa b Peiris	13	st Soysa b Prasanna	12
3	G.K.Amarasinghe	c B.A.W.Mendis b Rathnayake	13	lbw b Prasanna	28
4	W.S.D.Fernando	b Rathnayake	0	(5) c Soysa b B.A.W.Mendis	8
5	S.C.Serasinghe	b Rathnayake	0	(7) not out	27
6	†N.M.S.M.Sepala	c sub (R.D.I.A.Karunatilleke) b B.A.W.Mendis	28	(4) c Kaluarachchi b Palleguruge	29
7	R.S.A.Palliyaguruge	b Prasanna	14	(6) lbw b Prasanna	23
8	L.D.P.Nishantha	not out	28	c T.R.D.Mendis b B.A.W.Mendis	1
9	P.M.Pushpakumara	lbw b Prasanna	0	c de Zoysa b B.A.W.Mendis	17
10	L.A.S.Vishwaranga	lbw b B.A.W.Mendis	0	(11) c Prasanna b B.A.W.Mendis	1
11	M.I.Abdeen	b B.A.W.Mendis	0	(10) b B.A.W.Mendis	0
	Extras	b 4, lb 6, nb 7	17	b 1, nb 2	3
			188		164

FoW (1): 1-17 (2), 2-42 (3), 3-46 (4), 4-46 (5), 5-128 (1), 6-140 (6), 7-163 (7), 8-163 (9), 9-164 (10), 10-188 (11)
FoW (2): 1-15 (1), 2-56 (2), 3-61 (3), 4-90 (5), 5-98 (4), 6-122 (6), 7-123 (8), 8-143 (9), 9-150 (10), 10-164 (11)

Saracens Sports Club Bowling
	O	M	R	W	
Nishantha	19	4	49	1	8nb
Abdeen	13	1	68	2	1w
Vishwaranga	18	0	81	2	9nb
Pushpakumara	21	3	73	2	1nb
Palliyaguruge	2	0	19	0	
Serasinghe	12	1	31	1	
Alwis	12	3	43	1	
Amarasinghe	3	1	9	0	

Sri Lanka Army Sports Club Bowling
	O	M	R	W			O	M	R	W	
Rathnayake	10	3	30	3			5	0	37	0	1nb
Peiris	8	0	67	1	4nb		6	0	31	1	
B.A.W.Mendis	16	3	35	3	2nb	(4)	17.4	2	46	5	1nb
Prasanna	8	1	46	2	1nb	(3)	12	3	30	3	
Palleguruge						(5)	7	1	19	1	

Umpires: M.W.D.P.de Silva and K.M.Kottahachchi. Referee: B.C.Cooray.   Toss: Sri Lanka Army Sports Club

Close of Play: 1st day: Sri Lanka Army Sports Club (1) 366-9 (Prasad 134*, Palleguruge 16*, 90 overs); 2nd day: Saracens Sports Club (2) 132-7 (Serasinghe 4*, Pushpakumara 9*, 37 overs).

K.C.Prasad's 153 took 283 balls and included 20 fours and 1 six.

SRI LANKA AIR FORCE SPORTS CLUB v SEBASTIANITES CRICKET AND ATHLETIC CLUB

Played at Air Force Ground, Colombo, January 18, 19, 20, 2008.
Premier Championship 2007/08 - Tier B
Match drawn.   (Points: Sri Lanka Air Force Sports Club 3.4, Sebastianites Cricket and Athletic Club 11.78)

SEBASTIANITES CRICKET AND ATHLETIC CLUB

1	H.A.H.U.Tillakaratne	c Kularatne b Bandara	106	lbw b Bandara		5
2	B.Y.Arumathanthri	c and b Kumara	38	lbw b Rizan		31
3	R.H.T.A.Perera	lbw b Rizan	22	c Kumara b Madanayake		28
4	M.A.B.Peiris	c Kumara b Lakshitha	59	not out		53
5	A.D.Indunil	c Perera b Kumara	5			
6	†K.L.K.Fernando	c Lakshitha b Rizan	90	c and b Rizan		23
7	*M.A.P.Salgado	c Kumara b Lakshitha	7	(5) c Bandara b Rizan		0
8	D.G.C.Silva	c Kularatne b Wickrama	8	(7) not out		10
9	Y.I.S.Gunasena	c Rizan b Kumara	18			
10	A.B.L.D.Rodrigo	not out	41			
11	M.N.T.H.Kumara	not out	17			
	Extras	lb 11, w 3, nb 7	21	b 2, lb 3, nb 1		6
		(9 wickets, declared)	432	(5 wickets)		156

FoW (1): 1-99 (2), 2-142 (3), 3-211 (1), 4-226 (5), 5-260 (4), 6-273 (7), 7-323 (8), 8-366 (9), 9-377 (6)
FoW (2): 1-11 (1), 2-68 (3), 3-68 (2), 4-68 (5), 5-133 (6)

SRI LANKA AIR FORCE SPORTS CLUB

1	M.A.M.Faizer	b Salgado	108
2	†M.K.P.B.Kularatne	c Gunasena b Silva	33
3	A.Rizan	lbw b Salgado	0
4	P.A.R.C.Karunasena	lbw b Salgado	49
5	M.R.Porage	c Indunil b Salgado	12
6	*K.A.Kumara	not out	115
7	S.Madanayake	b Gunasena	34
8	W.P.Wickrama	lbw b Salgado	13
9	M.K.G.C.P.Lakshitha	lbw b Silva	2
10	A.M.C.M.K.Bandara	c Fernando b Kumara	8
11	W.C.M.Perera	c Rodrigo b Silva	18
	Extras	b 2, lb 7, nb 7	16
			408

FoW (1): 1-60 (2), 2-60 (3), 3-191 (4), 4-198 (1), 5-221 (5), 6-280 (7), 7-309 (8), 8-327 (9), 9-348 (10), 10-408 (11)

Sri Lanka Air Force Bowling	O	M	R	W			O	M	R	W	
Lakshitha	20	0	91	2	3w,5nb		4	1	12	0	1nb
Bandara	13	1	60	1	2nb		3	0	8	1	
Perera	3	0	18	0							
Wickrama	11	2	26	1		(5)	2	0	8	0	
Kumara	21	2	81	2		(3)	9	0	34	0	
Madanayake	19	1	57	0			13	1	45	1	
Rizan	19	0	88	3		(4)	14	3	44	3	

Sebastianites Bowling	O	M	R	W	
Kumara	10	0	48	1	
Gunasena	13	4	44	1	2nb
Silva	29.4	3	103	3	5nb
Rodrigo	23	5	58	0	
Salgado	27	7	92	5	
Peiris	3	0	11	0	
Indunil	17	5	37	0	
Perera	1	0	6	0	

Umpires: R.M.P.J.Rambukwella and S.H.Sarathkumara.   Toss: Sri Lanka Air Force Sports Club

Close of Play: 1st day: Sebastianites Cricket and Athletic Club (1) 382-9 (Rodrigo 9*, Kumara 0*, 94 overs); 2nd day: Sri Lanka Air Force Sports Club (1) 249-5 (Kumara 20*, Madanayake 19*, 76 overs).

H.A.H.U.Tillakaratne's 106 took 142 balls and included 13 fours and 2 sixes. M.A.M.Faizer's 108 took 178 balls and included 17 fours and 1 six. K.A.Kumara's 115 took 163 balls and included 18 fours.

COLOMBO CRICKET CLUB v BLOOMFIELD CRICKET AND ATHLETIC CLUB

Played at Colombo Cricket Club Ground, January 24, 25, 26, 27, 2008.
Premier Championship 2007/08 - Tier A
Colombo Cricket Club won by 257 runs.   (Points: Colombo Cricket Club 17.265, Bloomfield Cricket and Athletic Club 3.68)

COLOMBO CRICKET CLUB

1	M.G.Vandort	c Jayawardene b Gamage	7	b Gunaratne		91
2	†D.K.Ranaweera	c Masmulla b Lakshitha	24	c Masmulla b Ranasinghe		63
3	J.Mubarak	c Katipiarchchi b Dissanayake	121	c and b Mendis		49
4	*B.M.T.T.Mendis	c and b Gunaratne	27	lbw b Mendis		51
5	A.S.Polonowita	lbw b Ranasinghe	58	not out		52
6	P.D.G.Chandrakumara	c Masmulla b Ranasinghe	17	lbw b Dissanayake		0
7	A.C.Wethathasinghe	b Dissanayake	20	(9) not out		7
8	M.P.N.L.Perera	c Jayawardene b Ranasinghe	9	(7) c Mendis b Dissanayake		1
9	W.R.S.de Silva	b Gamage	18	(8) c Katipiarchchi b Dissanayake		5
10	N.S.Rupasinghe	lbw b Dissanayake	0			
11	M.I.Ratnayake	not out	8			
	Extras	b 2, lb 7, w 9, nb 1	19	lb 2, w 2, nb 2		6
			328	(7 wickets, declared)		325

FoW (1): 1-15 (1), 2-83 (2), 3-172 (4), 4-214 (3), 5-270 (5), 6-271 (6), 7-285 (8), 8-312 (7), 9-312 (10), 10-328 (9)
FoW (2): 1-159 (1), 2-161 (2), 3-253 (4), 4-268 (3), 5-269 (6), 6-281 (7), 7-291 (8)

BLOOMFIELD CRICKET AND ATHLETIC CLUB

1	T.S.Masmulla	c sub b de Silva	2	c Ranaweera b Ratnayake		43
2	A.U.Katipiarachchi	run out (sub [A.D.Solomons])	6	lbw b Ratnayake		9
3	M.T.Gunaratne	c Mendis b de Silva	0	c Polonowita b Rupasinghe		15
4	W.S.Jayantha	run out (sub [A.D.Solomons])	0	c Polonowita b Rupasinghe		33
5	†H.A.P.W.Jayawardene	c Polonowita b Chandrakumara	62	c Ranaweera b Ratnayake		15
6	*D.M.G.S.Dissanayake	c Ranaweera b Chandrakumara	89	c de Silva b Rupasinghe		32
7	G.A.S.K.Gangodawila	run out (de Silva)	1	c Ranaweera b Ratnayake		11
8	M.P.Ranasinghe	b Chandrakumara	6	(10) lbw b Rupasinghe		4
9	A.B.T.Lakshitha	c Vandort b Chandrakumara	4	not out		31
10	T.P.Gamage	st Ranaweera b Chandrakumara	2	(11) c Polonowita b Rupasinghe		4
11	Y.A.N.Mendis	not out	8	(8) lbw b Perera		6
	Extras	lb 1, nb 2	3	b 4, w 1, nb 1		6
			187			209

FoW (1): 1-9 (2), 2-9 (1), 3-9 (4), 4-11 (3), 5-134 (5), 6-144 (7), 7-162 (8), 8-169 (6), 9-176 (10), 10-187 (9)
FoW (2): 1-34 (2), 2-65 (1), 3-91 (3), 4-114 (4), 5-118 (5), 6-164 (7), 7-164 (6), 8-182 (8), 9-187 (10), 10-209 (11)

Bloomfield Bowling

	O	M	R	W			O	M	R	W	
Gamage	20.2	1	81	2	1w	(3)	8	0	33	0	
Ranasinghe	14	3	43	3		(1)	13	2	37	1	1w
Lakshitha	18	5	54	1	2w,1nb	(2)	14	0	39	0	1w,2nb
Katipiarchchi	7	2	30	0	1w						
Gunaratne	17	3	37	1		(4)	16	0	60	1	
Dissanayake	25	5	56	3		(5)	14.3	2	70	3	
Mendis	3	0	18	0		(8)	11	0	52	2	
Gangodawila						(6)	2	0	17	0	
Jayantha						(7)	5	0	15	0	

Colombo Cricket Club Bowling

	O	M	R	W			O	M	R	W	
de Silva	15	4	28	2	2nb		9	2	12	0	1w,1nb
Ratnayake	10	1	40	0			17	3	56	4	
Polonowita	4	0	15	0							
Rupasinghe	11	1	51	0		(5)	17	1	73	5	
Chandrakumara	12.1	2	23	5		(3)	9	0	26	0	
Perera	8	0	29	0		(4)	15	5	38	1	

Umpires: I.D.Gunawardene and R.Martinesz.   Referee: U.Warnapura.   Toss: Colombo Cricket Club
Close of Play: 1st day: Colombo Cricket Club (1) 275-6 (Wethathasinghe 1*, Perera 3*, 91 overs); 2nd day: Colombo Cricket Club (2) 37-0 (Vandort 24*, Ranaweera 12*, 11 overs); 3rd day: Bloomfield Cricket and Athletic Club (2) 24-0 (Masmulla 16*, Katipiarchchi 7*, 15 overs).
J.Mubarak's 121 took 187 balls and included 13 fours.

COLTS CRICKET CLUB v RAGAMA CRICKET CLUB

Played at Sinhalese Sports Club Ground, Colombo, January 24, 25, 26, 2008.
Premier Championship 2007/08 - Tier A
Colts Cricket Club won by four wickets. (Points: Colts Cricket Club 15.565, Ragama Cricket Club 3.155)

RAGAMA CRICKET CLUB

1	D.A.Ranatunga	c Kalavitigoda b Perera	0	c Pathirana b Prasad	1
2	H.E.Vithana	b Kulatunga	36	(6) c Mathews b Prasad	8
3	†R.S.S.S.de Zoysa	b Perera	0	(2) lbw b Prasad	2
4	*S.I.de Saram	lbw b Weerakoon	43	c Kulatunga b Silva	59
5	W.D.D.S.Perera	run out (Weerakoon)	7	b Prasad	22
6	C.M.Bandara	lbw b Weerakoon	2	(7) c Kulatunga b Perera	7
7	K.Weeraratne	c Pathirana b Perera	11	(8) c Peiris b Perera	18
8	K.R.N.U.Perera	st Peiris b Weerakoon	24	(3) lbw b Perera	0
9	S.A.D.U.Indrasiri	c Kulatunga b Silva	21	lbw b Silva	4
10	A.A.D.H.Nilantha	not out	2	not out	13
11	H.G.D.Nayanakantha	b Silva	4	c Prasad b Perera	9
	Extras	b 1, lb 5, nb 2	8	b 1, lb 7, w 1, nb 1	10
			158		**153**

FoW (1): 1-0 (1), 2-0 (3), 3-56 (2), 4-72 (5), 5-75 (6), 6-98 (7), 7-106 (4), 8-143 (9), 9-151 (8), 10-158 (11)
FoW (2): 1-1 (1), 2-2 (3), 3-8 (2), 4-66 (5), 5-96 (4), 6-100 (6), 7-124 (7), 8-129 (9), 9-131 (8), 10-153 (11)

COLTS CRICKET CLUB

1	T.P.Attanayake	c Ranatunga b Weeraratne	9	c de Saram b Weeraratne	5
2	S.Kalavitigoda	run out (de Zoysa)	0	b Bandara	31
3	*B.S.M.Warnapura	c Indrasiri b Nayanakantha	30	c W.D.D.S.Perera b Nayanakantha	1
4	H.G.J.M.Kulatunga	c sub (P.K.J.R.N.Nonis) b Nilantha	7	c Ranatunga b Nilantha	10
5	A.D.Mathews	c de Zoysa b Weeraratne	1	not out	52
6	D.N.Pathirana	c W.D.D.S.Perera b Weeraratne	8	(7) c Bandara b K.R.N.U.Perera	29
7	†T.R.Peiris	c Bandara b Weeraratne	37	(8) not out	10
8	S.Weerakoon	b Bandara	29	(6) c de Zoysa b Nayanakantha	36
9	A.A.S.Silva	c de Saram b Weeraratne	6		
10	U.M.A.Prasad	b Weeraratne	4		
11	P.D.R.L.Perera	not out	0		
	Extras	b 1, lb 4, nb 1	6	lb 1, nb 1	2
			137	(6 wickets)	**176**

FoW (1): 1-5 (2), 2-34 (1), 3-40 (3), 4-45 (5), 5-53 (6), 6-69 (4), 7-116 (7), 8-129 (9), 9-137 (8), 10-137 (10)
FoW (2): 1-10 (1), 2-23 (3), 3-40 (4), 4-48 (2), 5-125 (6), 6-166 (7)

Colts Cricket Club Bowling

	O	M	R	W		O	M	R	W	
Perera	14	4	34	3		9.2	2	23	4	
Prasad	10	0	43	0		14	3	42	4	1w
Mathews	6	1	17	0	2nb	4	0	21	0	1nb
Kulatunga	6	3	6	1		2	0	13	0	
Weerakoon	12	6	19	3		7	1	24	0	
Silva	6.5	1	33	2		8	1	22	0	

Ragama Cricket Club Bowling

	O	M	R	W			O	M	R	W	
Weeraratne	13.2	1	47	6			11	1	43	1	
Nayanakantha	6	1	36	1			11	1	52	2	
Nilantha	5	1	19	1	1nb		6	0	23	1	1nb
Indrasiri	5	0	14	0		(6)	2	0	13	0	
Bandara	9	1	16	1		(4)	13	5	17	2	
K.R.N.U.Perera						(5)	7.4	2	27	1	

Umpires: J.W.L.Nandana and T.H.Wijewardene. Referee: B.C.Cooray. Toss: Ragama Cricket Club

Close of Play: 1st day: Colts Cricket Club (1) 125-7 (Weerakoon 24*, Silva 4*, 34 overs); 2nd day: Colts Cricket Club (2) 124-4 (Mathews 39*, Weerakoon 36*, 36 overs).

The match was scheduled for four days but completed in three.

MOORS SPORTS CLUB v CHILAW MARIANS CRICKET CLUB

Played at Moors Sports Club Ground, Colombo, January 24, 25, 26, 27, 2008.
Premier Championship 2007/08 - Tier A
Chilaw Marians Cricket Club won by 226 runs.   (Points: Moors Sports Club 4.19, Chilaw Marians Cricket Club 17.62)

CHILAW MARIANS CRICKET CLUB

1	M.L.Udawatte	c Nawela b A.M.L.Perera	31	b Ranjith	9
2	D.N.A.Athulathmudali	c Boteju b Ranjith	26	run out	44
3	N.H.G.Cooray	c and b A.M.L.Perera	34	c Dilhara b Rideegammanagedera	49
4	*L.J.P.Gunaratne	c Ranjith b A.M.L.Perera	102		
5	K.H.R.K.Fernando	lbw b Rideegammanagedera	96	c Mudalige b Herath	96
6	W.M.G.Ramyakumara	lbw b Mudalige	10	lbw b A.M.L.Perera	43
7	†C.S.Fernando	run out (sub [P.U.M.Chanaka])	12	(4) c Mudalige b Rideegammanagedera	23
8	J.M.P.C.Jayasundera	c Sudarshana b Mudalige	36	(7) c Rideegammanagedera b Herath	45
9	R.M.S.Eranga	lbw b Herath	7	(8) not out	1
10	S.H.M.Silva	lbw b A.M.L.Perera	5		
11	D.Hettiarachchi	not out	4		
	Extras	b 20, lb 7, w 2, nb 8	37	b 6, lb 6, w 1, nb 1	14
			400	**(7 wickets, declared)**	**324**

FoW (1): 1-33 (2), 2-100 (1), 3-122 (3), 4-293 (5), 5-314 (6), 6-323 (4), 7-351 (7), 8-384 (9), 9-386 (8), 10-400 (10)
FoW (2): 1-14 (1), 2-68 (2), 3-124 (4), 4-131 (3), 5-224 (6), 6-322 (5), 7-324 (7)

MOORS SPORTS CLUB

1	T.K.D.Sudarshana	c sub (G.A.C.R.Perera) b Jayasundera	70	c C.S.Fernando b Hettiarachchi	55
2	N.M.N.P.Nawela	not out	124	b Hettiarachchi	2
3	J.W.H.D.Boteju	c Eranga b Ramyakumara	56	lbw b Ramyakumara	4
4	W.M.B.Perera	c C.S.Fernando b Jayasundera	5	lbw b Ramyakumara	4
5	A.Rideegammanagedera	c sub (M.M.D.N.R.G.Perera) b Jayasundera	1	c Jayasundera b Udawatte	35
6	*L.H.D.Dilhara	c Eranga b Jayasundera	8	b Hettiarachchi	17
7	†M.D.Randika	c C.S.Fernando b Ramyakumara	6	(8) not out	35
8	H.M.R.K.B.Herath	c Udawatte b Hettiarachchi	16	(7) c Jayasundera b Udawatte	19
9	A.M.L.Perera	c sub (M.M.D.N.R.G.Perera) b Hettiarachchi	0	(10) c Jayasundera b Hettiarachchi	0
10	C.R.B.Mudalige	c C.S.Fernando b Hettiarachchi	0	(9) lbw b Hettiarachchi	5
11	P.N.Ranjith	c K.H.R.K.Fernando b Hettiarachchi	13	lbw b Hettiarachchi	2
	Extras	b 5, lb 8, nb 2	15	b 1, lb 5	6
			314		**184**

FoW (1): 1-133 (1), 2-233 (3), 3-238 (4), 4-240 (5), 5-250 (6), 6-257 (7), 7-294 (8), 8-296 (9), 9-298 (10), 10-314 (11)
FoW (2): 1-3 (2), 2-8 (3), 3-22 (4), 4-106 (1), 5-106 (5), 6-126 (7), 7-150 (6), 8-166 (9), 9-166 (10), 10-184 (11)

Moors Bowling	O	M	R	W			O	M	R	W	
Ranjith	10.1	1	51	1			5	0	27	1	
Rideegammanagedera	22	4	56	1		(6)	16	2	35	2	
Dilhara	18	3	59	0	6nb		2	0	16	0	
A.M.L.Perera	21.3	2	74	4	2nb	(2)	11	1	66	1	1nb
Herath	34.5	8	71	1			18.1	5	59	2	
Boteju	2	0	7	0	2w	(8)	1	0	12	0	1w
Mudalige	19	5	46	2		(4)	21	1	78	0	
W.M.B.Perera	2	0	9	0		(7)	3	0	19	0	

Chilaw Marians Bowling	O	M	R	W			O	M	R	W	
Ramyakumara	9	1	36	2		(2)	5	2	13	2	
Eranga	17	1	65	0	2nb	(5)	2	0	9	0	
Hettiarachchi	18.3	3	44	4		(1)	20.3	8	58	6	
Silva	11	0	51	0		(3)	8	0	34	0	
K.H.R.K.Fernando	5	1	19	0							
Jayasundera	24	4	66	4		(4)	11	1	33	0	
Cooray	8	2	20	0							
Udawatte						(6)	6	1	31	2	

Umpires: P.G.Liyanage and M.G.Silva.   Referee: G.F.Labrooy.   Toss: Chilaw Marians Cricket Club
Close of Play: 1st day: Chilaw Marians Cricket Club (1) 314-5 (Gunaratne 95*, 96 overs); 2nd day: Moors Sports Club (1) 206-1 (Nawela 86*, Boteju 39*, 56 overs); 3rd day: Chilaw Marians Cricket Club (2) 206-4 (K.H.R.K.Fernando 43*, Ramyakumara 29*, 51 overs).
L.J.P.Gunaratne's 102 took 202 balls and included 13 fours. N.M.N.P.Nawela's 124 took 266 balls and included 10 fours and 1 six.

NONDESCRIPTS CRICKET CLUB v BADURELIYA SPORTS CLUB

Played at Nondescripts Cricket Club Ground, Colombo, January 24, 25, 26, 27, 2008.
Premier Championship 2007/08 - Tier A
Badureliya Sports Club won by 271 runs.   (Points: Nondescripts Cricket Club 3.89, Badureliya Sports Club 17.245)

BADURELIYA SPORTS CLUB

1	†D.W.A.N.D.Vitharana	c Ganegama b Suraj	62	lbw b Gajanayake	7
2	M.M.D.P.V.Perera	b Kulasekara	32	c Kulasekara b Gunawardene	90
3	T.M.N.Sampath	c Wessels b Ganegama	30	lbw b Gajanayake	1
4	*R.P.A.H.Wickramaratne	c Wijeratne b Suraj	114	c Ganegama b Gajanayake	91
5	W.J.S.D.Perera	b Kulasekara	22	c Wessels b Ganegama	4
6	K.A.D.M.Fernando	c Fernando b Suraj	11	c Wessels b Kulasekara	42
7	R.M.A.R.Ratnayake	c Gunawardene b Gajanayake	36	c Kulasekara b Ganegama	6
8	P.S.Liyanage	lbw b Kulasekara	13	c Gunawardene b Wijesinghe	13
9	M.R.C.N.Bandaratilleke	b Komasaru	7	lbw b Komasaru	26
10	K.L.S.L.Dias	b Kulasekara	4	not out	1
11	S.D.C.Malinga	not out	0	c Gajanayake b Komasaru	1
	Extras	b 1, lb 4, w 3	8	b 18, lb 8, w 1, nb 1	28
			339		**310**

FoW (1): 1-45 (2), 2-105 (3), 3-202 (5), 4-247 (1), 5-271 (6), 6-288 (4), 7-325 (7), 8-335 (8), 9-335 (9), 10-339 (10)
FoW (2): 1-14 (1), 2-18 (3), 3-189 (4), 4-213 (2), 5-215 (5), 6-231 (7), 7-260 (8), 8-306 (6), 9-308 (9), 10-310 (11)

NONDESCRIPTS CRICKET CLUB

1	K.D.Gunawardene	lbw b Malinga	10	c Vitharana b Fernando	7
2	W.L.P.Fernando	c M.M.D.P.V.Perera b Bandaratilleke	37	lbw b Dias	52
3	†M.H.Wessels	c Wickramaratne b Bandaratilleke	4	(6) c Bandaratilleke b Ratnayake	12
4	C.G.Wijesinghe	c Malinga b Ratnayake	29	lbw b Malinga	16
5	*M.K.Gajanayake	b Dias	51	c Fernando b Malinga	10
6	M.S.R.Wijeratne	lbw b Bandaratilleke	5	(3) c Sampath b Fernando	0
7	C.K.B.Kulasekara	c Ratnayake b Malinga	29	st Vitharana b Dias	3
8	M.M.M.Suraj	c Vitharana b Malinga	1	not out	53
9	W.C.A.Ganegama	lbw b Dias	14	lbw b Bandaratilleke	9
10	D.T.Kottehewa	run out (Sampath)	0	lbw b Bandaratilleke	17
11	N.C.Komasaru	not out	4	c Fernando b Bandaratilleke	0
	Extras	lb 5, w 1, nb 1	7	b 4, lb 1, w 1, nb 2	8
			191		**187**

FoW (1): 1-19 (1), 2-41 (3), 3-83 (4), 4-87 (2), 5-103 (6), 6-170 (7), 7-172 (5), 8-172 (8), 9-173 (10), 10-191 (9)
FoW (2): 1-29 (1), 2-29 (3), 3-61 (4), 4-77 (5), 5-91 (2), 6-103 (6), 7-117 (7), 8-131 (9), 9-168 (10), 10-187 (11)

Nondescripts Cricket Club Bowling

	O	M	R	W			O	M	R	W	
Ganegama	6	0	41	1	2w	(8)	7	1	21	2	
Kottehewa	14	0	58	0	1w	(6)	11	1	23	0	1w
Kulasekara	16.2	0	68	4		(1)	12	1	40	1	
Gajanayake	4	0	21	1		(3)	21	1	75	3	
Suraj	26	3	101	3		(2)	12	2	45	0	
Fernando	4	1	16	0		(5)	2	0	10	0	
Komasaru	16	2	29	1		(4)	19	7	58	2	
Gunawardene						(7)	4	2	2	1	
Wijesinghe						(9)	3	0	10	1	1nb

Badureliya Sports Club Bowling

	O	M	R	W			O	M	R	W	
Fernando	7	0	35	0	1nb	(2)	9	1	44	2	1nb
Malinga	13	3	52	3	1w	(1)	10	2	35	2	
Bandaratilleke	15	5	33	3			15.2	5	29	3	
Ratnayake	7	1	46	1		(5)	6	0	34	1	1w
Dias	6.4	4	20	2		(4)	13	0	40	0	1nb

Umpires: A.G.Dissanayake and R.R.Wimalasiri. Referee: C.T.M.Devaraj.   Toss: Nondescripts Cricket Club
Close of Play: 1st day: Nondescripts Cricket Club (1) 2-0 (Gunawardene 1*, Fernando 1*, 1 over); 2nd day: Badureliya Sports Club (2) 199-3 (M.M.D.P.V.Perera 78*, W.J.S.D.Perera 3*, 42 overs); 3rd day: Nondescripts Cricket Club (2) 133-8 (Suraj 18*, Kottehewa 1*, 39 overs).
R.P.A.H.Wickramaratne's 114 took 119 balls and included 12 fours and 2 sixes. D.W.A.N.D.Vitharana retired hurt in the Badureliya Sports Club first innings having scored 45 (team score 141-2) - he returned when the score was 202-3.

TAMIL UNION CRICKET AND ATHLETIC CLUB v SINHALESE SPORTS CLUB

Played at P.Saravanamuttu Stadium, Colombo, January 24, 25, 26, 2008.
Premier Championship 2007/08 - Tier A
Sinhalese Sports Club won by an innings and 104 runs.   (Points: Tamil Union Cricket and Athletic Club 3.05, Sinhalese Sports Club 18)

SINHALESE SPORTS CLUB

1	N.T.Paranavitana	lbw b Pushpakumara	27
2	B.M.A.J.Mendis	lbw b Pushpakumara	10
3	†J.K.Silva	lbw b Wijesiriwardene	9
4	*T.T.Samaraweera	c Sirisoma b Wijesiriwardene	125
5	S.H.T.Kandamby	lbw b Pushpakumara	163
6	E.D.J.Sriyapala	c Wijesiriwardene b Pushpakumara	5
7	K.S.Lokuarachchi	b Dias	23
8	M.T.T.Mirando	c Daniel b Maduwantha	29
9	K.T.G.D.Prasad	lbw b Rupasinghe	60
10	S.M.Senanayake	st G.T.de Silva b Rupasinghe	46
11	C.W.Vidanapathirana	not out	2
	Extras	b 5, lb 9, nb 1	15
			514

FoW (1): 1-33 (2), 2-42 (1), 3-52 (3), 4-313 (4), 5-372 (5), 6-372 (7), 7-374 (6), 8-426 (8), 9-499 (9), 10-514 (10)

TAMIL UNION CRICKET AND ATHLETIC CLUB

1	G.I.Daniel	c Silva b Vidanapathirana	8	c Paranavitana b Vidanapathirana	0
2	*H.M.Maduwantha	c Kandamby b Mirando	31	c Sriyapala b Senanayake	7
3	S.I.Fernando	c Samaraweera b Vidanapathirana	9	c Paranavitana b Senanayake	17
4	S.K.L.de Silva	c Silva b Mirando	11	b Mirando	85
5	†G.T.de Silva	c Silva b Prasad	19	b Senanayake	50
6	R.J.M.G.M.Rupasinghe	lbw b Senanayake	1	lbw b Senanayake	23
7	W.J.M.R.Dias	b Senanayake	8	c sub b Senanayake	6
8	M.Pushpakumara	st Silva b Senanayake	72	c sub (R.D.Abeydeera) b Prasad	6
9	R.M.G.K.Sirisoma	c Mendis b Prasad	5	c Mendis b Lokuarachchi	17
10	O.L.A.Wijesiriwardene	not out	0	not out	3
11	K.M.Fernando	absent hurt	0	absent hurt	0
	Extras	lb 3	3	b 12, lb 10, w 5, nb 2	29
			167		243

FoW (1): 1-18 (1), 2-32 (3), 3-54 (2), 4-65 (4), 5-78 (6), 6-80 (5), 7-104 (7), 8-147 (9), 9-167 (8)
FoW (2): 1-0 (1), 2-37 (2), 3-47 (3), 4-175 (5), 5-194 (4), 6-201 (7), 7-220 (6), 8-227 (8), 9-243 (9)

Tamil Union Cricket and Athletic Club Bowling

	O	M	R	W	
Wijesiriwardene	22	1	102	2	
Dias	19	1	86	1	
Maduwantha	26	9	62	1	
Pushpakumara	31	4	120	4	
Sirisoma	26	4	95	0	
Daniel	2	0	5	0	
Rupasinghe	5.3	2	14	2	1nb
S.I.Fernando	2	0	16	0	

Sinhalese Sports Club Bowling

	O	M	R	W		O	M	R	W	
Vidanapathirana	11	4	36	2		13	4	24	1	
Mirando	11	0	46	2	(4)	15	2	40	1	
Senanayake	12.3	3	34	3		21	3	70	5	
Prasad	8	2	27	2	(2)	15	0	53	1	1w,2nb
Lokuarachchi	6	1	21	0	(6)	9.2	1	33	1	
Paranavitana					(5)	1	0	1	0	

Umpires: S.S.K.Gallage and R.D.Kottahachchi. Referee: M.C.Mendis.   Toss: Tamil Union Cricket and Athletic Club
Close of Play: 1st day: Sinhalese Sports Club (1) 325-4 (Kandamby 143*, Sriyapala 3*, 90 overs); 2nd day: Tamil Union Cricket and Athletic Club (1) 151-8 (Pushpakumara 56*, Wijesiriwardene 0*, 44 overs).
The match was scheduled for four days but completed in three. T.T.Samaraweera's 125 took 202 balls and included 18 fours and 1 six. S.H.T.Kandamby's 163 took 262 balls and included 21 fours and 1 six. E.D.J.Sriyapala retired hurt in the Sinhalese Sports Club first innings having scored 3 (team score 325-4) - he returned when the score was 372-5.

445

LANKAN CRICKET CLUB v PANADURA SPORTS CLUB

Played at Bloomfield Cricket and Athletic Club Ground, Colombo, January 25, 26, 27, 2008.
Premier Championship 2007/08 - Tier B
Panadura Sports Club won by three wickets.   (Points: Lankan Cricket Club 3.75, Panadura Sports Club 16.055)

LANKAN CRICKET CLUB

1	†C.M.Withanage	b Dilukshan	2	c G.S.U.Fernando b Cooray	38
2	D.G.N.de Silva	lbw b Dilukshan	5	c M.T.T.Fernando b Wanasinghe	14
3	D.V.Gunawardene	lbw b Mendis	6	lbw b Cooray	29
4	G.A.L.W.Shantha	lbw b Dilukshan	0	(8) lbw b Cooray	0
5	B.A.R.S.Priyadarshana	lbw b Dilukshan	0	(6) c M.T.T.Fernando b Fonseka	1
6	E.F.M.U.Fernando	c M.T.T.Fernando b Wanasinghe	16	(5) run out	37
7	Y.N.Tillakaratne	c Peiris b Cooray	17	(4) c Fonseka b Perera	18
8	D.G.R.Dhammika	st M.T.T.Fernando b Cooray	0	(7) c Wanasinghe b Peiris	96
9	*S.H.S.M.K.Silva	not out	32	b Dilukshan	32
10	L.D.I.Perera	c M.T.T.Fernando b Perera	12	not out	15
11	D.R.F.Weerasinghe	c Niroshan b Cooray	4	run out	0
	Extras	b 3, lb 2, w 1, nb 2	8	b 19, lb 8, nb 1	28
			102		**308**

FoW (1): 1-4 (1), 2-9 (2), 3-9 (4), 4-9 (5), 5-32 (3), 6-34 (6), 7-42 (8), 8-64 (7), 9-91 (10), 10-102 (11)
FoW (2): 1-41 (2), 2-79 (1), 3-87 (3), 4-124 (4), 5-125 (6), 6-184 (5), 7-186 (8), 8-260 (9), 9-302 (7), 10-308 (11)

PANADURA SPORTS CLUB

1	G.K.M.Niroshan	lbw b Dhammika	10	lbw b S.H.S.M.K.Silva	9
2	†M.T.T.Fernando	lbw b Dhammika	38	b Dhammika	32
3	G.S.U.Fernando	lbw b Dhammika	13	lbw b Dhammika	58
4	*J.S.K.Peiris	b Dhammika	40	(5) c Tillakaratne b S.H.S.M.K.Silva	7
5	W.M.P.N.Wanasinghe	lbw b Dhammika	7	(6) c Tillakaratne b Weerasinghe	55
6	M.N.R.Cooray	lbw b Weerasinghe	14	(4) lbw b S.H.S.M.K.Silva	3
7	G.A.S.Perera	b Dhammika	40	not out	23
8	H.F.M.Fonseka	c Tillakaratne b Dhammika	18	c and b Weerasinghe	2
9	B.R.S.Mendis	st Withanage b Weerasinghe	0	not out	5
10	I.A.Y.Dilukshan	not out	0		
11	H.D.N.de Silva	c sub (K.G.D.Fernando) b Dhammika	7		
	Extras	lb 1, nb 6	7	lb 12, nb 6, pen 5	23
			194	**(7 wickets)**	**217**

FoW (1): 1-43 (2), 2-57 (3), 3-73 (1), 4-101 (5), 5-114 (4), 6-146 (6), 7-182 (7), 8-187 (8), 9-187 (9), 10-194 (11)
FoW (2): 1-27 (1), 2-49 (2), 3-62 (4), 4-72 (5), 5-147 (3), 6-196 (6), 7-198 (8)

Panadura Sports Club Bowling

	O	M	R	W			O	M	R	W	
Dilukshan	10	3	14	4	1nb		12	4	38	1	
de Silva	6	1	12	0	1w		2	2	0	0	
Mendis	8	1	22	1	1nb	(4)	3	0	22	0	
Wanasinghe	9	3	16	1		(5)	20	2	49	1	1nb
Fonseka	1	1	0	0		(3)	14	0	64	1	
Cooray	10.5	1	23	3			20.1	2	67	3	
Perera	5	0	10	1			11	2	34	1	
G.S.U.Fernando						(8)	1	0	2	0	
Peiris						(9)	2	0	5	1	

Lankan Cricket Club Bowling

	O	M	R	W			O	M	R	W	
Priyadarshana	9	3	26	0			10	0	35	0	2nb
Perera	7	2	17	0			6	0	28	0	
Weerasinghe	14	3	55	2	1nb	(5)	7	0	23	2	1nb
Dhammika	20.1	3	58	8	5nb		26	6	75	2	3nb
S.H.S.M.K.Silva	8	2	32	0		(3)	10	1	38	3	
Tillakaratne	1	0	5	0							
Withanage						(6)	0.1	0	1	0	

Umpires: D.Ekanayake and R.M.P.J.Rambukwella.   Referee: K.T.Francis.   Toss: Lankan Cricket Club

Close of Play: 1st day: Panadura Sports Club (1) 151-6 (Perera 22*, Fonseka 0*, 40 overs); 2nd day: Lankan Cricket Club (2) 257-7 (Dhammika 63*, S.H.S.M.K.Silva 30*, 68 overs).

MORATUWA SPORTS CLUB v SARACENS SPORTS CLUB

Played at Tyronne Fernando Stadium, Moratuwa, January 25, 26, 27, 2008.
Premier Championship 2007/08 - Tier B
Saracens Sports Club won by ten wickets. (Points: Moratuwa Sports Club 2.675, Saracens Sports Club 15.69)

MORATUWA SPORTS CLUB

1	R.C.Rupasinghe	b Nishantha	10	c and b Nishantha	5
2	R.A.A.I.Perera	lbw b Serasinghe	51	lbw b Nishantha	4
3	*W.S.T.Fernando	b Abdeen	5	c Niroshan b Abdeen	9
4	L.T.A.de Silva	c Niroshan b Serasinghe	1	b Nishantha	8
5	†R.M.Mendis	c Abeyratne b Pushpakumara	14	c Niroshan b Abdeen	36
6	H.U.K.de Silva	st Niroshan b Karunaratne	63	(7) lbw b Nishantha	30
7	M.D.S.Perera	b Karunaratne	1	(8) not out	26
8	A.L.D.M.Deshapriya	c Alwis b Karunaratne	1	(6) st Niroshan b Karunaratne	14
9	S.J.C.de Silva	not out	10	b Pushpakumara	8
10	S.P.Rupasinghe	lbw b Serasinghe	0	st Niroshan b Nishantha	0
11	P.C.M.Fernando	lbw b Nishantha	6	lbw b Karunaratne	9
	Extras	b 6, lb 1, nb 5	12	b 2, lb 7, nb 3	12
			174		**161**

FoW (1): 1-19 (1), 2-26 (3), 3-32 (4), 4-75 (2), 5-140 (5), 6-141 (7), 7-151 (8), 8-158 (6), 9-159 (10), 10-174 (11)
FoW (2): 1-5 (2), 2-18 (3), 3-19 (1), 4-39 (4), 5-62 (6), 6-104 (5), 7-110 (7), 8-119 (9), 9-122 (10), 10-161 (11)

SARACENS SPORTS CLUB

1	W.G.R.K.Alwis	run out (H.U.K.de Silva)	73	not out	62
2	P.K.Bodhisha	c R.C.Rupasinghe b Deshapriya	0	not out	50
3	M.I.Abdeen	lbw b Deshapriya	1		
4	P.M.Pushpakumara	lbw b P.C.M.Fernando	1		
5	N.M.S.M.Sepala	c Mendis b Deshapriya	7		
6	*G.N.Abeyratne	c M.D.S.Perera b Deshapriya	23		
7	W.S.D.Fernando	c Mendis b P.C.M.Fernando	36		
8	S.C.Serasinghe	c R.A.A.I.Perera b S.J.C.de Silva	34		
9	M.L.R.Karunaratne	not out	20		
10	†W.A.S.Niroshan	lbw b S.J.C.de Silva	6		
11	L.D.P.Nishantha	lbw b S.P.Rupasinghe	1		
	Extras	b 3, lb 3, w 2, nb 6	14	b 3, lb 3, nb 4	10
			216	(no wicket)	**122**

FoW (1): 1-4 (2), 2-23 (3), 3-24 (4), 4-51 (5), 5-94 (6), 6-131 (1), 7-166 (7), 8-204 (8), 9-211 (10), 10-216 (11)

Saracens Sports Club Bowling

	O	M	R	W			O	M	R	W	
Nishantha	13.1	4	33	2	2nb		23	7	53	5	3nb
Abdeen	5	1	21	1			14	6	33	2	
Serasinghe	22	6	44	3		(4)	8	2	14	0	
Alwis	2	0	5	0		(6)	3	0	9	0	
Pushpakumara	12	3	26	1			14	7	15	1	
Bodhisha	6	1	23	0							
Karunaratne	9	4	15	3		(3)	17.4	6	28	2	

Moratuwa Sports Club Bowling

	O	M	R	W			O	M	R	W	
P.C.M.Fernando	14	1	49	2	1w		4	0	21	0	
Deshapriya	11	0	52	4	3nb		2	0	14	0	2nb
S.J.C.de Silva	10	1	42	2			9.2	1	31	0	
S.P.Rupasinghe	7.4	0	42	1	2nb		6	1	29	0	2nb
M.D.S.Perera	15	6	25	0	1nb	(6)	2	0	14	0	
W.S.T.Fernando						(5)	5	2	7	0	

Umpires: R.A.Kottahachchi and S.H.Sarathkumara. Referee: N.Fredrick. Toss: Saracens Sports Club

Close of Play: 1st day: Saracens Sports Club (1) 42-3 (Alwis 33*, Sepala 5*, 12 overs); 2nd day: Moratuwa Sports Club (2) 99-5 (Mendis 32*, H.U.K.de Silva 24*, 46 overs).

POLICE SPORTS CLUB v SEBASTIANITES CRICKET AND ATHLETIC CLUB

Played at Police Park Ground, Colombo, January 25, 26, 27, 2008.
Premier Championship 2007/08 - Tier B
Police Sports Club won by nine wickets.　　(Points: Police Sports Club 16.09, Sebastianites Cricket and Athletic Club 3.185)

SEBASTIANITES CRICKET AND ATHLETIC CLUB

1	H.A.H.U.Tillakaratne	c Weerasinghe b Rasmijinan	8	c Nirmala b Rasmijinan		52
2	H.P.G.Perera	c Soysa b Weerasinghe	15	b Rasmijinan		13
3	R.H.T.A.Perera	c Nirmal b Rasmijinan	12	c Abeyratne b Rasmijinan		1
4	M.A.B.Peiris	c Weerasinghe b Soysa	71	c Nirmal b Weerasinghe		6
5	S.R.Kumar	c Nirmala b Rasmijinan	61	lbw b Soysa		44
6	†K.L.K.Fernando	c Soysa b Rasmijinan	7	(7) c Nirmala b Weerasinghe		48
7	*M.A.P.Salgado	c Abeyratne b Sanjeewa	6	(9) c Nirmala b Rasmijinan		10
8	D.G.C.Silva	not out	13	not out		31
9	Y.I.S.Gunasena	lbw b Soysa	3	(10) c Nirmala b Rasmijinan		0
10	A.B.L.D.Rodrigo	lbw b Rasmijinan	5	(6) c Sanjeewa b Weerasinghe		0
11	M.N.T.H.Kumara	c Jayawardene b Soysa	0	c Nirmala b Rasmijinan		0
	Extras	nb 4	4	lb 3, w 3, nb 1		7
			205			**212**

FoW (1): 1-22 (2), 2-24 (1), 3-46 (3), 4-156 (5), 5-168 (6), 6-182 (4), 7-184 (7), 8-193 (9), 9-204 (10), 10-205 (11)
FoW (2): 1-47 (2), 2-49 (3), 3-71 (4), 4-89 (1), 5-93 (6), 6-146 (5), 7-191 (7), 8-204 (9), 9-212 (10), 10-212 (11)

POLICE SPORTS CLUB

1	†P.H.K.S.Nirmala	st Fernando b Salgado	33	not out	43
2	S.A.Wijeratne	lbw b Gunasena	2	c Fernando b Silva	81
3	J.P.M.Abeyratne	run out (Rodrigo)	40	not out	3
4	W.N.M.Soysa	c Kumar b Peiris	37		
5	P.R.Nirmal	c Fernando b Salgado	0		
6	H.M.Jayawardene	c Rodrigo b Silva	77		
7	*R.G.D.Sanjeewa	c H.P.G.Perera b Rodrigo	45		
8	H.P.A.Priyantha	c Kumar b Rodrigo	34		
9	M.M.Rasmijinan	not out	12		
10	T.A.N.Weerasinghe	c Kumar b Peiris	2		
11	R.S.K.A.P.Dilantha	c Fernando b Rodrigo	1		
	Extras	lb 2, nb 1	3	lb 3, nb 2	5
			286	**(1 wicket)**	**132**

FoW (1): 1-6 (2), 2-68 (3), 3-78 (1), 4-78 (5), 5-175 (4), 6-213 (6), 7-269 (7), 8-280 (8), 9-283 (10), 10-286 (11)
FoW (2): 1-115 (2)

Police Sports Club Bowling

	O	M	R	W			O	M	R	W	
Dilantha	3	1	8	0	2nb		7	0	52	0	1nb
Rasmijinan	19	4	53	5		(3)	21.5	4	68	6	
Weerasinghe	13	2	51	1		(2)	19	1	70	3	3w
Soysa	14.5	0	45	3			5	2	11	1	
Priyantha	3	0	12	0	2nb						
Wijeratne	4	0	12	0							
Jayawardene	4	0	15	0		(5)	1	0	2	0	
Sanjeewa	3	0	9	1		(6)	1	0	6	0	

Sebastianites Cricket and Athletic Club Bowling

	O	M	R	W			O	M	R	W	
Kumara	3	0	20	0		(2)	2	0	15	0	
Gunasena	6	0	38	1	1nb	(1)	1	0	7	0	
Silva	11	1	61	1		(5)	5	0	29	1	2nb
Peiris	16	3	36	2							
Salgado	15	1	45	2		(4)	2	0	26	0	
Rodrigo	22	2	84	3		(3)	4	0	28	0	
Kumar						(6)	3	0	24	0	
R.H.T.A.Perera						(7)	0.1	0	0	0	

Umpires: H.D.P.K.Dharmasena and M.V.D.Zilva.　Referee: A.M.J.G.Amerasinghe.　　　　Toss: Police Sports Club

Close of Play: 1st day: Police Sports Club (1) 94-4 (Soysa 10*, Jayawardene 6*, 24 overs); 2nd day: Sebastianites Cricket and Athletic Club (2) 158-6 (Fernando 33*, Silva 3*, 39 overs).

SRI LANKA AIR FORCE SPORTS CLUB v SINGHA SPORTS CLUB

Played at Air Force Ground, Colombo, January 25, 26, 27, 2008.
Premier Championship 2007/08 - Tier B
Singha Sports Club won by seven wickets.   (Points: Sri Lanka Air Force Sports Club 3.09, Singha Sports Club 15.795)

SRI LANKA AIR FORCE SPORTS CLUB

1	M.A.M.Faizer	c Kavinga b Gamage	1	c Madanayake b Randunu	18
2	†M.K.P.B.Kularatne	c Zoysa b de Silva	0	(3) b Gamage	2
3	P.A.R.C.Karunasena	c Kumara b Gamage	3	(7) c Kavinga b Randunu	4
4	A.Rizan	lbw b Gamage	1	(2) c Zoysa b de Silva	2
5	M.R.Porage	c Kavinga b de Silva	48	(4) c Faux b Zoysa	48
6	M.D.S.Wanasinghe	lbw b de Silva	10	(9) c Zoysa b Randunu	1
7	M.D.R.Prabath	c Kavinga b de Silva	0	(5) c Vithana b de Silva	45
8	*K.A.Kumara	c Faux b de Silva	5	(6) b Randunu	26
9	S.Madanayake	c Kavinga b Gamage	17	(8) b Vithana	22
10	M.K.G.C.P.Lakshitha	not out	29	c Kavinga b Randunu	7
11	A.M.C.M.K.Bandara	c Kumara b Gamage	32	not out	3
	Extras	b 1, lb 3, w 1, nb 12	17	b 12, lb 1, nb 4	17
			163		195

FoW (1): 1-2 (1), 2-2 (2), 3-5 (4), 4-59 (6), 5-63 (7), 6-71 (8), 7-84 (5), 8-97 (9), 9-98 (3), 10-163 (11)
FoW (2): 1-3 (2), 2-13 (3), 3-57 (1), 4-116 (4), 5-154 (6), 6-154 (5), 7-176 (7), 8-184 (8), 9-186 (9), 10-195 (10)

SINGHA SPORTS CLUB

1	D.A.Faux	c sub (K.K.A.K.Lakmal) b Lakshitha	45	c Porage b Lakshitha	11
2	N.T.Thenuwara	b Madanayake	29	lbw b Bandara	3
3	T.J.Madanayake	b Prabath	21	lbw b Prabath	3
4	H.W.M.Kumara	c sub (K.K.A.K.Lakmal) b Bandara	28	not out	28
5	†H.H.R.Kavinga	not out	73	not out	25
6	H.S.M.Zoysa	lbw b Lakshitha	8		
7	*A.S.Wewalwala	b Lakshitha	31		
8	S.I.Vithana	lbw b Lakshitha	0		
9	S.K.C.Randunu	c Bandara b Lakshitha	15		
10	K.S.H.de Silva	lbw b Prabath	0		
11	P.L.S.Gamage	c Bandara b Lakshitha	19		
	Extras	b 2, lb 9, nb 7	18	w 1, nb 1	2
			287	(3 wickets)	72

FoW (1): 1-48 (2), 2-91 (3), 3-113 (1), 4-141 (4), 5-150 (6), 6-229 (7), 7-229 (8), 8-247 (9), 9-254 (10), 10-287 (11)
FoW (2): 1-11 (2), 2-18 (1), 3-20 (3)

Singha Sports Club Bowling

	O	M	R	W		O	M	R	W	
de Silva	13	2	41	5	4nb	13	3	39	2	
Gamage	12.3	1	61	5	1w,8nb	13	2	53	1	4nb
Randunu	17	4	33	0		20.3	5	44	5	
Vithana	8	0	23	0		8	0	31	1	
Madanayake	3	2	1	0		2	0	5	0	
Zoysa					(6)	3	0	10	1	

Sri Lanka Air Force Sports Club Bowling

	O	M	R	W		O	M	R	W	
Lakshitha	24	4	82	6	5nb	6	0	34	1	1w
Bandara	13	3	43	1	2nb	3	0	5	1	1nb
Madanayake	10	0	41	1		(5) 0.2	0	4	0	
Rizan	13	2	47	0						
Prabath	15	2	58	2		(3) 3	0	7	1	
Kumara	1	0	5	0						
Wanasinghe						(4) 1	0	22	0	

Umpires: W.Jayasena and K.M.Kottahachchi.   Referee: A.J.Samarasekera.   Toss: Sri Lanka Air Force Sports Club

Close of Play: 1st day: Singha Sports Club (1) 141-3 (Kumara 28*, Kavinga 10*, 32 overs); 2nd day: Sri Lanka Air Force Sports Club (2) 126-4 (Prabath 37*, Kumara 7*, 40 overs).

P.A.R.C.Karunasena retired hurt in the Sri Lanka Air Force Sports Club first innings having scored 0 (team score 2-1) - he returned when the score was 84-7.

SRI LANKA ARMY SPORTS CLUB v BURGHER RECREATION CLUB

Played at Army Ground, Panagoda, January 25, 26, 27, 2008.
Premier Championship 2007/08 - Tier B
Sri Lanka Army Sports Club won by ten wickets.   (Points: Sri Lanka Army Sports Club 16.19, Burgher Recreation Club 3.17)

BURGHER RECREATION CLUB

1	D.H.Sandagirigoda	c Prasanna b Peiris	26	c de Zoysa b Rathnayake	0
2	I.C.D.Perera	b Peiris	67	c Prasanna b B.A.W.Mendis	47
3	†P.H.M.G.Fernando	c de Zoysa b Peiris	2	c T.R.D.Mendis b B.A.W.Mendis	38
4	D.F.Arnolda	c de Zoysa b Peiris	22	lbw b Palleguruge	35
5	*V.S.K.Waragoda	c de Zoysa b Prasanna	21	c Soysa b Palleguruge	24
6	I.C.Soysa	c de Zoysa b B.A.W.Mendis	37	c Prasanna b Palleguruge	0
7	W.T.Abeyratne	c sub (A.D.L.Wijewardene)		c sub (A.D.L.Wijewardene)	
		b B.A.W.Mendis	0	b B.A.W.Mendis	14
8	M.S.T.Fernando	b Rathnayake	0	lbw b Prasanna	7
9	G.D.R.Eranga	c Palleguruge b Prasanna	33	lbw b B.A.W.Mendis	0
10	C.A.M.Madusanka	not out	13	not out	3
11	A.N.P.R.Fernando	c Prasanna b B.A.W.Mendis	0	lbw b Prasanna	0
	Extras	lb 4, w 1, nb 6	11	b 13, lb 4, w 1, nb 11, pen 5	34
			232		202

FoW (1): 1-41 (1), 2-43 (3), 3-75 (4), 4-100 (5), 5-175 (2), 6-183 (6), 7-183 (8), 8-183 (7), 9-231 (9), 10-232 (11)
FoW (2): 1-11 (1), 2-106 (3), 3-121 (2), 4-163 (4), 5-163 (6), 6-178 (5), 7-192 (7), 8-192 (9), 9-202 (8), 10-202 (11)

SRI LANKA ARMY SPORTS CLUB

1	S.Sanjeewa	c Soysa b M.S.T.Fernando	20	not out	56
2	R.D.I.A.Karunatilleke	lbw b Madusanka	8	not out	32
3	H.H.M.de Zoysa	c P.H.M.G.Fernando b M.S.T.Fernando	16		
4	S.Prasanna	lbw b Eranga	11		
5	K.C.Prasad	c P.H.M.G.Fernando b Arnolda	134		
6	B.A.W.Mendis	run out (Arnolda)	11		
7	T.R.D.Mendis	b Eranga	22		
8	†T.D.T.Soysa	run out (Arnolda)	58		
9	*P.K.N.M.K.Rathnayake	c P.H.M.G.Fernando b Soysa	24		
10	W.R.Palleguruge	not out	8		
11	P.P.M.Peiris	b Soysa	0		
	Extras	b 9, lb 6, nb 20	35	b 1, nb 2	3
			347	(no wicket)	91

FoW (1): 1-29 (1), 2-44 (2), 3-70 (4), 4-70 (3), 5-105 (6), 6-157 (7), 7-311 (8), 8-317 (5), 9-347 (9), 10-347 (11)

Sri Lanka Army Sports Club Bowling

	O	M	R	W			O	M	R	W	
Rathnayake	10	3	56	1	5nb		11	0	41	1	9nb
Karunatilleke	8	0	29	0	1w		7	2	24	0	1w
Peiris	15	2	64	4		(5)	7	1	12	0	
B.A.W.Mendis	18.5	3	41	3	1nb	(3)	30	9	45	4	2nb
Prasanna	9	3	27	2		(4)	14.2	5	25	2	
Palleguruge	5	0	11	0			13	1	33	3	

Burgher Recreation Club Bowling

	O	M	R	W			O	M	R	W	
Eranga	19	5	58	2	9nb		3	0	23	0	1nb
M.S.T.Fernando	15	3	49	2	3nb	(5)	2	0	15	0	
Madusanka	30	5	92	1			3	0	33	0	
A.N.P.R.Fernando	11	3	43	0	4nb		1	0	10	0	1nb
Arnolda	10	1	33	1	4nb						
Abeyratne	7	0	31	0							
Soysa	5.5	0	26	2		(2)	1	0	9	0	

Umpires: M.W.D.P.de Silva and E.J.A.P.A.M.Jayasuriya.   Referee: R.P.Samarasinghe.   Toss: Sri Lanka Army Sports Club

Close of Play: 1st day: Sri Lanka Army Sports Club (1) 67-2 (de Zoysa 14*, Prasanna 11*, 22 overs); 2nd day: Burgher Recreation Club (2) 46-1 (Perera 21*, P.H.M.G.Fernando 5*, 12 overs).

K.C.Prasad's 134 took 201 balls and included 18 fours and 2 sixes.

BURGHER RECREATION CLUB v SARACENS SPORTS CLUB

Played at Burgher Recreation Club Ground, Colombo, February 1, 2, 3, 2008.
Premier Championship 2007/08 - Tier B
Match drawn.   (Points: Burgher Recreation Club 3.655, Saracens Sports Club 11.6)

BURGHER RECREATION CLUB

1	D.H.Sandagirigoda	c Serasinghe b Karunaratne	104	c Alwis b Vishwaranga	5
2	I.C.D.Perera	c Alwis b Pushpakumara	72	b Pushpakumara	32
3	*D.F.Arnolda	c and b Karunaratne	0	c Serasinghe b Karunaratne	18
4	G.R.Perera	c Niroshan b Pushpakumara	22	lbw b Pushpakumara	0
5	H.D.P.S.Harischandra	not out	104	c Niroshan b Alwis	13
6	†M.F.H.Dawood	lbw b Nishantha	1	c Sepala b Karunaratne	11
7	L.A.H.de Silva	c Vishwaranga b Bodhisha	63	c Nishantha b Pushpakumara	0
8	M.S.T.Fernando	lbw b Pushpakumara	4	c Bodhisha b Nishantha	14
9	G.D.R.Eranga	b Pushpakumara	9	not out	25
10	C.C.J.Peiris			not out	3
11	A.M.S.Pushpakumara				
	Extras	b 5, lb 5, nb 29	39	b 5, lb 1, nb 4	10
		(8 wickets, declared)	418	(8 wickets)	131

FoW (1): 1-151 (1), 2-151 (3), 3-205 (4), 4-242 (2), 5-251 (6), 6-377 (7), 7-394 (8), 8-418 (9)
FoW (2): 1-17 (1), 2-41 (3), 3-41 (4), 4-68 (5), 5-82 (2), 6-82 (6), 7-82 (7), 8-118 (8)

SARACENS SPORTS CLUB

1	W.G.R.K.Alwis	c Dawood b Pushpakumara	33
2	P.K.Bodhisha	c Dawood b Pushpakumara	9
3	†W.A.S.Niroshan	c Peiris b Arnolda	46
4	*G.N.Abeyratne	c and b Arnolda	64
5	W.S.D.Fernando	b Arnolda	82
6	S.C.Serasinghe	c Fernando b Eranga	118
7	N.M.S.M.Sepala	lbw b Peiris	3
8	M.L.R.Karunaratne	c Eranga b de Silva	52
9	L.D.P.Nishantha	c I.C.D.Perera b Eranga	31
10	P.M.Pushpakumara	c Pushpakumara b Peiris	2
11	L.A.S.Vishwaranga	not out	4
	Extras	b 9, lb 7, w 8, nb 16	40
			484

FoW (1): 1-44 (2), 2-63 (1), 3-145 (3), 4-166 (4), 5-279 (5), 6-298 (7), 7-430 (8), 8-473 (6), 9-480 (9), 10-484 (10)

Saracens Sports Club Bowling

	O	M	R	W			O	M	R	W	
Nishantha	20	3	69	1	11nb		3	0	15	1	1nb
Vishwaranga	13	1	89	0	12nb		5	1	32	1	3nb
Karunaratne	17	2	67	2	2nb	(4)	11	3	37	2	
Serasinghe	17	3	53	0		(6)	1	0	4	0	
Pushpakumara	39.5	10	77	4		(3)	18	6	32	3	
Alwis	7	1	13	0		(5)	4	2	5	1	
Bodhisha	11	1	40	1							

Burgher Recreation Club Bowling

	O	M	R	W	
Eranga	16	0	85	2	1w
Fernando	14	0	51	0	1w,3nb
Pushpakumara	7	0	56	2	5nb
Peiris	38.3	9	120	2	
Arnolda	19	2	80	3	2w,8nb
de Silva	13	1	62	1	
G.R.Perera	1	0	14	0	

Umpires: D.Ekanayake and M.V.D.Zilva.   Referee: B.C.Cooray.   Toss: Saracens Sports Club

Close of Play: 1st day: Burgher Recreation Club (1) 301-5 (Harischandra 45*, de Silva 22*, 93 overs); 2nd day: Saracens Sports Club (1) 281-5 (Serasinghe 27*, Sepala 0*, 58 overs).

D.H.Sandagirigoda's 104 took 136 balls and included 18 fours. H.D.P.S.Harischandra's 104 took 195 balls and included 12 fours. S.C.Serasinghe's 118 took 251 balls and included 15 fours and 1 six.

MORATUWA SPORTS CLUB v SRI LANKA AIR FORCE SPORTS CLUB

Played at R.Premadasa Stadium, Colombo, February 1, 2, 3, 2008.
Premier Championship 2007/08 - Tier B<R>Match drawn.   (Points: Moratuwa Sports Club 3.795, Sri Lanka Air Force Sports Club 12.125)

SRI LANKA AIR FORCE SPORTS CLUB

1	M.A.M.Faizer	c R.C.Rupasinghe b S.J.C.de Silva	50	c H.U.K.de Silva b P.C.M.Fernando	2
2	A.Rizan	c M.D.S.Perera b S.P.Rupasinghe	77	lbw b P.C.M.Fernando	16
3	W.A.Eranga	b S.J.C.de Silva	1	lbw b M.D.S.Perera	39
4	M.R.Porage	c H.U.K.de Silva b S.J.C.de Silva	16	lbw b P.C.M.Fernando	5
5	M.D.R.Prabath	c R.A.A.I.Perera b M.D.S.Perera	29	(6) run out	29
6	*K.A.Kumara	lbw b M.D.S.Perera	7	(7) c H.U.K.de Silva b S.J.C.de Silva	44
7	S.Madanayake	c S.J.C.de Silva b Deshapriya	76	(8) c H.U.K.de Silva b P.C.M.Fernando	33
8	W.P.Wickrama	c W.S.T.Fernando b S.J.C.de Silva	26	(9) lbw b S.J.C.de Silva	10
9	†M.K.P.B.Kularatne	lbw b S.J.C.de Silva	0	(5) lbw b S.P.Rupasinghe	40
10	M.K.G.C.P.Lakshitha	c H.U.K.de Silva b P.C.M.Fernando	14	not out	21
11	A.M.C.M.K.Bandara	not out	0	st Wijemanne b S.P.Rupasinghe	0
	Extras	b 9, w 2, nb 10	21	b 13, lb 4, w 2, nb 10	29
			317		268

FoW (1): 1-74 (1), 2-82 (3), 3-122 (4), 4-188 (5), 5-188 (2), 6-196 (6), 7-256 (8), 8-256 (9), 9-317 (7), 10-317 (10)
FoW (2): 1-15 (1), 2-32 (2), 3-47 (4), 4-85 (3), 5-142 (6), 6-142 (5), 7-196 (8), 8-228 (9), 9-266 (7), 10-268 (11)

MORATUWA SPORTS CLUB

1	R.C.Rupasinghe	c Prabath b Rizan	121	b Madanayake	10
2	R.A.A.I.Perera	c Kularatne b Lakshitha	0	not out	20
3	*W.S.T.Fernando	c Kularatne b Lakshitha	7		
4	L.T.A.de Silva	c Kularatne b Rizan	26	not out	4
5	†D.S.Wijemanne	c and b Madanayake	62		
6	H.U.K.de Silva	c Kularatne b Rizan	13	(3) c sub (K.K.A.K.Lakmal) b Rizan	27
7	A.L.D.M.Deshapriya	b Rizan	8		
8	M.D.S.Perera	c Porage b Rizan	9		
9	S.J.C.de Silva	c Prabath b Rizan	20		
10	S.P.Rupasinghe	b Lakshitha	7		
11	P.C.M.Fernando	not out	5		
	Extras	b 2, lb 11, w 4, nb 1	18	nb 2	2
			296	(2 wickets)	63

FoW (1): 1-2 (2), 2-14 (3), 3-106 (4), 4-230 (5), 5-230 (1), 6-250 (6), 7-253 (7), 8-264 (8), 9-284 (10), 10-296 (9)
FoW (2): 1-15 (1), 2-58 (3)

Moratuwa Sports Club Bowling

	O	M	R	W		O	M	R	W	
P.C.M.Fernando	13.1	3	43	1		19	3	56	4	1w
Deshapriya	6	2	26	1	2nb	2	1	5	0	
L.T.A.de Silva	3	0	18	0	1w					
S.P.Rupasinghe	18	3	67	1	7nb	(3) 18	1	61	2	5nb
S.J.C.de Silva	24	3	74	5		(4) 18	1	68	2	1nb
M.D.S.Perera	14	2	56	2	1nb	(5) 14	0	61	1	1w,4nb
R.A.A.I.Perera	6	1	19	0	1w					
W.S.T.Fernando	1	0	5	0						

Sri Lanka Air Force Sports Club Bowling

	O	M	R	W		O	M	R	W	
Lakshitha	32	7	74	3	2w,1nb					
Madanayake	8	1	30	1		5	3	15	1	
Bandara	7	1	31	0		(1) 1	0	4	0	
Rizan	37.4	5	99	6	2w	1	0	12	1	
Wickrama	3	0	19	0						
Prabath	5	1	21	0		(5) 1	0	1	0	
Kumara	2	0	9	0						
Faizer						(3) 4	0	31	0	2nb

Umpires: M.W.D.P.de Silva and E.J.A.P.A.M.Jayasuriya. Referee: K.T.Francis.   Toss: Moratuwa Sports Club
Close of Play: 1st day: Moratuwa Sports Club (1) 1-0 (R.C.Rupasinghe 1*, R.A.A.I.Perera 0*, 2 overs); 2nd day: Moratuwa Sports Club (1) 284-9 (S.J.C.de Silva 15*, 91.3 overs).
R.C.Rupasinghe's 121 took 213 balls and included 12 fours.

PANADURA SPORTS CLUB v SEBASTIANITES CRICKET AND ATHLETIC CLUB

Played at Panadura Esplanade, February 1, 2, 3, 2008.
Premier Championship 2007/08 - Tier B
Match drawn.　(Points: Panadura Sports Club 12.815, Sebastianites Cricket and Athletic Club 4.135)

PANADURA SPORTS CLUB

1	G.Y.S.R.Perera	c Fernando b Kumar	6	lbw b Rodrigo		17
2	†M.T.T.Fernando	c Salgado b Kumar	5	st Fernando b Rodrigo		63
3	G.S.U.Fernando	c sub (D.A.J.S.de Silva) b Rajitha	39	c Silva b Rajitha		31
4	*J.S.K.Peiris	lbw b Rajitha	57	c Bennett b Silva		18
5	W.M.P.N.Wanasinghe	c Perera b Rodrigo	0	not out		101
6	M.N.R.Cooray	lbw b Salgado	40	c Rajitha b Silva		4
7	G.A.S.Perera	c Indunil b Rajitha	6	c Fernando b Silva		62
8	H.F.M.Fonseka	st Fernando b Rodrigo	30			
9	S.R.Abeywardene	b Silva	10	(8) not out		18
10	N.Quintaz	st Fernando b Rodrigo	29			
11	H.D.N.de Silva	not out	0			
	Extras	b 4, lb 8, w 4, nb 3	19	b 14, lb 4, w 3, nb 7		28
			241	(6 wickets, declared)		342

FoW (1): 1-11 (2), 2-17 (1), 3-98 (3), 4-100 (5), 5-133 (4), 6-163 (7), 7-172 (6), 8-189 (9), 9-234 (10), 10-241 (8)
FoW (2): 1-76 (1), 2-105 (2), 3-142 (4), 4-155 (3), 5-160 (6), 6-281 (7)

SEBASTIANITES CRICKET AND ATHLETIC CLUB

1	B.Y.Arumathanthri	c Abeywardene b Cooray	40	b Wanasinghe	101
2	R.H.T.A.Perera	lbw b Fonseka	13	c Cooray b Fonseka	57
3	A.D.Indunil	lbw b G.A.S.Perera	16	c M.T.T.Fernando b Wanasinghe	27
4	T.L.T.Peiris	lbw b Cooray	2	(5) lbw b G.S.U.Fernando	4
5	S.R.Kumar	c M.T.T.Fernando b Cooray	4	(4) run out	19
6	D.G.C.Silva	c M.T.T.Fernando b G.A.S.Perera	32	(8) b G.A.S.Perera	12
7	†K.L.K.Fernando	c Quintaz b Cooray	23	c Peiris b G.S.U.Fernando	22
8	G.A.Bennett	run out (G.S.U.Fernando)	6	(6) b Wanasinghe	0
9	*M.A.P.Salgado	c Abeywardene b Fonseka	7	not out	49
10	A.B.L.D.Rodrigo	b G.A.S.Perera	19	lbw b Wanasinghe	10
11	B.S.Rajitha	not out	9	not out	3
	Extras	b 1, lb 8, nb 1	10	b 18, nb 4	22
			181	(9 wickets)	326

FoW (1): 1-33 (2), 2-66 (1), 3-70 (4), 4-78 (3), 5-88 (5), 6-122 (6), 7-144 (8), 8-146 (7), 9-166 (10), 10-181 (9)
FoW (2): 1-105 (2), 2-188 (3), 3-191 (1), 4-213 (4), 5-213 (6), 6-213 (5), 7-242 (8), 8-251 (7), 9-283 (10)

Sebastianites Bowling	O	M	R	W		O	M	R	W	
Silva	12	1	42	1	1w,1nb	22	2	105	3	3w,7nb
Kumar	6	1	31	2	1w	2	0	11	0	
Bennett	1	0	2	0	1nb					
Salgado	11	2	34	1		(7) 2	0	10	0	
Indunil	4	1	19	0		5	0	36	0	
Rajitha	15	3	39	3	1nb	(3) 20	2	72	1	
Rodrigo	13.5	1	62	3	2w	(6) 10	0	54	2	
Arumathanthri						(4) 10	1	36	0	

Panadura Bowling	O	M	R	W		O	M	R	W	
Quintaz	5	0	24	0		(2) 3	0	22	0	
de Silva	5	0	22	0		(1) 3	0	22	0	
Wanasinghe	7	0	23	0		(7) 17	2	53	4	
Fonseka	6.2	0	24	2	1nb	15	2	61	1	
Cooray	15	2	43	4		10	2	33	0	
G.A.S.Perera	10	2	34	3		9	3	29	1	
Abeywardene	1	0	2	0		(8) 1	0	22	0	
Peiris						(3) 3	0	15	0	
G.S.U.Fernando						(9) 16	2	51	2	4nb

Umpires: W.Jayasena and K.M.Kottahachchi.　Referee: R.P.Samarasinghe.　Toss: Sebastianites Cricket and Athletic Club
Close of Play: 1st day: Sebastianites Cricket and Athletic Club (1) 89-5 (Silva 9*, Fernando 1*, 24 overs); 2nd day: Panadura Sports Club (2) 272-5 (Wanasinghe 66*, G.A.S.Perera 55*, 59 overs).
W.M.P.N.Wanasinghe's 101 took 127 balls and included 4 fours and 7 sixes. B.Y.Arumathanthri's 101 took 105 balls and included 14 fours and 3 sixes.

POLICE SPORTS CLUB v SINGHA SPORTS CLUB

Played at Bloomfield Cricket and Athletic Club Ground, Colombo, February 1, 2, 3, 2008.
Premier Championship 2007/08 - Tier B
Match drawn.   (Points: Police Sports Club 8.135, Singha Sports Club 8.07)

POLICE SPORTS CLUB

1	†P.H.K.S.Nirmala	b Liyanage	2	lbw b K.S.H.de Silva		0
2	S.A.Wijeratne	b Liyanage	0	(7) lbw b Gamage		13
3	J.P.M.Abeyratne	c Kavinga b Gamage	30	(2) lbw b Liyanage		3
4	*R.G.D.Sanjeewa	c Kavinga b Liyanage	0	(6) c Wewalwala b Randunu		157
5	W.N.M.Soysa	b Gamage	8	(3) c Kavinga b K.S.H.de Silva		0
6	H.P.A.Priyantha	c Randunu b Liyanage	12	(5) c Kavinga b Gamage		28
7	K.A.D.M.C.Kuruppu	lbw b Randunu	28	(4) c Kavinga b K.S.H.de Silva		25
8	M.M.Rasmijinan	c Liyanage b Randunu	56	c Zoysa b K.M.S.de Silva		5
9	H.M.Jayawardene	b Gamage	8	(10) c Zoysa b Liyanage		5
10	T.A.N.Weerasinghe	b Gamage	1	(9) c K.S.H.de Silva b Liyanage		72
11	G.S.G.Perera	not out	5	not out		0
	Extras	nb 5	5	b 9, lb 3, w 3, nb 4, pen 5		24
			155			332

FoW (1): 1-0 (2), 2-16 (1), 3-16 (4), 4-42 (5), 5-43 (3), 6-66 (6), 7-114 (7), 8-133 (9), 9-137 (10), 10-155 (8)
FoW (2): 1-0 (1), 2-4 (2), 3-12 (3), 4-55 (5), 5-72 (4), 6-98 (7), 7-116 (8), 8-316 (9), 9-328 (6), 10-332 (10)

SINGHA SPORTS CLUB

1	D.A.Faux	b Weerasinghe	24	c Kuruppu b Weerasinghe		61
2	K.M.S.de Silva	c Nirmala b Rasmijinan	10	lbw b Perera		13
3	T.J.Madanayake	c and b Jayawardene	22	b Soysa		63
4	H.W.M.Kumara	c Nirmala b Weerasinghe	18	b Perera		38
5	†H.H.R.Kavinga	c Wijeratne b Soysa	12	c Nirmala b Jayawardene		13
6	H.S.M.Zoysa	c Nirmala b Rasmijinan	10	b Abeyratne		26
7	A.S.Wewalwala	lbw b Soysa	0	c Abeyratne b Rasmijinan		1
8	S.K.C.Randunu	not out	32	not out		22
9	*N.C.K.Liyanage	c Weerasinghe b Sanjeewa	18			
10	K.S.H.de Silva	lbw b Jayawardene	0	(9) not out		1
11	P.L.S.Gamage	run out (Perera)	4			
	Extras	b 2, w 3	5	b 6, lb 2, nb 13		21
			155	(7 wickets)		259

FoW (1): 1-35 (2), 2-37 (1), 3-65 (4), 4-87 (3), 5-97 (5), 6-97 (7), 7-101 (6), 8-146 (9), 9-148 (10), 10-155 (11)
FoW (2): 1-36 (2), 2-125 (1), 3-168 (3), 4-195 (5), 5-218 (4), 6-220 (7), 7-257 (6)

Singha Sports Club Bowling	O	M	R	W		O	M	R	W	
K.S.H.de Silva	9	2	33	0		9	1	40	3	1w
Liyanage	8	1	45	4	3nb	18	4	58	3	3nb
Gamage	12	1	51	4	2nb	14	2	61	2	2w,1nb
Randunu	9.1	5	26	2		32	4	81	1	
K.M.S.de Silva					(5)	6	0	16	1	
Zoysa					(6)	2	1	4	0	
Madanayake					(7)	10	0	42	0	
Kumara					(8)	4	0	9	0	
Wewalwala					(9)	1	0	4	0	

Police Sports Club Bowling	O	M	R	W		O	M	R	W	
Perera	2	0	17	0	1w	12	1	54	2	11nb
Rasmijinan	8	0	43	2	1w	(4) 8	2	21	1	
Weerasinghe	11	2	28	2	1w	(2) 12	2	47	1	
Jayawardene	11.4	0	40	2		(3) 26	4	70	1	
Wijeratne	1	0	2	0		(7) 6	1	16	0	
Soysa	2	1	12	2		(5) 5	1	15	1	1nb
Sanjeewa	4	0	11	1		(6) 13	0	25	0	
Abeyratne						(8) 1	0	3	1	

Umpires: R.A.Kottahachchi and S.H.Sarathkumara. Referee: C.T.M.Devaraj. Toss: Singha Sports Club

Close of Play: 1st day: Singha Sports Club (1) 155 all out; 2nd day: Police Sports Club (2) 307-7 (Sanjeewa 142*, Weerasinghe 72*, 90.1 overs).
R.G.D.Sanjeewa's 157 took 210 balls and included 19 fours and 4 sixes.

SRI LANKA ARMY SPORTS CLUB v LANKAN CRICKET CLUB

Played at Army Ground, Panagoda, February 1, 2, 3, 2008.
Premier Championship 2007/08 - Tier B
Sri Lanka Army Sports Club won by three wickets.   (Points: Sri Lanka Army Sports Club 16.245, Lankan Cricket Club 3.935)

LANKAN CRICKET CLUB

1	†C.M.Withanage	c Soysa b Rathnayake	5	lbw b Prasanna	27
2	P.S.A.N.Shiroman	c Sanjeewa b Karunatilleke	5	c and b Peiris	4
3	D.V.Gunawardene	c Sanjeewa b B.A.W.Mendis	32	lbw b Prasanna	14
4	Y.N.Tillakaratne	c Sanjeewa b B.A.W.Mendis	27	c Rathnayake b Prasanna	121
5	B.A.R.S.Priyadarshana	lbw b B.A.W.Mendis	23	(6) b B.A.W.Mendis	11
6	E.F.M.U.Fernando	c Sanjeewa b Prasanna	0	(5) c de Zoysa b B.A.W.Mendis	40
7	D.G.R.Dhammika	lbw b B.A.W.Mendis	0	c Karunatilleke b Rathnayake	0
8	K.N.S.Fernando	c sub (W.M.V.Weerakoon)			
		b B.A.W.Mendis	18	lbw b Prasanna	12
9	*S.H.S.M.K.Silva	lbw b B.A.W.Mendis	2	c de Zoysa b Prasanna	6
10	L.D.I.Perera	b B.A.W.Mendis	20	c de Zoysa b Prasanna	24
11	K.G.D.Fernando	not out	21	not out	3
	Extras	lb 6, nb 5	11	b 6, lb 7, w 2, nb 6	21
			164		**283**

FoW (1): 1-7 (1), 2-11 (2), 3-74 (4), 4-75 (3), 5-78 (6), 6-79 (7), 7-111 (5), 8-113 (9), 9-129 (8), 10-164 (10)
FoW (2): 1-5 (2), 2-41 (1), 3-49 (3), 4-168 (5), 5-194 (6), 6-196 (7), 7-233 (8), 8-241 (9), 9-268 (4), 10-283 (10)

SRI LANKA ARMY SPORTS CLUB

1	S.Sanjeewa	b Perera	25	lbw b Priyadarshana	18
2	R.D.I.A.Karunatilleke	c Tillakaratne b Perera	3	lbw b Perera	10
3	H.H.M.de Zoysa	lbw b Silva	54	lbw b Perera	7
4	S.Prasanna	c Gunawardene b K.G.D.Fernando	12	lbw b K.N.S.Fernando	54
5	K.C.Prasad	lbw b Tillakaratne	22	lbw b Dhammika	32
6	B.A.W.Mendis	c Silva b K.G.D.Fernando	15	run out	27
7	T.R.D.Mendis	c Withanage b K.G.D.Fernando	5	not out	45
8	†T.D.T.Soysa	c Perera b Silva	10	c E.F.M.U.Fernando b Tillakaratne	33
9	*P.K.N.M.K.Rathnayake	b Silva	3		
10	W.R.Palleguruge	lbw b Dhammika	18	(9) not out	8
11	P.P.M.Peiris	not out	10		
	Extras	b 4, lb 8, w 1, nb 16	29	lb 3, nb 6	9
			206	(7 wickets)	**243**

FoW (1): 1-27 (2), 2-31 (1), 3-72 (4), 4-117 (5), 5-145 (6), 6-153 (3), 7-163 (7), 8-167 (8), 9-167 (9), 10-206 (10)
FoW (2): 1-29 (1), 2-31 (2), 3-47 (3), 4-124 (4), 5-128 (5), 6-161 (6), 7-232 (8)

Sri Lanka Army Sports Club Bowling

	O	M	R	W			O	M	R	W	
Rathnayake	8	2	33	1	3nb	(4)	20	5	51	1	2w,3nb
Karunatilleke	9	1	27	1			4	0	17	0	
Peiris	5	0	23	0		(1)	5	1	23	1	
Prasanna	16	2	28	1		(3)	25	7	76	6	
B.A.W.Mendis	18.1	2	37	7	2nb		28	5	69	2	
Palleguruge	2	0	10	0		(7)	9	2	22	0	2nb
de Zoysa						(6)	5	2	12	0	

Lankan Cricket Club Bowling

	O	M	R	W			O	M	R	W	
Priyadarshana	5	0	29	0	2nb		7	1	43	1	3nb
Perera	9	3	34	2	1w		9	1	40	2	
Dhammika	8.1	0	28	1	1nb	(5)	12.3	1	46	1	1nb
K.G.D.Fernando	13	2	45	3	10nb	(3)	7	1	39	0	2nb
Silva	12	3	41	3		(4)	9	0	38	0	
Tillakaratne	3	0	17	1		(7)	2	0	14	1	
K.N.S.Fernando						(6)	5	0	20	1	

Umpires: S.S.K.Gallage and R.R.Wimalasiri. Referee: N.S.H.M.R.Kodituwakku.   Toss: Sri Lanka Army Sports Club
Close of Play: 1st day: Sri Lanka Army Sports Club (1) 134-4 (de Zoysa 52*, B.A.W.Mendis 10*, 31 overs); 2nd day: Lankan Cricket Club (2) 194-5 (Tillakaratne 85*, 67.5 overs).
Y.N.Tillakaratne's 121 took 249 balls and included 15 fours.

BLOOMFIELD CRICKET AND ATHLETIC CLUB v CHILAW MARIANS CRICKET CLUB

Played at Bloomfield Cricket and Athletic Club Ground, Colombo, February 7, 8, 9, 10, 2008.
Premier Championship 2007/08 - Tier A
Chilaw Marians Cricket Club won by 285 runs.   (Points: Bloomfield Cricket and Athletic Club 3.84, Chilaw Marians Cricket Club 17.365)

CHILAW MARIANS CRICKET CLUB

1	M.L.Udawatte	lbw b Jayantha	23	b Dissanayake		168
2	D.N.A.Athulathmudali	c Jayawardene b Jayantha	77	c Mendis b Gamage		23
3	†N.H.G.Cooray	c Mendis b Jayantha	7	c Mendis b Lakshitha		4
4	L.J.P.Gunaratne	c Ranasinghe b Jayantha	24	c Ranasinghe b Gamage		10
5	K.H.R.K.Fernando	c Masmulla b Gunaratne	105	c Jayawardene b Katipiarchchi		9
6	W.M.G.Ramyakumara	lbw b Gunaratne	50	lbw b Masmulla		106
7	M.M.D.N.R.G.Perera	lbw b Gunaratne	7	c Gamage b Masmulla		9
8	*J.M.P.C.Jayasundera	not out	13	lbw b Dissanayake		11
9	G.A.C.R.Perera	c Gamage b Dissanayake	0	c Jayawardene b Dissanayake		0
10	R.M.S.Eranga	c Jayawardene b Lakshitha	2	not out		2
11	D.Hettiarachchi	c Mendis b Gamage	0			
	Extras	b 4, lb 1, w 1, nb 5	11	b 1, lb 2, w 4, nb 5		12
			319	(9 wickets, declared)		354

FoW (1): 1-96 (1), 2-113 (2), 3-128 (3), 4-176 (4), 5-280 (6), 6-292 (7), 7-306 (5), 8-309 (9), 9-314 (10), 10-319 (11)
FoW (2): 1-28 (2), 2-33 (3), 3-52 (4), 4-99 (5), 5-295 (6), 6-317 (7), 7-346 (8), 8-346 (9), 9-354 (1)

BLOOMFIELD CRICKET AND ATHLETIC CLUB

1	T.S.Masmulla	c Eranga b Gunaratne	41	b Ramyakumara		11
2	Y.S.S.Mendis	lbw b Hettiarachchi	14	b G.A.C.R.Perera		1
3	M.T.Gunaratne	run out (Eranga)	15	b Ramyakumara		41
4	W.S.Jayantha	c Fernando b Ramyakumara	12	b Hettiarachchi		15
5	†H.A.P.W.Jayawardene	lbw b G.A.C.R.Perera	62	(6) c sub (S.H.M.Silva) b Eranga		8
6	*D.M.G.S.Dissanayake	c and b Gunaratne	0	(7) st Cooray b Hettiarachchi		41
7	C.U.Jayasinghe	c Gunaratne b G.A.C.R.Perera	25	(8) lbw b Hettiarachchi		0
8	A.U.Katipiarachchi	st Cooray b Gunaratne	6	(5) b Eranga		34
9	A.B.T.Lakshitha	not out	10	c M.M.D.N.R.G.Perera b Hettiarachchi		13
10	M.P.Ranasinghe	c Ramyakumara b Hettiarachchi	1	c Udawatte b Eranga		4
11	T.P.Gamage	c Udawatte b Eranga	1	not out		0
	Extras	b 10, lb 8, nb 1	19	b 4, lb 4, nb 6		14
			206			182

FoW (1): 1-22 (2), 2-39 (3), 3-60 (4), 4-125 (1), 5-137 (6), 6-167 (5), 7-184 (7), 8-190 (8), 9-202 (10), 10-206 (11)
FoW (2): 1-14 (2), 2-16 (1), 3-39 (4), 4-103 (3), 5-119 (5), 6-138 (6), 7-143 (8), 8-167 (9), 9-180 (7), 10-182 (10)

Bloomfield Bowling	O	M	R	W			O	M	R	W	
Ranasinghe	6	2	29	0	2nb	(4)	7	0	40	0	1nb
Gamage	10.5	1	71	1	1w,2nb		12	1	39	2	
Lakshitha	8	1	51	1		(1)	13	1	63	1	2w,4nb
Dissanayake	23	2	74	1		(6)	15.5	2	79	3	
Jayantha	21	4	43	4	1nb		7	0	16	0	1w
Gunaratne	9	1	26	3		(7)	11	2	29	0	
Katipiarchchi	5	0	20	0		(3)	7	0	41	1	1w
Masmulla						(8)	7	0	44	2	

Chilaw Marians Bowling	O	M	R	W			O	M	R	W	
Ramyakumara	8	1	26	1			11	2	32	2	
G.A.C.R.Perera	12	4	21	2	1nb		10	0	51	1	6nb
Hettiarachchi	16	3	41	2			8	3	29	4	
Eranga	9.5	2	27	1			10.4	1	36	3	
Jayasundera	7	1	28	0		(6)	2	0	4	0	
Gunaratne	10	1	45	3		(5)	2	0	8	0	
Fernando						(7)	2	0	14	0	

Umpires: W.A.Senanayake and N.D.Withana. Referee: V.B.John.   Toss: Bloomfield Cricket and Athletic Club
Close of Play: 1st day: Chilaw Marians Cricket Club (1) 307-7 (Jayasundera 3*, G.A.C.R.Perera 0*, 76.3 overs); 2nd day: Chilaw Marians Cricket Club (2) 37-2 (Udawatte 7*, Gunaratne 1*, 6.5 overs); 3rd day: Bloomfield Cricket and Athletic Club (2) 72-3 (Gunaratne 24*, Katipiarchchi 11*, 21 overs).
K.H.R.K.Fernando's 105 took 145 balls and included 13 fours. M.L.Udawatte's 168 took 232 balls and included 19 fours and 3 sixes. W.M.G.Ramyakumara's 106 took 160 balls and included 10 fours and 3 sixes.

COLOMBO CRICKET CLUB v RAGAMA CRICKET CLUB

Played at Colombo Cricket Club Ground, February 7, 8, 9, 2008.
Premier Championship 2007/08 - Tier A
Colombo Cricket Club won by nine wickets.   (Points: Colombo Cricket Club 15.47, Ragama Cricket Club 2.565)

RAGAMA CRICKET CLUB

1	D.A.Ranatunga	b Chandrakumara	60	c Ranaweera b Rupasinghe	15
2	M.A.Sandaruwan	lbw b Ratnayake	0	lbw b de Silva	1
3	K.R.N.U.Perera	c Ranaweera b Ratnayake	0	(8) c Mendis b de Silva	0
4	†S.A.Perera	c Vandort b Chandrakumara	3	(3) b Ratnayake	0
5	*S.I.de Saram	c Ranaweera b Ratnayake	19	(4) lbw b de Silva	40
6	W.D.D.S.Perera	b Rupasinghe	0	b Rupasinghe	4
7	K.Weeraratne	c Vandort b Ratnayake	14	c Mendis b de Silva	5
8	C.M.Bandara	b Chandrakumara	27	(9) c Mubarak b Chandrakumara	49
9	A.A.D.H.Nilantha	c Ratnayake b Rupasinghe	0	(10) b Mubarak	7
10	P.A.S.S.Jeewantha	not out	3	(5) b de Silva	19
11	H.G.D.Nayanakantha	c Ratnayake b Rupasinghe	4	not out	0
	Extras	lb 8, w 5, nb 1	14	b 6, lb 1, w 2	9
			144		**149**

FoW (1): 1-3 (2), 2-3 (3), 3-25 (4), 4-60 (5), 5-65 (6), 6-90 (7), 7-130 (1), 8-137 (8), 9-139 (9), 10-144 (11)
FoW (2): 1-3 (2), 2-6 (3), 3-47 (1), 4-69 (4), 5-74 (6), 6-86 (7), 7-90 (8), 8-91 (5), 9-149 (9), 10-149 (10)

COLOMBO CRICKET CLUB

1	M.G.Vandort	b Bandara	42	(2) not out	23
2	†D.K.Ranaweera	lbw b Weeraratne	1	(1) b Weeraratne	0
3	J.Mubarak	c S.A.Perera b Nayanakantha	1		
4	*B.M.T.T.Mendis	c Ranatunga b Nayanakantha	2		
5	A.S.Polonowita	c de Saram b Jeewantha	113		
6	K.G.N.Randika	lbw b Bandara	8	(3) not out	7
7	A.D.Solomons	c Ranatunga b Bandara	0		
8	P.D.G.Chandrakumara	st S.A.Perera b Bandara	46		
9	W.R.S.de Silva	c Sandaruwan b Jeewantha	9		
10	N.S.Rupasinghe	c de Saram b Weeraratne	25		
11	M.I.Ratnayake	not out	3		
	Extras	lb 6, w 5, nb 3	14		
			264	(1 wicket)	**30**

FoW (1): 1-3 (2), 2-4 (3), 3-13 (4), 4-101 (1), 5-129 (6), 6-129 (7), 7-215 (5), 8-226 (9), 9-244 (8), 10-264 (10)
FoW (2): 1-0 (1)

Colombo Cricket Club Bowling

	O	M	R	W		O	M	R	W	
de Silva	7	1	31	0	1w,1nb	15	4	48	5	1w
Ratnayake	15	4	37	4	4w	9	0	36	1	1w
Chandrakumara	12	3	31	3		(4) 4	2	8	1	
Mendis	4	3	3	0						
Rupasinghe	10.3	5	21	3		(6) 13	5	30	2	
Mubarak	5	0	13	0		(7) 3.2	1	7	1	
Randika						(3) 3	1	11	0	
Polonowita						(5) 2	0	2	0	

Ragama Cricket Club Bowling

	O	M	R	W		O	M	R	W
Weeraratne	18.1	3	53	2	1nb	3	0	10	1
Nayanakantha	16	4	60	2	1w	2	0	16	0
Nilantha	5.3	2	16	0	1nb				
Jeewantha	9	0	32	2	1nb	(3) 0.3	0	4	0
Bandara	31	8	67	4					
W.D.D.S.Perera	0.3	0	0	0					
K.R.N.U.Perera	6	0	30	0					
de Saram	1	1	0	0					

Umpires: R.D.Kottahachchi and M.S.K.Nandiweera. Referee: S.Ranatunga.   Toss: Colombo Cricket Club
Close of Play: 1st day: Colombo Cricket Club (1) 43-3 (Vandort 20*, Polonowita 12*, 14 overs); 2nd day: Ragama Cricket Club (2) 58-3 (de Saram 33*, Jeewantha 4*, 21 overs).
The match was scheduled for four days but completed in three. A.S.Polonowita's 113 took 210 balls and included 14 fours.

COLTS CRICKET CLUB v TAMIL UNION CRICKET AND ATHLETIC CLUB

Played at Colts Cricket Club Ground, Colombo, February 7, 8, 9, 10, 2008.
Premier Championship 2007/08 - Tier A
Tamil Union Cricket and Athletic Club won by 9 runs.   (Points: Colts Cricket Club 4.01, Tamil Union Cricket and Athletic Club 16.055)

TAMIL UNION CRICKET AND ATHLETIC CLUB

1	G.I.Daniel	c Peiris b Perera	0	lbw b Perera	41
2	*H.M.Maduwantha	lbw b Prasad	0	(8) c Kulatunga b Prasad	0
3	S.I.Fernando	c Peiris b Perera	49	c Kulatunga b Prasad	19
4	S.K.L.de Silva	c Kulatunga b Weerakoon	73	lbw b Perera	0
5	†G.T.de Silva	lbw b Mathews	0	b Prasad	13
6	M.Pushpakumara	c Weerakoon b Silva	53	b Prasad	102
7	R.J.M.G.M.Rupasinghe	lbw b Weerakoon	0	st Peiris b Silva	5
8	T.R.Rasanga	c Peiris b Perera	9	(2) lbw b Weerakoon	4
9	O.L.A.Wijesiriwardene	lbw b Perera	7	lbw b Weerakoon	19
10	R.A.S.Lakmal	lbw b Silva	0	(11) not out	3
11	P.S.Jayaprakashdaran	not out	0	(10) lbw b Perera	0
	Extras	b 4, lb 1, w 1, nb 1	7	b 2, lb 3, nb 2	7
			198		213

FoW (1): 1-0 (2), 2-8 (1), 3-88 (3), 4-110 (5), 5-128 (4), 6-138 (7), 7-157 (8), 8-198 (6), 9-198 (10), 10-198 (9)
FoW (2): 1-36 (2), 2-50 (1), 3-50 (4), 4-81 (3), 5-84 (5), 6-109 (7), 7-110 (8), 8-148 (9), 9-156 (10), 10-213 (6)

COLTS CRICKET CLUB

1	*B.S.M.Warnapura	c G.T.de Silva b Maduwantha	33	c G.T.de Silva b Jayaprakashdaran	54
2	S.Kalavitigoda	c Fernando b Wijesiriwardene	0	lbw b Maduwantha	2
3	D.N.Pathirana	lbw b Rupasinghe	36	st G.T.de Silva b Pushpakumara	55
4	H.G.J.M.Kulatunga	c Rupasinghe b Maduwantha	0	c G.T.de Silva b Pushpakumara	9
5	A.D.Mathews	c Rasanga b Maduwantha	3	not out	59
6	K.A.S.Jayasinghe	c and b Pushpakumara	66	c Wijesiriwardene b Pushpakumara	7
7	A.A.S.Silva	lbw b Rupasinghe	0	(10) c G.T.de Silva b Lakmal	0
8	†T.R.Peiris	c G.T.de Silva b Pushpakumara	2	(7) st G.T.de Silva b Maduwantha	13
9	S.Weerakoon	lbw b Lakmal	16	(8) c Fernando b Wijesiriwardene	8
10	P.D.R.L.Perera	c Fernando b Pushpakumara	2	(9) c Pushpakumara b Jayaprakashdaran	1
11	U.M.A.Prasad	not out	0	b Rupasinghe	12
	Extras	b 1, lb 4, nb 2	7	lb 1, w 4, nb 12	17
			165		237

FoW (1): 1-15 (2), 2-46 (1), 3-46 (4), 4-58 (5), 5-103 (3), 6-103 (7), 7-112 (8), 8-163 (6), 9-165 (9), 10-165 (10)
FoW (2): 1-4 (2), 2-89 (3), 3-107 (4), 4-141 (1), 5-156 (6), 6-169 (7), 7-190 (8), 8-198 (9), 9-203 (10), 10-237 (11)

Colts Cricket Club Bowling

	O	M	R	W			O	M	R	W	
Perera	19.1	5	47	4			14.1	1	63	3	1nb
Prasad	11	2	46	1	1w		9.2	1	54	4	1nb
Mathews	16	4	40	1	1nb		6	2	9	0	
Kulatunga	8	0	29	0		(6)	1	0	5	0	
Weerakoon	11	3	31	2		(4)	9	2	36	2	
Silva	1	1	0	2		(5)	11	0	41	1	

Tamil Union Cricket and Athletic Club Bowling

	O	M	R	W			O	M	R	W	
Wijesiriwardene	6	1	29	1	1nb		8	0	33	1	3w,6nb
Lakmal	5	1	29	1		(3)	12	2	33	1	1nb
Maduwantha	16	5	34	3		(2)	13	0	41	2	
Jayaprakashdaran	4	0	20	0		(6)	8	0	34	2	1w
Pushpakumara	8.1	0	30	3			14	4	41	3	
Rupasinghe	8	3	18	2	1nb	(4)	10.1	1	54	1	5nb

Umpires: B.B.J.Nandakumar and R.R.Wimalasiri.   Referee: C.T.M.Devaraj.   Toss: Colts Cricket Club

Close of Play: 1st day: Tamil Union Cricket and Athletic Club (1) 64-2 (Fernando 37*, S.K.L.de Silva 27*, 16.3 overs); 2nd day: Colts Cricket Club (1) 133-7 (Jayasinghe 48*, Weerakoon 5*, 35 overs); 3rd day: Colts Cricket Club (2) 135-3 (Warnapura 50*, Mathews 9*, 23.1 overs).

M.Pushpakumara's 102 took 96 balls and included 14 fours and 3 sixes.

MOORS SPORTS CLUB v BADURELIYA SPORTS CLUB

Played at Moors Sports Club Ground, Colombo, February 7, 8, 9, 2008.
Premier Championship 2007/08 - Tier A
Moors Sports Club won by seven wickets.   (Points: Moors Sports Club 15.895, Badureliya Sports Club 3.19)

BADURELIYA SPORTS CLUB

1	†D.W.A.N.D.Vitharana	c Nawela b Dilhara	0	c Ranjith b Herath	71
2	M.M.D.P.V.Perera	c Herath b Dilhara	1	st Randika b Herath	60
3	T.M.N.Sampath	c Randika b Ranjith	0	(7) c and b Mudalige	0
4	*R.P.A.H.Wickramaratne	c Nawela b Dilhara	22	c Ranjith b Mudalige	83
5	W.J.S.D.Perera	c Randika b A.M.L.Perera	3	c and b Herath	20
6	K.A.D.M.Fernando	c Mudalige b Rideegammanagedera	1	c Boteju b Ranjith	21
7	R.M.A.R.Ratnayake	c Herath b Rideegammanagedera	0	(8) c W.M.B.Perera b Herath	37
8	P.S.Liyanage	not out	4	(3) lbw b Herath	5
9	M.R.C.N.Bandaratilleke	c Randika b A.M.L.Perera	0	b Ranjith	1
10	K.L.S.L.Dias	c Randika b A.M.L.Perera	0	(11) not out	2
11	S.D.C.Malinga	c W.M.B.Perera b A.M.L.Perera	18	(10) c Dilhara b Herath	8
	Extras			b 9, lb 2, nb 10	21
			49		**329**

FoW (1): 1-0 (1), 2-1 (3), 3-7 (2), 4-26 (4), 5-27 (6), 6-27 (7), 7-27 (5), 8-27 (9), 9-27 (10), 10-49 (11)
FoW (2): 1-145 (2), 2-146 (1), 3-155 (3), 4-240 (5), 5-279 (4), 6-279 (7), 7-281 (6), 8-283 (9), 9-320 (10), 10-329 (8)

MOORS SPORTS CLUB

1	N.M.N.P.Nawela	run out (M.M.D.P.V.Perera)	53	not out	39
2	G.R.P.Peiris	c Sampath b Fernando	7	c M.M.D.P.V.Perera b Dias	15
3	†M.D.Randika	b Bandaratilleke	21	c M.M.D.P.V.Perera b Dias	8
4	W.M.B.Perera	c W.J.S.D.Perera b Fernando	7	c Ratnayake b Sampath	14
5	A.Rideegammanagedera	c and b Bandaratilleke	26	not out	2
6	J.W.H.D.Boteju	c Vitharana b Malinga	29		
7	*L.H.D.Dilhara	c Vitharana b Fernando	94		
8	H.M.R.K.B.Herath	c Vitharana b W.J.S.D.Perera	14		
9	A.M.L.Perera	c W.J.S.D.Perera b Fernando	6		
10	C.R.B.Mudalige	c Wickramaratne b Fernando	0		
11	P.N.Ranjith	not out	14		
	Extras	b 5, lb 2, w 6, nb 11	24	b 3, nb 3	6
			295	**(3 wickets)**	**84**

FoW (1): 1-13 (2), 2-55 (3), 3-74 (4), 4-128 (1), 5-136 (5), 6-218 (6), 7-265 (8), 8-274 (7), 9-274 (10), 10-295 (9)
FoW (2): 1-26 (2), 2-46 (3), 3-67 (4)

Moors Sports Club Bowling

	O	M	R	W		O	M	R	W	
Dilhara	6	1	14	3		5	0	22	0	1nb
Ranjith	4	1	13	1		10	2	24	2	
Rideegammanagedera	4	3	4	2	(4)	14	3	54	0	
A.M.L.Perera	3	1	18	4	(3)	14	1	97	0	7nb
Mudalige					(5)	9	1	52	2	
Herath					(6)	24.1	4	69	6	1nb

Badureliya Sports Club Bowling

	O	M	R	W			O	M	R	W	
Malinga	15	0	71	1	2w						
Fernando	19.2	4	50	5	8nb	(1)	4	0	19	0	2nb
Ratnayake	8	0	40	0							
Bandaratilleke	15	4	49	2		(3)	2	0	11	0	
Dias	8	1	46	0		(2)	9	1	41	2	1nb
Liyanage	3	0	6	0	1nb						
W.J.S.D.Perera	3	0	25	1	1nb						
Sampath	1	0	1	0		(4)	3.3	0	10	1	

Umpires: I.D.Gunawardene and P.G.Liyanage. Referee: M.C.Mendis.   Toss: Moors Sports Club

Close of Play: 1st day: Moors Sports Club (1) 93-3 (Nawela 32*, Rideegammanagedera 13*, 27 overs); 2nd day: Badureliya Sports Club (2) 198-3 (Wickramaratne 31*, W.J.S.D.Perera 12*, 43 overs).

The match was scheduled for four days but completed in three.

SINHALESE SPORTS CLUB v NONDESCRIPTS CRICKET CLUB

Played at Sinhalese Sports Club Ground, Colombo, February 7, 8, 9, 10, 2008.
Premier Championship 2007/08 - Tier A
Match drawn.   (Points: Sinhalese Sports Club 12, Nondescripts Cricket Club 4.33)

NONDESCRIPTS CRICKET CLUB

1	K.D.Gunawardene	c Silva b Lokuarachchi	48	c Paranavitana b Senanayake	185
2	T.M.I.Mutaliph	c Paranavitana b Mirando	26	lbw b Lokuarachchi	36
3	W.L.P.Fernando	c Paranavitana b Senanayake	2	c Kandamby b Senanayake	1
4	C.G.Wijesinghe	c Samaraweera b Senanayake	18	c Silva b Prasad	22
5	*M.K.Gajanayake	c Paranavitana b Mirando	77	lbw b Mirando	22
6	G.D.D.Indika	c Silva b Lokuarachchi	22	b Mirando	54
7	C.K.B.Kulasekara	c Samaraweera b Vidanapathirana	44	b Lokuarachchi	19
8	†M.R.D.G.Mapa Bandara	c Samaraweera b Mirando	0	c Senanayake b Prasad	32
9	W.C.A.Ganegama	c Kandamby b Mirando	9	(10) b Senanayake	9
10	D.T.Kottehewa	c Samaraweera b Vidanapathirana	0	(9) lbw b Senanayake	4
11	N.C.Komasaru	not out	5	not out	0
	Extras	b 12, lb 1, w 7, nb 2	22	lb 2, w 6, nb 1	9
			273		393

FoW (1): 1-40 (2), 2-43 (3), 3-91 (4), 4-116 (1), 5-169 (6), 6-253 (7), 7-254 (8), 8-260 (5), 9-263 (10), 10-273 (9)
FoW (2): 1-56 (2), 2-61 (3), 3-115 (4), 4-158 (5), 5-278 (6), 6-320 (7), 7-376 (8), 8-384 (9), 9-385 (1), 10-393 (10)

SINHALESE SPORTS CLUB

1	N.T.Paranavitana	c Mapa Bandara b Kottehewa	92
2	*D.A.Gunawardene	lbw b Kottehewa	1
3	†J.K.Silva	c Mapa Bandara b Ganegama	71
4	T.T.Samaraweera	c Mutaliph b Komasaru	120
5	S.H.T.Kandamby	c Indika b Komasaru	17
6	K.S.Lokuarachchi	c Wijesinghe b Komasaru	20
7	K.P.S.P.Karunanayake	c Mapa Bandara b Ganegama	32
8	M.T.T.Mirando	lbw b Kulasekara	1
9	K.T.G.D.Prasad	c and b Kulasekara	50
10	S.M.Senanayake	c Gajanayake b Komasaru	16
11	C.W.Vidanapathirana	not out	4
	Extras	b 8, lb 6, w 4, nb 2	20
			444

FoW (1): 1-4 (2), 2-159 (3), 3-197 (1), 4-247 (5), 5-301 (6), 6-347 (4), 7-348 (8), 8-385 (7), 9-432 (10), 10-444 (9)

Sinhalese Sports Club Bowling

	O	M	R	W		O	M	R	W	
Vidanapathirana	14	1	52	2	2w	9	0	34	0	
Karunanayake	9	2	17	0		(7) 7	0	35	0	
Mirando	21.3	2	80	4	1w,2nb	(2) 12	0	48	2	1w,1nb
Senanayake	22	5	57	2		(3) 33.1	2	90	4	
Lokuarachchi	15	8	22	2		(4) 27	3	94	2	
Prasad	9	3	32	0		(5) 17	1	62	2	1w
Paranavitana						(6) 9	0	28	0	

Nondescripts Cricket Club Bowling

	O	M	R	W	
Ganegama	28	6	78	2	1w
Kottehewa	21	4	60	2	2w,2nb
Kulasekara	23	3	75	2	1w
Wijesinghe	2	0	6	0	
Komasaru	42	4	157	4	
Gajanayake	5	1	16	0	
Fernando	4	0	20	0	
Indika	4	1	18	0	

Umpires: H.D.P.K.Dharmasena and B.P.J.Mendis. Referee: U.Warnapura.   Toss: Nondescripts Cricket Club
Close of Play: 1st day: Nondescripts Cricket Club (1) 206-5 (Gajanayake 49*, Kulasekara 27*, 72.2 overs); 2nd day: Sinhalese Sports Club (1) 232-3 (Samaraweera 43*, Kandamby 12*, 64.2 overs); 3rd day: Nondescripts Cricket Club (2) 95-2 (Gunawardene 52*, Wijesinghe 6*, 29 overs).
T.T.Samaraweera's 120 took 179 balls and included 15 fours and 1 six. K.D.Gunawardene's 185 took 313 balls and included 18 fours and 3 sixes.

BLOOMFIELD CRICKET AND ATHLETIC CLUB v MOORS SPORTS CLUB

Played at Bloomfield Cricket and Athletic Club Ground, Colombo, February 14, 15, 16, 2008.
Premier Championship 2007/08 - Tier A
Moors Sports Club won by six wickets.   (Points: Bloomfield Cricket and Athletic Club 2.83, Moors Sports Club 15.445)

BLOOMFIELD CRICKET AND ATHLETIC CLUB

1	K.Y.de Silva	lbw b Dilhara	4	c Sudarshana b Ranjith	17
2	T.S.Masmulla	c Boteju b Rideegammanagedera	19	c Randika b Ranjith	4
3	M.T.Gunaratne	lbw b Perera	9	lbw b Mudalige	15
4	R.Rathika	b Ranjith	6	lbw b Ranjith	0
5	†H.A.P.W.Jayawardene	c Herath b Rideegammanagedera	0	b Ranjith	0
6	*D.M.G.S.Dissanayake	c Dilhara b Perera	13	c Nawela b Ranjith	69
7	C.U.Jayasinghe	c Randika b Dilhara	16	c Rideegammanagedera b Herath	18
8	G.A.S.K.Gangodawila	c Herath b Mudalige	15	c Herath b Ranjith	19
9	A.U.Katipiarachchi	c Randika b Mudalige	25	c Herath b Ranjith	0
10	A.B.T.Lakshitha	c Peiris b Mudalige	17	c Randika b Ranjith	0
11	T.P.Gamage	not out	0	not out	0
	Extras	b 2, lb 6, w 2, nb 1	11	b 6, lb 1, w 1, nb 1	9
			135		151

FoW (1): 1-4 (1), 2-28 (3), 3-34 (2), 4-34 (5), 5-53 (6), 6-65 (4), 7-85 (7), 8-102 (8), 9-134 (9), 10-135 (10)
FoW (2): 1-16 (2), 2-29 (1), 3-29 (4), 4-29 (5), 5-78 (3), 6-118 (7), 7-144 (8), 8-146 (9), 9-150 (10), 10-151 (6)

MOORS SPORTS CLUB

1	T.K.D.Sudarshana	c Gunaratne b Gangodawila	14	lbw b Gamage	0
2	N.M.N.P.Nawela	c Rathika b Gamage	4	c de Silva b Gangodawila	50
3	G.R.P.Peiris	lbw b Gamage	31	lbw b Gamage	1
4	†M.D.Randika	c de Silva b Gangodawila	5		
5	A.Rideegammanagedera	c Jayasinghe b Gangodawila	3	not out	57
6	J.W.H.D.Boteju	run out (Dissanayake)	13	(4) c Jayawardene b Gamage	5
7	*L.H.D.Dilhara	c Rathika b Gangodawila	0		
8	H.M.R.K.B.Herath	c Gangodawila b Gamage	37	(6) not out	7
9	A.M.L.Perera	c Jayasinghe b Lakshitha	12		
10	C.R.B.Mudalige	c de Silva b Gangodawila	10		
11	P.N.Ranjith	not out	14		
	Extras	b 4, lb 2, w 5, nb 7	18	b 1, lb 2, w 3, nb 2	8
			161	(4 wickets)	128

FoW (1): 1-4 (2), 2-58 (1), 3-60 (3), 4-68 (4), 5-76 (5), 6-84 (7), 7-101 (6), 8-125 (8), 9-145 (9), 10-161 (10)
FoW (2): 1-3 (1), 2-7 (3), 3-23 (4), 4-84 (2)

Moors Sports Club Bowling

	O	M	R	W			O	M	R	W	
Dilhara	8	2	18	2			12	1	39	0	1nb
Ranjith	14	3	22	1	1nb		18.1	3	48	8	1w
Perera	10	3	26	2	1w						
Rideegammanagedera	9	2	33	2		(3)	5	3	5	0	
Herath	8	2	19	0		(4)	15	6	26	1	
Mudalige	4.1	1	9	3		(5)	7	1	26	1	

Bloomfield Cricket and Athletic Club Bowling

	O	M	R	W			O	M	R	W	
Lakshitha	13	3	53	1	1w,4nb	11	3	35	0	1w,1nb
Gamage	9	0	33	3	4w	9	1	40	3	2w
Gangodawila	15.3	1	64	5	3nb	7.3	1	50	1	1nb
Dissanayake	1	0	5	0						

Umpires: R.D.Kottahachchi and B.B.J.Nandakumar.   Referee: S.Ranatunga.   Toss: Bloomfield Cricket and Athletic Club

Close of Play: 1st day: Moors Sports Club (1) 135-8 (Perera 5*, Mudalige 6*, 32 overs); 2nd day: Bloomfield Cricket and Athletic Club (2) 130-6 (Dissanayake 60*, Gangodawila 8*, 47 overs).

The match was scheduled for four days but completed in three.

CHILAW MARIANS CRICKET CLUB v RAGAMA CRICKET CLUB

Played at Moors Sports Club Ground, Colombo, February 14, 15, 16, 17, 2008.
Premier Championship 2007/08 - Tier A
Ragama Cricket Club won by an innings and 87 runs. (Points: Chilaw Marians Cricket Club 3.175, Ragama Cricket Club 18)

RAGAMA CRICKET CLUB

1	D.A.Ranatunga	c Jayasundera b Hettiarachchi	19
2	H.E.Vithana	lbw b Hettiarachchi	20
3	R.S.S.S.de Zoysa	st C.S.Fernando b Hettiarachchi	5
4	*S.I.de Saram	lbw b Hettiarachchi	156
5	W.D.D.S.Perera	lbw b Hettiarachchi	1
6	C.M.Bandara	c sub (M.M.D.N.R.G.Perera) b Perera	16
7	K.Weeraratne	c Udawatte b Hettiarachchi	135
8	†S.A.Perera	c sub (M.M.D.N.R.G.Perera) b Hettiarachchi	79
9	P.A.S.S.Jeewantha	not out	107
10	S.A.D.U.Indrasiri	not out	6
11	H.G.D.Nayanakantha		
	Extras	b 6, lb 7, w 1, nb 4	18
		(8 wickets, declared)	562

FoW (1): 1-40 (1), 2-43 (2), 3-56 (3), 4-58 (5), 5-93 (6), 6-360 (7), 7-367 (4), 8-555 (8)

CHILAW MARIANS CRICKET CLUB

1	M.L.Udawatte	c and b Weeraratne	0	b Vithana	16
2	N.H.G.Cooray	c S.A.Perera b Nayanakantha	1	(3) b Bandara	8
3	*L.J.P.Gunaratne	c S.A.Perera b Weeraratne	11	(4) c and b Indrasiri	8
4	†C.S.Fernando	c sub (R.D.Dissanayake) b Nayanakantha	24	(7) c Bandara b Vithana	32
5	K.H.R.K.Fernando	c Ranatunga b W.D.D.S.Perera	24	run out	6
6	W.M.G.Ramyakumara	lbw b Vithana	37	lbw b Bandara	48
7	D.N.A.Athulathmudali	c de Saram b W.D.D.S.Perera	16	(2) c Indrasiri b Jeewantha	56
8	J.M.P.C.Jayasundera	c W.D.D.S.Perera b Bandara	3	c S.A.Perera b Indrasiri	19
9	D.Hettiarachchi	not out	18	not out	48
10	G.A.C.R.Perera	c Ranatunga b Bandara	22	c de Saram b Bandara	18
11	R.M.S.Eranga	st S.A.Perera b Indrasiri	19	c S.A.Perera b Nayanakantha	21
	Extras	b 4, lb 2, w 1, nb 1	8	b 4, lb 4, w 1, nb 3	12
			183		292

FoW (1): 1-1 (1), 2-3 (2), 3-38 (4), 4-40 (3), 5-77 (5), 6-107 (6), 7-117 (7), 8-120 (8), 9-154 (10), 10-183 (11)
FoW (2): 1-50 (1), 2-65 (3), 3-91 (2), 4-94 (4), 5-125 (5), 6-164 (7), 7-191 (8), 8-218 (6), 9-242 (10), 10-292 (11)

Chilaw Marians Bowling	O	M	R	W	
Ramyakumara	8	0	36	0	
Perera	25	2	113	1	1w,4nb
K.H.R.K.Fernando	8	0	40	0	
Eranga	14	3	57	0	
Hettiarachchi	52	14	149	7	
Gunaratne	17	3	48	0	
Jayasundera	17	3	59	0	
Udawatte	4	0	28	0	
Cooray	7	2	19	0	

Ragama Bowling	O	M	R	W			O	M	R	W	
Weeraratne	11	1	54	2	1w,1nb		8	1	32	0	
Nayanakantha	8	0	36	2			5.3	0	34	1	1w
Jeewantha	5	0	32	0		(8)	11	2	34	1	3nb
W.D.D.S.Perera	7	0	21	2		(3)	3	2	3	0	
Vithana	3	0	13	1		(4)	15	4	53	2	
Bandara	7	1	21	2			31	6	89	3	
Indrasiri	0.4	0	0	1			14	6	20	2	
de Saram						(5)	3	0	19	0	

Umpires: A.G.Dissanayake and R.Martinesz. Referee: U.Warnapura. Toss: Chilaw Marians Cricket Club
Close of Play: 1st day: Ragama Cricket Club (1) 347-5 (de Saram 140*, Weeraratne 133*, 91 overs); 2nd day: Ragama Cricket Club (1) 562-8 (Jeewantha 107*, Indrasiri 6*, 152 overs); 3rd day: Chilaw Marians Cricket Club (2) 99-4 (K.H.R.K.Fernando 1*, Ramyakumara 4*, 43 overs).
S.I.de Saram's 156 took 204 balls and included 21 fours and 1 six. K.Weeraratne's 135 took 201 balls and included 16 fours and 2 sixes. P.A.S.S.Jeewantha's 107 took 136 balls and included 8 fours and 6 sixes.

COLOMBO CRICKET CLUB v TAMIL UNION CRICKET AND ATHLETIC CLUB

Played at Colombo Cricket Club Ground, February 14, 15, 16, 17, 2008.
Premier Championship 2007/08 - Tier A
Colombo Cricket Club won by 196 runs.　(Points: Colombo Cricket Club 16.825, Tamil Union Cricket and Athletic Club 3.745)

COLOMBO CRICKET CLUB

1	M.G.Vandort	c Pushpakumara b Wijesiriwardene	19	c G.T.de Silva b Wijesiriwardene	26
2	†D.K.Ranaweera	b Wijesiriwardene	0	lbw b Pushpakumara	7
3	J.Mubarak	lbw b Pushpakumara	26	b Maduwantha	55
4	*B.M.T.T.Mendis	lbw b Sirisoma	9	c G.T.de Silva b Wijesiriwardene	92
5	A.S.Polonowita	c Pushpakumara b Sirisoma	69	run out	45
6	K.G.N.Randika	lbw b Maduwantha	69	c K.M.Fernando b Sirisoma	41
7	A.C.Wethathasinghe	c G.T.de Silva b Jayaprakashdaran	30	b Maduwantha	32
8	P.D.G.Chandrakumara	lbw b Sirisoma	10	st G.T.de Silva b Sirisoma	0
9	N.S.Rupasinghe	b Sirisoma	7	c Pushpakumara b Maduwantha	4
10	M.I.Ratnayake	not out	0	not out	1
11	W.R.S.de Silva			absent hurt	0
	Extras	b 7, lb 2, w 1, nb 3	13	b 5, lb 2, w 1, nb 2	10
		(9 wickets, declared)	252		313

FoW (1): 1-3 (2), 2-42 (3), 3-58 (1), 4-58 (4), 5-189 (6), 6-209 (5), 7-226 (8), 8-238 (9), 9-252 (7)
FoW (2): 1-19 (2), 2-53 (1), 3-118 (3), 4-196 (5), 5-251 (4), 6-305 (7), 7-306 (8), 8-311 (9), 9-313 (6)

TAMIL UNION CRICKET AND ATHLETIC CLUB

1	T.R.Rasanga	c Ranaweera b Wethathasinghe	4	(7) c Randika b Rupasinghe	8
2	P.D.M.A.Cooray	c Mendis b Wethathasinghe	13	lbw b Ratnayake	2
3	R.M.G.K.Sirisoma	c Mubarak b Ratnayake	16	(8) lbw b Rupasinghe	2
4	S.I.Fernando	c Randika b Chandrakumara	10	(3) c Wethathasinghe b Ratnayake	13
5	S.K.L.de Silva	not out	106	(4) c Randika b Ratnayake	2
6	†G.T.de Silva	c Mubarak b Chandrakumara	0	(1) run out	22
7	M.Pushpakumara	b Wethathasinghe	11	(6) c Ranaweera b Mubarak	69
8	K.M.Fernando	c Vandort b Ratnayake	22	(5) c Ranaweera b Ratnayake	0
9	*H.M.Maduwantha	lbw b Chandrakumara	22	b Ratnayake	8
10	O.L.A.Wijesiriwardene	b Wethathasinghe	4	c Mendis b Mubarak	6
11	P.S.Jayaprakashdaran	st Ranaweera b Chandrakumara	4	not out	6
	Extras	b 2, lb 2	4	b 14, lb 2	16
			216		153

FoW (1): 1-9 (1), 2-24 (2), 3-41 (4), 4-59 (3), 5-70 (6), 6-95 (7), 7-153 (8), 8-202 (9), 9-209 (10), 10-216 (11)
FoW (2): 1-17 (2), 2-45 (3), 3-47 (4), 4-47 (5), 5-65 (1), 6-94 (7), 7-96 (8), 8-106 (9), 9-146 (6), 10-153 (10)

Tamil Union Cricket and Athletic Club Bowling

	O	M	R	W		O	M	R	W	
Wijesiriwardene	16	2	48	2	1w,3nb	18	1	70	2	1nb
Jayaprakashdaran	9.2	1	33	1		12	0	52	0	
Maduwantha	20	5	56	1		23	4	56	3	1w
Pushpakumara	20	2	54	1		11	2	44	1	
S.I.Fernando	3	0	6	0	(6)	7	1	18	0	
Sirisoma	13	1	46	4	(5)	27.4	6	62	2	
Cooray					(7)	2	1	4	0	1nb

Colombo Cricket Club Bowling

	O	M	R	W		O	M	R	W	
Ratnayake	16	4	48	2		16	3	42	5	
Wethathasinghe	18	6	35	4		7	2	16	0	
Chandrakumara	16.5	3	60	4		10	2	36	0	
Rupasinghe	10	1	40	0		7	0	30	2	
Randika	6	2	15	0	(6)	2	1	1	0	
Mubarak	4	0	14	0	(5)	5.2	1	12	2	

Umpires: B.P.J.Mendis and M.G.Silva.　Referee: M.C.Mendis.　　　Toss: Tamil Union Cricket and Athletic Club

Close of Play: 1st day: Tamil Union Cricket and Athletic Club (1) 18-1 (Sirisoma 1*, Cooray 12*, 6 overs); 2nd day: Tamil Union Cricket and Athletic Club (1) 187-7 (S.K.L.de Silva 89*, Maduwantha 18*, 64 overs); 3rd day: Colombo Cricket Club (2) 242-4 (Mendis 84*, Randika 16*, 81.4 overs).
S.K.L.de Silva's 106 took 145 balls and included 11 fours.

COLTS CRICKET CLUB v NONDESCRIPTS CRICKET CLUB

Played at Colts Cricket Club Ground, Colombo, February 14, 15, 16, 17, 2008.
Premier Championship 2007/08 - Tier A
Nondescripts Cricket Club won by 9 runs.   (Points: Colts Cricket Club 4.36, Nondescripts Cricket Club 16.405)

NONDESCRIPTS CRICKET CLUB

1	K.D.Gunawardene	run out (Weerakoon)	12	run out (Weerakoon)		1
2	T.M.I.Mutaliph	c Jayasinghe b Alwitigala	8	c Jayasinghe b Perera		14
3	W.L.P.Fernando	lbw b Perera	125	c Jayasinghe b Alwitigala		5
4	C.G.Wijesinghe	c Jayasinghe b Prasad	4	lbw b Perera		31
5	*M.K.Gajanayake	lbw b Prasad	4	(6) b Mathews		16
6	G.D.D.Indika	c sub (T.R.Peiris) b Kulatunga	37	(5) c Warnapura b Perera		19
7	C.K.B.Kulasekara	c Perera b Weerakoon	57	c Warnapura b Prasad		4
8	†M.R.D.G.Mapa Bandara	c Pathirana b Alwitigala	13	(9) not out		48
9	D.T.Kottehewa	b Alwitigala	0	(10) b Mathews		8
10	W.C.A.Ganegama	lbw b Perera	0	(8) c Kulatunga b Perera		20
11	N.C.Komasaru	not out	0	b Alwitigala		9
	Extras	b 11, lb 14, w 5, nb 5	35	b 1, lb 3, w 2, nb 5		11
			295			186

FoW (1): 1-20 (1), 2-20 (2), 3-41 (4), 4-45 (5), 5-121 (6), 6-239 (7), 7-291 (8), 8-295 (3), 9-295 (10), 10-295 (9)
FoW (2): 1-5 (1), 2-21 (2), 3-29 (3), 4-61 (4), 5-81 (5), 6-90 (7), 7-107 (6), 8-118 (8), 9-140 (10), 10-186 (11)

COLTS CRICKET CLUB

1	B.S.M.Warnapura	c Ganegama b Komasaru	77	lbw b Kulasekara		4
2	*S.Kalavitigoda	c Mapa Bandara b Kulasekara	14	c Wijesinghe b Komasaru		1
3	†D.N.Pathirana	st Mapa Bandara b Komasaru	42	run out		15
4	H.G.J.M.Kulatunga	c Gajanayake b Kulasekara	2	(6) b Kulasekara		71
5	A.D.Mathews	run out (Kottehewa)	6	(4) c Gajanayake b Ganegama		18
6	K.A.S.Jayasinghe	c Mapa Bandara b Gajanayake	25	(5) c Fernando b Gajanayake		40
7	S.Weerakoon	lbw b Gajanayake	8	c Fernando b Komasaru		9
8	K.G.Alwitigala	st Mapa Bandara b Komasaru	11	c Fernando b Komasaru		7
9	A.A.S.Silva	c Mapa Bandara b Kulasekara	14	(10) not out		3
10	U.M.A.Prasad	c and b Kulasekara	23	(11) b Kottehewa		0
11	P.D.R.L.Perera	not out	27	(9) b Kottehewa		15
	Extras	b 17, lb 3, w 2, nb 4	26	b 5, lb 4, w 2, nb 3		14
			275			197

FoW (1): 1-33 (2), 2-141 (3), 3-144 (1), 4-144 (4), 5-172 (6), 6-186 (5), 7-194 (7), 8-204 (8), 9-228 (9), 10-275 (10)
FoW (2): 1-6 (1), 2-18 (2), 3-31 (3), 4-52 (4), 5-114 (5), 6-150 (7), 7-166 (8), 8-186 (6), 9-197 (9), 10-197 (11)

Colts Cricket Club Bowling

	O	M	R	W			O	M	R	W	
Perera	18	6	51	2	2nb		16	2	40	4	4nb
Prasad	10	1	50	2	2nb	(4)	8	3	11	1	2w
Alwitigala	13.3	2	41	3	1w,1nb	(2)	12.1	2	25	2	1nb
Weerakoon	22	5	53	1		(3)	23	5	40	0	
Mathews	6	1	12	0		(7)	10	1	28	2	
Silva	12	1	38	0		(5)	7	0	20	0	
Kulatunga	12	5	25	1							
Warnapura						(6)	4	0	18	0	

Nondescripts Cricket Club Bowling

	O	M	R	W			O	M	R	W	
Ganegama	9	1	59	0		(5)	5	0	28	1	
Kottehewa	14	1	49	0	1w,2nb	(4)	11.2	1	38	2	2w,2nb
Kulasekara	20.3	4	43	4	1w,2nb	(1)	13	1	40	2	
Komasaru	23	7	63	3		(3)	21	1	61	3	1nb
Gajanayake	15	3	41	2		(2)	8	2	21	2	

Umpires: S.S.K.Gallage and M.S.K.Nandiweera. Referee: V.B.John.   Toss: Nondescripts Cricket Club

Close of Play: 1st day: Nondescripts Cricket Club (1) 291-6 (Fernando 125*, Mapa Bandara 13*, 90 overs); 2nd day: Colts Cricket Club (1) 183-5 (Mathews 5*, Weerakoon 5*, 50 overs); 3rd day: Nondescripts Cricket Club (2) 124-8 (Mapa Bandara 5*, Kottehewa 1*, 53 overs).

W.L.P.Fernando's 125 took 288 balls and included 15 fours and 1 six.

SINHALESE SPORTS CLUB v BADURELIYA SPORTS CLUB

Played at Sinhalese Sports Club Ground, Colombo, February 14, 15, 16, 17, 2008.
Premier Championship 2007/08 - Tier A
Sinhalese Sports Club won by an innings and 123 runs. (Points: Sinhalese Sports Club 18, Badureliya Sports Club 2.755)

BADURELIYA SPORTS CLUB

1	†D.W.A.N.D.Vitharana	c Samaraweera b Karunanayake	17	b Senanayake	39
2	M.M.D.P.V.Perera	c Silva b Karunanayake	18	c Silva b Zoysa	0
3	T.M.N.Sampath	b Prasad	2	c and b Senanayake	9
4	*R.P.A.H.Wickramaratne	c Karunanayake b Mirando	28	c Senanayake b Mirando	24
5	W.J.S.D.Perera	c Lokuarachchi b Mirando	10	b Senanayake	4
6	U.R.P.Perera	not out	71	run out	2
7	R.M.A.R.Ratnayake	c Paranavitana b Lokuarachchi	11	c Karunanayake b Lokuarachchi	16
8	P.S.Liyanage	run out (Zoysa)	44	c Mirando b Lokuarachchi	33
9	M.R.C.N.Bandaratilleke	lbw b Lokuarachchi	18	c Karunanayake b Lokuarachchi	1
10	S.D.C.Malinga	c Silva b Mirando	11	c Mirando b Senanayake	4
11	K.L.S.L.Dias	c Silva b Zoysa	4	not out	0
	Extras	b 4, lb 9, w 6	19	b 4, lb 1, w 1	6
			253		138

FoW (1): 1-35 (1), 2-36 (2), 3-62 (3), 4-74 (4), 5-85 (5), 6-107 (7), 7-189 (8), 8-217 (9), 9-230 (10), 10-253 (11)
FoW (2): 1-11 (2), 2-49 (3), 3-50 (1), 4-82 (4), 5-82 (5), 6-90 (6), 7-112 (7), 8-116 (9), 9-137 (10), 10-138 (8)

SINHALESE SPORTS CLUB

1	K.Magage	c Liyanage b Ratnayake	35
2	N.T.Paranavitana	c sub (K.A.D.M.Fernando) b U.R.P.Perera	112
3	†J.K.Silva	b Dias	45
4	*T.T.Samaraweera	c and b Bandaratilleke	31
5	S.H.T.Kandamby	lbw b Sampath	110
6	K.S.Lokuarachchi	c Vitharana b Ratnayake	0
7	K.P.S.P.Karunanayake	not out	122
8	K.T.G.D.Prasad	st Vitharana b Dias	27
9	D.N.T.Zoysa	c Malinga b Dias	18
10	M.T.T.Mirando		
11	S.M.Senanayake		
	Extras	b 4, lb 3, w 2, nb 5	14
	(8 wickets, declared)		514

FoW (1): 1-63 (1), 2-148 (3), 3-213 (4), 4-241 (2), 5-243 (6), 6-419 (5), 7-486 (8), 8-514 (9)

Sinhalese Bowling	O	M	R	W		O	M	R	W	
Zoysa	8.1	2	46	1	1w	4	0	20	1	
Karunanayake	9	1	31	2	1w					
Mirando	15	3	54	3		(5)	6	4	10	1
Prasad	15	2	41	1			6	1	34	0
Lokuarachchi	19.4	7	22	2		(6)	4.2	1	27	3
Senanayake	12.2	1	41	0		(3)	15	5	30	4
Paranavitana	2	0	5	0						
Magage						(2)	2	0	12	0	1w

Badureliya Bowling	O	M	R	W	
Malinga	12	3	46	0	
Ratnayake	17	0	69	2	2w
Sampath	15	1	67	1	
Bandaratilleke	18	2	89	1	
Liyanage	9	0	39	0	3nb
W.J.S.D.Perera	4	0	23	0	2nb
Dias	26.5	5	129	3	
U.R.P.Perera	6	2	35	1	
Wickramaratne	2	0	10	0	

Umpires: J.W.L.Nandana and W.A.Senanayake. Referee: G.F.Labrooy. Toss: Badureliya Sports Club
Close of Play: 1st day: Sinhalese Sports Club (1) 16-0 (Magage 12*, Paranavitana 3*, 6 overs); 2nd day: Sinhalese Sports Club (1) 242-4 (Kandamby 14*, Lokuarachchi 0*, 60 overs); 3rd day: Badureliya Sports Club (2) 138-9 (Liyanage 33*, Dias 0*, 37 overs).
N.T.Paranavitana's 112 took 139 balls and included 14 fours. S.H.T.Kandamby's 110 took 135 balls and included 12 fours and 2 sixes. K.P.S.P.Karunanayake's 122 took 152 balls and included 10 fours and 6 sixes.

465

BURGHER RECREATION CLUB v MORATUWA SPORTS CLUB

Played at Burgher Recreation Club Ground, Colombo, February 15, 16, 17, 2008.
Premier Championship 2007/08 - Tier B
Match drawn.   (Points: Burgher Recreation Club 11.825, Moratuwa Sports Club 3.41)

BURGHER RECREATION CLUB

1	D.H.Sandagirigoda	c Rupasinghe b Fernando	11	c L.T.A.de Silva b Fernando	12
2	I.C.D.Perera	c S.J.C.de Silva b de Mel	18	c Wijemanne b M.D.S.Perera	84
3	L.A.H.de Silva	c Fernando b S.J.C.de Silva	26	c Mendis b Fernando	12
4	G.R.Perera	c Wijemanne b de Mel	79	c Wijemanne b Fernando	29
5	*H.D.P.S.Harischandra	b M.D.S.Perera	18	lbw b Fernando	1
6	†M.F.H.Dawood	c L.T.A.de Silva b Fernando	2		
7	T.H.D.C.C.Kumara	c Fernando b de Mel	41	(6) c M.D.S.Perera b Fernando	45
8	M.S.T.Fernando	b Fernando	41	(7) not out	0
9	C.A.M.Madusanka	b Dammika	31	(8) not out	1
10	C.C.J.Peiris	not out	18		
11	A.M.S.P.Kumara	lbw b Dammika	0		
	Extras	b 9, lb 9, w 18, nb 4	40	b 2, lb 3, w 3, nb 3, pen 5	16
			325	(6 wickets, declared)	200

FoW (1): 1-41 (1), 2-45 (2), 3-108 (3), 4-148 (5), 5-164 (6), 6-212 (4), 7-243 (7), 8-290 (9), 9-322 (8), 10-325 (11)
FoW (2): 1-30 (1), 2-48 (3), 3-117 (4), 4-129 (5), 5-189 (2), 6-199 (6)

MORATUWA SPORTS CLUB

1	R.C.Rupasinghe	lbw b Madusanka	40	c A.M.S.P.Kumara b Fernando	40
2	R.A.A.I.Perera	b Madusanka	21	c Harischandra b T.H.D.C.C.Kumara	6
3	R.M.Mendis	c T.H.D.C.C.Kumara b Peiris	46	not out	4
4	L.T.A.de Silva	c T.H.D.C.C.Kumara b Madusanka	11		
5	†D.S.Wijemanne	c G.R.Perera b Madusanka	0		
6	H.U.K.de Silva	c I.C.D.Perera b Madusanka	75		
7	W.P.D.de Mel	lbw b Madusanka	7		
8	*M.D.S.Perera	lbw b Madusanka	25		
9	P.C.M.Fernando	b A.M.S.P.Kumara	26		
10	S.J.C.de Silva	b Madusanka	25		
11	S.D.Dammika	not out	2		
	Extras	b 9, lb 2, nb 11	22	lb 3, nb 9	12
			300	(2 wickets)	62

FoW (1): 1-66 (2), 2-67 (1), 3-96 (4), 4-96 (5), 5-203 (6), 6-215 (7), 7-223 (3), 8-257 (8), 9-287 (9), 10-300 (10)
FoW (2): 1-23 (2), 2-62 (1)

Moratuwa Sports Club Bowling

	O	M	R	W			O	M	R	W	
Fernando	21	2	88	3	2w,2nb		14	2	44	5	1w
de Mel	18	3	78	3	4w,1nb	(3)	5	0	16	0	2w
L.T.A.de Silva	5	1	17	0							
Dammika	18.2	7	28	2		(2)	8	1	23	0	
S.J.C.de Silva	17	5	52	1			10	0	47	0	
M.D.S.Perera	16	2	43	1	1nb		11	1	47	1	3nb
R.A.A.I.Perera	1	0	1	0							
Rupasinghe						(4)	3	0	8	0	
Mendis						(7)	2	0	5	0	

Burgher Recreation Club Bowling

	O	M	R	W			O	M	R	W	
A.M.S.P.Kumara	10	1	61	1	7nb	(3)	1	0	18	0	3nb
T.H.D.C.C.Kumara	4	0	30	0	4nb		2	0	17	1	
Fernando	9	1	43	0		(1)	3.2	0	24	1	1nb
Madusanka	35.5	10	76	8							
de Silva	13	4	47	0							
Peiris	14	4	32	1							

Umpires: R.A.Kottahachchi and R.M.P.J.Rambukwella.   Referee: C.T.M.Devaraj.   Toss: Moratuwa Sports Club

Close of Play: 1st day: Burgher Recreation Club (1) 189-5 (G.R.Perera 70*, T.H.D.C.C.Kumara 15*, 62 overs); 2nd day: Moratuwa Sports Club (1) 227-7 (Fernando 2*, M.D.S.Perera 8*, 56 overs).

LANKAN CRICKET CLUB v SARACENS SPORTS CLUB

Played at R.Premadasa Stadium, Colombo, February 15, 16, 17, 2008.
Premier Championship 2007/08 - Tier B
Match drawn.   (Points: Lankan Cricket Club 2.97, Saracens Sports Club 11.6)

SARACENS SPORTS CLUB

1	W.G.R.K.Alwis	c Weerasinghe b Dhammika	50
2	P.K.Bodhisha	not out	226
3	†W.A.S.Niroshan	lbw b Fernando	14
4	*G.N.Abeyratne	st Shantha b Weerasinghe	16
5	W.S.D.Fernando	run out (Namal)	7
6	S.C.Serasinghe	b Weerasinghe	113
7	N.M.S.M.Sepala	c S.L.Perera b Weerasinghe	18
8	M.L.R.Karunaratne	lbw b Kumara	13
9	L.D.P.Nishantha	lbw b Fernando	15
10	P.M.Pushpakumara	not out	11
11	L.A.S.Vishwaranga		
	Extras	b 1, lb 3, w 1, nb 15	20
		(8 wickets, declared)	**503**

FoW (1): 1-76 (1), 2-103 (3), 3-141 (4), 4-150 (5), 5-376 (6), 6-419 (7), 7-447 (8), 8-482 (9)

LANKAN CRICKET CLUB

1	C.M.Withanage	c Pushpakumara b Vishwaranga	5	c Nishantha b Karunaratne	30
2	D.G.N.de Silva	st Niroshan b Karunaratne	43	run out	31
3	†G.A.L.W.Shantha	b Pushpakumara	10	lbw b Pushpakumara	6
4	*Y.N.Tillakaratne	st Niroshan b Serasinghe	40	c sub (G.K.Amarasinghe) b Nishantha	67
5	J.R.G.Namal	run out (Alwis)	0	(6) c Niroshan b Nishantha	3
6	D.G.R.Dhammika	c Niroshan b Serasinghe	36	(5) c sub (R.S.A.Palliyaguruge) b Nishantha	86
7	S.L.Perera	c Vishwaranga b Serasinghe	1	not out	13
8	D.R.F.Weerasinghe	not out	22	not out	8
9	L.D.I.Perera	c Alwis b Serasinghe	0		
10	K.G.D.Fernando	b Pushpakumara	3		
11	P.D.M.P.N.Kumara	c Nishantha b Pushpakumara	1		
	Extras	b 1, lb 3, w 5, nb 9	18	b 5, lb 1, nb 5	11
			179	**(6 wickets)**	**255**

FoW (1): 1-9 (1), 2-49 (3), 3-73 (2), 4-78 (5), 5-142 (6), 6-145 (4), 7-146 (7), 8-146 (9), 9-153 (10), 10-179 (11)
FoW (2): 1-67 (2), 2-74 (1), 3-98 (3), 4-229 (4), 5-232 (5), 6-234 (6)

Lankan Cricket Club Bowling	O	M	R	W	
L.D.I.Perera	10.2	0	81	0	
Kumara	12	3	64	1	
Dhammika	29	5	95	1	1nb
Fernando	20	2	107	2	1w,13nb
Weerasinghe	27	4	86	3	1nb
Tillakaratne	7	0	27	0	
Namal	7	0	29	0	
Withanage	3	0	10	0	

Saracens Sports Club Bowling	O	M	R	W			O	M	R	W	
Nishantha	11	2	28	0	6nb	(2)	7	1	19	3	2nb
Vishwaranga	9	2	28	1	1w,2nb	(1)	3	0	15	0	3nb
Pushpakumara	13.4	3	32	3			13	3	47	1	
Alwis	1	0	5	0	1nb						
Serasinghe	15	4	39	4		(4)	15	4	69	0	
Karunaratne	9	1	43	1		(5)	15	1	69	1	
Abeyratne						(6)	6	1	22	0	
Bodhisha						(7)	3	0	8	0	

Umpires: W.Jayasena and R.R.Wimalasiri.   Referee: A.M.J.G.Amerasinghe.   Toss: Lankan Cricket Club

Close of Play: 1st day: Saracens Sports Club (1) 239-4 (Bodhisha 98*, Serasinghe 44*, 57.3 overs); 2nd day: Lankan Cricket Club (1) 73-3 (Tillakaratne 8*, Namal 0*, 18 overs).
P.K.Bodhisha's 226 took 351 balls and included 22 fours and 6 sixes. S.C.Serasinghe's 113 took 170 balls and included 18 fours and 1 six.

PANADURA SPORTS CLUB v SINGHA SPORTS CLUB

Played at Panadura Esplanade, February 15, 16, 17, 2008.
Premier Championship 2007/08 - Tier B
Panadura Sports Club won by 170 runs.   (Points: Panadura Sports Club 16.705, Singha Sports Club 3.355)

PANADURA SPORTS CLUB
1	†M.T.T.Fernando	c Ranatunga b Liyanage	0	b K.S.H.de Silva	15
2	M.R.Fernando	b Liyanage	64	c Gamage b Liyanage	4
3	G.S.U.Fernando	c Randunu b Gamage	17	c Randunu b K.S.H.de Silva	29
4	*J.S.K.Peiris	c K.S.H.de Silva b Liyanage	53	c Gamage b Randunu	46
5	W.M.P.N.Wanasinghe	c and b Randunu	67	(6) c and b Randunu	36
6	M.N.R.Cooray	lbw b Ranatunga	24	(5) not out	61
7	G.A.S.Perera	c Madanayake b Ranatunga	32		
8	H.F.M.Fonseka	lbw b Liyanage	28		
9	N.Quintaz	b Randunu	6		
10	B.R.S.Mendis	c Liyanage b Ranatunga	1		
11	I.A.Y.Dilukshan	not out	15		
	Extras	b 8, lb 8, w 1, nb 4	21	b 9, lb 6, w 1, nb 6	22
			328	**(5 wickets, declared)**	**213**

FoW (1): 1-3 (1), 2-39 (3), 3-120 (2), 4-150 (4), 5-181 (6), 6-273 (5), 7-281 (7), 8-290 (9), 9-291 (10), 10-328 (8)
FoW (2): 1-21 (2), 2-21 (1), 3-81 (3), 4-126 (4), 5-213 (6)

SINGHA SPORTS CLUB
1	D.A.Faux	c G.S.U.Fernando b Dilukshan	13	c M.T.T.Fernando b Fonseka	51
2	K.M.S.de Silva	c G.S.U.Fernando b Quintaz	11	c M.T.T.Fernando b Mendis	18
3	T.J.Madanayake	b Wanasinghe	9	c and b Fonseka	19
4	H.W.M.Kumara	lbw b Cooray	48	c Peiris b Perera	19
5	†H.H.R.Kavinga	lbw b Wanasinghe	7	c Perera b Fonseka	29
6	H.S.M.Zoysa	b Wanasinghe	18	b Cooray	4
7	S.K.C.Randunu	run out (Fonseka)	23	c M.T.T.Fernando b Perera	4
8	*N.C.K.Liyanage	lbw b Perera	4	c and b Perera	0
9	K.S.H.de Silva	c and b Cooray	35	not out	13
10	P.L.S.Gamage	b Perera	2	c sub (G.K.M.Niroshan) b Fonseka	0
11	C.Ranatunga	not out	0	c Peiris b Cooray	5
	Extras	b 8, lb 1, nb 4	13	b 12, lb 4, w 7, nb 3	26
			183		**188**

FoW (1): 1-20 (2), 2-26 (1), 3-52 (3), 4-65 (5), 5-98 (4), 6-126 (6), 7-139 (7), 8-158 (8), 9-178 (9), 10-183 (10)
FoW (2): 1-60 (2), 2-106 (3), 3-109 (1), 4-154 (4), 5-159 (6), 6-164 (7), 7-170 (8), 8-170 (5), 9-170 (10), 10-188 (11)

Singha Sports Club Bowling
	O	M	R	W		O	M	R	W	
K.S.H.de Silva	13	0	38	0		11	1	34	2	
Liyanage	18.4	3	83	4	1w,2nb	9	1	45	1	4nb
Gamage	10	2	42	1	2nb	6	0	26	0	1w,2nb
Randunu	20	3	66	2		12.1	1	55	2	
Ranatunga	21	2	61	3		5	0	28	0	
K.M.S.de Silva	7	0	22	0						
Zoysa					(6)	1	0	10	0	

Panadura Sports Club Bowling
	O	M	R	W			O	M	R	W	
Dilukshan	5	1	26	1			4	0	22	0	1w
Quintaz	5	1	16	1		(3)	3	0	10	0	
Mendis	3	0	24	0	4nb	(2)	10	2	30	1	2nb
Wanasinghe	12	4	40	3			4	0	17	0	
Peiris	2	1	1	0							
Cooray	10	4	35	2		(5)	13.4	1	41	2	2w
Fonseka	5	1	16	0		(6)	10	1	22	4	1nb
Perera	8.3	3	16	2		(7)	10	2	30	3	

Umpires: H.D.P.K.Dharmasena and E.J.A.P.A.M.Jayasuriya.   Referee: N.S.H.M.R.Kodituwakku.   Toss: Singha Sports Club

Close of Play: 1st day: Panadura Sports Club (1) 324-9 (Fonseka 27*, Dilukshan 13*, 88 overs); 2nd day: Panadura Sports Club (2) 71-2 (G.S.U.Fernando 20*, Peiris 21*, 15 overs).

SEBASTIANITES CRICKET AND ATHLETIC CLUB v SRI LANKA ARMY SPORTS CLUB

Played at St Sebastian's College Ground, Moratuwa, February 15, 16, 17, 2008.
Premier Championship 2007/08 - Tier B
Sri Lanka Army Sports Club won by eight wickets. (Points: Sebastianites Cricket and Athletic Club 2.835, Sri Lanka Army Sports Club 15.64)

SEBASTIANITES CRICKET AND ATHLETIC CLUB

1	H.A.H.U.Tillakaratne	lbw b Rathnayake	19	lbw b Rathnayake	16
2	B.Y.Arumathanthri	c Sanjeewa b Karunatilleke	9	b Rathnayake	0
3	R.H.T.A.Perera	b Peiris	5	c Palleguruge b Rathnayake	2
4	M.A.B.Peiris	c de Zoysa b Rathnayake	46	c Karunatilleke b Peiris	0
5	S.R.Kumar	b Rathnayake	0	(6) st Soysa b Prasanna	50
6	†K.L.K.Fernando	c Peiris b B.A.W.Mendis	34	(5) not out	40
7	D.G.C.Silva	lbw b Rathnayake	0	(9) c Prasad b Rathnayake	13
8	*M.A.P.Salgado	b B.A.W.Mendis	5	(7) lbw b Prasanna	11
9	Y.I.S.Gunasena	not out	11	(8) c Sanjeewa b B.A.W.Mendis	9
10	A.B.L.D.Rodrigo	lbw b B.A.W.Mendis	21	st Soysa b B.A.W.Mendis	0
11	B.S.Rajitha	b Rathnayake	0	c Palleguruge b B.A.W.Mendis	12
	Extras	b 4, lb 4, nb 4	12	b 5, lb 6, nb 1	12
			162		165

FoW (1): 1-18 (2), 2-25 (3), 3-56 (1), 4-57 (5), 5-106 (4), 6-106 (7), 7-114 (8), 8-124 (6), 9-161 (10), 10-162 (11)
FoW (2): 1-1 (2), 2-7 (3), 3-12 (4), 4-25 (1), 5-83 (6), 6-101 (7), 7-118 (8), 8-140 (9), 9-141 (10), 10-165 (11)

SRI LANKA ARMY SPORTS CLUB

1	S.Sanjeewa	c Arumathanthri b Silva	19	c Fernando b Rodrigo	20
2	R.D.I.A.Karunatilleke	c Fernando b Silva	20	not out	62
3	H.H.M.de Zoysa	lbw b Rajitha	13	c Perera b Rodrigo	19
4	K.C.Prasad	b Gunasena	9		
5	S.Prasanna	b Rajitha	19	(4) not out	26
6	B.A.W.Mendis	lbw b Salgado	23		
7	T.R.D.Mendis	c Gunasena b Rodrigo	38		
8	†T.D.T.Soysa	c Arumathanthri b Rodrigo	27		
9	W.R.Palleguruge	not out	14		
10	*P.K.N.M.K.Rathnayake	c Perera b Rodrigo	3		
11	P.P.M.Peiris	lbw b Salgado	0		
	Extras	b 1, lb 1, w 3, nb 8	13	lb 1, nb 2	3
			198	(2 wickets)	130

FoW (1): 1-35 (1), 2-48 (2), 3-61 (4), 4-89 (5), 5-102 (3), 6-129 (6), 7-179 (7), 8-182 (8), 9-186 (10), 10-198 (11)
FoW (2): 1-42 (1), 2-93 (3)

Sri Lanka Army Sports Club Bowling

	O	M	R	W			O	M	R	W	
Peiris	8	0	33	1		(2)	5	1	18	1	
Karunatilleke	5	1	26	1							
Rathnayake	12.2	1	36	5	4nb	(1)	17	3	43	4	1nb
Prasanna	7	0	26	0			15	5	33	2	
B.A.W.Mendis	12	2	33	3			21.5	9	39	3	
Palleguruge						(3)	5	0	21	0	

Sebastianites Cricket and Athletic Club Bowling

	O	M	R	W			O	M	R	W	
Silva	14	2	47	2	3w,3nb		3	0	13	0	1nb
Gunasena	12	1	50	1	5nb		2	0	12	0	1nb
Salgado	13.2	2	37	2		(4)	1	0	2	0	
Rajitha	10	1	22	2		(3)	6	1	22	0	
Rodrigo	9	0	36	3			9	1	32	2	
Peiris	1	0	4	0			1	0	11	0	
Kumar						(7)	2	0	13	0	
Perera						(8)	3	1	24	0	

Umpires: K.M.Kottahachchi and S.H.Sarathkumara. Referee: B.C.Cooray. Toss: Sebastianites Cricket and Athletic Club
Close of Play: 1st day: Sri Lanka Army Sports Club (1) 64-3 (de Zoysa 8*, Prasanna 0*, 16.5 overs); 2nd day: Sebastianites Cricket and Athletic Club (2) 112-6 (Gunasena 6*, Fernando 18*, 37.4 overs).

SRI LANKA AIR FORCE SPORTS CLUB v POLICE SPORTS CLUB

Played at Air Force Ground, Colombo, February 15, 16, 17, 2008.
Premier Championship 2007/08 - Tier B
Match drawn.   (Points: Sri Lanka Air Force Sports Club 11.485, Police Sports Club 2.775)

SRI LANKA AIR FORCE SPORTS CLUB

1	M.A.M.Faizer	c Kuruppu b Rasmijinan	3	c Nirmala b Rasmijinan	1
2	A.Rizan	c Nirmal b Weerasinghe	7	run out	8
3	W.A.Eranga	run out (Nirmala)	49	lbw b Soysa	25
4	†M.K.P.B.Kularatne	lbw b Jayawardene	51	b Jayawardene	39
5	M.D.R.Prabath	c Kuruppu b Jayawardene	29		
6	*K.A.Kumara	c Kuruppu b Weerasinghe	89		
7	M.W.B.Dissanayake	lbw b Soysa	18	(6) c Nirmal b Jayawardene	23
8	S.Madanayake	c Nirmala b Soysa	0	(5) not out	52
9	M.K.G.C.P.Lakshitha	run out (Nirmal)	19		
10	K.K.A.K.Lakmal	c Nirmal b Weerasinghe	18	(7) c Jayawardene b Perera	36
11	B.D.S.A.Rajapakse	not out	1	(8) not out	2
	Extras	b 10, lb 4, w 1, nb 9	24	b 2, lb 1	3
			308	**(6 wickets)**	**189**

FoW (1): 1-3 (1), 2-40 (2), 3-77 (3), 4-151 (4), 5-160 (5), 6-215 (7), 7-215 (8), 8-271 (9), 9-300 (10), 10-308 (6)
FoW (2): 1-8 (1), 2-9 (2), 3-73 (4), 4-73 (3), 5-118 (6), 6-181 (7)

POLICE SPORTS CLUB

1	†P.H.K.S.Nirmala	c sub (M.R.Porage) b Lakshitha	15
2	M.M.P.Kumara	lbw b Lakmal	15
3	P.R.Nirmal	c Kularatne b Lakshitha	55
4	K.A.D.M.C.Kuruppu	c Faizer b Rizan	6
5	H.P.A.Priyantha	run out (Lakshitha)	36
6	*R.G.D.Sanjeewa	c sub (M.R.Porage) b Rizan	66
7	W.N.M.Soysa	c Kularatne b Lakshitha	2
8	M.M.Rasmijinan	c Kularatne b Lakshitha	4
9	T.A.N.Weerasinghe	not out	17
10	H.M.Jayawardene	c Dissanayake b Rizan	3
11	G.S.G.Perera	c Dissanayake b Rizan	0
	Extras	b 2, lb 5, nb 9	16
			235

FoW (1): 1-29 (1), 2-34 (2), 3-47 (4), 4-127 (3), 5-186 (5), 6-192 (7), 7-203 (8), 8-220 (6), 9-232 (10), 10-235 (11)

Police Sports Club Bowling

	O	M	R	W			O	M	R	W
Perera	15	0	80	0	8nb	(7)	2	0	3	1
Rasmijinan	31	8	64	1		(1)	10	2	29	1
Weerasinghe	18.2	2	62	3	1w	(2)	9	1	34	0
Soysa	27	8	41	2	1nb		7	0	18	0
Jayawardene	20	5	34	2		(3)	12	2	51	0
Sanjeewa	5	1	13	0			5	0	35	0
Kumara						(5)	3	0	16	0

Sri Lanka Air Force Sports Club Bowling

	O	M	R	W	
Lakshitha	26	5	80	4	8nb
Lakmal	20	5	58	1	1nb
Rizan	23	2	63	4	
Rajapakse	8	2	21	0	
Madanayake	5	1	6	0	

Umpires: N.S.Bopage and D.Ekanayake. Referee: A.J.Samarasekera.   Toss: Sri Lanka Air Force Sports Club

Close of Play: 1st day: Sri Lanka Air Force Sports Club (1) 177-5 (Kumara 17*, Dissanayake 2*, 56 overs); 2nd day: Police Sports Club (1) 114-3 (Nirmal 43*, Priyantha 28*, 35 overs).

BLOOMFIELD CRICKET AND ATHLETIC CLUB v BADURELIYA SPORTS CLUB

Played at Bloomfield Cricket and Athletic Club Ground, Colombo, February 21, 22, 23, 24, 2008.
Premier Championship 2007/08 - Tier A
Bloomfield Cricket and Athletic Club won by 278 runs.   (Points: Bloomfield Cricket and Athletic Club 17.635, Badureliya Sports Club 4.21)

BLOOMFIELD CRICKET AND ATHLETIC CLUB

1	K.Y.de Silva	b Malinga	0	(4) c Malinga b Bandaratilleke	163
2	T.S.Masmulla	c Vitharana b Liyanage	68	(1) st Vitharana b U.R.P.Perera	16
3	W.S.Jayantha	c Wickramaratne b Ratnayake	6	b Dias	13
4	K.N.C.Fernando	c M.M.D.P.V.Perera b Malinga	8	(2) lbw b Dias	5
5	†H.A.P.W.Jayawardene	lbw b Dias	134	c Malinga b Bandaratilleke	57
6	*D.M.G.S.Dissanayake	c Wickramaratne b Dias	24	c U.R.P.Perera b Dias	17
7	C.U.Jayasinghe	b Dias	22	c Wickramaratne b Bandaratilleke	17
8	G.A.S.K.Gangodawila	c Liyanage b Malinga	46	st Vitharana b Dias	113
9	M.C.R.Fernando	c Wickramaratne b Dias	2	b Dias	0
10	A.B.T.Lakshitha	run out (Wickramaratne)	7	not out	1
11	T.P.Gamage	not out	1		
	Extras	lb 4, w 1, nb 4	9	b 2, lb 3, w 6	11
			327	(9 wickets, declared)	413

FoW (1): 1-0 (1), 2-11 (3), 3-29 (4), 4-129 (2), 5-182 (6), 6-259 (7), 7-282 (5), 8-290 (9), 9-316 (10), 10-327 (8)
FoW (2): 1-16 (2), 2-30 (3), 3-46 (1), 4-145 (5), 5-174 (6), 6-203 (7), 7-411 (8), 8-411 (9), 9-413 (4)

BADURELIYA SPORTS CLUB

1	M.M.D.P.V.Perera	c Gangodawila b Lakshitha	7	(2) c de Silva b Dissanayake	57
2	†D.W.A.N.D.Vitharana	c M.C.R.Fernando b Lakshitha	4	(1) c Jayantha b Lakshitha	12
3	D.N.Hunukumbura	c Jayawardene b Gamage	0	lbw b Jayantha	60
4	W.J.S.D.Perera	c Jayawardene b Gamage	0	(5) c Jayawardene b M.C.R.Fernando	33
5	U.R.P.Perera	c Jayawardene b Lakshitha	19	(6) c K.N.C.Fernando b Jayantha	20
6	*R.P.A.H.Wickramaratne	c Jayawardene b Gamage	5	(4) c Masmulla b Jayantha	46
7	R.M.A.R.Ratnayake	c Jayantha b Gamage	5	c K.N.C.Fernando b Dissanayake	105
8	P.S.Liyanage	c Gangodawila b Lakshitha	18	c Lakshitha b Dissanayake	5
9	M.R.C.N.Bandaratilleke	c de Silva b Lakshitha	4	lbw b Dissanayake	7
10	S.D.C.Malinga	b Lakshitha	4	lbw b Dissanayake	30
11	K.L.S.L.Dias	not out	4	not out	6
	Extras	lb 1	1	lb 4, w 2, nb 4	10
			71		391

FoW (1): 1-5 (2), 2-6 (3), 3-6 (4), 4-22 (1), 5-29 (6), 6-37 (5), 7-57 (8), 8-61 (9), 9-63 (7), 10-71 (10)
FoW (2): 1-14 (1), 2-112 (2), 3-160 (3), 4-203 (4), 5-223 (5), 6-274 (6), 7-288 (8), 8-303 (9), 9-367 (10), 10-391 (7)

Badureliya Bowling	O	M	R	W		O	M	R	W	
Malinga	13.5	2	47	3		13	1	58	0	2w
Ratnayake	9	0	49	1	1w,2nb	16	1	65	0	3w
Liyanage	15	3	45	1	(5)	5	0	38	0	
W.J.S.D.Perera	6	1	28	0	1nb	(7) 5	1	19	0	
Dias	21	1	90	4	1nb	(3) 20	1	78	5	
Bandaratilleke	12	0	46	0		19.3	4	71	3	
M.M.D.P.V.Perera	3	0	18	0						
U.R.P.Perera						(4) 15	2	79	1	

Bloomfield Bowling	O	M	R	W		O	M	R	W	
Lakshitha	8.4	2	36	6		13	0	69	1	1w,2nb
Gamage	8	1	34	4		7	0	36	0	
Jayantha						(3) 25	3	88	3	1w,2nb
Gangodawila						(4) 2	0	14	0	
M.C.R.Fernando						(5) 10	1	36	1	
Dissanayake						(6) 35.4	9	135	5	
Jayawardene						(7) 3	0	9	0	

Umpires: R.Martinesz and N.D.Withana. Referee: A.J.Samarasekera. Toss: Bloomfield Cricket and Athletic Club
Close of Play: 1st day: Badureliya Sports Club (1) 18-3 (M.M.D.P.V.Perera 7*, U.R.P.Perera 7*, 7 overs); 2nd day: Bloomfield Cricket and Athletic Club (2) 335-6 (de Silva 148*, Gangodawila 55*, 78 overs); 3rd day: Badureliya Sports Club (2) 371-9 (Ratnayake 91*, Dias 0*, 89 overs).
H.A.P.W.Jayawardene's 134 took 201 balls and included 15 fours and 1 six. K.Y.de Silva's 163 took 232 balls and included 21 fours and 2 sixes. G.A.S.K.Gangodawila's 113 took 134 balls and included 12 fours and 3 sixes. R.M.A.R.Ratnayake's 105 took 137 balls and included 6 fours and 9 sixes.

MOORS SPORTS CLUB v RAGAMA CRICKET CLUB

Played at Moors Sports Club Ground, Colombo, February 21, 22, 23, 24, 2008.
Premier Championship 2007/08 - Tier A
Moors Sports Club won by 36 runs.   (Points: Moors Sports Club 16.54, Ragama Cricket Club 4.36)

MOORS SPORTS CLUB

#	Batsman	Dismissal 1	R	Dismissal 2	R
1	†W.M.J.Wannakuwatta	c W.D.D.S.Perera b Weeraratne	0	(2) c Ranatunga b Nayanakantha	6
2	N.M.N.P.Nawela	c W.D.D.S.Perera b Jeewantha	26	(1) b Nayanakantha	12
3	G.R.P.Peiris	c W.D.D.S.Perera b Nayanakantha	24	lbw b Bandara	29
4	W.M.B.Perera	lbw b Jeewantha	85	c S.A.Perera b Indrasiri	113
5	A.Rideegammanagedera	c de Saram b Jeewantha	2	c Jeewantha b Indrasiri	30
6	A.S.A.Perera	c de Saram b Bandara	28	(7) b Indrasiri	9
7	*L.H.D.Dilhara	c S.A.Perera b Jeewantha	10	(8) c de Zoysa b Vithana	36
8	H.M.R.K.B.Herath	lbw b Nayanakantha	38	(6) c W.D.D.S.Perera b Indrasiri	13
9	P.N.Ranjith	c Weeraratne b Bandara	3	(10) b Vithana	8
10	A.M.L.Perera	c Bandara b Jeewantha	11	(11) not out	3
11	C.R.B.Mudalige	not out	9	(9) lbw b Indrasiri	4
	Extras	lb 2, w 1, nb 6	9		9
			245		**263**

FoW (1): 1-0 (1), 2-49 (3), 3-51 (2), 4-55 (5), 5-89 (6), 6-105 (7), 7-179 (8), 8-189 (9), 9-218 (10), 10-245 (4)
FoW (2): 1-12 (2), 2-23 (1), 3-75 (3), 4-151 (5), 5-167 (6), 6-183 (7), 7-240 (8), 8-248 (4), 9-257 (10), 10-263 (9)

RAGAMA CRICKET CLUB

#	Batsman	Dismissal 1	R	Dismissal 2	R
1	D.A.Ranatunga	c Herath b Dilhara	7	lbw b Dilhara	0
2	H.E.Vithana	c A.S.A.Perera b Dilhara	15	lbw b Herath	19
3	R.S.S.S.de Zoysa	b Herath	38	c Wannakuwatta b Ranjith	25
4	*S.I.de Saram	b Dilhara	28	c Wannakuwatta b Ranjith	10
5	W.D.D.S.Perera	c Wannakuwatta b Herath	4	(6) lbw b Herath	83
6	K.Weeraratne	b Herath	0	(7) b Herath	7
7	C.M.Bandara	c Wannakuwatta b Herath	15	(5) c A.M.L.Perera b Rideegammagedera	39
8	†S.A.Perera	c A.S.A.Perera b Dilhara	53	c Wannakuwatta b Herath	19
9	P.A.S.S.Jeewantha	c Nawela b Dilhara	65	not out	12
10	S.A.D.U.Indrasiri	c Wannakuwatta b Dilhara	9	lbw b A.M.L.Perera	1
11	H.G.D.Nayanakantha	not out	1	c Ranjith b Herath	3
	Extras	lb 2, w 5, nb 2	9	b 3, lb 6, nb 1	10
			244		**228**

FoW (1): 1-12 (1), 2-37 (2), 3-79 (4), 4-92 (5), 5-92 (6), 6-99 (3), 7-110 (7), 8-234 (8), 9-235 (9), 10-244 (10)
FoW (2): 1-4 (1), 2-45 (2), 3-55 (3), 4-60 (4), 5-153 (5), 6-161 (7), 7-211 (8), 8-212 (6), 9-215 (10), 10-228 (11)

Ragama Cricket Club Bowling

	O	M	R	W		O	M	R	W	
Weeraratne	11	1	51	1		13	0	52	0	
Nayanakantha	15	2	44	2	1w,1nb	14	2	41	2	
Jeewantha	13.4	2	54	5	5nb	(4) 8	2	23	0	
W.D.D.S.Perera	4	2	8	0						
Bandara	16	0	65	2		(3) 20	6	70	1	
Indrasiri	4	2	8	0		(5) 27.5	8	71	5	
Vithana	2	0	13	0		(6) 6	2	6	2	

Moors Sports Club Bowling

	O	M	R	W		O	M	R	W	
Dilhara	21.4	8	39	6		12	4	18	1	
Ranjith	16	2	58	0		11	3	27	2	
A.M.L.Perera	13	2	56	0		(5) 13	6	23	1	
Herath	27	15	30	4		(3) 34.3	4	85	5	1nb
Mudalige	7	0	26	0	1w,1nb	(6) 7	0	31	0	
Rideegammanagedera	12	3	24	0		(4) 13	3	30	1	
A.S.A.Perera	2	0	4	0	1nb					
Peiris	3	0	5	0		(7) 1	0	5	0	

Umpires: E.A.R.de Silva and S.S.K.Gallage. Referee: C.T.M.Devaraj. Toss: Moors Sports Club
Close of Play: 1st day: Ragama Cricket Club (1) 76-2 (de Saram 26*, de Zoysa 26*, 22 overs); 2nd day: Moors Sports Club (2) 34-2 (Peiris 6*, W.M.B.Perera 10*, 9 overs); 3rd day: Ragama Cricket Club (2) 22-1 (Vithana 11*, de Zoysa 6*, 12 overs).
W.M.B.Perera's 113 took 211 balls and included 9 fours and 3 sixes.

NONDESCRIPTS CRICKET CLUB v COLOMBO CRICKET CLUB

Played at Nondescripts Cricket Club Ground, Colombo, February 21, 22, 23, 24, 2008.
Premier Championship 2007/08 - Tier A
Match drawn.   (Points: Nondescripts Cricket Club 12.9, Colombo Cricket Club 3.92)

NONDESCRIPTS CRICKET CLUB

1	K.D.Gunawardene	b Wethathasinghe	13	c Rupasinghe b Mubarak	45
2	W.L.P.Fernando	c Mubarak b Ratnayake	9	c Chandrakumara b Perera	82
3	C.G.Wijesinghe	c Mubarak b Rupasinghe	109	c Mubarak b Randika	79
4	M.M.M.Suraj	run out (Mendis)	7		
5	C.K.B.Kulasekara	c Mendis b Ratnayake	111	(4) lbw b Mubarak	30
6	*M.K.Gajanayake	c Wethathasinghe b Rupasinghe	53	(5) c Vandort b Perera	27
7	G.D.D.Indika	c Vandort b Rupasinghe	10	(6) not out	52
8	†M.R.D.G.Mapa Bandara	c Ranaweera b Ratnayake	12	(7) not out	20
9	D.T.Kottehewa	c Mubarak b Rupasinghe	18		
10	A.A.C.E.Athukorala	c Randika b Rupasinghe	0		
11	N.C.Komasaru	not out	4		
	Extras	b 5, lb 5	10	b 1, lb 3, w 1, nb 4	9
			356	(5 wickets, declared)	344

FoW (1): 1-21 (2), 2-23 (1), 3-66 (4), 4-179 (3), 5-291 (5), 6-310 (7), 7-333 (6), 8-333 (8), 9-334 (10), 10-356 (9)
FoW (2): 1-78 (1), 2-172 (2), 3-224 (4), 4-265 (3), 5-291 (5)

COLOMBO CRICKET CLUB

1	M.G.Vandort	b Athukorala	34	b Fernando	33
2	†D.K.Ranaweera	lbw b Kottehewa	1	c Mapa Bandara b Suraj	10
3	J.Mubarak	run out (Wijesinghe)	22	(4) c Suraj b Fernando	9
4	*B.M.T.T.Mendis	lbw b Kottehewa	84	(6) not out	13
5	A.S.Polonowita	lbw b Komasaru	11		
6	K.G.N.Randika	st Mapa Bandara b Komasaru	7	(3) c Wijesinghe b Komasaru	49
7	A.C.Wethathasinghe	not out	136		
8	P.D.G.Chandrakumara	c Gunawardene b Kulasekara	6	(5) not out	16
9	M.P.N.L.Perera	b Kottehewa	1		
10	N.S.Rupasinghe	c Mapa Bandara b Kottehewa	22		
11	M.I.Ratnayake	c and b Komasaru	2		
	Extras	b 3, lb 7, w 2, nb 8	20	b 1, lb 4, nb 3	8
			346	(4 wickets)	138

FoW (1): 1-10 (2), 2-59 (1), 3-59 (3), 4-90 (5), 5-107 (6), 6-227 (4), 7-250 (8), 8-251 (9), 9-317 (10), 10-346 (11)
FoW (2): 1-22 (2), 2-68 (1), 3-80 (4), 4-121 (3)

Colombo Bowling	O	M	R	W		O	M	R	W	
Ratnayake	23	2	93	3		9	1	38	0	1w
Wethathasinghe	16	3	51	1		11	3	27	0	
Polonowita	12	2	22	0						
Chandrakumara	11	2	41	0	(3)	12	1	48	0	
Rupasinghe	27.5	3	83	5	(6)	0.5	0	14	0	2nb
Perera	7	1	32	0	(5)	20	2	104	2	
Mubarak	2	0	14	0	(4)	22	3	67	2	2nb
Randika	6	1	10	0		15	4	42	1	
Mendis					(7)	0.1	0	0	0	

Nondescripts Bowling	O	M	R	W		O	M	R	W	
Kottehewa	26	5	71	4	2w,2nb	5	1	12	0	1nb
Kulasekara	15	3	78	1		1	0	8	0	
Suraj	18	1	61	0	1nb	11	3	34	1	
Gajanayake	1	0	3	0	(7)	3	1	13	0	
Athukorala	16	2	57	1	5nb	(4)	3	0	22	0	1nb
Komasaru	28.3	11	56	3		10	3	17	1	
Indika	2	0	10	0						
Fernando					(5)	6	1	19	2	
Wijesinghe					(8)	1	0	8	0	1nb

Umpires: I.D.Gunawardene and P.G.Liyanage. Referee: V.B.John.   Toss: Colombo Cricket Club
Close of Play: 1st day: Nondescripts Cricket Club (1) 312-6 (Gajanayake 43*, Mapa Bandara 1*, 90 overs); 2nd day: Colombo Cricket Club (1) 223-5 (Mendis 80*, Wethathasinghe 54*, 73 overs); 3rd day: Nondescripts Cricket Club (2) 154-1 (Fernando 66*, Wijesinghe 37*, 48 overs).
C.G.Wijesinghe's 109 took 148 balls and included 13 fours and 1 six. C.K.B.Kulasekara's 111 took 205 balls and included 12 fours and 1 six. A.C.Wethathasinghe's 136 took 219 balls and included 15 fours and 2 sixes.

SINHALESE SPORTS CLUB v COLTS CRICKET CLUB

Played at Sinhalese Sports Club Ground, Colombo, February 21, 22, 23, 24, 2008.
Premier Championship 2007/08 - Tier A
Sinhalese Sports Club won by an innings and 104 runs.   (Points: Sinhalese Sports Club 18, Colts Cricket Club 3.24)

COLTS CRICKET CLUB

1	T.P.Attanayake	c and b Lokuarachchi	31	c Paranavitana b Lokuarachchi	23
2	*B.S.M.Warnapura	lbw b Vidanapathirana	30	lbw b Lokuarachchi	27
3	D.N.Pathirana	lbw b Prasad	1	lbw b Mirando	17
4	A.D.Mathews	c Paranavitana b Prasad	71	c Paranavitana b Senanayake	33
5	H.G.J.M.Kulatunga	c Samaraweera b Prasad	0	c Samaraweera b Prasad	6
6	K.A.S.Jayasinghe	b Senanayake	8	b Prasad	4
7	†T.R.Peiris	c Mirando b Prasad	45	c Prasad b Senanayake	34
8	S.Weerakoon	lbw b Senanayake	52	b Vidanapathirana	7
9	K.G.Alwitigala	c Silva b Lokuarachchi	5	b Vidanapathirana	0
10	A.A.S.Silva	not out	15	c Silva b Senanayake	12
11	U.M.A.Prasad	c Mirando b Senanayake	3	not out	2
	Extras	b 3, lb 4, w 5, nb 1	13	b 4, lb 3, w 1, nb 1	9
			274		174

FoW (1): 1-37 (2), 2-38 (3), 3-108 (1), 4-109 (5), 5-126 (6), 6-163 (4), 7-230 (8), 8-255 (7), 9-259 (9), 10-274 (11)
FoW (2): 1-47 (2), 2-50 (1), 3-101 (3), 4-111 (5), 5-115 (4), 6-115 (6), 7-134 (8), 8-134 (9), 9-171 (7), 10-174 (10)

SINHALESE SPORTS CLUB

1	K.Magage	lbw b Prasad	16
2	N.T.Paranavitana	c Weerakoon b Alwitigala	6
3	†J.K.Silva	c Kulatunga b Silva	59
4	*T.T.Samaraweera	c Kulatunga b Weerakoon	184
5	S.H.T.Kandamby	c Alwitigala b Weerakoon	202
6	K.S.Lokuarachchi	st Peiris b Weerakoon	3
7	K.P.S.P.Karunanayake	lbw b Warnapura	20
8	K.T.G.D.Prasad	lbw b Weerakoon	13
9	M.T.T.Mirando	c Alwitigala b Weerakoon	22
10	S.M.Senanayake	not out	8
11	C.W.Vidanapathirana	st Peiris b Silva	0
	Extras	b 1, lb 7, w 1, nb 10	19
			552

FoW (1): 1-13 (2), 2-40 (1), 3-155 (3), 4-403 (4), 5-407 (6), 6-455 (7), 7-491 (8), 8-543 (9), 9-544 (5), 10-552 (11)

Sinhalese Sports Club Bowling

	O	M	R	W			O	M	R	W	
Vidanapathirana	10	1	27	1	1w		11	1	48	2	1w,1nb
Karunanayake	6	1	31	0	1w		3	0	12	0	
Prasad	16	4	63	4	1w	(5)	9	2	23	2	
Mirando	11	2	50	0	1nb	(6)	11	1	26	1	
Lokuarachchi	20	2	52	2	1w	(4)	15	6	29	0	
Senanayake	15.2	6	44	3		(3)	15	6	29	3	

Colts Cricket Club Bowling

	O	M	R	W	
Alwitigala	15	4	54	1	3nb
Prasad	20	2	77	1	1w
Silva	31.5	2	141	2	
Mathews	13	1	61	0	6nb
Kulatunga	4	0	9	0	
Weerakoon	40	3	140	5	1nb
Jayasinghe	1	0	11	0	
Attanayake	5	0	22	0	
Pathirana	3	0	14	0	
Warnapura	7	0	15	1	

Umpires: A.G.Dissanayake and B.P.J.Mendis.   Referee: S.Ranatunga.   Toss: Colts Cricket Club
Close of Play: 1st day: Sinhalese Sports Club (1) 39-1 (Magage 16*, Silva 12*, 9 overs); 2nd day: Sinhalese Sports Club (1) 402-3 (Samaraweera 184*, Kandamby 121*, 99 overs); 3rd day: Colts Cricket Club (2) 134-7 (Peiris 10*, 47 overs).
T.T.Samaraweera's 184 took 264 balls and included 24 fours. S.H.T.Kandamby's 202 took 268 balls and included 20 fours and 4 sixes.

TAMIL UNION CRICKET AND ATHLETIC CLUB v CHILAW MARIANS CRICKET CLUB

Played at P.Saravanamuttu Stadium, Colombo, February 21, 22, 23, 24, 2008.
Premier Championship 2007/08 - Tier A
Tamil Union Cricket and Athletic Club won by six wickets. (Points: Tamil Union Cricket and Athletic Club 17.035, Chilaw Marians Cricket Club 4.405)

CHILAW MARIANS CRICKET CLUB

1	M.L.Udawatte	c K.M.Fernando b Lakmal	16	c G.T.de Silva b Lakmal	6
2	A.P.Jansze	c G.T.de Silva b Maduwantha	23	(9) lbw b Rupasinghe	5
3	N.H.G.Cooray	c Pushpakumara b Lakmal	3	c S.I.Fernando b Liyanagunawardene	14
4	*L.J.P.Gunaratne	c G.T.de Silva b Wijesiriwardene	61	run out	6
5	K.H.R.K.Fernando	c Rupasinghe b Lakmal	74	c K.M.Fernando b Lakmal	38
6	W.M.G.Ramyakumara	c Rupasinghe b Lakmal	11	b Pushpakumara	97
7	M.M.D.N.R.G.Perera	c Cooray b Pushpakumara	32	c Cooray b S.I.Fernando	48
8	†C.S.Fernando	lbw b S.I.Fernando	29	lbw b Pushpakumara	34
9	D.Hettiarachchi	lbw b Pushpakumara	1	(10) lbw b Liyanagunawardene	13
10	G.A.C.R.Perera	b Rupasinghe	13	(2) c Wijesiriwardene b Lakmal	11
11	S.H.M.Silva	not out	1	not out	1
	Extras	b 3, lb 7, w 9, nb 9	28	b 4, lb 15, w 2, nb 15	36
			292		309

FoW (1): 1-48 (2), 2-53 (1), 3-61 (3), 4-184 (4), 5-208 (6), 6-221 (5), 7-273 (8), 8-277 (7), 9-284 (9), 10-292 (10)
FoW (2): 1-23 (2), 2-23 (1), 3-37 (4), 4-61 (3), 5-133 (5), 6-221 (6), 7-254 (7), 8-267 (9), 9-305 (8), 10-309 (10)

TAMIL UNION CRICKET AND ATHLETIC CLUB

1	†G.T.de Silva	run out (Hettiarachchi)	91	c Udawatte b Gunaratne	15
2	S.I.Fernando	b Ramyakumara	16	c Udawatte b Silva	49
3	K.M.Fernando	lbw b Ramyakumara	9		
4	S.K.L.de Silva	lbw b Gunaratne	77	not out	97
5	R.J.M.G.M.Rupasinghe	lbw b Gunaratne	3	c Cooray b Hettiarachchi	91
6	M.Pushpakumara	c K.H.R.K.Fernando b Gunaratne	20	not out	37
7	P.D.M.A.Cooray	b G.A.C.R.Perera	1	(3) c C.S.Fernando b Hettiarachchi	30
8	S.C.Liyanagunawardene	c Udawatte b G.A.C.R.Perera	0		
9	*H.M.Maduwantha	b Hettiarachchi	19		
10	O.L.A.Wijesiriwardene	c sub (D.N.A.Athulathmudali) b Hettiarachchi	7		
11	R.A.S.Lakmal	not out	13		
	Extras	b 6, lb 2, nb 6	14	b 3, lb 4, w 2, nb 9	18
			270	(4 wickets)	337

FoW (1): 1-28 (2), 2-49 (3), 3-156 (4), 4-164 (5), 5-200 (6), 6-212 (7), 7-212 (8), 8-247 (9), 9-250 (1), 10-270 (10)
FoW (2): 1-29 (1), 2-95 (2), 3-117 (3), 4-279 (5)

Tamil Union Bowling	O	M	R	W			O	M	R	W	
Wijesiriwardene	10	3	45	1	2w		3	2	1	0	
Lakmal	18w,13nb	3	78	4	3w,7nb		17	2	92	3	
Maduwantha	15	3	48	1	1nb	(4)	10	1	26	0	
Rupasinghe	6.4	1	19	1	1nb	(3)	5	0	7	1	2nb
Liyanagunawardene	13	1	40	0			20	5	64	2	
Pushpakumara	14	1	44	2			13.1	1	44	2	
S.I.Fernando	4	0	8	1			19.5	4	56	1	

Chilaw Marians Bowling	O	M	R	W			O	M	R	W	
Ramyakumara	11	2	33	2			8	1	19	0	2w
G.A.C.R.Perera	18	2	68	2	6nb		11	3	46	0	9nb
Gunaratne	18	1	53	3		(4)	19	0	61	1	
Hettiarachchi	19.5	2	68	2		(3)	25.5	3	110	2	
K.H.R.K.Fernando	1	0	1	0		(8)	1	0	11	0	
Silva	9	2	39	0			7	0	48	1	
M.M.D.N.R.G.Perera						(5)	4	0	18	0	
Cooray						(7)	2	0	10	0	
Udawatte						(9)	1	0	7	0	

Umpires: B.B.J.Nandakumar and M.S.K.Nandiweera. Referee: U.Warnapura. Toss: Chilaw Marians Cricket Club
Close of Play: 1st day: Tamil Union Cricket and Athletic Club (1) 23-0 (G.T.de Silva 11*, S.I.Fernando 11*, 9 overs); 2nd day: Chilaw Marians Cricket Club (2) 44-3 (Cooray 10*, K.H.R.K.Fernando 2*, 19 overs); 3rd day: Tamil Union Cricket and Athletic Club (2) 40-1 (S.I.Fernando 19*, Cooray 6*, 19 overs).

BURGHER RECREATION CLUB v LANKAN CRICKET CLUB

Played at R.Premadasa Stadium, Colombo, February 22, 23, 24, 2008.
Premier Championship 2007/08 - Tier B
Burgher Recreation Club won by three wickets.   (Points: Burgher Recreation Club 16.36, Lankan Cricket Club 4.35)

LANKAN CRICKET CLUB

1	C.M.Withanage	c Peiris b A.M.S.P.Kumara	6	c Peiris b T.H.D.C.C.Kumara	33
2	D.G.N.de Silva	b Eranga	17	lbw b Madusanka	21
3	B.M.D.T.D.Ariyasinghe	b Madusanka	13	c Eranga b Peiris	32
4	*Y.N.Tillakaratne	c Fernando b de Silva	89		
5	J.R.G.Namal	c Fernando b Madusanka	30	(4) b Eranga	6
6	D.G.R.Dhammika	st Fernando b de Silva	100	b A.M.S.P.Kumara	14
7	†G.A.L.W.Shantha	c Peiris b A.M.S.P.Kumara	60	(5) b de Silva	7
8	K.N.S.Fernando	c Fernando b A.M.S.P.Kumara	37	(7) c and b de Silva	8
9	D.R.F.Weerasinghe	b Madusanka	16	(8) not out	0
10	L.D.I.Perera	not out	8		
11	P.D.M.P.N.Kumara	c Sandagirigoda b A.M.S.P.Kumara	6		
	Extras	b 7, lb 4, w 3, nb 3	17	b 6, lb 1, w 2, nb 1	10
			399	(7 wickets, declared)	131

FoW (1): 1-12 (1), 2-28 (2), 3-61 (3), 4-112 (5), 5-217 (4), 6-306 (6), 7-354 (7), 8-382 (8), 9-386 (9), 10-399 (11)
FoW (2): 1-41 (1), 2-88 (3), 3-96 (2), 4-103 (4), 5-117 (5), 6-131 (7), 7-131 (6)

BURGHER RECREATION CLUB

1	D.H.Sandagirigoda	lbw b Perera	1	c Tillakaratne b Perera	84
2	I.C.D.Perera	c Dhammika b Kumara	35	run out	124
3	L.A.H.de Silva	lbw b Perera	0	(4) b Perera	12
4	G.R.Perera	b Kumara	83	(6) not out	15
5	T.H.D.C.C.Kumara	b Kumara	0	(3) c Tillakaratne b Perera	4
6	*H.D.P.S.Harischandra	c Dhammika b Withanage	14	(7) run out	1
7	†P.H.M.G.Fernando	lbw b Tillakaratne	48	(5) c sub (S.L.Perera) b Perera	21
8	G.D.R.Eranga	run out (Kumara)	7		
9	C.A.M.Madusanka	c Tillakaratne b Dhammika	26	(8) b Kumara	1
10	C.C.J.Peiris	not out	9	(9) not out	1
11	A.M.S.P.Kumara	lbw b Dhammika	4		
	Extras	b 12, lb 7, w 2, nb 3	24	b 9, lb 6, nb 3	18
			251	(7 wickets)	281

FoW (1): 1-17 (1), 2-21 (3), 3-58 (2), 4-58 (5), 5-87 (6), 6-180 (7), 7-203 (8), 8-216 (4), 9-245 (9), 10-251 (11)
FoW (2): 1-182 (1), 2-198 (3), 3-223 (4), 4-256 (5), 5-274 (2), 6-275 (7), 7-276 (8)

Burgher Recreation Club Bowling

	O	M	R	W			O	M	R	W	
Eranga	16	1	60	1			11	3	29	1	
A.M.S.P.Kumara	18.4	3	59	4	1w,2nb		6.2	0	23	1	1nb
T.H.D.C.C.Kumara	13	3	44	0	1w,1nb		4	1	23	1	2w
Madusanka	24	4	95	3			5	1	23	1	
de Silva	13	3	48	2	1w	(6)	6	1	17	2	
G.R.Perera	4	0	24	0							
Peiris	9	0	58	0		(5)	2	0	9	1	
I.C.D.Perera	1	1	0	0							

Lankan Cricket Club Bowling

	O	M	R	W			O	M	R	W	
Perera	8	2	25	2			12	0	47	4	
Kumara	19	2	58	3	1w		6.4	0	53	1	
Fernando	13	0	40	0		(6)	3	0	15	0	
Dhammika	21.5	5	41	2	1nb	(3)	15	0	93	0	3nb
Weerasinghe	10	1	39	0	2nb		10	1	39	0	
Withanage	5	1	14	1		(4)	1	0	12	0	
Tillakaratne	3	0	15	1	1w						
Namal						(7)	2	0	7	0	

Umpires: H.D.P.K.Dharmasena and S.H.Sarathkumara. Referee: K.T.Francis. Toss: Lankan Cricket Club
Close of Play: 1st day: Lankan Cricket Club (1) 374-7 (Fernando 36*, Weerasinghe 7*, 90 overs); 2nd day: Burgher Recreation Club (1) 246-9 (Peiris 8*, A.M.S.P.Kumara 0*, 79 overs).
D.G.R.Dhammika's 100 took 111 balls and included 10 fours and 2 sixes. I.C.D.Perera's 124 took 161 balls and included 12 fours.

PANADURA SPORTS CLUB v SRI LANKA AIR FORCE SPORTS CLUB

Played at Panadura Esplanade, February 22, 23, 24, 2008.
Premier Championship 2007/08 - Tier B
Match drawn.   (Points: Panadura Sports Club 11.9, Sri Lanka Air Force Sports Club 3.84)

SRI LANKA AIR FORCE SPORTS CLUB

1	M.A.M.Faizer	b Perera	17	c M.R.Fernando b Dilukshan	5
2	A.Rizan	c M.T.T.Fernando b de Silva	10	b Cooray	43
3	P.A.R.C.Karunasena	c M.T.T.Fernando b de Silva	0	c Peiris b Cooray	9
4	W.A.Eranga	c de Silva b Fonseka	49	(5) c Cooray b Wanasinghe	24
5	†M.K.P.B.Kularatne	c Cooray b Perera	28	(7) c Peiris b Fonseka	4
6	*K.A.Kumara	st M.T.T.Fernando b Cooray	23	(8) c Abeywardene b Cooray	30
7	S.Madanayake	lbw b Cooray	4	(4) lbw b Perera	41
8	W.P.Wickrama	run out (sub [G.K.M.Niroshan])	10	(6) c de Silva b Cooray	42
9	M.K.G.C.P.Lakshitha	not out	15	(10) not out	8
10	K.K.A.A.K.Lakmal	lbw b Perera	7	(9) c Wanasinghe b Cooray	1
11	M.P.G.D.P.Gunatilleke	c Perera b Abeywardene	20	b Cooray	1
	Extras	b 16, lb 8, w 2	26	b 4, lb 6, nb 1	11
			209		219

FoW (1): 1-17 (2), 2-17 (3), 3-82 (4), 4-88 (1), 5-140 (6), 6-146 (7), 7-158 (8), 8-159 (5), 9-171 (10), 10-209 (11)
FoW (2): 1-11 (1), 2-57 (3), 3-62 (2), 4-113 (5), 5-144 (4), 6-155 (7), 7-209 (8), 8-209 (6), 9-215 (9), 10-219 (11)

PANADURA SPORTS CLUB

1	†M.T.T.Fernando	c Kularatne b Lakshitha	0	(2) lbw b Lakshitha	0
2	M.R.Fernando	c Gunatilleke b Lakmal	40	(1) c Kumara b Madanayake	7
3	G.S.U.Fernando	c Kumara b Lakshitha	33	b Madanayake	20
4	*J.S.K.Peiris	lbw b Gunatilleke	51	(6) lbw b Madanayake	13
5	W.M.P.N.Wanasinghe	lbw b Lakshitha	0	c Rizan b Lakshitha	8
6	M.N.R.Cooray	st Kularatne b Madanayake	44	(7) c Rizan b Madanayake	0
7	G.A.S.Perera	b Lakshitha	4	(8) not out	53
8	H.F.M.Fonseka	not out	29	(9) not out	28
9	S.R.Abeywardene	c Faizer b Gunatilleke	7	(4) c Kularatne b Lakshitha	4
10	I.A.Y.Dilukshan	c Rizan b Wickrama	8		
11	H.D.N.de Silva	c Wickrama b Rizan	2		
	Extras	b 2, lb 1, nb 7	10	b 8, lb 8, nb 3	19
			228	(7 wickets)	152

FoW (1): 1-0 (1), 2-66 (2), 3-76 (3), 4-80 (5), 5-175 (6), 6-179 (4), 7-179 (7), 8-194 (9), 9-223 (10), 10-228 (11)
FoW (2): 1-5 (2), 2-13 (1), 3-24 (4), 4-42 (3), 5-44 (5), 6-45 (7), 7-64 (6)

Panadura Sports Club Bowling

	O	M	R	W			O	M	R	W	
Dilukshan	5	1	12	0	1w	(2)	4	0	18	1	
de Silva	6	1	21	2		(1)	7	0	26	0	
Peiris	3	1	8	0							
Wanasinghe	10	1	40	0	1w	(3)	12	2	28	1	1nb
Abeywardene	5.4	1	10	1							
Cooray	15	4	35	2		(5)	20.1	2	57	6	
Fonseka	7	2	20	1			2	0	17	1	
Perera	22	7	39	3		(6)	16	2	46	1	
G.S.U.Fernando						(4)	3	0	17	0	

Sri Lanka Air Force Sports Club Bowling

	O	M	R	W			O	M	R	W	
Lakshitha	22	4	63	4	2nb		12	1	30	3	
Lakmal	13	4	31	1	3nb		1	0	7	0	
Rizan	13.3	2	53	1		(6)	8	2	28	0	
Madanayake	9	1	32	1		(3)	19	7	28	4	
Gunatilleke	14	4	34	2	2nb	(4)	9	2	26	0	3nb
Wickrama	4	1	12	1		(5)	5	1	17	0	

Umpires: R.A.Kottahachchi and R.R.Wimalasiri.   Referee: A.M.J.G.Amerasinghe.   Toss: Sri Lanka Air Force Sports Club

Close of Play: 1st day: Panadura Sports Club (1) 49-1 (M.R.Fernando 30*, G.S.U.Fernando 17*, 14 overs); 2nd day: Sri Lanka Air Force Sports Club (2) 69-3 (Madanayake 7*, Eranga 1*, 24 overs).

477

POLICE SPORTS CLUB v MORATUWA SPORTS CLUB

Played at Police Park Ground, Colombo, February 22, 23, 24, 2008.
Premier Championship 2007/08 - Tier B
Match drawn.   (Points: Police Sports Club 3.04, Moratuwa Sports Club 12.315)

MORATUWA SPORTS CLUB

1	R.C.Rupasinghe	lbw b Weerasinghe	30	c Sanjeewa b Dilantha		27
2	R.M.Mendis	c Rasmijinan b Dilantha	2	c Rasmijinan b Sanjeewa		89
3	W.P.D.de Mel	c Sanjeewa b Dilantha	2	(7) c Weerasinghe b Soysa		32
4	L.T.A.de Silva	c Nirmala b Weerasinghe	22	(3) c Soysa b Jayawardene		67
5	†D.S.Wijemanne	b Wijeratne	19	(4) b Jayawardene		0
6	H.U.K.de Silva	c Soysa b Rasmijinan	37	(5) c Weerasinghe b Soysa		116
7	S.J.C.de Silva	c Weerasinghe b Soysa	24	(8) not out		41
8	*M.D.S.Perera	lbw b Soysa	21	(6) c Wijeratne b Sanjeewa		13
9	P.C.M.Fernando	not out	67	lbw b Soysa		2
10	S.D.Dammika	c Wijeratne b Dilantha	21			
11	N.A.C.T.Perera	lbw b Weerasinghe	0	(10) not out		5
	Extras	b 5, lb 3, w 6, nb 4	18	b 7, lb 1, w 1, nb 4		13
			263	(8 wickets, declared)		**405**

FoW (1): 1-7 (2), 2-13 (3), 3-42 (4), 4-66 (1), 5-120 (6), 6-124 (5), 7-166 (7), 8-173 (8), 9-252 (10), 10-263 (11)
FoW (2): 1-38 (1), 2-145 (3), 3-145 (4), 4-279 (2), 5-323 (6), 6-330 (5), 7-370 (7), 8-374 (9)

POLICE SPORTS CLUB

1	†P.H.K.S.Nirmala	c Dammika b Fernando	1	not out		17
2	S.A.Wijeratne	b N.A.C.T.Perera	17	not out		22
3	J.P.M.Abeyratne	c Wijemanne b Fernando	7			
4	W.N.M.Soysa	c Wijemanne b Fernando	18			
5	P.R.Nirmal	c Wijemanne b N.A.C.T.Perera	8			
6	*R.G.D.Sanjeewa	c S.J.C.de Silva b N.A.C.T.Perera	19			
7	H.P.A.Priyantha	c de Mel b N.A.C.T.Perera	30			
8	T.A.N.Weerasinghe	c and b S.J.C.de Silva	36			
9	M.M.Rasmijinan	not out	37			
10	H.M.Jayawardene	c Rupasinghe b Fernando	24			
11	R.S.K.A.P.Dilantha	c Rupasinghe b S.J.C.de Silva	0			
	Extras	b 1, w 1, nb 8	10	lb 2		2
			207	(no wicket)		**41**

FoW (1): 1-1 (1), 2-10 (3), 3-28 (2), 4-53 (5), 5-63 (4), 6-73 (6), 7-126 (7), 8-166 (8), 9-202 (10), 10-207 (11)

Police Sports Club Bowling

	O	M	R	W		O	M	R	W	
Dilantha	23	2	76	3	1w,2nb	8	0	35	1	4nb
Rasmijinan	23	5	55	1	3w	(4) 11	1	42	0	1w
Weerasinghe	25	6	61	3	2w	(2) 4	1	18	0	
Soysa	14	1	32	2	2nb	(3) 23.5	2	81	3	
Jayawardene	8	0	13	0		23	2	113	2	
Wijeratne	7	2	12	1		(7) 7	0	30	0	
Sanjeewa	2	0	6	0		(6) 18	1	78	2	

Moratuwa Sports Club Bowling

	O	M	R	W		O	M	R	W	
N.A.C.T.Perera	16	2	63	4	1nb	(2) 2	0	20	0	
Fernando	17	4	53	4	2nb	(1) 2	0	13	0	
de Mel	4	1	18	0	1w					
Dammika	10	5	14	0		(3) 1	0	5	0	
M.D.S.Perera	2	0	8	0	1nb					
S.J.C.de Silva	13	1	50	2	4nb	(4) 1	0	1	0	

Umpires: E.J.A.P.A.M.Jayasuriya and M.V.D.Zilva.   Referee: N.Fredrick.   Toss: Police Sports Club

Close of Play: 1st day: Moratuwa Sports Club (1) 237-8 (Fernando 46*, Dammika 18*, 91 overs); 2nd day: Moratuwa Sports Club (2) 26-0 (Rupasinghe 21*, Mendis 4*, 7 overs).

H.U.K.de Silva's 116 took 101 balls and included 12 fours and 4 sixes.

SARACENS SPORTS CLUB v SEBASTIANITES CRICKET AND ATHLETIC CLUB

Played at Kadirana Cricket Grounds, Gampaha, February 22, 23, 24, 2008.
Premier Championship 2007/08 - Tier B
Saracens Sports Club won by six wickets. (Points: Saracens Sports Club 16.16, Sebastianites Cricket and Athletic Club 3.55)

SARACENS SPORTS CLUB

1	W.G.R.K.Alwis	c Tillakaratne b Kumara	34	b Arumathanthri	9
2	P.K.Bodhisha	c Fernando b M.A.B.Peiris	53	not out	45
3	†W.A.S.Niroshan	c Tillakaratne b Kumara	2	c Rajitha b M.A.B.Peiris	0
4	*G.N.Abeyratne	c Arumathanthri b Silva	74	(6) not out	29
5	W.S.D.Fernando	c Rodrigo b Rajitha	28	b M.A.B.Peiris	2
6	S.C.Serasinghe	c M.A.B.Peiris b Arumathanthri	63		
7	M.L.R.Karunaratne	c T.L.T.Peiris b Rajitha	13	(4) c and b M.A.B.Peiris	0
8	A.V.S.Nikethana	c Rodrigo b Arumathanthri	53		
9	L.D.P.Nishantha	lbw b Arumathanthri	6 ˙		
10	P.M.Pushpakumara	c M.A.B.Peiris b Arumathanthri	0		
11	M.I.Abdeen	not out	0		
	Extras	b 9, lb 2, nb 4	15	b 5, lb 1	6
			341	(4 wickets)	91

FoW (1): 1-50 (1), 2-53 (3), 3-145 (2), 4-190 (5), 5-206 (4), 6-228 (7), 7-331 (8), 8-334 (6), 9-338 (9), 10-341 (10)
FoW (2): 1-14 (1), 2-23 (3), 3-25 (4), 4-29 (5)

SEBASTIANITES CRICKET AND ATHLETIC CLUB

1	H.A.H.U.Tillakaratne	c Fernando b Abdeen	23	lbw b Pushpakumara	98
2	B.Y.Arumathanthri	c Niroshan b Abdeen	4	c Niroshan b Serasinghe	27
3	H.P.G.Perera	st Niroshan b Pushpakumara	8	c Pushpakumara b Karunaratne	18
4	M.A.B.Peiris	b Serasinghe	11	b Serasinghe	18
5	†K.L.K.Fernando	c Bodhisha b Serasinghe	15	(7) lbw b Nishantha	0
6	S.R.Kumar	c Nishantha b Pushpakumara	13	(8) b Nishantha	1
7	T.L.T.Peiris	lbw b Pushpakumara	12	(5) lbw b Nishantha	26
8	D.G.C.Silva	c Nikethana b Pushpakumara	3	(9) c and b Pushpakumara	10
9	A.B.L.D.Rodrigo	b Pushpakumara	8	(10) lbw b Serasinghe	54
10	B.S.Rajitha	not out	7	(6) lbw b Nishantha	0
11	*M.N.T.H.Kumara	lbw b Serasinghe	2	not out	36
	Extras	lb 5, nb 5	10	b 7, lb 10, nb 9	26
			116		314

FoW (1): 1-6 (2), 2-35 (1), 3-37 (3), 4-69 (4), 5-72 (5), 6-85 (6), 7-94 (8), 8-102 (9), 9-111 (7), 10-116 (11)
FoW (2): 1-64 (2), 2-102 (3), 3-140 (4), 4-199 (5), 5-199 (6), 6-206 (7), 7-206 (1), 8-208 (8), 9-220 (9), 10-314 (10)

Sebastianites Cricket and Athletic Club Bowling

	O	M	R	W			O	M	R	W	
Silva	13	1	68	1	4nb						
Kumara	9	1	48	2		(1)	1	0	8	0	
Kumar	3	0	23	0							
M.A.B.Peiris	29	6	77	1		(2)	13	1	47	3	
Rodrigo	15	1	60	0			1	0	12	0	
Rajitha	12	1	42	2		(4)	2	1	3	0	
Arumathanthri	6.4	2	12	4		(3)	10	4	15	1	

Saracens Sports Club Bowling

	O	M	R	W			O	M	R	W	
Nishantha	6	1	20	0	4nb		21	8	39	4	7nb
Abdeen	7	1	22	2	1nb		4	0	29	0	
Pushpakumara	18	6	35	5		(5)	36	8	95	2	
Serasinghe	10.1	2	26	3			22.2	5	68	3	
Karunaratne	3	1	8	0		(6)	10	0	39	1	1nb
Nikethana						(3)	2	0	9	0	1nb
Bodhisha						(7)	2	0	9	0	
Alwis						(8)	4	1	9	0	

Umpires: N.S.Bopage and D.Ekanayake. Referee: N.S.H.M.R.Kodituwakku. Toss: Sebastianites Cricket and Athletic Club

Close of Play: 1st day: Saracens Sports Club (1) 341 all out; 2nd day: Sebastianites Cricket and Athletic Club (2) 200-5 (Tillakaratne 92*, Fernando 0*, 53 overs).

SRI LANKA ARMY SPORTS CLUB v SINGHA SPORTS CLUB

Played at Army Ground, Panagoda, February 22, 23, 24, 2008.
Premier Championship 2007/08 - Tier B
Sri Lanka Army Sports Club won by 43 runs.　　(Points: Sri Lanka Army Sports Club 15.56, Singha Sports Club 3.345)

SRI LANKA ARMY SPORTS CLUB

1	S.Sanjeewa	c Kavinga b de Silva	0	(2) c Kumara b Gamage	25
2	R.D.I.A.Karunatilleke	b de Silva	9	(1) c Kavinga b Ranatunga	26
3	H.H.M.de Zoysa	lbw b Liyanage	0	c sub (K.M.S.de Silva) b Gamage	91
4	S.Prasanna	c Kavinga b Liyanage	2	c and b Ranatunga	18
5	K.C.Prasad	c Kumara b de Silva	0	c Kumara b Randunu	1
6	B.A.W.Mendis	b Liyanage	0	(8) b Ranatunga	8
7	T.R.D.Mendis	c Zoysa b Liyanage	1	c Faux b Madanayake	20
8	†T.D.T.Soysa	c Kavinga b Liyanage	6	(6) c Madanayake b Randunu	3
9	W.R.Palleguruge	lbw b Liyanage	9	b Liyanage	16
10	*P.K.N.M.K.Rathnayake	st Kavinga b Randunu	15	not out	19
11	P.P.M.Peiris	not out	1	lbw b Gamage	0
	Extras	lb 2, w 5, nb 2, pen 5	14	b 5, lb 8, w 5, nb 10	28
			57		**255**

FoW (1): 1-0 (1), 2-10 (3), 3-14 (2), 4-16 (4), 5-16 (5), 6-17 (7), 7-22 (6), 8-34 (8), 9-44 (9), 10-57 (10)
FoW (2): 1-42 (2), 2-88 (1), 3-116 (4), 4-117 (5), 5-137 (6), 6-176 (7), 7-194 (8), 8-215 (9), 9-255 (3), 10-255 (11)

SINGHA SPORTS CLUB

1	D.A.Faux	c de Zoysa b B.A.W.Mendis	20	lbw b Prasanna	14
2	†H.H.R.Kavinga	lbw b de Zoysa	50	c Rathnayake b Prasanna	0
3	T.J.Madanayake	lbw b B.A.W.Mendis	40	(4) c de Zoysa b B.A.W.Mendis	2
4	H.W.M.Kumara	c Peiris b de Zoysa	15	(5) b B.A.W.Mendis	4
5	H.S.M.Zoysa	lbw b B.A.W.Mendis	17	(3) lbw b Prasanna	16
6	A.S.Wewalwala	lbw b Palleguruge	6	lbw b de Zoysa	11
7	S.K.C.Randunu	c Rathnayake b B.A.W.Mendis	5	(8) b B.A.W.Mendis	4
8	K.S.H.de Silva	not out	8	(7) b de Zoysa	21
9	P.L.S.Gamage	c and b Palleguruge	1	(10) not out	1
10	*N.C.K.Liyanage	c Prasanna b Palleguruge	5	(9) b B.A.W.Mendis	0
11	C.Ranatunga	c Soysa b B.A.W.Mendis	0	c T.R.D.Mendis b B.A.W.Mendis	2
	Extras	b 4, nb 6	10	b 11, lb 1, w 1, nb 4	17
			177		**92**

FoW (1): 1-51 (1), 2-80 (2), 3-113 (4), 4-142 (5), 5-151 (3), 6-162 (6), 7-162 (7), 8-164 (9), 9-170 (10), 10-177 (11)
FoW (2): 1-1 (2), 2-34 (3), 3-41 (4), 4-41 (1), 5-46 (5), 6-79 (6), 7-89 (8), 8-89 (9), 9-89 (7), 10-92 (11)

Singha Sports Club Bowling

	O	M	R	W			O	M	R	W	
de Silva	6	1	15	3			3	0	13	0	1w
Liyanage	8	1	27	6	1w		11	4	31	1	1nb
Gamage	4	1	8	0	2nb		9	1	26	3	7nb
Randunu	0.2	0	0	1			35	12	65	2	
Ranatunga						(5)	25	1	98	3	2nb
Madanayake						(6)	3	1	9	1	

Sri Lanka Army Sports Club Bowling

	O	M	R	W			O	M	R	W	
Rathnayake	10	2	22	0	1nb	(4)	5	1	17	0	2nb
Karunatilleke	5	0	15	0							
Peiris	3	0	16	0	1nb		2	0	7	0	1w
B.A.W.Mendis	22.4	2	49	5	1nb	(2)	17	6	25	5	1nb
Prasanna	7	2	24	0		(1)	12	5	18	3	
de Zoysa	8	1	14	2	1nb	(5)	5	0	13	2	1nb
Palleguruge	11	1	33	3	2nb						

Umpires: K.M.Kottahachchi and R.M.P.J.Rambukwella.　Referee: B.C.Cooray.　Toss: Singha Sports Club

Close of Play: 1st day: Singha Sports Club (1) 177 all out; 2nd day: Singha Sports Club (2) 3-1 (Faux 1*, Zoysa 0*, 2 overs).

BURGHER RECREATION CLUB v SEBASTIANITES CRICKET AND ATHLETIC CLUB

Played at Burgher Recreation Club Ground, Colombo, February 29, March 1, 2, 2008.
Premier Championship 2007/08 - Tier B
Sebastianites Cricket and Athletic Club won by 170 runs.   (Points: Burgher Recreation Club 3.72, Sebastianites Cricket and Athletic Club 16.57)

SEBASTIANITES CRICKET AND ATHLETIC CLUB

1	H.A.H.U.Tillakaratne	lbw b Madusanka	79	lbw b Eranga	4
2	B.Y.Arumathanthri	lbw b Eranga	8	b Madusanka	57
3	T.M.N.Rajaratne	c Dawood b Mendis	23	c and b Eranga	1
4	M.A.B.Peiris	b Fernando	88	c Perera b Eranga	0
5	T.L.T.Peiris	c Sandagirigoda b Lakmal	33	c Dawood b Nishantha	8
6	†K.L.K.Fernando	c Dawood b Fernando	16	lbw b Madusanka	15
7	S.R.Kumar	c Nishantha b Fernando	13	c Dawood b Eranga	0
8	*M.N.T.H.Kumara	c Mendis b Eranga	7	(10) b Fernando	25
9	A.B.L.D.Rodrigo	c Dawood b Eranga	4	c Mendis b Eranga	36
10	P.W.L.R.Fernando	not out	9	(8) c Harischandra b Madusanka	6
11	B.S.Rajitha	lbw b Madusanka	7	not out	7
	Extras	b 9, lb 4, w 6, nb 13	32	b 8, lb 11, nb 17	36
			319		195

FoW (1): 1-31 (2), 2-94 (3), 3-134 (1), 4-232 (5), 5-266 (6), 6-272 (4), 7-291 (8), 8-295 (7), 9-299 (9), 10-319 (11)
FoW (2): 1-8 (1), 2-27 (3), 3-71 (5), 4-112 (2), 5-113 (7), 6-115 (6), 7-123 (8), 8-185 (9), 9-185 (4), 10-195 (10)

BURGHER RECREATION CLUB

1	D.H.Sandagirigoda	c Rodrigo b Kumara	1	lbw b P.W.L.R.Fernando	0
2	I.C.D.Perera	c Kumar b Kumara	21	c K.L.K.Fernando b Rodrigo	58
3	†M.F.H.Dawood	lbw b P.W.L.R.Fernando	43	(5) c K.L.K.Fernando b Rodrigo	38
4	*H.D.P.S.Harischandra	run out (Rodrigo)	6	(6) c Kumar b Rodrigo	1
5	B.M.S.N.Mendis	b Rajitha	1	(3) lbw b Rajitha	20
6	K.D.J.Nishantha	lbw b M.A.B.Peiris	5	(4) c Rajaratne b Rajitha	19
7	R.K.U.Lakmal	c Arumathanthri b Rodrigo	22	b Rajitha	15
8	C.A.M.Madusanka	lbw b Rodrigo	1	(10) b Rajitha	4
9	G.D.R.Eranga	c M.A.B.Peiris b Rodrigo	45	(8) c Rodrigo b Rajitha	3
10	D.S.Liyanage	run out (Rodrigo)	12	(9) b Rodrigo	0
11	A.N.P.R.Fernando	not out	11	not out	0
	Extras	lb 5, w 1, nb 3	9	b 2, lb 3, w 4	9
			177		167

FoW (1): 1-10 (1), 2-31 (2), 3-46 (4), 4-50 (5), 5-59 (6), 6-101 (3), 7-102 (8), 8-133 (7), 9-162 (10), 10-177 (9)
FoW (2): 1-1 (1), 2-39 (3), 3-86 (4), 4-140 (2), 5-142 (6), 6-145 (5), 7-150 (8), 8-163 (7), 9-167 (10), 10-167 (9)

Burgher Bowling	O	M	R	W			O	M	R	W	
Eranga	19	2	70	3	5nb		16	5	49	5	7nb
Liyanage	9	1	48	0		(3)	2	2	0	0	
Fernando	16	4	63	3	1w,4nb	(2)	8.1	0	49	1	6nb
Madusanka	18.3	6	39	2		(5)	16	7	35	3	
Mendis	8	1	42	1	1w	(4)	2	1	12	0	
Lakmal	15	3	34	1		(7)	6	1	11	0	
Nishantha	4	1	10	0		(6)	5	1	20	1	

Sebastianites Bowling	O	M	R	W			O	M	R	W	
Kumara	6	2	21	2			6	2	23	0	
P.W.L.R.Fernando	5	0	24	1	1w,3nb		7	0	21	1	
Kumar	3	1	8	0							
Arumathanthri	4	1	10	0		(3)	6	1	29	0	
Rajitha	14	3	22	1		(4)	19	4	34	5	
M.A.B.Peiris	12	0	36	1							
Rodrigo	18.5	3	51	3		(5)	16.1	3	55	4	3w

Umpires: E.J.A.P.A.M.Jayasuriya and R.R.Wimalasiri.   Referee: A.J.Samarasekera.   Toss: Sebastianites Cricket and Athletic Club

Close of Play: 1st day: Sebastianites Cricket and Athletic Club (1) 272-6 (Kumar 0*, Kumara 0*, 76.2 overs); 2nd day: Sebastianites Cricket and Athletic Club (2) 78-3 (Arumathanthri 43*, K.L.K.Fernando 2*, 18 overs).
M.A.B.Peiris retired hurt in the Sebastianites Cricket and Athletic Club second innings having scored 0 (team score 34-2) - he returned when the score was 185-8.

LANKAN CRICKET CLUB v MORATUWA SPORTS CLUB

Played at R.Premadasa Stadium, Colombo, February 29, March 1, 2, 2008.
Premier Championship 2007/08 - Tier B
Match drawn.   (Points: Lankan Cricket Club 11.845, Moratuwa Sports Club 3.31)

LANKAN CRICKET CLUB

1	D.G.N.de Silva	c H.U.K.de Silva b P.C.M.Fernando	17	(2) c Wijemanne b N.A.C.T.Perera	13
2	B.M.D.T.D.Ariyasinghe	lbw b Dammika	44	(1) c Wijemanne b Dammika	60
3	D.V.Gunawardene	c Wijemanne b de Mel	14	(4) lbw b N.A.C.T.Perera	18
4	Y.N.Tillakaratne	lbw b N.A.C.T.Perera	1	(5) lbw b de Mel	10
5	*†E.F.M.U.Fernando	not out	104	(6) c H.U.K.de Silva b M.D.S.Perera	16
6	J.R.G.Namal	c H.U.K.de Silva b P.C.M.Fernando	7	(3) c H.U.K.de Silva b M.D.S.Perera	66
7	G.A.L.W.Shantha	c Wijemanne b N.A.C.T.Perera	0	c Dammika b S.J.C.de Silva	6
8	J.D.M.de Silva	lbw b M.D.S.Perera	18	c Wijemanne b S.J.C.de Silva	1
9	D.R.F.Weerasinghe	lbw b P.C.M.Fernando	13	c Mendis b de Mel	49
10	K.G.D.Fernando	c Wijemanne b M.D.S.Perera	12	lbw b Dammika	55
11	P.D.M.P.N.Kumara	lbw b M.D.S.Perera	2	not out	6
	Extras	b 9, lb 7, w 2, nb 3	21	b 7, lb 1, w 1, nb 7	16
			253		**316**

FoW (1): 1-21 (1), 2-59 (3), 3-60 (4), 4-79 (2), 5-92 (6), 6-92 (7), 7-161 (8), 8-198 (9), 9-231 (10), 10-253 (11)
FoW (2): 1-20 (2), 2-110 (1), 3-157 (3), 4-166 (4), 5-176 (5), 6-198 (7), 7-199 (6), 8-199 (8), 9-305 (9), 10-316 (10)

MORATUWA SPORTS CLUB

1	R.M.Mendis	b K.G.D.Fernando	26	not out	11
2	W.S.T.Fernando	c and b K.G.D.Fernando	39	not out	31
3	L.T.A.de Silva	c Namal b Ariyasinghe	32		
4	†D.S.Wijemanne	c Gunawardene b Kumara	1		
5	H.U.K.de Silva	c E.F.M.U.Fernando b K.G.D.Fernando	25		
6	S.J.C.de Silva	lbw b K.G.D.Fernando	31		
7	W.P.D.de Mel	lbw b K.G.D.Fernando	5		
8	*M.D.S.Perera	c Gunawardene b Weerasinghe	18		
9	P.C.M.Fernando	c and b Tillakaratne	1		
10	S.D.Dammika	not out	8		
11	N.A.C.T.Perera	c E.F.M.U.Fernando b Kumara	2		
	Extras	lb 9, nb 16	25	b 4, lb 3	7
			213	(no wicket)	**49**

FoW (1): 1-69 (1), 2-75 (2), 3-76 (4), 4-130 (3), 5-142 (5), 6-151 (7), 7-184 (8), 8-185 (9), 9-203 (6), 10-213 (11)

Moratuwa Sports Club Bowling

	O	M	R	W			O	M	R	W	
P.C.M.Fernando	25	8	62	3	1w,1nb		24	4	72	0	
N.A.C.T.Perera	18	3	77	2			15	2	49	2	1nb
de Mel	8	2	17	1	1w	(7)	8	0	35	0	1w
Dammika	16	4	37	1			13.4	4	33	2	
S.J.C.de Silva	2	0	18	0		(3)	17	1	79	2	2nb
M.D.S.Perera	5.2	0	26	3	2nb	(5)	14	2	38	2	4nb
H.U.K.de Silva						(6)	1	0	2	0	

Lankan Cricket Club Bowling

	O	M	R	W			O	M	R	W	
Kumara	12	2	43	2	1nb		3	0	4	0	
J.D.M.de Silva	9	1	38	0			2	0	13	0	
Gunawardene	1	0	5	0			2	2	0	0	
Tillakaratne	8	3	21	1		(5)	1	0	4	0	
K.G.D.Fernando	17	2	57	5	12nb						
Weerasinghe	9	2	27	1							
Ariyasinghe	8	3	13	1	1nb						
E.F.M.U.Fernando						(4)	2	0	13	0	
D.G.N.de Silva						(6)	1	0	6	0	
Namal						(7)	1	0	2	0	

Umpires: N.S.Bopage and S.H.Sarathkumara. Referee: B.C.Cooray.   Toss: Moratuwa Sports Club
Close of Play: 1st day: Lankan Cricket Club (1) 195-7 (E.F.M.U.Fernando 70*, Weerasinghe 13*, 55 overs); 2nd day: Lankan Cricket Club (2) 36-1 (Ariyasinghe 19*, Namal 3*, 8 overs).
E.F.M.U.Fernando's 104 took 175 balls and included 12 fours and 2 sixes.

POLICE SPORTS CLUB v PANADURA SPORTS CLUB

Played at Police Park Ground, Colombo, February 29, March 1, 2, 2008.
Premier Championship 2007/08 - Tier B
Match drawn.   (Points: Police Sports Club 2.975, Panadura Sports Club 12.07)

PANADURA SPORTS CLUB

1	M.R.Fernando	c Kuruppu b Ramanayake	7	(2) c Kuruppu b Dilantha	11
2	†G.Y.S.R.Perera	c Nirmal b Weerasinghe	18	(1) c Nirmal b Sanjeewa	55
3	M.T.T.Fernando	c Rasmijinan b Dilantha	10	not out	126
4	G.S.U.Fernando	run out (Sanjeewa)	15	not out	10
5	*J.S.K.Peiris	c Kuruppu b Rasmijinan	8		
6	W.M.P.N.Wanasinghe	b Soysa	55		
7	M.N.R.Cooray	c Jayawardene b Ramanayake	28		
8	G.A.S.Perera	c Rasmijinan b Soysa	82		
9	H.F.M.Fonseka	c Soysa b Jayawardene	4		
10	J.K.D.Chathuranga	b Dilantha	20		
11	H.D.N.de Silva	not out	15		
	Extras	lb 3, w 1, nb 6	10		
			272	**(2 wickets, declared)**	**202**

FoW (1): 1-8 (1), 2-24 (3), 3-54 (2), 4-56 (4), 5-65 (5), 6-114 (7), 7-176 (6), 8-211 (9), 9-243 (8), 10-272 (10)
FoW (2): 1-21 (2), 2-150 (1)

POLICE SPORTS CLUB

1	M.M.P.Kumara	b Cooray	8	(8) c and b G.A.S.Perera	2
2	†K.A.D.M.C.Kuruppu	c G.Y.S.R.Perera b Wanasinghe	18	(1) c G.S.U.Fernando b G.A.S.Perera	13
3	P.R.Nirmal	lbw b Cooray	0	(2) c M.R.Fernando b G.A.S.Perera	78
4	W.N.M.Soysa	b de Silva	16	c Peiris b Fonseka	20
5	T.A.N.Weerasinghe	lbw b Cooray	1	(6) not out	19
6	*R.G.D.Sanjeewa	c Peiris b Cooray	4	(3) c Fonseka b G.S.U.Fernando	26
7	H.P.A.Priyantha	c G.Y.S.R.Perera b Wanasinghe	22	c Peiris b Cooray	40
8	M.M.Rasmijinan	not out	47	(5) c Peiris b Fonseka	14
9	H.M.Jayawardene	c G.Y.S.R.Perera b Wanasinghe	1	not out	0
10	R.S.K.A.P.Dilantha	lbw b Cooray	2		
11	W.C.K.Ramanayake	c and b Cooray	14		
	Extras	lb 3, w 1, nb 3	7	b 1, lb 2	3
			140	**(7 wickets)**	**215**

FoW (1): 1-31 (1), 2-31 (2), 3-31 (3), 4-39 (5), 5-44 (6), 6-68 (4), 7-87 (7), 8-93 (9), 9-104 (10), 10-140 (11)
FoW (2): 1-61 (1), 2-119 (3), 3-119 (2), 4-145 (5), 5-158 (4), 6-202 (7), 7-215 (8)

Police Sports Club Bowling

	O	M	R	W			O	M	R	W
Dilantha	14.4	1	59	2	1w,5nb		6	0	34	1
Ramanayake	15	6	31	2			8	2	20	0
Weerasinghe	17	5	44	1			4	1	14	0
Rasmijinan	23	4	69	1			2	0	13	0
Jayawardene	7	1	29	1		(7)	4	0	42	0
Sanjeewa	5	2	10	0		(5)	10.2	1	52	1
Soysa	14	5	27	2		(6)	6	0	27	0

Panadura Sports Club Bowling

	O	M	R	W			O	M	R	W
de Silva	15	6	20	1			3	0	20	0
Chathuranga	9	2	18	0	1w,2nb		1	0	12	0
Wanasinghe	14	4	23	3	1nb	(4)	3	0	20	0
Peiris	3	2	6	0		(8)	1	0	2	0
Cooray	25	9	49	6		(3)	14	2	44	1
G.A.S.Perera	9	4	12	0		(5)	15	3	53	3
Fonseka	4	0	9	0			10	1	36	2
G.S.U.Fernando						(6)	5	1	25	1

Umpires: K.M.Kottahachchi and R.M.P.J.Rambukwella.   Referee: R.P.Samarasinghe.   Toss: Police Sports Club

Close of Play: 1st day: Panadura Sports Club (1) 239-8 (G.A.S.Perera 79*, Chathuranga 5*, 81.2 overs); 2nd day: Police Sports Club (1) 131-9 (Rasmijinan 42*, Ramanayake 10*, 73 overs).
M.T.T.Fernando's 126 took 103 balls and included 10 fours and 5 sixes.

SARACENS SPORTS CLUB v SINGHA SPORTS CLUB

Played at Nondescripts Cricket Club Ground, Colombo, February 29, March 1, 2, 2008.
Premier Championship 2007/08 - Tier B
Match drawn.   (Points: Saracens Sports Club 3.14, Singha Sports Club 11.76)

SINGHA SPORTS CLUB

1	D.A.Faux	c Joseph b Nishantha	19	lbw b Nishantha	50
2	†P.M.U.Shirosh	lbw b Serasinghe	18	lbw b Nishantha	0
3	H.H.R.Kavinga	c Pushpakumara b Serasinghe	106	lbw b Nishantha	6
4	A.S.Wewalwala	b Alwis	44	lbw b Alwis	44
5	T.J.Madanayake	lbw b Karunaratne	9	run out	33
6	H.S.M.Zoysa	c Abeyratne b Serasinghe	16	lbw b Alwis	0
7	S.I.Vithana	c Joseph b Karunaratne	14	not out	36
8	R.S.R.de Zoysa	not out	16	not out	8
9	D.O.L.Silva	c Niroshan b Karunaratne	16		
10	*N.C.K.Liyanage	c Pushpakumara b Karunaratne	0		
11	P.L.S.Gamage	b Nishantha	0		
	Extras	b 2, lb 4, nb 5	11	b 6, lb 4, w 5, nb 11	26
			269	(6 wickets, declared)	203

FoW (1): 1-32 (1), 2-55 (2), 3-163 (4), 4-181 (5), 5-198 (6), 6-229 (3), 7-240 (7), 8-264 (9), 9-266 (10), 10-269 (11)
FoW (2): 1-19 (2), 2-30 (3), 3-116 (1), 4-130 (4), 5-130 (6), 6-177 (5)

SARACENS SPORTS CLUB

1	W.G.R.K.Alwis	c Shirosh b Silva	10	c sub (H.W.M.Kumara) b Silva	0
2	P.K.Bodhisha	b Gamage	13	c Gamage b Vithana	15
3	†W.A.S.Niroshan	lbw b Silva	14	c Silva b Gamage	23
4	*G.N.Abeyratne	lbw b Liyanage	26		
5	S.C.Serasinghe	c H.S.M.Zoysa b Liyanage	21	(6) not out	0
6	G.A.Joseph	c Shirosh b Gamage	3	(4) lbw b de Zoysa	8
7	M.L.R.Karunaratne	c H.S.M.Zoysa b Silva	67	(5) not out	1
8	L.D.P.Nishantha	c Faux b Liyanage	27		
9	A.V.S.Nikethana	not out	30		
10	P.M.Pushpakumara	c Wewalwala b Silva	24		
11	D.P.L.M.Liyanage	lbw b Liyanage	0		
	Extras	b 5, lb 6, nb 10	21	b 2, lb 2, nb 1	5
			256	(4 wickets)	52

FoW (1): 1-14 (1), 2-36 (3), 3-51 (2), 4-83 (4), 5-90 (5), 6-103 (6), 7-169 (8), 8-206 (7), 9-248 (10), 10-256 (11)
FoW (2): 1-0 (1), 2-42 (3), 3-50 (4), 4-50 (2)

Saracens Sports Club Bowling

	O	M	R	W			O	M	R	W	
Nishantha	20.3	7	51	2	5nb	(2)	34	8	77	3	9nb
Liyanage	7	0	41	0		(1)	2	0	14	0	1w
Serasinghe	18	5	38	3		(5)	6	0	22	0	
Pushpakumara	23	2	51	0							
Karunaratne	21	5	74	4		(6)	8	0	23	0	
Alwis	4	2	8	1		(4)	30	7	49	2	
Nikethana						(3)	3	0	8	0	2nb

Singha Sports Club Bowling

	O	M	R	W			O	M	R	W	
Silva	15	4	35	4	6nb		3	2	5	1	
Liyanage	23.3	5	83	4			2	0	28	0	
Gamage	11	4	40	2	3nb	(4)	2	0	6	1	1nb
de Zoysa	19	4	49	0		(5)	1	0	8	1	
Vithana	15	3	38	0		(6)	1	0	1	1	
Madanayake						(3)	1	1	0	0	

Umpires: W.Jayasena and K.M.Kottahachchi.   Referee: K.T.Francis.   Toss: Saracens Sports Club

Close of Play: 1st day: Singha Sports Club (1) 267-9 (de Zoysa 14*, Gamage 0*, 90 overs); 2nd day: Singha Sports Club (2) 9-0 (Faux 4*, Shirosh 0*, 2 overs).

H.H.R.Kavinga's 106 took 189 balls and included 11 fours and 1 six.

SRI LANKA AIR FORCE SPORTS CLUB v SRI LANKA ARMY SPORTS CLUB

Played at Air Force Ground, Colombo, February 29, March 1, 2, 2008.
Premier Championship 2007/08 - Tier B
Sri Lanka Army Sports Club won by four wickets. (Points: Sri Lanka Air Force Sports Club 3.105, Sri Lanka Army Sports Club 15.51)

SRI LANKA AIR FORCE SPORTS CLUB

1	M.A.M.Faizer	c Rathnayake b Karunatilleke	15	c T.R.D.Mendis b Rathnayake	2
2	A.Rizan	lbw b Palleguruge	36	lbw b Prasanna	16
3	W.A.Eranga	lbw b Prasanna	30	b B.A.W.Mendis	28
4	W.M.M.W.E.V.Gangoda	run out (Karunatilleke)	49	(5) c de Zoysa b Prasanna	20
5	†M.K.P.B.Kularatne	c Soysa b Palleguruge	0	(6) c Soysa b Prasanna	1
6	*K.A.Kumara	lbw b B.A.W.Mendis	9	(7) c de Zoysa b B.A.W.Mendis	0
7	S.Madanayake	b Prasanna	10	(8) lbw b B.A.W.Mendis	4
8	W.P.Wickrama	c Lawrance b Karunatilleke	20	(10) run out	4
9	M.K.G.C.P.Lakshitha	c Prasad b Rathnayake	14	c Prasad b B.A.W.Mendis	8
10	K.K.A.K.Lakmal	run out (Karunatilleke)	0	(11) not out	0
11	M.P.G.D.P.Gunatilleke	not out	4	(4) b B.A.W.Mendis	0
	Extras	b 16, lb 5, nb 1	22	b 1, lb 1, nb 7	9
			209		92

FoW (1): 1-19 (1), 2-58 (3), 3-110 (2), 4-110 (5), 5-141 (4), 6-147 (6), 7-155 (7), 8-191 (8), 9-192 (10), 10-209 (9)
FoW (2): 1-3 (1), 2-42 (3), 3-44 (4), 4-73 (2), 5-75 (6), 6-76 (7), 7-80 (8), 8-80 (5), 9-90 (10), 10-92 (9)

SRI LANKA ARMY SPORTS CLUB

1	R.D.I.A.Karunatilleke	c Lakshitha b Madanayake	13	(2) c Rizan b Lakshitha	2
2	D.A.Lawrance	lbw b Madanayake	12	(4) c Kularatne b Rizan	19
3	H.H.M.de Zoysa	lbw b Madanayake	0	c Madanayake b Rizan	14
4	S.Prasanna	c Gunatilleke b Lakshitha	1	(1) b Rizan	70
5	K.C.Prasad	lbw b Lakshitha	0	not out	37
6	B.A.W.Mendis	lbw b Madanayake	7	c Kularatne b Madanayake	0
7	T.R.D.Mendis	c Rizan b Gunatilleke	47	lbw b Madanayake	0
8	†T.D.T.Soysa	c Kularatne b Madanayake	33	not out	0
9	W.R.Palleguruge	c Faizer b Gunatilleke	21		
10	*P.K.N.M.K.Rathnayake	lbw b Gunatilleke	3		
11	P.P.M.Peiris	not out	10		
	Extras	b 2, lb 4, nb 3	9	b 3, lb 1	4
			156	(6 wickets)	146

FoW (1): 1-23 (1), 2-23 (3), 3-28 (2), 4-28 (4), 5-28 (5), 6-54 (6), 7-89 (7), 8-120 (9), 9-143 (10), 10-156 (8)
FoW (2): 1-28 (2), 2-78 (3), 3-93 (1), 4-141 (4), 5-142 (6), 6-142 (7)

Sri Lanka Army Sports Club Bowling

	O	M	R	W				O	M	R	W	
Rathnayake	14.1	2	39	1				9	0	40	1	7nb
Karunatilleke	9	2	17	2								
Lawrance	2	0	7	0								
Peiris	4	1	20	0		(5)	2	1	4	0	
Prasanna	24	11	38	2		(2)	15	6	22	3	
B.A.W.Mendis	24	5	44	1	1nb	(4)	14.3	1	23	5	
Palleguruge	14	7	15	0		(3)	5	4	1	0	
de Zoysa	4	1	8	0								

Sri Lanka Air Force Sports Club Bowling

	O	M	R	W				O	M	R	W	
Lakshitha	17	2	56	2	2nb	(3)	3	0	22	1	
Lakmal	4	0	13	0								
Madanayake	17	3	42	5		(1)	13.1	2	40	2	
Gunatilleke	8	1	37	3	1nb	(2)	5	0	24	0	
Rizan	1	0	2	0		(4)	12	2	37	3	
Wickrama						(5)	3	0	9	0	
Gangoda						(6)	3	0	10	0	

Umpires: H.D.P.K.Dharmasena and M.V.D.Zilva. Referee: N.S.H.M.R.Kodituwakku. Toss: Sri Lanka Army Sports Club

Close of Play: 1st day: Sri Lanka Air Force Sports Club (1) 197-9 (Lakshitha 10*, Gunatilleke 0*, 91.3 overs); 2nd day: Sri Lanka Air Force Sports Club (2) 44-3 (Rizan 7*, Gangoda 0*, 21 overs).

485

BADURELIYA SPORTS CLUB v RAGAMA CRICKET CLUB

Played at Colombo Cricket Club Ground, March 6, 7, 8, 9, 2008.
Premier Championship 2007/08 - Tier A
Match drawn.   **(Points: Badureliya Sports Club 3.075, Ragama Cricket Club 11.555)**

RAGAMA CRICKET CLUB
1	D.A.Ranatunga	run out (Ratnayake)	10
2	H.E.Vithana	c Perera b Sampath	32
3	R.S.S.S.de Zoysa	run out (Bandaratilleke)	35
4	*S.I.de Saram	c Vitharana b Bandaratilleke	188
5	C.M.Bandara	c Sampath b Malinga	4
6	W.D.D.S.Perera	c Perera b Malinga	1
7	K.Weeraratne	b Fernando	10
8	†S.A.Perera	run out (Perera)	15
9	P.A.S.S.Jeewantha	c Sampath b Bandaratilleke	7
10	S.A.D.U.Indrasiri	c Hunukumbura b Bandaratilleke	0
11	H.G.D.Nayanakantha	not out	12
	Extras	b 6, nb 11	17
			331

FoW (1): 1-21 (1), 2-73 (2), 3-88 (3), 4-95 (5), 5-101 (6), 6-120 (7), 7-161 (8), 8-190 (9), 9-190 (10), 10-331 (4)

BADURELIYA SPORTS CLUB
1	†D.W.A.N.D.Vitharana	c Weeraratne b W.D.D.S.Perera	49	st S.A.Perera b Bandara	79
2	M.M.D.P.V.Perera	b Vithana	17	c de Saram b Weeraratne	1
3	D.N.Hunukumbura	run out (de Saram)	9	lbw b Weeraratne	0
4	*R.P.A.H.Wickramaratne	c S.A.Perera b Jeewantha	24	c Jeewantha b Bandara	109
5	T.M.N.Sampath	b Bandara	10	(7) c and b Bandara	15
6	K.A.D.M.Fernando	b Jeewantha	1	lbw b Bandara	0
7	R.M.A.R.Ratnayake	c S.A.Perera b Jeewantha	12	(5) c de Zoysa b Bandara	10
8	P.S.Liyanage	c Indrasiri b Bandara	1	c sub (K.R.N.U.Perera) b Vithana	15
9	M.R.C.N.Bandaratilleke	not out	15	not out	6
10	S.D.C.Malinga	lbw b Bandara	12	b Bandara	2
11	K.L.S.L.Dias	b Jeewantha	8		
	Extras	lb 2, w 2, nb 4	8	lb 6, w 3, nb 3	12
			166	**(9 wickets)**	**249**

FoW (1): 1-39 (2), 2-73 (3), 3-83 (1), 4-108 (5), 5-112 (6), 6-119 (4), 7-129 (8), 8-130 (7), 9-143 (10), 10-166 (11)
FoW (2): 1-13 (2), 2-13 (3), 3-177 (1), 4-197 (5), 5-199 (6), 6-218 (4), 7-241 (8), 8-241 (7), 9-249 (10)

Badureliya Sports Club Bowling
	O	M	R	W	
Malinga	19	2	98	2	
Fernando	21	5	68	1	7nb
Ratnayake	11	2	35	0	3nb
Dias	18	6	70	0	
Sampath	8	3	17	1	
Bandaratilleke	7.4	1	37	3	1nb

Ragama Cricket Club Bowling
	O	M	R	W			O	M	R	W	
Weeraratne	2	0	19	0	2nb		16	2	62	2	1nb
Nayanakantha	3	0	35	0	1w	(5)	3	1	14	0	1w
Vithana	10	3	26	1		(4)	13	4	30	1	
W.D.D.S.Perera	8	0	30	1		(3)	5	1	9	0	
Bandara	9	0	26	3		(6)	22.1	7	47	6	
Jeewantha	5.3	1	18	4	1w,2nb	(2)	11	2	34	0	1w,2nb
Indrasiri	2	1	10	0		(8)	11	2	34	0	
de Saram						(7)	5	3	13	0	

Umpires: S.S.K.Gallage and R.D.Kottahachchi.   Referee: M.C.Mendis.   Toss: Badureliya Sports Club

Close of Play: 1st day: No play; 2nd day: Ragama Cricket Club (1) 95-3 (de Saram 6*, Bandara 4*, 39 overs); 3rd day: Badureliya Sports Club (1) 166-9 (Bandaratilleke 15*, Dias 8*, 39 overs).

S.I.de Saram's 188 took 152 balls and included 19 fours and 12 sixes. R.P.A.H.Wickramaratne's 109 took 184 balls and included 14 fours and 2 sixes.

BLOOMFIELD CRICKET AND ATHLETIC CLUB v TAMIL UNION CRICKET AND ATHLETIC CLUB

Played at Bloomfield Cricket and Athletic Club Ground, Colombo, March 6, 7, 8, 9, 2008.
Premier Championship 2007/08 - Tier A
Match drawn.   (Points: Bloomfield Cricket and Athletic Club 12.35, Tamil Union Cricket and Athletic Club 3.08)

BLOOMFIELD CRICKET AND ATHLETIC CLUB

1	T.S.Masmulla	c Cooray b Pushpakumara	25	b Pushpakumara	31
2	M.T.Gunaratne	lbw b Wijesiriwardene	4	(7) not out	1
3	S.T.Jayasuriya	c Pushpakumara b Wijesiriwardene	2	(2) c Pushpakumara	
				b Liyanagunawardene	75
4	K.Y.de Silva	lbw b Liyanagunawardene	55	c sub (W.J.M.R.Dias)	
				b Liyanagunawardene	11
5	†T.M.Dilshan	c sub (W.J.M.R.Dias)			
		b Liyanagunawardene	121		
6	L.P.C.Silva	lbw b Liyanagunawardene	25	(3) c and b Liyanagunawardene	49
7	*D.M.G.S.Dissanayake	b Maduwantha	24	(5) not out	74
8	C.U.Jayasinghe	c Wijesiriwardene b Liyanagunawardene	81	(6) c S.K.L.de Silva b Cooray	45
9	G.A.S.K.Gangodawila	b Liyanagunawardene	12		
10	A.B.T.Lakshitha	c Fernando b Liyanagunawardene	0		
11	T.P.Gamage	not out	3		
	Extras	b 3, lb 2, w 8, nb 5	18	b 5, lb 4, nb 5	14
			370	(5 wickets)	300

FoW (1): 1-7 (2), 2-10 (3), 3-50 (1), 4-158 (4), 5-187 (6), 6-250 (7), 7-292 (5), 8-341 (9), 9-351 (10), 10-370 (8)
FoW (2): 1-114 (1), 2-120 (2), 3-167 (4), 4-212 (3), 5-296 (6)

TAMIL UNION CRICKET AND ATHLETIC CLUB

1	†G.T.de Silva	c Dilshan b Lakshitha	59
2	G.I.Daniel	c L.P.C.Silva b Dissanayake	31
3	S.I.Fernando	lbw b Dissanayake	14
4	S.K.L.de Silva	c Dilshan b Jayasuriya	29
5	R.J.M.G.M.Rupasinghe	c de Silva b Gamage	121
6	M.Pushpakumara	c L.P.C.Silva b Jayasuriya	0
7	P.D.M.A.Cooray	lbw b Jayasuriya	11
8	*H.M.Maduwantha	lbw b Dilshan	17
9	S.C.Liyanagunawardene	lbw b Dilshan	0
10	O.L.A.Wijesiriwardene	c Dilshan b Lakshitha	7
11	P.S.Jayaprakashdaran	not out	0
	Extras	b 7, lb 10, w 6, nb 4	27
			316

FoW (1): 1-65 (2), 2-108 (3), 3-144 (1), 4-158 (4), 5-158 (6), 6-197 (7), 7-271 (8), 8-277 (9), 9-316 (10), 10-316 (5)

Tamil Union Bowling	O	M	R	W			O	M	R	W	
Wijesiriwardene	9.4	1	40	2	3w						
Jayaprakashdaran	11	0	73	0	1w,5nb	(1)	13	0	72	0	5nb
Fernando	0.2	0	2	0		(4)	3	1	4	0	
Pushpakumara	20	2	83	1		(3)	12	1	57	1	
Maduwantha	12	1	41	1		(2)	11	1	50	0	
Rupasinghe	6	1	32	0							
Liyanagunawardene	19.1	2	94	6		(5)	16	0	88	3	
Cooray						(6)	2	0	20	1	

Bloomfield Bowling	O	M	R	W	
Lakshitha	20	5	70	2	1w,4nb
Gamage	16.1	3	54	1	1w
Dissanayake	20	3	68	2	
Gangodawila	2	0	10	0	
Gunaratne	7	0	13	0	
Jayasuriya	17	3	71	3	
Dilshan	4	0	13	2	

Umpires: E.A.R.de Silva and J.W.L.Nandana.   Referee: U.Warnapura.   Toss: Bloomfield Cricket and Athletic Club
Close of Play: 1st day: No play; 2nd day: Bloomfield Cricket and Athletic Club (1) 178-4 (Dilshan 63*, L.P.C.Silva 17*, 35.2 overs); 3rd day: Tamil Union Cricket and Athletic Club (1) 187-5 (Rupasinghe 22*, Cooray 7*, 53 overs).
T.M.Dilshan's 121 took 121 balls and included 9 fours and 6 sixes. R.J.M.G.M.Rupasinghe's 121 took 173 balls and included 10 fours and 5 sixes.

487

CHILAW MARIANS CRICKET CLUB v SINHALESE SPORTS CLUB

Played at R.Premadasa Stadium, Colombo, March 6, 7, 8, 9, 2008.
Premier Championship 2007/08 - Tier A
Sinhalese Sports Club won by eight wickets.   (Points: Chilaw Marians Cricket Club 2.83, Sinhalese Sports Club 15.645)

CHILAW MARIANS CRICKET CLUB

1	†C.S.Fernando	st Silva b Senanayake	20	c Silva b Vidanapathirana	4
2	M.L.Udawatte	b Senanayake	21	lbw b Mirando	0
3	N.H.G.Cooray	b Mirando	56	c Jayawardene b Senanayake	7
4	*L.J.P.Gunaratne	c Paranavitana b Mirando	3	c Kandamby b Senanayake	8
5	K.H.R.K.Fernando	c Silva b Mirando	0	(6) c Paranavitana b Mirando	9
6	W.M.G.Ramyakumara	c Silva b Senanayake	31	(7) c Kandamby b Mirando	7
7	M.M.D.N.R.G.Perera	c Silva b Lokuarachchi	44	(8) c Paranavitana b Mirando	0
8	J.M.P.C.Jayasundera	lbw b Mirando	15	(9) c Mirando b Lokuarachchi	27
9	D.Hettiarachchi	c Paranavitana b Mirando	2	(5) b Prasad	36
10	G.A.C.R.Perera	c sub (K.Magage) b Mirando	11	c Kandamby b Senanayake	5
11	R.M.S.Eranga	not out	1	not out	2
	Extras	b 2, lb 2, w 1, nb 3	8	b 3, lb 3, nb 3	9
			212		**114**

FoW (1): 1-42 (1), 2-43 (2), 3-51 (4), 4-51 (5), 5-106 (6), 6-173 (7), 7-192 (3), 8-194 (9), 9-211 (10), 10-212 (8)
FoW (2): 1-2 (2), 2-10 (1), 3-14 (3), 4-62 (5), 5-62 (4), 6-76 (6), 7-76 (8), 8-79 (7), 9-98 (10), 10-114 (9)

SINHALESE SPORTS CLUB

1	N.T.Paranavitana	run out (Gunaratne)	36	c Cooray b Hettiarachchi	37
2	K.T.G.D.Prasad	lbw b Hettiarachchi	5		
3	†J.K.Silva	lbw b K.H.R.K.Fernando	110	not out	35
4	D.P.M.D.Jayawardene	lbw b Hettiarachchi	30		
5	*T.T.Samaraweera	c M.M.D.N.R.G.Perera b Eranga	1		
6	S.H.T.Kandamby	run out (Jayasundera)	24		
7	K.S.Lokuarachchi	b K.H.R.K.Fernando	4	(2) c Udawatte b G.A.C.R.Perera	3
8	K.P.S.P.Karunanayake	c C.S.Fernando b K.H.R.K.Fernando	0	(4) not out	21
9	M.T.T.Mirando	not out	3		
10	S.M.Senanayake	c C.S.Fernando b Jayasundera	1		
11	C.W.Vidanapathirana	c Gunaratne b K.H.R.K.Fernando	0		
	Extras	b 1, lb 1, w 1, nb 14	17	nb 2	2
			231	(2 wickets)	**98**

FoW (1): 1-11 (2), 2-93 (1), 3-162 (4), 4-167 (5), 5-215 (6), 6-220 (3), 7-221 (7), 8-229 (8), 9-230 (10), 10-231 (11)
FoW (2): 1-5 (2), 2-69 (1)

Sinhalese Sports Club Bowling

	O	M	R	W		O	M	R	W	
Vidanapathirana	11	2	39	0		7	2	10	1	
Karunanayake	6	2	16	0	1nb					
Senanayake	28	7	41	3		14	7	28	3	
Mirando	15.3	3	50	6	1w,2nb (2)	12	3	36	4	3nb
Prasad	9	1	38	0	(6)	6	1	26	1	
Lokuarachchi	12	3	24	1	(4)	4.5	1	7	1	
Paranavitana					(5)	1	0	1	0	

Chilaw Marians Cricket Club Bowling

	O	M	R	W		O	M	R	W	
G.A.C.R.Perera	12	0	48	0	10nb	5	0	22	1	2nb
Eranga	10	1	48	1	1w					
Hettiarachchi	18	0	66	2	(2)	10	2	33	1	
Gunaratne	4	1	6	0		2.3	0	23	0	
Jayasundera	15	3	44	1						
K.H.R.K.Fernando	7.3	1	17	4	(3)	3	0	20	0	

Umpires: A.G.Dissanayake and I.D.Gunawardene.   Referee: C.T.M.Devaraj.   Toss: Chilaw Marians Cricket Club

Close of Play: 1st day: Chilaw Marians Cricket Club (1) 11-0 (C.S.Fernando 3*, Udawatte 8*, 6.3 overs); 2nd day: Chilaw Marians Cricket Club (1) 211-8 (Jayasundera 15*, G.A.C.R.Perera 11*, 81 overs); 3rd day: Chilaw Marians Cricket Club (2) 15-3 (Gunaratne 0*, Hettiarachchi 0*, 14 overs).

J.K.Silva's 110 took 191 balls and included 11 fours.

COLTS CRICKET CLUB v COLOMBO CRICKET CLUB

Played at Colts Cricket Club Ground, Colombo, March 6, 7, 8, 9, 2008.
Premier Championship 2007/08 - Tier A
Match drawn.   (Points: Colts Cricket Club 3.44, Colombo Cricket Club 12.135)

COLOMBO CRICKET CLUB

1	M.G.Vandort	c Peiris b Kulatunga	30	c Perera b Kulasckara	1
2	J.Mubarak	c Warnapura b Mathews	0	(3) c Kulatunga b Kulasekara	0
3	K.G.N.Randika	c Peiris b Kulasekara	8	(6) c Attanayake b Weerakoon	6
4	*B.M.T.T.Mendis	lbw b Weerakoon	73	b Perera	14
5	C.K.Kapugedera	c Peiris b Kulasekara	13	c Perera b Mathews	101
6	A.S.Polonowita	b Weerakoon	104	(7) b Perera	79
7	A.C.Wethathasinghe	lbw b Weerakoon	30	(8) c Alwitigala b Perera	8
8	†D.K.Ranaweera	c Pathirana b Kulasekara	2	(2) lbw b Weerakoon	40
9	P.D.G.Chandrakumara	lbw b Mathews	2	not out	20
10	S.C.D.Boralessa	c Kulatunga b Weerakoon	0	lbw b Kulasekara	1
11	M.I.Ratnayake	not out	1	not out	27
	Extras	b 7, lb 8, w 7, nb 4	26	b 5, lb 7, nb 9	21
			289	**(9 wickets, declared)**	**318**

FoW (1): 1-5 (2), 2-29 (3), 3-67 (1), 4-87 (5), 5-220 (4), 6-222 (8), 7-236 (9), 8-272 (7), 9-276 (10), 10-289 (6)
FoW (2): 1-5 (1), 2-12 (3), 3-29 (4), 4-91 (2), 5-99 (6), 6-236 (5), 7-257 (8), 8-265 (7), 9-266 (10)

COLTS CRICKET CLUB

1	T.P.Attanayake	run out (Wethathasinghe)	1	run out (Wethathasinghe)	19
2	*B.S.M.Warnapura	c Vandort b Chandrakumara	37	not out	34
3	S.Weerakoon	c Kapugedera b Ratnayake	0		
4	A.D.Mathews	c Vandort b Boralessa	30		
5	H.G.J.M.Kulatunga	c Mendis b Boralessa	0		
6	K.G.Alwitigala	lbw b Chandrakumara	18		
7	M.D.K.Perera	c Ranaweera b Boralessa	20	(3) not out	18
8	K.A.S.Jayasinghe	not out	73		
9	D.N.Pathirana	b Boralessa	8		
10	K.M.D.N.Kulasekara	c Kapugedera b Boralessa	8		
11	†T.R.Peiris	c Ranaweera b Mubarak	37		
	Extras	nb 5	5		
			237	**(1 wicket)**	**71**

FoW (1): 1-4 (1), 2-4 (3), 3-50 (2), 4-51 (5), 5-83 (4), 6-108 (6), 7-108 (7), 8-126 (9), 9-163 (10), 10-237 (11)
FoW (2): 1-43 (1)

Colts Cricket Club Bowling

	O	M	R	W			O	M	R	W	
Kulasekara	20	2	70	3	4nb		18	2	70	3	7nb
Mathews	18	5	57	2	1w		12	3	29	1	2nb
Alwitigala	10	3	22	0	2w	(4)	11	2	35	0	
Kulatunga	6	1	22	1							
Weerakoon	27.2	6	72	4		(3)	27	4	101	2	
Perera	9	1	31	0		(5)	19	1	71	3	

Colombo Cricket Club Bowling

	O	M	R	W			O	M	R	W	
Ratnayake	15	4	43	1			4	1	19	0	
Wethathasinghe	4	1	16	0			7	2	21	0	
Randika	7	2	17	0							
Chandrakumara	15	2	48	2		(5)	3	1	5	0	
Mubarak	7.4	0	21	1							
Boralessa	24	5	92	5	5nb	(4)	5	0	21	0	
Kapugedera						(3)	2	1	5	0	

Umpires: M.G.Silva and N.D.Withana.   Referee: S.Ranatunga.   Toss: Colts Cricket Club

Close of Play: 1st day: Colombo Cricket Club (1) 67-3 (Mendis 18*, 20.5 overs); 2nd day: Colts Cricket Club (1) 70-4 (Mathews 24*, Alwitigala 7*, 26 overs); 3rd day: Colombo Cricket Club (2) 143-5 (Kapugedera 55*, Polonowita 22*, 40 overs).
A.S.Polonowita's 104 took 186 balls and included 14 fours. C.K.Kapugedera's 101 took 149 balls and included 10 fours and 1 six.
A.S.Polonowita retired hurt in the Colombo Cricket Club first innings having scored 70 (team score 220-5) - he returned when the score was 236-7.

NONDESCRIPTS CRICKET CLUB v MOORS SPORTS CLUB

Played at Nondescripts Cricket Club Ground, Colombo, March 6, 7, 8, 9, 2008.
Premier Championship 2007/08 - Tier A
Nondescripts Cricket Club won by ten wickets.   (Points: Nondescripts Cricket Club 16.045, Moors Sports Club 3.155)

MOORS SPORTS CLUB

1	T.K.D.Sudarshana	c Mapa Bandara b Kottehewa	15	c Wijesinghe b Athukorala	27
2	N.M.N.P.Nawela	lbw b Athukorala	35	c Kottehewa b Komasaru	26
3	G.R.P.Peiris	lbw b Athukorala	2	c Mapa Bandara b Kottehewa	50
4	W.M.B.Perera	c Sangakkara b Komasaru	52	c Gajanayake b Kottehewa	28
5	A.Rideegammanagedera	c Tharanga b Kottehewa	11	b Komasaru	30
6	*L.H.D.Dilhara	c Mapa Bandara b Varuna	14	(7) c Gajanayake b Komasaru	10
7	A.S.A.Perera	c Tharanga b Varuna	29	(8) c Gunawardene b Komasaru	35
8	H.M.R.K.B.Herath	c Mapa Bandara b Varuna	28	(9) c Wijesinghe b Komasaru	35
9	†W.M.J.Wannakuwatta	lbw b Athukorala	16	(6) c Gajanayake b Komasaru	17
10	U.W.M.B.C.A.Welagedara	not out	4	not out	6
11	P.N.Ranjith	c Mapa Bandara b Athukorala	2	st Mapa Bandara b Fernando	10
	Extras	b 3, lb 10, w 2, nb 2	17	lb 5, w 3, nb 4	12
			225		**286**

FoW (1): 1-26 (1), 2-33 (3), 3-112 (4), 4-120 (2), 5-137 (6), 6-159 (5), 7-196 (8), 8-219 (7), 9-221 (9), 10-225 (11)
FoW (2): 1-53 (2), 2-53 (1), 3-96 (4), 4-170 (5), 5-172 (3), 6-196 (7), 7-201 (6), 8-256 (8), 9-273 (9), 10-286 (11)

NONDESCRIPTS CRICKET CLUB

1	W.U.Tharanga	c Wannakuwatta b Welagedara	2	not out	1
2	K.D.Gunawardene	lbw b Dilhara	72	not out	4
3	W.L.P.Fernando	c W.M.B.Perera b Rideegammanagedera	26		
4	K.C.Sangakkara	c Herath b Rideegammanagedera	285		
5	C.G.Wijesinghe	c Dilhara b Herath	25		
6	*M.K.Gajanayake	c A.S.A.Perera b Peiris	77		
7	†M.R.D.G.Mapa Bandara	not out	1		
8	A.A.C.E.Athukorala				
9	H.W.U.Varuna				
10	D.T.Kottehewa				
11	N.C.Komasaru				
	Extras	b 1, lb 4, w 5, nb 5	15	b 4	4
		(6 wickets, declared)	503	(no wicket)	9

FoW (1): 1-6 (1), 2-79 (3), 3-148 (2), 4-208 (5), 5-484 (6), 6-503 (4)

Nondescripts Cricket Club Bowling

	O	M	R	W		O	M	R	W	
Kottehewa	26	8	73	2	1w,2nb	23	7	61	2	2w,3nb
Athukorala	20	5	44	4		18	3	59	1	
Tharanga	3	1	4	0						
Varuna	14	2	55	3	1w	9	1	43	0	1w
Komasaru	13	2	36	1	(3)	36	14	81	6	
Fernando					(5)	5.2	2	10	1	
Gunawardene					(6)	1	0	12	0	1nb
Gajanayake					(7)	5	1	15	0	

Moors Sports Club Bowling

	O	M	R	W		O	M	R	W	
Welagedara	25	1	125	1	4w,2nb	0.5	0	5	0	
Dilhara	12	1	44	1	1w,3nb					
Herath	23	1	106	1						
Ranjith	14	0	62	0						
Rideegammanagedera	28.4	2	108	2						
Peiris	6	0	24	1						
A.S.A.Perera	6	0	29	0						

Umpires: B.B.J.Nandakumar and M.S.K.Nandiweera. Referee: V.B.John.   Toss: Moors Sports Club
Close of Play: 1st day: Moors Sports Club (1) 69-2 (Nawela 20*, W.M.B.Perera 22*, 29 overs); 2nd day: Nondescripts Cricket Club (1) 138-2 (Gunawardene 68*, Sangakkara 38*, 38 overs); 3rd day: Moors Sports Club (2) 40-0 (Sudarshana 16*, Nawela 24*, 14 overs).
K.C.Sangakkara's 285 took 292 balls and included 31 fours and 3 sixes.

BURGHER RECREATION CLUB v SINGHA SPORTS CLUB

Played at Burgher Recreation Club Ground, Colombo, March 7, 8, 9, 2008.
Premier Championship 2007/08 - Tier B
Singha Sports Club won by five wickets. (Points: Burgher Recreation Club 3.015, Singha Sports Club 15.53)

BURGHER RECREATION CLUB

1	D.H.Sandagirigoda	c Zoysa b Silva	16	c Madanayake b Vithana	32
2	I.C.D.Perera	c Randunu b Liyanage	9	b Vithana	26
3	B.M.S.N.Mendis	c Kavinga b Gamage	5	(7) c Madanayake b Vithana	11
4	G.R.Perera	c Kavinga b Gamage	5	b Randunu	33
5	*H.D.P.S.Harischandra	b Silva	19	(3) b Vithana	5
6	K.D.J.Nishantha	b Liyanage	28	(5) lbw b Vithana	9
7	†P.H.M.G.Fernando	not out	12	(6) c Zoysa b Vithana	25
8	M.S.T.Fernando	lbw b Silva	0	not out	24
9	G.D.R.Eranga	b Liyanage	9	c Kavinga b Randunu	6
10	C.A.M.Madusanka	c Zoysa b Gamage	1	(11) lbw b Randunu	0
11	A.N.P.R.Fernando	lbw b Gamage	0	(10) c Zoysa b Randunu	5
	Extras	lb 4, w 1, nb 6	11	lb 7, nb 5	12
			115		**188**

FoW (1): 1-19 (1), 2-34 (3), 3-39 (4), 4-40 (2), 5-74 (5), 6-96 (6), 7-97 (8), 8-113 (9), 9-114 (10), 10-115 (11)
FoW (2): 1-63 (1), 2-64 (2), 3-80 (3), 4-112 (4), 5-114 (5), 6-134 (7), 7-161 (6), 8-175 (9), 9-187 (10), 10-188 (11)

SINGHA SPORTS CLUB

1	D.A.Faux	c Nishantha b M.S.T.Fernando	14	run out	34
2	N.T.Thenuwara	c Nishantha b Eranga	5	c Eranga b Madusanka	28
3	†H.H.R.Kavinga	lbw b Nishantha	25	(6) not out	53
4	A.S.Wewalwala	c Sandagirigoda b A.N.P.R.Fernando	22	c P.H.M.G.Fernando b Madusanka	10
5	T.J.Madanayake	c P.H.M.G.Fernando b Madusanka	23	b Madusanka	7
6	H.S.M.Zoysa	c Eranga b Madusanka	1	(3) c Harischandra b Madusanka	1
7	S.I.Vithana	not out	23	not out	27
8	D.O.L.Silva	b A.N.P.R.Fernando	0		
9	S.K.C.Randunu	run out (A.N.P.R.Fernando)	5		
10	*N.C.K.Liyanage	b Eranga	0		
11	P.L.S.Gamage	b Eranga	0		
	Extras	b 2, lb 4, nb 8	14	b 5, lb 1, w 2, nb 6	14
			132	(5 wickets)	**174**

FoW (1): 1-21 (2), 2-25 (1), 3-65 (4), 4-85 (3), 5-88 (6), 6-125 (5), 7-125 (8), 8-131 (9), 9-132 (10), 10-132 (11)
FoW (2): 1-58 (2), 2-60 (3), 3-78 (1), 4-86 (4), 5-93 (5)

Singha Sports Club Bowling

	O	M	R	W			O	M	R	W	
Silva	13	4	48	3	4nb		6	1	20	0	
Liyanage	13	1	37	3	1w		8	0	49	0	
Gamage	7	3	26	4	2nb		9	0	23	0	5nb
Vithana						(4)	20	4	52	6	
Randunu						(5)	11.4	4	37	4	

Burgher Recreation Club Bowling

	O	M	R	W			O	M	R	W	
Eranga	9.4	2	36	3	3nb		7	0	22	0	1w,2nb
Mendis	3	0	9	0							
M.S.T.Fernando	5	1	11	1	1nb	(2)	3	0	20	0	1nb
A.N.P.R.Fernando	10	2	33	2	4nb	(3)	8	2	29	0	1w,3nb
Madusanka	6	0	23	2		(4)	16	3	63	4	
Nishantha	6	1	14	1		(5)	8	3	30	0	
I.C.D.Perera						(6)	0.1	0	4	0	

Umpires: N.S.Bopage and K.M.Kottahachchi. Referee: K.T.Francis. Toss: Burgher Recreation Club

Close of Play: 1st day: Singha Sports Club (1) 125-6 (Vithana 22*, Silva 0*, 37.1 overs); 2nd day: Singha Sports Club (2) 61-2 (Faux 25*, Wewalwala 0*, 18 overs).

LANKAN CRICKET CLUB v SEBASTIANITES CRICKET AND ATHLETIC CLUB

Played at Kadirana Cricket Grounds, Gampaha, March 7, 8, 9, 2008.
Premier Championship 2007/08 - Tier B
Match drawn.   (Points: Lankan Cricket Club 11.17, Sebastianites Cricket and Athletic Club 3.76)

SEBASTIANITES CRICKET AND ATHLETIC CLUB

1	H.A.H.U.Tillakaratne	c Tillakaratne b Kumara	21	c S.L.Perera b B.M.S.Perera	164	
2	B.Y.Arumathanthri	c and b Gunawardene	25	(3) c Shantha b Weerasinghe	51	
3	T.M.N.Rajaratne	b Kumara	0	(2) b Weerasinghe	51	
4	U.L.K.D.Fernando	c Gunawardene b Kumara	2	c sub (C.M.Withanage) b B.M.S.Perera	67	
5	T.L.T.Peiris	c Tillakaratne b Maduranga	54	run out	0	
6	†K.L.K.Fernando	run out (Kumara)	25	not out	2	
7	A.D.Indunil	c Shamitha b Weerasinghe	37	not out	0	
8	D.G.C.Silva	lbw b Weerasinghe	2			
9	A.B.L.D.Rodrigo	run out (S.L.Perera)	4			
10	*M.N.T.H.Kumara	c Gunawardene b Tillakaratne	19			
11	B.S.Rajitha	not out	3			
	Extras	b 2, lb 8, nb 6	16	b 4, w 1, nb 4	9	
			208	(5 wickets)	344	

FoW (1): 1-32 (1), 2-44 (3), 3-49 (2), 4-51 (4), 5-100 (6), 6-163 (7), 7-180 (5), 8-184 (9), 9-188 (8), 10-208 (10)
FoW (2): 1-113 (2), 2-222 (3), 3-341 (4), 4-341 (5), 5-341 (1)

LANKAN CRICKET CLUB

1	H.L.S.Maduranga	c Peiris b Rodrigo	42
2	G.A.L.W.Shantha	run out (Peiris)	22
3	D.V.Gunawardene	c U.L.K.D.Fernando b Rajitha	111
4	*Y.N.Tillakaratne	c Tillakaratne b Arumathanthri	25
5	J.R.G.Namal	c Tillakaratne b Arumathanthri	18
6	D.R.F.Weerasinghe	c K.L.K.Fernando b Rodrigo	13
7	S.L.Perera	c Tillakaratne b Rajitha	11
8	B.M.S.Perera	lbw b Silva	23
9	†W.D.P.Shamitha	c K.L.K.Fernando b Rodrigo	21
10	P.D.M.P.N.Kumara	not out	24
11	E.A.D.Prasad	c Indunil b Rodrigo	0
	Extras	b 6, lb 12, w 2, nb 4	24
			334

FoW (1): 1-61 (2), 2-71 (1), 3-118 (4), 4-165 (5), 5-204 (6), 6-253 (3), 7-266 (7), 8-287 (8), 9-334 (9), 10-334 (11)

Lankan Cricket Club Bowling

	O	M	R	W		O	M	R	W	
Kumara	18	5	59	3	1nb	14	1	71	0	1nb
Gunawardene	10	0	48	1	3nb	3	0	22	0	
Weerasinghe	18	6	46	2	2nb	34	3	129	2	2nb
Maduranga	6	1	24	1						
Namal	3	2	6	0		26	1	81	0	1w
Tillakaratne	5.4	1	9	1	(4)	2	0	16	0	
Prasad	1	0	6	0						
B.M.S.Perera					(6)	8	1	21	2	1nb

Sebastianites Cricket and Athletic Club Bowling

	O	M	R	W	
Kumara	5	0	14	0	
U.L.K.D.Fernando	12	4	22	0	
Rajitha	24	3	65	2	1nb
Arumathanthri	18	5	43	2	1w
Silva	8	2	31	1	3nb
Rodrigo	30.5	5	125	4	1w
Indunil	6	1	16	0	

Umpires: R.A.Kottahachchi and R.M.P.J.Rambukwella.   Referee: B.C.Cooray.   Toss: Lankan Cricket Club

Close of Play: 1st day: Lankan Cricket Club (1) 17-0 (Maduranga 7*, Shantha 10*, 6 overs); 2nd day: Lankan Cricket Club (1) 334-9 (Kumara 24*, 103.1 overs).
D.V.Gunawardene's 111 took 145 balls and included 12 fours and 3 sixes. H.A.H.U.Tillakaratne's 164 took 255 balls and included 17 fours and 2 sixes.

PANADURA SPORTS CLUB v MORATUWA SPORTS CLUB

Played at Panadura Esplanade, March 7, 8, 9, 2008.
Premier Championship 2007/08 - Tier B
Match drawn.   (Points: Panadura Sports Club 11.615, Moratuwa Sports Club 2.615)

PANADURA SPORTS CLUB

1	†G.Y.S.R.Perera	b N.A.C.T.Perera	5	lbw b P.C.M.Fernando	19
2	M.T.T.Fernando	c H.U.K.de Silva b N.A.C.T.Perera	110	c S.J.C.de Silva b P.C.M.Fernando	5
3	G.S.U.Fernando	c Mendis b N.A.C.T.Perera	0	c L.T.A.de Silva b S.J.C.de Silva	15
4	*J.S.K.Peiris	lbw b S.J.C.de Silva	116	(6) not out	39
5	M.N.R.Cooray	c M.D.S.Perera b P.C.M.Fernando	2	(7) c Mendis b S.P.Rupasinghe	0
6	W.M.P.N.Wanasinghe	lbw b S.P.Rupasinghe	26	(5) c H.U.K.de Silva b M.D.S.Perera	30
7	S.N.Wijesinghe	run out (M.D.S.Perera)	12	(4) c R.A.A.I.Perera b S.J.C.de Silva	53
8	G.A.S.Perera	not out	27		
9	H.F.M.Fonseka	lbw b P.C.M.Fernando	6		
10	J.K.D.Chathuranga	b P.C.M.Fernando	0		
11	H.D.N.de Silva	c Mendis b N.A.C.T.Perera	17		
	Extras	b 5, lb 6, w 1, nb 19	31	lb 1, nb 9	10
			352	(6 wickets)	171

FoW (1): 1-10 (1), 2-10 (3), 3-202 (2), 4-208 (5), 5-251 (6), 6-292 (4), 7-296 (7), 8-316 (9), 9-320 (10), 10-352 (11)
FoW (2): 1-11 (2), 2-40 (1), 3-42 (3), 4-100 (5), 5-167 (6), 6-171 (7)

MORATUWA SPORTS CLUB

1	R.C.Rupasinghe	b de Silva	0
2	R.A.A.I.Perera	c G.S.U.Fernando b Chathuranga	8
3	W.S.T.Fernando	lbw b Chathuranga	1
4	†R.M.Mendis	c G.S.U.Fernando b Wanasinghe	35
5	L.T.A.de Silva	lbw b Wanasinghe	28
6	H.U.K.de Silva	c G.S.U.Fernando b Wanasinghe	8
7	S.J.C.de Silva	c Peiris b Cooray	8
8	*M.D.S.Perera	c G.Y.S.R.Perera b Cooray	68
9	P.C.M.Fernando	lbw b Wanasinghe	10
10	S.P.Rupasinghe	not out	12
11	N.A.C.T.Perera	b Wanasinghe	1
	Extras	b 9, lb 7, nb 3, pen 5	24
			203

FoW (1): 1-0 (1), 2-1 (3), 3-20 (2), 4-81 (5), 5-82 (4), 6-89 (6), 7-121 (7), 8-160 (9), 9-192 (8), 10-203 (11)

Moratuwa Sports Club Bowling

	O	M	R	W			O	M	R	W	
P.C.M.Fernando	17	3	80	3	1w,3nb		10	3	21	2	3nb
N.A.C.T.Perera	17.5	4	64	4	1nb		4	0	24	0	
S.P.Rupasinghe	15	0	65	1	10nb	(6)	10.3	1	49	1	4nb
L.T.A.de Silva	3	1	5	0		(3)	3	2	2	0	
S.J.C.de Silva	17	2	81	1	3nb	(4)	6	0	39	2	
M.D.S.Perera	10	1	41	0	2nb	(7)	5	0	35	1	2nb
R.A.A.I.Perera	2	1	5	0							
W.S.T.Fernando						(5)	1	1	0	0	

Panadura Sports Club Bowling

	O	M	R	W	
de Silva	8	2	21	1	
Chathuranga	6	0	18	2	
Wanasinghe	16.1	3	44	5	1nb
Cooray	19	2	51	2	
Fonseka	4	0	12	0	
G.A.S.Perera	11	5	23	0	2nb
G.S.U.Fernando	2	1	8	0	
Peiris	2	0	5	0	

Umpires: D.Ekanayake and M.V.D.Zilva.   Referee: A.M.J.G.Amerasinghe.   Toss: Moratuwa Sports Club
Close of Play: 1st day: Panadura Sports Club (1) 204-3 (Peiris 68*, Cooray 2*, 42.1 overs); 2nd day: Moratuwa Sports Club (1) 161-8 (M.D.S.Perera 51*, S.P.Rupasinghe 0*, 53.2 overs).
M.T.T.Fernando's 110 took 128 balls and included 12 fours and 3 sixes. J.S.K.Peiris's 116 took 183 balls and included 10 fours and 2 sixes.

SRI LANKA AIR FORCE SPORTS CLUB v SARACENS SPORTS CLUB

Played at Air Force Ground, Colombo, March 7, 8, 9, 2008.
Premier Championship 2007/08 - Tier B
Sri Lanka Air Force Sports Club won by three wickets.   **(Points: Sri Lanka Air Force Sports Club 16.065, Saracens Sports Club 3.84)**

SARACENS SPORTS CLUB

1	W.G.R.K.Alwis	c Perera b Rizan	29	c Kularatne b Lakshitha	11	
2	P.K.Bodhisha	lbw b Lakshitha	4	c Rizan b Madanayake	5	
3	†N.M.S.M.Sepala	lbw b Perera	1	b Madanayake	0	
4	*G.N.Abeyratne	c Kumara b Madanayake	22	(6) c Kularatne b Gunatilleke	20	
5	W.S.D.Fernando	c Wanasinghe b Rizan	45	(7) c Eranga b Rizan	79	
6	S.C.Serasinghe	c Eranga b Lakshitha	2	(8) c sub (W.P.Wickrama) b Perera	32	
7	M.L.R.Karunaratne	c Kularatne b Lakshitha	11	(5) c Rizan b Lakshitha	17	
8	A.V.S.Nikethana	st Kularatne b Madanayake	32	(11) not out	4	
9	L.D.P.Nishantha	c Kumara b Lakshitha	0	c Kularatne b Perera	9	
10	P.M.Pushpakumara	b Lakshitha	0	not out	7	
11	W.H.P.Chanditha	not out	14	(4) c Eranga b Rizan	68	
	Extras	b 1, nb 8	9	b 2, lb 4, w 1	7	
			169	**(9 wickets, declared)**	**259**	

FoW (1): 1-9 (2), 2-10 (3), 3-37 (4), 4-91 (1), 5-101 (6), 6-117 (5), 7-125 (7), 8-127 (9), 9-128 (10), 10-169 (8)
FoW (2): 1-16 (2), 2-16 (3), 3-16 (1), 4-44 (5), 5-78 (6), 6-164 (4), 7-231 (7), 8-245 (8), 9-245 (9)

SRI LANKA AIR FORCE SPORTS CLUB

1	†M.K.P.B.Kularatne	lbw b Nishantha	18	c sub (G.A.Joseph) b Bodhisha	78	
2	A.Rizan	b Serasinghe	57	c Abeyratne b Alwis	18	
3	W.A.Eranga	b Alwis	3	lbw b Pushpakumara	16	
4	W.M.M.W.E.V.Gangoda	c Serasinghe b Nishantha	5	(8) not out	7	
5	S.Madanayake	run out (Pushpakumara)	56	(4) b Serasinghe	13	
6	M.W.B.Dissanayake	c Chanditha b Serasinghe	2	(5) run out	12	
7	*K.A.Kumara	c Chanditha b Alwis	34	c Abeyratne b Bodhisha	10	
8	M.D.S.Wanasinghe	lbw b Bodhisha	30			
9	M.K.G.C.P.Lakshitha	lbw b Alwis	0	not out	12	
10	W.C.M.Perera	c Pushpakumara b Alwis	13	(6) lbw b Serasinghe	12	
11	M.P.G.D.P.Gunatilleke	not out	0			
	Extras	b 4, lb 5, w 6, nb 14	29	lb 2, w 1, nb 5	8	
			247	**(7 wickets)**	**186**	

FoW (1): 1-50 (1), 2-61 (3), 3-72 (4), 4-139 (2), 5-149 (6), 6-178 (5), 7-207 (7), 8-207 (9), 9-223 (10), 10-247 (8)
FoW (2): 1-38 (2), 2-81 (3), 3-106 (4), 4-125 (5), 5-147 (6), 6-163 (1), 7-169 (7)

Sri Lanka Air Force Sports Club Bowling

	O	M	R	W		O	M	R	W	
Lakshitha	23	2	61	5	8nb	25	3	77	2	1w
Perera	6	1	14	1	(6)	3	0	13	2	
Madanayake	10	1	28	2	(2)	15	4	49	2	
Gunatilleke	6	3	24	0		5	0	22	1	
Rizan	12	2	38	2	(3)	20	6	82	2	
Kumara	1	0	2	0						
Gangoda	2	1	1	0	(5)	2	0	10	0	

Saracens Sports Club Bowling

	O	M	R	W		O	M	R	W	
Pushpakumara	8	2	18	0	(4)	8	0	43	1	
Nishantha	28	7	64	2	10nb	(1)	5	0	34	0	2nb
Chanditha	4	0	31	0	2w,4nb	(2)	4	0	22	0	1w,3nb
Alwis	19	11	25	4	(3)	7.5	0	27	1	
Serasinghe	19	5	67	2	(6)	5	0	31	2	
Karunaratne	8	0	32	0						
Bodhisha	2.4	1	1	1	(5)	7	1	27	2	

Umpires: B.P.J.Mendis and S.H.Sarathkumara.   Referee: A.J.Samarasekera.   Toss: Saracens Sports Club

Close of Play: 1st day: Sri Lanka Air Force Sports Club (1) 1-0 (Kularatne 1*, Rizan 0*, 1 over); 2nd day: Saracens Sports Club (2) 32-3 (Chanditha 5*, Karunaratne 9*, 12 overs).

SRI LANKA ARMY SPORTS CLUB v POLICE SPORTS CLUB

Played at Army Ground, Panagoda, March 7, 8, 2008.
Premier Championship 2007/08 - Tier B
Sri Lanka Army Sports Club won by six wickets.   **(Points: Sri Lanka Army Sports Club 15.085, Police Sports Club 2.47)**

POLICE SPORTS CLUB

1	P.R.Nirmal	run out (B.A.W.Mendis)	5	lbw b B.A.W.Mendis	40
2	S.A.Wijeratne	c Prasad b Rathnayake	13	c Karunatilleke b Prasanna	12
3	J.P.M.Abeyratne	c de Zoysa b Karunatilleke	2	(6) c Palleguruge b de Zoysa	8
4	K.A.D.M.C.Kuruppu	b B.A.W.Mendis	10	(9) c T.R.D.Mendis b B.A.W.Mendis	5
5	H.P.A.Priyantha	c Soysa b Prasanna	23	(8) c Prasanna b de Zoysa	5
6	†P.H.K.S.Nirmala	lbw b Prasanna	10	(7) b B.A.W.Mendis	5
7	*R.G.D.Sanjeewa	b B.A.W.Mendis	18	(3) c B.A.W.Mendis b Prasanna	0
8	M.M.Rasmijinan	c and b Prasanna	9	(5) b de Zoysa	14
9	W.N.M.Soysa	b B.A.W.Mendis	8	(4) lbw b B.A.W.Mendis	8
10	T.A.N.Weerasinghe	not out	0	c Prasad b Prasanna	0
11	W.C.K.Ramanayake	c de Zoysa b B.A.W.Mendis	0	not out	0
	Extras	lb 4, w 1	5	b 4, lb 8, w 1, nb 1	14
			103		111

FoW (1): 1-5 (1), 2-24 (3), 3-24 (2), 4-53 (4), 5-59 (5), 6-86 (7), 7-86 (6), 8-101 (8), 9-103 (9), 10-103 (11)
FoW (2): 1-25 (2), 2-29 (3), 3-48 (4), 4-82 (1), 5-82 (5), 6-96 (7), 7-104 (6), 8-105 (8), 9-111 (9), 10-111 (10)

SRI LANKA ARMY SPORTS CLUB

1	S.Prasanna	lbw b Rasmijinan	26	not out	35
2	R.D.I.A.Karunatilleke	c Abeyratne b Rasmijinan	0	c Nirmal b Ramanayake	0
3	H.H.M.de Zoysa	c Rasmijinan b Sanjeewa	42	lbw b Rasmijinan	2
4	T.R.D.Mendis	lbw b Rasmijinan	5		
5	K.C.Prasad	lbw b Rasmijinan	1	(6) not out	14
6	D.A.Lawrance	b Wijeratne	20	(4) lbw b Soysa	2
7	B.A.W.Mendis	c Nirmala b Rasmijinan	34		
8	†T.D.T.Soysa	c Nirmal b Rasmijinan	14		
9	W.R.Palleguruge	b Rasmijinan	4	(5) lbw b Soysa	6
10	*P.K.N.M.K.Rathnayake	c Nirmal b Rasmijinan	4		
11	P.P.M.Peiris	not out	1		
	Extras	lb 2, w 2, nb 1	5	w 2	2
			156	(4 wickets)	61

FoW (1): 1-21 (2), 2-28 (1), 3-34 (4), 4-38 (5), 5-78 (6), 6-124 (3), 7-137 (7), 8-142 (9), 9-147 (10), 10-156 (8)
FoW (2): 1-16 (2), 2-19 (3), 3-28 (4), 4-34 (5)

Sri Lanka Army Sports Club Bowling

	O	M	R	W			O	M	R	W	
Rathnayake	8	3	14	1	1w		4	1	13	0	
Karunatilleke	6	3	23	1			3	1	6	0	1w
Peiris	2	1	4	0		(4)	2	0	13	0	
Prasanna	7	1	35	3		(3)	9.5	3	19	3	
B.A.W.Mendis	7	0	23	4			15	7	31	4	1nb
Palleguruge						(6)	1	0	11	0	
de Zoysa						(7)	8	6	6	3	

Police Sports Club Bowling

	O	M	R	W			O	M	R	W	
Rasmijinan	20.4	7	48	8	2w		7	1	38	1	2w
Ramanayake	12	2	28	0			3	0	14	1	
Soysa	9	2	24	0	1nb		3	1	9	2	
Sanjeewa	15	4	39	1							
Wijeratne	2	0	6	1							
Weerasinghe	2	0	6	0							

Umpires: H.D.P.K.Dharmasena and E.J.A.P.A.M.Jayasuriya.   Referee: N.S.H.M.R.Kodituwakku.   Toss: Sri Lanka Army

Close of Play: 1st day: Sri Lanka Army Sports Club (1) 146-8 (Soysa 6*, Rathnayake 3*, 55 overs).

The match was scheduled for three days but completed in two.

BLOOMFIELD CRICKET AND ATHLETIC CLUB v NONDESCRIPTS CRICKET CLUB

Played at Bloomfield Cricket and Athletic Club Ground, Colombo, March 13, 14, 15, 16, 2008.
Premier Championship 2007/08 - Tier A
Match drawn.   (Points: Bloomfield Cricket and Athletic Club 11.305, Nondescripts Cricket Club 3.04)

NONDESCRIPTS CRICKET CLUB

1	†W.U.Tharanga	b Lakshitha	17	lbw b Jayasuriya	34
2	K.D.Gunawardene	c Mendis b Gamage	6	(3) c Mendis b Gamage	14
3	W.L.P.Fernando	c Dissanayake b Lakshitha	38	(4) c Mendis b Gunaratne	7
4	C.G.Wijesinghe	c Mendis b Gamage	2	(5) c Jayasinghe b Jayasuriya	18
5	*M.K.Gajanayake	lbw b Gamage	21	(6) c Jayasuriya b Dissanayake	42
6	M.F.Maharoof	c Mendis b Katipiarchchi	0	(2) c Gangodawila b Gamage	14
7	M.M.M.Suraj	c Gangodawila b Katipiarchchi	2	(9) c Gunaratne b Katipiarchchi	17
8	D.T.Kottehewa	c Mendis b Gamage	14	lbw b Jayasuriya	1
9	W.C.A.Ganegama	not out	36	(7) c Mendis b Gamage	1
10	A.A.C.E.Athukorala	c Masmulla b Jayasuriya	2	c Jayasinghe b Jayasuriya	16
11	N.C.Komasaru	c and b Gamage	2	not out	0
	Extras	b 4, lb 3, nb 4	11	b 1, lb 9, nb 3	13
			151		177

FoW (1): 1-20 (2), 2-28 (1), 3-43 (4), 4-76 (5), 5-77 (6), 6-79 (7), 7-95 (3), 8-118 (8), 9-137 (10), 10-151 (11)
FoW (2): 1-43 (2), 2-59 (1), 3-70 (4), 4-95 (3), 5-95 (5), 6-98 (7), 7-105 (8), 8-142 (9), 9-165 (6), 10-177 (10)

BLOOMFIELD CRICKET AND ATHLETIC CLUB

1	T.S.Masmulla	c Tharanga b Ganegama	9	c Gunawardene b Suraj	14
2	S.T.Jayasuriya	lbw b Kottehewa	38	lbw b Gajanayake	36
3	M.T.Gunaratne	c Ganegama b Suraj	33	not out	9
4	K.Y.de Silva	c Ganegama b Suraj	8	c Suraj b Gajanayake	0
5	*D.M.G.S.Dissanayake	c Gajanayake b Kottehewa	6	(6) not out	9
6	C.U.Jayasinghe	c Maharoof b Komasaru	22	(5) st Tharanga b Komasaru	2
7	G.A.S.K.Gangodawila	lbw b Kottehewa	27		
8	A.U.Katipiarachchi	b Kottehewa	19		
9	†Y.S.S.Mendis	not out	2		
10	A.B.T.Lakshitha	c Suraj b Komasaru	1		
11	T.P.Gamage	lbw b Komasaru	0		
	Extras	b 6, lb 1, w 4, nb 5	16	b 4, lb 3, nb 3	10
			181	(4 wickets)	80

FoW (1): 1-12 (1), 2-76 (2), 3-100 (4), 4-103 (3), 5-109 (5), 6-136 (6), 7-177 (8), 8-180 (7), 9-181 (10), 10-181 (11)
FoW (2): 1-33 (1), 2-59 (2), 3-61 (4), 4-65 (5)

Bloomfield Cricket and Athletic Club Bowling

	O	M	R	W			O	M	R	W	
Lakshitha	15	3	45	2	2nb		4	0	26	0	1nb
Gamage	14.3	4	44	5			12	1	41	3	
Gangodawila	4	2	6	0							
Katipiarchchi	9	0	23	2	2nb		6	0	18	1	1nb
Jayasuriya	10	1	23	1		(3)	21.1	5	66	4	
Dissanayake	1	0	3	0			7	0	14	1	1nb
Gunaratne						(5)	3	2	2	1	

Nondescripts Cricket Club Bowling

	O	M	R	W			O	M	R	W	
Ganegama	13	3	41	1	4w	(6)	2	1	5	0	
Kottehewa	15	5	39	4	4nb	(1)	5	0	16	0	2nb
Athukorala	10	2	18	0	1nb	(4)	1	0	7	0	
Suraj	16	4	39	2		(3)	5	1	16	1	1nb
Komasaru	11	3	25	3		(7)	5.2	2	5	1	
Gajanayake	2	0	12	0		(5)	7	0	19	2	
Fernando						(2)	2	0	5	0	

Umpires: R.D.Kottahachchi and M.S.K.Nandiweera.   Referee: S.Ranatunga.   Toss: Nondescripts Cricket Club

Close of Play: 1st day: Bloomfield Cricket and Athletic Club (1) 76-1 (Jayasuriya 38*, Gunaratne 23*, 23 overs); 2nd day: Nondescripts Cricket Club (2) 72-3 (Gunawardene 8*, Wijesinghe 1*, 22 overs); 3rd day: Bloomfield Cricket and Athletic Club (2) 80-4 (Gunaratne 9*, Dissanayake 9*, 27.2 overs).
There was no play on the final day.

COLOMBO CRICKET CLUB v BADURELIYA SPORTS CLUB

Played at Colombo Cricket Club Ground, March 13, 14, 15, 16, 2008.
Premier Championship 2007/08 - Tier A
Colombo Cricket Club won by six wickets.   (Points: Colombo Cricket Club 15.805, Badureliya Sports Club 3.2)

BADURELIYA SPORTS CLUB

1	†D.W.A.N.D.Vitharana	b de Silva	40	c de Silva b Wethathasinghe	3
2	M.M.D.P.V.Perera	c Chandrakumara b de Silva	8	c Ranaweera b Chandrakumara	63
3	D.N.Hunukumbura	c Mubarak b Chandrakumara	0	lbw b Wethathasinghe	0
4	*R.P.A.H.Wickramaratne	c Wethathasinghe b Chandrakumara	14	c Ranaweera b Wethathasinghe	71
5	U.R.P.Perera	lbw b de Silva	0	(8) not out	7
6	K.A.D.M.Fernando	c Ranaweera b Boralessa	14	c and b Mubarak	29
7	R.M.A.R.Ratnayake	c Polonowita b de Silva	79	c Ranaweera b Wethathasinghe	2
8	W.J.S.D.Perera	c Polonowita b Boralessa	2	(5) c Polonowita b Chandrakumara	3
9	M.R.C.N.Bandaratilleke	c Ranaweera b Ratnayake	0	c Kapugedera b Mubarak	0
10	K.L.S.L.Dias	not out	16	c and b Mubarak	1
11	S.D.C.Malinga	c Ranaweera b de Silva	0	c Bandara b Mubarak	6
	Extras	lb 2	2		
			175		**185**

FoW (1): 1-19 (2), 2-24 (3), 3-52 (4), 4-58 (5), 5-65 (1), 6-105 (6), 7-125 (8), 8-126 (9), 9-175 (7), 10-175 (11)
FoW (2): 1-3 (1), 2-4 (3), 3-102 (5), 4-137 (4), 5-139 (7), 6-171 (2), 7-173 (6), 8-173 (9), 9-177 (10), 10-185 (11)

COLOMBO CRICKET CLUB

1	†D.K.Ranaweera	lbw b Fernando	1	c Vitharana b Fernando	1
2	H.B.C.C.Bandara	c Ratnayake b Malinga	8	c Ratnayake b Dias	46
3	J.Mubarak	c Dias b Fernando	2	c Vitharana b Wickramaratne	66
4	*B.M.T.T.Mendis	c Wickramaratne b Malinga	0	run out	23
5	C.K.Kapugedera	c U.R.P.Perera b Ratnayake	25	not out	3
6	S.C.D.Boralessa	run out (U.R.P.Perera/Vitharana)	4		
7	A.S.Polonowita	lbw b Dias	14	(6) not out	9
8	A.C.Wethathasinghe	b Ratnayake	13		
9	P.D.G.Chandrakumara	not out	61		
10	W.R.S.de Silva	b Fernando	11		
11	M.I.Ratnayake	c M.M.D.P.V.Perera b Bandaratilleke	45		
	Extras	b 5, lb 10, w 1, nb 4	20	b 4, lb 2, nb 3	9
			204	(4 wickets)	**157**

FoW (1): 1-5 (1), 2-9 (2), 3-9 (4), 4-15 (3), 5-23 (6), 6-58 (5), 7-68 (7), 8-72 (8), 9-89 (10), 10-204 (11)
FoW (2): 1-7 (1), 2-81 (2), 3-144 (3), 4-146 (4)

Colombo Cricket Club Bowling

	O	M	R	W		O	M	R	W
de Silva	16.3	4	41	5		7	0	34	0
Ratnayake	15	3	44	1	(7)	2	0	10	0
Polonowita	3	2	1	0		2	0	6	0
Chandrakumara	13	3	32	2	(8)	10	1	19	2
Boralessa	16	3	48	2	(4)	13	2	29	0
Mubarak	5	0	7	0	(5)	11.2	3	28	4
Wethathasinghe					(2)	15	1	45	4
Kapugedera					(6)	1	0	14	0

Badureliya Sports Club Bowling

	O	M	R	W		O	M	R	W	
Malinga	12	2	37	2		5	1	13	0	
Fernando	17	3	47	3	3nb	5	0	26	1	2nb
Dias	15	7	39	1		10	1	35	1	
Ratnayake	11	2	40	2	1nb	3	0	26	0	1nb
Bandaratilleke	8.1	3	12	1		6	0	43	0	
M.M.D.P.V.Perera	2	0	14	0	1w					
Wickramaratne						(6)	1.3	0	8	0

Umpires: P.G.Liyanage and J.W.L.Nandana. Referee: U.Warnapura.   Toss: Colombo Cricket Club
Close of Play: 1st day: Colombo Cricket Club (1) 15-4 (Kapugedera 4*, Boralessa 0*, 6.1 overs); 2nd day: Badureliya Sports Club
(2) 35-2 (M.M.D.P.V.Perera 12*, Wickramaratne 20*, 10 overs); 3rd day: Badureliya Sports Club (2) 185 all out.
M.M.D.P.V.Perera retired hurt in the Badureliya Sports Club second innings having scored 47 (team score 98-2) - he returned when
the score was 139-5.

COLTS CRICKET CLUB v CHILAW MARIANS CRICKET CLUB

Played at Colts Cricket Club Ground, Colombo, March 13, 14, 15, 2008.
Premier Championship 2007/08 - Tier A
Colts Cricket Club won by ten wickets.   (Points: Colts Cricket Club 15.705, Chilaw Marians Cricket Club 2.69)

CHILAW MARIANS CRICKET CLUB

1	M.L.Udawatte	lbw b Perera	21	lbw b Perera	20
2	D.N.A.Athulathmudali	c Peiris b Mathews	38	c Weerakoon b Alwitigala	22
3	N.H.G.Cooray	b Mathews	6	lbw b Kulatunga	30
4	A.P.Jansze	c Peiris b Prasad	30	(5) lbw b Weerakoon	21
5	K.H.R.K.Fernando	lbw b Weerakoon	6	(4) lbw b Perera	11
6	M.M.D.N.R.G.Perera	b Mathews	34	(7) c and b Weerakoon	14
7	*L.J.P.Gunaratne	lbw b Alwitigala	19	(6) c Kalavitigoda b Alwitigala	3
8	†C.S.Fernando	c Pathirana b Mathews	0	c Jayasinghe b Weerakoon	5
9	D.Hettiarachchi	not out	15	(10) b Kulatunga	6
10	G.A.C.R.Perera	run out (Pathirana)	0	(9) c Alwitigala b Weerakoon	12
11	S.H.M.Silva	c Pathirana b Mathews	2	not out	1
	Extras	lb 8, nb 2	10	b 4, lb 6, w 2	12
			181		157

FoW (1): 1-58 (2), 2-66 (3), 3-96 (1), 4-102 (5), 5-106 (4), 6-147 (6), 7-151 (8), 8-170 (7), 9-170 (10), 10-181 (11)
FoW (2): 1-33 (2), 2-48 (1), 3-70 (4), 4-98 (5), 5-101 (6), 6-133 (3), 7-133 (7), 8-142 (8), 9-154 (9), 10-157 (10)

COLTS CRICKET CLUB

1	T.P.Attanayake	c K.H.R.K.Fernando b Hettiarachchi	47	not out	40
2	M.D.K.Perera	lbw b G.A.C.R.Perera	6		
3	D.N.Pathirana	lbw b K.H.R.K.Fernando	1		
4	A.D.Mathews	lbw b G.A.C.R.Perera	18		
5	*H.G.J.M.Kulatunga	c Cooray b Silva	5		
6	S.Kalavitigoda	lbw b Hettiarachchi	22	(2) not out	32
7	K.A.S.Jayasinghe	b Gunaratne	1		
8	†T.R.Peiris	not out	71		
9	S.Weerakoon	b Gunaratne	1		
10	K.G.Alwitigala	c K.H.R.K.Fernando b M.M.D.N.R.G.Perera	60		
11	U.M.A.Prasad	run out (Udawatte)	1		
	Extras	lb 4, w 4, nb 24	32	b 2, nb 2	4
			265	(no wicket)	76

FoW (1): 1-13 (2), 2-15 (3), 3-53 (4), 4-64 (5), 5-115 (1), 6-116 (7), 7-118 (6), 8-119 (9), 9-237 (10), 10-265 (11)

Colts Cricket Club Bowling

	O	M	R	W		O	M	R	W	
Mathews	13.5	1	47	5	2nb	8	4	15	0	
Prasad	6	0	43	1		7	2	25	0	
Perera	11	1	36	1		17	4	41	2	
Alwitigala	7	2	16	1		10	3	21	2	1w
Weerakoon	11	1	31	1		14	8	20	4	
Kulatunga					(6)	4.3	0	25	0	1w

Chilaw Marians Cricket Club Bowling

	O	M	R	W		O	M	R	W	
K.H.R.K.Fernando	10	0	38	1	1w					
G.A.C.R.Perera	15	0	73	2	2w,16nb (1)	2	0	13	0	2nb
Hettiarachchi	24	6	64	2		5	0	28	0	
Silva	6	0	34	1						
Gunaratne	13	2	41	2	(4)	2	0	10	0	
M.M.D.N.R.G.Perera	4.1	0	11	1	1w,2nb (2)	4	0	23	0	

Umpires: E.A.R.de Silva and I.D.Gunawardene.   Referee: V.B.John.   Toss: Chilaw Marians Cricket Club

Close of Play: 1st day: Colts Cricket Club (1) 127-8 (Peiris 3*, Alwitigala 6*, 33.2 overs); 2nd day: Chilaw Marians Cricket Club (2) 76-3 (Cooray 9*, Jansze 4*, 32 overs).

The match was scheduled for four days but completed in three.

MOORS SPORTS CLUB v SINHALESE SPORTS CLUB

Played at Moors Sports Club Ground, Colombo, March 13, 14, 15, 16, 2008.
Premier Championship 2007/08 - Tier A
Match drawn.   (Points: Moors Sports Club 10.695, Sinhalese Sports Club 2.62)

SINHALESE SPORTS CLUB

1	K.Magage	c A.M.L.Perera b Rideegammanagedera	5	lbw b Dilhara	0
2	*N.T.Paranavitana	c Wannakuwatta b Rideegammanagedera	8	c Dilhara b Mudalige	38
3	†J.K.Silva	lbw b Dilhara	0	run out	0
4	B.M.A.J.Mendis	lbw b Dilhara	27	lbw b Mudalige	40
5	S.H.T.Kandamby	c Wannakuwatta b A.M.L.Perera	85	c Fernando b Dilhara	18
6	E.D.J.Sriyapala	c W.M.B.Perera b Mudalige	7	(7) not out	6
7	K.S.Lokuarachchi	c Wannakuwatta b A.M.L.Perera	1	(6) c W.M.B.Perera b Dilhara	5
8	K.P.S.P.Karunanayake	lbw b Dilhara	14	not out	18
9	D.N.T.Zoysa	not out	23		
10	S.M.Senanayake	c Nawela b Mudalige	8		
11	C.W.Vidanapathirana	lbw b A.M.L.Perera	7		
	Extras	b 4, lb 1, w 1, nb 2	8	lb 5, nb 1	6
			193	(6 wickets)	131

FoW (1): 1-13 (1), 2-15 (2), 3-23 (3), 4-74 (4), 5-99 (6), 6-110 (7), 7-142 (8), 8-165 (5), 9-184 (10), 10-193 (11)
FoW (2): 1-0 (1), 2-0 (3), 3-69 (2), 4-100 (5), 5-106 (4), 6-106 (6)

MOORS SPORTS CLUB

1	T.K.D.Sudarshana	lbw b Lokuarachchi	39
2	N.M.N.P.Nawela	c Paranavitana b Vidanapathirana	5
3	H.M.P.Fernando	b Vidanapathirana	0
4	W.M.B.Perera	b Zoysa	38
5	A.Rideegammanagedera	b Vidanapathirana	46
6	A.S.A.Perera	c Vidanapathirana b Zoysa	0
7	*L.H.D.Dilhara	c Silva b Zoysa	78
8	†W.M.J.Wannakuwatta	c Silva b Zoysa	0
9	A.M.L.Perera	lbw b Senanayake	1
10	C.R.B.Mudalige	not out	3
11	D.C.B.Keerthisinghe	b Senanayake	1
	Extras	b 6, lb 1, nb 1	8
			219

FoW (1): 1-18 (2), 2-22 (3), 3-86 (1), 4-89 (4), 5-89 (6), 6-199 (7), 7-199 (8), 8-200 (9), 9-218 (5), 10-219 (11)

Moors Sports Club Bowling

	O	M	R	W			O	M	R	W	
Dilhara	21	6	46	3	2nb		11	4	16	3	1nb
Rideegammanagedera	19	8	38	2			7	2	15	0	
A.M.L.Perera	9.4	1	42	3	1w	(4)	9	1	29	0	
A.S.A.Perera	2	0	13	0							
Mudalige	12	1	42	2		(3)	14	2	43	2	
Keerthisinghe	3	1	7	0			3	0	16	0	
Fernando						(5)	1	0	7	0	

Sinhalese Sports Club Bowling

	O	M	R	W	
Zoysa	15	3	47	4	1nb
Vidanapathirana	13	3	41	3	
Senanayake	12.2	2	46	2	
Karunanayake	6	0	21	0	
Lokuarachchi	13	2	54	1	
Mendis	1	0	3	0	

Umpires: S.S.K.Gallage and B.P.J.Mendis. Referee: M.C.Mendis.   Toss: Moors Sports Club

Close of Play: 1st day: Sinhalese Sports Club (1) 136-6 (Kandamby 71*, Karunanayake 12*, 51 overs); 2nd day: Moors Sports Club (1) 199-5 (Rideegammanagedera 32*, Dilhara 78*, 51 overs); 3rd day: Sinhalese Sports Club (2) 131-6 (Sriyapala 6*, Karunanayake 18*, 45 overs).

There was no play on the final day.

TAMIL UNION CRICKET AND ATHLETIC CLUB v RAGAMA CRICKET CLUB

Played at P.Saravanamuttu Stadium, Colombo, March 13, 14, 15, 16, 2008.
Premier Championship 2007/08 - Tier A
Ragama Cricket Club won by 195 runs. (Points: Tamil Union Cricket and Athletic Club 3, Ragama Cricket Club 16.375)

RAGAMA CRICKET CLUB

1	D.A.Ranatunga	b Liyanagunawardene	4	c G.T.de Silva b Pushpakumara	38
2	H.E.Vithana	c S.K.L.de Silva b Lakmal	16	b Liyanagunawardene	37
3	M.I.G.Senaratne	c Pushpakumara b Maduwantha	13	st G.T.de Silva b Pushpakumara	61
4	*S.I.de Saram	c S.K.L.de Silva b Wijesiriwardene	4	c G.T.de Silva b Lakmal	48
5	C.M.Bandara	c G.T.de Silva b Lakmal	1	(8) not out	36
6	W.D.D.S.Perera	b Pushpakumara	41	not out	60
7	K.Weeraratne	b Wijesiriwardene	6	run out	40
8	†S.A.Perera	b Maduwantha	22	(5) c Liyanagunawardene b Lakmal	0
9	P.A.S.S.Jeewantha	lbw b Maduwantha	8		
10	S.A.D.U.Indrasiri	c Fernando b Maduwantha	6		
11	H.G.D.Nayanakantha	not out	0		
	Extras	b 1, lb 2, nb 5	8	b 13, lb 4, w 3, nb 6	26
			129	(6 wickets, declared)	**346**

FoW (1): 1-18 (1), 2-37 (2), 3-37 (3), 4-40 (5), 5-47 (4), 6-53 (7), 7-104 (8), 8-115 (9), 9-127 (6), 10-129 (10)
FoW (2): 1-86 (2), 2-115 (1), 3-184 (3), 4-197 (5), 5-206 (4), 6-271 (7)

TAMIL UNION CRICKET AND ATHLETIC CLUB

1	†G.T.de Silva	c S.A.Perera b Nayanakantha	4	c de Saram b Nayanakantha	1
2	G.I.Daniel	c W.D.D.S.Perera b Weeraratne	10	c Weeraratne b Bandara	45
3	S.I.Fernando	c Vithana b Weeraratne	10	(5) c Vithana b Nayanakantha	4
4	P.D.M.A.Cooray	c Bandara b Nayanakantha	10	(3) c W.D.D.S.Perera b Nayanakantha	2
5	S.K.L.de Silva	b Weeraratne	2	(4) c Bandara b Nayanakantha	0
6	M.Pushpakumara	c de Saram b Nayanakantha	30	run out	34
7	*H.M.Maduwantha	c de Saram b Nayanakantha	42	(8) not out	37
8	R.J.M.G.M.Rupasinghe	not out	18	(7) c Weeraratne b Bandara	2
9	O.L.A.Wijesiriwardene	b Weeraratne	6	c Ranatunga b Bandara	4
10	S.C.Liyanagunawardene	c de Saram b Weeraratne	0	(11) c S.A.Perera b Weeraratne	0
11	R.A.S.Lakmal	lbw b Indrasiri	2	(10) c Senaratne b Weeraratne	5
	Extras	lb 3	3	b 2, lb 4, w 1, nb 2	9
			137		**143**

FoW (1): 1-13 (1), 2-17 (2), 3-34 (3), 4-36 (5), 5-36 (4), 6-110 (7), 7-111 (6), 8-134 (9), 9-134 (10), 10-137 (11)
FoW (2): 1-13 (1), 2-19 (3), 3-27 (4), 4-32 (5), 5-83 (6), 6-88 (7), 7-97 (2), 8-114 (9), 9-143 (10), 10-143 (11)

Tamil Union Cricket and Athletic Club Bowling

	O	M	R	W		O	M	R	W	
Wijesiriwardene	12	4	23	2		8	0	43	0	
Lakmal	13	1	32	2	5nb	13	3	71	2	2w,2nb
Maduwantha	21.5	10	45	4	(4)	11	1	53	0	1nb
Liyanagunawardene	9	4	26	1	(3)	23	4	75	1	1w,1nb
Pushpakumara	2	2	0	1		20	1	71	2	
Rupasinghe					(6)	2	0	16	0	2nb

Ragama Cricket Club Bowling

	O	M	R	W		O	M	R	W	
Weeraratne	13.4	3	53	5		9	1	34	5	
Nayanakantha	14	0	42	4		8	1	17	4	1w
Jeewantha	7.2	1	24	0		4	0	26	0	2nb
Vithana	3	1	6	0	(5)	10	3	19	0	
Indrasiri	2	0	9	1	(6)	3	1	2	0	
Bandara					(4)	17	2	39	3	

Umpires: A.G.Dissanayake and M.G.Silva. Referee: G.F.Labrooy. Toss: Ragama Cricket Club

Close of Play: 1st day: Tamil Union Cricket and Athletic Club (1) 79-5 (Pushpakumara 19*, Maduwantha 21*, 22 overs); 2nd day: Ragama Cricket Club (2) 186-3 (de Saram 31*, S.A.Perera 0*, 36 overs); 3rd day: Ragama Cricket Club (2) 346-6 (W.D.D.S.Perera 60*, Bandara 36*, 77 overs).

BURGHER RECREATION CLUB v SRI LANKA AIR FORCE SPORTS CLUB

Played at Burgher Recreation Club Ground, Colombo, March 14, 15, 16, 2008.
Premier Championship 2007/08 - Tier B
Match drawn.   (Points: Burgher Recreation Club 2.5, Sri Lanka Air Force Sports Club 11.015)

BURGHER RECREATION CLUB

1	*D.H.Sandagirigoda	c Eranga b Rizan	43	b Kumara	19
2	L.S.D.Perera	c Kularatne b Perera	0	st Kularatne b Madanayake	15
3	I.C.D.Perera	c Rizan b Lakshitha	27	(6) st Kularatne b Madanayake	2
4	G.R.Perera	c Gunatilleke b Rizan	6	(7) not out	5
5	T.H.D.C.C.Kumara	c Kularatne b Lakshitha	10	(4) c Rizan b Kumara	17
6	†P.H.M.G.Fernando	c Kularatne b Gangoda	30		
7	I.C.Soysa	lbw b Madanayake	26	(5) not out	17
8	L.A.H.de Silva	st Kularatne b Rizan	11	(3) st Kularatne b Madanayake	10
9	G.D.R.Eranga	not out	33		
10	C.A.M.Madusanka	c Kumara b Gunatilleke	24		
11	A.N.P.R.Fernando	c Dissanayake b Gangoda	0		
	Extras	lb 3, w 1, nb 1	5		5
			215	**(5 wickets)**	**85**

FoW (1): 1-10 (2), 2-61 (1), 3-72 (4), 4-87 (5), 5-88 (3), 6-143 (6), 7-145 (7), 8-166 (8), 9-214 (10), 10-215 (11)
FoW (2): 1-33 (2), 2-35 (1), 3-57 (3), 4-61 (4), 5-72 (6)

SRI LANKA AIR FORCE SPORTS CLUB

1	†M.K.P.B.Kularatne	c Soysa b Madusanka	64
2	A.Rizan	run out (L.S.D.Perera)	22
3	W.A.Eranga	c Madusanka b Soysa	0
4	W.M.M.W.E.V.Gangoda	c de Silva b Eranga	51
5	S.Madanayake	c de Silva b Madusanka	55
6	M.W.B.Dissanayake	b Madusanka	14
7	*K.A.Kumara	c sub (M.S.T.Fernando) b de Silva	27
8	M.K.G.C.P.Lakshitha	c Kumara b Eranga	11
9	M.D.S.Wanasinghe	lbw b de Silva	31
10	W.C.M.Perera	not out	5
11	M.P.G.D.P.Gunatilleke	c I.C.D.Perera b de Silva	8
	Extras	b 1, lb 9, w 2, nb 3	15
			303

FoW (1): 1-33 (2), 2-34 (3), 3-139 (4), 4-147 (1), 5-188 (6), 6-221 (5), 7-240 (8), 8-276 (7), 9-289 (9), 10-303 (11)

Sri Lanka Air Force Sports Club Bowling

	O	M	R	W		O	M	R	W
Lakshitha	24	4	99	2	1w,1nb				
Perera	4	0	16	1					
Madanayake	14	1	41	1	(1)	8	0	43	3
Rizan	14	1	46	3	(2)	2	0	21	0
Gunatilleke	4	3	1	1					
Gangoda	4.2	1	9	2					
Kumara					(3)	5	0	21	2

Burgher Recreation Club Bowling

	O	M	R	W	
Eranga	15	3	60	2	1w,1nb
Soysa	11	3	24	1	
A.N.P.R.Fernando	12	2	29	0	1w,2nb
Madusanka	27	3	77	3	
L.S.D.Perera	1	0	4	0	
de Silva	21	1	79	3	
Kumara	2	0	13	0	
G.R.Perera	1	0	7	0	

Umpires: E.J.A.P.A.M.Jayasuriya and R.M.P.J.Rambukwella. Referee: B.C.Cooray.   Toss: Burgher Recreation Club

Close of Play: 1st day: Burgher Recreation Club (1) 184-8 (Eranga 24*, Madusanka 3*, 53 overs); 2nd day: Sri Lanka Air Force Sports Club (1) 137-2 (Kularatne 61*, Gangoda 50*, 36 overs).

LANKAN CRICKET CLUB v SINGHA SPORTS CLUB

Played at Kadirana Cricket Grounds, Gampaha, March 14, 15, 16, 2008.
Premier Championship 2007/08 - Tier B
Match drawn.   (Points: Lankan Cricket Club 3.26, Singha Sports Club 11.145)

SINGHA SPORTS CLUB

1	D.A.Faux	b Weerasinghe	33	b Weerasinghe	17
2	N.T.Thenuwara	c Shantha b Pushpalal	25	lbw b Pushpalal	0
3	T.J.Madanayake	c Shazmil b Weerasinghe	22	c Shantha b Kumara	9
4	A.S.Wewalwala	c B.M.S.Perera b Weerasinghe	29	c Ariyasinghe b Kumara	25
5	†H.H.R.Kavinga	lbw b Weerasinghe	0	b Kumara	28
6	H.W.M.Kumara	c B.M.S.Perera b Pushpalal	61	run out	23
7	S.I.Vithana	lbw b Pushpalal	31	c Shazmil b Kumara	0
8	K.M.S.de Silva	lbw b Pushpalal	19	lbw b Pushpalal	2
9	S.K.C.Randunu	b Pushpalal	0	c S.L.Perera b Kumara	11
10	*N.C.K.Liyanage	b Weerasinghe	6	c Shantha b Kumara	10
11	P.L.S.Gamage	not out	14	not out	3
	Extras	b 5, lb 2, w 6, nb 1	14	b 4, lb 2, w 1	7
			254		**135**

FoW (1): 1-64 (2), 2-64 (1), 3-104 (4), 4-104 (5), 5-135 (3), 6-211 (7), 7-213 (6), 8-213 (9), 9-226 (10), 10-254 (8)
FoW (2): 1-4 (2), 2-19 (3), 3-43 (1), 4-61 (4), 5-109 (5), 6-109 (7), 7-111 (6), 8-111 (8), 9-126 (10), 10-135 (9)

LANKAN CRICKET CLUB

1	B.M.S.Perera	c Kavinga b Gamage	18		
2	*B.M.D.T.D.Ariyasinghe	c Faux b Liyanage	17	(1) c Randunu b Gamage	4
3	J.R.G.Namal	lbw b Randunu	19	(2) run out	21
4	K.D.C.Pushpalal	c Kavinga b Gamage	0	(3) not out	20
5	G.A.L.W.Shantha	b Vithana	14		
6	S.L.Perera	c Kavinga b Randunu	44		
7	D.R.F.Weerasinghe	c Faux b Vithana	1		
8	†W.D.P.Shamitha	lbw b Vithana	9		
9	J.S.M.Shazmil	c Wewalwala b Vithana	64	(4) not out	5
10	P.D.M.P.N.Kumara	not out	1		
11	C.M.Hathurusingha	lbw b Randunu	0		
	Extras	b 1, lb 2, nb 6	9	b 4, lb 1, w 1	6
			196	**(2 wickets)**	**56**

FoW (1): 1-40 (1), 2-40 (2), 3-41 (4), 4-75 (5), 5-75 (3), 6-76 (7), 7-90 (8), 8-189 (9), 9-196 (6), 10-196 (11)
FoW (2): 1-8 (1), 2-44 (2)

Lankan Cricket Club Bowling

	O	M	R	W		O	M	R	W	
Kumara	4	0	36	0	1w	17.2	4	52	6	
Hathurusingha	5	1	23	0	(6)	4	1	13	0	
Pushpalal	12.1	1	64	5	1w	(2) 12	3	25	2	1w
Weerasinghe	19	3	59	5		(3) 14.4	6	30	1	
Ariyasinghe	3	1	11	0		2	0	6	0	
Shazmil	5	0	17	0						
B.M.S.Perera	4	0	37	0	1nb					
S.L.Perera						(4) 1	0	2	0	
Namal						(7) 0.2	0	1	0	

Singha Sports Club Bowling

	O	M	R	W		O	M	R	W	
Gamage	9	0	46	2	4nb	5	0	22	1	1w
Liyanage	9	1	34	1	2nb	4.5	0	29	0	
Randunu	20.4	6	32	3						
Vithana	26	5	67	4						
de Silva	1	0	11	0						
Madanayake	3	1	3	0						

Umpires: W.Jayasena and M.V.D.Zilva.   Referee: N.S.H.M.R.Kodituwakku.   Toss: Singha Sports Club

Close of Play: 1st day: Lankan Cricket Club (1) 31-0 (B.M.S.Perera 14*, Ariyasinghe 12*, 6.4 overs); 2nd day: Singha Sports Club (2) 7-1 (Faux 4*, Madanayake 2*, 4.2 overs).

PANADURA SPORTS CLUB v SRI LANKA ARMY SPORTS CLUB

Played at Panadura Esplanade, March 14, 15, 16, 2008.
Premier Championship 2007/08 - Tier B
Match drawn.   (Points: Panadura Sports Club 1.885, Sri Lanka Army Sports Club 10.09)

PANADURA SPORTS CLUB

1	†G.Y.S.R.Perera	c Soysa b Rathnayake	1
2	M.T.T.Fernando	lbw b B.A.W.Mendis	44
3	G.S.U.Fernando	c T.R.D.Mendis b B.A.W.Mendis	13
4	*J.S.K.Peiris	b de Zoysa	0
5	W.M.P.N.Wanasinghe	c Sanjeewa b B.A.W.Mendis	0
6	S.N.Wijesinghe	c Peiris b B.A.W.Mendis	19
7	D.H.S.Pradeep	b B.A.W.Mendis	10
8	M.N.R.Cooray	lbw b Rathnayake	36
9	G.A.S.Perera	st Soysa b B.A.W.Mendis	33
10	H.F.M.Fonseka	not out	16
11	I.A.Y.Dilukshan	c Prasanna b B.A.W.Mendis	1
	Extras	b 9, lb 11, nb 4	24
			197

FoW (1): 1-2 (1), 2-69 (2), 3-70 (4), 4-70 (3), 5-71 (5), 6-97 (7), 7-128 (6), 8-168 (8), 9-195 (9), 10-197 (11)

SRI LANKA ARMY SPORTS CLUB

1	S.Prasanna	c G.S.U.Fernando b Wanasinghe	22
2	S.Sanjeewa	c G.Y.S.R.Perera b Pradeep	34
3	B.A.W.Mendis	b Wanasinghe	31
4	A.D.L.Wijewardene	run out (Wijesinghe)	8
5	K.C.Prasad	run out (G.S.U.Fernando)	53
6	T.R.D.Mendis	c G.Y.S.R.Perera b Wanasinghe	28
7	†T.D.T.Soysa	lbw b Wanasinghe	2
8	W.R.Palleguruge	c Wijesinghe b Pradeep	22
9	*P.K.N.M.K.Rathnayake	lbw b G.A.S.Perera	4
10	P.P.M.Peiris	not out	1
11	H.H.M.de Zoysa	not out	0
	Extras	b 4, lb 4, nb 5	13
	(9 wickets, declared)		218

FoW (1): 1-60 (1), 2-66 (2), 3-77 (4), 4-114 (3), 5-162 (6), 6-166 (7), 7-202 (8), 8-213 (9), 9-218 (5)

Sri Lanka Army Sports Club Bowling

	O	M	R	W	
Rathnayake	12	3	33	2	4nb
Prasanna	13	4	35	0	
de Zoysa	13	5	28	1	
Peiris	2	0	13	0	
B.A.W.Mendis	21.3	6	61	7	
Palleguruge	4	0	7	0	

Panadura Sports Club Bowling

	O	M	R	W	
Dilukshan	7	2	48	0	2nb
Pradeep	17	2	80	2	3nb
Wanasinghe	24	4	54	4	
Cooray	2	0	12	0	
G.A.S.Perera	7	2	16	1	

Umpires: S.H.Sarathkumara and R.R.Wimalasiri. Referee: K.T.Francis.   Toss: Panadura Sports Club

Close of Play: 1st day: Panadura Sports Club (1) 194-8 (G.A.S.Perera 32*, Fonseka 16*, 60 overs); 2nd day: Sri Lanka Army Sports Club (1) 194-6 (Prasad 43*, Palleguruge 15*, 48.2 overs).

POLICE SPORTS CLUB v SARACENS SPORTS CLUB

Played at Police Park Ground, Colombo, March 14, 15, 16, 2008.
Premier Championship 2007/08 - Tier B
Match drawn.   (Points: Police Sports Club 2.38, Saracens Sports Club 2.265)

SARACENS SPORTS CLUB

1	W.G.R.K.Alwis	c Sanjeewa b Dilantha	15
2	P.K.Bodhisha	c Nirmala b Rasmijinan	11
3	G.K.Amarasinghe	c Nirmala b Weerasinghe	17
4	*G.N.Abeyratne	c Nirmala b Priyantha	26
5	W.S.D.Fernando	c Abeyratne b Soysa	29
6	S.C.Serasinghe	c and b Soysa	80
7	W.H.P.Chanditha	c Soysa b Weerasinghe	11
8	A.V.S.Nikethana	c and b Sanjeewa	4
9	M.L.R.Karunaratne	not out	69
10	†W.A.S.Niroshan	b Wijeratne	51
11	L.A.S.Vishwaranga	lbw b Soysa	0
	Extras	lb 7, w 2, nb 11	20
			333

FoW (1): 1-19 (2), 2-33 (1), 3-72 (4), 4-73 (3), 5-126 (5), 6-160 (7), 7-174 (8), 8-226 (6), 9-322 (10), 10-333 (11)

POLICE SPORTS CLUB

1	P.R.Nirmal	c Niroshan b Vishwaranga	3
2	S.A.Wijeratne	c Bodhisha b Chanditha	24
3	J.P.M.Abeyratne	b Alwis	38
4	†P.H.K.S.Nirmala	c Abeyratne b Serasinghe	31
5	*R.G.D.Sanjeewa	c Amarasinghe b Serasinghe	16
6	H.P.A.Priyantha	c Nikethana b Karunaratne	26
7	W.N.M.Soysa	not out	58
8	M.M.Rasmijinan	not out	54
9	T.A.N.Weerasinghe		
10	R.S.K.A.P.Dilantha		
11	W.C.K.Ramanayake		
	Extras	b 2, lb 3, nb 21	26
		(6 wickets)	276

FoW (1): 1-24 (1), 2-40 (2), 3-112 (4), 4-133 (5), 5-133 (3), 6-197 (6)

Police Sports Club Bowling

	O	M	R	W	
Rasmijinan	24	2	99	1	1w
Dilantha	7	0	26	1	
Ramanayake	7	1	21	0	
Priyantha	17	0	49	1	3nb
Weerasinghe	9	1	38	2	1w
Soysa	23	5	64	3	6nb
Sanjeewa	10	1	29	1	
Wijeratne	1	1	0	1	

Saracens Sports Club Bowling

	O	M	R	W	
Vishwaranga	18.1	1	87	1	16nb
Chanditha	13	5	38	1	4nb
Serasinghe	22	6	66	2	
Karunaratne	23.5	6	65	1	1nb
Nikethana	0.1	0	0	0	
Alwis	5	0	15	1	

Umpires: N.S.Bopage and K.M.Kottahachchi.   Referee: M.Pethiyagoda.   Toss: Police Sports Club

Close of Play: 1st day: Saracens Sports Club (1) 226-8 (Karunaratne 20*, Niroshan 0*, 69.2 overs); 2nd day: Police Sports Club (1) 53-2 (Abeyratne 7*, Nirmala 5*, 15 overs).

SEBASTIANITES CRICKET AND ATHLETIC CLUB v MORATUWA SPORTS CLUB

Played at Tyronne Fernando Stadium, Moratuwa, March 14, 15, 16, 2008.
Premier Championship 2007/08 - Tier B
Match drawn.   (Points: Sebastianites Cricket and Athletic Club 2.03, Moratuwa Sports Club 10.06)

MORATUWA SPORTS CLUB

1	R.C.Rupasinghe	c Arumathanthri b Peiris	49	c Rajitha b Wijethilake		18
2	R.A.A.I.Perera	c Kumara b Peiris	43	c U.L.K.D.Fernando b Peiris		18
3	†R.M.Mendis	lbw b Wijethilake	4	not out		0
4	L.T.A.de Silva	c and b Peiris	28			
5	A.L.D.M.Deshapriya	c Rajaratne b Peiris	0			
6	H.U.K.de Silva	b Wijethilake	1			
7	*M.D.S.Perera	c K.L.K.Fernando b Peiris	5			
8	S.J.C.de Silva	b Rajitha	9			
9	P.C.M.Fernando	b Wijethilake	21			
10	S.P.Rupasinghe	b Rajitha	2			
11	N.A.C.T.Perera	not out	6			
	Extras	b 4, lb 2, w 1	7	w 1		1
			175	**(2 wickets)**		**37**

FoW (1): 1-83 (1), 2-98 (3), 3-100 (2), 4-100 (5), 5-101 (6), 6-124 (7), 7-138 (4), 8-146 (8), 9-148 (10), 10-175 (9)
FoW (2): 1-35 (2), 2-37 (1)

SEBASTIANITES CRICKET AND ATHLETIC CLUB

1	H.A.H.U.Tillakaratne	lbw b Fernando	2
2	T.M.N.Rajaratne	b N.A.C.T.Perera	1
3	B.Y.Arumathanthri	lbw b N.A.C.T.Perera	1
4	M.A.B.Peiris	c Mendis b N.A.C.T.Perera	0
5	U.L.K.D.Fernando	run out (Deshapriya)	52
6	A.D.Indunil	c Mendis b Deshapriya	33
7	†K.L.K.Fernando	c and b Fernando	36
8	G.M.Wijethilake	b Fernando	1
9	P.W.L.R.Fernando	c sub (W.S.T.Fernando) b M.D.S.Perera	7
10	*M.N.T.H.Kumara	c Deshapriya b S.P.Rupasinghe	23
11	B.S.Rajitha	not out	4
	Extras	b 1, lb 3, nb 2	6
			166

FoW (1): 1-3 (1), 2-4 (3), 3-4 (4), 4-7 (2), 5-74 (6), 6-101 (5), 7-102 (8), 8-122 (9), 9-161 (10), 10-166 (7)

Sebastianites Cricket and Athletic Club Bowling

	O	M	R	W		O	M	R	W	
Kumara	4	0	11	0						
U.L.K.D.Fernando	5	0	27	0		(3)	1	0	12	0
P.W.L.R.Fernando	4	1	10	0	1w	(1)	2	0	9	0	1w
Arumathanthri	6.5	1	25	0						
Rajitha	8	1	22	2						
Wijethilake	12	2	33	3		(4)	0.5	0	2	1
Peiris	12.1	1	41	5		(2)	3	0	14	1

Moratuwa Sports Club Bowling

	O	M	R	W	
Fernando	18.1	4	49	3	1nb
N.A.C.T.Perera	11	3	38	3	
S.P.Rupasinghe	15	5	25	1	
S.J.C.de Silva	3	1	10	0	
Deshapriya	9	2	16	1	
M.D.S.Perera	10	1	24	1	1nb

Umpires: M.W.D.P.de Silva and H.D.P.K.Dharmasena.   Referee: A.J.Samarasekera.   Toss: Moratuwa Sports Club

Close of Play: 1st day: Sebastianites Cricket and Athletic Club (1) 55-4 (U.L.K.D.Fernando 26*, Indunil 23*, 14 overs); 2nd day: Sebastianites Cricket and Athletic Club (1) 125-8 (K.L.K.Fernando 20*, Kumara 3*, 51.2 overs).

COLOMBO CRICKET CLUB v CHILAW MARIANS CRICKET CLUB

Played at Colombo Cricket Club Ground, March 20, 21, 22, 23, 2008.
Premier Championship 2007/08 - Tier A
Chilaw Marians Cricket Club won by four wickets.   (Points: Colombo Cricket Club 3.45, Chilaw Marians Cricket Club 15.855)

COLOMBO CRICKET CLUB

1	†D.K.Ranaweera	c and b Gunaratne	32	c Cooray b Perera	14	
2	H.B.C.C.Bandara	c Fernando b Ramyakumara	1	c sub (M.M.D.N.R.G.Perera)		
				b Hettiarachchi	4	
3	J.Mubarak	lbw b Ramyakumara	56	c Jansze b Silva	54	
4	*B.M.T.T.Mendis	c Cooray b Ramyakumara	4	(6) b Hettiarachchi	87	
5	C.K.Kapugedera	lbw b Ramyakumara	0	lbw b Perera	0	
6	A.S.Polonowita	b Perera	8	(4) c Cooray b Perera	4	
7	A.C.Wethathasinghe	c Perera b Silva	26	run out	4	
8	P.D.G.Chandrakumara	c Cooray b Silva	7	c Fernando b Siriwardene	3	
9	S.C.D.Boralessa	c Jansze b Silva	0	c Athulathmudali b Hettiarachchi	12	
10	M.I.Ratnayake	st Cooray b Hettiarachchi	18	lbw b Hettiarachchi	0	
11	W.R.S.de Silva	not out	17	not out	0	
	Extras	b 5, lb 6, w 1, nb 2	14	b 2, lb 1, nb 2	5	
			183		187	

FoW (1): 1-15 (2), 2-83 (1), 3-87 (4), 4-87 (5), 5-102 (6), 6-119 (3), 7-136 (8), 8-140 (9), 9-149 (7), 10-183 (10)
FoW (2): 1-6 (2), 2-38 (1), 3-44 (4), 4-44 (5), 5-105 (3), 6-111 (7), 7-137 (8), 8-184 (9), 9-184 (10), 10-187 (6)

CHILAW MARIANS CRICKET CLUB

1	M.L.Udawatte	c Ranaweera b Ratnayake	8	c Mubarak b Boralessa	28	
2	D.N.A.Athulathmudali	c Bandara b de Silva	5	c Ratnayake b de Silva	5	
3	†N.H.G.Cooray	c Ranaweera b Boralessa	68	c Bandara b Boralessa	5	
4	A.P.Jansze	lbw b Boralessa	49	(5) lbw b Boralessa	0	
5	K.H.R.K.Fernando	b Mubarak	45	(6) c sub (K.G.N.Randika) b de Silva	1	
6	W.M.G.Ramyakumara	run out (Boralessa)	47	(7) not out	52	
7	*L.J.P.Gunaratne	c Ranaweera b Boralessa	16	(8) not out	23	
8	T.A.M.Siriwardene	c Ranaweera b Boralessa	2			
9	D.Hettiarachchi	lbw b Mubarak	0	(4) b Boralessa	1	
10	G.A.C.R.Perera	c Kapugedera b Boralessa	0			
11	S.H.M.Silva	not out	2			
	Extras	b 9, lb 3, w 1	13	nb 1	1	
			255	(6 wickets)	116	

FoW (1): 1-9 (2), 2-14 (1), 3-92 (4), 4-173 (5), 5-203 (3), 6-229 (7), 7-233 (8), 8-238 (9), 9-239 (10), 10-255 (6)
FoW (2): 1-11 (2), 2-29 (3), 3-34 (4), 4-34 (5), 5-41 (6), 6-43 (1)

Chilaw Marians Bowling	O	M	R	W			O	M	R	W	
Ramyakumara	13	3	41	4			11	3	23	0	
Perera	10	1	36	1	2nb	(3)	11	1	38	3	2nb
Fernando	11	1	26	0	1w						
Silva	15	3	49	3		(5)	12	4	26	1	
Hettiarachchi	3.5	0	13	1		(2)	21.3	3	54	4	
Gunaratne	3	1	7	1		(4)	5	0	23	0	
Siriwardene						(6)	10	2	20	1	

Colombo Cricket Club Bowling	O	M	R	W			O	M	R	W	
de Silva	16	8	18	1	1w		8	1	29	2	
Wethathasinghe	7	4	12	0							
Ratnayake	12	0	37	1		(4)	1	0	9	0	
Chandrakumara	9	1	39	0							
Boralessa	31.1	7	79	5		(3)	15	2	43	4	
Mubarak	17	2	47	2		(2)	10	1	34	0	1nb
Kapugedera	3	0	11	0							
Polonowita						(5)	0.3	0	1	0	

Umpires: P.G.Liyanage and W.A.Senanayake. Referee: A.M.J.G.Amerasinghe.Toss: Chilaw Marians Cricket Club

Close of Play: 1st day: Colombo Cricket Club (1) 151-9 (Ratnayake 2*, de Silva 1*, 50 overs); 2nd day: Chilaw Marians Cricket Club (1) 235-7 (Ramyakumara 29*, Hettiarachchi 0*, 84 overs); 3rd day: Chilaw Marians Cricket Club (2) 34-2 (Udawatte 22*, Hettiarachchi 1*, 11 overs).

MOORS SPORTS CLUB v COLTS CRICKET CLUB

Played at Moors Sports Club Ground, Colombo, March 20, 21, 22, 23, 2008.
Premier Championship 2007/08 - Tier A
Moors Sports Club won by five wickets.   (Points: Moors Sports Club 15.425, Colts Cricket Club 3.505)

COLTS CRICKET CLUB

1	T.P.Attanayake	c W.M.B.Perera b Dilhara	26			
2	S.Kalavitigoda	c Peiris b Rideegammanagedera	1	(1) c sub (J.W.H.D.Boteju)		
				b A.M.L.Perera	6	
3	M.D.K.Perera	b Dilhara	1	c sub (J.W.H.D.Boteju)		
				b Rideegammanagedera	36	
4	A.D.Mathews	c sub (J.W.H.D.Boteju) b Mudalige	104	run out	21	
5	K.G.Alwitigala	c Wannakuwatta b Mudalige	23			
6	D.N.Pathirana	c Sudarshana b Dilhara	90			
7	*H.G.J.M.Kulatunga	c sub (J.W.H.D.Boteju) b W.M.B.Perera	15	(2) c Sudarshana b A.M.L.Perera	16	
8	K.A.S.Jayasinghe	lbw b Dilhara	10	(5) not out	24	
9	†T.R.Peiris	run out (A.S.A.Perera)	0			
10	S.Weerakoon	c Nawela b Rideegammanagedera	8			
11	U.M.A.Prasad	not out	1			
	Extras	b 4, lb 4, w 1, nb 4	13	b 4, lb 2	6	
			292	(4 wickets, declared)	109	

FoW (1): 1-2 (2), 2-4 (3), 3-56 (1), 4-110 (5), 5-196 (4), 6-225 (7), 7-260 (8), 8-267 (9), 9-290 (10), 10-292 (6)
FoW (2): 1-23 (2), 2-30 (1), 3-82 (3), 4-109 (4)

MOORS SPORTS CLUB

1	T.K.D.Sudarshana	lbw b Weerakoon	17	not out	90	
2	†W.M.J.Wannakuwatta	lbw b Mathews	0	st Peiris b Kulatunga	41	
3	G.R.P.Peiris	c Kulatunga b Perera	57	c Attanayake b Kulatunga	39	
4	W.M.B.Perera	c Peiris b Mathews	3	c Jayasinghe b Weerakoon	14	
5	N.M.N.P.Nawela	b Weerakoon	5			
6	A.Rideegammanagedera	lbw b Weerakoon	10	(7) not out	4	
7	*L.H.D.Dilhara	c Peiris b Alwitigala	37	(6) c Pathirana b Alwitigala	32	
8	A.S.A.Perera	run out (Perera)	22	(5) c and b Weerakoon	4	
9	C.R.B.Mudalige	c and b Weerakoon	9			
10	A.M.L.Perera	not out	0			
11	P.N.Ranjith	absent hurt	0			
	Extras	lb 2, w 1	3	b 6, lb 7, pen 5	18	
			163	(5 wickets)	242	

FoW (1): 1-3 (2), 2-35 (1), 3-48 (4), 4-68 (5), 5-89 (6), 6-109 (3), 7-150 (8), 8-161 (7), 9-163 (9)
FoW (2): 1-55 (2), 2-134 (3), 3-164 (4), 4-174 (5), 5-222 (6)

Moors Sports Club Bowling

	O	M	R	W			O	M	R	W
Dilhara	28.4	8	69	4	1w,4nb	(4)	3	0	20	0
Rideegammanagedera	14	5	17	2			7.1	0	43	1
Ranjith	12	2	42	0						
A.M.L.Perera	16	4	45	0		(1)	5	0	22	2
Mudalige	20	2	67	2		(3)	2	0	18	0
A.S.A.Perera	2	0	6	0						
W.M.B.Perera	14	2	38	1						

Colts Cricket Club Bowling

	O	M	R	W			O	M	R	W
Mathews	10	5	14	2			9	0	45	0
Prasad	9	2	24	0	1w	(5)	1	0	17	0
Perera	13	3	29	1		(4)	4	0	16	0
Alwitigala	10	4	19	1		(6)	2	0	12	1
Weerakoon	16.2	3	75	4		(2)	13	0	87	2
Kulatunga						(3)	10	0	47	2

Umpires: R.D.Kottahachchi and N.D.Withana. Referee: G.F.Labrooy.   Toss: Moors Sports Club

Close of Play: 1st day: No play; 2nd day: Colts Cricket Club (1) 65-3 (Mathews 25*, Alwitigala 6*, 34 overs); 3rd day: Moors Sports Club (1) 41-2 (Peiris 22*, W.M.B.Perera 1*, 23 overs).
A.D.Mathews's 104 took 208 balls and included 13 fours and 1 six.

NONDESCRIPTS CRICKET CLUB v RAGAMA CRICKET CLUB

Played at Nondescripts Cricket Club Ground, Colombo, March 20, 21, 22, 23, 2008.
Premier Championship 2007/08 - Tier A
Ragama Cricket Club won by five wickets.   (Points: Nondescripts Cricket Club 3.33, Ragama Cricket Club 15.845)

NONDESCRIPTS CRICKET CLUB

1	W.U.Tharanga	c Jeewantha b Vithana	40	c S.A.Perera b Weeraratne	61
2	K.D.Gunawardene	lbw b Weeraratne	0	c de Saram b Weeraratne	14
3	W.L.P.Fernando	lbw b Bandara	36	c S.A.Perera b Bandara	8
4	C.G.Wijesinghe	lbw b Jeewantha	1	run out	14
5	*M.K.Gajanayake	c Nayanakantha b Jeewantha	0	run out	0
6	C.K.B.Kulasekara	c Weeraratne b Bandara	9	(7) c de Saram b Indrasiri	0
7	G.D.D.Indika	b Weeraratne	18	(6) c de Saram b Weeraratne	7
8	†M.R.D.G.Mapa Bandara	not out	65	c and b Indrasiri	0
9	D.T.Kottehewa	lbw b Bandara	2	c de Saram b Jeewantha	8
10	W.C.A.Ganegama	c de Saram b Jeewantha	46	lbw b Weeraratne	10
11	N.C.Komasaru	c S.A.Perera b Jeewantha	9	not out	0
	Extras	b 5, lb 7, nb 5	17	lb 1	1
			243		**123**

FoW (1): 1-7 (2), 2-64 (1), 3-76 (4), 4-76 (5), 5-82 (3), 6-101 (6), 7-122 (7), 8-127 (9), 9-223 (10), 10-243 (11)
FoW (2): 1-31 (2), 2-46 (3), 3-85 (4), 4-85 (5), 5-97 (6), 6-100 (7), 7-100 (8), 8-108 (1), 9-122 (10), 10-123 (9)

RAGAMA CRICKET CLUB

1	H.E.Vithana	c Mapa Bandara b Kulasekara	17	(2) lbw b Kottehewa	56
2	D.A.Ranatunga	c Gajanayake b Kottehewa	44	(1) c Mapa Bandara b Ganegama	27
3	M.I.G.Senaratne	lbw b Komasaru	52	c and b Kulasekara	32
4	*S.I.de Saram	c Gajanayake b Komasaru	5	lbw b Kulasekara	0
5	†S.A.Perera	b Kottehewa	0		
6	W.D.D.S.Perera	lbw b Komasaru	27	c Wijesinghe b Kottehewa	7
7	K.Weeraratne	lbw b Ganegama	11	not out	9
8	C.M.Bandara	not out	27	(5) not out	27
9	P.A.S.S.Jeewantha	c Indika b Komasaru	0		
10	S.A.D.U.Indrasiri	run out (Ganegama)	0		
11	H.G.D.Nayanakantha	c Wijesinghe b Komasaru	2		
	Extras	lb 2, nb 9	11	b 1, lb 6, w 1, nb 7	15
			196	**(5 wickets)**	**173**

FoW (1): 1-50 (1), 2-81 (2), 3-95 (4), 4-99 (5), 5-138 (3), 6-157 (7), 7-174 (6), 8-174 (9), 9-181 (10), 10-196 (11)
FoW (2): 1-55 (1), 2-106 (3), 3-106 (4), 4-146 (2), 5-156 (6)

Ragama Cricket Club Bowling

	O	M	R	W			O	M	R	W	
Weeraratne	18	1	58	2			12	3	47	4	
Nayanakantha	12	0	56	0			3	0	14	0	
Jeewantha	20	4	49	4	5nb	(5)	8.3	2	17	1	
Vithana	4	2	15	1		(3)	7	2	6	0	
Bandara	21	5	50	3		(4)	5	0	26	1	
Indrasiri	2	1	3	0			5	3	12	2	

Nondescripts Cricket Club Bowling

	O	M	R	W			O	M	R	W	
Komasaru	22.4	5	60	5		(2)	16	3	47	0	3nb
Kottehewa	20	2	70	2	8nb	(1)	13	0	60	2	1w,4nb
Ganegama	11	4	27	1		(4)	6.2	2	25	1	
Kulasekara	10	0	36	1	1nb	(3)	10	3	21	0	
Gajanayake	2	1	1	0			2	0	8	0	
Indika						(6)	3	0	5	0	

Umpires: S.S.K.Gallage and I.D.Gunawardene.   Referee: C.T.M.Devaraj.   Toss: Ragama Cricket Club

Close of Play: 1st day: Nondescripts Cricket Club (1) 187-8 (Mapa Bandara 31*, Ganegama 37*, 60 overs); 2nd day: Ragama Cricket Club (1) 181-9 (Bandara 16*, Nayanakantha 0*, 53 overs); 3rd day: Ragama Cricket Club (2) 136-3 (Vithana 49*, Bandara 15*, 42 overs).

SINHALESE SPORTS CLUB v BLOOMFIELD CRICKET AND ATHLETIC CLUB

Played at Sinhalese Sports Club Ground, Colombo, March 20, 21, 22, 2008.
Premier Championship 2007/08 - Tier A
Sinhalese Sports Club won by ten wickets. (Points: Sinhalese Sports Club 15.865, Bloomfield Cricket and Athletic Club 2.855)

BLOOMFIELD CRICKET AND ATHLETIC CLUB

1	T.S.Masmulla	lbw b Zoysa	0	c Karunanayake b Senanayake		21
2	S.T.Jayasuriya	c Sriyapala b Karunanayake	16	c Silva b Zoysa		0
3	M.T.Gunaratne	lbw b Zoysa	0	lbw b Senanayake		19
4	K.Y.de Silva	c Silva b Zoysa	20	lbw b Senanayake		39
5	†Y.S.S.Mendis	c Silva b Zoysa	18	c Paranavitana b Senanayake		2
6	*D.M.G.S.Dissanayake	c Sriyapala b Zoysa	13	c Mendis b Senanayake		3
7	C.U.Jayasinghe	c Silva b Senanayake	34	c Kandamby b Lokuarachchi		97
8	G.A.S.K.Gangodawila	b Lokuarachchi	11	c Paranavitana b Senanayake		13
9	A.U.Katipiarachchi	lbw b Senanayake	6	not out		10
10	A.B.T.Lakshitha	c and b Senanayake	1	c Kandamby b Senanayake		26
11	T.P.Gamage	not out	1	st Silva b Lokuarachchi		1
	Extras	b 5, lb 5, w 1, nb 7	18	b 1, lb 1		2
			138			**233**

FoW (1): 1-2 (1), 2-2 (3), 3-30 (2), 4-70 (4), 5-79 (5), 6-88 (6), 7-117 (8), 8-134 (9), 9-137 (7), 10-138 (10)
FoW (2): 1-1 (2), 2-26 (3), 3-49 (1), 4-51 (5), 5-61 (6), 6-133 (4), 7-190 (7), 8-200 (8), 9-228 (10), 10-233 (11)

SINHALESE SPORTS CLUB

1	*N.T.Paranavitana	c Mendis b Gamage	177		
2	S.H.Fernando	c Jayasuriya b Gamage	6	(1) not out	4
3	†J.K.Silva	c Mendis b Gamage	34		
4	B.M.A.J.Mendis	c Mendis b Katipiarchchi	59		
5	S.H.T.Kandamby	lbw b Gunaratne	16		
6	E.D.J.Sriyapala	c Dissanayake b Jayasuriya	3	(2) not out	1
7	K.S.Lokuarachchi	b Dissanayake	16		
8	K.P.S.P.Karunanayake	lbw b Dissanayake	6		
9	D.N.T.Zoysa	c Masmulla b Dissanayake	4		
10	S.M.Senanayake	not out	21		
11	C.W.Vidanapathirana	lbw b Gamage	11		
	Extras	b 1, lb 4, w 1, nb 8	14	lb 1	1
			367	(no wicket)	**6**

FoW (1): 1-12 (2), 2-128 (3), 3-280 (4), 4-290 (1), 5-301 (6), 6-307 (5), 7-325 (8), 8-330 (7), 9-339 (9), 10-367 (11)

Sinhalese Sports Club Bowling

	O	M	R	W			O	M	R	W
Zoysa	12	3	39	5			14	3	37	1
Vidanapathirana	9	3	25	0	1w		14	2	48	0
Karunanayake	7	1	47	1	2nb	(5)	5	0	15	0
Senanayake	4	1	4	3	1nb	(3)	20	3	81	7
Lokuarachchi	5	1	13	1		(4)	8.1	2	50	2

Bloomfield Cricket and Athletic Club Bowling

	O	M	R	W			O	M	R	W
Gamage	24	2	95	4	1w		0.4	0	5	0
Lakshitha	15	2	46	0	4nb					
Katipiarchchi	9	1	43	1	2nb					
Jayasuriya	13	2	42	1						
Gangodawila	2	0	11	0						
Dissanayake	16	2	64	3	2nb					
Gunaratne	13	0	51	1						
Masmulla	2	0	10	0						

Umpires: E.A.R.de Silva and M.S.K.Nandiweera. Referee: U.Warnapura. Toss: Bloomfield Cricket and Athletic Club

Close of Play: 1st day: Sinhalese Sports Club (1) 76-1 (Paranavitana 47*, Silva 19*, 21 overs); 2nd day: Bloomfield Cricket and Athletic Club (2) 28-2 (Masmulla 7*, de Silva 2*, 13 overs).

The match was scheduled for four days but completed in three. N.T.Paranavitana's 177 took 219 balls and included 24 fours and 1 six.

TAMIL UNION CRICKET AND ATHLETIC CLUB v BADURELIYA SPORTS CLUB

Played at P.Saravanamuttu Stadium, Colombo, March 20, 21, 22, 2008.
Premier Championship 2007/08 - Tier A
Tamil Union Cricket and Athletic Club won by an innings and 104 runs.   (Points: Tamil Union Cricket and Athletic Club 18, Badureliya Sports Club 2.595)

BADURELIYA SPORTS CLUB

1	†D.W.A.N.D.Vitharana	c G.T.de Silva b Lakmal	13	c S.K.L.de Silva b Perera	1
2	M.M.D.P.V.Perera	lbw b Pushpakumara	16	(6) b Pushpakumara	30
3	D.N.Hunukumbura	c G.T.de Silva b Pushpakumara	6	(2) b Perera	8
4	*R.P.A.H.Wickramaratne	c Daniel b Lakmal	30	c Pushpakumara b Maduwantha	35
5	U.R.P.Perera	c S.K.L.de Silva b Lakmal	7	(3) c G.T.de Silva b Perera	0
6	R.M.A.R.Ratnayake	c Daniel b Lakmal	12	(5) c and b Pushpakumara	44
7	D.M.Gunathilake	lbw b Pushpakumara	0	(8) c G.T.de Silva b Lakmal	23
8	M.R.C.N.Bandaratilleke	c and b Pushpakumara	26	(7) c Rupasinghe b Pushpakumara	64
9	K.L.S.L.Dias	c G.T.de Silva b Lakmal	0	(10) b Lakmal	0
10	S.D.C.Malinga	c K.M.Fernando b Pushpakumara	5	(9) lbw b Pushpakumara	7
11	B.B.Sanjeewa	not out	0	not out	6
	Extras	lb 3, nb 8	11	b 7, lb 2, nb 6	15
			126		233

FoW (1): 1-21 (1), 2-35 (2), 3-70 (4), 4-82 (5), 5-95 (3), 6-95 (7), 7-95 (6), 8-102 (9), 9-107 (10), 10-126 (8)
FoW (2): 1-10 (1), 2-11 (2), 3-13 (3), 4-58 (4), 5-117 (5), 6-139 (6), 7-200 (8), 8-219 (9), 9-227 (7), 10-233 (10)

TAMIL UNION CRICKET AND ATHLETIC CLUB

1	†G.T.de Silva	c Ratnayake b Dias	7
2	G.I.Daniel	c Malinga b Sanjeewa	101
3	S.I.Fernando	st Vitharana b Bandaratilleke	131
4	S.K.L.de Silva	lbw b Malinga	36
5	R.J.M.G.M.Rupasinghe	lbw b Wickramaratne	96
6	M.Pushpakumara	lbw b Malinga	71
7	K.M.Fernando	c M.M.D.P.V.Perera b Malinga	2
8	*H.M.Maduwantha	c Ratnayake b Malinga	3
9	N.K.M.Perera	not out	0
10	S.C.Liyanagunawardene		
11	R.A.S.Lakmal		
	Extras	b 2, lb 9, nb 5	16
	(8 wickets, declared)		463

FoW (1): 1-21 (1), 2-238 (2), 3-252 (3), 4-339 (4), 5-437 (5), 6-457 (6), 7-463 (8), 8-463 (7)

Tamil Union Cricket and Athletic Club Bowling

	O	M	R	W		O	M	R	W	
Lakmal	15	1	78	5	7nb	11.3	2	84	2	3nb
Perera	3	0	16	0	1nb	6	0	31	3	3nb
Maduwantha	9	4	12	0		(4) 6	3	17	1	
Pushpakumara	14.5	8	12	5		(3) 18	2	56	4	
Rupasinghe	1	1	0	0		(6) 2	0	5	0	
Liyanagunawardene	1	0	5	0		(5) 5	0	31	0	

Badureliya Sports Club Bowling

	O	M	R	W	
Malinga	26	6	89	4	
Ratnayake	14	2	63	0	5nb
Dias	30	6	92	1	
Sanjeewa	14	3	65	1	
Bandaratilleke	13	2	48	1	
U.R.P.Perera	9	0	46	0	
Gunathilake	5	3	18	0	
Wickramaratne	7	0	31	1	

Umpires: B.B.J.Nandakumar and M.G.Silva.   Referee: N.S.H.M.R.Kodituwakku.   Toss: Badureliya Sports Club

Close of Play: 1st day: Tamil Union Cricket and Athletic Club (1) 40-1 (Daniel 22*, S.I.Fernando 8*, 12 overs); 2nd day: Tamil Union Cricket and Athletic Club (1) 443-5 (Pushpakumara 57*, K.M.Fernando 1*, 111 overs).
The match was scheduled for four days but completed in three. G.I.Daniel's 101 took 204 balls and included 6 fours and 2 sixes.
S.I.Fernando's 131 took 163 balls and included 17 fours and 4 sixes.

LANKAN CRICKET CLUB v SRI LANKA AIR FORCE SPORTS CLUB

Played at Burgher Recreation Club Ground, Colombo, March 21, 22, 23, 2008.
Premier Championship 2007/08 - Tier B
Sri Lanka Air Force Sports Club won by 198 runs.   (Points: Lankan Cricket Club 3.515, Sri Lanka Air Force Sports Club 16.805)

SRI LANKA AIR FORCE SPORTS CLUB

1	†M.K.P.B.Kularatne	c Shantha b Kumara	39	c Shantha b Shazmil	10	
2	A.Rizan	c M.H.H.Perera b Weerasinghe	54	b Shazmil	33	
3	M.A.M.Faizer	c Shantha b Kumara	8	c Weerasinghe b Kumara	2	
4	W.A.Eranga	c Maduranga b Kumara	19	(7) c B.M.S.Perera b Ariyasinghe	47	
5	W.M.M.W.E.V.Gangoda	c Maduranga b Kumara	34	lbw b Shazmil	4	
6	S.Madanayake	c B.M.S.Perera b Namal	49	c Shantha b Shazmil	12	
7	M.W.B.Dissanayake	c and b Weerasinghe	18	(8) c Pushpalal b Namal	50	
8	*K.A.Kumara	c Pushpalal b Weerasinghe	30	(4) not out	122	
9	M.D.S.Wanasinghe	c Maduranga b Weerasinghe	10			
10	M.K.G.C.P.Lakshitha	not out	1			
11	G.S.Priyankara	b Kumara	0			
	Extras	b 3, lb 6, nb 1	10	b 8, w 1	9	
			272	(7 wickets, declared)	289	

FoW (1): 1-53 (1), 2-65 (3), 3-101 (4), 4-145 (2), 5-177 (5), 6-221 (7), 7-233 (6), 8-264 (8), 9-271 (9), 10-272 (11)
FoW (2): 1-37 (2), 2-46 (3), 3-52 (1), 4-62 (5), 5-82 (6), 6-195 (7), 7-289 (8)

LANKAN CRICKET CLUB

1	H.L.S.Maduranga	lbw b Madanayake	17	b Madanayake	1	
2	J.R.G.Namal	c sub (M.P.G.D.P.Gunatilleke) b Gangoda	78	b Lakshitha	0	
3	K.D.C.Pushpalal	c Wanasinghe b Madanayake	2	(8) c Gangoda b Rizan	17	
4	*B.M.D.T.D.Ariyasinghe	c Faizer b Madanayake	0	(3) c Kumara b Madanayake	14	
5	B.M.S.Perera	b Madanayake	1	(6) lbw b Gangoda	42	
6	M.H.H.Perera	lbw b Gangoda	3	(11) c Eranga b Rizan	2	
7	†G.A.L.W.Shantha	lbw b Gangoda	7	(4) c Wanasinghe b Madanayake	19	
8	S.L.Perera	c Eranga b Madanayake	20	(7) c Kumara b Gangoda	34	
9	J.S.M.Shazmil	c sub (K.K.A.K.Lakmal) b Rizan	36	(5) c and b Madanayake	15	
10	D.R.F.Weerasinghe	c and b Rizan	17	(9) not out	1	
11	P.D.M.P.N.Kumara	not out	14	(10) c sub (K.K.A.K.Lakmal) b Madanayake	5	
	Extras	b 4, lb 1, nb 1	6	b 4, lb 3, nb 5	12	
			201		162	

FoW (1): 1-40 (1), 2-48 (3), 3-48 (4), 4-58 (5), 5-67 (6), 6-85 (7), 7-126 (2), 8-146 (8), 9-170 (9), 10-201 (10)
FoW (2): 1-2 (1), 2-2 (2), 3-39 (3), 4-40 (4), 5-79 (5), 6-108 (6), 7-142 (7), 8-154 (8), 9-159 (10), 10-162 (11)

Lankan Cricket Club Bowling	O	M	R	W		O	M	R	W	
Kumara	19.4	5	67	5		13	0	64	1	
Pushpalal	7	2	45	0		1	0	15	0	1w
Shazmil	1	0	11	0	1nb	11	1	45	4	
Weerasinghe	25	6	66	4		17	2	56	0	
Ariyasinghe	5	0	22	0	(8)	7	1	24	1	
B.M.S.Perera	2	0	16	0	(5)	2	0	4	0	
Namal	11	2	36	1	(9)	5.4	0	23	1	
M.H.H.Perera					(6)	8	0	41	0	
S.L.Perera					(7)	2	0	9	0	

Sri Lanka Air Force Bowling	O	M	R	W		O	M	R	W	
Lakshitha	5	0	24	0		14	4	33	1	5nb
Priyankara	3	0	13	0	1nb					
Madanayake	23	3	69	5	(2)	18	8	45	5	
Gangoda	18	4	47	3		7	2	21	2	
Rizan	11.5	0	43	2	(3)	9.5	0	56	2	

Umpires: N.S.Bopage and H.D.P.K.Dharmasena. Referee: A.C.M.Lafir.   Toss: Lankan Cricket Club

Close of Play: 1st day: Lankan Cricket Club (1) 59-4 (Namal 37*, M.H.H.Perera 0*, 17 overs); 2nd day: Sri Lanka Air Force Sports Club (2) 224-6 (Kumara 96*, Dissanayake 16*, 53 overs).
K.A.Kumara's 122 took 177 balls and included 11 fours and 1 six.

PANADURA SPORTS CLUB v SARACENS SPORTS CLUB

Played at Bloomfield Cricket and Athletic Club Ground, Colombo, March 21, 22, 23, 2008.
Premier Championship 2007/08 - Tier B
Match drawn.   (Points: Panadura Sports Club 3.9, Saracens Sports Club 12.215)

SARACENS SPORTS CLUB

1	W.G.R.K.Alwis	b Dilukshan	7	c G.Y.S.R.Perera b Pradeep	13
2	P.K.Bodhisha	c Mapatuna b Cooray	53	c G.Y.S.R.Perera b Wanasinghe	11
3	G.K.Amarasinghe	lbw b G.A.S.Perera	48	c G.Y.S.R.Perera b Wanasinghe	72
4	*G.N.Abeyratne	lbw b Cooray	26	b Pradeep	5
5	W.S.D.Fernando	c Mapatuna b Cooray	6	c Cooray b G.S.U.Fernando	21
6	A.V.S.Nikethana	run out (G.A.S.Perera)	4	c sub (J.K.D.Chathuranga)	
				b G.S.U.Fernando	0
7	S.C.Serasinghe	c G.A.S.Perera b Dilukshan	39	c G.Y.S.R.Perera b G.A.S.Perera	26
8	W.H.P.Chanditha	c G.Y.S.R.Perera b Wanasinghe	56	b Wanasinghe	35
9	†W.A.S.Niroshan	run out (Wanasinghe)	13	c G.A.S.Perera b G.S.U.Fernando	11
10	L.D.P.Nishantha	c G.A.S.Perera b G.Y.S.R.Perera	6	not out	3
11	L.A.S.Vishwaranga	not out	0		
	Extras	b 2, lb 5, w 1, nb 10	18	b 2, lb 3, nb 5	10
			276	(9 wickets, declared)	207

FoW (1): 1-13 (1), 2-114 (3), 3-118 (2), 4-132 (5), 5-140 (6), 6-159 (4), 7-232 (7), 8-258 (9), 9-268 (8), 10-276 (10)
FoW (2): 1-16 (2), 2-39 (1), 3-52 (4), 4-116 (5), 5-120 (6), 6-134 (3), 7-179 (7), 8-197 (8), 9-207 (9)

PANADURA SPORTS CLUB

1	†G.Y.S.R.Perera	lbw b Amarasinghe	11	b Vishwaranga	2
2	M.T.T.Fernando	st Niroshan b Amarasinghe	18	b Vishwaranga	0
3	G.S.U.Fernando	c Niroshan b Amarasinghe	23	lbw b Vishwaranga	8
4	D.H.S.Pradeep	lbw b Amarasinghe	4	(5) lbw b Bodhisha	57
5	W.M.P.N.Wanasinghe	c Niroshan b Alwis	2	(7) c Bodhisha b Alwis	29
6	C.P.Mapatuna	c Bodhisha b Amarasinghe	21	(4) c Chanditha b Fernando	120
7	S.N.Wijesinghe	c sub (G.A.Joseph) b Serasinghe	6	(9) not out	17
8	*J.S.K.Peiris	not out	21	b Serasinghe	11
9	M.N.R.Cooray	lbw b Amarasinghe	4	(10) not out	2
10	G.A.S.Perera	c Fernando b Serasinghe	12	(6) c Alwis b Serasinghe	1
11	I.A.Y.Dilukshan	lbw b Vishwaranga	1		
	Extras	b 2, lb 1, nb 15	18	lb 4, w 1, nb 7	12
			141	(8 wickets)	259

FoW (1): 1-36 (1), 2-39 (2), 3-45 (4), 4-51 (5), 5-84 (6), 6-95 (7), 7-102 (3), 8-106 (9), 9-129 (10), 10-141 (11)
FoW (2): 1-2 (2), 2-9 (1), 3-16 (3), 4-137 (5), 5-142 (6), 6-186 (7), 7-215 (8), 8-257 (4)

Panadura Sports Club Bowling	O	M	R	W			O	M	R	W	
Dilukshan	17	0	76	2	1w,5nb		3	1	12	0	
Wanasinghe	14	3	32	1			20	3	55	3	
Pradeep	6	0	25	0	2nb		12	1	46	2	5nb
Cooray	22	6	54	3			12	0	44	0	
G.A.S.Perera	22	3	57	1			20	8	32	1	
Mapatuna	3	1	12	0							
G.S.U.Fernando	1	0	5	0		(6)	8	2	13	3	
G.Y.S.R.Perera	1	0	8	1	2nb						

Saracens Sports Club Bowling	O	M	R	W			O	M	R	W	
Nishantha	7	1	23	0	5nb		5	0	16	0	4nb
Vishwaranga	10	0	31	1	5nb		5	0	23	3	2nb
Serasinghe	13	1	50	2		(7)	6	1	36	2	
Amarasinghe	19	8	34	6	1nb	(3)	7	1	28	0	1nb
Alwis	1	1	0	1	4nb		24	3	77	1	
Chanditha						(4)	1	0	10	0	1w
Bodhisha						(6)	16	0	63	1	
Fernando						(8)	1	0	2	1	

Umpires: E.J.A.P.A.M.Jayasuriya and R.A.Kottahachchi.   Referee: R.Punchihewa.   Toss: Panadura Sports Club

Close of Play: 1st day: Saracens Sports Club (1) 232-7 (Chanditha 37*, 77.2 overs); 2nd day: Saracens Sports Club (2) 120-5 (Amarasinghe 67*, 37.4 overs).
C.P.Mapatuna's 120 took 179 balls and included 14 fours.

POLICE SPORTS CLUB v BURGHER RECREATION CLUB

Played at Police Park Ground, Colombo, March 21, 22, 23, 2008.
Premier Championship 2007/08 - Tier B
Match drawn.   (Points: Police Sports Club 11.7, Burgher Recreation Club 3.73)

BURGHER RECREATION CLUB

#	Batsman	Dismissal	R	2nd innings	R
1	*D.H.Sandagirigoda	c Nirmal b Weerasinghe	6	c Abeyratne b Rasmijinan	1
2	I.C.D.Perera	c Weerasinghe b Rasmijinan	0		
3	B.M.P.D.Fernando	run out (Wijeratne)	59	(2) run out (Wijeratne)	17
4	L.S.D.Perera	lbw b Rasmijinan	0	(3) c and b Soysa	53
5	G.R.Perera	b M.R.Priyantha	31	(4) c Kuruppu b Soysa	65
6	†P.H.M.G.Fernando	c Kuruppu b Rasmijinan	52	(5) c Kuruppu b Sanjeewa	46
7	I.C.Soysa	c Kuruppu b M.R.Priyantha	43	(6) not out	60
8	K.D.J.Nishantha	c Abeyratne b Rasmijinan	39	(7) c Kuruppu b Weerasinghe	17
9	C.A.M.Madusanka	c Wijeratne b M.R.Priyantha	5	not out	2
10	H.O.Darshana	lbw b M.R.Priyantha	17	(8) lbw b Rasmijinan	19
11	G.D.R.Eranga	not out	7		
	Extras	lb 3	3	lb 2, w 2	4
			262	**(7 wickets)**	**284**

FoW (1): 1-3 (2), 2-15 (1), 3-18 (4), 4-71 (5), 5-113 (3), 6-181 (6), 7-201 (7), 8-208 (9), 9-246 (10), 10-262 (8)
FoW (2): 1-4 (1), 2-31 (2), 3-134 (4), 4-137 (3), 5-197 (5), 6-241 (7), 7-281 (8)

POLICE SPORTS CLUB

#	Batsman	Dismissal	R
1	P.R.Nirmal	b L.S.D.Perera	202
2	S.A.Wijeratne	c Eranga b Soysa	36
3	J.P.M.Abeyratne	c P.H.M.G.Fernando b Soysa	0
4	†P.H.K.S.Nirmala	lbw b L.S.D.Perera	38
5	W.N.M.Soysa	c G.R.Perera b L.S.D.Perera	2
6	*R.G.D.Sanjeewa	b Eranga	19
7	H.P.A.Priyantha	c Soysa b L.S.D.Perera	65
8	M.M.Rasmijinan	c Darshana b Nishantha	8
9	K.A.D.M.C.Kuruppu	st P.H.M.G.Fernando b Nishantha	26
10	T.A.N.Weerasinghe	not out	16
11	M.R.Priyantha	st P.H.M.G.Fernando b Nishantha	5
	Extras	lb 10, w 3, nb 11	24
			441

FoW (1): 1-73 (2), 2-79 (3), 3-207 (4), 4-219 (5), 5-284 (6), 6-336 (1), 7-371 (8), 8-403 (7), 9-435 (9), 10-441 (11)

Police Sports Club Bowling

	O	M	R	W		O	M	R	W	
Rasmijinan	20.1	6	58	4		18	1	69	2	1w
Weerasinghe	11	3	24	1		11	2	47	1	1w
Soysa	12	1	22	0		21	1	82	2	
M.R.Priyantha	27	3	106	4		8	0	57	0	
Sanjeewa	8	2	17	0	(6)	4	0	13	1	
Wijeratne	6	0	27	0						
H.P.A.Priyantha	1	0	5	0						
Nirmala					(5)	3	0	14	0	

Burgher Recreation Club Bowling

	O	M	R	W	
Eranga	19	2	88	1	1w,10nb
Darshana	10	1	63	0	2w
Madusanka	30	7	71	0	
Soysa	23	5	80	2	
Nishantha	17.5	4	52	3	
G.R.Perera	6	3	8	0	
L.S.D.Perera	21	4	69	4	

Umpires: M.W.D.P.de Silva and D.Ekanayake.   Referee: A.J.Samarasekera.   Toss: Police Sports Club

Close of Play: 1st day: Burgher Recreation Club (1) 262-9 (Nishantha 39*, Eranga 7*, 85 overs); 2nd day: Police Sports Club (1) 336-6 (H.P.A.Priyantha 20*, 94.4 overs).

P.R.Nirmal's 202 took 264 balls and included 28 fours and 3 sixes.

SEBASTIANITES CRICKET AND ATHLETIC CLUB v SINGHA SPORTS CLUB

Played at Colts Cricket Club Ground, Colombo, March 21, 22, 23, 2008.
Premier Championship 2007/08 - Tier B
Match drawn. (Points: Sebastianites Cricket and Athletic Club 4.26, Singha Sports Club 12.29)

SEBASTIANITES CRICKET AND ATHLETIC CLUB

1	B.Y.Arumathanthri	c Kavinga b Liyanage	20	c Kumara b Randunu	64
2	R.H.T.A.Perera	c Zoysa b Liyanage	30	lbw b Vithana	8
3	U.L.K.D.Fernando	run out (Randunu)	28	(4) c Kavinga b Vithana	4
4	M.A.B.Peiris	c Kavinga b Gamage	16	(7) c Zoysa b Randunu	29
5	T.L.T.Peiris	c Zoysa b Liyanage	0	c Zoysa b Gamage	16
6	A.D.Indunil	b Vithana	29	(3) c Kavinga b de Silva	51
7	†K.L.K.Fernando	b Randunu	16	(6) c Faux b Wewalwala	55
8	D.G.C.Silva	st Kavinga b Vithana	4	(9) not out	59
9	A.B.L.D.Rodrigo	not out	28	(8) lbw b Gamage	33
10	Y.I.S.Gunasena	run out (Kumara)	1	c Kavinga b Wewalwala	13
11	*M.N.T.H.Kumara	c Kumara b Randunu	8	c Gamage b Vithana	10
	Extras	lb 7, w 2, nb 12	21	b 22, lb 13, w 1, nb 13	49
			201		**391**

FoW (1): 1-35 (1), 2-85 (3), 3-85 (2), 4-86 (5), 5-133 (4), 6-148 (6), 7-162 (8), 8-162 (7), 9-164 (10), 10-201 (11)
FoW (2): 1-39 (2), 2-117 (1), 3-125 (4), 4-147 (3), 5-172 (5), 6-220 (7), 7-263 (8), 8-336 (6), 9-362 (10), 10-391 (11)

SINGHA SPORTS CLUB

1	D.A.Faux	c U.L.K.D.Fernando b Gunasena	56	c U.L.K.D.Fernando b Rodrigo	32
2	H.S.M.Zoysa	c K.L.K.Fernando b Gunasena	17	st K.L.K.Fernando b M.A.B.Peiris	4
3	A.S.Wewalwala	lbw b Gunasena	0	(5) not out	17
4	K.S.H.de Silva	c Silva b Kumara	5	(3) st K.L.K.Fernando b M.A.B.Peiris	8
5	H.W.M.Kumara	not out	164	(4) not out	34
6	†H.H.R.Kavinga	c Silva b Rodrigo	19		
7	S.I.Vithana	lbw b Rodrigo	3		
8	S.K.C.Randunu	c M.A.B.Peiris b Rodrigo	13		
9	*N.C.K.Liyanage	b Gunasena	46		
10	P.L.S.Gamage	c Silva b Gunasena	3		
11	R.L.S.Ananda	lbw b Rodrigo	1		
	Extras	b 9, lb 3, w 3, nb 14	29	w 1, nb 6	7
			356	(3 wickets)	**102**

FoW (1): 1-23 (2), 2-24 (3), 3-29 (4), 4-163 (1), 5-199 (6), 6-213 (7), 7-238 (8), 8-348 (9), 9-355 (10), 10-356 (11)
FoW (2): 1-28 (2), 2-49 (3), 3-51 (1)

Singha Bowling	O	M	R	W			O	M	R	W	
de Silva	4	1	11	0			9	0	42	1	
Liyanage	10	1	38	3	1w,3nb		11	2	52	0	1w,2nb
Ananda	3	1	16	0	1w,1nb	(8)	4	0	23	0	
Gamage	8	0	38	1	4nb	(3)	18	4	55	2	10nb
Vithana	15	2	61	2		(4)	22.1	4	74	3	
Randunu	12	3	30	2		(5)	38	7	82	2	
Zoysa						(6)	1	0	7	0	
Kumara						(7)	3	0	5	0	
Wewalwala						(9)	8	2	16	2	1nb

Sebastianites Bowling	O	M	R	W			O	M	R	W	
Kumara	4	0	26	1							
Gunasena	15	2	52	5	1w,7nb	(1)	2	0	12	0	2nb
Silva	9	0	59	0	1w,5nb	(2)	1	0	15	0	1w,3nb
U.L.K.D.Fernando	3	0	32	0	1w						
M.A.B.Peiris	9	1	50	0	2nb	(3)	4	0	31	2	1nb
Arumathanthri	9	1	20	0		(5)	2	0	7	0	
Rodrigo	21.3	0	88	4		(4)	6	0	37	1	
Indunil	6	1	17	0							

Umpires: W.Jayasena and K.M.Kottahachchi. Referee: N.Fredrick.   Toss: Singha Sports Club

Close of Play: 1st day: Singha Sports Club (1) 158-3 (Faux 51*, Kumara 77*, 34 overs); 2nd day: Sebastianites Cricket and Athletic Club (2) 131-3 (Indunil 44*, T.L.T.Peiris 0*, 42 overs).
H.W.M.Kumara's 164 took 228 balls and included 19 fours and 4 sixes.

SRI LANKA ARMY SPORTS CLUB v MORATUWA SPORTS CLUB

Played at Army Ground, Panagoda, March 21, 22, 23, 2008.
Premier Championship 2007/08 - Tier B
Sri Lanka Army Sports Club won by seven wickets. (Points: Sri Lanka Army Sports Club 15.64, Moratuwa Sports Club 2.92)

MORATUWA SPORTS CLUB

#	Batsman	Dismissal 1	R	Dismissal 2	R
1	R.C.Rupasinghe	c Prasanna b Rathnayake	5	(8) c Karunatilleke b B.A.W.Mendis	27
2	R.A.A.I.Perera	c T.R.D.Mendis b Rathnayake	48	b Prasanna	26
3	†R.M.Mendis	b Rathnayake	4	(1) c sub (D.A.Lawrance) b Prasanna	4
4	A.L.D.M.Deshapriya	lbw b B.A.W.Mendis	6	(3) c Sanjeewa b Prasanna	30
5	L.T.A.de Silva	c Soysa b Prasanna	6	lbw b B.A.W.Mendis	1
6	P.C.M.Fernando	c Soysa b B.A.W.Mendis	20	c Prasad b B.A.W.Mendis	30
7	H.U.K.de Silva	c Rathnayake b Palleguruge	58	c Rathnayake b Prasanna	2
8	*M.D.S.Perera	c Prasanna b B.A.W.Mendis	0	(4) c Soysa b Prasanna	7
9	S.J.C.de Silva	not out	8	c B.A.W.Mendis b Prasanna	2
10	S.P.Rupasinghe	c Soysa b Rathnayake	10	c Sanjeewa b B.A.W.Mendis	6
11	N.A.C.T.Perera	run out (T.R.D.Mendis)	0	not out	2
	Extras	lb 4, w 1, nb 4, pen 5	14	b 3, lb 4, nb 1	8
			179		**145**

FoW (1): 1-10 (1), 2-20 (3), 3-52 (4), 4-66 (2), 5-77 (5), 6-159 (6), 7-160 (8), 8-160 (7), 9-177 (10), 10-179 (11)
FoW (2): 1-25 (1), 2-32 (2), 3-58 (4), 4-63 (5), 5-69 (3), 6-75 (7), 7-118 (8), 8-130 (9), 9-138 (6), 10-145 (10)

SRI LANKA ARMY SPORTS CLUB

#	Batsman	Dismissal 1	R	Dismissal 2	R
1	S.Prasanna	c Fernando b N.A.C.T.Perera	0	c S.P.Rupasinghe b Fernando	18
2	R.D.I.A.Karunatilleke	lbw b N.A.C.T.Perera	28		
3	B.A.W.Mendis	lbw b Fernando	12		
4	S.Sanjeewa	c S.J.C.de Silva b Fernando	64	not out	28
5	K.C.Prasad	c H.U.K.de Silva b S.P.Rupasinghe	27	(3) c Mendis b Fernando	30
6	L.M.R.Suresh	run out (S.P.Rupasinghe)	0	(2) c L.T.A.de Silva b S.P.Rupasinghe	21
7	T.R.D.Mendis	c and b M.D.S.Perera	0	(5) not out	0
8	†T.D.T.Soysa	b Fernando	43		
9	W.R.Palleguruge	b N.A.C.T.Perera	8		
10	*P.K.N.M.K.Rathnayake	run out (M.D.S.Perera)	26		
11	P.P.M.Peiris	not out	1		
	Extras	b 2, lb 3, w 1, nb 10	16	b 2, lb 1, nb 3	6
			225	(3 wickets)	**103**

FoW (1): 1-2 (1), 2-39 (3), 3-49 (2), 4-136 (4), 5-139 (6), 6-140 (7), 7-153 (5), 8-163 (9), 9-220 (10), 10-225 (8)
FoW (2): 1-18 (1), 2-56 (3), 3-89 (2)

Sri Lanka Army Sports Club Bowling

	O	M	R	W			O	M	R	W	
Karunatilleke	3.5	1	8	0							
Peiris	6	2	15	0			1	0	16	0	
Rathnayake	10.2	2	38	4	1w,2nb	(1)	9	3	21	0	
B.A.W.Mendis	21	1	64	3	2nb		21.2	5	50	4	1nb
Prasanna	9	1	35	1		(3)	26	8	51	6	
Palleguruge	5	2	10	1							

Moratuwa Sports Club Bowling

	O	M	R	W			O	M	R	W	
Fernando	15.3	0	47	3	1w,2nb		5	1	18	2	
N.A.C.T.Perera	12	2	40	3			3	0	26	0	
Deshapriya	2	0	12	0		(4)	1	0	10	0	
S.P.Rupasinghe	11	1	66	1	5nb	(3)	5	0	27	1	3nb
M.D.S.Perera	5	0	29	1	3nb						
S.J.C.de Silva	5	0	26	0							
H.U.K.de Silva						(5)	2.5	1	19	0	

Umpires: R.M.P.J.Rambukwella and R.R.Wimalasiri. Referee: B.C.Cooray. Toss: Moratuwa Sports Club

Close of Play: 1st day: Sri Lanka Army Sports Club (1) 37-1 (Karunatilleke 23*, B.A.W.Mendis 10*, 12 overs); 2nd day: Moratuwa Sports Club (2) 141-9 (S.P.Rupasinghe 5*, N.A.C.T.Perera 2*, 55.4 overs).

BLOOMFIELD CRICKET AND ATHLETIC CLUB v RAGAMA CRICKET CLUB

Played at Bloomfield Cricket and Athletic Club Ground, Colombo, March 27, 28, 29, 30, 2008.
Premier Championship 2007/08 - Tier A
Match drawn.   (Points: Bloomfield Cricket and Athletic Club 13.125, Ragama Cricket Club 4.67)

BLOOMFIELD CRICKET AND ATHLETIC CLUB

1	K.N.C.Fernando	c Jeewantha b Weeraratne	3	(3) run out	15
2	T.S.Masmulla	lbw b Vithana	121	run out	25
3	†Y.S.S.Mendis	c Ranatunga b Jeewantha	22	(7) c W.D.D.S.Perera b Indrasiri	24
4	G.A.S.K.Gangodawila	c Weeraratne b Jeewantha	1	(6) c Indrasiri b Bandara	2
5	K.Y.de Silva	not out	164	(4) c S.A.Perera b Vithana	35
6	S.T.Jayasuriya	c Ranatunga b Vithana	4	(1) c W.D.D.S.Perera b Jeewantha	79
7	*D.M.G.S.Dissanayake	lbw b Vithana	35	(5) c Ranatunga b Bandara	57
8	R.Rathika	lbw b Weeraratne	7	c de Saram b Weeraratne	9
9	A.B.T.Lakshitha	run out (Vithana)	0	c W.D.D.S.Perera b Jeewantha	21
10	M.P.Ranasinghe	c Indrasiri b Vithana	58	c W.D.D.S.Perera b Jeewantha	26
11	T.P.Gamage	run out (de Saram)	0	not out	2
	Extras	b 7, lb 5, nb 4	16	b 4, lb 2, w 1, nb 3	10
			431		305

FoW (1): 1-4 (1), 2-56 (3), 3-64 (4), 4-192 (2), 5-196 (6), 6-275 (7), 7-313 (8), 8-331 (9), 9-422 (10), 10-431 (11)
FoW (2): 1-75 (2), 2-111 (3), 3-125 (1), 4-214 (5), 5-218 (4), 6-218 (6), 7-247 (8), 8-259 (7), 9-302 (10), 10-305 (9)

RAGAMA CRICKET CLUB

1	D.A.Ranatunga	lbw b Dissanayake	18	(2) c Masmulla b Ranasinghe	18
2	H.E.Vithana	c Mendis b Lakshitha	24	(1) c Masmulla b Dissanayake	20
3	M.I.G.Senaratne	run out (de Silva)	4	c Jayasuriya b Dissanayake	52
4	*S.I.de Saram	c Mendis b Dissanayake	19	run out	45
5	C.M.Bandara	b Ranasinghe	37	c Ranasinghe b Dissanayake	32
6	W.D.D.S.Perera	c Mendis b Dissanayake	18	not out	52
7	K.Weeraratne	c Jayasuriya b Ranasinghe	11	st Mendis b Dissanayake	89
8	†S.A.Perera	c de Silva b Dissanayake	24	not out	0
9	P.A.S.S.Jeewantha	lbw b Dissanayake	2		
10	S.A.D.U.Indrasiri	not out	19		
11	H.G.D.Nayanakantha	c Mendis b Dissanayake	12		
	Extras	b 2, lb 12, w 1, nb 5	20	b 3, lb 8, w 4, nb 3	18
			208	(6 wickets)	326

FoW (1): 1-36 (1), 2-45 (3), 3-56 (2), 4-97 (4), 5-136 (6), 6-142 (5), 7-149 (7), 8-161 (9), 9-190 (8), 10-208 (11)
FoW (2): 1-33 (2), 2-69 (1), 3-122 (3), 4-159 (4), 5-192 (5), 6-320 (7)

Ragama Bowling	O	M	R	W			O	M	R	W	
Weeraratne	23	1	117	2	2nb		17	2	85	1	1w,2nb
Nayanakantha	17	2	63	0		(3)	2	0	20	0	
Jeewantha	20	3	85	2	2nb	(6)	7	0	29	3	
Vithana	20	5	60	4		(2)	13	0	49	1	
de Saram	3	1	7	0		(4)	8	2	27	0	1nb
Bandara	19	2	55	0		(5)	16	1	56	2	
Indrasiri	7	1	32	0			8	1	33	1	
W.D.D.S.Perera	1	1	0	0							

Bloomfield Bowling	O	M	R	W			O	M	R	W	
Gamage	14	4	41	0	1w,1nb	(2)	13	2	63	0	1w
Ranasinghe	15	4	34	2	3nb	(1)	6	0	47	1	3w
Dissanayake	35.3	10	83	6		(4)	29	4	125	4	
Jayasuriya	4	0	21	0		(5)	3	0	24	0	
Lakshitha	6	1	15	1	1nb	(3)	9	2	36	0	
Fernando						(6)	2	0	10	0	3nb
Masmulla						(7)	2	0	10	0	

Umpires: A.G.Dissanayake and P.G.Liyanage.   Referee: M.C.Mendis.   Toss: Bloomfield Cricket and Athletic Club

Close of Play: 1st day: Bloomfield Cricket and Athletic Club (1) 330-7 (de Silva 126*, Lakshitha 0*, 90 overs); 2nd day: Ragama Cricket Club (1) 185-8 (S.A.Perera 20*, Indrasiri 14*, 65 overs); 3rd day: Bloomfield Cricket and Athletic Club (2) 303-9 (Lakshitha 20*, Gamage 1*, 70.3 overs).
T.S.Masmulla's 121 took 142 balls and included 16 fours and 3 sixes. K.Y.de Silva's 164 took 274 balls and included 25 fours and 3 sixes.

COLOMBO CRICKET CLUB v SINHALESE SPORTS CLUB

Played at Colombo Cricket Club Ground, March 27, 28, 29, 30, 2008.
Premier Championship 2007/08 - Tier A
Match drawn.   (Points: Colombo Cricket Club 3.515, Sinhalese Sports Club 12.715)

SINHALESE SPORTS CLUB

#	Batsman	Dismissal 1	R	Dismissal 2	R
1	*N.T.Paranavitana	c sub (P.D.G.Chandrakumara) b Perera	236	(6) not out	80
2	S.H.Fernando	b Wethathasinghe	4	(1) lbw b Boralessa	27
3	†J.K.Silva	b Boralessa	24	c Polonowita b Perera	46
4	B.M.A.J.Mendis	b Mubarak	53	c Bandara b Boralessa	115
5	S.H.T.Kandamby	run out (Randika)	56	c sub (P.D.G.Chandrakumara) b Perera	26
6	E.D.J.Sriyapala	b de Silva	25	(2) c Kapugedera b Wethathasinghe	6
7	K.P.S.P.Karunanayake	c Ranaweera b Boralessa	15	c Ranaweera b Randika	9
8	S.M.Senanayake	b Perera	62	run out	0
9	R.D.Abeydeera	b Mubarak	9	b de Silva	19
10	C.W.Vidanapathirana	not out	11	lbw b de Silva	0
11	C.Gunasinghe	c Mubarak b Boralessa	0	c and b de Silva	0
	Extras	b 7, lb 6, w 1, nb 4	18	b 7, lb 5, w 2, nb 1	15
			513		**343**

FoW (1): 1-20 (2), 2-44 (3), 3-130 (4), 4-228 (5), 5-302 (6), 6-334 (7), 7-447 (8), 8-479 (9), 9-507 (1), 10-513 (11)
FoW (2): 1-28 (2), 2-39 (1), 3-133 (3), 4-201 (5), 5-250 (4), 6-259 (7), 7-260 (8), 8-333 (9), 9-343 (10), 10-343 (11)

COLOMBO CRICKET CLUB

#	Batsman	Dismissal 1	R	Dismissal 2	R
1	†D.K.Ranaweera	c Abeydeera b Vidanapathirana	0	not out	3
2	H.B.C.C.Bandara	c Silva b Karunanayake	0	not out	12
3	J.Mubarak	lbw b Senanayake	33		
4	A.S.Polonowita	c and b Abeydeera	68		
5	C.K.Kapugedera	c Kandamby b Senanayake	96		
6	*B.M.T.T.Mendis	c Paranavitana b Abeydeera	13		
7	K.G.N.Randika	c Paranavitana b Abeydeera	9		
8	A.C.Wethathasinghe	st Silva b Senanayake	20		
9	S.C.D.Boralessa	b Abeydeera	6		
10	M.P.N.L.Perera	not out	28		
11	W.R.S.de Silva	c Paranavitana b Abeydeera	1		
	Extras	b 5, lb 2, w 1, nb 4	12	w 2	2
			286	(no wicket)	**17**

FoW (1): 1-0 (2), 2-11 (1), 3-51 (3), 4-166 (4), 5-200 (6), 6-231 (5), 7-233 (7), 8-247 (9), 9-269 (8), 10-286 (11)

Colombo Cricket Club Bowling	O	M	R	W			O	M	R	W	
de Silva	18	3	65	1	1w,3nb		12.3	0	47	3	1w
Wethathasinghe	27	6	74	1			8	0	27	1	1w
Bandara	2	0	3	0							
Randika	9	4	24	0		(7)	9	1	23	1	1nb
Boralessa	28.3	1	101	3		(3)	24	2	83	2	
Perera	32	1	109	2			22	6	53	2	
Mubarak	35	1	115	2	1nb	(5)	25	3	92	0	
Kapugedera	1	0	9	0							
Polonowita						(4)	3	0	6	0	

Sinhalese Sports Club Bowling	O	M	R	W			O	M	R	W	
Vidanapathirana	14	1	69	1	1nb						
Karunanayake	4	0	25	1	1w,3nb						
Senanayake	27	5	96	3		(2)	1	0	1	0	
Gunasinghe	5	0	21	0							
Abeydeera	19	4	55	5							
Mendis	4	0	13	0							
Kandamby						(1)	4	1	9	0	
Silva						(3)	2	0	7	0	1w

Umpires: R.D.Kottahachchi and T.H.Wijewardene.   Referee: V.B.John.   Toss: Sinhalese Sports Club
Close of Play: 1st day: Sinhalese Sports Club (1) 301-4 (Paranavitana 125*, Sriyapala 24*, 90 overs); 2nd day: Colombo Cricket Club (1) 77-3 (Polonowita 29*, Kapugedera 11*, 17 overs); 3rd day: Sinhalese Sports Club (2) 73-2 (Silva 20*, Mendis 19*, 24 overs).
N.T.Paranavitana's 236 took 392 balls and included 21 fours. B.M.A.J.Mendis's 115 took 205 balls and included 13 fours and 2 sixes. N.T.Paranavitana retired hurt in the Sinhalese Sports Club first innings having scored 5 (team score 5-0) - he returned when the score was 44-2.

COLTS CRICKET CLUB v BADURELIYA SPORTS CLUB

Played at Colts Cricket Club Ground, Colombo, March 27, 28, 29, 30, 2008.
Premier Championship 2007/08 - Tier A
Colts Cricket Club won by an innings and 57 runs.   (Points: Colts Cricket Club 18, Badureliya Sports Club 3.235)

BADURELIYA SPORTS CLUB

1	†D.W.A.N.D.Vitharana	c Kulatunga b Perera	79	(8) c Weerakoon b Perera	15
2	M.M.D.P.V.Perera	c Janoda b Prasad	31	(1) c Janoda b Perera	12
3	K.Vasudevadas	c Attanayake b Weerakoon	28	(4) st Peiris b Weerakoon	38
4	*R.P.A.H.Wickramaratne	c Peiris b Mathews	3	(6) c Pathirana b Prasad	3
5	X.T.Sargunam	b Weerakoon	18	(3) c Perera b Weerakoon	19
6	D.N.Hunukumbura	b Perera	3	(2) st Peiris b Perera	84
7	R.M.A.R.Ratnayake	c Mathews b Weerakoon	24	c Perera b Weerakoon	4
8	M.R.C.N.Bandaratilleke	b Weerakoon	6	(9) c Mathews b Perera	1
9	W.J.S.D.Perera	run out (Perera)	19	(5) st Peiris b Perera	31
10	K.L.S.L.Dias	not out	8	(11) not out	1
11	S.D.C.Malinga	lbw b Weerakoon	4	(10) c and b Perera	4
	Extras	lb 2	2	lb 10	10
			225		**222**

FoW (1): 1-53 (2), 2-106 (3), 3-115 (4), 4-154 (1), 5-162 (5), 6-162 (6), 7-187 (8), 8-194 (7), 9-218 (9), 10-225 (11)
FoW (2): 1-30 (1), 2-69 (3), 3-134 (4), 4-172 (2), 5-175 (6), 6-198 (7), 7-205 (5), 8-215 (9), 9-221 (10), 10-222 (8)

COLTS CRICKET CLUB

1	T.P.Attanayake	lbw b Dias	4
2	S.Kalavitigoda	lbw b Dias	8
3	M.D.K.Perera	c Sargunam b Dias	48
4	A.D.Mathews	st Vasudevadas b Wickramaratne	157
5	D.N.Pathirana	lbw b Dias	92
6	S.Weerakoon	c sub (D.M.Gunathilake) b Sargunam	83
7	*H.G.J.M.Kulatunga	c sub (T.M.N.Sampath) b Wickramaratne	56
8	K.A.S.Jayasinghe	c sub (U.R.P.Perera) b Wickramaratne	11
9	†T.R.Peiris	not out	6
10	J.G.A.Janoda	c Malinga b Sargunam	15
11	U.M.A.Prasad	b Dias	0
	Extras	b 9, lb 3, w 4, nb 8	24
			504

FoW (1): 1-12 (1), 2-36 (2), 3-98 (3), 4-290 (5), 5-389 (4), 6-472 (7), 7-472 (6), 8-484 (8), 9-503 (10), 10-504 (11)

Colts Bowling	O	M	R	W		O	M	R	W
Mathews	15	4	37	1		8	1	22	0
Janoda	3	0	21	0					
Perera	27	6	68	2		19	1	86	6
Prasad	7	0	20	1	(2)	12	0	49	1
Kulatunga	4	2	3	0					
Weerakoon	24.2	5	58	5	(4)	14	2	45	3
Pathirana	4	0	16	0	(5)	3	0	10	0

Badureliya Bowling	O	M	R	W	
Malinga	16	2	76	0	2w,2nb
Ratnayake	20	1	89	0	1w,4nb
Dias	64.4	16	152	5	2nb
Bandaratilleke	18	3	42	0	
Vasudevadas	3	0	13	0	
W.J.S.D.Perera	7	0	17	0	1w
Wickramaratne	15	1	62	3	
M.M.D.P.V.Perera	2	0	14	0	
Sargunam	10	2	27	2	

Umpires: E.A.R.de Silva and B.B.J.Nandakumar. Referee: S.Ranatunga.   Toss: Badureliya Sports Club

Close of Play: 1st day: Colts Cricket Club (1) 21-1 (Kalavitigoda 6*, Perera 7*, 5 overs); 2nd day: Colts Cricket Club (1) 291-4 (Mathews 124*, Weerakoon 0*, 97 overs); 3rd day: Badureliya Sports Club (2) 135-3 (Hunukumbura 60*, W.J.S.D.Perera 0*, 29.4 overs).
A.D.Mathews's 157 took 364 balls and included 9 fours and 6 sixes. K.Vasudevadas kept wicket in the Colts innings.

NONDESCRIPTS CRICKET CLUB v CHILAW MARIANS CRICKET CLUB

Played at Nondescripts Cricket Club Ground, Colombo, March 27, 28, 29, 30, 2008.
Premier Championship 2007/08 - Tier A
Chilaw Marians Cricket Club won by four wickets. (Points: Nondescripts Cricket Club 4.275, Chilaw Marians Cricket Club 16.71)

NONDESCRIPTS CRICKET CLUB

1	W.U.Tharanga	b Perera	26	b Ramyakumara		0
2	K.D.Gunawardene	c Fernando b Ramyakumara	8	c Athulathmudali b Perera		66
3	W.L.P.Fernando	c Cooray b Perera	27	c Athulathmudali b Silva		109
4	C.G.Wijesinghe	b Hettiarachchi	9	(6) c Cooray b Ramyakumara		53
5	*M.K.Gajanayake	c Jansze b Silva	2	(7) c Ramyakumara b Silva		6
6	M.F.Maharoof	b Hettiarachchi	46	(8) c Siriwardene b Gunaratne		104
7	M.S.R.Wijeratne	c Cooray b Silva	3	(9) c and b Hettiarachchi		5
8	C.K.B.Kulasekara	c Cooray b Perera	3	(4) c Cooray b Udawatte		28
9	†M.R.D.G.Mapa Bandara	c Siriwardene b Silva	9	(10) lbw b Hettiarachchi		0
10	D.T.Kottehewa	lbw b Hettiarachchi	0	(5) lbw b Silva		12
11	N.C.Komasaru	not out	0	not out		6
	Extras	nb 2	2	b 1, lb 5, nb 10		16
			135			405

FoW (1): 1-17 (2), 2-60 (3), 3-71 (4), 4-71 (1), 5-85 (5), 6-89 (7), 7-102 (8), 8-135 (6), 9-135 (9), 10-135 (10)
FoW (2): 1-0 (1), 2-130 (2), 3-177 (4), 4-222 (3), 5-235 (5), 6-249 (7), 7-309 (6), 8-322 (9), 9-322 (10), 10-405 (8)

CHILAW MARIANS CRICKET CLUB

1	M.L.Udawatte	c Gajanayake b Kottehewa	0	(2) c Gunawardene b Komasaru	22
2	D.N.A.Athulathmudali	c Gunawardene b Gajanayake	23	(1) lbw b Gajanayake	9
3	†N.H.G.Cooray	st Mapa Bandara b Gajanayake	13	c Gunawardene b Gajanayake	3
4	A.P.Jansze	c Mapa Bandara b Kulasekara	32	c Komasaru b Maharoof	6
5	K.H.R.K.Fernando	c Mapa Bandara b Kulasekara	6	c and b Komasaru	44
6	W.M.G.Ramyakumara	c Wijesinghe b Gajanayake	64	not out	114
7	*L.J.P.Gunaratne	b Gajanayake	31	c Fernando b Komasaru	57
8	T.A.M.Siriwardene	c Mapa Bandara b Komasaru	17	not out	32
9	D.Hettiarachchi	c Mapa Bandara b Kulasekara	31		
10	G.A.C.R.Perera	c Wijeratne b Komasaru	8		
11	S.H.M.Silva	not out	1		
	Extras	b 4, lb 5, nb 5	14	b 6, lb 2, w 4, nb 3	15
			240	(6 wickets)	302

FoW (1): 1-0 (1), 2-40 (3), 3-49 (2), 4-56 (5), 5-112 (4), 6-172 (7), 7-193 (6), 8-207 (8), 9-234 (10), 10-240 (9)
FoW (2): 1-9 (1), 2-25 (3), 3-40 (2), 4-40 (4), 5-123 (5), 6-232 (7)

Chilaw Marians Bowling	O	M	R	W		O	M	R	W	
Ramyakumara	6	1	26	1		11	1	48	2	1nb
Fernando	6	0	27	0	(8)	3	0	10	0	
Perera	7	0	35	3	2nb	(2) 18	1	85	1	8nb
Hettiarachchi	8.1	3	15	3		(3) 41	9	107	2	
Silva	10	3	32	3		21	4	67	3	
Gunaratne						(4) 12.1	1	31	1	
Siriwardene						(6) 10	0	44	0	1nb
Udawatte						(7) 4	0	7	1	

Nondescripts Bowling	O	M	R	W		O	M	R	W	
Kottehewa	18	3	30	1	2nb	8	0	49	0	2w,2nb
Maharoof	10	3	38	0	3nb	(5) 7	0	37	1	2w,1nb
Gajanayake	22	3	57	4		(2) 19	5	73	2	
Kulasekara	14.3	2	45	3		8	1	29	0	
Komasaru	18	4	55	2		(3) 20	3	71	3	
Fernando	2	0	6	0		4	0	16	0	
Wijesinghe						(7) 2	0	13	0	
Gunawardene						(8) 1	0	6	0	

Umpires: W.A.Senanayake and M.G.Silva. Referee: G.F.Labrooy. Toss: Nondescripts Cricket Club
Close of Play: 1st day: Chilaw Marians Cricket Club (1) 130-5 (Ramyakumara 34*, Gunaratne 9*, 43 overs); 2nd day: Nondescripts Cricket Club (2) 179-3 (Fernando 79*, Kottehewa 0*, 46 overs); 3rd day: Chilaw Marians Cricket Club (2) 16-1 (Udawatte 7*, Cooray 0*, 6 overs).
W.L.P.Fernando's 109 took 189 balls and included 12 fours. M.F.Maharoof's 104 took 187 balls and included 12 fours and 2 sixes.
W.M.G.Ramyakumara's 114 took 142 balls and included 10 fours and 1 six.

TAMIL UNION CRICKET AND ATHLETIC CLUB v MOORS SPORTS CLUB

Played at P.Saravanamuttu Stadium, Colombo, March 27, 28, 29, 30, 2008.
Premier Championship 2007/08 - Tier A
Tamil Union Cricket and Athletic Club won by six wickets.   (Points: Tamil Union Cricket and Athletic Club 16.885, Moors Sports Club 4.28)

MOORS SPORTS CLUB

1	T.K.D.Sudarshana	c G.T.de Silva b Irandika	65	lbw b Lakmal	28
2	N.M.N.P.Nawela	c Rupasinghe b Irandika	39	lbw b Irandika	6
3	G.R.P.Peiris	lbw b Lakmal	3	c Perera b Maduwantha	1
4	W.M.B.Perera	b Irandika	26	c S.K.L.de Silva b Pushpakumara	40
5	J.W.H.D.Boteju	c Pushpakumara b Lakmal	100	c Perera b Lakmal	28
6	A.Rideegammanagedera	c Irandika b Pushpakumara	48	b Irandika	65
7	*L.H.D.Dilhara	c sub (T.R.Rasanga) b Lakmal	46	c Daniel b Maduwantha	1
8	A.S.A.Perera	c Maduwantha b Lakmal	24	c Pushpakumara b Maduwantha	0
9	†M.D.Randika	lbw b Maduwantha	1	c Irandika b Lakmal	10
10	C.R.B.Mudalige	not out	10	b Irandika	0
11	D.C.B.Keerthisinghe	lbw b Maduwantha	14	not out	0
	Extras	b 6, lb 4, w 1, nb 9	20	nb 1	1
			396		**180**

FoW (1): 1-113 (1), 2-118 (2), 3-118 (3), 4-164 (4), 5-284 (6), 6-325 (5), 7-364 (7), 8-366 (9), 9-376 (8), 10-396 (11)
FoW (2): 1-19 (2), 2-20 (3), 3-74 (4), 4-84 (1), 5-149 (5), 6-155 (7), 7-155 (8), 8-180 (6), 9-180 (10), 10-180 (9)

TAMIL UNION CRICKET AND ATHLETIC CLUB

1	†G.T.de Silva	c sub (A.M.L.Perera) b Keerthisinghe	55	lbw b Mudalige	32
2	G.I.Daniel	c Mudalige b Dilhara	44	c Mudalige b Dilhara	53
3	S.I.Fernando	c Boteju b Mudalige	76	c Nawela b Mudalige	17
4	S.K.L.de Silva	c Randika b Dilhara	59	not out	75
5	R.J.M.G.M.Rupasinghe	lbw b Mudalige	9	c A.S.A.Perera b Mudalige	3
6	M.Pushpakumara	c Nawela b Rideegammanagedera	30	not out	24
7	K.M.Fernando	not out	49		
8	*H.M.Maduwantha	c sub (W.M.J.Wannakuwatta) b Dilhara	9		
9	N.K.M.Perera	c Randika b Mudalige	1		
10	R.A.S.Lakmal	c and b Keerthisinghe	2		
11	P.L.U.Irandika	lbw b Mudalige	7		
	Extras	b 7, lb 3, w 11, nb 5	26	lb 3, w 2, nb 1	6
			367	**(4 wickets)**	**210**

FoW (1): 1-112 (1), 2-164 (2), 3-223 (3), 4-240 (5), 5-288 (6), 6-302 (4), 7-318 (8), 8-335 (9), 9-344 (10), 10-367 (11)
FoW (2): 1-50 (1), 2-84 (3), 3-143 (2), 4-161 (5)

Tamil Union Cricket and Athletic Club Bowling

	O	M	R	W			O	M	R	W	
Lakmal	22	3	100	4	7nb		14.1	1	49	3	
Perera	6	1	9	0	1w		1	0	5	0	
Maduwantha	23.2	3	77	2		(4)	14	1	51	3	1nb
Irandika	29	0	125	3		(3)	14	2	47	3	
Pushpakumara	11	1	57	1			9	1	24	1	
Rupasinghe	1	0	12	0	2nb						
K.M.Fernando	1	0	6	0		(6)	2	0	4	0	

Moors Sports Club Bowling

	O	M	R	W			O	M	R	W	
Dilhara	26	4	69	3	5nb		15	0	68	1	1w,1nb
Rideegammanagedera	14.5	1	69	1			7	0	28	0	1w
Mudalige	40	9	100	4	1w		12	0	69	3	
A.S.A.Perera	2	0	12	0	2w	(5)	1.2	0	9	0	
Keerthisinghe	29.1	6	86	2							
Boteju	8	2	21	0	3w						
W.M.B.Perera						(4)	5	0	33	0	

Umpires: H.D.P.K.Dharmasena and I.D.Gunawardene. Referee: B.C.Cooray. Toss: Moors Sports Club
Close of Play: 1st day: Moors Sports Club (1) 382-9 (Mudalige 7*, Keerthisinghe 4*, 90 overs); 2nd day: Tamil Union Cricket and Athletic Club (1) 262-4 (S.K.L.de Silva 42*, Pushpakumara 16*, 85 overs); 3rd day: Moors Sports Club (2) 134-4 (Boteju 23*, Rideegammanagedera 36*, 39 overs).
J.W.H.D.Boteju's 100 took 145 balls and included 11 fours and 1 six.

JAMAICA v LEEWARD ISLANDS

Played at Sabina Park, Kingston, January 4, 5, 6, 2008.
Carib Beer Cup 2007/08
Jamaica won by five wickets.   (Points: Jamaica 12, Leeward Islands 0)

LEEWARD ISLANDS

1	J.S.Liburd	lbw b Brown	43	lbw b Brown	8
2	M.V.Hodge	c Bernard b Russell	6	c and b Brown	64
3	S.S.W.Liburd	lbw b Bernard	5	c and b Miller	28
4	T.A.Willett	c Marshall b Brown	53	(5) run out	19
5	*O.A.C.Banks	c Bernard b Brown	2	(4) c Lambert b Brown	11
6	†D.C.Thomas	c and b Brown	5	c Brown b Miller	1
7	M.Pipe	c Bernard b Miller	7	c Bernard b Miller	4
8	L.S.Baker	b Brown	5	c Russell b Brown	0
9	A.Sanford	c Baugh b Miller	2	not out	20
10	G.C.Tonge	c Hibbert b Miller	4	c and b Miller	1
11	A.Martin	not out	8	c Hinds b Brown	11
	Extras	lb 1, nb 14	15	lb 4, nb 12	16
			155		**183**

FoW (1): 1-21 (2), 2-40 (3), 3-80 (1), 4-82 (5), 5-94 (6), 6-109 (7), 7-133 (8), 8-139 (9), 9-145 (10), 10-155 (4)
FoW (2): 1-31 (1), 2-67 (3), 3-93 (4), 4-133 (5), 5-136 (6), 6-140 (7), 7-144 (8), 8-165 (2), 9-172 (10), 10-183 (11)

JAMAICA

1	X.M.Marshall	c Hodge b Sanford	53	c Baker b Tonge	0
2	K.H.Hibbert	c Thomas b Baker	18	c J.S.Liburd b Sanford	1
3	B.P.Nash	b Banks	4	c Thomas b Tonge	2
4	A.D.Russell	c Thomas b Sanford	15		
5	W.W.Hinds	c Tonge b Banks	0	(4) c S.S.W.Liburd b Martin	62
6	*T.L.Lambert	c and b Martin	36	(5) c Willett b Tonge	4
7	D.E.Bernard	not out	46	(6) not out	26
8	†C.S.Baugh	b Tonge	15	(7) not out	8
9	N.O.Miller	lbw b Martin	1		
10	O.V.Brown	lbw b Martin	2		
11	J.J.C.Lawson	lbw b Banks	6		
	Extras	b 10, lb 6, nb 12	28	b 5, lb 2, nb 5	12
			224	(5 wickets)	**115**

FoW (1): 1-48 (2), 2-58 (3), 3-90 (4), 4-91 (5), 5-115 (1), 6-172 (6), 7-199 (8), 8-202 (9), 9-208 (10), 10-224 (11)
FoW (2): 1-5 (2), 2-7 (1), 3-8 (3), 4-20 (5), 5-102 (4)

Jamaica Bowling

	O	M	R	W			O	M	R	W
Lawson	6	0	41	0	7nb		4	0	21	0
Russell	11	3	25	1	5nb		9	1	30	0
Bernard	10	3	15	1	2nb					
Miller	20	5	42	3			38	18	43	4
Brown	21.1	7	31	5		(3)	28.4	8	72	5
Lambert						(5)	3	0	3	0
Nash						(6)	4	2	10	0

Leeward Islands Bowling

	O	M	R	W			O	M	R	W
Sanford	17	4	57	2			7.3	2	20	1
Tonge	8	1	35	1			7	1	24	3
Baker	10	0	35	1			1	0	6	0
Martin	19	6	31	3		(5)	5	1	27	1
Banks	15.4	3	50	3		(6)	4	2	12	0
Willett						(4)	6	2	19	0

Umpires: A.L.Farrell and N.A.Malcolm.   Toss: Leeward Islands

Close of Play: 1st day: Jamaica (1) 59-2 (Marshall 27*, Russell 0*, 21 overs); 2nd day: Leeward Islands (2) 87-2 (Hodge 32*, Banks 9*, 40 overs).

Man of the Match: O.V.Brown.
The match was scheduled for four days but completed in three.

TRINIDAD AND TOBAGO v GUYANA

Played at Queen's Park Oval, Port of Spain, January 4, 5, 6, 7, 2008.
Carib Beer Cup 2007/08
Trinidad and Tobago won by nine wickets.   **(Points: Trinidad and Tobago 12, Guyana 0)**

GUYANA

1	S.Chattergoon	c Lara b D.Mohammed	130	c Simmons b Kelly	4
2	T.M.Dowlin	b Kelly	18	lbw b Emrit	28
3	L.R.Johnson	lbw b Jaggernauth	43	c G.Mohammed b Emrit	10
4	N.Deonarine	c Pollard b Jaggernauth	0	c Lara b Jaggernauth	46
5	*R.R.Sarwan	c Pollard b Kelly	63	not out	105
6	A.B.Fudadin	c Lara b D.Mohammed	43	c Emrit b Jaggernauth	18
7	†D.O.Christian	c G.Mohammed b Rampaul	0	c Kelly b Jaggernauth	2
8	E.A.Crandon	c D.Mohammed b Jaggernauth	20	c G.Mohammed b Jaggernauth	13
9	Z.Mohamed	c Kelly b Jaggernauth	1	c sub (J.C.Guillen) b Jaggernauth	8
10	V.Permaul	c G.Mohammed b D.Mohammed	4	lbw b D.Mohammed	5
11	B.J.Bess	not out	0	lbw b D.Mohammed	0
	Extras	b 1, lb 2, nb 9	12	b 1, lb 2, nb 7	10
			334		249

FoW (1): 1-36 (2), 2-125 (3), 3-125 (4), 4-251 (1), 5-267 (5), 6-268 (7), 7-322 (8), 8-324 (9), 9-329 (10), 10-334 (6)
FoW (2): 1-15 (1), 2-43 (2), 3-48 (3), 4-122 (4), 5-184 (6), 6-188 (7), 7-209 (8), 8-229 (9), 9-249 (10), 10-249 (11)

TRINIDAD AND TOBAGO

1	L.M.P.Simmons	c Permaul b Mohamed	25	lbw b Permaul	62
2	A.B.Barath	c and b Mohamed	36	not out	57
3	B.C.Lara	c and b Permaul	123	not out	53
4	D.M.Bravo	c Fudadin b Permaul	32		
5	K.A.Pollard	c Christian b Bess	85		
6	*R.R.Emrit	c Fudadin b Mohamed	0		
7	†G.Mohammed	c and b Sarwan	18		
8	R.A.Kelly	not out	30		
9	D.Mohammed	c Christian b Crandon	4		
10	R.Rampaul	c and b Mohamed	8		
11	A.S.Jaggernauth	c Mohamed b Crandon	4		
	Extras	b 8, lb 4, nb 24	36	b 5, lb 2, w 2, nb 4	13
			401	(1 wicket)	185

FoW (1): 1-64 (1), 2-91 (2), 3-187 (4), 4-293 (3), 5-312 (6), 6-340 (5), 7-359 (7), 8-373 (9), 9-391 (10), 10-401 (11)
FoW (2): 1-106 (1)

Trinidad and Tobago Bowling	O	M	R	W		O	M	R	W	
Rampaul	20	1	76	1	5nb	11	1	70	0	3nb
Kelly	20	6	57	2	3nb	16	2	65	1	
Emrit	13	3	35	0	1nb	7	2	35	2	4nb
Jaggernauth	34	7	84	4	(5)	18	3	52	5	
D.Mohammed	25.2	4	59	3	(4)	8	2	24	2	
Pollard	3	0	20	0						

Guyana Bowling	O	M	R	W		O	M	R	W	
Crandon	21.2	3	74	2	2nb	4	0	38	0	
Bess	17	3	102	1	22nb	4	1	13	0	2w,2nb
Mohamed	28	5	78	4		5	0	35	0	
Permaul	27	3	100	2		10	0	59	1	1nb
Deonarine	4	0	27	0		3	0	12	0	
Sarwan	1	0	8	1		3	0	16	0	
Johnson					(7)	0.1	0	5	0	1nb

Umpires: T.Birbal and V.Weekes.   Toss: Guyana

Close of Play: 1st day: Guyana (1) 267-4 (Sarwan 63*, Fudadin 4*, 88 overs); 2nd day: Trinidad and Tobago (1) 273-3 (Lara 115*, Pollard 41*, 66 overs); 3rd day: Guyana (2) 128-4 (Sarwan 31*, Fudadin 0*, 26 overs).

Man of the Match: B.C.Lara.

S.Chattergoon's 130 took 237 balls in 310 minutes and included 16 fours. B.C.Lara's 123 took 200 balls in 231 minutes and included 13 fours. R.R.Sarwan's 105 took 142 balls in 224 minutes and included 12 fours and 1 six.

WINDWARD ISLANDS v BARBADOS

Played at Arnos Vale Ground, Kingstown, St Vincent, January 4, 5, 6, 2008.
Carib Beer Cup 2007/08
Barbados won by nine wickets.   (Points: Windward Islands 0, Barbados 12)

WINDWARD ISLANDS

1	H.D.Campbell	c Morris b Collymore	9	lbw b Best	7
2	M.C.Bascombe	c Smith b Roach	5	lbw b Best	20
3	A.D.S.Fletcher	c Roach b Hinds	24	c Morris b Roach	14
4	H.C.R.Shallow	retired hurt	30	c Morris b Smith	14
5	D.B.Hector	run out	19	(6) run out	14
6	L.A.S.Sebastien	c Richards b Benn	68	(5) c Smith b Benn	18
7	†L.O.D.James	c Morris b Smith	7	not out	56
8	S.Shillingford	c Brooks b Benn	2	lbw b Benn	1
9	*D.K.Butler	c Richards b Benn	9	c sub b Hinds	3
10	M.Matthew	not out	0	b Smith	24
11	N.T.Pascal	lbw b Benn	0	lbw b Smith	0
	Extras	lb 8, nb 9	17	b 6, lb 3, nb 13	22
			190		193

FoW (1): 1-15 (1), 2-21 (2), 3-75 (3), 4-122 (5), 5-146 (7), 6-151 (8), 7-183 (6), 8-190 (9), 9-190 (11)
FoW (2): 1-22 (1), 2-35 (2), 3-55 (4), 4-73 (3), 5-87 (5), 6-104 (6), 7-113 (8), 8-131 (9), 9-193 (10), 10-193 (11)

BARBADOS

1	D.M.Richards	b Pascal	30	c Fletcher b Shillingford	80
2	J.A.M.Haynes	c Hector b Pascal	1	not out	36
3	D.R.Smith	lbw b Pascal	13	not out	26
4	R.O.Hinds	not out	95		
5	A.R.Holder	c Campbell b Pascal	10		
6	S.S.J.Brooks	b Shillingford	11		
7	†C.A.Morris	lbw b Shillingford	13		
8	S.J.Benn	b Sebastien	7		
9	T.L.Best	c Campbell b Butler	39		
10	K.A.J.Roach	c Hector b Shillingford	16		
11	*C.D.Collymore	c James b Shillingford	0		
	Extras	b 2, lb 4, nb 5	11		
			246	(1 wicket)	142

FoW (1): 1-19 (2), 2-38 (1), 3-52 (3), 4-74 (5), 5-111 (6), 6-131 (7), 7-142 (8), 8-210 (9), 9-246 (10), 10-246 (11)
FoW (2): 1-111 (1)

Barbados Bowling

	O	M	R	W		O	M	R	W	
Collymore	11	4	26	1		4	2	16	0	
Best	10	4	14	0	1nb	11	2	31	2	4nb
Roach	7	1	40	1	5nb	10.4	4	31	1	4nb
Smith	10	2	40	1	3nb	16.5	6	41	3	2nb
Benn	22.4	11	30	4		27	11	47	2	
Hinds	5	1	8	1		10	2	18	1	3nb
Brooks	5	0	24	0						

Windward Islands Bowling

	O	M	R	W			O	M	R	W	
Pascal	14.3	0	70	4	5nb		4	0	25	0	
Butler	13	2	49	1			4	0	17	0	
Matthew	6	1	20	0							
Shillingford	24.2	6	60	4		(3)	10	1	29	1	
Sebastien	18	2	35	1		(4)	8.4	0	60	0	
Fletcher	3	0	6	0		(5)	2	0	11	0	

Umpires: K.R.Davis-Whyttle and C.R.Duncan.   Toss: Barbados

Close of Play: 1st day: Barbados (1) 64-3 (Hinds 11*, Holder 2*, 17 overs); 2nd day: Windward Islands (2) 58-3 (Fletcher 8*, Sebastien 0*, 26 overs).
Man of the Match: R.O.Hinds.
The match was scheduled for four days but completed in three. H.C.R.Shallow retired hurt in the Windward Islands first innings having scored 30 (team score 76-3).

BARBADOS v GUYANA

Played at Kensington Oval, Bridgetown, January 11, 12, 13, 14, 2008.
Carib Beer Cup 2007/08
Barbados won by an innings and 57 runs.   (Points: Barbados 12, Guyana 0)

GUYANA

1	T.M.Dowlin	lbw b Roach	37	c Brooks b Roach	7
2	R.T.Crandon	c Morris b Best	0	c Morris b Roach	1
3	L.R.Johnson	c Hinds b Roach	19	c Holder b Benn	36
4	N.Deonarine	c Brooks b Roach	19	c Haynes b Benn	48
5	*R.R.Sarwan	c Hinds b Benn	55	c Richards b Benn	82
6	A.B.Fudadin	c Richards b Hinds	14	c Morris b Hinds	33
7	†D.O.Christian	c Brooks b Hinds	20	c Holder b Smith	39
8	E.A.Crandon	c Morris b Benn	6	lbw b Smith	3
9	Z.Mohamed	c Smith b Hinds	0	b Smith	21
10	V.Permaul	lbw b Hinds	0	c Hinds b Benn	2
11	J.O.A.Gordon	not out	0	not out	5
	Extras	b 2, lb 7, nb 6	15	lb 2, w 2, nb 8	12
			185		289

FoW (1): 1-12 (2), 2-42 (3), 3-74 (4), 4-89 (1), 5-144 (6), 6-178 (5), 7-178 (7), 8-178 (9), 9-184 (10), 10-185 (8)
FoW (2): 1-7 (1), 2-8 (2), 3-83 (4), 4-122 (3), 5-209 (6), 6-219 (5), 7-247 (8), 8-270 (7), 9-273 (10), 10-289 (9)

BARBADOS

1	D.M.Richards	b Mohamed	24
2	J.A.M.Haynes	c R.T.Crandon b Johnson	111
3	D.R.Smith	c Sarwan b Gordon	1
4	R.O.Hinds	lbw b E.A.Crandon	108
5	A.R.Holder	c Gordon b Permaul	58
6	S.S.J.Brooks	c Johnson b E.A.Crandon	39
7	†C.A.Morris	c and b Sarwan	70
8	S.J.Benn	not out	58
9	T.L.Best	st Christian b Mohamed	0
10	K.A.J.Roach	c Johnson b Sarwan	14
11	*C.D.Collymore	c Johnson b Deonarine	16
	Extras	b 10, lb 11, w 1, nb 10	32
			531

FoW (1): 1-42 (1), 2-43 (3), 3-255 (2), 4-263 (4), 5-349 (5), 6-381 (6), 7-472 (7), 8-473 (9), 9-514 (10), 10-531 (11)

Barbados Bowling	O	M	R	W			O	M	R	W	
Collymore	12	5	19	0		(3)	4	2	5	0	
Best	12	2	45	1	1nb	(1)	15	1	50	0	2nb
Roach	10	2	30	3	3nb	(2)	15	3	43	2	1w,1nb
Smith	11	6	24	0	1nb		18.3	4	66	3	1w,1nb
Benn	9.2	2	44	2		(6)	36	6	96	4	1nb
Hinds	8	3	14	4	1nb	(5)	18	5	26	1	3nb
Holder						(7)	2	1	1	0	

Guyana Bowling	O	M	R	W	
E.A.Crandon	26	4	125	2	1w
Gordon	17.4	2	86	1	9nb
Mohamed	22	3	90	2	
Permaul	27	2	88	1	
Deonarine	18.4	3	64	1	
R.T.Crandon	3	0	12	0	
Johnson	4	0	17	1	1nb
Sarwan	11.2	3	28	2	

Umpires: A.N.H.Corbin and C.E.Mack.   Referee: C.S.Brome.   Toss: Barbados

Close of Play: 1st day: Barbados (1) 58-2 (Haynes 22*, Hinds 11*, 21 overs); 2nd day: Barbados (1) 256-3 (Hinds 101*, Holder 0*, 77 overs); 3rd day: Guyana (2) 85-3 (Johnson 21*, Sarwan 2*, 35 overs).

Man of the Match: R.O.Hinds.
J.A.M.Haynes's 111 took 205 balls in 319 minutes and included 11 fours. R.O.Hinds's 108 took 226 balls in 256 minutes and included 13 fours.

JAMAICA v COMBINED CAMPUSES AND COLLEGES

Played at Kensington Park, Kingston, January 11, 12, 13, 2008.
Carib Beer Cup 2007/08
Jamaica won by ten wickets.   **(Points: Jamaica 12, Combined Campuses and Colleges 0)**

COMBINED CAMPUSES AND COLLEGES

1	R.K.Currency	b Lawson	0	(4) lbw b Lambert	1
2	S.Jackson	run out	31	c Baugh b Miller	49
3	K.J.Wilkinson	c Baugh b Nash	34	(6) lbw b Lambert	11
4	F.L.Reifer	lbw b Nash	0	(5) lbw b Lambert	4
5	N.Parris	b Brown	18	(3) b Brown	75
6	†C.A.K.Walton	lbw b Miller	2	(7) c Baugh b Brown	9
7	*S.M.Clarke	c Russell b Brown	4	(1) lbw b Miller	11
8	J.Robinson	c Baugh b Brown	0	c Hinds b Brown	9
9	J.P.Bennett	c Nash b Miller	1	c Hibbert b Miller	22
10	K.Kantasingh	c Hibbert b Brown	0	c Hibbert b Miller	3
11	J.Noel	not out	0	not out	4
	Extras	lb 3, nb 6	9	b 1, lb 4, w 2, nb 8	15
			99		**213**

FoW (1): 1-0 (1), 2-53 (3), 3-53 (4), 4-91 (2), 5-93 (6), 6-98 (7), 7-98 (5), 8-99 (8), 9-99 (10), 10-99 (9)
FoW (2): 1-25 (1), 2-116 (2), 3-127 (4), 4-147 (5), 5-161 (3), 6-163 (6), 7-183 (7), 8-188 (8), 9-206 (9), 10-213 (10)

JAMAICA

1	X.M.Marshall	c Walton b Noel	69	not out	20
2	K.H.Hibbert	c Walton b Bennett	15	not out	8
3	*T.L.Lambert	lbw b Bennett	30		
4	A.D.Russell	b Noel	33		
5	W.W.Hinds	c Clarke b Kantasingh	87		
6	B.P.Nash	c Clarke b Noel	22		
7	D.E.Bernard	lbw b Noel	8		
8	†C.S.Baugh	run out (Wilkinson)	6		
9	N.O.Miller	c Wilkinson b Kantasingh	2		
10	O.V.Brown	lbw b Kantasingh	1		
11	J.J.C.Lawson	not out	0		
	Extras	lb 3, w 2, nb 8	13		
			286	(no wicket)	**28**

FoW (1): 1-30 (2), 2-98 (3), 3-152 (4), 4-163 (1), 5-248 (6), 6-264 (7), 7-280 (8), 8-283 (5), 9-285 (9), 10-286 (10)

Jamaica Bowling

	O	M	R	W		O	M	R	W	
Lawson	6	0	24	1		10	1	35	0	2w,8nb
Russell	5	2	11	0		2	0	4	0	
Bernard	7	1	20	0						
Nash	10	4	7	2	(5)	4	2	5	0	
Miller	13.2	3	20	2	(4)	31.4	10	65	4	
Brown	9	2	14	4	(3)	21	8	40	3	
Lambert					(6)	20	3	59	3	

Combined Campuses and Colleges Bowling

	O	M	R	W	O	M	R	W
Bennett	24	9	41	2	3.1	0	21	0
Noel	25	5	80	4	3	1	7	0
Robinson	8	1	61	0				
Wilkinson	6	2	16	0				
Kantasingh	28.3	8	55	3				
Clarke	13	2	30	0				

Umpires: C.Fletcher and W.Mitchum.   Toss: Jamaica

Close of Play: 1st day: Jamaica (1) 103-2 (Marshall 50*, Russell 0*, 37 overs); 2nd day: Combined Campuses and Colleges (2) 36-1 (Jackson 17*, Parris 3*, 16 overs).

Man of the Match: W.W.Hinds.

The match was scheduled for four days but completed in three.

WINDWARD ISLANDS v LEEWARD ISLANDS

Played at Queen's Park (New), St George's, Grenada, January 11, 12, 13, 14, 2008.
Carib Beer Cup 2007/08
Leeward Islands won by 34 runs.   (Points: Windward Islands 0, Leeward Islands 12)

LEEWARD ISLANDS

1	M.V.Hodge	run out (Shallow)	22	c James b Butler	21
2	J.S.Liburd	lbw b Shillingford	16	(3) lbw b George	36
3	S.S.W.Liburd	run out (Shallow)	26	(2) c Shillingford b Pascal	24
4	T.A.Willett	b Shillingford	12	b Sebastien	18
5	*O.A.C.Banks	c Hector b Pascal	8	(6) c James b Butler	57
6	†D.C.Thomas	c and b Shillingford	26	(5) run out	0
7	C.J.K.Hodge	c Shallow b Shillingford	7	c James b Butler	16
8	A.Sanford	c Fletcher b Shillingford	0	c George b Sebastien	1
9	L.S.Baker	c and b Shillingford	3	(11) not out	21
10	G.C.Tonge	c Fletcher b George	57	(9) c Butler b Sebastien	7
11	A.Martin	not out	14	(10) c and b Butler	1
	Extras	b 3, lb 4, w 1, nb 2	10	b 8, lb 4, w 1, nb 6	19
			201		221

FoW (1): 1-36 (1), 2-64, 3-79, 4-82, 5-106, 6-124, 7-125, 8-125, 9-130, 10-201
FoW (2): 1-21, 2-86, 3-94, 4-154, 5-154, 6-187, 7-192, 8-197, 9-212, 10-221

WINDWARD ISLANDS

1	M.C.Bascombe	c Thomas b Willett	42	lbw b Martin	30
2	H.D.Campbell	c Thomas b Sanford	8	lbw b Martin	48
3	A.D.S.Fletcher	run out	1	c S.S.W.Liburd b Willett	57
4	H.C.R.Shallow	c Willett b Sanford	13	c Willett b Banks	10
5	D.M.George	c Banks b C.J.K.Hodge	9	(10) c Thomas b Willett	7
6	L.A.S.Sebastien	lbw b Sanford	15	(8) not out	54
7	†L.O.D.James	c Martin b Banks	0	(6) c M.V.Hodge b Banks	0
8	S.Shillingford	c S.S.W.Liburd b C.J.K.Hodge	3	(7) c sub (M.Pipe) b Martin	11
9	D.B.Hector	c S.S.W.Liburd b Martin	18	(5) c Thomas b Willett	0
10	*D.K.Butler	c S.S.W.Liburd b Sanford	10	(9) b Willett	17
11	N.T.Pascal	not out	2	lbw b Willett	0
	Extras	b 4, lb 5, w 1, nb 3	13	b 6, lb 7, w 1, nb 6	20
			134		254

FoW (1): 1-41 (2), 2-45 (3), 3-61 (1), 4-77 (4), 5-93, 6-104, 7-104, 8-122, 9-122, 10-134
FoW (2): 1-57 (1), 2-123 (2), 3-140 (4), 4-164 (3), 5-166 (5), 6-167 (6), 7-190 (7), 8-233 (9), 9-252 (10), 10-254 (11)

Windward Islands Bowling

	O	M	R	W			O	M	R	W
Pascal	13	2	40	1	1w,1nb		7	0	30	1
Shillingford	27	9	66	6		(3)	17	3	33	0
Butler	9	2	28	0		(2)	22.4	9	50	4
George	18.4	3	60	1	1nb		11	3	34	1
Sebastien						(5)	23	5	62	3

Leeward Islands Bowling

	O	M	R	W			O	M	R	W
Sanford	17.4	7	34	4	1w		16	4	36	0
Tonge	1	0	12	0	2nb					
Baker	4	0	16	0		(2)	6	1	21	0
Willett	6	2	17	1			15	0	31	5
Banks	13	1	29	1	1nb		19	3	52	2
C.J.K.Hodge	6	1	16	2			8	5	13	0
Martin	3	2	1	1		(3)	33	10	78	3
S.S.W.Liburd						(7)	2	0	10	0

Umpires: D.O.Holder and I.Lorde.   Toss: Leeward Islands

Close of Play: 1st day: Windward Islands (1) 71-3 (Shallow 10*, George 0*, 20 overs); 2nd day: Leeward Islands (2) 179-5 (Banks 51*, C.J.K.Hodge 10*, 60 overs); 3rd day: Windward Islands (2) 183-6 (Shillingford 9*, Sebastien 16*, 69 overs).

Man of the Match: T.A.Willett.

COMBINED CAMPUSES AND COLLEGES v BARBADOS

Played at Three Ws Oval, Bridgetown, January 18, 19, 20, 2008.
Carib Beer Cup 2007/08
Combined Campuses and Colleges won by 24 runs. (Points: Combined Campuses and Colleges 12, Barbados 0)

COMBINED CAMPUSES AND COLLEGES

1	R.K.Currency	b Collins	2	(2) c Benn b Best	35
2	S.Jackson	c Morris b Collins	0	(1) c Benn b Best	24
3	K.J.Wilkinson	b Collins	0	(4) c Collymore b Benn	14
4	J.Smith	lbw b Collins	5	(3) b Best	0
5	F.L.Reifer	c Morris b Best	70	c Benn b Best	22
6	N.Parris	st Morris b Best	52	lbw b Benn	16
7	*S.M.Clarke	c Richards b Best	7	lbw b Best	20
8	†C.A.K.Walton	c Collymore b Benn	6	c Morris b Benn	0
9	J.P.Bennett	b Best	8	b Best	3
10	K.Kantasingh	not out	12	c Collymore b Benn	10
11	J.Noel	c Holder b Benn	14	not out	2
	Extras	b 8, lb 13, w 2, nb 3	26	b 6, lb 4, nb 3	13
			202		**159**

FoW (1): 1-5 (2), 2-7 (3), 3-16 (1), 4-17 (4), 5-140 (6), 6-158 (7), 7-159 (5), 8-169 (8), 9-173 (9), 10-202 (11)
FoW (2): 1-60 (1), 2-60 (3), 3-61 (2), 4-93 (4), 5-115 (5), 6-125 (6), 7-125 (8), 8-146, 9-153, 10-159

BARBADOS

1	D.M.Richards	lbw b Bennett	0	b Noel	6
2	J.A.M.Haynes	run out	17	b Bennett	25
3	S.S.J.Brooks	lbw b Bennett	0	(6) c Walton b Bennett	6
4	A.R.Holder	c Parris b Bennett	2	(5) b Bennett	28
5	T.L.Best	lbw b Bennett	4	(9) b Bennett	0
6	R.O.Hinds	c Walton b Bennett	35	(4) c Reifer b Smith	9
7	D.R.Smith	c Walton b Wilkinson	35	(3) lbw b Wilkinson	85
8	†C.A.Morris	c Clarke b Kantasingh	12	(7) b Kantasingh	12
9	S.J.Benn	not out	15	(8) lbw b Bennett	3
10	P.T.Collins	c Walton b Bennett	0	(11) not out	10
11	*C.D.Collymore	c Wilkinson b Clarke	16	(10) lbw b Kantasingh	0
	Extras	lb 2, nb 1	3	b 4, lb 10	14
			139		**198**

FoW (1): 1-0 (1), 2-0 (3), 3-10 (4), 4-14 (5), 5-29 (2), 6-84 (7), 7-107 (6), 8-109 (8), 9-109 (10), 10-139 (11)
FoW (2): 1-16 (1), 2-69 (2), 3-92 (4), 4-162 (3), 5-162 (5), 6-181 (7), 7-181 (6), 8-181 (9), 9-182 (10), 10-198 (8)

Barbados Bowling

	O	M	R	W		O	M	R	W	
Collins	18	6	30	4		9	1	38	0	2nb
Collymore	12	5	24	0	(3)	1	0	11	0	
Best	16	4	37	4	(2)	16	5	47	6	
Smith	11	4	38	0	2w,3nb					
Benn	14.3	4	39	2	(4)	22.5	6	50	4	
Hinds	6	2	13	0	(5)	3	1	3	0	1nb

Combined Campuses and Colleges Bowling

	O	M	R	W		O	M	R	W	
Bennett	21	5	59	6		17.4	5	46	5	
Noel	2	1	4	0	(3)	6	1	33	1	
Kantasingh	19	7	25	1	(2)	17	5	46	2	
Clarke	7.5	1	25	1	(6)	3	0	21	0	
Wilkinson	7	1	19	1	1nb (4)	7	0	25	1	
Smith	1	0	5	0	(5)	4	1	13	1	

Umpires: T.O.Franklyn and E.A.Nicholls. Referee: M.Jones.   Toss: Barbados

Close of Play: 1st day: Barbados (1) 15-4 (Haynes 6*, Hinds 1*, 10 overs); 2nd day: Combined Campuses and Colleges (2) 138-7 (Clarke 17*, Bennett 1*, 42 overs).

Man of the Match: J.P.Bennett.

The match was scheduled for four days but completed in three.

JAMAICA v GUYANA

Played at Sabina Park, Kingston, January 18, 19, 20, 2008.
Carib Beer Cup 2007/08
Jamaica won by eight wickets.   **(Points: Jamaica 12, Guyana 0)**

GUYANA

1	T.M.Dowlin	c Marshall b Richardson	0	(6) run out		10
2	G.Singh	c Pagon b Lawson	5	lbw b Lawson		2
3	L.R.Johnson	c Baugh b Bernard	19	c Marshall b Lawson		73
4	N.Deonarine	c Brown b Lawson	39	c Pagon b Miller		14
5	*R.R.Sarwan	c Lambert b Richardson	9	lbw b Bernard		0
6	A.B.Fudadin	c Baugh b Lawson	13	(1) run out		31
7	†D.O.Christian	c Baugh b Miller	34	c Baugh b Brown		13
8	E.A.Crandon	b Lambert	11	c Lambert b Brown		0
9	Z.Mohamed	b Lawson	26	st Baugh b Brown		21
10	V.Permaul	b Lawson	11	b Lawson		0
11	T.C.Garraway	not out	0	not out		1
	Extras	lb 1, nb 3	4	b 1, w 1, nb 10		12
			171			**177**

FoW (1): 1-1 (1), 2-6 (2), 3-29 (3), 4-47 (5), 5-77 (6), 6-90 (4), 7-121 (8), 8-148 (7), 9-170 (9), 10-171 (10)
FoW (2): 1-9 (2), 2-79 (1), 3-96 (4), 4-99 (5), 5-108 (6), 6-133 (7), 7-133 (8), 8-171 (9), 9-176 (3), 10-177 (10)

JAMAICA

1	X.M.Marshall	b Crandon	0	not out		48
2	D.J.Pagon	b Garraway	0	c Dowlin b Crandon		4
3	*T.L.Lambert	c Sarwan b Garraway	9	c Christian b Garraway		1
4	W.W.Hinds	c sub (R.T.Crandon) b Garraway	53	not out		50
5	B.P.Nash	not out	91			
6	D.E.Bernard	c Johnson b Permaul	12			
7	†C.S.Baugh	lbw b Mohamed	0			
8	N.O.Miller	st Christian b Permaul	34			
9	O.V.Brown	c Johnson b Permaul	2			
10	J.J.C.Lawson	c Sarwan b Permaul	0			
11	A.P.Richardson	b Garraway	22			
	Extras	b 7, lb 2, nb 8	17	b 4, lb 1, nb 1		6
			240	**(2 wickets)**		**109**

FoW (1): 1-0 (1), 2-0 (2), 3-28 (3), 4-83 (4), 5-105 (6), 6-106 (7), 7-187 (8), 8-193 (9), 9-195 (10), 10-240 (11)
FoW (2): 1-10 (2), 2-11 (3)

Jamaica Bowling

	O	M	R	W		O	M	R	W
Lawson	12	1	41	5		17.4	1	61	3
Richardson	10	3	20	2		4	0	16	0
Bernard	12	3	22	1		13	2	33	1
Nash	4	2	6	0					
Miller	14	8	25	1	(4)	25	12	29	1
Brown	14	1	52	0	(5)	16	4	35	3
Lambert	1	0	4	1	(6)	2	1	2	0

Guyana Bowling

	O	M	R	W		O	M	R	W
Crandon	15	1	46	1		6	2	8	1
Garraway	13.3	2	45	4	7nb	6	1	14	1
Mohamed	18	2	36	1	(4)	6	0	40	0
Permaul	22	3	75	4	(3)	3	0	24	0
Deonarine	11	4	16	0		3.4	0	18	0
Sarwan	1	0	6	0					
Johnson	3	1	7	0	1nb				

Umpires: V.V.Bullen and M.A.Chung.   Toss: Guyana

Close of Play: 1st day: Jamaica (1) 56-3 (Hinds 37*, Nash 4*, 21 overs); 2nd day: Guyana (2) 59-1 (Fudadin 25*, Johnson 28*, 27 overs).
Man of the Match: B.P.Nash.
The match was scheduled for four days but completed in three.

LEEWARD ISLANDS v TRINIDAD AND TOBAGO

Played at Carib Lumber Ball Park, Philipsburg, St Maarten, January 18, 19, 20, 21, 2008.
Carib Beer Cup 2007/08
Match drawn.   (Points: Leeward Islands 4, Trinidad and Tobago 4)

TRINIDAD AND TOBAGO

1	L.M.P.Simmons	lbw b Martin	47
2	A.B.Barath	c Martin b Baker	2
3	B.C.Lara	retired hurt	9
4	D.M.Bravo	hit wkt b Sanford	0
5	K.A.Pollard	b C.J.K.Hodge	7
6	†G.Mohammed	not out	43
7	*R.R.Emrit	not out	56
8	S.Badree		
9	R.A.Kelly		
10	D.Mohammed		
11	A.S.Jaggernauth		
	Extras	b 2, lb 5, w 1, nb 6	14
		(4 wickets)	178

FoW (1): 1-14 (2), 2-29 (4), 3-47 (5), 4-87 (6)

LEEWARD ISLANDS

1	*O.A.C.Banks
2	M.V.Hodge
3	J.S.Liburd
4	S.S.W.Liburd
5	T.A.Willett
6	C.J.K.Hodge
7	A.Martin
8	L.S.Baker
9	B.A.DeFreitas
10	A.Sanford
11	†D.C.Thomas

Leeward Islands Bowling

	O	M	R	W	
Sanford	9	3	19	1	
Baker	10	2	34	1	5nb
C.J.K.Hodge	12	2	43	1	
Willett	8	0	33	0	1nb
Martin	6	0	21	1	
Banks	10	1	21	0	

Umpires: G.E.Greaves and A.L.Kelly.   Toss: Leeward Islands

Close of Play: 1st day: Trinidad and Tobago (1) 166-4 (G.Mohammed 38*, Emrit 49*, 49 overs); 2nd day: Trinidad and Tobago (1) 178-4 (G.Mohammed 43*, Emrit 56*, 55 overs); 3rd day: No play.

Man of the Match: No award made.

There was no play on the final day. B.C.Lara retired hurt in the Trinidad and Tobago first innings having scored 9 (team score 29-1). His arm was fractured by a ball from Baker.

LEEWARD ISLANDS v BARBADOS

Played at Salem Oval, Montserrat, February 29, March 1, 2, 3, 2008.
Carib Beer Cup 2007/08
Match drawn.   (Points: Leeward Islands 3, Barbados 6)

LEEWARD ISLANDS

1	A.C.L.Richards	b Benn	45
2	J.S.Liburd	b Hinds	14
3	*R.S.Morton	c Benn b Collins	137
4	T.A.Willett	c Richards b Benn	18
5	M.V.Hodge	c Browne b Hinds	4
6	S.S.W.Liburd	c Carter b Collins	17
7	†J.N.Hamilton	lbw b Collins	23
8	C.J.K.Hodge	c Richards b Hinds	0
9	L.S.Baker	not out	5
10	A.Martin	b Collins	5
11	A.Sanford	lbw b Collins	0
	Extras	b 8, lb 4, w 1, nb 14	27
			295

FoW (1): 1-126 (1), 2-152 (4), 3-170 (5), 4-206 (2), 5-231 (6), 6-265 (3), 7-283 (8), 8-285 (7), 9-295 (10), 10-295 (11)

BARBADOS

1	D.M.Richards	c Sanford b Martin	56
2	J.A.M.Haynes	c J.S.Liburd b Martin	92
3	†P.A.Browne	lbw b Baker	4
4	*D.R.Smith	c Martin b C.J.K.Hodge	51
5	R.O.Hinds	c S.S.W.Liburd b Martin	39
6	K.A.Stoute	lbw b C.J.K.Hodge	71
7	J.L.Carter	run out	19
8	A.R.Holder	not out	57
9	S.J.Benn	not out	17
10	P.T.Collins		
11	K.A.J.Roach		
	Extras	b 4, lb 2, w 1, nb 8	15
		(7 wickets)	421

FoW (1): 1-105 (1), 2-111 (3), 3-204 (4), 4-221 (2), 5-277 (5), 6-309 (7), 7-368 (6)

Barbados Bowling

	O	M	R	W	
Collins	11.4	1	49	5	5nb
Roach	5	0	33	0	7nb
Smith	5	0	27	0	
Benn	25	5	88	2	
Hinds	29	6	86	3	2nb

Leeward Islands Bowling

	O	M	R	W	
Sanford	10	0	60	0	
Baker	11	0	74	1	1w,5nb
Willett	3	0	39	0	3nb
Martin	24	1	129	3	
C.J.K.Hodge	15	0	113	2	

Umpires: G.E.Greaves and C.E.Mack. Referee: C.Shiell.   Toss: Leeward Islands

Close of Play: 1st day: Leeward Islands (1) 166-2 (Morton 73*, M.V.Hodge 3*, 40 overs); 2nd day: No play; 3rd day: No play.

Man of the Match: P.T.Collins , R.S.Morton.

R.S.Morton's 137 included 12 fours and 8 sixes. J.S.Liburd retired hurt in the Leeward Islands first innings having scored 10 (team score 24-0) - he returned when the score was 170-3. He was struck on the forearm by a ball from Roach.

TRINIDAD AND TOBAGO v JAMAICA

Played at Queen's Park Oval, Port of Spain, February 29, March 1, 2, 3, 2008.
Carib Beer Cup 2007/08
Match drawn.   (Points: Trinidad and Tobago 3, Jamaica 6)

TRINIDAD AND TOBAGO

#	Batsman	Dismissal 1	Score 1	Dismissal 2	Score 2
1	L.M.P.Simmons	c Parchment b Powell	2	lbw b Powell	4
2	W.K.D.Perkins	c Marshall b Nash	27	c Marshall b Powell	25
3	*D.Ganga	lbw b Miller	79	lbw b Taylor	40
4	D.J.Bravo	c Baugh b Taylor	15	(5) lbw b Miller	95
5	K.A.Pollard	c Parchment b Taylor	0	(6) c Bernard b Miller	2
6	J.N.Mohammed	lbw b Taylor	5	(4) c Marshall b Powell	7
7	†D.Ramdin	c Bernard b Powell	63	not out	106
8	R.R.Emrit	c Baugh b Miller	19	c Parchment b Miller	6
9	D.Mohammed	c Nash b Powell	26	c Hyatt b Gayle	18
10	R.Rampaul	lbw b Powell	2	c Marshall b Miller	8
11	A.S.Jaggernauth	not out	6	not out	9
	Extras	b 2, lb 2, w 1, nb 8	13	b 2, lb 5, nb 9	16
			257	(9 wickets, declared)	336

FoW (1): 1-11 (1), 2-59 (2), 3-90 (4), 4-94 (5), 5-102 (6), 6-194 (3), 7-218 (7), 8-226 (8), 9-236 (10), 10-257 (9)
FoW (2): 1-13 (1), 2-41 (2), 3-66 (4), 4-108 (3), 5-111 (6), 6-247 (5), 7-265 (8), 8-302 (9), 9-319 (10)

JAMAICA

#	Batsman	Dismissal 1	Score 1	Dismissal 2	Score 2
1	B.A.Parchment	run out	25	lbw b Bravo	28
2	*C.H.Gayle	lbw b Bravo	6	not out	100
3	X.M.Marshall	lbw b Jaggernauth	47	lbw b Emrit	8
4	D.P.Hyatt	c J.N.Mohammed b Jaggernauth	72	c Ramdin b Rampaul	31
5	B.P.Nash	c Ramdin b Rampaul	102	(6) run out	2
6	D.E.Bernard	c Jaggernauth b Emrit	14	(7) run out	0
7	†C.S.Baugh	b Emrit	0	(5) c Ramdin b Bravo	23
8	N.O.Miller	c Ramdin b Rampaul	6	not out	0
9	J.E.Taylor	c Simmons b Rampaul	11		
10	D.B.L.Powell	c Jaggernauth b Rampaul	30		
11	O.V.Brown	not out	5		
	Extras	b 5, lb 6, w 11, nb 5	27	b 2, lb 1, nb 4	7
			345	(6 wickets)	199

FoW (1): 1-36 (2), 2-64 (1), 3-107 (3), 4-224 (4), 5-262 (6), 6-262 (7), 7-271 (8), 8-290 (9), 9-336 (10), 10-345 (5)
FoW (2): 1-45 (1), 2-77 (3), 3-159 (4), 4-192 (5), 5-196 (6), 6-197 (7)

Jamaica Bowling	O	M	R	W		O	M	R	W	
Taylor	13	4	41	3	1nb	18	3	63	1	
Powell	16.4	2	60	4	1w,4nb	18	3	71	3	1nb
Bernard	9	0	40	0	3nb	10	2	26	0	
Nash	6	0	17	1						
Brown	18	2	57	0	(4)	16	3	58	0	2nb
Miller	19	6	38	2	(5)	39	7	81	4	
Gayle					(6)	10	1	30	1	

Trinidad and Tobago Bowling	O	M	R	W		O	M	R	W	
Rampaul	17.2	1	78	4	11w,5nb	11	0	58	1	4nb
Emrit	14	1	56	2	(3)	9	4	10	1	
Bravo	16	5	38	1	(2)	15.3	1	49	2	
Jaggernauth	25	3	73	2	(5)	11	1	32	0	
D.Mohammed	22	10	66	0	(4)	12	3	47	0	
Pollard	3	0	15	0						
J.N.Mohammed	5	1	8	0						

Umpires: C.E.Alfred and P.J.Nero.   Toss: Jamaica

Close of Play: 1st day: Jamaica (1) 41-1 (Parchment 18*, Marshall 1*, 8 overs); 2nd day: Jamaica (1) 330-8 (Nash 96*, Powell 27*, 98 overs); 3rd day: Trinidad and Tobago (2) 247-6 (Ramdin 59*, 81.5 overs).

Man of the Match: D.Ramdin.
B.P.Nash's 102 took 198 balls in 292 minutes and included 13 fours. D.Ramdin's 106 took 258 balls in 221 minutes and included 7 fours. C.H.Gayle's 100 took 182 balls in 260 minutes and included 10 fours and 1 six.

WINDWARD ISLANDS v COMBINED CAMPUSES AND COLLEGES

Played at Beausejour Stadium, Gros Islet, St Lucia, February 29, March 1, 2, 2008.
Carib Beer Cup 2007/08
Windward Islands won by ten wickets.   (Points: Windward Islands 12, Combined Campuses and Colleges 0)

WINDWARD ISLANDS

1	D.S.Smith	c Wilkinson b Wallace	159	not out	27
2	M.C.Bascombe	c Reifer b Wilkinson	36	not out	21
3	A.D.S.Fletcher	lbw b Wilkinson	0		
4	L.A.S.Sebastien	c Reifer b Kantasingh	0		
5	D.J.G.Sammy	c N.Parris b Wallace	37		
6	D.B.Hector	c Reifer b Clarke	46		
7	*R.N.Lewis	c Reifer b Noel	19		
8	†L.O.D.James	lbw b Noel	0		
9	S.Shillingford	c Wilkinson b Bennett	6		
10	D.K.Butler	c Reifer b Wallace	21		
11	N.T.Pascal	not out	4		
	Extras	b 5, lb 7, w 1, nb 6	19	nb 3	3
			347	(no wicket)	51

FoW (1): 1-58 (2), 2-66 (3), 3-69 (4), 4-128 (5), 5-207 (6), 6-244 (7), 7-244 (8), 8-277 (9), 9-331 (10), 10-347 (1)

COMBINED CAMPUSES AND COLLEGES

1	S.Jackson	b Sammy	13	c and b Shillingford	18
2	J.A.Parris	b Butler	15	b Butler	0
3	K.J.Wilkinson	c Sammy b Butler	1	c Lewis b Shillingford	50
4	F.L.Reifer	lbw b Pascal	9	run out	101
5	N.Parris	c James b Sammy	5	c James b Butler	26
6	*S.M.Clarke	c Hector b Sebastien	27	b Butler	0
7	†C.A.K.Walton	c Sammy b Shillingford	63	c Pascal b Shillingford	12
8	G.Wallace	c Bascombe b Sebastien	4	lbw b Pascal	1
9	J.P.Bennett	b Sebastien	1	c Sammy b Shillingford	12
10	K.Kantasingh	c Hector b Shillingford	0	b Sebastien	8
11	J.Noel	not out	0	not out	4
	Extras	b 4, lb 2, nb 5	11	b 3, lb 10, nb 3	16
			149		248

FoW (1): 1-23 (2), 2-27 (3), 3-35 (1), 4-50 (5), 5-50 (4), 6-144 (7), 7-144 (6), 8-148, 9-149, 10-149
FoW (2): 1-1 (2), 2-62 (1), 3-85 (3), 4-138 (5), 5-138 (6), 6-158 (7), 7-175 (8), 8-204 (9), 9-243 (4), 10-248 (10)

Combined Campuses and Colleges Bowling

	O	M	R	W		O	M	R	W	
Bennett	13	1	57	1		3.1	0	26	0	
Noel	10	0	58	2		3	0	25	0	3nb
Kantasingh	20	1	81	1						
Wilkinson	11	2	41	2						
Wallace	11.1	0	56	3						
Clarke	13	2	42	1						

Windward Islands Bowling

	O	M	R	W				O	M	R	W	
Pascal	9	0	49	1	5nb	(2)		9	0	57	1	1nb
Butler	10	3	20	2		(1)		22	4	65	3	
Sammy	15	7	22	2				16	2	42	0	2nb
Shillingford	17.3	7	38	2				31	6	69	4	
Sebastien	11	7	14	3				4.3	2	2	1	

Umpires: V.V.Bullen and N.A.Malcolm.   Toss: Combined Campuses and Colleges

Close of Play: 1st day: Windward Islands (1) 347-9 (Smith 159*, Pascal 4*, 78 overs); 2nd day: Combined Campuses and Colleges (2) 96-3 (Reifer 13*, N.Parris 10*, 34 overs).

Man of the Match: D.S.Smith.

The match was scheduled for four days but completed in three. D.S.Smith's 159 took 223 balls in 347 minutes and included 14 fours and 2 sixes. F.L.Reifer's 101 took 210 balls in 275 minutes and included 14 fours.

BARBADOS v JAMAICA

Played at Kensington Oval, Bridgetown, March 7, 8, 9, 10, 2008.
Carib Beer Cup 2007/08
Barbados won by 17 runs.   (Points: Barbados 12, Jamaica 4)

BARBADOS

1	D.M.Richards	c Baugh b Bernard	38	c Powell b Miller	98
2	J.A.M.Haynes	c Baugh b Taylor	0	c Lambert b Gayle	18
3	†P.A.Browne	c Marshall b Powell	15	c Baugh b Bernard	3
4	R.O.Hinds	b Powell	8	c Bernard b Gayle	33
5	*D.R.Smith	b Bernard	0	b Miller	8
6	K.A.Stoute	c Baugh b Bernard	9	c Parchment b Gayle	14
7	A.R.Holder	c Marshall b Bernard	27	c Baugh b Miller	55
8	S.J.Benn	c Baugh b Bernard	0	c Parchment b Gayle	20
9	K.A.J.Roach	c Baugh b Taylor	11	c Baugh b Miller	16
10	F.H.Edwards	c Parchment b Gayle	40	b Taylor	20
11	P.T.Collins	not out	5	not out	1
	Extras	b 2, lb 8, nb 4	14	b 3, nb 1	4
			167		290

FoW (1): 1-5 (2), 2-38 (3), 3-61 (1), 4-61 (5), 5-65 (4), 6-98 (6), 7-98 (8), 8-109 (7), 9-142 (9), 10-167 (10)
FoW (2): 1-54 (2), 2-71 (3), 3-155 (4), 4-155 (1), 5-163 (5), 6-195 (6), 7-241 (8), 8-255 (7), 9-276 (9), 10-290 (10)

JAMAICA

1	B.A.Parchment	b Collins	0	(2) c Richards b Collins	30
2	*C.H.Gayle	c Smith b Edwards	13	(1) c Holder b Edwards	5
3	X.M.Marshall	c sub (J.L.Carter) b Benn	27	c Browne b Collins	2
4	D.P.Hyatt	c Browne b Hinds	47	c Browne b Collins	12
5	B.P.Nash	c Browne b Collins	23	c Browne b Collins	37
6	T.L.Lambert	c Hinds b Smith	61	c Richards b Edwards	46
7	D.E.Bernard	lbw b Collins	4	(8) lbw b Benn	1
8	†C.S.Baugh	c Hinds b Collins	0	(7) lbw b Collins	1
9	N.O.Miller	lbw b Edwards	32	b Hinds	9
10	J.E.Taylor	c Benn b Smith	7	c Smith b Edwards	13
11	D.B.L.Powell	not out	1	not out	0
	Extras	b 12, lb 6, w 2, nb 22	42	lb 11, nb 16	27
			257		183

FoW (1): 1-0 (1), 2-31 (2), 3-62 (3), 4-123 (4), 5-128 (5), 6-132 (7), 7-136 (8), 8-219 (9), 9-256 (6), 10-257 (10)
FoW (2): 1-9 (1), 2-17 (3), 3-56 (2), 4-66 (4), 5-138 (5), 6-144 (7), 7-147 (8), 8-165 (9), 9-170 (6), 10-183 (10)

Jamaica Bowling

	O	M	R	W		O	M	R	W
Taylor	13	3	42	2		10.1	4	28	1
Powell	16	5	59	2		6	2	32	0
Bernard	14.1	1	44	5		10	2	55	1
Miller	6	3	8	0	(5)	39	11	86	4
Gayle	2	1	4	1	(4)	42	12	86	4

Barbados Bowling

	O	M	R	W		O	M	R	W
Collins	19	3	62	4		20	3	46	5
Edwards	11	0	43	2		8.3	0	37	3
Smith	13	0	49	2	(5)	5	0	14	0
Benn	21	11	36	1		18	4	39	1
Hinds	13	2	36	1	(6)	10	3	12	1
Roach	2	0	13	0	(3)	6	0	24	0

Umpires: T.Birbal and D.O.Holder. Referee: V.C.Carter.   Toss: Jamaica

Close of Play: 1st day: Jamaica (1) 149-7 (Lambert 13*, Miller 5*, 39 overs); 2nd day: Barbados (2) 177-5 (Stoute 8*, Holder 6*, 55 overs); 3rd day: Jamaica (2) 133-4 (Nash 35*, Lambert 26*, 44 overs).

Man of the Match: P.T.Collins.

GUYANA v COMBINED CAMPUSES AND COLLEGES

Played at Providence Stadium, March 7, 8, 9, 10, 2008.
Carib Beer Cup 2007/08
Match drawn.   (Points: Guyana 6, Combined Campuses and Colleges 3)

GUYANA

1	K.Arjune	lbw b Noel	0
2	S.Chattergoon	c Clarke b Wilkinson	38
3	*R.R.Sarwan	b Noel	0
4	L.R.Johnson	c Reifer b Clarke	94
5	S.Chanderpaul	not out	207
6	T.M.Dowlin	lbw b McClean	36
7	†D.O.Christian	c J.A.Parris b Noel	16
8	E.A.Crandon	c Walton b Noel	5
9	Z.Mohamed	c Walton b Noel	2
10	T.C.Garraway	lbw b Noel	5
11	D.Bishoo	c Noel b Kantasingh	4
	Extras	lb 7, w 4, nb 3	14
			421

FoW (1): 1-0 (1), 2-0 (3), 3-61 (2), 4-236 (4), 5-345 (6), 6-372 (7), 7-389 (8), 8-395 (9), 9-401 (10), 10-421 (11)

COMBINED CAMPUSES AND COLLEGES

1	S.Jackson	c Christian b Bishoo	38	c and b Bishoo	25
2	J.A.Parris	c Arjune b Garraway	21	c Crandon b Bishoo	33
3	K.J.Wilkinson	c Arjune b Garraway	0		
4	F.L.Reifer	c Christian b Crandon	17	not out	9
5	N.Parris	c Arjune b Bishoo	1	(3) not out	27
6	*S.M.Clarke	lbw b Bishoo	2		
7	K.R.McClean	c Christian b Bishoo	1		
8	†C.A.K.Walton	c Christian b Garraway	32		
9	K.Kantasingh	c Chattergoon b Mohamed	18		
10	J.Noel	lbw b Bishoo	10		
11	G.Moore	not out	1		
	Extras	b 4, lb 1, nb 5	10	lb 1, nb 1	2
			151	(2 wickets)	96

FoW (1): 1-35 (2), 2-35 (3), 3-71 (4), 4-78 (5), 5-78 (1), 6-88 (6), 7-94 (7), 8-133 (8), 9-150 (10), 10-151 (9)
FoW (2): 1-47 (1), 2-66 (2)

Combined Campuses and Colleges Bowling

	O	M	R	W
Noel	30	3	101	6
McClean	22	2	94	1
Moore	18	2	71	0
Wilkinson	13	2	38	1
Kantasingh	16.3	2	57	1
Clarke	13	1	53	1

Guyana Bowling

	O	M	R	W		O	M	R	W
Crandon	19	11	23	1		5	3	15	0
Garraway	16	3	48	3		5	0	24	0
Bishoo	18	6	29	5		12	6	18	2
Mohamed	13.1	3	33	1		5	0	27	0
Johnson	3	0	5	0					
Dowlin	4	2	8	0		2	0	5	0
Chattergoon					(5)	3	1	6	0

Umpires: V.V.Bullen and E.A.Nicholls.   Toss: Guyana

Close of Play: 1st day: Guyana (1) 338-4 (Chanderpaul 161*, Dowlin 31*, 86 overs); 2nd day: Combined Campuses and Colleges (1) 29-0 (Jackson 11*, J.A.Parris 16*, 12 overs); 3rd day: Combined Campuses and Colleges (2) 96-2 (N.Parris 27*, Reifer 9*, 32 overs).

Man of the Match: S.Chanderpaul.
There was no play on the final day. S.Chanderpaul's 207 took 272 balls in 448 minutes and included 17 fours and 1 six.

WINDWARD ISLANDS v TRINIDAD AND TOBAGO

Played at Windsor Park, Roseau, March 7, 8, 9, 10, 2008.
Carib Beer Cup 2007/08
Trinidad and Tobago won by three wickets.   (Points: Windward Islands 4, Trinidad and Tobago 12)

WINDWARD ISLANDS

1	D.S.Smith	lbw b Jaggernauth	52	c Ganga b Mohammed	33
2	M.C.Bascombe	c Ramdin b Rampaul	12	st Ramdin b Jaggernauth	36
3	A.D.S.Fletcher	lbw b Mohammed	19	c Simmons b Jaggernauth	18
4	L.A.S.Sebastien	run out	11	c Pollard b Jaggernauth	1
5	D.J.G.Sammy	c Pollard b Jaggernauth	5	c Ramdin b Jaggernauth	12
6	D.B.Hector	c Ramdin b Rampaul	43	c Bravo b Jaggernauth	9
7	*R.N.Lewis	c Ramdin b Pollard	19	c Rampaul b Mohammed	31
8	†L.O.D.James	c Kelly b Jaggernauth	66	st Ramdin b Mohammed	3
9	S.Shillingford	c Ganga b Jaggernauth	5	c Pollard b Jaggernauth	2
10	D.K.Butler	not out	41	c Ganga b Jaggernauth	6
11	N.T.Pascal	c Mohammed b Jaggernauth	0	not out	0
	Extras	b 9, lb 6, w 2, nb 4	21	b 2, lb 2, w 1, nb 2	7
			294		158

FoW (1): 1-28 (2), 2-72 (3), 3-97 (1), 4-108 (5), 5-110 (4), 6-155 (7), 7-191 (6), 8-209 (9), 9-280 (8), 10-294 (11)
FoW (2): 1-68 (2), 2-85 (1), 3-91 (3), 4-93 (4), 5-114 (6), 6-119 (5), 7-127 (8), 8-132 (9), 9-156 (10), 10-158 (7)

TRINIDAD AND TOBAGO

1	L.M.P.Simmons	c sub (M.Matthew) b Shillingford	39	c Sebastien b Butler	6
2	W.K.D.Perkins	c James b Sammy	52	c Fletcher b Butler	26
3	K.A.Pollard	c Bascombe b Pascal	28	(4) b Shillingford	22
4	*D.Ganga	c Pascal b Shillingford	24	(3) c Hector b Shillingford	37
5	D.J.Bravo	c Pascal b Butler	29	(6) not out	37
6	†D.Ramdin	c and b Shillingford	10	(7) c Hector b Pascal	31
7	R.R.Emrit	c James b Butler	14	(8) c James b Pascal	0
8	R.A.Kelly	c Fletcher b Sammy	29	(5) b Sebastien	17
9	D.Mohammed	b Pascal	11	not out	4
10	R.Rampaul	c Sebastien b Pascal	9		
11	A.S.Jaggernauth	not out	8		
	Extras	lb 5, nb 10	15	lb 7, w 1	8
			268	(7 wickets)	188

FoW (1): 1-97 (1), 2-97 (2), 3-150 (3), 4-182 (4), 5-186 (5), 6-206 (6), 7-222 (7), 8-250 (8), 9-250 (9), 10-268 (10)
FoW (2): 1-23 (1), 2-38 (2), 3-87 (4), 4-108 (5), 5-118 (3), 6-178 (7), 7-184 (8)

Trinidad and Tobago Bowling

	O	M	R	W		O	M	R	W
Rampaul	15	3	55	2		6	0	24	0
Kelly	8	0	36	0		1	0	11	0
Bravo	7	0	7	0	(6)	7	1	15	0
Jaggernauth	33	7	73	5	(3)	27	2	60	7
Mohammed	21	6	59	1		19.2	7	28	3
Emrit	7	1	17	0	(4)	4	1	16	0
Pollard	6	0	32	1					

Windward Islands Bowling

	O	M	R	W		O	M	R	W
Butler	23	8	54	2	(3)	10	1	35	2
Pascal	16.3	2	67	3	(1)	8.5	0	35	2
Sammy	21	4	50	2	(4)	6	0	23	0
Shillingford	35	4	81	3	(2)	23	7	58	2
Sebastien	4	1	11	0		13	4	30	1

Umpires: L.Abraham and N.A.Malcolm.   Toss: Windward Islands

Close of Play: 1st day: Windward Islands (1) 271-8 (James 60*, Butler 25*, 93 overs); 2nd day: Trinidad and Tobago (1) 211-6 (Emrit 11*, Kelly 4*, 81 overs); 3rd day: Trinidad and Tobago (2) 9-0 (Simmons 1*, Perkins 4*, 2 overs).

Man of the Match: A.S.Jaggernauth.

COMBINED CAMPUSES AND COLLEGES v TRINIDAD AND TOBAGO

Played at Three Ws Oval, Bridgetown, March 14, 15, 16, 2008.
Carib Beer Cup 2007/08
Trinidad and Tobago won by nine wickets.   (Points: Combined Campuses and Colleges 0, Trinidad and Tobago 12)

COMBINED CAMPUSES AND COLLEGES

1	*S.M.Clarke	c Jaggernauth b Rampaul	0	c Ramdin b Rampaul	4
2	S.Jackson	c Bravo b Rampaul	4	c Ramdin b Kelly	83
3	N.Parris	b Jaggernauth	27	c Simmons b Jaggernauth	31
4	F.L.Reifer	lbw b Rampaul	6	(5) c Ganga b Mohammed	64
5	K.J.Wilkinson	c Jaggernauth b Mohammed	21	(6) c Perkins b Kelly	0
6	†C.A.K.Walton	c and b Jaggernauth	1	(4) c Perkins b Kelly	58
7	C.W.Emmanuel	c Rampaul b Jaggernauth	24	c Pollard b Jaggernauth	15
8	K.R.McClean	run out (Pollard)	6	b Rampaul	3
9	J.P.Bennett	c Ganga b Mohammed	2	lbw b Rampaul	0
10	K.Kantasingh	c Pollard b Jaggernauth	0	c Simmons b Jaggernauth	1
11	J.Noel	not out	2	not out	4
	Extras	lb 2, nb 2	4	b 1, lb 6, w 1, nb 4	12
			___		___
			97		275

FoW (1): 1-4 (1), 2-7 (2), 3-29 (4), 4-41 (3), 5-43 (6), 6-71 (5), 7-82 (8), 8-92 (9), 9-94 (10), 10-97 (7)
FoW (2): 1-8 (1), 2-87 (3), 3-171 (2), 4-216 (4), 5-216 (6), 6-237 (7), 7-244 (8), 8-244 (9), 9-261 (10), 10-275 (5)

TRINIDAD AND TOBAGO

1	W.K.D.Perkins	c Walton b McClean	29	c Kantasingh b McClean	12
2	L.M.P.Simmons	c Walton b McClean	23	not out	11
3	*D.Ganga	c Walton b Bennett	46		
4	K.A.Pollard	c Noel b Bennett	85		
5	D.M.Bravo	c Walton b McClean	29	(3) not out	12
6	†D.Ramdin	b Clarke	18		
7	R.A.Kelly	c Reifer b Clarke	34		
8	R.R.Emrit	c Reifer b Clarke	0		
9	D.Mohammed	b McClean	1		
10	R.Rampaul	st Walton b Clarke	58		
11	A.S.Jaggernauth	not out	2		
	Extras	b 2, lb 3, w 1, nb 6	12	b 1	1
			___		___
			337	(1 wicket)	36

FoW (1): 1-44 (2), 2-58 (1), 3-175 (3), 4-197 (4), 5-224 (6), 6-262 (5), 7-263 (8), 8-264 (9), 9-294 (7), 10-337 (10)
FoW (2): 1-13 (1)

Trinidad and Tobago Bowling

	O	M	R	W		O	M	R	W	
Rampaul	10	5	22	3		19	4	51	3	4nb
Kelly	5	2	11	0		19	2	64	3	
Emrit	6	2	13	0		8	2	14	0	
Jaggernauth	11.2	1	35	4		34	2	88	3	1w
Mohammed	9	3	14	2		19.2	3	51	1	

Combined Campuses and Colleges Bowling

	O	M	R	W			O	M	R	W	
Bennett	12	1	69	2							
Noel	14	2	64	0	2nb	(1)	4	0	26	0	
McClean	16	1	54	4	2nb	(2)	3.4	1	9	1	
Emmanuel	9	0	59	0	1w,2nb						
Kantasingh	5	0	33	0							
Clarke	13.5	1	53	4							

Umpires: T.Birbal and D.Somwaru.   Toss: Trinidad and Tobago

Close of Play: 1st day: Trinidad and Tobago (1) 224-5 (Bravo 16*, 45.4 overs); 2nd day: Combined Campuses and Colleges (2) 185-3 (Walton 52*, Reifer 6*, 66 overs).

Man of the Match: R.Rampaul.

The match was scheduled for four days but completed in three.

JAMAICA v WINDWARD ISLANDS

Played at Alpart Sports Club, Nain, March 14, 15, 2008.
Carib Beer Cup 2007/08
Jamaica won by ten wickets.   (Points: Jamaica 12, Windward Islands 0)

JAMAICA

1	B.A.Parchment	c Lewis b Pascal	15	not out		9
2	*C.H.Gayle	c James b Butler	55	not out		8
3	D.P.Hyatt	c and b Pascal	4			
4	M.N.Samuels	b Pascal	28			
5	B.P.Nash	c Browne b Shillingford	22			
6	T.L.Lambert	c Browne b Shillingford	22			
7	D.E.Bernard	c Sammy b Shillingford	12			
8	†C.S.Baugh	c Browne b Butler	25			
9	N.O.Miller	b Shillingford	28			
10	J.E.Taylor	c James b Butler	0			
11	D.B.L.Powell	not out	3			
	Extras	b 4, lb 6, nb 8	18			
			232	(no wicket)		**17**

FoW (1): 1-38 (1), 2-57 (3), 3-95 (2), 4-119 (4), 5-152 (6), 6-159 (5), 7-181 (7), 8-210 (8), 9-210 (10), 10-232 (9)

WINDWARD ISLANDS

1	D.S.Smith	lbw b Powell	1	hit wkt b Powell		4
2	S.R.Browne	c Baugh b Powell	3	b Bernard		14
3	R.Casimir	b Powell	0	(10) c Gayle b Miller		6
4	A.D.S.Fletcher	lbw b Miller	25	(3) not out		103
5	D.B.Hector	lbw b Miller	17	(4) b Bernard		12
6	D.J.G.Sammy	c Baugh b Taylor	6	(5) lbw b Bernard		7
7	*R.N.Lewis	lbw b Miller	1	(6) lbw b Miller		5
8	†L.O.D.James	c Hyatt b Taylor	0	(7) c Nash b Miller		19
9	D.K.Butler	lbw b Taylor	0	(8) lbw b Gayle		2
10	S.Shillingford	not out	0	(9) lbw b Gayle		7
11	N.T.Pascal	lbw b Miller	0	c Baugh b Gayle		2
	Extras	b 6, lb 1, nb 1	8	lb 1, nb 5		6
			61			**187**

FoW (1): 1-1 (1), 2-1 (3), 3-8 (2), 4-42 (4), 5-60 (6), 6-60 (5), 7-61 (7), 8-61 (8), 9-61 (9), 10-61 (11)
FoW (2): 1-5 (1), 2-32 (2), 3-45 (4), 4-65 (5), 5-94 (6), 6-120 (7), 7-127 (8), 8-157 (9), 9-172 (10), 10-187 (11)

Windward Islands Bowling

	O	M	R	W		O	M	R	W	
Pascal	16	3	42	3		1.2	0	12	0	
Butler	17	3	35	3						
Sammy	20	4	53	0						
Shillingford	21.3	3	76	4						
Fletcher	2	2	0	0						
Casimir	7	2	16	0						
Smith					(2)	1	0	5	0	

Jamaica Bowling

	O	M	R	W		O	M	R	W	
Taylor	11	4	17	3		5	0	23	0	
Powell	8	4	13	3		8	2	21	1	
Bernard	6	2	14	0	(4)	5	0	39	3	5nb
Nash	1	0	4	0						
Miller	8.2	5	6	4	(3)	25	5	60	3	
Lambert					(5)	1	0	4	0	
Gayle					(6)	13	1	39	3	

Umpires: B.Ali and K.Barrasingha.   Toss: Windward Islands

Close of Play: 1st day: Windward Islands (1) 1-2 (Browne 0*, 3.1 overs).

Man of the Match: N.O.Miller.
The match was scheduled for four days but completed in two. A.D.S.Fletcher's 103 took 162 balls in 188 minutes and included 11 fours and 2 sixes.

LEEWARD ISLANDS v GUYANA

Played at Addelita Cancryn Junior High School Ground, Charlotte Amalie, St Thomas, US Virgin Islands, March 14, 15, 16, 17, 2008.
Carib Beer Cup 2007/08
Guyana won by an innings and 29 runs.   (Points: Leeward Islands 0, Guyana 12)

LEEWARD ISLANDS

1	A.C.L.Richards	c Mohamed b Crandon	0	c Christian b Crandon	17
2	S.M.Jeffers	c Chattergoon b Bess	37	c Dowlin b Garraway	5
3	*R.S.Morton	c sub (A.B.Fudadin) b Crandon	0	not out	96
4	T.A.Willett	c Chanderpaul b Bess	34	lbw b Garraway	8
5	O.Peters	c Sarwan b Mohamed	22	b Garraway	0
6	S.S.W.Liburd	c Sarwan b Mohamed	29	run out	30
7	†J.N.Hamilton	c Sarwan b Mohamed	28	c Chanderpaul b Crandon	0
8	G.C.Tonge	c Christian b Garraway	14	b Mohamed	1
9	L.S.Baker	c Christian b Bess	26	c Bess b Mohamed	4
10	B.A.DeFreitas	c Garraway b Mohamed	1	c Dowlin b Mohamed	1
11	A.Martin	not out	9	b Mohamed	4
	Extras	b 2, w 2	4	lb 5, w 2, nb 9	16
			204		**182**

FoW (1): 1-0 (1), 2-0 (3), 3-59 (4), 4-80 (2), 5-123, 6-128, 7-158, 8-195, 9-195, 10-204
FoW (2): 1-27, 2-27, 3-51, 4-51, 5-124, 6-126, 7-131, 8-148, 9-162, 10-182

GUYANA

1	S.Chattergoon	c Liburd b Baker	6
2	K.Arjune	lbw b Willett	35
3	L.R.Johnson	lbw b Baker	7
4	T.M.Dowlin	c Morton b DeFreitas	26
5	S.Chanderpaul	c Morton b Liburd	82
6	*R.R.Sarwan	c Jeffers b Liburd	150
7	†D.O.Christian	lbw b Martin	13
8	E.A.Crandon	c Hamilton b DeFreitas	16
9	Z.Mohamed	c Peters b Liburd	43
10	T.C.Garraway	c Hamilton b Martin	3
11	B.J.Bess	not out	6
	Extras	b 4, lb 5, w 2, nb 17	28
			415

FoW (1): 1-6 (1), 2-17 (3), 3-58 (2), 4-104 (4), 5-249 (5), 6-279 (7), 7-301 (8), 8-404, 9-407, 10-415

Guyana Bowling

	O	M	R	W		O	M	R	W
Crandon	9	1	35	2	1w	20	2	54	2
Garraway	11	1	44	1		11	0	56	3
Bess	8	2	35	3	1w	4	0	27	0
Johnson	4	0	24	0					
Mohamed	12.2	2	49	4	(4)	15	3	40	4
Sarwan	1	0	15	0					

Leeward Islands Bowling

	O	M	R	W
Baker	16	2	69	2
Tonge	15	0	63	0
DeFreitas	17	4	59	2
Martin	41.1	5	108	2
Willett	15	3	53	1
Peters	2	1	8	0
Liburd	11	1	46	3

Umpires: H.Gumbs and R.O.Richards.   Toss: Guyana

Close of Play: 1st day: Guyana (1) 138-4 (Chanderpaul 36*, Sarwan 16*, 44 overs); 2nd day: Guyana (1) 299-6 (Sarwan 89*, Crandon 15*, 88 overs); 3rd day: Leeward Islands (2) 160-8 (Morton 81*, DeFreitas 0*; 44 overs).

Man of the Match: R.R.Sarwan.
R.R.Sarwan's 150 took 230 balls in 336 minutes and included 16 fours and 1 six.

WEST INDIES v SRI LANKA

Played at Providence Stadium, March 22, 23, 24, 25, 26, 2008.
Sri Lanka in West Indies 2007/08 - 1st Test
Sri Lanka won by 121 runs.

SRI LANKA

1	M.G.Vandort	lbw b Taylor	52	c Ramdin b Gayle	24
2	B.S.M.Warnapura	c Ramdin b Bravo	120	c Ramdin b Bravo	62
3	K.C.Sangakkara	c Smith b Taylor	50	c sub (F.H.Edwards) b Bravo	21
4	*D.P.M.D.Jayawardene	lbw b Gayle	136	c Chanderpaul b Benn	33
5	T.T.Samaraweera	c sub (T.M.Dowlin) b Taylor	0	not out	56
6	T.M.Dilshan	lbw b Taylor	20	lbw b Taylor	4
7	†H.A.P.W.Jayawardene	b Powell	21	(9) not out	5
8	W.P.U.J.C.Vaas	not out	54	(7) c Ramdin b Benn	13
9	M.T.T.Mirando	c sub (T.M.Dowlin) b Gayle	0	(8) c Taylor b Benn	14
10	H.M.R.K.B.Herath	not out	13		
11	M.Muralitharan				
	Extras	lb 7, w 1, nb 2	10	b 2, lb 1, nb 5	8
		(8 wickets, declared)	476	(7 wickets, declared)	240

FoW (1): 1-130 (1), 2-205 (2), 3-243 (3), 4-243 (5), 5-277 (6), 6-331 (7), 7-457 (4), 8-459 (9)
FoW (2): 1-43 (1), 2-94 (3), 3-133 (2), 4-159 (4), 5-171 (6), 6-192 (7), 7-224 (8)

WEST INDIES

1	*C.H.Gayle	lbw b Vaas	0	(6) not out	51
2	D.S.Smith	c H.A.P.W.Jayawardene b Mirando	14	(1) c Mirando b Vaas	10
3	R.R.Sarwan	c H.A.P.W.Jayawardene b Vaas	80	lbw b Mirando	72
4	M.N.Samuels	c H.A.P.W.Jayawardene b Mirando	5	c Sangakkara b Vaas	10
5	S.Chanderpaul	c Warnapura b Muralitharan	23	b Vaas	3
6	D.J.Bravo	lbw b Muralitharan	8	(2) c and b Muralitharan	83
7	R.O.Hinds	c H.A.P.W.Jayawardene b Muralitharan	37	c Sangakkara b Muralitharan	10
8	†D.Ramdin	c Sangakkara b Vaas	38	c D.P.M.D.Jayawardene b Mirando	1
9	S.J.Benn	run out (Dilshan)	28	lbw b Muralitharan	7
10	J.E.Taylor	not out	27	c Dilshan b Vaas	12
11	D.B.L.Powell	c D.P.M.D.Jayawardene b Mirando	12	c Muralitharan b Vaas	14
	Extras	lb 4, nb 4	8	b 25, lb 3, nb 14	42
			280		315

FoW (1): 1-4 (1), 2-46 (2), 3-58 (4), 4-99 (5), 5-109 (6), 6-162 (3), 7-193 (7), 8-236 (8), 9-252 (9), 10-280 (11)
FoW (2): 1-22 (1), 2-156 (2), 3-171 (4), 4-178 (5), 5-212 (3), 6-229 (7), 7-231 (8), 8-244 (9), 9-291 (10), 10-315 (11)

West Indies Bowling

	O	M	R	W			O	M	R	W	
Powell	29	3	89	1			9	0	33	0	
Taylor	33	8	110	4			8	0	37	1	
Gayle	27	4	66	2		(5)	13	1	54	1	
Bravo	30	3	74	1	1w,2nb	(3)	14	0	54	2	1nb
Benn	40	6	120	0		(4)	13	0	59	3	
Hinds	3	0	10	0							

Sri Lanka Bowling

	O	M	R	W			O	M	R	W	
Vaas	25	7	48	3			22.2	7	61	5	
Mirando	20.5	3	59	3			17	2	70	2	8nb
Dilshan	1	0	2	0							
Muralitharan	40	6	112	3	2nb		45	6	112	3	1nb
Herath	25	6	55	0	2nb	(3)	22	7	44	0	1nb

Umpires: B.F.Bowden and S.J.A.Taufel. Third umpire: C.R.Duncan. Referee: B.C.Broad.　　　　Toss: Sri Lanka

Close of Play: 1st day: Sri Lanka (1) 269-4 (D.P.M.D.Jayawardene 25*, Dilshan 15*, 90 overs); 2nd day: West Indies (1) 29-1 (Smith 8*, Sarwan 21*, 16 overs); 3rd day: West Indies (1) 269-9 (Taylor 22*, Powell 6*, 106 overs); 4th day: West Indies (2) 96-1 (Bravo 46*, Sarwan 34*, 23 overs).

Man of the Match: W.P.U.J.C.Vaas.
B.S.M.Warnapura's 120 took 226 balls in 269 minutes and included 14 fours. D.P.M.D.Jayawardene's 136 took 234 balls in 369 minutes and included 13 fours.

LEEWARD ISLANDS v COMBINED CAMPUSES AND COLLEGES

Played at Grove Park, Charlestown, Nevis, March 28, 29, 30, 31, 2008.
Carib Beer Cup 2007/08
Match drawn.   (Points: Leeward Islands 6, Combined Campuses and Colleges 3)

LEEWARD ISLANDS

1	S.M.Jeffers	c Reifer b Wallace	41	(2) b Hutchinson	21
2	K.O.A.Powell	c McClean b Wallace	85	(1) c Reifer b Clarke	99
3	*R.S.Morton	c Phillips b Noel	59	(5) not out	122
4	S.S.W.Liburd	run out (Parris)	41	c Noel b McClean	18
5	O.Peters	b Wallace	0	(3) c Reifer b Wallace	12
6	T.A.Willett	c Jackson b Wallace	67	c Walton b Clarke	90
7	†D.C.Thomas	c Jackson b Hutchinson	66		
8	G.C.Tonge	c Jackson b Wallace	17		
9	L.S.Baker	run out (Jackson)	2		
10	B.A.DeFreitas	b Wallace	4		
11	A.Martin	not out	1		
	Extras	b 16, lb 10, w 1, nb 8	35	b 5, lb 5, w 1, nb 13	24
			418	(5 wickets, declared)	386

FoW (1): 1-135 (2), 2-140 (1), 3-239 (4), 4-240 (5), 5-242 (3), 6-354 (7), 7-386 (8), 8-388 (9), 9-403 (10), 10-418 (6)
FoW (2): 1-82 (2), 2-98 (3), 3-129 (4), 4-193 (1), 5-386 (6)

COMBINED CAMPUSES AND COLLEGES

1	S.Jackson	c and b Willett	75	c Jeffers b Willett	46
2	O.J.Phillips	c Thomas b Martin	38	c Morton b Baker	14
3	N.Parris	c Thomas b Baker	14	not out	28
4	F.L.Reifer	lbw b Tonge	26	not out	2
5	†C.A.K.Walton	run out (DeFreitas)	32		
6	*S.M.Clarke	c Baker b Tonge	13		
7	C.W.Emmanuel	c Jeffers b Tonge	0		
8	K.R.McClean	not out	24		
9	G.Wallace	b DeFreitas	2		
10	J.Noel	c Willett b Tonge	8		
11	B.Hutchinson	c Thomas b DeFreitas	0		
	Extras	lb 6, w 1, nb 9	16	lb 1, w 3, nb 5	9
			248	(2 wickets)	99

FoW (1): 1-122 (1), 2-128 (2), 3-145 (3), 4-197, 5-204, 6-206, 7-219, 8-236, 9-246, 10-248
FoW (2): 1-30 (2), 2-82 (1)

Combined Campuses and Colleges Bowling

	O	M	R	W		O	M	R	W
Noel	16	0	64	1	(2)	16	1	70	0
McClean	9	1	40	0	(1)	9	0	39	1
Emmanuel	5	2	26	0					
Clarke	25	5	87	0	(5)	17	4	76	2
Hutchinson	7	2	61	1	(3)	13	2	55	1
Wallace	32.2	6	108	6	(4)	24	1	129	1
Jackson	2	0	6	0	(6)	1	0	7	0

Leeward Islands Bowling

	O	M	R	W		O	M	R	W
Baker	13	2	61	1		5	0	28	1
Tonge	11	1	66	4		6	1	21	0
Liburd	2	1	20	0					
DeFreitas	7.1	0	29	2	(3)	4	1	19	0
Martin	12	2	54	1		3	0	11	0
Willett	6	1	12	1	(4)	6	2	20	1

Umpires: P.B.Grazette and C.Whittle.   Toss: Leeward Islands

Close of Play: 1st day: Leeward Islands (1) 402-8 (Willett 52*, DeFreitas 4*, 91 overs); 2nd day: Leeward Islands (2) 82-1 (Powell 52*, 13.5 overs); 3rd day: Combined Campuses and Colleges (2) 99-2 (Parris 28*, Reifer 2*, 24 overs).

Man of the Match: K.O.A.Powell.
There was no play on the final day. R.S.Morton's 122 took 134 balls and included 16 fours and 2 sixes.

TRINIDAD AND TOBAGO v BARBADOS

Played at Guaracara Park, Pointe-a-Pierre, March 28, 29, 30, 31, 2008.
Carib Beer Cup 2007/08
Trinidad and Tobago won by 250 runs.   (Points: Trinidad and Tobago 12, Barbados 0)

TRINIDAD AND TOBAGO

#	Batsman	Dismissal 1	R	Dismissal 2	R
1	W.K.D.Perkins	c Collymore b Edwards	41	lbw b Stoute	22
2	A.B.Barath	c Browne b Benn	39	c Browne b Stoute	50
3	*D.Ganga	lbw b Collymore	12	c Richards b Edwards	23
4	L.M.P.Simmons	c Holder b Benn	126	run out	18
5	K.A.Pollard	c Browne b Benn	22	b Stoute	25
6	†G.Mohammed	b Stoute	19	lbw b Stoute	13
7	R.A.Kelly	c Stoute b Smith	68	c and b Stoute	12
8	R.R.Emrit	c Benn b Smith	1	not out	27
9	D.Mohammed	run out	15	lbw b Benn	3
10	R.Rampaul	b Benn	38		
11	A.S.Jaggernauth	not out	1	(10) lbw b Stoute	0
	Extras	b 6, lb 7, w 4, nb 21	38	b 6, lb 8, w 3, nb 5	22
			420	(9 wickets, declared)	**215**

FoW (1): 1-88 (2), 2-94 (1), 3-115 (3), 4-150 (5), 5-182 (6), 6-296 (7), 7-300 (8), 8-321 (9), 9-419 (10), 10-420 (4)
FoW (2): 1-73 (1), 2-76 (2), 3-116 (4), 4-133 (3), 5-164 (5), 6-174 (6), 7-191 (7), 8-198 (9), 9-215 (10)

BARBADOS

#	Batsman	Dismissal 1	R	Dismissal 2	R
1	D.M.Richards	lbw b Jaggernauth	38	c Kelly b Jaggernauth	77
2	J.A.M.Haynes	c G.Mohammed b Kelly	8	c Simmons b D.Mohammed	41
3	K.A.Stoute	c Pollard b Rampaul	21	c sub (A.Browne) b Jaggernauth	0
4	S.S.J.Brooks	c sub (A.Browne) b Emrit	17	(8) lbw b Jaggernauth	11
5	D.R.Smith	c G.Mohammed b D.Mohammed	39	c Kelly b Jaggernauth	8
6	J.L.Carter	b D.Mohammed	4	(7) not out	32
7	A.R.Holder	b Jaggernauth	27	(6) c Perkins b Jaggernauth	1
8	†P.A.Browne	lbw b Emrit	7	(4) c Jaggernauth b D.Mohammed	20
9	S.J.Benn	c G.Mohammed b Emrit	0	c Ganga b Jaggernauth	0
10	F.H.Edwards	c Simmons b Jaggernauth	7	lbw b Jaggernauth	5
11	*C.D.Collymore	not out	5	c G.Mohammed b Kelly	1
	Extras	lb 3, nb 8	11	lb 4, nb 1	5
			184		**201**

FoW (1): 1-18 (2), 2-56 (1), 3-68 (3), 4-129 (5), 5-135 (6), 6-135 (4), 7-157 (8), 8-157 (9), 9-177 (7), 10-184 (10)
FoW (2): 1-97 (2), 2-97 (3), 3-134 (1), 4-146 (4), 5-147 (6), 6-156 (5), 7-170 (8), 8-170 (9), 9-192 (10), 10-201 (11)

Barbados Bowling

	O	M	R	W			O	M	R	W	
Collymore	20	6	46	1			8	3	23	0	
Edwards	20	0	94	1	1w,15nb		16	6	43	1	4nb
Smith	21	1	64	2	2w,4nb		9	3	29	0	1nb
Stoute	8	2	33	1	1w,2nb	(5)	24	8	64	6	3w
Benn	39	7	136	4		(6)	9	2	22	1	
Carter	11	3	34	0							
Brooks						(4)	5	0	20	0	

Trinidad and Tobago Bowling

	O	M	R	W			O	M	R	W	
Rampaul	10	0	54	1	5nb		3	0	24	0	
Kelly	4	1	23	1			5.5	0	32	1	1nb
Jaggernauth	11.3	1	34	3		(5)	18	2	45	7	
Emrit	10	2	37	3	3nb	(3)	3	0	28	0	
D.Mohammed	9	2	33	2		(4)	18	2	68	2	

Umpires: R.Laroque and P.J.Nero. Referee: C.M.Shaffralli.   Toss: Trinidad and Tobago

Close of Play: 1st day: Trinidad and Tobago (1) 301-7 (Simmons 63*, D.Mohammed 1*, 89 overs); 2nd day: Trinidad and Tobago (2) 31-0 (Perkins 6*, Barath 21*, 13 overs); 3rd day: Trinidad and Tobago (2) 175-6 (Kelly 7*, Emrit 1*, 54.2 overs).

Man of the Match: L.M.P.Simmons.

L.M.P.Simmons's 126 took 279 balls in 392 minutes and included 9 fours and 1 six.

GUYANA v WINDWARD ISLANDS

Played at Providence Stadium, March 29, 30, 31, April 1, 2008.
Carib Beer Cup 2007/08
Match drawn. (Points: Guyana 3, Windward Islands 6)

GUYANA

1	S.Chattergoon	c James b Shillingford	27	(2) lbw b Matthew	98
2	K.Arjune	b Matthew	18	(1) lbw b Matthew	5
3	L.R.Johnson	c James b Shillingford	46	b Matthew	80
4	*T.M.Dowlin	not out	176		
5	S.Chanderpaul	retired out	78		
6	G.Singh	b Shillingford	14	(4) c Matthew b Pascal	15
7	†D.O.Christian	c Matthew b Sammy	5	(5) not out	17
8	E.A.Crandon	c Smith b Sammy	1		
9	D.Bishoo	c Lewis b Sammy	0	(6) run out	5
10	T.C.Garraway	b Shillingford	2		
11	Z.Mohamed	c Bascombe b Shillingford	4		
	Extras	b 4, lb 5, w 1, nb 15	25	b 13, lb 1, w 1, nb 15	30
			396	**(5 wickets)**	**250**

FoW (1): 1-42 (2), 2-55 (1), 3-161 (3), 4-312 (5), 5-362 (6), 6-377 (7), 7-379 (8), 8-379 (9), 9-382 (10), 10-396 (11)
FoW (2): 1-19 (1), 2-202 (2), 3-209 (3), 4-226 (4), 5-250 (5)

WINDWARD ISLANDS

1	D.S.Smith	c Bishoo b Dowlin	58
2	M.C.Bascombe	b Mohamed	54
3	A.D.S.Fletcher	lbw b Bishoo	29
4	L.A.S.Sebastien	c Arjune b Singh	133
5	D.J.G.Sammy	c Christian b Crandon	72
6	D.B.Hector	st Christian b Crandon	0
7	*R.N.Lewis	c Bishoo b Garraway	18
8	†L.O.D.James	lbw b Chattergoon	0
9	M.Matthew	b Johnson	39
10	S.Shillingford	not out	18
11	N.T.Pascal	c Arjune b Bishoo	16
	Extras	b 7, lb 7, w 3, nb 13	30
			467

FoW (1): 1-104 (1), 2-138 (2), 3-166 (3), 4-275 (5), 5-277 (6), 6-311 (7), 7-312 (8), 8-393 (9), 9-428 (11), 10-467 (4)

Windward Islands Bowling	O	M	R	W		O	M	R	W
Pascal	17	1	82	0		13	1	54	1
Matthew	20	6	41	1		18	6	39	3
Sammy	24	3	78	3		32	9	65	0
Shillingford	34.5	6	115	5		9	2	15	0
Sebastien	12	0	51	0		23	4	48	0
Fletcher	4	0	20	0	(7)	1	0	4	0
Smith					(6)	1	0	3	0
Hector					(8)	1	0	1	0
Bascombe					(9)	0.3	0	7	0

Guyana Bowling	O	M	R	W
Crandon	24	3	79	2
Garraway	28	3	98	1
Bishoo	43	6	156	2
Dowlin	14	1	36	1
Mohamed	2	0	8	1
Johnson	15	1	37	1
Singh	8.5	3	22	1
Chattergoon	12	5	17	1

Umpires: D.Anandjit and T.Birbal. Referee: O.Bacchus. Toss: Guyana
Close of Play: 1st day: Guyana (1) 312-3 (Dowlin 121*, Chanderpaul 78*, 90 overs); 2nd day: Windward Islands (1) 267-3 (Sebastien 42*, Sammy 65*, 70 overs); 3rd day: Guyana (2) 29-1 (Chattergoon 14*, Johnson 3*, 9 overs).
Man of the Match: T.M.Dowlin. T.M.Dowlin's 176 took 267 balls in 405 minutes and included 21 fours. L.A.S.Sebastien's 133 took 331 balls and included 11 fours. L.A.S.Sebastien retired hurt in the Windward Islands first innings with cramp in his hand (team score 404-8). He returned when the score was 428-9. The start of the match was delayed for a day as the Windward Islands gear had not arrived.Chanderpaul was not out at the end of the first day overnight but was not at the ground the following day as he had left the country to attend a West Indies Players Association function in Trinidad. He returned to field after lunch on the third day, Guyana being forced to field with 10 men.

WEST INDIES A v SRI LANKANS

Played at Shaw Park, Scarborough, Tobago, March 29, 30, 31, 2008.
Sri Lanka in West Indies 2007/08
Match cancelled.

The match was cancelled because of flight problems.

WEST INDIES v SRI LANKA

Played at Queen's Park Oval, Port of Spain, April 3, 4, 5, 6, 2008.
Sri Lanka in West Indies 2007/08 - 2nd Test
West Indies won by six wickets.

SRI LANKA

1	M.G.Vandort	c Ramdin b Edwards	30	run out		1
2	B.S.M.Warnapura	c Chattergoon b Edwards	35	c Chattergoon b Taylor		0
3	†K.C.Sangakkara	c Ramdin b Edwards	10	c Samuels b Powell		14
4	*D.P.M.D.Jayawardene	b Taylor	26	b Edwards		12
5	T.T.Samaraweera	c Gayle b Taylor	6	run out		125
6	T.M.Dilshan	c Ramdin b Edwards	62	b Taylor		25
7	L.P.C.Silva	c Powell b Bravo	76	c Samuels b Taylor		13
8	W.P.U.J.C.Vaas	c Ramdin b Powell	1	c Ramdin b Gayle		45
9	M.T.T.Mirando	run out (Sarwan)	1	c Ramdin b Bravo		10
10	M.Muralitharan	c Bravo b Powell	8	c Powell b Taylor		4
11	M.K.D.I.Amerasinghe	not out	0	not out		0
	Extras	lb 8, w 5, nb 10	23	b 1, lb 10, w 6, nb 2		19
			278			**268**

FoW (1): 1-62 (2), 2-72 (3), 3-93 (1), 4-112 (5), 5-117 (4), 6-222 (6), 7-224 (8), 8-240 (9), 9-255 (10), 10-278 (7)
FoW (2): 1-2 (2), 2-4 (1), 3-32 (4), 4-32 (3), 5-73 (6), 6-99 (7), 7-237 (8), 8-252 (9), 9-268 (5), 10-268 (10)

WEST INDIES

1	*C.H.Gayle	c Vandort b Mirando	45	c Dilshan b Mirando		10
2	S.Chattergoon	b Vaas	46	lbw b Vaas		11
3	R.R.Sarwan	c Warnapura b Muralitharan	57	c Dilshan b Muralitharan		102
4	M.N.Samuels	lbw b Muralitharan	3	c Warnapura b Vaas		11
5	S.Chanderpaul	lbw b Mirando	18	not out		86
6	D.S.Smith	b Muralitharan	47	not out		14
7	D.J.Bravo	lbw b Amerasinghe	26			
8	†D.Ramdin	c Jayawardene b Muralitharan	13			
9	J.E.Taylor	lbw b Vaas	13			
10	D.B.L.Powell	lbw b Muralitharan	3			
11	F.H.Edwards	not out	1			
	Extras	lb 5, w 2, nb 15	22	b 11, lb 2, w 2, nb 5		20
			294	**(4 wickets)**		**254**

FoW (1): 1-58 (1), 2-137 (2), 3-141 (4), 4-177 (3), 5-199 (5), 6-246 (7), 7-266 (6), 8-289 (9), 9-291 (8), 10-294 (10)
FoW (2): 1-23 (1), 2-24 (2), 3-73 (4), 4-230 (3)

West Indies Bowling

	O	M	R	W			O	M	R	W	
Powell	17	7	59	2	1w		13	4	49	1	1w
Taylor	17.2	7	74	2	2nb		15.1	1	52	4	1w
Edwards	18	4	84	4	3w,3nb		14	1	62	1	2nb
Gayle	2	2	0	0		(5)	14	0	30	1	
Bravo	10.3	2	53	1	1w,1nb	(4)	19	5	64	1	

Sri Lanka Bowling

	O	M	R	W			O	M	R	W	
Vaas	23	1	76	2	8nb		17	2	52	2	
Amerasinghe	12	1	62	1		(3)	13	0	43	0	
Mirando	12	0	72	2	1w,5nb	(2)	12	3	49	1	2w,1nb
Muralitharan	29.2	4	79	5	2nb		24.3	4	92	1	4nb
Silva						(5)	2	0	5	0	

Umpires: B.F.Bowden and S.J.A.Taufel. Third umpire: G.E.Greaves. Referee: B.C.Broad.　　　　Toss: West Indies

Close of Play: 1st day: Sri Lanka (1) 217-5 (Dilshan 58*, Silva 37*, 46.3 overs); 2nd day: West Indies (1) 268-7 (Ramdin 5*, Taylor 1*, 63.5 overs); 3rd day: Sri Lanka (2) 268 all out.

Man of the Match: R.R.Sarwan.

The match was scheduled for five days but completed in four. T.T.Samaraweera's 125 took 199 balls and included 18 fours. R.R.Sarwan's 102 took 172 balls and included 15 fours.

JAMAICA v TRINIDAD AND TOBAGO

Played at Sabina Park, Kingston, April 24, 25, 26, 2008.
Carib Beer Challenge 2007/08
Jamaica won by nine wickets.

TRINIDAD AND TOBAGO

1	*D.Ganga	run out (Lambert/Baugh)	18	b Powell	27
2	A.B.Barath	b Taylor	9	c Samuels b Miller	33
3	D.M.Bravo	c Samuels b Miller	12	c Parchment b Miller	1
4	L.M.P.Simmons	c Hyatt b Miller	0	lbw b Taylor	13
5	K.A.Pollard	c Hyatt b Powell	5	c Taylor b Miller	20
6	†D.Ramdin	retired hurt	7	c Samuels b Miller	6
7	R.A.Kelly	c and b Miller	7	c Samuels b Lambert	50
8	D.Mohammed	not out	30	c and b Miller	57
9	R.Rampaul	c Parchment b Miller	0	c Miller b Brown	19
10	A.S.Jaggernauth	b Taylor	10	not out	4
11	M.Dillon	c Nash b Miller	17	b Powell	1
	Extras	lb 5, w 1	6	b 6, lb 3, nb 1	10
			121		**241**

FoW (1): 1-16 (2), 2-39 (3), 3-42 (4), 4-43 (1), 5-54 (5), 6-65 (7), 7-69 (9), 8-96 (10), 9-121 (11)
FoW (2): 1-50 (1), 2-51 (3), 3-80 (2), 4-90 (4), 5-104 (5), 6-128 (6), 7-165 (7), 8-199 (9), 9-240 (8), 10-241 (11)

JAMAICA

1	B.A.Parchment	c Bravo b Jaggernauth	34	c Simmons b Rampaul	4
2	D.P.Hyatt	run out (Jaggernauth)	3	not out	24
3	M.N.Samuels	c sub (W.K.D.Perkins) b Rampaul	9	not out	37
4	W.W.Hinds	c Mohammed b Dillon	0		
5	B.P.Nash	c Simmons b Rampaul	117		
6	*T.L.Lambert	c Ganga b Dillon	50		
7	†C.S.Baugh	c Simmons b Rampaul	17		
8	N.O.Miller	c Simmons b Kelly	11		
9	J.E.Taylor	not out	27		
10	D.B.L.Powell	c Mohammed b Dillon	14		
11	O.V.Brown	c Simmons b Kelly	4		
	Extras	w 1, nb 6	7	b 6	6
			293	**(1 wicket)**	**71**

FoW (1): 1-5 (2), 2-17 (3), 3-29 (4), 4-94 (1), 5-200 (6), 6-231 (7), 7-243 (5), 8-258 (8), 9-285 (10), 10-293 (11)
FoW (2): 1-9 (1)

Jamaica Bowling

	O	M	R	W			O	M	R	W	
Taylor	14	4	46	2			17	7	36	1	1nb
Powell	13	3	34	1	1w		13.3	1	42	2	
Miller	18.4	5	29	5		(4)	30	9	92	5	
Nash	4	0	7	0							
Brown						(3)	15	3	51	1	
Lambert						(5)	4	0	11	1	

Trinidad and Tobago Bowling

	O	M	R	W			O	M	R	W	
Rampaul	18	2	75	3	4nb		4	0	21	1	
Dillon	18	7	57	3	2nb		4	1	10	0	
Kelly	14.2	2	46	2			2	0	24	0	
Jaggernauth	29	8	56	1			2	0	10	0	
Mohammed	16	3	31	0							
Pollard	11	3	28	0	1w						

Umpires: V.V.Bullen and E.A.Nicholls. Third umpire: N.A.Malcolm. Referee: D.Bryan.   Toss: Jamaica

Close of Play: 1st day: Jamaica (1) 107-4 (Nash 56*, Lambert 3*, 37 overs); 2nd day: Trinidad and Tobago (2) 43-0 (Ganga 24*, Barath 19*, 21 overs).
Man of the Match: N.O.Miller.
The match was scheduled for five days but completed in three. B.P.Nash's 117 took 291 balls in 385 minutes and included 13 fours.
D.Ramdin retired hurt in the Trinidad and Tobago first innings having scored 7 (team score 57-5). He was hit in the face by a ball from Powell. L.M.P.Simmons kept wicket as Ramdin was injured.

ZIMBABWE SELECT XI v INDIA A

Played at Harare Sports Club, July 24, 25, 26, 27, 2007.
India A in Kenya and Zimbabwe 2007/08
India A won by nine wickets.

INDIA A

1	C.A.Pujara	c Chigumbura b Mpofu	8		
2	R.V.Uthappa	c Rainsford b Utseya	88	(1) c Masakadza b Brent	7
3	†P.A.Patel	c Brent b Chigumbura	67		
4	*M.Kaif	c Taibu b Utseya	63		
5	R.G.Sharma	lbw b Chigumbura	66	(3) not out	16
6	S.Badrinath	c Taibu b Rainsford	62		
7	I.K.Pathan	lbw b Mpofu	0	(2) not out	39
8	P.P.Chawla	c Taibu b Rainsford	58		
9	V.Y.Mahesh	c Taibu b Rainsford	10		
10	R.V.Pawar	not out	21		
11	V.R.Singh	c and b Mpofu	26		
	Extras	lb 3, w 4, nb 13	20	w 5, nb 2	7
			489	(1 wicket)	69

FoW (1): 1-56 (1), 2-133 (2), 3-201 (3), 4-274 (4), 5-331 (5), 6-332 (7), 7-422 (8), 8-430 (6), 9-444 (9), 10-489 (11)
FoW (2): 1-26 (1)

ZIMBABWE SELECT XI

1	T.M.K.Mawoyo	c Kaif b Mahesh	24	lbw b Singh	0
2	H.Masakadza	b Pawar	38	c Patel b Pathan	8
3	V.Sibanda	c Kaif b Singh	12	b Chawla	69
4	†T.Taibu	b Chawla	123	c Patel b Chawla	40
5	S.Matsikenyeri	b Chawla	21	lbw b Singh	0
6	E.C.Rainsford	b Mahesh	0	(10) b Pawar	0
7	E.Chigumbura	lbw b Pathan	0	(6) c and b Chawla	30
8	*P.Utseya	c Patel b Chawla	53	(7) lbw b Sharma	18
9	A.G.Cremer	c Patel b Pathan	13	(8) b Pawar	6
10	G.B.Brent	not out	15	(9) not out	13
11	C.B.Mpofu	b Chawla	0	lbw b Chawla	3
	Extras	b 5, lb 14, w 7, nb 13	39	b 4, lb 5, w 2, nb 18	29
			338		216

FoW (1): 1-45 (1), 2-72 (3), 3-82 (2), 4-129 (5), 5-135 (6), 6-136 (7), 7-264 (8), 8-283 (9), 9-334 (4), 10-338 (11)
FoW (2): 1-0 (1), 2-15 (2), 3-123 (4), 4-124 (5), 5-127 (3), 6-173 (6), 7-191 (7), 8-191 (8), 9-193 (10), 10-216 (11)

Zimbabwe Select XI Bowling

	O	M	R	W			O	M	R	W	
Mpofu	27	8	90	3	3w,3nb	(2)	3	0	19	0	
Rainsford	22	4	82	3	6nb	(1)	3.4	0	19	0	5w,2nb
Chigumbura	20	6	64	2	2nb	(4)	0.1	0	4	0	
Brent	14	7	30	0		(3)	3	0	27	1	
Utseya	32	2	126	2	1nb						
Cremer	22	2	88	0							
Matsikenyeri	1	0	6	0	1nb						

India A Bowling

	O	M	R	W			O	M	R	W	
Pathan	20	2	80	2	2w,11nb	(5)	12	3	43	1	4nb
Mahesh	24	3	67	2	1w	(4)	9	4	22	0	1w
Pawar	28	8	70	1		(2)	15	2	46	2	
Singh	19	4	57	1	3w,2nb	(1)	19.4	5	54	2	14nb
Chawla	22.2	2	40	4		(3)	21.1	8	30	4	
Sharma	3	0	5	0			5	0	12	1	

Umpires: K.C.Barbour and R.B.Tiffin.   Referee: B.Jackman.   Toss: India A

Close of Play: 1st day: India A (1) 331-5 (Badrinath 24*, 90 overs); 2nd day: Zimbabwe Select XI (1) 129-4 (Taibu 25*, 35.5 overs); 3rd day: Zimbabwe Select XI (2) 15-1 (Masakadza 8*, Sibanda 7*, 9 overs).

T.Taibu's 123 took 245 balls in 375 minutes and included 11 fours.

ZIMBABWE SELECT XI v INDIA A

Played at Queens Sports Club, Bulawayo, July 30, 31, August 1, 2007.
India A in Kenya and Zimbabwe 2007/08
India A won by an innings and 233 runs.

INDIA A

1	C.A.Pujara	c Taibu b Utseya	100
2	R.V.Uthappa	c Sibanda b Rainsford	67
3	†P.A.Patel	b Utseya	126
4	*M.Kaif	c Taibu b Brent	26
5	R.G.Sharma	c Taibu b Rainsford	14
6	S.Badrinath	not out	103
7	I.K.Pathan	lbw b Brent	0
8	P.P.Chawla	c Mpofu b Rainsford	50
9	Pankaj Singh	c Sibanda b Rainsford	4
10	V.Y.Mahesh	not out	8
11	P.P.Ojha		
	Extras	lb 1, w 3, nb 22	26
		(8 wickets, declared)	524

FoW (1): 1-110 (2), 2-224 (1), 3-296 (4), 4-318 (5), 5-378 (3), 6-379 (7), 7-484 (8), 8-488 (9)

ZIMBABWE SELECT XI

1	T.M.K.Mawoyo	lbw b Mahesh	20	c Patel b Chawla	33
2	H.Masakadza	c Uthappa b Ojha	24	lbw b Pathan	73
3	V.Sibanda	b Ojha	0	b Chawla	0
4	†T.Taibu	b Chawla	10	lbw b Ojha	19
5	S.Matsikenyeri	lbw b Ojha	18	lbw b Chawla	11
6	E.C.Rainsford	b Chawla	0	(10) c Uthappa b Chawla	0
7	E.Chigumbura	c Patel b Pankaj Singh	20	(6) c Sharma b Chawla	0
8	*P.Utseya	c Mahesh b Chawla	26	(7) lbw b Chawla	0
9	A.G.Cremer	lbw b Ojha	11	(8) c Patel b Pathan	4
10	G.B.Brent	lbw b Chawla	7	(9) lbw b Pathan	0
11	C.B.Mpofu	not out	0	not out	0
	Extras	b 1, lb 2, nb 4	7	b 4, lb 1, nb 3	8
			143		148

FoW (1): 1-45 (2), 2-45 (3), 3-45 (1), 4-67 (4), 5-67 (6), 6-89 (5), 7-101 (7), 8-122 (9), 9-141 (10), 10-143 (8)
FoW (2): 1-63 (1), 2-67 (3), 3-116 (4), 4-143 (5), 5-143 (6), 6-143 (7), 7-145 (2), 8-145 (9), 9-148 (8), 10-148 (10)

Zimbabwe Select XI Bowling

	O	M	R	W	
Rainsford	24	2	100	4	1w,17nb
Mpofu	26.5	3	108	0	1nb
Brent	33	8	74	2	
Cremer	27	1	123	0	
Utseya	32	6	80	2	4nb
Matsikenyeri	2	0	13	0	
Masakadza	8	0	25	0	2w

India A Bowling

	O	M	R	W			O	M	R	W
Pathan	11	2	46	0	3nb	(5)	10	6	12	3
Mahesh	8	3	19	1		(1)	6	0	30	0
Ojha	21	6	45	4	1nb		12	2	30	1
Chawla	5.1	1	12	4			15.3	3	46	6
Pankaj Singh	6	1	18	1		(2)	7	1	25	0

Umpires: K.C.Barbour and R.B.Tiffin.   Referee: D.W.Townshend.   Toss: India A

Close of Play: 1st day: India A (1) 291-2 (Patel 76*, Kaif 26*, 91 overs); 2nd day: Zimbabwe Select XI (1) 67-5 (Matsikenyeri 10*, Chigumbura 0*, 26 overs).

The match was scheduled for four days but completed in three. C.A.Pujara's 100 took 235 balls in 238 minutes and included 11 fours. P.A.Patel's 126 took 259 balls in 332 minutes and included 12 fours. S.Badrinath's 103 took 150 balls in 207 minutes and included 10 fours and 2 sixes.

ZIMBABWE SELECT XI v SOUTH AFRICA A

Played at Harare Sports Club, August 9, 10, 11, 12, 2007.
South Africa A in Zimbabwe 2007/08
South Africa A won by eight wickets.

ZIMBABWE SELECT XI

1	T.M.K.Mawoyo	c Tsolekile b Langeveldt	9	lbw b Nel	20
2	H.Masakadza	c Botha b Hall	40	run out	4
3	C.J.Chibhabha	c Tsolekile b Nel	18	b Langeveldt	3
4	V.Sibanda	lbw b Hall	68	(5) lbw b Harris	3
5	†T.Taibu	not out	63	(4) c Tsolekile b Hall	24
6	S.Matsikenyeri	c Tsolekile b Hall	10	not out	67
7	*P.Utseya	lbw b Harris	9	lbw b Harris	4
8	T.Maruma	b Langeveldt	5	b Hall	0
9	G.B.Brent	c Tsolekile b Langeveldt	4	c Langeveldt b Harris	18
10	T.Mupariwa	c Tsolekile b Nel	3	c Langeveldt b Harris	15
11	C.B.Mpofu	lbw b Langeveldt	0	lbw b Hall	0
	Extras	b 4, lb 1, w 5, nb 3	13	b 6, lb 1, w 2, nb 2	11
			242		**169**

FoW (1): 1-11 (1), 2-31 (3), 3-120 (2), 4-165 (4), 5-179 (6), 6-205 (7), 7-223 (8), 8-232 (9), 9-237 (10), 10-242 (11)
FoW (2): 1-25 (2), 2-25 (1), 3-48 (3), 4-61 (4), 5-61 (5), 6-71 (7), 7-78 (8), 8-128 (9), 9-169 (10), 10-169 (11)

SOUTH AFRICA A

1	M.N.van Wyk	c Taibu b Mpofu	12	not out	63
2	A.N.Petersen	b Brent	12	c Maruma b Mupariwa	14
3	H.M.Amla	lbw b Brent	15	(4) not out	9
4	*H.H.Dippenaar	c Matsikenyeri b Maruma	77		
5	J.L.Ontong	c Taibu b Mupariwa	101		
6	A.J.Hall	c Taibu b Brent	37		
7	†T.L.Tsolekile	run out (Mupariwa)	5		
8	J.Botha	not out	8		
9	P.L.Harris	c Matsikenyeri b Brent	0	(3) c Maruma b Matsikenyeri	40
10	A.Nel	c Taibu b Mpofu	1		
11	C.K.Langeveldt	c Mupariwa b Mpofu	0		
	Extras	b 4, lb 2, w 1, nb 5	12	b 4, lb 1, nb 1	6
			280	**(2 wickets)**	**132**

FoW (1): 1-20 (1), 2-24 (2), 3-39 (3), 4-190 (5), 5-255 (4), 6-261 (7), 7-278 (6), 8-279 (8), 9-280 (10), 10-280 (11)
FoW (2): 1-36 (2), 2-118 (3)

South Africa A Bowling

	O	M	R	W			O	M	R	W	
Nel	21	9	47	2	5w		12	3	30	1	
Langeveldt	24	6	62	4	2nb		18	3	30	1	2w
Hall	14	4	29	3	1nb	(4)	14	3	38	3	2nb
Harris	22	7	55	1		(3)	23	6	38	4	
Botha	17	3	44	0			10	1	26	0	
Ontong	1	1	0	0							

Zimbabwe Select XI Bowling

	O	M	R	W			O	M	R	W	
Mpofu	8.3	2	39	3	1w		8	1	25	0	
Brent	14	4	48	4			8	3	29	0	
Mupariwa	10	1	54	1	2nb		3	0	8	1	
Maruma	18	2	51	1	3nb	(5)	9	0	36	0	
Utseya	21	0	82	0		(6)	4	0	16	0	
Chibhabha						(4)	1	0	2	0	1nb
Matsikenyeri						(7)	4.2	1	11	1	

Umpires: K.C.Barbour and I.D.Robinson.   Referee: R.C.Strang.   Toss: Zimbabwe Select XI

Close of Play: 1st day: Zimbabwe Select XI (1) 223-7 (Sibanda 56*, 91 overs); 2nd day: Zimbabwe Select XI (2) 17-0 (Mawoyo 13*, Masakadza 4*, 6 overs); 3rd day: South Africa A (2) 44-1 (van Wyk 25*, Harris 0*, 17 overs).

J.L.Ontong's 101 took 86 balls in 98 minutes and included 14 fours and 1 six.

ZIMBABWE A v SOUTH AFRICA ACADEMY

Played at Harare Sports Club, August 15, 16, 17, 18, 2007.
South Africa Academy in Zimbabwe 2007/08
South Africa Academy won by eight wickets.

ZIMBABWE A

1	T.M.K.Mawoyo	c Walters b le Roux	39	lbw b le Roux	26	
2	E.Chauluka	run out (Razak)	1	c Walters b le Roux	8	
3	C.J.Chibhabha	run out (Swan)	98	(5) c Walters b Campher	23	
4	S.C.Williams	c Gray b Bhayat	11	c Gray b le Roux	25	
5	A.Maregwede	c Walters b Razak	16	(3) c Walters b Bhayat	4	
6	†R.W.Chakabva	b Campher	47	c Walters b van Wyk	32	
7	A.G.Cremer	b Campher	23	b van Wyk	21	
8	T.Mupariwa	not out	2	not out	28	
9	T.N.Garwe	c Walters b van Wyk	1	c Walters b van Wyk	6	
10	E.C.Rainsford	b van Wyk	0	c Gray b Mathebula	1	
11	T.Kamungozi	run out (van Wyk)	1	run out (van Wyk)	1	
	Extras	b 1, lb 13, w 2, nb 24	40	lb 5, w 10, nb 6	21	
			279		**196**	

FoW (1): 1-15 (2), 2-104 (1), 3-138 (4), 4-186 (3), 5-207 (5), 6-242 (7), 7-276 (6), 8-278 (9), 9-278 (10), 10-279 (11)
FoW (2): 1-41 (1), 2-43 (2), 3-51 (3), 4-81 (4), 5-102 (5), 6-156 (6), 7-161 (7), 8-173 (9), 9-186 (10), 10-196 (11)

SOUTH AFRICA ACADEMY

1	A.J.A.Gray	lbw b Rainsford	11	c Williams b Cremer	42	
2	M.Akoojee	lbw b Garwe	149	lbw b Cremer	11	
3	W.C.Swan	c Chakabva b Chibhabha	44	not out	9	
4	E.P.van Wyk	b Cremer	98	not out	1	
5	M.Bekker	c Kamungozi b Garwe	28			
6	H.W.le Roux	b Garwe	0			
7	†L.R.Walters	c Chakabva b Mupariwa	11			
8	R.Bhayat	run out (Mupariwa)	22			
9	A.H.Razak	run out (Chauluka)	9			
10	J.P.Campher	c Garwe b Cremer	3			
11	B.M.Mathebula	not out	0			
	Extras	b 2, lb 9, nb 24	35	nb 3	3	
			410	**(2 wickets)**	**66**	

FoW (1): 1-20 (1), 2-98 (3), 3-282 (4), 4-324 (5), 5-339 (6), 6-372 (7), 7-375 (2), 8-403 (9), 9-410 (8), 10-410 (10)
FoW (2): 1-49 (2), 2-62 (1)

South Africa Academy Bowling

	O	M	R	W		O	M	R	W	
Mathebula	12	2	33	0	10nb	20	5	55	1	7w,3nb
Campher	12	2	37	2	14nb	10.5	3	29	1	2w,2nb
Bhayat	18	3	61	1	2w,10nb	11	1	41	1	1w
le Roux	27	10	38	1		16	10	18	3	1nb
van Wyk	13.1	3	39	2	(6)	13	3	17	3	
Razak	20	4	57	1	(5)	15	2	31	0	

Zimbabwe A Bowling

	O	M	R	W		O	M	R	W	
Rainsford	13.4	1	76	1	14nb	1	0	7	0	
Garwe	19	3	51	3		5	1	15	0	
Mupariwa	18.1	5	54	1		4	0	17	0	
Chibhabha	13.1	1	56	1	6nb					
Cremer	31.4	5	103	2	4nb	(4)	4.1	1	11	2
Kamungozi	19	3	59	0		(5)	4	1	16	0

Umpires: O.Chirombe and T.J.Tapfumaneyi. Referee: S.Kombayi.   Toss: Zimbabwe A

Close of Play: 1st day: ; 2nd day: South Africa Academy (1) 282-3 (Akoojee 105*, Bekker 0*, 75 overs); 3rd day: .

M.Akoojee's 149 took 292 balls in 454 minutes and included 15 fours.

ZIMBABWE SELECT XI v SOUTH AFRICA A

Played at Queens Sports Club, Bulawayo, August 15, 16, 17, 18, 2007.
South Africa A in Zimbabwe 2007/08
South Africa A won by an innings and 219 runs.

SOUTH AFRICA A

1	M.N.van Wyk	lbw b Mpofu	30
2	I.Khan	run out (Chigumbura)	27
3	H.M.Amla	c Masakadza b Chigumbura	142
4	*H.H.Dippenaar	c Sibanda b Masakadza	189
5	A.G.Prince	b Brent	34
6	J.L.Ontong	c Chigumbura b Dabengwa	70
7	A.J.Hall	not out	28
8	†T.L.Tsolekile	run out (Utseya)	1
9	P.L.Harris		
10	Y.A.Abdulla		
11	A.Nel		
	Extras	b 1, lb 6, w 6, nb 8	21
		(7 wickets, declared)	542

FoW (1): 1-51 (2), 2-70 (1), 3-326 (3), 4-410 (5), 5-478 (4), 6-526 (6), 7-542 (8)

ZIMBABWE SELECT XI

1	H.Masakadza	c Tsolekile b Nel	15	c Prince b Harris	32
2	B.R.M.Taylor	c Khan b Harris	2	lbw b Harris	13
3	V.Sibanda	lbw b Harris	4	b Hall	7
4	†T.Taibu	b Nel	8	c Ontong b Nel	41
5	T.Maruma	lbw b Nel	8	(10) lbw b Harris	0
6	S.Matsikenyeri	c Hall b Harris	26	(5) c Abdulla b Harris	4
7	E.Chigumbura	c Tsolekile b Abdulla	18	(6) lbw b Nel	4
8	K.M.Dabengwa	lbw b Harris	9	(7) b Abdulla	31
9	*P.Utseya	c Nel b Harris	32	(8) c Tsolekile b Nel	0
10	G.B.Brent	not out	25	(9) lbw b Hall	15
11	C.B.Mpofu	b Hall	0	not out	15
	Extras	b 5, lb 1, nb 2	8	b 2, lb 3, nb 1	6
			155		168

FoW (1): 1-17 (1), 2-22 (2), 3-24 (3), 4-38 (4), 5-45 (5), 6-71 (7), 7-89 (6), 8-94 (8), 9-153 (9), 10-155 (11)
FoW (2): 1-24 (2), 2-39 (3), 3-95 (1), 4-95 (4), 5-103 (5), 6-103 (6), 7-105 (8), 8-144 (9), 9-148 (10), 10-168 (7)

Zimbabwe Select XI Bowling

	O	M	R	W	
Mpofu	32	4	117	1	2w,1nb
Brent	26	9	67	1	
Chigumbura	24	4	82	1	2w,5nb
Utseya	25	4	74	0	
Maruma	23	3	76	0	1nb
Dabengwa	15.2	1	65	1	
Masakadza	15	2	54	1	2w

South Africa A Bowling

	O	M	R	W			O	M	R	W	
Nel	16	7	23	3			16	11	18	3	
Abdulla	10	4	29	1	1nb	(3)	10.2	4	19	1	
Harris	32	11	67	5		(2)	31	10	77	4	
Hall	7.3	4	4	1	1nb		9	4	20	2	1nb
Ontong	5	0	15	0			4	1	14	0	
Khan	3	0	11	0			2	0	15	0	

Umpires: K.C.Barbour and R.B.Tiffin. Referee: D.W.Townshend.   Toss: South Africa A

Close of Play: 1st day: South Africa A (1) 287-2 (Amla 115*, Dippenaar 103*, 94 overs); 2nd day: Zimbabwe Select XI (1) 36-3 (Taibu 6*, Maruma 6*, 21 overs); 3rd day: Zimbabwe Select XI (2) 95-2 (Masakadza 32*, Taibu 41*, 42 overs).

H.M.Amla's 142 took 295 balls in 335 minutes and included 19 fours and 1 six. H.H.Dippenaar's 189 took 337 balls in 485 minutes and included 19 fours and 1 six.

ZIMBABWE A v SOUTH AFRICA ACADEMY

Played at Queens Sports Club, Bulawayo, August 23, 24, 25, 26, 2007.
South Africa Academy in Zimbabwe 2007/08
South Africa Academy won by nine wickets.

ZIMBABWE A

1	T.M.K.Mawoyo	c Bekker b Wagner	6	lbw b Mathebula	0
2	A.Tichana	c Ndlovu b Mathebula	9	c Ndlovu b McMillan	41
3	E.Chauluka	st Ndlovu b Serame	74	b McMillan	20
4	A.Maregwede	b McMillan	31	st Ndlovu b Serame	70
5	†R.W.Chakabva	lbw b McMillan	0	lbw b van Wyk	53
6	S.K.Nyamuzinga	b McMillan	53	c Ndlovu b Bennett	8
7	A.M.Manyumwa	b Wagner	10	c McMillan b Bennett	55
8	A.G.Cremer	lbw b Wagner	19	c Bennett b Wagner	25
9	N.B.Mahwire	lbw b Wagner	7	lbw b van Wyk	2
10	T.S.Chisoro	c Bekker b Wagner	9	b Wagner	14
11	T.Muzarabani	not out	0	not out	2
	Extras	b 1, lb 7, nb 2, pen 5	15	b 3, lb 7, nb 7	17
			233		307

FoW (1): 1-9 (1), 2-17 (2), 3-93 (4), 4-93 (5), 5-177 (3), 6-185 (6), 7-211 (7), 8-212 (8), 9-222 (9), 10-233 (10)
FoW (2): 1-1 (1), 2-42 (3), 3-115 (2), 4-151 (4), 5-173 (6), 6-252 (5), 7-265 (7), 8-271 (9), 9-296 (10), 10-307 (8)

SOUTH AFRICA ACADEMY

1	A.J.A.Gray	lbw b Mahwire	142	b Cremer	9
2	M.Akoojee	lbw b Mahwire	34	not out	58
3	B.L.Bennett	lbw b Nyamuzinga	88	not out	24
4	E.P.van Wyk	c Chakabva b Chisoro	59		
5	M.Bekker	c Chakabva b Nyamuzinga	4		
6	H.W.le Roux	b Mahwire	41		
7	R.D.McMillan	b Mahwire	41		
8	†A.L.Ndlovu	not out	5		
9	N.Wagner	not out	1		
10	N.M.Serame				
11	B.M.Mathebula				
	Extras	b 8, lb 9, w 2, nb 8	27	b 6, w 1, nb 1	8
		(7 wickets, declared)	442	(1 wicket)	99

FoW (1): 1-96 (2), 2-233 (1), 3-345 (3), 4-350 (4), 5-352 (5), 6-434 (7), 7-439 (6)
FoW (2): 1-19 (1)

South Africa Academy Bowling

	O	M	R	W			O	M	R	W	
Mathebula	14	2	41	1	1nb		13	2	38	1	2nb
Wagner	15.2	7	28	5			16.2	5	51	2	
le Roux	16	6	38	0			6	1	15	0	
van Wyk	16	5	39	0		(7)	5	0	17	2	
McMillan	15	3	44	3	1nb	(4)	14	5	28	2	
Serame	10	0	35	1			11	0	54	1	
Bennett						(5)	22	1	94	2	5nb

Zimbabwe A Bowling

	O	M	R	W			O	M	R	W	
Mahwire	26	4	73	4	1w		5	1	19	0	
Muzarabani	20	6	48	0	1w		2	0	8	0	1w,1nb
Chisoro	19	2	66	1	3w						
Manyumwa	27	7	74	0		(5)	3	0	18	0	
Cremer	40	5	99	0		(3)	13	3	27	1	
Tichana	4	0	18	0		(4)	8	1	21	0	
Nyamuzinga	9	0	47	2	3w						

Umpires: C.Bester and N.N.Singo. Referee: D.W.Townshend.   Toss: Zimbabwe A

Close of Play: 1st day: ; 2nd day: ; 3rd day: .

A.J.A.Gray's 142 took 233 balls in 336 minutes and included 2 sixes.

ZIMBABWE PROVINCES v GAUTENG

Played at Queens Sports Club, Bulawayo, October 11, 12, 13, 2007.
South African Airways Provincial Three-Day Challenge 2007/08 - Pool B
Gauteng won by nine wickets.　　(Points: Zimbabwe Provinces 6.38, Gauteng 19.92)

ZIMBABWE PROVINCES

1	T.M.K.Mawoyo	c Vilas b Burger	2	(2) c Vilas b Mafa	32
2	T.Duffin	lbw b Mathebula	0	(1) lbw b Cameron	21
3	E.Chauluka	c Ramela b Mathebula	0	c Vilas b Das Neves	13
4	A.Maregwede	c Vilas b Burger	8	st Vilas b Symes	58
5	†R.W.Chakabva	run out (Vilas)	64	c Makalima b Das Neves	48
6	S.K.Nyamuzinga	c Ramela b Mafa	34	c Makalima b Das Neves	0
7	A.G.Cremer	run out (Ramela)	3	c Makalima b Das Neves	38
8	*N.B.Mahwire	c Makalima b Burger	9	not out	14
9	T.N.Garwe	hit wkt b Das Neves	5	b Symes	1
10	P.M.Tsvanhu	lbw b Das Neves	19	c Mafa b Das Neves	2
11	T.Kamungozi	not out	11	run out	0
	Extras	lb 6, nb 8	14	b 1, lb 4, nb 5	10
			169		237

FoW (1): 1-2 (2), 2-2 (1), 3-2 (3), 4-20 (4), 5-93 (6), 6-105 (7), 7-122 (8), 8-133 (5), 9-155 (9), 10-169 (10)
FoW (2): 1-54 (2), 2-54 (1), 3-126 (4), 4-128 (3), 5-128 (6), 6-220 (7), 7-220 (5), 8-225 (9), 9-236 (10), 10-237 (11)

GAUTENG

1	J.Symes	lbw b Mahwire	2	not out	49
2	W.B.Motaung	c Mawoyo b Garwe	44	b Cremer	4
3	O.A.Ramela	c Nyamuzinga b Garwe	33	not out	6
4	W.C.Swan	lbw b Garwe	5		
5	D.L.Makalima	c and b Cremer	4		
6	*S.Burger	lbw b Kamungozi	53		
7	†D.J.Vilas	c Tsvanhu b Cremer	93		
8	R.Cameron	not out	66		
9	R.Das Neves	c Kamungozi b Cremer	32		
10	B.M.Mathebula	lbw b Cremer	7		
11	J.T.Mafa	c Cremer b Kamungozi	0		
	Extras	b 3, w 1, nb 3	7	w 1, nb 2	3
			346	(1 wicket)	62

FoW (1): 1-2 (1), 2-73 (3), 3-86 (4), 4-91 (5), 5-91 (2), 6-233 (6), 7-275 (7), 8-328 (9), 9-345 (10), 10-346 (11)
FoW (2): 1-42 (2)

Gauteng Bowling

	O	M	R	W			O	M	R	W	
Burger	14	7	36	3		(2)	10	4	30	0	
Mathebula	8	2	28	2	5nb	(1)	8	1	33	0	
Mafa	8	0	32	1	2nb		8	3	38	1	3nb
Cameron	5	0	30	0			6	2	30	1	1nb
Symes	10	3	26	0	1nb	(6)	14	5	35	2	1nb
Das Neves	2.5	0	11	2		(5)	19.1	4	52	5	
Swan						(7)	3	0	8	0	
Ramela						(8)	4	2	6	0	

Zimbabwe Provinces Bowling

	O	M	R	W			O	M	R	W	
Mahwire	10	2	38	1	1w		4	1	15	0	1w
Tsvanhu	11	2	52	0			4	1	23	0	1nb
Nyamuzinga	3	0	12	0	1nb						
Garwe	17	3	54	3		(3)	2	0	12	0	
Cremer	25	0	113	4	2nb	(4)	2.1	0	6	1	1nb
Kamungozi	14.3	1	74	2		(5)	1	0	6	0	

Umpires: S.George and N.N.Singo.　Referee: D.W.Townshend.　　　Toss: Zimbabwe Provinces

Close of Play: 1st day: Gauteng (1) 135-5 (Burger 24*, Vilas 20*, 41.1 overs); 2nd day: Zimbabwe Provinces (2) 237 all out.

Cameron scored his fifty off 48 balls in Gauteng's 2nd innings. Maregwede scored his fifty off 24 balls in Zimbabwe Provinces' 2nd innings.

ZIMBABWE SELECT XI v SRI LANKA A

Played at Harare Sports Club, October 16, 17, 18, 19, 2007.
Sri Lanka A in Zimbabwe 2007/08
Match drawn.

SRI LANKA A

1	M.L.Udawatte	c Taibu b Mpofu	1	hit wkt b Utseya	31	
2	N.T.Paranavitana	c Dabengwa b Utseya	48	c Taylor b Mupariwa	15	
3	B.S.M.Warnapura	c Taibu b Mupariwa	71	c Williams b Brent	55	
4	*T.M.Dilshan	c Taibu b Utseya	3	b Chibhabha	5	
5	†J.K.Silva	c Taylor b Mpofu	63	c Taibu b Utseya	2	
6	C.K.Kapugedera	c Matsikenyeri b Utseya	8	not out	58	
7	M.D.K.Perera	c Brent b Mpofu	75	not out	27	
8	K.T.G.D.Prasad	c Taibu b Brent	5			
9	H.M.R.K.B.Herath	not out	59			
10	K.M.D.N.Kulasekara	lbw b Brent	41			
11	W.C.A.Ganegama	c Taibu b Utseya	37			
	Extras	lb 11, w 1, nb 3	15	b 4, lb 2, w 2	8	
			426	**(5 wickets, declared)**	**203**	

FoW (1): 1-2 (1), 2-120 (2), 3-128 (3), 4-130 (4), 5-138 (6), 6-279 (7), 7-279 (5), 8-289 (8), 9-364 (10), 10-426 (11)
FoW (2): 1-33 (2), 2-55 (1), 3-64 (4), 4-73 (5), 5-150 (3)

ZIMBABWE SELECT XI

1	V.Sibanda	c Dilshan b Herath	55	c Warnapura b Herath	47	
2	B.R.M.Taylor	lbw b Herath	30	lbw b Kulasekara	21	
3	C.J.Chibhabha	c Kulasekara b Ganegama	40	b Prasad	103	
4	†T.Taibu	run out (Kulasekara)	9	not out	39	
5	S.Matsikenyeri	c Prasad b Perera	26			
6	S.C.Williams	b Perera	52			
7	T.Mupariwa	c Silva b Perera	0			
8	K.M.Dabengwa	not out	62			
9	*P.Utseya	c Dilshan b Perera	11			
10	G.B.Brent	lbw b Perera	4			
11	C.B.Mpofu	c Paranavitana b Kapugedera	6			
	Extras	b 2, lb 7, w 5, nb 4	18	b 7, lb 4	11	
			313	**(3 wickets)**	**221**	

FoW (1): 1-91 (1), 2-104 (2), 3-124 (4), 4-166 (3), 5-201 (5), 6-201 (7), 7-252 (6), 8-283 (9), 9-289 (10), 10-313 (11)
FoW (2): 1-38 (2), 2-105 (1), 3-221 (3)

Zimbabwe Select XI Bowling

	O	M	R	W			O	M	R	W	
Mpofu	18	3	87	3			12	0	44	0	1w
Brent	24	6	68	2			15	3	43	1	
Chibhabha	11	3	39	0	3nb	(5)	6	0	21	1	
Mupariwa	13	1	65	1	1w	(3)	12	2	39	1	1w
Utseya	30.5	4	100	4		(4)	13	1	37	2	
Dabengwa	18	1	56	0			2	0	13	0	

Sri Lanka A Bowling

	O	M	R	W			O	M	R	W	
Kulasekara	26	7	75	0	2nb		12	1	34	1	
Ganegama	16	1	67	1	5w,2nb		5	2	26	0	
Herath	16	4	39	2			22	4	55	1	
Prasad	18	2	54	0			6.2	0	27	1	
Dilshan	10	1	12	0		(6)	3	1	9	0	
Perera	25	6	56	5		(5)	13	1	52	0	
Kapugedera	1.5	1	1	1			3	0	7	0	

Umpires: T.J.Tapfumaneyi and R.B.Tiffin. Third umpire: T.J.Matibiri. Referee: S.Kombayi. Toss: Sri Lanka A

Close of Play: 1st day: Sri Lanka A (1) 330-8 (Herath 29*, Kulasekara 16*, 93 overs); 2nd day: Zimbabwe Select XI (1) 203-6 (Williams 27*, Dabengwa 1*, 67 overs); 3rd day: Sri Lanka A (2) 106-4 (Warnapura 34*, Kapugedera 17*, 42 overs).

C.J.Chibhabha's 103 took 165 balls in 195 minutes and included 10 fours and 2 sixes.

ZIMBABWE SELECT XI v SRI LANKA A

Played at Queens Sports Club, Bulawayo, October 22, 23, 24, 2007.
Sri Lanka A in Zimbabwe 2007/08
Sri Lanka A won by 224 runs.

SRI LANKA A

#	Batsman	1st innings	R	2nd innings	R
1	M.L.Udawatte	c and b Maruma	92	b Maruma	44
2	N.T.Paranavitana	c Taibu b Utseya	39	lbw b Brent	0
3	B.S.M.Warnapura	b Utseya	17	c Mupariwa b Utseya	7
4	*T.M.Dilshan	lbw b Maruma	8	c Taibu b Mupariwa	85
5	†J.K.Silva	c Taylor b Chibhabha	25	lbw b Brent	45
6	C.K.Kapugedera	c Taibu b Mpofu	4	c Taibu b Utseya	41
7	M.D.K.Perera	lbw b Chibhabha	11	c Sibanda b Utseya	5
8	H.M.R.K.B.Herath	c Taibu b Mupariwa	29	c Sibanda b Mupariwa	8
9	K.M.D.N.Kulasekara	lbw b Maruma	9	not out	10
10	W.R.S.de Silva	c Taibu b Brent	8	c Taylor b Maruma	10
11	M.K.D.I.Amerasinghe	not out	8	lbw b Utseya	0
	Extras	b 1, lb 4, w 1	6	b 6, lb 4, w 1, nb 1	12
			256		**268**

FoW (1): 1-98 (2), 2-134 (3), 3-143 (4), 4-171 (1), 5-178 (6), 6-196 (7), 7-203 (5), 8-228 (9), 9-248 (8), 10-256 (10)
FoW (2): 1-8 (2), 2-53 (1), 3-59 (3), 4-138 (5), 5-233 (6), 6-233 (7), 7-239 (4), 8-253 (8), 9-267 (10), 10-268 (11)

ZIMBABWE SELECT XI

#	Batsman	1st innings	R	2nd innings	R
1	V.Sibanda	run out (Dilshan)	14	b de Silva	10
2	B.R.M.Taylor	lbw b Kulasekara	6	lbw b Kulasekara	0
3	C.J.Chibhabha	c Udawatte b Kulasekara	0	c J.K.Silva b Kulasekara	60
4	†T.Taibu	c J.K.Silva b de Silva	0	c Kulasekara b Herath	20
5	S.Matsikenyeri	st J.K.Silva b Herath	20	c Paranavitana b Herath	0
6	K.M.Dabengwa	lbw b de Silva	13	c Herath b Perera	73
7	*P.Utseya	c J.K.Silva b de Silva	7	lbw b de Silva	4
8	G.B.Brent	not out	12	c Warnapura b de Silva	5
9	T.Maruma	c J.K.Silva b Herath	3	lbw b Kulasekara	14
10	T.Mupariwa	lbw b Herath	0	lbw b Herath	7
11	C.B.Mpofu	c Warnapura b Herath	6	not out	0
	Extras	lb 5, w 1, nb 9	15	lb 7, w 2, nb 2	11
			96		**204**

FoW (1): 1-15 (2), 2-20 (3), 3-21 (4), 4-23 (1), 5-51 (6), 6-72 (7), 7-74 (5), 8-81 (9), 9-81 (10), 10-96 (11)
FoW (2): 1-16 (2), 2-18 (1), 3-66 (4), 4-74 (5), 5-113 (3), 6-149 (7), 7-161 (8), 8-188 (6), 9-200 (10), 10-204 (9)

Zimbabwe Select XI Bowling

	O	M	R	W			O	M	R	W	
Mpofu	12	2	27	1		(3)	2	1	10	0	
Brent	14.2	5	31	1			15	2	41	2	
Mupariwa	14	2	59	1	1w	(1)	11	3	56	2	
Chibhabha	12	3	27	2		(7)	3	0	9	0	
Utseya	22	4	58	2		(4)	21.1	4	59	4	
Matsikenyeri	1	0	1	0							
Maruma	22	6	48	3		(5)	12	2	59	2	
Dabengwa						(6)	7	0	24	0	

Sri Lanka A Bowling

	O	M	R	W			O	M	R	W	
Kulasekara	9	4	14	2			11.5	2	38	3	
de Silva	10	0	36	3	6nb		12	3	40	3	2nb
Amerasinghe	6	1	16	0	1w,3nb		3	0	15	0	1w
Herath	11.4	3	25	4			14	2	43	3	
Kapugedera						(5)	3	1	6	0	1w
Perera						(6)	16	3	50	1	
Dilshan						(7)	2	0	5	0	

Umpires: K.C.Barbour and O.Chirombe. Referee: D.W.Townshend.   Toss: Sri Lanka A

Close of Play: 1st day: Sri Lanka A (1) 245-8 (Herath 27*, de Silva 8*, 92 overs); 2nd day: Sri Lanka A (2) 128-3 (Dilshan 30*, J.K.Silva 44*, 43 overs).
The match was scheduled for four days but completed in three.

ZIMBABWE PROVINCES v EASTERNS (SOUTH AFRICA)

Played at Queens Sports Club, Bulawayo, November 1, 2, 3, 2007.
South African Airways Provincial Three-Day Challenge 2007/08 - Pool B
Easterns (South Africa) won by 210 runs.   (Points: Zimbabwe Provinces 4, Easterns (South Africa) 17.6)

EASTERNS (SOUTH AFRICA)

1	I.C.Hlengani	c Chauluka b Tsvanhu	10	lbw b Manyumwa	22
2	A.J.Seymore	c and b Tsvanhu	8	lbw b Tsvanhu	29
3	†T.M.Bodibe	run out (Cremer/Chauluka)	38	(8) lbw b Manyumwa	3
4	E.Nyawo	lbw b Muzarabani	10	(3) c Chakabva b Manyumwa	1
5	G.Toyana	c Tsvanhu b Manyumwa	7	(4) c Masakadza b Cremer	37
6	J.J.Pienaar	b Cremer	32	(5) c Butterworth b Masakadza	27
7	P.P.van den Berg	c Kamungozi b Cremer	9	lbw b Muzarabani	15
8	*S.P.O'Connor	c Butterworth b Cremer	39	(6) c Chakabva b Kamungozi	33
9	J.C.Fourie	not out	46	not out	18
10	M.H.Robey	c Butterworth b Cremer	0	b Manyumwa	5
11	T.R.Plaatjie	c Masakadza b Cremer	21	b Manyumwa	1
	Extras	b 8, nb 2	10	lb 1	1
			230		192

FoW (1): 1-9 (2), 2-18 (1), 3-35 (4), 4-47 (5), 5-105 (6), 6-112 (3), 7-136 (7), 8-172 (8), 9-172 (10), 10-230 (11)
FoW (2): 1-39 (2), 2-48 (3), 3-55 (1), 4-112 (4), 5-116 (5), 6-149 (7), 7-155 (8), 8-173 (6), 9-188 (10), 10-192 (11)

ZIMBABWE PROVINCES

1	T.Duffin	lbw b Plaatjie	14	lbw b van den Berg	24
2	E.Chauluka	lbw b Robey	4	c Seymore b Hlengani	7
3	*H.Masakadza	c Nyawo b O'Connor	6	c Pienaar b O'Connor	34
4	†R.W.Chakabva	c Nyawo b Plaatjie	35	(5) lbw b van den Berg	1
5	S.K.Nyamuzinga	c Pienaar b O'Connor	8	(6) c and b Hlengani	38
6	R.E.Butterworth	c Plaatjie b O'Connor	0	(7) c Bodibe b O'Connor	2
7	A.G.Cremer	lbw b van den Berg	4	(8) c Toyana b Hlengani	6
8	A.M.Manyumwa	run out (Plaatjie/Nyawo)	2	(9) c O'Connor b Hlengani	2
9	P.M.Tsvanhu	not out	6	(4) lbw b Plaatjie	0
10	T.Muzarabani	lbw b Plaatjie	0	st Bodibe b Hlengani	16
11	T.Kamungozi	lbw b Plaatjie	0	not out	0
	Extras	lb 2	2	lb 1	1
			81		131

FoW (1): 1-17 (1), 2-21 (2), 3-33 (3), 4-48 (5), 5-48 (6), 6-57 (7), 7-64 (8), 8-81 (4), 9-81 (10), 10-81 (11)
FoW (2): 1-31 (1), 2-37 (2), 3-53 (4), 4-56 (5), 5-95 (3), 6-99 (7), 7-110 (8), 8-115 (6), 9-116 (9), 10-131 (10)

Zimbabwe Provinces Bowling

	O	M	R	W			O	M	R	W
Tsvanhu	9	3	27	2			5	2	27	1
Muzarabani	12	2	30	1			12	1	43	1
Manyumwa	11	0	63	1	1nb	(4)	8.4	1	29	5
Nyamuzinga	5	2	18	0	1nb	(3)	8	2	22	0
Cremer	17.2	2	64	5			8	0	32	1
Kamungozi	5	0	20	0			8	3	19	1
Masakadza						(7)	4	1	19	1

Easterns (South Africa) Bowling

	O	M	R	W			O	M	R	W
Robey	8	4	9	1		(2)	2.4	0	9	0
Plaatjie	8	3	13	4		(1)	9	3	31	1
O'Connor	11	3	30	3		(6)	8	1	25	2
Hlengani	1	1	0	0			16.2	5	45	5
van den Berg	10	2	27	1		(3)	12.2	7	11	2
Toyana						(5)	1	0	4	0
Fourie						(7)	2	1	5	0

Umpires: C.Bester and E.C.Hendrikse. Referee: D.W.Townshend.   Toss: Easterns (South Africa)

Close of Play: 1st day: Zimbabwe Provinces (1) 3-0 (Duffin 2*, Chauluka 0*, 1 over); 2nd day: Zimbabwe Provinces (2) 45-2 (Masakadza 14*, Tsvanhu 0*, 17 overs).

Nyawo replaced Bodide as wicketkeeper after 5.4 overs of Zimbabwe Provinces first innings.

ZIMBABWE PROVINCES v NORTHERNS (SOUTH AFRICA)

Played at Harare Sports Club, November 15, 16, 17, 2007.
South African Airways Provincial Three-Day Challenge 2007/08 - Pool B
Match drawn. (Points: Zimbabwe Provinces 8.8, Northerns (South Africa) 5.82)

ZIMBABWE PROVINCES

1	T.M.K.Mawoyo	c Dikgale b Masekela	15	b Engelbrecht		39
2	T.Duffin	c Viljoen b Mashimbyi	86	c Liebisch b Mashimbyi		35
3	*H.Masakadza	c Phangiso b Wagner	8	c Liebisch b Engelbrecht		0
4	B.Mujuru	run out (van Biljon)	32	(6) b Viljoen		21
5	S.Matsikenyeri	c Viljoen b Liebisch	30	(4) lbw b Phangiso		11
6	†R.W.Chakabva	b Wagner	61	(5) b Liebisch		66
7	K.O.Meth	c Engelbrecht b Liebisch	37	c Ndlovu b Viljoen		0
8	A.G.Cremer	c Malan b Liebisch	11	c Ndlovu b Viljoen		1
9	A.M.Manyumwa	c Engelbrecht b Liebisch	1	c van Biljon b Liebisch		38
10	T.N.Garwe	not out	1	not out		3
11	T.Muzarabani	not out	1			
	Extras	lb 4, nb 3	7	b 2, lb 4		6
		(9 wickets)	290	(9 wickets, declared)		220

FoW (1): 1-39 (1), 2-59 (3), 3-143 (2), 4-143 (4), 5-208 (5), 6-253 (6), 7-286 (8), 8-286 (7), 9-288 (9)
FoW (2): 1-68 (2), 2-69 (3), 3-88 (4), 4-94 (1), 5-116 (6), 6-116 (7), 7-120 (8), 8-211 (5), 9-220 (9)

NORTHERNS (SOUTH AFRICA)

1	P.J.Malan	c Cremer b Muzarabani	17	lbw b Cremer		30
2	A.F.Viljoen	c Chakabva b Manyumwa	11	c Meth b Cremer		37
3	W.T.Dikgale	b Manyumwa	0	lbw b Cremer		13
4	S.W.Liebisch	lbw b Manyumwa	2	lbw b Cremer		13
5	P.J.van Biljon	b Garwe	1	c Garwe b Cremer		23
6	L.M.G.Masekela	c Chakabva b Manyumwa	29	(10) not out		0
7	S.A.Engelbrecht	c Masakadza b Cremer	23	(6) c Mujuru b Cremer		30
8	*A.M.Phangiso	c Masakadza b Cremer	25	(7) c Garwe b Mawoyo		37
9	†A.L.Ndlovu	c Meth b Cremer	2	(8) c Mujuru b Matsikenyeri		10
10	M.A.Mashimbyi	not out	17	(9) not out		32
11	N.Wagner	b Cremer	4			
	Extras	b 1, lb 2, w 1, nb 6	10	b 11, lb 7, w 1, nb 6		25
			141	(8 wickets)		250

FoW (1): 1-25 (2), 2-25 (3), 3-32 (4), 4-32 (1), 5-41 (5), 6-86 (6), 7-94 (7), 8-116 (9), 9-133 (8), 10-141 (11)
FoW (2): 1-55 (2), 2-73 (3), 3-88 (1), 4-103 (4), 5-134 (5), 6-163 (6), 7-194 (8), 8-242 (7)

Northerns (South Africa) Bowling

	O	M	R	W				O	M	R	W	
Wagner	20	7	53	2				6	3	11	0	
Mashimbyi	14.4	2	49	1	1nb	(5)		12	3	32	1	
Masekela	10	3	31	1		(2)		5	2	7	2	
Liebisch	16.2	1	54	4		(3)		13.1	2	43	2	
Phangiso	17	2	66	0	2nb	(6)		13	1	38	1	
Engelbrecht	7	1	33	0		(4)		19	3	74	2	
Viljoen						(7)		4	1	9	3	

Zimbabwe Provinces Bowling

	O	M	R	W				O	M	R	W	
Muzarabani	11	2	34	1	2nb			11	1	29	0	
Garwe	9	2	28	1	1w,2nb			7	1	38	0	
Manyumwa	16	7	20	4	2nb			17	5	45	0	1w,2nb
Cremer	14.1	7	29	4				36	11	69	6	
Meth	6	1	15	0				12	4	27	0	
Masakadza	5	2	10	0								
Matsikenyeri	1	0	2	0			(6)	15	6	24	1	
Mawoyo							(7)	1	1	0	1	

Umpires: T.R.Matare and B.M.White. Referee: T.J.Matibiri and T.J.Matibiri. Toss: Northerns (South Africa)

Close of Play: 1st day: Northerns (South Africa) (1) 40-4 (van Biljon 1*, Masekela 5*, 17 overs); 2nd day: Zimbabwe Provinces (2) 123-7 (Chakabva 9*, Manyumwa 3*, 47 overs).

CENTRALS v WESTERNS

Played at Kwekwe Sports Club, April 17, 18, 19, 2008.
Logan Cup 2007/08
Centrals won by seven wickets.   (Points: Centrals 17, Westerns 5)

WESTERNS

1	B.Staddon	lbw b Muzarabani	5	lbw b Rainsford		32
2	†T.Ngulube	c Mugochi b Chinouya	112	b Mire		4
3	B.Mujuru	c Mahlunge b Chinouya	11	b Rainsford		1
4	M.M.Mabuza	b Mugochi	31	c Chauluka b Mugochi		3
5	*K.M.Dabengwa	c Waller b Mugochi	2	c Chauluka b Mugochi		41
6	R.T.Kasawaya	b Mugochi	0	c Rainsford b Mugochi		1
7	T.Mupariwa	c Mahlunge b Mugochi	0	c Waller b Mugochi		4
8	S.Kusano	b Waller	13	lbw b Chinouya		0
9	T.M.Mboyi	c Mahlunge b Rainsford	5	c Chauluka b Waller		14
10	J.Nyumbu	b Mugochi	0	(11) lbw b Rainsford		23
11	C.B.Mpofu	not out	0	(10) not out		29
	Extras	b 1, lb 1, w 1, nb 5	8	b 3, lb 1, w 1, nb 3		8
			187			**160**

FoW (1): 1-8, 2-26, 3-47, 4-116, 5-116, 6-120, 7-161, 8-186, 9-187, 10-187
FoW (2): 1-21, 2-37, 3-40, 4-50, 5-54, 6-78, 7-83, 8-101, 9-123, 10-160

CENTRALS

1	B.M.Chapungu	c Nyumbu b Mpofu	58	(2) lbw b Mupariwa		40
2	*E.Chauluka	run out	55	(5) not out		0
3	M.N.Waller	c Mboyi b Mupariwa	22	not out		20
4	I.Chikunya	run out	0			
5	S.F.Mire	lbw b Nyumbu	42	(4) c Kasawaya b Mupariwa		0
6	†T.Mahlunge	c Dabengwa b Nyumbu	14	(1) c Dabengwa b Mboyi		22
7	R.Nyathi	c Staddon b Kusano	16			
8	E.C.Rainsford	c Ngulube b Kusano	30			
9	T.Muzarabani	b Dabengwa	10			
10	B.Mugochi	c Mabuza b Kusano	5			
11	M.T.Chinouya	not out	0			
	Extras	lb 4, w 2, nb 7	13	lb 1, w 1, nb 1		3
			265	(3 wickets)		**85**

FoW (1): 1-97, 2-141, 3-141, 4-149, 5-193, 6-208, 7-232, 8-243, 9-262, 10-265
FoW (2): 1-61, 2-65, 3-74

Centrals Bowling

	O	M	R	W			O	M	R	W	
Rainsford	12.4	4	31	1			9	3	14	3	1nb
Muzarabani	13	2	37	1	1w,1nb		13	3	22	0	1w,2nb
Chinouya	19	8	22	2			9	4	15	1	
Nyathi	6	0	37	0	4nb	(7)	2	0	14	0	
Mugochi	19	6	48	5			15	2	55	4	
Waller	5	3	10	1			5	0	26	1	
Mire						(4)	7	1	10	1	

Westerns Bowling

	O	M	R	W			O	M	R	W	
Mpofu	18	6	41	1	1w	(4)	1	0	3	0	
Mupariwa	22	7	49	1	1w,1nb	(1)	8	1	16	2	1w
Kusano	19.4	6	46	3	5nb	(2)	3.2	1	22	0	1nb
Dabengwa	27	5	58	1	1nb	(6)	2	0	14	0	
Nyumbu	17	4	38	2		(3)	2	0	14	0	
Mboyi	6	0	29	0		(5)	7	0	17	1	

Umpires: O.Chirombe and T.R.Matare.   Referee: J.Chikange.   Toss: Centrals

Close of Play: 1st day: ; 2nd day: .

The match was scheduled for four days but completed in three. T.Ngulube's 112 took 213 balls and included 10 fours.

EASTERNS v NORTHERNS

Played at Mutare Sports Club, April 17, 18, 19, 2008.
Logan Cup 2007/08
Northerns won by 65 runs.   (Points: Easterns 6, Northerns 17)

NORTHERNS

1	K.Kondo	c Mawoyo b S.W.Masakadza	30	(2) c Marumisa b S.W.Masakadza	8
2	A.Tichana	c Mutizwa b S.W.Masakadza	5	(1) lbw b Maruma	15
3	†B.R.M.Taylor	lbw b Mujaji	62	(4) b Maruma	8
4	S.Mwakayeni	run out	2	(3) c H.Masakadza b Maruma	16
5	P.Masvaure	b Nyamuzinga	22	(6) lbw b Utseya	1
6	A.G.Cremer	c Mutizwa b Kadzitye	35	(7) lbw b Maruma	17
7	T.Chimbambo	c Mutizwa b Mujaji	25	(5) lbw b Utseya	5
8	R.W.Price	b S.W.Masakadza	28	lbw b Maruma	34
9	A.M.Manyumwa	c Mutizwa b H.Masakadza	7	b Maruma	14
10	T.N.Garwe	not out	22	not out	19
11	N.Chari	c Utseya b Mujaji	0	c Matsikenyeri b Maruma	8
	Extras	b 4, lb 15, w 6, nb 9	34	lb 3, w 4, nb 4	11
			272		**156**

FoW (1): 1-8, 2-109, 3-118, 4-138, 5-153, 6-196, 7-239, 8-241, 9-264, 10-272
FoW (2): 1-15, 2-44, 3-54, 4-60, 5-61, 6-68, 7-98, 8-125, 9-138, 10-156

EASTERNS

1	T.M.K.Mawoyo	c Chari b Manyumwa	27	(5) b Price	16
2	J.Marumisa	c Taylor b Garwe	52	(1) lbw b Manyumwa	4
3	*H.Masakadza	run out	60	b Cremer	58
4	S.Matsikenyeri	c Chimbambo b Chari	8	c Manyumwa b Cremer	0
5	†F.Mutizwa	c Tichana b Price	18	(2) c Garwe b Price	39
6	T.Maruma	b Manyumwa	15	run out	0
7	P.Utseya	st Taylor b Price	5	lbw b Price	5
8	S.K.Nyamuzinga	c and b Price	1	c sub (A.Mlambo) b Price	4
9	S.W.Masakadza	lbw b Price	0	c Garwe b Price	1
10	S.Mujaji	not out	0	c Price b Garwe	1
11	P.Kadzitye			not out	8
	Extras	lb 6, w 10, nb 3, pen 5	24	b 13, lb 1, w 2, nb 1	17
		(9 wickets, declared)	**210**		**153**

FoW (1): 1-75, 2-122, 3-137, 4-167, 5-186, 6-195, 7-201, 8-201, 9-210
FoW (2): 1-5, 2-70, 3-70, 4-134, 5-134, 6-134, 7-138, 8-143, 9-144, 10-153

Easterns Bowling

	O	M	R	W			O	M	R	W	
H.Masakadza	9	3	22	1			1	0	8	0	
S.W.Masakadza	12	1	32	3	3w,4nb		6	2	6	1	2w
Nyamuzinga	14	4	42	1	1w,1nb						
Utseya	19	7	26	0		(3)	13	5	23	2	
Mujaji	16.1	2	40	3	5w	(4)	6	1	14	0	2w
Maruma	8	1	19	0	1nb		17.3	3	82	7	4nb
Matsikenyeri	2	0	14	0							
Kadzitye	13	2	58	1		(5)	7	0	20	0	

Northerns Bowling

	O	M	R	W			O	M	R	W	
Garwe	13	2	63	1	2w,3nb		7	1	16	1	
Masvaure	5	0	33	0	6w		3	0	6	0	
Manyumwa	15	4	49	2	2w		11.4	1	34	1	1w
Cremer	3	0	15	0			14.2	1	42	2	1w,1nb
Chari	5	0	27	1			1	0	2	0	
Price	8	2	12	4			18	6	39	5	

Umpires: J.Muzeya and T.J.Tapfumaneyi. Referee: R.Kwari.   Toss: Easterns

Close of Play: 1st day: ; 2nd day: .

The match was scheduled for four days but completed in three.

NORTHERNS v WESTERNS

Played at Harare Sports Club, April 24, 25, 26, 27, 2008.
Logan Cup 2007/08
Northerns won by an innings and 83 runs.   (Points: Northerns 20, Westerns 2)

NORTHERNS

1	A.Tichana	c Takarusenga b Mupariwa	106
2	K.Kondo	c Ngulube b Mpofu	7
3	†B.R.M.Taylor	c Mupariwa b Nyumbu	40
4	*E.Chigumbura	c Dabengwa b Mupariwa	186
5	P.Masvaure	c Ngulube b Mpofu	50
6	T.Chimbambo	c Dabengwa b Mpofu	0
7	A.G.Cremer	not out	1
8	T.N.Garwe		
9	G.B.Brent		
10	R.W.Price		
11	A.M.Manyumwa		
	Extras	b 3, lb 3, w 17, nb 4	27
		(6 wickets, declared)	417

FoW (1): 1- (2), 2- (3), 3- (1), 4- (5), 5- (6), 6-417 (4)

WESTERNS

1	F.Takarusenga	c Manyumwa b Brent	6	b Brent	3
2	†T.Ngulube	c Price b Cremer	15	lbw b Price	51
3	B.Staddon	st Taylor b Price	7	c Brent b Chigumbura	41
4	*K.M.Dabengwa	c Chigumbura b Masvaure	67	c Brent b Price	0
5	T.M.Mboyi	c Kondo b Cremer	16	c Taylor b Price	0
6	T.Madhiri	run out	1	(7) run out	1
7	M.M.Mabuza	c Cremer b Price	4	(6) b Brent	31
8	T.Mupariwa	lbw b Cremer	5	c Manyumwa b Garwe	48
9	S.Kusano	c Brent b Price	4	b Brent	7
10	C.B.Mpofu	not out	6	c Taylor b Brent	2
11	J.Nyumbu	c Taylor b Price	0	not out	3
	Extras	lb 1, nb 5	6	b 5, lb 3, w 2	10
			137		197

FoW (1): 1- , 2- , 3- , 4- , 5- , 6- , 7- , 8- , 9- , 10-137
FoW (2): 1- (1), 2- (3), 3-101 (2), 4-101 (5), 5- , 6- , 7- , 8- , 9- , 10-197

Westerns Bowling

	O	M	R	W
Mupariwa	34.1	10	104	2
Kusano	25	8	50	0
Mpofu	33	9	73	3
Mboyi	11	3	41	0
Dabengwa	15	4	51	0
Nyumbu	20	2	69	1
Staddon	11	2	23	0

Northerns Bowling

	O	M	R	W		O	M	R	W
Brent	13	4	13	1	(2)	19	4	40	4
Chigumbura	11	2	30	0	(1)	8	3	15	1
Garwe	3	2	4	0	(8)	5.2	0	31	1
Manyumwa	3	2	7	0	(3)	4	1	11	0
Price	22.3	12	24	4		25	11	32	3
Cremer	16	2	51	3		21	4	40	0
Masvaure	5	2	7	1	(4)	7	0	17	0
Tichana					(7)	3	1	3	0

Umpires: K.C.Barbour and O.Chirombe. Referee: A.Hamid.   Toss: Northerns
Close of Play: 1st day: Northerns (1) 234-2 (Tichana 85*, Chigumbura 93*); 2nd day: Westerns (1) 46-3; 3rd day: Westerns (2) 101-2 (Ngulube 51*).
215 runs were added for the 3rd wicket in the Northerns first innings (A.Tichana and E.Chigumbura). 84 runs were added for the 2nd wicket in the Westerns second innings (T.Ngulube and B.Staddon). A.Tichana's 106 took 320 balls and included 13 fours. E.Chigumbura's 186 took 299 balls and included 19 fours and 1 six.

SOUTHERNS v EASTERNS

Played at Masvingo Sports Club, April 24, 25, 26, 2008.
Logan Cup 2007/08
Easterns won by an innings and 7 runs.   (Points: Southerns 7, Easterns 19)

SOUTHERNS

1	T.Machiri	b Masakadza	46	lbw b Masakadza	0
2	M.Chiturumani	lbw b Kadzitye	1	c Mutizwa b Masakadza	7
3	C.J.Chibhabha	c Maruma b Kadzitye	13	c Matsikenyeri b Mujaji	21
4	J.Chinyengetere	lbw b Kadzitye	0	b Kadzitye	6
5	R.Mutumbami	b Utseya	50	(8) not out	21
6	R.Chinyengetere	b Masakadza	50	run out	0
7	N.B.Mahwire	lbw b Masakadza	8	c Marumisa b Utseya	4
8	P.Charumbira	c Maruma b Masakadza	38	(5) b Utseya	26
9	T.Kamungozi	st Mutizwa b Utseya	20	b Utseya	0
10	H.Matanga	b Mujaji	16	c Maruma b Utseya	14
11	B.V.Vitori	not out	10	lbw b Maruma	1
	Extras	lb 7, w 2, nb 10	19	b 4, lb 4, w 1	9
			271		109

FoW (1): 1- , 2- , 3- , 4- , 5- , 6- , 7- , 8- , 9- , 10-271
FoW (2): 1- , 2- , 3- , 4- , 5- , 6- , 7- , 8- , 9- , 10-109

EASTERNS

1	T.M.K.Mawoyo	c Mutumbami b Vitori	10
2	J.Marumisa	lbw b Chibhabha	35
3	F.Mutizwa	c Machiri b Vitori	0
4	S.Matsikenyeri	c Chibhabha b Kamungozi	201
5	T.Maruma	c Mahwire b Kamungozi	25
6	P.Utseya	c Mahwire b Kamungozi	6
7	S.Matsika	c Mahwire b Kamungozi	3
8	S.K.Nyamuzinga	c R.Chinyengetere b Kamungozi	52
9	S.Mujaji	b Kamungozi	0
10	S.W.Masakadza	not out	27
11	P.Kadzitye	c Mutumbami b Kamungozi	6
	Extras	b 4, lb 9, w 3, nb 6	22
			387

FoW (1): 1- , 2- , 3- , 4- , 5- , 6- , 7- , 8- , 9- , 10-387

Easterns Bowling

	O	M	R	W		O	M	R	W
Masakadza	13	0	49	4		8	2	25	2
Utseya	22	4	62	2	(5)	11	2	25	4
Matsika	3	1	9	0	(4)	1	0	1	0
Kadzitye	10.3	4	26	3	(2)	6	2	17	1
Mujaji	7	1	31	1	(3)	6	2	12	1
Maruma	13	3	35	0		7.2	2	21	1
Nyamuzinga	7.3	1	27	0					
Matsikenyeri	7	1	25	0					

Southerns Bowling

	O	M	R	W
Charumbira	14	3	53	0
Matanga	11	1	55	0
Kamungozi	33	10	104	7
Mahwire	14	2	55	0
Vitori	9	0	37	2
Chibhabha	13	0	58	1
Machiri	2	0	12	1

Umpires: T.R.Matare and T.J.Tapfumaneyi. Referee: J.Chikange.   Toss: Southerns

Close of Play: 1st day: Easterns (1) 10-0; 2nd day: .

The match was scheduled for four days but completed in three. S.Matsikenyeri's 201 took 226 balls and included 21 fours and 3 sixes.

EASTERNS v CENTRALS

Played at Mutare Sports Club, May 3, 4, 5, 6, 2008.
Logan Cup 2007/08
Easterns won by 385 runs.　　(Points: Easterns 17, Centrals 5)

EASTERNS

1	T.M.K.Mawoyo	lbw b Chinouya	42	lbw b Muzarabani	4
2	J.Marumisa	b Mugochi	49	(3) lbw b Mugochi	42
3	*H.Masakadza	c Chikunya b Muzarabani	117	(5) c Mahlunge b Matigonda	67
4	S.Matsikenyeri	c Chikunya b Mugochi	0	(6) c Waller b Nyathi	35
5	S.Matsika	lbw b Mugochi	4	(7) b Mugochi	24
6	T.Maruma	c Mahlunge b Nyathi	2	(4) run out	16
7	†F.Mutizwa	c Muzarabani b Mugochi	37	(8) not out	102
8	P.Utseya	c Mahlunge b Mugochi	8	(2) c Mahlunge b Mugochi	44
9	S.W.Masakadza	c Mugochi b Muzarabani	7	b Muzarabani	1
10	S.Musoso	b Muzarabani	0	not out	4
11	S.Mujaji	not out	1		
	Extras	b 6, lb 2, w 12, nb 7	27	b 3, lb 6, w 12, nb 7	28
			294	(8 wickets, declared)	367

FoW (1): 1-85 (2), 2-133 (1), 3-134 (4), 4-138 (5), 5-164 (6), 6-244 (7), 7-257 (8), 8-278 (9), 9-278 (10), 10-294 (3)
FoW (2): 1-4 (1), 2-102 (3), 3-116 (2), 4-122 (4), 5-184 (6), 6-219 (7), 7-292 (5), 8-298 (9)

CENTRALS

1	B.M.Chapungu	c Mujaji b S.W.Masakadza	0	(2) c Maruma b S.W.Masakadza	20
2	†T.Mahlunge	lbw b Mujaji	0	(1) run out	17
3	M.N.Waller	c Mutizwa b S.W.Masakadza	16	(4) c Mawoyo b S.W.Masakadza	4
4	I.Chikunya	c Mutizwa b S.W.Masakadza	0	(6) c Mutizwa b S.W.Masakadza	0
5	*E.Chauluka	b Utseya	84	b Musoso	30
6	S.F.Mire	c Mutizwa b H.Masakadza	10	(8) st Mutizwa b Mujaji	7
7	R.Nyathi	c Musoso b Utseya	19	c Matsikenyeri b Musoso	4
8	T.Muzarabani	c Marumisa b Utseya	6	(3) lbw b Musoso	8
9	B.Mugochi	c H.Masakadza b Utseya	0	(11) not out	6
10	M.T.Chinouya	b Utseya	9	(9) c Mutizwa b Musoso	0
11	J.Matigonda	not out	0	(10) c Mutizwa b Musoso	2
	Extras	b 4, w 2, nb 19	25	lb 3, w 1, nb 5	9
			169		107

FoW (1): 1-4 (2), 2-24 (1), 3-24 (3), 4-27 (4), 5-42 (6), 6-82 (7), 7-88 (8), 8-97 (9), 9-145 (10), 10-169 (5)
FoW (2): 1-34 (2), 2-52 (1), 3-52 (3), 4-78 (4), 5-82 (5), 6-86 (6), 7-97 (7), 8-97 (9), 9-97 (8), 10-107 (10)

Centrals Bowling

	O	M	R	W			O	M	R	W	
Muzarabani	25.3	12	54	3	5nb		15	2	53	2	6w,2nb
Chinouya	26	7	73	1	6w		14.4	1	74	0	2w
Matigonda	16	6	55	0	1w,2nb	(5)	10	2	62	1	3w,4nb
Mire	4	0	19	0							
Mugochi	20	4	69	5	5w	(3)	26	5	89	3	
Nyathi	7	2	16	1		(4)	12	0	53	1	1nb
Waller						(6)	8	1	27	0	

Easterns Bowling

	O	M	R	W			O	M	R	W	
S.W.Masakadza	8	3	15	3	1w,5nb		11	5	31	3	2nb
Mujaji	6	1	44	1	10nb		4	1	13	1	1w
Musoso	5	2	20	0			11.3	3	43	5	3nb
H.Masakadza	5	1	20	1							
Utseya	14.2	6	28	5		(4)	5	2	9	0	
Maruma	11	2	33	0		(5)	3	0	8	0	
Matsikenyeri	5	2	5	0	1w						

Umpires: T.R.Matare and T.J.Matibiri.　Referee: J.Chikange.　　　　Toss: Centrals
Close of Play: 1st day: Easterns (1) 181-5 (H.Masakadza 54*, Mutizwa 13*); 2nd day: Easterns (2) 19-1 (Utseya 10*, Marumisa 5*); 3rd day: Centrals (2) 52-2 (Muzarabani 8*).
Man of the Match: H.Masakadza.
H.Masakadza's 117 took 205 balls and included 19 fours and 1 six. F.Mutizwa's 102 took 92 balls and included 13 fours and 4 sixes.

NORTHERNS v SOUTHERNS

Played at Harare Sports Club, May 3, 4, 2008.
Logan Cup 2007/08
Northerns won by an innings and 92 runs.   (Points: Northerns 17, Southerns 4)

SOUTHERNS

1	P.Charumbira	b Brent	1	c Masvaure b Brent		4
2	M.Chiturumani	lbw b Chigumbura	0	c Tichana b Brent		0
3	T.Machiri	b Manyumwa	24	b Brent		0
4	C.J.Chibhabha	b Garwe	22	(5) lbw b Chigumbura		4
5	†R.Mutumbami	c Kondo b Masvaure	6	(7) b Brent		0
6	J.Chinyengetere	c Taylor b Manyumwa	7	(4) c Chigumbura b Brent		12
7	R.Chinyengetere	c Cremer b Manyumwa	0	(6) b Price		9
8	*N.B.Mahwire	lbw b Brent	44	lbw b Cremer		1
9	T.Kamungozi	st Taylor b Cremer	8	c Masvaure b Price		0
10	H.Matanga	c Taylor b Brent	14	c sub (T.Chimbambo) b Cremer		0
11	B.V.Vitori	not out	4	not out		4
	Extras	b 2, lb 3, nb 6	11	b 6, lb 2		8
			141			**42**

FoW (1): 1-1 (1), 2-1 (2), 3-32 (3), 4-42 (4), 5-61 (5), 6-61 (6), 7-72 (7), 8-95 (9), 9-125 (10), 10-141 (8)
FoW (2): 1- , 2- , 3- , 4- , 5- , 6- , 7- , 8- , 9- , 10-42

NORTHERNS

1	K.Kondo	c J.Chinyengetere b Mahwire	16
2	A.Tichana	c Mutumbami b Chibhabha	10
3	†B.R.M.Taylor	c Mutumbami b Vitori	28
4	E.Chigumbura	c Matanga b Vitori	0
5	P.Masvaure	c Mutumbami b Kamungozi	31
6	T.N.Garwe	b Mahwire	1
7	S.Mwakayeni	c Machiri b Chibhabha	13
8	A.G.Cremer	b Chibhabha	0
9	G.B.Brent	c Mahwire b Kamungozi	51
10	*R.W.Price	lbw b Kamungozi	89
11	A.M.Manyumwa	not out	0
	Extras	b 8, lb 8, w 6, nb 14	36
			275

FoW (1): 1- , 2- , 3- , 4- , 5- , 6- , 7- , 8- , 9- , 10-275

Northerns Bowling

	O	M	R	W			O	M	R	W
Chigumbura	12	5	20	1			8	4	5	1
Brent	13.1	6	23	3			9	3	21	5
Garwe	5	1	11	1	1nb					
Masvaure	5	0	10	1	3nb					
Manyumwa	8	4	14	3						
Price	8	1	17	0		(3)	2.2	1	4	2
Cremer	11	0	41	1	2nb	(4)	1	0	4	2

Southerns Bowling

	O	M	R	W	
Chibhabha	16	3	60	3	7nb
Vitori	12	2	55	2	3w,5nb
Mahwire	13	2	22	2	
Charumbira	16	2	59	0	2nb
Kamungozi	13.2	3	38	3	
Matanga	6	0	25	0	

Umpires: O.Chirombe and N.N.Singo.   Referee: A.Hamid.   Toss: Southerns

Close of Play: 1st day: Northerns (1) 87-5.

Man of the Match: G.B.Brent.

The match was scheduled for four days but completed in two.

CENTRALS v NORTHERNS

Played at Kwekwe Sports Club, May 10, 11, 12, 13, 2008.
Logan Cup 2007/08
Northerns won by an innings and 98 runs. (Points: Centrals 4, Northerns 21)

NORTHERNS

1	A.Tichana	run out (Nyathi/Chikunya)	66
2	I.Senzere	c Nyathi b Waller	131
3	†B.R.M.Taylor	not out	150
4	*E.Chigumbura	c Chikunya b Chinouya	58
5	P.Masvaure	lbw b Chinouya	4
6	S.Mwakayeni	run out (Chinouya)	0
7	A.G.Cremer	c Chikunya b Rainsford	0
8	R.W.Price	c Waller b Nyathi	52
9	A.M.Manyumwa	not out	3
10	A.Mlambo		
11	T.N.Garwe		
	Extras	b 8, lb 10, w 1, nb 10	29
		(7 wickets, declared)	493

FoW (1): 1-193 (1), 2-248 (2), 3-347 (4), 4-366 (5), 5-366 (6), 6-378 (7), 7-478 (8)

CENTRALS

1	†I.Chikunya	c sub (C.Zhuwawo) b Chigumbura	2	(5) lbw b Price	35
2	S.P.Gupo	c Taylor b Mlambo	6	(1) c Mwakayeni b Manyumwa	35
3	*E.Chauluka	b Manyumwa	25	c Tichana b Mwakayeni	34
4	M.N.Waller	lbw b Cremer	27	c Price b Cremer	9
5	R.Nyathi	c Taylor b Manyumwa	9	(7) c and b Cremer	14
6	B.M.Chapungu	c Mwakayeni b Price	17	c Manyumwa b Garwe	32
7	S.F.Mire	not out	42	(2) c Taylor b Garwe	32
8	E.C.Rainsford	lbw b Garwe	5	c Cremer b Price	6
9	T.Muzarabani	c Cremer b Garwe	9	st Taylor b Cremer	5
10	M.T.Chinouya	c Masvaure b Price	1	(11) lbw b Garwe	6
11	B.Mugochi	c Taylor b Manyumwa	1	(10) not out	16
	Extras	b 4, lb 2, w 2, nb 6	14	b 1, lb 2, nb 5, pen 5	13
			158		237

FoW (1): 1-5 (1), 2-32 (2), 3-51 (3), 4-61 (5), 5-94 (6), 6-100 (4), 7-122 (8), 8-136 (9), 9-141 (10), 10-158 (11)
FoW (2): 1-40 (2), 2-86 (1), 3-96 (4), 4-157 (5), 5-159 (3), 6-200 (6), 7-207 (8), 8-215 (7), 9-215 (9), 10-237 (11)

Centrals Bowling	O	M	R	W	
Rainsford	30	10	94	1	6nb
Muzarabani	22	4	94	0	1w,1nb
Chinouya	21	3	67	2	
Mugochi	28	6	115	0	
Nyathi	13	2	45	1	3nb
Chauluka	11	1	36	0	
Waller	8	0	24	1	

Northerns Bowling	O	M	R	W			O	M	R	W	
Chigumbura	15	8	25	1			8	3	14	0	
Garwe	12	2	13	2	1nb		12.3	2	51	3	2nb
Mlambo	7	1	24	1	1w,2nb						
Manyumwa	7.3	3	24	3	1w		14	4	37	1	
Masvaure	2	0	11	0	2nb	(3)	2	0	6	0	1nb
Cremer	11	1	23	1	1nb	(5)	23	2	55	3	1nb
Price	11	4	32	2		(6)	20	5	41	2	
Senzere						(7)	2	0	9	0	1nb
Mwakayeni						(8)	6	1	16	1	

Umpires: O.Chirombe and T.J.Matibiri. Referee: A.Marodza.   Toss: Centrals

Close of Play: 1st day: ; 2nd day: Centrals (1) 114-6 (Mire 11*, Rainsford 3*); 3rd day: Centrals (2) 190-5 (Chapungu 23*, Nyathi 9*).
Man of the Match: B.R.M.Taylor.
I.Senzere's 131 took 265 balls in 318 minutes and included 11 fours and 2 sixes. B.R.M.Taylor's 150 took 182 balls in 259 minutes and included 19 fours and 2 sixes.

WESTERNS v SOUTHERNS

Played at Queens Sports Club, Bulawayo, May 10, 11, 12, 13, 2008.
Logan Cup 2007/08
Southerns won by nine wickets.　　(Points: Westerns 5, Southerns 17)

WESTERNS

1	F.Takarusenga	run out (Matanga)	34	b Vitori	0
2	†T.Ngulube	c Machiri b Vitori	14	run out	34
3	B.Staddon	lbw b Matanga	48	c R.Chinyengetere b Kamungozi	64
4	*K.M.Dabengwa	c Machiri b Matanga	21	(6) c Mutumbami b Chibhabha	24
5	M.L.Williams	c Machiri b Matanga	0	c J.Chinyengetere b Charumbira	5
6	M.M.Mabuza	lbw b Chibhabha	25	(4) b Charumbira	6
7	R.T.Kasawaya	lbw b Matanga	0	c sub (Mushayi) b Chibhabha	14
8	T.Mupariwa	c Mutumbami b Chibhabha	12	c Mutumbami b Matanga	41
9	C.B.Mpofu	lbw b Chibhabha	0	c R.Chinyengetere b Charumbira	3
10	K.Ntuli	not out	10	not out	4
11	B.Mukondiwa	c Machiri b Chibhabha	6	lbw b Matanga	0
	Extras	b 9, lb 6, w 1, nb 6	22	b 5, lb 13, w 2	20
			192		**215**

FoW (1): 1-33 (2), 2-99 (1), 3-110 (3), 4-110 (5), 5-154 (4), 6-154 (7), 7-173 (6), 8-173 (9), 9-176 (8), 10-192 (11)
FoW (2): 1-1 (1), 2-69 (2), 3-91 (4), 4-97 (5), 5-126 (6), 6-152 (3), 7-173 (7), 8-206 (9), 9-215 (8), 10-215 (11)

SOUTHERNS

1	C.Rizhibowa	lbw b Kasawaya	40	lbw b Mupariwa	4
2	T.Machiri	c Dabengwa b Ntuli	23	(3) not out	50
3	*C.J.Chibhabha	c Mabuza b Ntuli	0	(2) not out	73
4	†R.Mutumbami	lbw b Dabengwa	64		
5	R.Chinyengetere	c Dabengwa b Staddon	58		
6	J.Chinyengetere	b Mupariwa	1		
7	P.Charumbira	lbw b Mpofu	4		
8	I.M.Chinyoka	c Ngulube b Mpofu	27		
9	T.Kamungozi	not out	16		
10	H.Matanga	b Staddon	8		
11	B.V.Vitori	run out (Takarusenga)	0		
	Extras	b 10, lb 6, w 15	31	b 5, lb 2, w 2, nb 1	10
			272	**(1 wicket)**	**137**

FoW (1): 1-44 (2), 2-48 (3), 3-115 (1), 4-164 (4), 5-165 (6), 6-176 (7), 7-240 (8), 8-254 (5), 9-270 (10), 10-272 (11)
FoW (2): 1-15 (1)

Southerns Bowling

	O	M	R	W			O	M	R	W	
Chinyoka	9	3	26	0	3nb		7	5	6	0	
Vitori	10	3	28	1			5	0	19	1	
Charumbira	12	5	21	0	1w,2nb		15	2	39	3	
Chibhabha	9.2	3	25	4			10	1	44	2	1w
Kamungozi	20	8	39	0	1nb	(6)	18	6	29	1	1w
Matanga	21	3	36	4		(5)	24.5	6	60	2	
Machiri	1	0	2	0							

Westerns Bowling

	O	M	R	W			O	M	R	W	
Mpofu	30.4	8	60	2	4w		11	0	37	0	1w
Mupariwa	31	15	48	1	2w		7	2	27	1	
Dabengwa	16	2	37	1			2	0	10	0	
Ntuli	11	3	38	2	9w						
Mukondiwa	7	1	24	0		(4)	5.1	0	17	0	1w
Staddon	11	2	27	2							
Kasawaya	12	5	18	1		(5)	2	0	10	0	
Takarusenga	2	1	4	0							
Mabuza						(6)	6	0	29	0	1nb

Umpires: T.Phiri and T.J.Tapfumaneyi.　Referee: N.N.Singo.　Toss: Southerns
Close of Play: 1st day: Southerns (1) 10-0 (Rizhibowa 9*, Machiri 1*, 9 overs); 2nd day: Southerns (1) 222-6 (R.Chinyengetere 48*, Chinyoka 15*, 99 overs); 3rd day: Westerns (2) 191-7 (Mupariwa 0*, Mpofu 0*, 66 overs).
Man of the Match: H.Matanga.

SOUTHERNS v CENTRALS

Played at Masvingo Sports Club, May 17, 18, 19, 20, 2008.
Logan Cup 2007/08
Match drawn.   (Points: Southerns 14, Centrals 12)

CENTRALS

1	†T.Mahlunge	c Charumbira b Kamungozi	145	(4) lbw b Charumbira	37
2	S.P.Gupo	c Charumbira b Kamungozi	26	c and b Matanga	18
3	*E.Chauluka	b Kamungozi	31	c Chinyoka b Matanga	24
4	F.Kasteni	c Machiri b Kamungozi	32	(5) lbw b Matanga	29
5	L.K.Mutyambizi	c Matanga b Kamungozi	7	(6) lbw b Matanga	0
6	B.M.Chapungu	lbw b Kamungozi	3	(1) hit wkt b Matanga	20
7	J.Matigonda	lbw b Kamungozi	5	(9) not out	25
8	B.Mugochi	c Chinyoka b Kamungozi	27	(10) b Chibhabha	0
9	T.Chitongo	c Chinyoka b Matanga	0	(7) c Mutumbami b Chibhabha	14
10	T.Muzarabani	b Matanga	11	(8) b Matanga	0
11	M.T.Chinouya	not out	0	b Chibhabha	1
	Extras	b 3, lb 3, w 2, nb 14	22	b 5, lb 2, nb 2	9
			309		177

FoW (1): 1-62 (2), 2-112 (3), 3-180 (4), 4-196 (5), 5-212 (6), 6-236 (7), 7-236 (8), 8-291 (9), 9-301 (1), 10-309 (10)
FoW (2): 1-32 (1), 2-47 (2), 3-76 (3), 4-125 (5), 5-125 (6), 6-138 (4), 7-139 (8), 8-175 (7), 9-175 (10), 10-177 (11)

SOUTHERNS

1	C.Rizhibowa	b Mugochi	15	(7) b Mugochi	33
2	T.Machiri	lbw b Muzarabani	1	(1) c Mahlunge b Chinouya	1
3	*C.J.Chibhabha	c Chauluka b Mugochi	36	(2) c Chauluka b Chinouya	6
4	R.Chinyengetere	c Muzarabani b Mugochi	94	(6) not out	30
5	†R.Mutumbami	c Chauluka b Mugochi	14	c Gupo b Mugochi	30
6	T.S.Chisoro	c Gupo b Chinouya	29	(3) c Kasteni b Chinouya	12
7	P.Charumbira	c and b Mugochi	30	(9) not out	3
8	I.M.Chinyoka	c and b Chitongo	41	(4) c Kasteni b Chinouya	2
9	T.Kamungozi	st Mahlunge b Matigonda	27		
10	H.Matanga	run out (Chinouya)	1		
11	B.V.Vitori	not out	16	(8) c Chauluka b Muzarabani	2
	Extras	b 1, lb 6, nb 10	17	lb 1, w 10	11
			321	(7 wickets)	130

FoW (1): 1-6 (2), 2-47 (1), 3-62 (3), 4-78 (5), 5-111 (6), 6-186 (7), 7-271 (8), 8-281 (4), 9-287 (10), 10-321 (9)
FoW (2): 1-6 (1), 2-15 (2), 3-24 (3), 4-35 (4), 5-69 (5), 6-118 (7), 7-126 (8)

Southerns Bowling

	O	M	R	W		O	M	R	W	
Chisoro	6	3	13	0	3nb					
Vitori	8	2	25	0	2nb	(1) 5	2	5	0	
Charumbira	18	10	24	0	2nb	(4) 12	5	30	1	2nb
Chinyoka	4	1	11	0	1w,4nb					
Kamungozi	47	10	125	8	2nb	(2) 27	8	44	0	
Chibhabha	11	5	31	0	1w,1nb	(5) 3.3	2	1	3	
Matanga	29.4	10	74	2		(3) 38	8	90	6	

Centrals Bowling

	O	M	R	W		O	M	R	W	
Muzarabani	18	3	30	1	4nb	10	1	31	1	2w
Chinouya	18	6	44	1	1nb	9	2	22	4	3w
Matigonda	11.5	3	26	1	5nb	(4) 1	0	17	0	4w
Chitongo	22	4	84	1		(5) 9	0	38	0	1w
Mugochi	37	14	80	5		(3) 11	3	21	2	
Kasteni	2	0	14	0						
Chauluka	7	1	36	0						

Umpires: T.R.Matare and T.J.Tapfumaneyi. Referee: J.Chikange.   Toss: Centrals

Close of Play: 1st day: Centrals (1) 236-6 (Mahlunge 115*, Mugochi 0*, 90 overs); 2nd day: Southerns (1) 158-5 (Chinyengetere 25*, Charumbira 25*, 62 overs); 3rd day: Centrals (2) 81-3 (Mahlunge 13*, Kasteni 5*, 40 overs).
Man of the Match: T.Kamungozi.
T.Mahlunge's 145 took 360 balls and included 16 fours and 1 six.

WESTERNS v EASTERNS

Played at Queens Sports Club, Bulawayo, May 17, 18, 19, 20, 2008.
Logan Cup 2007/08
Easterns won by seven wickets.   **(Points: Westerns 6, Easterns 18)**

WESTERNS

#	Batsman	1st innings		2nd innings	
1	†T.Ngulube	b H.Masakadza	51	c Maruma b S.W.Masakadza	15
2	B.Mujuru	c Mutizwa b Musoso	6	c Mutizwa b S.W.Masakadza	90
3	B.Staddon	c Mutizwa b Nyamuzinga	29	run out	47
4	*K.M.Dabengwa	c Mutizwa b S.W.Masakadza	34	b Maruma	11
5	C.Ncube	lbw b Maruma	2	(9) st Mutizwa b Utseya	8
6	T.Mupariwa	b Maruma	36	(7) run out	17
7	T.Madhiri	c Matsikenyeri b Utseya	18	(8) b S.W.Masakadza	0
8	M.M.Dube	c Maruma b Matsikenyeri	6	(5) c Mutizwa b Musoso	7
9	R.T.Kasawaya	c Mutizwa b S.W.Masakadza	23	(10) not out	1
10	S.Kusano	not out	7	(11) lbw b Maruma	0
11	C.B.Mpofu	lbw b Musoso	5	(6) c Mutizwa b Musoso	4
	Extras	w 1, nb 12	13	b 8, lb 3, w 2, nb 13	26
			230		**226**

FoW (1): 1-15 (2), 2-60 (3), 3-125 (4), 4-129 (5), 5-145 (1), 6-188 (7), 7-188 (6), 8-213 (8), 9-222 (9), 10-230 (11)
FoW (2): 1-24 (1), 2-126 (3), 3-146 (4), 4-179 (5), 5-189 (6), 6-194 (2), 7-194 (8), 8-225 (7), 9-225 (9), 10-226 (11)

EASTERNS

#	Batsman	1st innings		2nd innings	
1	T.M.K.Mawoyo	c Ngulube b Mpofu	13		
2	B.Mlambo	c Kasawaya b Staddon	47	(1) c Ncube b Madhiri	47
3	*H.Masakadza	c Madhiri b Mpofu	69		
4	S.Matsikenyeri	c Ngulube b Kusano	15	(3) c Madhiri b Kasawaya	54
5	J.Marumisa	b Mupariwa	25	(4) not out	4
6	†F.Mutizwa	c Ncube b Mupariwa	11		
7	T.Maruma	run out (Mupariwa/Ngulube)	49		
8	P.Utseya	c Ngulube b Staddon	15	(2) c Dube b Mupariwa	6
9	S.K.Nyamuzinga	c Mupariwa b Staddon	0	(5) not out	1
10	S.W.Masakadza	not out	68		
11	S.Musoso	c Ncube b Kasawaya	2		
	Extras	b 8, lb 3, w 10, nb 3	24	b 4, lb 1, w 2	7
			338	(3 wickets)	**119**

FoW (1): 1-49 (1), 2-98 (2), 3-139 (4), 4-187 (3), 5-195 (5), 6-198 (6), 7-224 (8), 8-224 (9), 9-306 (7), 10-338 (11)
FoW (2): 1-13 (2), 2-100 (3), 3-118 (1)

Easterns Bowling

	O	M	R	W		O	M	R	W	
S.W.Masakadza	13	1	35	2	1w,4nb	19	4	58	3	2w,8nb
Musoso	12.5	0	46	2	8nb	18	5	46	2	3nb
Nyamuzinga	7	1	31	1						
H.Masakadza	10	1	25	1	(3)	6	4	10	0	
Maruma	24	5	52	2		27.4	11	52	2	1nb
Utseya	17	9	31	1	(4)	28	7	49	1	1nb
Matsikenyeri	3	0	10	1	(6)	1	1	0	0	

Westerns Bowling

	O	M	R	W		O	M	R	W	
Mupariwa	29	11	74	2	5w	7	0	27	1	2w
Mpofu	26	10	59	2	1w	9.1	0	35	0	
Kasawaya	18	2	56	1	(4)	4	0	37	1	
Staddon	17	6	46	3	2w					
Kusano	22	3	61	1	2w,3nb (3)	2	0	9	0	
Dabengwa	15	6	31	0						
Madhiri					(5)	1	0	6	1	

Umpires: O.Chirombe and T.Phiri. Referee: N.N.Singo.   Toss: Easterns

Close of Play: 1st day: Easterns (1) 4-0 (Mawoyo 0*, Mlambo 2*); 2nd day: Easterns (1) 202-6 (Maruma 0*, Utseya 4*, 89 overs); 3rd day: Westerns (2) 116-1 (Mujuru 40*, Staddon 48*, 50 overs).

Index of Matches